Tenth Edition

STRATEGIC MANAGEMENT
and BUSINESS POLICY

CASES

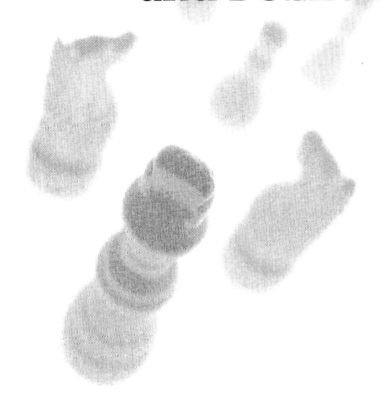

Tenth Edition

STRATEGIC MANAGEMENT
and BUSINESS POLICY

Thomas L. Wheelen
University of South Florida

J. David Hunger
Iowa State University

PEARSON

Prentice
Hall

Upper Saddle River, NJ 07458

Library of Congress Cataloging-in-Publication Data

Wheelen, Thomas L.
    Strategic management and business policy. Cases / Thomas Wheelen, J. David
Hunger.—10th ed.
        p. cm.
    Includes bibliographical references and index.
    ISBN 0-13-149460-0
    1. Strategic planning—Case studies. I. Hunger, J. David, 1941– II. Title.
HD30.28.W43 2005b
658.4′012—dc22

                                                                                    2005049246

Senior Acquisitions Editor: Jennifer Simon
VP/Editorial Director: Jeff Shelstad
Assistant Editor: Richard Gomes
Marketing Manager: Anne K. Howard
Associate Director, Production: Judy Leale
Managing Editor: Renata Butera
Production Editor: Marcela Boos
Permissions Supervisor: Charles Morris
Associate Director, Manufacturing: Vincent Scelta
Manufacturing Buyer: Diane Peirano
Design Director: Maria Lange
Design Manager: Pat Smythe
Interior Design: Jonathan Boylan
Cover Design: Jonathan Boylan
Cover Photo: Getty Images
Manager, Print Production: Christy Mahon
Composition/Full Service Project Management: GGS Book Services
Printer/Binder: Courier–Kendallville
Typeface: Times Roman 10 pt.

Credits and acknowledgments borrowed from other sources and reproduced, with permission, in this textbook appear on appropriate page within text.

Pearson Education LTD.   Pearson Education Australia PTY, Limited
Pearson Education Singapore, Pte. Ltd   Pearson Education North Asia Ltd
Pearson Education, Canada, Ltd   Pearson Educación de Mexico, S.A. de C.V.
Pearson Education–Japan   Pearson Education Malaysia, Pte. Ltd

10 9 8 7 6 5 4 3 2 1
ISBN 0-13-149460-0

Dedicated to

Kathy, Richard, and Tom

Betty, Kari and Jeff, Maddie and Megan, Suzi and Nick, Summer, Lori, Merry, and Smokey: Those for whom this book was written; and to Elizabeth Carey and Jackson S. Hunger—without whom there would be no book.

To the Prentice Hall sales representatives who work so hard to promote this book:

MICHELLE ABRELL
DAVID ALEVY
TARA ALGEO
PETER ANCONA
GRETCHEN ANDERSON
DAVID ARMSTRONG
LARRY ARMSTRONG
RACHAEL AVERY
LINDA BABAT
LORI BAKER
ALICE BARR
CORDELIA BARRERA
KELLIEANN BERLIN
BILL BEVILLE
JOAN BLASCO-PAUL
SARA BREDBENNER
CHARLENE BREWSTER
DANA BULBA
SHAUNA BURGMEIER
JULIE BURGMEIER
RUTH CARDIFF
MICHAEL CARRIGG
BEVERLY CHANNING
MATT CHRISTOPHERSON
CAROLINE COLLINS
CATHY COLUCCI
THAYNE CONRAD
SUSAN COTTENDEN
JONATHAN COTTRELL
CYNDI CRIMMINS

AMANDA CROTTS
DAN CURRIER
MEI LYNN D'ALESSANDRO
ANN DANIEL
NORA DAVIDSON
ERIN DAVIS
SCOTT DAY
CRISTINA DE LA CRUZ
CAROLINE DENNIS
IAN DESROSIERS
GEORGE DEVENNEY
BLAKE DeYOUNG
SUSAN DIKUN
DANA DUNCAN-ZGONC
CYNDI ELLER
VALERIE FANDL
JEFF FEAZELL
TREY FEIGLE
DENNIS FERNANDES
MARY FERNANDEZ
CHRIS FISHER
MYRIAH FITZGIBBON
EVELYN FORTE
YOLIETTE FOURNIER
MARY FRANCESCHINI
YVETTE FREEMAN
JOSIE GALL
AMBER GARDNER
CHERYL GARNER
CHERYL GEHRLICH

SYBIL GERAUD
CHIP GILLIKIN
KERI GOLDBERG-LEONARD
DOUG GREIVE
TRACI HAGELE OMS
REBECCA HAIRELSON
KATIE HANENBERG
VIRGINIA HARRIS
PAUL HARROLD
ALISON HARVEY
TERRY HAUGEN
THOMAS HAYWARD
STEVE HEASLEY
JESSICA HECTOR
AMANDA HEINL
KATHERINE HEPBURN
LYNN HICKS
KATIE HINKLE
SHANNON HOWARD
JULIE HULSEY
ELIZABETH IRVIN
HEATHER JACKSON
MAIREAD JACOBY
VINCE JANSEN
LEAH JOHNSON
ROBERT JOHNSTON
DAVID JURMAN
MOLLY KETCHERSIDE
CURT KETTERMAN
ERIC KRASSOW

DANIEL KRAUSS
NILA LABORIEL
MICHAEL LAMB
KELLY LAMBING
JEREMY LaMONTAGNE
PATRICE LEE
APRIL LEMONS
MICHELLE LIMOGES
TRICIA LISCIO
JENNIFER LUCKING
CARY LUNA
LAURA MANN
DEE DEE MARTINSON
JACK MAYLEBEN
MIKE McDONALD
RYAN McHENRY
RAY MEDINA
MOLLY MEINERS
MATT MESAROS
GREG MIDDLETON
LAURA MIDDLETON
DAVID MILLAGE
CHRIS MILLIKAN
ASHLEY MILLINOR
KATE MOORE
JULIE MOREL
KATIE MORGAN
WYATT MORRIS
JENNIFER MOYERS
MAGGIE MOYLAN
TOM NIXON

KIM NORBUTA
BRIAN NORMOYLE
CELESTE NOSSITER
TY OLDEN
TORI OLSON ALVES
SUE PALMER
ELLEN PALMINTERI
MIKE PERMAN
MICK PFAFF
MELISSA PFISTNER
JIM PORTER HAMANN
TACY QUINN
JULIE RESLER
MARY RHODES
MOLLY RIGGS
KATIE ROGERS
CHRISTIE ROSE
DOROTHY ROSENE
KELLY ROSS
RICHARD ROWE
JAMES SAWYER
SUSAN SCHAUM
LAUREN SCHUR
STEPHANIE SEERY
FUAD SHATARA
ROY SHAW
COLLETTE SIEVER
PHYLLIS SIMON
KARA SMITH
CARRIE SONGSTAD
JEFF SPENCER

MATTHEW SPIEGEL
JANA STAMBAUGH
ANGELA STONE
DAN SULLIVAN
LORI SULLIVAN
MARK SULLIVAN
CHUCK SYNOVEC
LORI SYPHER
LIBBY TEMPLE
MARK TEMPLEMAN
DEVORAH THARP
SARAH THOMAS
ROBERT THORESEN
FRANK TIMONEY
CATHERINE TRAYWICK
TARA TRIPP
JULIE TURLEY
KAREN VILLAGOMEZ
JENNIFER WALTERS
CARMEN WATSON
MARY WEATHERLY
LeDAWN WEBB
LIZ WEIR
TIFFANY WENDT
ERIN WILLIAMS
BRIAN WILLIFORD
MONICA WOLFF
TARA YAZINSKI
SHARON YOUNG
GEORGE YOUNG

Contents

ix

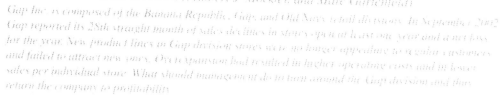

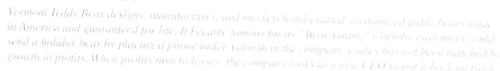

Preface

Welcome to the 10th edition of *Cases in Strategic Management and Business Policy*! We have added 25 new cases—some brand new and some updated versions of especially popular cases. This book contains 43 cases of well-known and not-so-well-known companies dealing with complicated strategic issues. Enjoy!

New Cases: Both Full-Length and Mini-Length

Thirteen full-length cases and 12 mini-cases are new to this edition, for a **total of 25 new cases**. Together with **18 cases carried forward** from past editions, this **edition contains a total of 43 cases.**

NEW FULL-LENGTH CASES

Thirteen full-length cases are new to this edition. Of the 31 full-length cases appearing in this book, 10 are exclusive and do not appear in other books.

Three new cases deal with international issues:

- *GlaxoSmithKline's Retaliation Against Cross-Border Sales of Prescription Drugs*
- *Starbucks' International Operations*
- *Turkcell: The Only Turk on Wall Street*

Three new cases deal with Internet companies:

- *eBay*
- *Amazon.com: An E-Commerce Retailer*
- *AOL Time Warner, Inc.: A Bad Idea from the Start?*

Three new cases deal with competitive issues in retailing:

- *Gap International: A Specialty Apparel Retailer*
- *Tiffany & Company: A Specialty Fine Jewelry Retailer*
- *Panera Bread Company: Rising Fortunes?*

Two new cases deal with entrepreneurial ventures:

- *Oprah Winfrey: The Story of an Entrepreneur*
- *JetBlue Airways' Success Story*

Two new cases deal with strategic issues in manufacturing and technology:

- *The Comeback of Caterpillar, 1985–2002*
- *Eastman Kodak: The Photography Segment of the Information Industry*

NEW MINI-CASES

Twelve new mini-cases are included. They can be quickly read for class discussion or used as Internet research assignments for students to update. They deal with companies in a wide range of industries, from food and health care to airlines and distribution:

Case	Industry
Airtran Holdings, Inc.	airlines
Boise Cascade/OfficeMax	paper/retailing
Eli Lilly & Company	health care
Hershey Foods Company	food
Tech Data Corporation	distribution
H.J. Heinz Company	food
Lowe's Companies, Inc.	retailing
Nike, Inc.	footwear/clothing
Stryker Corporation	health care
Walter Industries	housing
Sykes Enterprises	customer relationship management
Outback Steakhouse, Inc.	restaurants

Additional mini-cases are provided on the Internet, at *www.prenhall.com/wheelen*. They include *Palm, Pfizer, Williams-Sonoma*, and *Tyson Foods*.

All cases are about actual organizations. The firms range in size from large, established multinationals to small, entrepreneurial ventures, and they cover a broad variety of issues. As an aid to case analysis, we propose the strategic audit as an analytical technique.

Supplements

Supplemental materials are available to the instructor from the publisher. This includes the *Case Instructor's Manual*.

Case Instructor's Manual

To aid in case method teaching, the *Case Instructor's Manual* includes detailed suggestions for use, teaching objectives, and examples of student analyses for each of the 31 cases. This is the most comprehensive instructor's manual available in strategic management. A standardized format is provided for each of the comprehensive strategic management cases (cases 5–30):

- Case Abstract
- Case Issues and Subjects
- Steps Covered in the Strategic Decision-making Process
- Case Objectives
- Suggested Classroom Approaches
- Discussion Questions
- Case Author's Teaching Note
- Student-written Strategic Audit or Paper
- EFAS, IFAS, and SFAS Exhibits

- Financial Analysis—Ratios and Common-Size Income Statements
- Student Strategic Audit Worksheet

Examples of student papers are provided for each of the mini-cases included in the book.

COMPANION WEBSITE

The new Companion Website provides a customized course. It features an online study guide for students that includes Multiple Choice, True/False, and Essay Questions. Instructors may download files of both Instructor's Manuals, PowerPoint slides, and test bank files from the Instructor's Resource Center link at the Companion Website. It also includes additional mini-cases on Palm, Pfizer, Williams-Sonoma, and Tyson Foods. Point your browser to *www.prenhall.com/wheelen*.

Acknowledgments

We thank the many people at Prentice Hall who helped to make this edition possible. We thank our Editor, Jennifer Simon. We are especially grateful to Jennifer's Editorial Assistant, Richard Gomes, who managed to keep everything on an even keel. We also thank Marcela Boos and Heidi Allgair, who took the book through the production process.

We are also very grateful to Kathy Wheelen for her first-rate administrative support of the cases and the *Case Instructor's Manual*. We are especially thankful to the many students who tried out the cases we chose to include in this book. Their comments helped us find any flaws in the cases before the book went to the printer.

In addition, we express our appreciation to Dr. Labh Hira, Dean, and Dr. Thomas Chacko, Management Department Chair, of Iowa State University's College of Business, for their support and provision of the resources so necessary to produce a textbook. Both of us acknowledge our debt to Dr. William Shenkir and Dr. Frank S. Kaulback, former Deans of the McIntire School of Commerce of the University of Virginia, for the provision of a work climate most supportive to the original development of this book.

We offer a special thanks to the hundreds of case authors who have provided us with excellent cases for the 10 editions of this book. The adage is true: The path to greatness is through others. We consider many of these case writers to be friends. A special thanks to each of you!

We especially thank Mary Anne Rouse, an outstanding classroom teacher and case author. A true professional, Mary Anne believed in turning her students into lifelong learners. On her own, she wrote 24 mini-cases for our 9th and 10th editions. Retiring in 2005, she and her husband look forward to many years of new and exciting adventures.

Finally, to the many strategy instructors and students who have moaned to us about their problems with the strategy course: We have tried to respond to your problems and concerns as best we could by providing a comprehensive yet usable text coupled with recent and complex cases. To you, the people who work hard in the strategy trenches, we acknowledge our debt. This book is yours.

T. L. W.
Tampa, Florida

J. D. H.
Ames, Iowa

About the Contributors

Moustafa H. Abdelsamad, D.B.A. (George Washington University), is Dean of the College of Business at Texas A&M University–Corpus Christi. He previously served as Dean of the College of Business and Industry at University of Massachusetts—Dartmouth and as Professor of Finance and Associate Dean of Graduate Studies in Business at Virginia Commonwealth University. He is Editor-in-Chief of SAM *Advanced Management Journal* and International President of the Society of Advancement of Management. He is author of *A Guide to Capital Expenditure Analysis* and two chapters in the *Dow Jones—Irwin Capital Budgeting Handbook*. He is the author and co-author of numerous articles in various publications.

Hitesh (John) P. Adhia, CPA, B.A. and M.S. (University of South Florida), is the President and Chief Investment Officer of Adhia Investment Advisors, Inc. (the "Firm"). He is a C.P.A. and has been in the finance industry since 1982. He is the founder and Investment Manager for the Adhia Twenty Fund, the Adhia Health Care Fund, the Adhia Short Term Advantage Fund, the Adhia Arbitrage Fund, and the Adhia Derivative Fund. Prior to forming Adhia Investment Advisors, Mr. Adhia owned a Tampa-based public accounting practice and also served as Acting CFO and Independent Advisor to the Well Care Group of Companies. Mr. Adhia has over 20 years of experience managing fixed income strategies.

James W. Camerius, M.S. (University of North Dakota), is Professor of Marketing at Northern Michigan University. He has served as President of the Society for Case Research, Marketing Track Chair of the North American Case Research Association, and Workshop and Colloquium Director of the World Association for Case Method Research. He is a research grant recipient of the Walker L. Cisler College of Business at Northern Michigan University and also a 1995 recipient of the Distinguished Faculty Award of the Michigan Association of Governing Boards of State Universities. His cases appear in more than 90 management, marketing, and retailing textbooks in addition to *Annual Advances in Business Cases*, a publication of the Society for Case Research. His studies of corporate situations include Kmart Corporation; Tanner Companies, Inc.; Mary Kay Cosmetics, Inc.; Sasco Products, Inc.; The Fuller Brush Company; Wal-Mart Stores, Inc.; Longaberger Marketing, Inc.; Encyclopaedia Britannica International; and RWC, Inc. His writings include several studies of the case method of instruction. He is an award and grant recipient of the Direct Selling Educational Foundation, Washington, DC, and is listed in *Who's Who in the World, America, Midwest, American Education*, and *Finance and Industry*.

Marcia Chan is a Graduate Research Assistant at the Tobin School of Business at Saint John's University.

Isaac Cohen is a Professor of Organization and Management in San Jose State University. He has presented many cases on strategic management in the North American Case Research Association during the past seven years, all of which have appeared in multiple text books. He is now completing a case titled "The Rise and Rise of Airbus, 1970–2005."

Patrick Collins is a Graduate Research Assistant at the Tobin School of Business at Saint John's University.

Roy A. Cook, D.B.A. (Mississippi State University), is Associate Dean of the School of Business Administration and Professor of Management, Fort Lewis College, Durango,

xxii ABOUT THE CONTRIBUTORS

Colorado. He has written a best-selling textbook, *Tourism: The Business of Travel*, now in its second edition, and has two forthcoming textbooks: *Cases and Experiential Exercises in Human Resource Management* and *Guide to Business Etiquette*. He has authored numerous articles, cases, and papers based on his extensive experience in the hospitality industry and research interests in the areas of strategy, small business management, human resource management, and communication. Dr. Cook is the Director of Colorado's Center for Tourism Research and Editor of *The Annual Advances in Business Cases*, and he also serves on the Editorial Boards of the *Business Case Journal*, the *Journal of Business Strategies*, and the *Journal of Teaching and Tourism*. He is a member of the Academy of Management, Society for Case Research (past President), and the International Society of Travel and Tourism Educators. Dr. Cook teaches courses in Strategic Management, Small Business Management, Tourism and Resort Management, and Human Resource Management.

Richard A. Cosier, Ph.D. (University of Iowa), is Dean and Leeds Professor of Management at Purdue University. He was formerly the Dean and Fred B. Brown Chair at the University of Oklahoma and was Associate Dean for Academics and Professor of Business Administration at Indiana University. He served as Chairperson of the Department of Management at Indiana University. He was formerly a Planning Engineer with Western Electric Company and Instructor of Management and Quantitative Methods at the University of Notre Dame. He is interested in researching the managerial decision-making process, organization responses to external forces, and participative management. He has been published in *Behavior Science, Academy of Management Journal, Academy of Management Review, Organizational Behavior and Human Performance, Management Science, Strategic Management Journal, Business Horizons, Decision Sciences, Personnel Psychology, Journal of Creative Behavior, International Journal of Management, The Business Quarterly, Public Administration Quarterly, Human Relations*, and other journals. In addition, Dr. Cosier has presented numerous papers at professional meetings and has coauthored a management text. He has been active in many executive development programs and has acted as management-education consultant for several organizations. Dr. Cosier is the recipient of Teaching Excellence Awards in the M.B.A. Program at Indiana and a Richard D. Irwin Fellowship. He belongs to the Institute of Management, Sigma Iota Epsilon, and the Decision Sciences Institute.

David B. Croll, Ph.D. (Pennsylvania State University), is Professor Emeritus of Accounting at the McIntire School of Commerce, the University of Virginia. He was Visiting Associate Professor at the Graduate Business School, the University of Michigan. He is on the Editorial Board of *SAM Advanced Management Journal*. He has been published in the *Accounting Review* and the *Case Research Journal*. His cases appear in 12 accounting and management textbooks.

Dan R. Dalton, Ph.D. (University of California–Irvine), is Dean of the Graduate School of Business, Indiana University, and Harold A. Polipl Chair of Strategic Management. He was formerly with General Telephone & Electronics for 13 years. Widely published in business and psychology periodicals, his articles have appeared in the *Academy of Management Journal, Journal of Applied Psychology, Personnel Psychology, Academy of Management Review*, and *Strategic Management Journal*.

Sanjib Dutta, M.B.A. (University of Ljubljana, Slovenia), is a Professor at the ICFAI Center for Management Research (ICMR), Hyderabad, and Consulting Editor for *Effective Executive*, a monthly management magazine from ICFAI Publications. He has six years' experience in research activities related to case study development. He teaches Strategic Management at the ICFAI Business School, Hyderabad.

Cathy A. Enz, Ph.D. (Ohio State University), is the Lewis G. Schaeneman Jr. Professor of Innovation and Dynamic Management at Cornell University's School of Hotel Administration, where she is also the Executive Director of the Center for Hospitality Research. Her doctoral degree is in organization theory and behavior. Professor Enz has written numerous articles, cases, and books on corporate culture, value sharing, change management, and strategic human resource management effects on performance. Professor Enz consults extensively in the service sector and serves on the Boards of Directors for two hospitality-related organizations.

Thomas F. Flanagan (1934–1968), B.A. (Boston College), was a Ford Motor executive. He changed my life and so he is a true lifetime friend of Thomas L. Wheelen. He is greatly missed by his family—his wife, Patricia, and his children, William, Ellen, Susie, Michael, and Maureen—and his many friends and family.

Ellie A. Fogarty, M.L.S. (University of Pittsburgh), M.B.A. (Temple University), is the Executive Assistant to the Provost at The College of New Jersey in Ewing, New Jersey, where she supports the strategic planning and assessment efforts of the college. Prior to this position, she was the Business and Economics Librarian at the college for over 10 years.

Stacey Foster, B.A. (Saint Michael's College), M.B.A. (Bentley College), is a Strategic Marketing Manager at Textron Systems, Wilmington, Massachusetts. She has worked as a Senior Consultant for the competitive intelligence firms Fuld & Company, Cambridge, Massachusetts, and Fletcher/CSI, Williston, Vermont.

Gamewell D. Gantt, J.D., C.P.A., is Professor of Accounting and Management in the College of Business at Idaho State University in Pocatello, Idaho, where he teaches a variety of legal studies courses. He is past President of the Rocky Mountain Academy of Legal Studies in Business and a past Chair of the Idaho Endowment Investment Fund Board. His published articles and papers have appeared in journals including *Midwest Law Review, Business Law Review, Copyright World*, and *Intellectual Property World*. His published cases have appeared in several textbooks and in *Annual Advances in Business Cases.*

Marc Gartenfeld, B.S., M.B.A. (St. John's University), is the Associate Director of The Strategic Management Research Group and the Center for Case Development and Use. He has co-authored more than 75 books, monographs, instructor's guides, case studies, journal articles, conference presentations, and table topic papers in the areas of Multinational Strategic Management, E-Business, Expert Knowledge-Based Systems, Entrepreneurship, and Application Service Providers. One of his co-authored papers won a "Distinguished Paper Award," and various case studies won national and international awards. He was also the recipient of the 2001 "Teaching Excellence Award" and "Professor the Year Award," both from the Tobin College of Business, St. John's University.

Norman J. Gierlasinski, D.B.A., C.P.A., C.F.E., C.I.A., is Professor of Accounting at Central Washington University. He served as Chairman of the Small Business Division of the Midwest Business Administration Association. He has authored and co-authored cases for professional associations and the Harvard Case Study Series. He has authored various articles in professional journals and served as a contributing author for textbooks and as a consultant to many organizations. He also served as a reviewer for various publications.

Sue Greenfeld, D.B.A. (University of Southern California), is Professor of Management and Associate Dean for Student Affairs in the College of Business Administration, California State University–San Bernardino. She is a two-time recipient of a Fulbright Senior Fellowship, and she has taught at the National Chengchi University in Taipei, Taiwan, and at the Marmara University in Istanbul, Turkey. She has written numerous cases on business policy and strategic issues and has served on the Editorial Board of *Case Research Journal.*

Irene Hagenbuch Sanjana, B.S. (Bentley College), is currently working as an Operations Specialist for Warburg Dillon Read in Stamford, Connecticut. Among her various roles at Warburg Dillon Read, Irene has spent time with the Precious Metals, Domestic Equities, and Fixed Income Groups. Some of her responsibilities have included the reduction of settlement risk through operational controls, new product development, design and testing, and general project management. She is an avid skier and runner. In her spare time, she enjoys foreign travel.

Alan N. Hoffman, D.B.A. (Indiana University), is an Associate Professor of Management, Bentley College, Waltham, Massachusetts, and was formerly Assistant Professor of Business Environment and Policy at the University of Connecticut. He is co-author of *The Strategic Management Casebook and Skill Builder*, with Hugh O'Neill. Publications have appeared in the *Academy of Management Journal, Human Relations*, the *Journal of Business Research, Business Horizons*, and the *Journal of Business Ethics*. His cases appear in more than 20 strategy textbooks. He is co-author of the following strategic management cases: "Harley-Davidson: The Eagle Soars Alone," "The Boston YWCA: 1991," "Ryka Inc.: The Athletic Shoe with a 'Soul', " "Liz Claiborne: Troubled Times for the Women's Retail Giant," "Snapple Beverage," "NTN Communications: The Future is Now!," "Ben & Jerry's Homemade, Yo! I'm Your CEO," "Cisco Systems", "Sun Microsystems," "Chipcom, Inc.," "Palm Computing," "Handspring Inc.," "AOL/Time Warner," and "eBay, Inc."

J. David Hunger, Ph.D. (Ohio State University), is Professor of Strategic Management at Iowa State University. He previously taught at George Mason University, the University of Virginia, and Baldwin-Wallace College. His research interests lie in strategic management, corporate governance, and entrepreneurship. He served as Academic Director of the Pappajohn Center for Entrepreneurship at Iowa State University. He worked in brand management at Procter & Gamble Company, worked as a selling supervisor at Lazarus Department Stores, and served as a Captain in U.S. Army Military Intelligence. He has been active as a Consultant and Trainer to business corporations, as well as to state and federal government agencies. He has written numerous articles and cases that have appeared in the *Academy of Management Journal, International Journal of Management, Human Resource Management, Journal of Business Strategies, Case Research Journal, Business Case Journal, Handbook of Business Strategy, Journal of Management Case Studies, Annual Advances in Business Cases, Journal of Retail Banking, SAM Advanced Management Journal*, and *Journal of Management*, among others. Dr. Hunger is a member of the Academy of Management, North American Case Research Association, Society for Case Research, North American Management Society, Textbook and Academic Authors Association, and the Strategic Management Society. He is past President of the North American Case Research Association, Society for Case Research, and the Iowa State University Board of Directors. He also served as Vice President of the U.S. Association for Small Business and Entrepreneurship (USASBE). He has served on the Editorial Review Boards of *SAM Advanced Management Journal, Journal of Business Strategies*, and *Journal of Business Research*. He is also a member of the Board of Directors of the North American Case Research Association, the Society for Case Research, and the North American Management Society. He is co-author with Thomas L. Wheelen of *Strategic Management and Business Policy* and *Essentials of Strategic Management* plus *Concepts in Strategic Management and Business Policy* and *Cases in Strategic Management and Business Policy*, as well as *Strategic Management Cases* (PIC: Preferred Individualized Cases), and a monograph assessing undergraduate business education in the United States. The 8th edition of *Strategic Management and Business Policy* received the McGuffey Award for Excellence and Longevity in 1999 from the Text and Academic Authors Association. Dr. Hunger received the Best Case Award given by the McGraw-Hill Publishing Company and the Society for Case Research in 1991 for outstanding case development. He is listed in various versions of *Who's Who*, including *Who's Who in the United States* and *Who's Who in the World*. He was also recognized in 1999 by the Iowa State University College of Business with its Innovation in Teaching Award and was elected a Fellow of the Teaching and Academic Authors Association in 2001.

George A. Johnson, Ph.D., is Professor of Management and Director of the Idaho State University M.B.A. program. He has been published in the fields of management education, ethics, project management, and simulation. He is also active in developing and publishing case material for educational purposes. His industry experience includes several years as a Project Manager in the development and procurement of aircraft systems.

Michael J. Keeffe, Ph.D. (University of Arkansas), is Associate Professor of Management at Southwest Texas State University. He has served as Chair of the Department of Management and Marketing and Co-Director of AACSB—International Accreditation at SWT, and he has authored numerous cases in the field of strategic management, published in several journals, and served as an independent consultant since 1982. He currently teaches and conducts research in the fields of strategic management and human resource management.

John A. Kilpatrick, Ph. D. (University of Iowa), is Professor of Management and International Business, Idaho State University. He has taught in the areas of business and business ethics for over 25 years. He served as Co-Chair of the management track of the Institute for Behavioral and Applied Management from its inception and continues as a board member for that organization. He is author of *The Labor Content of American Foreign Trade*, and co-author of *Issues in International Business*. His cases have appeared in a number of organizational behavior and strategy texts and casebooks, as well as in *Annual Advances in Business Cases*.

Eric G. Kirby, Ph.D. (University of Kentucky), is Assistant Professor of Strategic Management at Southwest Texas State University. He previously held a joint appointment on the faculties of the College of Business Administration and Medicine at Texas Tech University. He has received numerous awards for his research in the areas of health care administration and sport management. He has published over a dozen articles in scholarly journals and presented many more at academic conferences. Most of his research examines how businesses understand and respond to their external environment. Prior to becoming an academic, he was a building contractor, a technical writer, and an information systems manager. He can be contacted online at *www.EricKirby.com*.

Donald F. Kuratko is the Jack M. Gill Chair of Entrepreneurship, Professor of Entrepreneurship, and Executive Director of the Johnson Center for Entrepreneurship & Innovation at The Kelley School of Business, Indiana University. Dr. Kuratko is considered a preeminent scholar and national leader in the field of entrepreneurship. He has published over 150 articles on aspects of entrepreneurship, new venture development, and corporate entrepreneurship. His work has been published in journals such as *Strategic Management Journal, Academy of Management Executive, Journal of Business Venturing, Entrepreneurship Theory & Practice, Journal of Small Business Management, Journal of Small Business Strategy, Family Business Review*, and *Advanced Management Journal*. Dr. Kuratko has authored 20 books, including the leading entrepreneurship book in American universities today, *Entrepreneurship: Theory, Process, Practice*, 7th ed. (South-Western/Thomson Publishers, 2007), as well as *Strategic Entrepreneurial Growth*, 2nd ed. (South-Western/Thomson Publishers, 2004), *Corporate Entrepreneurship* (South-Western/Thomson Publishers, 2007), and *Effective Small Business Management*, 7th ed. (Wiley & Sons Publishers, 2001). In addition, Dr. Kuratko has been Consultant on Corporate Entrepreneurship and Entrepreneurial Strategies to a number of major corporations, such as Anthem Blue Cross/Blue Shield, AT&T, United Technologies, Ameritech, The Associated Group (Acordia), Union Carbide Corporation, ServiceMaster, and TruServ.

Under his leadership, Indiana University's Entrepreneurship Program has recently been ranked 4th in the nation by *Entrepreneur* magazine, 11th in Graduate Business Schools for Entrepreneurship by *U.S. News & World Report,* 4th in Graduate Business Schools (Public Institutions) for Entrepreneurship by *U.S. News & World Report*, and one of the Top 5 Entrepreneurial Business Schools by the *Princeton Review* as reported in *Forbes* magazine. Before coming to Indiana University, he was the Stoops Distinguished Professor of Entrepreneurship and Founding Director of the Entrepreneurship Program at Ball State

University. In addition, he was the Executive Director of The Midwest Entrepreneurial Education Center. Dr. Kuratko was the first professor ever to be named a Distinguished Professor for the College of Business at Ball State University and held that position for 15 years. The Entrepreneurship Program that Dr. Kuratko developed at Ball State University continually earned national rankings including *Top 20* in *Business Week* and *Success* magazines; *Top 10* business schools for entrepreneurship research (*Journal of Management*); *Top 4* in *U.S. News & World Report's* elite ranking (including the #1 public university for entrepreneurship); and the *#1 Regional Entrepreneurship Program* in *Entrepreneur* magazine.

Dr. Kuratko's honors include earning the Ball State University College of Business Teaching Award 15 consecutive years as well as being the only professor in the history of Ball State University to achieve all four of the university's major lifetime awards, including *Outstanding Young Faculty* (1987); *Outstanding Teaching Award* (1990); *Outstanding Faculty Award* (1996); and *Outstanding Researcher Award* (1999). He was also honored as the *Entrepreneur of the Year* for the state of Indiana and was inducted into the *Institute of American Entrepreneurs Hall of Fame* (1990). He has been honored with *The George Washington Medal of Honor*; the *Leavey Foundation Award for Excellence in Private Enterprise*; the *NFIB Entrepreneurship Excellence Award*; and the *National Model Innovative Pedagogy Award for Entrepreneurship*. In addition, Dr. Kuratko was named the *National Outstanding Entrepreneurship Educator* (by the U.S. Association for Small Business and Entrepreneurship), and he was selected one of the *Top Three Entrepreneurship Professors in the U.S.* by the Kauffman Foundation, Ernst & Young, *Inc.* magazine, and Merrill Lynch. He received the *Thomas W. Binford Memorial Award for Outstanding Contribution to Entrepreneurial Development* from the Indiana Health Industry Forum. Dr. Kuratko has been named a *21st Century Entrepreneurship Research Fellow* by the National Consortium of Entrepreneurship Centers as well as the U.S. Association for Small Business & Entrepreneurship *Scholar for Corporate Entrepreneurship* in 2003. Finally, he has been honored by his peers in *Entrepreneur* magazine as one of the Top Two Entrepreneurship Program Directors in the nation for three consecutive years, including the *#1 Entrepreneurship Program Director* in 2003.

Darrin Kuykendall, M.B.A., M.S.F.P., is a consultant for PricewaterhouseCoopers in Boston. He is also a professional licensed realtor in the state of Massachusetts. He received his Information Age M.B.A. and Master's in Financial Planning from the McCallum Graduate School of Business at Bentley University. Bentley is the first business university that is distinguished by grooming knowledge professionals for today's information- and technology-driven business world. He also holds a bachelor's degree in Marketing and International Communications from Robert Morris University, located in Pittsburgh, Pennsylvania. He has also served in the U.S. Army National Guard in financial and administrative roles. He is a member of National Association of Realtors (NAR), Massachusetts Association of Realtors (MAR), and National Black MBA Association. In addition, he owns and operates his own firm, *Khamelian International*, LLC, a diversified portfolio firm positioned to engage in ventures in real estate investment, marketing consulting, and investment management.

William P. May, B. A. (McIntire School of Commerce, University of Virginia), after serving as an advisor in Vietnam, returned to his home in Charlottesville, Virginia. He enrolled in the McIntire School of Commerce, University of Virginia, where he studied under the direction of Dr. Wheelen, earning a degree in management. He has spent 33 years in real estate sales, investment, development, and real estate office management. He has invested countless hours in community service and seeks to direct all those with whom he comes in contact to get out of the stands and to play full out in the game of life. He is clear that he makes a positive contribution in the world because of mentors such as Dr. Thomas Wheelen who commit their lives to helping many like him understand that the true management of people is a listening. That special listening allows each person on the team of life to be all they can be using their individual talents in the successful achievement of bigger-than-life goals.

Bill J. Middlebrook, Ph.D. (University of North Texas), is Professor of Management at Southwest Texas State University. He has served as Acting Chair of the Department of Management and Marketing, been published in numerous journals, and served as a consultant in industry, and he is currently teaching and researching in the fields of Strategic Management and Human Resources.

Robert J. Mockler, Ph.D. (Columbia University), B.A. and M.B.A. (Harvard University) is the Joseph F. Adams Professor of Management at St. John's University's Graduate School of Business. He is the Director of the Strategic Management Research Group and its Centers of Knowledge-Based Systems for Business (one of the largest databases of prototype expert systems for management decision making in the United States), Case Study Development and Use Program (the third-largest case study development program in the United States), and Cross-Cultural Management. He has authored, co-authored, and edited over 50 books and monographs, some 230 case studies, over 70 articles, over 50 book chapters, and over 200 presentations covering such areas as strategic management, case study development and use, competitive market analysis, new venture management, multinational planning, business ethics, management decision making, modeling of cognitive and behavioral management processes, contingency theory, business process reengineering, computer information systems, group decision support systems for management, expert knowledge-base systems, and innovative teaching. His first articles on strategic management and situational decision theory were published in *Harvard Business Review* in 1970 and 1971. His first book on strategic management was published in 1969 (Prentice Hall). His books include three on expert systems and computer information systems development in 1992 (Macmillan), five on strategic management, information systems, and case study development and use in 1993 and 1994 (Addison-Wesley, Simon & Schuster, The Planning Forum); and four on multinational strategic management in 1997, 1998, 1999, and 2003 (John Wiley & Sons, Quorum Books, Haworth Press, and Strategic Management Research Group Publishing). Three of his books have been translated into Chinese and published in China, two into Romanian and published in Romania, one into Greek and published in Greece, and one into Russian and published in Russia. He has lectured, consulted, and taught worldwide in (China – Xian, Beijing, and Shanghai; Russia – Moscow and St. Petersburg; Finland; Japan; England; Poland; Germany; Brazil; Argentina; Costa Rica; Ireland; Italy; Taiwan; Philippines; India; Egypt; Mexico; Canada; and Romania). He has received national awards for innovative teaching (Decision Sciences Institute), been a Fulbright Scholar, and taught M.B.A. courses in Rome, Milan, Latin America, and Beijing, and won numerous other awards for his work. He has also successfully started, run, and eventually sold his own multi-million-dollar business ventures. He has developed and published over 120 presentations, case studies, and articles with other faculty at St. John's University. In addition, he has done over 80 joint publications with professors from other domestic and overseas universities.

Rebecca J. Morris, Ph.D. (University of Nebraska at Lincoln), is Associate Professor of Management, University of Nebraska at Omaha. She has published cases in the *Case Research Journal* and the *Business Case Journal*. Her cases have appeared in a number of strategic management, international management and business ethics textbooks. Dr. Morris is an active member of the North American Case Research Association (NACRA) and the Society for Case Research (SCR). She is currently serving as President-Elect of NACRA and on the Editorial Review Board for the *Journal of Business Strategies*. In 2004, Dr. Morris received the University of Nebraska at Omaha Excellence in Teaching Award. She is currently teaching and conducting case research in the fields of Strategic Management and International Management.

A. Mukund is a former Faculty Member at the ICFAI Center for Management Research.

Nathan Nebbe, M.B.A. and M.A. (Iowa State University), has significant interests in the indigenous peoples of the Americas. With an undergraduate degree in Animal Ecology, he served as a Peace Corps Volunteer in Honduras, where he worked at the Honduran national forestry school ESNAACIFORE (*Escuela National de Ciencias Forestales*). After the Peace Corps, Nathan worked for a year on a recycling project for the Town of Ignacio and the Southern Ute Indian Tribe in southwestern Colorado. Following his experience in Colorado, Nathan returned to Iowa State University, where he obtained an M.B.A. followed by an M.A. in anthropology. He is currently studying how globalization of the Chilean forestry industry is affecting the culture of the indigenous Mapuche people of south-central Chile.

Thomas M. Patrick, Ph.D. (University of Kentucky), is Professor of Finance at The College of New Jersey. He has also taught at Rider University and the University of Notre Dame. He has been published widely in the areas of commercial banking and small business finance. His research appears in such journals as *Journal of Consumer Finance, Journal of International Business Studies, Journal of Small Business Management,* and *Banker's Monthly.* He also serves on the Editorial Review Boards of a number of academic journals.

Laurence C. Pettit, Jr., D.B.A. (University of Virginia), B.S. and M.S. (Virginia Polytechnic Institute and State University), is Professor of Commerce at the McIntire School of Commerce, University of Virginia, where he specializes in corporate financing and banking. He was Associate Director of the Virginia-Maryland School of Bank Management and the founder and lead instructor for the National Banking School for the AICPA, and he teaches in the Virginia Bankers School, Stonier Graduate School of Banking, and Consumer Bankers School of Retail Bank Management. He has been Visiting Professor at Washington and Lee University, the University of Texas at Austin, and Emory University, and has taught at Virginia Polytechnic Institute and the University of Southwestern Louisiana. He has a special publishing interest in the valuation of the middle market firm and commercial banking. His articles have appeared in various banking and financial publications, including *Bankers Magazine, Financial Review, The Southern Banker,* the *Journal of Financial Education*, and the *Journal of Bank Accounting & Auditing.*

A. Neela Radhika is a former Faculty Associate at the ICFAI Center for Management Research.

Shirisha Regani is a Faculty Associate at the ICFAI Center for Management Research.

Ted Repetti, B.S. (The College of New Jersey), is currently a valuation analyst at Management Planning, Inc., in Princeton. Management Planning renders financial advice to corporations, and specializes in the valuation of closely held corporations.

John K. Ross, III, Ph.D. (University of North Texas), is Associate Professor of Management at Southwest Texas State University. He has served as SBI Director, Associate Dean, Chair of the Department of Management and Marketing; been published in numerous journals; and is currently teaching and researching in the fields of strategic management and human resource.

Maryanne M. Rouse, M.B.A. (University of South Florida), B.A. in English, Romance Languages, and Political Science (Syracuse University), is a C.P.A. in Florida. She joined the faculty of the College of Business Administration at the University of South Florida in 1971. She served as the college's Assistant Dean from 1974 to 1976 and as Director of Executive Education and Management Development from 1981 to 1994. Ms. Rouse's current teaching assignments include Strategic Management, the undergraduate capstone course, Measuring Organization Performance in the Graduate Leadership Program, Integrative Business Applications II in the MBA, and Managerial Accounting in the Executive MBA and the MBA Program for Physicians. She has also taught in the USF/EDC French executive M.B.A. program in Paris. The recipient of a number of MBA teaching awards, including MVP by the Physicians MBA class and Outstanding Professor for the Executive MBA program, she is a frequent program speaker and continuing education faculty member. A Consultant in strategic planning and accounting in several industries, including the not-for-profit sector and health care, she served as one of four international accreditation fellows for the Accreditation Commission for Education in Health Services Administration (ACEHSA). Maryanne is a member of the Board of Directors and Vice Chair of the Tampa Economic Development Corporation, and CDC, and serves on the board of the University's Small Business Development Center, and chairs the college's Undergraduate Programs Committee.

Patricia A. Ryan, Ph.D. (University of South Florida), is an Associate Professor of Finance, Colorado State University. She currently serves on the Board of the Midwest Finance Association and is the Associate Editor of the *Business Case Journal.* Her research interests lie in corporate finance, specifically initial public offerings, capital budgeting, and case writing. She has been published in the *Journal of Business and Management*, the *Business Case Journal, Educational and Psychological Measurement*, the *Journal of Research in Finance*, the *Journal of Financial and Strategic Decisions*, and the *Journal of Accounting and Finance Research.* Her research has been cited in the *Wall Street Journal, CFO Magazine*, and *Investment Dealers Digest.*

Sara Smith Shull, Pharm.D. (University of Nebraska Medical Center), M.B.A. (University of Nebraska at Omaha), is a Drug Policy and Economics Pharmacist Specialist at Nebraska Health Systems. In 2003, Sara received the Outstanding Student-Authored Case Award at the North American Case Research Association for her case on GlaxoSmithKline. She was further recognized for this achievement with the MBA Business Case Student Research Award at the University of Nebraska at Omaha in 2004. She received the Jack Hill Award for academic excellence in the MBA program at the University of Nebraska at Omaha in 2003. Sara's primary research and clinical interests include pharmacoeconomics, outcomes research, and the implementation of cost-effective programs.

Laurence J. Stybel, Ed.D. (Harvard University), is Co-founder of Stybel Peabody Lincolnshire, a Boston-based management consulting firm devoted to enhancing career effectiveness of executives who report to boards of directors. Services include search, outplacement, outplacement avoidance, and valued executive career consulting. Stybel Peabody Lincolnshire was voted "Best Outplacement Firm" by the readers of *Massachusetts Lawyers Weekly.* Its programs are the only ones officially endorsed by the Massachusetts Hospital Association and the Financial Executives Institute. He serves on the Board of Directors of the New England Chapter of the National Association of Corporate Directors and the Boston Human Resources Association. His home page can be found at *www.stybelpeabody.com.* The "Your Career" department of the home page contains downloadable back issues of his monthly *Boston Business Journal* column, "Your Career."

K. Subhadra is a former Faculty Associate at the ICFAI Center for Management Research.

John F. Talbot, B.S.E. (Fitchburg State College), retired mathematics teacher from Lunenburg High School in Lunenburg, Massachusetts, graduated from Gardner High School (MA) and Sacred Heart School in 1953 and 1949, respectively. We met in the first grade in 1941 at Sacred Heart School and still friends 64 years later—Thanks.

John J. Tarpey (1969–1996), M.A., M.Ed., and B.S. (Assumption College, Fitchburg State College, and University of Massachusetts), was a retired teacher and coach from Gardner High School in Gardner, Massachusetts. He was a true lifetime friend of Thomas Wheelen. He is greatly missed by his family—his wife, Gloria, and his children, John, Maureen, Carolyn, and Emily—and his many friends.

Joanna Tochowicz is a Graduate Research Assistant at the Tobin School of Business at Saint John's University.

Jossett Trewick is a Graduate Research Assistant at the Tobin School of Business at Saint John's University.

Joyce P. Vincelette, D.B.A. (Indiana University), is Professor of Management at The College of New Jersey. She was previously a faculty member at the University of South

Florida. She has authored and co-authored various articles, chapters, and cases that have appeared in management journals and strategic management texts and casebooks. She is also active as a consultant and trainer for a number of local and national business organizations as well as for a variety of not-for-profit and government agencies. She currently teaches and conducts research in the fields of strategic management and leadership.

Vineet Walia was an MBA student at Bentley College and is a Graduate Research Assistant at the Tobin School of Business at Saint John's University.

Kathryn E. Wheelen, B.A., L.M.T. (University of Tampa), has worked as an Administrative Assistant for case and textbook development with the Thomas L. Wheelen Company. She is the owner of Kathryn E. Wheelen, Inc., and works out of Meridian Wellness Centre, Tampa, Florida.

Richard D. Wheelen, B.S. (University of South Florida), has worked as a Case Research Assistant. He is currently studying in the field of health care and is getting married in the summer of 2005. He currently lives in Everett, Washington.

Thomas L. Wheelen II, B.A. (Boston College), has worked as a Case Research Assistant. He is currently working and living in Boulder, Colorado.

Thomas L. Wheelen, D.B.A. (George Washington University), M.B.A. (Babson College), M.B.A. (1961); Boston College, B.S. cum laude (1957). Teaching Experience: Visiting Professor, *Trinity College–University of Dublin* (Fall 1999); *University of South Florida,* Professor of Strategic Management (1983–present); University of Virginia–*McIntire School of Commerce*; Ralph A. Beeton Professor of Free Enterprise (1985–1981); Professor (1981–1974); Associate Professor (1974–1971); and Assistant Professor (1971–1968); Visiting Professor—*University of Arizona* (1980–1979) and *Northeastern University* (Summer 1979, 1977, and 1975). **Academic, Industry and Military Experience:** *University of Virginia College of Continuing Education:* (1) Coordinator for Business Education (1983–1978, 1976–1971)—approve all undergraduate courses offered at 7 Regional Centers and approved faculty; (2) Liaison Faculty and Consultant to the National Academy of the FBI Academy (1983-1972) and; (3) developed, sold, and conducted over 200 seminars for local, state, and national governments, and companies for McIntire School of Commerce and Continuing Education. *General Electric Company*—various management positions (1965–1961); *U.S. Navy Supply Corps* (SC)—Lt. (SC) USNR—assistant supply officer aboard nuclear support tender (1960–1957). **Publications** (1) *Monograph, An Assessment of Undergraduate Business Education in the United States* (with J.D. Hunger), 1980; (2) *Books*—60 books published; 14 books translated into 8 languages (*Arabic, Bahasa, Indonesia, Chinese, Chinese Simplified, Greek, Italian, Japanese, Portuguese and Thai*) (3) *Books*—co-author with J.D. Hunger - 5 active books: *Strategic Management and Business Policy*, 10th Edition (2006); *Cases in Strategic Management and Business Policy*, 10th Edition (2006); *Concepts in Strategic Management and Business Policy*, 10th Edition (2006); *Strategic Management and Business Policy,* 10th Edition; *International Edition* (2006); and *Essentials of Strategic Management*, 3rd Edition (2003). (3) *Co-editor*—Developments in Information Systems (1974) and Collective Bargaining in the Public Sector (1977) and (4) *Co-developer of software—ST*rategic *F*inancial *AN*alyzer (ST. FAN) (1993, 1990, 1989 - different versions.); (5) *Articles*—authored over 40 articles that have appeared in such journals as the *Journal of Management, Business Quarterly, Personnel Journal, SAM Advanced Management Journal, Journal of Retailing, International Journal of Management,* and the *Handbook of Business Strategy*. (6) *Cases*— have about 300 cases appearing in over 83 text and case books, as well as the *Business Case Journal, Journal of Management Case Studies, International Journal of Case Studies and Research and Case Research Journal*. *Awards:* (1) *Fellow* elected the *Society for Advancement of Management* in 2002 (2) *Fellow* elected by *North American Case Research Association* in 2000; (3) *Fellow* elected by *Text and Academic Authors Association* in 2000; (4) *1999 Phil Carroll Advancement of Management Award in Strategic Management* from the Society for

Advancement of Management; (5) *1999 McGuffey Award for Excellence and Longevity for Strategic Management and Business Policy - 6th Edition* from the Text and Academic Authors Association; (6) *1996/97 Teaching Incentive Program Award* for teaching undergraduate strategic management; (7) *Fulbright, 1996–97*, to Ireland but I had to turn it down; (8) *Endowed Chair, Ralph A. Beeton Professor*, at University of Virginia (1981–1985); (9) *Sesquicentennial Associateship* research grant from the Center for Advanced Studies at the University of Virginia, 1979–80; (10) *Small Business Administration* (Small Business Institute) supervised undergraduate team that won *District, Regional III, and Honorable Mention Awards*; and (11) awards for two articles. *Associations:* Dr. Wheelen currently serves on the Board of Directors of Adhia Mutual Fund, Society for Advancement of Management, and on the Editorial Board and the Associate Editor of *SAM Advanced Management Journal*. He served on the Board of Directors of Lazer Surgical Software, Inc, and Southern Management Association and on the Editorial Boards of the *Journal of Management* and *Journal of Management Case Studies, Journal of Retail Banking, Case Research Journal*, and *Business Case Journal*. He was Vice President of *Strategic Management* for the *Society for the Advancement of Management*, and President of the *North American Case Research Association*. Dr. Wheelen is a member of the *Academy of Management, Beta Gamma Sigma, Southern Management Association, North American Case Research Association, Society for Advancement of Management, Society for Case Research, Strategic Management Association, and World Association for Case Method Research and Application*. He has been listed in *Who's Who in Finance and Industry, Who's Who in the South and Southwest*, and *Who's Who in American Education*.

Cases in
Strategic Management

Cases in Strategic Management

CONTENTS

CASE 1

The Recalcitrant Director at Byte Products, Inc.:

Corporate Legality Versus Corporate Responsibility

Dan R. Dalton, Richard A. Cosier, and Cathy A. Enz

BYTE PRODUCTS, INC., IS PRIMARILY INVOLVED IN THE PRODUCTION OF ELECTRONIC components that are used in personal computers. Although such components might be found in a few computers in home use, Byte products are found most frequently in computers used for sophisticated business and engineering applications. Annual sales of these products have been steadily increasing over the past several years; Byte Products, Inc., currently has total sales of approximately $265 million.

Over the past six years, increases in yearly revenues have consistently reached 12%. Byte Products, Inc., headquartered in the midwestern United States, is regarded as one of the largest-volume suppliers of specialized components and is easily the industry leader, with some 32% market share. Unfortunately for Byte, many new firms—domestic and foreign—have entered the industry. A dramatic surge in demand, high profitability, and the relative ease of a new firm's entry into the industry explain in part the increased number of competing firms.

Although Byte management—and presumably shareholders as well—is very pleased about the growth of its markets, it faces a major problem: Byte simply cannot meet the demand for these components. The company currently operates three manufacturing facilities in various locations throughout the United States. Each of these plants operates three production shifts (24 hours per day), 7 days a week. This activity constitutes virtually all of the company's production capacity. Without an additional manufacturing plant, Byte simply cannot increase its output of components.

James M. Elliott, Chief Executive Officer and Chairman of the Board, recognizes the gravity of the problem. If Byte Products cannot continue to manufacture components in sufficient numbers to meet the demand, buyers will go elsewhere. Worse yet is the possibility that any continued lack of supply will encourage others to enter the market. As a long-term solution to this problem, the Board of Directors unanimously authorized the construction of a new, state-of-the-art manufacturing facility in the southwestern United States. When the planned capacity of this plant is added to that of the three current plants, Byte should be able to meet demand for many years to come. Unfortunately, an estimated three years will be required to complete the plant and bring it online.

Jim Elliott believes very strongly that this three-year period is far too long and has insisted that there also be a shorter-range, stopgap solution while the plant is under construction. The instability of the market and the pressure to maintain leader status are two factors contributing to Elliott's insistence on a more immediate solution. Without such a move, Byte management believes that it will lose market share and, again, attract competitors into the market.

Several Solutions

A number of suggestions for such a temporary measure were offered by various staff specialists but rejected by Elliott. For example, licensing Byte's product and process technology to other manufacturers in the short run to meet immediate demand was possible. This licensing authorization would be short term, or just until the new plant could come online. Top management, as well as the board, was uncomfortable with this solution for several reasons. They thought it unlikely that any manufacturer would shoulder the fixed costs of producing appropriate components for such a short term. Any manufacturer that would do so would charge a premium to recover its costs. This suggestion, obviously, would make Byte's own products available to its customers at an unacceptable price. Nor did passing any price increase to its customers seem sensible, for this too would almost certainly reduce Byte's market share as well as encourage further competition.

Overseas facilities and licensing also were considered but rejected. Before it became a publicly traded company, Byte's founders had decided that its manufacturing facilities would be domestic. Top management strongly felt that this strategy had served Byte well; moreover, Byte's majority stockholders (initial owners of the then privately held Byte) were not likely to endorse such a move. Beyond that, however, top management was reluctant to foreign license—or make available by any means the technologies for others to produce Byte products—as they could not then properly control patents. Top management feared that foreign licensing would essentially give away costly proprietary information regarding the company's highly efficient means of product development. There also was the potential for initial low product quality—whether produced domestically or otherwise—especially for such a short-run operation. Any reduction in quality, however brief, would threaten Byte's share of this sensitive market.

The Solution!

One recommendation that has come to the attention of the Chief Executive Officer could help solve Byte's problem in the short run. Certain members of his staff have notified him that an abandoned plant currently is available in Plainville, a small town in the northeastern United States. Before its closing eight years before, this plant was used primarily for the manufacture of electronic components. As is, it could not possibly be used to produce Byte products, but it could be inexpensively refitted to do so in as few as three months. Moreover, this plant is available at a very attractive price. In fact, discreet inquiries by Elliott's staff indicate that this plant could probably be leased immediately from its present owners because the building has been vacant for some eight years.

All the news about this temporary plant proposal, however, is not nearly so positive. Elliott's staff concedes that this plant will never be efficient and its profitability will be low. In addition, the Plainville location is a poor one in terms of high labor costs (the area is highly unionized), warehousing expenses, and inadequate transportation links to Byte's major markets and suppliers. Plainville is simply not a candidate for a long-term solution. Still, in the short run, a temporary plant could help meet the demand and might forestall additional competition.

The staff is persuasive and notes that this option has several advantages: (1) there is no need for any licensing, foreign or domestic, (2) quality control remains firmly in the company's hands, and (3) an increase in the product price will be unnecessary. The temporary plant, then, would be used for three years or so until the new plant could be built. Then the temporary plant would be immediately closed.

CEO Elliott is convinced.

Taking the Plan to the Board

The quarterly meeting of the Board of Directors is set to commence at 2:00 P.M. Jim Elliott has been reviewing his notes and agenda for the meeting most of the morning. The issue of the temporary plant is clearly the most important agenda item. Reviewing his detailed presentation of this matter, including the associated financial analyses, has occupied much of his time for several days. All the available information underscores his contention that the temporary plant in Plainville is the only responsible solution to the demand problems. No other option offers the same low level of risk and ensures Byte's status as industry leader.

At the meeting, after the board has dispensed with a number of routine matters, Jim Elliott turns his attention to the temporary plant. In short order, he advises the 11-member board (himself, 3 additional inside members, and 7 outside members) of his proposal to obtain and refit the existing plant to ameliorate demand problems in the short run, authorizes the construction of the new plant (the completion of which is estimated to take some three years), and plans to switch capacity from the temporary plant to the new one when it is operational. He also briefly reviews additional details concerning the costs involved, advantages of this proposal versus domestic or foreign licensing, and so on.

All the board members except one are in favor of the proposal. In fact, they are most enthusiastic; the overwhelming majority agree that the temporary plant is an excellent—even inspired—stopgap measure. Ten of the eleven board members seem relieved because the board was most reluctant to endorse any of the other alternatives that had been mentioned.

The single dissenter—T. Kevin Williams, an outside director—is, however, steadfast in his objections. He will not, under any circumstances, endorse the notion of the temporary plant and states rather strongly that "I will not be party to this nonsense, not now, not ever."

T. Kevin Williams, the senior executive of a major nonprofit organization, is normally a reserved and really quite agreeable person. This sudden, uncharacteristic burst of emotion clearly startles the remaining board members into silence. The following excerpt captures the ensuing, essentially one-on-one conversation between Williams and Elliott:

Williams: How many workers do your people estimate will be employed in the temporary plant?

Elliott: Roughly 1,200, possibly a few more.

Williams: I presume it would be fair, then, to say that, including spouses and children, something on the order of 4,000 people will be attracted to the community.

Elliott: I certainly would not be surprised.

Williams: If I understand the situation correctly, this plant closed just over eight years ago, and that closing had a catastrophic effect on Plainville. Isn't it true that a large portion of the community was employed by this plant?

Elliott: Yes, it was far and away the majority employer.

Williams: And most of these people have left the community, presumably to find employment elsewhere.

Elliott: Definitely, there was a drastic decrease in the area's population.

Williams: Are you concerned, then, that our company can attract the 1,200 employees to Plainville from other parts of New England?

Elliott: Not in the least. We are absolutely confident that we will attract 1,200—even more, for that matter virtually any number we need. That, in fact, is one of the chief advantages of this proposal. I would think that the community would be very pleased to have us there.

Williams: On the contrary, I would suspect that the community will rue the day we arrived. Beyond that, though, this plan is totally unworkable if we are candid. On the other hand, if we are less than candid, the proposal will work for us, but only at great cost to Plainville. In fact, quite frankly, the implications are appalling. Once again, I must enter my serious objections.

Elliott: I don't follow you.

Williams: The temporary plant would employ some 1,200 people. Again, this means the infusion of over 4,000 to the community and surrounding areas. Byte Products, however, intends to close this plant in three years or less. If Byte informs the community or the employees that the jobs are temporary, the proposal simply won't work. When the new people arrive in the community, there will be a need for more schools, instructors, utilities, housing, restaurants, and so forth. Obviously, if the banks and local government know that the plant is temporary, no funding will be made available for these projects and certainly no credit for the new employees to buy homes, appliances, automobiles, and so forth.

If, on the other hand, Byte Products does not tell the community of its "temporary" plans, the project can go on. But, in several years when the plant closes (and we here have agreed today that it will close), we will have created a ghost town. The tax base of the community will have been destroyed; property values will decrease precipitously; practically the whole town will be unemployed. This proposal will place Byte Products in an untenable position and in extreme jeopardy.

Elliott: Are you suggesting that this proposal jeopardizes us legally? If so, it should be noted that the legal department has reviewed this proposal in its entirety and has indicated no problem.

Williams: No! I don't think we are dealing with an issue of legality here. In fact, I don't doubt for a minute that this proposal is altogether legal. I do, however, resolutely believe that this proposal constitutes gross irresponsibility.

I think this decision has captured most of my major concerns. These along with a host of collateral problems associated with this project lead me to strongly suggest that you and the balance of the board reconsider and not endorse this proposal. Byte Products must find another way.

The Dilemma

After a short recess, the board meeting reconvened. Presumably because of some discussion during the recess, several other board members indicated that they were no longer inclined to support the proposal. After a short period of rather heated discussion, the following exchange took place:

Elliott: It appears to me that any vote on this matter is likely to be very close. Given the gravity of our demand capacity problem, I must insist that the stockholders' equity be protected. We cannot wait three years; that is clearly out of the question. I still feel that licensing—domestic or foreign—is not in our long-term interests for any number of reasons, some of which have been discussed here. On the other hand, I do not want to take this project forward on the strength of a mixed vote. A vote of 6–5 or 7–4, for example, does not indicate that the board is remotely close to being of one mind. Mr. Williams, is there a compromise to be reached?

Williams: Respectfully, I have to say no. If we tell the truth—namely, the temporary nature of our operations—the proposal is simply not viable. If we are less than candid in this respect, we do grave damage to the community as well as to our image. It seems to me that we can only go one way or the other. I don't see a middle ground.

CASE 2
The Wallace Group

Laurence J. Stybel

FRANCES RAMPAR, PRESIDENT OF RAMPAR ASSOCIATES, DRUMMED HER FINGERS ON THE desk. Scattered before her were her notes. She had to put the pieces together in order to make an effective sales presentation to Harold Wallace.

Hal Wallace was the President of The Wallace Group. He had asked Rampar to conduct a series of interviews with some key Wallace Group employees, in preparation for a possible consulting assignment for Rampar Associates.

During the past three days, Rampar had been talking with some of these key people and had received background material about the company. The problem was not in finding the problem. The problem was that there were too many problems!

Background on The Wallace Group

The Wallace Group, Inc., is a diversified company dealing in the manufacture and development of technical products and systems (see **Exhibit 1**). The company currently consists of three operational groups and a corporate staff. The three groups include Electronics, Plastics, and Chemicals, each operating under the direction of a Group Vice President (see **Exhibits 2, 3,** and **4**). The company generates $70 million in sales as a manufacturer of plastics, chemical products, and electronic components and systems. Principal sales are to large contractors in governmental and automotive markets. With respect to sales volume, Plastics and Chemicals are approximately equal in size, and both of them together equal the size of the Electronics Group.

Electronics offers competence in the areas of microelectronics, electromagnetic sensors, antennas, microwave, and minicomputers. Presently, these skills are devoted primarily to the engineering and manufacture of countermeasure equipment for aircraft. This includes radar detection systems that allow an aircraft crew to know that they are being tracked by radar

This case was prepared by Dr. Laurence J. Stybel. It was prepared for class discussion rather than to illustrate either effective or ineffective handling of an administrative situation. Unauthorized duplication of copyright materials is a violation of federal law. This case was edited for SMBP-9th and 10th Editions. The copyright holders are solely responsible for case content. Reprint permission is solely granted to the publisher, Prentice Hall, for the books, Strategic Management and Business Policy—10th Edition (and the International version of this book) and Cases in Strategic Management and Business Policy—10th Edition by copyright holders, Dr. Laurence J. Stybel. Any other publication of this case (translation, any form of electronic or other media), or sold (any form of partnership) to another publisher will be in violation of copyright laws, unless the copyright holder has granted an additional written reprint permission.

Exhibit 1
An Excerpt from
the Annual Report

To the Shareholders:

This past year was one of definite accomplishment for The Wallace Group, although with some admitted soft spots. This is a period of consolidation, of strengthening our internal capacity for future growth and development. Presently, we are in the process of creating a strong management team to meet the challenges we will set for the future.

Despite our failure to achieve some objectives, we turned a profit of $3,521,000 before taxes, which was a growth over the previous year's earnings. And we have declared a dividend for the fifth consecutive year, albeit one that is less than the year before. However, the retention of earnings is imperative if we are to lay a firm foundation for future accomplishment.

Currently, The Wallace Group has achieved a level of stability. We have a firm foothold in our current markets, and we could elect to simply enact strong internal controls and maximize our profits. However, this would not be a growth strategy. Instead, we have chosen to adopt a more aggressive posture for the future, to reach out into new markets wherever possible and to institute the controls necessary to move forward in a planned and orderly fashion.

The Electronics Group performed well this past year and is engaged in two major programs under Defense Department contracts. These are developmental programs that provide us with the opportunity for ongoing sales upon testing of the final product. Both involve the creation of tactical display systems for aircraft being built by Lombard Aircraft for the Navy and the Air Force. Future potential sales from these efforts could amount to approximately $56 million over the next five years. Additionally, we are developing technical refinements to older, already installed systems under Army Department contracts.

In the future, we will continue to offer our technological competence in such tactical display systems and anticipate additional breakthroughs and success in meeting the demands of this market. However, we also believe that we have unique contributions to make to other markets, and to that end we are making the investments necessary to expand our opportunities.

Plastics also turned in a solid performance this past year and has continued to be a major supplier to Chrysler, Martin Tool, Foster Electric, and, of course, to our Electronics Group. The market for this group continues to expand, and we believe that additional investments in this group will allow us to seize a larger share of the future.

Chemicals' performance, admittedly, has not been as satisfactory as anticipated during the past year. However, we have been able to realize a small amount of profit from this operation and to halt what was a potentially dangerous decline in profits. We believe that this situation is only temporary and that infusions of capital for developing new technology, plus the streamlining of operations, has stabilized the situation. The next step will be to begin more aggressive marketing to capitalize on the group's basic strengths.

Overall, the outlook seems to be one of modest but profitable growth. The near term will be one of creating the technology and controls necessary for developing our market offerings and growing in a planned and purposeful manner. Our improvement efforts in the various company groups can be expected to take hold over the years with positive effect on results.

We wish to express our appreciation to all those who participated in our efforts this past year.

Harold Wallace
Chairman and President

units on the ground, on ships, or on other aircraft. Further, the company manufactures displays that provide the crew with a visual "fix" on where they are relative to the radar units that are tracking them.

In addition to manufacturing tested and proven systems developed in the past, The Wallace Group is currently involved in two major and two minor programs, all involving display systems. The Navy-A Program calls for the development of a display system for a tactical fighter plane; Air Force-B is another such system for an observation plane. Ongoing production orders are anticipated following flight testing. The other two minor programs, Army-LG and OBT-37, involve the incorporation of new technology into existing aircraft systems.

Exhibit 2 Organizational Chart: The Wallace Group (Electronics)

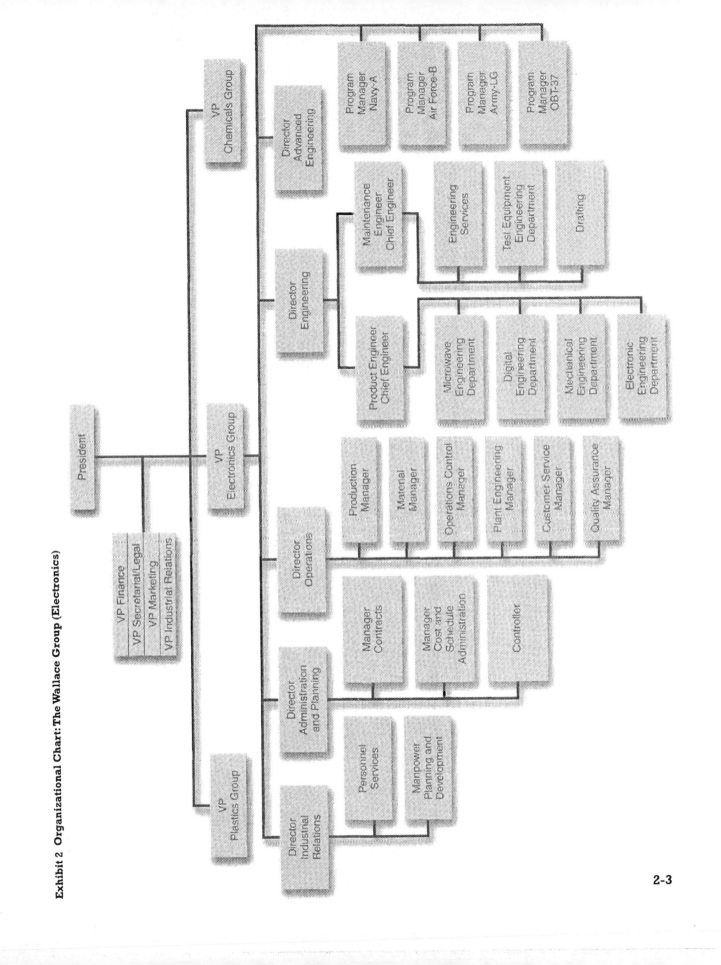

Exhibit 3
The Wallace Group
(Chemicals)

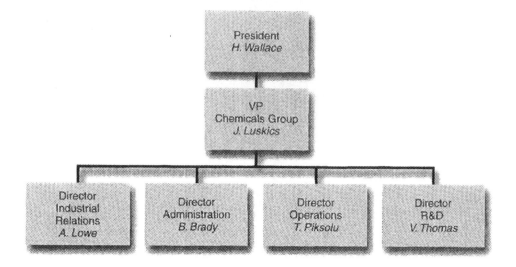

The Plastics Group manufactures plastic components utilized by the electronics, automotive, and other industries requiring plastic products. These include switches, knobs, keys, insulation materials, and so on, used in the manufacture of electronic equipment and other small made-to-order components installed in automobiles, planes, and other products.

The Chemicals Group produces chemicals used in the development of plastics. It supplies bulk chemicals to the Plastics Group and other companies. These chemicals are then injected into molds or extruded to form a variety of finished products.

Exhibit 4
The Wallace Group
(Plastics)

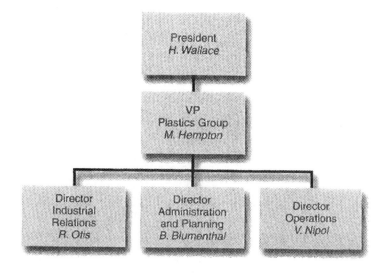

History of The Wallace Group

Each of the three groups began as a sole proprietorship under the direct operating control of an owner/manager. Several years ago, Harold Wallace, owner of the original electronics company, determined to undertake a program of diversification. Initially, he attempted to expand his market through product development and line extensions entirely within the electronics industry. However, because of initial problems, he drew back and sought other opportunities. Wallace's primary concern was his almost total dependence on defense-related contracts. He had felt for some time that he should take some strong action to gain a foothold in the private markets. The first major opportunity that seemed to satisfy his various requirements was the acquisition of a former supplier, a plastics company whose primary market was not defense-related. The company's owner desired to sell his operation and retire. At the time, Wallace's debt structure was such that he could not manage the acquisition and so he had to attract equity capital. He was able to gather a relatively small group of investors and form a closed corporation. The group established a Board of Directors with Wallace as Chairman and President of the new corporate entity.

With respect to operations, little changed. Wallace continued direct operational control over the Electronics Group. As holder of 60% of the stock, he maintained effective control over policy and operations. However, because of his personal interests, the Plastics Group, now under the direction of a newly hired Vice President, Martin Hempton, was left mainly to its own devices except for yearly progress reviews by the President. All Wallace asked at the time was that the Plastics Group continue its profitable operation, which it did.

Several years ago, Wallace and the board decided to diversify further because two-thirds of their business was still defense dependent. They learned that one of the major suppliers of the Plastics Group, a chemical company, was on the verge of bankruptcy. The company's owner, Jerome Luskics, agreed to sell. However, this acquisition required a public stock offering, with most of the funds going to pay off debts incurred by the three groups, especially the Chemicals Group. The net result was that Wallace now holds 45% of The Wallace Group and Jerome Luskics 5%, with the remainder distributed among the public.

Organization and Personnel

Presently, Harold Wallace serves as Chairman and President of The Wallace Group. The Electronics Group had been run by LeRoy Tuscher, who just resigned as Vice President. Hempton continued as Vice President of Plastics, and Luskics served as Vice President of the Chemicals Group.

Reflecting the requirements of a corporate perspective and approach, a corporate staff has grown up, consisting of Vice Presidents for Finance, Secretarial/Legal, Marketing, and Industrial Relations. This staff has assumed many functions formerly associated with the group offices.

Because these positions are recent additions, many of the job accountabilities are still being defined. Problems have arisen over the responsibilities and relationships between corporate and group positions. President Wallace has settled most of the disputes himself because of the inability of the various parties to resolve differences among themselves.

Current Trends

Presently, there is a mood of lethargy and drift within The Wallace Group. Most managers feel that each of the three groups functions as an independent company. And, with respect to group performance, not much change or progress has been made in recent years. Electronics and Plastics are still stable and profitable, but both lack growth in markets and profits. The infusion of capital breathed new life and hope into the Chemicals operation but did not solve most of the old problems and failings that had caused its initial decline. For all these reasons, Wallace decided that strong action was necessary. His greatest disappointment was with the Electronics Group, in which he had placed high hopes for future development. Thus he acted by requesting and getting the Electronics Group Vice President's resignation. Hired from a computer company to replace LeRoy Tuscher, Jason Matthews joined The Wallace Group a week ago.

As of last week, Wallace's annual net sales were $70 million. By group they were:

Electronics	$35,000,000
Plastics	$20,000,000
Chemicals	$15,000,000

Exhibit 5
Selected Portions of a Transcribed Interview with H. Wallace

Rampar: What is your greatest problem right now?

Wallace: That's why I called you in! Engineers are a high-strung, temperamental lot. Always complaining. It's hard to take them seriously.

Last month we had an annual stockholder's meeting. We have an Employee Stock Option Plan, and many of our long-term employees attended the meeting. One of my managers—and I won't mention any names—introduced a resolution calling for the resignation of the President—me!

The vote was defeated. But, of course, I own 45% of the stock!

Now I realize that there could be no serious attempt to get rid of me. Those who voted for the resolution were making a dramatic effort to show me how upset they are with the way things are going.

I could fire those employees who voted against me. I was surprised by how many did. Some of my key people were in that group. Perhaps I ought to stop and listen to what they are saying.

Businesswise, I think we're O.K. Not great, but O.K. Last year we turned in a profit of $3.5 million before taxes, which was a growth over previous years' earnings. We declared a dividend for the fifth consecutive year.

We're currently working on the creation of a tactical display system for aircraft being built by Lombard Aircraft for the Navy and the Air Force. If Lombard gets the contract to produce the prototype, future sales could amount to $56 million over the next five years.

Why are they complaining?

Rampar: You must have thoughts on the matter.

Wallace: I think the issue revolves around how we manage people. It's a personnel problem. You were highly recommended as someone with expertise in high-technology human resource management.

I have some ideas on what is the problem. But I'd like you to do an independent investigation and give me your findings. Give me a plan of action.

Don't give me a laundry list of problems, Fran. Anyone can do that. I want a set of priorities I should focus on during the next year. I want a clear action plan from you. And I want to know how much this plan is going to cost me!

Other than that, I'll leave you alone and let you talk to anyone in the company you want.

**Exhibit 6
Selected Portions
of a Transcribed
Interview with
Frank Campbell,
Vice President
of Industrial
Relations**

Rampar: What is your greatest problem right now?

Campbell: Trying to contain my enthusiasm over the fact that Wallace brought you in! Morale is really poor here. Hal runs this place like a one man operation, when it's grown too big for that. It took a palace revolt to finally get him to see the depths of the resentment. Whether he'll do anything about it, that's another matter.

Rampar: What would you like to see changed?

Campbell: Other than a new President?

Rampar: Uh-huh.

Campbell: We badly need a management development program for our group. Because of our growth, we have been forced to promote technical people to management positions who have had no prior managerial experience. Mr. Tuscher agreed on the need for a program, but Hal Wallace vetoed the idea because developing such a program would be too expensive. I think it is too expensive *not* to move ahead on this.

Rampar: Anything else?

Campbell: The IEWU negotiations have been extremely tough this time around, due to excessive demands they have been making. Union pay scales are already pushing up against our foreman salary levels, and foremen are being paid high in their salary ranges. This problem, coupled with union insistence on a no-layoff clause, is causing us fits. How can we keep all our workers when we have production equipment on order that will eliminate 20% of our assembly positions?

Rampar: Wow.

Campbell: We have been sued by a rejected candidate for a position on the basis of discrimination. She claimed our entrance qualifications are excessive because we require shorthand. There is some basis for this statement since most reports are given to secretaries in handwritten form or on audio cassettes. In fact, we have always required it and our executives want their secretaries to have skill in taking dictation. Not only is this case taking time, but I need to reconsider if any of our position entrance requirements, in fact, are excessive. I am sure we do not want another case like this one.

Rampar: That puts The Wallace Group in a vulnerable position, considering the amount of government work you do.

Campbell: We have a tremendous recruiting backlog, especially for engineering positions. Either our pay scales are too low, our job specs are too high, or we are using the wrong recruiting channels. Kane and Smith [Director of Engineering and Director of Advanced Systems] keep rejecting everyone we send down there as being unqualified.

Rampar: Gee.

Campbell: Being head of human resources around here is a tough job. We don't act. We react.

On a consolidated basis, the financial highlights of the past two years are as follows:

	Last Year	Two Years Ago
Net sales	$70,434,000	$69,950,000
Income (pre-tax)	3,521,000	3,497,500
Income (after-tax)	2,760,500	1,748,750
Working capital	16,200,000	16,088,500
Shareholders' equity	39,000,000	38,647,000
Total assets	59,869,000	59,457,000
Long-term debt	4,350,000	3,500,000
Per Share of Common Stock		
Net income	$.37	$.36
Cash dividends paid	.15	.25

Of the net income, approximately 70% came from Electronics, 25% from Plastics, and 5% from Chemicals.

Exhibit 7
Selected Portions
of a Transcribed
Interview with
Matthew Smith,
Director of
Advanced Systems

Rampar: What is your greatest problem right now?

Smith: Corporate brass keeps making demands on me and others that don't relate to the job we are trying to get done. They say that the information they need is to satisfy corporate planning and operations review requirements, but they don't seem to recognize how much time and effort is required to provide this information. Sometimes it seems like they are generating analyses, reports, and requests for data just to keep themselves busy. Someone should be evaluating how critical these corporate staff activities really are. To me and the Electronics Group, these activities are unnecessary.

An example is the Vice President, Marketing (L. Holt), who keeps asking us for supporting data so he can prepare a corporate marketing strategy. As you know, we prepare our own group marketing strategic plans annually, but using data and formats that are oriented to our needs, rather than Corporate's. This planning activity, which occurs at the same time as Corporate's, coupled with heavy work loads on current projects, makes us appear to Holt as though we are being unresponsive.

Somehow we need to integrate our marketing planning efforts between our group and Corporate. This is especially true if our group is to successfully grow in nondefense-oriented markets and products. We do need corporate help, but not arbitrary demands for information that divert us from putting together effective marketing strategies for our group.

I am getting too old to keep fighting these battles.

Rampar: This is a long-standing problem?

Smith: You bet! Our problems are fairly classic in the high-tech field. I've been at other companies and they're not much better. We spend so much time firefighting, we never really get organized. Everything is done on an ad hoc basis.

I'm still waiting for tomorrow.

Exhibit 8
Selected Portions
of a Transcribed
Interview with
Ralph Kane,
Director of
Engineering

Rampar: What is your greatest problem right now?

Kane: Knowing you were coming, I wrote them down. They fall into four areas:

1. Our salary schedules are too low to attract good, experienced EEs. We have been told by our Vice President (Frank Campbell) that corporate policy is to hire new people below the salary grade midpoint. All qualified candidates are making more than that now and in some case are making more than our grade maximums. I think our Project Engineer job is rated too low.

2. Chemicals Group asked for and the former Electronics Vice President (Tuscher) agreed to "lend" six of our best EEs to help solve problems it is having developing a new battery. That is great for the Chemicals Group, but meanwhile how do we solve the engineering problems that have cropped up in our Navy-A and OBT-37 programs?

3. As you know, Matt Smith (Director of Advanced Systems) is retiring in six months. I depend heavily on his group for technical expertise, and in some areas he depends heavily on some of my key engineers. I have lost some people to the Chemicals Group, and Matt has been trying to lend me some of his people to fill in. But he and his staff have been heavily involved in marketing planning and trying to identify or recruit a qualified successor long enough before his retirement to be able to train him or her. The result is that his people are up to their eyeballs in doing their own stuff and cannot continue to help me meet my needs.

4. IR has been preoccupied with union negotiations in the plant and has not had time to help me deal with this issue of management planning. Campbell is working on some kind of system that will help deal with this kind of problem and prevent them in the future. That is great, but I need help now—not when his "system" is ready.

Exhibit 9
Selected Portions
of a Transcribed
Interview with
Brad Lowell,
Program Manager,
Navy-A

Rampar: What is your . . .?

Lowell: . . . great problem? I'll tell you what it is. I still cannot get the support I need from Kane in Engineering. He commits and then doesn't deliver, and it has me quite concerned. The excuse now is that in "his judgment," Sid Wright needs the help for the Air Force program more than I do. Wright's program is one week ahead of schedule, so I disagree with "his judgment." Kane keeps complaining about not having enough people.

Rampar: Why do you think Kane says he doesn't have enough people?

Lowell: Because Hal Wallace is a tight-fisted S.O.B. who won't let us hire the people we need!

Exhibit 10
Selected Portions of a Transcribed Interview with Phil Jones, Director of Administration and Planning

Rampar: What is your greatest problem right now?

Jones: Wheel spinning—that's our problem! We talk about expansion, but we don't do anything about it. Are we serious or not?

For example, a bid request came in from a prime contractor seeking help in developing a countermeasure system for a medium-range aircraft. They needed an immediate response and concept proposal in one week. Tuscher just sat on my urgent memo to him asking for a go/no go decision on bidding. I could not give the contractor an answer (because no decision came from Tuscher), so they gave up on us.

I am frustrated because (1) we lost an opportunity we were "naturals" to win, and (2) my personal reputation was damaged because I was unable to answer the bid request. Okay, Tuscher's gone now, but we need to develop some mechanism so an answer to such a request can be made quickly.

Another thing, our MIS is being developed by the Corporate Finance Group. More wheel spinning! They are telling us what information we need rather than asking us what we want! E. Kay (our Group Controller) is going crazy trying to sort out the input requirements they need for the system and understanding the complicated reports that came out. Maybe this new system is great as a technical achievement, but what good is it to us if we can't use it?

Exhibit 11
Selected Portions of a Transcribed Interview with Burt Williams, Director of Operations

Rampar: What is your biggest problem right now?

Williams: One of the biggest problems we face right now stems from corporate policy regarding transfer pricing. I realize we are "encouraged" to purchase our plastics and chemicals from our sister Wallace groups, but we are also committed to making a profit! Because manufacturing problems in those groups have forced them to raise their prices, should we suffer the consequences? We can get some materials cheaper from other suppliers. How can we meet our volume and profit targets when we are saddled with noncompetitive material costs?

Rampar: And if that issue was settled to your satisfaction, then would things be O.K.?

Williams: Although out of my direct function, it occurs to me that we are not planning effectively our efforts to expand into nondefense areas. With minimal alteration to existing production methods, we can develop both end-use products (e.g., small motors, traffic control devices, and microwave transceivers for highway emergency communications) and components (e.g., LED and LCD displays, police radar tracking devices, and word processing system memory and control devices) with large potential markets.

The problems in this regard are:

1. Matt Smith (Director, Advanced Systems) is retiring and has had only defense-related experience. Therefore, he is not leading any product development efforts along these lines.
2. We have no marketing function at the group level to develop a strategy, define markets, and research and develop product opportunities.
3. Even if we had a marketing plan and products for industrial/commercial application, we have no sales force or rep network to sell the stuff.

Maybe I am way off base, but it seems to me we need a Groups/Marketing/Sales function to lead us in this business expansion effort. It should be headed by an experienced technical marketing manager with a proven track record in developing such products and markets.

Rampar: Have you discussed your concerns with others?

Williams: I have brought these ideas up with Mr. Matthews and others at the Group Management Committee. No one else seems interested in pursuing this concept, but they won't say this outright and don't say why it should not be addressed. I guess that in raising the idea with you I am trying to relieve some of my frustrations.

The Problem Confronting Frances Rampar

As Rampar finished reviewing her notes (see **Exhibits 5–11**), she kept reflecting on what Hal Wallace had told her:

> Don't give me a laundry list of problems, Fran. Anyone can do that. I want a set of priorities I should focus on during the next year. I want a clear action plan from you. And I want to know how much this plan is going to cost me!

Fran Rampar again drummed her fingers on the desk.

CASE 3

The Audit

John A. Kilpatrick, Gamewell D. Gantt, and George A. Johnson

SUE WAS PUZZLED AS TO WHAT COURSE OF ACTION TO TAKE. SHE HAD RECENTLY STARTED her job with a national CPA firm, and she was already confronted with a problem that could affect her future with the firm. On an audit, she encountered a client who had been treating payments to a large number, but by no means a majority, of its workers as payments to independent contractors. This practice saves the client the payroll taxes that would otherwise be due on the payments if the workers were classified as employees. In Sue's judgment this was improper as well as illegal and should have been noted in the audit. She raised the issue with John, the senior accountant to whom she reported. He thought it was a possible problem but did not seem willing to do anything about it. He encouraged her to talk to the partner in charge if she didn't feel satisfied.

She thought about the problem for a considerable time before approaching the partner in charge. The ongoing professional education classes she had received from her employer emphasized the ethical responsibilities that she had as a CPA and the fact that her firm endorsed adherence to high ethical standards. This finally swayed her to pursue the issue with the partner in charge of the audit. The visit was most unsatisfactory. Paul, the partner, virtually confirmed her initial reaction that the practice was wrong, but he said that many other companies in the industry follow such a practice. He went on to say that if an issue was made of it, Sue would lose the account, and he was not about to take such action. She came away from the meeting with the distinct feeling that had she chosen to pursue the issue, she would have created an enemy.

Sue still felt disturbed and decided to discuss the problem with some of her co-workers. She approached Bill and Mike, both of whom had been working for the firm for a couple of years. They were familiar with the problem because they had encountered the same issue when doing the audit the previous year. They expressed considerable concern that if she went over the head of the partner in charge of the audit, they could be in big trouble since they had failed to question the practice during the previous audit. They said that they realized it was probably wrong, but they went ahead because it had been ignored in previous years, and they knew their supervisor wanted them to ignore it again this year. They didn't want to cause problems. They encouraged Sue to be a "team player" and drop the issue.

This case was prepared by Professors John A. Kilpatrick, Gamewell D. Gantt, and George A. Johnson of the College of Business, Idaho State University. The names of the organization, individual, location, and/or financial information have been disguised to preserve the organization's desire for anonymity. This case was edited for SMBP-9th and the 10th Editions. Presented to and accepted by the refereed Society for Case Research. All rights reserved to the authors and the SCR. Copyright © 1995 by John A. Kilpatrick, Gamewell D. Gantt, and George A. Johnson. This case may not be reproduced without written permission of the copyright holders. Reprinted by permission.

CASE 4

GlaxoSmithKline's Retaliation Against Cross-Border Sales of Prescription Drugs

Sara Smith Shull and Rebecca J. Morris

WAR WAS IMMINENT WITH IRAQ, THE RELENTLESS BEAR MARKET WAS ENTERING ITS FOURTH year, personal savings were at an all-time low, and the American consumer was valiantly growing the economy at a meager 1.4% annually. Against this backdrop healthcare costs were spiraling upward year after year. The aging of the largest single population cohort in American history (the Baby Boomers) resulted in greater utilization of healthcare services. Concurrently, the cost of the services themselves (prescription drugs, physician visits, and hospitalizations) was increasing. Cumulatively, these services were responsible for a double-digit increase (10% per capita) in healthcare costs in 2001, the first time in more than a decade that healthcare costs had accelerated so rapidly.[1] Reaching $1.4 trillion, healthcare costs escalated to 14.1% of the gross domestic product (GDP).[2]

GlaxoSmithKline plc (GSK), a prescription drug and personal hygiene consumer products company based in Britain, found itself coping with a new challenge during this period as Americans, especially senior citizens, developed various tactics to deal with the rising drug costs. Discovering that prescription drugs could be acquired from Canadian pharmacies via the Internet at prices substantially lower than those available at pharmacies in the United States, resourceful Americans began to consistently adopt the practice.[3] The flow of drugs from Canadian pharmacies to American consumers captured the attention of GSK and their concern grew as the practice spread. Late in 2002 they attempted to curb the flow of prescription drugs out of Canada into the United States by limiting the drugs shipped to Canadian pharmacies.[4] This challenged pharmacies to provide adequate prescription product for their Canadian customers while shipping product to American customers south of the border. However, GSK discovered Americans, especially seniors, to be loud, persistent, and effective protesters when they threatened to limit drug supplies to Canadian pharmacies. Kate Stahl, the 83-year-old metro president of the Minnesota Senior Federation was defiant: "People in America, including Minnesotans, pay the world's highest prices for drugs. Now, if they (GSK) are going to boycott us, we're going to boycott them."[5] Una Moore echoed support for sanctions against GSK. A retired licensed practical nurse with no pension, she had been compelled to purchase drugs from Canada for years. "I'm terrified that the other companies will follow Glaxo. We have to get together and find a way to beat these guys."[6]

The Basis for GlaxoSmithKline's Decision

The late 1990s and the early years of the 21st century set the stage for GSK's decision. Seeking relief from escalating healthcare costs, many Americans, especially senior citizens, sought alternate channels for acquiring the prescription medicines upon which they increasingly relied. Publicizing the increasing costs and promoting a political agenda, U.S. congressmen from states along the Canadian border began to host bus trips for senior citizens across the border in order to procure prescription drugs at costs as much as 80% lower than those available in the United States. Logistically, relatively small numbers could participate in this practice and make savings on drugs worth the cost of the trip. Americans traveling in Europe, Canada, and Mexico might also acquire small amounts of prescription drugs for personal use at a cost much lower than that available in the United States. However, it was not until the Internet became routinely available in homes, public libraries, and kiosks that prescription drugs from around the world were available at the touch of a button to Americans. In a relatively simple process, seniors and others could take a prescription written by an American physician, send it to a Canadian pharmacy, and within days receive their drugs at home at a substantial discount to what that product cost in the United States.[7] The practice grew rapidly in the early years of the 21st century, as political agendas and budgetary constraints stalled a Medicare prescription drug benefit in the United States. By late 2002, over a million senior citizens indicated that they were seeking prescription drugs over the Internet from an estimated 123 Canadian pharmacies. Precise sales figures attributed to the practice were private record; however, Manitoba pharmacies alone claimed $250 million in sales from approximately 400,000 U.S. customers during 2002.[8] Prices for GSK drugs from a variety of sources are provided in **Exhibit 1**.

GlaxoSmithKline was beginning to feel the economic effects of American consumers acquiring prescription drugs from Canada at lower cost, circumventing the traditional pre-

Exhibit 1 Comparative Patient Drug Costs for GlaxoSmithKline Products (Dollar amounts in U.S. dollars)

Drugs	U.S.A	Canada (In $US)	Insurance Copay
Advair 50/500mcg diskus	$206.99	$103.18	$30.00–$45.00
Augmentin 875/125mg X28 tabs	66.76	38.72	15.00–25.00
Avandia 8mg X 100 tabs	313.52	219.46	30.00–45.00
Flovent 250mcg inhaler	121.99	63.27	30.00–45.00
Imitrex 50mg X6 injections	117.99	67.84	30.00–45.00
Paxil 30 mg X30 tabs	107.99	47.41	$30.00–$45.00

Note: U.S. prices were taken from a Walgreens Pharmacy in the Minneapolis, Minnesota, area on February 19, 2003. Prices for Augmentin and Avandia were taken from the RailwayRxAssist web site (*www.RailwayRxAssist.com*). Canadian prices do not include shipping. The Canadian exchange rate for U.S. dollars on February 19, 2003, was 0.656938.

scription drug market. Therefore, responding to the growing popularity of cheaper Canadian drugs among American consumers, GSK defended premium pricing in America. "Prescription drugs are generally cheaper in Canada (than the U.S.) primarily because prices are controlled and capped by Canada's Patented Medicines Prices Review Board (through a national health insurance plan)," reiterated the management of GSK on a corporate Website.[9] "But even without price controls, prescription medicines, like most other products, would probably still be cheaper in Canada due to lower wages and buying power there. A Dodge Caravan costs $31,000 in the U.S. but just $21,000 in U.S. dollars in Canada," the site continued. Also, in January 2003 in an action GSK closely compared to that of other consumer good manufacturers, they threatened to stop supplying drug wholesalers and retailers in Canada, unless Canadian pharmacies ceased their cross-border sales. "In response to (U.S.) dealers importing cars from Canada to resell, some U.S. auto-makers threatened to void their warranties or hold back other incentives from the (offending) dealers," declared GSK,[10] ostensibly providing a rationale for their own actions. GSK delayed the deadline once, allowing Canadian pharmacies more time to "self-certify" that they were not exporting drugs to the United States. Then GSK finally cut off the product supply near the end of February 2003. GSK was the only pharmaceutical manufacturer that initiated such action, although all companies selling prescription drugs in America were affected.[11]

The reaction to the GSK decision was immediate and vocal, affecting the public image of the company worldwide. Perceived as mean-spirited, bullying, greedy, and insensitive, GSK faced angry consumers, who for years had tolerated double-digit price increases for their medicines.[12] Detroit resident William Finton, a 65-year-old semi-retired accountant who purchased chronic medications from Canadian pharmacies, remarked, "It really doesn't take a rocket scientist to figure out that they are making excessive profits. Of course they have a lot of expenses in producing these drugs, but once they make the cost back, it really shouldn't be this expensive."[13] "They are beginning to make the tobacco companies look good," quipped Todd Lebor, an equity analyst for Morningstar.[14] Joe Graedon, an author of a syndicated column dedicated to drug issues, wrote of GSK's crackdown to limit Canadian drug supply, "It's like attacking apple pie, Mom, and Chevrolet."[15]

A coalition of ten leading American and Canadian healthcare and business organizations began a national advertising campaign harshly criticizing the drug maker for its ban (Exhibit 2). They maintained that GSK was keeping Americans, especially seniors, from accessing more affordable prescription medications than could be acquired in the United States.[16] Peter Wyckoff, executive director of the Minnesota Senior Federation, a coalition member, declared, "we see this as an issue of unbridled greed, hurting the health and safety of American citizens who have no choice but to look at less costly alternatives (than drugs available in the United States)."[17] The coalition members collectively purchased a full-page ad in the New York Times encouraging healthcare professionals and consumers to pressure GSK to reverse their decision. They insisted that GSK renew delivery of their products to Canadian pharmacies, despite a high likelihood of exportation across the border to the United States. The coalition encouraged readers to contact their legislators and the CEO of GSK, Jean Pierre Garnier, to complain about the ban. They also encouraged senior citizens to consult with their pharmacists and physicians to investigate whether comparable generic agents were available, or whether patients could be switched to drugs manufactured by GSK's competitors and achieve the same therapeutic goal. Consumers were encouraged to sell off GSK stock and boycott over-the-counter or personal hygiene products manufactured by GSK. Jimm Axline, president of the National Association of the Terminally Ill, a nonprofit organization serving families facing terminal illness said,

> With this campaign, we're delivering our message loud and clear to Glaxo, that you cannot steal access to affordable drugs from those who are dying and expect to get away with it. We're urging consumers and healthcare professionals to call their Senators and Congressmen and Glaxo's U.S. CEO, and tell them to give our patients back their affordable drugs.[18]

Exhibit 2
Coalition Ad
Critical of Glaxo

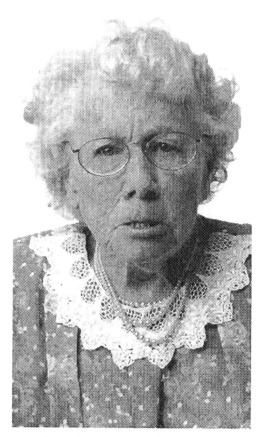

Glaxo is taking away your right to affordable prescription drugs!

The world's second largest drug maker, GlaxoSmithKline, has stopped providing its drugs to Canadian pharmacies and wholesalers who supply an estimated one million uninsured and underinsured American seniors with affordable, high quality medications. If Glaxo gets its way, all drugmakers will likely follow its lead and eventually strip seniors of their well-established right to access affordable drugs from alternative sources.

Fight Back to Stop Glaxo Now:

1 Contact the U.S. Congress switchboard in Washington, DC at 1-202-224-3121, ask for the names and phone numbers of your House and Senate members, and call them to share your concerns. Or, visit www.congress.org to learn your legislators' e-mail addresses and send them a note.

2 Call Glaxo's toll-free consumer hotline at 1-888-825-5249, press 3, then press 2, and give your views to the live operator.

3 Write Glaxo's U.S. CEO and tell him to stop the restrictions being placed on Canadian drugs:
Mr. Jean-Pierre Garnier, CEO, GSK U.S. Pharmaceuticals, Five Moore Drive, P.O. Box 13398, Research Triangle Park, NC. 27709

4 If you have been buying your Glaxo drugs from a Canadian pharmacy and cannot afford the high U.S. pharmacy prices, check with your doctor to see if there is a comparable drug made by another drugmaker that you can switch to.

5 Consider selling any Glaxo stock that you currently hold either directly or through a pension fund. Glaxo stock is listed as "GSK" on the New York Stock Exchange.

6 You may want to consider switching from these Glaxo over-the-counter treatments to those made by other manufacturers. The company's products include the following brands: Beano, Citrucel, Contac, Geritol, Sominex, Sensodyne, Polident, Poligrip, Nytol, Nicoderm, Nicorette, Tegrin, Tums and Vivarin.

This message is brought to you by these American and Canadian organizations who work to keep affordable alternative-sourced drugs available as a safe, reliable and low-cost option for all Americans. The person depicted is a model and the photo is used for illustrative purposes only.

For more information or if your organization is interested in joining the coalition, call 1-773-769-1616

GSK spokeswoman Nancy Pekarek maintained,

> This is not a financial issue for GlaxoSmithKline. The amount of money we estimate is involved with Internet sales from Canada is less than one percent of our sales in the United States. But, obviously Internet sales are growing, and, as the business increases, so does the potential risk to patients.[19]

Meanwhile, the press and coalition sought to portray GSK as a powerful company more concerned with profits than the health and well-being of American and Canadian consumers. Elizabeth Wennar, MD, spokesperson for the Coalition for Access to Affordable Prescription Drugs, a Vermont-based advocacy group said,

> Strong profit growth is Glaxo's chief concern, not the quality care and the well-being of seniors who cannot pay the exorbitant American prices for their life-saving drugs. If patient care was a genuine worry, Glaxo would have come forward much earlier. They wouldn't have waited nearly three years (during Internet growth) while Canadian pharmacies have grown to serve millions of uninsured and underinsured Americans. Simply put, Glaxo wants a much bigger piece of the sales action.[20]

Glaxo insisted that the decision was simply a tactical maneuver to protect American patients' safety from risks attributed to quality assurance lapses in the reimportation process. However, the Minnesota Senior Federation believed that the drug company was really concerned with the "safety of its sales and profits." Barbara Kaufman, president of the senior group, declared, "The idea that shipping drugs north to Canada . . . and throughout the United States . . . is safe, while shipping drugs south to the U.S. is dangerous is ludicrous."[21] Joe Graedon, in his syndicated column, cast even further doubt on the patient safety rationale for the crackdown, calling it "smoke and mirrors" and emphasizing Canada's own interest in protecting its citizens. "Canadian authorities have rigorous federal supervision of medicines," he said. "You have to assume that if you shop for your Advair at a pharmacy in Toronto, it's going to be just as good as Advair in downtown Durham (North Carolina)."[22] Kris Thorkelson, representing the Manitoba International Pharmacists Association, agreed saying,

> The shipping of drugs across the border and elsewhere has always been and will continue to be safe, ensuring product integrity, and Glaxo's claims about safety are without foundation. Drugs are shipped great distances in similar circumstances every day with no threat to their integrity. The same thing happens in the U.S. and elsewhere, yet the manufacturer is not raising the issue there. Glaxo uses the same shipping techniques to move its products to wholesalers and retailers all over North America.[23]

Industry watchers suggested that the most obvious motivation for the GSK action was the erosion of its American profit picture. A PR newswire out of St. Paul, Minnesota, reinforced this notion by suggesting that Glaxo was attempting to take away the rights of senior citizens under the guise of safety.[24] Formal legal implications were also raised.[25] "What they are doing is restraint of trade,"[26] said Phil Mamber, president of the Massachusetts Senior Action Council.

GlaxoSmithKline, while spending hundreds of millions of dollars annually to advertise its drugs, was losing control over something it couldn't buy: its image. The crackdown on reimportation of Canadian drugs via the Internet had become a lightning rod of controversy, featuring vulnerable, typically elderly patients on one side and a large, multinational, and successful corporation on the other. "(Ironically) GSK is feeding a climate of antipathy toward drug companies that could, in the long term, result in new laws that could have an impact on their sales,"[27] warned Frances Cloud, a pharmaceutical analyst with London's Nomura Securities. Joe Graedon, co-hosting the public radio program, "The People's Pharmacy," agreed,

> (The crack-down) risks alienating a lot of Canadians, and it risks alienating Americans who are fed up with subsidizing the cost of drugs for the rest of the world. The only explanation I can

imagine for why GSK would be willing to risk that is because so many people are now buying their medicines from Canada that GSK is starting to see the effect on the bottom line.[28]

In 2003, the pharmaceutical industry introduced their products into a marketplace decidedly different than other industries. Individuals did not enter the healthcare services marketplace for discretionary purchases. Healthcare services, at one juncture or another, were essential in the lives of most people to maintain optimal health or to treat acute and chronic diseases. However, access to healthcare services and prescription drugs was variable, based on gender, geographic location, socioeconomic factors, and race. Complicating the data interpretation was the weak economy and the prolonged ennui of the American stock markets. While many seniors partook of an active, secure, and stimulating retirement, others, just years short from anticipating a secure retirement, were contemplating remaining at or returning to work, unwillingly, to make ends meet.[29]

GlaxoSmithKline plc

GlaxoSmithKline plc (GSK) was a multinational concern formed from the acquisition of SmithKline Beecham by Glaxo in late 2000. Headquartered in London, England, the company employed more than 100,000 people and distinguished itself as the largest pharmaceutical company in Europe and the second largest pharmaceutical company in the world. Seeing the United States as a key market, GSK struggled to establish itself as the fastest-growing pharmaceutical company there. The 2000 merger resulted in a broad product line that included prescription drugs, vaccines, and consumer health products. Therapeutic targets for GSK products included depression, infectious disease, asthma and chronic obstructive pulmonary disease, migraine headaches, non-insulin dependent diabetes mellitus, chemotherapy-induced nausea and vomiting, and congestive heart failure. Blockbuster products (global sales > £1 billion per annum) included Paxil (depression), Augmentin (Gram positive aerobic bacterial infection), Advair (asthma), Flovent (asthma), Imitrex (migraine headache), and Avandia (non-insulin dependant diabetes mellitus). Consumer health products included Aquafresh toothpaste, Nicorette patches and gum (smoking cessation), and Tums (calcium supplement/ heartburn relief).

GSK was in strong financial condition[30] as shown in **Exhibit 3**. In 2002, they experienced an increase of 7.8% in global sales of pharmaceutical products to nearly $27 billion. U.S. sales of pharmaceutical products increased by 13%. An essential market, the United States represented 54% of all GSK sales. GSK commanded 8.8% of the market share for prescription

Exhibit 3
Profit and Loss Summary: GlaxoSmithKline, plc (Dollar amounts in millions, except per-share data)

Year Ending Dec. 31	2002	2001	Change (%)
Sales			
Pharmaceuticals	$26,993	$24,775	9.0
Consumer health	4,826	4,729	2.1
Total sales	31,819	29,504	7.8
Gross profit	24,906	22,688	9.7
Operating profit	8,327	6,817	22.2
Profit before taxation	8,259	6,504	28.0
Earnings	5,873	4,396	33.5
Earnings per share	$1.99	$1.45	38.0
Shares outstanding	5,912	6,064	(2.5)

Source: GlaxoSmithKline Annual Report, 2002, released February 12, 2003.

**Exhibit 4
Global Sales
and Growth
Rates for Key
GlaxoSmithKline
Therapeutic Drug
Groups and
Individual Agents
(Dollar amounts in
millions)**

Therapeutic Class	Global Sales	Global Growth (%)
Central Nervous System	$6.8 billion	17
Paxil	3.1 billion	15 (18% in U.S.)
Respiratory System—Advair	4.4 billion	25
	2.4 billion	96
Anti-infectives—HIV	2.2 billion	13
Metabolic/gastrointestinal—	2.1 billion	1
Avandia	1 billion	19 (15% in U.S.)
Oncology—Zofran	1.1 billion	22 (28% in U.S.)
Cardiovascular—Coreg	459 million	27

drugs in 2001.[31] See GlaxoSmithKline's 2002 Annual Report for complete financial statements at *www.gsk.com*.

Six therapeutic drug groups experienced significant global growth in 2002. Within categories, individual agents also demonstrated significant sales growth. Key figures for these drugs are shown in **Exhibit 4**.

GlaxoSmithKline devoted $4.35 billion to research and development expenditures in 2002, an increase of 14% over 2001. The product "pipeline" included 123 products in clinical development, which consisted of 61 new chemical entities, 23 new vaccines, and 39 line extensions. One agent was in Phase III clinical trials for the prevention of prostate cancer. Five new products were expected to be launched for marketing over the next two years.

In a practice defined as "innovative lifecycle management," GSK's research organization also sought to extend the patent life of established agents by releasing slightly altered forms of already marketed agents. Wellbutrin, an antidepressant, was reformulated as a long-acting, once daily formulation, and was expected to be released in 2003.

Research and development was also committed to extending product lines. Pharmaceutical manufacturers were allowed to resubmit drug applications to the U.S. Food and Drug Administration (FDA) for already marketed agents in order to advertise the drug for expanded uses. GSK expected that new indications approved by the FDA for established agents would contribute to future growth. While physicians often prescribed drugs for "off-label" use, FDA approval legitimized such use and decreased attendant liability. Also, pharmaceutical manufacturers were prohibited by the FDA from encouraging the use of agents for non-approved indications, severely limiting marketing potential. Finally, acquiring new indications for older agents could effectively extend the period of patent protection and discourage generic competition. GSK aggressively sought expanded indications for Paxil, Coreg, Augmentin, and Advair during 2002.[32]

Marketing and general administration costs decreased in 2002 to $12,062 million, a decrease of 0.4%. GSK continued to expand their sales force with a particular focus on new product launches.

Emphasizing an international presence, GSK participated in community service initiatives around the world. Working with the United Nations, the company established fixed, not-for-profit pricing for anti-retroviral (HIV/AIDS) and anti-malarial drugs to public sector customers and nonprofit organizations in the least developed countries and in sub-Saharan Africa. GSK also established preferential pricing to employers that provided HIV/AIDS treatment to their employees in the sub-Sahara. In the United States, GSK initiated the Orange Card program in January 2002, in order to provide medications to the poor that did not have public or private prescription drug coverage. GSK reported worldwide community investment and charitable donations of $104 million in 2001, 2.3% of net income.

The Pharmaceutical Industry

In 2001, prescription drug spending was the fastest growing component of national health expenditures, totaling $141 billion, or 10%, of U.S. national health expenditures.[33] Prescription drug spending had grown 15.7% from the $122 billion spent in 2000. In 2002, drug sales growth slowed but still rose 12%, essentially due to the industry's ability to raise drug prices in the United States by an average of 4%, nearly double the rate of inflation.[34] Two sectors comprised the industry: research-based pharmaceutical companies that developed new branded agents, and generic houses that marketed previously branded drugs that had lost patent protection.

The average revenue growth for the branded pharmaceutical industry slowed from 9.5% in 2001 to 4.5% in 2002.[35] The top ten companies accounted for 60% of all U.S. drug sales. Slowing revenue growth was primarily due to the entry into the market of generic formulations of previous blockbuster products,[36] such as Prilosec (omeprazole) and Prozac (fluoxetine). Concurrent with eroding profits, research and development costs were rising, accelerating to nearly a 17% increase in 2001 up from 8% in 1999. Research and development spending increased 16.6% to $30.3 billion from 2000 to 2001, claiming 13% of revenues. However, the rate at which branded pharmaceutical manufacturers were launching blockbuster products appeared to be slowing.[37] New molecular entities (unique active ingredients at their initial introduction to the pharmaceutical marketplace that had the potential to become blockbuster products) declined to 15 in 2002 compared with the 23 entities brought to market in 1990. Concerns developed that revenue loss to generic formulations was not being offset by the introduction of new agents. Therefore, branded pharmaceutical companies sought strategies to sustain growth that were less research intensive. "Life cycle management" became a strategy to leverage the potential of existing, already marketed agents.[38] This strategy included line extension, the introduction of slightly altered formulations in order to gain patent protection. Aggressive protection of intellectual property through litigation against encroaching generic competitors was another strategy commonly used to manage the life cycle of existing agents.

In 2001, the average branded pharmaceutical company committed 31% of revenues for selling, general, and administrative expenses. Few companies specified the advertising and promotion component of this expense; however, it was estimated to be as high as 12% of revenue in 2001. Marketing spending was divided into direct to consumer advertising (DTC), physician advertising and detailing, and provision of free drug samples as shown in **Exhibit 5**. DTC grew the fastest of the three categories, at a rate of 33% between 1996 and 2000. Marketing dollars were committed to free samples in the hope that patients would not be switched to competing products when a formal prescription was written.

Branded pharmaceutical manufacturers remained highly profitable throughout 2002, with an average 20% profit margin, and were predicted to experience accelerated growth in 2003. Analyst David Reisinger stated, "Despite earnings disappointments, the pharmaceutical

Exhibit 5
Promotional Activity Spending of Pharmaceutical Companies as a Percentage of Total Promotional Spending

Promotional Activity	1996 (%)	2000 (%)
Free samples	53.5%	50.6%
Physician detailing	32.8	30.6
Direct-to-Consumer advertising (DTC)	8.6	15.7
Advertising in professional journals	5.0	3.1
Total promotional spending, in millions	$9,164.3	$15,708.2

Note: As estimated by IMS Health. The 1996 figures add to 99.9%.

industry maintains a very healthy financial position and generates healthy cash flow."[39] Variance in financial performance of individual companies was predicted to continue, however, ultimately separating winners and losers.

The generic drug industry enjoyed explosive growth of 55% in 2001, to nearly $6 billion, and benefited from the patent expirations on several blockbuster branded agents. Although growth slowed in 2002, the fundamentals of the industry remained strong. Cost containment efforts by insurance plans and healthcare systems routinely encouraged the utilization of generic products. In order to encourage use of generic products, such plans offered low out-of-pocket co-payments for these agents, significantly lower than the out-of-pocket cost for comparable, branded agents. However, no generic manufacturer had yet to be included in the top ten U.S. drug companies as of 2001. Indeed, generic drugs accounted for 47% of the dispensed prescriptions in the United States, but only 8% of dollar sales, highlighting the cost differential between generic and branded agents.

Both sectors continued to experience high profits and healthy cash flows. Both outperformed the S&P during the period 1998–2002. While the average stock price to earnings (P/E) multiple for the S&P 500 during that period was 24 times, the average P/E multiple for branded companies was 28 times, while generic manufacturers experienced a stock price that was 29 times earnings.

Health Insurance Coverage in America

The vast majority of Americans in 2003 relied on healthcare insurance benefits to shield them from the major financial impact of illness or accident. In general, Americans that had access to prescription drug coverage during this period did so as part of general healthcare insurance coverage. The Henry Kaiser Family Foundation tracked annual changes in health insurance coverage for all Americans, and in January 2003 released annual statistics for 2001.[40] On average, one in six non-elderly Americans was uninsured during the year. Also, the probability of becoming uninsured varied depending on age, income, work status, race, ethnicity, and other demographic factors. Despite the economic boom of the 1990s, approximately one million adults joined the ranks of the uninsured each year during the decade. The rate slowed perceptibly, even decreased in 1999 and 2000, but began to increase again with the economic downturn in 2001, as the percentage of Americans with employer-sponsored health insurance decreased for the first time since 1993. At the end of 2001, the number of uninsured individuals reached 40.9 million, while the total of uninsured was estimated to be over 43 million in 2003. The 2001 census counted 281.4 million Americans. Hence, 15.3% of Americans were uninsured in 2003. Meanwhile, family incomes for the poor (< 100% of poverty level) and near-poor (between 100%–200% of poverty) shifted downward after 2000.

Non-elderly adults with low incomes were the least likely to have job-based insurance during 2001. Less than half of the persons in low-income families that had two full-time workers had job-based coverage and over 25% were completely uninsured. As a group, only 17% of the poor and 43% of the near poor received a health insurance benefit. Finally, employees in service and labor jobs were far more likely to be uninsured than those with technical, professional, sales, and managerial jobs, even within the same industry and employer.

While Medicaid eligibility requirements for children were more relaxed, adults faced higher hurdles. Therefore, nearly 20% of American adults under the age of 65 were uninsured during 2001, compared to only 12% of children. Racial and ethnic disparities were also detected in patterns of healthcare coverage. Even after adjusting for income differences, minority groups were less likely to have access to health insurance. While minority groups comprised 30% of the non-elderly population in America, they represented nearly 53% of the uninsured.

The Weak Economy Affects Healthcare Benefits

Employers succeeded in modifying insurance benefits during the stagnant economy by transferring greater out-of-pocket costs to employees, or simply declining to contribute to a premium for health insurance at all. More than 43 million Americans were essentially without healthcare insurance. Many of these people were working but unable to afford their contribution to the insurance premium. Caught in a paradox, they had incomes too high to be eligible for public healthcare coverage, such as Medicaid. At the same time, middle class senior citizens that relied on Medicare supplemental insurance benefits as part of a pension package watched as one company after another, old-guard and new, discontinued such coverage. In 1998, 66% of large employers offered retiree health and prescription benefits to retirees. By 2000, less than 40% of such employers did so. Of those that continued to provide health benefits, only 79% offered any type of prescription coverage.[41] By 2003, only 30% of retired seniors carried Medicare supplemental health insurance provided by a former employer.[42] At the same time, 9% of large employers reported in a 2003 survey that they were very likely to eliminate retiree benefits by 2004 for new and current employees that had not yet retired and 6% reported that they would eliminate employee health benefits entirely.[43] A study by the Employee Benefit Research Institute published in 2003 provided some insight into the financial ramifications of being elderly and insured only by Medicare.[44] They estimated that individuals retiring at 65 in 2003 and living until age 85 could expect to pay $100,000 per person out-of-pocket for healthcare over that period. Those that would retire in 2013 (at 65 years and surviving 20 years) could expect to pay at least twice that amount when including Medicare premiums, drugs, and all other out-of-pocket costs.

Prescription Drug Utilization and Spending for Prescription Drugs

Prescription drug use accounted for only 5% of national health expenditures as late as the 1970s. Most insurers did not cover the prescription drug costs. Individuals paid for the relatively few agents that were available out of their own pocket. Perhaps ironically, prescription drug coverage was introduced as a benefit with the advent of managed care in the 1980s. In fact, many beneficiaries of managed care health benefits received pharmaceutical products for no cost. Others paid nominal co-payments of $5–$10 per prescription. Under this system, the out-of-pocket costs contributed by individuals to acquire prescriptions remained low, resulting in burgeoning demand for and utilization of prescription drug products. Private insurance pay-out for prescription drugs was $45 billion in 1991, or 26% of retail drug revenues. By 2001 this figure had ballooned to $141 billion, now 47% of retail drug revenues.[45]

The average individual spent $449 out of his or her own pocket for prescription drugs in 2001, representing 0.9% of personal income. However, the out-of-pocket cost increased significantly with increasing age as portrayed in the **Exhibits 6 and 7**.[46] The American Association for Retired Persons estimated that 80% of Americans 65 years old or older used at least one prescription drug every day. The typical Medicare beneficiary filled a prescription eighteen times per year, a rate of one prescription every twenty days.[47]

A study published by the Department of Health and Human Services in 2001 indicated that customers that paid out-of-pocket paid nearly 15% more for prescription drugs than customers

**Exhibit 6
Average Annual
Out-of-Pocket
Expenditure by Age**

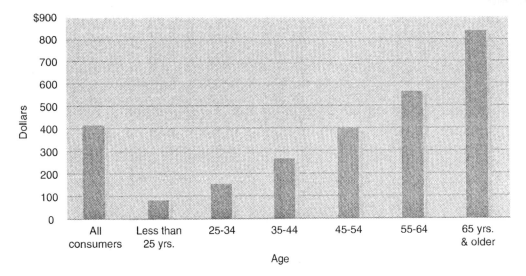

with prescription drug insurance coverage.[48] For the 25% of the most commonly prescribed drugs, this differential was even higher, over 20%. This differential was attributed to the bargaining potential of pharmacy benefit managers (PBMs) that represented prescription drug plans in negotiations with pharmaceutical manufacturers over drug prices. Intense competition between companies to control market share for common therapeutic drug classes resulted in even greater influence of the PBM when negotiating prices for these commonly used agents. The resulting differential outcome strongly reinforced the value of prescription drug insurance coverage.

Medicare was originally created to provide a safety net against rising hospitalization costs for senior citizens. It had never included a benefit for prescription drugs used in the out-patient setting. Few prescription medications were available prior to 1965, the year Medicare was unveiled, and few envisioned the explosion in products resulting from pharmaceutical research. While some Medicare beneficiaries enjoyed prescription drug benefits from other

**Exhibit 7
Percentage of
Annual Income
Spent on Drugs,
by Age**

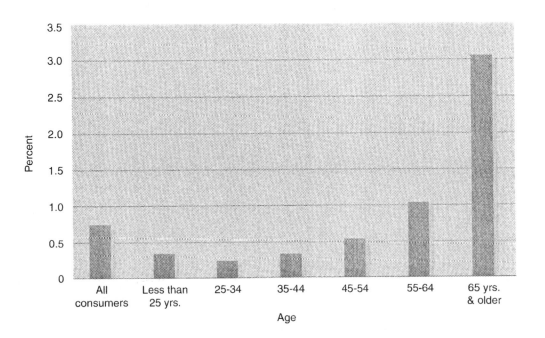

Exhibit 8
Sources of
Prescription Drug
Coverage for
Medicare
Beneficiaries

Source of Coverage	1999
Employer sponsored	30.4%
Medicare managed care	15.4%
Medicaid	11.1%
Medigap (privately purchased policies)	11.0%
Other public sources	1.7%
No drug coverage	23.8%

public and private sources, 23.8% of Medicare beneficiaries lacked any type of prescription coverage in 1999. These seniors were more likely to live in rural areas, were 85 years of age or older, and were near poor (income between $10,000–$20,000 per annum). Sources of prescription drug coverage for Medicare beneficiaries in 1999 are summarized in **Exhibit 8**. The beneficiaries with supplementary prescription coverage received an average of $1,131 worth of product, paying 31% or $352 out of their own resources. In contrast, the beneficiary with no supplementary coverage received 45% less, or an average of $617 worth of product, 100% of it covered out of pocket.

In 2002, 13% of Medicare beneficiaries enrolled in managed care programs had no drug coverage, 15% could elect drug coverage for an additional premium, and 72% had limited drug coverage included in the Medicare managed care plan. Almost 1/3 of these plans limited drug choice to generic formulations and enforced relatively low coverage limits, often less than $500.[49]

The Food and Drug Administration's Role

The U.S. Food and Drug Administration (FDA) was responsible for ensuring that drug products made available in the United States were safe and effective. The Division of Import Operations and Policy, a department of the FDA, administered the United States Federal Food, Drug, and Cosmetic Act,[50] which prohibited the interstate shipment (including importation) of unapproved new drugs whether for personal use or otherwise. Unapproved drugs included foreign-made versions of U.S.-approved drugs that had not been manufactured in accordance with and pursuant to FDA approval. Under this act, the FDA could refuse to admit into the United States any drug that "appeared" to be unapproved, placing the burden of proof on the importer to prove that the drug sought to be imported was approved by the FDA. However, the FDA was cognizant of its limited resources in enforcing this act and, therefore, developed a policy regarding its enforcement priorities related to the personal importation of prescription drugs. Under the "Coverage of Personal Importation,"[51] the focus of the FDA was to confiscate only products obviously intended for the commercial resale market (determined by volume), fraudulent products, and those that posed obvious health risks. In other words, small amounts of prescription products (enough for ninety days) destined for personal use and personally carried across the border from outside the United States or mailed into the United States would not normally draw scrutiny as violating the Food, Drug, and Cosmetics Act. In fact, the FDA allowed their own and customs personnel to consider a more permissive policy when assessing such drug products for entry into the United States. In order to understand the impetus for the growth of imported drugs from Canada, one must read the careful wording of the FDA "general guidance" detailed in the "Personal Importation" subchapter of the Regulatory Procedures Manual:

> The statements in this chapter are intended only to provide operating guidance for FDA personnel and are not intended to create or confer any rights, privileges, or benefits on or for any private person.

> FDA personnel may use their discretion to allow entry of shipments of violative FDA regu-
> lated products when the quantity and purpose are clearly for personal use, and the product does not
> present an unreasonable risk to the user. Even though all products that appear to be in violation of
> statutes administered by the FDA are subject to refusal (for entry), FDA personnel may use their
> discretion to examine the background, risk, and purpose of the product before making a final deci-
> sion (to allow entry). Although FDA may use discretion to allow admission of certain violative
> items, this should not be interpreted as a license to individuals to bring in such shipments.[52]

Under this guidance, the product and its intended use were to be identified, the intended
use could not be for the treatment of a serious condition, and the product could not be known
to represent a significant health risk.

Alternatively, drugs imported for personal use could be used to treat more serious conditions as long as an effective treatment was not available domestically, there was no known
commercialization or promotion of the product to those residing in the United States, the
product was not considered to pose an unreasonable risk, the individual importing the drug
verified that it was for personal use and included no more than a ninety-day supply, and a U.S.
physician was involved in the person's medical care. In such cases, "persons were still breaking the law by acquiring drugs from outside the country, however, the FDA was letting them
get away with it," according to an anonymous FDA attorney. Emphasizing that the personal
use importation guidance was meant to save FDA resources, and to generally permit medical
treatments sought by individuals that were not otherwise available in the United States, the
FDA stated that "foreign-made chemical versions of drugs available in the U.S. were not
intended to be covered by the personal use policy."[53]

Adopting a relaxed stance under the "personal use guidance," the FDA did little to dis-
suade the importation of prescription drug products throughout the period from 1995-2003.
Despite the growing popularity of Internet pharmacies among Americans, (especially
Canadian pharmacies) the FDA did little to inhibit the practice of purchasing foreign drug
products online, ostensibly because it did not want to appear unsympathetic to American consumers, especially the elderly.[54] In fact, in the fall of 2002, when American employers and
insurers began advocating the use of Canadian pharmacies by covering claims generated
there, the FDA associate commissioner for policy and planning, William Hubbard, stated, "If
they are not actually importing drugs, I don't know what enforcement role we (FDA) would
have."[55] However, the FDA stance appeared to change dramatically in response to
GlaxoSmithKline's retaliation to cross-border sales. Quickly, the FDA indicated it would
change its regulatory stance and crack down on the importation of drugs, even those clearly
destined for personal use.[56] Seeking to distance the agency's harder line from the consumer,
Mr. Hubbard implied that insurers that helped Americans import drugs might come under fire.
In a February 2003 letter sent to address the questions of an attorney representing health
plans, Mr. Hubbard stated,

> Those who aid and abet a criminal violation of the (Food, Drug, and Cosmetic) Act, or conspire
> to violate the act can also be found criminally liable. Any party participating in an import plan
> in which a health insurer or claims processor helps arrange a purchase (of drugs) from Canada,
> does so at its own legal risk.[57]

At the same time, the FDA echoed GSK by citing safety reasons for enforcing the Food,
Drug, and Cosmetic Act.[58] Imported drugs might be less likely to be manufactured under
exacting specifications and might be mislabeled or otherwise without specific directions for
use. The FDA established that this was a public health risk, because Americans had little, if
any, recourse if they were exposed to tainted drug product. Sources at the FDA also expressed
concern that Canadian pharmacies were diverting drugs from deserving Canadian citizens in
order to capture a tidy profit by selling prescription products to Americans. The spread
between acquisition cost from pharmaceutical companies and selling price to Americans was

enhanced by the attractive exchange rate between American and Canadian dollars at the time. This was true despite the fact that Americans were often purchasing products for as much as 80% less than they would pay for the products in the United States.

European Influence on Pharmaceutical Pricing

The European pricing for prescription drug products influenced pricing of the products in the United States. Due to the administration of national healthcare systems, the European governments set price controls for prescription drug products. In June 2002, the German Health Ministry attempted to cut by 4% the prices it would pay for prescription products to provide public health services.[59] Drug companies balked, as the public health system purchased 80% of all drugs in the country. In a compromise, Chancellor Gerhardt Schroeder agreed to veto the price cut if major drug companies would establish a trust fund designed to finance Germany's soaring healthcare costs. GlaxoSmithKline, along with 37 other multinational pharmaceutical companies, reluctantly agreed to the plan. Worried that other European countries that administer nationalized health systems would follow suit and make the same demands for price cuts, the drug companies had little leverage in Germany and were highly motivated to accept the establishment of the trust fund in lieu of price cuts.

Across the ocean, the outcome of these negotiations directly affected Americans and the prices they paid for prescription drug products. The United States was the only major industrialized country that did not administer some sort of governmental price control for drug products. Pharmaceutical manufacturers openly admitted that as European governments mandated price cuts and eroded the profitability of the European markets, they increased prescription prices in the United States. "Step-by-step, the profitability of European markets is decreasing, and we're depending on the U.S. market more and more," said Jean-Francois Dehecq, chief executive of the French drug maker, Sanofi-Synthelabo.[60] In each of the years prior to 2003, the cost of drugs in the United States had increased by 2%-3% annually, sometimes more, as European governments mandated price cuts in Europe. One company increased prices in the United States by 5.9% annually for three popular medications used to treat heart disease, asthma, and osteoporosis. The result was large differences in the prices that Americans paid for prescriptions versus those paid in other markets. While Europe accounted for the largest single market in the world for prescription drugs, it accounted for just 22% of the dollar sales in the global market. Meanwhile the United States, with fewer people, contributed more than 46% of global dollar sales, and more than 60% of profits.

Donna Shalala, U.S. Secretary of Health and Human Services under President Clinton, commented on the situation. While pointing out that U.S. taxpayers financed much of the basic research that supported the pharmaceutical industry, she remarked, "We have been subsidizing this research and in return we get to pay higher prices (than Europeans)? It's not fair."[61]

Employers and Insurers Join the Debate

Americans were not always acting independently when they acquired necessary prescription medications from Canadian pharmacies via the Internet. Various retirement plans and insurers endorsed the practice to varying degrees. United Health Group, in conjunction with the American Association of Retired Persons (AARP), announced in October 2002 that it was waiving its policy requiring prescriptions eligible for Medicare supplemental insurance coverage to be purchased in the United States, or a U.S. territory.[62] Therefore, it would cover the cost of prescription drugs acquired from pharmacies not just in Canada, but also around the world. While not explicitly encouraging the practice of shopping for prescriptions outside the country, the announcement educated more than 400,000 AARP beneficiaries to the possibility.

Meanwhile, some employers and insurers overtly encouraged their retired employees and beneficiaries to purchase prescription drugs from Canadian Internet pharmacies in order to take advantage of cost savings. The National Association of Retired and Veteran Railway Employees Inc.[63] provided a hyperlink to a Canadian Internet pharmacy on its own Web site. The pharmacy site included a catalog of available medications (narcotics were not available) and the cost, in American dollars, of each agent. A selection of "frequently asked questions" instructed users how to use the site and reassured users of the similarity between drug agents available in the United States and Canada. Users were informed that, "prescription drugs coming from Canada are made by the same manufacturers, often at the same plants, as those sold in the U.S." In order to protect Canadian citizens, "Health Canada, the equivalent of the U.S. FDA, provides strict oversight of prescription drugs." The site continued by informing users that a report issued by the Congressional Research Service in Washington DC found that, "pharmaceutical manufacturing practices required by Health Canada and the U.S. FDA are equivalent." The site also informed users of the FDA "general guidance" on personal importation of medication. "While it is technically illegal to purchase medicines from a Canadian pharmacy, the FDA exercises enforcement discretion to allow individuals to import up to a ninety-day supply of prescription drugs for personal use."

Where Elected Officials Stood

Congress had made several attempts to legalize the personal importation of prescription drugs by early 2003, largely due to concern about rapidly rising drug costs for senior citizens.[64] However, the drug industry, applying an aggressive lobbying campaign, had succeeded in preventing the passage of such legislation. During 2002, the Senate voted to allow importation of prescription drugs from Canada, but the proposition never came to a vote in the House of Representatives. A bill legalizing importation from Canadian pharmacies passed both the Senate and the House in 2000. However, the Clinton administration declined to implement the legislation, ostensibly over worries about verifying product safety and little documentation that the practice would actually save money.[65]

Individual elected officials reacted quickly to GSK's policy of limiting drug product to Canadian pharmacies that exported to the United States. Russ Feingold, U.S. Senator from Wisconsin, introduced a bill in Congress to deny tax breaks to pharmaceutical companies that restricted shipment of drugs to Canada.[66] Vermont Representative Bernard Sanders also introduced a bill specifically penalizing GSK for its attempt to cut off U.S. consumer access to Canadian drugs, citing restriction of free trade.[67] Congressman Gil Gutknecht, a Republican from the first district in Minnesota, responded to the shipment restriction,

> Glaxo's brazen attempt to prevent Americans from obtaining lower cost medications from Canada is a textbook example of brazen abuse of monopolistic power. Glaxo is attempting to fix prices. If this isn't a classic example of anti-trust abuse, it should be. It is time for our attorney general to dust off anti-trust laws and enforce them.[68]

By April 2003, legislators were actively accusing the FDA and GlaxoSmithKline of "scaring seniors that are trying to get more affordable medicines."[69] In a raucous hearing, members of the recently formed House Subcommittee on Human Rights and Wellness said the FDA had no evidence of safety problems with drug reimportation and that the agency was shifting its personal importation policy because of drug industry pressure. The committee insisted the FDA should use its efforts to find a way to allow safe importation of drugs from Canada instead. Vermont Representative Sanders criticized the FDA by saying, "You should be putting out pamphlets saying people have been going across the border . . . and there hasn't been one problem."[70]

Meanwhile, busloads of constituents, with their elected officials on-board, continued to make the trip to Canada with the explicit purpose of acquiring prescription drugs at lower cost than was available in the United States. Most prominent, perhaps, was Minnesota Senator Mark Dayton, who donated his annual Senate salary of $145,000 to subsidize monthly trips for senior citizens to purchase drugs in Canada.[71]

GlaxoSmithKline Attempted Discount Card

GSK, in cooperation with other large pharmaceutical manufacturers, began to offer a discount card in 2001 to provide assistance to low-income American families that earned less than $28,000 annually. The card, named Together RX, provided a variable discount for prescription products up to 40% off retail prices. However, in the autumn of 2002, GSK cut the discount, maintaining that the U.S. government would use the low retail prices to demand even lower prices for Medicaid beneficiaries.[72] GSK referred to legislation enacted in 1990 which stipulated that drug manufacturers must treat the Medicaid program as a most-favored customer, meaning that no other buyer could have access to lower prices for prescription product than the Medicaid program. Anxious that the government would accuse GSK of selling prescription drugs to low-income families at a cost lower than that available to Medicaid, they decreased the program discounts to reflect Medicaid pricing. The result was a significant increase in prices for participants in the GSK discount program, while Medicaid beneficiaries continued to pay nominal co-payments to acquire drug products. (Federal and state administrators of the Medicaid program then reimbursed intermediaries for the cost of the prescription at most-favored pricing.) After that time, GSK encouraged concerned Americans to urge Congress to enact a Medicare prescription drug benefit in order to help resolve issues relating to the affordability of medicines.[73]

GSK also provided drugs to qualifying persons through a Patient Assistance Program. In 2002, the program provided free medications valued at $168 million to 400,000 Americans with incomes below $24,000 for a household of two.[74]

Public Perception

The Wall Street Journal conducted a non-scientific, Web-based poll of its readers on March 11, 2003, in order to elicit opinion about Americans that acquired prescription drugs from Internet pharmacies in Canada.[75] The responses to the poll provided some insight into the public image of GSK and other pharmaceutical corporations. The *Journal* received 1,665 answers in response to the question, "Should regulators try to stop Americans from buying prescription drugs from Canada?" Eighty-four percent of respondents said "No," while 16% said "Yes." The poll also provided respondents an opportunity to provide editorial comment on the question. Fifty-two written responses were generated in answer to the preceding question. All but two of the respondents referred negatively to the pharmaceutical industry in their editorial answer. Most respondents complained of "price fixing" by pharmaceutical companies, specifically GSK, in the United States. Others referred to "restraint of free trade," when U.S. citizens were prevented from purchasing prescriptions from Canada. Other editorials suggested that the FDA had altered its stance regarding the personal importation of medications due to political pressure from pharmaceutical companies. Campaign contributions to high-profile officials by pharmaceutical companies were suggested several times as one reason why a price differential for drugs remained between America and the rest of the world. In general, the safety rationale provided by GSK for more stringently regulating imports from Canada was dismissed as rhetorical and not believed to be the authentic reason for GSK's actions.

Two respondents referred to the high cost of pharmaceutical research and Americans' ability to pay higher prices as the primary reason for the cost differential. One respondent worried that the ultimate response by the pharmaceutical industry to the importation issue would be to increase the costs of drugs in Canada, ultimately limiting access for that country as well.

Meanwhile, *The Wall Street Journal* mocked the abrupt crackdown by the FDA with a characterization of the typical "drug trafficker" bringing in medications from abroad.[76] Dubbing elderly Americans as "not your generic smugglers," they described a typical "profile" as "white, elderly, often wearing Bermuda shorts, and American Legion baseball caps." Ostensibly, the detailed "profile" would make it easier for these "traffickers" to be spotted by the FDA. Adopting a serious tone, the author described the motivation of the traffickers. "For many elderly shoppers, cutting the cost of medications is a crucial part of budgeting for retirement." A 76-year-old woman was blunt about her need to leave the country to acquire medicine, "I live on less than $1,200 per month and I saw a $50,000 stock portfolio evaporate since 2000. If I couldn't get cheap meds, I couldn't live."[77]

Americans, especially the elderly, paid the highest prices in the world for prescription drugs.[78] Even though they represented the biggest market for drugs, they had no ability to negotiate prices. Like the 76-year-old woman forced to leave the United States to acquire medicine, a large contingent of the elderly simply could not afford the medications they required to stay alive. But unlike most other developed countries, they received no help from their government to acquire necessary prescriptions.

The Tradeoffs: Health vs. Profits vs. Safety

What was the responsibility of GlaxoSmithKline to see that American patients, especially those with limited means, could have regular access to prescription drug products? Glaxo maintained that patient safety was their primary motivation for the retaliation against cross-border sales from Canada into the United States. Company officials stated, "GSK decided to block the reimportation from Canada out of concern for patient safety. Although consumers may be getting the very same drugs they would buy in the U.S., the drugs may be damaged in transport, mislabeled, or otherwise adulterated."[79]

But was safety the most relevant issue when the product was not a consumer good but rather necessary for health, perhaps even life, but was too expensive for a significant portion of the American population? As University of Minnesota professor Barbara Kaufmann reiterated, "A drug that is not affordable is neither safe nor effective."[80]

What sort of power differential separated GSK from their customers? Did GSK damage their public image through their action? If so, what strategic resources must be committed to repair the resulting damage and restore good public relations to the commerce of GSK?

Notes

1. B. Strunk, P. Ginsburg, and J. Gabel, "Tracking Health Care Costs: Growth Accelerates Again in 2001," *Health Affairs* (September 25, 2002), pp. W299–W310.

2. K. Levit, C. Smith, C. Cowan, et al., "Trends in U.S. Health Care Spending, 2001," *Health Affairs* Vol. 22, No. 1 (2003), pp. 154–164.

3. J. Baglole, "What's New at the Mall of America? Cheaper Drugs from Canada," *The Wall Street Journal* (November 8, 2002).

4. S. Lueck and J. Baglole, "Glaxo Says It Will Retaliate Against Cross-Border Sales," *The Wall Street Journal* (January 13, 2003); J. Baglole, "Glaxo Presses Canadian Firms Not to Resell Its Drugs to U.S.," *The Wall Street Journal* (January 22, 2003); J. Fisher, "GSK Fighting Border Battle," *The News and Observer* (February 13, 2003).

5. W. Wolf, "Seniors Groups Boycott Glaxo over Canada Move," *Star Tribune* (February 23, 2003).

6. A. Dembner, "Rallies Aim to Save Canadian Drug Sales," *The Boston Globe* (February 20, 2003).

7. E. Reguly, "Drugstores That Are Hard to Swallow," *Time Canada* Vol. 16, No. 5 (2003), p. 29.

8. *Ibid.*

9. GlaxoSmithKline, Important Facts Patients Should Know About Cross-Border Internet Sales, *www.gsk.com/media/ca_key.html.*

10. *Ibid.*

11. S. Lueck and J. Baglole, "Glaxo Says It Will Retaliate Against Cross-Border Sales," *The Wall Street Journal* (January 13, 2003); J. Baglole, "Glaxo Presses Canadian Firms Not to Resell Its Drugs to U.S.," *The Wall Street Journal* (January 22, 2003); W. Wolf, "Seniors Groups Boycott Glaxo over Canada Move," *Star Tribune* (February 23, 2003).

12. C. Serres, "Drug Titan Draws Ire," *The News and Observer* (February 14, 2003); A. Krishnan, "GlaxoSmithKline Fights War of Perceptions over Flow of Drugs from Canada," *The (Durham, North Carolina) Herald-Sun* (February 4, 2003).

13. A. Taylor, "Seniors Find Drug Relief in Canada: Congress Will Push Again for Law to Allow Pharmacists to Import Cheaper Medications," *The Detroit News* (August 21, 2001).

14. C. Serres, "Drug Titan Draws Ire," *The News and Observer* (February 14, 2003).

15. A. Krishnan, "GlaxoSmithKline Fights War of Perceptions over Flow of Drugs from Canada," *The (Durham, North Carolina) Herald-Sun* (February 4, 2003).

16. PR Newswire, *Philadelphia Seniors' Organizations Protest Glaxo's Ban on Affordable Drugs* (February 19, 2003), "U.S. & Canadian Organizations Slam Glaxo's Ban Against Affordable Prescription Drugs for American Seniors in Need," *Today's Seniors Network* (February 12, 2003), *http://todayseniornetwork.com/glaxo_ad_campaign.html*; T. Agovino, "Pharmacy Seeks Boycott of Glaxo Products," Associated Press Online (February 4, 2003).

17. A. Dembner, "Rallies Aim to Save Canadian Drug Sales," *The Boston Globe* (February 20, 2003).

18. PR Newswire, *GlaxoSmithKline Actions Threaten Thousands* (February 20, 2003).

19. A. Dembner, "Rallies Aim to Save Canadian Drug Sales," *The Boston Globe* (February 20, 2003).

20. PR Newswire, *GlaxoSmithKline Actions Threaten Thousands* (February 20, 2003).

21. *Ibid.*

22. A. Krishnan, "GlaxoSmithKline Fights War of Perceptions over Flow of Drugs from Canada," *The (Durham, North Carolina) Herald-Sun* (February 4, 2003).

23. Canada NewsWire, *Manitoba On-line Pharmacies Slam Glaxo Drug Ban* (January 12, 2003).

24. PR Newswire, *GlaxoSmithKline Actions Threaten Thousands* (February 20, 2003).

25. T. Cohen, "Wholesaler Cuts GlaxoSmithKline Supplies," Associated Press Online (January 29, 2003).

26. A. Dembner, "Rallies Aim to Save Canadian Drug Sales," *The Boston Globe* (February 20, 2003).

27. C. Serres, "Drug Titan Draws Ire," *The News and Observer* (February 14, 2003).

28. J. Fisher, "GSK Fighting Border Battle," *The News and Observer* (February 13, 2003).

29. K. Green, "Retiree Returns to Early Shift, but This Time at Half Pay," *The Wall Street Journal* (March 5, 2003).

30. GlaxoSmithKline, *Annual Report* (2001); G. Naik and H. Hovey, "Glaxo Profit Rose 28% in 2002: Protest Against Company Urged," *The Wall Street Journal* (February 13, 2003); D. Ranii, "GSK Profit Increases, on This Side of Atlantic," *The News and Observer* (February 13, 2003).

31. T. Scully, L. vander Walde, K. Choi, and J. Higgins, *Health Care Industry Market Update* (Baltimore, MD: Centers for Medicare & Medicaid Services, January 10, 2003), *www.cms.hhs.gov/marketupdate.*

32. GlaxoSmithKline, *Annual Report* (2002).

33. T. Scully, L. vander Walde, K. Choi, and J. Higgins, *Health Care Industry Market Update* (Baltimore, MD: Centers for Medicare & Medicaid Services, January 10, 2003), *www.cms.hhs.gov/marketupdate.*

34. G. Harris, "Drug Sales Growth Slowed, but Still Rose 12% in 2002," *The Wall Street Journal* (February 23, 2003).

35. T. Scully, L. vander Walde, K. Choi, and J. Higgins, *Health Care Industry Market Update* (Baltimore, MD: Centers for Medicare & Medicaid Services, January 10, 2003), *www.cms.hhs.gov/marketupdate.*

36. C. Adams and G. Harris, "Drug Firms Face Growing Pressure over Extensions of Their Patents," *The Wall Street Journal* (March 19, 2002).

37. G. Harris, "Why Drug Makers Are Failing in the Quest for New Blockbusters," *The Wall Street Journal* (April 18, 2002).

38. G. Harris, "Prilosec's Maker Switches Users to Nexium, Thwarting Generics," *The Wall Street Journal* (June 6, 2002).

39. T. Scully, L. vander Walde, K. Choi, and J. Higgins, *Health Care Industry Market Update* (Baltimore, MD: Centers for Medicare & Medicaid Services, January 10, 2003), *www.cms.hhs.gov/marketupdate.*

40. C. Hoffman and M. Wang, *Health Insurance Coverage in America: 2001 Data Update* (The Kaiser Commission on Medicaid and the Uninsured, January 2003), *www.kkf.org.*

41. L. McCormack, J. Gabel, H. Whitmore, et al., "Trends in Retiree Health Benefits: Health Benefits for Retirees Are Eroding Even in the Best of Times," *Health Affairs*, Vol. 21, No. 6 (2003), pp. 169–176.

42. H. Gleckman, "Old, Ill, and Uninsured," *Business Week* (April 7, 2003), pp. 78–79.

43. L. McCormack, J. Gabel, H. Whitmore, et al., "Trends in Retiree Health Benefits: Health Benefits for Retirees Are Eroding Even in the Best of Times," *Health Affairs*, Vol. 21, No. 6 (2003), pp. 169–176.

44. H. Gleckman, "Old, Ill, and Uninsured," *Business Week* (April 7, 2003), pp. 78–79.

45. D. Kreling, D. Mott, J. Wiederholt, et al., *Prescription Drug Trends: A Chartbook Update* (The Kaiser Family Foundation, 2001).

46. T. Scully, L. vander Walde, K. Choi, and J. Higgins, *Health Care Industry Market Update* (Baltimore, MD: Centers for Medicare & Medicaid Services, January 10, 2003), *www.cms.hhs.gov/marketupdate.*

47. Medicare Prescription Drugs: Just the Facts. American Association of Retired Persons. *www.aarp.org/prescriptiondrugs/facts.html*; D. Gross, *Trends in Costs, Coverage, and Use of Prescription Drugs by Medicare Beneficiaries* (AARP, 2001), *http://research.aarp.org/health/dd63_trends.html.*

48. T. Scully, L. vander Walde, K. Choi, and J. Higgins, *Health Care Industry Market Update* (Baltimore, MD: Centers for Medicare & Medicaid Services, January 10, 2003), *www.cms.hhs.gov/marketupdate.*

49. Medicare Prescription Drugs: Just the Facts. American Association of Retired Persons. *www.aarp.org/prescriptiondrugs/facts.html*;

D. Gross, *Trends in Costs, Coverage, and Use of Prescription Drugs by Medicare Beneficiaries* (AARP, 2001), *http://research.aarp.org/health/dd63_trends.html.*

50. M. Blumberg, *Information on Importation of Drugs Prepared by the Division of Import Operations and Policy* (Washington, DC: Office of Regulatory Affairs, U.S. Food and Drug Administration, 1998), *www.fda.gov/ora/import/pipinfo.htm.*

51. "Coverage of Personal Importations," Regulatory Procedures Manual (Washington, DC: Office of Regulatory Affairs, U.S. Food and Drug Administration), *www.fda.gov/ora/compliance_ref/rpm_news2/ch9pers.htm.*

52. *Ibid.*

53. *Ibid.*

54. T. Burton, "FDA Is Cracking Down on Drugs from Canada," *The Wall Street Journal* (March 12, 2003).

55. *Ibid.*

56. J. Baglole, "FDA Effort to Halt Drugs from Canada Stirs Uproar," *The Wall Street Journal* (March 13, 2003).

57. W. Hubbard, *Letter to Robert P. Lombardi Esq. The Kullman Firm, New Orleans La.* (Washington, DC: U.S. Food and Drug Administration, February 12, 2003), *www.fda.gov.*

58. M. Meadows, "Imported Drugs Raise Safety Concerns," *FDA Consumer Magazine* (September/October 2002), *www.fda.gov/fdac/features/2002/502_import.html.*

59. V. Fuhrmans and G. Naik, "In Europe, Drug Makers Fight Against Mandatory Price Cuts," *The Wall Street Journal* (June 7, 2002).

60. *Ibid.*

61. *Ibid.*

62. T. Burton and S. Lueck, "AARP Insurer to Cover Drugs Purchased Outside the U.S.," *The Wall Street Journal* (October 11, 2002).

63. *Low-cost Safe Medicines from Canada: Frequently Asked Questions.* RRxA Railway Rx Assistant, *www.RailwayRxAssist.com/faq.htm.*

64. T. Burton and S. Lueck, "AARP Insurer to Cover Drugs Purchased Outside the U.S.," *The Wall Street Journal* (October 11, 2002).

65. L. McGinley, "Shalala Declines to Implement Law on Importing Prescription Drugs," *The Wall Street Journal* (December 27, 2000).

66. PR Newswire, *GlaxoSmithKline Actions Threaten Thousands* (February 20, 2003).

67. E. Kelly, "Sanders Introduces Prescription Drug Bill," Gannett News Service (February 18, 2003).

68. PR Newswire, *GlaxoSmithKline Actions Threaten Thousands* (February 20, 2003).

69. S. Lueck, "FDA Defends Tougher Stance on Drug Imports," *The Wall Street Journal* (April 4, 2003).

70. *Ibid.*

71. J. Baglole, "What's New at the Mall of America? Cheaper Drugs from Canada," *The Wall Street Journal* (November 8, 2002).

72. J. Graham, "Canada's Mail-Order Drug Houses Plague Glaxo," *The Wall Street Journal* (February 28, 2003).

73. *GlaxoSmithKline Calls for Passage of Medicare Prescription Drug Benefit* (GlaxoSmithKline, February 20, 2003), *www.gsk.com/press2003/press_02202003.htm.*

74. J. Graham, "Canada's Mail-Order Drug Houses Plague Glaxo," *The Wall Street Journal* (February 28, 2003).

75. "Reader Poll: Should Regulators Try to Stop Americans from Buying Prescription Drugs from Canada?" *The Wall Street Journal Online* (March 11, 2003), *www.wsj.com.*

76. J. Millman, "Not Your Generic Smugglers," *The Wall Street Journal* (March 20, 2003).

77. *Ibid.*

78. PR Newswire, *GlaxoSmithKline Actions Threaten Thousands* (February 20, 2003).

79. A. Dembner, "Rallies Aim to Save Canadian Drug Sales," *The Boston Globe* (February 20, 2003).

80. PR Newswire, *GlaxoSmithKline Actions Threaten Thousands* (February 20, 2003).

CASE 5

Starbucks' International Operations

Sanjib Dutta and K. Subhadra

"Internationally, we are in our infancy."
> Howard Schultz, Chairman and Chief Global Strategist, Starbucks, March 2003

"The expansion strategy internationally is not bulletproof as it is in the U.S."
> Mitchell J. Speiser, Analyst, Lehman Brothers, June 2003

All's Not Well with Starbucks

IN MARCH 2003, *FORTUNE* CAME OUT WITH ITS ANNUAL LIST OF *FORTUNE 500* COMPANIES. For Howard Schultz, Chairman of Starbucks Corp., this list was special as Starbucks featured in the list. It was a dream come true for the Seattle-based entrepreneur.

Though the U.S. economy was reeling under recession and many major retailers were reporting losses and applying for bankruptcy, Starbucks announced a 31% increase in its net earnings and a 23% increase in sales for the first quarter of 2003. Analysts felt that the success of Starbucks showed that a quality product speaks for itself. The fact that Starbucks spent less than 1% of its sales on advertising and marketing strengthened this view. In addition to being a popular brand among customers, Starbucks was also considered the best place to work due to its employee-friendly policies.[1] **Exhibit 1** shows Starbucks' income statement. See Starbucks' 2002 Annual Report, at *http://www.starbucks.com/aboutus/financials.asp*, for complete financial statements.

Exhibit 1
Consolidated Statement of Earnings Starbucks Corporation (Dollar amounts in millions, except per share data)

	Year Ending		
	Sept. 29 2002	Sept. 30 2001	Oct. 1 2000
Net revenues:			
Retail	$2,792,904	$2,229,594	$1,823,607
Specialty	496,004	419,386	354,007
Total net revenues	3,288,908	2,648,980	2,177,614
Cost of sales and related occupancy costs	1,350,011	1,112,785	961,885
Store operating expenses	1,121,108	875,473	704,898
Other operating expenses	127,178	93,326	78,445
Depreciation and amortization expenses	205,557	163,501	130,232
General and administrative expenses	202,161	151,416	110,202
Income from equity investees	35,832	28,615	20,300
Operating income	318,725	281,094	212,252
Interest and other income, net	9,300	10,768	7,110
Internet-related investment losses	–	2,940	58,792
Gain on sale of investment	13,361	–	–
Earnings before income taxes	341,386	288,922	160,570
Income taxes	126,313	107,712	66,006
Net earnings	$ 215,073	$ 181,210	$ 94,564
Net earnings per common share—basic	$ 0.56	$ 0.48	$ 0.25
Net earnings per common share—diluted	$ 0.54	$ 0.46	$ 0.24
Weighted average shares outstanding:			
Basic	385,575	380,566	371,191
Diluted	397,526	394,349	385,999
Ratios (%)			
Cost of sales (%)	41.0	42.0	44.2
Operating income margin (%)	9.7	10.6	9.7
Net profit margin (%)	6.5	6.8	4.3

Source: Starbucks Corporation "2002 Annual Report."

However, analysts felt that the success of Starbucks was due to its profitable domestic operations. It was reported that most of Starbucks' international operations were running into losses. In May 2003, Starbucks' Japanese operations reported a loss of $3.9 million (Japan constituted the largest market for the company outside the United States), and the company also performed badly in Europe and the Middle East. Analysts pointed out that Starbucks' international operations were not as well planned as its U.S. operations. They also observed that the volatile international business environment made it difficult for the company to effectively manage its international operations.

Many analysts felt that it was important for the company to focus on its international operations. With the U.S. market getting saturated, Starbucks would be forced to look outside the United States for revenues and growth.

Background Note

The history of Starbucks dates to 1971, when Jerry Baldwin, Zev Siegl, and Gordon Bowker launched a coffee bean retailing store named Starbucks to sell specialty whole-bean coffee in Seattle. By 1981, the number of Starbucks stores had increased to five, and Starbucks had also established a small roasting facility in Seattle. Around the same time, Schultz, who was working with Hammarplast—a Swedish housewares company that marketed coffee makers—noticed that Starbucks, a small company from Seattle, was ordering more coffee makers than anyone else. In order to find out more about the company, Schultz visited Seattle. Schultz was so impressed by the company and its founders that he offered to work for the company.

In 1982, Schultz joined Starbucks as marketing manager, with an equity stake in the company. During his first year at Starbucks, he studied the various types of coffee and the intricacies of the coffee business. The turning point came in 1983, when Schultz was sent to Milan, Italy, for an international housewares show. There he observed that every street in the city had an espresso coffee bar where people met and spent time. Schultz realized that Starbucks could introduce espresso coffee bars in the United States. He put forward this idea to his partners, but they did not like the idea of selling espresso coffee. However, after a lot of persuasion from Schultz, they agreed to allow him to sell espresso coffee in their retail shop. The business picked up, and by the weekend, they were making more money by selling the beverage than by selling coffee beans. Still, the partners refused to venture into the beverage business, so Schultz decided to quit the company and start out on his own.

In April 1985, Schultz opened a coffee bar called Il Giornale in Seattle, with a seed capital of $150,000 invested by Jerry Baldwin and Gordon Bowker. The rest of the capital was raised through private placement. Soon, the second and third stores were opened in Seattle and Vancouver respectively. During 1987, when Schultz heard that Starbucks' owners were selling off six stores along with a roasting plant and the Starbucks brand name, he raised $3.8 million through private placements and bought Starbucks. Because Starbucks was a more established name, Schultz decided to retain it instead of Il Giornale.

Schultz expanded Starbucks to Chicago, Los Angeles, and other major cities. But with increasing overhead expenses, the company reported a loss of $1.2 million in 1990. However, Schultz was confident of his business plan and continued his expansion spree. He even hired employees from companies such as PepsiCo. By 1991, the number of Starbucks stores had increased to 116, and Starbucks became the first privately owned company to offer employee stock options. In 1992, Starbucks was listed on the New York Stock Exchange at a price of $17 per share.

The strategy Starbucks adopted was to blanket a region with its new stores. By doing so, it could reduce the customers' rush in one store and also increase its revenues through new stores. This helped the company to reduce its distribution costs and the waiting period for customers in its stores, thereby increasing the number of customers. It was reported that on average, a customer visited Starbucks stores 18 times a month, a very high number compared to other American retailers. By 1993 there were around 100 Starbucks stores, which increased to 145 in 1994.

Along with serving coffee, Starbucks also sold merchandise. In 1995, it started selling CDs of its famous in-house music program. It also entered into alliances with various players such as Canadian Airlines, United Air Lines, Starwood Hotels, and Barnes & Noble, Inc., to serve Starbucks coffee.

Analysts attributed the success of Starbucks not only to its aggressive expansion but also to its product innovation. Starbucks came out with new products to attract customers. For instance, in 1995, to cater to the needs of diet-conscious young people, it launched Frappuccino—a low fat creamy iced coffee. In 1996, it launched ice cream and ice cream bars through its subsidiary Starbucks and Dreyer's Grand Ice Cream, Inc. In the same year, it also entered into an agreement with PepsiCo to launch bottled Starbucks Frappuccino. Due to all these initiatives, Starbucks has recorded an average growth of 20% per year since 1991, and its store traffic has increased 6%–8% per year.

However, in the mid 1990s, with the market reaching saturation, Starbucks could no longer depend on the U.S. market for growth. Analysts felt that to maintain its growth rates and to boost revenues, Starbucks should venture abroad. In 1995, Starbucks formed Starbucks

Exhibit 2
Starbucks'
International
Presence

Country	Type of Entry	Name of Partner	Year
Canada	Wholly owned subsidiary	Starbucks Coffee Canada	1996
Japan	Joint Venture	Sazaby Inc.	1996
Malaysia	Licensee	Berajaya Group bhd	1998
New Zealand	Licensee	Restaurant Brands	1998
Taiwan	Joint Venture	President Coffee Corp.	1998
Kuwait	Licensee	Alshaya	1999
Philippines	Licensee	Rustan's Coffee Corp.	2000
Australia	Joint Venture	Markus Hofer	2000
Israel	Joint Venture	Delek Corporation[2]	2001
Austria	Licensee	Bon Appetit Group[2]	2001
Switzerland	Licensee	Bon Appetit Group[2]	2001
Germany	Joint Venture	Karstadt Qualle AG	2002
Greece	Joint Venture	Marinopoulos Brothers	2002
Mexico	Joint Venture	SC de Mexico	2002
Hawaii	Joint Venture	Café Hawaii Partners	2002
Hong Kong	Joint Venture	Maxim's Caterers Ltd	2000
Indonesia	Joint Venture	PT Mitra A diperkasa	2002
Puerto Rico	Joint Venture	Puerto Rico Coffee Partners LLC	2002
Lebanon	Licensee	Alshaya	N/A
Spain	Joint Venture	Grupo Vips	2002

Notes:
1. This list is not exhaustive.
2. Starbucks closed its operations in Israel and bought out the stakes of its partners in Austria and Switzerland in 2003.

Source: Compiled from various newspaper articles.

Coffee International, a wholly owned subsidiary, to monitor the company's international expansion. In 1996, Starbucks entered Japan through a joint venture with Sazaby Inc. (a leading Japanese teashop and interior-goods retailer), and over the years it expanded into southeast Asia, Europe, and the Middle East. By March 2003, Starbucks had 1,532 stores (23% of its total stores) outside the United States. (See **Exhibit 2** for Starbucks' international presence.)

International Expansion Strategies

Starbucks decided to enter the Asia/Pacific Rim markets first.[2] Growing consumerism in the Asia Pacific countries and eagerness among the younger generation to imitate Western lifestyles made these countries attractive markets for Starbucks.

Starbucks decided to enter international markets by using a three-pronged strategy: joint ventures, licensing, and wholly owned subsidiaries (see **Exhibit 3** for the modes of entry in international markets). Prior to entering a foreign market, Starbucks focused on studying the market conditions for its products in the country. It then decided on the local partner for its business. Initially, Starbucks test-marketed with a few stores that were opened in trendy places, and the company's experienced managers from Seattle handled the operations.

After successful test-marketing, local baristas (brew masters) were given training for 13 weeks in Seattle. Starbucks did not compromise on its basic principles. It ensured similar coffee beverage lineups and *No Smoking* rule in all its stores around the globe.

When Starbucks entered into a joint venture with Sazaby Inc. to open Starbucks stores in Japan, analysts felt that Starbucks was unlikely to succeed. They even advised Starbucks to forego its principles such as its *No Smoking* rule and ensure that the size of the stores would

Exhibit 3
Modes of Entry into
International
Markets

There are six ways to enter a foreign market: through exporting, turnkey projects, licensing, franchising, joint venture with a host country firm, and setting up a wholly owned subsidiary in the host country. Each mode of entry has advantages and disadvantages. The method a company chooses depends on a variety of factors, including the nature of the particular product or service and the conditions for market penetration in the foreign target market.

Exporting

Most firms begin their global expansion with exports and later switch over to another mode. In the 1990s, the volume of exports in the world economy had increased significantly due to the decline in trade barriers. However, exporting still remains a challenge for smaller firms. Firms planning to export must identify foreign market opportunities, familiarize themselves with the mechanics of exports, and learn to deal with foreign exchange risk.

Turnkey Projects

In a turnkey project, the contractor handles every aspect of the project for a foreign client, including the training of operating personnel. After the completion of the contract, the foreign client is handed the "key" to the plant that is ready for operation. Turnkey projects are common in the chemical, pharmaceutical, and petroleum refining industries.

Licensing

Licensing is an arrangement whereby a company (licenser) grants the rights to intangible property such as patents, inventions, formulas, processes, designs, copyrights, and trademarks to another company (licensee) for a specified period of time. The licenser receives a royalty fee from the licensee. For example, in the early 1960s, Xerox licensed its patented xerographic know-how to Fuji-Xerox. It was initially meant for 10 years, but the license was extended several times. In return, Fuji-Xerox paid Xerox a royalty fee equal to 5% of the net sales revenue that it earned.

Franchising

Franchising is similar to licensing except that it requires long-term commitments. In franchising, the franchiser not only sells intangible property to the franchisee but also insists that the franchisee abide by the rules of the business. In some cases, the franchiser also assists the franchisee in running the business. The franchiser receives a royalty payment that is usually a percentage of the franchisee's revenues. Service companies usually opt for franchising. For example, McDonald's pursues its expansion abroad through franchising. McDonald's sets down strict rules for the franchisees to operate their restaurants. The rules extend to cooking methods, staffing policy, and design and location of the restaurants. McDonald's also organizes the supply chain and provides management training and financial assistance to the franchisees.

Joint Ventures

In contrast to licensing and franchising arrangements, joint ventures allow companies to own a stake and play a role in the management of the foreign operation. Joint ventures require more direct investment and training, management assistance, and technology transfer. Joint ventures can be equity or non-equity partnerships. Equity joint ventures are contractual arrangements with equal partners. Non-equity ventures are ones where the host country partner has a greater stake. In some countries, a joint venture is the only way for a foreign company to set up operations.

**Exhibit 3
(continued)**

Wholly Owned Subsidiaries

In a wholly owned subsidiary, the firm owns 100% of the stock of the subsidiary. Wholly owned subsidiaries can be established in a foreign country in two ways. A firm can set up new operations in the foreign country or it can acquire a firm and promote its products through that firm. The following are the advantages and disadvantages of various entry modes.

Exporting

Advantage:

Ability to realize location and experience curve economies

Disadvantages:

High Transport Costs
Trade Barriers
Problems with local marketing agents

Turnkey Contracts

Advantages:

Ability to earn returns from process technology skills in countries where FDI is restricted
Creating efficient competitors

Disadvantage:

Lack of long term market presence

Licensing

Advantage:

Low development costs and risks

Disadvantages:

Lack of control over technology
Inability to realize location and experience curve economies
Inability to engage in global strategic coordination

Joint Ventures

Advantages:

Access to local partner's knowledge
Sharing development costs and risks
Politically acceptable

Disadvantages:

Lack of control over technology
Inability to engage in global strategic coordination
Inability to realize location and experience economies

Wholly owned subsidiaries

Advantages:

Protection of technology
Ability to engage in global strategic coordination

Disadvantages:

Ability to realize location and experience economies
High costs and risks

Source: ICFAI Center for Management Research.

not be more than 500 square feet due to the high rents in Japan. However, Starbucks stuck to its *No Smoking* principle, which attracted young Japanese women to the Starbucks stores, and the size of the stores was 1200–1500 square feet—similar to the stores in the United States. Proving analysts wrong, Starbucks became successful and, in the first year, it opened more than 100 stores in Japan.

According to Starbucks sources, listening to its local partner also helped. Starbucks took advantage of its local partner Sazaby's knowledge about Japanese coffee drinking habits and introduced new products such as Green Tea Frappucino, which became popular.

Starbucks was successful in attracting a young crowd in all its Asian markets, as young people in these markets were eager to imitate the American culture. It even adapted itself to the local culture to gain market acceptance. For instance, Starbucks offered curry puffs and meat buns in Asian markets as Asians generally prefer to eat something while having coffee.

Analysts felt that the strong coffee-drinking culture in Europe posed both challenges and opportunities for Starbucks. It would face tough competition from the sidewalk cafes of France, coffeehouses of Vienna, and espresso bars of Italy that had developed a strong coffee-drinking culture across the continent, exposing Europeans to some of the best coffee in the world. However, Starbucks executives commented that Europe used to make great coffees but by the late 1990s, the taste had gone awry. In 1998, Starbucks opened its first store in England, and it soon expanded its presence to Switzerland, Germany, and Greece.

It was generally felt that though old people would stick to the existing coffee houses, the young would be attracted to Starbucks. Said Helmut Spudich, Editor, *Der Standard* (a Vienna-based paper), "The coffeehouses in Vienna are nice, but they are old. Starbucks is considered hip."[3] Another important factor that could lead to the success of Starbucks in Europe was its ambience and *No Smoking* environment, unlike traditional European coffee bars. The self-service mode of operation also attracted the young crowd as it was observed that youngsters did not like to wait for the waiter to come and take orders. According to Starbucks sources, it was successful because it was not selling just coffee but an experience that was unique only to Starbucks stores. Maslen, President of Starbucks International, said, "The coffee is good, but it's just the vehicle. The romance of coffee, the occasion, the community, is what Starbucks is selling."[4] In the Middle East, Starbucks went for licensing (except in Israel, where it had a joint venture). Respecting the culture in the Middle East, Starbucks stores offered segregated sections for women.

In September 2002, Starbucks announced that by 2005 it would increase the number of international stores to 10,000. However, analysts pointed out that it would be difficult for Starbucks to make profits in international markets, and they were soon to be proved right.

Problems in International Markets

From the early 2000s, Starbucks faced many problems in its international operations. (See **Exhibit 4** for the types of risks in international business.) The volatile political environment in the Middle East created serious problems for Starbucks. In July 2002, Arab students called for a boycott of American goods and services, due to the alleged close relationship between the United States and Israel. The boycott targeted U.S. companies including Starbucks, Burger King, Coca-Cola and Estée Lauder. Starbucks topped the list of companies to be boycotted due to Schultz's alleged closeness to the Jewish community.[5]

The problem was aggravated when it was reported that, in one of his lectures to students at the University of Washington, Schultz had said, "One of my missions is to sensitize you; you should not be immune to what is happening in the world. I travel a great deal and one of the things that I see is the rise of anti-Semitism in Europe, especially France and England."[6] His address to Jewish-Americans made matters worse. Schultz said, "What is going on in the Middle East is not an isolated part of the world. The rise of anti-Semitism is at an all time high

Exhibit 4
Types of Risk in
International
Business

Typically, a firm operating internationally is exposed to different types of risk. These can be listed as environmental, financial, organizational, or strategic risks.

Strategic Risk

MNCs typically face a diverse set of risks, and not all of them can be assessed quantitatively. Michael Porter defines five forces impacting a firm's competitiveness—threat of substitutes, threat of new entrants in the industry, bargaining power of suppliers, bargaining power of customers, and the intensity of competition within the industry. A firm's strategic decisions to respond to these five forces are a source of risk.

Operational Risk

Operational risk arises out of factors internal to the company, such as machinery breakdown, industrial strife, supply and distribution imperfections, excess or shortfall in inventory, etc. It causes downtime in the day-to-day operations of the enterprise. Reducing costs by eliminating waste and reducing variances and lead time by improving processes are important to bring about global efficiency. The greater the number of parts and processes involved in production, the greater the risk of not achieving the desired quality and productivity standards.

Political Risk

Political risk refers to political actions that have a negative impact on the firm's value. The process of establishing a cause-and-effect relationship between political factors and business income is called *political risk analysis*. Political risk is not confined to developing countries. It exists even in highly industrialized economies. While macro-political risks such as war and anti-globalization efforts affect the value of all firms in the country, micro-political risks such as regulation of certain industries adversely affect the value of a firm or firms within that industry.

Country Risk

Country risk is a wider concept that encompasses economic conditions, government policies, political conditions, and security factors. The challenge of country risk analysis is in the aggregation of risk factors.

Technological Risk

Technological risk means the probability of adverse effects on business due to factors such as obsolescence of an existing technology, development costs of new technology, failure of a new technology, and security concerns of electronic transactions.

Environmental Risk

Environmental risk can be of two forms. The company may incur regulators' wrath because it polluted the environment, or there may be a public outcry in the event of environmental damage caused by the company. Environmental risk management might not provide short-term gains like financial risk management does, but in the long run, it can certainly become a source of competitive advantage and also enhance the corporate image.

Source: ICFAI Center for Management Research.

since the 1930s. Palestinians aren't doing their job, they're not stopping terrorism."[7] These comments from Schultz resulted in angry protests from the Arab countries and pro-Palestinian groups across the Middle East and Europe. Analysts felt that Schultz's comments strengthened the feeling that he was acting as an Israeli mouthpiece.

Starbucks distanced itself from Schultz's comments, saying that they represented his personal beliefs and not those of the company. Schultz also denied allegations that he was anti-Palestinian and released a personal statement, saying "My position has always been pro-peace and for the two nations to co-exist peacefully."[8] In addition to these incidents, the U.S. declaration of war on Iraq in early 2003 made matters worse for the company. Due to increasing security threats, Starbucks closed down its six stores in Israel.

Starbucks also faced criticism from Non Governmental Organizations (NGOs) that urged the company to acquire certified coffee beans, ensuring that those coffee beans were grown and marketed under certain economic and social conditions. Furthermore, Starbucks faced problems due to economic recession in countries such as Switzerland, Germany, and Japan in the early 2000s, where it experienced declining sales and revenues.

Starbucks faced stiff competition, high business development costs, and resistance from customers in international markets. Especially in Europe, it was reported that Starbucks faced stiff competition from well-established local players that offered specialty coffee at lower prices than Starbucks. For example, in England, a Starbucks tall latte was sold at $2.93, and a similar drink was available for $2.12 at a local coffee shop.

By the late 1990s, Starbucks noticed that store traffic in Japan, its largest overseas market, had been reducing. It was observed that over a period of time, customers opted for different stores because they did not like the taste of Starbucks coffee. Commented a customer, "I never go to Starbucks if I can help it. The coffee tastes artificial."[9] Starbucks sales in Japan declined by over 17% in 2002. In order to boost its sales, Starbucks introduced food items such as rice and salmon wraps and white peach muffins, yet it failed to gain market acceptance.

Analysts observed that Starbucks was unable to earn enough revenues from its international operations due to its complex joint ventures and licensing agreements. While the company invested huge amounts in imparting training to the employees and promoting its products, it earned only a percentage share in total profits and royalty fees. It was further felt that the company did not have any control over the operational costs.

In addition to its problems in international markets, Starbucks experienced operational problems due to lack of a trained workforce and suitable real estate for its stores. Commenting on the operational hindrances Starbucks faced, Maslen said, "If we could train the people and find the real estate, the expansion could happen tomorrow, almost. There is demand."[10]

Future Prospects

In order to have better control over operational costs, Starbucks decided to go to new suppliers for items such as mugs. It was reported that the company was thinking of sourcing mugs from low-cost Japanese vendors rather than importing them from the United States and that it was planning to source its paper goods (such as plates and cups) from Southeast Asia.

Starbucks also announced that it would slow down its pace of expansion by opening around 80 stores in 2003 (compared to the 115 stores opened in 2002). Company sources also revealed that Starbucks would close down its loss-making stores. However, analysts pointed out that closing the loss-making stores and adopting cost cutting could increase profitability only in the short run and not drive future growth.

Analysts pointed out that Starbucks should rethink its entry strategy in international markets and focus on pricing. They also felt that because the company was relatively debt free and had around $300 million in free cash flows, it should be able to rebuild its foreign operations.

However, they cautioned Starbucks against the external risks resulting from volatile political and business environments around the world. They felt that with increasing tensions between the United States and the rest of the world, the business environment, especially in the Middle East and Southeast Asia, was becoming increasingly volatile. Acknowledging the risks involved in the international markets, Schultz said, "We're not taking our success for granted. We also understand that the burden of proof at times is on us given the fact that a lot is being written and there's more sensitivity than ever before about America and American companies. These are the very early days for the growth and development of the company internationally. Clearly there's a big world out there for Starbucks to expand in."[11]

Only time can tell whether Starbucks will be able to brew its success in the international markets.

Notes

1. Starbucks was the first organization in the United States to offer stock options and health care coverage to part-time employees.
2. Asia/Pacific Rim markets consist of Japan, the Philippines, Indonesia, Thailand, Taiwan, Malaysia, Singapore, China, South Korea, North Korea, New Zealand, Australia, Vietnam, Cambodia, and Papua New Guinea.
3. S. Holmes, D. Bennett, K. Carlisle, and C. Dawson, "Planet Starbucks," *Business Week* (September 9, 2003).
4. "Starbucks Jolts Europe's Coffee Houses," *Seattle Times* (May 19, 2002).
5. In 1998, Schultz was honored with the Israeli 50th Anniversary Tribute Award by the Jerusalem Fund of Aish Ha-Torah (a group supporting Israel).
6. W. McDougall, *Starbucks: The Cup That Cheers*, www.zmag.org/content/Mideast/99110687698 (July 11, 2002).
7. *Ibid.*
8. *Ibid.*
9. S. Holmes, M. I. Kunii, J. Ewing, and K. Capell, "For Starbucks, There's No Place Like Home," *BusinessWeek* (June 9, 2003).
10. "Starbucks Jolts Europe's Coffee Houses," *Seattle Times* (May 19, 2002).
11. H. Jung, *Starbucks Backlash: The Java Giant's Expansion Brews Dissent Overseas*, www.globalexchange.org/campaigns/fairtrade/coffee/673.html (April 16, 2003).

Additional Readings and References

J. Reese, "Starbucks," *Fortune* (December 9, 1996).

L. Ioannau, "King Bean," *Fortune* (May 5, 1998).

"Perky People," *The Economist* (May 28, 1998).

Stone, "Starbucks: The Jolt Is Still There—and Not Just from Java," *BusinessWeek* (April 6, 1999).

N. Schwartz, "Still Perking After All These Years," *Fortune* (May 24, 1999).

M. Gimein, "Behind Starbucks' New Venture: Beans, Beatniks, and Booze," *Fortune* (May 15, 2000).

D. Yang Jones, "An American (Coffee) in Paris—and Rome," www.ups.edu (February 19, 2001).

S. Holmes, "Starbucks: Keeping the Brew Hot," *BusinessWeek* (August 6, 2001).

"Coffee with Your Tea?" *The Economist* (October 4, 2001).

S. Erlanger, "Starbucks Proves a Hit in Vienna, Even with Smoking Banned," www.naplesnews.com (June 1, 2002).

"Israel to Back out of Starbucks Venture As Arab Boycotts Rage On," www.inminds.co.uk (July 11, 2002).

C. Dawson and S. Holmes, "Is Japan Losing Its Taste for Latte Already?" *BusinessWeek* (December 9, 2002).

C. Daniels, "Mr. Coffee," *Fortune* (March 30, 2003).

P. Patsuris, "Can Starbucks Get It Wholesale?" *Forbes* (April 25, 2003).

www.starbucks.com
www.starbucks.co.jp
www.hoovers.com
www.businesswire.com
www.seattletimes.com

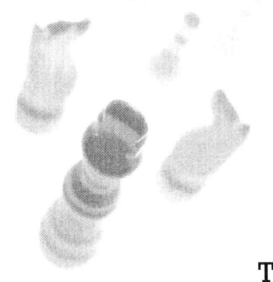

CASE 6
Turkcell:
The Only Turk on Wall Street

Sue Greenfeld

WITH MORE THAN 60% OF THE TURKISH MARKET FOR MOBILE PHONES AND 16.3 MILLION subscribers as of March 31, 2003, Turkcell İletişim Hizmetleri A.Ş., or Turkcell (TKC) for short, is the only Turkish company listed on the New York Stock Exchange. As stated on TKC's web site, "we . . . have developed the premier mobile brand in Turkey by differentiating ourselves from our competition based on quality of service . . . [We] have introduced a wide range of mobile services intended to attract and retain customers with various service needs." Simply put, there is no company in the world like Turkcell. It is a vibrant, full-of-life, and energetic firm that is all over Turkey. This is especially amazing because Turkcell only began operations in 1994.

With more than 100 different consumer services, Turkcell considers itself the leading mobile telecommunications operator in Turkey. Having launched its General Packet Radio Service (GPRS) in 2001 and a Multimedia Messaging Service (MMS) in 2002, Turkcell has believed in remaining at the forefront of technological innovation since its inception. MMS is an application that combines videotext, graphics, and voice into a single message. According to company literature, Turkcell was one of the first mobile operators in Europe to promote MMS technology to its subscribers.

By the end of 2002, Turkcell had total assets of $3.2 billion, revenues of $1.97 billion, net income of $101 million, and more than 2,000 employees. With three additional Turkish market players created since 1994, including Aycell, a state-owned company, and an onerous 66% tax burden, Turkcell wonders what steps it should take to position itself for the twenty-first century. For example, how can it reduce economic risk if the Turkish lira (TRL) takes a nosedive as it did in the year 2000? How can it increase usage per customer aside from increasing its subscriber base? Also, can it afford to take a leadership role in introducing 3G, the third generation of mobile phone systems, into Turkey? Is there anything it can do to influence the Turkish government in order to reduce its 66% tax burden? And with the Turkish government moving toward privatization of numerous industries, why would the government set up a state-owned company in the first place? These are just a few of the questions that the managers of Turkcell are asking as they think about the company and its future.

Country Background

Turkey is a fascinating country with more than 19 civilizations that date back thousands of years. Hittites, Phrygians, Urartians, Lydians, Greeks, and Romans are just a few among the many people who once roamed the rolling landscape. However, the history of modern Turkey begins October 29, 1923, with the revolution and the creation of the Republic of Turkey. This was accomplished through the inspirational leadership of Mustafa Kemal Atatürk, the "Father of the Turks," who transformed and secularized the country.

Turkey is the successor to the great Ottoman Empire, which started in the late thirteenth century but was slowly dismantled throughout the nineteenth century via wars and by the Allied powers during World War I, when the Turks sided with Germany. In fact, one of the worst battles occurred at Gallipoli, when the Australian, British, and New Zealand Armies struggled to destroy the remnants of the Ottoman Empire. More than 100,000 Allied forces and Turks lost their lives at Gallipoli, but the Allied forces were unable to vanquish the Turkish spirit. From this gruesome despair of World War I, Mustafa Kemal Atatürk emerged as a new leader for Turkey, and he quickly realized the need for a new type of government, one more democratic and more secular than had previously existed.

From 1923 to 1929, the Turkish government focused on reducing illiteracy, latinizing the language, nationalizing the economy, and decreasing the 80% dependency on agriculture as a primary source of employment. Some foreign capital was encouraged in the areas of construction and railways. This focus changed during the world depression years of 1929 to 1939, when the emphasis shifted to protectionism, nationalization of foreign firms, and the building up of financial institutions. At that time, the government created its first Five-Year Plan for industrial development, including the establishment of factories for steel, cement, paper, chemicals, sugar, and textiles. The Second Five-Year Plan of 1936 added mines, facilities in natural resources, and other heavier industry, but World War II interrupted this development. During the war years of 1939 to 1945, the government was engaged in a major land reform effort, against the wishes of Turkey's largest landholders.

During World War II, Turkey remained neutral until 1945, when it joined the Allies, and it subsequently became part of the United Nations. It was admitted into the North American Treaty Organization (NATO) in 1952. From 1947 to 1962, Turkey received funds from the Marshall Plan to mechanize agricultural output. Strong encouragement of foreign capital investment began in 1954, while 1963 to 1979 saw rapidly growing international debt. This debt was incurred in part from Turkey's low level of exports in comparison to its high dependence on imported raw material. Since 1986, Turkey has been an associate member of the European Union (EU), and it has since applied for full membership. In December 2002, Turkey received a date from the EU for accession talks to begin in December 2004.

In 2002, Turkey's economy still had a strong 40% agricultural base. Other industries were clothing, textiles, ceramics, food processing, automobiles, mining, steel, petroleum, construction, and glass. About 18.7% of Turkey's exports went to Germany, while 11.4% were directed to the United States. Turkey is highly dependent on oil imports.

Nevertheless, Turkey continues to struggle with an inflation rate that has hovered around 40% for 20 years. **Exhibit 1** indicates the exchange rate of the U.S. dollar for the TRL.

In 2001, there was a major economic crisis when overnight the Turkish lira was drastically devaluated. According to the 2001 Annual Report letter from Chairman Mehmet Emin Karamehmet to Turkcell's shareholders, "the Turkish Lira lost 114% of its value against the U.S. dollar, [Turkish] gross national product decreased by approximately 9.4%, [and] consumer infla-

**Exhibit 1
Exchange Rate of
the U.S. Dollar for
the Turkish Lira**

Year	U. S. Dollar ($)	Turkish Lira (TRL)
1996	$1.00	81,405
1997	1.00	151,865
1998	1.00	260,724
1999	1.00	418,783
2000	1.00	677,621
2001	1.00	1,176,560
2002	1.00	1,650,000

Source: www.odci.gov/cia/publications/factbook/geos/tu.html (September 10, 2002).

tion rose by 68% by year end." It was also the first time that Turkcell had posted a net income loss of more than $186 million. Some have blamed the crisis in part on the government printing too much money and having too many state-supported programs, inadequate collection of tax revenues, the severe drop in the Turkish stock market, insufficient privatization of industries, and inadequate reform in the banking area. In 2000, the government took over 22 different Turkish banks that had gone bankrupt and/or were considered corrupt. The International Monetary Fund (IMF) has stepped in more than one time to help assist Turkey. By the end of 2002, Turkey held $16 billion in IMF loans. To make up for lost tax revenues and the underreporting of income, the Turkish government decided to place heavy tax burdens on both the petroleum and mobile communications industries. In the case of petroleum, there is a user tax at the gas pump. In 2002, the equivalent U.S. price for a gallon of gasoline in Turkey was $4.50, and after 1999 the government added a 25% earthquake tax on mobile communications. The 2002 tax rate on Global System for Mobile Communication (GSM) communications operators/subscribers in Turkey, including Turkcell, was approximately 66% of earnings before interest charges.

To enhance foreign investment opportunities in Turkey, a foreign economic relations board (DEIK) was created in 1986. This nonprofit, private organization "attempts to improve the external economic relations with Turkish enterprises and to contribute to the integration of the Turkish economy into the world economy." According to Başak Kızıldemir from DEIK, there are 30 individuals on staff working with business councils in 59 different countries. The Turkish–U.S. Business Council is a part of DEIK. Some member organizations include Microsoft, CNN Türk, Boeing, JPMorgan, and Delta Air Lines, among many others. Literature from the DEIK reminds readers that Turkey is one of the 10 largest emerging economies, has great resiliency, is a long-term trading partner with the United States, and is one of the most trusted allies of the United States. Turkey played a major role in the 1991 Gulf War, helping the United States.

In terms of demographics, Turkey has about 70 million people in a land space approximately the size of Texas (see **Exhibit 2**). Seventy percent of the population is under the age of 35. While the country is secular, without a state-supported religion, 98.8% of Turks identify themselves as Muslim, with less than 1% Jewish or Christian. Turkey has 53 government and 19 private trust-funded universities, and students are admitted through a central placement system. Entry is extremely competitive, and students have to score very well on the multidisciplinary university entrance exam. On the university campus and elsewhere, the Turkish population dresses casually, in Western-style clothing.

History of Telecommunications in Turkey

Like the rest of the world, Turkey has embraced the mobile telephone communication age with a ravenous appetite, and as in many other countries, the postal service and telecommunications in Turkey have been the sole domain of the government. Except for the GSM com-

Exhibit 2
Map of Turkey

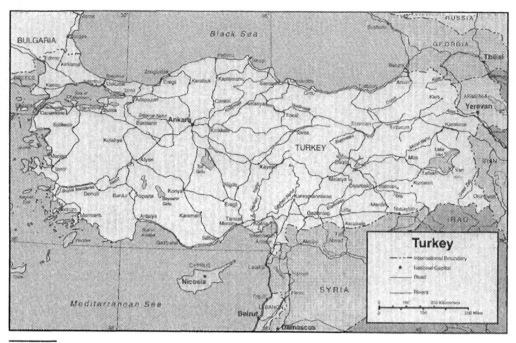

Source: Lonely Planet.

munications, the state-owned Türk Telecom is the only authorized supplier of telecommunications. The Telecommunication Authority regulates all telecommunications activity in Turkey. Telegram and Telephone Law No. 406 was the principal law governing telecommunication, and it gave Turk Telecom complete monopoly power until December 31, 2003. Then the communications world in Turkey became a different ballgame, but the mobile telephone world of GSM had changed 16 years earlier.

In 1987, GSM was created to assist in the unification and integration of mobile communications within the EU, and it is one of four basic digital standards for mobile communications. A key component of GSM is the subscriber's identity, or SIM card. The SIM card allows the user of a handset or mobile phone to be identified. Without a valid SIM card inside, a handset does not function. Under a revenue-sharing agreement with Türk Telecom, Turkcell was formed in 1993 as Turkey's first GSM company. Turkcell started operations the following year, at the same time that a second mobile phone company, TelSim, began. In 1998, upon payment of an up-front license fee of $500 million, Turkcell was a granted a 25-year GSM license to operate in Turkey.

In the mid-1990s, the only services provided were the basic handsets for the sole mobile vocal communication market, but mobile phones in Turkey, as elsewhere, have become personal digital assistants (PDAs), among other features. The infrastructure in Turkey has been constantly updated as new technologies have emerged to provide for better mobile phone services. Turkcell introduced Dual Numbering Service, which enables the creation of two separate numbers on an individual mobile phone. Another technological advance has been the Wireless Application Protocol (WAP), which allows Internet access to anyone with a mobile phone. More specifically, WAP is an application environment and a set of communication protocols for wireless devices, designed to enable manufacturer-, vendor-, and technology-independent access to the Internet and advanced telephony services.

In 2000, the government of Turkey issued two new GSM 1800 licenses. One was to the İştim consortium, operating under the name Aria. The other new GSM 1800 license was awarded to Türk Telecom, operating under its wholly owned subsidiary Aycell. Aria began offering services on March 21, 2001, and Aycell became operational in December 2001. By the end of 2002, there were four major players in the highly competitive Turkish market: Turkcell, TelSim, Aria, and state-owned Aycell. Each has its own marketing style, and each is working hard to become a household name in Turkey.

While TelSim also started operations in 1994 and held a respectable market share in 2002, it has become embroiled in a long-standing controversy with Motorola, the U.S. communications giant, and Nokia, the Swedish handset vendor. Both Motorola and Nokia have claimed in court papers that TelSim defaulted on $2 billion of vendor financing to help set up TelSim's infrastructure. Motorola wanted the top TelSim CEO to go to jail for up to 24 months for contempt.

Aria is a smaller player and a fast-rising star in Turkey. It is composed of a major consortium of Turkey's largest bank, Işbank, and Telecom Italia. Together, they paid $2.5 billion for the GSM 1800 license, but the real threat to the mobile communications market has been the government's entry, Aycell. Aycell has undercut prices and offers services lower than cost, especially to its own customers calling from an Aycell phone to another Aycell phone, but so far it has gotten away with it. The Turkish government covers any losses of Aycell. Through its lawyers, Turkcell has issued concerns to the regulatory body in Turkey, but wonders whether there is anything else it can do to halt what it thinks is unfair competition.

A new threat from Aycell surfaced in May 2003. The news agency Reuters announced that the Italian telecommunication giant TIM, part of the Telecom Italia group, was merging with Aycell in Turkey. Reuters reported that the two companies "agreed to merge their Turkish wireless operation in a move that would solve TIM's escalating regulatory dispute in the country." The merger of TIM with Aycell would give the Italian company entry into Turkey and would eliminate the need for roaming access to its rivals' networks, which is an important facet of the dispute in Turkey. To combat this challenge, Turkcell realizes that it must be vigilant in case there is an opportunity to merge with or acquire another company itself.

At the end of 2002, it was believed that market penetration of mobile phones ran around 34% in Turkey. This means a lot more growth can be expected if Turkey is to reach the saturation levels of other industrial countries, such as Italy (92%), Finland (82%), Portugal (91%), Spain (81%), the United Kingdom (83%), Greece (83%), Germany (69%), or France (62%). See **Exhibit 3** for mobile phone etiquette.

**Exhibit 3
Mobile Phone
Etiquette**

1. When answering or making a mobile telephone call, it is important to remember a few simple rules. Being polite is the first step.
2. Receiving or making calls should not be disruptive, intrusive, or take priority over face-to-face conversations.
3. Mobile phones should be switched off in meetings, in places of worship, in libraries, and at the cinema, the theater, or a concert.
4. Using a mobile phone should be avoided in elevators, buses, trains, and other small places where the conversation can be overheard.
5. Phones *must* be switched off on airplanes, on sea buses, and in hospitals.
6. Using a mobile phone while driving can be very dangerous. Some U.S. states have made a law against using a phone while driving. Drivers should never endanger themselves or others by using a handheld phone. Only under a dire emergency should a mobile phone be used while driving a car. It is better to pull off to the side of the road to make the call.
7. If calling for business purposes, always call during business hours.

Source: Adapted from S. Delin, "Mobile Manners Maketh Man," Turkcell World: The International Magazine of Turkey's Leading GSM Operator, Issue 2 (Winter 2001).

Company Background

Starting with only 94 employees, Turkcell commenced operations in 1994 under a revenue-sharing agreement with Türk Telecom, the state-owned fixed-line network operator. At that time, there were only 63,500 subscribers in the customer base. This number grew significantly each year to about 2.3 million in 1998, when upon a payment of an up-front license fee of $500 million, Turkcell was granted a 25-year GSM license to operate in Turkey. From 1994 to 1998, Turkcell operated with only TelSim as a primary competitor. Since 1998, the customer base has continued to grow considerably: 5.5 million at the end of 1999, 10.1 million at the end of 2000, 12.2 million at the end of 2001 and 16.3 million by the end of March 2003.

There are two basic types of Turkcell customers: prepaid and postpaid. A prepaid customer purchases a voucher card at a gas station, newsstand, kiosk, retail store, Turkcell's web site, or a bank ATM. He or she scratches the card to reveal the secret 12-digit number. When the customer calls an authorized Turkcell number and provides the 12-digit number, the service is activated or continued for a particular mobile phone. A postpaid customer receives a bill. Both types of customers have risen steadily for Turkcell, to the point where the customer base is two-thirds prepaid and one-third postpaid. By March 21, 2002, there was a nationwide network of more than 520 exclusive handset dealers selling only Turkcell services, and about 13,300 sales points (such as newspaper kiosks) for voucher cards.

In 1999, Turkcell became the first GSM operator in Turkey to be awarded the prestigious ISO 9001. The International Organization for Standardization (ISO) created worldwide guidelines to promote operating efficiency, improve productivity, and reduce costs. The ISO 9000 concept took off in the early 1990s and has helped to define world-class quality systems. There are four levels of ISO 9000: 9001, 9002, 9003, and 9004. The most rigorous of the ISO standards is ISO 9001, which has 20 components. ISO 9001 means the company has certification in design, engineering, and manufacturing.

However, one of Turkcell's most momentous events occurred on July 11, 2000, when the company completed its initial public offering (IPO) of more than 25 billion shares, in the form of ordinary shares on the Istanbul Stock Exchange and American Depository shares on the New York Stock Exchange. There was quite a bit of excitement at Turkcell as numerous company employees were on hand to make the day a big success. Turkcell took over Wall Street with a carnival-like atmosphere. A small Turkish village with street fair tents and kiosks was set up. It featured Turkish food, Turkish coffee and tea, and authentic Turkish crafts. The air had a festive feeling of celebration. There was a man on stilts whose legs were covered with long yellow pants and purple trim saying Turkcell. He wore a matching blue jacket with the Turkcell snabbit logo and a tall hat. It was a sight to behold. And who could forget the blue and white balloons tied together in a gigantic arch overreaching the tents and the wonderful Turkcell banner hanging from the sober columns of the New York Stock Exchange building? None of the Turkcell employees who attended can forget that day. By the end of 2002, they were still talking about the grand Turkcell entrance and quite proud to be the first Turkish company ever listed on the New York Stock Exchange.

In 2001, the company launched one of the world's largest mobile portals, called GPRSLand. GPRS means General Packet Radio Service; it is a data transmission service that provides faster mobile access to the Internet than WAP. GPRS is a standard for wireless communications that runs at speeds up to 115 kilobits per second, compared to GSM's speed of 9.6 kilobits per second. GPRS, which supports a wide range of bandwidths, is an efficient use of limited bandwidth and is particularly suited for sending and receiving small bundles of data, such as in e-mail and web browsing, as well as large volumes of data. GPRS allows Turkcell postpaid customers to have permanent access to their e-mail and the Internet. GPRSLand is a collaborative effort between Turkcell and Ericsson, one of Sweden's largest companies and a supplier of mobile phones. Four software companies have worked to develop the 15 applications included in GPRSLand. GPRSLand is a unique service that has provided Turkcell customers with access to a host of data applications. The applications were segmented into information and entertainment offerings. The launch of GPRSLand was supported by an extensive advertising campaign that made it a well-known service among Turkcell customers. In October 2002, GPRSLand won the "best new service" award at the World Communications Awards in the United Kingdom. "This is how everyone should do it," said the judges of Turkcell's GPRSLand. A panel of judges, including industry leaders, consultants, and representatives from industry groups, also commented, "Turkcell has done a great job putting a package together, not just a network. They've really thought it through and it's great to hear of this kind of sophistication." Currently there are 27 applications on GPRSLand. The business model provides financial incentives for third-party developers as well, encouraging them to create successful applications.

In 2002, Turkcell and Microsoft created another new service, called Office Mobile Service. This service allows subscribers access to Microsoft Outlook and Exchange by using a Microsoft Mobile Information Server (MMIS). Turkcell also provided 100% comprehensive coverage for all cities in Turkey that had populations of 5,000 or more. Turkcell had international roaming agreements with 319 operators in 136 countries as of June 3, 2003. Turkcell started the year 2002 with the appointment of new Chief Executive Officer Muzaffer Akpinar. He became Turkcell's second CEO, following the visionary leadership of CEO Cüneyt Türktan.

The Story of Snabbit

Snabbit is the 1994 creation of Mengül Ertel, a famous Turkish contemporary graphic designer who passed away on March 15, 2000. When Turkcell was about to be launched, the company approached Ertel to design a company logo and emblem that would be very unique and quite memorable. He turned to the animal world and created an animal like no other animal: the snabbit, partly a snail (because of its antennae) and partly a rabbit (because of its speed). According to company literature, the snabbit "reflects the energy, dynamism and total uniqueness that define Turkcell." The snabbit is featured in every Turkcell retail store. It graces numerous promotional items and can be seen at many sporting events. What Ertel produced has become a Turkish icon.

Initially, only one snabbit existed, and he was named Sinyal Bebek. For an important telecommunication fair to be held in September 2001, Sinyal Bebek was renamed Cell-O and given a whole new family. Later, in a *Turkcell World* article, Sevil Delin, a writer and translator, described all the family members. Cell-O is pictured as a technophile and joker, but he is kind-hearted and a visionary. His wife, Celly, is cautious and very economical. She is interested in astrology, and she is a great businesswoman and a great mother. Cellita, the daughter, is environmentally and fashion conscious. She needs her freedom, while Cell, Jr., the son, is an Internet addict, obsessed with soccer, voracious, and enterprising. Finally, the grandfather, Celldede, is just a teenager in his 70s who is an adventurer, a philanderer, and a generous man. By establishing an entire family, Turkcell believed that the Cell family would increase the value of the Turkcell brand and help to ensure brand loyalty to retain subscribers. Each member of the Cell family represents a different segment of Turkcell's customer base. The idea was to target products for those various market segments. Some individuals in Turkey believe the Cell family with its dad, mom, daughter, son and grandfather may have some similarity to the popular show *The Simpsons*, which is shown on TV in English but with Turkish subtitles in Turkey.

Facilities

Turkcell's main headquarters is located at the Turkcell Plaza in Istanbul, Turkey. The highly commercial area is a mixture of upscale retail stores, various types of businesses, mosques, churches, schools, and a tramway. One side of the Turkcell offices faces the famous İstiklal Caddesi (or Independence Street) of Taksim. The headquarters building is nine stories and includes offices, underground parking, a gym, a cafeteria, and a sauna. All lunches are provided by the company through lunch tickets that are given to employees each month. The company pays for parking, and various shops in the nearby area give Turkcell employees special discounts. In the main lobby area is a display case that contains the dozens of awards that Turkcell has received. Among the awards are plaques and certificates from Ericsson, Interpro, and the Lions Club, along with Turkcell's ISO 9001 certification. The building is mostly dedicated to Turkcell's administration, finances, marketing, training, investor relations, and corporate communications.

Maltepe (on the outskirts of Istanbul) is the home of the "brains" of Turkcell—the $10 million Network Control Center, with its state-of-the-art computer technology. It houses 42 technical staff who work in shifts for the 24/7 coverage. Similar to the Houston control center that monitors space shuttle flights, the Turkcell Network Control Center has a series of curved interconnected workstations facing multifaceted sets of maps. When a red light appears, a Turkcell team of technicians is immediately sent to the location to investigate the problem. These 7,500 base stations allow Turkcell to provide 100% mobile communications coverage in Turkey for all cities in Turkey with populations of 5,000 or more. Turkcell also has numerous Turkcell customer care centers throughout Turkey, where subscribers can sign up for various services or resolve their mobile communications or billing issues.

Organizational Philosophy and Social Responsibility

The Turkcell company philosophy has been strongly influenced by the first Turkcell CEO, Cüneyt Türktan, who received bachelor's and master of business administration (MBA) degrees from Bosphorus University in Turkey. In 1980, he joined PriceWaterhouse in New York as an accountant, and then he returned to Turkey in 1985 as an audit supervisor for KPMG, and he worked for Interbank as the Head of Corporate Finance. Then in 1992, he became the Area Finance Director of PepsiCo International, in charge of Turkey and Israel. In 1994, he led the organizational team that created Turkcell.

According to Türktan, writing in a 2002 issue of *Turkcell World*, Turkcell values five structural principles: proactive approach, result orientation, minimum hierarchy, full accountability, and simplicity. The company strongly espouses both creating high employee loyalty and providing extensive employee training. Once a year in Istanbul, the company holds a major Turkcell information day that is designed strictly for the employees, and through its own educational classrooms, Turkcell provides training programs on individual development, functional, conference attending, computer and language training, and organization. The courses are given in English and Russian. Turkcell has more than 2,000 employees, divided into 49% technical, 26% customer care, 16% finance and administration, and 9% marketing. The average age of a Turkcell employee is 28. More than 80% of Turkcell's employees are university educated. Turkcell pays all its employees slightly above industry average.

Carrying on with the organizational philosophy of Turkcell is the second CEO, Muzaffer Akpinar, who was born in 1962 and has worked in the telcom sector since 1993. Akpinar speaks Turkish, French, and English, and he took part in the restructuring of Fintur. He was a founder and managing director of Penta Textile, and he worked as the CEO for KVK Mobil Telfon Hizmetleri, a major importer and distributor of handsets, as well as MV Holding Company. Like the first CEO, Akpinar is a graduate of Bosphorus University in Turkey. He started as the second CEO of Turkcell in January 2002.

Part of Turkcell's philosophy involves good customer relations and social responsibility. This means stressing the importance of customer care and being a good corporate citizen in Turkey. The company wants to increase its customer base and retain its current customers through both marketing and its visibility as a responsible company. For example, in conjunction with the Foundation for Supporting Modern Life, Turkcell has provided 5,000 young girls with scholarships and training in Eastern Turkey. Turkcell targets girls in this program because in rural Turkey, most families prefer to spend their limited funds on their sons. Daughters' educations are generally neglected. For its efforts in this area, Turkcell has received Institute of Public Relations (IPR) excellence awards in the category *Corporate Social Responsibility*. Turkcell also achieved the Cystal Obelisk award for the same project from the Foundation of Women Executives (WEPR) in New York.

As stated by A. Cüneyt Türktan, the former CEO, in an issue of *Turkcell World*, "Turkcell understands and is proud of its role as a corporate citizen and will continue to sponsor important programs." It has also sponsored the restoration of school gyms in Istanbul and the "Sharing Our Toys" campaign for children in rural areas of Turkey, and it helped set up computer laboratories in 53 schools in less developed provinces of Turkey.

Marketing

Turkcell engages in extensive marketing within Turkey. Not only does Turkcell want to increase the number of subscribers, but it wants to increase the call minutes per customer as well. Globally, the year 2001 was a difficult year for mobile telecom operators. These difficulties were compounded in Turkey by economic upheaval that led to a steep depreciation of the currency, lower purchasing power, and a contraction of economic activity. Turkcell had to manage the economic crisis with flexibility and sensitivity by taking decisive measures to control operating and capital expenditures. In order to keep up with the currency's depreciation, Turkcell had to raise the tariffs to subscribers in reasonable increments throughout the year while remaining sensitive to customer expectations and usage patterns.

In addition, Turkey's economic crisis seriously affected the monthly minutes used by subscribers. While subscribers had been using on average more than 100 minutes per month, that number drastically fell to 56.2 minutes monthly as of year end 2003. Ideally, Turkcell would like the monthly minutes per month to match the average of other industrialized or developing countries. The average U.S. subscriber spends more than 430 minutes monthly on a mobile phone, Hong Kong 350, Israel 237, China 199, Egypt 188, Norway 181, Brazil 105, and Greece 105. Turkcell wonders: Are there certain marketing campaigns that might help to achieve an improvement in the average monthly minutes? What type of marketing segmentation should we try? How can Turkish mobile phone users be encouraged to spend more time monthly on a mobile phone? Would educational campaigns be helpful?

For example, some subscribers, especially those in rural areas, appear to be quite resistant to newer technologies such as cell phones and do not know how to best use mobile communication. If an educational campaign were conducted, how much time and effort should Turkcell spend on it? One effort in the year 2000 was quite successful. Should Turkcell do it again? In that year, Turkcell sponsored the "Signal Tour 2000" project, which lasted six months. In this project, a truck was used as a symbol of wireless communication. The truck tour traveled to 82 locations throughout Turkey, met with more than 500,000 people, and covered about 18,000 miles. After the completion of this campaign, Turkcell received the Direct Marketing Association (DMA) International ECHO award, which was presented in Chicago at a gala event in 2001. But such campaigns take time and money. Would sponsorship of other events be more worthwhile? To illustrate, Turkcell also sponsors numerous athletic, cultural, theater, film, and/or music events, including the International Istanbul Jazz Festival and the International Istanbul Film Festival. Which campaigns are best geared at customer retention, getting new subscribers, or getting current consumers to use their mobile phones and services more often?

Financial Issues

The financial structure of Turkcell is highly sophisticated and involves a number of holdings inside and outside Turkey. To illustrate, on August 21, 2002, Turkcell, Sonera, and Cukurova Group, the shareholders of Fintur Holdings B.V., finalized the restructuring of two business divisions of Fintur: the international GSM businesses and the technology businesses. In line with the terms of the transaction, Turkcell bought 16.45% of Fintur International from the Cukurova Group, increasing its stake in Fintur International to 41.45%. At the same time, Sonera bought 23.24% of Fintur International from the Cukurova Group, increasing its holding to 58.8%. As part of this transaction, Turkcell and Sonera sold their entire interest in Fintur Technologies (Internet service providers, digital television, etc.) to the Cukurova Group. But because Cukurova Group is the majority shareholder of Turkcell, it will continue to create group synergies via various projects. Thus Turkcell is one of the major shareholders of Fintur Holdings B.V., which in turn holds a 51.3% interest in Azercell of Azerbaijan, an 83.2% interest in Geocell of Georgia (formerly part of the U.S.S.R.), a 51% interest in K'Cell of Kazakhstan, and a 77% interest in Moldcell of Moldova. Most of these countries have very low penetration of mobile phone usage. For example, only 3% of the Georgian market has mobile phones. Fintur International's GSM business in Azerbaijan, Kazakhstan, Georgia, and Moldova added approximately 500,000 new subscribers and reached a total of approximately 1.6 million subscribers in 2002. The combined revenue of the business was US$240 million in 2002, and the business was EBITDA positive in all countries.

Other holdings of Turkcell outside Turkey include Kuzey Kibris Turkcell (KKTCell) in the Republic of Northern Cyprus. Thus outside Turkey, there is great opportunity for Turkcell to increase its subscriber base, and this explains why Russian is one of the languages included by Turkcell in its training facilities. Should Turkcell expand into other European countries, and, if yes, which ones?

In 2001, Turkcell's loss of more than $186 million was attributed to the severe deflation of the TRL and the subsequent currency translation. Turkcell has to use U.S. funds to repay bank loans, licensing agreements, and purchasing of infrastructure, while revenues from subscribers are received in TRL. Although Turkcell raised its rates to subscribers by 101% in 2001, this was not sufficient to cover the 114% inflation and devaluation of the lira. However, Turkcell announced a $101.8 million net profit as of year end 2002. In 2002, Turkcell made debt repayments of $474.3 million in both principal and interest. At the end of 2002, Turkcell's total outstanding financial debt was reduced to approximately US$1.3 billion at the end of 2002. In addition, during the first quarter of 2003, Turkcell paid a total of $313 million of debt in principal and interest. As of March 31, 2003, Turkcell's total outstanding financial debt was reduced to approximately US$1.0 billion from US$1.3.

Also problematic for Turkcell is the fact that records have to be maintained using two vastly different accounting standards. As a company quoted on the NYSE, Turkcell has to follow U.S. Generally Accepted Accounting Principles (GAAP), while as a firm listed on the Istanbul Stock Exchange, the company also uses the Turkish SPK system. The latter does not allow for any inflation accounting, and this does not make sense to Turkcell, especially given Turkey's historical inflation rates. **Exhibits 4 and 5** are Turkcell's balance sheet and operations statement information, given in U.S. dollars.

**Exhibit 4
Consolidated
Balance Sheets:
Turkcell (TKC)
(Dollar amounts in
thousands, except
share data)**

Year Ending December 31	2001	2000
Assets		
Current Assets:		
Cash and cash equivalents	$243,114	$363,365
Trade receivables	256,143	325,636
Due from related parties	164,448	113,860
Inventories	12,154	16,402
Prepaid expenses	20,843	22,484
Other current assets	46,965	44,476
Total current assets	$743,667	$886,223
Advances to related parties		1,020
Due from related parties	10,085	
Prepaid expenses	3,300	11,765
Investments	58,329	60,068
Fixed assets	1,655,110	1,762,168
Construction in progress	119,363	233,299
Intangibles	916,920	892,995
Other long-term assets	28,996	37,382
Total Assets	$3,536,043	$3,884,920
Liabilities and Shareholders' Equity		
Current Liabilities:		
Short-term borrowings	$383,167	$438,081
Trade payables	302,039	208,890
Due to related parties	3,626	2,811
Tax payable	130	
Deferred tax liability		21,103
Other current liabilities and accrued expenses	303,425	271,194
Total Current Liabilities	992,387	942,079
Long-term lease obligations	1,218,903	1,600,676
Long-term lease obligations	37,103	34,472
Retirement pay liability	4,737	3,545
Deferred tax liabilities		3,491
Minority interest	896	12
Other long-term liabilities	6,792	5,838
Shareholders' equity:		
Common Stock	636,116	458,239
Additional paid in capital	178	
Advances for common stock	119	141
Legal reserves	5	5
Accumulated other comprehensive loss	(1,875)	(1,049)
Retained earnings	650,682	837,471
Total shareholders' equity	1,285,225	1,294,807
Total Liabilities and Shareholders' Equity	3,536,043	$3,884,920

Source: Turkcell, "2001 Annual Report," p. 46.

Exhibit 5
Consolidated
Statements of
Operations:
Turkcell (TKC)
(Dollar amounts in
thousands, except
share data)

Year Ending December 31	2001	2000
Revenues	$1,786,910	$2,224,940
Direct cost of revenue	(1,173,743)	$1,197,175
Gross profit	613,167	1,027,765
General administrative expenses	(130,681)	(187,878)
Selling and marketing expenses	(265,249)	(414,250)
Operating Income	217,237	425,637
Income from related parties	2,508	2,450
Interest income	97,268	94,654
Interest expense	(305,069)	(251,174)
Other income (expenses)	(5,135)	9,703
Equity in net loss of unsoiled investees	(51,316)	(31,645)
Gain on sale of affiliates		44,244
Minority interest	389	(316)
Translation loss	(151,454)	(21,953)
Income (loss) before taxes	(195,572)	271,600
Net Income (loss)	($186,789)	$ 227,907
Basic and dilute earnings (loss) per common share	($0.00040)	$0.00051
Weighted average number of common shares outstanding	470,348,717,330	443,740,603,721

Source: Turkcell, "2001 Annual Report," p. 4.

Future Challenges and Issues

As Turkcell looks toward the future, it wants to maintain its leadership in the Turkish communications market, but how should it do that? Turkcell has to consider both Turkish competitors and other European competitors. Even though there are high barriers to entry, the mobile phone industry has been quite competitive. With 15.7 million mobile phone subscribers as of year end 2002, Turkcell is one of the largest operators in Europe in terms of the number of users. Besides TIM of the Telecom Italia group, other European competitors are Germany's T-Mobile, Norway's Vodafone, Spain's Telfonica, France's Orange, and Italy's Omnitel Vodafone.

In February 2003, Turkcell joined the Board of Directors of the GSM Association (GSMA), an association of the world's mobile operators, infrastructure producers, telephone manufacturers, and procurers. The GSMA, whose 700 members originate from 192 countries, with a total customer base of almost 788 million subscribers, represents 77% of the world's mobile communications market. In addition to Turkcell, the other members of the Board are well known, large, mobile operators, including Vodafone and Orange from the United Kingdom, NTT DoCoMo from Japan, Telecom Italia Mobile from Italy, and AT&T Wireless from the United States. The GSMA is established as the mobile communications sector's global trade organization, and in coming periods, the association is to focus on a series of commercial enterprises that should have significant effects on the development of the sector.

Of the major competitors on the GSMA Board, Turkcell is closely watching the mobile operators Orange, Vodafone, and Telecom Italia because these firms are expanding beyond their national borders. Orange has operations in 33 countries, Vodafone 29 countries, and Telecom Italia 20 countries. To hook the younger market, Vodafone advertises heavily on MTV Europe. Industry authorities believe that Vodafone wants to be considered the Coca-

Cola of cell phone communications. A major consolidation might occur, and mergers may occur across continents, such as the partnership between Sony (Japan) and Ericsson (Sweden) or a partnership between Telia (Sweden) and Sonera (Finland). Turkcell wants to be a major player in the European market, but should it go it alone? Should it merge with another company or allow itself to become a subsidiary of a major communications giant?

One leadership approach would be to be the first to offer 3G, the third generation of mobile cell technology, in Turkey. At the end of 2002, Turkcell's infrastructure was at 2.5G. This technology allows a subscriber to use a mobile phone for data transmission, including the sending and receiving of digital pictures, as well as for the provision of wireless Internet services. The 3G technology would allow a subscriber to download and watch videos. The problem is that expected revenues would not cover the cost of adding the required infrastructure. In Europe, mobile communications companies that have moved to the 3G technology have already paid more than $150 billion for the licenses. Industry analysts believe it may take 10 years for them to get back their investments in this technology. Also, the Turkish government has not issued a license allowing Turkcell to move into the 3G technology, but given the risks, should it? Not going to 3G technology may allow another company to get an advantage in future years. The increasing demand for voice is creating capacity problems, and the quality of the service will be diminished. Going to 3G technology will help to build a better infrastructure, but will revenues be enough to cover the costs?

Thus as managers at Turkcell sip their Turkish coffee after finishing a meal at a cafe on Istiklal, they think about this vibrant and dynamic company that they have joined. They wonder: What strategies will allow us to stay a market leader, be one of the largest mobile communications operators in Europe and position ourselves for the ever-increasing communication battle that is bound to come?

Bibliography

M. Bentley and W. Schomberg, "TIM: Turk Telkom Merge Turkish Mobile Units," *Reuters* (May 13, 2003).

T. Brosnahan and P. Yale, *Turkey*, 5th edition (Australia: Lonely Planet, 1997).

E. Cülcuoğlü, "Upgrading Services: A Technological Imperative," *Turkcell World: The International Magazine of Turkey's Leading GSM Operator*, Issue 1 (Autumn 2000).

DEIK, *Business Guide to Turkey* (Istanbul, Turkey: Foreign Relations Board, March 2002).

S. Delin, "And Snabbit Was Created," *Turkcell World: The International Magazine of Turkey's Leading GSM Operator*, Issue 2 (Winter 2001).

S. Delin, "Congratulations! It's a Family," *Turkcell World: The International Magazine of Turkey's Leading GSM Operator*, Issue 4 (2002).

S. Delin, "Mobile Manners Maketh Man," *Turkcell World: The International Magazine of Turkey's Leading GSM Operator*, Issue 2 (Winter 2001).

H. Dyck and S. Greenfeld, "Inland Technologies, Inc: An ISO 9001 Certified Company" (Case Study), in C. W. L. Hill and G. Jones, *Strategic Management: An Integrated Approach*, 4th ed. (Boston: Houghton Mifflin, 1998).

IGEME—Export Promotion Center of Turkey, *Turkey* (Republic of Turkey: Prime Ministry, Undersecretariat for Foreign Trade, December 2000).

O. Karagoz, Interviews and PowerPoint presentations from the office of the CEO Turkcell. (November 2002–January 2003).

A. Liel, *Turkey in the Middle East: Oil, Islam and Politics* (Boulder, CO: Lynne Riener Publishers, 2001).

N. Taits, "Uzan Fails to Appear for Questioning," *Durrants* (December 2002), p. 26.

R. B. Tekin, "Turkish Economic Conditions," unpublished paper (Marmara University, 2002).

Turkcell, *Annual Reports*, 1999 through 2001.

Turkcell, "Corporate Profile" (brochure).

"Turkey," *Encyclopedia Americana International Edition*, Vol. 27, pp. 247–254.

Turkish–U.S. Business Council (TUSBC) of DEIK, "Turkish–U.S. Economic Relations" brochure (March 2002).

www.odci.gov/cia/publications/factbook/geos/tu.html (September 10, 2002).

www.turkcell.com.tr/english/history.html (November 15, 2002).

CASE 7

Waterford Wedgwood plc (2000):

The Millennium (Revised)

Kathryn E. Wheelen

ON MARCH 14, 2000, P. REDMOND O'DONOGHUE, CHIEF EXECUTIVE OFFICER (CEO) of Waterford Crystal Limited, was chairing a meeting. The focus of the meeting was on the sale of Millennium products. A Millennium Waterford Crystal ball, the "Star of Hope," was used in Times Square to ring in the New Year and the Millennium. The 500-pound Waterford crystal ball was lowered down a 77-foot flag pole that was 22 stories above the ground. It took a team of 40 designers and 10 months to assemble the 6-foot-diameter geodesic sphere. O'Donoghue was curious about the impact the Millennium crystal ball had on the sale of the company's products.

Overview of the Crystal Business and History of Waterford Crystal[1]

Manufacturing of Crystal

The crystal manufacturing business was by nature very labor intensive. Each piece of crystal had to go through the processes of mixing, blowing, cutting, and polishing. Mixing involved the heating of raw materials in a furnace to temperatures in excess of 1400 degrees Centigrade to create molten crystal. Blowing formed the molten crystal into a basic item such as a wine goblet or vase. The cutting process etched a design pattern into the blank piece. Finally, the piece was polished to smoothen the edges of the cuts and give the piece the luster and sparkle for which crystal is known. Labor costs typically represented 50%–55% of the cost of manufacturing crystal.

Blowing was done either by machine or was mouth-blown by a skilled craftsman. Similarly, crystal pieces could be cut by machine or hand-cut. Three different technologies were used in the crystal cutting process. They were (1) fully hand-cut, (2) semi-automated and slow speed-automated, and (3) high speed-automated. Crystal pieces which were both mouth-blown and hand-cut had the highest image of quality of all crystal products.

Developing craft skills was a key element in a manufacturer's ability to increase its production output. This was particularly critical in the case of mouth-blown and hand-cut products. In addition to the wages paid to craftsmen (i.e., blowers and cutters), an intensive apprenticeship program must be maintained. Apprenticeships typically lasted for four or more years. Each craftsman usually oversaw several apprentices. The availability of craft and design skills was a major factor in establishing and maintaining competitive advantage. Relative to the labor component involved in manufacturing crystal, raw materials were inexpensive and readily available.

Labor cost efficiency was not a significant issue until the late 1970s. At that time, pressure on prices forced manufacturers to focus on costs in order to maintain gross profit margins. The pressure on prices came from multiple sources. Primary among these were general economic conditions, an increasing number of competitors (most of them European), and new technology. The technology of glass blowing had changed little since crystal making began. The traditional tools, hollow irons and wooden templates, were still used by glass blowers to create the crystal pieces that were then passed on to cutters and hand-cut in the design patterns. Recently, improved processing of machine-cut crystal had been introduced into the industry.

While the quality of machine-cut crystal had improved, its level varied and was not equal to hand-cut crystal. Machine-cut crystal was lower in price relative to hand-cut crystal.

Lead crystal manufacturing was not a fixed capital intensive business. However, it did require a significant level of investment, and its working capital needs are high. High-valued finished inventories had to be maintained throughout the distribution channels. In addition, work-in-progress inventories contained a high value-added component which must be financed, reflecting significant cash requirements.

The technology differences used in the manufacture of crystal products translate into three market segments: *high-end, medium,* and *low-end*. These three segments were based on price and brand name recognition

History of Waterford

In 1783, businessmen George and William Penrose founded the Waterford Glass House in the busy port of Waterford, Ireland, and began to make crystal "as fine a quality as any in Europe . . . in the most elegant style." The Penroses knew the secret of mingling minerals and glass to create crystal with beauty and mystery. When tapped, it sang sweetly. When touched, it felt warm and soft. Yet it possessed strength and durability and, most wonderful of all, the crystal shone with a romantic, silvery brilliance. Patience, skill, and artistry had forged a triumph.

In 1851, Waterford Crystal won several gold medals and universal acclaim at the Great Exhibition in London, but just as Waterford's art was reaching its full bloom, the financial climate turned grim. In the same year, the Waterford factory was forced to close, largely due to heavy excise duties.

Waterford Crystal's great tradition lay dormant for 100 years. But when Irish independence rekindled a passion for the Irish arts in the 1940s and 1950s, a group of businessmen resolved to bring back to life the legacy that had made Waterford synonymous with the finest crystal in the world.

In 1947, they recruited a small group of artisans and, under the guidance of these masters, young apprentices learned the art of Waterford Crystal made famous by their skilled countrymen decades before. By 1951, Waterford Crystal was again launched on the world market. When, in the early 1960s, demand began to exceed supply, a larger glass works was built. This was later expanded until, by the 1980s, Waterford Crystal was the largest producer of hand-crafted crystal in the world.

In 1991, Waterford launched Marquis by Waterford Crystal, the first new brand in the company's 200-year history fine enough to carry the name Waterford Crystal. Today, Marquis by Waterford Crystal is the most successful new entry in the tabletop industry . . . and the number four brand. Marquis offers innovative crystal patterns ranging from contemporary to traditional design, designed by Waterford and brought to life by the great crystal makers in Europe.

In 1992, after extensive consumer research, Waterford learned that many consumers desired Waterford Crystal in less formal designs. In a move to broaden Waterford's design and consumer appeal, some new products were successfully introduced from the finest crystal facilities in Europe—all manufactured to the same exacting standards of Waterford, Ireland.

Each piece of Waterford Crystal stands today as a testament to the traditions and standards of excellence that have survived with the Waterford name for more than 200 years ". . . to be enjoyed and displayed now . . . to be cherished as an heirloom for generations to come."

Corporate Governance: Board of Directors

The Annual Report stated the Directors' responsibilities:

> The Directors are required by Irish company law to prepare financial statements for each financial year which give a true and fair view of the state of affairs of the Company and the Group and of the profit or loss of the Group for that financial year.
>
> In preparing those financial statements, Directors are required to: select appropriate accounting policies and apply them consistently; make reasonable and prudent judgments and estimates; and state that all accounting standards which they consider to be applicable have been followed.
>
> The Directors have responsibility for ensuring that the Group keeps accounting records which disclose with reasonable accuracy at any time the financial position of the Group and which enable them to ensure that the financial statements are prepared in accordance with accounting standards generally accepted in Ireland and comply with Irish statute, comprising the Companies Acts 1963 to 1999 and the European Communities (Companies: Group Accounts) Regulations, 1992. The Directors confirm that the financial statements comply with the above requirements. The Directors also have responsibility for taking such steps as are reasonably open to them to safeguard the assets of the Group and to prevent and detect fraud and other irregularities.[2]

Exhibit 1 provides the names of the 17 board members. Eight are internal members. Eight are classified as Non-executive Independent Directors. Dr. O'Reilly announced that Lord Wedgwood would join the Board as an Executive Director at the next board meeting. Lord Wedgwood was a direct descendant of Josiah Wedgwood, founder of Wedgwood, and has served for years as Wedgwood's International Ambassador.

In February 2000, Dr. O'Reilly announced the appointment of Peter John Goulandris as Executive Chairman of Ceramics. Goulandris was a major shareholder (see **Exhibit 2**) and had been Deputy Chairman of Waterford Wedgwood since 1999. He was the Chairman's brother-in-law.

R. A. Barnes, O. C. Küsel, C. J. McGillivary, K. C. McGoran, and F. A. Wedgwood were reelected at the 2000 Annual Meeting.

Exhibit 2 shows the stock ownership of Dr. A. J. F. O'Reilly, Mrs. C. J. O'Reilly, and P. J. Goulandris, Mrs. O'Reilly's brother, and other substantial ordinary shareholders.

Exhibit 1 Board of Directors: Waterford Wedgwood plc

Dr. Anthony J. F. O'Reilly[1]
Chairman, had been a Director of the Group since 1990 and was appointed Chairman on 1 January 1994. He was Chairman of H.J. Heinz Company and Executive Chairman of Independent News & Media plc.

Peter John Goulandris
Joined the Group as a Director in 1996. He was Deputy Chairman of the Group and Executive Chairman, Ceramics. His other directorships included Fitzwilton Limited.

Chryssanthie J. O'Reilly[1]
Joined the Group as a Director in 1995. She was also Chairperson of the Irish National Stud Company Limited.

Richard A. Barnes
Joined the Group in 1988. He was appointed a Director in 1993. He was Waterford Wedgwood Group Finance Director and a Director of West Midlands Regional Development Agency, a U.K. Government appointment.

P. Redmond O'Donoghue
Joined the Group as a Director in 1985. He was Chief Executive Officer of Waterford Crystal Limited. Additionally he was Nonexecutive Chairman of Bord Failte (Irish Tourist Board) and Nonexecutive Director of Greencore plc.

Brian D. Patterson
Joined the Group in 1987. He was appointed a Director in 1992. He is Chief Executive Officer of Wedgwood and Chairman of Competitiveness Council of Ireland, a Government appointment.

Ottmar C. Küsel
Is Chief Executive Officer of Rosenthal AG. He was appointed a Director of the Group in 1997. He was Chairman of the Ceramics Industry Association in Germany and of the Ambiente/Tendence Trade Show Committee in Frankfurt.

Christopher J. McGillivary
Joined the Group in 1990. He was appointed a Director in 1996. He was Chief Executive Officer of Waterford Wedgwood U.S.A., Inc. He was also Co-Chairman of All-Clad Holdings, Inc.

Sam Michaels
Joined the Group as a Director on 2 July 1999. He was Co-Chairman and Chief Executive Officer of All-Clad Holdings, Inc., and Chairman of Pittsburgh Annealing Box Company.

Robert H. Niehaus[1]
Joined the Group as a Director in 1990. He was Chairman of Waterford Wedgwood U.K. plc. He was also Chairman and Managing Partner of Greenhill Capital Partners, a private equity investment fund in New York. His other directorships included the American Italian Pasta Company.

David W. Sculley[1]
Is a partner in the New York based investment firm, Sculley Brothers. He joined the Group as a Director in 1997. He serves on the board of a number of private companies.

Tony O'Reilly, Jr.[1]
Joined the Group as a Director in 1998. He was a Director and Chief Executive Officer of Arcon International Resources plc. His other directorships included Tedcastle Holdings Limited, Lockwood Financial Group, Inc. (U.S.A.), Providence Resources plc, and Independent News & Media plc.

Dr. F. Alan Wedgwood[1]
Joined the Group as a Director in 1986 and before that was a Director of Josiah Wedgwood & Sons Limited since 1966. He was also a Director of Waterford Wedgwood U.K. plc.

Kevin C. McGoran[1]
Joined the Group as a Director in 1990. He was Deputy Chairman of Fitzwilton Limited, and Chairman of Waterford Crystal Limited.

Gerald P. Dempsey[1]
Joined the Group as a Director in 1986. His other directorships included UNM Financial Services Ireland and Design and Project Management Limited.

Christopher J. S. Johnson
Joined Wedgwood in 1968. He was appointed a Group Director in 1988. He was Manufacturing and Technical Director of Wedgwood.

Lewis L. Glucksman[1]
Joined the Group as a Director in 1998. He acted as a senior adviser at Salomon Smith Barney, New York, and was a member of the Advisory Committee of the National Treasury Management Agency in Ireland—a Government appointment. His directorships included Risk Capital Holdings (U.S.A.).

Note: 1. Non-executive Independent Director.

Source: Waterford Wedgwood plc, Annual Report *(1999), p. 11.*

**Exhibit 2
Substantial
Ordinary
Shareholders:
Waterford
Wedgwood plc
March 7, 2000**

A. General Ownership

Name	Holding	Percentage
Greater than 10%		
Stoneworth Investment Ltd.	119,666,795	16.20%
Bank of Ireland Nominees Ltd.	112,016,276	15.17%
Between 5% and 10%		
Allied Irish Banks plc & its subsidiaries	42,136,373	5.71%
Ulster Bank Markets (Nominees) Ltd.	37,293,695	5.05%
Between 3% and 5%		
Irish Life Assurance plc	29,541,431	4.00%
Araquipa International Ltd.	27,111,201	3.67%
Albany Hill Ltd.	26,778,362	3.63%

B. A. J. F. O'Reilly, Mrs. C. J. O'Reilly, and P. J. Goulandris (Mrs. O'Reilly's brother) Stock Ownership

Name	Stock Owner	Percentage	Shares
Indexia Holdings Ltd.	A. J. F. O'Reilly	100%	250,000
Mystic Investments (Cayman) Ltd.			420,097
Albany Hill Limited	A. J. F. O'Reilly	100%	26,778,362
	Mrs. C. J. O'Reilly combined		
	P. J. Goulandris		
Stoneworth Investments Ltd.	A. J. F. O'Reilly	49%	119,666,795
	P. J. Goulandris	49%	
	L. L. Glucksman	2%	

Source: Waterford Wedgwood plc, Annual Report (1994), pp. 7 and 10.

Top Management

The Executive Directors are P. J. Goulandris, Richard A. Barnes, P. R. O'Donoghue, B. D. Patterson, O. C. Küsel, C. J. McGillivary, S. Michaels, and C. J. S. Johnson (see **Exhibit 1**).

Group Structure and Organization

Exhibit 3 shows the four product lines for the company. The principal executives of these units are:

Name	Title	Unit
P. R. O'Donoghue	CEO	Waterford Crystal Ltd.
B. D. Patterson	CEO	Wedgwood
O. C. Küsel	CEO	Rosenthal
C. J. McGillivary	CEO	Waterford Wedgwood, U.S.A., Inc.
S. Michaels	CEO Co-chairman	All-Clad Holdings
C. J. S. Johnson	Manufacturing and Technical Director	Wedgwood
P. J. Goulandris	Deputy Chairman Executive Chairman	Ceramics

Exhibit 3
Product Lines:
Waterford
Wedgwood plc

Source: Waterford Wedgwood plc, Annual Report *(1999), backside of cover page.*

Exhibit 4 shows principal subsidaries of the company.

Strategic Group Units

Waterford Crystal CEO's Strategic Report

"Group Crystal sales increased by 31.5% in 1999, an all time record year for the peerless Waterford and our other luxury crystal brands."[3]

P. R. O'Donoghue, CEO

I am delighted to report that Group Crystal operating profit in 1999 was €57.0 million, an increase of no less than 39% (see **Exhibit 5**). Sales were €395.2 million, up 31.5% (€395.2 million [IR£501.8 million]). Our record 1999 performance was based on many things, but most particularly on our successful design and marketing of exciting new products, on reaping the benefits of investments, over the past several years, in reducing unit costs and on manufacturing and logistics skills.

Waterford Crystal is the only truly global luxury crystal brand. Last year's success was repeated in all of our major international markets, with the sole exception of Japan where consumer demand remained depressed. In the world's largest market, the United States, our outstandingly professional team, under the inspired leadership of Chris McGillivary, increased sales by 37%. Working closely with Ireland, the products development effort in America has gone from strength to strength. At home in Ireland sales increased by 28%, while the United Kingdom showed 17% growth and Europe grew 8%. Furthermore, we achieved strong growth in Australia and Canada with sales up by 42% and 39% respectively.

Exhibit 4 Principal Subsidiaries, 2000: Waterford Wedgwood plc

Company	Registered office and country of incorporation	Nature of business
A. Manufacturing		
Waterford Crystal (Manufacturing) Ltd.	Kilbarry, Waterford, Ireland	Crystal glass manufacturer
Josiah Wedgwood & Sons Ltd.	Barlaston, Stoke-on-Trent, England	Ceramic tableware/giftware manufacturer
Rosenthal AG	Selb, Germany	Ceramic tableware/giftware manufacturer
All-Clad Metalcrafters LLC	Delaware, U.S.A.	Kitchenware manufacturer
Stuart & Sons Ltd.	Stourbridge, West Midlands, England	Kitchenware manufacturer
B. Distribution		
Waterford Crystal Ltd.	Kilbarry, Waterford, Ireland	Distributor
Waterford Crystal Gallery Ltd.	Kilbarry, Waterford, Ireland	Product display and sales center
Waterford Wedgwood Australia Ltd.	Barlaston, Stoke-on-Trent, England	Distributor
Waterford Wedgwood Canada, Inc.	Toronto, Canada	Distributor
Waterford Wedgwood U.S.A., Inc.	New York, U.S.A.	Distributor
Waterford Wedgwood Japan Ltd.	Tokyo, Japan	Distributor
Waterford Wedgwood Retail Ltd.	Barlaston, Stoke-on-Trent, England	Retailer
Josiah Wedgwood & Sons (Exports) Ltd.	Barlaston, Stoke-on-Trent, England	Exporter
Josiah Wedgwood (Malaysia) Sdn Bhd.	Kuala Lumpur, Malaysia	Retailer
Waterford Wedgwood Trading Singapore Pte. Ltd.	Singapore	Distributor
Waterford Wedgwood (Taiwan) Ltd.	Taipei, Taiwan	Distributor
Wedgwood GmbH	Selb, Germany	Sales office
C. Finance		
Stanim Limited	Barlaston, Stoke-on-Trent, England	Finance
Waterford Wedgwood International Financial Services	Dublin, Ireland	Finance
D. Other		
Waterford Wedgwood U.K. plc	Barlaston, Stoke-on-Trent, England	Subsidiary holding company
Wedgwood Ltd.	Barlaston, Stoke-on-Trent, England	Subsidiary holding company
Waterford Wedgwood, Inc.	Delaware, U.S.A.	Subsidiary holding company
Waterford Glass Research and Development Ltd.	Kilbarry, Waterford, Ireland	Research and development
Dungarvan Crystal Ltd.	Kilbarry, Waterford, Ireland	Dormant
Waterford Wedgwood Employee Share Ownership Plan (Jersey) Ltd.	St. Helier, Jersey	Trustee company
Waterford Wedgwood GmbH	Dusseldorf, Germany	Subsidiary holding company
All-Clad Holdings, Inc.	Canonsburg, Pennsylvania, U.S.A.	Subsidiary holding company

One of the key factors in our success in recent years has been the continuous introduction of innovative, market-led new products, which have attracted new consumers to our brands at the same time as keeping existing consumers loyal. On top of the success of new products we have been able to maintain and increase sales of existing products. This unique combination of new contemporary products and traditional products has been the driving force behind our sales growth rate which has been so dramatic year after year since the early 1990's. In 1999, however, we elevated our performance onto an entirely new plane with a range of Waterford Crystal Millennium products. These were a particular success for two main reasons. Firstly, they appealed to gift buyers by providing attractively packaged, well priced gift solutions.

Exhibit 5 Segment Information: Waterford Wedgwood plc (Stated in pounds)

Year Ending December 31	1999			1998				
	Turnover	Operation Profit	1999 Net Assets	Turnover	Operating Profit Before Exceptional Cost	Exceptional Costs	Operating Profit/ (Loss)	1998 Net Assets Restated
Crystal	£395.2	£57.0	£213.5	£300.5	£41.0	(£4.5)	£36.5	£182.8
Ceramics	396.8	14.0	227.2	382.1	13.9	(26.7)	(12.8)	186.9
Other	87.6	11.9	110.2	47.9	8.8	—	8.8	4.9
Group Net Borrowings	—	—	(311.8)	—	—	—	—	(190.8)
Minority Interests	879.6	82.9	239.1	730.5	63.7	(31.2)	32.5	183.8
Total Group	579.6	82.9	236.0	730.5	63.7	(31.2)	32.5	180.0

Note:
1. The segmental analysis provided has been changed from business segment to product category analysis reflecting the greater integration of the Group's ceramic businesses and the acquisition of All-Clad. Crystal includes the manufacture and distribution of the Group's crystal products. Ceramics includes the manufacture and distribution of the group's ceramic products. "Other" includes products manufactured and distributed by All-Clad together with the Group's other non-crystal and ceramic products.

Source: Waterford Wedgwood plc, Annual Report (1999), p. 19.

Secondly, they were linked by a series of related themes and collectors were delighted to own several pieces or, indeed, the whole collection.

In addition to the growth in our core crystal business, line and brand extensions have continued to expand and are now making a valuable contribution to our overall performance. Thus a combination including John Rocha at Waterford, Waterford China, Waterford Holiday Heirlooms, the newly launched Waterford Jewelry and our licensed products (table linen, cutlery and writing instruments) accounted for retail sales in 1999 of €70 million. And none of these products existed before mid 1997! The John Rocha line was particularly strong showing 1999 growth of 75%.

Marquis and Stuart Crystal brands also had a successful year. Stuart launched the Jasper Conran at Stuart range designed to appeal to more contemporary taste and attract younger consumers. It was greeted with acclaim and immediate sales success. The 'livery' and identity of the core Stuart brand was tastefully rejuvenated and has already won a national U.K. design award. At home in Waterford the Visitor Center remained one of Ireland's most popular tourist attractions with 315,000 visitors and sales up 24%.

Waterford has continued its strategy of investing in appropriate manufacturing technology, together with maintaining the largest team of traditional craftspeople in our industry. Our three Waterford plants have now been smoothly consolidated into two, the Kilbarry tank furnace rebuilt, while the Stuart plant in Stourbridge has been fully integrated into Waterford's manufacturing organization. As a result of this streamlining, we were able to meet last year's record consumer demand and so achieve our remarkable sales and profit results.

Waterford's greatest public highlight of last year—indeed of the last century—was, of course, the Times Square Millennium crystal ball, which received front page coverage in hundreds of newspapers and was watched by around 1.4 billion television viewers around the world. The visual excitement of this spectacular event was literally overwhelming for every member of the Waterford family and a source of pride for Irish people everywhere. It was the emotional zenith of a stunningly successful year and I want to thank everyone, both in Ireland and in America, who worked on the ball and, in doing so, met a near impossible challenge—in terms of crystal making, engineering and logistics—in record time and to glorious effect. At the same time, my sincere thanks go to all of Waterford's employees everywhere whose talent, determination and skill produced the finest year in our company's history.

The next challenge is to use the platform of our 1999 achievements as a base for further innovation, more growth and ever wider Waterford brand awareness. Even though our Millennium products remain on sale in 2000 (and are selling well) we already have in the pipeline a broad range of exciting new products to maintain and extend sales momentum. These will replicate the key attributes of the Millennium Collection and will appeal to consumers looking for the ideal gift and to collectors who enjoy owning a series of beautiful pieces of crystal linked by a theme or story. Additionally there is significant potential for further expansion of line and brand extensions which are still at an early stage of their lives. Our recently launched Waterford Jewelery is a particularly exciting prospect. Given the proven creativity of our people and the responsiveness of our organization to market trends we are sure of continued success.

Waterford Crystal has been a great brand for a long time. In the past decade, we have nurtured and promoted our brand with the utmost care and thoughtfulness. We have made it more accessible to many more consumers. We continue to refuse to sell seconds and we discourage discounting, while insisting that we distribute only in the finest stores. We have extended the brand carefully, protectively, intelligently. We have invested in effective advertising and wonderful, indeed spectacular, public relations. We have maintained the highest standards of craftsmanship which, allied to the most suitable technology available, assures the breathtaking beauty and quality of our products. We have transformed a brand that was once heavily identified with stemware (i.e. drinking glasses), into a multi faceted brand that today provides our consumers all over the world with perfect solutions to gift giving challenges. We have made a great international luxury brand even greater which allows us to look forward with confidence to the continuing profitable growth of Waterford in the years ahead.[4]

We have extended the brand carefully, protectively, intelligently.

Waterford Crystal Products *Waterford Crystal product offerings are crystal and table lamps; ceiling and wall fixtures; crystal chandeliers; table items; candle sticks; cutlery; hurricane lamps; collectibles (baby, sport, religious); vanity (picture frames, vanity items, bridal items); executive desk items; crystal animals; clocks and time pieces; vases and bowls.[5]*

Waterford Linens *In spring, 1996, Waterford Linens were introduced. W-C Design of New York manufactured these linens. The label bore Waterford name and W-C Design name in smaller letters. The initial linens were tested in the Irish market before being sold in the U.S. The prices varied from $450 for a tablecloth and $8 for napkins. These linens were sold through selected department stores with limited advertising.*

Waterford Writing Instruments *In April 1996, Lodis Corporation of Los Angeles was granted exclusive rights to manufacture and distribute writing instruments with the Waterford name.*

Waterford Holiday Heirlooms *In December 1996, the company introduced a line of crystal and glass holiday ornaments and tree toppers. Each Christmas (dated-year), new items offered.[6]*

Wedgwood—CEO's Strategic Report

"Happily, Wedgwood today stands more firmly than ever at the top of its league, leaner, hungrier, stronger, the world's pre-eminent luxury ceramic brand."[7]

B. Patterson, CEO

In a tough global ceramics industry, Wedgwood is doing well. Several years ago, we determined that our prime strategic goal was to increase and maintain our international competitiveness in the face of an industry increasingly under pressure from over capacity, widespread discounting and cheap, imported products. We recognized that the Wedgwood brand was unique in its international appeal, its centuries-old reputation for quality and craftsmanship and because of its symbolic stature as one of the greatest of all English brands.

In order to generate the oxygen to power the Wedgwood brand, we initiated early action—starting in 1997—to take substantial costs out of our business. This included further investment in—and radical restructuring of—our manufacturing and supply chain operations. We are now the leader in applying appropriate technology in manufacturing, while preserving the traditional hand-crafted element that makes Wedgwood so desirable to discerning consumers. Our restructuring program included over 100 different projects.

I am pleased to report this is now virtually complete. It has not been easy. We now manufacture in five rather than eight factories and we employ 1,800 fewer people, as a result of restructuring, than we did at the end of 1996. Our costs of manufacturing have decreased greatly, while our customer service is more efficient and cost-controlled than ever before in the company's history. We know that had we not acted decisively and in time, Wedgwood might be in a similar unfortunate position to some of our competitors. Happily, Wedgwood today stands more firmly than ever at the top of its league, leaner, hungrier, stronger, the world's pre-eminent luxury ceramic brand.

Total sales in 1999 increased by 5.4%. Our sales in the U.K. increased by an encouraging 6.2%. In the widest context, Wedgwood remains the number one premium ceramic brand in the nation. We continue to have wonderful relationships with the best British and Irish retailers and we are confident the success of recently launched product lines like Sarah's Garden and Contrasts will be repeated with new lines such as Time for Wedgwood, Fruit Symphony and the exclusive ceramic creations of leading designers Nick Munro and Paul Costelloe.

Japan's prolonged recession did not abate during 1999, although there were several encouraging signs. In common with overall retail sales, Wedgwood sales in Japan were down 4% year on year. The effect of the recession is felt far beyond the national boundaries of Japan itself, for Japanese tourists have in the past spent considerable sums on Wedgwood products in foreign markets from Hong Kong to London, from Singapore to Hawaii. However, research shows that these same consumers continue to hold the Wedgwood brand in the highest esteem, which has allowed us over the past decade to extend our brand into food, crystal, cutlery and linen. But the Japanese consumer is changing as well and, as a result, the traditional gifting market is evolving too. Hence we have taken a number of major steps to strengthen our brand—and our distribution efforts—in Japan, aimed at encouraging consumers to self-buy our products as well as purchase for gifts. To this end, we have an outstanding team in place, led by company President Hanspeter Kappeler. Our network of retail shops is being focused and strengthened and our advertising and promotion reinvigorated. The prestige accorded to Wedgwood in Japan continues to flourish, most recently evident in a series of exclusive high-end gift items—some costing £15,000 [IR£19,046]—currently being produced for Takashimaya, the leading department store chain. We are confident that the economy will continue to improve in Japan during the course of 2000 and, as a result of our wide-ranging efforts in 1999, we will be ideally placed to meet the rise in consumer demand.

We made excellent sales progress in the United States, up 14.5%. In this market, which still holds enormous potential for Wedgwood, our brand is perceived in more traditional terms than in either the U.K. or Europe, hence the continuing success of our formal bone china lines. During the year we introduced ranges of specially designed giftware along with new tableware lines at more affordable price points. Plans for 2000 include innovative marketing initiatives, improved merchandising and the penetration of new distribution channels. The dedicated efforts of our Wedgwood spokesperson, Sarah, Duchess of York, paid handsome dividends for us throughout America in both brand awareness and customer loyalty. I continue to receive a stream of letters from Americans who admire and respect the Duchess of York and who are impressed by Wedgwood's association with her.

Outside our three main markets, Wedgwood achieved some outstanding results. In Australia, sales increased by a record 13% in 1999. As one of the official licensees for the Sydney Olympic Games, opening in September 2000, we foresee even greater rewards ahead in Australia where our brand has been virtually adopted by a nation, which first started trading with Josiah Wedgwood back in the 18th century. In Canada, too, we enjoyed a second great year of sales in a market that ranks Wedgwood at the very highest level of premium desirability.

In Continental Europe, despite the difficult conditions in the German market, we achieved some important new sales breakthroughs. Italy, thanks to our integration with the highly successful existing Rosenthal marketing and distribution team, saw Wedgwood firmly establish itself as one of the best-selling brands of premium ceramics. In Holland, always a strong national market for Wedgwood, we saw sales grow significantly. We developed new distribution in the Scandinavian countries—which hold great promise—and we re-established our position in the promising Spanish market, through our relationship with leading retail chain El Corte Ingles.

During 1999, we made an important step into Taiwan—a sophisticated market of 22 million people with high disposable income. Setting up our own operation under Michael Boyle in Taipei, we already operate eight stores with more to come. The results so far are very encouraging.

The world of distribution and retailing is being shaken by rapid developments in e-commerce. We already use the Internet for business-to-business transactions with our key customers and in 1999, Wedgewood opened its own e-commerce site promoting initially a limited range of giftware items.

Wedgwood is now emerging from some years of rationalization and investing in manufacturing and supply chain operations—making us the least cost manufacturer with leading customer service. In the years ahead the focus of investment can now shift to the front end of the business—our retail partners and our consumers.

In the last year we have carried out some important work on the Wedgwood brand. Working with the London consultancy, The Partners, we sought to refresh our emotional conviction about its consumer appeal—and to renew ourselves with the qualities that make Wedgwood so special. Working through a 'right brain' process of visualization and emotional cues, we arrived at a three word summation that epitomizes for all of us the essence of our brand—"Authentic English Style."

- *Authentic* because in the age of "hype," consumers increasingly value things that are real. And with its roots going back nearly 250 years to the founder Josiah Wedgwood, our brand has a heritage and tradition which is truly genuine. For Wedgwood, authenticity is a given.

- *English* because, Englishness is aspirational in all of our markets—from the United States to Germany to Japan.

- *Style* has within it a dynamic which can embrace both the traditional and the modern—and English style has a unique capability of taking an old idea and re-expressing it in a modern way—often with a twist of humor or surprise. Style then, is dynamic—and positions us as highly desirable in today's fashion conscious world.

"Authentic English Style" is the message which Wedgwood will consistently communicate to our consumers as we advance as one of the world's leading luxury lifestyle brands in the century ahead.[8]

We plan to increase our brand advertising in lifestyle magazines and other media, in keeping with our long-term strategy of being a global luxury brand.

If we look at recent Wedgwood brand achievements, there are a number of outstanding success stories. At home, British Airways has chosen Wedgwood to provide the special gift which all Concorde passengers will receive as they fly through the Millennium date change and Wedgwood is the sole licensee for premium ceramics in the U.K.'s Millennium Experience. Also in the U.K., we have embarked on a major study of our national retailing perspectives.

In the United States, Sarah, Duchess of York has begun her active association with Wedgwood to very favorable press reaction. We are confident that she will bring to our brand the same kind of excellent U.S. consumer awareness that she achieved for Weight Watchers through her energetic, high profile endorsement.

In Australia, Wedgwood—like Waterford—has been selected as an official licensee for next year's Olympic Games in Sydney. While such licenses were open only to Australian companies, our innovative enterprise—and the strong historical links with Wedgwood, dating back to the 18th century (when Joseph Banks sent back to Josiah Wedgwood clay from Sydney Cove)—resulted in the manufacturing processes incorporating Australian materials in a line of luxury gifts, thus opening the door to a unique Australian–U.K.–Irish partnership, in keeping with the international Olympic spirit.

Wedgwood sells 35% of its products worldwide through its own 320 retail shops, outlets and shops-in-shops. We have embarked on a program of refurbishment to ensure that the Wedgwood shopping environment will appeal to the affluent, younger consumer targeted by our marketing strategy.

In Tokyo, our flagship store in the Ginza will be used to test future retail environments for the Japanese market, including "super boutiques" and other new concepts.

Our strategy calls for increased "relationship" marketing of our products, with direct marketing in appropriate areas, including the Internet, and through expanding our presence in lifestyle retail shops. We plan to increase our brand advertising in lifestyle magazines and other media, in keeping with our long-term strategy of being a global luxury brand.

It would be remiss not to mention the dedication and energy of Lord Wedgwood, our international ambassador, who has travelled the globe for week after week to promote the brand with his own unique combination of knowledge, eloquence and conviction. His appearances on television and radio and in the press around the world have won many new friends for Wedgwood. In addition to his efforts, our public relations achievements include numerous craft events, the Wedgwood Chef & Potter competition in Ireland and the United Kingdom and a host of other PR successes.

In July, Wedgwood Brand Director, Gavin Haig and I met in Barlaston, together with other Wedgwood marketing colleagues from around the world, for the Strategic Marketing and International Marketing meetings. Held over a three day period, this was a most constructive series of reporting and planning sessions. We were particularly encouraged by the support and direction provided over the entire three days by Deputy Chairman Peter John Goulandris.

All the above can be seen in the context of our three-part strategy to achieve our medium and long term goals for the Wedgwood brand. First, we have been working hard to develop new products, which will reach the right markets at the optimum price. Second, we have been concentrating on enhancing our existing retail distribution network and on expanding in a manner consistent with a successful modern premium lifestyle brand. Finally, we have taken a number of important steps to communicate directly with consumers the contemporary excitement and appeal of today's Wedgwood products—and the relevance to their lives of the great Wedgwood brand.[9]

Rosenthal—CEO's Strategic Report

"Last year was a very exciting one for us at Rosenthal."[10]

O. C. Küsel, CEO

Though conditions in our home consumer market of Germany were difficult, particularly in the first half of the year, there were definite signs of improvement in the second half. At the same time, we increased our leading market share in Germany, crossing the significant 25% hurdle for the first time in our history. Overall the German ceramics market was down about 13%, while Rosenthal managed to hold its sales decrease to just 2.5%.

The forecasts for the German economy in 2000 are good, predicting double the growth of last year, and we know from past history that, if correct, this should make a substantial impact on Rosenthal's sales, particularly in the second half of this year.

Looking at our other markets offers a more comprehensive and realistic view of where Rosenthal truly stands some two years after joining the Waterford Wedgwood group. Thanks to the successful integration which has been achieved, Rosenthal saw double digit sales growth in the United States and in Continental Europe (outside Germany). In Japan, where conditions remain difficult, sales growth was less dramatic but this should improve in 2000 as that market improves and as major steps are completed in our integration with the powerful Wedgwood marketing organization in that country.

Italy, in particular, is one market that stood out as a major success story for Rosenthal in 1999. Not only are we the market leader in Italy, but now that we have completed integration with Wedgwood, we find ourselves on-par in the Italian ceramics rankings and, collectively, miles ahead of any other challenger. This is a model that I am confident we will see repeated in many other European countries in the next few years.

Our single proudest achievement of last year, of course, came with the overwhelming success of the new Bulgari luxury tableware and gifts lines. Following much the same trajectory as our earlier phenomenally successful partnership with Versace, the elegant new Bulgari range sold a total of DM 10 million [German marks] by year end, which was 2.5 times more than we had forecast. Not only have discerning consumers in the major markets around the world taken our Bulgari products to their hearts, but they have also received fantastic coverage in the most important lifestyle publications.

We fully intend to develop the Bulgari range in future as we have done with the Versace range and look forward to many years of handsome returns from both partnerships. Naturally, we are also currently exploring other possible collaborative relationships with a handful of the world's leading luxury goods designers.

"Design Your Life" remains our corporate and consumer rallying cry and nowhere in our product range is this better expressed than in both our medium-market Thomas line of products and the distinguished new additions to our famous Rosenthal Studio Line. The latter is in brilliant accord with an international consumer trend today towards what is to be called "emotional purism": simple, elegant, functional and highly desirable. The reception to these products had been very favorable, most particularly in Germany, and as the consumer market recovers there, we are confident that we have the exciting new products to take full advantage of improved conditions.

I am pleased to report that our major restructuring efforts are now almost 100% completed. The strategy set out in 1997 called for a number of goals to be achieved: reduction in capacity, a re-focus on our key businesses and an improvement in the profitability of our retail business. To these ends, four factories have either been closed or sold; we have disposed of our other non-ceramics related businesses and completed the high-tech modernization of our Rothbuhl factory. The program at our factory at Thomas am Kulm, including new cup and plate lines, will be completed in a matter of weeks as I write this.

Our 1997 strategy called for an investment of DM 65.8 million in our manufacturing process to effect cost savings of DM 17.6 million per annum. By last summer, having invested slightly more—DM 66.9 million—we had achieved our goal and were saving at a rate of DM 17.6 million. Our strategy also called for us to outsource 20% of our production in order to increase our global competitiveness and maintain maximum production and price-structure flexibility. We have now achieved that goal as well.

By the end of 1999, I was very pleased by the progress Rosenthal had made in reaching the above and many other goals, first set two years earlier. The restructuring program has been successfully implemented with immediately conclusive results. Our concept of Rosenthal "meets" some of the world's leading luxury designer brands—Bulgari and Versace—has been an absolute triumph, and will continue to be developed.

Finally, and above all, Rosenthal has traveled an immense distance in a very short time towards becoming one of the world's leading premium lifestyle brands in table and giftware. As our reputation begins to soar ever higher in markets like the United States and the Far East, and together with our Waterford Wedgwood partners, I look forward to the next century as one that offers almost unlimited opportunity to our company and our great brand.[11]

Waterford Wedgwood and Rosenthal: Chairman O'Reilly's Financial Report

Waterford Wedgwood's operating profit increased by 19.7% to a record-breaking €21.3 million [IR£27.0 million] up from €17.8 million [IR£22.6 million] in 1998. Total Group sales increased 5.5% to €342.6 million (from €324.7 million [IR£435.2 million] in 1998), with Waterford sales growing particularly strongly. Interest costs were up by 23.3% on 1998, reflecting the cash outflow of the Rosenthal acquisition, restructuring and capital expenditure. Our group pre-tax profits increased by 17.5% to €13.4 million [IR£17.0 million], from €11.4 million [IR£14.4 million] in 1998. The Group ROS of 6.2% showed a gain of 0.7% points on 1998.

Earnings per share before goodwill amortization increased by 13.8% to 1.73¢; this represents a compound growth of 18% in the past five years. The Directors are proposing an interim dividend of 0.5714¢ (IR 0.45p) up 12.5%, to be paid to shareholders on the register on 15 October 1999. A scrip dividend alternative will be available to shareholders.[12]

Acquisition of All-Clad

In June 1999, the management acquired All-Clad, which was a premier U.S. luxury cookware company. The acquisition price was $100 million, which was more than double last year's sales of $51.6 million, and 11.2 times operating profits. The goodwill cost was estimated to be $80 million. All-Clad sales had increased more than three fold from $51.5 million in 1993 to $51.5 million in 1998.[13]

Waterford Wedgwood provided figures to show All-Clad's premium sector growth rate of more expensive cookware and kitchen was about 18% from 1990 to 1998, while overall sector grew about 7% during the same period.[14]

Chairman O'Reilly said, "The single most important strategic decision by Waterford Wedgwood last year [1999] was the acquisition of All-Clad."[15] He further stated, "At the heart of any successful luxury brand, of course, are truly great products."[16]

At acquisition time, 97% of All-Clad sales were in the U.S. An executive said, "All-Clad is an important brand in the United States and we are going to make it important elsewhere be it U.K. or Japan, Australia or Italy."[17]

Chairman O'Reilly said, "Our strategy is based firmly on a long tradition of quality, style and confidence—embodied in our existing luxury brands in all the world's markets—and on a dynamic approach to promoting and strengthening them in the future."[18] Thus became a crucial criteria for the selection of companies to acquire or invest in.

All-Clad: Co-Chairman's Strategic Report

"Record sales in 1999 continued the outstanding growth which has made All-Clad the envy of the rest of its industry."

C. McGillivary, Co-chairman

On behalf of my Co-chairman, Sam Michaels, I [C. McGillivary] am delighted to report that All-Clad's total sales reached US$69.2 million in 1999, representing a rise in our cookware sales of 39%. With the overall U.S. cookware industry growing by between 4 and 6% per year, All-Clad has averaged 32% a year growth over the past five years. This truly outstanding achievement is a result of All-Clad's success in distinguishing and separating itself from the rest of its market. Indeed, the company has virtually created its own category at the very top end of the market.

Innovative new products, strong relationships with leading U.S. retailers and a distinct vision of its future: these are the three key elements which first attracted Waterford Wedgwood to All-Clad and, subsequently, have produced another record year in 1999. It is remarkable but true that, while averaging 32% sales growth, we see enormous promise for All-Clad to sustain and advance its growth in the U.S. market—at an even faster rate. Having already taken so much market share from our competitors, the All-Clad team is full of enthusiasm, ideas and determination.

I strongly dispute those who say that the gourmet cookware sector is a trend that will peak in a few years. In fact, it seems clear that if you take the sales trend of All-Clad over the past five years together with the huge popularity of celebrity chefs on television, the high sales of cookbooks, and the continuing expansion of fine restaurants around the world, you must conclude that this category is on the upside of the bell curve, far from having peaked.

Breaking down our sales in terms of product lines, Stainless increased by 34%, LTD by 24% and Master Chef was up 20%. In its first year, our All-Clad Kitchen Tools range sold $2.90 million worth of product. When Waterford Wedgwood acquired All-Clad in June 1999, the strategy was to enhance its growth capabilities and improve its ability to better service the U.S. market. Thereafter, in careful stages, we look to expand into selected foreign markets where Waterford Wedgwood already has a strong presence. One of our first decisions was to invest about $5 million in order to increase the manufacturing capacity of the Pittsburgh plant by 33%. Second, we decided to expand the shopping warehouse in order to increase its capacity by 50%. Both of these programs are on track, with the manufacturing increase due to be completed by the summer of 2000.

We fully expected to find a great deal of synergy between All-Clad and the Waterford Wedgwood group, and we have not been disappointed. Distribution and purchasing are two of the most important areas in which we have already begun to merge our efforts. However, the Waterford Wedgwood philosophy is firm in its determination to allow each brand considerable independence. We don't want to homogenize a new business. On the other hand, both Waterford Wedgwood and All-Clad have considerable influence on major U.S. retailers and, working together, expect this influence only to increase.

For instance, both Waterford and Wedgwood have outstanding relations with the leading U.S. department stores' bridal registry departments. Brides are, above all, seeking information. Surely there is no better company to advise a new bride on setting up her first home kitchen than All-Clad. We foresee marketing several starter kits of All-Clad cookware that will enable a bride to receive, along with her heirloom bone china and crystal tableware, the finest cookware available in the land. Our WW group clout with bridal registry departments will enable this marketing plan to become reality.

I believe that new ideas are what really drive successful businesses, and I have been very pleased by the quality of innovative thinking that I have found within All-Clad. I am particular optimistic about the launch of the new line of Emeril Ware in co-partnership with America's leading gourmet television chef, Emeril Lagasse. When the idea was first presented to us at Waterford Wedgwood, it met our own thinking exactly, based on our previous success in launching the Marquis sub-brand for Waterford Crystal. Just as Marquis has been an outstanding success and allowed Waterford to move into the middle market without in any way tarnishing its own prestige value, so I believe the Emeril Ware product line can rapidly and profitably expand All-Clad's market presence.

When it comes to the great opportunities for foreign expansion outside the United States, we are determined to make this move in a manner that will ensure a solid, long-term success for our brand. Rather than leak product into a market, we will have full business plans, full marketing strategies and, when we enter a market, it will be with a splash. All-Clad is an important brand in the United States and we are going to make it equally important elsewhere, be that the U.K. or Japan, Australia or Italy. No doubt we will look to All-Clad's previously successful strategy of seeding its products with top professionals who recognize that this is truly an outstanding, high-performance range of cookware. These professionals have gone on to be our most loyal and enthusiastic advocates.

Ideally, we want to make All-Clad a very strong supplier to a number of categories of housewares. The outstanding thing about the All-Clad brand is that it carries a real emotion with the consumer. Its strongest advocate is the user, whether a professional chef or an enthusiastic amateur, who actually owns All-Clad products, who endorse them to friends, who shows them off in the kitchen. This emotional strength residing in the All-Clad brand—the same kind of emotional strength possessed by Waterford Crystal and Wedgwood—should enable a carefully planned and innovative expansion into new categories and, as a result, even higher levels of growth in sales and profits in what is already a lucrative business.

Finally, I want to thank all of the people at both All-Clad and Waterford Wedgwood who have worked hard and intelligently to make this union between the two companies a success. I have discovered that the All-Clad team, led by my Co-chairman and CEO Sam Michaels, is very similar to the Waterford Wedgwood team: highly professional, thoughtful, not easily satisfied, aggressive and excellent at working together. I am confident that, thanks to our new products, the new resources brought by Waterford Wedgwood, and our new strategic thinking, All-Clad has only just begun its journey towards becoming one of the world's leading home lifestyle brands.[19]

At All-Clad, each and every item of cookware is individually built and finished. As part of the process, we have recently installed our Canonsburg, Pennsylvania facility state-of-the art buffing equipment. These buffers enhance our staff's productivity; at the same time this new technology helps our experienced team to hone and perfect All-Clad's finished quality, already renowned as the best in the world.[20]

All-Clad: Chairman O'Reilly's Financial Report

All-Clad Inc. is the leading premium cookware brand in the United States. Its acquisition was another major step towards achieving Waterford Wedgwood's strategic goals. Not only is All-Clad a company with a strong reputation and unique products, its financial performance over the past five years has been outstanding. Sales have gone up more than 300% in that period, to U.S. $51.5m in 1998. The company has 300 employees at its two plants outside Pittsburgh, Pennsylvania. All-Clad has superb relationships with the top premium lifestyle retail groups in the United States.

All-Clad's products are based on a special process of metal bonding. Its high-quality cookware has been widely hailed by the top U.S. professional chefs and food writers and is the fastest growing product range in a very fast-growing sector in the U.S. We see enormous opportunities to take it to new markets in the U.K. Continental Europe and the Far East markets where Waterford Wedgwood has great presence and expertise.

In specific terms, Waterford Wedgwood currently derives 46% of its sales in Europe, 12% in Australia and 40% in North America. All-Clad has no significant market presence outside the U.S. With Continental Europe the fastest growing market in the world for cookware, there is an enormous opportunity for our Group, particularly Rosenthal and Wedgwood, to bring All-Clad into this dynamic new European market. In Japan, Wedgwood's great brand strength will lend a very important helping hand to All-Clad. At the same time, All-Clad's market share in the United States will further strengthen all our Group's brands in that important retail arena. Adding All-Clad products to our Waterford, Wedgwood and Rosenthal contemporary ranges will extend our Group's presence across a fuller spectrum of the premium lifestyle marketplace.

The European launch of All-Clad is scheduled for the year 2000, with other world markets to follow.

Sam Michaels will continue as Chairman and CEO of All-Clad—a role which he has held since 1988. I am very pleased that he has also joined the main Board of Waterford Wedgwood plc as an Executive Director. His past success and vast business experience will be extremely valuable in guiding the future development of All-Clad within our Group.

All-Clad sales and profits are not included in these interim results, as All-Clad was acquired on 30 June 1999.[21]

Other Irish Crystal Companies

Galway Crystal Ltd. was part of Fermanagh-based Belleek Pottery Group. Galway Crystal was established over 25 years ago. In June 1993, Belleek Galway Irish Crystal. At the time of purchase, Galway Crystal "was struggling with 35 employees and heavy financial losses." The company went into receivership on April 17, 1993. George Moore, who owned Belleek, turned the company around. It now employed 80 and was profitable. Moore purchased Belleek Pottery in 1990, when it was losing money. Moore established "strong links with U.S. distributors, aggressive marketing and improved brand image were the ingredients which led to a turnaround in that business."[22] These are basically the same strategies he employed in the mid-1990s.

Tipperary Crystal was purchased in 1992 by Ray Stafford and had a debt of IR£1 million in 1996. The company was sold. During October–December of 1997, the business was at break-even. In 1998, Yeoman International Holdings reduced their 100% stake to 52%. Two minority partners, Irelandia Investments and Nial Wall, acquired 30% and 18%, respectively. In September, 1999, Louise Kennedy, noted Irish designer, agreed to create a new range of products. Kennedy was compared with John Rocha, who designed a modern line of products for Waterford Crystal. Kennedy said, my work will be "a different look and appeal to a different consumer."[23]

Some 60,000 visitors come yearly to the thatched cottage style showroom in the Tipperary Crystal plant. There are several small regional crystal companies.

Royal Doulton Investment

On November 19, 1999, Waterford Wedgwood management bought 12,380,000 shares of Royal Doulton at £90 sterling. The shares opened on the previous day at £78. The shares were garnered from five institutions.

Royal Doulton expected losses for 1999 to be £16 million; the company had recorded a £14.4 million tax loss for the first half of the year. A new software system delivery was delayed for 10 weeks. This cost Royal Doulton to lose about 5% of its annual turnover; the estimated loss was between £10 to £12 million.[24]

Royal Doulton has been undergoing "a major rationalization program, announcing the laying off of 1,200 employees, a fifth of its workforce, last December [1998]."[25] Royal Doulton raised £31 million by issuing shares.

Royal Doulton generated £225 million in sales. The company's premier products are Royal Crown Derby, Minton, Royal Doulton, and Royal Albert. The company had three plants in Stoke-on-Trent and one in Indonesia.

Richard Barnes, Group Finance Director for Waterford Wedgwood, said, "the purchase represented 'good value,' provided closer cooperation between the two companies and gave it 'flexibility'. [Barnes was] adamant the group had 'no intention' of making a bid for the whole company." He further stated, "We are pursuing our strategy of becoming the world's largest luxury lifestyle group."[26]

Royal Doulton's management remained neutral on their reaction to the purchase of a 14.9% equity stake by Waterford Wedgwood.

Royal Doulton's management stressed that the company had "outstanding brand portfolio and strong positions in major markets worldwide and stressed its determination to realize the values of those brands and strategic market positions to the benefit of all its shareholders, employees, and customers."[27]

Waterford Wedgwood management did not seek board representation and described the investment as a "strategic investment."

An analyst said Waterford Wedgwood and Royal Doulton brands each have suffered from "grandmother's inheritance syndrome." A young bride or couple will not purchase these brands, since the couple will inherit these family treasures. This has been hurting these brands for a decade or more. This has acted as a stimulant for these companies to make new designs (Jasper Conran by Stuart, John Rocha by Waterford). This is their future—new brands and products for the modern couple who want luxury.

Technology/Research and Product Development

How had advanced technology been adapted to Waterford Crystal's requirements? For centuries glass was formed by pot-melting, then hand-gathered. This method resulted in wastage of up to 75%, and glass pulled from the surface was of necessity marred with impurities. At Waterford we have installed three of the most advanced continuous-melt, automatically gathered furnaces in the world, at a cost of tens of millions of euros. Operating this state-of-the-art technology, we have more than doubled our previous yield. More importantly, special gathering equipment (inelegantly called "gob-feeders") pulls glass from the purest part of the molten stream of liquid crystal—eliminating all inclusions, air, or foreign matter—and delivers it to Waterford's master blowers and cutters. As a benefit of our investment in sophisticated technology, our craftspeople are therefore not only more productive, but they are today creating crystal pieces unprecedented in their quality and purity, each one a masterwork.

But our application of technology is much more than a mathematical exercise. At Waterford Wedgwood we also assure that the science to be applied is befitting of our product, consistent with our traditions, supportive of our craftspeople, and enhancing of quality. This is one of our Group's true marks of genius. Building upon a heritage of several centuries, our Irish, English, German and American engineers, a brilliant team, are without rival in adapting the latest technology to ensure that it is appropriate to the Group's special production needs.

Rosenthal's facility on the outskirts of Selb in southern Bavaria, designed by Walter Gropius, is architecture of great sensitivity—a work environment of harmony and light. Here, Ralf Kuhn and his team have put in place state-of-the-art mechanical-handling equipment. This equipment eliminates tedious and heavy manual work, avoids breakage and other handling damage, and frees up Rosenthal's superb manufacturing craftspeople to concentrate their full attention on the making of their product. The result is greater efficiency with improved production quality.[28]

The company spent £5.6 million on design and development in 1999.[29]

Internet Strategy

With the market for business to business e-commerce predicted to rise from US$145 billion in 1999 to $7.29 trillion in 2004, Waterford Wedgwood's excellent corporate web sites are a vital asset for safeguarding the future of the leading luxury home lifestyle brand company in the 21st century.

Since the launch of *www.wreview.com* last year, Waterford Wedgwood has expanded its corporate presence on the Internet to two more sites: *www.wwinterim.com* and *www.wwelegance.com*. All have proved extremely popular, with *www.wwreview.com* registering over half a million users in just four months.

As any visitor can quickly see, the Waterford Wedgwood group sites contain highly useful information in a very stylish format for both investors and consumers alike. As well as the most up-to-date Waterford Wedgwood financial news, including annual and interim reports, analyst presentations, statements from Chairman Dr. Tony O'Reilly, fascinating features about our products and our co-partners like Bulgari and Versace, users can access detailed information on each individual brand within the WW group.

Waterford Crystal, Wedgwood, Rosenthal, and All-Clad: if you are searching for company history, product information, and news on the latest happenings for each of these brands, check out the group site first. Visitors can also watch video footage of special statements and events, access the latest press releases, and e-mail a request for corporate literature or any comments or inquiries. Soon other useful information, including contact details for retail stockists in each market, details of regional or national Waterford Wedgwood headquarters, and even advice on caring for your product, will be available.

Click us up today, and soon you will be a regular visitor to one of the Internet's most informative, exciting, and easy-to-use corporate sites.

Key Facts about the Internet and Today's Business

- Britain is the market leader for e-commerce in Europe, accounting for an amazing 95% of EU companies claiming web sites, and more than half of business leaders use the Net for buying and selling.

- Total global sales transactions will reap $105 trillion in revenue by 2004, with e-commerce accounting for 7% of those.

- The Internet grows by 10,900 people a day in the United Kingdom. Currently, there are 10.6 million people with Internet access in the United Kingdom.

- By 2004, 58.5 million people in the United States will have access to the Internet. (That's 55% of all households and 89% of PC-owning households.)

- Three million people in the United Kingdom search for financial information on the Net every year.

- Spending on Internet infrastructure is expected to quadruple to $41.5 trillion by 2003, surpassing the $1.3 trillion spent on e-commerce that year.[30]

The Internet site has proved extremely popular, with *www.wwreview.com* registering over half a million users in just four months.[31]

Financial Report by Chairman O'Reilly

Regional Financial Information

North America—40% of Group Sales

Waterford continues to make great gains in the United States with sales up 26% over the same period in 1998 (see **Exhibit 6**). As the American economy continues to thrive, Waterford Crystal has increased its U.S. market share to well over 50% of the premium crystal market.

The Times Square New Year's Eve Ball by Waterford Crystal that will be lowered to mark the Millennium celebrations has already captured the imagination of the American people and hundreds of millions of people around the world will observe, via television and other media, the start of the new Millennium in New York City, focusing on the magnificent Waterford Crystal ball.

This momentous event, and the imaginative new crystal products created to celebrate it, are winning huge numbers of new customers for the Waterford brand—seed corn for new sales opportunities in the years ahead.

I am glad to report that Wedgwood's sales in the U.S. have reached double digit growth rates, up by 11%. In April we appointed Sarah, Duchess of York as our official Wedgwood ambassador in the United States. As her program of events begins in Fall 1999, we expect further growth arising from this exciting alliance. I am also pleased to report that Rosenthal's sales in the U.S. have increased by 5%.

I have already discussed the benefits that All-Clad's strong position in its sector of the premium homewares market will bring to our Group. I am sure these benefits will lead not only to increased sales for our Waterford, Wedgwood and Rosenthal brands, but also to a further increase in All-Clad's advancing market share in the U.S.

Were All-Clad sales consolidated into the first half, sales in the continuingly robust North American market would be close to 45% of the worldwide total.

U.K. and Ireland—24% of Group Sales

Wedgwood's sales remained steady during the first six months and a growth trend is already apparent for the second half of 1999. Highly successful product lines like *Sarah's Garden*, *Variations* and our new *Weekday Weekend*, have enjoyed steady sales increases. The upcoming launch of a new Paul Costelloe range of ceramic tableware, new giftware and jewelry lines and Wedgwood's appointment as sole premium ceramics licensee for the U.K.'s Millennium Experience will underpin the growth trend. The completion and launch of our state-of-the-art Global Processing Center (distribution facility) in Staffordshire is already bringing significant benefits to our cost efficiency and customer service.

Waterford Crystal had an excellent year in the U.K. and Ireland, echoing its success in the U.S., with sales up 18%. With the John Rocha range continuing to grow strongly and the imminent launch of the superb new Jasper Conran–designed range of crystal from Stuart, Waterford's subsidiary in the U.K., we expect even greater returns by the end of 1999.

Exhibit 6 Selected Financial Information: Waterford Wedgwood plc
(Geographical segment by country of operation. Amounts stated in millions of pounds)

Year Ending December 31	Turnover by Destination	Turnover by Country of Operation	Operating Profit/(Loss)	1999 Net Assets	Destination	Turnover by Country of Operation	Operating Profit Before Exceptional Costs	Exceptional Costs	Operating Profit/(Loss)	1998 Net Assets Restated
Europe	€356.8	€651.6	€68.1	€421.7	€354.9	€579.4	€55.5	(€28.4)	€27.1	€288.6
North America	406.9	399.8	14.3	96.8	283.4	276.2	7.1	(1.1)	6.0	58.8
Asia Pacific	79.8	63.2	(1.1)	24.4	58.7	54.8	—	(1.3)	(1.3)	21.4
Rest of World	36.1	25.2	1.6	8.0	33.5	20.7	1.1	(0.4)	0.7	5.8
	879.6	1,139.8	82.9	550.9	730.5	931.1	63.7	(31.2)	32.5	374.6
Inter Segment Sales[1]	—	(260.2)	—	—	—	(200.6)	—	—	—	—
Group Net Borrowings				(311.8)						(190.8)
	879.6	879.6	82.9	239.1	730.5	730.5	63.7	(31.2)	32.5	183.8
Minority Interest				(3.1)						(3.8)
Total Group	879.6	879.6	82.9	236.0	730.5	730.5	63.7	(31.2)	32.5	180.0

Exchange rates used between the euro and the principal foreign currencies in which the Group does business were as follows:

Profit and Loss Transactions

	1999	1998
U.S. Dollar	$1.06	$1.13
Sterling	£0.66	£0.68
Yen	¥121.33	¥146.91

Balance Sheet

	1999	1998
U.S. Dollar	$1.00	$1.17
Sterling	£0.62	£0.71
Yen	¥102.93	¥132.80

Note:
1. All intersegment sales originate from Europe.

Source: Waterford Wedgwood plc, 1999 Accounts, p. 19.

Continental Europe—22% of Group Sales

The Group's sales in Europe, particularly Rosenthal in Germany, reflected difficult market conditions there. Despite this, several of our new product launches were very successful. The Bulgari collection from Rosenthal has been a fantastic success and has already sold €2.6 million in three months, the figure originally estimated for its first year's sales, and Versace remains strong. The lower cost Benetton range, designed to introduce the Rosenthal brand to a new younger consumer group, has begun to take off—all indications show that sales will exceed our expectations.

Wedgwood sales in Europe were affected by restructuring of distribution in order to change from third party distribution to joint Rosenthal/Wedgwood distribution to our customers. In Holland, Scandinavia and Spain, Wedgwood continued to report strong growth.

Australia—12% of Group Sales

Overall Australian sales declined by 3.6%, continuing to recognize the slowdown in Japan but gaining in the rest of this region.

In Australia, our Waterford Wedgwood team achieved a considerable triumph with the appointment of both Waterford and Wedgwood brands as licensees for the creation of commemorative ranges for the next Olympic Games in Sydney. I am proud that Waterford and Wedgwood will both be linked to the Olympics in 2000.

In the difficult Japanese economy of recent years, Wedgwood has held market share and is continuing to invest in the brand, to develop new products—both ceramic and licensed non-ceramic ranges—and to position at price points to meet customer needs. The economy in Japan is now showing signs of picking up momentum and we are looking to an expanding market in 2000.

Wedgwood is planning two major exhibitions of prestige products in Japan in the year 2000: the first with leading store group Takashimaya and the second with one of Japan's top daily newspapers, *Sankei Shimbun*.[32]

Chairman O'Reilly believes people who come to the games will want true heirlooms to remember them by, not just tee-shirts or caps.[33]

Overall

During the first half the Group has invested €25 million [IR£31.7 million] in advertising and marketing its brands. This represents 7.3% of revenue, maintaining the 1998 standard. Gross capital investment at €16.7 million [IR£21.2 million] primarily reflects the completion of the Rosenthal capital expenditure programs. At both Wedgwood and Rosenthal the extensive restructuring is nearing completion. We have now, we believe, the three most modern and progressive ceramic manufacturing locations in the world. The Group has again shown its growth capability in both sales and profits, as well as through acquisition. Our Group today is twice the size it was in 1994 in sales and profitability, and our brand portfolio is more widely spread by category and these brands are more widely known for their "luxury living" qualities. We shall continue this strategy.

The sustained nature of the Group's growth encourages me for the future. The opportunity for top line improvements presented by All-Clad, the strong performance of our brands in the U.S., the global exposure of the Times Square New Year's Eve Ball by Waterford Crystal for the Millennium, the success of our wide ranging new product development and the easing of the Asian economies all point to the Group increasing its momentum.[34]

**Exhibit 7
Consolidated Profit
and Loss Account
(1999–1995):
Waterford
Wedgwood plc
(Amounts stated in
millions of euros,
except per share
data)**

Year Ending December 31	1999	1998	1997	1996	1995
Turnover	€879.6	€730.5	€529.7	€477.8	€437.4
Operating profit before exceptional charge	82.9	63.7	57.4	49.8	42.3
Operating profit after exceptional charge	82.9	32.5	22.1	49.8	42.3
Share of profits of associated undertaking	—	—	0.6	—	—
Net interest cost	(17.4)	(13.6)	(7.2)	(5.5)	(6.6)
Profit on ordinary activities before taxation	65.5	18.9	15.5	44.3	35.7
Taxation on profit on ordinary activities	(9.4)	(2.5)	(7.4)	(7.5)	(5.1)
Profit on ordinary activities after taxation	56.1	16.4	8.1	36.8	30.6
Minority interests	0.9	(0.3)	—	—	—
Profit attributable to members of parent company	57.0	16.1	8.1	36.8	30.6
Dividends	(19.1)	(16.1)	(14.1)	(12.8)	(11.2)
Retained profit/(loss) for the year	37.9	—	(6.0)	24.0	19.4
Earnings per share (cents)	7.82¢	2.21¢	1.12¢	5.08¢	4.30¢
Diluted earnings per share (cents)	7.80¢	2.18¢	1.10¢	5.03¢	4.23¢
Earnings per share (before exceptional charge and goodwill amortization) (cents)	8.26¢	6.59¢	5.97¢	5.08¢	4.30¢

Source: Waterford Wedgwood plc, Annual Report (1999), p. 34.

Other Selected Financial Information

Exhibits 7 and 8 are consolidated profit and loss accounts. **Exhibit 7** was stated in millions of Euros (€) for 1999–1995, and **Exhibit 8** was stated in millions of Irish pounds (IR£) for 1998–1995. In 1999, the company started stating its financial statements in Euros (€), **Exhibit 9** shows the company's consolidated profit and loss account in millions of euros (€). **Exhibit 10** shows the company's consolidated balance sheet in millions of Euros (€),

**Exhibit 8
Consolidated Profit
and Loss Account
(1998–1995):
Waterford
Wedgwood plc
(Amounts stated in
millions of Irish
pounds [IR£],
except per share
data)**

Year Ending December 31	1998	1997	1996	1995
Turnover	£575.3	£417.2	£376.3	£344.5
Operating profit before exceptional charge	50.2	45.2	39.2	33.3
Operating profit after exceptional charge	25.6	17.4	39.2	33.3
Share of profits of associated undertaking	—	0.5	—	—
Net interest cost	(10.7)	(5.7)	(4.3)	(5.2)
Profit on ordinary activities before taxation	14.9	12.2	34.9	28.1
Taxation on profit on ordinary activities	(2.0)	(5.8)	(5.9)	(4.0)
Profit on ordinary activities after taxation	12.9	6.4	29.0	24.1
Minority interests	(0.2)	—	—	—
Profit attributable to members of parent company	12.7	6.4	29.0	24.1
Dividends	(12.7)	(11.1)	(10.1)	(8.8)
Retained profit/(loss) for the year	0.0	(4.7)	18.9	15.3
Earnings per share	1.74p	0.88p	4.00p	3.39p
Diluted earnings per share	1.72p	0.87p	3.96p	3.33p
Earnings per share (before exceptional charge and goodwill amortization)	5.19p	4.70p	4.00p	3.39p

Source: Waterford Crystal plc, 1999 Accounts, p. 32.

**Exhibit 9
Consolidated Profit
and Loss Account:
Waterford
Wedgwood plc
(Amounts stated in
millions of euros
[€], except per
share data)**

Year Ending December 31	Continuing Operations 1999	Acquisitions All-Clad 1999	Total 1999	1998 Restated
Turnover	€842.9	€36.7	€879.6	€730.5
Cost of sales	(425.4)	(20.1)	(445.5)	(389.7)
Gross profit	417.5	16.6	434.1	340.8
Distribution costs	(250.6)	(7.5)	(258.1)	(233.5)
Administrative expenses	(89.7)	(4.7)	(94.4)	(74.9)
Other operating income	1.3	—	1.3	0.1
	(339.0)	(12.2)	(351.2)	(308.3)
Operating profit	78.5	4.4	82.9	32.5
Net interest payable			(17.4)	(13.6)
Profit on ordinary activities after taxation			65.5	18.9
Taxation on profit on ordinary activities			(9.4)	(2.5)
Profit on ordinary activities after taxation			56.1	16.4
Minority interests			0.9	(0.3)
Profit attributable to members of the parent company			57.0	16.1
Dividends			(19.1)	(16.1)
Retained profit for the year			37.9	0.0
Transfer to/(from) reserves and translation adjustments			16.9	(17.8)
Increase/(decrease) in balance during year			54.8	(17.8)
Balance at beginning of year			(62.9)	(45.1)
			(8.1)	(62.9)
Earnings per share			7.82¢	2.21¢
Diluted earnings per share			7.80¢	2.18¢
Earnings per share before exceptional charge and goodwill amortization			8.26¢	6.59¢

Note: Notes were deleted.

Source: Waterford Wedgwood plc, Annual Report *(1999), p. 14.*

Exhibit 10 Consolidated Balance Sheet: Waterford Wedgwood plc (Amounts stated in millions of euros [€])

Year Ending December 31	1999	1998 Restated
Fixed assets		
Intangible assets	104.8	16.8
Tangible assets	259.5	226.6
Financial assets	22.6	6.7
Total of fixed assets	386.9	250.1
Current assets		
Stocks	238.8	203.9
Debtors	167.0	132.9
Cash and deposits	87.4	68.2
Total of current assets	493.2	405.0
Creditors (amount falling due within 1 year)	(202.3)	(171.6)
Net current assets	290.9	233.4
Total assets less current liabilities	677.8	483.5
Creditors (amounts falling due after more than 1 year)	(430.1)	(291.5)
Provisions for liabilities and charges	(8.6)	(8.2)
Total assets	239.1	183.8
Capital and reserves		
Called up share capital	56.6	56.5
Share premium account	176.7	175.6
Revaluation reserve	10.8	10.8
Revenue reserves	(8.1)	(62.9)
Shareholders' funds—equity interests	236.0	180.0
Minority interests—equity interests	3.1	3.8
Shareholders' funds	239.1	183.8

Note: Notes were deleted.

Source: Waterford Wedgwood plc, Annual Report *(1999), p. 15.*

**Exhibit 11
Summary
Financial
Statements:
Waterford
Wedgwood plc**

To assist overseas investors, the consolidated financial statements of Waterford Wedgwood plc are presented in summary form below, prepared in accordance, with generally accepted accounting principles applicable in the Republic of Ireland ("Irish GAAP"), translated at the year-end exchange rates of €1 = STG£0.62 and US$1.00.

**Statement stated in euros (€), Irish pounds (IR£), and U.S. dollars ($):
Waterford Wedgwood plc**

A. Consolidated Income Statement	1999 €mils	1999 STG£mils	1999 US$mils
Net sales	879.6	545.4	879.6
Net income before taxes	65.5	40.6	65.5
Taxes on income	(9.4)	(5.8)	(9.4)
Minority interests	0.9	0.6	0.9
Net income	57.0	35.4	57.0
Income per ordinary share	7.82c	4.85p	7.82c
Diluted income per ordinary share	7.80c	4.84p	7.80c
Income per ordinary share before exceptional charge and goodwill amortization	8.26c	5.12p	8.26c

B. Consolidated Balance Sheet	1999 €mils	1999 STG£mils	1999 US$mils
Fixed assets	386.9	239.9	386.9
Current assets	493.2	305.8	493.2
Total assets	880.1	545.7	880.1
Current liabilities	202.3	125.4	202.3
Long-term liabilities	438.7	272.1	438.7
Shareholders' funds	236.0	146.3	236.0
Minority interests	3.1	1.9	3.1
Total liabilities, shareholders' funds, and minority interests	880.1	545.7	880.1

Note: 1998 conversion rates were based on IR£ (not € as in 1999). The exchange rates were IR£1 = US$1.43 and STG£0.86.

Source: Waterford Wedgwood plc, Accounts 1999, *p. 36.*

Exhibit 11 provides selected financial information in three currencies—euros (€), British pound sterling (STG) (£), and U.S. dollars ($).

Notes

1. This case was written in the present tense to directly represent the quoted materials of Waterford Wedgwood executives. This section—Overview of the Crystal Business and History of Waterford Crystal—from Philip H. Anderson's case, "Waterford Crystal Ltd." These sections were directly quoted with minor editing, and "History of Waterford Crystal" was from *www.wwreview.com.*
2. Waterford Wedgwood plc, *1999 Accounts,* p. 9. The above paragraphs were directly quoted with minor editing.
3. Waterford Wedgwood plc, *Interim Review 1999,* p. 22. Just this sentence.

4. Waterford Wedgwood plc, *Review of 1999,* pp. 72, 74, and 75. The above nine paragraphs were directly quoted with minor editing.
5. Waterford Crystal, 2000 *Give the Gift You Love to Receive,* back side of the cover.
6. *Ibid.*
7. Waterford Wedgwood plc, *Review of 1999,* p. 81. Just this sentence.
8. Waterford Wedgwood plc, *Review of 1999,* pp. 81–83. The above 16 paragraphs were directly quoted with minor editing.
9. Waterford Wedgwood plc, *Interim Review 1999,* p. 19. The above nine paragraphs were directly quoted with minor editing.

10. *Ibid., Review of 1999*, p. 89. Just this sentence.

11. *Ibid.*, pp. 89–90. The above 11 paragraphs are directly quoted with minor editing.

12. Waterford Wedgwood plc, *Interim Review 1999*, p. 1 of the Chairman's Statement. These two paragraphs were directly quoted with minor editing.

13. "All-Clad Has Right Ingredient for Waterford," *Irish Times*, May 31, 1999, p. 12.

14. *Ibid.*, p. 10.

15. Waterford Wedgwood plc, *Review of 1999*, p. 9.

16. *Ibid.*, p. 10.

17. *Ibid.*, p. 95.

18. *Ibid.*, p. 12. Waterford Wedgwood plc, *Interim Review 1999*, p. 1 of the Chairman's Statement. The above six paragraphs were directly quoted with minor editing.

19. *Ibid.*, p. 93.

20. *Ibid.*, pp. 93–96. The above 11 paragraphs were directly quoted with minor editing.

21. Waterford Wedgwood plc, *Interim Review 1999*, p. 1 of the Chairman's Statement. The above six paragraphs were directly quoted with minor editing.

22. Alex Meehan, "Hordes Expected at Galaway Crystal Centre," *Sunday Business* (May 5, 1996); Eddie Doyle, "Moore Plans £2.5m Galaway Centre," *Sunday Business* (May 8, 1994).

23. "Crystal Firm Hoping Things Will Take Shape with Louise Kennedy Designs," *Irish Times* (September 16, 1999).

24. Bill Murdock, "Waterford Wedgwood Takes 14.9% Equity Stake in Royal Doulton," *Irish Times* (November 20, 1999).

25. *Ibid.*

26. *Ibid.*

27. *Ibid.*

28. Waterford Wedgwood plc, *Review of 1999*, p. 65. The above four paragraphs were directly quoted with minor editing.

29. Waterford Wedgwood plc, *Accounts 1999*, p. 10.

30. Waterford Wedgwood plc, *Review of 1999*, pp. 34–35. The above six paragraphs were directly quoted with minor editing.

31. *Ibid.*, p. 35.

32. Waterford Crystal plc, *Interim Review 1999*, pp. 1–2 of the Chairman's Statement. The above 14 paragraphs were directly quoted with minor editing.

33. Waterford Wedgwood plc, *Review of 1999*, p. 25.

34. Waterford Crystal plc, *Interim Review 1999*, p. 2 of the Chairman's Statement. The above two paragraphs were quoted with minor editing.

CASE 8

Guajilote Cooperativo Forestal, Honduras

Nathan Nebbe and J. David Hunger

GUAJILOTE (PRONOUNCED WA-HEE-LOW-TAY) COOPERATIVO FORESTAL WAS A FORESTRY cooperative that operated out of Chaparral, a small village located in the buffer zone of La Muralla National Park in Honduras' Olancho province. Olancho was one of 18 Honduran provinces and was located inland, bordering Nicaragua. The cooperative was one result of a relatively new movement among international donor agencies promoting sustainable economic development of developing countries' natural resources.[1] A cooperative in Honduras was similar to a cooperative in the United States: It was an enterprise jointly owned and operated by members who used its facilities and services.

Guajilote was founded in 1991 as a component of a USAID (United States Agency for International Development) project. The project attempted to develop La Muralla National Park as an administrative and socioeconomic model that COHDEFOR (the Honduran forestry development service) could transfer to Honduras' other national parks. The Guajilote Cooperativo Forestal was given the right to exploit naturally fallen (not chopped down) mahogany trees in La Muralla's buffer zone. Thus far, it was the only venture in Honduras with this right. A buffer zone was the designated area within a park's boundaries but outside its core protected zone. People were allowed to live and engage in economically sustainable activities within this buffer zone.

In 1998, Guajilote was facing some important issues and concerns that could affect not only its future growth but its very survival. For one thing, the amount of mahogany wood was limited and was increasingly being threatened by forest fires, illegal logging, and slash-and-burn agriculture. If the total number of mahogany trees continued to decline, trade in its wood could be restricted internationally. For another, the cooperative had no way to transport its wood to market and was thus forced to accept low prices for its wood from the only distributor in the area. What could be done to guarantee the survival of the cooperative?

This case was prepared by Nathan Nebbe and Professor J. David Hunger of Iowa State University. Copyright © 1999 and 2005 by Nathan Nebbe and J. David Hunger. This case was edited for SMBP–9th and 10th editions. Presented to the Society for Case Research and published in *Annual Advances in Business Cases 1999*. The copyright holders are solely responsible for its content. Further use or reproduction of this material is strictly subject to the express permission of copyright holders. Reprinted by permission of the copyright holders, Nathan Nebbe and J. David Hunger, for the 10th Edition of SMBP and Cases in SMBP.

Operations

Guajilote's work activities included three operations using very simple technologies. First, members searched the area to locate appropriate fallen trees. This, in itself, could be very difficult since mahogany trees were naturally rare. These trees were found at elevations up to 1,800 meters (5,400 feet) and normally were found singly or in small clusters of no more than four to eight trees per hectare (2.2 acres).[2]

Finding fallen mahogany in La Muralla's buffer zone was hampered due to the area's steep and sometimes treacherous terrain. (*La Muralla* means "steep wall of rock" in Spanish.) The work was affected by the weather. For example, more downed trees were available during the wet season due to storms and higher soil moisture—leading to the uprooting of trees.

Second, the cooperative set up a temporary hand-sawmill as close as possible to a fallen tree. Due to the steep terrain, it was often difficult to find a suitable location nearby to operate the hand-sawmill. Once a suitable work location was found, men used a large cross-cut saw to disassemble the tree into various components. The disassembling process was a long and arduous process that could take weeks for an especially large tree. The length of time it took to process a tree depended on the tree's size—mature mahogany trees could be gigantic. Tree size thus affected how many trees Guajilote was able to process in a year.

Third, after a tree was disassembled, the wood was either carried out of the forest using a combination of mule and human power or floated down a stream or river. Even if a stream happened to be near a fallen tree, it was typically usable only during the wet season. The wood was then sold to a distributor who, in turn, transported it via trucks to the cities to sell to furniture makers for a profit.

Guajilote's permit to use fallen mahogany was originally granted in 1991 for a 10-year period by COHDEFOR. The permit was simply written, and stated that if Guajilote restricted itself to downed mahogany, its permit renewal should be granted automatically. The administrator of the area's COHDEFOR office indicated that if things remained as they were, Guajilote should not have any problem obtaining renewal in 2001. Given the nature of Honduran politics, however, nothing could be completely assured.

In 1998, Guajilote's mahogany was still sold as a commodity. The cooperative did very little to add value to its product. Nevertheless, the continuing depletion of mahogany trees around the world meant that the remaining wood should increase in value over time.

Management and Human Resources

Santos Munguia, 29 years old, had been Guajilote's leader since 1995. Although Munguia had only a primary school education, he was energetic and intelligent and had proven to be a very skillful politician. In addition to directing Guajilote, Munguia farmed a small parcel of land and raised a few head of cattle. He was also involved in local politics.

Munguia had joined the cooperative in 1994. Although he had not been one of Guajilote's original members, he quickly became its de facto leader in 1995, when he renegotiated a better price for the sale of the cooperative's wood.

Before Munguia joined the cooperative, Guajilote had been receiving between 3 and 4 lempiras ($0.37, or 11 lempiras to the dollar) per foot of cut mahogany from its sole distributor, Juan Suazo. No other distributors were available in this remote location. The distributor transported the wood to Tegucigalpa or San Pedro Sula and sold it for 16 to 18 lempiras per foot. Believing that Suazo was taking advantage of the cooperative, Munguia negotiated a price increase to 7 to 8 lempiras per foot ($0.60 to $0.62 per foot at the July 15, 1998, exchange rate) by putting political pressure on Suazo. The distributor agreed to the price increase only after a police investigation had been launched to investigate his business dealings. (Rumors circulated that Suazo was transporting and selling illegally logged mahogany by mixing it with that purchased from Guajilote.)

Munguia: El Caudillo

After renegotiating successfully with the cooperative's distributor, Munguia quickly became the group's caudillo (strong man). The caudillo was a Latin American political and social institution. A caudillo was a (typically male) purveyor of patronage. All decisions went through, and were usually made by, him. A caudillo was often revered, feared, and hated at the same time because of the power he wielded. Munguia was viewed by many in the area as an ascending caudillo because of his leadership of Guajilote.

Guajilote did not operate in a democratic fashion. Munguia made all the decisions—sometimes with input from his second in command and nephew, Miguel Flores Munguia—and handled all of Guajilote's financial matters. Guajilote's members did not seem to have a problem with this management style. The prevailing opinion seemed to be that Guajilote was a lot better off with Munguia running the show by himself than with more involvement by the members. One man put the members' view very succinctly: "Santos, he saved us (from Suazo, from COHDEFOR, from ourselves)."

Guajilote's organizational structure emphasized Munguia's importance. He was alone at the top in his role as decision maker. If, in the future, Munguia became more involved in politics and other ventures that could take him out of Chaparral (possibly for long periods of time), he would very likely be forced to spend less time with Guajilote's operations. Munguia's leadership has been of key importance to Guajilote's maturing as both a work group and as a business. In 1998, there did not seem to be another person in the cooperative that could take Munguia's place.

Guajilote's Members

When founded, the cooperative had been composed of 15 members. Members were initially selected for the cooperative by employees of USAID and COHDEFOR. The number of employees has held steady over time. Since the cooperative's founding, 3 original members have quit; 4 others were allowed to join. Although no specific reasons were given for members leaving, they appeared to be because of personality differences, family problems, or differences of opinion. No money had been paid to them when they left the cooperative. In 1998 there were 16 members in the cooperative.

None of Guajilote's members had any education beyond primary school. Many of the members had no schooling at all and were illiterate. As a whole, the group knew little of markets or business practices.

Guajilote's existence has had an important impact on its members. One member stated that before he had joined Guajilote, he was lucky to have made 2,000 lempiras in a year, whereas he made around 1,000 to 1,500 in one month as a member of the cooperative. He stated that all five of his children were in school, something that he could not have afforded previously. Before joining the cooperative, he had been involved in subsistence farming and other activities that brought in a small amount of money and food. He said that his children had been required previously to work as soon as they were able. As a simple farmer, he often had to leave his family to find work, mostly migrant farm work, to help his family survive. Because of Guajilote, his family now had enough to eat, and he was able to be home with his family.

This was a common story among Guajilote's members. The general improvement in its members' quality of life also appeared to have strengthened the cooperative members' personal bonds with each other.

Financial Situation

No formal public financial records were available. As head of the cooperative, Munguia kept informal records. Guajilote's 1997 revenues were approximately 288,000 lempiras (US$22,153). (Revenues for 1996 were not available.) Guajilote processed around 36,000 feet of wood during 1997. Very little of the money was held back for capital improvement purchases due to the operation's simple material needs. Capital expenditures for 1997 included a mule plus materials needed to maintain Guajilote's large cross-cut saws.

Each of Guajilote's 16 members was paid an average of about 1,500 lempiras (US$113) per month in 1997 and 1,300 lempiras (US$100) per month in 1996. 1998 payments per month had been similar to 1997's payments, according to Guajilote's members. Money was paid to members based on their participation in Guajilote's operations.

There was conjecture, among some workers, that Munguia and his second in charge were paying themselves more than the other members were receiving. When Munguia was asked if he received a higher wage than the others because of his administrative position in the group, he responded that everything was distributed evenly. An employee of COHDEFOR indicated, however, that Munguia had purchased a house in La Union—the largest town in the area. That person conjectured, based on this evidence, that Munguia was likely receiving more from the cooperative than were the other members.

Issues Facing the Cooperative

Guajilote's size and growth potential were limited by the amount of mahogany it could produce in a year. Mahogany was fairly rare in the forest, and Guajilote was legally restricted to downed trees. Moreover, with the difficulties of finding, processing by hand, and then moving the wood out of the forest, Guajilote was further restricted in the quantity of wood it could handle.

Lack of transportation was a major problem for Guajilote. The cooperative had been unable to secure the capital needed to buy its own truck; lending through legitimate sources was very tight in Honduras and enterprises like Guajilote did not typically have access to lines of credit. Although the prices the cooperative was receiving for its wood had improved, the men still thought that the distributor, Juan Suazo, was not paying them what the wood was worth. It was argued that when demand was high for mahogany, the cooperative gave up as much as 10 lempiras per foot in sales to Suazo. Guajilote could conceivably double its revenues if it could somehow haul its wood to Honduras' major market centers and sell it without use of a distributor. The closest market center was Tegucigalpa—three to four hours from Chaparral on dangerous, often rain soaked, mountain roads.

A Possibility

Some of the members of Guajilote wondered if the cooperative could do better financially by skipping the distributor completely. It was possible that some specialty shops (chains and independents) and catalogs throughout the world might be interested in selling high-quality mahogany furniture, i.e., chests or chairs, that were produced in an environmentally friendly manner. Guajilote, unfortunately, had no highly skilled carpenters or furniture makers in its membership. There were, however, a couple towns in Honduras with highly skilled furniture makers who worked on a contract basis.

A U.S. citizen with a furniture export business in Honduras worked with a number of independent furniture makers on contract to make miniature ornamental chairs. This exporter reviewed Guajilote's situation and concluded that the cooperative might be able to make and market furniture very profitably—even if it had to go through an exporter to find suitable markets. Upon studying Guajilote's operations, he estimated that Guajilote might be able to more than treble its revenues. In order to do this, however, the exporter felt that Guajilote would have to overcome problems with transportation and upgrade its administrative competence. Guajilote would need to utilize the talents of its members more if it were to widen its operational scope. It would have to purchase trucks and hire drivers to transport the wood over treacherous mountain roads. The role of administrator would become much more demanding, thus forcing Munguia to delegate some authority to others in the cooperative.

Concerns

In spite of Guajilote's improved outlook, there were many concerns that could affect the cooperative's future. A serious concern was the threat of deforestation through fires, illegal logging (i.e., poaching of mahogany as well as clear cutting), and slash-and-burn agriculture.

Small fires were typically set to prepare soils for planting and to help clear new areas for cultivation. Often these fires were either not well supervised or burned out of the control of the people starting them. Due to the 1998 drought, the number of out-of-control forest fires had been far greater than normal. There seemed to be a consensus among Hondurans that 1998 would be one of the worst years for forest fires. Mahogany and tropical deciduous forests are not fire resistant. Fires not only kill adult and young mahogany trees, but they also destroy their seeds.[3] Mahogany could therefore be quickly eliminated from a site. Each year, Guajilote lost more area from which it could take mahogany.

To make matters worse, many Hondurans considered the area around La Muralla National Park to be a frontier open to settlement by landless campesinos (peasant farmers). In fleeing poverty and desertification, people were migrating to the Olancho province in large numbers.[4] Not only did they clear the forests for cultivation, but they also cut wood for fuel and for use in building their homes. Most of the new settlements were being established in the area's best mahogany growing habitats.

Another concern was that of potential restrictions by CITIES (the international convention on trade in endangered species). Although trade in mahogany was still permitted, it was supposed to be monitored very closely. If the populations of the 12 mahogany species continued to decrease, it was possible that mahogany would be given even greater protection under the CITIES framework. This could include even tighter restrictions on the trade in mahogany or could even result in an outright ban similar to the worldwide ban on ivory trading.

Notes

1. K. Norsworthy, *Inside Honduras* (Albuquerque, NM: Inter-Hemispheric Education Resource, 1993), pp. 133–138.
2. H. Lamprecht, *Silviculture in the Tropics* (Hamburg, Germany: Verlag, 1989), pp. 245–246.
3. *Ibid.*
4. K. Norsworthy, *Inside Honduras* (Albuquerque, NM: Inter-Hemispheric Education Resource, 1993), pp. 133–138.

CASE 9

eBay, Inc.

Darrin Kuykendall, Vineet Walia, and Alan N. Hoffman

"We intend to achieve our mission of becoming the world's most efficient and abundant marketplace by creating marketplace conditions that enable our users' success. By continuing to foster the vibrancy of the world's largest network of buyers and sellers and by making the online trading experience faster, easier and safer, we better enable the success of our user community."

eBay, Annual Report (2002)

ONE OF THE TREMENDOUS ADVANTAGES OF E-COMMERCE IS THAT TRULY ALL OF THE world's shoppers are potential customers for a vendor, no matter their physical location. Not only has eBay handsomely captured a lion's share of the American online auction consumer market, but eBay's offerings also extend to some 18 countries, as well as Latin America.[1] As a result, eBay has emerged as a global organization able to reach a significant customer base. Given its electronic medium, eBay is able to expand its reach much less expensively than a traditional brick-and-mortar business. Philosophically speaking, eBay has created a marketplace where one person's trash is another person's treasure.

In the Beginning: Scarce Resources and Unlimited Wants

Economics is the study of scarce resources and unlimited human wants. Pierre Omidyar, founder of eBay, had a vision of a utopian community founded on the basis of fundamental economics. The vision underlined the concept of having a *self-sustaining platform* that would be able to adapt to user needs without any heavy intervention from a central authority. Omidyar began the business as an online hobby in September 1995, calling it AuctionWeb. The enterprise started out as a sole proprietorship. It was some individual's desired want to own a "broken laser pointer." This *scarce resource* was provided by Omidyar, through his own personal web site auction that he developed. The site was satisfying this individual's want, but Omidyar knew that there was more to his AuctionWeb than met the eye.

AuctionWeb was incorporated in California in May 1996 with partner Jeff Skoll, a Stanford MBA. The company then became known as eBay (for "Electronic Bay"). When Omidyar and Skoll began generating a large amount of traffic and charging customers only $0.25 for listings, their mailboxes were overflowing with checks, and they did not have time to even open the mail. In 1996, eBay then grew to a one-room office, a part-time employee to handle payments, and a salary of $25,000 each for Omidyar and Skoll. eBay, Inc., was reincorporated in Delaware in 1998 and completed its IPO.

As eBay evolved, Omidyar envisioned a world of buyers where scarce resources were reduced. Through an Internet platform and the auction-based business model, this would be very possible. eBay has grown to become a consumer-driven buyer–seller platform. The idea was to develop a community-driven process, where the *community*—an organic, evolving, self-organizing web of individual relationships, formed around shared interests—would handle tasks that other companies handle with customer service operations.

On May 7, 1998, eBay's founder, Omidyar, now former CEO, became Chairman of the Board and brought in a seasoned veteran of consumer marketing, a Harvard Business School MBA, Meg Whitman. Whitman was brought in to direct corporate strategy to continue the accelerated growth rate of eBay. Whitman brought global management and marketing experience through years of service in brand management of Playskool and Mr. Potato Head. Upon Whitman's arrival at eBay, her focus was on expansion and global development: "With more than 10 million auctions completed since eBay's inception, we are changing the face of traditional commerce by giving power to individual consumers, as well as by allowing them to extend their buying and selling reach around the world. I am delighted to be joining eBay,"[2] she said.

Company Background

Whitman followed Omidyar's vision, believing that eBay's success is attributable to the notion that people are inherently good. eBay, Inc., incorporated in May 1996, operates a marketplace in which anyone, anywhere, can buy or sell practically anything. Through eBay's PayPal service, any business or consumer with e-mail and a credit card or bank account can send and receive online payments securely, conveniently, and cost-effectively. Whitman's goal is to create, maintain, and expand the technological functionality, safety, ease of use, and reliability of the trading platform while at the same time supporting the growth and success of its community of users.

Technology is another factor in eBay's success. eBay's trading platform is a fully automated, topically arranged, intuitive, and easy-to-use online service that is available 24 hours a day, 7 days a week (subject to a weekly scheduled two-hour maintenance period). The platform includes software tools and services that are available for free or for a fee and that allow buyers and sellers to more easily trade with one another. Its software tools are designed to make its trading process easy and efficient.

"The depth, breadth and potential of our business gives us great confidence in the future," said Whitman, now President and CEO of eBay. "The eBay marketplace is thriving across geographies, trading categories, pricing formats, listed items, user growth, and the services we offer our community." For Whitman and her executives, this was a major challenge—to uncover eBay's potential.

Corporate Governance

The success of the eBay community and company are fundamentally based on openness, honesty, integrity, and trust. eBay must have a strong board and management team to be effective toward not only stockholders but also stakeholders of the company. eBay's focus is on the effective use of building and strengthening the tools for online relationships. **Exhibit 1** shows biographies of the members of the Board of Directors of eBay, Inc.

Exhibit 1
Board of Directors:
eBay, Inc.

Name	Age	Position
Pierre M. Omidyar	35	Founder, Chairman of the Board and Director
Margaret C. Whitman	46	President, Chief Executive Officer and Director
		Senior Vice President and General Manager, Global Online
Matthew J. Bannick	38	Payments
William C. Cobb	46	Senior Vice President and General Manager, eBay International
Rajiv Dutta	41	Senior Vice President and Chief Financial Officer
Michael R. Jacobson	48	Senior Vice President, Legal Affairs, General Counsel and Secretary
Jeffrey D. Jordon	44	Senior Vice President and General Manager, U. S. Business
Maynard G. Webb, Jr.	47	Chief Operating Officer
Philippe Bourguignon	55	Director
Scott D. Cook	50	Director
Robert C. Kagle	47	Director
Dawn G. Lepore	49	Director
Howard D Schultz	49	Director
Thomas J. Tierney	49	Director

Pierre M. Omidyar founded eBay as a sole proprietorship in September 1995. He has been a director and Chairman of the Board since eBay's incorporation in May 1996 and also served as its Chief Executive Officer, Chief Financial Officer, and President from inception to February 1998, November 1997 and August 1996, respectively. Prior to finding eBay, Mr. Omidyar was a developer services engineer at General Magic, a mobile communication platform company from December 1994 to July 1996. Mr. Omidyar co-founded Ink Development Corp. (later renamed eShop) in May 1991 and served as a software engineer there from May 1991 to September 1994. Prior to co-founding Ink, Mr. Omidyar was a developer for Claris, a subsidiary of Apple Computer, and for other Macintosh-oriented software development companies. Mr. Omidyar is currently Chairman and CEO of Omidyar Network. He also serves on Board of Trustees of Tufts University, The Santa Fe Institute, and as a director of several private companies. Mr. Omidyar holds a B.S. degree in Computer Science from Tufts University.

Margaret C. Whitman serves eBay as President and Chief Executive Officer. She has served in that capacity since February 1998 and as a director since March

(continued)

Exhibit 1
(continued)

1998. From January 1997 to February 1998, she was General Manager of the Preschool Division of Hasbro Inc., a toy company. From February 1995 to December 1996, Ms. Whitman was employed by FTD, Inc., a floral products company, most recently as President, Chief Executive Officer and a director. From October 1992 to February 1995, Ms. Whitman was employed by the Stride Rite Corporation, a footwear company, in various capacities, including President, Stride Rite Children's Group and Executive Vice President, Product Development, Marketing & Merchandising, Keds Division. From May 1989 to October 1992, Ms. Whitman was employed by The Walt Disney Company, an entertainment company, most recently as Senior Vice President, Marketing, Disney Consumer Products. Before joining Disney, Ms. Whitman was at Bain & Co., a consulting firm, most recently as a Vice President. Ms. Whitman also serves on the board of directors of The Procter & Gamble Company and Gap Inc. Ms. Whitman holds an A.B. degree in Economics from Princeton University and an M.B.A. degree from the Harvard Business School.

Philippe Bourguignon has served as a director of eBay since December 1999. Mr. Bourguignon has been the Chairman of Aegis Media France, a media communications and market research company since April 2004. From September 2003 to March 2004, Mr. Bourguignon was Co-Chief Executive Officer of The World Economic Forum (The DAVOS Forum). From August 2003 to October 2003, Mr. Bourguignon served as Managing Director of The World Economic Forum. From April 1997 to January 2003, Mr. Bourguignon served as Chairman of the Board of Club Mediterranee S.A., a resort operator. Prior to his appointment at Club Mediterranee S.A., Mr. Bourguignon was Chief Executive Officer of Euro Disney S.A., the parent company of Disneyland Paris, since 1993, and Executive Vice President of The Walt Disney Company (Europe) S.A., since October 1996. Mr. Bourguignon was named President of Euro Disney in 1992, a post he held through April 1993. He joined The Walt Disney Company in 1988 as head of Real Estate development. Mr. Bourguignon holds a Masters Degree in Economics at the University of Aix-en-Provence and holds a post-graduate diploma from the Institut d'Administration des Enterprises (IAE) in Paris.

Scott D. Cook has served as a director of eBay since June 1998. Mr. Cook is the founder of Intuit Inc., a financial software developer. Mr. Cook has been a director of Intuit since March 1984 and is currently Chairman of the Executive Committee of the Board of Intuit. From March 1993 to July 1998, Mr. Cook served as Chairman of the Board of Intuit. From March 1984 to April 1994, Mr. Cook served as President and Chief Executive Officer of Intuit. Mr. Cook also serves on the board of directors of The Procter & Gamble Company. Mr. Cook holds a B.A. degree in Economics and Mathematics from the University of Southern California and an M.B.A. degree from the Harvard Business School.

Robert C. Kagle has served as a director of eBay since June 1997. Mr. Kagle has been a Member of Benchmark Capital, the General Partner of Benchmark Capital Partners, L.P. and Benchmark Founders' Fund, L.P., since its founding in May 1995. Mr. Kagle also has been a General Partner of Technology Venture Investors since January 1984. Mr. Kagle also serves on the board of directors of E-LOAN, Inc. and ZipRealty, Inc. Mr. Kagle holds a B.S. degree in Electrical and Mechanical Engineering from the General Motors Institute (renamed Kettering University in Jaunuary 1998) and an M.B.A. degree from the Stanford Graduate School of Business.

Exhibit 1
(continued)

Dawn G. Lepore has served as a director of eBay since December 1999. Ms. Lepore has served as Chief Executive Officer and Chairman of the Board of drugstore.com, inc., a leading online provider of health, beauty, vision, and pharmacy solutions, since October 2004. From August 2003 to October 2004, Ms. Lepore served as Vice Chairman of Technology, Active Trader, Operations, Business Strategy, and Administration for the Charles Schwab Corporation and Charles Schwab & Co, Inc., a financial holding company. Prior to this appointment, she held various positions with the Charles Schwab Corporation including: Vice Chairman of Technology, Operations, Business Strategy, and Administration from May 2003 to August 2003; Vice Chairman of Technology, Operations, and Administrations from March 2002 to May 2003; Vice Chairman of Technology and Administration from November 2001 to March 2002; and Vice Chairman and Chief Information Officer from July 1999 to November 2001. She also serves on the board of directors of Catalyst, a research and advisory organization working to expand opportunities for women in business, and as a trustee of Smith College. Ms. Lepore holds a B.A. degree from Smith College.

Howard D. Schultz has served as a director of eBay since June 1998. Mr. Schultz is the founder of Starbucks Corporation, a provider of gourmet coffee, and has been its Charirman of the Board and Chief Global Strategist since June 2000. From Starbucks' inception in 1985 to June 2000, he served as its Charirman of the Board and Chief Executive Officer. From 1985 to June 1994, Mr. Schultz also served as President of Starbucks. Mr. Schultz is also one of two founding members of Maveron LLC, a company providing advisory services to consumer-based businesses, and is a member of two LLCs that serve as General Partners of Maveron LLC's affiliated venture capital funds, Maveron Equity Partners LP and Maveron Equity Partners 2000 LP. Mr. Schultz has announced that he will step down from the board when his current term expires at our Annual Meeting in June 2003.

Thomas J. Tierney has served as a director of eBay since March 2003. Mr. Tierney is the founder of The Bridgespan Group, a non-profit consulting firm serving the non-profit sector, and has been its Chairman of the Board since late 1999. Prior to founding Bridgespan, Mr. Tierney served as Chief Executive Officer of Bain & Company, a consulting firm, from June 1992 to January 2000. Mr. Tierney holds a B.A. degree in Economics from the University of California at Davis and an M.B.A. degree with distinction from the Harvard Business School. Mr. Tierney is the co-author of a book about organization and strategy called *Aligning the Stars*.

Executive Officers
Matthew J. Bannick serves eBay as Senior Vice President and General Manager, Global Online Payments and Chief Executive Officer of PayPal. He has served in those capacities since October 2002. From December 2000 to October 2002, Mr. Bannick served as eBay's Senior Vice Persident and General Manager, eBay International. From February 1999 to December 2000, Mr. Bannick served in a variety of other executive positions at eBay. From April 1995 to January 1999, Mr. Bannick was an executive for Navigation Technologies (NavTech), the leading provider of digital map databases for the vehicle navigation and internet mapping industries. Mr. Bannick was President of NavTech North America for three years and also served as

(continued)

Exhibit 1
(continued)

Senior Vice President of Marketing and Vice President of Operations. From June 1992 to August 1992, Mr. Bannick served as a consultant for McKinsey & Company, in Europe and from June 1993 to April 1995 in the U.S. Mr. Bannick also served as a U.S. diplomat in Germany during the period of German unification. Mr. Bannick holds a B.A. in Economics and International Studies from Univeristy of Washington and an M.B.A. degree from the Harvard Business School.

Scott D. Cook has served as a director of eBay since June 1998. Mr. Cook is the founder of Intuit Inc., a financial software developer. Mr. Cook has been a director of Intuit since March 1984 and is currently Chairman of the Executive Committee of the Board of Intuit. From March 1993 to July 1998, Mr. Cook served as Chairman of the Board of Intuit. From March 1984 to April 1994, Mr. Cook served as President and Chief Executive Officer of Intuit. Mr. Cook also serves on the board of directors of The Procter & Gamble Company. Mr. Cook holds a B.A. degree in Economics and Mathematics from the University of Southern California and an M.B.A. degree from the Harvard Business School.

Rajiv Dutta serves eBay as Senior Vice President and Chief Financial Officer. He has served in that capacity since January 2001. From August 1999 to January 2001, Mr. Dutta served as eBay's Vice President of Finance and Investor Relations. From July 1998 to August 1999, Mr. Dutta served as eBay's Finance director. From February 1998 to July 1998, Mr. Dutta served as the World Wide Sales Controller of KLA-Tencor, a manufacturer of semiconductor equipment. Prior to KLA-Tencor, Mr. Dutta spent ten years, from January 1988 to February 1998, at Bio-Rad Laboratories, Inc., a manufacturer and distributor of life science and diagnostic products with operations in over 24 countries. Mr. Dutta held a variety of positions with Bio-Rad, including the group controller of the Life Science Group. Mr. Dutta also serves on the board of directors of Jamadat Mobile Inc., a global publisher of wireless entertainment applications. Mr. Dutta holds a B.A. degree in Economics from St. Stephen's College, Delhi University in India and an M.B.A. degree from Drucker School of Management.

Michael R. Jacobson serves eBay as Senior Vice President, Legal Affairs, General Counsel and Secretary. He has served in that capacity or as Vice President, Legal Affairs, General Counsel, since August 1998. From 1986 to August 1998, Mr. Jacobson was a partner with the law firm of Cooley Godward LLP, specializing in securities law, mergers and acquisitions, and other transactions. Mr. Jacobson holds an A.B. degree in Economics from Harvard College and a J.D. degree from Stanford Law School.

Jeffrey D. Jordan serves eBay as President, PayPal. He has served in that capacity since December 2004. From April 2000 to December 2004, Mr. Jordan served as eBay's Senior Vice President, eBay North America. From September 1999 to April 2000, Mr. Jordan served as eBay's Vice President, Regionals and Services. From September 1998 to September 1999, Mr. Jordan served as Chief Financial Officer for Hollywood Entertainment Corporation, a video rental company, and President of their subsidiary, Reel.com. From September 1990 to September 1998, Mr. Jordan served in various capacities including most recently Senior Vice President and Chief Financial Officer of the Disney Store Worldwide, a subsidiary of the Walt Disney Company. Mr. Jordan holds a B.A. degree in Political Science and Psychology from Amherst College and an M.B.A. degree from the Stanford Graduate School of Business.

Exhibit 1
(continued)

> *Maynard G. Webb, Jr.* serves eBay as Chief Operating Officer. He has served in that capacity since June 2002. From August 1999 to June 2002, Mr. Webb served as President, eBay Technologies. From July 1998 to August 1999, Mr. Webb was Senior Vice President and Chief Information Officer at Gateway, Inc., a computer manufacturer. From February 1995 to July 1998, Mr. Webb was Vice President and Chief Information Officer at Bay Networks, Inc., a manufacturer of computer networking products. From June 1991 to January 1995, Mr. Webb was Director, IT at Quantum Corporation. Mr. Webb also serves on the board of directors of Gartner, Inc., a high technology research and consulting firm and Peribit Networks, a networking company. Mr. Webb holds a B.A.A. degree from Florida Atlantic University.

Source: Adapted from eBay, Inc. (www.ebay.com), SEC 10-K (March 31, 2003), pp. 77–80.

Services

Customer Support

There is intrinsic value in the customer service that eBay provides. eBay does not necessarily provide customer service to buyers and sellers; however, it provides the tools that allow buyers and sellers to easily trade with one another. These software tools are available to buyers and sellers for free or for a fee (see **Exhibit 2**).

eBay prides itself on giving buyers and sellers the opportunity to be able to contact each other through the use of e-mail, text messaging, and phone. eBay enhances the user experience through pretrade and posttrade services. The listing process is simplified through pretrade services including photo hosting, authentication, and seller productivity applications. Posttrade services include insurance, payment processing, vehicle inspections, shipping and postage, and escrow. Services such as these are provided through third-party contracts.

Trust and Safety Programs

The Feedback Forum allows users to provide comments on other eBay users. Feedback is related to specific transactions of trades they personally dealt with. Positive representations are color coded. Users are encouraged to review feedback before making trades with other

Exhibit 2
Software Tools

- eBay Anywhere: Provides wireless connectivity to eBay.
- Seller's Assistant: Allows one to automate e-mail, project management, and list and track listing; provides pictures and HTML and formatting for sellers.
- Turbo Lister: This desktop-based selling tool facilitates creating listings to post on the eBay site. Turbo Lister helps a seller list items on eBay more quickly and easily.
- Selling Manager: Automates the selling process.
- Freight Resource Center: Allows users to calculate shipping costs.
- PayPal: Facilitates online exchange of funds.

Source: Adapted from eBay, Inc. (www.ebay.com), company document.

users. This creates trust within a community of users. The Feedback Forum reduces anonymity and uncertainty of dealing with unknown trading users.

Safeharbor™ Program

This program provides trading guidelines and information regarding disputes and the misuse of the eBay service. In this program, eBay staff are investigators of inappropriate behavior:

> The SafeHarbor™ group is organized into three areas: Investigations, Fraud Prevention and Community Watch. The Investigations team investigates reported trading infractions and misuse of the eBay service. The Fraud Prevention department provides information to assist users with disputes over the quality of the goods sold or potentially fraudulent transactions and, upon receipt of an officially filed, written claim of fraud from a user, will generally suspend the offending user from the eBay service or take other action as appropriate. The Community Watch department investigates the listing of illegal, infringing or inappropriate items on the eBay.com site and our international websites and violations of certain of our policies.[3]

My eBay

This program allows users to receive information about their online eBay activity. This information report includes recent activity, bidding, selling, account balances, favorite categories, and a feedback report. eBay users can also link their personal web pages to the "My eBay" portal. "The About Me home page can include personal information, items listed for sale, eBay feedback ratings, images and links to other favorite sites."[4]

Competitors

> *"We expect competition to intensify in the future as the barriers to entry into these channels are relatively low, as current offline and new competitors can easily launch online sites at a nominal cost using commercially available software or partnering with any one of a number of successful electronic commerce companies."*

> eBay, Annual Report (2002)

eBay is in an intensely competitive industry. Profitability can be maintained through preserving and expanding the abundance and diversity of the user community as well as enhancing the user experience. However, Whitman, President and CEO, faces the challenge of high operating expenses, which can lead to declines in net income. The Internet provides new, rapidly evolving and intensely competitive channels for the sale of all types of goods. eBay's broad list of competitors is listed in **Exhibit 3**. In addition, features of eBay's fixed-price business compete with the major Internet portals, such as AOL, MSN, Yahoo!, Amazon.com, and others.

Seasonality is a factor in eBay's globally competitive environment. Users reduce their online activities during holidays such as Thanksgiving and Christmas as well as the change from spring to summer.

**Exhibit 3
Competitors by
Product Area:
eBay, Inc.**

Antiques: Bonhams, Christie's, eHammer, Sotheby's, Phillips (LVMH), antique dealers and sellers

Coins & Stamps: Collectors Universe, Heritage, U.S. Mint, Bowers and Merena

Collectibles: Franklin Mint, Go Collect, Collectiblestoday.com, wizardworld.com, Russ Cochran Comic Art Auctions, All Star Auctions

Musical Instruments: Guitar Center, Musician's Friend, Sam Ash, Gbase.com, musical instrument retailers and manufacturers

Sports Memorabilia: Beckett, Collectors Universe, Mastro, Leylands, ThePit.com

Toys, Hobbies, Dolls, Bears: Toys "R" Us, Amazon.com/Toysrus.com, KB Toys/KBToys.com, FAO Inc. (FAO Schwarz, Zany Brainy, the Right Start), Lego, TY Inc.

Premium Collectibles: Bonhams, Christie's, DuPont Registry, Greg Manning Auctions, iCollector, Lycos/Skinner Auctions, Millionaire.com, Phillips (LVMH), Sotheby's, other premium collectibles dealers and sellers

Automotive (used cars and parts): Advance Auto Parts, Autonation.com, AutoTrader.com, Autozone, Barrett-Jackson, California Classics, CarMax, Cars.com, CarsDirect.com, Collectorcartraderonline.com, Dealix, Discount Auto Parts, Dupont Registry, eClassics.com, Edmunds, General Parts (Carquest), Genuine/NAPA, Hemmings, imotors.com, JC Whitney, TraderOnline, Trader Publishing, vehix.com, Wal-Mart, newspaper classifieds, used car dealers, swap meets, car clubs

Books, Movies, Music: Amazon.com, Barnes & Noble/Barnesandnoble.com, Alibris.com, Blockbuster, BMG, Columbia House, Best Buy, CDNow, Express.com, Emusic.com, Tower Records/TowerRecords.com

Clothing and Accessories: Abercrombie.com, AE.com, Amazon.com, Bluefly.com, ColdwaterCreek.com, Delias.com, Dockers.com, Eddie Bauer, The Gap/gap.com, J. Crew/JCrew.com, LandsEnd.com, The Limited, LLBean.com, Macy's, The Men's Wearhouse, Payless.com, Ross, Urbanq.com, VictoriasSecret.com

Computers & Consumer Electronics: Amazon.com, Best Buy, Buy.com, Circuit City, CNET, CompUSA, Dell, Electronics Boutique, Fry's Electronics, Gamestop, Gateway, The Good Guys, MicroWarehouse, PC Connection, Radio Shack, Ritz Camera, Tech Depot, Tiger Direct, Tweeter Home Entertainment, uBid, Computer Discount Warehouse, computer, consumer electronics and photography retailers

Home & Garden: IKEA, Crate & Barrel, Home Depot, Williams-Sonoma Inc. (Pottery Barn, Williams-Sonoma), Bed, Bath & Beyond, Lowes, Linens 'n Things, Pier One, Ethan Allen, Frontgate, Burpee.com

Jewelry: Bluenile.com, Diamond.com, Macy's

Pottery & Glass: Just Glass, Pottery Auction, Pottery Barn, Go Collect, Pier 1 Imports, Restoration Hardware

Sporting Goods/Equipment: Bass Pro Shops, Cabela's, dsports.com, Footlocker, Gear.com, Global Sports, golfclubexchange, MVP.com, Play It Again Sports, REI, Sports Authority, Sportsline.com

Tickets: Ticketmaster, Tickets.com, other ticket brokers

Tool/Equipment/Hardware: Home Depot, HomeBase, Amazon.com, Ace Hardware, OSH

Business-to-Business: Ariba, BidFreight.com, Bid4Assets, BizBuyer.com, Buyer Zone, CloseOutNow.com, Commerce One, Concur Technologies, DoveBid, FreeMarkets, Iron Planet, labx.com, Oracle, Overstock.com, PurchasePro.com, RicardoBiz.com, Sabre, SurplusBin.com, Ventro, Vertical Net

Global Business Strategy

Whitman has seen key opportunities for growth in the United States as well as internationally. Whitman cited international acquisitions, online merchandising, and marketing as levers to achieve the company goals. Overall, eBay receives three major sources of revenue growth: U.S. business, International business, and online payments.

For future expansion, Whitman wants to focus on new user acquisition and marketing. Online auctions, like many online communities, rely on positive relationships among those transacting business. One area of concern for eBay is the threat from fraudulent auctions (e.g., seller has no intention of shipping item), counterfeits, and knock-offs. Each of these areas erodes the trust needed for eBay to flourish. Even though eBay has in place various monitoring measures and de-listing capabilities, unscrupulous individuals or criminals are often one step ahead of eBay and likely will continue to identify means to undermine the trust-based marketplace. As a result, unethical behavior will continue to be a threat to eBay, and its ability to manage such acts, however strong, must be considered a weakness as potential customers may harbor concern about the eBay environment. For example, Jed Conboy, a district attorney in New York, purchased a baseball he believed was signed by Ted Williams for $367 on eBay.[5] The autograph was a fake, and Conboy decided to sue eBay. As in many similar cases, the court ruled in favor of eBay. The primary question is whether eBay is an auction house or a marketplace. If the courts view eBay as a classic auctioneer, the company would have to vouch for the products sold on its site. However, eBay's lawyers have argued successfully that eBay is no more than an independent intermediary that does not take sides in the transaction. Up to this point, the courts have accepted this defense. This legal precedent has allowed eBay to grow and prosper without paying penalties for fraudulent products sold on its site.

Acquisition of PayPal

As a result of the 2001 financial analysts' conference, on October 3, 2002, eBay acquired PayPal, Inc. PayPal enabled any business or consumer with e-mail access and a credit card or bank account in 38 countries to send and receive online payments securely, conveniently, and cost-effectively. Whitman noted, "eBay and PayPal have complementary missions. We both empower people to buy and sell online."[6] eBay's intentions were to accelerate the velocity of trade on eBay by eliminating the various obstacles presented by traditional payment methods. Based on the same financial infrastructure of bank accounts and credit cards, PayPal and eBay created an international payment system. In July 2002, eBay announced plans to acquire PayPal, an online payment company, for $1.5 billion.[7] Although the acquisition provided many opportunities, $7 billion in annual sales on eBay are completed using something other than online payment. And the acquisition of PayPal also came with some legal baggage.

A suit was brought against PayPal by First USA Bank in September 2002 alleging infringement of two patents pertaining to assigning an alias to a credit card. PayPal has a solid defense against this accusation, but even if successful in court, the defense will be costly and divert management's time. A class action suit was also brought against PayPal in February 2002, claiming that the company violated the state's consumer protection laws by restricting customer accounts and failing to promptly unrestrict legitimate accounts. If unsuccessful in its defense, PayPal will have to change its anti-fraud operations in a way that could harm the business in addition to paying significant damages. Even if PayPal is successful in this suit, the trial has damaged the company's reputation and will be costly in terms of legal fees and management's time.

Technology

Much of eBay's success is based on the company's ability to quickly analyze sales trends and capitalize on the movement in specific product categories. In order to compete in this area, eBay requires extensive data mining and data storage software. By taking advantage of the latest product offerings and implementing the software in a coherent architecture, eBay is able to process millions of transactions a day while gathering information on specific segments. It also revamped its application development architecture to support the Java 2, Enterprise Edition, framework. This programming environment adds a new level of flexibility that was not available with the older C++ development tools. Buyers and sellers on eBay make an average of 30 million searches a day.[8] Due to this volume, eBay is constantly trying to improve its search capability. Bidding on items increases dramatically when eBay adds a new search feature; therefore, eBay has constantly invested in improving technology to provide more accurate results as quickly as possible.

Marketing

eBay is recognized as one of the few successful dot-com companies. To realize such achievements, eBay has developed a great number of marketing strengths. Although eBay has advantages as a first mover, to maintain its competitive edge, the company has identified several ways to create and sustain customer relationships. In particular, the company tries to achieve strengths in each of the four P's—price, promotion, product, and place. The fruits of these endeavors is demonstrated by one of the longest "customer hang-times"[9] on the Internet.[10] Furthermore, a strong argument could be made that eBay is synonymous with online auctions and vice versa. eBay's offerings are related to pull rather than push marketing. eBay's product offerings are a result of this user demand. eBay's customers must sell products successfully in order for the digital marketplace to be economically viable; therefore, it is in eBay's best interest to ensure that buyers and sellers alike are satisfied. eBay does not produce the items sold on its site, but it provides the tools and forums that enable the efficient interaction between buyers and sellers. These tools and forums are the keys to eBay's success. For eBay to gain competitive advantage, customers must perceive a value from eBay that exceeds the values of potential rivals or alternatives.

Tremendous brand recognition enables eBay to draw an ever-expanding array of customers. With tens of millions registered users and listings of some 16 million items worldwide, clearly eBay has realized strong product promotion.[11] Surely those wishing to sell or buy items are more inclined to enter a marketplace that has the most significant listing of items. Thus, eBay currently attracts a growing cascade of customers because it appears to be the sensible site for the world of online auctions. Another marketing strength of eBay is its protection of trademarks, copyrights, patents, domain names, trade dress, and trade secrets. eBay employs confidentiality and invention agreements with employees and contractors, as well as nondisclosure agreements with business contacts. Registration and upkeep of these intellectual properties are critical to success.

The value that eBay offers is to make inefficient markets more efficient. Traditional offline marketplaces can be inefficient because:

- They are fragmented and regional in nature, making it difficult and expensive for buyers and sellers to meet, exchange information, and complete transactions
- They offer a limited variety and breadth of goods
- They often have high transaction costs due to intermediaries
- In particular, large markets with broad buyer and seller bases, wide product ranges, and moderate shipping costs have been successful on eBay. Its marketplace is most effective, relative to available alternatives, at addressing markets of new and scarce goods, end-of-life products, and used and vintage items.

eBay has several core competencies that translate into competitive advantages. Competitive advantages are subject to becoming outdated and irrelevant if a company does not work to continuously adapt its strategic outlook. eBay has been able to enable its users to have successful trading experiences through continuous improvements. eBay has also been able to provide exceptional customer service through its Power Seller Program, where people who sell over a certain total dollar value per month receive personal support through an exclusive toll-free phone number.

Financial Performance

eBay's income is mainly generated from transactions fees, third-party advertising, end-to-end services, and offline services in its U.S., International, and Payments segments. eBay's sales have increased every year, from $224.7 million in 1999 to $1,213 million in 2002. This yields a compounded annual growth rate (CAGR) of 75%. Over the same period, net income increased from $9.6 million to $249.9 million. This is a CAGR of 196%. The higher growth rate of net income over sales can probably be attributed to expenses growing at a slower rate than sales.

During the period from 2001 to 2002, eBay's cash holdings have more than doubled from $524 million to $1,109.3 million. This amount of cash is more than enough to cover debt obligations. From 1999 to 2002, long-term debt has decreased from $15 million to $13.8 million, a CAGR of 3%. From 2001 to 2002, long-term debt increased from $12 million to $13.8 million. In eBay's global arena, international sales increased 165% over sales in 2001. International sales make up 26% of total revenues, up from 7% in 2000. **Exhibits 4 and 5** are eBay's income statement and balance sheet, respectively.

The Future

Whitman now faces some critical issues. She notes that eBay's core competencies and competitive advantages are what allow eBay to be successful. Whitman is confident that eBay's business model is sound and the vision of becoming the world's online marketplace is a matter of enhancing the efficient use and effectiveness of eBay's products and services. Whitman faces problems in that eBay needs to be able to develop new services, features,

**Exhibit 4
Consolidated
Income Statement:
eBay, Inc. (Dollar
amounts in thou-
sands, except per
share amount)**

Year Ending December 31	2000	2001	2002
Net revenues	$1,214,100	$748,821	$431,424
Cost of net revenue:	213,876	134,816	95,453
Gross Profit:	1,000,224	614,005	335,971
Operating expenses:			
Sales and marketing	349,650	253,474	166,767
Product development	104,636	75,288	55,863
General and administrative	171,785	105,784	73,027
Payroll taxes on stock option gains	4,015	2,442	2,337
Amortization of intangible assets	15,941	36,591	1,433
Merger related costs	—	—	1,550
Total operating expenses	646,027	473,579	300,977
Income from operations	354,197	140,426	34,994
Interest and other income, net	49,209	41,613	46,337
Interest expenses	(1,492)	(2,851)	(3,374)
Impairment of certain equity investments	(3,781)	(16,245)	—
Income before income taxes and minority interests	398,133	162,943	77,957
Provision for income taxes	(145,946)	(80,009)	(32,725)
Minority interests in consolidated companies	(2,296)	7,514	3,062
Net income	$ 249,891	$ 90,448	$ 48,294
Net income per share:			
Basic	$ 0.87	$ 0.34	$ 0.19
Diluted	$ 0.85	$ 0.32	$ 0.17
Weighted average shares:			
Basic	287,496	268,971	251,776
Diluted	292,820	280,595	280,346

Note: Notes were deleted.

Source: eBay, Inc., SEC Form 10-K (December 2002), p. 95.

and functions in order to stay ahead of its increasing competition. Whitman needs to decide how eBay can exploit its potential and consider the following approaches to ensure future growth of the company:

1. Invest large portions of revenue in research and development in order to develop new service features and functions

2. Make acquisitions and strategic partnerships to increase success in new categories and specialty stores

3. Recruit personnel familiar with certain market segments to allow eBay to develop services better suited to those particular segments

4. Enter the business-to-business auctions market to allow eBay to offer higher-priced items and collect higher commissions

5. Make strategic alliances with shipping companies such as FedEx

In growing, eBay's management will have to take care not to destroy brand value and image as well as remain an auction site, eBay's area of core competence.

Exhibit 5
Consolidated
Balance Sheets:
eBay, Inc. (Dollar
amounts in thou-
sands, except per
share amounts)

Year Ending December 31	2002	2001
Assets		
Current assets:		
Cash and cash equivalents	$1,109,313	$ 523,969
Short-term investments	89,690	199,450
Accounts receivable	131,453	101,703
Funds receivable	41,014	—
Other current assets	96,988	58,683
Total current assets	1,468,458	883,805
Long-term investments	470,227	286,998
Restricted cash and investments	134,644	129,614
Property and equipment net	218,028	142,349
Goodwill	1,456,024	187,829
Intangible assets net	279,465	10,810
Deferred tax assets	84,218	21,540
Other assets	13,380	15,584
	$4,124,444	$1,678,529
Liabilities and Stockholders' Equity		
Current liabilities		
Accounts payable	$ 47,424	$ 33,235
Funds payable and amounts due to customers	50,396	—
Accrued expenses and other current liabilities	199,323	94,593
Deferred revenue and customer advances	18,846	15,583
Short-term debt	2,970	16,111
Income taxes payable	67,265	20,617
Total current liabilities	386,224	180,139
Long-term debt	12,008	13,798
Deferred tax liabilities	3,629	111,843
Other liabilities	15,864	22,874
Minority interests	37,751	33,232
Total liabilities	249,391	567,971
Commitment		
Stockholders' equity:		
Convertible Preferred Stock, $0.001 par value; 10,000 shares authorized; no shares issued or outstanding	—	—
Common Stock, $0.001 par value; 900,000 shares authorized; 277,259 and 311,277 shares issued and outstanding	311	277
Additional paid-in capital	3,108,443	1,275,240
Unearned stock-based compensation	(5,253)	(2,367)
Retained earnings	414,474	164,633
Accumulated other comprehensive income (loss)	38,498	(8,645)
Total stockholders' equity	3,556,473	1,429,138
Total liabilities and stockholders' equity	$4,124,444	$1,678,529

Note: Notes were deleted.

Source: eBay, Inc., SEC Form 10-K (December 2002), p. 94.

Notes

1. eBay web site, *http://pages.ebay.com/community/aboutebay/overview/index.html* (July 2003).
2. Whitman, 1998.
3. eBay.com, 2003.
4. eBay.com, 2003.
5. M. Mannix, "Sure It's a Great Deal. But Is It Real? Fraud Online Threatens eBay's Money Model," *U.S. News and World Report* (December 11, 2000).
6. Whitman, 2002.
7. M. Richtel, "eBay to Buy PayPal, a Rival in Online Payments," *The New York Times* (July 9, 2002).
8. R. Hof, "Desperately Seeking Search Technology," *BusinessWeek* (September 24, 2001).
9. *Customer hangtime* is an e-commerce term that evaluates the length of time a customer spends on a site at each visit. The greater the length of time per visit, the greater the customer hangtime.
10. eBay web site, *http://pages.ebay.com/community/aboutebay/overview/index.html* (July 2003).
11. *Ibid.*

CASE 10

Amazon.com:

An E-Commerce Retailer

Patrick Collins, Robert J. Mockler, and Marc Gartenfeld

HEADING INTO THE SECOND QUARTER OF 2003, JEFF BEZOS, FOUNDER AND CEO OF Amazon.com, could look back over the last couple sets of quarterly numbers for Amazon.com and be proud. Under pressure from the financial markets to abandon the company's oft-stated goal of sacrificing short-term profits for building long-term growth, market share, and increased shareholder value, Bezos proved that his online retail business model could produce operating profits. Now that Bezos had that issue taken care of, there were a number of new ones that needed to be addressed. Outside the overall economic malaise of the U.S. and world economies, the Internet Tax Moratorium law was up for renewal in November, with no assurance of its being extended, and online stalwarts eBay and Yahoo! were expanding into Amazon.com's markets. Bezos was faced with the task of developing an effective differentiating enterprisewide strategy if Amazon.com was to survive and prosper against aggressive competition over the intermediate and long-term futures.

Amazon.com is considered to be the premier online retailer in the world. Although it originally started out selling only books, it has expanded into numerous other product lines, as shown in **Exhibit 1**. Some of these product lines include CDs, DVDs, and videos. However, in order to offer as large a product line as possible, Amazon.com has entered into contracts with numerous retail partners, such as The Gap and Eddie Bauer, to sell their goods through Amazon.com's web site. Some of these partnership agreements involve Amazon.com running another company's own web site. This type of partnership, known as "powered by Amazon," allows companies to use Amazon.com technology and patented web site capabilities, such as 1-Click Ordering. Two well-known retailers who have participated in this type of arrangement are Target and Toys 'R' Us.

With the number of households having broadband access expected to increase to 29 million by the end of 2003 and the number of Internet users worldwide estimated at 500 million,

**Exhibit 1
Product
Categories:
Amazon.com**

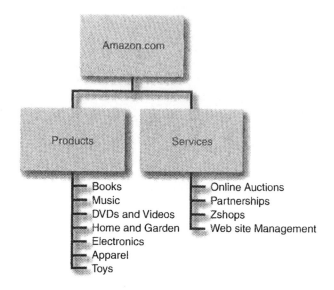

it was becoming easier and easier for a person to shop from the comfort of home.[1] As defined by the Federal Communications Commission (FCC), *broadband* is a new generation of high-speed transmission services that allows users to access the Internet and Internet-related services at significantly higher speeds than by using traditional modems. It has the potential technical capability to meet customers' broad communication, entertainment, information, and commercial needs and desires. And with online retailers commanding a small percentage of retail sales, there is plenty of market to go after.

In an earnings statement announcement released January 23, 2003, Amazon.com showed some outstanding financial numbers. For the fourth quarter, which was the busiest time of year for retailers due to the holiday season, Amazon.com reported record sales of $1.43 billion, an increase of 28% over 2001 fourth quarter sales of $1.12 billion. For the fiscal year ending December 31, 2002, Amazon.com showed an increase of 26% in yearly sales, reporting $3.94 billion in sales for 2002, compared to $3.12 billion for 2001. In addition, for the year ending December 31, 2002, Amazon.com managed its first operating profit of $64.1 million, as compared to a $412.2 million operating loss in 2001. And overall, Amazon.com cut its losses from $567 million to $149 million, an improvement of $418 million.[2] Even though Amazon.com continued to meet its internal goals of focusing on increased market share, expanded product offerings, and overall sales growth, the company was still facing pressure from the stock market to produce consistent operating profits and to prove that its business model worked financially over the long term. This pressure, combined with a decreasing customer confidence level and an increased unemployment rate, had made the retail future look uncertain. The main question for Bezos was how to turn Amazon.com into a consistent moneymaker in the immediate, intermediate, and long-term time frames, while continuing to pursue its corporate objective of expansion at reasonable costs.

History

After graduating from Princeton with a bachelor's degree in electrical engineering and computer science in 1986, Jeff Bezos went to work for a company called Fitel, a startup financial communications firm. From there, Bezos went to Banker's Trust and finally to D. E. Shaw.

While he was in these jobs, Bezos gained invaluable experience in computer programming, finance, and international markets. During his time at D. E. Shaw, Bezos was assigned the job of exploring possible Internet business opportunities. He looked for the best products to sell through the web and put together a list of products that could easily be sold online, including books, computer software, office supplies, apparel, and music.[3] After examining how the retail book business was set up and the fact that there was not a single company that had a stranglehold on the industry, Bezos felt that setting up an online bookstore was the best way to go. He made this recommendation to his company, but his recommendation was rejected. However, the idea of opening an online bookstore became something that Bezos could not let go of, and in 1994 he left D. E. Shaw to chase his dream of commerce on the Internet.

In starting his company, Bezos was faced with a number of questions. Although he had the financial and computer background to run his company, Bezos needed to think about where he was going to establish his company. In doing this analysis, Bezos came up with three criteria for the location of his business. The location had to be an area with people who had the necessary programming talent to develop the software, closeness to a major book wholesaler, and a state with little or no sales tax. After narrowing his options down to four areas that fit his criteria, Bezos decided on Seattle, Washington, as being the best place to start his company.

By the time Bezos got settled in Seattle and went about the process of starting his company, there were a number of online booksellers already in business. Because most people were not familiar with the World Wide Web and were just focusing on using e-mail, their business process model was to take book orders via e-mail, fill them, and ship them—a rather labor-intensive process. To help overcome their first-mover advantage and differentiate his company from the competition, Bezos decided to make his company mission to use the Internet to transform book buying into the fastest, easiest, and most enjoyable shopping experience possible.[4] The competition method was not very cost-effective and was in fact very labor intensive and did not fully maximize the capabilities of the Internet. The second selling method was to develop an online store so that people who had access to the Internet and a web browser, such as Netscape Navigator or Microsoft Explorer, could go and purchase books. To help defray some of the costs for setting up this web store, open-source programming code (which was free) was used.

In 1995, the Internet was becoming easier to use, and Amazon.com's method of sales through its web site started to take off. It was the perfect time to become an online retailer. When Sun Microsystems released Java, a programming language that made it possible to run interactive web pages, web sites became easier for customers to use. This, combined with the increasing number of personal computers, formed a market that was there for the taking. By being one of the first companies to go online and embrace the idea of taking orders through a web site, Amazon.com enjoyed a tremendous first-mover advantage, which it continues to enjoy today. Amazon.com has gone through a number of different changes in its short history, including dividing the company into four different operating segments, as shown in **Exhibit 2**.

**Exhibit 2
Operating
Segments:
Amazon.com**

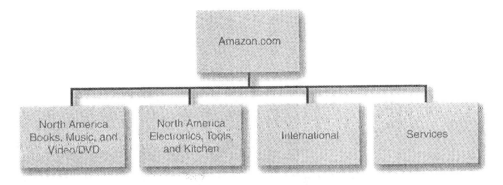

Exhibit 3 Business Model: Amazon.com

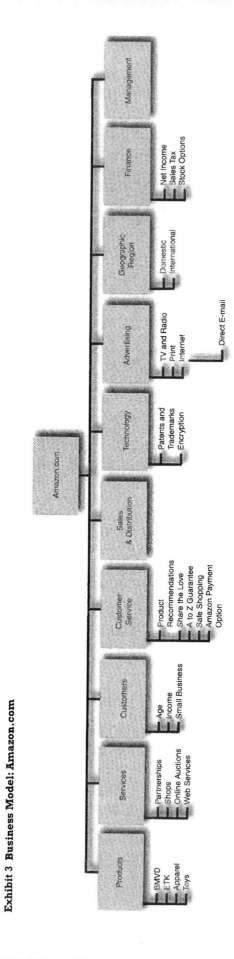

One theme always remained consistent: to get big fast, at all costs. This philosophy, which was stated in Amazon.com's 1997 Letter to Its Shareholders, was developed because it was seen as the best way to spread out costs. Due to its low overhead, the more sales that Amazon.com had, the bigger the increase in profit margin on the items it sold. Amazon.com, like all other retailers, had inventory and administrative costs. But by collecting payments immediately for its sales and floating vendor payments 30 to 40 days, Amazon.com was able to generate a large amount of working capital. Amazon.com also enjoyed an additional competitive advantage over traditional brick-and-mortar retailers in that it did not have to operate physical stores in order to sell its goods and services. Although there were some similarities with brick-and-mortar retailers, there were some unique factors with the online environment, as shown in **Exhibit 3**.

Products

Amazon.com sold a wide variety of products online for both itself and its retail partners. Amazon.com broke down its product line into four areas. The first area was called the Books, Music, and Video/DVD Segment, or BMVD. The second area was called the Electronics, Tools, and Kitchen Segment, or ETK. Apparel and toys made up the remaining two areas.

Books, Music, Video/DVD Segment

The BMVD segment offered books, music, and videos/DVDs for sale. Amazon.com offered these items for sale directly and did not use any of its affiliated partners.

Books

Selling books is what made Amazon.com famous. Amazon.com had more than 5 million titles in stock and available for purchase everyday. Some of the more popular categories included Arts & Photography, Biographies & Memoirs, Business & Investing, Children's Books, Cooking, History, Home & Garden, Horror, Literature & Fiction, Mystery & Thrillers, Nonfiction, Romance, Science Fiction & Fantasy, Sports, and Travel. Books could be purchased in hardcover, paperback, audio, and downloadable formats. Amazon.com offered significant discounts on most categories of books, including those on the *New York Times* bestseller list. To help customers in their selection process, Amazon.com posted book cover art, sample chapters, editorial staff reviews, and professional reviews of the book. In addition to professional reviews, Amazon.com allowed its customers to review books and had them posted online, alongside the professional reviews.

Music

In addition to its wide selection of books, Amazon.com offered a wide selection of music titles. The music could be purchased in a variety of formats, including tapes, compact discs, and downloadable formats, such as MP3s. Some of the more popular categories included Alternative Rock, Blues, Box Sets, Children's Music, Classic Rock, Classical, Country and Western, Hard Rock & Metal, Jazz, Latin, New Age, Opera & Vocal, Pop, Motown, R&B, Rap & Hip-Hop, and Soundtracks. To help customers in their selection process, Amazon.com posted short music clips for customers to listen to. For the more popular music categories, Amazon.com posted its own editorial reviews, as well as customer reviews.

Videos/DVDs

Amazon.com offered a large selection of video and DVD titles for sale. Some of the more popular categories included Action & Adventure, Boxed Sets of Television Series, Classics, Comedy, Cult Movies, Disney Home Video, Documentary, Drama, Horror, Kids & Family,

Musicals, Mystery & Suspense, Science Fiction & Fantasy, Sports, and Westerns. To help customers in their selection process, Amazon.com posted movie summaries as well as movie credits, such as actor and director information. To further help customers, Amazon.com posted its own editorial reviews, as well as customer reviews.

Electronics, Tools, and Kitchen Segment

The ETK segment offered electronic goods, tools, and kitchen supplies. Both Amazon.com and some of its retail partners offered these items for sale.

Electronics

Through its web site, Amazon.com sold a wide variety of electronic goods, including offerings from some of its affiliated partners, such as Target. Some of the categories included Audio & Video Products, Cameras, Camcorders, Cell Phones, Computers, Computer & Video Games, and Software. Amazon.com sold all the major national brands, including Sony, Panasonic, and Canon. Because of the number of accessories needed with some of the electronic goods, such as home theatre systems, Amazon.com posted a list of accessories on the same web page as the main item. To further help customers, Amazon.com made available both professional and staff reviews of products. As it did for books and music, Amazon.com posted product reviews by other customers.

Tools

In order to attract self-proclaimed do-it-yourselfers, Amazon.com offered a wide variety of tools, most of which were carried by its affiliate partners, such as Home Depot. Some of the hardware and tools available for sale included cordless screwdrivers and drills, electric saws and drills, circular saws, and sanders. Some of the brands carried included Black & Decker, Dewalt, and Stanley. Amazon.com posted product information as well as product reviews by its staff and other customers.

Kitchen

To complement its selection of cookbooks, Amazon.com offered a wide selection of kitchen products on its web site, from both itself and its partners, such as Target. Some of the products included small kitchen appliances, cookware, fine china, and flatware. Some of the brands available included Corningware, Calphalon, and Kitchenaid. To help customers make decisions on what products to buy, Amazon.com made available both professional and staff reviews of products. As it did for its other product lines, Amazon.com allowed customers to review and post their reviews online.

Apparel

Because most people were interested in name-brand clothing, Amazon.com did not sell any of its own line of apparel but focused on offering clothing and accessories through its numerous partners. Amazon.com had partnered with some of the country's leading clothing retailers, including The Gap, Target, Eddie Bauer, and Nordstrom.

For women, some of the categories that were available for sale included Lingerie, Sleepwear & Hosiery, Maternity, Outerwear, Pants & Shorts, Shirts & Tops, Skirts & Dresses, Suits & Separates, Sweaters & Sweatshirts, Swim & Athletic Wear, Shoes, and Accessories. All sizes, including petite and plus sizes, were available. Nationally known product lines sold by The Gap, Target, and Mimi Maternity were available, as were the retailers' own private-label brands. For men, some of the categories available for sale included Outerwear, Pants &

Shorts, Shirts, Suits & Sport Coats, Sweaters & Sweatshirts, Swim & Athletic Wear, Underwear, Socks & Sleepwear, Accessories, and Shoes. All sizes, including big and tall, were available. Nationally known product lines sold by companies such as Foot Locker and Eddie Bauer were available, as were the retailers' own private-label brands. For children, a full line of products was made available, the categories including Pants & Shorts, Shirts & Tops, Shoes & Sneakers, Outerwear, Sweaters & Sweatshirts, and Skirts & Dresses. All children's sizes, including infants' and toddlers', were available. Nationally known product lines sold by companies such as OshKosh B'Gosh and Babies 'R' Us, were available, as were the retailers' own private-label brands.

Toys

In order to have as complete a selection of toys as possible, Amazon.com teamed up with the world's biggest toy store, Toys 'R' Us, to offer a wide variety of toys. Some of the categories available included Action Figures, Bikes, Scooters, Dolls, Games, Learning Toys, Preschool Toys, Sports & Outdoor Play, and Video Games. Old favorites such as Lego, Barbie, and G.I. Joe were available, as were more modern games such as Sony PlayStation 2, Nintendo, and Xbox. To help customers in their selection of toys, Amazon.com made available on its web site complete product information and descriptions. In addition, Amazon.com posted both professional and staff reviews of products. As it did for its other product categories, Amazon.com allowed customers to review and post their own product reviews.

Web Operations

Due to its vast selection, Amazon.com was considered to be an online mall. Because of the cost associated with carrying such a large inventory, Amazon.com made use of partnership and affiliation agreements to supplement its own product lines of books, music, videos and DVDs, electronics, tools, and kitchen products. Because it operated online, Amazon.com accepted all major credit cards for payments. Because it did not operate retail stores, Amazon.com had very little overhead and was able to pass these savings along to customers in the form of low prices.

To help customers determine what to buy, Amazon.com posted product reviews from both its staff and outside experts. In addition to these product reviews, Amazon.com allowed its customers to post their own reviews for viewing by other customers. Because all its products were shipped, Amazon.com offered a number of shipping options, including free shipping on many orders over $25. Amazon.com also posted links to shipping companies so its customers could easily track their orders. Product returns needed to be shipped back to Amazon.com by the customer. To help with this, Amazon.com posted shipping instructions and labels on its web site. For those items purchased from its affiliates, in-store product returns were possible.

Services

In order to be the most complete retailer possible, Amazon.com realized that it needed to expand beyond offering its own products for sale. The best way to accomplish this was to use the Amazon.com selling platform as a basis to offer additional goods and services for sale. By turning its focus away from just selling books, music, and movies, some wondered whether Amazon.com would be distracted. However, this was something that the company had always envisioned it would do. In the words of Bezos:

We want to build a place where people can come to find and discover anything they might want to buy online. You realize very quickly that you can't sell everything people want directly. So instead you need to do that in partnership with thousands and indeed millions of third party sellers in different ways. To try to do that alone, in strictly a traditional retailing model, isn't practical.[5]

Aside from having partnership agreements with other retailers and investing in other online retailers, Amazon.com offered auction services and a store-hosting program for small and medium-sized businesses, called zShops.

Partnerships

In the beginning of 1999, Amazon.com wanted to expand the number of product offerings available on its web site to its customers. Amazon.com decided to go about this in two different ways. The first way was to invest in other online companies that could benefit from the high traffic generated from Amazon.com's web site. To help pay for these investments, Amazon.com used its high stock prices to purchase ownership stakes in other online retailers. Some of the companies that Amazon.com invested in included Pets.com, Homegrocer.com, and Drugstore.com.[6] However, due to the collapse of the stock market, in particular Internet stocks, and years of cumulative losses, most of these companies, in particular Pets.com and Homegrocer.com, ended up going bankrupt and out of business, leading Amazon.com to write off most of these investments, causing a loss of close to $135 million in 2000. In addition to partnering with other online retailers, Amazon.com, due to its patented technology and strategically placed distribution centers, looked at partnering with brick-and-mortar retailers that did not have the e-commerce expertise that Amazon.com had. In 2001, Amazon.com signed deals with brick-and-mortar retailers such as Target, Circuit City, and Borders. These deals called for Amazon.com to run all or part of the other companies' e-commerce operations, selling their products on its own web site.[7]

zShops

Amazon.com got into the store hosting business with its offering called zShops. This was similar to the services offered by Internet portal companies such as Yahoo! and MSN. This service gave small and midsized companies a web site to sell their products. In order to attract people to use this service, Amazon.com offered a guarantee, called A-to-Z Guarantee, which insured the buyer in the event of nondelivery or the supply of a defective product. Both Amazon.com and the merchants benefited from this arrangement. Merchants were given an inexpensive way to sell their products to an already established, loyal customer base. Amazon.com benefited from getting a sales presence in products that it did not carry, which helped to reinforce Amazon.com's motto of offering the earth's largest selection.

Amazon.com made money from sellers in its zShops program in a number of ways. Every seller was required to pay a monthly fee of $39.99 for the right to list as many as 40,000 items. If the number of listed items exceeded 40,000, the seller was charged an additional listing fee of $0.10 per additional item.[8] In addition to the monthly listing fee, if they were willing to pay a merchandising fee, merchants were able to have their listing placed in conjunction with other Amazon.com offerings. Finally, when a sale was completed, a closing fee was charged. It was based on the selling price of the item. If the product sold for between $0.01 and $25.00, Amazon.com collected a 5% closing fee. If the product sold between $25.01 and $1,000.00, Amazon.com collected $1.25 plus a 2.5% commission of any amount above $25. If the product sold for more than $1,000.01, Amazon.com collected $25.63 plus a 1.25% commission on any amount above $1,000. In order to help facilitate the payment for goods purchased in the zShops program (as well as its auction services), Amazon.com set up a program called Amazon Payments, which is explained in the "Customer Service" section of this case study.

Offering this type of service provided many advantages for Amazon.com. It allowed Amazon.com to increase the number of items available on its web site, without the costs of carrying the inventory. By charging monthly management fees and commissions on completed purchases, Amazon.com developed a steady revenue stream without incurring much expense. By offering buyer insurance, Amazon.com was able to protect its loyal customers from fraudulent sellers. Although there were some major advantages of offering this service, there were some potential disadvantages that could materialize in the future. These included the possibility of zShops' merchants offering lower-quality goods, which could dilute Amazon.com's image. It was possible that the zShops could offer goods that competed with the items that Amazon.com sold for itself. There was always the potential of fraudulent sellers. Even though there was buyers' insurance, any fraudulent activity could cause bad public relations for Amazon.com. Finally, there was the possibility that this type of program could distract Amazon.com from its core competencies used in selling its own products.

Online Auctions

In response to the continued profitability and financial success of online auction companies, in particular eBay, Amazon.com announced its own online auction service, Amazon.com Auctions, on March 30, 1999. When online auctions continued to improve in popularity, it seemed to be a natural avenue of expansion for Amazon.com. In order to differentiate itself from established companies and to emphasize that the customer was the important part of retailing, Amazon.com offered a money-back guarantee on goods purchased under $350.

Amazon.com made money from sellers in its online auction program in a number of ways. Every seller was required to pay a listing fee. This fee was $0.10 per listing. Frequent sellers were eligible for the Pro Merchant Subscription monthly fee of $39.99, which gave them the right to list as many as 40,000 items. If the number of listed items exceeded 40,000, the sellers were charged an additional listing fee of $0.10 per additional item.[9] In addition to the listing fee, sellers, if they wanted to draw attention to their listing, were allowed to pay a merchandising fee, which ranged anywhere from $0.05 per item per day to $2.00 per listing. This fee enabled the seller to either promote his or her listing higher in its category or to have it stand out in boldface whenever someone did a search for it. And as in zShops, when a sale was completed, a closing fee was charged, based on the selling price of the item. If the product sold for between $0.01 and $25.00, Amazon.com collected a 5% closing fee. If the product sold between $25.01 and $1,000.00, Amazon.com collected $1.25 plus a 2.5% commission on any amount above $25. If the product sold for $1,000.01 or more, Amazon.com collected $25.63 plus a 1.25% commission on any amount above $1,000.

Amazon Web Services

As a way to help with the interaction with its zShops participants, Amazon.com offered web services, allowing merchants to use some of Amazon.com's patented technology on their own web sites. For bigger merchants, it was a way to help interact with Amazon.com regarding product descriptions and inventory availability.

Amazon.com had developed an online shopping platform that was the envy of the retail world. This platform allowed customers to store billing information and shipping addresses so that each time the customer shopped, it became a one-click process. Amazon.com used this platform to first dominate the online bookselling business and then the online music and movie product industry. When Amazon.com tried to use this platform to sell other goods for itself, such as clothing and toys, it was not as successful. Realizing that trying to sell everything to everyone by using their own fulfillment and shipping centers was a no-win situation, Amazon.com decided to license out its technology to other retailers. Amazon.com wanted to partner with national retailers that had sufficient domestic coverage so as to attain its stated motto of offering the earth's largest selection. Companies such as Target, Toys 'R' Us, Office Depot, and Circuit City decided to partner with Amazon.com. These retailers used Amazon.com's technology on their own web sites as well as offering their wares through Amazon.com's web site. This type of arrangement has worked out for all the parties involved and was something that Amazon.com would continue to do, as evidenced by its announcement of a partnership agreement with the NBA and WNBA.

Customers

Amazon.com catered to people of all ages and descriptions. Amazon.com sold a wide range of products and services that offered something for everyone. Although Amazon.com did not track the demographics of its customers, it had noticed signs that online shopping was starting to become more mainstream. This was evidenced by its best-seller lists reflecting more mainstream tastes, as opposed to its earlier days, when the best-seller titles reflected a more technological focus.[10]

Seniors

Born before or during World War II, seniors accounted for more than 12% of the U.S. population in 2002. By 2015, this age group is expected to comprise nearly 15% of the U.S. population. To entice them to buy, Amazon.com offered low prices and excellent customer service.

Baby Boomers

The baby boom generation, comprising individuals born between 1946 and 1964, constituted some 77 million Americans. In 2002, the baby boomers were in their 40s and 50s. Product lines that appealed to this category included books, home and garden products, kitchenware, and apparel.

Generation X

Generation X comprised approximately 45 million people born between 1965 and 1976. These individuals had reached adulthood in the mid-1980s, and in 2002 were in their 20s and 30s. Product lines that appealed to this category included books, kitchenware, and apparel.

Generation Y

Generation Y included individuals born between 1977 and 1994, representing about 25% of the population in 2002. Product categories that interested this group were apparel, music, books, and toys, in particular electronic games such as Xbox and PlayStation 2 games.

Customer Service

One of the reasons Amazon.com became successful was the tremendous emphasis that the company placed on customer service. From its founding, Amazon.com sought to become the earth's most customer-centric company, where customers could find and discover anything they might have wanted to buy online. Because of the empowerment of the customer, maintaining a high level of customer service was necessary. Being an Internet-only retailer made the job a lot easier. Some of the ways that Amazon.com accomplished great customer service were as follows:

1. It informed the customers, when they purchased, of the predicted and actual shipping times. On larger orders, customers were asked if they would like to wait for the entire order or have it sent piecemeal as the items were ready.

2. It allowed the customers to review products. This helped to build a sense of loyalty among its users.

3. It sent e-mails offering suggestions on other products that they may be interested in purchasing, based on past purchases.

4. By offering numerous ways to search for products (by title, subject, or author), the company made its web site very easy to use.

5. By developing and patenting cutting-edge technology such as its 1-Click Ordering process, the online shopping experience became an easy one.

By having this high level of customer service, combined with an easy-to-use web site, Amazon.com was able to differentiate itself from its competition.

Product Recommendations

As a way to promote sales, while at the same time letting customers know when a certain product was available, Amazon.com sent e-mails out to customers, stating possible recommendations. Amazon.com offered this as a way of making sure that a customer didn't miss the perfect item. Amazon.com determined a customer's interests by examining the items he or she had purchased, items the customer had told Amazon.com he or she owned, and items the customer rated; then it compared the customer's activity on the Amazon.com web site with that of other customers. Using this comparison, Amazon.com was able to recommend other items that may interest the customer. These recommended items would appear in several areas throughout the web site. If the customer needed more information about one area in particular, he or she could click the appropriate link. These recommendations would change when the customer purchased or rated a new item. Changes in the interests of other customers might also affect these recommendations. Because the recommendations would fluctuate, Amazon.com suggested that a customer add items of interest to his or her Wish List or Shopping Cart.

Share the Love

Amazon.com established the Share the Love program to get customers to recommend products to their friends. Each time a customer placed an order for books, music, DVDs, or videos with Amazon.com, the customer was given the opportunity to e-mail friends and give them an additional 10% off the items bought. (The customer selected which items and which friends.) If any of those people purchased one of these items within a week, that customer received a credit to use the next time he or she shopped at Amazon.com. This credit was equal to the dollar amount of the friend's 10% discount. For example, if the customer bought a CD for $15 and decided to Share the Love with a friend on that purchase, that friend would be able to buy the same CD for $13.50. If that friend did purchase the item, the customer would receive a credit for $1.50 (the difference) to use any time in the next 30 days. The customer was eligible to receive one credit per item shared. This was an excellent way for

Amazon.com to build loyalty among its users while offering customers the opportunity to achieve greater discounts.

A-to-Z Guarantee

When a customer bought an item from Amazon Marketplace, Auctions, and zShops sellers, Amazon.com wanted the buyer to feel safe. To address this concern, Amazon.com developed a program called A-to-Z Guarantee. This guarantee concerned the condition of the item purchased and its timely delivery. The buyer was covered as long as he or she provided payment to the seller and either the seller failed to deliver the item or the item was materially different from what was depicted in the seller's description. Buyers who purchased items using Amazon Payments were eligible to receive up to $2,500 of the purchase price, including shipping charges. If the buyer did not pay using Amazon Payments, he or she was eligible to receive up to $250 of the purchase price. Amazon.com provided this coverage at no cost to its buyers, as a demonstration of how committed it was to creating a safe buying experience.

Safe Shopping Guarantee

To address concerns raised about the theft of credit card numbers, Amazon.com started a program called Amazon.com Safe Shopping Guarantee. This guarantee offered protection to the customers while they shopped at Amazon.com so that they never had to worry about credit card safety. In addition to the use of encryption technology called Secure Sockets Layer to process customer transactions, this guarantee covered any liability on unauthorized use of a customer's credit card, up to $50, which was the legal amount a person was liable for under the Fair Credit Billing Act for fraudulent credit card transactions.

Amazon Payment Option

In order to help its loyal customers make payments when they were dealing with a zShops merchant or a seller in the Auctions section, Amazon.com developed a plan called Amazon Payments. Amazon Payments allowed an Amazon.com customer with an account to use the same credit card on file with Amazon.com to pay for other purchases. There were no additional fees involved. And by using this program, the buyer was eligible for both the A-to-z Guarantee and the Safe Shopping Guarantee. All sellers on Auctions or zShops accepted Amazon Payments.

Because it only sold its products online, Amazon.com needed to put its customers at ease when they shopped. Amazon.com had worked to develop numerous programs to accomplish this. Evidence of how successful Amazon.com has been with these customer service initiatives can be seen in the recent score it received from the American Customer Satisfaction Index (ACSI), a customer satisfaction survey. This survey is conducted annually by the National Quality Research Center at the University of Michigan Business School in partnership with the American Society of Quality and the CFI Group, an Ann Arbor, Michigan–based management-consulting group. It measures customer satisfaction when dealing with companies within certain business sectors, such as banking, retail, and e-commerce companies. In the survey conducted for the fourth quarter of 2002, Amazon.com achieved a score of 88, which was the highest ever recorded in the history of the survey.[11] Rather than rest on its laurels, however, Amazon.com was committed to do even better on the next year's survey.

Sales and Distribution

Because selling over the Internet was its only means of contact with customers, Amazon.com needed to ensure that its web site was one that its customers could easily navigate and would feel secure with. In addition to these concerns, Amazon.com had to make sure that the process of ordering an item was not difficult. Part of the way Amazon.com did this was by developing the 1-Click Ordering method, which it patented. The 1-Click Ordering method allowed its customers to store their billing and shipping information on the company's web site. Customers could choose how to pay for their purchases, such as by using credit cards, and choose among multiple shipping addresses, such as home and work. Amazon.com liked customers using this feature because with data mining software, it was able to develop profiles of a customer's buying habits that would help it to develop future product recommendations and marketing programs.

In order to make it as easy as possible for customers, online retailers such as Amazon.com offered a variety of shipping options with the major shipping companies, such as the U.S. Postal Service, UPS, and FedEx. The charges for shipping varied, depending on the level and speed of service chosen. To entice increased order amounts and to address concerns about shipping costs, most online companies, such as Amazon.com and Barnes & Noble.com, offered free shipping when customers ordered over a minimum level and chose normal shipping methods, which could take up to seven days. To help a customer track his or her purchases and determine when an order would be delivered, Amazon.com included on its web site links with their shipping companies, allowing customers to easily monitor the progress of their purchases. To address concerns with product returns, Amazon.com made available on its web site all the necessary shipping information, including mailing labels, for the customer to download and use.

Technology

Because Amazon.com was strictly an online retailer, technology played a significant role in the company's success. Amazon.com implemented numerous web site management, search, customer interaction, recommendation, transaction-processing and fulfillment services, and other systems, using a combination of proprietary technologies and commercially available, licensed technologies. Amazon.com's strategy in 2003 was to focus its development efforts on creating and enhancing the specialized, proprietary software that was unique to its business and to license or acquire commercially developed technology for other applications where available and appropriate. Amazon.com used a set of applications for accepting and validating customer orders, placing and tracking orders with suppliers, managing and assigning inventory to customer orders, and ensuring proper shipment of products to customers. Its transaction-processing systems handled millions of items, a number of different status inquiries, gift-wrapping requests, and multiple shipment methods. These systems allowed the customer to choose whether to receive single or several shipments based on availability and to track the progress of each order. These applications also managed the process of accepting, authorizing, and charging customer credit cards.

Patents and Trademarks

Amazon.com regarded its trademarks, service marks, copyrights, patents, domain names, trade dress, trade secrets, proprietary technologies, and similar intellectual property as critical to its success, and it relied on trademark, copyright, and patent law; trade-secret protection; and confidentiality and/or license agreements with its employees, customers, partners, and others to protect its proprietary rights.[12] Amazon.com had registered a number of domain names and been issued a number of trademarks, service marks, patents, and copyrights by U.S. and foreign governmental authorities. Amazon.com had also applied for the registration of other trademarks, service marks, and domain names and copyrights in the United States and internationally, and it had filed U.S. and international patent applications covering certain parts of its proprietary technology. Amazon.com had licensed in the past, and expected to license in the future, certain aspects of its proprietary rights, such as trademarks, patents, technologies, or copyrighted materials, to third parties. An example of Amazon.com's patented technology that provided a considerable competitive advantage was its 1-Click Ordering method. Amazom.com recognized that one of the biggest drawbacks to online shopping was that the speed of the purchase was slowed if each time a purchase was made, all billing and shipping information had to be entered again. To overcome this, Amazon.com developed a system in which relevant billing and shipping information about the customer was stored for future uses. Amazon.com sued and won a case against Barnes & Noble.com for violating this patent.

Encryption Technology

One of the biggest concerns online shoppers had was that their billing and credit card information were not secure and could be hacked into during the course of a transaction. To help allay this fear, Amazon.com used Secure Sockets Layer (SSL) software, an encryption technology program. This software was the industry standard and considered to be among the best software available at the time for secure online commerce transactions. It encrypted all of a customer's personal information, including credit card number, name, and address, so that it could not be read as it traveled over the Internet.

Wireless Selling Platform

Due to the widespread use of cell phones and PDAs, Amazon.com developed a stripped-down version of its main web site for customers to download and store on their cellular phones and PDAs. With the growing popularity of these devices, Amazone.com needed to address the potential for people to go online through wireless technologies.

Advertising

In order to increase brand recognition, Amazon.com, like most online retailers in 1999 and 2000, spent tremendous amounts of money on advertising. Amazon.com was willing to sacrifice short-term profits for the chance of acquiring greater market share. Because online retailing was a new way of doing business, Amazon.com felt that the best way to differentiate itself from the competition was to spend a tremendous amount of money on advertising its goods and services across all advertising media. However, due to the increasing pressure of producing an operating profit while still offering low prices and free shipping, Amazon was forced to consider cutting operating expenses, in particular advertising. By investing in more online ad activities, such as product recommendations and search engines, Amazon.com had successfully been able to cut back significantly on its marketing budget over the previous two years, as shown in **Exhibit 4**.

Television and Radio

During the 2002 holiday season, Amazon.com spent approximately $5 million on television ads making fun of the hassles of mall shopping. After reevaluating the effectiveness of its ads, Amazon.com decided to suspend all forms of television and radio advertising.

Exhibit 4
Marketing
Expenses:
Amazon.com
(Dollar amounts in
thousands)

Marketing Expenses				
2002	2001	2000	1999	1998
$125,383	$138,283	$179,980	$175,838	$67,427

Source: Amazon.com, Form 10-K (2003).

According to Amazon.com's Diego Piacentini, the company realized "that spending money on improving customer experience by dropping prices is definitely more effective than spending the same amount of money to do advertising on TV."[13]

Print

A great cost-effective way to get information out about product offerings is by using circulars, direct mail, and newspaper advertisements, particularly in Sunday newspapers. While it suspended its television advertising campaign, Amazon.com continued to use such inserts to help promote current offerings and coupons touting discounts on future purchases.

Internet

Amazon.com had successfully used the Internet to advertise itself, to both new and old customers. Through the use of data mining software programs and direct e-mail advertisements, Amazon.com was able to notify customers of products that they might be interested in purchasing. The company developed these recommendations based on the customers' prior purchases and comparisons with similar customers with the same purchasing habits. With programs such as Amazon.com Alerts, users could sign up to be notified when the latest releases of authors and artists they were interested in were made available for sale. Through deals with Internet service providers such as AOL and search engine companies such as Google, Amazon.com was able to effectively and directly market its goods and services over the Internet. By signing up more than 900,000 web sites into its Amazon.com Associates program, Amazon.com was able to advertise on a number of individual web sites at a minimal cost.

Because of the cost of running television and radio ad campaigns and concerns over the effectiveness of this type of advertising, Amazon.com focused its attention on advertising through the Internet. Through the use of data mining software programs and prior buying patterns, Amazon.com had developed extensive profiles of its customers. It used the profiles to develop a successful direct e-mail marketing program, alerting customers to items that they might be interested in. In addition, Amazon.com worked with search engine companies such as Google to make sure that its ads were prominently placed on web pages when people got the results of searches. Through its online partners, Amazon.com continually promoted its own web site and products. Because of the low cost of this type of advertising, Amazon.com used money that had previously been spent on ad campaigns to offer free shipping to its customers on many orders of $25 or more. The "buzz" from offering free shipping was better than the "buzz" from any ad campaign.

Geographic Region

Because of its online selling model, Amazon.com was available throughout the entire domestic U.S. market through its web site. Outside the United States, Amazon.com operated web sites in five international markets—Canada, France, Germany, Japan, and the United

Exhibit 5 Geographic Markets: Amazon.com

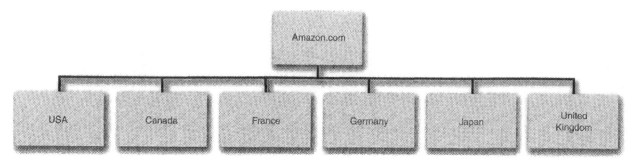

Kingdom, as shown in **Exhibit 5**. In 2002, Amazon.com was not present in any other additional international market.

Domestic

The corporate headquarters for Amazon.com was located in Seattle, Washington. Because Amazon.com conducted all its business over the Internet and did not have the need for any retail outlets, all its orders were processed through fulfillment centers. These fulfillment centers were strategically located throughout the country, to facilitate the delivery of merchandise both to Amazon.com from its distributors and to Amazon.com's customers in a timely fashion. These fulfillment sites were located in states that had low or no sales tax, to limit any potential sales tax expense for Amazon.com's customers. These U.S. centers were located in New Castle, Delaware; Coffeyville, Kansas; and Campbellsville and Lexington, Kentucky. Amazon.com continually evaluated all its real estate holdings to ensure that it had the necessary geographic coverage. In order to provide a high level of customer service, Amazon.com operated four separate customer service centers, located in the following places: Tacoma, Washington; Grand Forks, North Dakota; and Huntington, West Virginia. In addition to these centers, Amazon.com had customer service outsourcing agreements with certain vendors in India, Northern Ireland, and the United States.

International

As shown in **Exhibit 5**, the international markets in which Amazon.com conducted operations included Canada, Japan, France, Germany, and the United Kingdom. Due to the complexities of operating in foreign markets, such as local laws and customs, Amazon.com had set up a separate web site in each country. These international sites shared the common Amazon.com platform but were localized in terms of language, products, customer service, and fulfillment.

Because Amazon.com was an online retailer and did not have the need for any retail outlets, all its orders were taken over the Internet and then processed through fulfillment centers. These fulfillment centers were strategically located throughout its international markets, to facilitate the delivery of merchandise both to Amazon.com from its distributors and to Amazon.com's customers in as timely a fashion as possible. In Japan, Amazon.com outsourced its order fulfillment functions to Nippon Express, and in Canada it outsourced its order fulfillment operations to Assured Logistics. In its other international markets, Amazon.com operated local distribution centers. For these international fulfillment centers, Amazon.com leased and operated the sites in Marston Gate, United Kingdom; Orleans, France; and Bad Hersfeld, Germany.

In order to provide a high level of customer service to its international customers, Amazon.com operated customer service centers in Slough, United Kingdom; Regensburg,

Germany; and Sapporo, Japan. In addition to these centers, Amazon.com had customer service outsourcing agreements with certain vendors in India, Northern Ireland, and the United States.

Financial Position

Amazon.com's first goal was not to produce a profit but to gain market share. Management was willing to sacrifice profits for the potential for growth. As can been seen in its shareholders' deficit on the balance sheet in **Exhibit 6**, Amazon.com did exactly that. It was not until the dot-com bubble burst that Amazon.com began to focus on controlling expenses and producing an operating profit according to generally accepted accounting principles. See Amazon.com's 2002 Annual Report (at *www.amazon.com*) for complete financial statements.

Net Income

Starting in 2001, Amazon.com began to focus on increasing sales and reducing expenses so that it would be able to produce an operating profit. As is shown in **Exhibit 7**, Amazon.com was able to increase its gross profit margin in 2001 and 2002, finally showing an operating profit in 2002. Amazon.com cut advertising expenses tremendously by no longer advertising on television. The costs associated with offering free shipping were evaluated and limited to purchases over $99. However, due to pressure from other online booksellers such as Buy.com offering free shipping, Amazon.com was forced to follow suit and lowered the minimum amount of purchases needed for free shipping to most orders over $25. Despite these pressures, Amazon.com was able to generate sufficient cash to service its debt and capital obligations.

Sales Tax

One of the most important issues facing online retailers in the early 2000s was the issue of sales tax. In early 2003, there was a moratorium on the taxation of e-commerce transactions. But due to the tremendous pressure that state budgets were experiencing at the time, governments were looking for new, recurring revenue streams. The problems with the taxation of

Exhibit 6 Balance Sheet: Amazon.com (Dollar amounts in millions)

Year ending December 31	2002	2001	2000		2002	2001	2000
Cash and Cash equivalents	$ 738	$ 540	$ 822	Accounts payable	$ 618	$ 445	$ 485
Marketable securities	563	456	278	Accrued expenses	315	305	273
Inventories	202	144	175	Unearned revenue	48	88	131
Prepaid exp. + other current assets	113	68	86	Interest payable	72	68	69
Total current assets	1,616	1,208	1,361	Short term debt	13	15	17
Fixed assets, net	239	272	366	Total current liabilities	1,066	921	975
Goodwill, net	71	45	159	Long term debt	2,277	2,156	2,127
Other intangibles, net	3	34	96	Shareholders' deficit	(1,353)	(1,440)	(967)
Other assets	61	78	153	Total liabilities and stockholders' deficit	$1,990	$1,637	$2,135
Total Assets	$1,990	$1,637	$2,135				

Sources: *Amazon.com, Annual Report (2001); Amazon.com, Form 10-K (2003); and Amazon.com, www.amazon.com (2003).*

Exhibit 7
Income Statement:
Amazon.com
(Dollar amounts in
millions)

Year ending December 31,	2002	2001	2000
Sales	$3,932.9	$3,122.4	$2,762.0
Cost of goods sold	2,858.0	2,375.0	2,105.2
Gross profit	1,074.9	747.4	656.8
Gross profit margin (%)	27.3%	23.9%	23.8%
SG&A expense[1]	881.4	848.2	997.6
Depreciation & amortization	87.8	129.9	322.8
Operating income	105.7	(230.7)	(663.6)
Operating margin (%)	2.7%	—	—
Non-operating income	(71.2)	(5.2)	(273.9)
Non-operating expense	142.9	139.2	130.9
Income before taxes	(150)	(556.7)	(1,411.4)
Income taxes	0.0	0.0	0.0
Net loss	(150)	(556.7)	(1,411.4)
Diluted earnings per share	(0.40)	(1.53)	(4.02)

Note:
1. SG&A expenses—Selling, general, and administrative expenses include all salaries, indirect production, marketing, and general corporate expenses.

Source: *Hoover's Online, "Company Profiles—Amazon.com," www.hoovers.com.*

online transactions had nothing to do with the charging of the tax rates. The issue had to do with how different states categorized products. A recent agreement by 33 states to simplify and help develop a consistent tax platform was pointing in the direction of taxes being levied on these transactions, so a significant competitive advantage was possibly coming to an end. However, the agreement might not succeed if the U.S. Supreme Court issued another ruling forbidding the taxation of interstate commerce by individual states.

Stock Options

As the Financial Accounting Standards Board (FASB) looked at the issue of determining whether to show employee stock options as an expense, companies such as Amazon.com worried. Part of the appeal of working for online companies was the opportunity of striking it rich through stock options. Companies had no problem with issuing the stock options because they were not an expense on the income statement. But with the issue of excessive compensation and financial gimmicks being brought to a head, the FASB was close to issuing a directive on this issue. And with a number of prominent companies such as Citicorp and Coca-Cola already agreeing to show these options as an expense, the stock options situation for Amazon.com needed to be addressed.

Management Strategy

Amazon.com's management has shown a tremendous amount of flexibility in its strategy. In Amazon.com's first years of existence, Bezos had the company solely focused on increasing market share and offering superior customer service. However, once the dot-com bubble burst, along with it Amazon.com's stock price, Bezos had to strike a balance between the company's stated goal of increasing market share and producing a profit.

Although it started out with books and moved into related fields such as movies and music, Amazon.com also wanted to continue to expand the number of products available to its customers. In 1999, by using its high stock price to fund purchases, Amazon.com invested in other online retailers, such as Drugstore.com, Homegrocer.com, and Pets.com. However, none of these formats were ever as successful as Amazon.com, and most were not able to survive the collapse of the dot-com industry in 2000. Doubts were raised in regard to Amazon.com's future survival. So Bezos changed strategies once again.

Bezos focused on proving the viability of his business model. In developing this new strategy, Bezos first had to determine what products to offer for sale and the best way to incorporate them into Amazon.com's sales model. Rather than investing and running web sites in addition to its own, as it had done in the past, Amazon.com decided to form partnerships with other retail companies to cross-sell their products on either Amazon.com's own web sites or on the partners' web sites. Bezos saw this as part of his philosophy to offer everything to everyone. Amazon has been so successful with this strategy that it was running other retailers' web sites in early 2003, earning not only a percentage of sales but also a management fee.

Bezos attempted to produce an operating profit by cutting expenses, in particular advertising expenses. He looked at eliminating the use of expensive television and radio ads and focused on the more inexpensive and personal e-mail ads and reminders. This reduction, along with other cost-saving initiatives, paid off. In the year ending December 31, 2002, Amazon.com produced its first operating profit.

Looking Toward the Future

Although Amazon.com had established itself as one of the premier online retailers in the world, pressure from increased competition, an overall poor economic environment, and the possible repeal of the sales tax exemption afforded e-commerce transactions had put pressure on Amazon.com to evaluate and possibly formulate new strategies in order to remain competitive. CEO Bezos and his management team were faced with two alternatives in order to keep the company ahead of the competition. Both alternatives focused on the services offered by Amazon.com, and both recognized the continued need to expand. However, each one had a different vision to accomplish this.

The **first alternative** was to expand Amazon.com's business in online auctions. Because of the continued need for an intermediary in these types of transactions, Amazon.com would be able to market this additional service to both its current customer base, through the use of personalized e-mails, and to new customers, through a general advertising campaign, including television and print ads.

The benefit of this alternative was that Amazon.com would be expanding on an existing service offering and would not incur any developmental or startup expenses. An additional benefit would be that by aggressively promoting this service, Amazon.com would be able to attract new visitors to its web sites, and these customers might also purchase additional goods and services, such as new books and music that Amazon.com offered.

This alternative was feasible because of the prior experience Amazon.com had developed in expanding and marketing other product lines and services. By learning from past mistakes and successes, Amazon.com would be able to formulate the correct marketing campaign to attract additional traffic to its web sites. The alternative could work because Amazon.com had become one of the premier online brands and had a large enough customer base to compete against eBay and other established online auction services such as Ubid.com and Yahoo! Auctions. In addition to its name recognition, Amazon.com would look to use its large number of customer service programs, such as Amazon Payments and Safe Shopping Guarantee, to address buyer and seller concerns about privacy, fraud, and security while also expanding the number of payment options available to both parties.

The first drawback within this alternative was that Amazon.com would be competing against its own product offerings, as well as those of its retail partners. A second drawback was the fact that it was going head-to-head with one of the few other profitable online companies, eBay. eBay had built a considerably large base of loyal customers who would possibly be reluctant to go to a competitor.

A way around the first drawback was to either set up the auction services in a separate and distinct section on the web site, away from the retail aspect, or set up a new web address for this service line. A way around the second drawback was for Amazon.com to market itself as a less expensive alternative to eBay, setting its pricing structure at a level that was lower than eBay's.

The **second alternative** was to develop and implement a business-to-business (B2B) exchange for suppliers, manufacturers, distributors, and retailers to use. Because the largest percentage of e-commerce sales resulted from transactions conducted on B2B exchanges, this opened up a large potential market for Amazon.com to expand into.

The benefit of this alternative was that Amazon.com could easily market this service to its large number of affiliates and partners that it conducted business with. Having its partners' suppliers and distributors participate in this online exchange would allow their affiliates to achieve greater operational efficiencies in their supply chain. These efficiencies would translate into lower prices for Amazon.com. A second additional benefit for Amazon.com would be the steady cash flow it would receive through the charging of hosting fees and commissions on completed transactions.

This alternative was feasible because Amazon.com would use its past experiences and patented technology to develop a secure, easy-to-use platform that its customers would be comfortable with. It was also feasible because of the large number of midsize to small companies that did not have the necessary capital to develop or run their own exchanges but wished to participate in these auctions in order to increase their own sales and market coverage. This alternative could win against the competition because these additional offerings would be available to all companies—not just companies from one specific industry, which most existing B2B exchanges did (for example, Covisint in the automotive industry). And because Amazon.com would only be acting as an intermediary with these exchanges, costs would be kept to a minimum because Amazon.com would only be the host of the exchange and would not have to hold any inventory.

The drawback to this was that Amazon.com would be entering a business that would require more intense customer service than its other lines of business. This was due to the high dollar amounts of the transactions, as well as the issue of product specifications. An additional drawback would be the issue of payment processing and concerns with the shipping and receiving of goods.

A way around the first drawback was to assign specific customer service personnel to each exchange category. By having an assigned customer service representative handle all aspects of the exchange transaction, Amazon.com's employees would be able to build an excellent relationship with the involved parties, which would help to address any issues that might occur. The way around the second drawback could be broken down into two categories. First, Amazon.com would use its escrow payment service to hold all monies until the goods were received and all parties were satisfied. To help address shipping concerns, Amazon.com, because of its relationship with shipping companies, could negotiate discounted deals with them for their exchange partners to use.

Both alternatives seemed to make sense. They both seemed to have advantages and disadvantages. Both offered ways to increase sales and market share while staying ahead of the competition. Bezos and his management team decided to study both alternatives further, especially within present financial situations, as well as other alternatives in other strategic areas, in order to decide which would be most appropriate.

Notes

1. H. Green, "Retail: The Cart Is Half Full," *BusinessWeek*, No. 3815 (January 13, 2003), pp. 124–125.
2. Hoover's Online, *Company Profiles—Amazon.com*, *www.hoovers.com*. IRS, *www.irs.gov*.
3. R. Spector, *Amazon.com—Get Big Fast* (New York, NY: HarperCollins Publishers, Inc., 2000)
4. Amazon.com, *www.amazon.com*.
5. R. D. Hof, "Q & A: Jeff Bezos: Amazon.com," *BusinessWeek*, No. 3631 (May 31, 1999), p. 137.
6. R. Saunders, *Business the Amazon.com Way* (Milford, CT: Capstone Publishing Limited, 1999).
7. M. Warner, "Can Amazon Be Saved?" *Fortune*, Vol. 144, No. 11 (November 25, 2001), pp. 156–158.
8. Amazon.com, *www.amazon.com*.
9. Ibid.
10. M. Totty, "E-Commerce: Selling Strategies—Demographics: The Masses Have Arrived . . . And E-Commerce Will Never Be the Same," *The Wall Street Journal* (January 27, 2003), p. R8.
11. American Customer Satisfaction Index (ACSI), *www.theacsi.org*.
12. Amazon.com, Form 10-K (2003).
13. N. Wingfield, "eBay Earnings More Than Double—A Surge in Revenue Results from Purchase of PayPal, Big Gains in Core Business," *The Wall Street Journal* (April 23, 2003), p. B7.

References

Amazon.com, Annual Report (2001).

G. Anders and R. Quick, "Amazon.com Files Suit Over Patent on 1-Click Against Barnesandnoble.com," *The Wall Street Journal* (October 25, 1999), p. B18.

Barnes & Noble.com, Form 10-K (2003).

Barnes & Noble.com, *www.barnesandnoble.com*.

C. Bialik, "E-Commerce: B2B—Advertising: Sell First, Advertise Later," *The Wall Street Journal* (October 21, 2002), p. R11.

D. Brady, "How Barnes & Noble Misread the Web," *BusinessWeek*, No. 3667 (February 7, 2000), p. 63.

R. Clarke, "Electronic Data Interchange (EDI): An Introduction," *Business Credit*, Vol. 103, No. 9 (October 2001), pp. 23–25.

J. C. Cooper and K. Madigan, "A Lasting Postwar Surge Will Hinge on the Labor Markets," *BusinessWeek*, No. 3829 (April 21, 2003), pp. 31–32.

E. D. Cordy, "The Legal Regulation of E-Commerce Transactions," *Journal of American Academy of Business*, Vol. 2, No. 2 (March 2003).

J. C. Dooren, "Retail Sales Increase Sharply As Customer Confidence Rises," *The Wall Street Journal* (April 14, 2003), p. A2.

eBay, *www.ebay.com*.

"Amazon Settles Suit Against Online Rival over Buying Shortcut," *The Wall Street Journal* (March 8, 2002), p. B5.

B. Elgin, L. Himelstein, R. Grover, and H. Green, "Inside Yahoo!" *BusinessWeek*, No. 3733 (May 21, 2001), pp. 114–123.

B. Elgin, "Can Yahoo Make 'em Pay? The Net Portal's Turnaround Reaches a Critical Pass," *BusinessWeek*, No. 3798 (September 9, 2002), pp. 92–94.

B. Elgin, "Two Cheers for Yahoo!" *BusinessWeek*, No. 3817 (January 27, 2003) p. 44.

B. Elgin, "Can Yahoo! Make the Bounce Last?" *BusinessWeek*, No. 3820 (February 17, 2003), p. 41.

B. Garrity, "Amazon Now Powering Virgin's Retail Site," *Billboard Magazine*, Vol. 114, No. 27 (July 6, 2002), p. 55.

R. Gavin, "E-Commerce (A Special Report): The Rules—Rules & Regs," *The Wall Street Journal* (January 27, 2003), p. R10.

R. Gold, "E-Commerce: The Rules—Rules & Regs," *The Wall Street Journal* (December 9, 2002), p. R6.

E. Goodridge, "Yahoo's Not Just for Customers Anymore," *InformationWeek*, No. 80 (March 18, 2002), pp. 106–108.

R. Greenspan, "Surfing with Seniors and Boomers," *Cyberatlas*, *www. clickz.com/stats/sectors/demographics/article.ph/157-621* (January 23, 2003).

C. Guglielmo, "Don't Write Off Barnes & Noble," *Upside*, Vol. 12, No. 6 (June 2000).

L. Himelstein, "Q&A: Meg Whitman: eBay," *BusinessWeek*, No. 3631 (May 31, 1999), pp. 134–135.

L. Himelstein and G. Khermouch, "Webvan Left the Basics on the Shelf," *BusinessWeek*, No. 3742 (July 23, 2001), p. 43.

R. Hof and M. Roman, "Pets.com: Putting a Sock in It," *BusinessWeek*, No. 3708 (November 20, 2000).

R. D. Hof, "eBay Rules: The Online Marketplace Thrives in Good Times and Bad," *BusinessWeek*, No. 3825A (March 25, 2003), p. 172.

R. D. Hof, "The People's Company," *BusinessWeek*, No. 3760 (December 3, 2001), pp. EB14–EB21.

M. Janofsky, "Deep Cuts Have Not Closed Deficit in Many States, Report Says," *New York Times* (April 26, 2003), p. A20.

F. Keenan, S. Holmes, J. Greene, and R. O. Crockett, "A Mass Market of One," *BusinessWeek*, No. 3810 (December 2, 2002), pp. 68–72.

D. Kirkpatrick, "In the Hands of Geeks, Web Advertising Actually Works," *Fortune*, Vol. 147, No. 7 (April 14, 2003), p. 388.

T. Kontzer, "Amazon's E-Commerce Technology Is on Target," *Information Week*, No. 902 (August 19, 2002), p. 22.

D. J. Lipke, "Mystery Shoppers," *American Demographics*, Vol. 22, No. 12 (December 2000), pp. 41–43.

J. Maness, "Using Pricing Optimization," *Chain Store Age*, Vol. 9, No. 1 (January 2003), p. 109.

T. J. Mullaney, "The Web Is Finally Catching Profits," *BusinessWeek*, No. 3820 (February 17, 2003), p. 68.

S. Patton, "Barnesandnoble.com Settles for Lower Shelf," *CIO*, Vol. 16, No. 4 (November 15, 2002), pp. 64 65.

M. Prior, "eBay Acquires PayPal for $1.5B on Eve of Strong 2Q Report," *DSN Retailing Today*, Vol. 41, No. 14 (July 29, 2002), p. 8.

R. Quick, "Barnes & Noble and Its Online Sibling Enter Alliance Linking Bricks and Clicks," *The Wall Street Journal* (October 27, 2000), p. B10.

S. Reyes, "Tapping Girl Power," *Brandweek*, Vol. 43, No. 16 (April 22, 2002), pp. 26–30.

S. Shepard, "A Talk with Meg Whitman," *BusinessWeek*, No. 3724 (March 19, 2001), pp. 98–99.

J. Soat, "Ah, Spring! Love, Basketball and Taxes," *Information Week*, No. 934 (April 7, 2003), p. 82.

Standard & Poor's, "Retailing: Specialty," *http://netadvantage. standardpoor.com*.

J. Tessler, "E-Commerce: The Basics—Small Investment, Big Results: Entrepreneurs Need Very Little Money—Or Technical Know-how—To Launch a Web Business," *The Wall Street Journal* (November 22, 1999), p. R16.

M. Totty, "E-Commerce: Selling Strategies—So Much Information and So Much Confusion on What It All Means," *The Wall Street Journal* (December 9, 2002), p. R4.

M. Totty, "E-Commerce: The Rules—Regulations: Taming the Frontier—The Internet Was Going to Be a Place Without Rules, Without Borders; A Place Where Anything Goes; Well, Guess What Happened," *The Wall Street Journal* (January 27, 2003), p. R10.

D. Tynan, "The Rebirth of Online Advertising," *Chief Executive*, No. 185 (January/February 2003), pp. 13 14.

UCLA Center for Communication Policy, *Surveying the Digital Future—Year Three*, *www.ccp.ucla.edu/pages/internet-report.asp*.

U.S. Census Bureau, Department of Commerce, *www.census.gov*.

E. White, "Web, Direct Mail Get Larger Share of Marketers' Pie," *The Wall Street Journal* (December 18, 2002), p. B2.

L. Windham and K. Orton, *The Soul of the New Customer* (New York, NY: Allworth Press, 2000).

N. Wingfield, "eBay Conceding Missteps, Will Close Its Site in Japan," *The Wall Street Journal* (February 27, 2002), p. B4.

N. Wingfield, "E-Commerce (A Special Report): Selling Strategies—Delivery—Click and . . . Drive?" *The Wall Street Journal* (July 15, 2002), p. R11.

N. Wingfield, "TV Advertising: Why Web Firms Love It, Hate It," *The Wall Street Journal* (April 24, 2003), p. B1.

Yahoo! Form 10-K (2003).

Yahoo! *www.yahoo.com*.

J. G. S. Yang and W. W. Poon, "Taxable Base of Internet Commerce," *Journal of State Taxation*, Vol. 20, No. 4 (Spring 2002), pp. 70–80.

A. Yegyazarian, "Sales Taxes Hit the Web," *PC World*, Vol. 21, No. 3 (March 2003), p. 34.

AOL Time Warner, Inc.:
A Bad Idea from the Start?

Vineet Walia, Irene Hagenbuch Sanjana, Stacey Foster, and Alan N. Hoffman

"To become the world's most respected and valued company by connecting, informing and entertaining people everywhere in innovative ways that will enrich their lives."

AOL Time Warner mission statement

Time Warner

THE MEDIA AND ENTERTAINMENT GIANT TIME WARNER IS THE RESULT OF A MERGER OF two companies that have grown through mergers and acquisitions. The AOL Time Warner story began in 1918, when Henry Luce and Briton Hadden got the idea for *Time* magazine (incorporated as Time Inc. in 1922) and the Warner brothers opened their first West Coast studio. During the next 50 years, both companies grew to become industry leaders. Time Inc. launched various magazines and acquired a Boston publishing house called Little, Brown and Company. The Warner studio, on the other hand, released the first talking movie in the entertainment industry (Al Jolson's *The Jazz Singer*) and created Warner Bros. Records in 1958. In 1969, the Warner studio (then called Warner-Seven Arts) was acquired by Kinney National Co. and became Warner Communications Inc.

AOL

With the cable industry booming, the computer industry followed suit in 1985, when Steve Case, Jim Kimsey, and Marc Seriff founded Quantum Computer Services to send online information and other services to consumers via PC modems. At that time, the use and knowledge of the possibilities of the World Wide Web did not exist. Over the next four years, Quantum Computer Services was renamed Quantum Online and then America Online. At the same time, Time Inc. acquired Warner Communications Inc., to become Time Warner Inc., the world's largest media and entertainment company.

By the end of the 20th century, AOL reached 27 million members, was an industry leader in its industry, and was continuing its acquisition strategy by purchasing brands such as Netscape, MovieFone, CompuServe, and MapQuest. Time Warner Inc. also further expanded its market potentials in its industry and agreed to its latest and possibly most controversial merger with AOL in January 2001, to become AOL Time Warner.

The Merger That Wasn't

The merger between America Online and Time Warner Inc. was the largest corporate merger in U.S. history. When the merger was made public in January 2001, the transaction was valued at $183 billion. It was the first stock purchase whereby an Internet company—created through the Internet boom—utilized its sky-high stock value to acquire an older, more traditional *Fortune 500* company.

AOL offered $166 billion in stock for Time Warner's real assets and assumed Time Warner's $17 billion debt. This included a 71% premium for former Time Warner stockholders, who received 1.5 shares of AOL Time Warner stock for each Time Warner share they owned at that time. America Online offered a stock value of $110 for each Time Warner share that was selling at $64.75 in the market.[1] AOL shareholders then controlled 55% of the new company's stock, and Time Warner shareholders controlled 45%, which appeared to have left AOL in the driver's seat of the new corporation. While the deal was an amazing offer for Time Warner, analysts in the industry feared that the offer overvalued Time Warner by a tremendous amount. It was felt that this could eventually grow into a costly deal for AOL, particularly because AOL was responsible for paying the corporation's combined debts and meeting overly confident market expectations about future growth.[2]

The merged AOL Time Warner brands included AOL, *Time*, CNN, CompuServe, Warner Bros., Netscape, *Sports Illustrated*, *People*, HBO, ICQ, AOL Instant Messenger, AOL MovieFone, TBS, TNT, Cartoon Network, Digital City, Warner Music Group, Spinner, Winamp, *Fortune*, AOL.com, *Entertainment Weekly*, and Looney Tunes.[3] Before the merger, Time Warner Inc. had been the leading media, entertainment, and news monopoly in the United States. It owned Warner Bros. studio, Warner Music, CNN, HBO, and other cable television networks, and it controlled magazines with a circulation of 130 million. America Online Inc., on the other hand, had grown into the largest dial-up Internet service provider (ISP) and its name had become almost synonymous with the Internet in the public eye. It was the leading e-commerce service, interactive service, Internet technologies, and web brands provider in the world. It held a reputation as the most easy-to-use and convenient interactive service.

America Online and Time Warner believed that their merger was a merger of two synergistic companies. Their marketing concept was to combine new and old media vehicles in order to strengthen overall total position in the market. America Online needed technical capabilities to move into the broadband business. Time Warner, on the other hand, was the second largest cable television operator in the nation. It was a major content provider in the industry that had previously wanted to expand its media empire to become an Internet player. So the merger made perfect theoretical sense to both AOL and Time Warner. In an environment where online services, entertainment, and media meet, the new company's resources would be unparalleled.

The combined company's strategic objectives were:

1. To continue making technology simple for its customers
2. To continue offering simple e-business solutions to the market
3. To accelerate the growth of its cable broadband assets

These objectives were thought to be attainable because of the new combined core competencies, such as Time Warner's cable infrastructure, AOL's ease-of-use trademark, their globally trusted brands, traditional journalistic integrity, and vast Internet expertise.

The Competitive Environment

AOL Time Warner was a distinctive company with multiple business units that spanned many markets. There were numerous national and global competitors in each market, all varying in size and number of years of experience in the marketplace. Most of these competitors were large companies with deep pockets. Similarly to AOL Time Warner, their competitive growth strategy involved mergers and acquisitions of companies with new ideas and promising products or services. The key direct competitors of AOL Time Warner by business line were:

- **Cable Systems:** AT&T Broadband, Cablevision Systems, DIRECTV, Cox Communications, Comcast.
  Barriers to entry—A large up-front investment is required to establish and then maintain the required cable network system. In addition, the large number of already established competitors forces participants to upgrade their equipment and introduce new technology to their product and service lines on a regular basis to stay in the game.

- **Internet:** Earthlink, Prodigy, Terra, Lycos, Yahoo!, Microsoft.
  Barriers to entry—In the Internet arena, a small investment allows any firm to operate its own ISP and to provide e-commerce solutions and online content. Nonetheless, establishing a successful online portal to the world of consumers requires substantial capital to market the new site, maintain and update its content, and ensure efficient operation. Thus, any new entrant to the Internet world needs to weigh the benefits of low entry fees against the need for continuous innovation, maintenance, and updates; operational efficiencies; and strategic positioning of the firm's products and services.

- **Filmed Entertainment:** Vivendi Universal, Viacom, Walt Disney, Sony.
  Barriers to entry—The capital requirements for the film and entertainment industry are very high. While it is not necessary to have high levels of funding for production, this type of business is highly dependent on the talent of the writers, directors, producers, stunt coordinators, actors and actresses, and so forth. In addition, a smaller budget limits promotion capabilities and threatens the success and popularity of any piece produced.

- **Publishing, Music, and Media:** Advance Publications, Bertelsmann, Virgin Group, Sony, News Corp., Primedia, Dow Jones, Tribune, McGraw-Hill, NBC, EMI Group, Pearson, Reed Elsevier Group, Hachette Filipacchi Medias
  Barriers to entry—In the publishing, music, and media industries, the availability of writers, musicians, and ideas for publications is virtually inexhaustible. In all three industries, the already existing players are established in the market and have the necessary capital to find new talent, publish a new book, produce a new record, or print a new publication. In addition, it would be very difficult for a new entrant to gain enough market presence to

sustain the occasional one-off success story over a longer period of time, which thus limits the number of new entrants to this industry segment as well.

Corporate Governance

Richard D. Parsons was Chairman of the Board and Chief Executive Officer of AOL Time Warner Inc., whose businesses included interactive services, cable systems, filmed entertainment, television networks, music, and publishing. He became CEO in May 2002 and Chairman of the Board in May 2003.

Exhibit 1 provides the complete list of the company's Board of Directors.

Ken Novack was Vice Chairman of AOL Time Warner Inc. As a member of the Office of the Chairman, Novack provided strategic counsel and handled special assignments for the Chairman, and he assumed a leading role in major corporate transactions. Formerly the Vice Chairman of America Online and a member of its Board of Directors, he had also served as Vice Chairman of Time Warner, Inc. Novack had played a number of critical roles for the company during the past 11 years. In addition to having broad strategic responsibilities, he oversaw America Online's Legal Department as well as AOL Investments, and he was a key architect of the merger between AOL and Time Warner.

The Marco Environment

One of AOL Time Warner's greatest advantages was that its very brand stood for strong customer service. The company held the unique status of being the only one-stop broadband, Internet, entertainment, media, and communications company in the world.

Exhibit 1
Board of Directors: AOL Time Warner, Inc.

Richard D. Parsons
Chairman of the Board and CEO, Time Warner, Inc.

James L. Barksdale
President and CEO, Barksdale Management Corporation and Co-founder of Netscape

Stephen F. Bollenbach
Co-chairman and CEO, Hilton Hotels Corporation

Stephen M. Case
Co-founder, America Online, Inc.

Frank J. Caufield
Co-founder, Kleiner Perkins Caufield & Byers

R. E. Turner
Founder, Turner Broadcasting System, Inc.

Miles R. Gilburne
Managing Member, ZG Ventures, L.L.C.

Carla A. Hills
Chairman and CEO, Hills & Company, and Former United States Trade Representative

Reuben Mark
Chairman and CEO, Colgate-Palmolive Company

Michael A. Miles
Former Chairman and CEO, Philip Morris Companies Inc.

Kenneth J. Novack
Vice Chairman, Time Warner Inc.

Franklin D. Ranes
Chairman and CEO, Fannie May

Francis T. Vincent, Jr.
Chairman, Vincent Enterprises

Source: AOL Time Warner.

By combining assets and creating new enhanced products and services, the merged corporation was able to increase consumer usage, cross-marketing, and promotion capabilities:

- **eCommerce:** E-commerce and online shopping capabilities can stimulate growth and value for shareholders.

- **Copyright:** Prevailing global copyright advantages let the company produce, distribute, and sell its intellectual property through books, music, movies, entertainment, and broadcasting at a premium price.

- **Connection:** Its established broadband network affords AOL Time Warner the ability to deliver digital content via high-speed Internet access such as cable modems, DSL, satellite, and wireless.

Furthermore, the new AOL Time Warner did not target only a niche market segment or a specific demographic group; instead, it provided products and services to a vast array of consumers. Many of these segments had shifted from being suspicious of technology and e-commerce to being savvy online users.

FCC Changes in Broadband Regulations

Since the late 1990s, analyst and industry experts had predicted that broadband connections would be the future of the Internet and the computing world. It was projected to become the standard connection method for most homes and businesses, delivering new streams of multimedia content,[4] and it could become the most quickly adopted technology in history. Even though the large majority of Internet users in the United States used standard dial-up connections, such projections were worrisome to the more than 6,000 local and national dial-up Internet Service Providers (ISPs). The former America Online was the largest dial-up provider in the country, and numerous other dial-up ISPs felt that the future of their business looked very grim. Those who fell behind in the broadband revolution were at risk of never catching up.[5] The leading player in the broadband market was the cable industry, which in 2002 had a presence in more than two-thirds of all U.S. households and was in the process of upgrading its systems to allow for two-way Internet access.

Lobbying Against Broadband Service Providers

With bleak industry forecasts for dial-up ISPs, major ISPs—including former America Online, one of its most vigorous supporters—were urging the Federal Communications Commission (FCC) to change cable industry regulations. AOL wanted existing cable monopolies, such as AT&T (including its recently acquired TCI and MediaOne), to open their cable networks to unaffiliated ISPs. They demanded that cable industry regulations be adjusted to match the telephone system industry, which until early 2003 was required by law to host the more than 6,000 online access providers on its networks. Cable companies, on the other hand, joined forces in "the battle cry of 'deregulation,'"[6] largely as a means of maintaining business-as-usual in the closed, captive-audience world of cable.

The FCC Ruling

After many months of deliberation and speculation (during which time the former America Online and Time Warner merged), the FCC finally announced its decision on the cable network access issue in February 2002. It ruled that, unlike telephone companies, cable service companies do not have to open and share their networks with other ISPs. It announced the decision "to treat cable-based broadband service as an information service rather than a telecommunications service."[7] This allowed the FCC to work within an industry that had a lower degree of government regulations.

The FCC's second decision came in February 2003. The ruling was in favor of the regional Bell companies, and this resulted in vast changes of the phone and broadband competition rules for the telecommunication services industry. While it did not meet all of the Bell companies' deregulation demands, the FCC declared that the Bells would no longer be required to share their (existing or those planned to be built in the future) high-speed fiber networks with other broadband competitors in residential or business areas. The Bell companies were required to continue leasing a portion (though how much was not specified) of their local copper line networks to independent ISPs at the already existing, deeply discounted price. With such a solution, the FCC believed it was creating a deregulated and competitive broadband industry, which made "it easier for companies to invest in new equipment and deploy the high-speed services that consumers desire."[8]

Financial Performance

In 2002, AOL Time Warner was proud of what it had achieved in its first year of operating as a merged entity. Total revenues rose from $32.2 billion in 2001 to $40.9 billion in 2002 (see **Exhibit 2**). While revenues were on the increase, operating income and net income decreased significantly during this period. In 2002, the net loss was an astounding $98.69 billion in comparison to a loss of $4.93 in 2001 and a profit of $1.12 in 2000 (see **Exhibit 2**). AOL Time Warner attributed the loss in 2002 to a one-time charge due to accounting changes and impairment of goodwill generated at the time of the merger that aggregated to approximately $100 billion. These results illustrated the extremely difficult financial situation that AOL Time Warner was facing. While some difficulties could be attributed to difficult economic and financial times, internal management and cultural turmoil resulting from the merger proved to have more of an effect on the company's performance than originally anticipated. By 2003, the vast potential this firm held through its various publishing, media, entertainment, and Internet businesses was yet to be realized financially. **Exhibit 3** shows the company's consolidated balance sheet.

Leadership Crisis and Management Changes

Many critics argued that AOL should never have acquired Time Warner. Unfortunately, many of them now work for AOL Time Warner. The only reason that AOL was even able to make the acquisition was its inflated stock price during the Internet boom. Today, the "old media" side of the business is keeping the company afloat. This has caused animosity between the AOL and Time Warner units. " 'These companies never should have been merged in the first place,' said veteran media analyst Hal Vogel. 'The Warner side feels cheated and robbed.' "[9]

The main weakness of AOL Time Warner in the human resource area has been its instability in the ranks of upper management, leading to a lack of strategic leadership and infighting among those remaining. Gerald Levin, former Chief Executive at Time Warner, announced his

**Exhibit 2
Consolidated
Statement of
Operations: AOL
Time Warner, Inc.
(Dollar amounts in
millions, except
per share data)**

Year ending December 31,	2002	2001	2000
Revenues			
Subscriptions	$18,959	$15,657	$4,777
Advertising and commerce	7,680	8,260	2,273
Content and other	14,322	13,249	555
Total revenues[1]	40,961	37,166	7,605
Cost of revenues[1]	(23,315)	(20,533)	(3,866)
Selling, general and administrative[1]	(9,916)	(9,079)	(1,864)
Amortization of goodwill and other intangible assets	(732)	(7,186)	(99)
Impairment of goodwill and other intangible assets	(45,538)	—	—
Merger and restructuring costs	(335)	(250)	(10)
Operating income (loss)	(39,875)	118	1,766
Interest expense, net	(1,783)	(1,353)	275
Other expense, net[1]	(2,498)	(3,567)	(208)
Minority interest income (expense)	(278)	46	—
Income (loss) before income taxes, discontinued operations and cumulative effect of accounting change	(44,434)	(4,756)	1,833
Income tax provision	(140)	(139)	(712)
Income (loss) before discontinued operations and cumulative effect of accounting change	(44,574)	(4,895)	1,121
Discontinued operations, net of tax	113	(39)	—
Income (loss) before cumulative effect of accounting change	(44,461)	(4,934)	1,121
Cumulative effect of accounting	(54,235)	—	—
Net income (loss)	($98,696)	($4,934)	$1,121
Basic income (loss) per common share before discontinued operations and cumulative effect of accounting change	($10.01)	($1.11)	$0.48
Discontinued operations	0.03	—	—
Cumulative effect of accounting change	−12.17	—	—
Basic net income (loss) per common share	($22.15)	($1.11)	$0.48
Average basic common shares	4,545.90	4,429.10	2,323.00
Average diluted common shares	4,521.80	4,584.40	2,595.00

Note:
1. Includes the following income (expenses) resulting from transactions with related companies:

Revenue	$678	$721	$99
Cost of revenues	(130)	(296)	—
Selling, general and administrative	−83	10	10
Interest income (expense), net	14	30	—
Other income (expense), net	(9)	(19)	—

Source: AOL Time Warner, Inc., "2002 Annual Report," p. 17.

surprise retirement less than a year after the merger. Levin was the driving force behind the decision to sell to AOL, and his departure left few allies of the merger on the Time Warner side. The AOL Time Warner Board ousted Robert Pittman, former Chief Operating Officer, shortly after Levin's exit. Richard Parsons, current CEO of AOL Time Warner restructured the business after Pittman left, splitting the business into two large chunks—the Media & Entertainment Group and the Entertainment & Networks Group. Don Logan and Jeff Bewkes (both from the Time Warner side of the business) took over the management of these two groups. In September 2003, there was a house cleaning in the AOL unit. Jonathan Miller was put in charge

**Exhibit 3
Consolidated
Balance Sheet: AOL
Time Warner, Inc.
(Dollar amounts in
millions, except
per share data.)**

Year ending December 31	2002	2001
ASSETS		
Current assets		
Cash and equivalents	$1,730	$719
Receivables, less allowances of $2.379 and $1.889 billion	5,667	6,054
Inventories	1,896	1,791
Prepaid expenses and other current assets	1,862	1,687
Total current assets	11,155	10,251
Noncurrent inventories & film costs	3,351	3,490
Investments, including available-for-sale securities	5,138	6,886
Property, plant & equipment	12,150	12,669
Intangible assets subject to amortization	7,061	7,289
Intangible assets not subject to amortization	37,145	37,708
Goodwill	36,986	127,420
Other assets	2,464	2,791
Total assets	$115,450	$208,504
LIABILITIES AND SHAREHOLDERS' EQUITY		
Current liabilities		
Accounts payable	$2,459	$2,266
Participations payable	1,689	1,253
Royalties and programming costs payable	1,495	1,515
Deferred revenue	1,209	1,451
Debt due within one year	155	48
Other current liabilities	6,388	6,443
Total current liabilities	13,395	12,976
Long-term debt	27,354	22,792
Deferred income taxes	10,823	11,231
Deferred revenue	990	1,048
Other liabilities	5,023	4,839
Minority interests	5,048	3,591
Shareholders' equity		
Series LMCN-V Common Stock, $0.01 par value, 171.2 million shares outstanding in each period	2	2
AOL Time Warner Common Stock, $0.01 par value, 4.305 and 4.258 billion shares outstanding	43	42
Paid-in capital	155,134	155,172
Accumulated other comprehensive income (loss), net	(428)	49
Retained earnings (loss)	(101,934)	(3,238)
Total shareholders' equity	52,817	152,027
Total liabilities and shareholders' equity	$115,450	$208,504

Source: AOL Time Warner, Inc., "2002 Annual Report," p. 16.

of the unit, and several key executives were asked to step down, including Jan Brandt, the architect behind AOL's successful strategy of inundating the nation with free AOL CDs. AOL Time Warner also shut down its controversial Business Affairs office, headed by David Colburn, under suspicion of shady advertising and commerce deals. Many analysts saw these management changes as confirmation that Time Warner management was taking over the company.

Steve Case, the mastermind behind AOL and Time Warner's merger, was blamed for making a bad deal, and several major shareholders wanted him out. John C. Malone, the

Chairman of Liberty Media; Gordon Crawford, a Senior Vice President and Portfolio Manager for the investment firm Capital Research and Management; Fay Vincent, the former Baseball Commissioner; and Stephen F. Bollenbach, the Chief Executive of Hilton Hotels all supported Case's removal. Even Ted Turner, a former supporter of Case, backed his ouster. The 70% decline in AOL Time Warner's stock price had diminished Ted Turner's wealth, which had been over $9 billion at the time of the merger.[10] Case's job became largely advisory; he was removed from the day-to-day operations of the company. Case admitted that there had been a lack of leadership at the AOL unit after the merger, but he continued to believe that his job was safe and that the company was taking steps in the right direction.

What did not appear in the public financial statements was the additional time the newly merged AOL Time Warner began spending on the analysis and integration of the company's differing cultures, employee and management personalities, and operations. All external signs pointed toward a massive AOL Time Warner with combined services and operations that could not be paralleled, but other factors were at play. The combined stock market valuation that was projected, the combined profits and revenues, and the outlined synergies did not happen as expected.

Several factors could be blamed for the worsening AOL Time Warner Internet unit: possible ego and boardroom clashes, the slow-down of the economy, a three-year bear market, the burst of the Internet bubble, the September 11, 2001, terrorist attack, the slow realization of synergy, and the corporation's accounting issues. As one person said, "AOL is a victim of its own success, placing too much faith in the idea that it, like too many others in the dot.com boom, could defy economic gravity."[11] While the unit's poor performance had been linked to vanishing ad revenues, other probable issues included slowing subscriber growth, accounting troubles, investigation by the Department of Justice, impairment of goodwill, and the company's slow move into the broadband business. Furthermore, decreasing value left AOL Time Warner with a tremendous financial loss and high debt levels. This greatly contributed to the internal cultural and managerial tension, and it eventually led to the departures of former AOL Time Warner Chairman of the Board Steve Case and Vice Chairman Ted Turner.

Some analysts argued, "Synergies between traditional media and new media don't exist. Consumers use them for different purposes and to obtain entirely different things."[12] The Internet was used to match one's personal interest with content and to converse with others via specific web sites, chat rooms, or e-mail. Traditional media, on the other hand, were not able to fulfill these requirements. The fundamental limitation of traditional media was the inability to individualize. It was impossible to produce each edition to one user's specific mix of interests. The advantages of traditional media lay in the ability to produce and distribute the same information to everyone, satisfying a generic interest.

Time Warner Drops AOL from Its Name

If and how AOL Time Warner can succeed in the long term is yet to be seen. Until today, the company has held an exceptional position and has always had the potential of turning its business around and becoming very profitable again. The new company must quickly determine how to settle its outstanding battles, including FCC regulations, its approach on traditional versus new distribution and media channels, the Securities and Exchange Commission investigation, the broadband struggle and court case, and anti-trust issues, and it must soothe the bitterness among the company's employees and investors. Potential lenders are not interested in making loans to a company with skyrocketing debt levels, and Wall Street will not see much appeal in floating new stock. Furthermore, AOL Time Warner's new corporate strategy needed to overcome the harsh situation in the financial market, "a lack of qualified buyers [and] a new CEO who insists the merger still will pay off."[13]

On October 16, 2003, AOL Time Warner changed its name to Time Warner Inc., and the earlier Time Warner Inc.'s named was changed to Historic Time Warner Inc. This change confirmed management's belief that the business segments of the merged entity could not be managed under one name and needed their own identities. While its core business was in entertainment, the network, cable, and publishing units continued their steady financial performance. Therefore, the company's brands remained strong, but attention needed to be brought to the Internet division.

There was mixed feedback from the market about the company changing its name from AOL Time Warner to the old Time Warner or Time Warner AOL. Supporters of the change believed that it would encourage investors and employees to concentrate more on the profitable old Time Warner media, publishing, and entertainment properties and less on the downward spiral of the Internet unit. For supporters, employees and investors were the ones the company's name was designed to appeal to. "To them, the AOL ticker symbol is probably synonymous with gut-wrenching stock dives and aggressive accounting practices."[14]

With Case and Turner's departures from the newly renamed Time Warner, the company had various options for the future. The company could choose "a more conservative approach (in other words, the old Time Warner way)"[15] in the future, while its focus was on reducing the debt load and redirecting capital investments. This approach might not be that far-fetched, as more and more former Time Warner senior executives were assuming control over the company. Second, Time Warner could reestablish and redefine guidelines of corporate responsibilities under the current organizational structure. Even with new management's "faith in the recently announced strategy to revamp AOL"[16]—actively growing the number of broadband Internet subscribers, attaining exclusive content deals, and providing premium services—a new corporate concept was required. Despite senior executives' decisions on the firm's future moves, the entire Time Warner corporation will "keep government trust busters busy as they investigate what this new multimedia powerhouse is all about."[17] Time Warner must work to develop and implement the necessary strategies and concepts for a successful future.

In the end, a look at the unaudited 2003 third quarter of Time Warner Inc. indicated that the company was developing a plan—a plan to reduce debt, increase profitability, and raise its stock price. Most importantly, for the nine months ended September 30, 2003, Time Warner Inc. had announced a net profit of $2 billion and positive cash flow from operations.[18] There seemed to be significant reduction in debt. As for the stock price, which at the time hovered around $18, it was better than $9.9, the 52-week low, but it was still not good enough for investors to buy. A lot would depend on the financial results for the fiscal year 2003 yet to be announced by the company.

Notes

1. "AOL Buyout of Time Warner: Merger Frenzy Sweeping Corporate America," www.wsws.org/articles/2000/jan2000/merg-j14.shtml (January 14, 2000).
2. Ibid.
3. "AOL Time Warner Merger," www.antiessays.com/show.php?eid=1538.
4. www.cme.org/access/broadband/printer.html.
5. "The Broadband Revolution—Broadband, Networks and Narrow Visions: The Internet at Risk," www.democraticmedia.org/issues/openaccess/at_risk.html.
6. www.cme.org/access/broadband/end_to_end.html.
7. M. Lewis, "FCC Declines to Hobble Cable Broadband," www.forbes.com/2002/03/15/0315broadband.html (March 15, 2002).
8. R. Mark, "FCC Frees Bells of Broadband Restrictions," http://dc.internet.com/news/article.php/1588441 (February 20, 2003).
9. P. Furman, "AOLTW Feels Pressure to Split into Separate Companies," Knight Ridder Tribune Business News (July 16, 2002).
10. D. D. Kirkpatrick, "AOL Chairman's No. 1 Ally Turns into His Biggest Foe," New York Times (October 1, 2002).

11. D. Gardner, "Media: Hype Can't Save AOL Time Warner from Scandal," *www.sundayherald.com/26475* (July 28, 2002).
12. V. Crosbie, "AOL Time Warner: It's a New Media, Baby," *http://clickz.com/design/freefee/print.php/1434921* (July 30, 2002).
13. B. Johnson, "Breaking Up AOL Time Warner?" *www.adage.com/news.cms?newsId=35530* (July 23, 2002).
14. J. Glasner, "The Case for AOL Name Change," *www.wired.com/news/business/0,1367,57197,00.html* (January 14, 2003).
15. D. Gardner, "Media: Hype Can't Save AOL Time Warner from Scandal," *www.sundayherald.com/26475* (July 28, 2002).
16. S. Pruitt, "Analysis: AOLTW's Post-merger Depression Lingers On," *www.infoworld.com/article/03/01/30/030130hnaolloss_1.html?business* (January 30, 2003).
17. "AOL Time Warner Merger," *www.antiessays.com/show.php?eid=1538.*
18. *www.timewarner.com/investors/quarterly_earnings/index.adp*

References

"Timeline—Milestones and Key Dates in AOL Time Warner History," *www.aoltimewarner.com/corporate_information/timeline.adp.*

AOL, "Mission and Values," *www.aoltimewarner.com/corporate_information/mission_and_values.adp.*

AOL Time Warner, Annual Report, *www.aoltimewarner.com/investors/annual_reports/pdf/2001ar.pdf* (2001).

S. Lawson, "AOL Raises Red Flags over Three Past Deals," *http://archive.infoworld.com/articles/hn/xml/02/08/14/020814hnaolflag.xml* (August 14, 2002).

D. Gardner, "Media: Hype Can't Save AOL Time Warner from Scandal," *www.sundayherald.com/26475* (July 28, 2002).

"AOL Time Warner Execs Play Down Big Loss," *www.informationweek.com/story/IWK20030129S0009* (January 29, 2003).

AOL, "Board of Directors," *www.aoltimewarner.com/corporate_information/board_of_directors.adp.*

S. Pruitt, "Analysis: AOLTW's Post-merger Depression Lingers On," *www.infoworld.com/article/03/01/30/030130hnaolloss_1.html?business* (January 30, 2003).

"America Online Names AOL Time Warner Insider as New Chief Financial Officer," *www.siliconvalley.com/mld/siliconvalley/business/companies/aol/5286646.htm.*

"AOL Buyout of Time Warner: Merger Frenzy Sweeping Corporate America," *www.wsws.org/articles/2000/jan2000/merg-j14.shtml* (January 14, 2000).

S. Junnarkar and J. Hu, "AOL Buys Time Warner in Historic Merger," *http://news.com/2100-1023-235400.html?legacy=cnet* (January 10, 2000).

J. Pelline and M. Yamamoto, "Can New Empire Avoid Titanic Clashes?" *http://news.com/2100-1023-235448.html?legacy=cnet* (January 10, 2000).

J. Hu, S. Junnarkar, and B. Lipton Krigel, "How America Online Became a Superpower," *http://news.com/2100-1023-235444.html?legacy=cnet* (January 10, 2000).

V. Crosbie, "Viewpoint: AOL Time Warner: It's a New Media, Baby," *www.clickz.com/design/freefee/print.php/1434921* (July 30, 2002).

"AOL Time Warner Merger," *www.antiessays.com/show.php?eid=1538.*

D. Faber, "Clash of Cultures at AOL Time Warner," *http://moneycentral.msn.com/content/CNBCTV/Articles/TVReports/P37848.asp* (January 9, 2003).

S. F. Gale, "Memo to AOL Time Warner: Why Mergers Fail," *www.workforce.com/section/09/feature/23/39/96/* (February 2003).

B. Johnson, "Breaking Up AOL Time Warner?" *www.adage.com/news.cms?newsID=35530* (July 23, 2003).

J. Glasner, "The Case for AOL Name Change," *www.wired.com/news/business/0,1367,57197,00.html* (January 14, 2003).

L. Takeuchi Cullen, "Dialing Up a Departure," *www.time.com/time/archive/preview/from_redirect/0,10987,1101030127-409506,00.html* (January 27, 2003).

www.timewarneraustin.com/company/corporate_information/.

E. Millard, "Time Warner's AOL Problem," *www.newsfactor.com/perl/story/story-start#story-start* (June 4, 2002).

"Dial-Up Vs Broadband," *www.telesolutions.com.au/internet/dialvbroadband.asp.*

"Broadband Vs Dial-Up Internet; What Is DSL?" *http://hankfiles.pcvsconsole.com/answer.php?file=506* (October 21, 2002).

M. Carr, "Dial-up Computer Connections vs. Broadband," *www.gazettearchives.com/cyberspace2001/_disc4/000000cc.htm* (March 19, 2001).

"White Paper: Broadband—Bigger Pipes Mean Better Serving," *Smart Computing*, Vol. 9, No. 6 (June 2001).

K. Schurman, "White Paper: Broadband—Bigger Pipes Mean Better Surfing," *www.smartcomputing.com/editorial/article.asp?article=articles%2Farchive%2Fg0906%2F36g06%2F36g06%2Easp* (June 2001).

L. E. Saris, "White Paper Issues and Statistics on the Subject of Digital Divide," *www.salemcyberspace.org/whitepaper.htm* (July 29, 2002).

M. Cooper, "Consumer Group Kicks Off 'Broadband' Internet Campaign," *www.consumerfed.org/launch1099.htm* (October 7, 1999).

"The Broadband Revolution—What It Is and Why It Matters," *www.cme.org/access/broadband/primer.html.*

"The Broadband Revolution—The End-to-End Internet: No Room for Monopolies," *www.cme.org/access/broadband/end_to_end.html.*

"What the Market Will Bear: Cisco's Vision for Broadband Internet," *www.democraticmedia.org/issues/openaccess/whatthemarketwillbear.html.*

"The Broadband Revolution—Broadband Networks and Narrow Visions: The Internet at Risk," *www.democraticmedia.org/issues/openaccess/at_risk.html.*

G. Larson and J. Chester, "Song of the Open Road: Building a Broadband Network for the 21st Century," *www.democraticmedia.org/resources/articles/openroad4.html* (1999).

"Talking Points on the Broadband Future: Open Access or Closed Networks?" *www.democraticmedia.org/issues/openaccess/AFLTP.html.*

G. O. Larson and J. Chester, "How to Prepare for the Era of the Speedy Internet," *www.democraticmedia.org/resources/articles/prepareforspeedyinternet.html* (2000).

M. Freedman, "Is Broadband All It's Cracked Up to Be?" *http://216.239.37.100/search?q=cache:SvRCk5C0-QMC:www.nop.co.uk/technology/PDF%27s/White%2520Paper%2520-%2520broad-*

band.pdf+broadband%2Binternet%2Bwhite+paper&hl=en&ie= UTF-8 (July 2001).

D. McClure, "The Future of Residential Dial-up Access," *www. internetindustry.com/mag/01_02su/05fut/index.shtml.*

N. Garcia, "How It Works: Dial-Up Networking," *www.pcworld.com/ resource/printable/article/0,aid,48467,00.asp* (May 2, 2001).

M. Pastore, "Broadband Technology Boom Predicted," *cyberatlas. internet.com/markets/broadband/article/0,1323,10099_151341,00. html* (January 6, 1999).

"Broadband—High Speed Internet Access," *www.fcc.gov/cgb/ broadband.html.*

J. Borland, "Broadband Defectors on the Rise," *http://zdnet.com. com/2100-1106-814343.html* (November 7, 2001).

R. Mark, "FCC Frees Bells of Broadband Restrictions," *http:// dc.internet.com/news/article.php/1588441* (February 20, 2003).

M. Lewis, "FCC Declines to Hobble Cable Broadband," *www. forbes.com/2002/03/15/0315broadband.html* (March 15, 2002).

B. Charny, "FCC Loosens Broadband Rules," *http://news.com.com/ 2100-1033-985313.html* (February 20, 2003).

"New Regulations Could Spur Broadband Investment but Limit Choices," *www.hindustantimes.com/news/181_193657,00030010. htm* (February 22, 2003).

CASE 12

Harley-Davidson, Inc., 2002:

The 100th Anniversary

Patricia A. Ryan and Thomas L. Wheelen

"The year 2001 was our 16th consecutive year of record revenue and income, in spite of the weaker global economy,' said Jeffrey L. Bleustein, Chairman and Chief Executive Officer of Harley-Davidson, Inc. 'Worldwide retail sales of Harley-Davidson motorcycles in the fourth quarter were strong with 12.9 percent unit growth over last year.' "[1]

THE THEME FILLED THE ROOM AS THE PLANNING COMMITTEE FOR THE 100TH ANNIVER-sary Celebration met in preparation of the year-long event. It was a hot day in mid-July, and committee members were planning the final stages of the year-long 100th anniversary celebration of Harley-Davidson. The culmination would entail an open tour starting in mid-August in Portland, Las Vegas, Baton Rouge, and New York City and end in Milwaukee on August 29, 2003, in time for the three-day party and celebration. **Exhibit 1** shows the motorcycle routes for the participants. Company officials were expecting upward of 250,000 to participate in the final 100-year anniversary party celebration. At the end of the meeting, the committee discussed how to make the celebration one that Harley riders would never forget while at the same time encouraging a new, younger customer base to add to their aging baby boomer clientele.

History[2]

In 1903, William Harley (age 21), a draftsman, and his friend, Arthur R. Davidson, began experimenting with ideas to design and build their own motorcycles. They were joined by Arthur's brothers, William, a machinist, and Walter, a skilled mechanic. The Harley-Davidson Motor Company started in a 10×15-foot shed in the Davidson family's backyard in Milwaukee, Wisconsin.

Exhibit 1
Map of Harley-Davidson 100th Anniversary Celebration Roadtrip, 2003

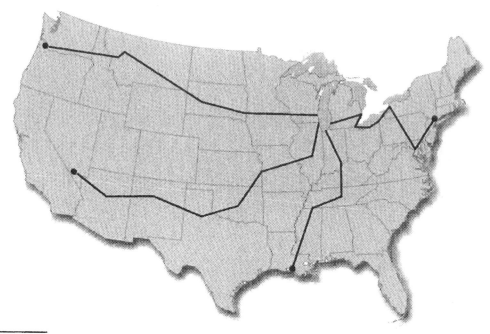

Source: www.harleydavidson.com.

In 1903, three motorcycles were built and sold. The production increased to eight in 1904. The company then moved to Juneau Avenue, which is the site of the company's present offices. In 1907, the company was incorporated.

In 1969, AMF, Inc., a leisure and industrial products conglomerate, acquired Harley-Davidson. The management team expanded production from 15,000 in 1969 to 40,000 motorcycles in 1974. AMF favored short-term profits instead of investing in research and development and retooling. During this time, Japanese competitors continued to improve the quality of their motorcycles, while Harley-Davidson began to turn out noisy, oil-leaking, heavily vibrating, poorly finished, and hard-to-handle machines. AMF ignored the Japanese competition. In 1975, Honda Motor Company introduced its Gold Wing, which became the standard for large touring motorcycles. Harley-Davidson had controlled that segment of the market for years. There was a $2,000 price difference between Harley's top-of-the-line motorcycles and Honda's comparable Gold Wing. This caused American buyers of motorcycles to start switching to Japanese motorcycles. The Japanese companies (Suzuki and Yamaha) from this time until the mid-1980s continued to enter the heavyweight custom market with Harley lookalikes.

During AMF's ownership of the company, sales of motorcycles were strong, but profits were weak. The company had serious problems with poor-quality manufacturing and strong Japanese competition. In 1981, Vaughn Beals, then head of the Harley Division, and 13 other managers conducted a leveraged buyout of the company for $65 million.

New management installed a Materials as Needed (MAN) system to reduce inventories and stabilize the production schedule. Also, this system forced production to work with marketing to create more accurate forecasts. This led to precise production schedules for each month, allowing only a 10% variance. The company forced its suppliers to increase their quality in order to reduce customer complaints.

Citicorp, Harley's main lender, refused to lend the company more money in 1985. On New Year's Eve, four hours before a midnight that would have meant Harley's demise, the company inked a deal with Heller Financial that kept its doors open. Seven months later, amid a hot market for new stock, Harley-Davidson went public again. James L. Ziemer, the CFO, puts it bluntly: "You throw cash at it, try to grow too fast, you'd destroy this thing."[3]

During the time Harley-Davidson was a privately held firm, management invested in research and development. Management purchased a Computer-Aided Design (CAD) system that allowed the company to make changes in the entire product line and still maintain its traditional styling. These investments by management had a quick payoff in that the break-even point went from 53,000 motorcycles in 1982 to 35,000 in 1986.

In June 1993, over 100,000 members of the worldwide Harley-Davidson family came home (Milwaukee) to celebrate the company's 90th anniversary. Willie G. Davidson, Vice President–Styling, grandson of the Co-founder, said, "I was overwhelmed with emotion when our parade was rolling into downtown Milwaukee. I looked up to heaven and told the founding fathers, 'Thanks, guys.'"

During 1993, the company acquired a 49% interest in Buell Motorcycle Company, a manufacturer of sport/performance motorcycles. This investment in Buell offered the company the possibility of gradually gaining entry into select niches within the performance motorcycle market. In 1998, Harley-Davidson owned most of the stock in Buell. Buell began distribution of a limited number of Buell motorcycles during 1994 to select Harley-Davidson dealers. Buell sales were:

Year	Sales	Units (thousands)
1994	$6 million	576
1995	$14 million	1,407
1996	$23 million	2,762
1997	$40 million	4,415
1998	$53.5 million	6,334
1999	$63.5 million	7,767
2000	$58.1 million	10,189
2001	$61.9 million	9,925

Buell's mission "is to develop and employ innovative technology to enhance 'the ride' and give Buell owners a motorcycle experience that no other brand can provide." The European sport/performance market was four times larger than its U.S. counterpart. In 1997, there were 377 Buell dealers worldwide.

On November 14, 1995, the company acquired substantially all of the common stock and common stock equivalents of Eaglemark Financial Services, Inc., a company in which it had held a 49% interest since 1993. Eaglemark provided credit to leisure product manufacturers, their dealers, and customers in the United States and Canada. The transaction was accounted for as a step acquisition under the purchase method. The purchase price for the shares and equivalents was approximately $45 million, which was paid from internally generated funds and short-term borrowings. The excess of the acquisition cost over the fair value of the net assets purchased resulted in approximately $43 million of goodwill, which was amortized on a straight-line basis over 20 years.

On January 22, 1996, the company announced its strategic decision to discontinue the operations of the Transportation Vehicles segment in order to concentrate its financial and human resources on its core motorcycle business. The Transportation Vehicles segment was comprised of the Recreation Vehicles division (Holiday Rambler trailers), the Commercial Vehicles division (small delivery vehicles), and B & B Molders, a manufacturer of custom or standard tooling and injection-molded plastic pieces. During 1996, the company completed the sale of the Transportation Vehicles segment for an aggregate sales price of approximately $105 million—approximately $100 million in cash and $5 million in notes and preferred stock.

In the fall of 1997, GT Bicycles manufactured and distributed 1,000 Harley Limited Edition bicycles at a list retail price of $1,700. The pedal-powered bike had a real Harley paint job, signature fenders, a fake gas tank, and the chrome of a Harley Softail motorcycle. GT Bicycles manufactured the Velo Glide bikes and was licensed by Harley to produce the limited version. The four-speed bike weighed 40-plus pounds. Kcn Alder, cycle shop owner, said, "It's a big clunker that no one would really want to ride." Nevertheless, the bicycles sold out to buyers in less than four months. The resale price for the Limited Edition jumped to $3,500, and one collector advertised his for $5,000. In comparison, a person could purchase an actual Harley XHL 883 Sportster motorcycle for $5,245.

Since 1997, Harley-Davidson had created an internal makeover. The unsung hero of Harley-Davidson's supply-chain makeover was an intense procurement expert named Garry Berryman, 48, Vice President of Materials Management/Product Cost. He came to Harley by way of John Deere and Honda Motors. Berryman joined the company in 1995 to find that its supply-chain management has been neglected. There were nine different purchasing departments operating from different plant locations, 14 separate sets of representative terms and conditions, and nearly 4,000 suppliers. Engineers with little or no expertise in supply management were doing the bulk of the buying. To top it off, "the voice of supply management was buried three layers deep in the corporate hierarchy," said Berryman.

While at Honda, Berryman studied Japanese *keiretsu*—huge, vertically integrated companies that fostered deep, trusting relationships with suppliers. He wanted to form similar strategic alliances with Harley's top suppliers, bringing them into the design and planning process. Berryman felt that new technology and the Web would make it easier than ever to form these bonds and collaborate. He made it clear that relationship and strategy should drive applications, not vice versa. As Dave Cotteleer, the company's manager of planning and control, explained, "We're using technology to cut back on communication times and administrative trivia, like invoice tracking, so we can focus the relationships on more strategic issues. We're not saying, 'Here's a neat piece of technology. Let's jam it into our model.'"[4]

Also, in the 1990s, Harley-Davidson saw the need to build a motorcycle to try to appeal to the younger and international markets, which preferred sleeker, faster bikes. Harley-Davidson spent an undisclosed amount of research and development dollars over several years to develop the $17,000 V-Rod motorcycle. The V-Rod, introduced in 2001, had 110 horsepower, nearly double that of the standard Harley bike. The V-Rod was the quickest and fastest production model the company had ever built, capable of reaching 60 miles per hour in 3.5 seconds and 100 mph in a little over 8 seconds. Its top speed was about 140 mph. All in all, the V-Rod was faster and handled better than the traditional bulky Harley bikes.

All other Harley models were powered by 45-degree V-twin air-cooled engines with camshafts in the block; the new V-Rod had a 1,130cc 60-degree engine with double overhead cams and four values for each cylinder. The V-Rod had a very long 67.5-inch wheelbase, and it handled better than other Harleys because it was so much lighter. Furthermore, the V-Rod was only 26 inches off the ground, so it would accommodate a wide range of riders.[5] Harley-Davidson hoped to gain some of the younger markets with this new bike.

Corporate Governance

Board of Directors

The Board of Directors consisted of nine members, of which only two were internal members—Richard E. Terlink, past Chairman, and Jeffrey L. Bleustein, Chairman and CEO. **Exhibit 2** highlights board members before the 2002 vote. In accordance with company bylaws, two of the directors, Richard J. Hermon-Taylor and Teerlink, whose term would expire at the 2002 meeting, were not eligible for reelection. The board recommended George

Exhibit 2 Board of Directors: Harley-Davidson, Inc.

Barry K. Allen, *President, Allen Enterprises, LLC*
Barry has been a member of the Board since 1992. His distinguished business career has taken him from the telecommunications industry to leading a medical equipment and systems business and back again. Barry's diverse experience has been particularly valuable to the Board in the areas of marketing and organization transformation.

Richard I. Beattie, *Chairman of the Executive Committee, Simpson, Thacher & Bartlett*
Dick has been a valued advisor to Harley-Davidson for nearly 20 years. His contributions evolved and grew with the company over time. In the early 1980s, he provided legal and strategic counsel to the 13 leaders who purchased Harley-Davidson from AMF, taking it back to private ownership. He also advised the team when it was time to take the company public again in 1986. Dick was elected to the Board in 1996.

Jeffrey L. Bleustein, *Chairman and CEO, Harley-Davidson, Inc.*
Jeff began his association with Harley-Davidson in 1975, when he was asked to oversee the Engineering Group. During Jeff's tenure as Vice President–Engineering, Harley-Davidson developed the Evolution engine and established the foundations of its current line of cruiser and touring motorcycles. Jeff has demonstrated creativity and vision across a wide range of senior leadership roles. In 1996 he was elected to the Board, and in June 1997, he was appointed to his current position.

Richard J. Hermon-Taylor, *President, BioScience International, Inc. (term expires in 2002; not eligible for reelection)*
Richard joined the Board in 1986 and has been advising on marketing and manufacturing strategy for Harley-Davidson for nearly 20 years. His association with the company began when he was with the Boston Consulting Group in the mid-1970s and has been valued through the intervening years.

Donald A. James, *Vice Chairman and CEO, Fred Deeley Imports, Inc.*
Don's wisdom and knowledge of the motorcycle industry has guided the Board since 1991. As a 31-year veteran of Harley-Davidson's exclusive distributor in Canada, he has a strong sense for our core products. Don has a particularly keen understanding of the retrial issues involved with motorcycles and related products and the competitive advantage inherent in strong, long-lasting dealer relationships.

Richard G. LeFauve, *President, GM University; Senior Vice President, General Motors Corporation, retired*
Skip joined the Board in 1993. He has generously shared his vehicle industry experience with Harley-Davidson, including learning from his prior role as President of Saturn. Parallels in durable goods manufacturing, consumer trends, and lifelong customer marketing strategy has provided considerable creative stimuli for Board discussions.

Sara L. Levinson, *ChairMom and CEO, ClubMom, Inc.*
Sara joined the Board in 1996. She understands the value and power of strong brands, and her current senior leadership role in marketing and licensing, together with her previous experience at MTV, give her solid insights into the entertainment industries and younger customer segments.

James A. Norling, *Executive Vice President, Motorola, Inc.; President, Personal Communications Sector, retired*
Jim has been a Board member since 1993. His career with Motorola has included extensive senior leadership assignments in Europe, the Middle East, and Africa, and he has generously shared his international experience and understanding of technological change to benefit Harley-Davidson.

Richard F. Teerlink, *Former Chairman and CEO, Harley-Davidson, Inc., retired (term expires in 2002; not eligible for reelection)*
Rich joined Harley-Davidson in 1981 and was elected to the Board in 1982. In 1988 he was appointed President of the company; in 1989, CEO. In 1996 he was named Chairman of the Board. Rich is credited with the financial restructuring of Harley-Davidson from private to public during the mid-1980s. His leadership was instrumental in creating at the company a values-based culture that revolves around developing mutually beneficial relationships with all stakeholders.

Source: Harley-Davidson, Inc., 2001 Annual Report, p. 83.

H. Conrades, 63, to fill one of those seats. Conrades had been Chairman and CEO of Akamai Technologies since April 1999, and since August 1998, he has been associated with Polaris Venture Partners, an early-stage investment company. Previously, he had served as Executive Vice President of GTE. The other seat would remain empty, dropping the board size from nine to eight members.

The terms of the Board of Directors were on a three-year stagger system: (a) The term expiring in 2002 was Sara L. Levinson (51); (b) terms expiring in 2003 were Bleustein (62), Donald James (58), and James A. Norling (60); and (c) terms expiring in 2004 were Barry K. Allen (53), Richard I. Beattie (62), and Richard G. LeFauve (67).

Directors who were employees of Harley-Davidson did not receive any special compensation for their services as directors. Directors who are not employees of Harley-Davidson receive an annual fee of $25,000 plus $1,500 for each regular meeting of the board, $750 for each special meeting of the board, $750 for each board committee meeting and a clothing allowance of $1,000 to purchase Harley-Davidson® MotorClothes™ apparel and accessories. Pursuant to the 1998 Director Stock Plan, an outside director could elect to receive 50% or 100% of the annual fee to be paid in each calendar year in the form of stock based on the fair market value at the time of the annual meeting. In 2001, each outside Director received an option to purchase 600 shares of common stock.[6]

All directors and executive officers as a group (19 individuals) owned 4,311,178 shares (1.4%). Jeffrey E. Bleustein owned the largest block with 1,785,993 shares, which was 0.5% of the outstanding stock. AXA Assurance I.A.R.D. Mutuelle owned 22,324,662 shares (7.4%) and was the largest shareholder.

The company's mission statement was as follows: "We fulfill dreams through the experience of motorcycling by providing to motorcyclists and to the general public an expanding line of motorcycles, branded products and services in selected market segments."[7]

Top Management

Jeffrey E. Bleustein had been a director of the company since 1986. He was appointed Executive Vice President in 1991 and President and Chief Operating Officer of the Motor Company in 1993. In 1997, Bleustein succeeded Richard E. Teerlink as Chairman and CEO. Bleustein, a former Yale engineering professor, joined AMF in the early 1970s. In 1981, he joined Harley-Davidson. Thirteen Harley executives, including Bleustein, bought the company in a highly leveraged buyout—$80 of debt for every $1 of equity—in February 1981. "Before the ink had dried on our paper we were in violation of most of our loan covenants," he said. His current stake, at less than 1%, was worth $40 million.[8]

Exhibit 3 shows the corporate officers for Harley-Davidson and its business segments—Motor Company, Buell, and Financial Services.

The 100th Anniversary Celebration

Forbes named Harley-Davidson its "Company of the Year" for 2001, and it was selected by *BusinessWeek* as one of the nation's "Most Admired Companies." Additionally, in 2001, it was named to *Fortune*'s list of the "Top 100 Companies to Work For" for the fourth time in five years. The company unveiled its newest bike, the V-Rod, aimed at younger, affluent riders with a list price of $16,995. The V-Rod was named *Motorcycle News* "Bike of the Year" the same year. Retail sales of Harley-Davison bikes were up 14.4% in 2001 in the United States. In Japan, Harley-Davidson celebrated its 17th consecutive year of growth with retail sales up 10.7% in 2001. In 2000 and 2001, Harley-Davidson was the best-selling heavyweight motorcycle in Japan.[9] With all this going for the company, they were moving to their year-long 100th Anniversary Celebration with excitement, hope for the future, and satisfaction for past accomplishments. The party was planned to be a year-long celebration, from summer 2002, culminating in a three-day party in Milwaukee in late August 2003.

All was not rosy for the century-old company. Harley-Davidson, which had fought back from near demise in the 1980s, was to face new rivals in the competitive market, the aging customer base, and the lasting recession. The projected sales figures looked strong through 2003,

Exhibit 3 Corporate Officers, Harley-Davidson, Inc.

Jeffrey L. Bleustein *Chairman and CEO*	William G. Davidson *Vice President, Styling*	Steven R. Phillips *Vice President, Quality, Reliability, and Technical Services*
James M. Brostowitz *Vice President, Controller, and Treasurer*	Karl M. Eberle *Vice President and General Manager, Kansas City Operations*	John Russell *Vice President and Managing Director, Europe*
Gail A. Lione *Vice President, General Counsel, and Secretary*	Jon R. Flickinger *Vice President, North American Sales and Dealer Services*	Harold A. Scott *Vice President, Human Resources*
James L. Ziemer *Vice President and Chief Financial Officer*	John A. Hevey *Vice President*	W. Kenneth Sutton, Jr. *Vice President, Continuous Improvement*
Motor Company Leadership	Jorge F. Hidalgo *General Manager, Pilgrim Road Operations*	Earl K. Werner *Vice President, Engineering*
Jeffrey L. Bleustein *CEO*	Timothy K. Hoelter *Vice President, Government Affairs*	Jerry G. Wilke *Vice President and General Manager, Asia/Pacific and Latin America Regions*
Garry S. Berryman *Vice President, Materials Management/Product Cost*	Ronald M. Hutchinson *Vice President, Parts and Accessories*	**Harley-Davidson Financial Services Leadership**
Joanne M. Bischmann *Vice President, Marketing*	Michael D. Keefe *Vice President and Director, Harley Owners Group®*	Lawrence G. Hund *Vice President and Chief Financial Officer*
James M. Brostowitz *Vice President and Controller*	Donald C. Kieffer *General Manager, Capitol Drive Operations*	Donna F. Zarcone *President and Chief Operating Officer*
Roy Coleman *General Manager, Tomahawk Operations*	Kathleen A. Lawler *Vice President, Communications*	**Buell Motorcycle Company Leadership**
Ruth M. Crowley *Vice President, General Merchandise*	Gail A. Lione *Vice President and General Counsel*	Erik F. Buell *Chairman and Chief Technical Officer*
William B. Dannehl *Vice President and General Manager, York Operations*	James A. McCaslin *President and Chief Operating Officer*	John A. Hevey *President and Chief Operating Officer*

Source: Harley-Davidson, Inc., 2001 Annual Report, p. 84.

but after the collectors' editions were sold, what would 2004 hold for Harley-Davidson? It was losing market share to Japanese rivals such as Honda Motors Co., seeing lower prices for some older bikes that used to trade at a premium, and facing a peculiar marketing headache stemming from its upcoming 100th anniversary. Buyers seemed to be hanging back, awaiting 2003's collector-edition models.[10] The coming year was less certain. These were issues management wrestled with during the celebration gala. One theme during the attention-getting celebration was to gain new, younger customers to move Harley-Davidson into its second century.

Harley-Davidson, the marvel of Milwaukee, which roared back from near-ruin in 1986 to dazzle investors and bikers alike with its marketing artistry, financial savvy, and sheer mystique may be facing a patch of rough road.

Harley Owners Group (H.O.G.)

A special kind of camaraderie marked the Harley Owners Group (H.O.G.) rallies and other motorcycle events. At events and rallies around the world, members of H.O.G. came together for fun, adventure, and a love of their machines and the open road. As the largest motorcycle

Exhibit 4
2002 Profile of H.O.G. and BRAG: Harley-Davidson, Inc.

H.O.G.-Sponsored Events: In 2001 H.O.G. continued to sponsor motorcycling events on local, regional, national, and international levels, including U.S. national rallies in Worcester, Maine, and Milwaukee, Wisconsin, as well as a special touring journey rally that took participants through Americana on legendary Route 66 from Chicago, Illinois, to Santa Monica, California. The 11th annual international H.O.G. Rally, held in Saint-Tropez, France, drew tens of thousands of members.

H.O.G. Membership: Any Harley-Davidson motorcyclist could become a member of H.O.G. In fact, the first year of membership was included with the purchase of a new Harley-Davidson motorcycle. The number of H.O.G. members had grown rapidly since the motorcycle organization began in 1983 with 33,000 members. There were 660,000 H.O.G. members in 115 countries worldwide. Sponsorship of H.O.G. chapters by Harley-Davidson dealers grew from 49 chapters in 1985 to 1,200 chapters at the close of 2001.

A Snapshot of H.O.G.

Worldwide members	660,000
Worldwide dealer-sponsored chapters	1,200
Countries with members	115

A Snapshot of BRAG (Buell Riders Adventure Group)

Created in	1995
Worldwide members	10,000
Number of clubs	55

Source: Harley-Davidson, Inc., 2001 Annual Report, pp. 28–29.

club in the world, H.O.G. offered customers organized opportunities to ride their famed bikes. H.O.G. rallies visibly promoted the Harley-Davidson experience to potential new customers and strengthened the relationships among members, dealers, and Harley-Davidson employees.

William G. Davidson, grandson of the Co-founder, biker to the core, and known to all as Willie G., dismissed the charge without quite denying it. "There's a lot of beaners, but they're out on the motorcycles, which is a beautiful thing," he says, noting that he had recently co-led a national rally of Canadian H.O.G. groups with Harley's top executive, CEO Jeff Bleustein.[11]

In 1995, the Buell Riders Adventure Group (BRAG) was created to bring Buell motorcycle enthusiasts together and to share their on-road experiences. In 2001, BRAG held a homecoming event in East Troy, Wisconsin. Harley-Davidson plans to grow both organizations with new members and chapters in the years to come.

Exhibit 4 provides a profile of H.O.G and BRAG clubs. As of 2001, there were about 660,000 H.O.G. members in about 1,200 clubs. The newer BRAG club for Buell riders numbered 10,000 members in more than 55 clubs.

Foreign Operations[12]

Europe/Middle East/Africa

In the European Region there were currently 381 independent Harley-Davidson dealerships serving 32 country markets. This included 280 combined Harley-Davidson and Buell dealerships. Buell was further represented by 10 dealerships that did not sell Harley-Davidson motorcycles. It had an established infrastructure in Europe, based out of its headquarters in the United Kingdom, and it operated through a network of independent dealers served by eight independent distributors and by five wholly owned sales and marketing subsidiaries in France, Germany, Italy, the Netherlands, and the United Kingdom. The European management team was continuing to focus on the expansion and improvement of distributor and dealer relationships through the dealer development team, specialized training programs, retail financing initiatives, ongoing product development, and coordinated Europe-wide and local marketing programs aimed at attracting new customers. Other initiatives included the development of information systems linking European subsidiaries directly with each of the major independent distributors and most of the dealers located in the subsidiary markets.

Asia-Pacific

There were currently 240 Harley-Davidson outlets serving eight country markets, of which 82 were combined Harley-Davidson/Buell dealerships and 27 were service-only outlets. In addition, there were currently only 2 Buell dealerships. Management expected the majority of its growth opportunities in the Asia-Pacific region to come from its existing markets in Japan and Australia. Harley-Davidson would continue to support its objectives of maintaining and growing its business in southeast Asia, where markets had continued to stabilize over recent years.

Latin America

This market consisted of 15 country markets managed from Milwaukee, Wisconsin. The Latin American market had a diverse dealer network including 28 Harley-Davidson dealerships. Management planned to continue developing its distribution in Brazil and Mexico, its two biggest Latin American markets, as well as broaden brand management and marketing activities across the entire region.

Canada

In Canada, there were currently 75 independent Harley-Davidson dealerships and 1 independent standalone Buell dealership served by a single independent distributor. This network included 25 combined Harley-Davidson and Buell dealerships, resulting in a total of 26 Buell dealerships in Canada.

Business Segments

"Running a company is like riding a motorcycle. Go too slow, and you tip over. Go too fast, and you crash. At the moment, Harley has a perfect balance."[13]

Harley-Davidson operates in two principal business segments: Motorcycles and Related Products (Motorcycles) and Financial Services. The segments will be discussed in that order. **Exhibit 5** provides financial information on the company's two business segments.

Motorcycles and Related Products Segment

"The longer the waits, the more Wall Street loved Harley.[14]

The primary business of the Motorcycles segment was to design, manufacture, and sell premium motorcycles for the heavyweight market. It was best known for its Harley-Davidson®

Exhibit 7
2002 Motorcycles
Product Line:
Harley-Davidson,
Inc.

Motorcycle	Suggested Selling Price ($)
Buell Blast[1]	4,595
XLH Sportster 883	6,145
XLH Sportster 883 Hugger®	6,545
XL Sportster 883R	6,795
XL883C Sportster 883 Custom	7,690
XLM Sportster 1200	8,425
XL 1200S Sportster 1200 Sport	9,130
XB9S Buell Lightning[1]	9,995
XB9R Buell Firebolt[1]	9,995
XL 1200C Sportster 1200 Custom	10,040
FXD Dyna Glide Super Glider®	12,490
FXST Softail® Standard	13,870
FXDX Dyna Glide Super Glide® Sport	14,510
FLHT/FLHTI Electra Glide® Standard	14,710
FXDXT Dyna Glide Super Glide® T-Sport	15,520
FXSTB Softail® Night Train®	15,575
FXDL Dyna Glide Low Rider®	16,090
FLSTS/FLSTSI Springer®	16,630
FLHR/FLHRI Road King®	16,650
VRSCA V-Rod	16,995
FLSTF/FLSTFI Fat Boy®	17,100
FXDWG Dyna Glide Wide Glider®	17,215
FXSTD Softail® Deuce	17,870
FLTSC/FLSTCI Heritage Softail® Classic	17,870
FLHTC/FLHTCI Electra Glide® Classic	18,070
FLHRCI Road King® Classic	18,310
FLTR/FLTRI Road Glide	18,520
FLSTS/FLSTSI Heritage Springer®	18,615
VRSC V-Rod® VRSCA	18,695
FLHTCUI Ultra Classic®	21,065

Note:

1. The Buell Blast, Buell Lightning, and Buell Firebolt are manufactured by Buell Motorcycle Company, which partnered with Harley-Davidson in 1993 and was purchased by Harley-Davidson in 1998.

Source: www.harley-davidson.com payment calculator schedule.

Although there were some accessory differences between the top-of-the-line touring motorcycles and those of its competitors, suggested retail prices were generally comparable. The prices for the high end of the Harley-Davidson custom product line ranged from being competitive to 50% more than its competitors' custom motorcycles. The custom portion of the Harley-Davidson product line represented its highest unit volumes and continued to command a premium price because of the features, styling, and high resale value associated with Harley-Davidson custom products. The smallest displacement custom motorcycle (the 883cc Sportster®) was directly price competitive with comparable motorcycles available in the market. The surveys of retail purchasers indicated that, historically, over three-quarters of the purchasers of its Sportster model either had previously owned competitive-brand motorcycles or were completely new to the sport of motorcycling or had not participated in the sport for at least five years. Since 1988, research had consistently shown that purchasers of Harley-Davidson motorcycles had a repurchase intent in excess of 90%, and management expected to see sales of its 883cc Sportster model partially translated into sales of its higher-priced products in the normal two- to three-year ownership cycle.

The major Parts and Accessories (P&A) products were replacement parts (Genuine Motor Parts) and mechanical and cosmetic accessories (Genuine Motor Accessories). Worldwide P&A net sales comprised 15.1%, 15.4%, and 14.8% of net sales in the Motorcycles segment in 2001, 2000, and 1999, respectively.

Worldwide net sales of General Merchandise, which included MotorClothes™ apparel and collectibles, comprised 4.9%, 5.2%, and 5.4% of net sales in the Motorcycles segment in 2001, 2000, and 1999, respectively.

Management also provided a variety of services to its dealers and retail customers, including service training schools, customized dealer software packages, delivery of its motorcycles, an owners' club membership, a motorcycle rental program, and a rider training program that was available in the United States through a limited number of authorized dealers.

President and CEO's Comments[17]

President Jeffrey L. Bluestein said in the 2001 *Annual Report*,

> It is a legacy forged by generations of people with a passion for motorcycling, a commitment to honor and build on the past, and the determinations to seek out new opportunities for the future. In 2001, despite the global economic downturn, Harley-Davidson achieved its 16th consecutive year of record revenue and earnings. Consolidated revenue for Harley-Davidson, Inc. was $3.36 billion, a 15.7% increase over 2000, while net income was $437.7 million, a 25.9% increase over the previous year. As a result, diluted earnings per share climbed from $1.13 to $1.43—a 26.4% increase. [see **Exhibits 8** and **9**]

Overview

The venerable motorcycle company was anything but set in its ways.[18] Consider Harley customer Bob Johnson, 52, Vice-President of an Oren, Utah, maker of oil-industry tools. Back in 2000, when Johnson bought his Softail Fat Boy, he had to wait five months and pay $1,000 over suggested retail. Even then, he considered himself lucky: In Texas, Harleys were fetching $4,000 to $5,000 over list. But last December, he snared an Electra Glide Classic for $1,200 below retail and rode away on his tricked-out $16,770 touring machine. "They had inventory, and they were actually discounting," he crowed.[19]

The customer waiting list for new motorcycles had shrunk from as much as two years to a matter of months. Dealer premiums that used to range between $2,000 and $4,000 had disappeared for most models. Dealers were grateful the company was playing the centennial to the hilt. But the question, said a dealer, was "What's going to happen in 2004?" The answer: Harley needed to get ahead of the demographics curve with new customers while somehow keeping faith with its fanatical old ones. If it didn't, the born-to-be-wild company would begin its second century with profit growth that was doomed to be mild.[20]

New Bikes: The Buell and the V-Rod

Harley's new V-Rod was introduced in the Los Angeles Convention Center on July 12, 2001. More than 4,000 packed into the center for the company's long-awaited announcement. The cavernous room went black. The engines roared in the darkness. Spotlights clicked on and followed two glinting new hot rods as they roared onto center stage.[21]

Harley-Davidson deviated from its traditional approach to styling with the introduction of the V-Rod™ motorcycle. The new, liquid-cooled V-Rod, inspired by Harley-Davidson's drag racing heritage, combines the characteristics of a performance motorcycle with the

Exhibit 8 Selected U.S. and World Financial and Sales Information: Harley-Davidson, Inc.

A. Motor Company Revenue, 2001
(Dollar amounts in millions)

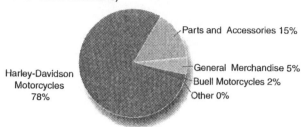

Harley-Davidson Motorcycles	$2,630.1
Parts and Accessories	507.3
General Merchandise	163.9
Buell Motorcycles	61.9
Other	0.2
Total	**$3,363.4**

Parts and Accessories 15%

General Merchandise 5%

Buell Motorcycles 2%

Other 0%

Harley-Davidson Motorcycles 78%

B. Worldwide Motorcycle Shipments
(Units in thousands)

	1997	1998	1999	2000	2001
Exports	36.1	38.8	41.6	45.8	46.7
Total Motorcycle Shipments	132.3	150.5	177.2	204.6	234.5
Export Percentage	27.3%	25.8%	23.5%	22.4%	19.9%

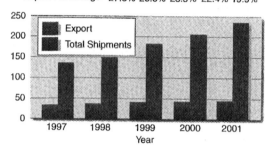

C. Worldwide Parts and Accessories and General Merchandise Revenue
(Dollar amounts in millions)

	1997	1998	1999	2000	2001
General Merchandise	95.1	114.5	132.7	151.4	163.9
Parts and Accessories	241.9	297.1	362.6	447.9	507.3

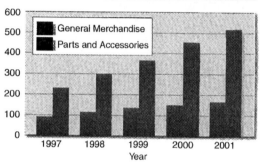

D. Operating Income
(Dollar amounts in millions)

1997	1998	1999	2000	2001
$270.0	$333.6	$415.8	$514.9	$662.5

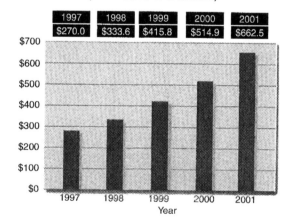

Source: Harley-Davidson, Inc., 2001 Annual Report and 10-K.

Exhibit 9 World Registrations: Harley-Davidson, Inc.

A. North American 651+CC Motorcycle Registrations
(Units in thousands)

	1992	1993	1994	1995	1996	1997	1998	1999	2000	2001
Total industry	112.0	132.8	150.4	163.1	182.7	206.1	246.2	297.9	365.4	422.8
Harley-Davidson	56.0	63.4	69.5	77.0	86.3	99.3	116.1	142.0	163.1	185.6
Harley-Davidson market share	50.0%	47.7%	46.2%	47.2%	47.2%	48.2%	47.2%	47.7%	44.6%	43.9%

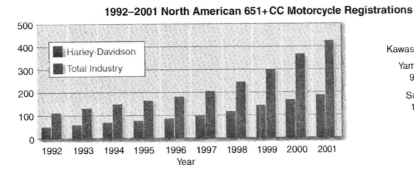

1992–2001 North American 651+CC Motorcycle Registrations

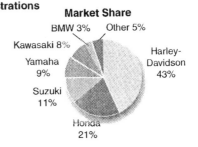

Market Share

B. European 651+CC Motorcycle Registrations
(Units in thousands)

	1992	1993	1994	1995	1996	1997	1998	1999	2000	2001
Total industry	212.1	218.6	201.9	207.2	224.7	250.3	270.2	306.7	293.4	293.6
Harley-Davidson	12.1	13.2	14.4	15.4	15.3	15.1	15.7	17.8	19.9	19.6
Harley-Davidson market share	5.7%	6.1%	7.1%	7.4%	6.8%	6.0%	5.8%	5.8%	6.8%	6.7%

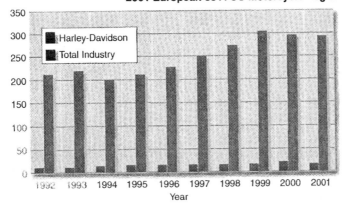

2001 European 651+CC Motorcycle Registrations

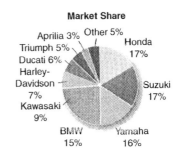

Market Share

Source: Harley-Davidson, Inc., 2001 Annual Report, p. 40.

Exhibit 9 (continued)

C. Asia/Pacific 651+CC Motorcycle Registrations
(Units in thousands)

	1992	1993	1994	1995	1996	1997	1998	1999	2000	2001
Total industry	37.5	35.7	39.1	39.4	37.4	58.9	69.2	63.1	62.7	62.1
Harley-Davidson	6.2	6.7	7.6	7.9	8.2	9.7	10.3	11.6	12.2	12.7
Harley-Davidson market share	16.1%	18.7%	19.4%	20.1%	21.9%	16.4%	14.8%	18.5%	19.5%	20.4%

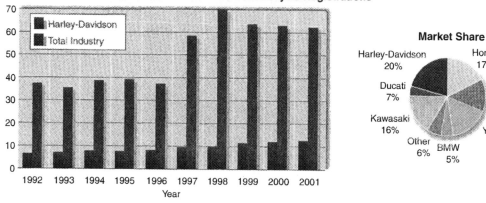

2001 Asia/Pacific 651+CC Motorcycle Registrations

Market Share

Harley-Davidson 20%
Honda 17%
Ducati 7%
Suzuki 13%
Kawasaki 16%
Other 6%
BMW 5%
Yamaha 16%

styling of a custom.[22] Liquid cooling allowed riders to rev a little higher and hotter in each gear, boosting acceleration. This was a giant step for a company so stubbornly conservative that it had made only air-cooled engines for 100 years; its designers just couldn't bear the idea of hanging a radiator on the front of the bike.[23]

The V-Rod was Milwaukee-based Harley-Davison Inc.'s first truly new motorcycle in more than 50 years. A sleek machine in the making for more than 6 years, the V-Rod was designed more for speed and handling, unlike the company's immensely popular touring bikes. The V-Rod was one factor behind Harley-Davidson's strong financial performance.

Harley-Davidson's Chief Executive Officer Jeffrey Bleustein was well aware of the popularity. He was on a local dealer's list, eagerly awaiting the arrival of the V-Rod he had ordered a few months earlier.[24]

As the company ramped up production, premiums on many models disappeared. Chief Financial Officer James L. Ziemer said Harley wanted to "narrow the gap" between supply and demand in order to curb the long-standing—but fast-diminishing—practice of selling bikes at a premium.[25] The new V-Rod's $17,000 price tag had also failed to win younger buyers.[26] To that end, Harley had poured money into developing new, youth-oriented models. The $17,000 Harley V-Rod—a low-slung, high-powered number known formally as a sport performance vehicle and colloquially as a crotch rocket—was meant for hard-charging youths. Harley had also tried to go young with the Buell Firebolt ($10,000), its answer to Japanese sport bikes, and the Buell Blast ($4,400), a starter motorcycle. But Buell, a subsidiary Harley bought in 1998, had captured just 2% of the sport-bike market, and Harley would make only 10,000 V-Rods in 2002. Bleustein insisted that those numbers weren't the point: "These aren't one-shot deals. These are whole new platforms from which many models will proliferate."[27]

At the Detroit Harley-Davidson/Buell dealership in Center Line, Owner Jim Loduca commented: "This is the first time in 10 years that I've actually had product on the floor available, but our sales are also up by 14 percent this year. The company has watched this demand curve very carefully. They are simply riding the wave. They know full well that it would be catastrophic to saturate the market." He was also encouraged by Harley's biggest product departure in recent decades—the V-Rod muscle bike.[28]

Clay Wilwert, whose family has owned a dealership in Dubuque since 1959, said, "But guess what, as they rode it, they loved it. They said, 'Hey, this is really cool that it doesn't shake my hands asleep.' "[29]

Some Harley traditionalists say the V-Rod, styled to compete with super-fast European bikes, strayed too far from the company's all-American roots, which tend to favor heavier cruising machines. Dealerships sold them for several thousand dollars over the $16,995 list price, and they're the talk of *Bike Week*.[30]

Licensing[31]

Harley-Davidson endeavored to create an awareness of the "Harley-Davidson" brand among the nonriding public and provided a wide range of products for enthusiasts by licensing the name "Harley-Davidson" and numerous related trademarks. Harley-Davidson had licensed the production and sale of a broad range of consumer items, including t-shirts, jewelry, small leather goods, toys, and numerous other products (Licensed Products). It had also licensed the use of the name in connection with a cafe located in Las Vegas. Although the majority of licensing activity occurred in the United States, Harley-Davidson continued to expand these activities in international markets.

The licensing activity provided a valuable source of advertising and goodwill. Licensing has also proven to be an effective means for enhancing the corporate image with consumers, and it provided an important tool for policing the unauthorized use of the trademarks, thereby protecting the Harley-Davidson brand and its use. Royalty revenues from licensing, included in motorcycle segment net sales, were approximately $32 million, $31 million, and $26 million during 2001, 2000, and 1999, respectively. While royalty revenues from licensing activities were relatively small, the profitability of this business was relatively high.

Inventory

There was the question about the inventory lag. In the past, there was up to a two-year wait for a new Harley-Davidson bike. Current trends predicted that the lag will drop to nearly zero, potentially leaving inventory on the dealers' floor, a concept new to Harley-Davidson. "In the end, there's more inventory out there," says Dean Gianoukos, JPMorgan leisure-industry analyst. "The question is, is it because of the economy? Because of people waiting to get the 2003's so they're not buying the 2002 models? Or is it that, if you increase production every year by 15%, you're going to eventually hit a wall?" He has a "long-term buy" on the shares, JPMorgan's second-highest rating.[32] (See **Exhibit 10** for Motorcycle Unit Shipments and Unit Sales for 2000 and 2001.)

Critics saw deeper problems for Harley. They said sales had slowed and that Harley had tried to mask the slowdown by pushing dealers to buy bikes they didn't need—known as channel stuffing—and allowing them to borrow to fund the purchases through Harley's financial arm. Dealers may feel the need to take on more inventory because their future allocations of hot models depend on past purchases, analysts said. "There's no question there's a lot more inventory on the dealer floor and the parent company has basically shoved merchandise into the dealer network," said Doug Kass of Seabreeze Partners, a hedge fund, who has sold shares of Harley stock short. The company disagreed.[33]

Marketing and Distribution[34]

"It's hard to put into words," said Joanne Bischmann, Vice President of Marketing for Harley-Davidson. "We knew that kicking-off Harley-Davidson's next 100 years was going to call for something that couldn't easily be described in words, but would be an unforget-

Exhibit 10

A. Motorcycle Unit Shipments and Net Sales: Harley-Davidson, Inc.

	2001	2000	Increase (Decrease)	Percentage Change
Motorcycle unit shipments				
Harley-Davidson motorcycle units	234,461	204,592	29,869	14.6
Buell motorcycle units	9,925	10,189	(264)	(2.6)
Total motorcycle units	244,386	214,781	29,605	13.8
Net Sales ($thousands)				
Harley-Davidson motorcycles	$2,630.1	$2,246.4	$383.7	17.1
Buell motorcycles	61.9	58.1	3.8	6.6
Total motorcycles	2,692.0	2,304.5	387.5	16.8
Motorcycle parts and accessories	507.3	447.9	59.4	13.3
General merchandise	163.9	151.4	12.5	8.2
Other	0.2	2.6	(2.4)	(92.3)
Total motorcycles and related parts	$3,363.4	$2,906.4	$457.0	15.7

B. 2001 Quarterly Motorcycle Shipments: Harley-Davidson, Inc.

	Q1	Q2	Q3	Q4	2001
Shipping days	60	64	59	62	245
Harley-Davidson units					
Sportster	11,455	12,849	12,819	13,691	50,814
Custom	28,149	30,202	27,632	32,320	118,303
Touring	14,550	17,110	16,160	17,524	65,344
Total	54,154	60,161	56,611	63,535	234,461
Domestic	40,210	48,018	45,071	53,616	186,915
International	13,944	12,143	11,540	9,919	47,546
Total	54,154	60,161	56,611	63,535	234,461
Buell units					
Buell (excluding Blast)	1,593	1,757	1,878	1,208	6,436
Buell Blast	854	711	961	963	3,489
Total	2,447	2,468	2,839	2,171	9,925

Source: Harley-Davidson, Inc., 2001 Annual Report, p. 42.

table Harley-Davidson experience for anyone who participated. We think the Open Road Tour fits the bill."[35]

Marketing efforts are divided among dealer promotions, customer events, magazine and direct-mail advertising, public relations, cooperative programs with Harley-Davidson/Buell dealers, and, beginning in 2002, television advertising. In 1999, the Harley-Davidson began a five-year strategic alliance with the Ford Motor Company that brought together resources to focus on a series of technical and marketing ventures. Harley-Davidson also sponsored racing activities and special promotional events and participated in all the major motorcycle consumer shows and rallies.

The Harley Owners Group®, or "H.O.G.®", had approximately 660,000 members worldwide in 2002 and was the industry's largest company-sponsored motorcycle enthusiast organization. Harley-Davidson formed this riders' club in 1983, in an effort to encourage Harley-Davidson owners to become more actively involved in the sport of motorcycling. The Buell Riders Adventure Group, or "BRAG®", was formed in recent years and had grown to approximately 10,000 members. BRAG sponsored events, including national rallies and rides, across the United States for Buell motorcycle enthusiasts.

Total expenditures on worldwide marketing, selling, and advertising were approximately $203.1 million, $189.8 million, and $164.3 million during 2001, 2000, and 1999, respectively.

E-commerce[36]

Harley-Davidson's e-commerce capability had its first full year of operation in 2001. Its model was unique in the industry in that, while the online catalog was viewed from the Harley-Davidson web site, orders were actually distributed to the participating authorized Harley-Davidson dealer that the customer selected. In turn, the dealer filled the order and handled any after-sale services that the customer may require. In addition to purchasing, customers actively browsed the site, created and shared product wish lists, and utilized the dealer locator.

International Sales[37]

International sales were approximately $597 million, $585 million, and $537 million, accounting for approximately 18%, 20%, and 22% of net sales of the Motorcycles segment, during 2001, 2000, and 1999, respectively. In 2001, Japan, Canada, and Germany, in that order, represented the largest international markets and together accounted for approximately 56% of international sales. Harley-Davidson ended 2001 with a 6.7% share of the European heavyweight (651cc+) market and a 20.4% share of the Asia-Pacific (Japan and Australia) heavyweight (651cc+) market.

Distribution[38]

The basic channel of distribution in the United States for its motorcycles and related products consisted of approximately 633 independently owned full-service Harley-Davidson dealerships to which Harley-Davidson sold directly. This included 412 combined Harley-Davidson and Buell dealerships. There are no Buell-only dealerships. With respect to sales of new motorcycles, approximately 82% of the U.S. dealerships sold Harley-Davidson motorcycles exclusively. All dealerships stocked and sold genuine replacement parts, accessories, and MotorClothes™ apparel and collectibles, and performed service for the Harley-Davidson motorcycles.

The company also sold a smaller portion of its parts and accessories and general merchandise through "non-traditional" retail outlets. The non-traditional outlets, which are extensions of the main dealership, consisted of Secondary Retail Locations (SRLs), Alternate Retail Outlets (AROs), and Seasonal Retail Outlets (SROs). SRLs, also known as Harley Shops, were satellites of the main dealership and were developed to meet the service needs of riding customers. Harley Shops also provide replacement parts and accessories and MotorClothes apparel and collectibles and were authorized to sell new motorcycles. AROs were located primarily in high-traffic areas such as malls, airports, or popular vacation destinations and focus on selling the MotorClothes apparel and collectibles and Licensed

Products. SROs were located in similar high traffic areas, but operated on a seasonal basis out of temporary locations such as vendor kiosks. AROs and SROs were not authorized to sell new motorcycles. Presently, there were approximately 65 SRLs, 50 AROs, and under 20 SROs located in the United States.

Retail Customer and Dealer Financing

Management believed Harley-Davidson Financial Services (HDFS) and other financial services companies provided adequate retail and wholesale financing to Harley-Davidson's domestic and Canadian dealers and customers. In Europe, HDFS provided wholesale financing to dealers through a joint venture agreement with Transamerica Distribution Finance Corporation. HDFS had exercised its option to terminate the joint venture effective August 2002 and began serving the wholesale financing needs of Harley-Davidson's European dealers at that time.[39]

Harley-Davidson Customer Base

" 'Fads don't have 100th birthdays,' boasts CEO Jeffrey Bleustein."[40]

Harley-Davidson's customers were not what some people expected. They expected rough-and-tumble riders and did not expect that a good proportion of Harley-Davidson riders were white-collar workers and executives who take weekend relaxation on their bikes. Selected quotes from customers follow:

"It's about an image—freedom of the road, hop on your bike and go, independent living, the loosing of the chains," said Dave Sarnowski, a teacher and Harley rider from La Farge, Wisconsin.[41]

"The Harley people I know go to church, have jobs, shop at the mall, just like everyone else," said Angie Robison, 68, of Daytona Beach, who helps her husband Joe run a motorcycle repair shop and Harley memorabilia/accessories store. "I can wear my silks over here and my leathers over there, and I'm still the same person."[42]

"I worked at a computer all day for the city, and for me it's pure relaxation. I wear the leathers because they're protective."[43]

Impact of President Bush's Steel Tariffs

Steel tariffs put in place in 2002 posed a threat to Harley-Davidson and other users of steel. Sanctions were to "induce that party that would be subject to them to bring itself in line" with international trade rules, Spokesman Anthony Gooch said. "The best way to avoid them is to compensate," he said, adding that the tariffs would take effect in May 2002. The 15-nation EU was protesting U.S. tariffs of as much as 30% on some steel imports, which it said broke World Trade Organization rules.[44] Domestic steel buyers eager to circumvent the three-year tariffs were sending lobbyists to make their case to the President's administration. Combine that with threats from Europe to retaliate against American steel and other goods—from Florida oranges to Harley-Davidson motorcycles—and the result could be loopholes big enough to drive a flatbed of cold-rolled sheet metal through.[45]

Recession Resistance?

Harley had seen tremendous sales and stock price growth in spite of the recession. However, some analysts questioned whether Harley-Davidson would be hit by the deep recession the nation is facing, albeit later than most U.S. companies. "For years, Harley-Davidson and the analysts that cover the company have reported that the business is recession-resistant. Given the recent changes in the economic and political landscape, this assertion is being put to the test, and from what we can tell, is ringing true. . . . Among 17 Wall Street analysts tracked by Bloomberg who cover the stock, 16 rate it *buy* and one *hold*."[46] But if the recession persists, motorcycles, the critics say, are easily deferred purchases. Harley's Ziemer said, "We always said we feel we are recession-resistant, not recession-proof."[47]

Competition[48]

The heavyweight (651cc+) motorcycle market was highly competitive. Major competitors were based outside the United States and generally had more financial and marketing resources. They also had larger worldwide sales volumes and were more diversified. In addition to these larger, established competitors, a growing segment of competition had emerged in the United States. The new U.S. competitors generally offered heavyweight motorcycles with traditional styling that competed directly with many of Harley-Davidson's products. These competitors currently had production and sales volumes that were lower than Harley-Davidson's and did not hold significant market share (see **Exhibits 11, 12**, and **13**.)

Exhibit 11 Worldwide Heavyweight Motorcycle Registration Data (Engine Displacement of 651+cc)
(Units in thousands)

	2001 % Share	2001 Units	2000 % Share	2000 Units	1999 % Share	1999 Units
North America[1]						
Harley-Davidson new registrations	43.9%	185.6	44.6%	163.1	47.7%	142.1
Buell new registrations	0.6%	2.7	1.2%	4.3	1.3%	4.0
Total company registrations	44.5%	188.3	45.8%	167.4	49.0%	146.1
Total market new registrations		422.8		365.4		297.9
Europe[2]						
Harley-Davidson new registrations	6.7%	19.6	6.8%	19.9	5.8%	17.8
Buell new registrations	0.7%	2.2	0.6%	1.9	1.7%	2.1
Total company registrations	7.4%	21.8	7.4%	21.8	7.5%	19.9
Total market new registrations		293.6		293.4		306.7
Japan/Australia[3]						
Harley-Davidson new registrations	20.4%	12.7	19.5%	12.2	2.5%	11.6
Buell new registrations	1.0%	0.7	0.7%	0.7	0.7%	0.7
Total company registrations	21.4%	13.4	20.5%	12.9	3.6%	12.3
Total market new registrations		62.1		62.7		63.1
Total						
Harley-Davidson new registrations	28.0%	217.9	27.1%	195.2	25.7%	171.5
Buell new registrations	0.7%	5.6	0.9%	6.9	1.0%	6.8
Total company registrations	28.7%	223.5	28.0%	202.1	26.7%	178.3
Total market new registrations		778.5		721.5		667.7

Notes:
1. Includes the United States and Canada. Data provided by the Motorcycle Industry Council (MIC). MIC revised its data for 2000.
2. Includes Austria, Belgium, France, Germany, Italy, the Netherlands, Spain, Switzerland, and the United Kingdom. Data provided by Giral S.A.
3. Data provided by JAMA and ABS.

Source: Harley-Davidson, Inc., Form 10-K, p. 10.

Exhibit 12
Market Share of U.S. Heavyweight Motorcycles (Engine Displacement of 651+cc)[1]

	2001	2000	1999	1998
New U.S. registrations (thousands of units)				
Total market new registrations	394.3	340.0	275.6	227.1
Harley-Davidson new registrations	177.4	155.1	134.5	109.1
Buell new registrations	2.6	4.2	3.9	3.2
Total company new registrations	180.0	159.3	138.4	112.3
Percentage market share				
Harley-Davidson motorcycles	45.0%	45.6%	48.8%	48.1%
Buell motorcycles	0.7	1.2	1.4	1.4
Total company	45.7	46.8	50.2	49.5
Honda	20.5	18.5	16.4	20.3
Suzuki	10.8	9.3	9.4	10.0
Kawasaki	8.0	9.0	10.3	10.1
Yamaha	7.9	8.4	7.0	4.2
Other	7.1	8.0	6.7	5.9
Total	100.0%	100.0%	100.0%	100.0%

Note:

1. Motorcycle registration and market share information has been derived from data published by the Motorcycle Industry Council (MIC). MIC revised its data for 1997 and 2000, and this table reflects the revised data.

Source: Harley-Davidson, Inc., Form 10-K, p. 9.

Competition in the heavyweight motorcycle market was based on a number of factors, including price, quality, reliability, styling, product features, customer preference, and warranties. Harley-Davidson emphasized quality, reliability, and styling in its products and offered a one-year warranty for its motorcycles. It regards its support of the motorcycling lifestyle in the form of events, rides, rallies, H.O.G.®, and its financing through HDFS, as a competitive advantage. In general, resale prices for used Harley-Davidson motorcycles, as a percentage of prices when new, are significantly higher than resale prices for used motorcycles of competitors.

Domestically, Harley-Davidson competed most heavily in the touring and custom segments of the heavyweight motorcycle market, which together accounted for 79%, 78%, and 79% of total heavyweight retail unit sales in the United States during 2001, 2000, and 1999, respectively. The custom and touring motorcycles were generally the most expensive vehicles in the market and the most profitable. During 2001, the heavyweight segment including standard, performance, touring, and custom motorcycles represented approximately 50% of the total U.S. motorcycle market (on- and off-highway motorcycles and scooters) in terms of new units registered.

For the last 14 years, Harley-Davidson has led the industry in domestic (U.S.) unit sales of heavyweight motorcycles. The market share in the heavyweight market was 45.7% in 2001, compared to 46.8% in 2000. The market share decreased slightly in 2001 as a result of the ongoing capacity constraints, however, this share is still significantly greater than the largest competitor in the domestic market, which ended 2001 with a 20.5% market share.

Rider Training and Safety

"Increasingly, the motorcycle riders who are getting killed are in their 40s, 50s, and 60s," said Susan Ferguson, vice president for research at the Insurance Institute for Highway Safety, which did the study.[49] Riders over 40 accounted for 40% of all fatalities in 2000, up

Exhibit 13 Motorcycle Industry Registration Statistics (Units): Harley-Davidson Inc.

U.S. and Canada	2001	2000	1999	1998	1997
651+cc volume	422,787	365,399	297,900	246,214	205,407
H-D volume	185,571	163,136	142,042	116,110	99,298
Buell volume	2,695	4,306	4,022	3,333	1,912
HDI total volume	188,266	167,442	146,064	119,443	101,210
% change 651+cc volume	15.7%	22.7%	21.0%	19.9%	15.1%
% change HDI total volume	12.4%	14.6%	22.3%	18.0%	16.6%
HDI market share	44.5%	45.8%	49.0%	48.5%	49.3%

Europe	2001	2000	1999	1998	1997
651+cc volume	293,554	293,424	306,748	270,212	250,293
H-D volume	19,563	19,870	17,836	15,650	15,286
Buell volume	2,171	1,912	2,079	1,600	771
HDI total volume	21,734	21,782	19,915	17,250	16,057
% change 651+cc volume	0.4%	−4.3%	13.5%	8.0%	11.4%
% change HDI total volume	−0.2%	9.4%	15.4%	7.4%	4.6%
HDI market share	7.4%	7.4%	6.5%	6.4%	6.4%

Japan and Australia	2001	2000	1999	1998	1997
651+cc volume	62,069	62,667	63,097	69,222	58,880
H-D volume	12,662	12,213	11,642	10,273	9,686
Buell volume	651	658	701	532	426
HDI total volume	13,313	12,871	12,343	10,805	10,112
% change 651+cc volume	−0.9%	−0.7%	−8.8%	17.6%	57.4%
% change HDI total volume	3.4%	4.3%	14.2%	6.9%	20.8%
HDI market share	21.4%	20.5%	19.6%	15.6%	17.2%

Total	2001	2000	1999	1998	1997
651+cc volume	778,410	721,490	667,694	585,648	514,580
H-D volume	217,796	195,219	171,520	142,033	124,270
Buell volume	5,517	6,876	6,802	5,465	3,109
HDI total volume	223,313	202,095	178,322	147,498	127,379
% change 651+cc volume	7.9%	8.1%	14.0%	13.8%	16.8%
% change HDI total volume	10.5%	13.3%	20.9%	15.8%	15.3%
HDI market share	28.7%	28.0%	26.7%	25.2%	24.8%

Notes:
1. Data provided by R.L. Polk & Company (1991–1996), Motorcycle Industry Council (1997–1998), Motorcycle and Moped Industry Council, Giral S.A., Australian Bureau of Statistics, and Japan Automobile Manufacturers Association.
2. Total HDI volume includes Portugal. Total 651+cc volume does not include Portugal.
3. These are actual registrations of motorcycles. The Harley-Davidson, Inc., registrations are typically lower than actual sales due to the timing differences.

Source: www.harley-davidson.com.

from 14% in 1990. Part of the reason for the dramatic increase in older bikers' deaths is the growing number of men and women over 40 buying motorcycles, IIHS says.

In 2000, Harley-Davidson launched an instruction program called Rider's Edge, run through dealers. Rookies paid $225 or so for a 25-hour class. The program had grown to 42 dealers in 23 states and graduated 3,800 riders in 2002. Forty-five percent were women, 86%

bought something, and 25% bought a Harley-Davidson or a Buell within three months. "Going into a Harley dealership can be intimidating," said Lara Lee, who ran the program. "We give them a home base and get them riding."[50]

Motorcycle Manufacturing[51]

The ongoing manufacturing strategy was designed to increase capacity, improve product quality, reduce costs, and increase flexibility to respond to changes in the marketplace. Harley-Davidson incorporated manufacturing techniques focused on the continuous improvement of its operations designed to control costs and maintain quality. These techniques, which included employee involvement, just-in-time inventory principles, partnering agreements with the local unions, high-performance work organizations, and statistical process control, were designed to improve product quality, productivity, and asset utilization in the production of Harley-Davidson motorcycles.

The use of just-in-time inventory principles allowed it to minimize its inventories of raw materials and work in process, as well as scrap and rework costs. This system also allowed quicker reaction to engineering design changes, quality improvements, and market demands. Harley-Davidson has trained the majority of its manufacturing employees in problem-solving and statistical methods.

The company's management believed the worldwide heavyweight (651cc+) market would continue to grow and planned to continue to increase its Harley-Davidson motorcycle production to have the capacity to sustain its growth for units shipped. During 2001, Harley-Davidson began work on plans for capacity expansion that would take place at two of the existing manufacturing facilities. These plans included a 350,000-square-foot expansion at the York, Pennsylvania, assembly facility and a 60,000-square-foot expansion at the Tomahawk, Wisconsin, facility. The company began its investment in these plans during 2001 and continued to invest capital related to these plans during 2002 and 2003. Based on the results achieved in 2001, the 2002 annual production target increased to 258,000 Harley-Davidson units.

The manufacturing techniques employed at Buell, BMC, which were similar to those of the rest of the company, were designed to provide cost control and quality products in a lower-volume environment. Its product development staff was located in close proximity to the production facilities to ensure that new product and model-year change activities were coordinated prior to and during launch. The manufacturing techniques employed included employee involvement with an emphasis on a highly flexible and participative workforce. The new powertrain was produced at the manufacturing facility in Kansas City, Missouri, through its joint venture with Porsche AG of Stuttgart, Germany, formed in 1997.

Finally, Harley-Davidson operated an assembly operation in Brazil that imported U.S.-made components and subassemblies for final assembly in Brazil. Assembling imported U.S.-made components increased the availability of Harley-Davidson motorcycles in Brazil and reduced duties and taxes, making them more affordable to a larger group of Brazilian customers. The facility, which had been operational since mid-1999, assembled select motorcycle models for the Brazilian market, with 2002 volumes less than 1,000 units per year.

Raw Material and Purchase Components[52]

Harley-Davidson has worked to establish long-term, mutually beneficial relationships with its suppliers. Through these relationships, Harley-Davidson gained access to technical and commercial resources for application directly to product design, development, and manufacturing initiatives. This strategy was resulting in improved product technical integrity, application of new features and innovations, reduced lead times for product development, and smoother/faster manufacturing ramp-up of new vehicle introductions.

Harley-Davidson purchased all its raw materials, principally steel and aluminum castings, forgings, sheets and bars, and certain motorcycle components, including carburetors, batteries, tires, seats, electrical components, and instruments. It hasn't anticipated significant difficulties in obtaining raw materials or components for which it relied on a limited source of supply.

As part of its strategic plan for sustainable growth, the Harley-Davidson Motor Company announced plans to move assembly of its Dyna Glide family of motorcycles to its facility in Kansas City, Missouri. All Dyna Glide models were currently assembled in York, Pennsylvania. "In our continuing efforts to narrow the gap between supply and demand, Harley-Davidson will relocate the Dyna line from York to Kansas City, Missouri," noted Motor Company President and Chief Operating Officer, Jim McCaslin. "The move is being made at this time to enable Harley-Davidson to more fully utilize these assets and increase capacity over time," said McCaslin. The Dyna Glide family was one of five families of motorcycles produced by Harley-Davidson: Sportster, Softail, Dyna, Touring, and the new VRSC family. Dyna models represented approximately 15% of their total production.[53]

Ultimately, Harley hoped to develop its supplier web portal, *www.H-dsn.com*. Launched in July 2000, it had primarily been an accounts-payable network. Suppliers could log on and review their accounts and do their own reconciliation. Harley's payables department reported that since the portal was launched, it had seen a 90% drop in supplier phone calls from users. In 2001, 83 suppliers were using the portal. They clicked in to review shipping specifications or access forms for product testing. In 2002, the site posted 12 months' worth of forecasted volumes and schedules for all suppliers. Also, H-dsn.com was expected to gain transaction capabilities. This was especially helpful for smaller suppliers that had been unable to hook up to Harley's existing EDI system. "Our goal," said Cotteleer, "is to have the supplier doing their own replenishing, using the site. They can see what our consumption rates are, rather than trying to project based on historical information."[54]

Research and Development[55]

Harley-Davidson viewed research and development as significant in its ability to lead the market definition of touring and custom motorcycling and to develop products for the performance segment. In recent years, it has established a 218,000-square-foot Motor Company Product Development Center (PDC), which is currently in the process of receiving a 165,000-square-foot addition. It also owned and operated a 43,000-square-foot Buell research and development facility. The innovative design of the PDC brought together employees from styling, purchasing, and manufacturing with regulatory professionals and supplier representatives to create a concurrent product and process development methodology. They incurred research and development expenses of approximately $80.7 million, $75.8 million, and $70.3 million during 2001, 2000, and 1999, respectively.

Patents and Trademarks[56]

Harley-Davidson owned patents that relate to its motorcycles and related products and processes for their production. It had increased its efforts to patent its technology and certain motorcycle-related designs and to enforce those patents. Management saw such actions as important as the money moved forward with new products, designs, and technologies.

Trademarks were important to Harley-Davidson's motorcycle business and licensing activities. It had a vigorous global program of trademark registration and enforcement to strengthen the value of the trademarks associated with its products and services, prevent the unauthorized use of those trademarks, and enhance its image and customer goodwill. Management believed the Harley-Davidson trademark and its Bar and Shield trademark were each highly recognizable by the public and were very valuable assets. The Buell trademark is well known in performance motorcycle circles, as is the associated Pegasus logo. Management was making efforts to ensure that each of these brands would become better known as the Buell business expanded. Additionally, the company uses numerous other trademarks, trade names, and logos, which are registered both in the United States and abroad. The following were among the trademarks of H-D Michigan, Inc.: Harley-Davidson, H-D, Harley, the Bar & Shield logo, MotorClothes, the MotorClothes logo, Rider's Edge, Harley Owners Group, H.O.G., the H.O.G. logo, Softail, Sportster, and V-Rod. The Harley-Davidson trademark had been used since 1903 and the Bar and Shield trademark since 1910. The following are among the trademarks of Buell Motorcycle Company: Buell, the Pegasus logo, and BRAG. The Buell trademark had been used since 1984.

Seasonality[57]

In general, the Motor Company had not experienced significant seasonal fluctuations in its sales. This had been primarily the result of a strong demand for the Harley-Davidson motorcycles and related products, as well as the availability of floor plan financing arrangements for its North American and European independent dealers. Floor plan financing allowed dealers to build their inventory levels in anticipation of the spring and summer selling seasons.

Regulations[58]

Federal, state, and local authorities had various environmental control requirements relating to air, water, and noise pollution that affect the business and operations. Harley-Davidson endeavored to ensure that its facilities and products complied with all applicable environmental regulations and standards.

The motorcycles were subject to certification by the U.S. Environmental Protection Agency (EPA) for compliance with applicable emissions and noise standards and by the State of California Air Resources Board (CARB) with respect to CARB's more stringent emissions standards. Motorcycles sold in California were also subject to certain tailpipe and evaporative emissions standards that were unique to California. Its motorcycle products had been certified to comply fully with all such applicable standards. CARB's motorcycle emissions standards would become more stringent in model years 2004 and 2008, respectively. Additionally, the European Union was considering making its motorcycle emissions standards more stringent and was considering making its motorcycle noise standards more stringent, which already were more stringent than those of the EPA. Similarly, motorcycle noise and emissions levels were becoming more stringent in Japan, as well as in certain emerging markets. Consequently, Harley-Davidson would continue to incur some level of research and development and production costs related to motorcycle emissions and noise in the foreseeable future.

Harley-Davidson, as a manufacturer of motorcycle products, was subject to the National Traffic and Motor Vehicle Safety Act, which were administered by the National Highway Traffic Safety Administration (NHTSA). It had certified to NHTSA that its motorcycle products complied fully with all applicable federal motor vehicle safety standards and related regulations. Harley-Davidson has, from time to time, initiated certain voluntary recalls. During the last three years, it initiated 24 voluntary recalls at a total cost of approximately $16.5 million. Management maintained reserves for all estimated costs associated with recalls in the period that the recalls were announced.

Employees[59]

As of December 31, 2001, the Motorcycles segment had approximately 8,100 employees. Unionized employees at the motorcycle manufacturing and distribution facilities in Wauwatosa, Menomonee Falls, Franklin, and Tomahawk, Wisconsin, and Kansas City, Missouri, were represented principally by the Paper Allied–Industrial Chemical and Energy Workers International Union (PACE) of the AFL-CIO, as well as the International Association of Machinist and Aerospace Workers (IAM). Production workers at the motorcycle manufacturing facility in York, Pennsylvania, were represented principally by IAM. The collective bargaining agreement with the Wisconsin-PACE and IAM will expire on March 31, 2008, the collective bargaining agreement with the Kansas City-PACE and IAM will expire on August 1, 2007, and the collective bargaining agreement with the Pennsylvania-IAM will expire on February 2, 2007.

Approximately 50% of Harley-Davidson's 8,000 employees rode Harley-Davidsons. All employees, including Bleustein, went through dealers to get their bikes. This way, the employees saw the customer experience firsthand.

Commitments and Contingencies[60]

Harley-Davidson was subject to lawsuits and other claims related to environmental, product, and other matters. In determining required reserves related to these items, management and legal counsel analyzed each individual case and considered the likelihood of adverse judgments or outcomes, as well as the potential range of probable loss. The required reserves were monitored on an ongoing basis and were updated based on new developments or new information in each matter.

Lawsuits[61]

In January 2001, Harley-Davidson, on its own initiative, notified each owner of 1999 and early-2000 model year Harley-Davidson motorcycles equipped with Twin Cam 88 and Twin Cam 88B engines that Harley-Davidson was extending the warranty for a rear cam bearing to 5 years or 50,000 miles. Subsequently, on June 28, 2001, a putative nationwide class action suit was filed against Harley-Davidson in state court in Milwaukee County, Wisconsin; it was amended by a complaint filed September 28, 2001. The complaint alleged that this cam bearing was defective and asserted various legal theories. The complaint sought unspecified compensatory and punitive damages for affected owners, an order compelling Harley-Davidson to repair the engines, and other relief. Management believed that the warranty extension it announced in January 2001 adequately addressed the condition for affected owners. Management had established reserves for this extended warranty. Harley-Davidson filed a motion to dismiss the amended complaint, and on February 27, 2002, the motion was granted by the court, and the amended complaint was dismissed in its entirety.

In addition, Harley-Davidson was involved with government agencies in various environmental matters, including a matter involving soil and groundwater contamination at its York, Pennsylvania, facility (the Facility). The Facility had formerly been used by the U.S. Navy and AMF (the predecessor corporation of Minstar). Harley-Davidson purchased the Facility from AMF in 1981. Although management was not certain as to the extent of the environmental contamination at the Facility, it had been working with the Pennsylvania Department of Environmental Protection in undertaking certain investigation and remediation activities, including a sitewide remedial investigation/feasibility study. In January 1995, management entered into a settlement agreement (the Agreement) with the Navy. The Agreement called for the Navy and Harley-Davidson to contribute amounts into a trust equal to 53% and 47%, respectively, of future costs associated with investigation and remediation activities at the Facility (response costs). The trust administered the payment of the response costs at the Facility as covered by the Agreement. Recently, the U.S. Environmental Protection Agency (EPA) advised the management that it considered some of the Harley-Davidson's remediation activities at the Facility to be subject to the EPA's corrective action programs and had offered Harley-Davidson the option of addressing corrective action under a facility-led agreement. The objectives and procedures for facility-led corrective action were consistent with the investigation and remediation already conducted under the agreement with the Navy. Although substantial uncertainty existed concerning the nature and scope of the environmental remediation that will ultimately be required at the Facility, based on preliminary information currently available to management and taking into account Harley-Davidson's agreement with the Navy, the management estimated that it will incur approximately $5 million of future response costs at the Facility. The company had established reserves for this amount. Management's estimate of future response costs was based on reports of independent environmental consultants retained by the company, the actual costs incurred to date, and the estimated costs to complete the necessary investigation and remediation activities. Response costs were expected to be incurred over a period of several years, ending in 2009.

Properties[62]

The following is a summary of the principal operating properties of Harley-Davidson, as of March 15, 2002. Seven facilities performed manufacturing operations: Wauwatosa and Menomonee Falls, Wisconsin, suburbs of Milwaukee (motorcycle powertrain production); Tomahawk, Wisconsin (fiberglass parts production and painting); York, Pennsylvania (motorcycle parts fabrication, painting, and big-twin assembly); Kansas City, Missouri (Sportster assembly); East Troy, Wisconsin (Buell motorcycles assembly); and Manaus, Brazil (assembly of select models for the Brazilian market) (see **Exhibit 14**).

Financial Services Segment[63]

The Financial Services segment consisted of Harley-Davidson's wholly owned subsidiary, Harley-Davidson Financial Services, Inc. (HDFS). HDFS was engaged in the business of financing and servicing wholesale inventory receivables, consumer retail installment sales contracts (primarily motorcycles and noncommercial aircraft). In addition, HDFS was an agency for certain unaffiliated insurance carriers providing property/casualty insurance and extended service contracts to motorcycle owners. HDFS conducts business in the United States, Canada, and Europe. The Financial Services segment had four office facilities: Chicago, Illinois (corporate headquarters); Carson City, Nevada, and Reno, Nevada (retail operations); and Plano, Texas (wholesale operations).

Harley-Davidson and Buell[64]

HDFS, operating under the trade name Harley-Davidson Credit and Insurance, provided wholesale financial services to Harley-Davidson and Buell dealers and retail financing to consumers. Wholesale financial services included floorplan and open account financing of motorcycles and motorcycle parts and accessories, real estate loans, computer loans, showroom remodeling loans, and the brokerage of a range of commercial insurance products. HDFS offered wholesale financial services to all Harley-Davidson dealers in the United States and Canada, and during 2001, approximately 96% of such dealers utilized those services. European

**Exhibit 14
Principal
Operating
Facilities: Harley-
Davidson, Inc.**

Type of Facility	Location	Approximate Square Feet	Status
Corporate office	Milwaukee, WI	523,000	Owned
Product development center	Wauwatosa, WI	218,000	Owned
Manufacturing	Wauwatosa, WI	422,000	Owned
Manufacturing	Menomonee Falls, WI	479,000	Owned
Manufacturing	Tomahawk, WI	179,000	Owned
Manufacturing	York, PA	1,033,000	Owned
Manufacturing	Kansas City, MO	330,000	Owned
Materials velocity center	Kansas City, MO	87,000	Lease expiring 2004
Manufacturing	East Troy, WI	40,000	Lease expiring 2003
Product development and office	East Troy, WI	48,000	Lease expiring 2003
Distribution center	Franklin, WI	250,000	Owned
Distribution center	York, PA	86,000	Lease expiring 2006
Motorcycle testing	Talladega, AL	24,000	Lease expiring 2004
Office	Ann Arbor, MI	3,000	Lease expiring 2004
Office	Morfelden-Waldorf, Germany	22,000	Lease expiring 2005
Office	Brackley, England	3,000	Lease expiring 2005
Warehouse	Brackley, England	1,000	Lease expiring 2005
Office	Windsor, England	10,000	Owned
Office	Liederdorp, The Netherlands	8,000	Lease expiring 2006
Office	Paris, France	6,000	Lease expiring 2004
Office	Arese, Italy	9,000	Lease expiring 2006
Warehouse	Arese, Italy	8,000	Lease expiring 2006
Office	Tokyo, Japan	14,000	Lease expiring 2004
Warehouse	Yokohama, Japan	15,000	Lease expiring 2004
Manufacturing and office	Manaus, Brazil	30,000	Lease expiring 2003

Source: Harley-Davidson, Inc., Form 10-K, p. 15.

dealers were currently serviced through a joint venture with another finance company. In August 2002, HDFS began serving the wholesale financing needs of Harley-Davidson's European dealers, as HDFS has exercised its option to terminate the joint venture effective August 2002. The wholesale finance operations of HDFS were located in Plano, Texas.

Retail financial services included installment lending for new and used Harley-Davidson and Buell motorcycles and the brokerage of a range of motorcycle insurance policies and extended service warranty agreements. HDFS acted as an insurance agent and did not assume underwriting risk with regard to insurance policies and extended service warranty agreements. Prior to the sale of Harley-Davidson Chrome Visa Card business in March 2000, HDFS financed and serviced revolving charge receivables. HDFS's retail financial services were available through virtually all Harley-Davidson and Buell dealers in the United States and Canada. HDFS's retail finance operations were located in Carson City, Nevada, and Reno, Nevada.

Other Manufacturers[66]

HDFS' retail and wholesale aircraft financial service programs were similar to the programs for Harley-Davidson and Buell dealers and consumers described above. During 1999, HDFS ceased offering retail financial services to consumers of marine and recreational vehicles.

Funding[66]

HDFS has been financed by operating cash flow, advances and loans from Harley-Davidson, asset-backed securitizations, commercial paper, revolving credit facilities, senior subordinated debt, and redeemable preferred stock.

Competition[67]

The ability to offer a package of wholesale and retail financial services was a significant competitive advantage of HDFS. Competitors competed for business based largely on price and, to a lesser extent, service. HDFS competed based on convenience, service, strong dealer relations, industry experience, terms, and price.

During 2001, HDFS financed 31% of new Harley-Davidson motorcycles retailed in the United States, as compared to 21% in 2000. HDFS faced minimal national competition for its retail motorcycle financing business. Competitors were primarily banks and other financial institutions that provided retail financing to local or regional markets. Competition to provide retail financial services to aircraft consumers include aircraft manufacturers' captive finance companies, such as Cessna Finance Corp., Debis Financial Services, and other financial entities, including MBNA and First Source Bank. Credit unions, banks, other financial institutions, and insurance agencies also competed for retail financial services business in segmented markets.

HDFS faced little national competition for Harley-Davidson's wholesale motorcycle financing business. Competitors were primarily regional and local banks and other financial institutions that provide wholesale financing to Harley-Davidson and Buell dealers in their local markets. Competition to provide wholesale financial services to aircraft dealers included aircraft manufacturers' captive finance companies.

Trademarks

HDFS used several trademarks and trade names licensed from Harley-Davidson. In addition to the above-mentioned licenses, HDFS had a registered trademark for the "Eaglemark and Design logo" used in aircraft financing programs.

Seasonality[68]

In the northern United States and Canada, motorcycles were primarily used during warmer months, generally March through August. Accordingly, HDFS experienced significant seasonal variations. Retail customers typically did not buy motorcycles until they can ride them. From mid-March through August, retail financing volume increased and wholesale financing volume decreased as dealers depleted their inventories. From September through mid-March, there was a decrease in retail financing volume, while dealer inventories build and turn over more slowly, substantially increasing wholesale financing volume.

Employees

At the end of 2001, the Financial Services segment had approximately 550 employees, none of which were unionized.

Regulation[69]

The operations of HDFS were subject, in certain instances, to supervision and regulation by state, federal, and various foreign governmental authorities and may be subject to various laws and judicial and administrative decisions imposing various requirements and restrictions, which among other things (a) regulated credit-granting activities, including establishing licensing requirements, if any, in applicable jurisdictions; (b) established maximum interest rates, finance charges, and other charges; (c) regulated customers' insurance coverages; (d) required disclosure to customers; (e) governed secured transactions; (f) set collection, foreclosure, repossession, and claims handling procedures and other trade practices; (g) prohibited discrimination in the extension of credit and administration of loans; and (h) regulated the use and reporting of information related to a borrower's credit experience.

A subsidiary of HDFS, Eaglemark Savings Bank, formerly known as Eaglemark Bank, N.A., was a Nevada state bank. Therefore, the activities of this subsidiary were restricted by federal and State of Nevada banking laws and were subject to examination by federal and state examiners.

Corporate Financial and Stock Price Performance

At a time when auto makers were whacking at their profit margins with 0% financing, Harley sold every bike it made, and dealers often charged $2,000 to $4,000 above the sticker price.[70] This was fueled mainly by continued strong demand for most of Harley's bikes, including the Sportster (entry-level motorcycle), Custom (carried the highest margins), Touring (highest selling price, although also the costliest to manufacture), and the Buell lines. Further, management's focus on trimming costs, also with increased sales of parts and accessories, resulted in an improved operating margin for the quarter and the full year. The outlook was quite promising for Harley at the time. (**Exhibits 15, 16, 17,** and **18** provide the company's summary of revenue, operating income, and assets, the balance sheet, the income statement, and the statement of cash flows. **Exhibit 19** provides a geographic breakdown of sales.)[71]

Since Harley went public, its shares had risen 15,000%. Harley-Davidson stock had remained strong, even when the general market has weakened. (**Exhibit 20** provides a comparison of Harley-Davidson stock and the Standard and Poor's 500 since the 1986 initial public offering and a second comparison from 1997 to 2002.) What did the future hold for Harley-Davidson? It really depended on how one viewed the strengths, weaknesses, opportunities, and threats facing the company. Two analysts viewed the future prospects of Harley-Davidson's stock differently:

"It's an upper-middle-class toy," said Chad Hudson of the Prudent Bear fund, one of a number of prominent short-sellers convinced that Harley will skid. "As people run out of disposable income, that's going to hurt."[72]

Short-sellers—bearish investors who sell borrowed shares, hoping to replace them later with cheaper ones—"are banking on at some point the story cracking," said Chris Cox, a Goldman Sachs analyst who is bullish on Harley shares. "My point is that, if it does, it's not happening any time soon."[73]

How should Harley-Davidson ride out the recession? How should it maintain interest in the 2004 model bikes? How should it grapple with the aging baby boomers, who are generally the individuals who could afford a Harley-Davidson motorcycle? These were but a few of the questions in the minds of the 100th Anniversary Planning Committee members as they strategized about the 2003 celebration.

Exhibit 15 Revenues, Operating Income, and Assets: Harley-Davidson, Inc.
(Dollar amounts in thousands)

	Motorcycles and Related Products	Financial Services	Corporate	Consolidated
2001				
Revenue	$3,363,414	$181,545	—	$3,544,959
Operating income (loss)	$613,311	$61,273	$(12,083)	$662,501
Identifiable assets as of December 31	$1,385,932	$1,096,239	$636,324	$3,118,495
2000				
Revenue	$2,906,365	$140,135	—	$3,046,500
Operating income (loss)	$487,485	$37,178	$(9,691)	$514,972
Identifiable assets as of December 31	$1,158,813	$856,961	$420,630	$2,436,404
1999				
Revenue	$2,452,939	$132,741	—	$2,585,680
Operating income (loss)	$397,601	$27,685	$(9,427)	$415,859
Identifiable assets as of December 31	$1,058,934	$868,711	$184,432	$2,112,077

Source: Harley-Davidson, Inc., 2001 Annual Report, pp. 55 and 81, and 2000 Form 10-K, pp. 19 and 54.

Exhibit 16 Balance Sheet, 1997–2001: Harley-Davidson, Inc.
(Dollar amounts in thousands)

	2001	2000	1999	1998	1997
Assets					
Current assets					
Cash and cash equivalents	$ 439,438	$ 419,736	$ 183,415	$ 165,170	$ 147,462
Marketable securities	196,011	0	0	0	0
Account receivable, net	118,843	98,311	101,708	113,417	102,797
Current portion of finance receivables, net	656,421	530,859	440,951	360,341	293,329
Inventories	181,115	191,931	168,616	155,616	117,475
Deferred income taxes	38,993	28,280	29,434	29,076	24,941
Prepaid expenses and other current assets	34,443	28,147	24,870	21,343	18,017
Total current assets	1,665,264	1,297,264	948,994	844,963	704,021
Finance Receivables, net	379,335	234,091	354,888	319,427	249,346
Property, plant and equipment, net	891,820	754,115	681,741	627,759	528,869
Goodwill, net	49,711	54,331	55,408	51,197	38,707
Other assets	132,365	96,603	71,046	76,863	77,958
Total assets	$3,118,495	$2,436,404	$2,112,077	$1,920,209	$1,598,901
Liabilities & shareholders' equity					
Current liabilities					
Accounts payable	$ 194,683	$ 169,844	$ 137,660	$ 122,722	$ 106,112
Accrued expenses and other liabilities	304,376	238,390	199,331	199,051	164,938
Current portion of finance debt	217,051	89,509	181,163	146,742	90,638
Total current liabilities	716,110	497,743	518,154	468,515	361,688
Finance debt	380,000	355,000	280,000	280,000	280,000
Other long-term liabilities	158,374	81,707	65,093	67,376	62,131
Postretirement health care benefits	89,912	80,666	75,719	72,083	68,414
Deferred income taxes	17,816	15,633	12,031	2,324	0
Total liabilities	$1,362,212	$1,030,749	$950,997	$890,298	$772,233
Shareholders' equity					
Common stock	3,242	3,210	1,592	1,584	1,572
Additional PIC	359,165	285,390	236,540	211,960	187,180
Retained earnings	1,833,335	1,431,017	1,113,376	873,171	683,824
Accumulated other comprehensive income	(13,728)	308	(2,067)	1,128	(2,835)
Less					
Treasury stock	(425,546)	(313,994)	(187,992)	(57,133)	(41,959)
Unearned compensation	(185)	(276)	(369)	(799)	(1,114)
Total shareholders' equity	1,756,283	1,405,655	1,161,080	1,029,911	826,668
Total liabilities and shareholders' equity	$3,118,495	$2,436,404	$2,112,077	$1,920,209	$1,598,901

Source: Harley-Davidson, Inc., 2001 Annual Report, pp. 56–57.

Exhibit 17 Income Statement, 1997–2001: Harley-Davidson, Inc.
(Dollar amounts in thousands)

	2001	2000	1999	1998	1997
Net sales	$3,363,414	$2,906,365	$2,452,939	$2,063,956	$1,762,569
Cost of goods sold	2,183,409	1,915,547	1,617,253	1,373,286	1,176,352
Gross profit	1,180,005	990,818	835,686	690,670	586,217
Financial services income	181,545	140,135	132,741	102,922	66,998
Financial services interest and operating expense	120,272	102,957	105,056	82,711	54,643
Operating income from financial services	61,273	37,178	27,685	20,211	12,355
Selling, admin, and engineering expense	(578,777)	(513,024)	(447,512)	(377,265)	(328,569)
Income from operations	662,501	514,972	415,859	333,616	270,003
Gain on sale of credit card business	0	18,915	0	0	0
Interest income, net	17,478	17,583	8,014	3,828	7,871
Other, net	(6,524)	(2,914)	(3,080)	(1,215)	(1,572)
Income before provision for income taxes	673,455	548,556	420,793	336,229	276,302
Provision for income taxes	235,709	200,843	153,592	122,729	102,232
Net income	$ 437,746	$ 347,713	$ 267,201	$ 213,500	$ 174,070

Source: Harley-Davidson, Inc., 2001 Annual Report, p. 41.

Exhibit 18 Statement of Cash Flows, 1997–2001: Harley-Davidson, Inc.
(Dollar amounts in thousands)

	2001	2000	1999	1998	1997
Cash flow from operating activities					
Net income	$ 437,746	$ 347,713	$ 267,201	$ 213,500	$ 174,070
Adjustments to reconcile net income to					
net cash provided by operating activities					
Depreciation and amortization	153,061	133,348	113,822	87,422	70,178
Gain on sale of credit card business	0	(18,915)	0	0	0
Tax benefit of stock options	44,968	35,876	15,504	0	0
Provision for finance credit losses	22,178	9,919	17,919	10,338	6,547
Deferred income taxes	(3,539)	1,363	11,393	1,190	2,748
Long-term employee benefits	21,588	4,631	(8,480)	5,302	1,275
Other	3,500	1,945	1,781	3,180	1,766
Net changes in current assets and					
current liabilities	77,761	49,609	12,502	(2,870)	53,151
Total adjustments	319,517	217,776	164,441	104,562	135,665
Net cash provided by operating activities	$ 757,263	$ 565,489	$ 431,642	$ 318,062	$ 309,735
Cash flow from investing activities:					
Net capital expenditures	$(290,381)	$(203,611)	$(165,786)	$(182,770)	$(186,171)
Finance receivables acquired or originated	(4,387,371)	(3,556,195)	(3,321,382)	(2,722,768)	(1,618,307)
Finance receivables collected	3,123,941	2,727,746	2,616,857	2,105,684	1,107,157
Finance receivables sold	987,676	723,928	574,997	469,653	300,000
Net proceeds from sale of credit card business	0	170,146	0	0	0
Purchase of marketable securities	(247,989)	0	0	0	0
Sales and redemptions of marketable securities	51,978	0	0	0	0
Purchase of Italian distributor	(1,873)	(18,777)	0	0	0
Other, net	(7,943)	(14,269)	(4,308)	(9,952)	(9,189)
Net cash used in investing activities	$(771,962)	$(171,032)	$(299,622)	$(340,153)	$(406,510)
Cash flow from financing activities					
Net increase (decrease) in notes payable	0	0	0	(773)	(2,580)
Net increase (decrease) in finance debt	152,542	(16,654)	34,421	56,104	112,573
Dividends paid	(35,428)	(30,072)	(26,996)	(24,153)	(21,028)
Purchase of common stock for treasury	(111,552)	(126,002)	(130,284)	(15,175)	0
Issuance of common stock under employee					
stock plans	28,839	14,592	9,084	23,796	12,793
Net cash provided by (used in)					
financing activities	$ 34,401	$(158,136)	$(113,775)	$ 39,799	$ 101,758
Net increase in cash and cash equivalents	19,702	236,321	18,245	17,708	4,983
Cash and cash equivalents					
At beginning of year	419,736	183,415	165,170	147,462	142,479
At end of year	$ 439,438	$ 419,736	$ 183,415	$ 165,170	$ 147,462

Source: Harley-Davidson, Inc., 2001 Annual Report, p. 47.

Exhibit 19
Geographic
Information:
Harley-Davidson,
Inc. (Amounts in
thousands)

	2001	2000	1999
Net Sales[1]			
United States	$2,766,391	$2,320,991	$1,915,631
Europe	301,729	285,372	274,737
Japan	141,181	148,684	135,589
Canada	96,928	93,352	80,271
Other foreign countries	57,185	57,966	46,711
Total	$3,363,414	$2,906,365	$2,452,939
Long-lived assets[2]			
United States	$1,021,946	$ 856,746	$ 775,764
Other foreign countries	33,234	27,844	8,948
Total	$1,055,180	$ 884,590	$ 784,712

Notes:

1. Net sales are attributed to geographic regions based on location of customer.

2. Long-lived assets include all long-term assets except those specifically excluded under SFAS Number 131, such as deferred income taxes and finance receivables.

Source: Harley-Davidson, Inc. Form 10-K, p. 59.

**Exhibit 20
Comparison of the
S&P 500 Annual
Return and Harley-
Davidson Annual
Stock Return at the
Company's 1986
Initial Public
Offering**

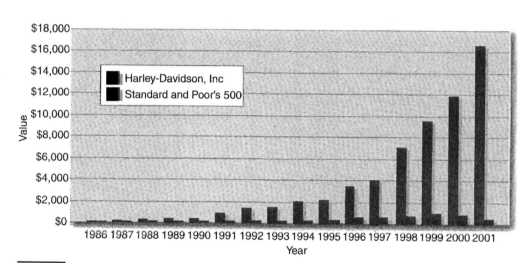

Source: www.harleydavidson.com.

**Recent Comparison
of Harley-Davidson
Stock Performance
Compared to S&P
500, 1997–2002**

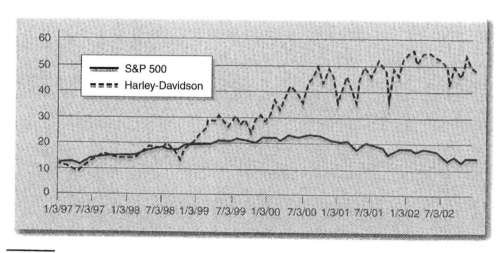

Source: www.yahoo.finance.

Notes

1. Buell Motorcycle Press Release "Harley-Davidson Reports Record Fourth Quarter" (January 17, 2002).

2. T. L. Wheelen, K. E. Wheelen, T. L. Wheelen II, and R. D. Wheelen, "Harley-Davidson: The 95th Anniversary," Case 16, *Strategic Management and Business Policy*, 8th Edition (Upper Saddle River, NJ: Prentice Hall, 2002), pp. 16-1–16-31.

3. J. Fahey, "Love into Money," *Forbes* (January 7, 2002), pp. 60–65.

4. M. Sullivan, "High-Octane Hog," *Forbes* (September 10, 2002), pp. 8–10. The preceding two paragraphs are directly quoted, with minor editing.

5. "A Harley Takes an Engine From Porsche" *New York Times* (May 26, 2002). Accessed at *www.nytimes.com*. This paragraph is directly quoted, with minor editing.

6. Harley-Davidson, Inc., *2002 Proxy Statement*. This paragraph is directly quoted, with minor editing.

7. Harley-Davidson, Inc., *Annual Report* (2002), back cover.

8. J. Fahey, "Love into Money," *Forbes* (January 7, 2002), pp. 60–65.

9. Harley-Davidson, Inc., *Annual Report* (2001), pp. 5–8.

10. J. Weber, "Harley Investors May Get a Wobbly Ride," *BusinessWeek* (February 11, 2002), p. 65.

11. J. Helyar, "Will Harley-Davidson Hit the Wall?" *Fortune* (August 12, 2002), pp. 120–124.

12. Harley-Davidson Inc., *Form 10-K* (2001). The following four paragraphs are directly quoted, with minor editing.

13. J. Fahey, "Love into Money," *Forbes* (January 7, 2002), pp. 60–65.

14. J. Weber, "Harley Investors May Get a Wobbly Ride," *BusinessWeek* (February 11, 2002), p. 65.

15. J. Fahey, "Love into Money," *Forbes* (January 7, 2002), pp. 60–65.

16. Discover Today's Motorcycling, Press Release "Rockefeller Center Motorcycle Show Opens with 'Today Show' segment and Giant Preview Party" (April 6, 2002).

17. Harley-Davidson, Inc., *Annual Report* (2001), pp. 5–8. This section is directly quoted from President Bluestein's letter to the shareholders, with minor editing.

18. M. Schifrin, "100 Years Young," *Forbes* (September 10, 2001), p. 6.

19. J. Weber, "Harley Investors May Get a Wobbly Ride," *BusinessWeek* (February 11, 2002), p. 65.

20. J. Helyar, "Will Harley-Davidson Hit the Wall?" *Fortune* (August 12, 2002), pp. 120–124.

21. M. Sullivan, "High-Octane Hog," *Forbes* (September 10, 2002), pp. 8–10.

22. Harley-Davidson, Inc. *Form 10-K* (2001).

23. J. Fahey, "Love into Money," *Forbes* (January 7, 2002), pp. 60–65.

24. R. Rovito, "No Revving Needed for Sales of Harley's V-Rod Motorcycle," *The Business Journal Serving Greater Milwaukee* (January 14, 2002). Accessed at *http://milwaukee.bizjournals. com/milwaukee/stories/2002/01/14/story8.html.*

25. J. Weber, "Harley Investors May Get a Wobbly Ride," *BusinessWeek* (February 11, 2002), p. 65.

26. "The Business Week 50 Ranking," *BusinessWeek* (Spring 2002), p. 54.

27. J. Helyar, "Will Harley-Davidson Hit the Wall?" *Fortune* (August 12, 2002), pp. 120–124.

28. J. V. Higgins, "All Hail, Harley-Davidson," *The Detroit News* (February 22, 2002). Accessed at *http://detnews.com.*

29. J. Fahey, "Love into Money," *Forbes* (January 7, 2002), pp. 60–65.

30. J. Shiver, "Richer, Older Harley Riders 'Like Everyone Else,' " *USA Today* (March 8, 2002) pp. 1A–2A.

31. Harley-Davidson, Inc., *Form 10-K* (2001). The following two paragraphs are directly quoted, with minor editing.

32. K. Brown, "Heard on the Street: Harley-Davidson Growth Engine May Be Stalling," *Wall Street Journal* (February 12, 2002), p. C2.

33. *Ibid.*

34. Harley-Davidson, Inc., *Form 10-K* (2001). The second, third, and fourth paragraphs are directly quoted, with minor editing.

35. Harley-Davidson, Inc., *Harley-Davidson 100th Anniversary Open Road Tour Is a Treat for Every Sense, Sound, and the Sensesational*, Harley-Davidson Press Release (May 8, 2002).

36. Harley-Davidson, Inc., *Form 10-K* (2001). This paragraph is directly quoted, with minor editing.

37. *Ibid.* This paragraph is directly quoted, with minor editing.

38. *Ibid.* The following two paragraphs are directly quoted, with minor editing.

39. *Ibid.* Directly quoted, with minor editing.

40. J. Shiver, "Richer, Older Harley Riders 'Like Everyone Else,' " *USA Today* (March 8, 2002) pp. 1A–2A.

41. "Harley Roars into Its Second Century," *The (Ames Iowa) Tribune* (July 26, 2002), p. A2.

42. J. Shiver, "Richer, Older Harley Riders 'Like Everyone Else,' " *USA Today* (March 8, 2002) pp. 1A–2A.

43. *Ibid.*, pp. 1A–2A.

44. A. Cox, "Levi, Harley-Davidson May Face EU Retaliation Over U.S. Steel," Bloomberg.com (March 23, 2002).

45. P. Magnusson, "Those Steel Tariffs Look Anything but Ironclad," *BusinessWeek* (May 6, 2002), p. 45.

46. D. Wells, "Lehman's Kantor Bets on Harley Davidson: Call of Day," Bloomberg.com (November 14, 2001).

47. *Ibid.*

48. Harley-Davidson, Inc., *Form 10-K* (2001). The following four paragraphs are directly quoted, with minor editing.

49. E. Eldrige, "More Over-40 Motorcyclists Die in Crashes," *USA Today* (January 10, 2002), p. 1B.

50. J. Fahey, "Love into Money," *Forbes* (January 7, 2002), pp. 60–65.

51. Harley-Davidson, Inc., *Form 10-K* (2001). The following five paragraphs are directly quoted, with minor editing.

52. *Ibid.* The first two paragraphs are directly quoted, with minor editing.

53. Harley-Davidson web site press release, "Harley-Davidson Motor Company to Move Dyna Assembly to Kansas City" (September 19, 2001).

54. M. Sullivan, "High-Octane Hog," *Forbes* (September 10, 2002), pp. 8–10.

55. Harley-Davidson, Inc., *Form 10-K* (2001). The following paragraph is directly quoted, with minor editing.

56. *Ibid.* The following two paragraphs are directly quoted, with minor editing.

57. *Ibid.* The following paragraph is directly quoted, with minor editing.

58. *Ibid.* The first three paragraphs are directly quoted, with minor editing.

59. *Ibid.* The first paragraph is directly quoted, with minor editing.

60. *Ibid.* The following paragraph is directly quoted, with minor editing.

61. *Ibid.* The following two paragraphs are directly quoted, with minor editing.

62. *Ibid.* The following paragraph is directly quoted, with minor editing.

63. *Ibid.* The following paragraph is directly quoted, with minor editing.
64. *Ibid.* The following two paragraphs are directly quoted, with minor editing.
65. *Ibid.* The following paragraph is directly quoted, with minor editing.
66. *Ibid.* The following paragraph is directly quoted, with minor editing.
67. *Ibid.* The following three paragraphs are directly quoted, with minor editing.
68. *Ibid.* The following paragraph is directly quoted, with minor editing.
69. *Ibid.* The following two paragraphs are directly quoted, with minor editing.
70. J. Fahey, "Love into Money," *Forbes* (January 7, 2002), pp. 60–65.
71. A. G. House, "Harley-Davidson," *ValueLine* 1830 (February 23, 2001).
72. J. Helyar, "Will Harley-Davidson Hit the Wall?" *Fortune* (August 12, 2002), pp. 120–124.
73. K. Brown, "Heard on the Street: Harley-Davidson Growth Engine May Be Stalling," *Wall Street Journal* (February 12, 2002), p. C2.

CASE 13

Carnival Corporation:

Acquiring Princess Cruise Line (2002)

Michael J. Keeffe, John K. Ross III, and Bill J. Middlebrook

CARNIVAL CORPORATION, IN TERMS OF PASSENGERS CARRIED, REVENUES GENERATED, and available capacity, was the largest cruise line in the world and considered the leader and innovator in the cruise travel industry. Carnival had grown from two converted ocean liners into an organization with multiple cruise brands, including Carnival Cruise Lines, Holland America Lines and Windstar Cruises, Costa Cruise Lines, Seabourn Cruise Lines, and Cunard Lines Limited, along with a chain of Alaskan hotels and tour coaches to complement Alaska Cruises. Corporate revenues for fiscal 2001 reached $4.5 billion with net income from operations of $926 million. Carnival had several "firsts" in the cruise industry—with over one million passengers carried in a single year and the first cruise line to carry five million total passengers by fiscal 1994. In 2002, its market share of the cruise travel industry was approximately 32% overall.

Carnival Corporation CEO and Chairman, Micky Arison, and the Carnival Corporation executive management team continually strove to maintain Carnival's reputation as the industry's leader and innovator. They had assembled one of the newest fleets catering to cruisers, with the introduction of several "superliners" built specifically for the Caribbean and Alaskan cruise markets. Management planned to invest over $6 billion in new ships by 2005 to be distributed among various cruise brands under the corporate umbrella.

In early December 2002, Arison reflected on the internal and external factors that had impacted the firm since the terrorist events of September 11, 2001. After these events, cruise bookings were negatively impacted but started to recover late in the year, indicating that leisure travel could rebound in 2002. Still, Carnival Corporation had to offer deep discounts to lure back passengers and experienced a 10% performance decline with a net income of $129.6 million on revenues of $905.8 million in the first quarter of calendar 2002. Additionally, cumulative advanced bookings for 2002 were 7% behind bookings received in the previous year. Overall profitability for fiscal 2001 was down only $40 million from fiscal 2000, given an increase in revenues of almost $800 million.

On a high note, Carnival Corporation's offer for Princess Cruise Lines had been accepted by the stockholders of P&O, the parent of Princess Cruises. Carnival had been in a long battle with Royal Caribbean Cruises Ltd. to acquire Princess Cruises. Combining Royal Caribbean, second in cruise market share, with Princess, third in market share, would have created the largest cruise operator in the industry, displacing Carnival as the largest cruise operator in the world. Carnival's offer of approximately $5.67 billion was accepted by P&O stockholders and had passed regulatory approval in Germany and the United States, and was expected to be approved by other countries as well. The combination of Princess Cruises' market share of 11.9% with Carnival's 31.9% would create a dominant organization in the cruise segment of the leisure travel industry.

In addition to rebounding from the events of September 11 and the successful pursuit of Princess Cruises during 2001, Carnival Corporation received some negative publicity. In April 2002, for example, Carnival pleaded guilty to federal ocean pollution charges stemming from bilge water discharges from six ships under the Carnival brand. (Carnival had falsified records related to the dumping.) The company agreed to pay $18 million in fines and restitution as part of the settlement, but the most worrisome aspect to management was the negative publicity for the company and cruise vacations in general. During the summer of 2002, passengers on a Holland America ship contracted a virus, and in November a virus struck passengers of Holland America, Carnival, and Disney Cruise Line ships. It was labeled a "Norwalk-like" virus, and some ships had to cancel sailings in order to clean the ships; many passengers had to be reimbursed or offered berths on other sailings. How the publicity of passengers getting sick on cruise outings would affect the industry and Carnival Corporation in particular was not yet known.

Management believed that cruises were taken by only a small portion of the North American vacation market, defined as persons who travel for leisure purposes on trips of three nights or longer, involving at least one night's stay in a hotel. The Boston Consulting Group, in a 1989 study, estimated that only 5% of persons in the North American target market had taken a cruise for leisure purposes and estimated the market potential to be in excess of $50 billion. Carnival Corporation's management believed that this percentage had increased to 12%–15% by 2002. Various cruise operators, including Carnival Corporation, had based their expansion and capital spending programs on the possibility of capturing part of the 85%–88% of the North American population who had yet to take a cruise vacation.

The Evolution of Cruising

With the replacement of ocean liners by aircraft in the 1960s as the primary means of transoceanic travel, the opportunity for developing the modern cruise industry was created. Ships no longer required to ferry passengers from destination to destination became available to investors with visions of a new vacation alternative to complement the increasing affluence of Americans. Cruising, once the purview of the rich and leisure class, was targeted to the middle class, with service and amenities similar to those of the grand days of first-class ocean travel.

According to Robert Meyers, Editor and Publisher of *Cruise Travel* magazine, the increasing popularity of taking a cruise as a vacation can be traced to two serendipitously timed events. First, television's *Love Boat* series dispelled many myths associated with cruising and depicted people of all ages and backgrounds enjoying the cruise experience. This show was among the top 10 shows on television for many years, according to Nielsen ratings, and provided extensive publicity for cruise operators. Second, the increased affluence of Americans and the increased participation of women in the workforce gave couples and families more disposable income for discretionary purposes, especially vacations. As the myths were dispelled and disposable income grew, younger couples and families "turned on" to the benefits of cruising as a vacation alternative, creating a large new target market for the cruise product, which accelerated the growth in the number of Americans taking cruises as a vacation.

Carnival History

In 1972 Ted Arison, backed by American Travel Services (AITS), Inc., purchased an aging ocean liner from Canadian Pacific Empress Lines for $6.5 million. The new AITS subsidiary, Carnival Cruise Line, refurbished the vessel from bow to stern and renamed it the *Mardi Gras* to capture the party spirit. (Also included in the deal was another ship later renamed the *Carnivale*.) The company's start was not promising, however, as on the first voyage the *Mardi Gras*, with over 300 invited travel agents aboard, ran aground in Miami Harbor. The ship was slow and guzzled expensive fuel, limiting the number of ports of call and lengthening the minimum stay of passengers on the ship to reach break-even. Arison then bought another older vessel from Union Castle Lines to complement the *Mardi Gras* and the *Carnivale* and named it the *Festivale*. To attract customers, Arison began adding diversions onboard such as planned activities, a casino, nightclubs, discos, and other forms of entertainment designed to enhance the shipboard experience.

Carnival lost money for the next three years, and in late 1974 Ted Arison bought out the Carnival Cruise subsidiary AITS, Inc., for $1 cash and the assumption of $5 million in debt. One month later, the *Mardi Gras* began showing a profit and through the remainder of 1975 operated at more than 100% capacity. (Normal ship capacity was determined by the number of fixed berths available. Ships, like hotels, can operate beyond this fixed capacity by using rollaway beds, pullmans, and upper bunks.)

Ted Arison (then Chairman), along with Bob Dickinson (who was then Vice President of Sales and Marketing) and his son Micky Arison (then President of Carnival), began to alter the current approach to cruise vacations. Carnival went after first-time and younger cruisers with a moderately priced vacation package that included airfare to the port of embarkation and home after the cruise. Per diem rates were very competitive with other vacation packages, and Carnival offered passage to multiple exotic Caribbean ports, several meals served daily with premier restaurant service, and all forms of entertainment and activities included in the base fare. The only things not included in the fare were items of a personal nature, liquor purchases, gambling, and tips for the cabin steward, table waiter, and busboy. Carnival continued to add to the shipboard experience with a greater variety of activities, nightclubs, and other forms of entertainment and varied ports of call to increase its attractiveness to potential customers. It was the first modern cruise operator to use multimedia-advertising promotions and established the theme of "Fun Ship" cruises, primarily promoting the ship as the destination and ports of call as secondary. Carnival told the public that it was throwing a shipboard party and everyone was invited. Today, the "Fun Ship" theme still permeates all Carnival Cruise brand ships.

Throughout the 1980s, Carnival was able to maintain a growth rate of approximately 30%, about three times that of the industry as a whole, and between 1982 and 1988 its ships sailed with an average capacity of 104%. Targeting younger, first-time passengers by promoting the ship as a destination proved to be extremely successful. Carnival's customer profile showed that approximately 30% of the passengers were between the ages of 25 and 39, with household incomes of $25,000 to $50,000.

In 1987, Ted Arison sold 20% of his shares in Carnival Cruise Lines and immediately generated over $400 million for further expansion. In 1988, Carnival acquired the Holland America Line, which had four cruise ships with 4,500 berths. Holland America was positioned to the higher-income travelers with cruise prices averaging 25%–35% more than similar Carnival cruises. The deal also included two Holland America subsidiaries, Windstar Sail

Cruises and Holland America Westours. This purchase allowed Carnival to begin an aggressive "superliner" building campaign for its core subsidiary. By 1989, the cruise segments of Carnival Corporation carried more than 750,000 passengers in one year, a first in the cruise industry.

Ted Arison relinquished the role of Chairman to his son Micky in 1990, a time when the explosive growth of the 1980s began to subside. Higher fuel prices and increased airline costs began to affect the industry as a whole. The Persian Gulf War caused many cruise operators to divert ships from European and Indian ports to the Caribbean area of operations, increasing the number of ships competing directly with Carnival. Carnival's stock price fell from $25 in June of 1990 to $13 late in that year. The company also incurred a $25.5 million loss during fiscal 1990 for the operation of the Crystal Palace Resort and Casino in The Bahamas. In 1991, Carnival reached a settlement with the Bahamian government (effective March 1, 1992) to surrender the 672-room Riveria Towers to the Hotel Corporation of The Bahamas in exchange for the cancellation of some debt incurred in constructing and developing the resort. The corporation took a $135 million write-down on the Crystal Palace for that year.

The early 1990s, even with industrywide demand slowing, were still a very exciting time. Carnival took delivery of its first two "superliners," the *Fantasy* (1990) and the *Ecstasy* (1991), which were to further penetrate the three- and four-day cruise market and supplement the seven-day market. In early 1991, Carnival took delivery of the third "superliner," *Sensation* (inaugural sailing November 1, 1993) and later in the year contracted for the fourth "superliner," to be named the *Fascination* (inaugural sailing 1994).

In 1991, Carnival attempted to acquire Premier Cruise Lines, which was then the official cruise line for Walt Disney World in Orlando, Florida, for approximately $372 million. The deal was never consummated since the involved parties could not agree on price. In 1992, Carnival acquired 50% of Seabourn, gaining the cruise operations of K/S Seabourn Cruise Lines, and formed a partnership with Atle Byrnestad. Seabourn served the ultra-luxury market with destinations in South America, the Mediterranean, Southeast Asia, and the Baltics.

The 1993 to 1995 period saw the addition of the "superliner" *Imagination* for Carnival Cruise Lines and the Ryndam for Holland America Lines. In 1994, the company discontinued operations of Fiestamarina Lines, which attempted to serve Spanish-speaking clientele. Fiestamarina was beset with marketing and operational problems and never reached continuous operations. Many industry analysts and observers were surprised at the failure of Carnival to successfully develop this market. In 1995 Carnival sold a 49% interest in the Epirotiki Line, a Greek cruise operation, for $25 million and purchased $101 million (face amount) of senior secured notes of Kloster Cruise Limited, the parent of competitor Norwegian Cruise Lines, for $81 million.

Carnival Corporation also expanded through internally generated growth, as evidenced by the number of new ships on order (see **Exhibit 1**). Additionally, Carnival seemed to be willing to continue with its external expansion through acquisitions if the right opportunity arose.

In June 1997, Royal Caribbean made a bid to buy Celebrity Cruise Lines for $500 million and assumption of $800 million in debt. Within a week, Carnival had responded by submitting a counter offer to Celebrity for $510 million and the assumption of debt. Two days later, Carnival raised the bid to $525 million. Nevertheless, Royal Caribbean announced on June 30, 1997, the final merger arrangements with Celebrity. The resulting company had 17 ships with more than 30,000 berths.

Not to be thwarted in its attempts at continued expansion, Carnival announced in June 1997 the purchase of Costa, an Italian cruise company and the largest European cruise line, for $141 million. The purchase was finalized in September 2000. External expansion continued when Carnival announced the acquisition of Cunard Line for $500 million from Kvaerner ASA on May 28, 1998. Cunard was then operationally merged with Seabourn Cruise Line.

**Exhibit 1
Carnival
Corporation Ships
Under Construction**

Vessel	Expected Delivery	Shipyard	Passenger Capacity[1]	Cost ($mils)
Carnival Cruise Lines				
Carnival Conquest	12/02	Fincantieri	2,974	$ 500
Carnival Glory	8/03	Fincantieri	2,974	500
Carnival Miracle	4/04	Masa-Yards	2,124	375
Carnival Valor	11/04	Fincantieri	2,974	500
Total Carnival Cruise Lines			**11,046**	**$1,875**
Holland America Line				
Zuiderdam	12/02	Fincantieri	1,848	410
Oosterdam	7/03	Fincantieri	1,848	410
Newbuilt	5/04	Fincantieri	1,848	410
Newbuilt	11/05	Fincantieri	1,848	410
Total Holland America Line			**7,392**	**$1,640**
Costa Cruise Lines				
Mediterranea	7/03	Masa-Yards	2,114	335
Fortuna	1/04	Fincantieri	2,720	390
Magica	12/04	Fincantieri	2,720	390
Total Costa Cruise Lines			**7,554**	**$1,115**
Cunard Line				
Queen Mary II	12/03	l'Alantique	2,620	780
Newbuilt	2/05	Fincantieri	1,968	410
Total Cunard Cruise Line			**4,588**	**$1,190**
Total all vessels			**30,580**	**$5,820**

Note:
1. In accordance with industry practice, all capacities indicated within this document are calculated based on two passengers per cabin, even though some cabins can accommodate three or four passengers.

Carnival owned 100% of the resulting Cunard Line in fiscal 2000. In an attempt at further expansion, Carnival announced on December 2, 1999, a hostile bid for NCL Holding ASA, the parent company of Norwegian Cruise Lines. Carnival was unsuccessful in this acquisition attempt. Its latest external acquisition would be the Princess Cruise Line, once all approvals had been received.

The Cruise Product

Ted and Mickey Arison envisioned a product in which the classical cruise elegance, along with modern convenience, could be had at a price comparable to that of a land-based vacation package sold by a travel agent. Carnival's all-inclusive package, when compared to resorts or a theme park, such as Walt Disney World, often was priced below these destinations, especially considering the array of activities, entertainment, and meals.

A typical vacation on a Carnival cruise ship began when the bags were tagged for the ship at the airport. Upon arriving at the port of embarkation, passengers were ferried by air-conditioned buses to the ship for boarding. Baggage was taken from the terminal to the cabin of the passenger by cruise-ship staff. Waiters on the ship offered tropical drinks to guests while the cruise staff oriented passengers to the various decks, cabins, and public rooms. In a few hours (most ships sail in the early evening), dinner was served in the main dining rooms, where the wine selection rivaled those of the finest restaurants and the variety of main dishes was designed to suit every palate. Diners could order a double portion if they decided not to save room for the variety of desserts and after-dinner specialties.

After dinner, cruisers could choose between many forms of entertainment, including live music, dancing, nightclubs, and a selection of movies; or they could sleep through the midnight buffet until breakfast. (Most ships had five or more distinct nightclubs.) During the night, a daily program for the next day of activities arrived at the passengers' cabins. The biggest decisions to be made for the duration of the vacation were what to do (or not to do), what to eat and when (usually eight separate serving times, not including the 24-hour room service), and when to sleep. Service in all areas from dining to housekeeping was upscale and immediate. The service was so good that a common shipboard joke stated that if you leave your bed during the night to visit the head (sea talk for bathroom), your cabin steward will have made the bed and placed chocolates on the pillow by the time you return.

After the cruise, passengers were transported back to the airport in air-conditioned buses for the flight home. Representatives of the cruise line were on hand at the cruise terminal and airport to help cruisers in meeting their scheduled flights. When all amenities were considered, most vacation packages would be hard pressed to match Carnival's per diem prices, which ranged from $125 to $300 per person per day, depending on accommodations. (Holland America and Seabourn were higher, ranging from $157 to $725 per person per day.) Specials and discounts allowed for even lower prices. Special suite accommodations could be purchased for an additional payment.

Carnival Operations

Carnival Corporation, headquartered in Miami, was composed of Carnival Cruise Lines, Holland America Lines (which included Windstar Sail Cruises as a subsidiary, Holland America Westours, and Westmark Hotels), Costa Cruise Lines, Seabourn Cruise Lines, Gray Line of Alaska and Seattle, Cunard Line Limited, and, in the near future, Princess Cruise Line. Carnival Corporation was a Panamanian corporation, and its subsidiaries were incorporated in Panama, the Netherlands Antilles, the British Virgin Islands, Liberia, and The Bahamas. The ships were subject to inspection by the U.S. Coast Guard for compliance with the Convention for the Safety of Life at Sea (SOLAS), which required specific structural requirements for safety of passengers at sea, and by the U.S. Public Health Service for sanitary standards. The company was also regulated in some aspects by the Federal Maritime Commission.

At its helm, Carnival Corporation was led by CEO and Chairman of the Board Micky Arison. The Carnival Cruise Lines President and COO was Bob Dickinson, and A. Kirk Lanterman was the President and CEO of the Holland America cruise division, which included Holland America Westours and Windstar Sail Cruises. (A listing of corporate officers is presented in **Exhibit 2**.)

The company's product positioning stemmed from its belief that the cruise market was actually comprised of three primary segments with different passenger demographics, passenger characteristics, and growth requirements. The three segments were the contemporary, premium, and luxury segments. The contemporary segment was served by Carnival ships for cruises that were seven days or shorter in length and featured a casual ambiance. The premium segment, served by Holland America, served the seven-day and longer market and appealed to more affluent consumers, and Costa Cruises offered an Italian cruise experience in this segment. The luxury segment, while considerably smaller than the other segments, catered to experienced cruisers for seven-day and longer sailings and was served by Seabourn and Cunard. Specialty sailing cruises were provided by Windstar Sail Cruises, a subsidiary of Holland America.

Exhibit 2
Corporate Officers
of Carnival
Corporation

Micky Arison Chairman of the Board and Chief Executive Officer	**Howard S. Frank** Vice Chairman and Chief Operating Officer
Gerald R. Cahill Senior Vice President, Finance, and CFO	**Ian Gaunt** Senior Vice President, International
Lowell Zemnick Vice President and Treasurer	**Kenneth D. Dubbin** Vice President, Corporate Development
Richard D. Ames Vice President, Audit Services	**Arnaldo Perez** Vice President, General Counsel, and Secretary
Robert H. Dickinson President and COO, Carnival Cruise Lines	**A. Kirk Lanterman** Chairman of the Board and CEO, Holland America Line
Pier Luigi Foschi Chairman and CEO, Costa Cruise Lines	**Pamela C. Conover** President and COO, Cunard Line

Source: Carnival Corporation, 2002.

Corporate structure was built around the profit center concept and was updated periodically when needed for control and coordination purposes. The cruise subsidiaries of Carnival Corporation had a presence in most of the major cruise segments and provided for worldwide operations.

Carnival always placed a high priority on marketing in an attempt to promote cruises as an alternative to land-based vacations. It wanted customers to know that the ship itself was the destination and the ports of call were important, but secondary, to the cruise experience. Education and the creation of awareness were critical to corporate marketing efforts. Carnival was the first cruise line to successfully break away from traditional print media and use television to reach a broader market. Even though other lines have followed Carnival's lead in selecting promotional media and were close to Carnival in total advertising expenditures, the organization still led all cruise competitors in advertising and marketing expenditures.

Carnival wanted to remain the leader and innovator in the cruise industry and intended to do this with sophisticated promotional efforts and by gaining loyalty from former cruisers, by refurbishing ships, varying activities and ports of call, and being innovative in all aspects of ship operations. Management intended to build on the theme of the ship as a destination given their historical success with this promotional effort.

Financial Performance

Carnival retained PricewaterhouseCoopers LLP as independent accountants and the First Union National Bank as its registrar and stock transfer agent. Its Class A Common stock traded on the New York Stock Exchange under the symbol CCL. The consolidated financial statements for Carnival Cruise Lines, Inc., are shown in **Exhibits 3** and **4**, and selected financial data are presented in **Exhibit 5**.

Customer cruise deposits, which represent unearned revenue, were included in the balance sheet (current liability account) when received and recognized as cruise revenues on completion of the voyage. Customers also were required to pay the full cruise fare (minus deposit) 60 days in advance, with the fares being recognized as cruise revenue on completion of the voyage.

Exhibit 3 Consolidated Statements of Operations: Carnival Corporation (Dollar amounts in thousands)

Year Ending November 30	2001	2000	1999	1998	1997	1996	1995	1994	1993	1992
Revenues	$4,535,751	$3,778,542	$3,497,470	$3,009,306	$2,447,468	$2,212,572	$1,998,150	$1,806,016	$1,556,919	$1,473,614
Costs and expenses										
Operating expense	2,468,730	2,058,342	1,862,636	1,619,377	1,322,669	1,241,269	1,131,113	1,028,475	907,925	865,587
Selling and administrative	618,664	487,403	447,235	69,469	296,533	274,855	248,566	223,272	207,995	194,298
Depreciation & amortization	375,224	287,667	243,658	200,668	167,287	144,987	128,433	110,595	93,333	88,833
Impairment charge	140,378	—	—	—	—	—	—	—	—	—
	$3,599,996	$2,833,412	$2,553,529	$2,189,514	$1,786,489	$1,661,111	$1,508,112	$1,362,342	$1,209,253	$1,148,718
Operating income before affiliated	935,755	945,130	943,941	819,792	660,979	551,461				
Income from affiliated (loss)	(44,024)	37,828	75,758	76,732	53,091	45,967				
Operating income	891,731	982,958	1,019,699	896,524	714,070	597,428	490,038	443,674	347,666	324,896
Other income (expense)										
Interest income	34,255	16,506	41,932	10,257	8,675	18,597	14,403	8,668	11,527	16,946
Interest expense, net of capitalized interest	(120,692)	(41,372)	(46,956)	(57,772)	(55,898)	(64,092)	(63,080)	(51,378)	(34,325)	(53,792)
Other income (expense)	108,649	8,460	29,357	1,793	5,436	23,414	19,104	(9,146)	(1,201)	2,731
Income tax benefit (expense)	12,257	(1,094)	(2,778)	(3,815)	(6,233)	(9,045)	(9,374)	(10,053)	(5,497)	(9,008)
Minority interest			(14,014)	(11,102)						
	34,469	(17,500)	7,541	(60,639)	(48,020)	(31,126)	(38,947)	(61,909)	(29,496)	(43,123)
Income before extraordinary item	926,200	965,458	1,027,240	835,885	666,050	566,302	451,091	381,765	318,170	281,773
Extraordinary item										
Loss on early extinguishment of debt	—	—	—	—	—	—	—	—	—	(5,189)
Net Income	$ 926,200	$ 965,458	$1,027,240	$ 835,885	$ 666,050	$ 566,302	$ 451,091	$ 381,765	$ 318,170	$ 276,584

Source: Carnival Corporation, 1992–2001 Form 10-K and 10Q forms.

Exhibit 4 Consolidated Balance Sheets: Carnival Corporation (Dollar amounts in thousands)

Year Ending November 30	2001	2000	1999	1998	1997	1996	1995	1994	1993
Assets									
Current assets									
Cash & cash equivalents	$ 1,421,300	$ 189,282	$ 521,771	$ 137,273	$ 139,989	$ 111,629	$ 53,365	$ 54,105	$ 60,243
Short-term investments	36,784	—	—	5,956	9,738	12,486	50,395	70,115	88,677
Accounts receivable	90,763	95,361	62,887	60,837	57,090	38,109	33,080	20,789	19,310
Consumable inventories [average cost]	91,996	100,451	84,019	75,449	54,970	53,281	48,820	45,122	37,245
Prepaid expenses & other	113,798	164,388	122,959	90,764	74,238	75,428	70,718	50,318	48,323
Fair value of hedged firm commitments	204,347	—	—	—	—	—	—	—	—
Total current assets	$ 1,958,988	$ 549,482	$ 791,636	$ 370,279	$ 336,025	$ 290,933	$ 256,378	$ 240,449	$ 253,798
Property and Equipment [at cost]									
Less accumulated depreciation & amortization	8,390,230	8,001,318	6,410,527	5,768,114	4,327,413	4,099,038	3,414,823	3,071,431	2,588,009
Other assets									
Goodwill [less accumulated amortization]	651,814	701,385	462,340	437,464	212,607	219,589	226,571	233,553	237,327
Long-term notes receivable	—	—	—	—	—	—	78,907	76,876	29,136
Investment in affiliates & other assets	188,915	437,391	586,922	546,693	479,329	430,330	128,808	47,514	21,097
Other assets	—	141,744	34,930	56,773	71,401	61,998	—	—	89,553
Fair value of hedged firm commitments	373,605	—	—	—	—	—	—	—	—
Total assets	$11,563,552	$9,831,320	$8,286,355	$7,179,323	$5,426,775	$5,101,888	$4,105,487	$3,669,823	$3,218,920
Liabilities and equity									
Current liabilities									
Current portion of long-term debt	21,764	248,219	206,267	67,626	59,620	66,369	$72,752	$84,644	$91,621
Accounts payable	269,467	322,694	195,879	168,546	106,783	84,748	90,237	86,750	81,374
Accrued liabilities	298,032	302,585	262,170	206,968	154,253	126,511	113,483	114,868	94,830
Customer deposits	627,698	770,425	675,816	638,383	420,908	352,698	292,606	257,505	228,153
Dividends payable	61,548	61,371	64,781	53,590	44,578	32,416	25,632	21,190	19,763
Reserve for discontinued operations	—	—	—	—	—	—	—	—	34,253
Fair value of derivative contracts	201,731	—	—	—	—	—	—	—	—
Total current liabilities	$ 1,480,240	$1,705,294	$1,404,913	$1,135,113	$ 786,142	$ 662,742	$ 594,710	$ 564,957	$ 549,994
Long-term debt	2,954,854	2,099,077	867,515	1,563,014	1,015,294	1,277,529	1,035,031	1,046,904	916,221
Convertible notes and	—	—	—	—	—	39,103	115,000	115,000	115,000
Other long-term liabilities	157,998	146,322	82,680	63,036	20,241	91,630	15,873	14,028	10,499
Fair value of derivative contracts	379,683	—	—	—	—	—	—	—	—
Minority interest	—	—	—	132,684	—	—	—	—	—
Shareholders' equity									
Class A common stock [1 vote share]	6,200	6,176	6,170	5,955	2,972	2,397	2,298	2,276	2,274
Class B common stock [5 votes share]	—	—	—	—	—	550	550	550	550
Paid in capital	1,805,248	1,772,897	1,757,408	880,488	866,097	819,610	594,811	544,947	541,194
Retained earnings	5,556,296	4,844,023	4,176,498	3,379,628	2,731,213	2,207,781	1,752,140	1,390,589	1,089,323
Unearned stock compensation	(12,398)	—	—	—	—	—	—	—	—
Accumulated other comprehensive loss	(36,932)	—	—	—	—	—	—	—	—
Treasury stock	(727,637)	(752,497)	—	—	—	—	—	—	—
Other	—	—	(8,829)	19,405	4,816	546	(4,926)	(9,428)	(6,135)
Total shareholders' equity	6,590,777	5,870,599	5,931,247	4,285,476	3,605,098	3,030,884	2,344,873	1,928,934	1,627,206
Total liabilities and shareholders' equity	$11,563,552	$9,831,320	$8,286,355	$7,179,323	$5,426,775	$5,101,888	$4,105,487	$3,669,823	$3,218,920

Source: Carnival Corporation 1993–2001 Form 10-K.

Exhibit 5 Selected Financial Data by Segment: Carnival Corporation
(Dollar amounts in thousands)

Year Ending November 30	2001	2000	1999[1]	1998[1]	1997	1996	1995	1994
Revenues								
Cruise	$4,357,942	$3,578,372	$3,286,701	$2,797,856	$2,257,567	$2,003,458	$1,800,775	$1,623,069
Tour	229,483	259,662	271,828	274,491	242,646	263,356	241,909	227,613
Intersegment elimination	(51,674)	(59,592)	(61,059)	(63,041)	(52,745)	(54,242)	(44,534)	(44,666)
Total	$4,535,751	$3,778,542	$3,497,470	$3,009,306	$2,447,468	$2,212,572	$1,998,150	$1,806,016
Depreciation & amortization								
Cruise	359,314	276,483	232,942	189,345	157,454	135,694	120,304	101,146
Tour	11,474	10,825	10,716	9,491	8,862	8,317	8,129	9,449
Corporate	1,436	359	—	—	971	976	—	—
Total	$ 372,224	$ 287,667	$ 243,658	$ 198,836	$ 167,287	$ 144,987	$ 128,433	$ 110,595
Operating income								
Cruise	958,273	957,226	947,452	822,242	656,009	535,814	465,870	425,590
Tour	(10,357)	7,664	10,403	9,248	13,262	21,252	24,168	18,084
Affiliated operations	(44,024)	37,828	5,758	—	—	—	—	—
Corporate	(12,161)	(19,760)	(13,914)	65,034	44,799	40,362	—	—
Total	$ 891,731	$ 982,958	$1,019,699	$ 896,524	$ 714,070	$ 597,428	$ 490,038	$ 443,674

Note:
1. Includes acquisitions.

Source: Carnival Corporation, 1995–2001 Form 10-K.

Property and equipment on the financial statements was stated at cost. Depreciation and amortization were calculated using the straight-line method over the following estimated useful lives: vessels 25–30 years, buildings 20–40 years, equipment 2–20 years, and leasehold improvements at the shorter of the "term of lease" or "related asset life." During 1995, Carnival received $40 million from the settlement of litigation with Metra Oy, the former parent company of Wartsila Marine Industries, related to losses suffered in connection with the construction of three cruise ships. (Wartsila declared bankruptcy in late 1994.) Of this amount, $14.4 million was recorded as "other income," with the remainder used to pay legal fees and reduce the cost basis of the three ships.

On June 25, 1996, Carnival reached an agreement with the trustees of Wartsila and creditors for the bankruptcy, resulting in a cash payment of approximately $80 million. Of the $80 million received, $5 million was used to pay costs, $32 million was recorded as other income, and $43 million was used to reduce the cost basis of ships, which had been affected by the bankruptcy.

By the end of fiscal 2001, Carnival had outstanding long-term debt of almost $3 billion. According to the Internal Revenue Code of 1986, Carnival was considered a "Controlled Foreign Corporation" (CFC) since 50% of its stock was held by individuals who were residents of foreign countries and its countries of incorporation exempt shipping operations of U.S. persons from income tax. Because of its CFC status, Carnival expected that all of its income (with the exception of U.S. source income from the transportation, hotel, and tour businesses of Holland America) would be exempt from U.S. federal income taxes at the corporate level.

The primary financial consideration of importance to Carnival management involved the control of costs, both fixed and variable, for the maintenance of a healthy profit margin.

Carnival had the lowest breakeven point of any organization in the cruise industry (ships break even at approximately 60% of capacity) due to operational experience and economies of scale. Unfortunately, fixed costs, including depreciation, fuel, insurance, port charges, and crew costs, represented more than 33% of the company's operating expenses. These costs could not be significantly reduced in relation to decreases in passenger loads and aggregate passenger ticket revenue. Major expense items were air fares (25%–30%), travel agent fees (10%), and labor (13%–15%). Increases in these costs could negatively affect the profitability of the organization.

Principle Subsidiaries

Carnival Cruise Line

At the end of fiscal 2001, Carnival operated 16 ships (excluding the *Tropicale*, which was transferred to Costa), with a total berth capacity of over 33,154. Carnival operated principally in the Caribbean and had an assortment of ships and ports of call serving the three-, four-, and seven-day cruise markets (see **Exhibit 6**).

Each ship was a floating resort including a full maritime staff, shopkeepers and casino operators, entertainers, and complete hotel staff. Approximately 14% of corporate revenue was generated from shipboard activities such as casino operations, liquor sales, and gift shop items. At various ports of call, passengers could also take advantage of tours, shore excursions, and duty-free shopping at their own expense.

Shipboard operations were designed to provide maximum entertainment, activities, and service. The size of the company and the similarity in design of the new cruise ships had allowed Carnival to achieve various economies of scale, and management was very cost-conscious.

Although the Carnival Cruise Lines division was increasing its presence in the shorter cruise markets, its general marketing strategy was to use three-, four-, or seven-day moderately price cruises to fit the time and budget constraints of the middle class. Shorter cruises cost less than $500 per person (depending on accommodations). Longer cruises cost up to $3,000 per person in a luxury suite on a seven-day cruise, including port charges. (Per diem rates for shorter cruises were slightly higher, on average, than per diem rates for seven-day cruises.) Average rates per day were approximately $180, excluding gambling, liquor and soft drinks, and items of a personal nature. Guests were expected to tip their cabin steward and waiter at a suggested rate of $3.50 per person/per day, and the busboy at $2 per person/per day.

Some 97% of all Carnival cruises were sold through travel agents, who received a standard commission of 10% (15% in Florida). Carnival worked extensively with travel agents to help promote cruises as an alternative to a Disney or European vacation. In addition to training travel agents from nonaffiliated travel/vacation firms to sell cruises, a special group of employees regularly visited travel agents posing as prospective clients. If the travel agent specified a Carnival cruise before other options, he or she received $100 on the spot. In calendar 2000, Carnival took reservations from about 29,000 of the approximately 45,000 travel agencies in the United States and Canada, and no one travel agency accounted for more than 2% of Carnival revenues.

Onboard service was labor intensive, employing help from some 51 nations—mostly third-world countries—with reasonable returns to employees. For example, waiters on the *Jubilee* could earn approximately $18,000 to $27,000 per year (base salary and tips), significantly greater than could be earned in their home countries for similar employment. Waiters typically worked 10 hours per day with approximately one day off per week for a specified contract period (usually 3 to 9 months). Carnival records showed that employees remained with the company for approximately 8 years and that applicants exceeded demand for all

Exhibit 6 The Ships of Carnival Corporation

Name	Registry	Year Built	First in Company	Service Capacity[1]	Areas of Operation
Carnival Cruise Lines					
Pride	Panama	2001	2001	2,124	Caribbean
Spirit	Panama	2001	2001	2,124	Caribbean
Victory	Panama	2000	2000	2,758	Caribbean
Triumph	Panama	1999	1999	2,758	East Coast, Caribbean
Paradise	Panama	1998	1998	2,040	Caribbean
Elation	Panama	1998	1998	2,040	Mexican Rivera
Destiny	Panama	1996	1997	2,642	Caribbean
Inspiration	Panama	1996	1996	2,040	Caribbean
Imagination	Panama	1995	1995	2,040	Caribbean
Fascination	Panama	1994	1994	2,040	Caribbean
Sensation	Panama	1993	1993	2,040	Caribbean
Ecstasy	Liberia	1991	1991	2,040	Caribbean
Fantasy	Liberia	1990	1990	2,044	Bahamas
Celebration	Liberia	1987	1987	1,486	Caribbean
Jubilee	Panama	1986	1986	1,486	Mexican Riviera
Holiday	Panama	1985	1985	1,452	Mexican Riviera
Tropicale	Liberia	1982	1982	1,022	Alaska, Caribbean

Total Carnival ship capacity = 34,196

Name	Registry	Year Built	First in Company	Service Capacity[1]	Areas of Operation
Holland America Line					
Zaandam	Netherlands	2000	2000	1,440	Worldwide
Amsterdam	Netherlands	2000	2000	1,380	Worldwide
Volendam	Netherlands	1999	1999	1,440	Europe, Worldwide
Rotterdam	Netherlands	1997	1997	1,316	Europe, Worldwide
Veendam	Bahamas	1996	1996	1,266	Alaska, Caribbean
Ryndam	Netherlands	1994	1994	1,266	Alaska, Caribbean
Maasdam	Netherlands	1993	1993	1,266	Europe, Caribbean
Statendam	Netherlands	1993	1993	1,266	Alaska, Caribbean
Westerdam	Netherlands	1986	1988	1,494	Canada, Caribbean
Noordam	Netherlands	1984	1984	1,214	Alaska, Caribbean

Total Holland America Line ship capacity = 13,348

Name	Registry	Year Built	First in Company	Service Capacity[1]	Areas of Operation
Windstar Cruises					
Wind Surf	Bahamas	1990	1990	312	Caribbean
Wind Spirit	Bahamas	1988	1988	148	Caribbean, Mediterranean
Wind Song	Bahamas	1987	1987	148	Costa Rica, Tahiti
Wind Star	Bahamas	1986	1986	148	Caribbean, Mediterranean

Total Windstar ship capacity = 756

Name	Registry	Year Built	First in Company	Service Capacity[1]	Areas of Operation
Cunard Line					
Caronia	England	1973	1973	24,500	Europe
Queen Elizabeth II	England	1969	1969	70,327	Worldwide

Total Cunard ship capacity = 94,827

Name	Registry	Year Built	First in Company	Service Capacity[1]	Areas of Operation
Seabourn Cruise Line					
Seabourn Legend	Norway	1992	1996	208	Pacific
Seabourn Spirit	Norway	1989	1989	208	Asia
Seabourn Pride	Norway	1988	1988	208	South America

Total Seabourn ship capacity = 624

Total capacity = 50,265

cruise positions. Nonetheless, the American Maritime union had cited Carnival (and other cruise operators) several times for exploitation of its crews because of low wages.

Holland America Lines

On January 17, 1989, Carnival acquired all the outstanding stock of HAL Antillen N.V. from Holland America Lines N.V. for $625 million in cash. Carnival financed the purchase through $250 million in retained earnings (cash account) and borrowed the other $375 million from banks at .25% over the prime rate. Carnival received the assets and operations of the Holland America Lines, Westours, Westmark Hotels, and Windstar Sail Cruises. In 2002, Holland America had 10 cruise ships with a capacity of 13,348 berths, with new ships to be delivered in the future.

Founded in 1873, Holland America Lines was an upscale (it charged an average of 25% more than similar Carnival cruises) line with principal destinations in Alaska during the summer months and the Caribbean during the fall and winter, with some worldwide cruises of up to 98 days. Holland America targeted an older, more sophisticated cruiser and offered fewer youth-oriented activities. On Holland America ships, passengers can dance to the sounds of the Big Band era and avoid the more recent music played on Carnival ships. Passengers on Holland America ships enjoyed more service (a higher staff-to-passenger ratio than at Carnival) and had more cabin and public space per person, and a "no tipping" shipboard policy. Holland America had not enjoyed the spectacular growth of Carnival cruise ships but had sustained constant growth over the decade of the 1980s and 1990s with high occupancy. The operation of these ships and the structure of the crew were similar to the Carnival cruise ship model, and the acquisition of the line gave the Carnival Corporation a presence in the Alaskan market where it had none before.

Holland America Westours was the largest tour operator in Alaska and the Canadian Rockies and provided vacation synergy with Holland America cruises. The transportation division of Westours included motor coaches comprised of the Gray Line of Alaska, the Gray Line of Seattle, Westours motorcoaches, the McKinley Explorer railroad coaches, and three-day boats for tours to glaciers and other points of interest. Carnival management believed that Alaskan cruises and tours should increased in the future due to a number of factors. These included the aging population wanting relaxing vacations with scenic beauty coupled with the fact that Alaska was a U.S. destination.

Westmark Hotels consisted of 16 hotels in Alaska and the Yukon territories, and it provided synergy with cruise operations and Westours. Westmark was the largest group of hotels in the region providing moderately priced rooms for the vacationer.

Windstar Sail Cruises was acquired by Holland America Lines in 1988 and consisted of four computer-controlled sailing vessels with a berth capacity of 756. Windstar was very upscale and offered an alternative to traditional cruise liners with a more intimate, activity-oriented cruise. The ships operated primarily in the Mediterranean and the South Pacific, visiting ports not accessible to large cruise ships. Although catering to a small segment of the cruise vacation industry, Windstar helped with Carnival's commitment to participate in all segments of the cruise industry.

Seabourn Cruise Lines

In April 1992, the company acquired 25% of the capital stock of Seabourn. As part of the transaction, the company also made a subordinated secured 10-year loan of $15 million to Seabourn and a $10 million convertible loan to Seabourn. In December 1995, the $10 million convertible loan was converted by the company into an additional 25% equity interest in

Seabourn. Full ownership was completed in 2000, with 100% ownership of Cunard Line Limited, which now operated both the Cunard and Seabourn brands.

Seabourn targeted the luxury market with three vessels providing 200 passengers per ship with all-suite accommodations. Seabourn was considered the "Rolls Royce" of the cruise industry and in 1992 was named the "World's Best Cruise Line" by the prestigious *Conde Nast Traveler*'s fifth annual readers' choice poll. Seabourn cruised the Americas, Europe, Scandinavia, the Mediterranean, and the Far East.

Costa Crociere S.P.A.

In June 1997, Carnival purchased the equity securities of Costa from the Costa family at a cost of approximately $141 million and completed the purchase of the remainder in September 2000. Costa was headquartered in Italy and was considered Europe's largest cruise line, with eight ships and approximately 10,000 passenger capacity. Costa operated primarily in the Mediterranean, Northern Europe, the Caribbean, and South America. The major market for Costa in southern Europe was mainly Italy, Spain, and France.

Cunard Line

Another Carnival acquisition was the Cunard Line, announced on May 28, 1998. Comprised of two ships, the Cunard Line was considered a luxury line with strong brand name recognition. Cunard had two ships (including the *Queen Elizabeth II*) in 2002, with two new ships on order.

Future Considerations

Carnival's management had to continue to monitor several strategic factors and issues for the next few years. The industry itself was expected to see further growth in passengers; consolidation through mergers, buyouts, and smaller cruise operator failures; and the expansion of the industry worldwide. Another factor of concern to management was how to reach the large untapped North American market.

With the industry maturing, cruise competitors had become more sophisticated in their marketing efforts, and price competition was the norm in most cruise segments. (For a partial listing of major industry competitors, see **Exhibit 7**.) Royal Caribbean Cruise Lines had also instituted a major shipbuilding program and was successfully challenging Carnival Cruise Lines in the contemporary segment. The emergence of the Walt Disney Company in the cruise market with two 80,000-ton cruise liners in 1998 and the prospect of new ships on the horizon could significantly impact the "family" cruise vacation segment.

With competition intensifying, industry observers believed the wave of failures, mergers, buyouts, and strategic alliances would increase. Regency Cruises ceased operations on October 29, 1995, and filed for Chapter 11 bankruptcy. American Family Cruises, a spin-off from Costa Cruise Lines, failed to reach the family market, and Carnival's *Fiestamarina* failed to reach the Spanish-speaking market. EffJohn International sold its Commodore Cruise subsidiary to a group of Miami-based investors, which then chartered one of its two ships to World Explorer Cruises/Semester at Sea. Commodore later folded and liquidated its

Exhibit 7
Major Industry
Competitors

Celebrity Cruises, 5200 Blue Lagoon Drive, Miami, FL 33126

Celebrity Cruises operated six modern cruise ships on 4-, 7-, and 10-day cruises to Bermuda, the Caribbean, the Panama Canal, and Alaska. Celebrity attracted first-time cruisers as well as seasoned cruisers. Purchased by Royal Caribbean on July 30, 1997.

Norwegian Cruise Lines, 95 Merrick Way, Coral Gables, FL 33134

Norwegian Cruise Lines (NCL), formally Norwegian Caribbean Lines, was the first company to base a modern fleet of cruise ships in the Port of Miami. It operated eight modern cruise liners on 3-, 4-, and 7-day eastern and western Caribbean cruises and cruises to Bermuda. A wide variety of activities and entertainment attracted a diverse array of customers. NCL had just completed reconstruction of two ships, and its newest ship, *Norwegian Sky*, a 2,000-passenger ship, was delivered in summer 1999.

Disney Cruise Line, 500 South Buena Vista Street, Burbank, CA 91521

Disney had just recently entered the cruise market, with the introduction of the *Disney Magic* and *Disney Wonder*. Both ships catered to both children and adults and featured 875 state-rooms each. Each cruise included a visit to Disney's private island, Castaway Cay. Although Disney had only two ships and the cruise portion of the vacation was small, its potential for future growth was substantial.

Princess Cruises, 10100 Santa Monica Boulevard, Los Angeles, CA 90067

Princess Cruises, with its fleet of 10 *Love Boats*, offered 7-day and extended cruises to the Caribbean, Alaska, Canada, Africa, the Far East, South America, and Europe. Princess's primary market was the upscale 50-plus experienced traveler, according to Mike Hannan, Senior Vice President for Marketing Services. Princess ships had ambiance best described as casual elegance and were famous for their Italian-style dining rooms and onboard entertainment.

Royal Caribbean Cruise Lines, 1050 Caribbean Way, Miami, FL 33132

Royal Caribbean's ships had consistently been given high marks by passengers and travel agents over the past 21 years. Royal Caribbean's ships were built for the contemporary market, were large and modern, and offered 3-, 4-, and 7-day as well as extended cruises.

Source: Cruise Line International Association (2001) and company 10K forms and annual reports.

ships. Sun Cruise Lines merged with the Epirotiki Cruise Line under the name Royal Olympic Cruises, and Cunard bought the Royal Viking Line and its name from Kloster Cruise Ltd., with one ship of its fleet being transferred to Kloster's Royal Cruise Line.

The increasing industry capacity was also a source of concern to cruise operators. The slow growth in industry demand was occurring during a period when industry berth capacity continued to grow at a faster rate. The entry of Disney and the ships already on order by current operators were expected to increase industry berth capacity by over 10,000 per year for the next four years, a significant increase. Combined with the lingering effects of September 11 and the recent negative publicity, the danger lies in cruise operators using the "price" weapon in their marketing campaigns to fill cabins, especially in the next few years. If cruise operators could make a reasonable return on investment, operating costs would have to be reduced (affecting quality of services) to remain profitable. This would increase the likelihood of further industry acquisitions, mergers, consolidations, and failures. Long-term implications concerned the addition of capacity faster than the growth in customer demand.

Exhibit 8
Board of Directors of Carnival Corporation

Mickey Arison
Chairman of the Board and Chief
Executive Officer
Carnival Corporation

Maks L. Birnbach
Chairman of the Board
Fullcut Manufacturers, Inc.

Robert H. Dickinson
President and Chief Operating Officer
Carnival Cruise Lines

James M. Dublin
Senior Partner
Paul, Weiss, Rifkind, Wharton & Garrison

A. Kirk Lanterman
Chairman of the Board and Chief
Executive Officer
Holland America Line-Westours Inc.

Stuart Subotnick
General Partner and Executive Vice President
Metromedia Company

Meshulam Zonis
Former Senior Vice President Operations
Carnival Cruise Lines

Shari Arison
Chairman
Arison Holdings (1998) Ltd.

Richard G. Capen, Jr.
Former United States
Ambassador to Spain

Arnold W. Donald
Chairman and Chief Executive Officer
Merisant Company

Howard S. Frank
Vice Chairman of the Board and Chief
Operating Officer
Carnival Corporation

Modesto A. Maidique
President
Florida International University

Sherwood M. Weiser
The Continental Companies, LLC
Chairman of the Board and Chief
Executive Officer

Uzi Zucker
Senior Managing Director
Bear Stearns & Co. Inc.

Source: Carnival Corporation, 2002 Annual Report, p. 35.

Carnival's management and Board of Directors (see **Exhibit 8**) believed that demand would continue to increase well into the future. Considering that only a small percentage of the North American market had taken a cruise vacation, reaching more of the North American target market would improve industry profitability. Industry analysts stated that the "assessment of market potential" was only an "educated guess." What if the current demand did not grow according to industry and cruise line projections?

CASE 14

Reebok International, Ltd. (2002)

*Thomas L. Wheelen, Moustafa H. Abdelsamad,
Richard D. Wheelen, and Thomas L. Wheelen II*

Report of Chairman Fireman

PAUL FIREMAN, CHAIRMAN AND CHIEF EXECUTIVE OFFICER (CEO) OF REEBOK, reviewed the accomplishments, highlights of 2001, and issues facing the company in his letter to shareholders in the *2001 Annual Report*:

> 2001 was another solid year for our company. Our profits increased 27% over the prior year despite some difficult economic declines in many of our key markets and a strong U.S. dollar which adversely impacted our margins in most foreign countries. Two years ago when I returned to managing the day-to-day operations of the company, I established several key objectives and committed to you that they would be achieved within two years. I committed to you that we would 1) establish a result-oriented culture, 2) strengthen our management team, 3) contemporize our products, 4) create relevant advertising and effective retail and consumer marketing campaigns, and as a result of these efforts, 5) grow quality market share. I am very pleased that we have made substantial progress on all of these fronts.
>
> Our management team has been enhanced significantly with the promotions of Jay Margolis to the newly created position of President and Chief Operating Officer of Reebok International Ltd., and David Perdue as President and CEO of the Reebok Brand. Jay will be responsible for the day-to-day oversight of our company-wide operations. He has over 25 years of experience leading highly visible, fashion-oriented footwear and apparel brands. Jay has strong leadership skills and has already begun to provide invaluable product, marketing and operational support to our brand presidents. David has a wealth of international experience and understands the complexity of a global marketplace. He has earned the respect and trust of our retailers and employees.

In addition to enhancing our leadership team, we have significantly improved the style and fashionability of our products and the quality and effectiveness of our marketing platforms. These initiatives provide us with a solid foundation from which we can grow quality market share.

Our Reebok Brand management team had an excellent year in 2001 making solid progress in their quest to make the Brand more relevant and aspirational to young men and women. During 2001, we further strengthened the Reebok Brand management team by filling several key positions with industry veterans who are all well respected, seasoned professionals. In our largest market, the United States, the Reebok Brand grew market share in the key athletic specialty channel each month during 2001. This channel is very influential as it sets the fashion tone for the U.S. market, particularly among young men and women.

In order to generate even greater focus on our targeted consumer segments during 2001, we realigned and restructured our product creation teams. Under our new structure, individual teams design and develop products specifically geared toward the needs of each of our primary channels of distribution and each of our targeted consumer groups. As a result of this new structure, our product and marketing teams are much more connected with the ultimate consumer and are, therefore, more successful at creating product and marketing initiatives that are relevant to both the individual retailer and the specific consumer.

In order to support our product focus, we have launched three marketing campaigns to reach our core consumers. Our Classic campaign, which we began in 2000, has been very successful in growing this important segment of our business. Our new women's campaign called "It's a Woman's World," which we launched in October 2001, is centered around a contemporary and inspirational message designed to further attract young women to our Brand.

In January 2002 in New York City, we launched our newest marketing campaign, "The Sounds & Rhythm of Sport." This campaign has already begun to energize the Reebok Brand among the critically important fashion consumer, particularly young men. These campaigns provide us with a solid marketing platform for the Reebok Brand that will continue for the next several years.

In 2001 we began our exciting new business venture with the National Football League ("NFL"), by outfitting 26 NFL teams. Beginning with the 2002 season, and for the next 10 years, the Reebok Brand will be exclusively worn by all 32 NFL teams, on the field and on the sidelines. Each week, the NFL attracts more than 110 million spectators in the United States. During 2002 we will broaden our consumer reach by developing and bringing to market new performances and lifestyle product collections, such as "NFL Equipment" and "NFL Classics."

Also in 2001, we entered into a 10-year agreement with the National Basketball Association ("NBA") under which Reebok will design, manufacture, sell, and market licensed merchandise for the NBA, the Women's National Basketball Association ("WNBA") and the National Basketball Development League ("NBDL"), the NBA's new minor league. Over the next three years, we will expand our exclusive agreement with the NBA to include all 29 teams in the league.

Our partnerships with NFL and NBA are strategically aligned with our objective to build the most successful sports licensing business in the world. And, it appears that we are very timely in re-entering the sports licensing business. We have recently seen a return to fashionability for sports licensed apparel and retailers are currently enjoying improved profitability and sell-through for these product categories.

Our new NFL and NBA partnerships allow Reebok Brand to leverage its core competencies and significantly increase its Brand visibility and product sales. The increased visibility of the Reebok Brand on thousands of professional athletes is sending a very positive message to our consumers every day. To date, sales of these apparel licenses have exceeded our expectations and we are very optimistic about the long-term potential for growth.

Our Rockport, Ralph Lauren Footwear and Greg Norman brands had a somewhat difficult year due in large part to their dependency on the department store channel in the United States. This channel was very promotional and hard hit throughout 2001. We are optimistic that the performance of these brands will improve during 2002. The leadership at all of these brands was changed over the past year. We believe this new leadership is capable of driving future revenue growth by gaining quality market share. During 2002 these businesses will be launching several new initiatives in order to improve sales performances. These initiatives include the introduction of new product and segmentation strategies that are designed to maximize our opportunity in the various trade channels we serve. We believe that there is a long-term opportunity for revenue and profit growth for all of these brands and we intend to vigorously pursue these over the next several years.

Our multi-brand strategy continues to provide us with a strong foundation from which we can drive greater synergies and improve our operating performance. During 2001, we successfully integrated our Rockport and Ralph Lauren brands into our domestic shared service operation. We have now integrated all of our brands into this center. Our shared services philosophy enables us to leverage our core competencies and, as a result, we reduced our general and administrative type expenses for the year. This is the third consecutive year in which we have reduced these types of expenses by utilizing our shared services platform.

Our overall balance sheet remains strong. In 2001, we generated $176 million of cash flow from operations, and during the past four years we've generated approximately $800 million of operating cash flow. These are very solid cash flow results driven by the continual improvement of all our key balance sheet metrics. Our capital structure is sound and provides us with significant financial flexibility. Over the next several years we intend our free cash flow to grow our business and improve shareholder value.

In all that we do, Reebok remains committed to corporate social responsibility, led by our stand for human rights. The most recent Reebok Human Rights Award ceremony was held as part of the Cultural Olympiad of the Salt Lake Olympic Winter games in February 2002. Over the last 14 years Reebok has honored 67 young men and women from around the world who

**Exhibit 1
Human Rights
Production
Standards: Reebok
International, Ltd.**

Nondiscrimination
Reebok will seek business partners that do not discriminate in hiring and employment practices on grounds of race, color, national origin, gender, religion, or political or other opinion.

Working Hours/Overtime
Reebok will seek business partners who do not require more than 60-hour workweeks on a regularly scheduled basis, except for appropriately compensated overtime in compliance with local laws, and we will favor business partners who use 48-hour workweeks as their maximum normal requirement.

Forced or Compulsory Labor
Reebok will not work with business partners that use forced or other compulsory labor, including labor that was required as a means of political coercion or as punishment for peacefully expressing political views, in the manufacture of its products. Reebok will not purchase materials that were produced by forced prison or other compulsory labor and will terminate business relationships with any sources found to utilize such labor.

Child Labor
Reebok will not work with business partners that use child labor. The term *child* generally refers to a person who was less than 14 years of age, or younger than the age for completing compulsory education if that age was higher than 14. In countries where the law defines *child* to include individuals who were older than 14, Reebok will apply that definition.

Freedom of Association
Reebok will seek business partners that share its commitment to the right of employees to establish and join organizations of their own choosing. Reebok will seek to assure that no employee was penalized because of his or her nonviolent exercise of that right. Reebok recognizes and respects the right of all employees to organize and bargain collectively.

Fair Wages
Reebok will seek business partners who share our commitment to the betterment of wage and benefit levels that address the basic needs of workers and their families.

Safe and Healthy Work Environment
Reebok will seek business partners that strive to assure employees a safe and healthy workplace and that do not expose workers to hazardous conditions.

Source: Reebok International, Ltd., "Reebok Human Rights Production Standards," company document.

have displayed uncommon courage and leadership. Our unwavering respect for individual human dignity guides the way we discharge our responsibilities to all our stakeholders, including our customers, business partners, employees and their families, suppliers, community neighbors and to our shareholders. This core value is expressed in our policies and our practices and is intrinsic to our company's identity. [See **Exhibit 1** for Reebok's Human Right's Production Standards.] We believe that pursuing this philosophy is a prudent business decision that aids customer loyalty, enhances employee motivation and retention and helps protect our corporate image.

In summary, I believe we have the management team in place that is capable of driving our brands forward by executing our long-term strategic plans. We will continue to create fashionable, high quality products that, at all times, meet and exceed our consumers' expectations. We will communicate marketing themes and relevant messages that speak directly to our various consumer segments thereby generating greater consumer demand for our products. We will work with all of our retail partners to ensure that our products are readily accessible at retail and that our brands are properly presented. Our goal is to grow quality market share for all our brands and to generate long-term improvement in the value we create for our shareholders. I look forward to meeting the challenges, which lie ahead, and delivering improved performance during 2002. I want to take this opportunity to thank our employees for their tireless efforts and unwavering commitment to our success. Our employees are our greatest assets and it is through their dedication to excellence that will continue to succeed.[1]

Background and History

The history of Reebok began in England in the 1890s. Athletes wanted to run faster. To meet this demand, Joseph William Foster developed cleated running shoes. By 1895, he had formed J.W. Foster and Sons, which made hand-stitched athletic shoes for many of the top athletes of that time.

In 1958, two of J. W. Foster's grandsons started a companion company that they named Reebok International after an African gazelle. In time this new company would absorb the parent company.

In 1979, Paul Fireman purchased an exclusive North American distribution license from Reebok. That year he marketed three running shoes in the United States, and at $60 a pair, they were the most expensive on the market. Sales increased slowly, exceeding $1.3 million in 1981, and eventually outgrew the production capacity of the UK plant. In 1981, needing financing for expansion, Reebok USA swapped 56% of its stock for $77,500 with Pentland Industries, a British shoe distributor, and established production facilities in Korea. That year, in a move that was to characterize the company, Reebok noted the popularity of a new fitness craze called aerobic dancing. It also noted that no one was making a shoe for this purpose. Thus it was the first company to market an athletic shoe just for women. Shortly, the "Freestyle" line, a fashion-oriented aerobic shoe, was introduced and sales took off. Company sales increased from $3.5 million in 1982 to $3.6 billion in 1997.

In 1985, Reebok USA and Reebok International merged to become Reebok International, Ltd. Four million shares of stock were offered to the public, and Pentland became a large shareholder. Paul Fireman continued as CEO and Chairman. This share offering was used to finance the company's growth strategy.

Reebok pursued a strategy of line extensions and acquisitions. In 1986, it acquired the Rockport Company for $118.5 million in cash. In 1987, Reebok purchased the outstanding common stock of Avia Group International for $181.0 million in cash and 194,000 shares of Reebok common shares. It also acquired ESE Sports for $18 million in cash. Rockport purchased John A. Frye Co. for $10 million cash. In 1988 and 1989, it acquired Ellesse USA, Inc. (for $25 million in cash) and Boston Whaler, respectively. In 1981, it purchased a large portion of Pentland Group's holdings in Reebok (Pentland still had an ownership interest of about 13% after the Reebok purchase) and acquired the assets of Above the Rim International. The following year, Reebok acquired Perfection Sports Fashions, which marketed under the Tinley brand name. In 1993, Reebok sold Ellesse USA and Boston Whaler, Inc.

In the late 1980s, after five years of phenomenal growth in the United States, the decision was made to aggressively pursue expansion into overseas markets and achieve an objective of 50% sales internationally. In 1997, Reebok products were available in 140 countries, and about 45.1% of total sales were generated from international sales.

In 1992, Paul Fireman set a bold goal for the company—to displace Nike as the top sports and fitness brand and become number one by 1995. By the end of 1994, Reebok's market share was 21.3%, a 3.4% increase over 1993. Nike's market share decreased by 6.3% from 31.7% to 29.7% during the same time. Since Fireman had established this goal to be number one, public perceptions of the brand had noticeably changed. Reebok started out as a brand that focused on aerobics, walking, and women. Eventually, it began to receive real credence from serious athletes–but not to the extent received by Nike. "We've lost the Michael Jordan generation. That battle has been lost—Nike owns them,"[2] said Tom Carmody, Reebok's General Manager–North America. The next step was a two-year marketing offensive designed to bump Nike from number one. The project included more inspired and focused advertising, expansion of the apparel, business, and more cross-promotion with other marketers, like Wheaties, to enhance Reebok's image as a leading sports brand.[3] Reebok intended to establish a worldwide reputation in sports as a supplier of innovative, high-performance athletic footwear, apparel, and equipment.

In late 1995, Reebok was facing an open revolt by a group of institutional shareholders who owned about 15% of Reebok's stock. This group included Warren Buffet's Government Employees Insurance Company (GEICO) and Chieftain Capital Management. These groups "were fed up with management missteps, rising costs, earning disappointments, and a sagging stock."[4] Some of the groups wanted Fireman to resign as CEO. Fireman said that he "isn't opposed to a new chief executive officer or chief operating officer." He further stated, "Titles don't mean anything."[5] Earlier in 1995, both joint presidents had resigned. Fireman announced that there had been "a consolidation of leadership and a focus."[6] Glenn Greenberg, Money Manager of Chieftain Capital, indicated that Chieftain had dumped 4.5 million shares of Reebok. Warburg Pincus Asset Management and GEICO had reportedly sold Reebok shares. Over the next year, the management team stabilized.

On June 7, 1996, Reebok sold its subsidiary Avia Group International, Inc. The company recorded a special charge of $54,064,000 in the fourth quarter of 1995 for this sale. In 1987, Reebok had paid $181 million in cash and 194,000 shares of Reebok stock for Avia. The company sold the Avia Group to refocus the company's strategies back to its core brands. As part of this strategy, the company discontinued its Bok Division in November 1996. Bok products were aimed at four segments and targeting the 16- to 24-year-old market: "Freesport," characterized by activities such as skateboarding, surfing, snowboarding; "Clubsport," a fashion-oriented line; "Utility," with worker-boot influence; and "Classic," updated popular designs from earlier seasons.

On July 28, 1996, the Board of Directors authorized the repurchase of up to 24.0 million shares of the company's common stock. The offer to repurchase commenced on July 30, 1996, and expired on August 27, 1996, and the price range for repurchasing stock was $30.00 to $36.00 net per share in cash. The company repurchased approximately 17.0 million common stock at a price of $36.00. Reebok's Board of Directors also suspended the quarterly dividend.[7] An analyst felt these measures resulted from the earlier revolt by the institutional shareholders.

The mid-1990s until today has been characterized by 'Y' Generation revolt. The Y Generation moved from athletic shoes to brown shoes provided by companies like Van, Airwalk, Etonic, and DC. Both Reebok and Nike were caught flat footed on this change.

Fireman said, "Consumers appear to be turning their backs on marketing type and super-heroes. . . . Every 10 years or so, consumers get bored with the status quo. People change, fashions change, sports trends change. Without much warning a fundamental [Y Generation] market shift occurs. And things are never the same again."[8] The impact of the shift was still being felt. Intially, the Y generation revolt resulted in a "worldwide product glut."[9]

During this period, there was an Asian financial crisis, which caused serious decline in athletic shoes and apparel sales in this region of the world. This lasted for several years.

On March 9, 2001, the company purchased selected assets of LogoAthletic ("Logo") for $14.2 million. Included in the assets purchased were inventory, equipment, facility leases, and the rights to Logo's trademarks. The acquisition did not materially affect the company's consolidated financial statements.[10]

Effective January 1, 2001, the company increased its ownership in one of its European subsidiaries and acquired majority ownership in one of its Latin American distributors. The impact of these events was not material to the consolidated financial statements. Also effective January 1, 2001, the company sold its interest in its South African subsidiary to an independent distributor. The sale price and historical operating results of the company's South African subsidiary were not material to the consolidated financial results or consolidated financial position of the company.[11]

In fall of 2001, the company signed Allen Iverson, 2001 NBA Most Valuable Player and star guard of the Philadelphia 76ers, to a lifetime spokesperson contract for $50 million. On July 16, 2002, Iverson pleaded not guilty to 14 charges in a Philadelphia court. All charges were later dropped.

Corporate Governance

Board of Directors

The Board of Directors of Reebok International, Ltd., as of December 31, 2001, included[12]:

Name	Company
Paul B. Fireman	Chairman, President, & Chief Operating Officer, & CEO Reebok International, Ltd.
Norman Axelrod	Chairman of the Board & Chief Executive Officer Linens 'N Things, Inc.
Paul R. Duncan	Retired Executive Vice President Reebok International, Ltd.
Mannie L. Jackson	Chairman of the Board & Chief Executive Officer Harlem Globetrotters International, Inc.
Richard G. Lesser	Senior Corporate Advisor & Director TJX Companies, Inc.
Jay Margolis	President & Chief Operating Officer Reebok International Ltd.
Geoffrey Nune	Retired Senior Vice President & General Counsel Millipore Corporation
David L. Patrick	Executive Vice President & General Counsel The Coca-Cola Company
Dorothy E. Puhy	Chief Financial Officer & Assistant Treasurer Dana-Farber Cancer Institute
Thomas M. Ryan	Chairman of the Board, President & Chief Executive Officer CVS Corporation

Exhibit 2 contains a brief biographical sketch on each board member, lists the committees and membership, and describes compensation and stock options for the board members.

During 2001, each director who was not an officer or employee of the company received $25,000 annually plus $2,000 for each committee chairmanship held, $2,000 for each directors' meeting, and $1,000 for each committee meeting attended, plus expenses. Beginning in 1998, as a part of a new policy adopted by the Board of Directors that required each director to own Reebok Common Stock with a market value of at least four times the amount of the annual retainer within five years from the date of the director's first election to the Board, a minimum of 40% of the annual retainer was paid to the directors in Reebok's common stock.[13]

Top Management[14]

Paul B. Fireman (58) founded the company and has served as its Chief Executive Officer and a Director since the company's founding in 1979 and its Chairman of the Board since 1986. With the exception of 1988, Fireman served as President of the company from 1979 until December 2001, with the appointment of Jay Margolis as President. In the mid and late 1980s, Fireman was one of the highest paid executives in the country. His salary package included base pay of $357,200 plus 5% of the amount by which Reebok's pretax earnings topped $20 million. He averaged $13.6 million a year. In 1990, the Board of Directors decided that Fireman's compensation should be more closely tied to increases in value for Reebok shareholders. Fireman had a new employment contract that determined his annual salary, plus an annual bonus based on the company's earnings, with a maximum of $1 million. He also was given a one-time grant of options to purchase 2.5 million Reebok common shares. The options become exercisable over a period of five years at exercise prices ranging from $17.32 to $18.37 per share and were exercisable until July 24, 2000. In 1991, Reebok paid a $513,601 premium on a $50 million life insurance policy for Fireman and his wife, Phyllis. This was reduced to only $46,162 in 1996. Fireman paid the remainder of the premiums. There had been some shareholder criticism of the high level of Fireman's compensation.

Paul Fireman and his wife Phyllis owned 8,298,377 (14.0%) and 6,412,000 (10.9%) shares, respectively. This represented about a 24.9% ownership interest. This left the company insiders and board members (excluding Fireman) with a 5.6% ownership interest.

Fireman was known to have a problem with delegation, which contributed to management turnover. A former executive who was highly recruited and lasted less than a year said that "Paul was the sort of fellow who would make a great neighbor. . . . But he was absolutely convinced that no one can do a job better than he can."[15] The institution investment groups felt that this caused some of the turmoil in the company management team. Fireman was a strong advocate of "est training," the human-potential program founded by Werner Erhart in the 1970s. The Forum was the current version of est. His admiration for est was best summarized when he said, "I believe in anything that allows you to look at yourself and see what's possible."[16] A former Reebok executive said that "the company sometimes divides up between those who buy into the est message and those who don't." He further said, "Key employees, even top management, at times seem to be kept out of the loop, denied crucial new research or excluded from strategy meetings unless they accept the est outlook and methods. Fervent est adherents, meanwhile, form a sort of subculture with its own attitudes and jargon."[17]

On June 28, 2002, Paul Fireman and his wife announced that they had adopted a common stock trading contract plan under which they would sell up to two million shares of Reebok stock through variable common prepaid forward contracts at three pre-determined price levels. The Firemans had not sold any of their stock since 1994. These shares were to be sold

Exhibit 2 Board of Directors: Reebok International

A. BOARD MEMBERSHIP

1. Class I members whose terms will expire at the 2005 Annual Meeting of Shareholders:

Name	Business Experiences and Current Directorships	Age	Director Since
Paul B. Fireman	CEO and Chairman of the Board of Directors of the company; President of the company (1979 to March 1987 and December 1989 through December 2001); and Director of Abiomed, Inc., a manufacturer of medical devices.	58	1979
Dorothy E. Puhy	Chief Financial Officer and Assistant Treasurer, Dana-Farber Cancer Institute (since 1994), a leading health care provider and research concern; Chief Financial Officer, New England Medical Center Hospitals, Inc. (from 1989 to 1994), a major health care provider.	50	2000
Thomas M. Ryan	President and CEO (since May 1998) and Chairman of the Board (since April 1999) of CVS Corporation ("CVS"), a company in the chain drug store industry; President and Chief Executive Officer of CVS Pharmacy Inc. (since 1994); Director of FleetBoston Financial Corporation, a financial services company; and Directors, Tricon Global Restaurants, Inc., the world's largest quick-serve restaurant company.	49	1998

2. Class II members whose terms will expire at the 2003 Annual Meeting of the Shareholders:

Name	Business Experiences and Current Directorships	Age	Director Since
Norman Axelrod	Chief Executive Officer of Linens 'N Things, Inc. (LNT), a national retailer of home textiles, housewares, and home accessories (since 1988); Chairman of the Board of Directors for LNT (since 1996); President and CEO of LNT, a division of Melville Corp. (1996 to 1998); various senior management positions at Bloomingdale's, a national department store (1976 to 1988); and Director of Jaclyn, Inc., a handbags and apparel company.	49	1979
Paul R. Duncan	Retired Executive Vice President of the company (February 1990 to December 1998 and January 2000 to January 2001), with various executive responsibilities, including President of the company's Specialty Business Groups (October 1995 to November 1996 and January 2000 to January 2001); Chief Financial Officer of the company (1985 to June 1995); and Director of Entersays Networks, successor to Cabletron System, Inc., a computer networking company.	61	1989
Richard G. Lesser	Senior Corporate Advisor (since February 2002) and Director (since 1994) of TJX Companies, Inc., an off-price apparel and home furnishings retailer; Chief Operating Officer of TJX Companies (November 1994 to February 2000) and Executive Vice President (February 1991 through December 2001); Chairman, The Marmaxx Group, a division of TJX Companies that operates TJ Maxx and Marshalls (February 2001 to December 2001); President, The Marmaxx Group (February 1996 to February 2001); Director of A.C. Moore Arts & Crafts, Inc., an operator of arts and crafts stores; and Director of Dollar Tree Stores, Inc., a national chain of variety stores selling merchandise at $1.	67	1988
Deval L. Patrick	Executive Vice President and General Counsel, The Coca-Cola Company, a beverage sales company (since April 2001); Vice President and General Counsel, Texaco, Inc., an energy company (1999 to March 2001); Partner,	45	2001

Exhibit 2 *(continued)*

Day, Berry & Howard (1997 to 1999), a law firm; Assistant Attorney General, Civil Rights Division of the U.S. Department of Justice (1994 to 1997); and Director, Coca-Cola Enterprises, Inc., which markets, distributes, and produces bottled and canned beverages.

3. Class I members whose terms will expire at the 2003 Annual Meeting of the Shareholders:

Name	Business Experiences and Current Directorships	Age	Director Since
Mannie L. Jackson	Chairman, CEO, and majority owner of Harlem Globetrotters International, Inc., a sports and entertainment entity (since August 1992); retired Senior Vice President, Corporate Marketing and Administration, Honeywell, Inc., a manufacturer of control systems, and prior to that served in various executive capacities for Honeywell, Inc., beginning in 1968; Director of Ashland Inc., a vertically intergrated petroleum and chemical company; and Director of The Stanley Works, a commercial, consumer, and specialty tools company.	62	1996
Jay Margolis	President and Chief Operating Officer of the company (since December 2001); Executive Vice President and President of the Specialty Business Groups of the company (December 2000 to December 2001); Chairman and CEO of E7th.com, a business-to-business supply solution for the footwear industry, linking wholesalers with retailers (August 2000 to November 2000); Chairman and CEO of Esprit de Corporation (June 1995 to January 1999); President and Vice Chairman of the Board of Tommy Hilfiger (January 1992 to June 1995); Vice Chairman of the Board of Liz Claiborne (January 1982 to January 1992).	53	2002
Geoffrey Nunes	Retired Senior Vice President and General Counsel for Millipore Corporation, a leader in the field of separation technology.	71	1986

B. BOARD COMMITTEES

During 2001 the Board of Directors held six meetings. All the directors attended at least 75% of the Board and relevant committee meetings during 2001, except for Mr. Ryan, who attended 63% of the meetings.

The Audit Committee, composed of Ms. Puhy (Chair), Mr. Lesser, and Mr. Nunes, held three meetings during 2001. The Audit Committee recommended to the Board of Directors the independent public auditors to be engaged by the company; reviewed with such auditors and management the company's internal accounting procedures and controls; and reviewed with such auditors the audit scope and results of their audit of the consolidated financial statements of the company.

The Compensation Committee, composed of Mr. Nunes (Chair), Mr. Ryan, and Mr. Axelrod (starting May 1, 2001), held four meetings during 2001 and acted once by unanimous written consent. The Compensation Committee administered the company's stock option and compensation plans, set compensation for the CEO, reviewed the compensation of the other executive officers, and provided recommendations to the Board regarding compensation matters.

The Board Affairs Committee, composed of Mr. Lesser (Chair), Messrs. Jackson, Ryan, Nunes (until May 1, 2001), and Mr. Patrick (starting May 1, 2001), held two meetings during 2001. The Board Affairs Committee was responsible for considering Board governance issues. The Board Affairs Committee also recommended individuals to serve as Directors of the company and will consider nominees recommended by shareholders. Recommendations by shareholders should be submitted in writing to the Board Affairs Committee, in care of the President of the company.

The Executive Committee, composed of Mr. Fireman (Chair), Messrs. Duncan, and Nunes, did not meet during 2001. The Executive Committee may take certain action permitted by law and the bylaws in the intervals between meetings of the full Board, and in fact, it did take action once by unanimous written consent during 2001.

(continued)

Exhibit 2 *(continued)*

C. BOARD COMPENSATION and STOCK OPTIONS

During 2001 each director who was not an officer or employee of the company received an annual retainer of $25,000, plus $2,000 for each committee chairmanship held and $2,000 for each directors' meeting and $1,000 for each committee meeting attended, plus expenses. As part of a policy adopted by the Board of Directors in 1998 that requires each director to own Reebok's common stock with a market value of at least four times the amount of the annual retainer within five years after the director's first election to the Board, a minimum of 40% of the annual retainer was paid to the directors in Reebok's common stock.

The company's Equity and Deferred Compensation Plan for Directors provided for the issuance of stock options to directors and provides a means by which directors may defer all or a portion of their directors' fees. In addition, the shareholders of Reebok approved the 2001 Equity Incentive and Director Deferred Compensation Plan at the 2001 Annual Meeting. These two plans shall be referred to as the "Directors' Plan" for purposes of this section.

Source: "2002 Notice of Annual Meeting of Shareholders" (March 28, 2002), pp. 3–5.

over a three-year period under provisions of the contract. The contract provided flexibility to the Firemans in the timing of their transactions and allowed them to participate fully in the upscale potential of Reebok stock up to a level 40% above the predetermined price level. The first million shares were sold in June 2002 at the current market price. Fireman said, "These contracts allow my wife and me to diversify our holdings and meet some long time estate planning goals." He further stated, "We both remain committed to Reebok, as evidenced by our substantial stock interests."[18]

On August 9, 2002, Paul Fireman, Chairman and CEO, and Ken Watchmaker, CFO, both signed sworn statements and submitted the statements to the United States Securities and Exchange Commission (SEC), pursuant to Commission Order No. 4-460 (new legislation by Congress, in light of the Enron, WorldCom, Tyco, and Global Crossing scandals requiring the personal signatures of top management on financial statements).

Jay M. Margolis (53) became President and Chief Operating Officer in December 2001. Margolis joined the company as Executive Vice President and President of the Specialty Business Groups in December 2000. Margolis was responsible for overseeing the management of the Reebok Brand (including its league licensing business), the Greg Norman Collection, Ralph Lauren Footwear Co., and the Rockport Company. Pior to joining the company, he served as the Chairman and CEO of E7th.com, a business-to-business supply solution for the footwear industry that linked wholesalers with retailers. Margolis also served as Chairman and CEO of Esprit de Corporation (1995–1999). From 1992 to 1994, he was President and Vice Chairman of the Board of Directors of Tommy Hilfiger. Margolis spent nine years at Liz Claiborne, Inc. where he held several positions including Vice Chairman of the Board of Directors (1989–1992), President of Liz Claiborne Sportswear (1986–1989), and President of Liz Claiborne Menswear (1983–1986).

Martin Cole was promoted from Executive Vice President to President and CEO of Reebok Brand on June 12, 2002. Cole joined the company in December, 2001. He previously was employed by Nike. He served five years as the Nike's general manager for Europe. He and his team were credited with increasing European sales from under $1 billion to over $2 billion during his five-year tenure. He replaced David Perdue, who accepted the position of Chairman and CEO of Pillowtex Corporation.

Kenneth I. Watchmaker (59) has been an Executive Vice President of the company since February 1994 and was appointed Chief Financial Officer in June 1995. Prior to his appointment as Chief Financial Officer, he was Executive Vice President with responsibility for finance, footwear production, and management information systems. He joined the company in July 1992 as Executive Vice President, Operations and Finance, of the Reebok Brand. Prior to joining the company, Watchmaker was a Senior Partner of Ernst & Young LLP.

James R. Jones III (57) has been Senior Vice President of Human Resources for the company since May 1998. Jones joined the company as Senior Vice President of Human Resources for Reebok Brand in April 1997. Prior to that, Jones was Vice President of Inova Health System from May 1996 through April 1997. From July 1995 through May 1996, Jones was the Senior Vice President of Human Resources of Franciscan Health System. Prior to that, since 1991, Jones was the Vice President of Human Resources of Johns Hopkins University.

David A. Pace (41) became a Senior Vice President of the company in February 2001, having been appointed Vice President and General Counsel, and elected Clerk, in December 1999. From May 1999 until his promotion, Pace was Vice President, Global Alliances and Endorsements for the Reebok Brand. Prior to this position, Pace was Assistant General Counsel from January 1997 until May 1999. In June 1995, Pace joined the company's legal department as Counsel–Marketing. Prior to joining the company, Pace was Vice President and General Counsel of Applied Extrusion Technologies, Inc. from June 1994 to June 1995, prior to which he was an associate of the law firm of Ropes & Gray.

Richard Paterno (44) became Senior Vice President of the company and President of The Rockport Company in June 2001. Paterno was initially hired as Executive Vice President for Sales and General Merchandise Manager of Women's for Rockport in May 2001. Prior to joining Rockport, Paterno worked for Easy Spirit since its inception in 1987 in various capacities. Paterno was Executive Vice President of Sales and Marketing from 1996 until October 1999 when he was promoted to President of Easy Spirit. Paterno held this position until May 2001 when he joined Rockport.

Terry R. Pillow (48) became President and Chief Executive Officer of Ralph Lauren Footwear in June 2001. Pillow joined the company as Senior Vice President of the company and President and Chief Executive Officer of the Rockport Company in 1999. Prior to joining the company, Pillow was President of the apparel division of Coach Leatherware, a subsidiary of Sara Lee Corporation. From 1989 to 1994, Pillow served as President of A/X Armani Exchange, New York.[19]

Executive Compensation

Exhibits 3 and 4 show the aggregate compensation paid or accrued by the company for service rendered during the years ended December 1999, 2000, and 2001 for the Chief Executive Officer and the company's four other most highly compensated executive officers.

Managements' Views on the Future

Managements' views on 14 issues and uncertainties facing the company in 2002 are cited below:[20]

- **Issue 1: The company's business is subject to economic conditions in its major markets.** Such factors included without limitation, recession, inflation, general weakness in retail markets, and changes in consumer purchasing power and preferences. Adverse changes in such economic factors could have a negative effect on the company's business. In 2001, the company saw a considerable slowdown in worldwide growth, particularly following the September 11 terrorist attacks in the United States. Generally weak economic conditions have led to fluctuations in investor confidence, a softening in consumer demand, and a retrenchment in overall spending. It is anticipated that actions taken in the U.S. economy during 2002 will improve the situation. It is hoped that similar stimulus

Exhibit 3 Summary Compensation Table: Reebok International, Ltd.

| Name and Principal Position | Year | Annual Compensation | | | Securities Underlying Options(#)(2) | All Other Compensation ($) |
		Salary ($)	Bonus ($)	Restricted Stock Awards	Long-Term Compensation Awards	
Paul B. Fireman	2001	$1,000,012	$2,075,000	None	None	$55,254
Chairman, President, and CEO	2000	1,000,012	2,100,000	None	2,000,000	55,254
	1999	1,000,012	None	None	500,000	81,539
Jay Margolis	2001	600,002	474,000	2,400,000	400,000	86,325
President and Chief Operating Officer	2000	23,077	200,000	None	150,000	None
Kenneth I. Watchmaker	2001	600,002	976,310	None	198,000	57,743
Executive Vice President and	2000	592,310	980,866	393,750	100,000	44,865
Chief Financial Officer	1999	542,308	457,542	None	101,000	44,062
David A. Perdue	2001	600,002	694,310	None	228,400	37,744
Executive Vice President and	2000	434,624	604,597	393,750	100,000	9,962
President & CEO, Reebok Division	1999	350,012	215,250	None	None	274,291
James R. Jones, III	2001	329,992	238,014	None	90,500	30,906
Senior Vice President and	2000	328,456	229,919	196,875	75,000	25,596
Chief Human Resources Officer	1999	316,928	145,333	None	70,000	13,077

Note: All notes were deleted.

Source: Reebok International, Ltd., "2002 Notice of Annual Meeting of Shareholders" (March 28, 2002), p. 10.

measures in Europe, the United Kingdom, and Asia/Pacific will energize the economies of those regions and contribute to a broader global recovery. However, such a recovery was contingent on a variety of factors and remains uncertain. Thus we expected the market for our business during 2002 to be challenging, at least in the near term.

- **Issue 2: The market for athletic footwear and apparel was intensely competitive and if we failed to compete effectively, we could lose our market position.** The athletic

Exhibit 4 Aggregated Option Exercises in 2001 and Option Values as of December 31, 2001: Reebok International, Ltd.

Name	Acquired on Exercise	Shares Value Realized	Number of Unexercised Options at 12/31/01[1] Exercisable/Unexercisable	Value of Unexercised In-the-Money Options at 12/31/01[1] Exercisable/Unexercisable
Paul B. Fireman	—	—	611,150/2,000,000	4,245,000/17,250,000
Jay Margolis	—	—	37,50/512,500	137,250/1,000,000
Kenneth I. Watchmaker	—	—	175,500/383,500	2,430,938/3,264,633
David A. Perdue	—	—	25,400/294,600	411,888/2,075,973
James R. Jones	—	—	66,250/174,250	963,047/1,586,366

Note:
1. Based on a fair market value as of December 31, 2001, of $26.50 per share. Values are stated on a pretax basis.

Source: Reebok International, Ltd., "2002 Notice of Annual Meeting of Shareholders" (March 28, 2002), p. 13.

footwear and apparel industry was intensely competitive. The principal methods of competition in the industry include price, quality, product design, brand name, marketing and promotion, and our ability to meet delivery commitments to retailers. We competed against a number of domestic and international companies, some of which had greater financial resources than we do. A major marketing or promotional success or technological innovation by one of our competitors could adversely impact our competitive position. Additionally, in countries where the athletic footwear market was mature, our ability to maintain and increase our market share can principally come at the expense of our competitors, which may be difficult to accomplish. Our results of operations and market position may be adversely impacted by our competitors and the competitive pressure in the athletic footwear and apparel industries.

- **Issue 3: Our athletic footwear and apparel business was subject to consumer preferences and unanticipated shifts in consumer preferences could adversely affect our sales and results of operations.** The footwear and apparel industry is subject to rapid changes in consumer preferences. Consumer demand for athletic footwear and apparel is heavily influenced by brand image. Our initiatives to strengthen our brand image, which include conducting extensive market research, introducing new and innovative products that emphasize fashion, and initiating focused advertising campaigns, may not be successful. Additionally, consumers place an emphasis on the "performance" aspect of our athletic footwear. Consequently, we must utilize current and future technology to continue to offer performance-enhancing products. Our failure to anticipate, identify, and react to shifts in consumer preferences and maintain a strong brand image could have an adverse effect on our sales and results of operations.

- **Issue 4: If we fail to accurately forecast consumer demand, we may experience difficulties in handling customer orders or in liquidating excess inventories and our sales and brand image may be adversely affected.** The athletic footwear industry has relatively long lead times for the design and production of products. Consequently, we must commit to production tooling and in some cases to production, in advance of orders based on our forecasts of consumer demand. If we fail to forecast consumer demand accurately, we may under-produce or over-produce a product and encounter difficulty in handling customer orders or in liquidating excess inventory. Additionally, if we overproduce a product based on an aggressive forecast of consumer demand, retailers may not be able to sell the product and may return the unsold quantities and cancel future orders. These outcomes could have an adverse effect on our sales and brand image.

- **Issue 5: Our advertising and marketing expenditures are based on sales forecasts and our failure to achieve these sales forecasts could adversely affect our profitability.** Our advertising and marketing expenditures are based on sales forecasts. These expenditures are made in advance of actual sales. Because the markets in which we do business are highly competitive and our sales are affected by a variety of factors, including brand awareness, changing consumer preferences, and retail market conditions, we may be unable to achieve our sales forecasts. Our failure to achieve our sales forecasts would result in our advertising and marketing expenditures representing a higher percentage of revenues and we could experience higher inventory levels and associated carrying costs, all of which could adversely affect our profitability.

- **Issue 6: If we are required to decrease the price that we charge for our products, we may earn lower gross margins and our revenues and profitability may be adversely affected.** The prices that we are able to charge for our products depend on the type of product offered, the consumer and retailer response to the product, and the prices charged by our competitors. To the extent that we are forced to lower our prices, our gross margins will be lower and our revenues and profitability may be adversely affected.

- **Issue 7: Our report of our backlog of open orders may not be indicative of our level of future sales.** We report our backlog of open orders for our Reebok brand. Our backlog position may not be indicative of future sales because many customer orders are cancelable with little or no penalty. In addition, our backlog position does not reflect "at once" shipments, sales by retail stores that we own and sales made by independent distributors.

- **Issue 8: Our sales and profitability may be adversely affected if our investments in advertising and marketing and our athlete endorsements and athletic sponsorships do not have the effect of increasing retailer acceptance and consumer purchases of our products.** Because consumer demand for athletic footwear and apparel is heavily influenced by brand image, our business requires substantial investments in marketing and advertising, as well as athlete endorsements, athletic sponsorships, and retail presence. In the event that these investments do not achieve the desired effect of increasing consumer purchases and retailer acceptance of our products, our sales and profitability may be adversely affected.

- **Issue 9: Our international sales and manufacturing operations are subject to the risks of doing business abroad, which could affect our ability to sell or manufacture our products in international markets, obtain products from foreign suppliers or control the cost of our products.** We operate facilities and sell products in numerous countries outside the United States. Additionally, a substantial portion of our products is manufactured abroad and we have suppliers located in China, Indonesia, Thailand, and the Philippines. Our athletic footwear and apparel sales and manufacturing operations are subject to the risks of doing business abroad. These risks include:
  - Fluctuations in currency exchange rates;
  - Political instability;
  - Limitations on conversion of foreign currencies into U.S. dollars;
  - Restrictions on dividend payments and other payments by our foreign subsidiaries;
  - Withholding and other taxes on dividend payments and other payments by our foreign subsidiaries;
  - Import duties, tariffs, quotas, and other restrictions on free trade, particularly as these regulations may affect our operations in China;
  - Hyperinflation in some foreign countries; and
  - Investments regulation and other restrictions by foreign governments.

  If these risks limit or prevent us from selling or manufacturing products in any significant international market, prevent us from acquiring products from our foreign suppliers, or significantly increase the cost of our products, our operations could be seriously disrupted until alternative suppliers are found or alternative markets are developed. Although we may enter into forward currency exchange contracts and options to hedge the risk of exchange rate fluctuations, these steps may not fully protect us against this risk and we may incur losses.

- **Issue 10: Because we rely on independent manufacturers to produce most of our products, our sales and profitability may be adversely affected if our independent manufacturers fail to meet pricing, product quality and timeliness requirements or if we are unable to obtain some components used in our products from limited supply sources.** We depend upon independent manufacturers to manufacture our products in a timely and cost-efficient manner while maintaining specified quality standards. We also rely upon the availability of sufficient production capacity at our manufacturers. Additionally, it is essential that our manufacturers deliver our products in a timely manner because our orders are cancelable by customers if agreed-upon delivery windows are not met. A failure by one or more of our manufacturers to meet established criteria for pricing, product quality, or timely delivery could adversely impact our sales and profitability. In addition, some of the components used in our products are obtained from only one or two sources. A loss of one of these supply sources could disrupt and delay production and adversely affect our sales and profitability.

- **Issue 11: We have substantial existing debt and may incur additional debt in the future.** We have substantial amounts of outstanding indebtedness. Our substantial level of indebtedness increases the possibility that we may be unable to generate cash sufficient to pay the principal of, interest on, and other amounts due in respect of our indebtedness when due. We may also obtain additional long-term debt and working capital lines of credit to meet future financing needs, which would have the effect of increasing our total leverage. Our substantial leverage could have significant negative consequences, including:

  - Increasing our vulnerability to general adverse economic and industry conditions;
  - Limiting our ability to obtain additional financing;
  - Requiring the dedication of a substantial portion of our cash flow from operations to service our indebtedness, thereby reducing the amount of our cash flow available for other purposes, including capital expenditures;
  - Limiting our flexibility in planning for, or reacting to, changes in our business and the industries in which we compete; and
  - Placing us at a possible competitive disadvantage with less leveraged competitors and competitors that may have better access to capital resources.

- **Issue 12: Our competitive position could be harmed if we are unable to protect our intellectual property rights.** We believe that our trademarks, patents technologies and designs are of great value. From time to time, third parties have challenged, and may in the future try to challenge, our ownership of our intellectual property. In addition, our business is subject to the risk of third parties counterfeiting our products or infringing on our intellectual property rights. We may need to resort to litigation in the future to enforce our intellectual property rights. The litigation could result in substantial costs and diversion of resources. Our failure to protect our intellectual property rights, and in particular, the loss of the Reebok, Rockport, Ralph Lauren, Greg Norman, or NFL and NBA trademark rights, could have an adverse impact on our business and our competitive position.

- **Issue 13: We may not be able to realize the full extent of our deferred tax assets.** We have approximately $120 million of net deferred tax assets, of which approximately $65 million is attributable to the expected utilization of tax net operating loss carry forwards and tax credit carry forwards. Our ability to realize the full value of the deferred tax assets will depend on several factors including the level of taxable income we generate, the countries in which taxable income is generated, and the effectiveness of our tax planning strategies. If our estimates of future taxable income are not realized in the near term, the value of the deferred tax assets and our future net income could be reduced.

- **Issue 14: A strengthening U.S. dollar reduces our reported results of operations from our international business.** In 2001, we derived approximately 37.1% of our revenue from sales in foreign currencies. In our combined financial statements, we translate local currency financial results into U.S. dollars based on average exchange rates prevailing during a reporting period. During times of a strengthening U.S. dollar, our reported gross margins for merchandise purchased in U.S. dollars and sold in other currencies may be negatively impacted.

Corporate Organization

The four principal business group units of Reebok were Reebok Division, Rockport Company, Inc., Ralph Lauren Footwear Co., Inc., and Greg Norman Division.

The Reebok Brand

The Reebok division designed, produced, and marketed sports, fitness, and casual footwear, apparel, and accessories that combined the attributes of athletic performance and style, as well as related sports and fitness products. Reebok's products included footwear for a variety of sports and fitness categories, lifestyle footwear marketed under the Reebok classic brand, and sports and fitness apparel and accessories. The products also included footwear and apparel for children sold under both the Reebok and Weebok® brands. Reebok continued to expand its product scope through a strategic licensing program, pursuant to which our technologies and/or trademarks were licensed to third parties for fitness equipment, sporting goods, accessories, sports and fitness videos, enhanced fitness water, and related products and services.

Reebok footwear products were designed to meet the demands of specific consumer types: image- and fashion-conscious athletes, sports and fitness enthusiasts, and casual athletic shoe buyers. In 2001, Reebok realigned the product creation teams to reflect this strategy—to focus more closely on consumers and the distribution channels that reach those consumers. Management's aim was to improve the product delivery cycle from design to delivery of the finished product by focusing on the consumers' needs. As part of this strategy, management had also aligned its product creation teams with the distribution channels that served those customer groups, such as athletic specialty stores and "urban" athletic outlets, sporting goods stores and independent specialty shops, as well as volume accounts. In 2002, management expected to drive the same strategy through Reebok's apparel product development cycles in order to achieve similar consumer and distribution alignments. Reebok's U.S. operations unit was responsible for all Reebok footwear and apparel products sold in the United States. Sales of footwear in the United States totaled approximately $930.5 million in 2001, compared to $925.1 million in 2000. Reebok brand apparel sales (including sales of Greg Norman Collection) in the United States in 2001 totaled approximately $395.1 million, compared to approximately $235.0 million in 2000.[21]

Rockport Company

Rockport designed, produced, and distributed specially engineered comfort footwear for men and women worldwide under the Rockport brand, and in 2001 produced, and distributed apparel through a licensee. In 2001, in furtherance of the company's shared services objective, Rockport cosolidated its corporate headquarters into Reebok's Canton facility and sold its former headquarters building in Marlborough, Massachusetts.

Rockport's net sales decreased to $399.6 million in 2001 from approximately $422.4 million in 2000, a reduction of approximately 5.4%. In 2001 Rockport's international revenues increased approximately 5.2% from its international revenues in 2000.

Designed to address the different aspects of consumers' lives, Rockport's product line included performance, casual, and dress shoes. In 2001, Rockport focused on contemporizing its men's product offerings with the introduction in spring 2001 of the Dressports® 2.0 collection, featuring updated, modern silhouettes while retaining the engineered comfort of its classic Dressports line, and the launch in fall 2001 of the premium "circle r" line, featuring sophisticated, fashion-forward styling. Rockport continued to use proprietary technologies to enhance comfort, incorporating into women's walking products its "Sole Identity" footbed, a microwaveable footbed that custom molds to a wearer's foot shape. Finally, in 2001 Rockport signed a license agreement for the development of a children's footwear line under the Rockport trademark, expected to launch in Fall 2002.

Rockport marketed its products to authorized retailers throughout the United States primarily through a locally-based employee sales staff, although Rockport utilized independent sales agencies in certain distribution channels. Internationally, Rockport marketed its products through approximately 30 distributors in approximately 50 foreign countries and territories. Many of the international distributors were subsidiaries of the company, the others were joint venture partners or independent distributors that also sold Reebok branded products. Rockport's direct consumer purchase program allowed consumers to purchase select Rockport products through Rockport's website located at *rockport.com*.

Rockport distributed its products in the United States predominantly through select higher-quality national and local shoe store chains, department stores, independent shoe stores, and outdoor outfitters, emphasizing retailers that provide substantial point-of-sale assistance and carry a full product line. Rockport also sold its products in Rockport concept or company stores in San Francisco (California), Newport (Rhode Island), King of Prussia (Pennsylvania), Boston (Massachusetts), New York (New York), Santa Monica (California), Braintree (Massachusetts), and Las Vegas (Nevada). In addition there were a number of Rockport shops—independent stores that sold Rockport products exclusively—in and outside the United States. Rockport had not pursued mass merchandisers or discount outlets for the distribution of its products.[22]

Ralph Lauren Footwear

Net sales for Ralph Lauren Footwear decreased to approximately $97.3 million in 2001 from approximately $106.7 million in 2000, a reduction of 8.8%. In 2001, a new management team was appointed to run the Ralph Lauren footwear business. Its product line featured traditional classics in addition to Polo Sport®, the Polo Jean Co.® line, a more fashion forward collection targeted to males between the ages of 16 and 25, and a children's line targeted to boys and girls between the ages of 5 and 12. Ralph Lauren Footwear also featured dress and casual silhouettes influenced by the Lauren® product line. Ralph Lauren Footwear sold Ralph Lauren® and Polo Ralph Lauren® products through top-tier retailers. The Polo Jeans Co. and Polo Sport lines were sold through major department stores and through Polo Jean Co. and Polo Sport specialty stores, respectively.

Internationally, Ralph Lauren Footwear had distributors in Japan, Canada, and Central America that marketed Ralph Lauren Footwear products in approximately eight foreign countries and territories while products were distributed primarily through independent agents in Europe. Ralph Lauren Footwear marketed its products to authorized retailers principally through an employee staff. Products were also sold through space licensing arrangements at approximately 29 Ralph Lauren/Polo-owned retail stores. Ralph Lauren Footwear operated concept footwear departments in Polo Ralph Lauren stores in a number of locations in the United States, including New York (New York), Beverly Hills (California), Chicago (Illinois), and Palm Beach (Florida). In addition, Ralph Lauren Footwear had footwear retail operations in approximately 17 Polo Ralph Lauren factory direct stores and operated four factory direct stores: Ellenton (Florida), Orlando (Florida), Freeport (Maine), and Wrentham (Massachusetts).[23]

Greg Norman Division

The company's Greg Norman Collection produced a range of men's apparel and accessories marketed under the Greg Norman name and logo. Originally a golf apparel line, the Greg Norman Collection had grown its line of men's sportswear to include products ranging from leather jackets and sweaters to activewear and swimwear. In addition, the Greg Norman Collection offered Greg Norman belts, small leather goods, and hosiery products, which were sold through licensees of the company. Products were sold principally at upper-end price points in department and men's specialty stores, on-course pro shops and golf specialty stores, as well as in Greg Norman–dedicated shops.

In December 1999, the Greg Norman Collection expanded its line of products by assuming responsibility for the golf footwear business from Reebok. During 2001, the Greg Norman Collection continued its marketing on the DMX Trac technology used in Reebok golf shoes, accentuated by a new fixturing and point-of-sale introduced in spring 2001.

In 2001, the Greg Norman Collection further expanded it product offerings with the introduction of Reebok branded men's golf apparel for mid-tier distribution. Also during 2001, the Greg Norman Collection continued to offer a line of moisture management golf shirts marketed under the trademark Play Dry™. Additional Play Dry branded products, including shorts, socks, hats, and outerwear, were added throughout the course of 2001.

The Greg Norman Collection engaged in licensing arrangements for three categories of products: hat and accessories, leather goods and travel goods, and corporate sales. Licensing its corporate sales business offered the Greg Norman Collection an opportunity to gain royalties and increase brand exposure without incurring the risk of maintaining a large inventory, as would typically be required in this channel. Additionally, the Greg Norman Collection utilized a combination of distributors and licensees to market and distribute Greg Norman branded products internationally. The brand was represented in Australia, Singapore, Malaysia, and Indonesia in the Far East; in several Middle East countries; in England, Ireland, Scotland, Portugal, Germany, France, and the Benelux countries in Europe; in Canada; and in Mexico. During 2002, the Greg Norman Collection planned to further develop the Far East and Latin American markets.

During 2002, the Greg Norman Collection continued to offer a broad variety of lifestyle products and to expand into international markets, as well as corporate accounts, through various licensing and distribution arrangements.

The Greg Norman Collection was marketed through its endorsement by professional golfer Greg Norman, and a marketing and advertising campaign designed to reflect his multi-faceted, powerfully active and elegant lifestyle. Marketing activities included print advertising in consumer and trade periodicals, retail in-store promotions, trade shows, and worldwide merchandise fixturing program that ensures a consistent aesthetic presentation on a global basis. The Greg Norman Collection products were sold by a combination of independent sales representatives and employee account executives.[24]

International Operations

Reebok's international sales were coordinated from corporate headquarters in Canton, Massachusetts, which was also where its regional operations responsible for Latin America were located. There were also regional offices in Lancaster and London, England, which were responsible for operations in Europe, the Middle East and Africa, and in Hong Kong and Tokyo, which were responsible for Far East operations. Reebok's Canadian operations were managed through its wholly owned subsidiary headquartered outside of Toronto. Management marketed Reebok branded products internationally through wholly owned subsidiaries of the company in Austria, Belgium, France, Germany, Ireland, The Netherlands, Italy, Poland, Portugal, Sweden (covering Sweden, Denmark and Norway), the United Kingdom, Japan and South Korea; and through majority-owned subsidiaries in India, Mexico, and Spain. Reebok also marketed products internationally through 26 independent distributors and two joint ventures in which the company held a minority equity interest. Through this international distribution network, products bearing the Reebok brand were actively marketed in approximately 170 countries and territories.

Additionally, there were approximately 25 Reebok factory direct stores owned by the company, its subsidiaries, joint ventures, or independent distributors. Reebok management planned to continue opening retail stores, either directly or through our distributors, in numerous international markets, as such shops were an important means of presenting the brand in various international markets.

During 2001 the contribution of Reebok's international operations unit to overall sales of Reebok branded products (including the Greg Norman Collection) decreased to $1.170 billion from $1.176 billion in 2000. Reebok's 2001 international sales were adversely impacted by the weakening of various foreign currencies. Effective January 1, 2001, the company sold its South African subsidiary to an independent distributor and acquired a majority interest in its Mexico distributor. The sales figures noted above did not reflect the full wholesale value of all Reebok branded products sold outside the United States in 2001 and 2000 because some of the company's distributors were not subsidiaries and thus their sales to retailers were not included in the calculation of the company's international sales. If the full wholesale value of all international sales of Reebok branded products were included, total sales of Reebok branded products outside the United States represented approximately $1.267 billion in wholesale value, consisting of approximately 29.9 million pairs of shoes totaling approximately $728.0 million in wholesale value of footwear sold outside the United States in 2001 (compared with approximately 29.1 million pairs totaling approximately $719.6 million in 2000) and approximately $539.5 million in wholesale value of Reebok apparel (including the Greg Norman Collection) sold outside the United States in 2001 (compared with approximately $550.4 million in 2000).[25]

Trade Policy

With the recent admission of China into the World Trade Organization (WTO), the threat of U.S. restrictions on the import of shoes from China had receded substantially. Management did not believe import restrictions would be imposed during 2002. China remained the largest source of footwear for Reebok and its major competitors. Should trade between China and the United States be interrupted, Reebok, as well as its competitors would face similar challenges to locate alternative manufacturing sources for its products.

The United States had increased enforcement of apparel/textile import quotas, as well as surveillance of working conditions relating to the manufacture of apparel overseas. This has resulted in additional inspection and documentation requirements upon entry of the products into the United States, and in some cases, delays in delivery to customers. This was a concern of trade associations representing the entire U.S. apparel import industry. Management believed that due to Reebok's diversified apparel sourcing and careful selection of vendors and factories, consistent with Human Rights Production Standards (see **Exhibit 1**), import enforcement would not require its change in sourcing, although delivery delays could occur while documentation was processed. However, such delays should not impact the company to a greater extent than Reebok's major competitors.

The European Union (EU) imposed import quotas on certain footwear from China in 1994. The effect of such quota scheme on the company had not been significant because the quota scheme provided an exemption for certain higher-priced special technology athletic footwear, which exemption was available for most Reebok branded products and some Rockport branded products. The EU and individual EU member states continued to review the athletic footwear exemption, which applied to both the quota scheme and antidumping duties discussed below. The company, on its own as well as through relevant trade associations, was working to prevent imposition of a more limited athletic footwear exception. Should revisions be adopted narrowing such exemption, certain of Reebok's product lines could be affected adversely, requiring sourcing from countries other than China or minor design modification. Should any narrowing of the exemption be imposed, management did not expect that its products would be more severely affected than those of major competitors.

In addition to the quotas on China-sourced footwear, the EU had imposed antidumping duties against certain textile-upper footwear from China and Indonesia. A broad exemption from the dumping duties was provided for athletic textile footwear, which covered most

Exhibit 8
Industry Average
Price per Pair

	1998	1999	2000	2001[1]	Change, 2000–2001
Men's	$54.58	$49.72	$48.35	$48.80	+0.9%
Women's	37.10	36.24	35.60	36.83	+3.5%
Children's	21.90	22.60	21.43	23.00	+7.3%
Average	**$40.07**	**$38.27**	**$37.05**	**$38.36**	**+3.5%**

Note:
1. 2001 figures are estimated.

Source: The NPD Group, Inc.

In 2001, the athletic shoe industry spent more than $5.9 billion on advertising and celebrity endorsements. New Balance had replaced Nike as the brand with the most loyal customers.

Athletic Footwear Market Share

Exhibit 9 shows the U.S. market share for the first quarter of 2000 versus the first quarter of 1999. The major shift was in the sales of Nike, which had its market share decrease from 48.9% in 1999 to 39.2% in 2000. New Balance, which was in fourth place, had its market share increase from 3.7% in 1999 to 9.4% in 2000.

Competition

Nike

Nike's market share declined from 48.9% in 1999 to 39.2% in 2000 (see **Exhibit 9**). New Balance was the main winner (9.4% in 2000 versus 3.7% in 1999) of Nike's loss market share. Nike still had 8 out the top 10 basketball shoes while Adidas and Reebok each had one shoe in the top 10. Basketball (16.6%) was second to running shoes (25.1%) in sales by shoe category. Nike's revenues were $9.9 billion, $9.5 billion, $9.0 billion, $8.8 billion, and $9.6 billion, and net income was $666.3 million, $580.7 million, $579.1 million, $451.4 million, and $399.6 million for 2002, 2001, 2000, 1999, and 1998, respectively. The sales were basically flat over these five years. Michael Jordan and Tiger Woods were Nike's two main spokespersons.

Exhibit 9
Market Share of the U.S. Athletic Footwear Market

Manufacturer	2000	Manufacturer	1999
Nike	39.2%	Nike	48.9%
Adidas	15.1	Adidas	16.9
Reebok	10.9	Reebok	10.9
New Balance	9.4	New Balance	3.7
K-Swiss	3.6	K-Swiss	3.1
Timberland	2.9	Timberland	2.1
Asics	2.1	Asics	1.5
Saucony	1.4	Lugz	1.4
Skechers	1.4	And1	0.9
And1	1.2	Saucony	0.9

Source: "Sports Trend Info.," Business Wire (April 7, 2000).

Nike acquired North Face for $240 million in 2001, which catapulted Nike into the top ranks of outdoor-gear (shoes and boots) maker. Gordon O. McFadden, Vice President for Outdoor Products, spent months courting North Face and fiercely lobbying for the acquisition. Phil Knight, CEO, and his top executives had favored Nike developing the business internally, instead of adding the problems of integrating another company. McFadden said, "The decision not to act stemmed from an insecurity of moving outside the Nike domain." Former Nike executives, analysts, and rivals said, "the company was in serious need of new blood and new ideas." They further believed that Nike's insular mindset was a major reason for current troubles. The company's inward decision-making culture caused highly recruited new outside talent to leave the company. They were recruited to bring new perception and views to assist the company to get out of its rut. Critics said Nike needed to revitalize its core U.S. footwear business, which was about 30% of the company's revenue, with new products and brands. Faye L. Landers, analyst, said Nike's culture will make it hard to do. He said, "The feeling is 'what we do is so special, no outsider can ever understand it.' . . . That's flawed thinking." Leslie L. Mundy, a Nike spokesperson, denied Nike's insularity by pointing out that nearly 40% of the Vice Presidents have been with Nike less than five years. In March 2001, Knight realigned Nike's top management.[28]

Adidas

Adidas–Solomon AG was the world's number two athletic footwear company (see **Exhibit 9**). Adidas' U.S. market share had grown steadily from 3.1% in 1993 to 15.1% in 2000. Adidas' sales were $5.5 billion and its net income was $188 million in 2001. Sales were up approximately 5%, which was the result of lowering costs, and net income was up 15% for 2001. Sales in Adidas' largest market, Europe, were $2.7 billion, which was an increase of 7%. Both Nike and Reebok traditionally outmarketed Adidas in Germany. Adidas was weakest in the United States, where sales dropped 5% to $1.6 billion in 2001. This decrease was expected since the company repositioned its products into the higher-end and sports specialty stores. Kobe Bryant, star basketball player for the Los Angeles Lakers, was the company's main endorser. Management expected increased sales in 2002.[29]

New Balance

New Balance Athletic Shoe, Inc., was a privately held corporation. The company's sales for 2001 were $1,160 million, which was 5.5% growth over 2000. The company's U.S. market share was 9.4% and 3.7% in 2000 and 1999, respectively (see **Exhibit 9**). This growth can be attributed to the company's differentiation strategy, which resulted in the most loyal customers in the athletic shoe industry.[30]

New Balance had no celebrity endorsers, did minimal advertising, and yet in the past five years had gained more customer loyalty than any other athletic shoe brand. Michael Jordan, Tiger Woods, and Mia Hamm held court for Nike. "NBA MVP Allen Iverson opined his hip-hop, straight-from-the-playground style for Reebok." Jordan's air-apparent, L.A. Lakers wonderkid Kobe Bryant, dunks for Adidas. All told, athletic footwear makers spent more than $5.9 billion on advertising and celebrity endorsements last year. None of these companies however, commanded the most broad loyalty. The highest levels of customer devotion in one of the most volatile and hotly contested product categories on the planet belonged to a small New England company that was proudly endorsed by no one. According to market research firm Brand Keys, Boston-based New Balance Athletic Shoes hadn't simply replaced Nike as the footwear brand with the most loyal customers. It was also the only athletic shoe brand in the Brand Keys index's top 20, and during the past five years, its high-performance shoes had gained more loyalty than had any other competitive brand.

More remarkable, New Balance had accomplished all of this in a period during which brand loyalty in general had been eroding. To create the Brand Keys brand loyalty index, Robert Passikoff, Brand Keys President, surveyed 16,000 consumers twice a year about their level of satisfaction with nearly 150 U.S. companies. Since the index began in 1997, Passikoff had seen significant erosion not just in athletic footwear but also in financial services, telecommunications, and airlines, among other categories. He attributed this to the sheer volume of products on the market. There were nearly 10,000 athletic shoe models, filling every niche from $15 Keds to $200 Nike Air Jordan XVII basketball shoes. Measured by market share, New Balance was number four in this standing-room-only category, behind Nike, Adidas, and Reebok, but it had been gaining rapidly. Between 1999 and 2001, its domestic share climbed from 3.7% to 9.4%, while revenues jumped from $550 million to $813 million (see **Exhibit 9**). What's more, the growth came from only $13 million in national advertising in 2001. Nike, by comparison, spent $155 million and Reebok $49 million, according to Competitive Media Reporting.

How did New Balance do it? The company gave customers a truly unique product: athletic shoes in varying widths. No other athletic footwear manufacturer made shoes for wide or narrow feet, while New Balance covered all sizes from AA to extra-wide 6E. "I can't tell you how many people tell me that we make the only shoes they can wear," says Paul Heffernan, New Balance Vice President for Global Marketing. The company supported its product with a marketing strategy that emphasized consistency and subtlety and targeted serious athletes between the ages of 25 and 45. These customers spent less on sports shoes than teens did—$2.3 billion compared with $3.5 billion—but according to Heffernan, they were far easier to keep. "Our customers are upwardly mobile, settled, very intense people," said New Balance marketing services manager John Donovan. "They're serious about fitness and their desire to achieve. Let me put it this way: Our customers don't really think they can win the Boston Marathon. But they believe they can beat last year's time."

New Balance ads featured unknown athletes and ran in niche magazines like *Outside*, *New England Runner*, and *Prevention* and on cable-TV channels favored by older viewers such as CNN, the Golf Channel, and A&E. New Balance's low-key slogan was "Achieve New Balance." It hadn't changed for five years. Even its ad tag lines go right after the Gen X and boomer mind-set: "Life sucks, go for a run." Or "Turn off your phone and fax . . . achieve New Balance."

The company's advertising didn't always play it so quietly. In fact, New Balance was the first athletic footwear company to offer a multimillion-dollar endorsement deal, to L.A. Lakers star James Worthy, in the mid-1980s. But after sales of its basketball shoes did not increase with Worthy's endorsement, New Balance canceled its celebrity deals and has shied away from mass-market advertising ever since. "I don't have a poster of Michael Jordan in my bedroom anymore," Heffernan says, "and neither do our customers."[31]

K-Swiss

K-Swiss, Inc., designed, developed, and marketed a growing array of athletic footwear for high-performance sport use, fitness activities, and casual wear under the K-Swiss brand. During 2001, the company acquired two additional footwear brands: National Geographic (via license) and Royal Elastics. Sales of these two brands were insignificant during 2001. All footwear categories came in both men's (approximately 52% of 2001 revenues) and women's (approximately 27% of 2001 revenues). Most styles within each footwear category were offered in men's, women's, and children's.

In May 2001, the company formed a joint venture with Rugged Shark, a designer and manufacturer of young, active-oriented footwear, to license, produce, and market a men's, women's, and children's collection of National Geographic outdoor-oriented and casual footwear. The joint venture launched a full-scale line of outdoor and casual footwear in fall 2002. Under the terms of the joint venture, the company owned 75% of the new company and provided the infrastructure to design and develop, manufacture, distribute, and market the line of National Geographic footwear. Rugged Shark owned 25% of the venture.

In November 2001, the company acquired the worldwide rights and business of Royal Elastics (Royal), an Australian-based designer and manufacturer of elasticated footwear. The purchase excluded distribution rights in Australia, which were retained by Royal Management Pty, Ltd.

The company's product line through 1987 consisted primarily of the Classic. The Classic was originally developed in 1966 as a high-performance tennis shoe. In 2000, the company launched Classic Luxury Edition, which sold for slightly more than the original version. The Classic, fueled by new products, had evolved into a category of shoes referred to as the Classic category. The Classic category was comprised of the Classic originals, the K-Swiss Collection, the Limited Edition series, and the Davos Collection.

K-Swiss revenues were $236.1 million, $221.6 million, $285.5 million, and $161.5 million, and net income was $23.3 million, $21.1 million, $34.3 million, and $12.5 million for 2001, 2000, 1999, and 1998, respectively. U.S market share was 3.6% in 2000 and 3.1% in 1999 (see **Exhibit 9**).[32]

Fila

Fila Holding S.P.A. (Fila) was a holding company with direct or indirect control over 40 other companies in 24 different countries, active in the development, production, and distribution of activewear, sportswear and athletic footwear under the brands Fila, Ciesse, and Enyce. Fila's sports apparel, accessory, and footwear lines included gear for tennis, skiing, swimming, mountain climbing, sailing, soccer, basketball, golf, fitness, and running. The company's products were sold in approximately 60 countries and were manufactured by independent subcontractors in the Far East.

Fila's footwear collection offered a wide variety of products ranging from active sport styles designed for basketball, running, tennis, cross-training, fitness, and soccer, to sportswear products that were sports inspired and fashion oriented. The footwear lines, which blended design, performance, quality, and function, included designs and sizes for men, women, and children. The company's product range offered a combination of design and style (characteristics of a brand with an Italian stylistic sensibility) and performance, through its carbon-Kevlar and cushioning technologies. The company's two design and development centers, one in Italy and one in the United States, constantly incorporated new trends and innovations to create a footwear line that addressed market needs.

In 2001, Pininfarina, a manufacturer of high-performance sports cars, worked with the company to develop the Fila-Pininfarina shoe, which evokes the Italian design of one of its cars with Fila's expertise in footwear production. For 2001, the company's highest-volume footwear categories were sportswear, running, cross-training, basketball, and tennis.[33]

Fila's revenues were $947.4 million, $976.3 million, $881.7 million, and $971.0 million, and losses were $135.9 million, $71.3 million, $57.3 million, and $125.5 million for 2001, 2000, 1999, and 1998, respectively.[34]

Puma

Puma, a venerable German athletic shoe manufacturer, nearly collapsed in the 1990s. The company had suffered many years of losses. Nevertheless, Puma had recently returned to profitability. The company in 2002 expected sales to increase by 40% to $845 million, and pretax profits up 70% to more than $100 million. Puma signed Serena Williams, world-class tennis player, to an endorsement contract. Puma sales were 60% from Western Europe and needed to increase U.S. market sales to maintain growth and profitability. Puma was hedging its bets with product mix ranging from athletic products sold at traditional sports stores to upscale stores (Henri Bendel Ltd.) for its Platinum line of $250 leather shoes. Jochen Zeitz, CEO, said, "Puma's in no rush to expand." He further stated, "Growth is easy. Growth based on brand—that's the challenge." One analyst said, "The Company's revenue size could allow it to get lost in the pack of also-rans."[35]

Converse

On January 22, 2001, Converse, a 93-year-old company, filed for Chapter 11 bankruptcy and closed three plants by March 31, 2001. The company was facing a January 31 deadline to creditors. The company missed a $25 million interest payment in June 2000, and had more than $183 million in debt due in July 2002. The company sold its products in 110 countries through about 5,500 stores. The company planned to become exclusively a licensor of Converse brand products.[36]

Marketing and Promotional Activity[37]

Reebok devoted significant resources to advertising its products to a variety of audiences through television, radio, print, and other media. The company also utilized relationships with major sports figures and leagues to enhance visibility for the Reebok-brand and created awareness of, and demand for, Reebok branded products. The marketing mix included advertising (television, print, radio, and outdoor), sports endorsements and sponsorships, public relations, in-store marketing, grassroots activities, and use of the Internet.

Reebok continued its sponsorship of the CBS television show *Survivor* with sponsorship of *Survivor 2—The Australian Outback* and *Survivor Africa*. As with the original *Survivor* series, Reebok was the official apparel supplier to contestants appearing on the series. During the second *Survivor* series, Reebok featured an advertising campaign entitled "Defy Convention," which was aimed at young men and women and consisted of a series of vignettes depicting various athletic and outdoor lifestyle situations set to the music of Rossini's *William Tell Overture*. During *Survivor Africa*, Reebok created and launched a television campaign aimed at women, called "It's a Woman's World." This campaign, which *Time* magazine recognized as one of the "10 best" advertising campaigns of the year, featured women in stereotypically male contexts or roles and included participants from previous *Survivor* shows, as well as sports stars such as Venus Williams and Jennifer Azzi. The campaign also featured music from James Brown's 1960s Rhythm and Blues classic "It's a Man's World" and a specially recorded version of the song by current R&B singer Missy Elliot. Reebok continued its sponsorship of *Survivor* for the show's fourth season, which debuted at the end of February 2002.

In October 2001, Reebok announced its most aggressive women's advertising campaign, "It's a Woman's World." Reebok's strategy was to leverage the enormous popularity of the hit CBS series, *Survivor*, which was the top-rated program among women in the U.S. Company spokespersons were some of the world's most dynamic and inspirational women hired to launch the company's most aggressive product and marketing women's program in the company's 22-year history.

Reebok built on past marketing success during 2001 with the continuation of its "Classics" print campaign, which showed Reebok Classic shoes in a striking black-and-white print campaign. The Classics campaign featured such music celebrities as Ice Cube, Iggy Pop, and Common and also tied into movies such as *Planet of the Apes*. The campaign appeared in magazines such as *Slam*, *Source*, *Vibe*, *In Style*, *GQ*, *Teen People*, and *Details*. A special promotion, featuring Common, was also run at the retailer Foot Action to launch the Arctic Ice range of Classic Footwear.

Consistent with its strategy of aligning product offerings with specific consumer preferences, Reebok continued in 2001 to focus its sports marketing efforts on key athletic icons who exemplified distinct lifestyles, other athletes who were either at the pinnacle of their profession or rising stars, and select team and league sponsorships.

Reebok's marquis athletes were:

- *Allen Iverson*, charismatic Philadelphia 76ers point guard and 2001 National Basketball Association Most Valuable Player, with whom Reebok marketed a signature line of footwear and apparel. Reebok extended and restructured its endorsement arrangement with Iverson in 2001 and had the right to use his name and image both throughout his playing career and beyond.

- *Venus Williams*, two-time winner of Wimbledon and U.S. Open, and an Olympic gold medallist in single and doubles, which Reebok featured as a lifestyle icon in its "Defy Convention" campaign during 2001.

To promote the sale of its basketball products in 2001, Reebok utilized athlete endorsements with:

- *Steve Francis* of the Houston Rockets, co-winner of the 2000 Rookie of the Year award, whom Reebok featured in connection with its Blacktop® line of basketball shoes;

- *Jalen Rose* of the Indiana Pacers, winner of the 2000 Most Improved Player award; and

- The college basketball programs at the *University of Utah*, *University of Memphis*, and *Boston College*.

To promote the sale of cross-training cleated baseball and football shoes during 2001, Reebok maintained sponsorship arrangements with:

- NFL Pro Bowl players *Edgerrin James* and *Jevon Kearse*;

- Major League Baseball stars *Andy Pettite* and *Kevin Brown*, and six-time Cy Young Award winner *Roger Clemens*; and

- The college football programs at *Boston College* and the *Air Force Academy*.

In soccer, Reebok had a number of sponsorship agreements, both with individuals and teams, including those with:

- *Julie Foudy*, member of the U.S. national team;

- *Ryan Giggs* (of current English-league champion Manchester United);

- *Iker Casillas* (goalkeeper with Real Madrid and Spain);

- *Liverpool FC*, one of the world's best-known soccer teams;

- *Bolton Wanderers of England* (which includes the naming rights to the Wanderers' soccer arena, the "Reebok Stadium"); and

- The *Colombian national team*.

To promote its running and tennis footwear and apparel, Reebok had endorsement agreements with:

- Runners *Abel Anton* and *Christine Arron*; and

- Professional tennis players *Patrick Rafter* and *Andy Roddick*.

In addition to advertising and sports marketing, Reebok also used grassroots marketing and in-store merchandising to promote its products and enhance brand awareness, particularly among a younger and more urban audience. In 2002, Reebok was sponsoring events such as the Entertainers Basketball Classic tournament at Rucker Park, the largest street basketball competition in the United States, and continued to support various local running clubs and races. Beginning in March 2002, Reebok planned a series of product displays in more than 1,000 music stores across the United States. These displays gave customers an opportunity to preview new, innovative products before they become available at retail stores and also tell customers where they could buy the products when they arrived in stores.

NFL and NBA Business Ventures

During 2001, Reebok entered into an exclusive licensing agreement with the NFL for apparel, footwear, equipment, and certain accessories commencing in 2002. Beginning with the 2002–2003 season, Reebok supplied uniforms, sideline apparel, and coaches' wear for all 32 NFL teams. Reebok also developed a new line of performance apparel designed for young male athletes and marketed under the brand name "NFL Equipment," launched in April 2002. Additionally in 2002, Reebok introduced "Gridiron Classics," a line of lifestyle apparel evoking the history of the NFL. Reebok planned an integrated marketing campaign throughout the year in order to extend the selling season for its NFL-licensed products beyond the traditional NFL season. In connection with its marketing efforts, Reebok had the right to depict Reebok athletes in their NFL uniforms for advertising purposes and in point-of-purchase displays.

Also during 2001, Reebok entered into a license agreement with the NBA covering apparel, footwear, and certain accessories. Under the agreement, Reebok was the official supplier of uniforms to 12 teams during the 2001–2002 season, became the official supplier of uniforms to 19 teams for the 2002–2003 season, and became the semi-exclusive supplier to all teams in the league for the 2004–2005 season. In addition, Reebok had the right to depict Reebok athletes in their NBA uniforms for advertising purposes and in point-of-purchase displays. Reebok also provided player uniforms and footwear to the NBDL (National Basketball Development League), the NBA's new minor league showcasing up-and-coming talent, and to all WNBA teams. During 2002, Reebok sponsored several NBA and WNBA events in order to leverage its new relationship with those leagues.[38]

Other Major Marketing Events

In 2000, Reebok and Liverpool Football Club, a member of the English Premier League announced a multi-million-dollar extension of its endorsement contract. Steve Barcewell, Reebok's global head of football, said, "Reebok is delighted to have extended our sponsorship [started 1996] of the Liverpool Football Club, which reaffirms Reebok's commitment to football and the club itself."[39]

In 2000, Reebok outfitted 2,500 athletes and coaches head-to-toe in training apparel and athletic shoes for the 2000 Summer Olympic Games. Reebok was the sponsor of several National Olympic Committees including Russia, Jamaica, Poland, New Zealand, South Africa, Trinidad, and Tobago.

In September 2001, the Reebok Sports Club opened at Canary Wharf complex in London. The club was the largest one in the United Kingdom. It occupied 100,000 square feet.

In February 2002, the Indy Racing League (IRL) and Reebok announced a multi-year partnership naming Reebok the official outfitter of the IRL. Fireman said, "Auto racing continues to be one of the most popular and exciting spectator sports. . . . The partnership will further drive Reebok's growing sports licensing business."[40]

Sports and Fitness Equipment

Reebok continued its promotional and educational efforts in 2001 in the fitness area, seeking to leverage and expand Reebok's position as a leading source of fitness programming and education. Reebok's multi-tiered Global Fitness Program, created by Reebok University® and driven by Reebok's website, encompassed strategic alliances, retail partnerships, interactive fitness programming, e-commerce, interactive marketing, consumer initiatives, and product offerings. Central to the development of the Global Fitness Program was the latest Reebok fitness program called Core Training. Core Training, which launched during the summer of 2000, was designed to improve cardiovascular performance and enhance functional strength, balance, and flexibility. The training utilized the Reebok Core Board, the first exercise board that tilted, twisted, torqued, and recoiled 360° in three dimensions in response to a user's movements. Reebok continued to promote Core Training by bringing Reebok Core Training and the Reebok Core Board to local facilities for the education of club owners, fitness instructors, personal trainers, and club members on the techniques and benefits of Core Training.

In addition, through Reebok University, its network of Master Trainers (including Gin Miller and Petra Kolber), and its Alliance fitness instructors, Reebok continued to develop and promote numerous other fitness programs. These programs were complemented by the marketing and sale of a line of Reebok fitness videos, as well as the marketing and sale of Reebok fitness equipment products such as the Step Reebok® exercise platform and the Reebok home exercise bike collection. Members of the Reebok Professional Alliance Program, a worldwide organization consisting of more than 200,000 fitness professionals, could access industry news, register for Reebok University seminars, and purchase Reebok products through Reebok's website, *reebok.com*. Reebok primarily used its web site as a relationship building platform through the delivery of fitness-based information and services such as Reebok University programs and instructions. The unique content of the Reebok University site on reebok.com was developed in partnership with the American College of Sports Medicine.

Reebok also ran marketing promotions and brand extension programs on its website in order to drive sales to Reebok's retail partners. Planned initiatives for 2002 increased direct-to-consumer marketing, including e-mail direct marketing and posting a direct order catalog on its new site devoted exclusively to women, reebokwomen.com, which launched in late February 2002. Reebok was also the exclusive sponsor of the NBA "All Access Pass.com" on the NBA's web site, *NBA.com*, through June 2002.[41]

Distribution

Foot Locker

Foot Locker, Inc. (formerly Woolworth's athletic division), was the world's leading retailer of athletic footwear and apparel, operating retail stores and selling direct-to-customers through catalogs and the Internet. The company's approximately 3,600 retail stores comprised complementary formats under the brand names Foot Locker, Lady Foot Locker, Kid's Foot Locker, and Champs Sports (the number one athletic footwear retailer in United States). The stores were primarily mall-based and were located in 14 countries in North America, Europe, and Australia. The company's direct-to-customer operation, Footlocker.com/Eastbay, was the largest Internet and catalog retailer of athletic footwear, apparel, and equipment in the world. The company changed its name to Foot Locker to focus on athletic retailing and then sold its noncore interests (San Francisco Music Box Co. and more than a dozen Burger King and Popeye's fast-food franchises) after years of disappointing sales. Investment group Greenway Partners owned 9% of Foot Locker; FMR Corp owned 8%.[42]

The company's stores by global location were (1) 2,929 U.S. stores, (2) 323 European stores, (3) 158 Canadian stores, (4) 73 Puerto Rico and Virgin Islands stores, (5) 73 Australian stores, (6) 21 Hawaiian stores, and (7) 5 Guam stores. Lady Foot Locker was the only national chain that specialized in women's athletic footwear, apparel, and accessories. The company planned to open 400 in-stores in Foot Lockers and Champs Stores. These boutiques were to sell Adidas merchandise endorsed by Tracy McGrady of the NBA's Orlando Magic.[43]

Sales had been flat over the past three fiscal years (FY). Sales were $4,379,000,000, $4,356,000,000 and, $4,647,000,000, respectively for FY 2002, 2001, and 2000. Net income was $92,000,000 for FY 2002, loss of $240,000,000 for FY 2001, and a profit of $48,000,000 for FY 2000. The company's profit margins were 2.1% and 1.0% for FY 2002 and FY 2000, respectively. The sales corresponded to the troubles the major athletic shoe companies had suffered over the previous five years.[44]

In August 2002, management announced a re-alignment of shoes. The company reduced its inventory of shoes selling for over $120, the target market that Nike dominated. Customers were changing their preference from expensive to less expensive athletic shoes. The company could reduce its 2003 purchases from Nike by $150 million to $250 million, or about 37.5%.[45]

Reebok and Nike had been battling over dominance in sales in Foot Locker since the 1980s. At that time, Reebok's aerobic shoe sales were not in the stores. So, Foot Locker management asked Reebok to turn out a specialty line for Foot Locker. Josie Esquivel, an analyst at Morgan Stanley, said that "Reebok basically thumbed its nose" at the retailer. Reebok "was selling to whomever it wanted, including the discounter down the street from Foot Locker."[46] Foot Locker's strategy was to offer exclusive lines as a weapon against discounters and was receiving exclusive lines from other athletic shoe manufacturers. Nike agreed to make exclusive lines for Foot Locker. In 1996, Nike introduced Flight 65 and Flight 67, which were high-priced basketball shoes that sold only at Foot Locker. These shoes came in Nike's trademark black and white. Earlier in the year, Reebok had agreed to make shoes exclusively for Foot Locker, but none of the shoes had reached the store.

Fireman's views on the rocky relations with Foot Locker were that "Reebok wasn't as good a listener to [Foot Locker], which happens to have a good ear as to what's happening on the street and consumers."[47] Fireman tried to repair the relationship by spending a few days with buyers of Foot Locker. He said, we are "trying to discern their needs."

Over the past few years, "Reebok had hired an army of testers at [Foot Locker's] shoe chains . . . to find out whether Reebok was getting equal treatment with other brands." Reebok was disappointed with their findings. They found that Reebok had the most shoes on display in the stores but got little positive help from the stores' salespeople. A salesperson told one 17-year-old customer that "Nikes were hip."

Reebok recognized that Foot Locker's customers were not Reebok's core clients, who were older customers and preteens unable to spend $80 to $90 for shoes. Foot Locker's target market were teens and Generation X customers, who spent $80 to $90 for shoes. Fireman said, "There's no question Nike owns that market," and "there's no one really in that market to compete against them in the high-end niche."[48]

Nike had a special salesforce, Elkins, which called on stores and spread the gospel of Nike. They were enthusiastic sponsors of Nike's product lines. They provided the company with excellent information on market trends and competition.

William DeVrues, who headed Woolworth's footwear units, dismissed talk about bad relations with Reebok. He said, "We're only selling what the customer wants."[49]

Footlocker had 18% market share of U.S. sales of athletic shoes and 8% of European sales.

Footstar, Inc.

Footstar, Inc., was a holding company that directly or indirectly, through its wholly owned subsidiaries, owned the capital stock of its subsidiaries. The retailer's Meldisco division, which accounted for about 60% of sales, operated leased footwear departments in about 5,800 U.S. stores, the majority of its sales came from about 1,800 Kmart stores. Meldisco offered shoes under private labels as well as licensed brands Everlast, Route 66, and Thom McAn. Footstar's athletic division, which sold shoes and apparel, included Footaction (about 500 stores, mostly in U.S. malls) and Just for Feet (about 90 stores in the southern United States). Thom McAn will soon be sold in about 300 Wal-Mart stores.

On March 8, 2002, Kmart announced its intention to close 283 stores. Meldisco operated licensed footwear departments in all of those stores. The 283 stores had been removed from Meldisco's comparable store sales base as of April sales. The store closings were progressing in an orderly fashion, and all 283 stores were currently expected to be closed during June.

Footstar's sales had increased by $620,000,000 over the past three years. Sales were $2,460,000,000, $2,237,100,000, and $1,880,000,000, respectively, for 2001, 2000, and 1999. The operating income decreased over the same three years from $153,900,000 in 1999, to $171,400,000 in 2000, to $97,000,000 in 2001. The operating margins were 3.9%, 7.7%, and 8.2%, respectively, for 2001, 2000, and 1999.

On May 30, 2002, Footstar reported that comparable stores sales results for the four-week period ended May 25, 2002, decreased 9.6%.

Comparable store sales at Meldisco declined 16.1%, and comparable store sales for the athletic segment increased 2.1%.

For the month of May 2002, total sales were $178.4 million, a decrease of 11.7% from the $202.1 million posted in the same period last year. Total sales for the Meldisco division declined 17.7% to $107.9 million from $131.1 million, and total sales in the company's athletic segment decreased 0.6% to $70.5 million from $71.0 million.[50]

Mickey Robinson, Footstar's Chairman and Chief Executive Officer, commented, "Our athletic segment posted a comparable store sales increase for May, however, Footstar's overall performance was impacted by disappointing results at Meldisco. Strong sales at both Footaction and Just for Feet contributed to the athletic segment's gain for the month, although the overall environment continued to be very promotional. At Meldisco, the sales performance was negatively affected by lower sales of summer-related product, particularly sandals and canvas shoes, due to cooler than normal weather for most of the month. However, sales were less promotional than planned.[51]

The other major competitors were Wal-Mart and Target. An analyst said, "the slow down and consumer spending were likely to hurt mall-based retailers more than discounters such as Wal-Mart Stores and Target."

Reebok's Retail Stores

Reebok also operated approximately 201 factory direct store fronts in the United States (including Reebok, Rockport, Ralph Lauren Footwear, and Greg Norman stores and counting multiple store fronts in combination stores as separate store fronts) that sold a variety of footwear, apparel, and accessories marketed under our various brands. These factory direct stores were an extension of the firm's wholesale business that allowed Reebok to control the disposition of excess inventory without compromising our primary channels of distribution. Management did not anticipate any significant expansion in the number of factory direct stores in the United States.

In addition to these factory direct stores, Reebok operated a full-price "concept," or company retail, store in New York City, another at the company's Canton, Massachusetts headquarters, and approximately 10 Rockport concept stores. All of these concept stores showcased a wide selection of current, in-line Reebok or Rockport branded footwear, apparel, and accessories.[52]

Reebok E-Commerce Store

On July 9, 2002, Reebok management announced an alliance between Reebok and GSI Commerce, a leading outsource solution provider for e-commerce, to develop and operate an e-commerce store that would be accessible at *www.reebok.com*.

GSI Commerce was to develop and operate all facets of the online store, including website design, customer service, order processing, fulfillment, and merchandising, while Reebok featured a broad selection of Reebok's top-tier footwear, apparel, equipment, and accessories, including NFL, NBA, Classic, and Reebok merchandise. It was expected to launch in the United Sates during the third quarter of 2002.

"This online retail store reflects our desire to offer consumers our most exciting products and marketing initiatives in one place," said Reebok Chief Marketing Officer Micky Pant. "It will complement our traditional 'bricks and mortar' distribution with a virtual offering of key products that will enhance our brand images."[53]

Manufacturing and Production

Virtually all of the company's products were produced by independent manufacturers, almost all of which were outside the United States, except that some of the company's apparel and some of the component parts used in the company's footwear were sourced from independent manufacturers located in the United States. Each of the company's operating units generally contracted with its manufacturers on a purchase order basis, subject in most cases to the terms of a formal manufacturing agreement between the company and such manufacturers. All contract manufacturing was performed in accordance with detailed specifications furnished by the operating unit, subject to strict quality control standards, with a right to reject products that did not meet specifications. To date, the company had not encountered any significant problem with product rejection or customer returns. The company generally considered its relationships with its contract manufacturers to be good.

As part of Reebok's commitment to human rights, the management required agents and/or manufacturers of Reebok products to apply the Reebok Human Rights Standards, which set forth acceptable factory policies and procedures regarding workplace conditions (see **Exhibit 1**). The company used a global monitoring program to implement these standards. Through its human rights initiatives, Reebok had an ongoing program to provide technical assistance to improve air quality in factories producing its footwear, had implemented a worker communication system to resolve conflicts in such factories, and had taken other steps to improve workplace conditions consistent with the company's Human Rights Production Standards. In conjunction with its human rights program, Reebok required suppliers of soccer balls in Pakistan to end the use of child labor by centralizing all production, including ball stitching, so that the labor force could be adequately monitored to prevent the use of child labor. Reebok-branded soccer balls were sold with a guarantee that the balls were made without child labor.

Similarly, Reebok was cognizant of the need to monitor carefully the substances used in the manufacture of its products and to assure that the health of the consumer, as well as the overall environment, was protected. To this end, management maintained a comprehensive list of restricted substances, the use of which was either limited or prohibited in any product manufactured. Vendors whose materials were used in the production of Reebok's products, and factories that assembled the products, were required to certify that they were in compliance with *Reebok Restricted Substances Policy*. The company continued to monitor governmental restrictions worldwide, which were then incorporated into the Restricted Substances Policy. However, the Restricted Substances Policy exceeded the mandated governmental restrictions in many respects. For example, although not required to do so by any laws or governmental regulations, the company was in the final stages of eliminating PVC from its products, a process management anticipated would be substantially completed during 2002.

China, Indonesia, and Thailand were Reebok's primary sources for footwear, accounting for approximately 51%, 28%, and 15%, respectively, of total footwear production during 2001 (based on the number of units produced). The firm's largest manufacturer accounted for approximately 19% of total footwear production in 2001.

Reebok maintained a network of affiliates in China, Hong Kong, Indonesia, Thailand, Taiwan, and South Korea to inspect certain components and materials purchased by manufacturers for use in footwear production, facilitate the shipment of footwear from the shipping point to the point of destination, and to help arrange for the issuance of letters of credit or wire transfers, the primary means used to pay the footwear manufacturers for finished products. Reebok's apparel group utilized the services of independent third parties, as well as its Hong Kong subsidiary and its affiliates in the Far East, to assist in the placement, inspection, and shipment of apparel and accessories orders internationally. The apparel group retained and managed those independent contractors responsible for production of apparel in the United States. The remainder of Reebok's order placement, quality assurance, and inspection work was handled by a combination of employees and independent contractors for the various countries in which its products were made.[54]

Research and Development

In 2001, the company spent approximately $41.7 million on product research, development, and evaluation, compared to $49.8 million in 2000 and $55.4 million in 1999.[55]

The company placed a strong emphasis on technology and had continued to incorporate various proprietary performance technologies in its products, focusing on cushioning, stability, and lightweight features in its footwear and on comfort and moisture management in its apparel.

As part of its commitment to offer leading footwear technologies, Reebok engaged in product research, devlopment, and design activities in its headquarters, where state-of-the-art product development facility was dedicated to the design and development of technologically advanced athletic and fitness footwear. Reebok also had product development centers in Korea, China, and Taiwan to enable development activities to be more closely integrated with production.

The company's most significant technologies were DMX®, the Pump®, and 3D Ultralite. The DMX technology provided cushioning utilizing a heel-to-forefoot, active airflow system that delivered cushioning when and where it was needed. Originally introduced in 1995, Reebok had enhanced and expanded this technology by developing multiple versions of DMX to meet the performance demanded of various activities, taking into account performance-attributed aesthetics and price among the various versions. Current versions included: a 6-pod system [the DMX (6)], a 10-pod system [the DMX (10)], two 2-pod systems [the DMX (2)], a DMX sockliner, and the DMX "Stimpak." Throughout 2001, Reebok continued to increase the range of products featuring DMX technology with the introduction of numerous new shoe models. The company also continued to incorporate 3D Ultralite, a proprietary material allowing midsole and outsole to be combined in a simple, injection-molded unit, in performance footwear. 3D Ultralite provided a unique blend of lightweight, flexible, and durable properties. In 2001 the company began to redevelop its proprietary inflatable shoe technology, the Pump®, exploring broader and more varied applications for this technology in its footwear. It was expected that new inflatable shoe products would be introduced in late 2002.

Reebok had also incorporated advanced technologies into certain of its apparel products with the Hydromove® and more advanced Play Dry™ moisture-management systems. These moisture-wicking technologies helped to keep athletes dry and thereby facilitate regulation of the wearer's body temperature. Management planned to expand the range of apparel products incorporating moisture-management technologies going forward.[56]

Sources of Supply

The principal materials used in the company's footwear products were leather, nylon, rubber, ethylvinyl acetate, and polyurethane. Most of these materials could be obtained from a number of sources, although a loss of supply could temporarily disrupt production. Some of the components used in the company's technologies were obtained from only one or two sources, and thus a loss of supply could disrupt production. The principal materials used in the company's apparel products were cotton, fleece, nylon, and spandex. These materials could be obtained from a number of sources.

The footwear products of the company that were manufactured overseas and shipped to the United States for sale were subject to U.S. Customs duties. Duties on the footwear products imported by the company ranged from 5.1% to 66% (plus a unit charge, in some cases, of $1.58), depending on whether the principal component was leather or some other material and depending on the construction.

As with its international sales operations, the company's footwear and apparel production operations were subject to the usual risks of doing business abroad, such as import duties, quotas and other threats to free trade, foreign currency fluctuations and restrictions, labor unrest, and political instability. Management believed that it had the ability to develop, over time, adequate substitute sources of supply for the products obtained from present foreign suppliers. If, however, events should prevent the company from acquiring products from its suppliers in China, Indonesia, Thailand, or the Philippines, or significantly increase the cost to the company of such products, the company's operations could be seriously disrupted until alternative suppliers were found, with a significant negative impact.[57]

Backlog

As of December 31, 2001, the backlog of orders that management believed to be firm (though cancelable by the purchaser) totaled approximately $979.4 million, compared to $967.4 million as of December 31, 2000. The backlog position was not necessarily indicative of future sales because the ratio of future orders to "at once" shipments and sales by company-owned retail stores varied from year to year. In addition, many markets in South America and Asia Pacific were not included in the backlog, since sales were made in those regions through Reebok's independent distributors.[58]

Seasonality

Sales by the company of athletic and casual footwear tended to be seasonal in nature, with the strongest sales occurring in the first and third quarters. Apparel sales also generally vary during the course of the year, with the greatest demand occurring during the spring and fall seasons.[59]

Single Customer

There was no single customer of the company that accounted for 10% or more of overall net sales in 2001. Nevertheless, the company did have certain significant customers, the loss of any one of which could have an adverse effect on its business. There could also be a negative effect on business if any significant customer became insolvent or otherwise failed to pay its debts.[60]

Human Resource Management

As of December 31, 2001, the company had approximately 6,700 employees in all operating units. None of these employees were represented by a labor union, except for the approximately 200 employees in France who had a workers' committee. Reebok had never suffered a material interruption of business caused by labor disputes with employees, and it considered employee relations to be good.[61]

On July 1, 2002, Reebok and Bright Horizons Family Solutions announced the opening of a new child care center on the site of the 44-acre landscape surrounding Reebok's World Headquarters in Canton, Massachusetts. Designed, built, and owned by Reebok, Bright Horizons Family Solutions was to manage the center's day-to-day operations. Scheduled to open September 3, 2002, the center had the capacity to serve 14 infants, 18 toddlers, and 40 pre-school children. Demand for the center's 72 spots had been high since Reebok began accepting pre-enrollment registration forms in January.

"Many of our employees were having a difficult time finding quality child care, so we set out to find a solution," said Leslie Abrahamson, Reebok's Director of Compensation and Benefits. "Managed by Bright Horizons, Reebok's new center will provide our employees with consistent, reliable, quality child care in a safe and nuturing environment."[62]

Outsourcing HRM Problems

Protests in Jakarta against Footwear Companies Fleeing Indonesia

Foreign footwear firms were scaling back their presence in Indonesia because of the country's deteriorating business environment and the lower labor costs offered by its neighbors. As an indication of this trend, Indonesia's footwear exports declined to $1.5 billion last year from nearly $2.2 billion in 1996, when the country accounted for 38% of Nike's production volume. Indonesia's share of the footwear giant's output is now at 30%. In contrast, Vietnam, which offered lower wages and a more stable business climate, had seen its share of Nike's production volume grow to 15% from 2%. The exodus of footwear firms to other countries had grave implications for the "flying geese" theory of development, which was followed by Indonesia. The theory stated that less-developed countries go up the production hierarchy as they pursue industrialization. According to Hal Hill, an expert on Indonesia at Australian National University, if the country "can't do it in footwear, you've have got to wonder whether it can do it in similar industries" like electronics and garments.[63]

Protests Against Reebok

On June 29, 2002, around 1,200 workers of PT Primarindo Asia Infrastructure, an Indonesian supplier of U.S. shoe manufacturer Reebok, staged rallies near the U.S. embassy. The demonstrators protested the unprovoked halt of purchasing order by the Reebok Trading International (RTI) without a tolerable period for Primarindo to find substitute buyers. They also demanded RTI to hold negotiations with Primarindo, located in Bandung, capital of West Java province, around 150 kilometers south of Jakarta. At around 13:00 local time (0600 GMT) the rally moved to Monas square and started to burn down a six-meter-long shoe replica and dozens of Reebok shoes while shouting simultaneously "expel Reebok out from here." Around 5,400 Primarindo workers faced the threat of losing their jobs since 100% of their products were sold only to Reebok. Two weeks ago a local newspaper reported some representatives of Primarindo's labor union met Reebok's country manager to Indonesia, Chris Barnett, but apparently failed to achieve any important deal. Indonesia was among other developing countries where Reebok sets up factories. It had five Reebok companies but all are subcontracted, mostly by South Korean companies. Labor activists, however, criticized Reebok for its low standard wage implemented on local workers. Dita Sari, an organizer with the National Front for Workers Struggle in Indonesia, rejected in January this year the 13th Annual Human Rights Award hosted by Reebok in Salt Lake City of the United States, because in her country Reebok workers get only around U.S.$1.50 a day.[64]

Protest Against Nike

On August 20, 2002, around 3,000 workers of PT Doson Indonesia, subcontractor of U.S. sportswear company Nike, packed onto the major street of Sudirman to protest against the withdrawal order by Nike.

The mob's main target was the BRI building where Nike leases its representative office in Jakarta. An employee even threatened to lead the others to the U.S. embassy. They claimed to have been laid off by the company due to the absence of purchase orders. The angry workers carried a banner that said "Nike runs uncivilized business, clear evidence of capitalism and liberalism."

Earlier Monday, the labor union of PT Doson failed to reach an agreement with the management over the amount of separation pay.

The union demanded a five-month separation pay for around 6,800 workers following the mass layoff at PT Doson, which has served Nike since 1993. Nike's General Manager to Indonesia, Jeff DuMont, announced on August 7 the discontinuance of orders from PT Doson, on grounds that the company's performance had been the poorest among other subcontractors here.

Nike began full production in Indonesia in 1988, and by 1996 one third of its shoes were produced here. In 2001, the sportswear giant bought shoes and sportswear from a total of 25 factories in Indonesia.

Similar to the Nike case, U.S. athletic apparel giant Reebok also halted orders from one of its subcontractors in West Java, forcing around 5,400 workers out of their jobs.[65]

Human Rights

Reebok History

In 1988, Amnesty International invited Reebok to be the sponsor of its Human Rights Now! World Tour. That tour, which featured artists Peter Gabriel, Bruce Springsteen, Sting, Tracy Chapman, and Youssou N'Dour, carried messages of freedom and justice to millions of people in 23 cities on four continents. That experience inspired Reebok to place human rights at the center of its corporate culture. That same year, it established the Reebok Human Rights Award program. Since then, it has become a leader in incorporating human rights into its business practices and making it an integral part of its corporate identity.

Understanding Human Rights

The following human rights information is directly from Reebok's web site.

- On December 10, 1948, the General Assembly of the United Nations adopted and proclaimed the UNIVERSAL DECLARATION OF HUMAN RIGHTS as the common standard of achievement for all peoples and all nations. At Reebok, we believe that as individuals we all have the responsibility to understand what human rights are and to GET

INVOLVED with the critical issues that impact our fellow human beings across the globe as well as in our own neighborhoods.

■ Please familiarize yourself with the Universal Declaration of Human Rights, learn about the extraordinary efforts of the Reebok Human Rights Awards recipients, and find ways to get involved with the many organizations that work to ensure dignity and rights of all human beings.

Reebok's Business Practices

"We believe that the incorporation of internationally recognized human rights standards into our business practice improves worker morale and results in a higher quality working environment and higher quality products."

Reebok Human Rights Production Standards

■ A commitment to human rights is an integral part of Reebok's corporate culture and identity. As a company operating in a global marketplace, we believe we have an obligation to act in a socially responsible way. In 1986, we were the first in our industry to pull out of South Africa in support of the anti-apartheid movement. Since then, we have implemented a number of programs and policies aimed at IMPROVING CONDITIONS for workers involved in making Reebok products. Some of these key initiatives include: the adoption of STANDARDS for production to protect the rights of workers who produce Reebok products; a comprehensive program to ensure that NO CHILD LABOR is used in the production of soccer balls; and an innovative WORKER COMMUNICATION SYSTEM that provides employees with a safe way to voice concerns or report violations. In addition, Reebok sponsored an independent assessment of working conditions in Indonesia and released a report entitled PEDULI HAK/CARING FOR RIGHTS. As a result of this report, many improvements in the factories have been implemented.

■ Such actions have helped to define Reebok as a corporation that is willing to follow its conscience. To learn more about current human rights programs, please visit NEWS AND NOTES. (*www.reebok.com*)

Reebok Human Rights Award

Standing up for human rights is a REEBOK hallmark—as much a part of our corporate culture and identity as our products. We believe that we all have a responsibility to UNDERSTAND HUMAN RIGHTS, to expose injustice, and to support efforts that ensure dignity and rights for all human beings. The BUSINESS PRACTICES we have developed and implemented around the world and OUR HISTORY, are a reflection of our commitment. Grants provided by the REEBOK HUMAN RIGHTS FOUNDATION help support human rights initiatives around the globe. The REEBOK HUMAN RIGHTS AWARD gives recognition and financial support to young activists who have made significant contributions to human rights through non-violent means. For more information about the REEBOK HUMAN RIGHTS PROGRAM please explore this website, or CONTACT US.[66]

2002 Human Rights Recipients

The four winners were women, the first time all winners were women. Kavwumbu Hakachima (age 27) of Zambia was an ardent spokesperson and advocate for victims of child abuse in Zambia, a country ravaged by poverty and AIDS. Ms. Hakachima now heads Children in Crisis, an organization dedicated to helping abused children.

Over the past eight years, Dita Sari (age 29) has been harassed, arrested, imprisoned, and tortured for her efforts to improve the deplorable labor conditions for thousands of factory workers, primarily women, in Indonesia. Today, Ms. Sari leads a union that is 22,000 strong and growing. She refused to accept the award because Reebok workers earned only around US$1.50 per day. She rejected her award. (See Protests Against Reebok.)

Babita Maili Lama (age 25) was a young mother who was abducted from her village in Nepal and sold into forced prostitution in Bombay. After surviving two years of unspeakable horrors, she escaped and now risks her own life to rescue other girls who suffer a similar fate.

A second-generation civil rights activist, Malika Asha Sanders (age 27) is Executive Director of the 21st Century Youth Leadership Movement, an innovative organization dedicated to developing leadership and community building skills for young African-Americans.

Award recipients received a $50,000 grant from the Reebok Human Rights Foundation to help further their work. They also became members of Forefront, a network of former recipients that helps each other gain skills and resources, share strategies and opportunities, communicate with the international community, and respond to cries.[67]

Financial Performance

Management Report on 2001 Operating Results[68]

During calendar year 2001, net income for the company increased to $102.7 million, or $1.66 per diluted share, from $80.9 million, or $1.40 per diluted share, for the calendar year 2000. Net sales for the company increased by 4.5%, from $2.865 billion in 2000 to $2.993 billion in 2001.

Net sales for the year ended December 31, 2001, were $2.993 billion (see **Exhibit 10**), a 4.5% increase from the year ended December 31, 2000, sales of $2.865 billion. Sales comparisons were adversely affected by the weakening of most foreign currencies against the U.S. dollar. On a constant-dollar basis, net Reebok brand sales (including the sales of the Greg Norman Collection) were $2.496 billion in 2001 an increase of 6.8% from the year ended

Exhibit 10 Consolidated Statements of Income: Reebok International, Ltd. (Dollar amounts in thousands, except per share data)

Year Ending December 31	2001	2000	1999
Net Sales	$2,992,878	2,865,240	$2,899,872
Costs and expenses			
Cost of sales	1,894,497	1,799,686	1,783,914
Selling, general and administrative expenses	913,941	915,387	971,945
Special charges	(532)	3,289	61,625
Interest expense, net	17,630	22,126	40,532
Other expenses, net	11,536	8,947	13,818
Total costs and expenses	$2,837,072	$2,729,435	$2,871,834
Income before income taxes and minority interest	155,806	135,805	28,038
Income taxes	48,300	49,000	10,093
Income before minority interest	107,506	86,805	17,945
Minority interest	4,780	5,927	6,900
Net income	$ 102,726	$ 80,878	$ 11,045
Basic earnings per share	$ 1.75	$ 1.42	$ 0.20
Diluted earnings per share	$ 1.66	$ 1.40	$ 0.20
Dividends per common share	$ 0.00	$ 0.00	$ 0.00
Common shares	98,049,605	96,208,558	92,985,737

Source: Reebok International, Ltd., 2001 Annual Report.

December 31, 2000, sales of $2.336 billion. On a constant-dollar basis, the Reebok brand's worldwide sales increased $219.5 million or 9.6%.

U.S. footwear sales of the Reebok brand increased 0.6% to $930.5 million in 2001 from $925.1 million in 2000. During the year, U.S. footwear sales to the athletic specialty channel of distribution increased 11%. The company believed its retail presence in this channel had improved compared to the prior year and that this improvement was strategically important to its long-term objective of growing quality market share in the United States. Sales increased 33% in the key strategic category of basketball. The company believed that its basketball increase was being fueled by a general resurgence in this category in the United States and by the strong presence of its endorsed athletes, led by the previous season's MVP, Allen Iverson. U.S. sales of the company's Classic product line increased approximately 10% for the year. The company believed this increase was partially attributable to a strong positive consumer response to its Classic advertising campaign. During 2001, U.S. footwear sales in the children's category also increased, whereas sales in the cross-training and running categories declined. U.S. apparel sales of the Reebok brand (including the sales of the Greg Norman Collection) increased by 68.1% to $395.1 million from $235.0 million in 2000. During 2001, the company entered into new licensing agreements with the National Football League ("NFL") and the National Basketball Association ("NBA"). In order to support its new sports licensing business, in February 2001 the company purchased selected assets of LogoAthletic ("Logo"). Included in the assets purchased were inventory, equipment, the assumption of certain facility leases, and the rights to Logo's trademarks. The total purchase price was $14.2 million. Much of the increase in U.S. apparel sales was from sales of this licensed product, however, wholesale sales of Reebok branded apparel also increased by 13.3% during the year as the result of some new apparel silhouettes with a strategic focus on women's fitness, Allen Iverson–inspired street wear, and Classics.

International sales of the Reebok brand (including footwear and apparel) were $1.170 billion in 2001, a decrease of 0.5% from sales of $1.176 billion in 2000. On a constant-dollar basis, international sales of the Reebok brand increased $54.0 million or 4.8%. On a reported-dollar basis, net sales in Europe increased 1.3% and net sales in Asia Pacific region decreased 10.3% for the year. On a constant-dollar basis, net sales in Europe increased $48.7 million or 6.1% for the year, and sales in the Asia Pacific region increased 1.2%. In Latin America, the company's sales to its independent distributors increased approximately 7.0% for the year. In constant dollars, international footwear sales increased approximately 6.8%, and international apparel sales increased by approximately 2.5%. Effective January 1, 2001, the company sold its South African subsidiary to an independent distributor and purchased a majority interest in its Mexican distributor. These changes did not have a material impact on sales or earnings during 2001.

Rockport's sales for 2001 decreased by 5.4% to $399.6 million from sales of $422.4 million in 2000. Domestic sales for the Rockport brand decreased by 9.0%. A significant portion of this decline occurred post-9/11 as a result of a decline in Rockport's business in the department store channel of distribution, as well as with the independent shoe stores. In the fourth quarter of 2001, Rockport's domestic business declined by 25%. The company believed that some of the decline was attributable to retailers adjusting down their model stock positions post-9/11 and that the decline was not indicative of a major deterioration in Rockport's U.S. market share. The company estimated that Rockport's market share in the United States declined by only 50–75 basis points in the fourth quarter. International revenues, which grew by 5.2%, accounted for approximately 28.4% of Rockport's sales in 2001 as compared to 25.5% in 2000. During 2002, Rockport was launching several new initiatives in order to improve sales performance, including a focused product strategy to enhance Rockport's women's business and a new product segmentation strategy to address the needs of its retailers and consumers.

**Exhibit 11
Consolidated
Balance Sheets:
Reebok
International, Ltd.
(Dollar amounts in
thousands, except
per share data)**

Year Ending December 31	2001	2000
Assets		
Current assets		
Cash and cash equivalents	$ 413,281	$ 268,665
Accounts receivable, net of allowance for doubtful accounts (2001, $55,240; 2000, $48,016)	383,372	423,830
Inventory	362,927	393,599
Deferred income taxes	104,280	101,715
Prepaid expenses and other current assets	30,835	37,396
Total current assets	1,294,695	1,225,205
Property and equipment, net	133,952	141,835
Other noncurrent assets		
Intangibles, net of amortization	76,686	64,288
Deferred income taxes	16,094	18,110
Other	21,746	13,608
Total assets	$1,543,173	$1,463,046
Liabilities and stockholders' equity		
Current liabilities		
Notes payable to banks	$ 11,779	$ 8,878
Current portion of long-term debt	97	13,813
Accounts payable	127,286	172,035
Accrued expenses	269,738	272,076
Income taxes payable	40,506	21,337
Total current liabilities	449,406	488,139
Long-term debt, net of current portion	351,210	345,015
Minority interest and other long-term liabilities	22,619	22,029
Commitments and contingencies		
Stockholders' equity		
Common stock, par value $.01; authorized 250,000,000 shares; issued shares: 98,049,605 in 2001; 96,208,558 in 2000	981	962
Retained earnings	1,453,348	1,301,269
Less 39,010,827 shares in 2001 and 38,716,227 shares in 2000 in treasury at cost	(660,422)	(653,370)
Unearned compensation	(2,736)	(1,402)
Accumulated other comprehensive income (expense)	(71,233)	(39,596)
Total stockholders' equity	719,938	607,863
Total liabilities and stockholders' equity	$1,543,173	$1,463,046

Source: Reebok International, Ltd., 2001 Annual Report.

Exhibit 12 Geographical Sales: Reebok International, Ltd. (Dollar amounts in thousands)

Net Sales	2001	%	2000	%	1999	%
United States	$1,721,834	57.53	$1,599,406	55.82	$1,609,697	55.51
United Kingdom	511,426	17.09	514,722	17.96	545,562	18.81
Europe	467,207	15.61	462,342	16.14	476,695	16.44
Other countries	292,411	9.77	288,770	10.08	267,918	9.24
Total net sales	$2,992,878	100.00	$2,865,240	100.00	$2,899,872	100.00

Source: Reebok International, Ltd., 2001 Annual Report, p. 63.

Ralph Lauren Footwear had sales of $97.3 million in 2001, a decrease of 8.8% from $106.7 million in 2000. The decline was partially attributable to the weak department store business during most of 2001 and partially due to the re-aligning of the company's product strategy to conform with that of Polo Ralph Lauren corporate.

The company's overall gross margin was 36.7% of sales for 2001, as compared to 37.9% for 2000, a decrease of 120 basis points. The company's margins were adversely affected by currency, the promotional retail climate in certain key markets, particularly in United States, and by the general slowdown in business that occurred post-9/11. Business had gradually rebounded from post-9/11 lows. Based on foreign currency exchange rates on December 31, 2001, and the company's hedging strategy, currency should continue to adversely impact margins throughout 2002. The company believed that 2002 gross margins should improve from fourth quarter 2001 levels. This improvement was based on the company's belief that this along with an assumed stabilization of foreign exchange rates should cause margins to improve from those experienced in the fourth quarter of 2001.

Selling, general, and administrative expenses for the year ended December 31, 2001, were $913.9 million, or 30.5% of sales, as compared to $915.4 million, or 31.9% of sales for 2000, a decline of $1.5 million or 140 basis points as a percentage of sales. The company continued to improve its expense leverage while at the same time increasing its Reebok Brand advertising and marketing investments. The company's shared service operation, which supported its multiple-brand strategy, continued to generate improved expense leverage as core services are implemented across all brands. As a result the company was able to reduce general and administrative type expenses by approximately 7% during 2001.

Net interest expense was $17.6 million for the year ended December 31, 2001, a decrease of $4.5 million as compared to 2000, as a result of strong cash flow generation and the refinancing of the company's long-term debt. In the first quarter of 2001, the company refinanced its term loan, which was due August 31, 2002, with the sale of $250 million in 20-year convertible debentures.

For the year ended December 31, 2001, the net other expenses were $11.5 million. During the year, the company identified an under accrual of buying agent's commissions of approximately $10.6 million was recorded in other expense during the second quarter of 2001. Also included in other expenses, net, are the gains from the sale of certain real estate assets of $8.2 million, the amortization of intangibles of $4.0, the write-off of $5.2 million of unamortized debt costs associated with the early extinguishment of the company's term loan, foreign currency losses, and other non-operating income and expenses.

Exhibit 11 shows Reebok's consolidated balance sheet.

Acquisition of Common Stock

Under various share repurchase programs from 1992 to 1995, the Board of Directors authorized the repurchase of up to $800,000 of the company's common stock in the open market or privately negotiated transactions. During the year ended December 31, 2001, the company acquired 294,600 shares of treasury stock for approximately $7,100. During the year ended December 31, 2000, the company acquired 2,000,000 shares of treasury stock in a noncash exchange pursuant to a stock option exercise by a major shareholder. As of December 31, 2001, the company had approximately $119,500 available for future repurchases of common stock under these programs.

Exhibit 12 shows sales of Reebok products by geographic regions. **Exhibit 13** shows sales by product type.

Exhibit 13 Net Sales by Product Type: Reebok International, Ltd. (Dollar amounts in thousands)

Net Sales	2001	%	2000	%	1999	%
Footwear	$2,081,393	69.54	$2,098,028	73.22	$2,071,768	71.44
Apparel	911,485	30.46	767,212	26.78	828,104	28.56
Total net sales	**$2,992,878**	**100.00**	**$2,865,240**	**100.00**	**$2,899,872**	**100.00**

Source: Reebok International, Ltd., 2001 Annual Report, p. 61.

Notes

1. Reebok International, Ltd., Form 10K (December 31, 2001), pp. i–iv. This letter was directly quoted.
2. *Footwear News* (May 8, 1995).
3. *Ibid.*
4. J. Perira, "In Reebok–Nike War, Big Woolworth Chain Was a Major Battle Ground," *Wall Street Journal* (September 22, 1995), p. A-1.
5. *Ibid.*
6. *Ibid.*
7. Reebok International Ltd., *1996 Annual Report*, p. 16.
8. *Ibid.*, p. i.
9. *Ibid.*
10. *Ibid.*, p. 62.
11. *Ibid.*
12. *Ibid.*, p. 67.
13. Reebok International, Ltd., "2001 Notice of Annual Meeting of Shareholders," p. 5. This was directly quoted.
14. Reebok International, Ltd., Form 10-K (December 31, 2001), pp. 18–19.
15. K. Labich, "Nike vs. Reebok," *Fortune* (September 18, 1995), p. 104.
16. *Ibid.*
17. *Ibid.*
18. "Reebok Press Release" (June 28, 2002).
19. Reebok International, Ltd., Form 10-K (December 31, 2001), pp. 30–34.
20. *Ibid.*, p. 4. This was directly quoted.
21. *Ibid.*, pp. 8–9. These six paragraphs were directly quoted.
22. *Ibid.*, pp. 10–11. These two paragraphs were directly quoted.
23. *Ibid.*, pp. 11–12. These six paragraphs were directly quoted.
24. *Ibid.*, pp. 12–13. These six paragraphs were directly quoted.
25. *Ibid.*, pp. 8–9. These three paragraphs were directly quoted.
26. *Ibid.*, pp. 17–18. These seven paragraphs were directly quoted.
27. *Ibid.*
28. *Ibid.*
29. *www.forbes.com.*
30. *www.hoovers.com* and *www.yahoo.com.*
31. D. Robson, "Just Do Something," *BusinessWeek* (July 2, 2001), pp. 70–71; Reebok International, Ltd., Form 10-K, pp. 2–5. This section was directly quoted.
32. *www.yahoo.com*
33. *www.theonlineinvestor.com* and *www.yahoomarketing.com.*
34. *www.yahoo.com.*
35. C. Matlack, "Puma Sharpens Its Claws," *BusinessWeek* (September 16, 2002), p. 46.
36. *www.espn.go.com/moresports/news* and *www.itochu.co.jp/main/news.*
37. Reebok International, Ltd., Form 10-K, pp. 4–7. This entire section was directly quoted.
38. *Ibid.*, pp. 9–14. These two paragraphs were directly quoted.
39. Reebok Press Release (May 4, 2000).
40. *Ibid.* (February 22, 2002).
41. Reebok International, Ltd., Form 10-K, p. 7. These three paragraphs were directly quoted.
42. *www.footlocker.com.*
43. *www.hoovers.com.*
44. *www.footlocker.com.*
45. *www.hoovers.com.*
46. J. Perira, "In Reebok–Nike War, Big Woolworth Chain Was a Major Battle Ground," *Wall Street Journal* (September 22, 1995), p. A-1.
47. *Ibid.*
48. K. Labich, "Nike vs. Reebok," *Fortune* (September 18, 1995), p. 104.
49. J. Perira, "In Reebok–Nike War, Big Woolworth Chain Was a Major Battle Ground," *Wall Street Journal* (September 22, 1995), p. A-1.
50. *www.yahoo.com.*
51. *Ibid.*
52. *www.hoovers.com.*
53. Reebok Press Release (July 9, 2002).
54. Reebok International, Ltd., Form 10-K, pp.13–14. These five paragraphs were quoted directly.
55. *Ibid.*, p. 13. These two paragraphs were directly quoted.
56. *Ibid.*, pp. 11–12. These four paragraphs were directly quoted.
57. *Ibid.*, pp. 14–15. These three paragraphs were directly quoted.
58. *Ibid.*, p. 16.
59. *Ibid.*, p. 12. This paragraph was directly quoted.
60. *Ibid.* This paragraph was directly quoted.
61. *Ibid.* This paragraph was directly quoted.
62. Reebok Press Release (July 1, 2002).
63. *www.WSNR.com/apps/art.*
64. *Ibid.*
65. *Ibid.*
66. *www.reebok.com.* The above five paragraphs were directly quoted.
67. *www.reebok.com.*
68. Reebok International, Ltd., Form 10-K, pp. 24–26. This entire section was directly quoted.

CASE 15

U.S. Major Home Appliance Industry in 2002:

Competition Becomes Global

J. David Hunger

THE U.S. MAJOR HOME APPLIANCE INDUSTRY IN 2002 IS AN EXAMPLE OF A VERY SUCCESSFUL industry. Contrasted with the U.S. automobile and consumer electronics industries, U.S. major appliance manufacturers had been able to successfully ward off strong foreign competition and were actually on the offensive internationally. The industry had been very successful in keeping prices low and in improving the value of its products. Compared to 1982, major home appliance prices had increased more slowly than the increase in U.S. earnings and the Consumer Price Index. Thus, the average American consumer in 2002 could earn a new appliance in fewer hours on the job than a half-century ago. From 1991 to 2001, after adjusting for inflation, retail prices actually declined—washers fell 12.7%, dryers dropped 9.8%, cooking equipment dropped 0.4%, and refrigerators/freezers fell 9.2%.[1] In addition, the energy efficiency of the most common major appliances had increased every year since 1972. Sales had also been increasing. More appliances were made and sold in the United States in 2001 than in any preceding year (see **Exhibit 1** for U.S. shipments of major home appliances). The Association of Home Appliance Manufacturers were predicting slight increases during 2002 in each category of "white goods"—refrigerators, freezers, washing machines, dryers, ranges, microwave ovens, and dishwashers.[2]

The major home appliance industry faced some significant threats as well as opportunities. After more than 50 years of rising sales, both in units and dollars, the U.S. and Canadian markets had reached maturity. (Annual unit shipments of appliances in the United States were a little over 70 million compared to 4.3 million units in Canada.) Aside from some normal

---

Exhibit 1
U.S. Manufacturers'
Unit Shipments of
Major Home
Appliances[1]
(Amounts in thousands)

Product	2001	2000	1999	1995	1990	1980
Compactors	117	118	115	98	185	235
Dishwashers, built-in	5,478	5,663	5,542	4,327	3,419	2,354
Dishwashers, portable	149	164	170	226	217	384
Disposers	5,547	5,485	5,369	4,519	4,137	2,962
Dryers, compact	NA	NA	170[2]	160[2]	275	207
Dryers, electric	5,117	5,095	4,865	4,020	3,318	2,287
Dryers, gas	1,384	1,480	1,443	1,205	1,002	682
Freezers, chest	1,285	1,075	1,058	934	723	963
Freezers, compact[2]	490	473	433	357	351	310
Freezers, upright	930	888	929	757	573	789
Microwave ovens, in ranges[2]	82	82	81	80	146	265
Microwave ovens, countertop	10,220	10,114	9,264	7,760	8,193	3,320
Microwave/convection ovens	200	196	155	115	303	N/A
Microwave ovens, over range	2,946	2,334	2,162	1,100	780	N/A
Range/oven hoods	3,200	3,150	3,000	2,740	2,450	2,400
Ranges, electric, built-in	723	706	704	619	631	555
Ranges, electric, freestanding	3,842	3,826	3,785	3,004	2,358	1,975
Ranges, electric, surface cooking	498	494	493	425	455	N/A
Ranges, electric, glass/ceramic[2]	2,314	2,057	2,035	955	85	155
Ranges, gas, built-in	71	70	72	86	106	102
Ranges, gas, freestanding	2,850	2,729	2,698	2,490	2,061	1,437
Ranges, gas, surface cooking	384	377	367	278	262	N/A
Ranges, gas, glass/ceramic[2]	58	34	—	—	—	—
Refrigerators, built-in	137	133	116	83	—	N/A
Refrigerators, compact[2]	1,355	1,530	1,497	1,032	932	543
Refrigerators, standard	9,305	9,217	9,099	8,670	7,101	5,124
Washers, automatic	7,362	7,495	7,313	6,901	6,192	4,426
Washers, compact	N/A	N/A	195[2]	200[2]	344	266
Water heaters, electric	4,333	4,257	4,281	3,917	3,226	2,451
Water heaters, gas	4,931	4,907	4,934	4,453	3,906	2,818
Water softeners	935	989	951	718	574	N/A
Total	73,300	72,492	70,381	60,476	53,726	37,010

Notes:
1. Exports not included.
2. Figures not included in industry total.

Source: "Statistical Review," Appliance (April 2002, 1998, and 1990), p. 50.

short-term fluctuations, future unit sales were expected to grow only 1.9% annually from 2000 to 2005 in the U.S. and Canadian markets. Operating margins had been dropping as appliance manufacturers were forced to keep prices low to be competitive even though costs kept increasing. The situation was the same in Western Europe, a market 25% larger than the U.S. major home appliance market, where unit sales were expected to grow only 1.7% annually during the same period. Markets in Asia, Eastern Europe, and Latin America had become more important to world trade as more countries changed to a free market economy. Industry analysts expected appliance markets in these areas to grow at a rate of 5%–6% annually between 2000 and 2005.[3] The industry was under pressure from governments around the world to make environmentally safe products plus significantly improve appliance efficiency in terms of energy usage and water consumption.

Development of the U.S. Major Home Appliance Industry

In 1945, there were approximately 300 U.S. major appliance manufacturers in the United States. By 2002, however, the "big four"—Whirlpool, General Electric, Maytag, and AB Electrolux—controlled 99% of the U.S. market. Although the German-based Bosch-Siemens entered the U.S. major home appliance industry in 1996, it had yet to earn a significant market share in any appliance category. The consolidation of the industry over the period was a result of fierce domestic competition. Emphasis on quality and durability coupled with strong price competition drove the surviving firms to increased efficiencies and a strong concern for customer satisfaction.

Industry History

All of the major U.S. automobile firms except Chrysler had participated at some time in the major home appliance industry. Giants in the consumer electronics industry had also been involved heavily in appliances. Some of the major auto, electronics, and diversified companies active at one time in the appliance industry were General Motors (Frigidaire), Ford (Philco), American Motors (Kelvinator), Studebaker (Franklin), Bendix, International Harvester, General Electric, RCA, Emerson Electric, Westinghouse, McGraw Edison, Rockwell, United Technologies, Raytheon, Litton, Borg-Warner, and Dart & Kraft. Only General Electric and Emerson Electric remained in major home appliances in 2002. Emerson Electric continued through its In-Sink-Erator line of disposers as well as being a major supplier of electronic parts (primarily motors) to the remaining appliance makers. Most of the other firms divested their appliance business units, many of which were acquired by White Consolidated Industries, which itself was acquired by the Swedish firm AB Electrolux in 1986 and subsequently renamed Frigidaire as its North American Division.

Prior to World War II, most appliance manufacturers produced a limited line of appliances derived from one successful product. General Electric made refrigerators. Maytag focused on washing machines. Hotpoint produced electric ranges. Each offered variations of its basic product, but not until 1945 did firms begin to offer full lines of various appliances. By 1955, the major appliance industry began experiencing overcapacity, leading to mergers and acquisitions and a proliferation of national and private brands.

The industry almost doubled in size during the 1960s, as sales of several products grew rapidly. Dishwasher unit sales almost quadrupled. Unit sales of clothes dryers more than tripled. Product reliability improved even though real prices (adjusted for inflation) declined around 10%.

Although the 1970s were a time of high inflation and high interest rates, the major home appliance industry continued to increase its unit sales. Profit margins were squeezed even more, and the industry continued to consolidate around fewer firms. Although antitrust considerations prevented GE and Whirlpool from acquiring other appliance units, White was able to buy the troubled appliance divisions of all the automobile manufacturers, along with Westinghouse's, as they were put up for sale.

The market continued to expand in the 1980s, thanks partially to the acceptance by the U.S. consumer of the microwave oven. By the 1990s, U.S. appliance manufacturers offered a full range of products even if they did not make the item themselves. A company would fill the gaps in its line by putting its own brand name on products it purchased from another manufacturer. For example, Whirlpool made trash compactors for Frigidaire (AB Electrolux), In-Sink-Erator (Emerson Electric), Jenn-Air (Maytag), Magic Chef (Maytag), and Sears (Kenmore). Caloric (Amana) not only made gas ranges for its in-house Amana brand, but also for Whirlpool. General Electric made some microwave ovens for Caloric (Amana), Jenn-Air (Maytag), Magic Chef (Maytag), and its own Hotpoint and RCA brands.

Product and Process Design

Innovations in the industry tended to be of four types: (1) new products that expanded the appliance market, (2) new technologies and designs to increase efficiency and effectiveness, (3) new customer-oriented features, and (4) process improvements to reduce manufacturing costs.

New products historically drove the growth of major home appliances. The washing machine and the refrigerator were the founding products of the industry. A survey by the Harris Corporation in 1999 revealed that the top technological achievements of the 20th century were the computer and television, followed closely by the refrigerator, microwave oven, and washing machine.[4] New home appliances that had strongly increased industry unit sales were dishwashers in the 1960s and microwave ovens in the 1980s.

New technologies and designs were being introduced into major home appliances. Due to governmental pressure, appliance manufacturers were introducing energy-efficient versions of refrigerators and washing machines at the dawn of the 21st century. Examples of these were Maytag's Neptune front-loading clothes washer and Whirlpool's top-loading Calypso washing machine. Both of these used less energy and water and resulted in more effective cleaning action than traditional washers. Research was being conducted to replace current technologies with more efficient ones. One example was the use of microwave energy in clothes dryers so that clothes could be dried faster, at a lower temperature (thus less shrinkage and damage), with less energy use than a conventional dryer. Unfortunately, the technology needed further development before it could be marketed: Microwaves had a tendency to heat metal objects to such a point that they caused fabric damage. In another example, researchers at Iowa State University, in cooperation with Astronautics Corporation of America, were developing a refrigerator using magnets. The cooling apparatus consisted of a wheel containing gadolinium powder moving through a high-powered, rare earth permanent magnet. The result was a virtually silent, vibration-free refrigerator instead of the traditional ozone-depleting refrigerant and noisy, energy-consuming compressor.[5] Other researchers were experimenting with sound waves to clean clothes.

Customer-oriented features included the self-cleaning oven, pilot-less gas range, automatic ice-cube-making refrigerator, warming drawers in ranges, and dishwashers with half-load washing capability. In most cases, features were introduced on top-of-the-line models and made available on lower-priced models later. Manufacturers' own brands usually had the newest and most elaborate features, followed by those from national retailers such as Sears, whose offerings usually copied the most successful features from the previous year. In this competitive industry, aside from patented features, no one producer could successfully keep a new innovation to itself for more than a year.

In 2002, three trends continued to be evident in customer-oriented features. First, design aesthetics were becoming more important in product development and marketing. Appliances were being given a more prominent place in the home. For example, washers and dryers were increasingly being placed not in the basement, but on the main floor. As a result, the washer and dryer were expected to be quieter and more aesthetically pleasing, complementing the decor of the room in which they resided. As the kitchen evolved into a hub of household activity, the refrigerator and range began to take on a greater importance in the household. European visual product design was having a strong impact on appliance design worldwide. Stainless steel was used like a color in high-end appliances to connote quality—especially to those people desiring ranges similar to those used by professional cooks. Refrigerators could be built in to various parts of the kitchen as drawers for distinct uses instead of as a large box with a door.

Second, manufacturers were introducing "smart" appliances with increasingly sophisticated electronic controls and self-diagnostic features. The Japanese firms Matsushita, Hitachi, Toshiba, and Mitsubishi had pioneered the use of "fuzzy logic" computer software in the 1980s to replace the many selector switches on an appliance with one start button. By 2000 all of the U.S. major home appliance manufacturers were using fuzzy logic to some extent in the making and marketing of their products. Whirlpool's "Sixth Sense" oven could determine the necessary settings for reheating or defrosting food, with no guesswork from the cook. The user simply pressed a single button for defrost—the oven then calculated on its own the correct time and power output. By 2002, these "smart appliances" were being connected to the Internet. For example, Haier, a Chinese appliance maker, demonstrated Internet-enabled refrigerators, washing machines, dishwashers, microwave ovens, air conditioners, and water heaters at the 2001 Domotechnica trade show in Cologne, Germany. These appliances could call for service, download programs, contact security providers in case of gas leaks or fire, pay utility bills, and be programmed remotely to start and stop when needed.

Third, there was an increasing global emphasis on environmentally safe products, such as the use of CFC-free refrigerant, and on greater efficiency in the use of water and energy. Since 1980, U.S. appliance makers have invested more than $1 billion to improve refrigerator energy efficiency. For the average home appliance customer, the appliance would cost less to operate and be better for the environment.

Process improvements for more efficient manufacturing of current products (compared to new-product development) tended to dominate research and development efforts in the U.S. major home appliance industry. Although modern appliances were much more effective and efficient, a refrigerator or a stove in 2002 still looked and acted very much the same as it did in the 1950s. It was built in a far different manner, however. The appliance industry historically had been characterized by low intensity in product research and development because of intense cost competition and demand for higher reliability. Until the late 1990s, the basis for effective competition had been producing the fewest basic components necessary in the most efficient plants. Although individual designs might vary, the components inside the appliances were becoming more universal and were being produced in highly automated plants, using computer-integrated manufacturing processes. Examples of this emphasis on product simplification were Maytag's "Dependable Drive" and Whirlpool's frame fabrication for its "Eye Level" ranges. Maytag's washer transmission was designed to have 40.6% fewer parts than the transmission it replaced. Fewer parts meant simplified manufacturing and less chance of breakdown. The result was lower manufacturing costs and higher product quality.

Most industry analysts agreed that continual process improvements had kept U.S. major home appliance manufacturers dominant in their market and competitive globally. The emphasis on quality and durability, coupled with a reluctance to make major design changes simply for the sake of change, resulted in products with long average life expectancy. The average useful life of a refrigerator or range was 15 to 20 years and those of washers, dryers, and dishwashers were around 12 to 14 years. (See **Exhibit 2** for life expectancy by appliance.)

Manufacturing and Purchasing

Although many manufacturing operations took place in an appliance factory, much of the process focused on proper preparation of the metal frame within which the washing, drying, or cooking components and elements would be attached. Consequently, appliance manufacturers could be characterized as "metal benders" who fabricated different shapes of metal boxes out of long coils of metal. As a result, the U.S. major home appliance industry purchased 22% of total coated-coil metals, second only to the building and construction industry.[6] Sophisticated machines would form and even weld the frames, and automated assembly lines and robots would add porcelain to protect the metal and add color to the finish. People were usually still needed to install the internal components in the frame and to wire sophisticated electronic controls. Quality control was often a combination of electronic diagnostics and personal inspection by employees.

Manufacturing costs were generally in the range of 65%–75% of total operating costs. Although direct labor costs were still an important part of the cost of completed goods

**Exhibit 2
Average Life
Expectancy of
Major Home
Appliances**

Appliance	Life Expectancy (Years)
Compactor	10
Dishwasher	12
Disposer	10
Dryer, electric	14
Dryer, gas	13
Freezer	16
Microwave oven	11
Range, electric	15
Range, gas	21
Range hood	14
Refrigerator, compact	7
Refrigerator, standard	15
Washer	12
Vacuum cleaner	8
Shampooer/steam cleaner	11
Water heater, electric	11
Water heater, gas	9

Source: "20th Annual Portrait of the U.S. Appliance Industry,"
Appliance *(September 2001), Special Insert, pp. 5–6.*

(around 10%), most companies were carefully examining material costs, general administration, and overhead for cost reduction. Traditionally, the optimal size of an assembly plant was considered to be an annual capacity of 500,000 units for refrigerators, ranges, washers, dryers, and dishwashers. Even though production costs were believed to be 10%–40% higher in smaller-sized plants, the use of robots suggested that the optimal plant could be even smaller than previously believed.[7]

The trend continued toward "dedicated" manufacturing facilities combining product line production in fewer larger plants to gain economies of scale. Although a plant's production line dedicated to the production of washing machines could be adjusted to make many different models, it could still only be used to make washing machines. Each product category required its own specialized manufacturing equipment.

All of the major home appliance manufacturers were heavily engaged in renovating and building production facilities to gain economies of scale, improve quality, and reduce labor and materials costs. For example, Electrolux's Frigidaire division in the United States spent over $600 million upgrading its current factories and building new refrigerator and dishwasher plants. It then invested $100 million each in its Anderson, South Carolina, and Greenville, Michigan, plants in 2001 to manufacturer its new Next Generation line of refrigerators. The General Electric Appliance (GEA) division spent around $1 billion over a four-year period (1994–1998) in product development and capital equipment (a 50% increase over previous spending levels) to upgrade its 40-year-old "appliance park" in Louisville, Kentucky. It then invested over $800 million during 2001 and 2002 in its 42 manufacturing plants in Mexico.[8] To ensure global quality standards, appliance manufactures have been going through the process of International Organization for Standardization (ISO) 9000 series certification.

Key materials purchased by the U.S. appliance industry were steel (primarily in sheets and coils), plastics, coatings (paint and porcelain), motors, glass, insulation, wiring, and fasteners. By weight, major appliances consisted of about 75% steel. Sales to the major home appliance industry of steel and aluminum together accounted for 10% of total industry sales.[9]

As the major home appliance industry had consolidated, so too had its suppliers. A. O. Smith, best known in the United States for its water heaters, acquired MagneTek's worldwide electric motor operations in 1999. Siebe and BTR merged in 2000 to form Invensys Appliance Controls and Invensys Climate Controls. Siebe had already purchased Eaton Corporation's worldwide controls business, Robertshaw Controls, Paragon Electric, and Ranco. The purchasing function and relationship with suppliers had changed considerably from the 1980s as more companies used fewer suppliers and more long-term contracts to improve quality and ensure JIT (just-in-time) delivery.

The 2000 update to the ISO 9000 series pushed appliance manufacturers to further integrate their supply chains to ensure total quality management. Along with its increasing global orientation, Whirlpool was putting emphasis on working with global suppliers. Appliance companies used certification programs to ensure that their smaller supplier bases were able to supply both the needed quantity and quality of materials, parts, and subassemblies when they were needed. Full-line, full-service suppliers had an advantage over one-dimensional suppliers. Appliance makers continued to put pressure on their suppliers to institute cost-saving productivity improvements. On the other hand, they were much more willing to involve suppliers earlier in the design stage of a product or process improvement.

Alliances between appliance makers and their suppliers were one way to speed up the application of new technology into new products and processes. For example, Maytag Corporation was approached by Honeywell, one of its suppliers, which offered its expertise in fuzzy logic technology—a technology Maytag did not have at that time. The resulting partnership in product development resulted in Maytag's new IntelliSense dishwasher. Unlike previous dishwashers, which had to be set by the user, Maytag's fuzzy logic dishwasher automatically selected the proper cycle to get the dishes clean based on a series of factors, including the amount of dirt and presence of detergent.

Although most U.S. appliance makers used both the Internet and extranets to communicate with their suppliers and distributors, there was no overall electronic marketplace between appliance makers and their suppliers (as there was in the auto industry) currently in existence in the United States.

Marketing and Distribution Channels

Due to relatively high levels of saturation in the United States, the market for major home appliances was driven primarily by the demand for replacements. Washers, ranges, refrigerators, and even microwave ovens were in more than 90% of U.S. households. (see **Exhibit 3** for saturation by product category.) Generally speaking, replacements accounted for 75% of sales, new housing for 20%, and new household formation for about 5% of sales of major home appliances. Replacement demand was usually driven by existing housing turnover, remodeling, changes in living arrangement trends, introduction of new features, and price levels in the economy. Although each new house had the potential to add four to six new appliances, the sale of an existing house also had an impact. According to J. Richard Stonesifer, President and CEO of GE Appliances, "About 4 million existing homes are sold each year, and approximately one new appliance is sold for every existing home that changes hands."[10] The National Kitchen and Bath Association estimated that about $4 billion of the total $25 billion spent annually on kitchen remodeling was for home appliances.

Both the new housing and remodeling markets currently tended to emphasize more upscale appliances in contrast to the previous tendency for builders to economize by buying the cheapest national brand appliances. A study by Simmons Market Research Bureau for *New Home* magazine revealed that more than $13 billion was spent annually by new-home owners on household goods, especially appliances. In order of importance, the appliances typically bought within the first 3 months of owning a new home were the refrigerator,

Exhibit 3
Saturation of
Selected Major
Home Appliances
in the United States,
Western Europe,
and Japan[1]
(Percentage of
households with at
least one of a par-
ticular appliance)

Appliance	United States	Western Europe	Japan
Compactor	5	N/A	N/A
Cooker	N/A	95	N/A
Dishwasher	59	39	N/A
Disposer	46	N/A	N/A
Dryer	59 (E), 20 (G)	28	22
Freezer	44	51	N/A
Microwave oven	96	60	N/A
Range	60 (E), 40 (G)	N/A	N/A
Refrigerator	99	98	98
Vacuum cleaner	99	N/A	98
Washer	93	94	99

Note:
1. (E) = electric, (G) = natural gas.

Source: "24th Annual Portrait of the U.S. Appliance Industry," Appliance *(September 2001), Special Insert;* "Portrait of the European Appliance Industry," Appliance *(November 2001), p. 50; "Portrait of the Japanese Appliance Industry,"* Appliance *(March 2002), p. 50.*

washer, dryer, microwave oven, vacuum cleaner, dishwasher, coffeemaker, and range.[11] This phenomenon provided sales opportunities for well-positioned appliance makers because brand loyalty in the appliance industry was only 35%.[12]

Changes in U.S. demographics favored the highly profitable, high-end, high-profile segment of the business. This trend was detrimental to the mass-market business, which emphasized cost over features. The aging of the baby boomers and the increase of two-income families had increased the upscale market, which demanded more style and costly features. According to Ken Gronbach, president of KGA Advertising, appliance manufacturers should continue to court the 80 million aging baby boomers because generation X contains only 50 million people. "[Baby boomers] want the high-end appliances and that's why companies that cater to that generation are doing well."[13] Appliance manufacturers responded by expanding product lines that emphasized quality and features. Those brands most identified in customers' minds with high product quality, such as Maytag and KitchenAid, were achieving good sales. (See **Exhibit 4** for ratings of brands by perceived quality.) Gronbach further proposed that the best way for appliance makers to appeal to the younger generation X was to offer new and unique products. "If your product is neither unique nor new it will be sold only on price because the demand will be pale compared to the supply."

Exporting was reasonably strong for high-quality U.S.-made refrigerators, vacuum cleaners, and laundry appliances but was much less than the importing of microwave ovens from Asia. For a number of reasons, exporting was not a significant factor for the U.S. major home appliance industry. The weight of most of these appliances meant high transportation costs, which translated into higher prices to the consumer. In addition, U.S.-made major appliances tended to be fairly large, whereas European and Asian markets preferred smaller appliances. As a result, most people around the world tended to buy appliances made locally, if they were available. Thus, those appliance companies wanting a significant presence in other parts of the world were either acquiring local companies, engaging in joint ventures, or building new manufacturing facilities in those regions in order to have a local presence.

There were two major distribution channels for major home appliances in the United States: contract and retail. A third, but less important, distribution channel was the commercial market, comprising laundromats and institutions.

Contract sales were made to large home builders and to other appliance manufacturers. Direct sales accounted for around 80% of contract sales. Firms sold appliances to the contract

Exhibit 4
Ratings of Brands in Terms of Consumer Perception of Quality According to U.S. Dealers (Percentage of responses by 300 appliance dealers from excellent to poor quality)

Appliance Brand[1]	Dealers Stocking Brand (%)	Excellent (%)	Poor (%)
Maytag	50	77	1
KitchenAid (Whirlpool)	45	76	2
Jenn-Air (Maytag)	45	66	3
Whirlpool	59	41	2
Amana (Maytag)	38	32	4
Profile (GE)	28	39	13
GE	44	24	3
Monogram (GE)	4	36	17
Frigidaire (Electrolux)	45	13	7
Magic Chef (Maytag)	36	8	10
RCA (GE)	28	6	10
Speed Queen [inactive]	8	6	1
Tappan (Electrolux)	29	5	15
White-Westinghouse (Electrolux)	28	6	15
Hotpoint (GE)	22	4	13
Gibson (Electrolux)	18	2	22
Roper (Whirlpool)	34	1	19
Kelvinator (Electrolux)	14	5	29
Caloric [inactive]	11	3	26
Admiral (Maytag)	7	0	30

Note:
1. Owners of brands shown in parentheses.

Source: J. Jancsurak, "What Retailers and Consumers Want Most," Appliance Manufacturer (May 1998), pp. 39–40.

segment both directly to the large builders and indirectly through local builder suppliers. Since builders were very cost conscious, they liked to buy at the middle to low end of a well-known appliance brand. Consequently, appliance manufacturers with strong offerings in this range, such as General Electric, Whirlpool, and Frigidaire, tended to do very well in this market. (See **Exhibit 5** for appliance sales by market segment.) In contrast, companies such as Maytag (except for the lower-priced Magic Chef brand) and Bosch-Siemens, which traditionally emphasized high-end products, sold little to builders. Whirlpool and GE designed whole kitchen concepts and sold the entire package—including their appliances—to builders. To further its advantage, Whirlpool opened a 35,000-square-foot customer center at its Benton

Exhibit 5
Revenue by Market Segment of Major White Goods Producers (Dollar amounts in billions)

Appliance Manufacturer	Discount Segment	Middle Segment	Premium Segment	Super-Premium Segment
Electrolux	$1.7	$2.9	1.3	—
Whirlpool	0.4	5.3	0.8	—
General Electric	0.2	1.1	1.4	—
Bosch-Siemens		0.5	3.7	$0.9
Maytag	—	0.3	2.5	0.1

Source: Goldman Sachs, "Brand Challenge," The Economist (April 6, 2002), p. 54.

Harbor, Michigan, headquarters in 1993 to demonstrate its offerings to retailers and contractors—the first such customer center in the industry.

Retail sales in the United States were made to three major kinds of outlets: (1) national chain stores and mass merchandisers; (2) department, furniture, and discount stores; and (3) independent appliance dealers.

National chain stores and mass merchandisers usually sold the most well-known brands and private brands promoted by the retailers. For example, Whirlpool has traditionally been the sole supplier of Kenmore washers and dryers to Sears Roebuck. Magic Chef sold similar private brand appliances to Montgomery Ward until Ward's bankruptcy in 1998. Almost half of U.S. white goods were traditionally sold through this mass merchandiser channel. Sears Roebuck has been so strong in major home appliance sales that it alone sold nearly two out of every five major appliances sold in the United States.[14]

Department stores, furniture stores, and discount stores were another important channel for major appliances, selling about 25% of white goods sold in the United States. These stores usually purchased well-known brands to offer their customers. As department stores tended to alter their product offerings to more soft goods (clothing items) and fewer hard goods (furniture and appliances) during the 1980s, discount stores became more important in major home appliance sales. Their concern with price, however, put even more pressure on manufacturers to sell in large quantity at low price. Lowe's, Home Depot, and Best Buy were becoming important outlets for appliances. Home Depot, for example, sold appliances not only from in-stock products, but also by using Internet-connected kiosks on the sales floor. Although Circuit City decided in 2001 to no longer sell major appliances, Wal-Mart's decision to offer selected GE appliances in a low-cost format suggests that appliance sales through discount and home improvement stores should continue to increase.

Independent appliance dealers had traditionally been an important retail outlet for white goods. Around 25% of major home appliances continued to be sold through this channel, although the amount was steadily declining. Many locally owned stores were being replaced by national chains and discount stores. By 2000, the so-called "power retailers"—Sears, national chains, and discount stores—were selling over 60% of all retail appliances in the United States.

Commercial sales were through an additional distribution channel. Never as important to manufacturers as the contract and retail channels, this channel nevertheless provided an important set of customers for sales of washing machines and dryers. Laundromats and institutions, such as colleges for their dormitories, typically bought the most durable appliances made for the home market. Manufacturers simply added coin meters to the tops of the washers and dryers destined for use in these commercial or public establishments. Although these home laundry appliances adapted for the commercial market comprised over 50% of sales to this channel, there were some indications that this market might be moving to commercial washers built to last two to three times longer than would a home washer used commercially. With regard to the makers of freezers, refrigerators, and ranges for use in business establishments such as restaurants, these were usually a different group of U.S. manufacturers (for example, Welbilt, Traulsen, Hobart, and Glenco) from those manufacturing home appliances. Contrasted with home appliances, commercial appliances were typically larger and more durable, with fewer convenience features. They were sold through different marketing channels. In addition, the commercial market was far smaller than the home market. Unit shipments of commercial major appliances in 2001 totaled only 2.6 million in the United States, compared to 73.3 million major home appliances.

By 2002, all of the major U.S. appliance makers used their own web sites to market their products and provide consumer-related information via whirlpool.com, maytag.com, ge.com, and frigidaire.com. The independent applianceadvisor.com provided industry information regarding individual brands for potential buyers, with links to manufacturer Web sites.

Maytag introduced online appliance shopping in 2001 to enable consumers to purchase Maytag appliances online from local dealers. Sears was said to have the busiest appliance e-commerce site at sears.com.[15] In 2001, Bosch-Siemens Hausgerate, AB Electrolux, and Whirlpool formed a business-to-business (B2B) electronics marketplace for European household appliance makers, distributors, and retailers called *Tradeplace*. For the convenience of the dealers, *Tradeplace* provided one common access point connected to the manufacturers' existing portals without having to log in every time.[16] BuildNet, Inc., offered Internet commerce for homebuilders in the United States. General Electric, the top supplier of major home appliances to builders, owned a part of BuildNet and sold its appliances through that web site.[17] Nevertheless, a true B2B electronic marketplace similar to *Tradeplace* had yet to be established in North America.

Appliance manufacturing shifted in the 1990s from its primary emphasis on quality and reliability to speed and agility. (See **Exhibit 6** for reliability data by appliance brand.) This meant that manufacturers worked to improve their use of logistics in order to provide better service to their distributors. Concepts similar to JIT had been applied in the 1990s to distribution and marketing. For example, Whirlpool introduced "Quality Express" in 1992 as part of its revamped distribution system. Quality Express used dedicated trucks, personnel, and warehousing to deliver Whirlpool appliances to 90% of all dealer and builder customers within 24 hours and 100% within 48 hours. As part of the service, drivers delivering product unloaded units from the truck and put them where the customer wanted them. This service even included uncrating, customizing, and installation if desired. Other appliance companies soon followed Whirlpool's lead. A 1998 survey of 2,000 North American appliance dealers ranked appliance manufacturers in terms of how well they serviced retailers:

1. Whirlpool Corporation
2. Maytag Corporation
3. GEA
4. Frigidaire (AB Electrolux's U.S. appliance unit)
5. Goodman (Amana; subsequently sold to Maytag)[18]

In the early years of the 21st century, U.S. appliance manufacturers were moving toward a stronger product-market orientation. Appliance makers had long known that their emphasis on quality and reliability meant that people replaced their appliances only when the appliances wore out or when they changed houses.

By 2002, a survey of 500 residential U.S. households found that energy efficiency had replaced price as the top appliance-purchasing consideration. Roughly 25% of the population said that they would be willing to pay 15%–25% above the standard price for higher-energy-saving appliances.[19]

Uniquely differentiated products, such as Maytag's Neptune washer, Gemini double oven, and Accellis range, Whirlpool's Calypso washer, and GE's Advantium oven, were successfully motivating people to replace their current working appliances. To continue to compete successfully in the 21st century, it had become essential to invest heavily in product development (not just process R&D) and in more sophisticated marketing. This meant that appliance makers could no longer rely on their traditional engineering orientation to create a competitive advantage. When the Wolf Appliance Company, an affiliate of Sub-Zero Freezer Company (a niche manufacturer of premium, built-in refrigerators and freezers), launched a new upscale built-in cooking appliance line, it conducted significant market research, using focus groups and conjoint analysis, to determine which combination of attributes and features would be most attractive to a specific market segment. To build its competence in marketing, Whirlpool had begun to hire brand management people from consumer products firms such as Kraft and General Foods to oversee the development of new brands.

Exhibit 6 Reliability Ratings of Selected Major U.S. Home Appliance Brands
(Listed in order of frequency, from fewest to most repairs, by percentage of appliances purchased)

Washers (Top Loaders)	Dryers (Electric)	Dryers (Gas)
Roper (7%)	Whirlpool (6%)	Whirlpool (7%)
Whirlpool—tied for 2nd	Roper	Kenmore
Maytag—tied for 2nd	Maytag	KitchenAid
Kenmore	Kenmore	Maytag
Hotpoint—tied for 5th	KitchenAid	Amana
Frigidaire—tied for 5th	Hotpoint	General Electric (10%)
Amana	Amana	
KitchenAid	Frigidaire	
General Electric (14%)	General Electric (9%)	

Refrigerator (Top Freezer/No Ice Maker or Dispenser)	Refrigerator (Top Freezer/Ice Maker Only)	Refrigerator (Side-By-Side/Icemaker & Dispenser)
Hotpoint—tied for 1st (4%)	Kenmore (7%)	Whirlpool (9%)
KitchenAid—tied for 1st	Whirlpool	KitchenAid
Whirlpool—tied for 1st	KitchenAid	Kenmore
Kenmore—tied for 1st	General Electric	General Electric
General Electric	Amana	Amana
Amana: bottom freezer	Maytag	Frigidaire
Maytag	Amana: bottom freezer	Maytag (33%)
Frigidaire	Frigidaire	
Amana (7%)	Sub-Zero: built-in bottom freezer (26%)	

Ranges (Gas)	Ranges (Electric)	Dishwashers
General Electric—tied for 1st (8%)	General Electric (5%)	Whirlpool (7%)
Hotpoint—tied for 1st	Hotpoint	Kenmore
Kenmore	Kenmore—tied for 3rd	KitchenAid
Frigidaire	Whirlpool—tied for 3rd	Maytag
Whirlpool	Frigidaire	Hotpoint
Tappan	Magic Chef—tied for 6th	GE Monogram—tied for 6th
Magic Chef	Amana—tied for 6th	Bosch—tied for 6th
KitchenAid	Maytag	Magic Chef
Maytag	KitchenAid	General Electric
Jenn-Air	Jenn-Air (15%)	Jenn-Air—tied for 10th
Amana (21%)		Amana—tied for 10th
		Asko—tied for last
		Frigidaire—tied for last (18%)

Sources: "Washing Machines and Dryers," Consumer Reports *(July 2002), pp. 42, 44; "Refrigerators,"* Consumer Reports *(January 2002), p. 47;* *"Ranges,"* Consumer Reports *(February 2002), p. 34.*

Environmental Issues and Government Regulation

Home appliance manufacturers around the world faced increasing regulation regarding their products. One example was refrigerators and freezers. On the one hand, governments were requiring less use of refrigerants, which might cause global warming. On the other hand, the U.S. Department of Energy (DOE) was requiring energy conservation improvements for refrigerators and freezers. These appliances had traditionally been notorious energy hogs—consuming about 20% of the electricity used in the American home. The appliance industry had worked significantly to make products more energy efficient over the decades. For example, from 1972 to 1990 for a typical top-mount, automatic-defrost refrigerator (the most popular U.S. refrigerator), the amount of energy consumed declined from 1,986 kilowatt hours per year to 950 kilowatt hours per year (kwh/yr). Chest freezer energy consumption dropped during the same period, from 1,268 kwh/yr to 575 kwh/yr. Nevertheless, the U.S. DOE standard in effect on July 1, 2001, required that the amount of energy used by a typical refrigerator equal no more than that used by a 55-watt light bulb.[20] According to a 2001 DOE minimum energy efficiency standard, U.S. clothes washers manufactured in 2004 were to be 22% more efficient than those in 2001 and 35% more efficient by 2007.[21] Units imported into the United States were also required to meet the regulations.

Another issue facing appliance manufacturers was the presence of widely different standards for major appliances in countries around the world. The emergence of a true global market in major home appliances required the development of common world standards. There were at least three categories of standards: safety/environmental, energy efficiency, and testing procedures. Existing standards had been drafted by such bodies as the British Standards Institute (BSI) in the United Kingdom, Japanese Industrial Standards Committee (JISC), AFNOR in France, DIN in Germany, CSA in Canada, and UL in the United States. These standards had traditionally created entry barriers that served to fragment the major home appliance industry by country. The International Electrotechnical Commission (IEC) standards were created to harmonize standards in the European Union and eventually to serve as worldwide standards, with some national deviations to satisfy specific needs. In addition, the ISO was tasked with preparing and publishing international standards. These standards provided a foundation for regional associations to build upon. CANENA, the Council for Harmonization of Electrotechnical Standards of the Nations of the Americas, was created in 1992 to further coordinate the harmonization of standards in North and South America. Efforts were also under way in Asia to harmonize standards. By 2002, it appeared that the industry was working toward achieving international standards with some allowance being made for regional differences.[22]

With the dawn of the 21st century, major home appliance manufacturers faced a new set of certification standards beyond the ISO 9000 series. While ISO 9000 standards dealt with quality management systems, ISO 14001 covered environmental management systems and addressed the need for one international environmental management standard. Some international markets, such as the European Union, could require certification as a prerequisite for doing business.

Products

Major home appliances, or white goods, as they were commonly called, were generally classified as laundry (washers and dryers), refrigeration (refrigerators and freezers), cooking (ranges and ovens), and other (dishwashers, disposals, and trash compactors) appliances. (See **Exhibit 7** for U.S. market share by appliance category.) In addition to making white goods, some appliance manufacturers also made and sold floor care appliances (Maytag), room air conditioners (Whirlpool and Electrolux), or lawn and garden equipment (Electrolux). The majority of U.S. heating and cooling appliances (water heaters, furnaces, and central air conditioning) were made by other manufacturers, such as Rheem, A.O. Smith, Lennox, and Carrier.

Exhibit 7 U.S. Major Home Appliance Market Shares by Category (By percentage of total U.S. sales)

Appliance	2001	1996[1]	Appliance	2001	1996[1]
Compactor			**Microwave oven**		
Whirlpool	88%	90%	Samsung	26	18
Broan NuTone	11	10	Sharp	24	29
Others	1	0	LG Electronics (Goldstar)	11.5	12
Dishwasher			Matsushita	10	15
Whirlpool	48	37	Whirlpool	7.5	5
Maytag	21	19	Sanyo Fisher	6.5	7
GEA	19	40	Daewoo	4.5	3
Electrolux	11	4	Maytag	3	3
Others	1	0	Others	7	8
Disposer			**Range Hood**		
In-Sink-Erator	75	70	Broan NuTone	85	65
Anaheim/Watertown/WKing	25	30	Watertown Metal Prod.	6	11
Dryer			Vent Line	5	24
Whirlpool	50.5	54	Others	4	5
Maytag	24	20	**Range (gas)**		
GEA	19	19	GEA	31	40
Electrolux	5.5	6	Electrolux	27	19
Others	1	1	Whirlpool	24	—
Freezer			Maytag	17	34
Whirlpool	63	60	Others	1	7
W.C. Wood	24	35	**Range (electric)**		
Haier	8	—	GEA	41	49
Sanyo Fisher	1	3	Whirlpool	26	19
Others	4	2	Electrolux	18	9
Refrigerator			Maytag	14	20
Whirlpool	28.5	27	Others	1	3
Electrolux	24.5	14	**Washer**		
GEA	23	37	Whirlpool	51.5	52
Maytag	23	20	Maytag	25	24
Others	1	2	GEA	15	17
			Electrolux	7.5	7
			Others	1	0

Note:
1. Raytheon's 1996 Amana appliance share totals included with Maytag share totals.

Source: *"Special Report: 2002 Market Profile,"* Appliance Manufacturer *(April 2002), p. 11.*

Competitors

Four major home appliance manufacturers controlled around 99% of the U.S. market for white goods. In order of 2001 market share, Whirlpool led, with 39.2%; followed by General Electric, with 23.2%; Maytag, with 21.6%; and A.B. Electrolux (Frigidaire), with 15.0%. The remaining 1% belonged to the foreign firms of Bosch-Siemens and Haier, which had recently begun to produce in North America, and to various manufacturers of a single type or category of appliance, such as Sub-Zero (built-in refrigerators and freezers and Wolf's professional ranges) and Emerson Electric (garbage disposals). (See **Exhibit 8** for overall U.S. and Western European market shares by company.) The strongest competitors in the United States during the five-year period from 1996 to 2001 were Whirlpool, Maytag, and Electrolux.

Exhibit 8
Shares of U.S. and
Western European
Market in White
Goods
(Including dish-
washers, dryers,
ranges, refrigera-
tors, and washers)

U.S. Combined Market Share by Company

Company	2001	1996	Brands
Whirlpool	39.2%	34.9%	Estate, Inglis, KitchenAid, Roper, Whirlpool
GEA	23.2%	32.0%	GE, Hotpoint, Monogram, Profile, RCA
Maytag[1]	21.6%	15.2%	Admiral, Amana, Jenn-Air, Magic Chef, Maytag
Electrolux	15.0%	9.6%	Frigidaire, Gibson, Kelvinator, Tappan, White-Westinghouse
Raytheon	—	6.7%	Amana, Caloric, Speed Queen
Others	1.0%	1.6%	

Western Europe Combined Market Share by Company

Company	Home Country	2000	1996
Electrolux	Sweden	16.2%	22.3%
Bosch-Siemens	Germany	14.4%	15.9%
Whirlpool	U.S.	9.4%	10.5%
Merloni Bonferraro	Italy	9.4%	6.0%
Groupe Brandt	France	4.1%	6.0%
Miele	Germany	4.0%	6.0%
Arcelik	Turkey	4.0%	6.0%
Ardo Merloni	Italy	4.0%	—
GDA	UK	3.6%	3.8%
Candy	Italy	3.4%	4.8%
Fagor	Spain	3.4%	—
Others		24.1%	18.7%

Note:
1. Includes Amana.

Source: "Special Report: 2002 Market Profile," Appliance Manufacturer (April 2002 and 1997), Special Insert; "Portrait of the European Appliance Industry," Appliance (November 2001), pp. 49–53, and (November 1997), pp. 59–64.

Whirlpool had increased its market share by almost five points, from 34.9% five years earlier. Maytag had been steadily increasing its market share (about 1% per year), from 15.2% in 1996 to 20.8% in 2000. Its purchase of Amana's home appliances from Goodman in 2001 raised Maytag's total market share an additional point, to 21.6% in 2001. Frigidaire, AB Electrolux's North American home appliance division, increased its market share over five points from 9.6% in 1996. In contrast, General Electric had lost about nine points of market share (almost 2% each year!), from 32.0% in 1996. By the time Maytag bought Amana home appliances, Amana's market share had been 2.9% in 2000, down from 6.7% in 1996.

When viewed in terms of total world sales, the U.S. major home appliance manufacturers were major contributors. The top 10 global appliance makers, in order of units sold worldwide, were Whirlpool (U.S.), AB Electrolux (Sweden), General Electric (U.S.), Matsushita (Japan), Bosch-Siemens (Germany), Maytag (U.S.), Sharp (Japan), Toshiba (Japan), Haier (China), and Hitachi (Japan).[23] Of these 10, only Whirlpool and AB Electrolux had strong positions in all the key world markets of North America, Western Europe, Latin America, and Asia (particularly China and India). For example, AB Electrolux was first in market share in Western Europe, with 16.2% in 2000. Whirlpool was third, with 9.4% share, following Bosch-Siemens, with 14.4%. General Electric placed ninth, with 3.6% market share, before it sold its half ownership of the British joint venture General Domestic Appliances (GDA) to the Italian appliance maker Merloni Electrodomestici in 2002. The

GDA joint venture had been successful in the United Kingdom but had achieved only minimal sales to the European continent.

The Japanese appliance firms were well entrenched in Asia but had no real competitive presence (outside of microwave ovens) in the rest of the world. This was similar to Maytag's being strong only in North America. Earlier Maytag had purchased Hoover to obtain Hoover's major appliance facilities in the United Kingdom (thus gaining access to the European market), but the enormous cost of upgrading the plants combined with Hoover's low sales outside Britain caused Maytag to sell Hoover's European operations to Candy, the Italian appliance firm. Although Bosch-Siemens was attempting to grow its presence throughout the world, it was overshadowed outside Europe by Whirlpool and Electrolux and by various strong regional competitors, such as Maytag in the United States and Haier in China. Nevertheless, Bosch-Siemens's recent investments in the Americas was likely to soon move it to fourth place in global unit sales. Haier, the dominant appliance maker of China, followed the Bosch-Siemens strategy by working diligently to establish itself in Europe and the Americas. Since 1987, Haier's sales had increased faster than those of any other home appliance company in the world.

In terms of their competitive orientation in 2002, major home appliance manufacturers could be placed in one of the following categories:

Global Players

Whirlpool (U.S.)
AB Electrolux (Sweden)
General Electric (U.S.)

Global Aspirants

Bosch-Siemens (Germany)
Haier (China)
LG Electronics (Korea)

Strong Regional Players

Matsushita, Sharp, Toshiba, and Hitachi (Japan) in Asia
Maytag (U.S.) in North America
Candy and Merloni (Italy) in Western Europe
Miele (Germany) in Western Europe
Samsung and Daewoo (Korea) in Asia

Strong Local Players with Some Regional Presence

Arcelik (Turkey)
Mabe (Mexico)
Multibras (Brazil)
Fisher & Paykel (New Zealand)

Domestic and Niche Players

Sub-Zero/Wolf (U.S.)
Guangdong Midea Group (China)
Many others

Many of the major home appliance manufacturers, such as Whirlpool and Maytag, had fairly narrow product lines, concentrating on home appliances. Some, like Electrolux and Haier, also sold related appliances such as air conditioning and commercial appliances. Other competitors were part of a larger, highly diversified corporation. General Electric Appliances, for example, was a division of the General Electric Company. Bosch-Siemens Hausgerate was a joint subsidiary of Robert Bosch GmbH and Siemens AG. Matsushita, Sharp, Toshiba, and Hitachi of

Japan and Samsung and Daewoo of Korea were appliance units of larger, much diversified, global corporations. Even though the Japanese and Korean appliance firms did not have strong positions in major home appliances in every key world market in 2002, they were broadly diversified and well established globally in brown goods (consumer electronics) and other product lines.

As the major home appliance industry became increasingly global, industry analysts wondered if regional and domestic major home appliance companies concentrating on white goods, such as Maytag in North America and Miele in Western Europe, would continue to be successful as independent firms. Appliance expert Paul Roggema wondered if such a company was big enough to play the global game, in terms of purchasing and advertising power. Would Miele's technological leadership and quality brands allow it to survive, despite globalization, or would it be the perfect fit for Electrolux's brand portfolio?[24]

The construction in 1997 of a 200,000-unit-capacity dishwasher plant in New Bern, North Carolina, by the powerful German-based Bosch-Siemens Hausgerate to serve the North American market signaled that the U.S. major home appliance industry was changing significantly. This aggressive move was soon followed by Haier, the number-one Chinese appliance manufacturer. Haier's construction of a refrigerator plant in Camden, South Carolina (with plenty of room for expansion), in 2000 was one indication of the company's desire to join Bosch-Siemens as a major player in the U.S. market.[25]

Until the entry of Bosch-Siemens, the only foreign home appliance manufacturing presence had been in floor care. Whirlpool Corporation had arranged a joint venture in 1990 with Matsushita Electric Industrial Company, Ltd., to own and operate Whirlpool's current manufacturing plant in Danville, Kentucky, to provide vacuum cleaners for Sears.

Whirlpool

Whirlpool and General Electric had traditionally dominated the U.S. major home appliance industry. (In 1991, Whirlpool's U.S. market share had been 33.8%; GE's had been 28.2%.) Unlike General Electric, major home appliances were Whirlpool's primary business. Whirlpool's market share had been steadily increasing to almost 40% in 2001, whereas GE's share had recently fallen to 23%. Whirlpool owed its leadership position to its 50-plus-year relationship with Sears, to which it has been the sole supplier of Kenmore (Sears' own brand label) washers and dryers, the principal supplier of trash compactors and microwave/hood combinations, and a major supplier of dishwashers, ranges, refrigerators, and freezers. Sears's movement away from a heavy reliance on its Kenmore brands toward offering all lines of major home appliances had serious implications for Whirlpool. Nevertheless, even though it no longer dominated Whirlpool's sales, Sears continued to be the firm's largest single customer in 2002 and accounted for around 21% of Whirlpool's sales.

With the completion of its purchase of Dutch-based Philips Electronics's appliance operations in 1991, Whirlpool became a serious competitor in the emerging global major home appliance industry. Sales and market share consistently increased annually in every geographic section of the company—North America, Europe, Latin America, and Asia. It was first in North America and third in Western Europe in terms of market share. The company's marketing strategy was to focus on making the Whirlpool name a global brand. (Even though the company ranked only third in Europe in terms of overall market share of its Philips, Whirlpool, Backnecht, and Ignis brands, management liked to point out that the Whirlpool brand alone had the highest share of any brand in Europe.) In 2002, Whirlpool purchased Polar SA, a leading appliance maker in Poland, and was in the process of bidding for the washing machine and cooking appliance plants of the bankrupt French appliance maker Moulinex-Brandt.[26]

Whirlpool manufactured appliances in 44 locations, 34 of which were outside the United States, in 12 countries. Whirlpool had developed a series of joint ventures and equity arrangements with appliance manufacturers throughout Asia and South America. Although its share of the Asian market was still fairly small, Whirlpool, together with its affiliates in Argentina and Brazil, had the largest manufacturing base and market share in South America. (Whirlpool owned 94% of the Brazilian appliance companies Brasmotor and Multibras.) In cooperation with its affiliates in Brazil and joint venture partners in India and Mexico, Whirlpool built facilities in those countries to produce what the company called the "world washer." Five years after acquiring Kelvinator of India in 1995 to gain entry into the Indian market, Whirlpool had established itself as the market leader in refrigerators and washing machines.[27]

Fifty-nine percent of Whirlpool's 2001 sales were in North America. The company's top management believed that the firm's global position provided a competitive advantage "by reason of its ability to leverage engineering capabilities across regions, transfer best practices, and economically purchase raw materials and component parts in large volumes."[28]

Whirlpool's global expansion carried a significant cost in efficiency. It posted losses of $70 million in 1996 and $55 million in 1997 in Asia. Consequently, the company undertook a global restructuring program in 1997 to revive its sagging European and Asia operations. It cut 10% of its 46,000-person workforce, increased its presence in South America, pulled out of two troubled joint ventures in China (leaving it with two remaining joint ventures), and sold its financing business.[29]

Whirlpool revealed its excellence in product development when it successfully built a prototype to win the Super Efficient Refrigerator Program (SERP) award. Another example of new product development was in washing machines—the category in which Whirlpool owned over half of the U.S. market. Even when Frigidaire and Maytag announced that they were developing radically new front-loading washing machines to meet tightening energy and water usage requirements, Whirlpool chose to build a new type of top-loading machine. The resulting washing machine, to reach the market in late 2000, was a huge success, both as the Whirlpool Calypso and the Kenmore Elite. Like Maytag's front-loading Neptune washer, the Calypso/Elite used less energy and water and was gentler on clothes than traditional top loaders.[30]

Even though Whirlpool continued to expand throughout the world, it was also diversifying into other products. Whirlpool began this process with the introduction in 2000 of its Cielo brand plumbing and bath appliance line, including jetted and soaking spas. According to Kelley Akre, National Accounts Manager for the Cielo brand, "The vision for Whirlpool Corporation is to be in 'Every Home, Everywhere' on the appliance side of the business. . . . We're taking on rooms in every home, everywhere."[31] It was rumored that the company would soon be introducing a line of products for the garage, such as workbenches, sinks, and storage systems. (See **Exhibit 9** for operating financial results for primary U.S. competitors.)

General Electric Appliances

General Electric, with a U.S. major home appliance market share of 23.2% in 2001, was a strong and profitable competitor in many industries but was failing to keep up with the industry in major home appliances. As a business unit, GE Appliances accounted for 4.6% of the corporation's total sales in 2001, down from 14% in 1996. General Electric had a powerful name and brand image and was the most vertically integrated of the major home appliance manufacturers. For example, General Electric Plastics was an important supplier to the industry. GEA was the only appliance producer to own its entire distribution and service facilities.

Realizing that GE's manufacturing facilities at its 40-year-old Appliance Park near Louisville, Kentucky, were slowly losing their competitiveness, management spent $100 million in the mid-1990s to modernize the washing machine plant. The Park's refrigerator plant was next in line for a $70 million makeover. Overall, the company invested around $1 billion over a four-year period in appliance product development and capital equipment—a 50% increase over previous spending levels. It then invested over $800 million during 2001 and 2002 in its 42 plants in Mexico. Committed to performing its own research, the company

**Exhibit 9
Major Home
Appliance
Operating Results
for Primary U.S.
Competitors[1]
(Dollar and
Swedish krona
amounts in mil-
lions)**

Company[2]	Category	2001	2000	1999
A.B. Electrolux	Revenue	SEK108,990	SEK98,488	SEK91,689
	Operating income	4,629	5,779	4,997
	Assets	30,510	27,444	26,224
General Electric	Revenue	$5,810	$5,887	$5,671
	Operating income	643	684	655
	Assets	3,100	2,775	2,463
Maytag	Revenue	4,093	3,713	3,706
	Operating income	324	478	562
	Assets	2,264	1,794	1,792
Whirlpool	Revenue	10,343	10,325	10,511
	Operating income	306	807	875
	Assets	6,967	6,902	6,826

Notes:
1. Figures for Electrolux given in Swedish kronor (SEK). US$1 roughly equals SEK9.
2. Results for Electrolux's consumer durables area, GE's appliance business unit, and Maytag's home appliances segment. Above results include worldwide sales, profits, and assets in home appliances area.

Source: 10-K reports of companies.

invested $100 million in 2002 to modernize its corporate research and development center in Niskayuna, New York.

Thirty percent of GE's appliance sales were currently outside the United States.[32] In 1989, GE paid $580 million for a joint appliance venture and other ventures with the UK's General Electric Corporation (GEC). Perhaps frustrated by the venture's inability to make significant sales inroads in the rest of Europe and by the growing saturation of the Western Europe appliance market, General Electric sold its half interest in the venture to Merloni Electrodomestici in 2002. Nevertheless, the company was heavily involved with international partners in Mexico (48% of MABE), Venezuela (Madosa), Brazil (majority interest in DAKO S.A.), India (40% of joint venture with Godrej & Boyce), the Philippines (Philacor), and Japan (Toshiba). These ventures have generally been successful. Although most appliances manufactured by the joint ventures were planned originally for sale in the country of origin, MABE gas stoves had been heavily exported into the United States, significantly cutting into Magic Chef's (a Maytag unit) dominance in this product line. More than one-third of all gas ranges and mini-refrigerators sold in the United States were being manufactured in MABE plants in northern Mexico.[33]

Since 1995, GE Appliances had been actively implementing a Six Sigma quality initiative throughout its many operations. Partly as a consequence of this program, GE refrigerators were rated in 1999 by U.S. property management personnel as being number one in quality compared to all other brands.[34] This rating further reinforced GE's reputation as the appliance sales leader to the North American builder market.

Maytag

Maytag Corporation, with a U.S. market share of 21.6% in 2002, had been steadily growing its share from 14.2% in 1991. It had moved past Electrolux into third place in the industry in 1995 and was now nipping at the heels of GE for second place in the North American home appliance market.

Realizing that the company could not successfully compete in the major home appliance industry as just a manufacturer of high-quality laundry products, the company embarked during the 1980s on the acquisition of Hardwick Stoves, Magic Chef, and Jenn-Air. These acquisitions provided Maytag the full line of laundry, cooking, and refrigeration appliances it needed to compete effectively in the U.S. market. Realizing that the industry was going global as well, Maytag purchased Hoover Company, a successful floor care company in the United States and a strong white goods producer in the United Kingdom and Australia. Increased debt from the acquisition, coupled with the heavy amount of investment needed to upgrade and integrate its newly acquired facilities and operations, put a big strain on Maytag's profitability. Consequently, Maytag sold as losses Hoover Australia in 1994 and Hoover Europe in 1995. Maytag then undertook a joint venture with the Rongshida appliance company of China in 1996 but ended its involvement in 2001, after continuous losses.

In 1995, Maytag invested $13.7 million to expand its recently completed state-of-the art dishwasher plant in Tennessee. At that time dishwasher sales were increasing at twice the rate of the rest of the industry.[35] This investment plus the corporation's decisions to spend $160 million upgrading its Admiral refrigerator plant (part of the Magic Chef purchase) and $50 million to build a new plant for its front-loading, horizontal-axis Neptune washer plant indicated that Maytag had no intention of being outmaneuvered by others in North America. The company finally decided in 1998 to offer its full line of Maytag brand appliances through Sears. (It was the last major U.S appliance maker to do so.) Maytag also established 10 Maytag retail stores in the late 1990s for the purpose of allowing consumers to use Maytag's appliances before buying them. The stores were independently owned but supplied by Maytag and were larger on average than the 550 independently owned Maytag dealers. Management decided to open 16 more stores in 2002. These stores were to also offer brands from other manufacturers.

Uninterested in being a takeover target, Maytag spent $325 million in 2001 to acquire Amana, a respected major home appliance brand noted for its excellence in refrigeration technology. Amana had earlier been the major home appliance unit of Raytheon before being sold to the Goodman Global Holding Company, a Texas heating and air conditioning company, in 1997. As a unit of Raytheon, the Amana appliance unit had been composed of the Amana, Speed Queen, and Caloric brands. (Speed Queen's commercial appliance unit was sold separately.) Goodman's Amana and Caloric brands posted a market share of 5.2% in 1998 but dropped to only 2.9% in 2000.

Maytag had purchased in 1997 the G. S. Blodgett Company, a leading commercial food service equipment maker in Burlington, Vermont. Blodgett made ovens, fryers, and charbroilers for restaurants and hotels. After the acquisition of Amana, Maytag sold Blodgett in order to reduce its debt and to concentrate on North American major home appliances. As part of its consolidation of Amana and Maytag operations, management sold the firm's components parts business in Jefferson City, Missouri, and moved limited refrigeration manufacturing to Amana's refrigeration plant in Amana, Iowa, in 2002. To further reduce manufacturing costs, management invested $2 million in a new subassembly plant in Mexico in 2002. Until this decision, subassembly work had either been done at Maytag's U.S. facilities or by outside suppliers.

According to William Beer, President of Maytag Appliances, Maytag's strategy was to focus on delivering a constant stream of innovative products, such as the Neptune washer, Gemini oven, and Wide-by-Side refrigerator. Although CEO Ralph Hake agreed that innovative products were very important, he felt that for the company to return to sustainable and attractive levels of profitability would require shoring up channels of distribution and even thinking beyond the "Core 5" major appliance product categories: dishwashers, dryers, ranges, refrigerators, and washers. "We're not going to have product hits each and every year like Neptune and Gemini," warned Hake.[36]

AB Electrolux

Along with Whirlpool, AB Electrolux of Sweden was an established global competitor. With its purchase of White Consolidated Industries in 1986, Electrolux became a major part of the U.S. major home appliance industry. Electrolux sold approximately 17 million appliances with over 40 brand names in countries around the world. Electrolux had a strong presence in every European country from Finland to Portugal and extended eastward with production facilities in Hungary, Estonia, and Russia. With Electrolux's purchase of Brazil's second largest appliance maker, Refrigeracao Parana (Refripar); Email, Ltd., the largest producer of appliances in Australia; and the Indian appliance firm Voltas, the company had a solid presence in Latin America and Asia.

In 1991, the WCI Major Appliance Group was renamed Frigidaire Company in order to provide AB Electrolux's U.S. subsidiary the recognition earned by its pioneering namesake brand. Previously, the company's brands had competed against one another and had not been designed for automated manufacturing. Consequently, the quality of many of its well-known branded products had deteriorated over time. Its share of the U.S. market dropped significantly from 16.9% in 1994 to 13.5% in 1995 and had caused the company to drop from its traditional third place in the U.S. market to fourth place, behind Maytag. To reverse this situation, the company invested more than $600 million to upgrade its existing plants and build new refrigerator and dishwasher plants. Top management also introduced benchmarking and total quality management to boost production quality and efficiency. The company aggressively advertised its products and was successful in regaining some of the market share it had earlier lost.

Electrolux was heavily involved in restructuring its many activities. For example, it cut 2,800 jobs worldwide in 2001 and closed or relocated four plants in Europe and Asia as a way to cut costs and boost productivity. This brought the total cuts to 4,900 jobs, roughly 5.6% of the company's total workforce. It also sold its three motor operations plants in Europe and its compressor plant in Mexico.

The Electrolux Group was divided into two business areas: consumer durables and professional products. The consumer durables business unit included American Yard Products, Frigidaire, and Poulan/Weed Eater and was composed of white goods (including room air conditioners) plus floor care, sewing machines, garden equipment, and light-duty chain saws. White goods composed 75% of sales in the consumer durables area. Management indicated that the marked decline in U.S. white goods operating income was due to retail stock-outs and to the phase-in of a new generation of refrigerators—costing the firm SEK (Swedish krona) 1,050 million (US$100 million).[37]

In 2002, Electrolux was first in white goods market share in Western Europe, with a 16.2% market share (down from 23.9% in 1994), and fourth in North America, with a 15.0% market share (up from 13.5% in 1995). Europe accounted for about 50% of its major home appliance sales. North America accounted for approximately 35%. The rest was scattered throughout Asia, Latin America (especially Brazil), Oceania, and Africa.

Careful planning was needed by Electrolux to properly take advantage of a proliferation of brands worldwide without getting bogged down with competing internal demands for attention to each brand. After noticing Whirlpool's success with one brand across all of Europe, the company began the introduction of its own pan-European brand using the Electrolux name. The company spent SEK 600 million over a five-year period to market the Electrolux products throughout Europe. It also invested $50 million in Southeast Asia, with an objective of becoming one of the top three suppliers of white goods in the region. The company then acquired the Electrolux name and trademark in North America in 2000 from Electrolux LLC, maker of canister vacuum cleaners. AB Electrolux had given up the name when it had sold its share of the U.S. vacuum manufacturer in 1968. The much-smaller American vacuum cleaner company changed its name to Aerus, and the Swedish firm once again had full worldwide control of the company name and brand. Rumors had circulated in 2000 that Electrolux pursued Maytag as an acquisition in order to add a high-quality brand to its stable of mid- to low-quality brands in the United States. Electrolux's commitment to use the Electrolux name throughout the world suggested that the company would likely introduce the Electrolux brand as its premium line of home appliances in North America.

Other Competitors

The remaining 1% of U.S. market share in major home appliances was accounted for by a number of other competitors. Two of these, Bosch-Siemens and Haier, were large, global competitors recently establishing themselves in North America. Others were smaller firms manufacturing one or more unique products sold to a premium niche in the market.

Global Competitors

Although not new to North America, Bosch-Siemens and Haier had recently switched from importing to manufacturing in North America.

Bosch-Siemens Hausgerate GmbH (BSH) BSH was an equally held joint venture of Robert Bosch GmbH and Siemens AG. Like Whirlpool and Maytag, it concentrated on manufacturing and selling major home appliances. With 32,000 employees distributed among 90 companies around the world, BSH viewed itself as a global competitor marketing 15 brands. Although its market share in North America was very small in 2002, it had the second largest market share (14.4%) in Western Europe. Over the past 20 years, BSH has acquired 400 companies, some of which have since been sold or closed. The company earned around 60% of its profits outside of its base in Germany. According to Dr. Herbert Worner, Chairman of BSH, "Right from its inception, with just four German production facilities, BSH pledged itself to the path of internationalization."[38]

The construction in 1997 of a 200,000-unit-capacity dishwasher plant in New Bern, North Carolina, initiated Bosch-Siemens' entry into the North American market. As the European market leader in dishwashers, BSH intended to expand sales of its high-end dishwashers from the 40,000 units it was exporting to North America in 1995 to a 5% dishwasher market share.[39] The company optimistically expanded its New Bern location with a washing machine plant in 2000, even though it not yet accomplished its share objective in dishwashers.

BSH management claimed in 2001 that the company had achieved third position in the world rankings of major home appliance manufacturers since 2000. (A report in 2000 placed Bosch-Siemens fifth, after GE and Matsushita.) According to company sources, BSH claimed to be behind Electrolux and Whirlpool but just ahead of General Electric. The company also intended to be the market leader in Europe.[40] BSH reported total net earnings for 2001 had leaped by 47.3%, from €311.8 million to €459.4. The company posted a total sales figure for 2001 of €6.1 billion.

Haier Electrical Appliance International Ranked China's number-one consumer electronics maker, Haier accounted for nearly 40% of China's refrigerator sales and one-third of its washing machine and air conditioner sales. According to President Zhang Ruimin, it wanted to become "a famous global brand like Japan's Matsushita." During the period from 1987 to 2001, Haier's sales had increased faster than those of any other home appliance company in the world. By 1997, the company was selling washing machines to Japan, air conditioners to France, and refrigerators to the United States.[41] A poll of Chinese executives revealed Haier to be the domestic company most respected by Chinese executives. Respondents admired the company's business globalization, advanced management methodologies and systems, brand recognition, and consistent business strategy.[42]

In 2000, Haier built a brand new refrigerator plant in Camden, South Carolina, followed by its purchase of an Italian refrigerator manufacturing plant. Previously, it had established a research center in Los Angeles and a U.S. sales network. It had also formed an alliance with India's Bestavision to manufacture and market clothes washers in India. As a result of these and other actions, Haier operated 48 manufacturing plants and sold products in more than 160 countries. Haier took the lead in China by establishing a B2B service and selling Haier products on the Internet. In 2002, Haier opened its $15 million U.S. headquarters in New York City. The offices housed corporate offices, R&D labs, a restaurant, and showrooms.

Haier announced that profits for 2001 were more than 50% higher than in 2000. As part of CEO Zhang Ruimin's strategy to join the *Fortune* Global 500, Haier has continuously expanded its business scope. Growing from a small regional refrigerator factory in China through a series of joint ventures, it had expanded to appliances in every category and had a strong presence throughout China. It was not only expanding globally, it was diversifying into other products, such as kitchen cabinets, life insurance, personal computers, and mobile phones.[43] The company attempted to transfer some of the technology used in one part of its organization to another. For example, it was the first major home appliance company to introduce a complete line of Internet-enabled appliances at the 2001 Domotechnica trade show.

Niche Competitors

There were a number of smaller major home appliance companies operating in North America, such as Sub-Zero, Viking Range, W.C. Wood, and Brown Stove Works. Most of them manufactured and sold one category of appliance, such as specialized ranges or freezers.

Sub-Zero Freezer Company   Founded in Madison, Wisconsin, in 1945, the company made high-end built-in refrigerator and freezers. It offered a comprehensive line of built-in refrigerators and freezers, including under-the-counter models and wine storage drawers. In 2000, it bought Wolf Gourmet, premier maker of residential ranges, cook tops, grills, and ventilation equipment. Wolf stated that its products were hand-built for exceptional quality. Like Sub-Zero, Wolf's products appealed to the super-premium niche of the home appliance market.

Viking Range Corporation   Founded in 1984 to manufacture a commercial-type range for the home, Viking Range offered a complete line of super-premium, professional-type kitchen appliances, including ranges, ventilation equipment, and dishwashers. The company added refrigerators in 2000, with the purchase of Amana's built-in refrigeration unit. Viking owned a cooking products plant, a ventilation products plant, and a newly opened refrigeration plant in Greenwood, Mississippi.

A Global Future?

According to an analysis by The Freedonia Group, world demand for major home appliances was expected to increase 3.6% annually through 2005, reaching 337 million units. Particularly favorable prospects would be in the Asia/Pacific region, where there would be above-average urban population growth and increasing personal incomes. Latin America should also provide growth opportunities because of continuing industrialization and urbanization of the region. Above-average growth was also expected in the Africa/Middle East region and in most of Eastern Europe. Gains in the developed nations should result more from consumer demand for more convenient and energy-efficient appliances. Rising consumption expenditures in Europe should boost demand. The gains in the developed nations should be modest because of the increasingly saturated market and because demographics should not result in a high level of new household formation. Microwave ovens should post strong sales gains through 2005 due to untapped market potential in the developing regions. Conventional ranges were expected to post only modest gains due to market saturation. Dishwashers and clothes dryers should also exhibit growth, although price, size, and cultural considerations should prevent these items from becoming commonplace in areas where they were not

Exhibit 10
Actual (1998) and
Forecasted (2008)
Major Home
Appliance Demand
by Region and by
Product

World Demand by Region (In millions of units)		
Region	1998	2008
World	256.4	355.0
North America	58.4	64.4
United States	49.3	51.8
Canada & Mexico	9.1	12.6
Latin America	18.0	25.4
Western Europe	64.9	73.9
Eastern Europe	18.1	31.9
Africa/Mideast	16.9	24.2
Asia/Pacific	80.1	135.2
Japan	18.6	19.1
China	35.1	75.2
Other Asia/Pacific	26.4	40.9

World Demand by Product (In thousands of units)		
Product	1998	2008
Households	1,474	1,728
World demand	256,300	354,900
Refrigerators & freezers	77,530	110,350
Clothes washers & dryers	66,595	89,850
Washers	55,005	73,600
Dryers	11,590	16,250
Cooking	98,135	134,150
Ranges & ovens	61,540	78,050
Microwave ovens	36,595	56,100
Dishwashers	14,040	20,550

Source: J. Jancsurak, "Majors: Good (Not Great) Times Ahead Worldwide,"
Appliance Manufacturer *(February 2001), p. G–15.*

already established. Because of rising industrialization and personal income levels in the developing nations, refrigerators and freezers should experience above-average sales gains.[44] (See **Exhibit 10** for forecasted major home appliance demand by region and by product line.)

According to Robert Holding, president of the Association of Home Appliance Manufacturers (AHAM), several industry trends were defining the industry's future in North America:

- Industry consolidation was raising the competitive stakes.
- Market maturity was leaving limited avenues for home market growth. A greater emphasis on new products was emerging.
- Free trade opened market opportunities but brought new competition. International standards and nontariff trade barriers were becoming more important.
- Globalization by some manufacturers created significant differences in strategic situations.
- Stronger niche producers were emerging in traditional product categories.
- Much faster product development times and the need to have unique features accelerated time frames for industry decision making when government regulations or product standards were involved.[45]

Even though the major home appliance industry continued to become more global, cultural differences should continue to make it impossible to create one type of appliance for all markets. Whirlpool's concept of one "world washer" that it could make and sell around the world collapsed when not only did the manufacturing processes have to be changed to suit local conditions, but also local preferences demanded a differentiated product. In cooking appliances, for example, over 90% of the ranges purchased in Germany were electric, whereas gas prevailed through the rest of Europe. Also, 65% of German ranges were built-in, while the percentage of built-ins outside Germany was considerably less. Top-loading washers dominated North America, but front-loaders dominated Europe, where washers and dryers must fit into a kitchen under a work surface or in a bathroom. Although built-in refrigerators formed only a small part of refrigerator sales in most of Europe, they comprised over 50% of the German market. The large, freestanding home appliances preferred by Americans were much less popular in Europe and Asia, where smaller, energy-efficient units were generally preferred. The Japanese market was most interested in appliances that minimized water usage. Top-loading washers using agitators to clean the clothes were not preferred in India because they tended to tear the long saris preferred by women. The cooking habits in Asia, Africa, and many other parts of the world dictated that the distance between burners be larger and the control knobs be put on the same surface as the burners.[46]

Hans G. Backman, President of Frigidaire Company and Vice-President of AB Electrolux, commented on industry globalization:

> Globalization of the product and globalization of the company are two different things. The appliance industry is becoming global, but the products and the consumers are still local. The more the world comes together, the more national differences get emphasized.[47]

Notes

1. U.S. Department of Labor, as reported by D. Delano, "It's Official; Now What?" *Appliance Manufacturer* (January 2002), p. 82.
2. J. Jancsurak, "It's All Good," *Appliance Manufacturer* (July 2002), p. 5. "White goods" is the traditional term used for major home appliances. The contrasting term "brown goods" refers to home electronics products, such as radios and televisions.
3. Freedonia Group, *World Major Household Appliances*, summarized in *Appliance* (April 2002), p. 19.
4. Harris web site, at *www.harris.com* (July 11, 2002).
5. "Ames Laboratory Testing First Magnetic Refrigerator," *Appliance* (February 2002), p. 14.
6. N. C. Remich, Jr., "Appliances Use About 20% of Coated Coil," *Appliance Manufacturer* (December 1996), p. 14.
7. C. R. Christensen, K. R. Andrews, J. L. Bower, R. G. Hamermesh, and M. Porter, "Note on the Major Home Appliance Industry in 1984 (Condensed)," *Business Policy*, 6th ed. (Homewood, IL: Irwin, 1987), p. 340.
8. "GE to Invest in Mexico," *Appliance* (November 2001), p. 13.
9. D. Ritchey, "Recycle America?" *Appliance* (July 2002), p. 9; "For Appliances, Coated Coil Grows by 14.6%," *Appliance Manufacturer* (June 1993), p. 10.
10. D. Davis, "1996: A Soft Landing," *Appliance* (January 1996), p. 52.
11. "Buying Power—Home Purchase Triggers Sales of Appliances," *Appliance Manufacturer* (February 1989), p. 31.
12. C. Miller, Vice President of Marketing, North American Appliance Group, Whirlpool Corporation, quoted by R. J. Babyak and J. Jancsurak in "Product Design & Manufacturing Process for the 21st Century," *Appliance Manufacturer* (November 1994), p. 59.
13. D. Ritchey, "The Worst Consumer?" *Appliance* (May 2002), p. 11.
14. D. Ritchey, "Appliance Retail Speaks," *Appliance* (March 2001), p. 11. Kenmore is Sears' private-label appliance brand.
15. *Ibid.*, p. 11.
16. L. Bonnema, "Tradeplace—A Retailer's Dream Come True," *Appliance* (April 2002), p. 49.
17. "GE to Begin Selling Appliances Online," *Daily (Ames, IA) Tribune* (June 22, 1999), p. C8.
18. J. Jancsurak, "What Retailers and Consumers Want Most," *Appliance Manufacturer* (May 1998), pp. 39–44.
19. D. Ritchey, "Craving for Energy," *Appliance* (February 2002), p. 9.
20. J. M. McGuire, "Energy Use an AHAM Priority," *Appliance Manufacturer* (August 2001), p. 14.
21. "Manager's Update," *Appliance Manufacturer* (March 2001), p. 13.
22. L. Swatkowski, "Building Towards International Standards," *Appliance* (December 1999), p. 30.
23. J. Jancsurak, "Majors: Good (Not Great) Times Ahead Worldwide," *Appliance Manufacturer* (February 2001), p. G-13.
24. P. Roggema, "European Consolidation," *Appliance* (June 2001), p. 30.
25. D. Ritchey, "Aiming Haier and Haier . . . ," *Appliance* (November 2001), p. 8.
26. "Whirlpool Corporation Bids for Parts of Brandt," *Appliance* (January 2002), p. 13; "Whirlpool News," *Appliance* (May 2002), p. 15.
27. A. Chatterjee, "Whirlpool's Market Leadership Gameplan," *Appliance* (May 2000), p. 24.
28. Whirlpool Corporation, *2001 Form 10-K*, p. 3.

29. C. Quintanilla and J. Carlton, "Whirlpool Unveils Global Restructuring Effort," *Wall Street Journal* (September 19, 1997), pp. A3, A6.

30. R. J. Babyak, "The Sway of Calypso," *Appliance Manufacturer* (February 2001), pp. 35–40.

31. L. Bonnema, "The Luxury Appliance," *Appliance* (July 2002), p. 32.

32. S. Stevens, "Executing Stretch," *Appliance* (June 1997), pp. GE-1–GE-6.

33. H. W. Lane, M. B. Brechu, and D. T. A. Wesley, "MABE's President Luis Berrondo Avalos on Teams and Industry Competitiveness," *Academy of Management Executive* (August 1999), pp. 8–14.

34. "GE Refrigerators Rated Highest Quality in U.S.," *Appliance* (January 2000), p. 19.

35. "Maytag to Expand Dishwasher Plant," *Appliance* (December 1994), p. 29.

36. J. Jancsurak, "New CEO; New Agenda Signal Changes Ahead," *Appliance Manufacturer* (November 2001).

37. AB Electrolux, *2001 Annual Report*, pp. 23–25.

38. H. Worner, "Newsquotes," *Appliance* (May 1998), p. 32.

39. "BSH to Build U.S. Plant," *Appliance* (January 1996), p. 17; "Bosch Targets U.S. Niche," *Appliance Manufacturer* (April 1996), p. 26.

40. "Bosch-Siemens Hausgerate: Saturated? Innovate!" *Appliance* (August 2001), p. 24.

41. K. Chen, "Global Cooling: Would America Buy a Refrigerator Labeled 'Made in Qingdao'?" *Wall Street Journal* (September 17, 1997), pp. A1, A14.

42. D. Ritchey, "Aiming Haier and Haier . . . ," p. 8.

43. C. Stevens, "Top of the Pile and Going Haier in China," *Appliance* (April 2002), p. 22.

44. The Fredonia Group, *World Major Household Appliances* (January 2002), as reported in "World Major Household Appliances," *Appliance* (April 2002), p. 19.

45. R. L. Holding, "30th Anniversary Reflections," *Appliance Manufacturer* (April 1997), p. 16.

46. M. Ashjaee, "Newsquotes," *Appliance* (November 1999), p. 34.

47. J. Jancsurak, "Global Trend for 1995–2005," *Appliance Manufacturer* (June 1995), p. A-3.

CASE 16

Maytag Corporation 2002:

Focus on North America

J. David Hunger

DRIVING 30 MILES EAST FROM DES MOINES ON INTERSTATE 80 THROUGH BRIGHT SUNSHINE, a traveler nears the Newton exit. It has been a mild winter in the upper Midwest, and by mid-April the surrounding fields already appear ready for the plow. It is easy to visualize the rich black soil of the rolling Iowa countryside in its future summer abundance of ripening corn and soybean plants. Motoring north from the I80 exit for a mile and then east on U.S. route 6, one enters the quiet town of Newton—population 16,000 and location of the headquarters for Maytag Corporation. Approaching the town square, a left turn puts the visitor on course for the Sodexho Marriott Conference Center, site of this year's annual shareholders' meeting. Even though the Center adjoins company facilities, it is on a street lined with the well-kept houses and flower gardens typical of small-town Iowa. A right turn followed by a quick left into the Conference Center's spacious parking lot locates the visitor only a few feet from the entrance. Walking from cars into the building, people exude an air of anticipation. Another beautiful spring day is predicted for May 9, 2002. It is 8:15 A.M. The meeting is scheduled to begin at 8:30 A.M.

Notices at the door direct people to a large stairway leading to the second floor. The foyer at the top of the stairs is filled with people chatting and munching on coffee and pastries. Women sitting at the "proxy station" table at the far side of the foyer provide copies of annual reports (each including the 10-K report) to any shareholder wishing one. Maytag executives, with their distinctive blue nametags, mingle with the crowd. The mood is relatively friendly but anticipatory of Ralph Hake's chairing his first shareholders' meeting since becoming CEO and Chairman of the Board. Although the company seems to have stabilized after much executive turnover and some confusion over Maytag's future, shareholders want some reassurance that their investment is in good hands. Anticipating an interesting meeting, people move toward the auditorium entrance, hoping to get a "good" seat. A group of visiting high school students is ushered to the back of the auditorium as a combination of young and old, known and unknown, wander into the room in their coats and ties and heels and hose. From their comments and age, a significant number of the stockholders appear to be retired Maytag employees living in the area. Seated in the first row are the members of Maytag Corporation's Board of Directors. Immediately behind them are the company's top managers. The auditorium is filled to capacity but hushes respectfully as Ralph Hake makes the short climb to the stage, walks to the podium, and begins to speak.

Corporate Governance

One by one, Chairman Hake introduces the nine other members of the Board of Directors and briefly describes each person's background. Each stands briefly as his or her name is announced. The present Board had shrunk in size to 10, from 17 members in 1989 and 14 members in 1996. One-third of the Board is elected every year for a three-year term. The audience notes the presence of Lester Crown and Neele Stearns, previous directors of the former Chicago Pacific Corporation who had joined Maytag's board when Maytag acquired Chicago Pacific (for Hoover's appliance business) in 1989. Crown personally owns 3.9% of Maytag's stock, but through holdings by associates and family members effectively controls 7% of the stock (5,486,850 shares)—far more than any other member of the board. Although more than 60% of Maytag's 77,122,582 shares of com-

Exhibit 1 Board of Directors: Maytag Corporation (2002) (Listed in order of time served)

Director	Age	Joined Board	Position	Term Expires	Shares Owned[1]
Howard L. Clark[3]	58	1986	Vice Chairman, Lehman Brothers, Inc.	2002[2]	39,836
W. Ann Reymolds[4]	64	1988	President, U. of Alabama, Birmingham	2004	18,619
Lester Crown[4]	76	1989	Chairman, Material Services Corporation	2002[2]	3,064,403
Neele E. Stearns, Jr.[3]	66	1989	Chairman, Financial Investments Corp	2003	28,801
Fred G. Steingraber[4]	63	1989	Chairman Emeritus, CC Industries, Inc.	2004	26,000
Wayland R. Hicks	59	1994	Vice Chair & CEO, United Rentals, Inc.	2004	25,000
Bernard G. Rethore[5]	60	1994	Chairman Emeritus, Flowserve Corporation	2003	16,000
Barbara R. Allen[3,5]	49	1995	Past CEO, Women's United Soccer Assoc.	2002[2]	14,845
William T. Kerr[3,5]	60	1998	Chair & CEO, Meredith Corporation	2002	9,100
Ralph F. Hake	52	2001	Chair & CEO, Maytag Corporation	2003	470,168

Notes:
1. Includes stock options not yet exercised.
2. Up for reelection May 9, 2002.
3. Members of Audit Committee.
4. Members of Governance & Nominating Committee.
5. Members of Compensation Committee.

Source: Maytag Corporation, Notice of Annual Meeting and Proxy Statement (April 2, 2002), pp. 4–7.

mon stock is owned by individual shareowners, 14.9% of the stock is owned by FMR Corporation (an investment company) and 5.9% by the State Street Bank and Trust Company (as trustee).

The Board is a mixture of long-term members and more recent arrivals. (See **Exhibit 1** for a list of the Board of Directors.) Counting only personally owned shares (including Crown's), all officers and directors owned only 6.1% of Maytag's outstanding shares. The Board meets quarterly, with additional meetings as needed (plus committee meetings). Non-Maytag directors receive $30,000 per year and $1,250 plus expenses for each Board and committee meeting attended. Non-Maytag directors also receive an annual option to purchase 3,000 shares of common stock.

Chairman Hake introduces the executive officers seated next to and behind the Board members in the first two rows of the auditorium. (See **Exhibit 2** for a listing of corporate officers.) Each stands briefly as he or she is presented. Hake, Craig Breese, Ernest Park, and Thomas Piersa joined Maytag during the past two years. Hake had previously served as Executive Vice President and CFO for Whirlpool until 1999, when he failed to be named President of Whirlpool. Hake then joined Fluor Corporation as its Executive VP and CFO until being offered the top position at Maytag in June 2001. The audience was pleased to acknowledge the presence of William Beer, the President of Maytag Appliances, the second-most-important position after CEO. Beer had been with Maytag since 1974 but had resigned in 1998, when Lloyd Ward, Maytag's previous CEO, had replaced him with Lawrence Blanford as President of the Major Appliance Division. Upon Ward's departure from Maytag in 2000, Beer had been rehired in his old position.

Once the introductions are completed, Corporate Secretary Patricia Martin, sitting at a table next to the podium, reports that a quorum is present and that the minutes of last year's meeting are available at the proxy station in the auditorium foyer. A quorum requires the presence either in person or by proxy of a majority of the 77,122,582 shares of common stock, not including 40,028,011 shares of treasury stock. Martin then turns to Hake, who reads the first three shareholder proposals. The first proposal deals with the election of the nominated slate of four directors. Since the board of directors is a staggered board elected for renewable three-year terms, the four directors whose term is up in 2002 (Allen, Clark, Crown, and Kerr) are the nominees to be elected. The second proposal deals with ratifying the selection of Ernst &

Exhibit 2
Executive Officers: Maytag Corporation (2002)

Officer	Age	Position	Year Became Maytag Officer	Shares Owned[1]
Ralph F. Hake	52	Chairman & CEO	2001	470,168
William L. Beer	49	President, Maytag Appliances	1993	48,715
Craig Breese	49	President, Maytag International	2001	N/A
Thomas A. Briatico	54	President, Dixie-Narco	1985	N/A
Steven J. Klyn	36	VP & Treasurer	2000	N/A
Keith G. Minton	54	President, Hoover Company	1989	61,989
Jon O. Nicholas	62	Senior VP, HRM	1993	N/A
Ernest Park	49	Senior VP & CIO	2000	N/A
Thomas J. Piersa	50	VP, Global Procurement	2000	N/A
Roger K. Scholten	47	Senior VP & General Counsel	2000	15,286
Vitas A. Stukes	48	VP & Controller	1989	N/A
Steven H. Wood	44	Executive VP & CFO	1992	66,833

Note:
1. Includes options not yet exercised.

Source: Maytag Corporation, 2001 Annual Report, p. 5, and Notice of Annual Meeting and Proxy Statement (April 2, 2002), p. 8.

Young as the corporation's auditors for 2002. The third proposal is to approve the Maytag 2002 Employee and Director Stock Incentive Plan. (Among other things, the proposal gives each director the right to annually purchase 10,000 shares of Maytag common stock, 7,000 more shares than was allowed currently.)

The audience leans forward in their seats as Hake introduces the last three stockholder proposals: elect each director annually, replace the super-majority provisions with simple majority shareholder voting, and allow shareholders to vote on poison pills proposed by the board of directors. A person in the audience who represents the initiating shareholders is recognized and stands to read the rationale for each proposal. It is clear to the audience that the proposals are attempts to eliminate some of the anti-takeover devices put in place over the years by the board of directors. Maytag had introduced a classified board in 1977, a super-majority provision in 1984, and a share purchase rights plan (poison pill) in 1986. The current super-majority voting provision requires an 80% vote of outstanding shares when a potential acquirer offers a premium price only to some shareholders. Interestingly, similar proposals had been approved by a majority vote at past shareholders' meetings but had never been implemented by the board. The board of directors had earlier presented its rationale why the passed proposals had not been implemented in the 2002 proxy statement. According to the board, although the first proposal received 55.7% of the shares voting in 2001, those shares represented only 38.7% of all shares outstanding. Even though the third proposal had received 61.6% of shares voted at the 2001 meeting, the votes only accounted for 42.8% of shares outstanding, according to the board statement. Although similar proposals to the second proposal had been approved in 2000 and 2001, the board had not chosen to implement them. According to the board, "super-majority provisions assure that carefully considered corporate governance rules are not replaced without a substantial consensus majority for change." The board has strongly argued that these provisions continue to be necessary "to protect the shareowners against takeover tactics that do not treat all shareholders fairly and equally, such as partial and two-tiered tender offers and creeping stock accumulation programs." The results of this year's votes are to be announced later in the meeting.

With the completion of the introductions and the reading of the shareholder proposals, Chairman and CEO Ralph Hake looks over the packed auditorium and presents his report on the state of the corporation. He first presents two goals that he has set for himself during his time as CEO:

1. Return the corporation to the historic earnings levels under Leonard Hadley.

2. Exceed those earnings results.

His remarks echo his Letter to the Shareholders in Maytag's *2001 Annual Report*:

In June of 2001, the Maytag board of directors entrusted me with the leadership of this company. After 12 years in the household appliance industry, I was extremely excited about joining a company with a multitude of opportunities. Although I was cognizant of the challenges, I was enamored by Maytag's powerful group of brands and distinguished heritage of quality, innovation, and achievement.

My first nine months at Maytag have only increased my enthusiasm. After meeting with my co-workers, visiting our manufacturing facilities, interacting with customers, and developing our business plans, I am confident we will attain our corporate goals of delivering sustainable profitable growth, achieving operational excellence, and creating value for our shareholders in 2002 and beyond.

We have challenges ahead of us, however. In terms of financial performance, 2001 was disappointing. We sold more and earned less than we did in 2000. Our sales grew 8.2% to $4.3 billion due to our acquisition of Amana in August and good volume in our major appliance lines.

During the year, we took a number of special charges against income, including those for discontinuing some operations and a restructuring that primarily involved a salaried workforce reduction. However, even when you exclude those charges, our comparative net income still fell 45% to $139 million, and comparative earnings per share were down 42% to $1.77.

There were a number of reasons for this performance: On the major appliance front, a combination of low price points and increased marketing, distribution and support costs had an adverse effect. Our floor care business suffered from reduced volume, and income from our vending business failed to meet expectations. We fully understand that this is not acceptable performance, and we have been addressing the issues before us.[1]

As Hake continues his speech, it becomes increasingly apparent that Maytag Corporation has come a long way from the days when F. L. Maytag sold agricultural machinery to local farmers.

History of the Company

Fred L. Maytag (or F. L., as he was commonly called), who came to Newton, Iowa, as a farm boy in a covered wagon, joined three other men in 1893 to found the Parsons Band Cutter and Self Feeder Company. The firm produced attachments invented by one of the founders to improve the performance of threshing machines. The company built its first washing machine, the Pastime, in 1907 as a sideline to its farm equipment. The founders hoped that this product would fill the seasonal slumps in the farm equipment business and enable the company to have year-round production.

In 1909, F. L. Maytag became sole owner of the firm and changed its name to The Maytag Company. Farm machinery was soon phased out as the company began to focus its efforts on washing machines. With the aid of Howard Snyder, a former mechanic whose inventive genius had led him to head Maytag's development department, the company generated a series of product and process improvements. Its gasoline-powered washer (pioneered by Maytag), for example, became so popular with rural customers without electricity that Maytag soon dominated the small town and farm markets in the United States.

Under the leadership of Lewis B. Maytag, a son of the founder, the company expanded from 1920 to 1926 into a national company. Using a radically new gyrator to move clothes within its tub, the Model 80 was introduced in 1922. F. L. Maytag, then serving as Chairman of the Board, was so impressed with the new product that he personally took one of the first four washers on a western sales trip. Sales of the Model 80 jumped from 16,000 units in 1922 to more than 258,000 units in 1926! The company went from a $280,000 loss in 1921 to profits exceeding $6.8 million in 1926. Throughout the 1920s and 1930s, Maytag Company had an average U.S. market share of 40%–45% in washing machines. During the Great Depression of the 1930s, Maytag never suffered a loss.

From Market Leader to Niche Manager

Unfortunately, the innovative genius and entrepreneurial drive of the company's early years seemed to fade after the death of its founder. Top management became less interested in innovation and marketing than it was with quality and cost control practices. Bendix, a newcomer to the industry, introduced an automatic washing machine at the end of World War II that used a spin cycle instead of a wringer to squeeze excess rinse water out of the clothes. Maytag, however, was slow to convert to automatic washers. Management felt that the automatic washer needed more research before it could meet Maytag quality standards. The company still had a backlog of orders for its wringer washer, and management was reluctant to go into debt to finance new manufacturing facilities. This reluctance cost the company its leadership of the industry. Even with its own automatic washers, Maytag's share of the U.S. washer market fell to only 8% in 1954. Nevertheless, the company continued to be a profitable manufacturer of high-quality, high-price home laundry appliances.

During the 1960s and 1970s, Maytag reaped the benefits of its heavy orientation on quality products and cost control. *Consumer Reports* annually ranked Maytag washers and dryers as the most dependable in the U.S. market. Maytag washers lasted longer, needed fewer repairs, and had lower service costs when they did require service. The Leo Burnett advertising agency dramatized the concept of Maytag brand dependability by showing that Maytag products were so good, repairmen had nothing to do and were thus "lonely." The company's "Ol' Lonely" ads, which first aired in 1967 and featured the lonely Maytag repairman, were consistently ranked among the most effective on television. Profit margins were the highest in the industry. The company invested in building capacity, improved its dishwasher line, and changed the design of its clothes dryers. Maytag's plants were perceived at that time to be the most efficient in the industry. By the end of the 1970s, Maytag's share of the market had increased to approximately 15% in both washers and dryers.

Revitalization: Growth Through Acquisitions

In 1978 top management, under the leadership of CEO Daniel Krumm, decided that the company could no longer continue as a specialty manufacturer operating only in the higher-priced end of the laundry market. Consequently, Maytag adopted a strategy to become a full-line manufacturer and develop a stronger position in the U.S. appliance industry. Up to this point the company had been able to finance its growth internally. The strategic decision was made to grow by acquisition within the appliance industry through debt and the sale of stock.

In 1981, Maytag purchased Hardwick Stove Company, a low-priced manufacturer of gas and electric ranges with an estimated 5% share of the range market. In 1982, the company acquired Jenn-Air, a niche manufacturer of high-quality built-in electric grill ranges. In 1986, Maytag purchased Magic Chef, Inc., a successful manufacturer of mass-marketed appliances in the mid-price segment of the market. The acquisition included not only Magic Chef's best-selling ranges and other products but also appliances sold under the Admiral, Norge, and Warwick labels, plus Dixie-Narco, a leading manufacturer of soft-drink vending equipment. Maytag Company and the Magic Chef family of companies were then merged under a parent Maytag Corporation on May 30, 1986, headed by Chairman and CEO Daniel Krumm. Maytag-brand products continued to be produced by Maytag Company, now just a part of the larger Maytag Corporation.

In 1988, realizing that the U.S. major home appliance market had reached maturity, the top management of the new Maytag Corporation decided to extend the corporation's growth strategy to the international arena. Maytag offered close to $1 billion in cash and Maytag stock for Chicago Pacific Corporation (CP), the owner of Hoover Company. In this one step, Maytag Corporation moved into the international home appliance marketplace, with nine manufacturing operations in the United Kingdom, France, Australia, Mexico, Colombia, and Portugal. Hoover was known worldwide for its floor care products and throughout Europe and Australia for its washers, dryers, dishwashers, microwave ovens, and refrigerators. Prior to the acquisition, Maytag's international revenues had been too small to even report.

Reluctant Retrenchment

By 1995, Maytag Corporation had achieved its goal of becoming an internationally oriented, full-line major home appliance manufacturer. However, its profits had deteriorated significantly. Although Hoover's North American operations had always been very profitable, Hoover Europe had not shown a profit since being acquired by Maytag, until 1994, when it earned a modest one. Hoover Australia had also incurred significant losses during this time. Unknown to Maytag Corporation's top management before the acquisition, Hoover's UK facilities had been in desperate need of renovation, and the product line badly needed upgrading. Some weaknesses at the South Wales facility were apparent before the purchase but had been discounted. CEO Leonard Hadley, who had served earlier as COO under CEO

Daniel Krumm, later admitted that the corporation's top management had been too preoccupied with learning about the vacuum cleaner business to investigate further into Hoover's major home appliance business. Once it realized the need to modernize the U.K. facilities, Maytag's top management committed many millions of dollars to renovate the laundry and dishwasher plant in South Wales and its floor care plant in Scotland.

Although some former executives talked of a culture clash between the collegial Hoover and the more rigid Maytag executives, CEO Leonard Hadley blamed Hoover's woes purely on the poor UK business environment. However, industry analysts concluded that the Hoover acquisition had been a strategic error. To pay for the acquisition, management had not only increased long-term debt to its highest level in the company's history, it also had to sell more stock. These actions combined with a high level of investment in the unprofitable overseas facilities to result in lower corporate profits and decreasing earnings per share. Since other major home appliance companies continued to operate profitably during this time period, some analysts were beginning to question management's ability to run an international corporation.

After concluding that there was no way the corporation could recoup its overseas investments, Maytag sold its Hoover operations in Australia and New Zealand in December 1994 and Hoover Europe in May 1995. The sale of the Australian/New Zealand operations for $82 million resulted in a 1994 after-tax loss of $16.4 million. The sale of Hoover Europe to Candy S.p.a of Monza, Italy for $180 million resulted in a more significant 1995 after-tax loss of $135.4 million. In evaluating the strength of both Hoover Europe and Hoover Australia, Chairman Hadley commented, "Each lacked the critical mass alone to be strong players in their respective global theaters. As a result, we sold both businesses to focus on growth from our North American–based businesses." The sales enabled the corporation to reduce the long-term debt it had acquired in the Chicago Pacific purchase.

Cautious Expansion

Although the corporation continued to focus on North America, the firm's entry into the 21st century was characterized by several new product initiatives and by the acquisitions of Blodgett, Jade Range, and Amana. With the retirement of Leonard Hadley in 1998 as CEO, the company was led first by Lloyd Ward and subsequently by Hake.

Consistent with its commitment to North America, Maytag's top management decided in 2001 to end its 1996 joint venture with China's Hefei Rongshida (RSD). Although the joint venture to make washers and dryers had been originally considered an opportunity to be in "one of the greatest growth markets in the world,"[2] the venture had not been profitable, and its market share had failed to grow.

Maytag successfully introduced its revolutionary Neptune front-loading washer and dryer, followed by other well-received new products, such as the Maytag Gemini double-oven range and lower-price Maytag Performa and Atlantis laundry lines. According to Chairman and CEO Hake, Maytag had become the industry's most innovative maker of household appliances. The firm's Wide-by-Side refrigerator earned a New Product *Best of Show* award at the 2001 Kitchen and Bath Industry Show.

In a strategic move to diversify into the commercial side of major appliances, Maytag Corporation acquired G. S. Blodgett Corporation in 1997 for $148.3 million. Blodgett had 1997 sales of $135 million. Headquartered in Burlington, Vermont, Blodgett was a profitable manufacturer of commercial ovens, fryers, charbroilers, and other food service equipment. Its customers included major hotel and restaurant chains and institutions. Following CEO Ward's statement in early 1998 that Maytag intended to use Blodgett to increase its presence in commercial major appliances, Maytag purchased Jade Range in January 1999 for a little over $20 million. Jade made ultra-premium commercial ranges and outdoor grills. In addition, Maytag began buying a line of premium-quality commercial clothes washers from Primus, a Belgian family-owned appliance company. In August 2001, however, Maytag sold Blodgett to

Middleby Corporation for $95 million. According to Hake, the sale of Blodgett reflected a strategic decision to focus on the basics. "Our core home appliance and vending businesses will be the focus of our growth strategy going forward. Activities and operations that don't directly support and complement this foundation will be de-emphasized, if not eliminated."[3] The company used the proceeds of the sale to reduce corporate debt. Although management was quiet on the subject, Lawrence Horan, an analyst at Parker Hunter, Inc., commented that Maytag had not been able to grow the commercial side of the business because it had more competence in household appliances. This was exasercated by the poorer economy of 2001.[4]

In July 2001, Maytag purchased Amana Appliances (including its major home appliance and commercial microwave businesses) for $325 million. Approximately 95% of the purchase was in cash and the remainder in Maytag stock. The Amana purchase added about $900 million to Maytag's total annual sales. Maytag's acquisition of Amana announced to the industry that, although Maytag had withdrawn from international operations, it intended to be aggressive in its home base in North America. Hake explained the rationale for the Amana purchase:

> We acquired Amana Appliances, a company with a premium brand strategy remarkably similar to Maytag's. This move not only strengthened our major appliance business by adding a leading refrigeration brand, it also has provided the basis for greater cost efficiencies throughout the organization. The integration of Amana into Maytag's major appliance division went well, and we entered 2002 with a single, successful major appliance business unit, operating under one leadership team. We are taking major appliance orders on one system, and one national sales force is handling all of our brands. Additionally, we are implementing an integrated brand strategy that will better position us in the kitchen using both the Jenn-Air and Amana brands, along with Maytag. This will lead to enhanced profits for both our company and our dealers.[5]

The U.S. Major Home Appliance Industry

The U.S. major home appliance industry in 2002 was a very successful industry. More appliances were made and sold in the United States in 2001 than in any preceding year. The Association of Home Appliance Manufacturers was predicting slight increases during 2002 in each category of "white goods"—refrigerators, freezers, washing machines, dryers, ranges, microwave ovens, and dishwashers.[6]

The major home appliance industry faced some significant threats as well as opportunities. After more than 50 years of rising sales, both in units and dollars, the U.S. and Canadian market had reached maturity. (Total unit shipments of appliances in the U.S. were a little over 70 million compared to 4.3 million units in Canada.) Aside from some normal short-term fluctuations, future unit sales were expected to grow only 1.9% annually from 2000 to 2005 in the U.S. and Canadian market. Operating margins had been dropping as appliance manufacturers had been forced to keep prices low to be competitive even though costs kept increasing. The situation was the same in Western Europe, a market 25% larger than the U.S. major home appliance market, where unit sales were expected to grow only 1.7% annually during the same period. Markets in Asia, Eastern Europe, and Latin America had become more important to world trade as more countries had changed to a free market economy. Industry analysts expected appliance markets in these areas to grow at a rate of 5%–6% annually between 2000 and 2005.[7] The industry was under pressure from governments around the world to make environmentally safe products plus significantly improve appliance efficiency in terms of energy usage and water consumption.

The U.S. major home appliance industry had consolidated from around 300 manufacturers in 1945 to only a few major players in 2002. This consolidation of the industry over the period was a result of fierce domestic competition. Emphasis on quality and durability coupled with strong price competition drove the surviving firms to increased efficiencies and a strong concern for customer satisfaction. Four major home appliance manufacturers controlled around 99% of the U.S. market for white goods. In order of 2001 market share, Whirlpool led, with 39.2%; followed by General Electric, with 23.2%; Maytag, with 21.6%; and AB Electrolux (Frigidaire), with 15.0%. The remaining 1% belonged to the foreign firms Bosch-Siemens and Haier, which had recently begun to produce in North America, and to various manufacturers of a single type or category of appliance, such as Sub-Zero (built-in refrigerators and freezers and Wolf professional ranges) and Emerson Electric (garbage disposals).

The strongest competitors in the United States during the five-year period from 1996 to 2001 were Whirlpool, Maytag, and Electrolux. Whirlpool had increased its market share by almost five points, from 34.9% five years earlier, in 1996. Maytag had been steadily increasing its market share (about 1% per year), from 15.2% in 1996 to 20.8% in 2000. Its purchase of Amana's home appliances from Goodman Global Holdings of Houston in 2001 raised Maytag's total market share an additional point, to 21.6% in 2001. Frigidaire, AB Electrolux's North American home appliance division, increased its market share over five points, from 9.6% in 1996. In contrast, General Electric had lost about nine points of market share (almost 2% each year!), from 32.0% in 1996. By the time Maytag bought Amana home appliances, Amana's market share had been 2.9% in 2000, down from 6.7% in 1996.

Both Whirlpool and AB Electrolux were global competitors, with strong positions in the Americas, Europe, and Asia. General Electric was also strong in North and South America but was much weaker in Europe and Asia. Bosch-Siemens was a newcomer to the Americas but was second in European market share and a very aggressive competitor. Haier, the largest appliance maker in China, was expanding rapidly—with new manufacturing facilities in Europe and North America. The major home appliance industry was clearly changing from a purely domestic industry with each country having its own appliance makers to one in which global competitors were engaging in battles for market share and economies of scale. Although Maytag was the only major competitor without any operations outside of North America, there were similar geographically focused companies in Europe, such as Candy and Merloni of Italy and Miele of Germany. The Asian appliance industry was still fragmented, with multiple domestic appliance manufacturers (especially Japanese) exporting to other countries within the region.

(For additional industry information, see Case 15, "U.S. Major Home Appliance Industry in 2002: Competition Becomes Global.")

Maytag Corporation Business Segments and Products

In 2002, Maytag Corporation was organized for official reporting purposes into two business segments: home appliances and commercial appliances. Home appliances constituted 94.7% of consolidated net sales in 2001. For practical purposes, however, Maytag Corporation was managed as three distinct businesses: major home appliances (Maytag, Jenn-Air, Amana, and Magic Chef brands), floor care appliances (Hoover), and commercial appliances (Dixie-Narco and Jade Range).

Major Home Appliances

Compared to its primary competitors, Maytag's home appliances ranked third, with a total U.S. market share of 21.6%. Washers and dryers were Maytag's traditional strength. Market surveys consistently found Maytag brand laundry appliances to be not only the brand most desired by consumers (when price was not considered) but also the most reliable. Refrigeration was a traditional strength of Amana. Gas ranges had always been a particular strength of Magic Chef and were perceived to be very reliable in surveys.

Exhibit 3
Maytag
Corporation's 2001
Share of U.S.
Market Compared
to Market Leaders'
Shares by Home
Appliance
Category[1]

Appliance Category	Market Leader	Leader Share	Maytag Share	Maytag Rank
Dishwashers	Whirlpool	48%	21%	2
Dryers	Whirlpool	50.5%	24%	2
Refrigerators	Whirlpool	28.5%	23%	3 (tied with GE)
Microwave ovens	Samsung	26%	3%	8
Ranges (gas)	GE	31%	17%	4
Ranges (electric)	GE	41%	14%	4
Washers	Whirlpool	51.5%	25%	2

Note:

1. Data for compactors, disposers, freezers, and range hoods not given because Maytag does not participate significantly in these appliance categories.

Source: "Special Report: 2002 Market Profile," Appliance Manufacturer (April 2002), p. 11.

Exhibit 3 lists Maytag's 2001 share of the U.S. market by home appliance category compared to that of the market leader. Contrasted with 1996, Maytag's share had increased in dishwashers, washing machines, clothes dryers, and refrigerators but had dropped in electric and gas ranges.

Headquartered in Newton, Iowa, the original Maytag Company was the flagship of the corporation and manufactured Maytag brand washing machines and dryers in its Newton plant. It also marketed Maytag brand cooking products made in the Cleveland, Tennessee, Magic Chef plant, a refrigerator line manufactured in the Galesburg, Illinois, Admiral plant, and dishwashers manufactured at the Jackson, Tennessee, manufacturing facility. Market emphasis was on the premium price segment and the upscale builder market. A survey of Americans found the Maytag brand to be 15th in a list of the strongest brand names, based on consumer recognition and perception of quality.

Located in Galesburg, Illinois, the Admiral plant manufactured refrigerators for Maytag, Jenn-Air, Admiral, and Magic Chef brands. The corporation had originally invested $60 million in the Galesburg plant to improve production efficiencies, enhance product quality, and increase capacity, plus another $160 million in 1995 to further upgrade the facility.

Jenn-Air specialized in electric and gas downdraft grill ranges and cooktops. The brand also marketed Jenn-Air brand refrigerators, freezers, dishwashers, and disposers manufactured by the Admiral plant, the corporation's Jackson plant, and other non-Maytag appliance manufacturers, such as Emerson Electric. Jenn-Air billed itself as "The Kitchen Equipment Expert" and believed that its high-quality cooking expertise complemented Maytag Company's high-quality image in laundry appliances. Jenn-Air's Indianapolis manufacturing plant had been closed when production of ranges was concentrated at Magic Chef's Cleveland, Tennessee, facilities.

Magic Chef manufactured gas and electric ranges for the Admiral, Magic Chef, Jenn-Air, and Maytag brands in its Cleveland, Tennessee, facilities. It also marketed refrigerators, dishwashers, laundry equipment, and microwave ovens under the Magic Chef brand to the mid-price segment and to certain private-label businesses. Prior to its purchase by Maytag, Magic Chef had been a small, family-run business. Its product development strategy had been to be a very fast follower. Maytag Corporation had invested $50 million in the Cleveland facilities. From this investment came new lines of Magic Chef and Maytag brand ranges. The medium-to low-price orientation of the Magic Chef and Admiral brands had enabled them to be successfully sold to builders.

Located in Jackson, Tennessee, Jackson Dishwashing Products was a $43 million, 400,000-square-foot state-of-the-art manufacturing facility dedicated to producing dishwashers for the Maytag, Admiral, Jenn-Air, and Magic Chef brands. It was designed as a "team plant," with little distinction made between hierarchical levels. Upon the completion of this plant in 1992, dishwasher production was phased out at Maytag's Newton plant, and the company no longer had to purchase dishwashers from General Electric for Magic Chef or Jenn-Air.

Floor Care Appliances

Headquartered in North Canton, Ohio, The Hoover Company manufactured and marketed to all price segments upright and canister vacuum cleaners, stick and handheld vacuum cleaners, disposable vacuum cleaner bags, floor polishers and shampooers, central cleaning systems, commercial vacuum cleaners, and washing machines in Mexico. It heavily advertised to the consumer. The company was almost totally vertically integrated. In addition to the North Canton headquarters and three Stark County, Ohio, manufacturing plants, Hoover North America controlled four other facilities, in El Paso, Texas; Ciudad Juarez, Mexico (a maquiladora assembly plant); Burlington, Ontario (Hoover Canada); and Industrial Vallejo, Mexico (Hoover Mexicana). Praised by industry experts in 1990 as one of the best manufacturing facilities in the United States, the new North Canton "factory within a factory" was designed by an interdisciplinary team to reduce costs and improve quality. In 1996, Hoover invested $7 million in two of its Ohio plants to increase manufacturing capacity for its Steam Vac line of extractors. At the same time, Hoover also spent $44 million to double the capacity of its El Paso and Ciudad Juarez vacuum cleaner maquiladora production plants.

Hoover held a 26.5% share of the very competitive U.S. market for residential full-size vacuum cleaners and 72% of the floor polisher market in 2001. It was in first place in both categories. Nevertheless, its share of the market for full-size vacuum cleaners had significantly dropped from 40% in 1983 when it led the industry. Eureka (part of AB Electrolux of Sweden) was a close second in 2001 full-sized cleaner sales, with a U.S. market share of 26%. Royal was third in full-sized cleaner sales in 2001, with a declining market share of 17%. Hoover only held 4% of the handheld market, compared to Black & Decker's 39% and Royal's 30%. Hoover's share of the extractor market was 39.5%, down from 49% in 1996. See **Exhibit 4** for details.

Exhibit 4
U.S. Floor Care Market Shares by Category
(By percentage of total U.S. sales)

Appliance	2001	1996	Appliance	2001	1996
Vacuum cleaners (upright, canister, stick)			**Vacuum cleaners (handheld)**		
Hoover	26.5	37	Applica (Black & Decker)	39	30
Eureka	26	24	Royal	30	42
Royal	17	11	EuroPro	14.5	—
Matsushita	9	12	Eureka	7.5	5
Bissell	6.5	4	Hoover	4	11
Oreck	5	—	Bissell	2	8
Iona	3	2	Others	3	4
Kirby	2.5	5	**Extractors**		
Aerus (Electrolux)	2	2	Bissell	44.5	41
Rexaire	1.5	2	Hoover	39.5	49
Others	1	1	Royal	15	—
Floor polishers			Others	1	10
Hoover	72	70			
Thorne Electic	19	20			
Electrolux	9	10			

Source: "Special Report: 2002 Market Profile," Appliance Manufacturer *(April 2002), p. 12.*

Growth in the U.S. floor care market generally exceeded that of many other appliance segments. Close to 20 million vacuum cleaners (upright, canister, and stick), 3.4 million extractors, and 162 thousand polishers were sold in the United States in 2001. Compared to the 10%–12% sales increases of 1999 and 2000, only moderate growth was predicted for the near future. Although 99% of U.S. households had at least one vacuum cleaner, many had two to three full-sized vacuums plus handheld vacuums. The average life expectancy of full-size vacuum cleaners was eight years.

Commercial Appliances

Maytag's commercial appliances were composed of Jade Range's commercial cooking and refrigeration equipment, Dynasty's commercial washers and dryers, and Dixie-Narco's vending equipment. The primary product lines of Jade Range were ultra-premium commercial ranges sold under the Jade brand and outdoor grills sold for residential use under the Dynasty brand. The Jade and Dynasty appliances were made in a plant in Commerce, California. When Jade Range was purchased in 1999, then-CEO Hadley stated that he expected Jade to add to Maytag's cooking product knowledge in both residential and commercial appliances.[8]

Dixie-Narco, Inc., made canned and bottled soft drink and juice vending machines sold to soft drink syrup bottlers and distributors, canteen owners, and others. Headquartered in Williston, South Carolina, Dixie-Narco manufactured vending machines in its factory there. The unit sold vending equipment directly to independent bottlers and full-service operators who installed banks of vending machines in offices and factories. It also marketed through bottlers directly to syrup company-owned bottlers. Sales of vending machines continued to be relatively flat in the United States, but due to strong demand for Dixie-Narco products, the company was able to hold its solid share of the U.S. market. International sales had been increasing, thanks to the introduction in 1994 of its glass-front merchandiser without coin slots. Traditional coin-fed vending machines had not been well accepted outside North America. In 2001, Dixie-Narco expanded beyond Coke and Pepsi products to market Eastman Kodak film and cameras and to test-market milk vending machines in schools. It also formed an alliance with Nippon Conlux, Ltd., to be the exclusive distributor of electronic payment systems for vending machines in the United States and Canada.

When asked why Dixie-Narco remained a part of Maytag Corporation, past-CEO Hadley had responded:

> Mechanically, a vending machine is a refrigerator, and we build thousands of refrigerators per day at our plant in Galesburg, Illinois. . . . As a marketing assignment, our Dixie-Narco customers have the same needs as our Maytag commercial laundry customers. . . . Dixie-Narco's great value to us is that it has a different set of competitors than the major home appliance business or the floor care industry. It allows us an important earnings stream from a business that our largest two major appliance competitors don't have. . . . It provides us with an important supplement to our U.S. business by allowing us an international export opportunity.[9]

Role of Strategic Planning

Strategic planning had led to many of the recent changes in Maytag Corporation. In 1978, when Leonard Hadley was working as Maytag Company's Assistant Controller, CEO Daniel Krumm asked him and two others from manufacturing and marketing to serve as a strategic planning task force. Krumm asked the three people the question "If we keep doing what we're now doing, what will the Maytag Company look like in five years?" The question posed a challenge—considering that the company had never done financial modeling and none of the three knew much of strategic planning. Hadley worked with a programmer in his MIS section to develop "what if" scenarios. The task force presented its conclusion to the board of directors: A large part of Maytag's profits (the company had the best profit margin in the industry) was coming from products and services with no future: repair parts, portable washers and dryers, and wringer washing machines.

Looking back to 1978, Hadley felt that this was a crucial time for the company. The Board of Directors was becoming less conservative as more outside directors came from companies that were growing through acquisitions. With the support of the board, Krumm promoted Hadley to the new position of Vice President of Corporate Planning. Hadley was given the task of analyzing the industry to search for acquisition candidates. Until that time, most planning had been oriented internally, with little external analysis. From that time forward, the job of the Director of Corporate Strategy has been to work closely with the company's business units to coordinate and facilitate strategic planning throughout the company. Maytag's current President of Maytag Appliances, William Beer, had served in this position earlier in his career.

Marketing

Of the four major home appliance brands—Maytag, Amana, Magic Chef, and Jenn-Air—only the Maytag and Amana brands had been heavily advertised to consumers. The Magic Chef and Jenn-Air brands usually received cooperative advertising, promotions through the dealers, and some print advertising. Both sold well to house and apartment builders, in contrast to the relatively poorer sales to this channel by Maytag and Amana. The lower-priced Admiral brand received little advertising. Norge and Hardwick were low-end brands used for special opportunities and received little to no marketing effort. Advertising expenses were $164 million in 1999, $158.5 in 2000, and $187.2 in 2001. Corporate selling, general, and administrative expenses (of which advertising expenses were a part) had risen from $609.3 million in 2000 to $704.6 million in 2001.[10] A single corporate sales force handled the Maytag, Amana, Jenn-Air, Magic Chef, and Admiral brands.

According to Beer, President of Maytag Appliances, Maytag had three "power" brands—Maytag, Amana, and Jenn-Air—and two "value" brands—Magic Chef and Admiral. The acquisition of Amana in 2001 created a challenge in positioning the brands. "Jenn-Air is at one end [upscale] and is sold through select distribution channels. Maytag is broadly distributed and will continue to be. And Amana is somewhere between those two guideposts." Beginning in mid-2002, the ad/marketing campaigns were to play to the strengths of these power brands. "For Maytag, it will be dependability and performance. For Amana, it will be clever conveniences and styling. And for Jenn-Air, innovation, elegance, and high-end performance," explained Beer.[11]

Chris Wignall, Vice President of Marketing, further explained how advertising was being used to differentiate the power brands. The Maytag brand ads featured the "Ol' Lonely" repairman and his younger sidekick in humorous situations. Some print ads were used in addition to the usual heavy television ads. Amana's campaign emphasized print ads in the home-and-shelter magazines but also used television. Humor was also used. One example was for the Amana Messenger refrigerator, with message-record capabilities in which the message said, "Touch the cake and you're toast.—Love, Mom." Jenn-Air's ad campaign targeted an upscale audience through print ads in city magazines and special interest publications.

Maytag and the Leo Burnett USA advertising agency (originator of the "Ol' Lonely" ad) were honored by the New York chapter of the American Marketing Association in 1998, with a gold EFFIE award for the "Keeping Your Cool" advertising campaign featuring "I Scream" and "U.F.O." (Unidentified Frozen Objects). The campaign was designed to let consumers know that the food they were throwing out prematurely would have stayed fresh longer if they had a Maytag refrigerator. This award was Maytag's fourth gold EFFIE in eight years.[12] The 1995 award was for the campaign featuring the Maytag repairman, Ol' Lonely, and included TV commercials, print advertising, and point-of-purchase materials.[13] Few people realized that appliance manufacturers such as Maytag did not do their own repair work. It was contracted out to independent dealers. According to Dale Reeder, Vice President of Customer Service at Maytag Appliances, "For Maytag, effective customer service is absolutely critical, not just to our retail partners, but to our customers." Reeder pointed out that research indicated that if the level of service was strong when a product failed, consumer loyalty was actually higher than before the sale[14] (see **Exhibit 5**).

Distribution channels were another challenge for Maytag, especially for the company's power brands. According to Wignall, "Maytag is broad-based [Maytag Home Appliance Centers, Lowe's, Home Depot, Sears, etc.]. Amana is less so, and tends to be distributed through more of the independent retailers. Jenn-Air is more tightly focused, with builders and upscale retailers being the main channels." The Maytag brand sponsored the Women's United Soccer Association (WUSA) and the uniforms of the Atlanta Beat soccer team. Management hoped to use the WUSA sponsorship to gain greater access to a key target market: affluent women. Although the corporation was currently satisfied with its interim brand positioning/distribution strategy, longer-term marketing strategies needed to be developed. "We need a higher degree of precision around the consumers we are targeting, in terms of demographics, psycho-graphics, and societal trends," stated Wignall.[15]

Through the 1990s, the Maytag brand sales slowly changed from being distributed only through its 725 independent dealers to being heavily sold through the "power retailers" of Sears, Best Buy, Circuit City, Sam's Club, Home Depot, and Lowe's. Although this change

Exhibit 5
The Real Maytag
Repairman

The "Ol' Lonely" Maytag repairman created for television ads in 1967 had little to do with the actual daily life of a real Maytag repairman. Michael Headlee of Michael's Maytag Home Appliance Center in Des Moines, Iowa, repaired approximately 40 malfunctioning machines per week. On average, only three of them were Maytags. Although Headlee sold only Maytag, he serviced all brands. No one exclusively repaired Maytag-brand appliances. "You won't find one because he would starve," explained Headlee. Headlee had been working as an independent service contractor until 1991, when Maytag Company asked him to open a Maytag store.

Headlee enjoyed doing stunts to show off the quality built into Maytag-brand appliances. In 1992 he started a Maytag and a Kenmore washer after rigging both to run continuously. Although Maytag officials weren't too excited about this project, Headlee went ahead to see for himself which product would last longer. The Kenmore died in six months; the Maytag continued for two years.

When a customer walked into Headlee's store one day to look at refrigerators, Headlee showed him the fine points of a floor model. According to Headlee, Maytag built for the "what ifs." For example, what if a neighbor boy used the door as a step ladder and knocked out one of the storage bins? No problem, said Headlee. The bins were removable and adjustable. No need to replace the $180 liner or the $35 bin—only a $2 breakaway clip. "The hinges are heavier than any other in the industry. . . . Rollers? We've got the fattest rollers in the industry." To demonstrate, Headlee took out the meat-cheese drawer, turned it over on the floor, and jumped on it. According to Headlee, a person could do aerobics on the meat-cheese drawer!

Competition from "super stores" kept profit margins low, so Headlee depended on repair work to stay in business. "We got a deck of cards. We got a cribbage board. And that keeps us pretty well occupied when we're not working on . . . a Kenmore or a Whirlpool," joked Headlee.

Source: M. A. Lickteig, "A Real Repairman Juggles Calls and Sales," Des Moines Register (November 1, 1994), p. M1.

antagonized the independent dealers, it significantly boosted sales. For example, sales to Sears alone increased from 11% of the corporation's consolidated annual net sales in 1999 to 18% in 2001. Part of these sales included providing Kenmore brand appliances to Sears. Michael Headlee, a veteran Maytag appliance dealer, expressed the views of most appliance dealers when he stated that the prices charged by super-sized competitors pushed down profit margins, making it difficult for the small dealer to survive. For example, Headlee's largest store had 4,000 square feet of space, compared to the giant electronics or home improvement stores that can have more than 100,000 square feet. "You'll see independent dealers dropping like flies in the next couple of years," commented Headlee. "They can't compete against the super-stores."[16]

In 1999, the corporation opened in Des Moines, Iowa, a new style of Maytag brand appliance store designed to be more inviting to customers who want to "test drive" the equipment. The concept was developed by Maytag in conjunction with Maytag appliance dealer Headlee. According the Steve Anderson, Maytag's Manager of Survey Research, the old approach to selling appliances was to fill the store with appliances lined up in rows. The new approach, in contrast, involved setting up appliances in a more home-like setting. "It's more of a come and look at me type atmosphere," commented Patti Beatty of West Des Moines. Although Headlee later closed his two test stores, by 2001 the company had successfully opened 11 "Maytag Stores" in other states.[17]

Some industry analysts argued that the company strategy for the Maytag brand was confusing. Efraim Levy, an analyst with S&P Equity Group, said that the Maytag brand was positioned as a higher-end line, but the brand was also being sold through discounters, such as Sam's Club and Home Depot. He contended that higher-end brands should be limited to independent dealers and mass merchandisers, like Sears, and lower-priced models, such as the Maytag Proforma line, should be sold through discount stores.[18]

Hoover floor care products had traditionally received strong advertising in all the media. The business unit continued its successful "Nobody Does It Like Hoover" consumer-oriented advertising. After noting that 70 dealers accounted for approximately 80% of Hoover's North American floor care sales, management restructured the sales organization in 1992 to better serve these "power retailers."

Corporate Culture

Much of Maytag Corporation's corporate culture derived from F. L. Maytag's personal philosophy and from lessons the founder learned when starting the Maytag Company at the turn of the century. His greatest impact was still felt in Maytag's (1) commitment to quality, (2) concern for employees, (3) concern for the community, (4) concern for innovation, (5) promotion from within, (6) dedication to hard work, and (7) emphasis on performance:

- **Commitment to quality:** Concerned when almost half the farm implements sold were defective in some way, F. L. Maytag vowed to eliminate all defects. Maytag's employees over the years had taken great pride in the company's reputation for high-quality products and being a part of "the dependability company."

- **Concern for employees:** Long before it was required to do so by law, Maytag Company established safety standards in the workplace and offered its employees accident and life insurance policies. Wages have traditionally been some of the highest in the industry.

- **Concern for the community:** Following F. L. Maytag's example, Maytag management has been active in community affairs and concerned about pollution. The decision to build its new automatic washer plant in Newton after World War II indicated the company's loyalty to the town.

- **Concern for innovation:** From its earliest years, the company was not interested in cosmetic changes for the sake of sales, but in internal improvements related to quality, durability, and safety.

- **Promotion from within:** F. L. Maytag was very concerned about building company loyalty and trust. The corporation's policy of promoting from within was an extension of that concern.

- **Dedication to hard work:** In tune with the strong work ethic permeating the Midwestern United States, F. L. Maytag put in huge amounts of time to establish and maintain the company. His fabled trip west, while chairman of the board, to sell personally a train-car load of washers set an example to his sales force and became a permanent part of company lore.

- **Emphasis on performance:** Preferring to be judged by his work rather than by his words, F. L. Maytag was widely regarded as a good example of the Midwestern work ethic.

This intense Maytag corporate culture had traditionally been one of the company's key strengths. It was seen by many to be an important contributor to the company's reputation and ability to make and sell high-quality products. This devotion to quality was exemplified by a corporate policy that no cost reduction proposal would be approved if it reduced product quality in any way. A 2000 survey of 26,000 people from all walks of life ranked Maytag second in corporate reputation (after Johnson & Johnson) of all U.S. firms.[19]

Maytag management expected any acquired company to adopt Maytag's culture. This first became an issue when Maytag acquired Admiral's refrigeration plant as part of its Magic Chef purchase in 1986. A prime reason for the acquisition had been to obtain the expertise and facilities to make a Maytag brand refrigerator. Unfortunately, the Admiral plant had been allowed by previous management to deteriorate. The employees had little pride in what they were doing, and refrigerators rolled off the line with screws driven in crooked and temperature balances askew.[20] Worried about their jobs, Admiral employees were very pleased when the company became part of Maytag. Nevertheless, they weren't sure how they would be treated by new management. When Leonard Hadley, then serving as Maytag Company President, first visited Admiral's plant in Galesburg, he was concerned that the Admiral plant would not be able to produce the level of quality needed for Maytag products. During the discussion, Admiral personnel asked Hadley when the name on the plant water tower would be changed from Admiral to Maytag. Hadley responded, "When you earn it." It was very clear to all that the Admiral plant needed to adopt the values of the Maytag culture if it was to have any future. Admiral's labor union worked closely with Maytag management to help ensure the future of the plant and its employees. The refrigerator resulting from the Maytag–Admiral collaboration was a huge success. The project crystallized corporate management's philosophy for forging synergies among the Maytag companies, while simultaneously allowing the expertise among those units to flourish.

The successful integration of Jenn-Air and Magic Chef (including Admiral) into the Maytag corporate culture did not prepare Maytag's management for dealing with its acquisition of Hoover in 1989. There was little difficulty with Hoover North America since the company had always been the leader in the vacuum cleaner business. Its management and employees had pride in their work and endorsed many of Maytag's core values (such as being involved in its local community and making quality products). Since Maytag's management had little knowledge of the floor care business, it allowed Hoover North America to operate fairly autonomously. Hoover's European operations were, however, a very different matter. Visiting Maytag executives were perceived by their British counterparts as being too rigid and uptight. The Maytag executives, for their part, saw the British managers as being "laid back" and too collegial. Even after pouring millions of dollars into the UK plants to make them more competitive, Maytag was unable to adequately deal with the Hoover Europe culture (among other things) and sold Hoover's European holdings in 1995.

Maytag's management hoped that the integration of Amana with Maytag would go smoothly. According to Arthur Learmonth, Vice President of Manufacturing and Engineering of Maytag Appliances, "The Amana acquisition has been more of a blending than it has been an assimilation. The cultures are very much the same and the strengths of Maytag and Amana complement each other, with Amana's strengths tending to be in refrigeration and Maytag being more focused on laundry and wet products."[21] Even though Amana had been losing market share recently, Maytag management and employees generally respected this appliance maker—located less than 50 miles from Newton, in Amana, Iowa. Founded in 1934, Amana pioneered the side-by-side refrigerator freezer and the counter-top microwave oven—the Radarange. Amana's overall market share had been dropping since the mid-1990s. Soon after Maytag's purchase of Amana's home appliance business in June 2001, 22 top executives left Amana because of job duplication with Maytag management. Although the typical Amana employees had some concern for their jobs, they accepted Maytag as being a good company.[22]

Executive Succession

Until the mid-1990s, most of the Maytag Corporation executive officers had worked their way up through the corporation and had spent most their careers immersed in the Maytag Company culture. This had certainly been the case for Leonard Hadley, Chair and CEO, who since joining the company as a cost accountant, had served the company continuously until his retirement in 1999. Hadley came out of retirement in 2000 and served an additional year during the search for a new Maytag CEO. Once Hake was hired as CEO, Hadley retired for the second time but remained on the Board until January 2002.

In a move to diversify top management backgrounds in 1993, then-CEO Hadley hired John Cunningham to serve as Corporate Executive Vice President and Chief Financial Officer (CFO) and Joseph Fogliano to serve as Corporate Executive Vice President and President of North American Operations. These were the second and third, respectively, most powerful corporate executive officers after Hadley. Cunningham had previously been Vice President and Assistant General Manager of IBM's Mainframe Division. Fogliano previously had served as President and CEO of Thomson Electronics.

In a surprise move, North American President Fogliano resigned from the corporation in August 1995. In an interview, Fogliano (age 55) stated that he had joined the corporation with the understanding that he would be a leading candidate to replace Hadley. As time went by, according to Fogliano, it became apparent that this was not to be. He further explained that there may have been a lack of fit between himself and the Maytag culture.[23] Four months later, John Cunningham announced that he was leaving the corporation to take a similar position with Whirlpool Corporation.

The corporation hired Lloyd D. Ward in 1996 to serve as Executive Vice President and President of Maytag Appliances. Ward had previously served as president of PepsiCo's western and central Frito-Lay sales divisions. Armed with a strong background in marketing, Ward was instrumental in creating the successful introduction extravaganza for Maytag's innovative front-loading Neptune washer in 1997. Heralded by the press as the top U.S. African-American executive, Ward replaced Leonard Hadley as CEO and Chair of Maytag Corporation in 1999. Ward was a charismatic speaker who stood in stark contrast to the quiet-spoken style of Hadley. Ward worked to speed up the corporation's traditionally slow product development efforts in order to get new products more quickly to the market. He also proposed that corporate headquarters might be moved out of Iowa and that many corporate administrative jobs be outsourced. He also added a group president structure so that division presidents would no longer report directly to the CEO. He replaced veteran executives, such as Beer, with people he had worked with earlier at PepsiCo and Procter & Gamble. These actions, among others, served to antagonize the workforce and the Newton community. Newton assembly line workers complained that the emphasis on getting to market faster meant that quality production standards were being unnecessarily lowered. Some in the community had been disturbed that Ward had chosen to live in Des Moines instead of in Newton—even after becoming CEO and Chair of the corporation. When combined with the rumor circulating in the summer of 2000 that AB Electrolux was thinking of purchasing Maytag, employees, shareholders, and the local community were emotionally shaken and uncertain of the company's future. The average share of Maytag stock had fallen from its high of $70 in mid-1999 to under $30 during the fourth quarter of 2000. Concerned about differences over strategy and the direction of the company, the board of directors asked for Ward's resignation at its November 2000 meeting. The board also asked Hadley to return to the CEO and Chair position while they searched for Ward's replacement.

Immediately dismantling Ward's group structure, Hadley stated, "The group president structure duplicated many of the functions and expenses that exist already at the business unit level. A structure that has division presidents reporting directly to the CEO is one that has worked well in the past and, I believe, is a proven model for a corporation our size." Hadley also reversed centralized research and development in favor of handling it within business units. Ward's outsourcing plan was also canceled. According to Hadley, "We must prudently, but smartly, measure our resources and deploy those resources against the core businesses in our most critical areas. This is also a model that has worked for us in the past."[24] Hadley also stated that Maytag would be staying in Newton. Said Hadley, "I'm disappointed that so much time, money, and effort were devoted to the project, that so many people were distracted, and that so much work in our business was disrupted by it."[25] With Hadley's return to power, three executives hired by Ward also tendered their resignations. In February 2001, Hadley announced the return of William Beer, the former head of the Maytag Appliance Group, to his former position as President of Major Appliances.

Maytag employees at all levels were pleased to have Beer back with the company. Beer had joined Maytag in 1974 as a market analyst. He then served as Director of Corporate Strategy in 1991. In 1993 he was named Vice President of Marketing for Maytag and Admiral products. In 1996 he was promoted to Senior Vice President for Product Supply for Maytag Appliances. Beer first served as President of Maytag Appliances from 1998 to 2000. He had a bachelor's degree in business administration from University of Nebraska, Lincoln, and had done graduate work at Drake University.

With the arrival of Hake as the new CEO and Chairman of the board, Hadley retired once again. Most employees and shareholders seemed to be pleased that the board had found someone like Hake who had significant experience in the major home appliance industry. While at Whirlpool, Hake had led the company's North American region operations, served as President of Whirlpool's Bauknecht Appliance Group, Vice President of Whirlpool Europe, and Whirlpool's CFO, before being passed over for the CEO position. Hake was a business and economics graduate of the University of Cincinnati and held an MBA from the University of Chicago. In early 2002, Hake reiterated Hadley's earlier announcement that Maytag's headquarters would remain in Newton. The local community was pleased to note that Hake was building a $750,00 home within Newton. "We love that," said Bill Jensen, a retired "Maytager," the local term for anyone who works or has worked for the company. Hake stated that he looked forward to walking home for lunch once his new home was finished sometime in late 2002. Hake and his wife, Robin, quickly involved themselves in the local community. They donated several thousand dollars to a downtown beautification project. Hake's wife volunteered to chair a Chamber of Commerce committee. Newton's Mayor David Aldridge stated that Hake had been readily accessible to city officials, businesses, and community leaders. "He gives you time to sit and visit. He's a very open, easy person to converse with," commented Aldridge.[26]

R&D and Purchasing

Research and development (R&D) at Maytag Company (long before it acquired other firms to become Maytag Corporation) had always been interested in internal improvements related to quality, durability, and safety. This orientation traditionally dominated the company's view of product development. One example was the careful way the company chose to replace in 1989 the venerable Helical Drive transmission with a new Dependable Drive transmission for its automatic washers. The new drive was delivered in 1975, patented in 1983, and put into test markets in 1985, after it was demonstrated that the drive would contribute to a 20-year product life. The Dependable Drive contained only 40 parts, as compared to the previous drive's 65, and allowed the agitator to move 153 strokes a minute compared to only 64 previously.

However, this methodical approach to R&D meant that Maytag Corporation might miss out on potential innovations. Realizing this dilemma, the corporation began to emphasize closer relationships with its key suppliers in both product development and process engineering. Joe Thomson, Vice President of Purchasing at Galesburg Refrigeration Products (Admiral), provided one example:

> We made an arrangement with a large steel supplier that led to a team effort to establish hardness specifications on our cabinet and door steel to improve fabrication. This team was very successful and the quality improvement and reduction in cost reached all our expectations. The company is now supplying all of our steel requirement.[27]

These strategic alliances between appliance makers and their suppliers were one way to speed up the application of new technology to new products and processes. For example, Maytag Company was approached by one of its suppliers, Honeywell's Microswitch Division, offering its expertise in fuzzy logic technology—a technology Maytag did not have at that time. The resulting partnership in product development resulted in Maytag's new IntelliSense dishwasher. Unlike previous dishwashers, which had to be set by the user, Maytag's fuzzy logic dishwasher automatically selected the proper cycle to get the dishes clean based on a series of factors such as the amount of dirt, presence of detergent, and other factors.[28] Terry Carlson, Vice President of Procurement for Maytag Corporation, stressed the importance of close relationships with suppliers:

> Strategic partnerships are a developing reality in our organization. . . . By paring our supplier base down by more than 50% in the past three years, we are encouraging greater supplier participation in our product design and production-planning processes. We're making choices to establish preferred supplier directions for our technical groups. These groups interact with their supplier counterparts. We are assigning joint task teams to specific projects, be they new-product-design oriented or continuous improvement of current products or processes.[29]

Prior to 1996, the various Maytag manufacturing plants acted independently and autonomously in their sourcing of components and materials. Since that time, corporate headquarters coordinated purchasing decisions to reach higher efficiencies but has allowed the plants significant leeway. According to Carlson, purchasing "signaled" the preferred suppliers to the engineering groups but didn't issue directives. The groups then worked together with the suppliers on new designs.[30] According to Doug Ringger, Director of Product Planning for Admiral and Maytag products, the use of cross-functional teams has helped cut development time in half from what it used to be. He states, "By having input from all areas early in the development cycle, issues are resolved before becoming problems."[31]

During the second half of the 1990s, the corporation poured significant money and effort into new technology and product development. In 1998, for example, the company spent $28 million to develop innovations in its traditional line of clothes washers and dryers and to upgrade its laundry manufacturing operations in Newton. In September 1999, Maytag announced the formation of its World Innovation Network, an integrated set of strategic partnerships, alliances, and engineering resources focused on delivering continuous discovery, invention, and rapid deployment of innovation. Through relationships with Arthur D. Little, Rhode Island School of Design, and the Battelle Institute, the company was attempting to further new technology development and application.[32] In early 2000, Maytag acquired an ownership position in e-Vend.net, a company making technology to control vending machines and appliances over the Internet. The company also formed an agreement with Microsoft to develop "smart" appliances that can interact with each other and the Internet. Representatives of Maytag served on a special committee with Microsoft to define how refrigerators, microwaves, and ovens will communicate with one another.

The corporation's R&D expenses were $58.3 million in 1999, $71.8 million in 2000, and $84.8 million in 2001. In 2001, the company announced that it was investing $8 million to expand three laundry products' R&D laboratories in Newton. Referring to the company's recent successful stream of new product introductions, William Beer stated that Maytag would launch a product in 2003 "that will rival Neptune in terms of innovation and success." Other recent successful new products were the Maytag Jetclean II Dishwasher (the first dishwasher with three full racks), the Jenn-Air Luxury Series Built-in Refrigerator (capable of being personalized for the buyer), and the Maytag Gemini Gas and Electric Ranges (containing twin ovens that operate independently). Beer said that Maytag will focus its efforts on designing in technology that improves the quality of life without complicating daily living. Such features, he stated, included turbidity sensors in dishwashers, adaptive defrost control systems in refrigerators, or, perhaps, a "smart" dryer that would be interconnected with a washer, thus enabling it to know what types of clothing were washed. The dryer could then set itself based on this information.[33]

Maytag applied new market research methodologies to define the benefits most desired by the consumer. In the past Maytag would prototype a new appliance or new features and ask the consumer, "What do you think?" Maytag recently applied the science of ethnography, literally having researchers live in a consumer's home to understand his or her lifestyle, then designing products to serve that lifestyle. "Before, all we cared about was how consumers used their dishwasher," said Beer. "Today we are just as interested in knowing they have to pick up Suzi for soccer and deliver Tommy to piano lessons. We weren't putting the refrigerator or dishwasher in a wide enough context to drive pure innovation. We could drive product development, but we couldn't truly change the game."[34] In recognition for its efforts, Maytag received the 1999 Outstanding Corporate Innovator Award by the Product and Development Association. The award, which recognizes firms for sustained success in the introduction of new products, was the first in its 12-year history to be awarded to an appliance manufacturer.[35]

According to T. Brent Freese, Director of Industrial Design at Maytag, it takes 4 to 12 ideas to get to one that can be developed into a new product. "Ideas are confirmed through consumer research, with some value assigned to them as they line up in a business model.

Then that model would be reviewed for execution of resources before moving forward." One example, said Freese, was "the zig-zag configuration of the Maytag Wide-by-Side Refrigerator which was designed around how people want to store party trays, pizza boxes, etc." One task that faced Freese and his staff was to create a "family look" for each of the different brands. "We need to differentiate our Jenn-Air, Maytag, and Amana brands so that they aren't competing."[36]

Although President Beer envisioned Maytag's future as having a continuous stream of innovative new products, CEO Hake was more reserved. "We're not going to have product hits each and every year like Neptune and Gemini," cautioned Hake. "Therefore we have to look at what we can do from a channel standpoint, from an individual dealer standpoint, and what we can do outside the Core five products that is tangential or similar, and that will enable us to grow." In a recession, Hake was concerned about trimming costs to stay competitive. "Right now we're running at about 17% SGA [selling, general, and administrative expenses as a percentage of sales], and we want that at 15%."[37]

Manufacturing

The Maytag Appliances unit contained the original Maytag Company plus the manufacturing plants of Admiral, Magic Chef, and Amana, in addition to the Jackson dishwasher plant, for a total of nine plants. (Jenn-Air's Indianapolis plant was not included since it had recently been closed and consolidated with Magic Chef's Cleveland facilities.) Four of the nine current manufacturing plants served as "Centers of Excellence," in which engineering and R&D activities were centralized. These were:

- Refrigeration—Amana, Iowa (Amana plant)
- Laundry—Newton, Iowa (Maytag plant)
- Cooking—Cleveland, Tennessee (Magic Chef plant)
- Dishwashers—Jackson, Tennessee

Additional manufacturing plants were in Galesburg, Illinios (Admiral refrigeration); Herrin, Illinios (Magic Chef laundry); Searcy, Arkansas (Amana laundry); Florence, Kentucky (Amana cooking); and Jefferson City, Missouri (components). Given the corporation's interest in obtaining synergy in production and marketing among the various products, there was no attempt to identify or isolate Admiral, Jenn-Air, Magic Chef, or Amana as separate profit centers. The Admiral Galesberg plant made refrigerators for all the brands. Magic Chef's Cleveland facilities made cooking products for Maytag, and so on.

Like other major home appliance manufacturers, Maytag Corporation had been investing millions of dollars in upgrading its plants and other facilities. Once considered to be the most efficient in the nation, Maytag's Newton, Iowa, plant had shown its age by the late 1980s. Consequently, top management made a controversial decision to move dishwasher production from its Newton plant to a new plant in Jackson, Tennessee. This new plant was dedicated to the manufacturing of dishwashers for all the corporation's brands. This was in line with the industry trend to build "dedicated" highly efficient plants to produce only one product line, with variations for multiple brands and price levels. Previously, only Maytag brand dishwashers had been made in Newton. Dishwashers had been purchased from General Electric for the Jenn-Air and Magic Chef brands. After only two years of operation, Maytag spent $13.7 million to add two more assembly lines to its successful Jackson dishwasher plant. The corporation also invested $160 million to further update the old Admiral refrigeration plant in Galesburg, Illinois, from 1995 to 1998. It also invested $12 million in 1998 plus $3 million in 2001 to upgrade and increase production capacity in its Herrin, Illinois, plant. In addition to making washing machines, the Herrin plant made transmissions used in the Newton and Herrin laundry plants.

Community leaders and union officials who had been discouraged by the corporation's dishwasher decision were jubilant in January 1994, when top management announced that it had chosen Newton as the production site for its new line of horizontal-axis (H-axis) clothes washing machines. (The Iowa Department of Economic Development had offered Maytag a $1 million forgivable loan if it built the plant in Newton.[38]) A front-loader, the new Neptune washer used 40% less water than comparable top-loaders (vertical axis) and significantly less electricity. Like Frigidaire, Maytag concluded that only a horizontal axis washer would meet future U.S. Department of Energy (DOE) standards. In contrast, GE and Whirlpool were unsure about the superiority of this design and instead designed more efficient vertical-axis washers. According to John Jansen, Vice President and General Manager of Newton Laundry Products, "We had to make the critical investment decision without knowing how the DOE would decide. It was an environment of tremendous uncertainty. We didn't know whether the washer would be a niche product or a dominant product. So we had to develop a strategy from an investment and manufacturing standpoint that offered us the flexibility to support a range of scenarios, from the H-axis being a niche product all the way to 100% conversion."[39] The company had invested another $11 million to add a second assembly line for increased manufacturing capacity of the Neptune washers and dryers.

The plan for centralizing the engineering and R&D activities within each of the appliance division's four product categories (cooking, laundry, refrigeration, and dishwashers) was implemented once Amana became a part of Maytag Corporation. According to Arthur Learmonth, Vice President of Manufacturing and Engineering of Maytag Appliances, "We had to make a choice between a decentralized or centralized approach, and to a certain extent we came up with a middle approach with the four Centers of Excellence and with key individuals sprinkled around at all the plants." Each of the core businesses, explained Learmonth, had a vice president and general manager headquartered at the Centers, to whom engineering reported. Maytag also had two senior directors of R&D and manufacturing for overall coordination of these areas. "This approach gives us the advantages of having decentralized engineering, while the strategists are able to tie everything together."[40]

Maytag Corporation launched a Lean Sigma initiative in 1998. The program combined "lean" manufacturing with the Six Sigma process utilized by Motorola. The focus of Lean Manufacturing was on reducing waste, managing shorter lead times, and increasing flexibility. The emphasis in Six Sigma was on process improvement—that is, defining, measuring, analyzing, improving, and controlling results. During the first quarter of 2002, the company held 800 training programs, each involving groups of 10–12 hourly and salaried employees for as much as a week in length. According to Vice President Learmonth, the program had resulted in 20%–30% productivity cost savings. The use of the program at the Jackson dishwasher plant increased productivity by 22% an hour and improved quality by 55%.[41] By simply reducing the work flow in the Cleveland, Tennessee, plant, more than $25 million was saved.

Management hoped that the Lean Sigma initiative would enable the company to provide consumers with made-to-order appliances delivered within a week of the initial order. The corporation hired TBM Consulting Group in early 2000 to help link the manufacturing process via computer, allowing for changes to be made at each step. "Once lean manufacturing systems are in place, linking various parts of the supply chain electronically is relatively easy," stated Anand Sharma, President and CEO of TBM. "It will lead directly to improved responsiveness to the market and reduced lead times, and virtually eliminate unsold physical inventories."[42]

Human Resources and Labor Relations

Throughout the corporation, employees were organized into various labor unions. The bargaining unit representing Maytag's unionized employees in Newton, Iowa, was the United Auto Workers. The unions representing employees at other Maytag Corporation companies were the International Brotherhood of Electrical Workers (Hoover North America) and the International Association of Machinists and Aerospace Workers (Magic Chef and Amana facilities). All the presidents of local unions belonged to the Maytag Council, which met once a year to discuss union issues.

Traditionally, the Maytag Company had had cordial relations with its local union, but the change to a large corporation seemed to alter that union relationship. Nevertheless, until 2000, the corporation had not had any strikes by any of its unions since a 1974 one-day walkout at Maytag Company. This was worthy of note considering that during the three-year period 1990–1992 the corporation reduced employment by 4,500 people.

In June 2000, 1,200 members of the International Association of Machinist and Aerospace Workers at Maytag's Herrin, Illinois, washing machine plant went on strike for nine days while disagreements with a proposed five-year contact were settled. In September 2001, the International Association of Machinists and Aerospace Workers Local 1526 went on a two-month strike after its Amana, Iowa, refrigeration plant workers rejected a new three-year contract. The union disagreed with mandatory overtime provisions, increasing insurance costs, and a two-tier wage system in which new hires would make $1.50 less than the current employees. Workers at the Amana, Iowa, plant had previously gone on strike for four days in 1995, in response to threats of company relocation, and for 16 days in 1992 for health insurance issues.

Following the Amana acquisition, Maytag eliminated 225 salaried jobs nationwide as part of integrating Amana Appliances into its major appliances division. Maytag's major appliance division had 4,600 salaried employees nationwide.[43] Some concern had been expressed among Maytag employees in Newton with the manner in which some long-time white-collar workers were being laid off. They were being escorted from the building shortly after they were informed that they were losing their jobs. When Hake was asked about this new procedure, he responded that he didn't know where the idea came from but that layoff procedures would be modified.[44]

Financial Situation

By the time of the shareholders' meeting on May 9, 2002, most of the corporation's shareholders knew how much the company had changed since the days when Maytag sold washing machines only as a sideline. Most appreciated management's attempts to build the company but were concerned with how executives were managing such a large company. Sales had steadily grown from $3 billion in 1991 to $4.3 billion in 2001, but profits had often fluctuated. Maytag Corporation showed a net loss in both 1992 and 1995 but had been profitable since then. Excluding special items, operating income had increased from $79 million in 1991 to $572.5 million in 1999 but then dropped to $479.6 in 2000 and to $289 million in 2001. Return on assets increased from 7.4% in 1997 to 13.8% in 1999 but then fell to 10.5% in 2000 and 5.4% in 2001. Maytag's stock price had dropped from a high of $70 in mid-1999 to under $30 during the fourth quarter of 2000 and was selling at $46.07 on May 9, 2002. (See **Exhibits 6–10** for Maytag's financial information.) After admitting the disappointing financial results of 2001, Hake stated that first quarter 2002 operating income was up and that earning per share was up 63% since last quarter.

Exhibit 6 Consolidated Statements of Income: Maytag Corporation (Dollar amounts in thousands)

Year Ended December 31	2001	2000	1999	1998	1997
Net sales	$4,323,713	$3,994,918	$4,053,185	$4,069,290	$3,407,911
Cost of sales	3,320,209	2,906,019	2,870,739	2,887,663	2,471,623
Gross profit	1,003,504	1,088,899	1,182,446	1,181,627	936,288
Selling, general and administrative expenses	704,596	609,284	609,958	658,889	578,015
Special charges	9,756	39,900	—		
Operating income	289,152	439,715	572,488	522,738	358,273
Interest expense	(64,828)	(60,309)	(48,329)	(62,765)	(58,995)
Loss on securities	(7,230)	(17,600)	—		
Other, net	(5,010)	(5,152)	8,193	10,912	1,277
Income from continuing operations before income taxes, minority interests, extraordinary item, and cumulative effect of accounting change	212,084	356,654	532,352	470,885	300,555
Income taxes	30,089	119,719	192,520	176,100	109,800
Income from continuing operations before minority interests, extraordinary item, and cumulative effect of accounting change	181,995	236,935	339,832	294,785	190,755
Minority interests	(14,457)	(20,568)	(11,250)	(8,275)	(7,265)
Incomes from continuing operations before extraordinary item and cumulative effect of accounting change	167,538	216,367	328,582	286,510	183,490
Discontinued operations:					
Income (loss) from operations of discontinued Blodgett and China joint venture	(7,987)	(19,919)	2,526	—	—
Income tax (benefit) on discontinued operations	1,113	(4,519)	(2,580)	—	—
Provision for impairment of China joint venture	42,304	—	—	—	—
Loss on sale of Blodgett	59,500	—	—	—	—
Loss from discontinued operations.	(110,904)	(15,400)	(54)	—	—
Income before extraordinary item and cumulative effect of accounting change	56,634	200,967	328,528	—	—
Extraordinary item—loss on early retirement of debt	(5,171)	—	—	(5,900)	(3,200)
Cumulative effect of accounting change	(3,727)	—	—		
Net income	$ 47,736	$ 200,967	$ 328,528	$ 280,610	$ 180,290

Source: Maytag Corporation, 2001 Annual Report, p. 19, and 1999 Annual Report, p. 39.

The Shareholders' Meeting

Chairman Hake continues his speech on the state of the corporation. He points to last year's strategic acquisition of Amana Appliances as a key part of Maytag's growth strategy. The corporation is currently following three key initiatives to better position itself in the industry:

1. Quality
2. Product development
3. Cost reduction

Exhibit 7 Consolidated Balance Sheet: Maytag Corporation (Dollar amounts in thousands)

Year Ending December 31	2001	2000	1999	1998	1997
ASSETS					
Current Assets					
Cash & cash equivalents	$ 109,370	$ 6,073	$ 28,815	$ 28,642	$ 27,991
Accounts receivable, less allowance for doubtful accounts (2001—$24,121; 2000—$15,583; 1999—$22,327; 1998—$22,305)	618,101	476,211	494,747	472,979	473,741
Inventories	447,866	325,313	404,120	383,753	350,209
Deferred income taxes	63,557	45,616	35,484	39,014	46,073
Other current assets	40,750	51,895	58,350	44,474	36,703
Discontinued current assets	89,900	171,451	—	—	—
Total current assets	1,369,544	1,076,559	1,021,516	968,862	934,717
Noncurrent assets					
Deferred income taxes	227,967	110,393	106,600	120,273	118,931
Prepaid pension cost	1,532	1,526	1,487	1,399	2,160
Intangible pension assets	101,915	49,889	48,668	62,811	33,819
Other intangibles, less allowance for amortization (2001—$123,395; 2000—$112,790; 1999—$112,006; 1998—$98,106; 1997—$85,071)	296,909	272,431	427,212	424,312	433,595
Other noncurrent assets	62,548	42,910	54,896	44,412	49,660
Discontinued noncurrent assets	60,001	251,154	—	—	—
Total noncurrent assets	750,872	728,303	638,863	653,207	638,165
Property, plant, and equipment					
Land	20,854	19,616	19,660	19,317	19,597
Buildings and improvements	352,447	320,545	349,369	333,032	309,960
Machinery and equipment	1,812,446	1,607,006	1,622,764	1,499,872	1,427,276
Construction in progress	146,335	84,980	74,057	102,042	59,376
	2,332,082	2,032,147	2,065,850	1,954,263	1,816,209
Less accumulated depreciation	1,296,347	1,168,085	1,089,742	988,669	874,937
Total property, plant, and equipment	1,035,735	864,062	976,108	965,594	941,272
Total assets	$3,156,151	$2,668,924	$2,636,487	$2,587,663	$2,514,154

Year Ending December 31	2001	2000	1999	1998	1997
Liabilities and shareowners' equity					
Current liabilities					
Notes payable	$ 148,247	$ 299,603	$ 133,041	$ 112,898	$ 112,843
Accounts payable	316,050	229,998	277,780	279,086	221,417
Compensation to employees	78,281	56,439	77,655	81,836	62,758
Accrued liabilities	285,627	176,289	194,074	176,701	161,344
Current portion of long-term debt	133,586	64,181	170,473	140,176	8,276
Discontinued current liabilities	112,702	145,177	—	—	—
Total current liabilities	1,074,493	971,687	853,023	790,697	566,638
Noncurrent liabilities					
Deferred income taxes	25,100	21,463	22,842	21,191	23,666
Long-term debt, less current portion	932,065	444,652	337,764	446,505	549,524
Postretirement benefit liabilities	497,182	479,452	467,386	460,599	454,390
Accrued pension costs	352,861	50,265	56,528	69,660	31,308

(continued)

Exhibit 7 *(continued)*

Year Ending December 31	2001	2000	1999	1998	1997
Other noncurrent liabilities	128,084	107,614	101,776	117,392	99,096
Discontinued noncurrent liability	22,678	72,018	—	—	—
Total noncurrent liabilities	1,957,970	1,175,464	986,296	1,115,347	1,157,984
Company obligated manditorily redeemable preferred capital securities of subsidiary trust holding solely the company's debentures	—	200,000	200,000	—	173,723
Minority interests	100,142	100,097	169,788	174,055	—
Temporary equity: Put options	—	200,000	—	—	—
Shareowners' equity					
Preferred stock					
Authorized—24,000,000 shares (par value $1.00)					
Issued—none	—	—	—	—	—
Common stock:					
Authorized—200,000,000 shares (par value $1.25)					
Issued—117,150,593 shares, including shares in treasury	146,438	146,438	146,438	146,438	146,438
Additional paid-in capital	450,683	285,924	503,346	467,192	494,646
Retained earnings	1,164,021	1,171,364	1,026,288	760,115	542,118
Cost of common stock in treasury (2001—40,286,575 shares; 2000—40,910,458 shares; 1999—34,626,316 shares; 1998—27,932,506 shares; 1997—22,465,256 shares)	(1,527,777)	(1,539,163)	(1,190,894)	(805,802)	(508,115)
Employee stock plans	(23,522)	(31,487)	(38,836)	(45,331)	(48,416)
Accumulated other comprehensive income (losses)	(186,297)	(11,400)	(18,962)	(15,048)	(10,862)
Total shareowners' equity	23,546	21,676	427,380	507,564	615,809
Total liabilities and shareowners' equity	$3,156,151	$2,668,924	$2,636,487	$2,587,663	$2,514,154

Source: Maytag Corporation, 2001 Annual Report, *pp. 20–21,* 1999 Annual Report, *pp. 40–41, and* 1997 Annual Report, *pp. 36–37.*

Exhibit 8
Business Segment Financial Information: Maytag Corporation (Dollar amounts in thousands)

	2001	2000	1999
Net sales			
Home appliances	$4,093,552	$3,712,708	$3,706,357
Commercial appliances	230,161	282,210	346,828
Operating income			
Home appliances	$324,646	$478,137	$562,288
Commercial appliances	5,755	29,532	51,891
Capital expenditures			
Home appliances	$131,777	$133,809	$117,765
Commercial appliances	7,919	3,665	2,826
Total assets			
Home appliances	$2,264,575	$1,793,626	$1,792,185
Commercial appliances	103,034	104,964	106,870

Source: Maytag Corporation, 2001 Annual Report, *p. 46.*

**Exhibit 9
Common Stock
Data: Maytag
Corporation
(Amounts in
dollars)**

Year	High	Low	Annual Dividends per Share
2001	$37.40	$22.25	$0.72
2000	47.75	25.00	0.72
1999	74.81	31.25	0.72
1998	64.50	35.44	0.66
1997	37.50	19.75	0.64

Source: Maytag Corporation Annual Reports.

As part of the product development initiative, the company has established a cross-functional new product development team for innovation. To show examples of some of the corporation's new products, Hake gives the signal to turn down the lights. Videos are shown of the company's latest television commercials. They show the new "sidekick" of the Maytag repairman carrying the Maytag Wide-by-Side refrigerator through a grocery store, Hoover's commercials for the Windtunnel vacuum and for its wet machine Floor MATE, and for The Maytag Store.

Hake also describes the formation of a quality improvement team whose job is to check all plants and make recommendations. After mentioning the introduction of a "strategic sourcing initiative" to complement the current Lean Sigma program, Hake contends that Maytag Corporation is well positioned versus the competition. Through new product innovation, the company's ultimate goal is to "Own the Kitchen." "Demographics are with us. The baby boomers are in their peak spending years. We have confidence in our ability to execute well. We enter 2002 with a stronger company."

Hake then introduces Maytag Appliances President Beer, who steps up to the stage to present his new products. According to Beer, "2001 was a rebuilding year for Maytag Corporation." He goes on to say that we are in a "wear out" industry. People have traditionally not purchased a new appliance until it wears out. We must change to a "want in" industry in which people buy a new appliance before the old wears out. He points to the Neptune washer and dryer as one example. "We have sold over 2.5 million Neptune washers—saving enough energy to light Des Moines for eleven years! We successfully established a $1095 retail price for the new Neptune and were able to attain a 1000 rpm spin cycle." Beer then describes the new Gemini range, with two ovens, and the new three-rack dishwasher. Jenn-Air has just developed a built-in refrigerator to compete with Sub-Zero. It has a stainless steel front, and its interior is completely customizable, says Beer. It is being built in the Amana, Iowa, facility.

Beer then introduces the President of Hoover Floor Care, Keith Minton, who takes over center stage to describe Hoover's new products. According to Minton, "Hoover is a strong name, one synonymous with floor care. Hoover has been identified as one of the 100 brands

**Exhibit 10
Inventory Data:
Maytag
Corporation
(Dollar amounts in
thousands)**

	2001	2000	1999	1998	1997
Raw materials	$ 62,587	$ 42,393	$ 66,731	$ 69,039	$ 61,740
Work in progress	76,524	60,588	72,162	66,578	53,069
Finished goods	382,925	303,249	325,844	317,331	229,450
Supplies	9,659	7,451	9,615	8,856	5,950
Total FIFO cost	$531,695	$413,681	$484,352	$461,804	$350,209

Source: Maytag Corporation Annual Reports.

that changed America in the 20th century. It has the highest brand awareness in the industry, a dependable reputation, and its upright vacuum is rated as requiring the least repair." To point out the importance of innovation to Hoover, Minton tells the audience of the company's new central vacuum system, its WindTunnel bagless upright, and its replacement of belts with a new gear-train drive system. "For any price point, we deliver better performance than the competition." He describes Hoover's new extractor line, the Floor MATE, for hard surface cleaning, and its experimentation with a robotic vacuum cleaner.

Minton relinquishes the stage to Hake. Hake moves to the podium to present the results of the voting. "The four nominees for a three-year term (expiring 2005) on the board of directors, Barbara Allen, Howard Clark, Lester Crown, and William Kerr, have been elected." The audience politely applauds. Hake continues. "Ernst & Young has been ratified as the independent auditors to audit the 2002 financial results." The Chairman then announces that the proposed 2002 employee and director stock incentive plan has been approved. After a slight pause, he states that propositions 4, 5, and 6 have passed. Hake then states that the board will review the results and determine the best course of action. (Maytag management had always contended that the shareholder votes were advisory only. That is why past votes had never been implemented.)

Hake than opens the meeting for questions from the audience. A shareholder in the back of the auditorium stands and moves to the aisle. An usher with a microphone joins him. He asks, "Has Maytag outsourced its internal audit function to Ernst & Young?" Hake responds in the affirmative, but states that the company intends to hire another firm to handle the internal part of the job so that the functions will have separate oversight. Another shareholder, seated in the front of the auditorium, stands to ask two questions: "We know that economies of scale through large, dedicated manufacturing plants help to cut costs. Now that Maytag has purchased Amana with its various plants, what is the future of Maytag's manufacturing facilities? Will you be building large, dedicated plants to replace the current plants, or will you be consolidating the manufacturing of each type of appliance, like refrigerators, in one existing plant? As a second question, we know that the big appliance manufacturers like Whirlpool and Electrolux are becoming internationally oriented, just at a time when Maytag seems to be retreating to North America. Will Maytag continue to be economically viable as a domestic maker of appliances in an increasingly global industry?" The Chairman ponders the questions for a moment and then responds: "We know that cost competitiveness is key at the retail level. We must have highly efficient factories to compete. It is important to note, however, that 50% to 70% of our manufacturing costs are from purchased materials. To reduce some of these costs, we are opening a component plant in Mexico." Hake states that the company has already announced plans to sell its Jefferson City, Missouri, parts business to a leading powdered metal manufacturer. The parts assembly for major appliances that will be moving to Reynosa, Mexico, is now being performed in Maytag plants or by outside suppliers. Planned to open late in 2002, the Mexican plant will enable the company's appliance manufacturing operations to focus more on parts fabrication and final assembly. Operating a plant in Mexico will save the company money because of lower labor costs and lower costs of some materials. Hake then moves his attention to the second question. "Our focus will continue to be in North America. We do have an international subsidiary that exports our top-end products. That will continue." (For the years 1999, 2000, and 2001, net sales to countries outside the United States by Maytag Corporation ranged from 9.3% to 10.1% of consolidated total net sales.[45])

With no more questions from the audience, Chairman Hake declares this year's annual shareholders' meeting to be adjourned. He then motions to the members of the board of directors to join him leaving the auditorium. It is 9:30 A.M. when the board walks out the front side door for its quarterly meeting a block away at Maytag Corporation headquarters.

As the shareholders and visitors wend their way out of the auditorium, down the stairs, and into the parking lot, a number of them comment on the meeting. Shareholder Lewis Rowles of

West Des Moines gives Hake good marks for his performance thus far. "He's been here a short time, but I think he's going to make a good CEO." Shareholder John Chevedden, a self-described shareholder activist from Los Angeles, explains to a reporter from the *Des Moines Register* why he had submitted the proposal for the annual election of directors. He wants "better corporate governance, which should translate into better management." Shareholder Bob Koch voices a concern that Maytag has had three CEOs in the past three years.

Financial analysts were still cautious in their judgment of Maytag's recent performance. Lawrence Horan, an analyst with Parker/Hunter, says that Maytag hasn't turned the corner yet, noting that the Amana acquisition largely contributed to the increased sales in 2001. According to Horan, the company needs to get more products in the pipeline, improve efficiency, and grow in the high-end business. Pointing out that Amana's figures for April though December 2001 had been included in Maytag's 2001 financial statements, Horan added, "They're basically admitting that they're losing market share." Doug West, a Vice President at the Urbandale, Iowa, office of A. G. Edwards & Sons, comments that Maytag is back on track but that it could take a few years for the company to return to record earnings levels and stock prices.[46]

One shareholder wonders: Does Maytag Corporation have what it takes to succeed in this increasingly competitive industry? Is this a good time to buy or to sell Maytag stock?

Notes

1. R. F. Hake, "Letter to Shareholders," Maytag Corporation *2001 Annual Report*, p. 2.
2. L. A. Hadley, "Letter to Shareholders," Maytag Corporation *1996 Annual Report*, p. 6.
3. R. F. Hake, "Letter to Shareholders," Maytag Corporation *2001 Annual Report*, p. 5.
4. C. Schlisserman, "Maytag Agrees to Sell Commercial Cooking Unit," *Des Moines Register* (September 1, 2001), p. D1.
5. R. F. Hake, "Letter to Shareholders," Maytag Corporation *2001 Annual Report*, p. 2.
6. J. Jancsurak, "It's All Good," *Appliance Manufacturer* (July 2002), p. 5. "White goods" is the traditional term used for major home appliances. The contrasting term "brown goods" refers to home electronics products, such as radios and televisions.
7. Freedonia Group, *World Major Household Appliances*, summarized in *Appliance* (April 2002), p. 19.
8. W. Ryberg, "Maytag Will Buy Jade Range," *Des Moines Register* (January 16, 1999), p. 10S.
9. Maytag Corporation, "Interview with Leonard Hadley," *1994 Annual Report*, p. 10.
10. Maytag Corporation, *2001 Annual Report*, p. 43.
11. J. Jancsurak, "Maytag Revs Up Innovation, Execution Engines," *Appliance Manufacturer* (August 2002).
12. "Maytag Honors," *Appliance Manufacturer* (September 1998), p. 19.
13. Maytag Corporation News Release, 1995.
14. D. Ritchey, "Service Friendly Appliances," *Appliance* (April 2002), p. 11.
15. J. Jancsurak, "Marketing Challenges," *Appliance Manufacturer* (August 2002), pp. Maytag 15–17.
16. W. Ryberg, "2nd Maytag Store Expects to Close," *Des Moines Register* (September 30, 2000), p. 1D.
17. W. Ryberg, "2nd Maytag Store Expects to Close," *Des Moines Register* (September 30, 2000), p. 1D; W. Ryberg, "Maytag Invites Customers to Take Hands-on Approach," *Des Moines Register* (March 14, 1999), pp. 1G, 2G.
18. W. Ryberg, "Maytag Urged to Review Retail Focus," *Des Moines Register* (November 11, 2000), p. D1.
19. "You've Got a Corporate Reputation—Now Don't Blow It," *U.S. News & World Report* (February 19, 2001), p. 12.
20. R. L. Rose, "Maytag's Acquisitions Don't Wear as Well as Washers and Dryers," *Wall Street Journal* (January 31, 1991), p. A6.
21. J. Jancsurak, "Excellence in Manufacturing," *Appliance Manufacturer* (August 2002), pp. Maytag-10–11.
22. P. Johnson and T. Meeser, "Maytag to Purchase Amana: Workers Weigh Effect on Jobs," *Des Moines Register* (June 6, 2001), pp. 1D, 6D.
23. W. Ryberg, "Maytag's No. 2 Officer Resigns," *Des Moines Register* (August 12, 1995), p. 10S.
24. "Maytag Announces Changes," *The (Ames, IA) Tribune* (December 9, 2000), p. B3.
25. "Hadley: Maytag Will Stay in Newton," *The (Ames, IA) Tribune* (December 7, 2000), p. B9.
26. W. Ryberg, "Maytag Chief Happy to Call Newton Home," *Des Moines Register* (April 11, 2002), pp. 1D, 6D.
27. M. Sanders, "Purchasing Power," *Appliance* (June 1993), pp. 45–46.
28. A. Baker, "Intelligent Dishwasher Outsmarts Dirt," *Design News* (April 10, 1995), pp. 69–73.
29. N. C. Remich, Jr., "The Power of Partnering," *Appliance Manufacturer* (August 1994), p. A-1.
30. R. J. Babyak, "The Power of One," *Appliance Manufacturer* (August 1997), pp. M-29–M-30.
31. R. Dzierwa, "The Permanent Press," *Appliance* (September 1995), p. 48.
32. D. Topping, "Innovation and the Internet," *Appliance* (January 2001), p. 87.
33. J. Jancsurak, "Maytag Revs Up Innovation, Execution Engines," *Appliance Manufacturer* (August 2002), pp. Maytag 3–6.

34. T. Stevens, "From Reliable to 'Wow,'" *Industry Week* (June 22, 1998).

35. "Maytag Wins Innovator Award," *Appliance Manufacturer* (October 1999), p. 18.

36. J. Jancsurak, "Multifaceted Industrial Design," *Appliance Manufacturer* (August 2002), pp. Maytag 12–13.

37. J. Jancsurak, "New CEO; New Agenda Signal Changes Ahead," *Appliance Manufacturer* (November 2001), pp. Maytag 5–9.

38. "Maytag, Fawn, Lennox, Parsons Get State Aid," *The (Ames, Iowa) Daily Tribune* (June 23, 1995), p. 1A.

39. R. J. Babyak, "The Washer Watch," *Appliance Manufacturer* (August 1997), p. M-11.

40. J. Jancsurak, "Excellence in Manufacturing," *Appliance Manufacturer* (August 2002), pp. Maytag 8–12.

41. P. Johnson, "Quality Counts," *Des Moines Register* (November 5, 2001), pp. 1D, 4D.

42. "Maytag to Customize Service," *Des Moines Register* (March 22, 2000), p. 1D.

43. W. Ryberg, "Maytag to Cut Salaried Jobs," *Des Moines Register* (October 11, 2001), p. 1D.

44. W. Ryberg, "Maytag Chief Happy to Call Newton Home," *Des Moines Register* (April 11, 2002), pp. 1D, 6D.

45. Maytag Corporation, *2001 Annual Report*, p. 47.

46. W. Ryberg, "Maytag Sees Turning Point," *Des Moines Register* (April 17, 2002), pp. 1D, 6D.

CASE 17

Kmart Corporation:
Seeking Survival in a Changing Marketplace (2002)

James W. Camerius

ON JANUARY 22, 2002, TROY, MICHIGAN–BASED KMART CORPORATION BECAME THE largest retailer in the history of the United States to seek bankruptcy protection. In its voluntary petition for reorganization under Chapter 11 of the U.S. Bankruptcy Code, Kmart management announced that it would outline a plan for repaying its creditors, reducing its size, restructuring its business, and emerging from court protection in July 2003. "After considering a wide range of alternatives, it became clear that this course of action was the only way to truly resolve the company's most challenging problems," Kmart Chief Executive Charles C. Conway said in a prepared statement. He promised that the nation's third-largest discount retailer would reemerge "as a stronger, more dynamic, more profitable enterprise with a well-defined position in the discount retail sector."

On March 11, 2002, Kmart announced that Charles Conaway had resigned. He was replaced as Chief Executive Officer (CEO) by James B. Adamson, who also would continue as Chairman of the Board of Kmart, a position he was elevated to just prior to the bankruptcy. Upon assuming the position, Adamson indicated that Kmart would emerge from bankruptcy protection "as a strong and healthy competitor, with a clearly defined place in the discount retail sector." On his first day as CEO, Adamson said he would initially be focusing on basics, such as cleaning up stores and making sure shelves were full of merchandise. He knew that he must develop a strategic plan of action that would guide the long-run performance of the organization following bankruptcy protection.

The early years of the 21st century were problematic and difficult ones for Kmart and the entire retail industry. Sluggish consumer spending, rising unemployment, the energy crisis, increased competitive pressures, battle for market share, a dismal holiday season, halts in shipments from wary vendors, problems in the securities and bond market, liquidity issues, and the events of September 11, 2001, all came together to make this period a very challenging time in which to operate. Several historic retail chains had also filed for bankruptcy protection and had either been reorganized or liquidated. Some analysts doubted if Kmart could survive in a changing marketplace and felt it would face eventual liquidation. Others felt that the firm needed an entirely new strategy that would reorganize and reposition the company in an extremely competitive marketplace. Retail analysts agreed that Kmart management had a huge task to undertake in the immediate future and the years ahead.

Kmart Corporation was one of the world's largest mass merchandise retailers. After several years of restructuring, it was composed largely of general merchandise businesses in the form of Kmart discount department stores (general merchandise and convenience items) and large Kmart Supercenters (food and general merchandise). It also merchandised though an e-

**Exhibit 1
Consolidated
Balance Sheet:
Kmart
Corporation[1]
(Dollar amounts in
millions except per
share data)**

Fiscal Year Ending January[2]	2001	2000
Assets		
Current assets		
Cash and cash equivalents	$ 1,245	$ 401
Merchandise inventories	5,822	6,412
Other current assets	817	939
Total current assets	7,884	7,752
Property and equipment, net	6,161	6,557
Other assets and deferred charges	253	523
Total assets	$14,298	$14,832
Liabilities and Shareholders' Equity		
Current liabilities		
Long-term debt due within 1 year	$ —	$ 68
Accounts payable	103	2,159
Accrued payroll and other liabilities	378	1,587
Taxes other than income taxes	143	187
Total current liabilities	624	4,001
Long-term debt and notes payable	330	2,084
Capital lease obligations	857	943
Other long-term liabilities	79	834
Total liabilities not subject to compromise	1,890	7,862
Liabilities subject to compromise	8,060	—
Company obligated mandatorily redeemable convertible preferred securities of a subsidiary trust holding solely 7¾ convertible junior subordinated debentures of Kmart (redemption value of $898 and $898, respectively)	889	887
Common stock, $1 par value, 1,500,000,000 shares authorized: 503,294,515 and 486,509,736 shares issued, respectively	503	487
Capital in excess of par value	1,695	1,578
Retained earnings	1,261	4,018
Total liabilities and shareholders' equity	$14,298	$14,832

Notes:
1. Fiscal Year is February to January.
2. FY2001 ended on January 31, 2002, and FY2000 ended on January 31, 2001.

Source: Kmart Corporation, 10-K Report (May 1, 2002).

commerce site, *www.bluelight.com.* It operated in all 50 of the United States and in Puerto Rico, Guam, and the U.S. Virgin Islands. It had equity interests as well in Meldisco subsidiaries of Footstar, Inc., that operated Kmart footwear departments. Measured in sales volume in 2001, it was the third largest retailer and the second largest discount department store chain in the United States. Kmart financial summaries are shown in **Exhibits 1, 2**, and **3**.

The discount department store industry was perceived by many to have reached maturity. Kmart, as part of that industry, had a retail management strategy that was developed in the late 1950s and revised several times in the 1990s. The firm was in a dilemma in terms of corporate strategy. The problem was how to lay a foundation to provide a new direction that would reposition the firm in a fiercely competitive environment. Analysts had noted, however, that the firm was without a definable niche in discount retailing. Studies had shown that number one ranked Wal-Mart, originally a rural retailer, had continued to be known for lower prices. Target Corporation, number three in sales, had staked out a niche as a merchandiser of dis-

Exhibit 2 Consolidated Statement of Operations: Kmart Corporation[1]
(Dollar amounts in millions, except per share data)

Fiscal Year Ending January[1]	2001[2]	2000[2]	1999[2]
Sales	$36,151	$37,028	$35,925
Cost of sales, buying, and occupancy	29,936	29,658	28,111
Gross margin	6,215	7,370	7,814
Selling, general, and administrative expenses	7,588	7,402	6,558
Equity income (loss) in unconsolidated subsidiaries	—	(13)	44
Restructuring, impairment, and other charges	1,099	—	—
Continuing income (loss) before interest, income taxes, reorganization items, and dividends on convertible preferred securities of subsidiary trust	(2,472)	(45)	1,300
Interest expense, net (contractual interest for fiscal year 2001 was $352)	344	287	280
Reorganization items	(184)	—	—
Income tax provision (benefit)	(115)	(134)	337
Dividends on convertible preferred securities of subsidiary trust, net of income taxes of $0, $25, and $27, respectively (contractual dividend for fiscal year 2001 was $72)	70	46	50
Net income (loss) from continuing operations	(2,587)	(244)	633
Discontinued operations, net of income taxes of $0 and $124	169	—	(230)
Net income (loss)	$(2,418)	$ (244)	$ 403
Basic earnings (loss) per common share			
Net income (loss) from continuing operations	$ (5.23)	$ (0.48)	$ 1.29
Discontinued operations	0.34	—	(0.47)
Net income (loss)	$ (4.89)	$ (0.48)	$ 0.82
Diluted earnings (loss) per common share			
Net income (loss) from continuing operations	$ (5.23)	$ (0.48)	$ 1.22
Discontinued operations	0.34	—	(0.41)
Net income (loss)	$ (4.89)	$ (0.48)	$ 0.81
Basic weighted average shares (millions)	494.1	482.8	491.7
Diluted weighted average share (millions)	494.1	482.8	561.7

Note:
1. The company's Fiscal Year is January through February.
2. FY 2001 ended on January 31, 2002; FY 2000 ended on January 31, 2001; and FY 1999 ended on January 26, 2000.

Source: Kmart Corporation, 10-K Report *(May 1, 2002).*

Exhibit 3 Selected Financial Data: Kmart Corporation (Dollar amounts in millions, except per share data)

Fiscal Year Ending[1]	2001[2]	2000[2]	1999[2]	1998[2]	1997[2]
Summary of operations[2]					
Total sales	$36,151	$37,028	$35,925	$33,674	$32,183
Comparable sales %	(0.1%)	1.1%	4.8%	4.8%	4.8%
Total sales %	(2.4%)	3.1%	6.6%	4.6%	2.4%
U.S. Kmart total sales %	(2.4%)	3.1%	6.6%	5.6%	5.0%
Cost of sales, buying, and occupancy	29,936	29,658	28,111	26,319	25,152
Selling, general, and administrative expenses	7,588	7,402	6,558	6,283	6,178
Restructuring, impairment, and other charges	1,099	—	—	19	114
Interest expense, net	344	287	280	293	363
Continuing income (loss) before income taxes, preferred dividend, and reorganization items	(2,816)	(332)	1,020	798	418
Chapter 11 reorganization items	184	—	—	—	—
Net income (loss) from continuing operations(3)	(2,587)	(244)	633	518	249
Discontinued operations	169	—	(230)	—	—
Net income (loss)	(2,418)	(244)	403	518	249
Per common share					
Basic					
Continuing income (loss)	$ (5.23)	$ (0.48)	$ 1.29	$ 1.05	$ 0.51
Discontinued operations	$ 0.34	$ —	$ (0.47)	$ —	$ —
Net income (loss)	$ (4.89)	$ (0.48)	$ 0.82	$ 1.05	$ 0.51
Diluted					
Continuing income (loss)	$ (5.23)	$ (0.48)	$ 1.22	$ 1.01	$ 0.51
Discontinued operations	$ 0.34	$ —	$ (0.41)	$ —	$ —
Net income (loss)	$ (4.89)	$ (0.48)	$ 0.81	$ 1.01	$ 0.51
Book value	$ 6.87	$ 12.50	$ 13.10	$ 12.12	$ 11.15
Financial data					
Working capital	$ 7,260	$ 3,751	$ 4,083	$ 4,174	$ 4,237
Total assets	14,298	14,832	15,208	14,255	13,625
Liabilities subject to compromise	8,060	—	—	—	—
Long-term debt	330	2,084	1,759	1,538	1,725
Long-term capital lease obligations	857	943	1,014	1,091	1,179
Trust convertible preferred securities	889	887	986	984	981
Capital expenditures	1,456	1,089	1,277	981	678
Depreciation and amortization	824	777	770	671	660
Current ratio	12.6	1.9	2.0	2.1	2.3
Basic weighted average shares outstanding (millions)	494	483	492	492	487
Diluted weighted average shares outstanding (millions)	494	483	562	565	492
Number of stores	2,114	2,105	2,171	2,161	2,136
U.S. Kmart store sales per comparable selling square footage	$ 235	$ 236	$ 233	$ 222	$ 211
U.S. Kmart total selling square footage (millions)	154	153	155	154	151

Notes:

1. The company's Fiscal Year is February through January.

2. FY2001 ended on January 31, 2002; FY2000 ended on January 31, 2001; FY1999 ended on January 26, 2000; FY1998 ended on January 27, 1999; and FY1997 ended on January 28, 1998.

3. Notes were deleted.

Source: Kmart Corporation, 10-K Report (May 1, 2002).

counted stylish upscale products. Kmart was left without a feature that would give it competitive distinction in the marketplace.

Corporate Governance

Charles C. Conaway

June 1, 2000, the search for the new Chairman and CEO of Kmart Corporation was over. Charles C. Conaway, a 39-year-old drugstore chain executive, was selected to fill the position vacated by retiring Chief Executive Floyd Hall. His appointment meant that the strategic direction of Kmart would come from a man who was previously unknown outside of the drugstore industry. He would have to provide an answer to a crucial question: How can Kmart respond to the challenges of industry leader Wal-Mart Stores, Inc., in the extremely competitive arena of discount retailing?

As President and Chief Operating Officer (COO) of CVS Corporation, Conaway was the number-two executive at the nation's largest drugstore chain, whose annual sales were about half those of Kmart's annual revenue of $36 billion. By all accounts, Conaway had made a sizable contribution in sales, earnings, and market value at CVS, Inc., headquartered in Woonsocket, Rhode Island. CVS had 1999 sales of $18 billion with 4,100 stores. Conaway, who became president and COO of CVS in 1998, was responsible for merchandising, advertising, store operations, and logistics. After joining the firm in 1992, he helped engineer the restructuring of the then-parent Melville Corporation, a diversified retailer, into a successful drugstore chain. Conaway said in an interview upon assuming his new position with Kmart that his primary task would be to improve customer service, productivity of resources, and problems with out-of-stock merchandise. Setting the stage for a new direction, Conaway said, "Customer service is going to be at the top. We're going to measure it and we're going to tie incentives around it," he noted. Following the implementation of this part of the comeback plan, he made big investments in computerized inventory systems and logistics to make the company more efficient. He revived Kmart's old trademark Blue Light Special that promoted an instant markdown on a particular item and at the same time cut back on weekly circulars that always had drawn traffic into stores.

Conaway also challenged Wal-Mart directly by lowering prices on 50,000 items as part of a "BlueLight Always" program and introduced an ill-fated "Dare to Compare" advertising campaign. The campaign contrasted Kmart prices on selected items with Target and Wal-Mart prices. Target sued for false advertising. Wal-Mart cut prices some more. Kmart dropped the "Dare to Compare" campaign.

Some industry analysts concluded that the Kmart Board of Directors held Charles Conway and President Mark S. Schwartz, who left the company on January 17, 2002, largely responsible for the lack of clearly defined turnaround plans and a number of strategic missteps that drained the company of cash and left it millions of dollars in debt and unable to pay its vendors, precipitating the bankruptcy. Some speculated that Conway would leave Kmart with at least $9.5 million. This included a severance package three times his base salary, which was $4.5 million. It also included forgiving a $5 million loan made to him in 2001 and, subject to court approval, one-third of previously promised bonuses worth $6.5 million and some stock options. An internal review in 2002, which initially focused in accounting irregularities at Kmart, was later extended to include a variety of issues, including executive loans, misuse of company funds by executives, and whether these employees performed any illegal acts or violated Kmart's policies during their tenure with the company.

New Leadership

James B. Adamson, 54, an outside Kmart director with firsthand experience in managing distressed companies, was appointed Chairman of the Board of Directors of Kmart on January 18, 2002. He was appointed CEO, as well, on March 11, 2002. Adamson was CEO of

Advantica Restaurant Group, Inc., which operated 2,400 Denny's, CoCo's, and Carrow's franchises, when he joined Kmart's board in 1996. During his tenure at Advantica, then known as Flagstar Cos., the firm filed for Chapter 11 protection to relieve debt from a leveraged buyout. The company emerged in 1998, after eliminating more than $1 billion in debt.

Adamson had previously served as Executive Vice President of Marketing at drugstore chain Revco, Inc., and was instrumental in bringing it out of bankruptcy. He also served as Executive Vice President of Merchandising at Target Stores, as a Senior Executive at B. Dalton Bookseller, and as the Chief Executive of Burger King Corporation.

To signal the beginning of a new era at Kmart, Julian Day, 49, former Executive Vice President and Chief Executive Operating Officer of Sears, Roebuck and Co. was named President and COO of Kmart on March 11, 2002. Albert A. Koch, 59, Chairman of the turnover firm Jay Alix & Co. became CFO, replacing John McDonald. Edward Stenger, 44, a principal of Jay Alix, was named the new Kmart Treasurer. In an earlier announcement, Kmart said it hired Ronald B. Hutchison, 51, to fill the new position of Chief Restructuring Officer. Mr. Hutchison was considered "one of the key architects" of an earlier reorganization at Advantica Restaurant Group, Inc. Since the filing of bankruptcy at the beginning of 2002, several other executives had either left the firm voluntarily or had been dismissed and replaced as part of the reorganization. A list of the Board of Directors, Executive Vice Presidents, and Senior Vice Presidents on May 1, 2002, is shown in **Exhibit 4**.

The Early Years

Kmart was the outgrowth of an organization founded in 1899 in Detroit by Sebastian S. Kresge. The first S.S. Kresge store represented a new type of retailing that featured low-priced merchandise for cash in low-budget, relatively small (4,000- to 6,000-square-foot) buildings with sparse furnishings. The adoption of the "5 and 10 cents" or "variety store" concept, pioneered by F.W. Woolworth Company in 1879, led to the rapid and profitable development of what was then the S.S. Kresge Company.

Kresge believed it could substantially increase its retail business through centralized buying and control, developing standardized store operating procedures, and expanding with new stores in heavy traffic areas. In 1912, the firm was incorporated in Delaware. It had 85 stores, with sales of $10,325,000, and, next to Woolworth's, was the largest variety chain in the world. In 1916 it was reincorporated in Michigan. Over the next 40 years, the firm experimented with mail-order catalogues, full-line department stores, self-service, a number of price lines, and the opening of stores in planned shopping centers. It continued its emphasis, however, on variety stores.

By 1957, corporate management became aware that the development of supermarkets and the expansion of drug store chains into general merchandise lines had made inroads into market categories previously dominated by variety stores. It also became clear that a new form of store with a discount merchandising strategy was emerging.

The Cunningham Connection

In 1957, in an effort to regain competitiveness and possibly save the company, Frank Williams, then President of Kresge, nominated Harry B. Cunningham as General Vice President. This maneuver was undertaken to free Mr. Cunningham, who had worked his way up the ranks in the organization, from operating responsibility. He was being groomed for the presidency and was given the assignment to study existing retailing businesses and recommend marketing changes.

**Exhibit 4
Corporate
Directors and
Officers, May 1,
2002: Kmart
Corporation**

Directors

James B. Adamson, Chair and CEO
Kmart Corporation
Director since 1996

Lilyan H. Affinito, Past Vice Chair
Maxxam Group, Inc.
Director since 1990

Richard G. Cline, Chairman
Hawthorne Investors, Inc.
Director since 1995

Willie D. Davis, President
All Pro Broadcasting, Inc.
Director since 1986

Joseph P. Flannery, Chair and CEO
Uniroyal Holding, Inc.
Director since 1985

Robert D. Kennedy, Past CEO
Union Carbide Corporation
Director since 1996

Robin B. Smith, Chair and CEO
Publishers Clearing House
Director since 1996

Thomas T. Stallkamp, CEO
MSX International
Director since 1999

Richard J. Statuto, CEO
St. Joseph Health System
Director since 2001

Executive and Senior Corporate Officers

James B. Adamson
Chairman of the Board and CEO

Julian D. Day
President and Chief Operating Officer

Albert A. Koch
Chief Financial Officer

Randy L. Allen
EVP Strategic Initiatives and
Chief Diversity Officer

Ronald B. Hutchison
EVP Chief Restructuring Officer

Cecil B. Kearse
EVP Merchandising

Janet G. Kelley
EVP General Counsel

Michael T. Macik
EVP Human Resources

Karen A. Austin
SVP Chief Information Officer

Richard Blunck
SVP and CEO, Bluelight.com

James E. Defebaugh, IV
SVP Chief Compliance Officer and Secretary

Steve Feuling
SVP Operations Administration

Paul J. Hueber
SVP Operations Administration

Keith A. Jelinek
SVP Inventory Management

Nicholas J. Just
SVP GMM Apparel

Lori McTavish
SVP Communications

James P. Mixon
SVP Logistics

Paula Paquette
SVP GMM Home

Steve Ryman
SVP Global Operations

Source: Kmart Corporation, 2001 10K Annual Report (May 1, 2002).

In his visits to Kresge stores, and those of the competition, Cunningham became interested in discounting—particularly in a new operation in Garden City, Long Island. Eugene Ferkauf had recently opened large discount department stores called E.J. Korvette. The stores had a discount mass-merchandising emphasis that featured low prices and margins, high turnover, large free-standing departmentalized units, ample parking space, and a location typically in the suburbs.

Cunningham was impressed with the discount concept, but he knew he had to first convince the Kresge Board of Directors, whose support would be necessary for any new strategy to succeed. He studied the company for two years and presented it with the following recommendation:

> We can't beat the discounters operating under the physical constraints and the self-imposed merchandise limitations of variety stores. We can join them—and not only join them, but with our people, procedures, and organization, we can become a leader in the discount industry.

In a speech delivered at the University of Michigan, Cunningham made his management approach clear by concluding with an admonition from the British author Sir Hugh Walpole: "Don't play for safety; it's the most dangerous game in the world."

The Board of Directors had a difficult job. Change is never easy, especially when the company had established procedures in place and a proud heritage. Before the first presentation to the Board could be made, rumors were circulating that one shocked senior executive had said:

> We have been in the variety business for 60 years—we know everything there is to know about it, and we're not doing very well in that, and you want to get us into a business we don't know anything about.

The Board of Directors accepted Cunningham's recommendations. When President Frank Williams retired, Cunningham became the new President and CEO and was directed to proceed with his recommendations.

The Birth of Kmart

Management conceived the original Kmart as a conveniently located one-stop-shopping unit where customers could buy a wide variety of quality merchandise at discount prices. The typical Kmart had 75,000 square feet, all on one floor. It generally stood by itself in a high-traffic, suburban area, with plenty of parking space. All stores had a similar floor plan.

The firm made an $80 million commitment in leases and merchandise for 33 stores before the first Kmart opened in 1962 in Garden City, Michigan. As part of this strategy, management decided to rely on the strengths and abilities of its own people to make decisions rather than employing outside experts for advice.

The original Kresge 5 & 10 variety store operation was characterized by low gross margins, high turnover, and concentration on return on investment. The main difference in the Kmart strategy would be the offering of a much wider merchandise mix.

The company had the knowledge and ability to merchandise 50% of the departments in the planned Kmart merchandise mix and contracted for operation of the remaining departments. In the following years, Kmart took over most of those departments originally contracted to licensees. Eventually all departments, except shoes, were operated by Kmart.

By 1987, the 25th anniversary year of the opening of the first Kmart store in America, sales and earnings of Kmart Corporation were at all-time highs. The company was the world's largest discount retailer, with sales of $25.6 billion, and operated 3,934 general merchandise and specialty stores.

On April 6, 1987, Kmart Corporation announced that it agreed to sell most of its remaining Kresge variety stores in the United States to McCrory Corporation, a unit of the closely held Rapid American Corporation of New York.

The Nature of the Competitive Environment

A Changing Marketplace

The retail sector of the U.S. economy went through a number of dramatic and turbulent changes during the 1980s and 1990s. Retail analysts concluded that many retail firms were negatively affected by increased competitive pressures, sluggish consumer spending, slower-than-anticipated economic growth in North America, and recessions abroad. As one retail consultant noted:

> The structure of distribution in advanced economies was currently undergoing a series of changes that are as profound in their impact and as pervasive in their influence as those that occurred in manufacturing during the 19th century.

This changing environment affected the discount department store industry. Nearly a dozen firms, such as E.J. Korvette, W.T. Grant, Arlans, Atlantic Mills, Bradlees, and Ames, passed into bankruptcy or reorganization. Some firms, such as Woolworth (Woolco Division), had withdrawn from the field entirely after years of disappointment. St. Louis–based May Department Stores sold its Caldor and Venture discount divisions, each with annual sales of more than $1 billion. Venture announced liquidation in early 1998. After declaring bankruptcy twice, New England regional discounter Ames Department Stores, Inc., announced in the summer of 2002 that it was closing all 237 of its stores, dismissing all of its employees, and liquidating its inventory. Many historic retailers, such as Chicago-based Montgomery Ward and Company and Jackson, Michigan–based Jacobson's Stores, Inc., also went out of business during this period.

Senior management at Kmart felt that most of the firms that had difficulty in the industry faced the same situation. First, they had been very successful 5 or 10 years earlier but had not changed and, therefore, had become somewhat dated. Management that had a historically successful formula, particularly in retailing, was perceived as having difficulty adapting to change, especially at the peak of success. Management would wait too long when faced with a threat in the environment and then would have to scramble to regain competitiveness.

Wal-Mart Stores, Inc., based in Bentonville, Arkansas, was an exception. It was especially growth oriented and had emerged in 1991 and continued in that position through 2002 as the nation's largest retailer as well as largest discount department store chain in sales volume. Operating under a variety of names and formats, nationally and internationally, it included Wal-Mart stores, Wal-Mart Supercenters, Sam's Warehouse Clubs, and Neighborhood Markets. The firm found early strength in cultivating rural markets, merchandise restocking programs, "everyday low-pricing," and the control of operations through companywide computer programs that linked cash registers to corporate headquarters. In early 2002, Wal-Mart became the largest company in the world, as measured by annual revenue.

Sears, Roebuck and Co., in a state of stagnated growth for several years, completed a return to its retailing roots by spinning off to shareholders its $9 billion controlling stake in its Allstate Corporation insurance unit and the divestment of financial services. After unsuccessfully experimenting with an "everyday low-price" strategy, management chose to refine its merchandising program to meet the needs of middle-market customers, who were primarily women, by focusing on product lines in apparel, home, and automotive. In 2001, Sears again revised this strategy to "position Sears in the retail marketplace as not a department store, not a discount store, but a broad line retailer with outstanding credit and service capabilities."

Many retailers, such as Target Corporation (formerly Dayton-Hudson), that adopted the discount concept, attempted to go generally after an upscale customer by emphasizing stylish merchandise. The upscale customer tended to have a household income of $25,000 to $44,000 annually. Other segments of the population were served by firms such as Ames Department Stores (Rocky Hill, Connecticut), which appealed to outsize, older, and lower-income workers, and by Shopko Stores, Inc. (Green Bay, Wisconsin), which attempted to serve the upscale rural consumer. Kohl's Corporation, a relatively new firm based in Menominee Falls, Wisconsin, which operated 420 family-focused, value-oriented department stores in 32 states in 2002, and the JCPenney Company, which operated 1,075 value-based department stores in all 50 states, were also considered competitors of Kmart in most markets.

Kmart executives found that discount department stores were being challenged by several other retail formats. Some retailers were assortment oriented, with a much greater depth of assortment within a given product category. To illustrate, Toys 'R' Us was an example of a firm that operated 20,000-square-foot toy supermarkets. Toys 'R' Us prices were very competitive within an industry that was very competitive. When the consumers entered a Toys 'R' Us facility, there was usually no doubt in their minds if the product wasn't there no one else had it. In the late 1990s, Toys 'R' Us was challenged by Wal-Mart and other firms that offered higher service levels, more aggressive pricing practices, and more focused merchandise selections. In 2001, Toys 'R' Us introduced a new strategy designed to update its stores to make them more convenient, open, and fun to shop.

Some retailers, such as Value City, were experimenting with the "off price" apparel concept, where name brands and designer goods were sold at 20%–70% discounts. Others, such as Home Depot, Lowe's, and Menards, operated home improvement centers that were warehouse-style stores with a wide range of hard-line merchandise for both do-it-yourselfers and professionals. Still others opened drug supermarkets that offered a wide variety of high-turnover merchandise in a convenient location. In these cases, competition was becoming more risk oriented by putting $3 or $4 million in merchandise at retail value in an 80,000-square-foot facility and offering genuinely low prices. Jewel-Osco stores in the Midwest, Rite Aid, CVS, Eckerd, and a series of independents were examples of organizations employing the entirely new concept of the drug supermarket. The Walgreen Company maintained its position as number one in drug sales by emphasizing prescription and general merchandise and by building its own stores in prime, high-traffic locations.

The competition was offering something that was new and different in terms of depth of assortment, competitive price image, and format. Kmart management perceived this as a threat because these were viable businesses and hindered the firm in its ability to improve and maintain share of market in specific merchandise categories. An industry competitive analysis is shown in **Exhibit 5**.

Expansion and Contraction

When Joseph E. Antonini was appointed Chairman of Kmart Corporation in October 1987, he was charged with the responsibility of maintaining and eventually accelerating the chain's record of growth, despite a mature retail marketplace.

He moved to string experimental formats into profitable chains. He noted:

> Our vision calls for the constant and never-ceasing exploration of new modes of retailing, so that our core business of U.S. Kmart stores can be constantly renewed and reinvigorated by what we learn from our other businesses.

In the mid-1970s and throughout the 1980s, Kmart became involved in the acquisition or development of several smaller new operations. Kmart Insurance Services, Inc., acquired as Planned Marketing Associates in 1974, offered a full line of life, health, and accident insurance centers located in 27 Kmart stores, primarily in the South and Southwest.

In 1982, Kmart initiated its own off-price specialty apparel concept called Designer Depot. A total of 28 Designer Depot stores were opened in 1982, to appeal to customers who wanted quality upscale clothing at a budget price. A variation of this concept, called Garment

**Exhibit 5
An Industry
Competitive
Analysis, 2001
(Dollar amounts in
millions)**

	Kmart	Wal-Mart	Sears	Target	Kohl's
Sales	$36,151	$217,799	$41,078	$39,888	$7,489
Net income	($2,418)	$6,671	$735	$1,368	$496
Sales growth	(0.1%)	14%	.99%	8%	22.0%
Profit margin	N/A	3.1%	1.78%	3.4%	6.6%
Sales/sq.ft.	$235	$455	$319	$247	$262
Return/equity	N/A	19.0%	12.0%	17.4%	17.1%

Number of stores:
  Kmart Corporation
    Kmart discount stores—2,114
    Kmart Supercenters—105
  Wal-Mart Stores, Inc.
    Wal-Mart discount stores—1,647
    Supercenters—1,066
    Sam's Clubs—500
    Neighborhood Markets—31
    International Stores—1,170
  Sears, Roebuck and Company
    Full-line department stores—867
    Hardware Stores—248
    Sears dealer stores—793
    Home supply stores (The Great Indoors)—13
    National Tire & Battery stores—223
    Outlet stores—35
  Target Corporation
    Target—1,053
    Mervyn's—264
    Marshall Field's department stores—64
  Kohl's Corporation
    Kohl's department stores—382

Note: The company's Fiscal Year (FY) is February through January.

Source: Company annual reports.

Rack, was opened to sell apparel that normally would not be sold in Designer Depot. A distribution center was added in 1983, to supplement them. Neither venture was successful.

Kmart also attempted an unsuccessful joint venture with the Hechinger Company of Washington, DC, a warehouse home center retailer. However, after much deliberation, Kmart chose instead to acquire, in 1984, Home Centers of America of San Antonio, Texas, which operated 80,000-square-foot warehouse home centers. The new division, renamed Builders Square, had grown to 167 units by 1996. It capitalized on Kmart's real estate, construction, and management expertise and on Home Centers of America's merchandising expertise. Builders Square was sold in 1997 to the Hechinger Company. On June 11, 1999, Hechinger filed for Chapter 11 bankruptcy protection. As a result, Kmart recorded a noncash charge of $354 million that reflected the impact of lease obligations for former Builders Square locations that were guaranteed by Kmart.

Waldenbooks, a chain of 877 bookstores, was acquired by Kmart from Carter, Hawley, Hale, Inc., in 1984. It was part of a strategy to capture a greater share of the market with a product category that Kmart already had in its stores. Kmart management had been interested in the book business for some time and took advantage of an opportunity in the marketplace to build on its common knowledge base. Borders Books and Music, an operator of 50 large-format superstores, became part of Kmart in 1992, to form the "Borders Group," a division that would include Waldenbooks. The Borders Group, Inc., was sold during 1995.

The Bruno's, Inc., joint venture in 1987 formed a partnership to develop large combination grocery and general merchandise stores, or "hypermarkets," called American Fare. The giant, one-stop-shopping facilities of 225,000 square feet, traded on the grocery expertise of Bruno's and the general merchandise of Kmart to offer a wide selection of products and services at discount prices. A similar venture, called Super Kmart Center, represented later thinking on combination stores with a smaller size and format. In 2001, these stores were renamed Kmart Supercenters.

In 1988, the company acquired a controlling interest in Makro, Inc., a Cincinnati-based operator of warehouse club stores. Makro, with annual sales of about $300 million, operated member-only stores that were stocked with low-priced fresh and frozen groceries, apparel, and durable goods in suburbs of Atlanta, Cincinnati, Washington, and Philadelphia. PACE Membership Warehouse, Inc., a similar operation, was acquired in 1989. The club stores were sold in 1994.

PayLess Drug Stores, a chain that operated super drugstores in a number of western states, was sold in 1994 to Thrifty PayLess Holdings, Inc., an entity in which Kmart maintained a significant investment. Interests in The Sports Authority, an operator of large-format sporting goods stores, which Kmart acquired in 1990, were disposed of during 1995.

On the international level, an interest in Coles Myer, Ltd., Australia's largest retailer, was sold in November 1994. Interests in 13 Kmart general merchandise stores in the Czech and Slovak Republics were sold at the beginning of 1996 to Tesco PLC, one of the United Kingdom's largest retailers. In February 1998, Kmart stores in Canada were sold to Hudson's Bay Co., a Canadian chain of historic full-service department stores. The interest in Kmart Mexico, S.A.de C.V. was disposed of in fiscal year 1997.

Founded in 1988, OfficeMax, with 328 stores, was one of the largest operators of high-volume, deep-discount office products superstores in the United States. It became a greater than 90% owned Kmart unit in 1991. Kmart's interest in OfficeMax was sold during 1995.

In November 1995, Kmart also sold its auto service center business to a new corporation controlled by Penske Corporation. In connection with the sale, Kmart and Penske entered into a sublease arrangement concerning the operation of Penske Auto Service Centers.

During 1999, Kmart signed agreements with SuperValu, Inc., and Fleming Companies, Inc., under which they would assume responsibility for the distribution and replenishment of grocery-related products to all Kmart stores. Kmart also maintained an equity interest in Meldisco subsidiaries of Footstar, Inc., operators of footwear departments in Kmart stores.

The Maturation of Kmart

Early corporate research revealed that on the basis of convenience, Kmart served 80% of the population. One study concluded that one out of every two adults in the United States shopped at a Kmart at least once a month. Despite this popular appeal, strategies that had allowed the firm to have something for everybody were no longer felt to be appropriate for the new millennium. Kmart found that it had a broad customer base because it operated on a national basis. Its early strategies had assumed that the firm was serving everyone in the markets where it was established. The financial community believed the Kmart customer was blue-collar, low-income, and upper lower class.

Although Kmart had made a major commitment in more recent years to secondary or rural markets, these were areas that had previously not been cultivated. The firm, in its initial strategies, perceived the rural consumer as different from the urban or suburban customer. In re-addressing the situation, it discovered that its assortments in rural areas were too limited, and there were too many preconceived notions regarding what the rural customer really wanted. The firm discovered that the typical farmer didn't always shop for bib overalls and shovels, but shopped for microwave ovens and the same things everyone else did.

One goal was not to attract more customers but to get the customer coming in the door to spend more. Once in the store, the customer was thought to demonstrate more divergent tastes. The upper-income consumer would buy more health and beauty aids, cameras, and sporting goods. The lower-income consumer would buy toys and clothing.

In the process of trying to capture a larger share of the market and get people to spend more, the firm began to recognize a market that was more upscale. When consumer research was conducted and management examined the profile of the trade area and the profile of the person who shopped at Kmart in the past month, they were found to be identical. Kmart was predominately serving the suburban consumer in suburban locations. In 1997, Kmart's primary target customers were women, between the ages of 25 and 45 years old, with children at home and with household incomes between $20,000 and $50,000 per year. The core Kmart shopper averaged 4.3 visits to a Kmart store per month. The purchase amount per visit was $40. The purchase rate was 95% during a store visit. The firm estimated that 180 million people shopped at Kmart in an average year.

In "lifestyle" research in markets served by the firm, Kmart determined there were more two-income families, families were having fewer children, there were more working wives, and customers tended to be homeowners. Customers were very careful how they spent their money and were perceived as wanting quality. This was a distinct contrast to the 1960s and early 1970s, which tended to have the orientation of a "throwaway" society. Customers wanted better-quality products but still demanded competitive prices. According to a Kmart *Annual Report*, "Consumers today are well educated and informed. They want good value and they know it when they see it. Price remains a key consideration, but the consumers' new definition of value includes quality as well as price."

Corporate management at Kmart considered the discount department store to be a mature idea. Although maturity was sometimes looked on with disfavor, Kmart executives felt that this did not mean a lack of profitability or lack of opportunity to increase sales. The industry was perceived as having been "reborn." It was in this context, in the 1990s, that a series of new retailing strategies, designed to upgrade the Kmart image, were developed.

The 1990 Renewal Program

The strategies that emerged to confront the changing environment were the result of an overall reexamination of existing corporate strategies. This program included accelerated store expansion and refurbishing, capitalizing on dominant lifestyle departments, centralized merchandising, more capital investment in retail automation, an aggressive and focused advertising program, and continued growth through new specialty retail formats.

The initial 1990, five-year, $2.3 billion program involved virtually all Kmart discount stores. There would be approximately 250 new full-size Kmart stores, 620 enlargements, 280 relocations, and 30 closings. In addition 1,260 stores would be refurbished to bring their layout and fixtures up to new store standards. Another program, introduced in 1996, resulted in an additional $1.1 billion being spent to upgrade Kmart stores. By year-end 1999, 1,860 new Big Kmart stores offered more pleasant shopping experiences, thanks to the updated and easy-to-shop departmental adjacencies, better signing and lighting, wider aisles, and more attractive in-store presentation.

One area receiving initial attention was improvement in the way products were displayed. The traditional Kmart layout was by product category. Often these locations for departments were holdovers from the variety store. Many departments would not give up prime locations. As part of the new marketing strategy, the shop concept was introduced. Management recognized that it had a sizable do-it-yourself store. As planning management discussed the issue, "nobody was aware of the opportunity. The hardware department was right smack in the center of the store because it was always there. The paint department was over here and the electrical department was over there." "All we had to do," management contended, "was put them all in one spot and everyone could see that we had a very respectable 'do-it-yourself' department." The concept resulted in a variety of new departments, such as Soft Goods for the Home, Kitchen Korners, and Home Electronic Centers. The goal behind each department was to sell an entire lifestyle-oriented concept to consumers, making goods complementary so shoppers would want to buy several interrelated products rather than just one item.

Name brands were added in soft and hard goods as management recognized that the customer transferred the product quality of branded goods to perceptions of private-label merchandise. In the eyes of Kmart management, "If you sell Wrangler, there is good quality. Then the private label must be good quality."

The company increased its emphasis on trusted national brands such as Rubbermaid, Procter & Gamble, and Kodak, and put emphasis of major strategic vendor relationships. In addition, it enhanced its private label brands such as Kathy Ireland, Jaclyn Smith, Route 66, and Sesame Street in apparel. Additional private label merchandise included K Gro in home gardening, American Fare in grocery and consumables, White-Westinghouse in appliances and Penske Auto Centers in automotive services. Some private labels were discontinued following review.

Kmart hired Martha Stewart, an upscale Connecticut author of lavish best-selling books on cooking and home entertaining, as its "life-style spokesperson and consultant." Martha Stewart was featured as a corporate symbol for housewares and associated products in advertising and in-store displays. Management visualized her as the next Betty Crocker, a fictional character created some years ago by General Mills, Inc., and a representative of its interest in "life-style" trends. The "Martha Stewart Everyday" home fashion product line was introduced in 1995 and expanded in 1996 and 1997. A separate division was established to manage strategy for all Martha Stewart label goods and programs. Merchandise was featured in the redesigned once-a-week Kmart newspaper circular that carried the advertising theme: "The quality you need, the price you want."

Several thousand prices were reduced to maintain "price leadership across America." As management noted, "it is absolutely essential that we provide our customers with good value—quality products at low prices." Although lowering of prices hurt margins and contributed importantly to an earnings decline, management felt that unit turnover of items with lowered prices increased significantly to "enable Kmart to maintain its pricing leadership that will have a most positive impact on our business in the years ahead."

A centralized merchandising system was introduced to improve communication. A computerized, highly automated replenishment system tracked how quickly merchandise sold and, just as quickly, put fast-moving items back on the shelves. Satellite capability and a point-of-sale (POS) scanning system were introduced as part of the program. Regular, live satellite communication from Kmart headquarters to the stores would allow senior management to communicate with store managers and allow for questions and answers. The POS scanning system allowed a record of every sale and transmission of the data to headquarters. This enabled Kmart to respond quickly to what's new, what's in demand, and what would keep customers coming back.

The company opened its first Kmart Supercenter (originally called Super Kmart Centers) in 1992. The format combined general merchandise and food with emphasis upon customer service and convenience and ranged in size from 135,000 to 190,000 square feet, with more than 40,000 grocery items. A typical Supercenter operated 7 days a week, 24 hours a day and generated high traffic and sales volume. The centers also featured wider shopping aisles, appealing displays, and pleasant lighting to enrich the shopping experience. Kmart Supercenters featured in-house bakeries, USDA fresh meats, fresh seafood, delicatessens, cookie kiosks, cappuccino bars, in-store eateries and food courts, and fresh carry-out salad bars. In many locations, the center provided customer services like video rental, dry cleaning, shoe repair, beauty salons, optical shops, express shipping services, and a full line of traditional Kmart merchandise. To enhance the appeal of the merchandise assortment, emphasis was placed on "cross-merchandising." For example, toasters were featured above the fresh baked breads, kitchen gadgets were positioned across the aisle from produce, and baby centers featured everything from baby food to toys. At the end of 2001, the company operated 105 Supercenter stores.

The Planning Function

Corporate planning at Kmart during the 1980s and 1990s was the result of executives, primarily the senior executive, recognizing change. The role played by the senior executive was to get others to recognize that nothing is good forever. "Good planning" was perceived as the result of those who recognized that at some point they would have to get involved. "Poor planning" was done by those who didn't recognize the need for it. When they did, it was too late to survive. Good planning, if done on a regular and timely basis, was assumed to result in improved performance. Kmart's Michael Wellman, then Director of Planning and Research, contended, "Planning, as we like to stress, is making decisions now to improve performance tomorrow. Everyone looks at what may happen tomorrow, but the planners are the ones who make decisions today. That's where I think too many firms go wrong. They think they are planning because they are writing reports and are aware of changes. They don't say, 'because of this, we must decide today to spend this money to do this to accomplish this goal in the future.' "

Kmart management believed that the firm had been very successful in the area of strategic planning. "When it became necessary to make significant changes in the way we were doing business," Wellman suggested, "that was accomplished on a fairly timely basis." When the organization made changes in the 1960s, it recognized there was a very powerful investment opportunity and capitalized on it—far beyond what anyone else would have done. "We just opened stores," he continued, "at a great, great pace. Management, when confronted with a crisis, would state, 'It's the economy, or it's this, or that, but it's not the essential way we are doing business.' " He noted, "Suddenly management would recognize that the economy may stay like this forever. We need to improve the situation and then do it." Strategic planning was thought to arise out of some difficult times for the organization.

Kmart had developed a reasonably formal planning organization that involved a constant evaluation of what was happening in the marketplace, what competition was doing, and what kinds of opportunities were available. Management felt a need to diversify because it would not be a viable company unless it was growing. Management felt it was not going to grow with the Kmart format forever. It needed growth and opportunity, particularly for a company that was able to open 200 stores on a regular basis. Wellman, Director of Planning and Research, noted, "Given a 'corporate culture' that was accustomed to challenges, management would have to find ways to expend that energy. A corporation that is successful," he argued, "has to continue to be successful. It has to have a basic understanding of corporate needs and be augmented by a much more rigorous effort to be aware of what's going on in the external environment."

A planning group at Kmart represented a number of functional areas of the organization. Management described it as an "in-house consulting group" with some independence. It was made up of financial planning, economic and consumer analysis, and operations research. The CEO was identified as the primary planner of the organization.

Early Reorganization and Restructuring

Kmart financial performance for 1993 was clearly disappointing. The company announced a loss of $974 million on sales of $34,156,000 for the fiscal year ended January 26, 1994. Chairman Antonini, noting the deficit, felt it occurred primarily because of lower margins in the U.S. Kmart stores division. "Margin erosion," he said, "stemmed in part from intense industrywide pricing pressure throughout 1993." He was confident, however, that Kmart was on track with its renewal program to make the more than 2,350 U.S. Kmart stores more "competitive, on-trend, and cutting-edge merchandisers." Tactical Retail Solutions, Inc., estimated that during Antonini's seven-year tenure with the company, Kmart's market share in the discount arena fell to 23% from 35%. Other retail experts suggested that because the company had struggled for so long to have the right merchandise in the stores at the right time, it had lost customers to competitors. An aging customer base was also cited.

In early 1995, following the posting of its eighth consecutive quarter of disappointing earnings, Kmart's Board of Directors announced that Joseph Antonini would be replaced as chairman. It named Donald S. Perkins, former Chairman of Jewel Companies, Inc., and a Kmart director, to the position. Antonini relinquished his position as President and CEO in March. After a nationwide search, Floyd Hall, 57, former Chairman and CEO of the Target discount store division of the Dayton Hudson Corporation, was appointed Chairman, President, and CEO of Kmart in June 1995.

The company concluded the disposition of many noncore assets in 1996, including the sale of the Borders group, OfficeMax, The Sports Authority, and Coles Myer. During the 1990s, it also closed a large number of underperforming stores in the United States and cleared out $700 million in aged and discontinued inventory in the remaining stores.

In 1996, Kmart converted 152 of its traditional stores to feature a new design that was referred to as the "high-frequency format." These stores were named Big Kmart. The stores emphasized those departments that were deemed the most important to core customers and offered an increased mix of high-frequency, everyday basics and consumables in the pantry area located at the front of each store. These items were typically priced at a one- to three-percentage differential from the leading competitors in each market and served to increase inventory turnover and gross margin dollars. In addition to the pantry area, Big Kmart stores featured improved lighting, new signage that was easier to see and read, and adjacencies that created a smoother traffic flow. In 1999, 588 stores were converted to the new Big Kmart format, bringing the total to 1,860. Other, smaller stores were updated to a "best of Big Kmart" prototype, as resources permitted.

Kmart launched its first e-commerce site in 1998. The initial Kmart.com offered a few products and was not considered a successful venture. In 1999, it partnered with SOFTBANK Venture Capital, which provided technical expertise, experienced personnel, and initial capital to create an Internet site 60% owned by Kmart. BlueLight.com increased the number of Kmart products it offered online to about 65,000 from 1,250. It planned to boost the number to 100,000 by year end 2000 and possibly to millions of items in the future. The name was changed to Kmart.com in 2002.

At the end of his tenure, Floyd Hall announced in 2000 that the company mandate in the year and century ahead was to create sustained growth that would profitably leverage all of the core strengths of the firm. The corporate mission was "to become the discount store of choice for low- and middle-income households by satisfying their routine and seasonal shopping needs as well as or better than the competition." Management believed that the actions taken by Charles Conaway during his tenure as CEO, would have a dramatic impact on how customers perceived Kmart, how frequently they shopped in the stores, and how much they would buy on each visit. Increasing customers' frequency and the amount they purchased each visit were seen as having a dramatic impact on the company's efforts to increase its profitability.

Restructuring and Repositioning a Bankrupt Company

The major objective of Kmart management in 2002 was to eventually emerge from bankruptcy protection as a strong and healthy competitor with a clearly defined place in the discount retail sector.

The bankruptcy filing had the immediate effect of stopping the loss of goods from suppliers no longer confident of Kmart's ability to pay. Dallas, Texas–based Fleming Companies, Inc., had announced that it was discontinuing shipments of groceries and other types of products to Kmart stores. Fleming resumed shipments once the bankruptcy court assured it of payment of bills outstanding.

On March 20, 2002, the bankruptcy court approved the closure of 283 Kmart stores, or approximately 13% of the 2,114 stores operating at the end of 2001. The closures included 270 Kmart discount stores and 12 Kmart Supercenters in 40 states and one Kmart store in Puerto Rico. Stores were selected by evaluating the market and financial performance of every store and the terms of every lease. Candidates for closure were stores that did not meet management's financial requirements for ongoing operations. In some cases, lease terms were renegotiated to attempt to improve store profitability and avoid the need for closure. Approximately 22,000 employees were affected by the store closures. The move also involved terminating leases on 350 Kmart stores that were closed prior to the bankruptcy.

On April 9, 2002, management announced that it had reached an agreement with Penske Corporation to close all of its auto service centers at more than 563 Kmart stores in 44 states.

Kmart management earlier announced that it would work on a marketing strategy to become "the authority for what moms value" and also be "the store that understands what really matters in life." This was later changed to suggest that Kmart featured "The stuff of life," in an attempt to focus on family values. A key component of this strategy was to invest in merchandise and marketing initiatives to enhance the firm's strategic positioning by offering exclusive brands that would differentiate it from competition. These exclusive brands included Martha Stewart Everyday home, garden, colors, baby, kitchen, keeping, and decorating products, along with candles and accessories; Jaclyn Smith women's apparel, jewelry, and accessories; Kathy Ireland apparel for infants and children; Route 66 men's and women's apparel and accessories; and Joe Boxer apparel, accessories, and home furnishings. As part of the new brand emphasis, displays of Disney, Sesame Street, and Joe Boxer were moved to the front of stores, where parents might be more tempted to browse. In 2002, Martha Stewart was in court fighting accusations of insider trading, a scandal that some analysts said could affect sales of the brand.

Management concluded that the "BlueLight Always" campaign had significantly affected Kmart's gross margin. The campaign, which had initially lowered prices on over 30,000 items, was therefore scaled back to approximately 18,000 items. Several other changes were made in an attempt to reduce gross margin erosion.

In October 2002, Kmart unveiled a store in White Lake, Michigan, that would serve as a prototype while management decided on a final strategy on how to move forward in repositioning itself in the marketplace. The prototype store featured a new logo, sleekly designed signs, brighter lighting, lower shelves, and wider aisles to encourage shoppers to buy more. A new color scheme was a key to the new design. The fire-engine-red Kmart logo, which had graced the outside of all the chain's stores since 1990, was replaced by a lime-green K logo. The new green, which Kmart management said suggested growth and nature, was also used on employee aprons and color decorating accents in the stores. Mr. Adamson said that the company would study the prototype and focus on changes that increase sales the most.

In addition to developing a new look for stores, management also experimented with how it controlled store operations and merchandising in an attempt to position Kmart as the "store of the neighborhood." Store operations traditionally were decisions made by Kmart management at corporate headquarters in Troy, Michigan. Inventory and merchandise were ordered centrally for the stores, and managers were told how to arrange the goods. In a pilot program involving about 40 stores in the Chicago metropolitan area, store managers were given the freedom to customize inventory, store hours, and displays based on customer preferences. During the first 10 weeks, sales at the stores in the test program outperformed the overall company by 12%.

Kmart's financial results reported in the fiscal second quarter of 2002 noted that it lost $377 million as spending cuts and layoffs failed to offset declines in sales and shrinking profit margins. Sales fell 15.7%, or nearly $1.4 billion, for the 13-week period ended July 31, 2002. The company lost an additional $126 million in August, the seventh consecutive month of losses at the company since it filed for bankruptcy protection. Kmart posted net sales of $7.2 billion for the second quarter, down from $8.92 billion during the same quarter of 2001. Same-store sales, a measurement that factors out stores that had been opened or closed and other changes, were down 11.9%. The profit margin dropped to 17.6% from 18.7% in the second quarter of 2001.

Kmart's ongoing financial losses, combined with its failure to sustain any kind of sales momentum, had many retail experts speculating on whether the company could successfully emerge from bankruptcy. "Kmart appears to be directionless," indicated one retail consultant. "What we're seeing is a bunch of tactical moves that don't have much substance to them, which is why they don't resonate with consumers for very long," he noted.

Most retail analysts believed that in addition to closing stores, lowering costs, and improving efficiency while in bankruptcy, Kmart management needed to develop a strategy for differentiating itself from Wal-Mart, Target, and other major competitors in the marketplace. In addition, some suggested that a leaner, more efficient Kmart should seek a buyer such as a general merchandiser and/or food distributor. Others proposed that Kmart merge with an international retailer eager to enter the U.S. market.

Financial Situation and Issues

Kmart's financial position is shown in **Exhibits 1, 2, 3,** and **6.** A 12-year (1990–2001) record of Kmart's financial performance is shown in **Exhibit 6.** In fiscal year 1990, Kmart's sales were $32,070,000,000, and Wal-Mart's sales were $32,601,594,000. In fiscal year 2001, Kmart's sales were $36,151,000,000 (an increase of $4,081,000,000 or 12.72%), while Wal-Mart's sales increased to $217,799,000,000 (an increase of $185,197,406,000 or 568.1%). Wal-Mart's fiscal year 2001 net income was $6,671,000,000 compared with Kmart's net loss of $2,418,000,000. Kmart had 105 Kmart Supercenters and 2,114 discount stores, for a total of 2,219. Wal-Mart had 2,295 Wal-Mart stores, 564 Sam's Clubs, 1,521 Supercenters, and 34 Neighborhood Markets, for a total of 4,414 stores.

Toward the end of 2002, Kmart's management announced that it was restating the company's financial statements for three prior fiscal years and for the first two quarters of 2002. Problems had been discovered as part of the company's review of its accounting practices. The adjustments were likely to reduce the company's net loss for the first two quarters of the year by less than $100 million. For fiscal years 1999–2001, it was likely to reduce total earnings during the period by nearly $100 million. (These adjustments are *not* reflected in case exhibits.) The adjustments derived from a software programming error in Kmart's accounts payable system, an understatement of historical accruals for certain leases with varying rent payments, and a related understatement of historical rent expenses.

**Exhibit 6
Financial
Performance:
Wal-Mart and
Kmart, 1990–2001
(Dollar amounts in
thousands)**

A. Kmart Financial Performance

Fiscal Year[1]	Sales	Assets	Net Income[2]	Stores[3]
2001	$ 36,151,000	$14,298,000	($2,418,000)	$2,114
2000	37,028,000	14,832,000	(244,000)	2,105
1999	35,925,000	15,104,000	403,000	2,171
1998	33,674,000	14,166,000	518,000	2,161
1997[3]	32,183,000	13,558,000	249,000	2,136
1996[3]	31,437,000	14,286,000	(220,000)	2,201
1995[3]	31,713,000	15,033,000	(571,000)	2,161
1994	34,025,000	17,029,000	296,000	2,481
1993	34,156,000	17,504,000	(974,000)	2,486
1992	37,724,000	18,931,000	941,000	2,435
1991	34,580,000	15,999,000	859,000	2,391
1990	$ 32,070,000	$13,899,000	$756,000	2,350

B. Wal-Mart Financial Performance

Fiscal Year[1]	Sales	Assets	Net Income	Stores[4]
2001	$217,799,000	$83,451,000	$6,671,000	$4,414
2000	191,329,000	78,130,000	6,295,000	4,189
1999	165,013,000	70,349,000	5,377,000	3,996
1998	137,634,000	49,996,000	4,430,000	3,999
1997	117,958,000	45,384,000	3,526,000	3,406
1996	104,859,000	39,604,000	3,056,000	3,054
1995	93,627,000	37,541,000	2,740,000	2,943
1994	82,494,000	32,819,000	2,681,000	2,684
1993	67,344,000	26,441,000	2,333,000	2,400
1992	55,484,000	20,565,000	1,995,000	2,136
1991	43,886,900	15,443,400	1,608,500	1,928
1990	$ 32,601,594	$11,388,915	$1,291,024	1,721

Notes:
1. The company's Fiscal Year is February through January.
2. Net income from discontinued operations.
3. Kmart, 2,114 discount stores (not including Supercenters).
4. Wal-Mart, all category of stores.

Source: Fortune *financial analysis and Wal-Mart annual reports.*

One financial analyst (Konicki—1/28/02—*Information Week.com*) cited specific facts and his perception of the issues facing Kmart:

Facts:

    a. The average customer spends 17 minutes in a Kmart store vs. 36 minutes in a Wal-Mart.

    b. Half the U.S. population has been inside a Kmart in the past three months.

    c. Someone from 45% of U.S. households was in a Kmart in the past week.

    d. Asians, blacks and Hispanics represent 31% of the population but 36% of Kmart traffic and 39% of Kmart sales.

Perception:

Formula: A discount store uses the lure of lower prices to sell huge volumes of the most popular items of general merchandise. Chains pull this off by wrangling volume discounts from suppliers, narrowing the selection of a product only to best sellers and operating on a skinnier profit margin. If the most popular brand won't supply products to a discount chain, the chain produces its own. The big discount chains are getting into the grocery business to increase customer frequency.

Recent Troubles: Kmart's bargain-basement image hit bottom when Dustin Hoffman's autistic character in the 1988 movie Rain Man learned how to say "Kmart sucks." That pop culture moment confirmed Kmart had become synonymous with cheapness, not value. An unwillingness to invest in technology made Kmart less competitive while its stores developed a reputation for listless clerks. Kmart gave up on its warehouse clubs and its venture in grocery-laden supercenters remains stuck in first gear.

Governance Issues: Regulators and the U.S. Attorney's Office are investigating the previous management group for forgiving tens of millions of dollars in loans to keep a dozen key executives who resigned anyway. Also probing accounting irregularities, including one that restated 2001 earnings because of $500-million accounting error that had artificially inflated results. Current CEO James Adamson, then an outside director, was head of the audit committee at the time.

Compared to Wal-Mart, Kmart's distribution and inventory system was inefficient and outdated. CEO Conaway tried to remedy this by unveiling an IT project based on Manhattan Associates' software, estimated at $600 million, to manage the flow of goods. In the process, he wrote off two distribution centers and IT assets, reportedly including some supply-chain and warehouse management software purchased the previous year, worth $130 million. A Kmart spokesperson stated that the software was so heavily modified that it cost too much to maintain. Due to problems with the system, inventory planners were unable to learn what was selling. Thus, many items were left on clearance racks and not enough of the items that customers wanted were available. Store clerks were forced to spend time dealing with paperwork in the back room instead of working with customers. The average store clerk only spent 22% of his/her time interacting with customers—leading customers to perceive Kmart as being less helpful and out-of-date. According to ex-CEO Charles Conaway, "That number should be 60% or 70%." In addition, Kmart was no longer able to effectively compete on price. A March 2001 survey by the *Minneapolis Star Tribune* of 21 identical items in Minneapolis discount stores found Kmart's total price to be $5.00 above Target's and $10.00 above Wal-Mart's.

References

Albright, Mark (December 1, 2002) "Kmart Bank on a Happy Holiday," *St. Petersburg Times,* pp. 1H, 11H.

Albright, Mark (January 23, 2002), "Kmart's Effort to Compete a Case of Too Little, Too Late," *St. Petersburg Times,* 1A.

Bussey, John (April 6, 1987), "Kmart Is Set To Sell Many of Its Roots to Rapid-American Corp's McCrory," *Wall Street Journal,* 24.

Carruth, Eleanore (July 1977), "Kmart Has To Open Some New Doors On The Future," *Fortune,* 143–150, 153–154.

Coleman, Calmetta (June 19, 2000), "BlueLight.com Aims to Coax Kmart Shoppers Online," *Wall Street Journal,* B4.

Coleman, Calmetta (July 27, 2000), "Kmart's New CEO Outlines Plans for Fast Changes," *Wall Street Journal,* B4.

Coleman, Calmetta (July 26, 2000), "Kmart Sees $740 Million Pretax Charge from Closing 72 Stores, Other Changes," *Wall Street Journal,* B10.

Coleman, Calmetta (June 1, 2000), "Kmart Selects CVS President to Be Its CEO," *Wall Street Journal,* June 1, 2000.

Cuneo, Alice (July 29, 2002), "Kmart Still Struggles to Find Its Way out of Darkness," *Advertising Age,* 13.

Dewar, Robert E. (July 2, 1975), "The Kresge Company and the Retail Revolution," *University of Michigan Business Review,* 2.

Dixon, Jennifer (March 20, 2002), "Martha Stewart Talks, Kmart Boss Listens," *Detroit Free Press,* E1.

Elmer, Vickie, and Joann Muller (March 22, 1995), "Retailer Needs Leader, Vision," *Detroit Free Press,* 1A, 9A.

Ewoldt, J. (March 1, 2001), "Discounter Encounter: Comparing Target, Wal-Mart, and Kmart," *Minneapolis Star Tribune.*

Grant, Lorrie (January 23, 2002), "Sticking by Kmart," *USA Today,* 5B.

Grant, Lorrie (January 25, 2002), "Kmart Food Supplier Resumes Shipments," *USA Today,* 7B.

Grant, Lorrie (March 12, 2002), "Kmart Cleans Its Executive House," *USA Today*, B1.

Grant, Lorrie (March 11, 2002), "Kmart Takes Aim at 284 Underperforming Stores," *USA Today*, 4B.

Guiles, Melinda G. (September 8, 1987), "Kmart, Bruno's Join to Develop 'Hypermarkets'," *Wall Street Journal*, 17.

Horovitz, Bruce (January 23, 2002), "With Image Crumbling, Kmart Files Chapter 11," *USA Today*, B1.

Ingrassia, Paul (October 6, 1987), "Attention Non-Kmart Shoppers: A Blue-Light Special Just for You," *Wall Street Journal*, 42.

"Kmart Adjustments," *Des Moines Register* (December 10, 2002), 3D.

Kmart Corporation, *Annual Report*, Troy, Michigan, 1999.

Kmart Corporation, *Annual Report*, Troy, Michigan, 2000.

Kmart Corporation, *Annual Report (10-K)*, Troy, Michigan, 2001.

Kmart Corporation, *Kmart Fact Book*, Troy, Michigan, 1997

"Kmart Board Weighs Bankruptcy-Court Filing" (January 22, 2002), *Wall Street Journal*, A3.

"Kmart Declares Bankruptcy," *St. Petersburg Times* (January 23, 2002), E1.

"Kmart Runs Out of Money Options" (February 22, 2002), *St. Petersburg Times*, 1A, 11A.

Konicki, S. (January 28, 2002), "Now in Bankruptcy, Kmart Struggled with Supply Chain," *Information Week.com*.

Kranhold, Kathryn (July 27, 2000), "Kmart Hopes to Steer Teens to Route 66," *Wall Street Journal*, B14.

Main, Jerry (September 21, 1981), "Kmart's Plan to Be Born Again," *Fortune*, 74–77, 84–85.

Merrick, Amy (January 23, 2002), "Kmart Lays Out Plans to Trim Its Size, Increase Efficiency in Bankruptcy Filing," *Wall Street Journal*, A3.

Merrick, Amy (February 6, 2002), "Kmart, Seeking Focus, Demotes Chief of Store Operations, Reorganizes Units," *Wall Street Journal*, B13.

Merrick, Amy (March 12, 2002) "Kmart Says CEO Conaway Resigned, Adds Post to Plate of Chairman Adamson," *Wall Street Journal*, A3.

Merrick, Amy (April 5, 2002) "Kmart Store Closures Will Include Many of Its New Ones," *Wall Street Journal*, B4.

Merrick, Amy (June 20, 2002) "Kmart, Turned Off by BlueLight.com, Renames Web Site," *Wall Street Journal*, B8.

Merrick, Amy (October 8, 2002), "Can Martha Deliver Merry?" *Wall Street Journal*, B1.

Merrick, Amy (October 15, 2002), "Turning Red Ink to Green," *Wall Street Journal*, B1.

Merrick, Amy (May 2, 2002), "Kmart Announces It May Restate Financial Results," *Wall Street Journal*, B2.

Muller, J. (September 4, 2002), "A Kmart Special: Better Service," *BusinessWeek Online*.

Rice, Faye (October 9, 1989), "Why Kmart Has Stalled," *Fortune*, 79.

Saporito, Bill (May 6, 1991), "Is Wal-Mart Unstoppable?," *Fortune*, 50–59.

Sellers, Patricia (February 4, 2002), "First It's (Not) a Good Thing," *Fortune*, 22–23.

Smith, Joel J. (June 11, 2002), "Kmart Widens Corruption Investigation," detnews.com.

Talaski, Karen (January 11, 2002), "Kmart Reorganizes as Troubles Mount," *The Detroit News*, 2A.

Talaski, Karen (August 11, 2000), "Kmart to Invest $2 Billion," *The Detroit News*, 1C.

Talaski, Karen (May 12, 2000), "Kmart Profits Plunge Sharply," *The Detroit News*, 1B.

Yue, Lorene (May 16, 2002), "Kmart Reports Its Biggest Loss," *Detroit Free Press*, 1E.

Wellman, Michael (August 6, 1984), Interview with Director of Planning and Research, Kmart Corporation.

Woodruff, David (January 22, 1990), "Will Kmart Ever Be a Silk Purse?" *BusinessWeek*, 46.

CASE 18

Wal-Mart Stores, Inc.:

On Becoming the World's Largest Company (2002)

James W. Camerius

REFLECTING ON THE EVENTS OF 2001, LEE SCOTT, PRESIDENT AND CEO OF WAL-MART Stores, Inc., was struck not only by how disappointing a year it was, but also how positively the company had responded to one of the most challenging times in its history. The year began after one of the worst holiday seasons (end-2000) in recent memory. Sluggish consumer spending, rising unemployment, the energy crisis, and the terrorist events of September 11, 2001, all had converged to make the year a very difficult time in retailing.

Scott was only the third CEO in the entire history of Wal-Mart when he was elected to the position in 2000. Its first CEO, Sam Walton, built the company from the ground up. During the 12 years that David Glass, the previous CEO, held the position, sales grew from $16 billion to $165 billion. Scott had been personally recruited by Glass 21 years before, from a Springdale, Arkansas, trucking company to come to Wal-Mart as the manager of the truck fleet. In his years at Wal-Mart, Glass had established himself as a leader, an innovator, and a team player. He had served as Chief Operating Officer (COO) and Vice Chairman of the company. He was aware that there were tremendous opportunities to serve new markets with the company's stores. His management mandate was to drive the company to a new level of success in domestic and international markets. Glass continued to be active in the firm as Chairman of the firm's executive committee.

Wal-Mart: A Maturing Organization

In 2002, Wal-Mart Stores, Inc., of Bentonville, Arkansas, operated mass merchandising retail stores under a variety of names and retail formats, including Wal-Mart discount department stores; Sam's Wholesale Clubs, wholesale/retail membership warehouses;

Neighborhood Markets, small grocery/drug store formats; and Wal-Mart Supercenters, large combination grocery and general merchandise stores in all 50 states. In the International Division, it operated its own stores in Canada, Mexico, Argentina, Brazil, Germany, South Korea, United Kingdom, and Puerto Rico, plus stores in China operated through joint ventures. It was not only the nation's largest discount department store chain but also had surpassed the retail division of Sears, Roebuck, and Co. in sales volume as the largest retail firm in the United States. It was also considered the largest retailer in the world, with sales of $217.8 billion in 2001. The McLane Company, Inc., a Wal-Mart sub-

Exhibit 1 Consolidated Income Statements: Wal-Mart Stores, Inc.[1]
(Dollar amounts in millions except per share data)

Fiscal Years Ending January 31[1]	2002	2001	2000
Revenues			
Net sales	$217,799	$191,329	$165,013
Other income, net	2,013	1,966	1,796
Total revenues	219,812	193,295	166,809
Costs and expenses			
Cost of sales	171,562	150,255	129,664
Operating, selling, and general and administrative expenses	36,173	31,550	27,040
Interest costs			
Debt	1,052	1,095	756
Capital leases	274	279	266
	209,061	183,179	157,726
Income before income taxes, minority interest, and cumulative effect of accounting change	10,751	10,116	9,083
Provision for income taxes			
Current	3,712	3,350	3,476
Deferred	185	342	(138)
	3,897	3,692	3,338
Income before minority interest and cumulative effect of accounting change	6,854	6,424	5,745
Minority interest	(183)	(129)	(170)
Income before cumulative effect of accounting change	6,671	6,295	5,575
Cumulative effect of accounting change, net tax benefit of $119	—	—	(198)
Net income	$ 6,671	$ 6,295	$ 5,377
Net income per common share			
Basic net income per common share			
Income before cumulative effect of accounting change	$ 1.49	$ 1.41	$ 1.25
Cumulative effect of accounting change, net of tax	—	—	(0.04)
Net income per common share	$ 1.49	$ 1.41	$ 1.21
Average number of common shares	4,465	4,465	4,451
Diluted net income per common share			
Income before cumulative effect of accounting change	$ 1.49	$ 1.40	$ 1.25
Cumulative effect of accounting change, net of tax	—	—	(0.04)
Net income per common share	$ 1.49	$ 1.40	$ 1.20
Average number of common shares (millions)	4,481	4,484	4,474

Note:
1. The company's fiscal year is February through January.

Source: Wal-Mart annual reports.

sidiary, sold a wide variety of groceries, nongrocery products, and institutional food services to a variety of retailers, including selected Wal-Marts, Sam's Clubs, and Supercenters. In 1999, *Discount Store News* honored Wal-Mart as "Retailer of the Century." In 2000, *Fortune* magazine named it as one of the "100 Best Places to Work." In 2001, it was ranked number three in *Fortune*'s annual list of "America's Most Admired Companies" and fifth on the list of *Fortune*'s "Global Most Admired Companies." Sales for the year ending January 31, 2002, were approximately $218 billion, making Wal-Mart Stores, Inc., the largest company in the world, as measured by annual revenue.

A financial summary of Wal-Mart Stores, Inc., for the fiscal years ended January 31, 2002, and January 31, 2001, is shown in **Exhibits 1** and **2**. An 11-year financial summary for the fiscal years ended January 31, 1992, to January 31, 2002, is shown in **Exhibit 3**.

The Sam Walton Spirit

Much of the success of Wal-Mart was attributed to the entrepreneurial spirit of its founder and Chairman of the Board, Samuel Moore Walton (1918–1992). Many considered him one of the most influential retailers of the century.

Sam Walton, or "Mr. Sam," as some referred to him, traced his down-to-earth, old-fashioned, home-spun, evangelical ways to growing up in rural Oklahoma, Missouri, and Arkansas. Although he appeared to be remarkably unconcerned about his roots, some suggested that it was his simple belief in hard work and ambition that had "unlocked countless doors and showered upon him, his customers, and his employees . . . the fruits of . . . years of labor in building [this] highly successful company."

"Our goal has always been in our business to be the very best," Sam Walton said in an interview, "and, along with that, we believe that in order to do that, you've got to make a good situation and put the interests of your associates first. If we really do that consistently, they in turn will cause . . . our business to be successful, which is what we've talked about and espoused and practiced." "The reason for our success," he said, "is our people and the way that they're treated and the way they feel about their company." Many have suggested it was this "people first" philosophy, that guided the company through the challenges and setbacks of its early years and allowed the company to maintain its consistent record of growth and expansion in later years.

A unique, enthusiastic, and positive individual, Sam Walton was "just your basic home-spun billionaire," a columnist once suggested. "Mr. Sam is a life-long small-town resident who didn't change much as he got richer than his neighbors," he noted. Walton had tremendous energy, enjoyed bird hunting with his dogs, and flew a corporate plane. When the company was much smaller, he could boast that he personally visited every Wal-Mart store at least once a year. A store visit usually included Walton leading Wal-Mart cheers that began, "Give me a W, give me an A . . . " To many employees, he had the air of a fiery Baptist preacher. Paul R. Carter, a Wal-Mart Executive Vice President, was quoted as saying, "Mr. Walton has a calling." He became the richest man in America and by 1991 had created a personal fortune for his family in excess of $21 billion. In 1999, despite a division of wealth, five family members were still ranked among the richest individuals in the United States.

In late 1989 Sam Walton was diagnosed as having multiple myeloma, or cancer of the bone marrow. He remained active in the firm as Chairman of the Board of Directors until his death in 1992. A son, S. Robson Walton, held the position of Chairman of the Board of Directors in 2002.

**Exhibit 2
Consolidated
Balance Sheets:
Wal-Mart Stores,
Inc. (Dollar
amounts in
millions)**

Fiscal Year Ending January 31[1]	2002	2001
Assets		
Current assets		
Cash and cash equivalents	$2,161	$2,054
Receivables	2,000	1,768
Inventories		
At replacement cost	22,749	21,644
Less LIFO reserve	135	202
Inventories at LIFO cost	22,614	21,442
Prepaid expenses and other	1,471	1,291
Total current assets	28,246	26,555
Property, plant, and equipment, at cost		
Land	10,241	9,433
Building and improvements	28,527	24,537
Fixtures and equipment	14,135	12,964
Transportation equipment	1,089	879
	53,992	47,813
Less accumulated depreciation	11,436	10,196
Net property, plant, and equipment	42,556	37,617
Property under capital lease		
Property under capital lease	4,626	4,620
Less accumulated amortization	1,432	1,303
Net property under capital leases	3,194	3,317
Other assets and deferred charges		
Net goodwill and other acquired intangible assets	8,595	9,059
Other assets and deferred charges	860	1,582
Total assets	$83,451	$78,130
Liabilities and shareholders' equity		
Current Liabilities		
Commercial paper	$743	$2,286
Accounts payable	15,617	15,092
Accrued liabilities	7,174	6,355
Accrued income taxes	1,343	841
Long-term debt due within 1 year	2,257	4,234
Obligations under capital leases due within 1 year	148	141
Total current liabilities	27,282	28,949
Long-term debt	15,687	12,501
Long-term obligations under capital leases	3,045	3,154
Deferred income taxes and other	1,128	1,043
Minority interest	1,207	1,140
Shareholders' equity		
Preferred stock ($0.10 par value; 100 shares authorized, none issued)		
Common stock ($0.10 par value; 11,000 shares authorized, 4,453 and 4,470 issued and outstanding in 2002 and 2003, respectively)	445	447
Capital in excess of par value	1,484	1,411
Retained earnings	34,441	30,169
Other accumulated comprehensive income	(1,268)	(684)
Total shareholders' equity	35,102	31,343
Total liabilities and shareholders' equity	$83,451	$78,130

Note:
1. The company's fiscal year is February through January.

Exhibit 3 Financial Summary: Wal-Mart Stores, Inc.[1] (Dollar amounts in millions except per share data)

11-Year Financial Summary

Fiscal Year Ending January 31	2002	2001	2000
Net sales	$217,799	$191,329	$165,013
Net sales increase	14%	16%	20%
Domestic comparative store sales increase	6%	5%	8%
Other income, net	2,013	1,966	1,796
Cost of sales	171,562	150,255	129,664
Operating, selling, and general and administrative expenses	36,173	31,550	27,040
Interest costs			
Debt	1,052	1,095	756
Capital leases	274	279	266
Provision for income taxes	3,897	3,692	3,338
Minority interest and equity in unconsolidated subsidiaries	(183)	(129)	(170)
Cumulative effect of accounting change, net of tax	—	—	(198)
Net income	6,671	6,295	5,377
Per share of common stock			
Basic net income	1.49	1.41	1.21
Diluted net income	1.49	1.40	1.20
Dividends	0.28	0.24	0.20
Financial position			
Current assets	$ 28,246	$ 26,555	$ 24,356
Inventories at replacement cost	22,749	21,644	20,171
Less LIFO reserve	135	202	378
Inventories at LIFO cost	22,614	21,442	19,793
Net property, plant, and equipment and capital leases	45,750	40,934	35,969
Total assets	83,451	78,130	70,349
Current liabilities	27,282	28,949	25,803
Long-term debt	15,687	12,501	13,672
Long-term obligations under capital leases	3,045	3,154	3,002
Shareholders' equity	35,102	31,343	25,834
Financial ratios			
Current ratio	1.0	0.9	0.9
Inventories/working capital	23.5	(9.0)	(13.7)
Return on assets	8.5%	8.7%	9.5%
Return on shareholders' equity	20.1%	22.0%	22.9%
Other year-end data			
Number of U.S. Wal-Mart stores	1,647	1,736	1,801
Number of U.S. Supercenters	1,066	888	721
Number of U.S. Sam's Clubs	500	475	463
Number of U.S. Neighborhood Markets	31	19	7
International units	1,170	1,071	1,004
Number of associates	1,383,000	1,244,000	1,140,000
Number of shareholders of record (as of March 31)	324,000	317,000	307,000

(continued)

Exhibit 3 *(continued)*

1999	1998	1997	1996	1995	1994	1993	1992
$137,634	$117,958	$104,859	$93,627	$82,494	$67,344	$55,484	$43,887
17%	12%	12%	13%	22%	21%	26%	35%
9%	6%	5%	4%	7%	6%	11%	10%
1,574	1,341	1,319	1,146	914	645	497	404
108,725	93,438	83,510	74,505	65,586	53,444	44,175	34,786
22,363	19,358	16,946	15,021	12,858	10,333	8,321	6,684
529	555	629	692	520	331	143	113
268	229	216	196	186	186	180	153
2,740	2,115	1,794	1,606	1,581	1,358	1,171	945
(153)	(78)	(27)	(13)	4	(4)	4	(1)
—	—	—	—	—	—	—	—
4,430	3,526	3,056	2,740	2,681	2,333	1,995	1,609
0.99	0.78	0.67	0.60	0.59	0.51	0.44	0.35
0.99	0.78	0.67	0.60	0.59	0.51	0.44	0.35
0.16	0.14	0.11	0.10	0.09	0.07	0.05	0.04
$ 21,132	$ 19,352	$ 17,993	$17,331	$15,338	$12,114	$10,198	$ 8,575
17,549	16,845	16,193	16,300	14,415	11,483	9,780	7,857
473	348	296	311	351	469	512	473
17,076	16,497	15,897	15,989	14,064	11,014	9,268	7,384
25,973	23,606	20,324	18,894	15,874	13,176	9,793	6,434
49,996	45,384	39,604	37,541	32,819	26,441	20,565	15,443
16,762	14,460	10,957	11,454	9,973	7,406	6,754	5,004
6,908	7,191	7,709	8,508	7,871	6,156	3,073	1,722
2,699	2,483	2,307	2,092	1,838	1,804	1,772	1,556
21,112	18,503	17,143	14,756	12,726	10,753	8,759	6,990
1.3	1.3	1.6	1.5	1.5	1.6	1.5	1.7
3.9	3.4	2.3	2.7	2.6	2.3	2.7	2.1
9.6%	8.5%	7.9%	7.8%	9.0%	9.9%	11.1%	12.0%
22.4%	19.8%	19.2%	19.9%	22.8%	23.9%	25.3%	26.0%
1,869	1,921	1,960	1,995	1,985	1,950	1,848	1,714
564	441	344	239	147	72	34	10
451	443	436	433	426	417	256	208
4	—	—	—	—	—	—	—
715	601	314	276	226	24	10	—
901,000	825,000	728,000	675,000	622,000	528,000	434,000	371,000
261,000	246,000	257,000	244,000	259,000	258,000	181,000	150,000

Note:
1. Notes were deleted.

Source: Wal-Mart annual reports.

Corporate Governance

Exhibit 4 lists the 16 members of Wal-Mart's board of directors. Four are internal members: (1) S. Robson Walton, Chairman, (2) David D. Glass, Chairman, Executive Committee of the Board, (3) Thomas M. Coughlin, Executive Vice President and President & CEO of Wal-Mart Store Division, and (4) H. Lee Scott, President and CEO.

Exhibit 4
Board of Directors and Executive Officers: Wal-Mart Stores, Inc., January 31, 2002

Directors

James W. Breyer, Managing Partner
Accel Partners
Director since 2001

John T. Chambers, CEO
Cisco Systems
Director since 2000

Thomas M. Coughlin, CEO
Wal-Mart Stores, Inc.
Director since 2001

Stephen Friedman, Past Chair
Goldman Sachs & Company
Director since 1996

Stanley C. Gault, Past CEO
Goodyear Tire & Rubber Co.
Director since 1996

David D. Glass, Past CEO
Wal-Mart Stores, Inc.
Director since 1977

Roland Hernandez, Past CEO
Telemundo Group, Inc.
Director since 1998

Dawn G. Lepore, Vice Chair
Charles Schwab Corporation
Director since 2001

J. Paul Reason, CEO
Metro Machine Corporation
Director since 2001

Elizabeth A. Sanders, Past VP
Nordstrom, Inc.
Director since 1992

H. Lee Scott, President and COO
Wal-Mart Stores, Inc.
Director since 1999

Jack C. Shewmaker, Past Executive
Wal-Mart Stores, Inc.
Director since 1977

Donald G. Soderquist, Past COO
Wal-Mart Stores, Inc.
Director since 1980

Jose Villarreal, Law Partner
Akin, Gump, Struass, Hauer and Fied
Director since 1998

John T. Walton, Chairman[1]
True North Partners
Director since 1992

S. Robson Walton, Chairman[1]
Wal-Mart Stores, Inc.
Director since 1978

Officers

S. Robson Walton
Chairman of the Board

H. Lee Scott
President and CEO

David D. Glass
Chairman, Executive
Committee of the Board

Thomas M. Coughlin
Executive Vice President;
President and CEO,
Wal-Mart Stores Division

Michael Duke
Executive Vice President, Administration

Thomas Grimm
Executive Vice President;
President and CEO,
SAM'S Club Division

Thomas Hyde
Executive Vice President,
Legal and Corporate Affairs

John B. Menzer
Executive Vice President;
President and CEO,
International Division

Coleman Peterson
Executive Vice President,
People Division

Thomas M. Schoewe
Executive Vice President and CFO

Note:
1. Sons of founder, Sam Walton.

Source: Wal-Mart Stores, Inc., 2002 Annual Report *(January 31, 2002).*

The Marketing Concept

Genesis of an Idea

Sam Walton started his retail career in 1940 as a management trainee with the JCPenney Co. in Des Moines, Iowa. He was impressed with the Penney method of doing business and later modeled the Wal-Mart chain on "The Penney Idea," as reviewed in **Exhibit 5**. The JCPenney Company found strength in calling employees "associates" rather than clerks. Penney's, founded in Kemerer, Wyoming, in 1902, located stores on the main streets of small towns and cities throughout the United States.

Following service in the U.S. Army during World War II, Sam Walton acquired a Ben Franklin variety store franchise in Newport, Arkansas. He operated this store successfully with his brother, James L. "Bud" Walton (1921–1995), until losing the lease in 1950.

The early retail stores owned by Sam Walton in Newport and Bentonville, Arkansas, and later in other small towns in adjoining southern states, were variety store operations. They were relatively small operations of 6,000 square feet, were located on "main streets," and displayed merchandise on plain wooden tables and counters. Operated under the Ben Franklin name and supplied by Butler Brothers of Chicago and St. Louis, they were characterized by a limited price line, low gross margins, high merchandise turnover, and concentration on return on investment. The firm, operating under the Walton 5 & 10 name with 15 stores, was the largest Ben Franklin franchisee in the country in 1962. The variety stores were phased out by 1976 to allow the company to concentrate on the growth of Wal-Mart discount department stores.

Foundations of Growth

The original Wal-Mart discount concept was not a unique idea. Sam Walton became convinced in the late 1950s that discounting would transform retailing. He traveled extensively in New England, the cradle of "off-pricing." After he had visited just about every discounter in the United States, he tried to interest Butler Brothers executives in the discount store concept. The first Kmart, as a "conveniently located one-stop shopping unit where customers could buy a wide variety of quality merchandise at discount prices" had just opened in Garden City, Michigan. Walton's theory was to operate a similar discount store in a small community and in that setting, he would offer name brand merchandise at low prices and would add friendly service. Butler Brothers executives rejected the idea. Undeterred, Walton opened the first "Wal-Mart Discount City" in late 1962 in Rogers, Arkansas.

Wal-Mart stores sold nationally advertised, well-known-brand merchandise at low prices in austere surroundings. As corporate policy, Wal-Mart cheerfully gave refunds, credits, and

Exhibit 5
The Penney Idea
(1913)

1. To serve the public, as nearly as we can, to its complete satisfaction.
2. To expect for the service we render a fair remuneration and not all the profit the traffic will bear.
3. To do all in our power to pack the customer's dollar full of value, quality, and satisfaction.
4. To continue to train ourselves and our associates so that the service we give will be more and more intelligently performed.
5. To improve constantly the human factor in our business.
6. To reward men and women in our organization through participation in what the business produces.
7. To test our every policy, method, and act in this way: "Does it square with what is right and just?"

Source: V. H. Trimble, Sam Walton: The Inside Story of America's Richest Man *(New York: Dutton, 1990).*

rain checks. Management conceived the firm as a "discount department store chain offering a wide variety of general merchandise to the customer." Early emphasis was placed upon opportunistic purchases of merchandise from whatever sources were available. Heavy emphasis was placed upon health and beauty aids in the product line and "stacking it high" in a manner of merchandise presentation. By the end of 1979, there were 276 Wal-Mart stores located in 11 states.

The firm developed an aggressive expansion strategy. New stores were located primarily in communities of 5,000 to 25,000 in population. The stores' sizes ranged from 30,000 to 60,000 square feet, with 45,000 being the average. The firm also expanded by locating stores in contiguous geographic areas. When its discount operations came to dominate a market area, it moved to an adjoining area. While other retailers built warehouses to serve existing outlets, Wal-Mart built the distribution center first and then spotted stores all around it, pooling advertising and distribution overhead. Most stores were less than a six-hour drive from one of the company's warehouses. The first major distribution center, a 390,000-square-foot facility, opened in Searcy, Arkansas, outside Bentonville in 1978.

Becoming National

At the beginning of 1991, the firm had 1,573 Wal-Mart stores in 35 states, with expansion planned for adjacent states. Wal-Mart had become the largest retailer and the largest discount department store in the United States.

As a national discount department store chain, Wal-Mart Stores, Inc., offered a wide variety of general merchandise to the customer. The stores were designed to offer one-stop shopping with 40 departments that included family apparel, health and beauty aids, household needs, electronics, toys, fabric and crafts, automotive supplies, lawn and patio, jewelry, and shoes. A pharmacy, automotive supply and service center, garden center, or snack bar were also operated at certain locations. The firm operated its stores with "everyday low prices" as opposed to putting heavy emphasis on special promotions, that called for multiple newspaper advertising circulars. Stores were expected to "provide the customer with a clean, pleasant, and friendly shopping experience."

Although Wal-Mart carried much the same merchandise, offered similar prices, and operated stores that looked much like the competition, there were many differences. In the typical Wal-Mart store, employees wore blue vests to identify themselves, aisles were wide, apparel departments were carpeted in warm colors, store employees followed customers to their cars to pick up their shopping carts, and the customer was welcomed at the door by a "people greeter" who gave directions and struck up conversation. In some cases, merchandise was bagged in brown paper sacks rather than plastic bags because customers seemed to prefer them. The "Wal-Mart" and the slogan "Always Low Prices" on the front of the store served to identify the firm. Yellow smiley faces were used on in-store displays along with the slogan "Watch for Falling Prices." In consumer studies it was determined that the chain was particularly adept at striking the delicate balance needed to convince customers its prices were low without making people feel that its stores were too cheap. In many ways, competitors like Kmart sought to emulate Wal-Mart by introducing people greeters, by upgrading interiors, by developing new logos and signage, and by introducing new inventory response systems.

A "satisfaction guaranteed" refund and exchange policy was introduced to allow customers to be confident of Wal-Mart's merchandise and quality. Technological advancements like scanner cash registers, handheld computers for the ordering of merchandise, and computer linkages of stores with the general office and distribution centers improved communications and merchandise replenishment. Each store was encouraged to initiate programs that would make it an integral part of the community in which it operated. Associates were encouraged to "maintain the highest standards of honesty, morality, and business ethics" in dealing with the public.

The External Environment

In 2002, Wal-Mart management was aware that its business operations on a national and international level were subject to a number of factors outside of its control. Any one, or a combination, of these factors could materially affect the financial performance of the firm. These factors included the costs of goods, the cost of electricity and other energy require- ments, competitive pressures, inflation, consumer debt levels, interest rate levels, and unem- ployment levels. They also included currency exchange fluctuations, trade restrictions, changes in tariff and freight rates, and other capital market and economic conditions.

Industry analysts labeled the 1980s and the 1990s as eras of economic uncertainty for retailers. Although the United States had experienced one of the longest periods of economic expansion in its history during this period, increased competitive pressures, sluggish con- sumer spending, the energy crisis, lack of worldwide economic growth, and the terrorist events of September 11, 2001, all converged to create a very challenging environment for all retailers at the beginning of the new century.

Many retail enterprises confronted heavy competitive pressure by restructuring. Sears was one example. Sears, Roebuck and Company, based in Chicago, became a more focused retailer by divesting itself of Allstate Insurance Company and its real estate subsidiaries. In 1993, the company announced it would close 118 unprofitable stores and discontinue the unprofitable Sears general merchandise catalog. It eliminated 50,000 jobs and began a $4 bil- lion, five-year remodeling plan for its remaining multiline department stores. After unsuc- cessfully experimenting with an "everyday low-price" strategy, management chose to realign its merchandise strategy to meet the needs of middle-market customers, who were primarily women, by focusing on product lines in apparel, home, and automotive. The new focus on apparel was supported with the advertising campaign "The Softer Side of Sears." A later com- panywide campaign broadened the appeal: "The many sides of Sears fit the many sides of your life." Sears completed its return to its retailing roots by selling off its ownership in Dean Witter Financial Services, Discover Card, Coldwell Banker Real Estate, and Sears mortgage banking operations. In 1999, Sears refocused its marketing strategy with a new program that was designed to communicate a stronger whole-house and event message. A new advertising campaign introduced the slogan "The good life at a great price. Guaranteed." In 2000, a new store format was introduced that concentrated on five focal areas: appliances, home fashions, tools, kids', and electronics. Other departments, including men's and women's apparel, assumed a support role in these stores. In 2001, Sears developed another plan to reposition and restructure its core business: the full-line stores. Alan J. Lacy, Chairman and CEO, announced that this strategy would position Sears in the retail marketplace as "not a depart- ment store, not a discount store, but a broad-line retailer with outstanding credit and service capabilities."

The discount department store industry by the late 1990s had changed in a number of ways and was thought by many analysts to have reached maturity. Several formerly success- ful firms like E.J. Korvette, W.T. Grant, Atlantic Mills, Arlans, Federals, Zayre, Heck's, and Ames had declared bankruptcy and as a result either liquidated or reorganized. Venture announced liquidation in early 1998. Firms like Target and Shopko began carrying more fash- ionable merchandise in more attractive facilities and shifted their emphasis to more national markets. Specialty retailers, such as Toys 'R' Us, Pier 1 Imports, and Oshman's had matured and were no longer making big inroads in toys, home furnishing, and sporting goods. The "superstores" of drug and food chains were rapidly discounting increasing amounts of general merchandise. Some firms like May Department Stores Company with Caldor and Venture and Woolworth Corporation with Woolco had withdrawn from the field by either selling their discount divisions or closing them down entirely. Woolworth's remaining 122 Woolco stores in Canada were sold to Wal-Mart in 1994. All remaining Woolworth variety stores in the United States were closed in 1997.

Several new retail formats had emerged in the marketplace to challenge the traditional discount department store format. The superstore, a 100,000- to 300,000-square-foot operation, combined a large supermarket with a discount general-merchandise store. Originally a European retailing concept, these outlets where known as "malls without walls." Kmart's Super Kmart, Target's SuperTarget, and Wal-Mart's Supercenter stores were examples of this trend toward large operations. Warehouse retailing, which involved some combination of warehouse and showroom facilities, used warehouse principles to reduce operating expenses and thereby offer discount prices as a primary customer appeal. Home Depot combined the traditional hardware store and lumberyard with a self-service home improvement center to become the largest home center operator in the nation.

Some retailers responded to changes in the marketplace by selling goods at price levels 20%–60% below regular retail prices. These off-price operations appeared as two general types: (1) factory outlet stores, like Burlington Coat Factory Warehouse, Bass Shoes, and Manhattan's Brand Name Fashion Outlet, and (2) independents, like Loehmann's, T.J. Maxx, Marshall's, and Clothestime, which bought seconds, overages, closeouts, or leftover goods from manufacturers and other retailers. Other retailers chose to dominate a product classification. Some super specialists, like Sock Appeal, Little Piggie, Ltd., and Sock Market, offered a single narrowly defined classification of merchandise with an extensive assortment of brands, colors, and sizes. Others, as niche specialists, like Kids Foot Locker and Champs Sports, a division of Foot Locker, Inc. (formerly Woolworth Corporation), targeted an identified market with carefully selected merchandise and appropriately designed stores.

Some retailers, like Silk Greenhouse (silk plants and flowers), Office Club (office supplies and equipment), and Toys 'R' Us (toys), were called "category killers" because they had achieved merchandise dominance in their respective product categories. Stores like The Limited, Limited Express, Victoria's Secret, and Banana Republic became mini-department specialists by showcasing new lines and accessories alongside traditional merchandise lines.

Kohl's Corporation, a relatively new firm based in Menominee Falls, Wisconsin, operated 420 family-focused, value-oriented department stores in 32 states as of April 2002. The company's stores offered moderately priced national brand-name apparel, shoes, accessories, and home products targeted to middle-income consumers in convenient neighborhood locations. During the period 1992–2001, Kohl's operation grew from 76 stores to 382 stores; its net sales increased nearly seven-fold, from $1.1 billion in 1992 to $7.5 billion in 2001.

Kmart Corporation, headquartered in Troy, Michigan, had been in 1990 the industry's third largest retailer and second largest discount department store chain in the United States. By 2001, Kmart operated 2,114 stores and had sales of $36,151 million but had fallen to fourth largest retailer and third largest discounter. (See **Exhibit 6**.) The firm was perceived by many industry analysts and consumers in several independent studies as a laggard. In the same studies, Wal-Mart was perceived as the industry leader, even though according to the *Wall Street Journal*: "They carry much the same merchandise, offer prices that are pennies apart and operate stores that look almost exactly alike." "Even their names are similar," noted the newspaper. The original Kmart concept of a "conveniently located, one-stop shopping unit where customers could buy a wide variety of quality merchandise at discount prices," had lost its competitive edge in a changing market. As one analyst noted in an industry newsletter: "They had done so well for the past 20 years without paying attention to market changes, now

**Exhibit 6
An Industry
Comparative
Analysis, 2001
(Dollar amounts in
millions, except
per share data)**

	Wal-Mart	Sears	Kmart	Target	Kohl's
Sales	$217,799	$41,078	$36,151	$39,888	$7,489
Net income	$ 6,671	$ 735	$(2,418)	$ 1,368	$ 496
Sales/sq. ft	$ 455	$ 319	$ (235)	$ 247	$ 262
Profit margin	3.1%	1.78%	N/A	3.4%	6.6%
% sales change	14.0%	.99%	(0.1)%	8.0%	22.0%

Number of stores:
Wal-Mart United States
   Discount stores—1,647
   Sam's Clubs—500
   Supercenters—1,066
   Neighborhood Markets—31
Wal-Mart International
   Discount stores—648
   Sam's Clubs—64
   Supercenters—455
   Neighborhood Markets—3
Sears, Roebuck and Company (all divisions)
   Sears Merchandise Group
      Full-line department stores—867
      Hardware stores—248
      Sears dealer stores—793
      Home supply stores—13
      NTB (National Tire & Battery) stores—223
      Outlet stores—35
Kmart Corporation
   Kmart discount stores—2,114
   Kmart Supercenters—105
Target Corporation
   Target—1,053
   Mervyn's—264
   Marshall Field's department stores—64
Kohl's Corporation
   Kohl's department stores—382

Source: Corporate annual reports.

they have to." Kmart acquired a new President and CEO in 2000. The firm filed for bankruptcy under Chapter 11 of the federal bankruptcy laws on January 22, 2002, but continued to operate as an ongoing business while reorganizing.

Wal-Mart and Kmart sales over the period 1990–2001 are reviewed in **Exhibit 7**.

Some retailers, like Kmart, had initially focused on appealing to professional, middle-class consumers who lived in suburban areas and who were likely to be price sensitive. Other firms, like Target, which had adopted the discount concept early, attempted to go generally after an upscale consumer. Some firms, such as Fleet Farm and Pamida, served the rural consumer, while firms like Value City and Ames Department Stores chose to serve the urban consumer.

In rural communities Wal-Mart success often came at the expense of established local merchants and units of regional discount store chains. Hardware stores, family department stores, building supply outlets, and stores featuring fabrics, sporting goods, and shoes were among the first to either close or relocate elsewhere. Regional discount retailers in the Sunbelt

Exhibit 7
Competitive Sales
and Store
Comparison,
1990–2001
(Dollar amounts in
thousands)

Fiscal Year[1]	Kmart			Wal-Mart		
	Sales	Net Income[2]	Stores[3]	Sales	Net Income	Stores[4]
2001	$36,151,000	($2,418,000)	2,114	$217,799,000	$6,671,000	4,414
2000	37,028,000	(244,000)	2,105	191,329,000	6,295,000	4,189
1999	35,925,000	403,000	2,171	165,013,000	5,377,000	3,996
1998	33,674,000	518,000	2,161	137,634,000	4,430,000	3,999
1997	32,183,000	249,000	2,136	117,958,000	3,526,000	3,406
1996	31,437,000	(220,000)	2,261	104,859,000	3,056,000	3,054
1995	31,713,000	(521,000)	2,161	93,627,000	2,740,000	2,943
1994	34,025,000	296,000	2,481	82,494,000	2,681,000	2,684
1993	34,156,000	(974,000)	2,486	67,344,000	2,333,000	2,400
1992	37,724,000	941,000	2,435	55,484,000	1,995,000	2,136
1991	34,580,000	859,000	2,391	43,886,900	1,608,000	1,928
1990	32,070,000	756,000	2,350	32,601,594	1,291,000	1,721

Notes:
1. Fiscal year is February through January.
2. Net income from discontinued operations.
3. Number of general merchandise stores (excludes Supercenters).
4. Total Wal-Mart Stores.

Source: Corporate annual reports.

states, like Roses, Howard's, T.G.& Y., and Duckwall-ALCO, which had once enjoyed solid sales and earnings, were forced to reposition themselves by renovating stores, opening bigger and more modern units, and re-merchandising. In many cases, stores like Coast-to-Coast and Ben Franklin closed upon a Wal-Mart announcement that it was planning to build in a specific community. "Just the word that Wal-Mart was coming made some stores close up," indicated one local newspaper editor. Ames Department Stores, Inc., which sought bankruptcy protection in 2001, announced in the summer of 2002 that it would close all 237 of its stores and liquidate inventory.

Domestic Corporate Strategies and Programs

The corporate and marketing strategies that emerged at Wal-Mart were based upon a set of two main goals that had guided the firm through its growth years. In the first goal the customer was featured: "Customers would be provided what they want, when they want it, all at a value." In the second objective team spirit was emphasized: "treating each other as we would hope to be treated, acknowledging our total dependency on our Associate-partners to sustain our success." The approach included aggressive plans for new store openings; expansion to additional states; upgrading, relocation, refurbishing, and remodeling of existing stores; and opening of new distribution centers. For Wal-Mart management, the 1990s were considered an era in which the firm grew to become a truly nationwide retailer that operated in all 50 states. At the beginning of 2000, Wal-Mart management predicted that over the next five years, 60%–70% of sales and earnings growth would come from domestic markets with Wal-Mart stores and Supercenters and another 10%–15% from Sam's Club and McLane. The remaining 20% of the growth would come from planned growth in international markets. As Glass once noted, "We'll be fine as long as we never lose our responsiveness to the customer."

During the 1980s, Wal-Mart developed a number of new retail formats. The first Sam's Club opened in Oklahoma City, Oklahoma, in 1983. The wholesale club was an idea that had been developed by other firms earlier but that found its greatest success and growth in acceptability at Wal-Mart. Sam's Clubs featured a vast array of product categories with limited selection of brand and model; cash-and-carry business with limited hours; large (100,000-square-foot), bare-bones facilities; rock-bottom wholesale prices; and minimal promotion. The limited membership plan permitted wholesale members who bought membership and others who usually paid a percentage above the ticket price of the merchandise. A revision in merchandising strategy resulted in fewer items in the inventory mix, with more emphasis on lower prices. A later acquisition of 100 PACE warehouse clubs, which were converted into Sam's Clubs, increased that division's units by more than one-third. At the beginning of 2002, there were 500 Sam's Clubs in operation in the United States and 64 in other countries. A new Sam's Club format was introduced with the opening of a 154,000-square-foot store in 2001 in East Plano, Texas. The store featured an expanded product line with emphasis on fresh food, an open layout, a café, and an Internet kiosk where customers were invited to shop at the *www.sams.com* Web site. A new Sam's Club slogan, "It's a Big Deal!" referred to the size of the facility and the features of the prototype store.

Wal-Mart Supercenters were large combination stores. They were first opened in 1988 as Hypermarket*USA, a 222,000-square-foot superstore that combined a full general merchandise discount store with a large full-line grocery supermarket, a food court of restaurants, and other service businesses, such as banks or videotape rental stores. A scaled-down version of Hypermarket*USA was called Wal-Mart Supercenter, and was similar in merchandise offerings, but with about 180,000 to 200,000 square feet of space. The company proceeded slowly with these plans and later suspended its plans for building any more hypermarkets in favor of the Supercenter concept. At the beginning of 2002, Wal-Mart operated 1,066 Supercenters.

Wal-Mart also tested a new concept called the Neighborhood Market in a number of locations in Arkansas. Identified by the company as "small-marts," these green-and-white stores were stocked with fresh fruits and vegetables, a drive-up pharmacy, a 24-hour photo shop, and a selection of classic Wal-Mart hard goods. Management elected to move slowly on this concept, planning to open no more than 10 a year. The goal was to ring the Superstores with these smaller stores to attract customers who were in hurry and wanted only a few items. At the end of 2001, the firm operated 31 Neighborhood Markets.

The McLane Company, Inc., a provider of retail and grocery distribution services for retail stores, was acquired by Wal-Mart in 1991. It was not considered a major segment of the total Wal-Mart operation.

Several programs were launched in Wal-Mart stores to highlight popular social causes. The "Buy American" program was a Wal-Mart retail program initiated in 1985. The theme was "Bring It Home to the USA," and its purpose was to communicate Wal-Mart's support for American manufacturing. In the program, the firm directed substantial influence to encourage manufacturers to produce goods in the United States rather than import them from other countries. Vendors were attracted into the program by encouraging manufacturers to initiate the process by contacting the company directly with proposals to sell goods that were made in the United States. Buyers also targeted specific import items in their assortments on a state-by-state basis to encourage domestic manufacturing. According to Haim Dabah, president of Gitano Group, Inc., a maker of fashion discount clothing that imported 95% of its clothing and now makes about 20% of its products in the United States: "Wal-Mart let it be known loud and clear that if you're going to grow with them, you sure better have some products made in the U.S.A." Farris Fashion, Inc. (flannel shirts), Roadmaster Corporation (exercise bicycles), Flanders Industries, Inc. (lawn chairs), and Magic Chef (microwave ovens) were examples of vendors that chose to participate in the program.

From the Wal-Mart standpoint, the "Buy American" program centered around value—producing and selling quality merchandise at a competitive price. The promotion included television advertisements featuring factory workers, a soaring American eagle, and the slogan "We buy American whenever we can, so you can too." Prominent in-store signage and store circulars were also included. One store poster read: "Success Stories—These items, formerly imported, are now being purchased by Wal-Mart in the U.S.A."

Wal-Mart was one of the first retailers to embrace the concept of "green" marketing. The program offered shoppers the option of purchasing products that are better for the environment in three respects: manufacturing, use, and disposal. It was introduced through full-page advertisements in the *Wall Street Journal* and *USA Today*. In-store signage identified those products that were environmentally safe. As Wal-Mart executives saw it, "customers are concerned about the quality of land, air, and water, and would like the opportunity to do something positive." To initiate the program, 7,000 vendors were notified that Wal-Mart had a corporate concern for the environment and asked for their support in a variety of ways. Wal-Mart television advertising showed children on swings, fields of grain blowing in the wind, and roses. Green and white store signs, printed on recycled paper, marked products or packaging that had been developed or redesigned to be more environmentally sound.

The Wal-Mart private brand program began with the "Ol' Roy" brand, the private-label dog food named for Sam Walton's favorite hunting companion. Introduced to Wal-Mart stores in 1982 as a low-price alterative to national brands, Ol' Roy became the biggest seller of all dog-food brands in the United States. "We are a [national] brand-oriented company first," noted Bob Connolly, Executive Vice President of Merchandising of Wal-Mart. "But we also use private label to fill value or pricing voids that, for whatever reason, the brands left behind." Wal-Mart's private-label program included thousands of products that had brand names, such as Sam's Choice, Great Value, Equate, and Spring Valley.

With almost $40 billion in "soft good" sales in 2001, Wal-Mart was the largest clothing seller in the world. Although most of the sales of its clothing business were in basics such as socks, underwear, t-shirts, and blue jeans, the firm developed a 100-member development team to begin to focus its clothing lines on fashion and style in all sizes. Claire Watts was hired from Limited, Inc., to become the first Director of Product Development. The company also made a significant investment in technology so that all the factors of the development process, from design to production, were coordinated online among Wal-Mart, its suppliers, and factories. Rather than wait for suppliers to bring products to Wal-Mart, merchandise teams traveled to Europe four times a year to visit trendy boutiques and fashion shows and bring back racks of clothes to be evaluated at corporate headquarters on the basis of quality, fashion, and style. In 2002, Wal-Mart introduced a contemporary brand nationwide called George. George, a stylish line of clothing for women and men, had been sold exclusively for 10 years in England's ASDA supermarkets, which Wal-Mart acquired in 1999.

In 2000, according to DSR Marketing Systems, Wal-Mart became the largest retailer of groceries in the United States, surpassing traditional grocery retailers such as Cincinnati, Ohio–based Kroger, Boise, Idaho–based Albertsons, and Pleasanton, California–based Safeway. Wal-Mart's 2001 discount store grocery sales, which included candy, paper towels, dog food, and tobacco, were estimated at $30.6 billion and amounted to 22% of overall store sales. Food sales, in 2001, at Sam's Club were $8.8 billion or 30% of sales.

Wal-Mart had become the channel commander in the distribution of many brand name items. As the nation's largest retailer and in many geographic areas the dominant distributor, it exerted considerable influence in negotiation for the best price, delivery terms, promotion allowances, and continuity of supply. Many of these benefits could be passed on to consumers in the form of quality name brand items available at lower-than-competitive prices. As a matter of corporate policy, management often insisted on doing business only with producers' top sales executives rather than going through a manufacturer's representative. Wal-Mart had been accused of threatening to buy from other producers if firms refused to sell directly to it. In the ensuing power struggle, Wal-Mart executives refused to talk about the controversial policy or admit that it existed. As a representative of an industry association representing a group of sales agencies representatives suggested, "In the Southwest, Wal-Mart's the only show in town." An industry analyst added, "They're extremely aggressive. Their approach has always been to give the customer the benefit of a corporate saving. That builds up customer loyalty and market share."

Another key factor in the mix was an inventory control system that was recognized as the most sophisticated in retailing. A high-speed computer system linked virtually all the stores to headquarters and the company's distribution centers. It electronically logged every item sold at the checkout counter, automatically kept the warehouses informed of merchandise to be ordered, and directed the flow of goods to the stores and even to the proper shelves. Most importantly for management, it helped detect sales trends quickly and sped up market reaction time substantially. According to Connolly, Executive Vice President of Merchandising, "Wal-Mart has used the data gathered by technology to make more inventory available in the key items that customers want most, while reducing inventories overall."

At the beginning of 2000, Wal-Mart set up a separate company for its web site, with plans to go public. Wal-Mart.com, Inc., based in Palo Alto, California, was jointly owned by Wal-Mart and Accel Partners, a Silicon Valley venture-capital firm. The site included a wide range of products and services that ranged from shampoo to clothing to lawn mowers, as well as airline, hotel, and rental car bookings. After launching and then closing a Sam's Club web site, Wal-Mart reopened the site in mid-June 2000, with an emphasis on upscale items such as jewelry, housewares, and electronics and full product lines for small business owners. SamsClub.com was operated by Wal-Mart from the company's Bentonville, Arkansas, headquarters.

International Corporate Strategies

In 1994, Wal-Mart entered the Canadian market with the acquisition of 122 Woolco discount stores from Woolworth Corporation. When acquired, the Woolco stores were losing millions of dollars annually, but operations became profitable within three years. At the end of 2001, the company had 196 Wal-Mart discount stores in Canada. The company's operations in Canada were considered as a model for Wal-Mart's expansion into other international markets. With 35% of the Canadian discount and department store market, Wal-Mart was the largest retailer in that country.

With a tender offer for shares and mergers of joint ventures in Mexico, the company in 1997 acquired a controlling interest in Cifra, Mexico's largest retailer. Cifra, later identified as Wal-Mart de Mexico, operated stores with a variety of concepts in every region of Mexico, ranging from the nation's largest chain of sit-down restaurants to a softline department store. Retail analysts noted that the initial venture involved many costly mistakes. Time after time it sold the wrong products, including tennis balls that wouldn't bounce in high-altitude Mexico City. Large parking lots at some stores made access difficult as many people arrived by bus. In 2002, Wal-Mart operated 443 discount stores, 62 Supercenters, and 46 Sam's Clubs in Mexico. The Cifra outlets in Mexico included 106 Bodegas, 51 Suburbias, 44 Superamas, and 242 VIPS stores.

When Wal-Mart entered Argentina in 1995, it also initially faced challenges adapting its U.S.-based retail mix and store layouts to the local culture. Although globalization and U.S. cultural influences had swept through the country in the early 1990s, the Argentine market did not accept U.S. cuts of meat, bright-colored cosmetics, and jewelry that gave prominent placement to emeralds, sapphires, and diamonds, even though most Argentine women preferred wearing gold and silver. The first stores even had hardware departments full of tools wired for 110-volt electric power; the standard throughout Argentina was 220. Compounding the challenges was store layout that featured narrow aisles; stores appeared crowded and dirty. In 2002, Wal-Mart operated 11 Supercenters in Argentina.

Wal-Mart management concluded that Brazil offered great opportunities for Wal-Mart because it had the fifth largest population in the world and a population that had a tendency to follow U.S. cultural cues. Although financial data were not broken out on South American operations, retail analysts cited the accounts of Wal-Mart's Brazilian partner, Lojas Americanas SA, to suggest that Wal-Mart lost $100 million in start-up costs for the initial 16 stores. Customer acceptance of Wal-Mart stores was mixed. In Canada and Mexico, many customers were familiar with the company from cross-border shopping trips. Many Brazilian customers were not familiar with the Wal-Mart name. In addition, local Brazilian markets were already dominated by savvy local and foreign competitors, such as Grupo Pao de Acucar SA of Brazil and Carrefour SA of France. Wal-Mart's insistence on doing things "the Wal-Mart way" initially alienated many local suppliers and employees. The country's continuing economic problems also presented a challenge. In 2002, Wal-Mart operated 12 Supercenters and 8 Sam's Clubs in Brazil and planned to expand its presence in that country.

Wal-Mart entered the European market by acquiring three retail chains. Because of stubborn local regulations, management felt it would be easier for Wal-Mart to buy existing stores in Europe than to build new ones. Wal-Mart moved into Germany at the end of 1997 by acquiring 21 stores from hypermarket operator Wertkauf. Also as part of its expansion efforts in Germany, Wal-Mart acquired 74 stores that were a part of the Interspar chain. Soon after the takeover, Wal-Mart quickly filled the top management positions with U.S. expatriates. Within weeks of the purchase, most of the top German managers left the company. Management also discovered that these stores were either cramped, unattractive, or poorly located and needed to be entirely renovated.

All of these German stores were identified with the Wal-Mart name and restocked with a new and revamped selection of merchandise. In response to local laws that forced early store closings and forbid Sunday sales, the company simply opened stores earlier, to allow shopping to begin at 7 A.M. In January 2000, the company launched its first big "rollback" by cutting prices on several hundred items by up to 23%. Germany was well populated with discounters such as Aldi and Lidl, which ran no-frills, cheap supermarkets. These discounters responded fiercely to price challenge by cutting their prices by up to 25%. As a result, price cuts did not have a dramatic impact on sales. A decrease in the International segment's operating income as a percentage of sales in 2001 resulted primarily from the continued negative impact of store remodeling cost, costs related to the start-up of a new distribution system to serve the stores, excess inventory, and related expenses in the company's German units. Despite Wal-Mart's lackluster performance in Germany, management remained positive and committed to serving this market.

Wal-Mart acquired ASDA, Britain's third largest supermarket group, for $10.8 billion in July 1999. With its own price rollbacks, people greeter, "permanently low prices," and even "smiley" faces, ASDA had emulated Wal-Mart's store culture for many years. Based in Leeds, England, the firm had 232 stores in England, Scotland, and Wales. While the culture and pricing strategies of the two companies were nearly identical, there were differences, primarily the size and product mix of the stores. The average Wal-Mart Supercenter was 180,000 square feet in size and had about 30% of its sales in groceries. In contrast, the average ASDA store had only 65,000 square feet and did 60% of sales in grocery items.

The response in Europe to Wal-Mart was immediate and dramatic. Competitors scrambled to match Wal-Mart's low prices, long hours, and friendly service. Some firms combined to strengthen their operations. For example, France's Carrefour SA chain of hypermarkets combined forces with competitor Promodes in a $16.5 billion deal. In 2002, Carrefour dominated the European market with three leading formats: hypermarket, supermarket, and hard discount (small food stores with low prices). It was also one of the world's largest retailers, with more than 9,200 stores not only in Europe, but in Latin America and Asia as well. It was widely speculated that Wal-Mart might eventually target other European retailers, such as Metro of Germany, Jernimo Martins of Portugal, Casino or Auchan of France, and Safeway of

Exhibit 8
Wal-Mart
International
Division, 2002

Country	Stores
Mexico	551
United Kingdom	250
Canada	196
Germany	95
Brazil	22
Puerto Rico	17
Argentina	11
China	19
South Korea	9

Source: Wal-Mart Stores, Inc., 2002 Annual Report.

the United Kingdom for acquisition. Wal-Mart's decision to expand to Europe had been widely considered to be a catalyst for the defensive merger between Carrefour and Promodes.

Wal-Mart's initial effort to enter China fell apart in 1996, when Wal-Mart and Thailand's Charoen Pokphand Group terminated an 18-month-old joint venture because of management differences. Wal-Mart decided to consolidate its operations with five stores in the Hong Kong border city of Shenzhen, one in Dalian, and another in Kumming. Analysts concluded that the company was taking a low-profile approach because of possible competitive response and government restrictions. Beijing restricted the operations of foreign retailers in China, requiring them, for instance, to have government-backed partners. In Shenzhen, it limited the number of stores Wal-Mart could open. Planned expansion in the China market came as China prepared to enter the World Trade Organization and its economy showed signs of accelerating. At the beginning of 2002, the company operated 15 Supercenters, three Sam's Clubs, and 1 Neighborhood Market in China. It also operated 9 Supercenters in South Korea.

The international expansion accelerated management's plans for the development of Wal-Mart as a global brand along the lines of Coca-Cola, Disney, and McDonald's. "We are a global brand name," said Bobby Martin, an early President of the International Division of Wal-Mart. "To customers everywhere it means low cost, best value, greatest selection of quality merchandise and highest standards of customer service," he noted. Some changes were mandated in Wal-Mart's international operations to meet local tastes and intense competitive conditions. "We're building companies out there," said Martin. "That's like starting Wal-Mart all over again in South America or Indonesia or China." Although stores in different international markets would coordinate purchasing to gain leverage with suppliers, developing new technology and planning overall strategy would be done from Wal-Mart headquarters in Bentonville, Arkansas. At the beginning of 2002, the International division of Wal-Mart operated 648 discount stores, 455 Supercenters, 64 Sam's Clubs, and three Neighborhood Markets.

Wal-Mart's International unit accounted for $35.5 billion in sales in 2001. **Exhibit 8** shows the countries in which stores were operated and the number of units in each country at the beginning of 2002.

Decision Making in a Market-Orientated Firm

One principle that distinguished Wal-Mart was the unusual depth of employee involvement in company affairs. Corporate strategies put emphasis on human resource management. Employees of Wal-Mart became "associates," a name borrowed from Sam Walton's early association with the JCPenney Co.

Input was encouraged at meetings at the store and corporate levels. The firm hired employees locally, provided training programs, and through a "Letter to the President" program, management encouraged employees to ask questions and made words like "we," "us," and "our" a part of the corporate language. A number of special award programs recognized individual, department, and division achievement. Stock ownership and profit-sharing programs were introduced as part of a "partnership" concept.

The corporate culture was recognized by the editors of the trade publication *Mass Market Retailers*, when it recognized all 275,000 associates collectively as the "Mass Market Retailers of the Year." "The Wal-Mart associate," the editors noted, "has come to symbolize all that is right with the American worker, particularly in the retailing environment and most particularly at Wal-Mart." The "store within a store" concept, as a Wal-Mart corporate policy, trained individuals to be merchants by being responsible for the performance of their own departments as if they were running their own businesses. Seminars and training programs afforded them opportunities to grow within the company. "People development is not just a good 'program' for any growing company but a must to secure our future," was how Suzanne Allford, Vice President of the Wal-Mart People Division, explained the firm's decentralized approach to retail management development.

"The Wal-Mart Way" was a phase that was used by management to summarize the firm's unconventional approach to business and the development of the corporate culture. As noted in a report referring to a recent development program: "We stepped outside our retailing world to examine the best managed companies in the United States in an effort to determine the fundamentals of their success and to 'benchmark' our own performances. The name 'Total Quality Management' (TQM) was used to identify this vehicle for proliferating the very best things we do while incorporating the new ideas our people have that will assure our future." In 1999, *Discount Store News* honored Wal-Mart Stores, Inc., as *Retailer of the Century*, with a commemorative 200-page issue of the magazine.

The Growth Challenge

Lee Scott indicated that he would never forget his first meeting with Sam Walton. "How old are you?" Walton asked the then 30-year-old Scott, who had just taken a job managing Wal-Mart's trucking fleet. "Do you think you can do this job?" asked Walton. When Scott said yes, Walton agreed and said, "I reckon you can." More than 20 years later, as Wal-Mart's new CEO, Scott was facing his toughest challenge yet: keeping the world's biggest retailer on its phenomenal roll and delivering the huge sales and earnings increases that investors had come to expect from Wal-Mart over the years. Analysts had correctly projected that Wal-Mart would surpass General Motors to be ranked number one in revenue on the *Fortune* 500 list in 2000. The combination of growth and acquisition had caused revenue increases every year. In 2001, it increased 14%, from $191 billion in 2000 to $218 billion. Earnings also increased in 2001 by 9%, to nearly $6.67 billion. Industry analysts noted that this growth was on top of an 18% compound annual growth rate over the past decade.

Wal-Mart Stores, Inc., revolutionized American retailing with its focus on low costs, high customer service, and everyday low pricing to drive sales. Although the company had suffered through some years of lagging performance, it experienced big gains from its move into the grocery business with one-stop Supercenters and into international markets with acquisitions and new ventures. To keep it all going and growing was a major challenge. As the largest retailer and firm in the world, the company and its leadership were challenged to find new areas to continue to grow sales and profits into the future. Lee Scott knew that an ambitious expansion program was called for to allow the company to meet these objectives.

Continued growth could exasperate some problems Wal-Mart was facing. For example, Wal-Mart has always suffered from annual employee-turnover of approximately 65%. To deal with this problem, management initiated a program called People Asset Review (PAR) in which senior management and division presidents reviewed areas in the firm where development was needed, tracked promotable individuals, and developed specific succession plans. In addition, critics contend that Wal-Mart discriminated against women, underpaid workers, and used illegal tactics to stop unionization efforts. Some 40 lawsuits have been filed by employees who said that they had been forced to work overtime for no pay. The company was also facing a sexual discrimination lawsuit in California that could become the largest case in U.S. history. Although more than 70% of Wal-Mart's sales associates were women, fewer than one-third were in management positions. Men held 90% of Wal-Mart store manager positions, and only 1 woman was among the company's 20 top officers. Even after accounting for seniority, store location, and other factors, women earned from 5% to 15% less than men in each year from 1996 to 2001. Since Wal-Mart's 1.3 million employees made it the world's largest private employer, both its reputation and profits were at stake. Overtime and sexual bias lawsuits could cost the company millions of dollars. These came at a time when the company was planning to hire more than one million employees between 2002 and 2007. Although none of Wal-Mart's employees were unionized in 2002, Wal-Mart was a defendant in 28 complaints brought by the U.S. National Labor Relations Board citing anti-union activities such as threats, interrogations, or disciplining. Critics contend that the company moved quickly to block organizing. For example, when a majority of meat cutters at a store in Jacksonville, Texas, voted to organize, the company closed its butcher departments at Jacksonville and other stores.

Financial Situation

In fiscal year 1990, Kmart's sales were $32,070,000,000, and Wal-Mart's sales were $32,601,594,000. In fiscal year 2001, Kmart's sales were $36,151,000,000 (an increase of $4,081,000,000, or 12.73%, while Wal-Mart's sales increased to $217,799,000,000 (an increase of $185,197,406,000, or 568.1%). Wal-Mart's fiscal year 2001 net income was $6,671,000, compared with Kmart's net loss of $2,418,000,000. Kmart had 105 Super Kmart Centers and 2,114 discount stores, for a total of 2,219 stores. Wal-Mart had 2,295 Wal-Mart stores, 564 Sam's Clubs, 1,521 Supercenters, and 34 Neighborhood Markets, for total of 4,414 stores.

References

Albright, Mark, "Changes in Store," *New York Times* (May 17, 1999), pp. 10, 12.

Armour, S., "Wal-Mart Takes Hits on Worker Treatment," *USA Today* (February 10, 2003), p. B1.

Bergman, Joan, "Saga of Sam Walton," *Stores* (January 1988), pp. 129–130.

Berner, Robert, and Stephanie Anderson Forest, "Wal-Mart Is Eating Everybody's Lunch," *Business Week* (April 15, 2002), p. 43.

Boudette, Neil E., "Wal-Mart Plans Major Expansion in Germany," *The Wall Street Journal* (July 20, 2000), p. A21.

Cummins, Chip, "Wal-Mart's Net Income Increases 28%, but Accounting Change Worries Investors," *Wall Street Journal* (August 10, 2000), p. A6.

"David Glass's Biggest Job Is Filling Sam's Shoes," *Business Month* (December 1988), p. 42.

Feldman, Amy, "How Big Can It Get?" *Money* (December 1999), pp. 158+.

Friedland, Johnathan and Louise Lee, "The Wal-Mart Way Sometimes Gets Lost in Translation Overseas," *Wall Street Journal* (October 8, 1997), pp. A1, A12.

Gimein, Mark, "Sam Walton Made Us a Promise," *Fortune* (March 18, 2002), pp. 121–130.

Grant, Lorrie, "Wal-Mart Bagging Success as Grocer," *USA Today* (June 6, 2002), p. 3B.

Gustke, Constance, "Smooth Operator," *Worth* (March 2000), pp. 41+.

Helliker, Kevin, "Wal-Mart's Store of the Future Blends Discount Prices, Department-Store Feel," *Wall Street Journal* (May 17, 1991), pp. B1, B8.

"How the Stores Did," *Wall Street Journal* (May 5, 2000), p. B4.

Huey, John, "America's Most Successful Merchant," *Fortune* (September 23, 1991) pp. 46–48+.

Johnson, Jay L., "The Supercenter Challenge," *Discount Merchandiser* (August 1989), pp. 70+.

Kmart Corporation, *Annual Report*, Troy, Michigan, 2001.

Kohl's Corporation, *Annual Report*, Menominee Falls, Wisconsin, 2001.

Komarow, Steven, "Wal-Mart Takes Slow Road in Germany," *USA Today*, (May 5, 2000), p. 3B.

Krauss, Clifford, "Wal-Mart Learns a Hard Lesson," *International Herald Tribune* (December 6, 1999), p. 15.

Larrabee, John, "Wal-Mart Ends Vermont's Holdout," *USA Today* (September 19, 1995), p. 4B.

Lee, Louise, "Discounter Wal-Mart Is Catering to Affluent to Maintain Growth," *Wall Street Journal* (February 7, 1996), p. A1.

Lee, Louise, and Joel Millman, "Wal-Mart to Buy Majority Stake in Cifra," *Wall Street Journal* (June 4, 1997), pp. A3+.

Loomis, Carol J., "Sam Would Be Proud," *Fortune* (April 17, 2000), pp 131+.

"Management Style: Sam Moore Walton," *Business Month* (May 1989), p. 38.

Marsch, Barbara, "The Challenge: Merchants Mobilize to Battle Wal-Mart in a Small Community," *Wall Street Journal* (June 5, 1991), pp. A1, A4.

Mason, Todd, "Sam Walton of Wal-Mart: Just Your Basic Homespun Billionaire," *Business Week* (October 14, 1985), pp. 142–143+.

Mitchener, Brandon, and David Woodruff, "French Merger of Hypermarkets Gets a Go-Ahead," *Wall Street Journal* (January 26, 2000), p. A19.

Murphy, Cait, "Now That Wal-Mart Is America's Largest Corporation, the Service Economy Wears the Crown," *Fortune* (April 15, 2002), pp. 95–98.

Nelson, Emily, "Wal-Mart to Build a Test Supermarket in Bid to Boost Grocery-Industry Share," *Wall Street Journal* (June 19, 1998), p. A4.

Nelson, Emily, and Kara Swisher, "Wal-Mart Eyes Public Sale of Web Unit," *Wall Street Journal* (January 7, 2000), p. A3.

O'Keefe, Brian, "Meet Your New Neighborhood Grocer," *Fortune* (May 13, 2002) pp. 93–96.

"Our People Make the Difference: The History of Wal-Mart," videocassette (Bentonville, Arkansas: Wal-Mart Video Productions, 1991).

Peters, Tom J., and Nancy Austin, *A Passion for Excellence* (New York: Random House), pp. 266–267.

Rawn, Cynthia Dunn, "Wal-Mart vs. Main Street," *American Demographics* (June 1990), pp. 58–59.

"Retailer Completes Purchase of Wertkauf of Germany," *Wall Street Journal* (December 31, 1997), p. B3.

Rudnitsky, Howard, "How Sam Walton Does It," *Forbes* (August 16, 1982), pp. 42–44.

"Sam Moore Walton," *Business Month* (May 1989), p. 38.

Schwadel, Francine, "Little Touches Spur Wal-Mart's Rise," *Wall Street Journal* (September 22, 1989), p. B1.

Sears, Roebuck and Co., *Annual Report* (2001).

Sheets, Kenneth R., "How Wal-Mart Hits Main St.," *U.S. News & World Report* (March 13, 1989), pp. 53–55.

Target Corporation, *Annual Report* (2001).

"The Early Days: Walton Kept Adding 'a Few More' Stores," *Discount Store News* (December 9, 1985), p. 61.

Tomlinson, Richard, "Who's Afraid of Wal-Mart?" *Fortune* (June 26, 2000), p. 186.

Trimble, Vance H., *Sam Walton: The Inside Story of America's Richest Man* (New York: Dutton, 1990).

Troy, M., "Finding Successors to the Dynasty Starts by Winning the Turnover War," *DSN Retailing Today* (June 5, 2000).

Voyle, Susanna, "ASDA Criticised for Price Claims," *Financial Times* (December 8, 1999), p. 3.

"Wal-Mart Spoken Here," *BusinessWeek* (June 23, 1997), pp. 138+.

Wal-Mart Stores, Inc., *Annual Report* (2000).

Wal-Mart Stores, Inc., *Annual Report* (2001).

Wal-Mart Stores, Inc., *Annual Report* (2002).

Wal-Mart's ASDA Says CEO to Head Europe Expansion," *Wall Street Journal Europe* (December 3, 1999), p. 6.

"Wal-Mart Takes a Stand," *The Economist* (May 22, 1999), p. 31.

"Wal-Mart: The Model Discounter," *Dun's Business Month* (December 1982), pp. 60–61.

"Wal-Mart Wins Again," *The Economist* (October 2, 1999), p. 33.

Walton, Sam, with John Huey, *Sam Walton: Made in America* (New York: Doubleday Publishing Company), 1992.

Wonacott, Peter, "Wal-Mart Finds Market Footing in China," *Wall Street Journal* (July 17, 2000), p. A31.

"Work, Ambition—Sam Walton," Press Release, Corporate and Public Affairs, Wal-Mart Stores, Inc.

Zellner, W., "No Way to Treat a Lady," *Business Week* (March 3, 2003), pp. 63–66.

Zellner, Wendy, "Someday, Lee, This May All Be Yours," *Business Week* (November 15, 1999), pp. 84+.

Zimmerman, Ann, and Teri Agins, "Pinstripes and Motor Oil: Wal-Mart Attempts Chic Although Still on the Cheap, with Fresh, Hipper Apparel," *Wall Street Journal* (September 3, 2002), p. B1.

Zimmerman, Ann, "Wal-Mart to Open Reworked Web Site for SamsClub.com," (June 6, 2000), p. B8.

CASE 19

The Home Depot, Inc.:
Growing the Professional Market (Revised)

Moustafa H. Abdelsamad, Hitesh (John) P. Adhia,
David B. Croll, William P. May, Laurence C. Pettit Jr.,
John F. Talbot, and Thomas L. Wheelen

ON APRIL 23, 1988, ARTHUR M. BLANK, PRESIDENT AND CHIEF EXECUTIVE OFFICER (CEO), was presiding over a strategic planning session for new strategies for each of Home Depot's six regional divisions (see "Organizational Structure") for the professional contractor market. Home Depot's management estimated this market to be $215 billion in 1997. Home Depot has been concentrating on the Do-It-Yourself/Buy-It-Yourself market sector, which Home Depot management had estimated to be $100 billion in 1997. Home Depot sales were $24.1 billion in 1997. **Exhibit 1** shows the combined sales for the Do-It-Yourself/Buy-It-Yourself sector and the professional sector to be $365 billion. The heavy industry sector was treated as a separate market sector. In 1998, Home Depot had less than 4% of the $215 billion professional sector.

In early April 1998, the company's management announced a new store format. In 1998, the company planned to build four new smaller stores with about 25% (25,000 square feet) of the existing store size. These stores would be similar to local hardware stores or Ace Hardware stores.

**Exhibit 1
Total Market for
Do-It-Yourself/Buy-
It-Yourself Sector,
Professional Sector,
and Heavy Industry
Sector**

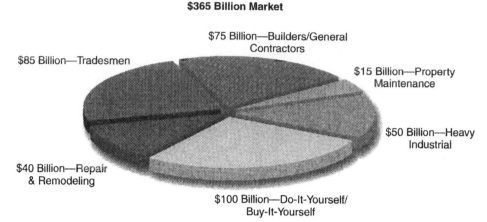

$365 Billion Market

$75 Billion—Builders/General Contractors

$85 Billion—Tradesmen

$15 Billion—Property Maintenance

$50 Billion—Heavy Industrial

$40 Billion—Repair & Remodeling

$100 Billion—Do-It-Yourself/ Buy-It-Yourself

Note: Home Improvement Research Institute, 1997 Product Sales Estimates; U.S. Census Bureau Product Sales Estimates.

Source: The Home Depot, Inc., 1997 *Annual Report, p. 3.*

The Home Depot, Inc.

Founded in Atlanta, Georgia, in 1978, Home Depot was the world's largest home improvement retailer and ranked among the 10 largest retailers in the United States. At the close of fiscal year 1997, the company was operating 624 full-service, warehouse-style stores—555 stores in 44 states and 5 EXPO Design Center stores in the United States, plus 32 in four Canadian provinces (see **Exhibit 2**).

The average Home Depot store had approximately 106,300 square feet of indoor selling space and an additional 16,000–28,000 square feet of outside garden center, including house-plant enclosures. The stores stocked approximately 40,000–50,000 different kinds of building materials, home improvement products, and lawn and garden supplies. In addition, Home Depot stores offered installation services for many products. The company employed approximately 125,000 associates, of whom approximately 7,900 were salaried, and the remainder of the employees were paid on an hourly basis.

Retail industry analysts had credited Home Depot with being a leading innovator in retailing, by combining the economies of warehouse-format stores with a high level of customer service. The company augmented that concept with a corporate culture that valued decentralized management and decision making, entrepreneurial innovation and risk taking, and high levels of employee commitment and enthusiasm.

The stores served primarily the Do-It-Yourself (DIY) repair person, although home improvement contractors, building maintenance professionals, interior designers, and other professionals have become increasingly important customers.

Home Depot also owned two wholly owned subsidiaries, Maintenance Warehouse and National Blind & Wallpaper Factory. The company also owned Load 'N Go™, an exclusive rental truck service for customers.

History[1]

Home Depot's Chairman, Bernard Marcus, began his career in the retail industry in a small pharmacy in Millburn, New Jersey. He later joined the Two Guys discount chain to manage its drug and cosmetics departments and eventually became the Vice President of Merchandising

Exhibit 2 Store Locations: The Home Depot, Inc.

The Home Depot Canada
32 stores

Western Division
153 stores

Midwest Division
63 stores

Northeast Division
137 stores

Southwest Division
86 stores

Southeast Division
148 stores

Western Division	153
Location	**Number of Stores**
Arizona	18
Phoenix	14
Prescott	1
Tucson	3
California	**96**
Bakersfield	1
Fresno	3
Los Angeles	51
Modesto	1
Sacramento	5
San Diego	11
San Francisco	23
Stockton	1
Colorado	**10**
Colorado Springs	2
Denver	7
Pueblo	1
Idaho	**1**
Boise	1
Nevada	**5**
Las Vegas	3
Reno	2
Oregon	**7**
Eugene	1
Portland	6
Utah	**4**
Salt Lake City	4
Washington	**12**
Seattle/Tacoma	11
Spokane	1

Southeast Division	148
Location	**Number of Stores**
Alabama	**6**
Birmingham	3
Huntsville	1
Mobile	1
Montgomery	1
Florida	**63**
Daytona Beach/ Melbourne/ Orlando	10
Ft. Lauderdale/Miami/ West Palm Beach	25
Ft. Myers, Naples	6
Ft. Walton	1
Gainesville/Ocala	3
Jacksonville	4
Pensacola	1
Tallahassee	1
Tampa/ St. Petersburg	12
Georgia	**32**
Athens	1
Atlanta	24
Augusta	1
Columbus	1
Dalton	1
Macon	1
Rome	1
Savannah	1
Valdosta	1
Indiana	**1**
Clarksville	1
Kentucky	**3**
Lexington	1
Louisville	2
Mississippi	**1**
Horn Lake	1
North Carolina	**18**
Asheville	1
Charlotte	6
Fayetteville	1
Greensboro/ Winston-Salem	3
Hickory	1
Raleigh	5
Wilmington	1
South Carolina	**7**
Charleston	1
Columbia	2
Greenville/ Spartanburg	4
Tennessee	**17**
Chattanooga	2
Johnson City/ Kingsport	2
Knoxville	3
Memphis	3
Nashville	7

Northeast Division	137
Location	**Number of Stores**
Connecticut	**13**
Hartford	6
New Haven	3
Danbury/Fairfield/ Norwalk	4
Delaware	**1**
Christana	1
Maine	**2**
Bangor	1
Portland	1
Maryland	**14**
Baltimore	8
Washington, DC area	**6**
Massachusetts	**17**
Boston	13
Southern Mass.	3
Springfield	1
New Hampshire	**4**
Manchester	1
Nashua	1
Portsmouth	1
Salem	1
New Jersey	**25**
Northern New Jersey	19
Southern New Jersey	6
New York	**32**
Albany	2
Buffalo	4
Hudson Valley	4
Johnson City	1
New York City/ Long Island	16
Rochester	3
Syracuse	2
Pennsylvania	**20**
Allentown/ Bethlehem	2
Harrisburg/ Reading	3
Philadelphia	10
Pittsburgh	3
Scranton/ Wilkes Barre	2
Rhode Island	**1**
Warwick	1
Vermont	**1**
Williston	1
Virginia	**7**
Washington, DC area	7

Southwest Division	86
Location	**Number of Stores**
Arkansas	**2**
Little Rock	2
Illinois	**1**
O'Fallon	1
Kansas	**1**
Kansas City	1
Louisiana	**9**
Baton Rouge	1
Lafayette	1
Lake Charles	1
New Orleans	5
Shreveport	1
Mississippi	**3**
Gulfport	1
Jackson	2
Missouri	**7**
Columbia	1
Kansas City	2
St. Louis	4
New Mexico	**3**
Albuquerque	3
Oklahoma	**6**
Oklahoma City	4
Tulsa	2
Texas	**54**
Austin	5
Beaumont	1
Corpus Christi	1
Dallas/Ft. Worth	21
El Paso	2
Houston	16
Lubbock	1
Midland	1
San Antonio	6

Midwest Division	63
Location	**Number of Stores**
Illinois	**24**
Chicago	23
Quincy	1
Indiana	**2**
Evansville	1
Hobart	1
Iowa	**1**
Waterloo	1

Michigan	22
Detroit	14
Flint/Saginaw	3
Grand Rapids	2
Kalamazoo	1
Lansing	1
Traverse City	1
Minnesota	**10**
Minneapolis/ St. Paul	10
Ohio	**4**
Boardman	1
Cleveland	2
Toledo	1

Home Depot Canada	32
Location	**Number of Stores**
Alberta	**4**
Calgary	2
Edmonton	2
British Columbia	**8**
Vancouver	8
Manitoba	**1**
Winnipeg	1
Ontario	**19**
Kitchener	1
London	1
Ottawa	2
Toronto	14
Windsor	1

EXPO Design Center	5
Location	**Number of Stores**
Atlanta	1
Dallas	1
Long Island	1
Miami	1
San Diego	1
Total Stores	**624**

Source: The Home Depot, Inc., 1994 Annual Report, *p. 32, and* 1997 Annual Report, *p. 36.*

and Advertising for the parent company, Vornado, Inc. In 1972 he moved into the Do-It-Yourself home improvement sector as President and Chairman of the Board at Handy Dan/Handy City. The parent company, Daylin, Inc., was chaired by Sanford Sigoloff. He and Marcus had a strong difference of opinion over control, and one Friday at 5:00 P.M. in 1978, Marcus and two other Handy Dan top executives were discharged.

That weekend, Home Depot was born, when the three men—Bernard Marcus, Arthur Blank, and Kenneth G. Langone—laid out plans for the Do-It-Yourself chain. Venture capital was provided by investment firms that included Inverned of New York as well as private investors. Two key investors were Joseph Flom, a takeover lawyer, and Frank Borman, then Chairman of Eastern Airlines.

When the first stores opened in Atlanta in 1979, the company leased space in three former Treasury Discount Stores with 60,000 square feet each. All three were suburban locations in the northern half of the city. Industry experts gave Home Depot 10-to-1 odds it would fail.

In 1980, a fourth Atlanta stored opened, and the company had annual sales of $22.3 million. The following year, Home Depot ventured beyond Atlanta to open four stores in South Florida and also had its first public offering at $12 a share. By early 1990, its stock had soared by 7,019% and split eight times. In May 1995, an original share was worth $26,300.

In the early 1980s, inflation rose over 13%, and unemployment was as high as 9.5%. These were rough times for most startup companies, but Home Depot prospered as hard-pressed shoppers sought out the best buy. The company was voted the Retailer of the Year in the home center industry in 1982 and had its first stock splits.

By 1983, Marcus was a nationally recognized leader in the Do-It-Yourself industry. New Orleans was a strong market with many homeowners and young people, so Home Depot moved in with three stores. Other additions were in Arizona and Florida. Two stores opened in Orlando, in the backyard of the Winter Haven–based Scotty's, and one more opened in South Florida. Home Depot's strong drawing power became evident as customers passively waited in long checkout lines.

In 1984, Home Depot's common stock was listed on the New York Stock Exchange. It was traded under the symbol "HD" and was included in the Standard & Poor's 500 Index. Marcus believed about the only restraint Home Depot faced that year was its ability to recruit and train new staff fast enough. However, Home Depot was soon to face other problems. In December, things briefly turned sour when Home Depot bought the nine-store Bowater Warehouse chain with stores in Texas, Louisiana, and Alabama. Bowater had a dismal reputation. Its merchandise didn't match Home Depot's, and nearly all its employees had to be dismissed because they were unable to fit into the company's strong customer service orientation.

Of the 22 stores opened in 1985, most were in eight new markets. Going into Houston and Detroit were moves into less hospitable terrain. The company lost money with promotional pricing and advertising costs. This rapid expansion into unknown territories also took management's attention away from the other stores. The media quickly noted that Home Depot was having problems and suggested that its troubles could be related to rapid expansion into the already crowded home center business. Home Depot's earnings dropped 40% in 1985.

Marcus had to regroup in 1986. He slowed Home Depot's growth to 10 stores in existing markets, including the first supersized store with 140,000 square feet. Home Depot withdrew from the Detroit market, selling its five new stores. By 1987, six California stores and two Tennessee stores had opened, and the company had sales of $1 billion. In that same year, Home Depot introduced an advanced inventory management system; as a result, inventory was turned 5.4 times a year instead of the 4.5 times for 1986. The company also paid its first quarterly dividend.

In 1988, 21 stores opened, with heavy emphasis in California. For the second time, Home Depot was voted the Retailer of the Year in the home center industry.

Home Depot expanded its market beyond the Sunbelt in early 1989 by opening two stores in the northeast—East Hanover, New Jersey, and New Haven, Connecticut. By the end of the year, there were five stores in the Northeast.

The year 1989 was also a benchmark year for technological developments. All stores began using Universal Product Code (UPC) scanning systems to speed checkout time.

The Company's satellite data communications network installation improved management communication and training. Sales of the year totaled $2.76 billion, and plans were made to open its initial contribution of $6 million to the Employee Stock Ownership Plan (ESOP). On its tenth anniversary, Home Depot opened its 100th store (in Atlanta) and by the year's end had become the nation's largest home center chain.

Thirty stores opened in 1990, bringing the total to 147, with sales of $3.8 billion. The largest store—140,000 square feet—was in San Diego. To handle more volume per store, Home Depot developed and tested a new store productivity improvement (SPI) program designed to make more effective use of existing and new store space and to allow for more rapid replenishment of merchandise on the sales floor. The SPI program involved the renovation of portions of certain existing stores and an improved design for new stores with the goal of enhanced customer access, reducing customer shopping time, and streamlining merchandise stocking and delivery. As part of SPI, the company also experimented with modified store layouts, materials handling techniques, and operations.

Home Depot continued its expansion by opening an additional 29 stores to bring the total number of stores to 174 in 1991, which generated total sales of $5.1 billion. In addition, the company's SPI program proved successful and was implemented in substantially all new stores and in selected existing stores. Home Depot also continued to introduce or refine a number of merchandising programs during fiscal 1991. Included among such programs were the introduction of full-service, in-store interior decorating centers staffed by designers and an expanded assortment in its lighting department. In 1991, management created a new division, EXPO Design Centers. The first store was opened in San Diego. EXPO Design Centers' niche was the extensive use of computer-aided design technology that the store's creative coordination used. It was targeted to upscale homeowners. These features were of assistance to customers remodeling their bathrooms and kitchens. To assist this strategy further, Home Depot offered a selection of major kitchen appliances. The product line offered was the top of the line. This allowed Home Depot to remain a leading-edge merchandiser.

From 1991 through 1995, many of the new merchandising techniques developed for the Home Depot EXPO were transferred to the entire chain. In 1994, the second EXPO store opened in Atlanta and was mostly dedicated to offering design services. The Atlanta store was 117,000 square feet, and the San Diego store was 105,000 square feet. In 1995 these stores were expanded in California, New York, and Texas. This division was expected to grow to 200 to 400 stores.

By the end of fiscal year 1992, Home Depot had increased its total number of stores to 214, with annual sales of $7.1 billion. Earlier that year, the company had begun a company-wide rollout of an enlarged garden center prototype, which had been successfully tested in 1991. These centers, which were as large as 28,000 square feet, featured 6,000- to 8,000-square-foot greenhouses or covered selling areas, providing year-round selling opportunities and significantly expanded product assortment. Also during 1992, the company's "installed sales program," which it began testing in three selected markets in 1990, became available in 122 stores in 10 markets. This program targeted the buy-it-yourself (BIY) customer, who would purchase an item but either did not have the desire or the ability to install the item. Finally, the company announced its national sponsorship of the 1994 and 1996 U.S. teams at the Winter and Summer Olympics.

During 1993, Home Depot introduced Depot Diners on a test basis in Atlanta, Seattle, and various locations in South Florida. Depot Diners were an extension of the company's commitment to total customer satisfaction and were designed to provide customers and employees with a convenient place to eat. The company continued to develop innovative merchandising programs that helped to grow the business further. The installed sales program became available in 251 stores in 26 markets, with approximately 2,370 installed sales vendors who, as independent, licensed contractors, were authorized to provide service to customers. By the end of fiscal year 1993, Home Depot had opened an additional 50 stores and sales were $9.2 billion, up by 30% from 1992.

From the end of fiscal year 1989 to the end of fiscal year 1994, the company increased its store count by an average of 24% per year (from 118 to 340) and increased the total store square footage by 28% per year (from 10,424,000 to 35,133,000). Home Depot entered the Canadian market on February 28, 1994. The company entered into a partnership with and, as a result, acquired 75% of Aikenhead's Home Improvement Warehouse. At any time after the sixth anniversary of the purchase, the company had the option to purchase, or the other partner had the right to cause the company to purchase, the remaining 25% of the Canadian company. Home Depot Canada commenced operations with seven stores previously operated by Aikenhead's. Five additional stores were built during fiscal 1994, for a total of 12 stores at fiscal year-end. Approximately 9 additional new Canadian stores were planned, for a total of 21 by the end of fiscal year 1995.

The company also made its initial entry into the Midwest by opening 11 stores in the region's two largest markets: Chicago, Illinois, and Detroit, Michigan. Approximately 16 new stores were scheduled for 1995, and by the end of 1998, the company expected approximately 112 stores to open.

During fiscal year 1994, Home Depot began developing plans to open stores in Mexico. The first store was scheduled to open in 1998. Although the company was already building relationships with key suppliers in Mexico, entry into the market was to be cautious and slow, paying special attention to Mexico's volatile economy. On a long-term basis, however, the company anticipated that success in Mexico could lead to more opportunities throughout Central and South America. Home Depot planned to expand its total domestic stores by about 25% per year, on average, over the foreseeable future. The international openings were to be above and beyond this figure. Management felt that its growth was optimal, given its financial and management resources.

In 1995, the company offered more private-label products. The company used the "Homer" character on all its private products and its advertisements. The first 24-hour store was opened in Flushing, New York. Ben Sharon of *Value Line* said, "[Home Depot's] ability to adopt different characteristics among regions and markets should keep Home Depot ahead of the industry in the years ahead."[2] By the end of 1995, the company had a total of 423 stores, of which 400 were Home Depot stores, 19 were Canadian stores in 3 provinces, and 4 were EXPO stores.

In March 1995, *Fortune* announced that Home Depot had made its list of America's Most Admired Corporations. Home Depot ranked 8.24, or fifth overall in the competition. In 1996, Home Depot ranked second. The company ranked first for rate of return (39.0%) for the past 10 years. The top four companies were Rubbermaid (8.65), Microsoft (8.42), Coca-Cola (8.39), and Motorola (8.38). *Fortune* stated, "The winners chart a course of constant renewal and work to sustain culture that produces the very best products and people."[3] More than 1,000 senior executives, outside directors, and financial analysts were surveyed. Each corporation was rated in 10 separate areas.

Home Depot had encountered local opposition to locating one of its stores in a small community in Pequannock Township, New Jersey. A group called "Concerned Citizens for Community Preservation" mobilized to prevent Home Depot from opening a store in the town. Members of the group posted flyers and signs throughout the township. These flyers documented Home Depot's alleged "legacy of crime, traffic, and safety violations." The flyers stated, "Our kids will be crossing through this death trap," referring to Home Depot's proposed parking lot. Another flyer asked, "How will we be protected?"[4]

In July 1995, Home Depot filed a lawsuit against Rickel Home Centers, a closely held competitor based in South Plainfield, New Jersey, claiming that "[Rickel] used smear tactics in a concerted effort to block Home Depot from opening stores in Pequannock and

Bloomfield, about 25 miles to the south."[5] The suit stated that Rickel had published false statements "impugning Home Depot's name, reputation, products, and services." The suit named Rickel and Bloomfield citizens' groups as defendants.

This was not the first time that citizens' groups had tried to stop a new store or development. Wal-Mart had a severe challenge when it was trying to open a new store in Bennington, Vermont. In 1997, the company opened its first store in Williston, Vermont.

On July 20, 1995, Dennis Ryan, President of CrossRoads, announced the opening of the first of Home Depot's new rural chain, CrossRoads, in Quincy, Illinois. A second store was planned to be opened in Columbus, Missouri, in January or February 1996. The target market for this chain was farmers and ranchers who shopped in smaller, rural towns across America. At that time, there were about 100 farm and home retailers, with about 850 stores and annual sales of $6 billion. A typical CrossRoads store would have about 117,000 square feet of inside retail space, plus a 100,000-square-foot lumberyard. In contrast, the average size of a Tractor Supply Company (a competitor) store was about one-tenth the size of a CrossRoads store and did not have a lumberyard. Dennis Ryan said, "This really is a Home Depot just tailored to this [Quincy] community."[6]

The store carried the typical products of Home Depot. In addition, CrossRoads carried pet supplies, truck and tractor tires and parts, work clothing, farm animal medicines, feed, and storage tanks, barbed wire, books (such as *Raising Sheep the Modern Way*), and other items. Employees would install engines and tires and go to the farm to fix a flat tractor tire.[7] The company soon terminated this strategy because the stores did not generate sales and profits that Home Depot expected. The existing CrossRoads stores were renamed Home Depot stores.

By year-end 1996, the company acquired Maintenance Warehouse/America Corporation, which was the leading direct mail marketer of maintenance, repair, and operating products to the United States building and facilities management market. The company's 1996 sales were approximately $130 million in an estimated $10 billion market. Home Depot management felt this was "an important step towards strengthening our position with professional business customers."[8] The company's long-term goal was to capture 10% of this market.

At the end of 1996, the company had 512 stores, including 483 Home Depot stores and 5 EXPO Design Centers in 38 states, and 24 stores in Canada.

In 1997, the company added 112 stores, for a total of 624 stores in 41 states. Stores in the United States were 587 Home Depot stores and 5 EXPO Design Center stores plus 32 stores in 4 Canadian provinces. This was a 22% increase in stores over 1996. Two-thirds of the new stores in fiscal 1997 were in existing markets. The company "continues to add stores to even its most mature markets to further penetrate and increase its presence in the market."[9]

The company planned to add new stores at a 21% to 22% annual growth rate, which would increase stores from 624 at the end of 1997 to 1,300 stores at the end of fiscal 2001. This meant the company would have to increase its associates from approximately 125,000 at the end of 1997 to 315,000 in four years (2001).

During 1998, Home Depot planned to open approximately 137 new stores, which would be a 22% increase in stores. The company planned to enter new markets—Anchorage, Alaska; Cincinnati and Columbus, Ohio; Milwaukee, Wisconsin; Norfolk and Richmond, Virginia; San Juan, Puerto Rico; Regina, Saskatchewan, and Kingston, Ontario in Canada; and Santiago, Chile. The company intended to open two stores in Santiago during fiscal 1998. To facilitate its entry into Chile, Home Depot entered into a joint venture agreement, in fiscal 1997, with S.A.C.I. Falabella, which was the largest department store retailer in Chile. The company's position on the joint venture was that it "was proving to be beneficial in expediting The Home Depot's startup in areas such as systems, logistics, real estate, and credit programs."[10]

This global expansion fit the company's stated vision to be one of the most successful retailers in the next millennium. According to management, "the most successful retailers . . . will be those who, among other things, can effectively profitably extend their reach to global markets."[11] Home Depot management "plans to employ a focused, regional strategy, establishing platform markets for growth into other markets."[12]

Corporate Culture

The culture at Home Depot was characterized by the phrase, "Guess what happened to me at Home Depot?" This phrase showed Home Depot's bond with its customers and the communities in which it had stores and was a recognition of superb service. Home Depot called this its "orange-blooded culture."

The orange-blooded culture emphasized individuality, informality, nonconformity, growth, and pride. These traits reflected those of the founders of the company, who within hours of being fired from Handy Dan, were busily planning the Home Depot stores to go into competition with the company from which they had just been summarily dismissed. The culture was "really a reflection of Bernie and me," said Blank. "We're not formal, stuffy folks. We hang pretty loose. We've got a lot of young people. We want them to feel comfortable."[13]

The importance of the individual to the success of the whole venture was consistently emphasized at Home Depot. Marcus' statements bear this out: "We know that one person can make a difference, and that is what is so unique about The Home Depot. It doesn't matter where our associates work in our company, they can all make a difference."[14] While emphasizing the opportunities for advancement at Home Depot, Marcus decried the kind of "cradle to grave" job that used to be the ideal in America and is the norm in Japan. To him, this was "a kind of serfdom."[15] Home Depot attempted to provide excellent wages and benefits, and superior training and advancement opportunities, while encouraging independent thinking and initiative.

Informality was always in order at Home Depot—"spitballs fly at board meetings"—and there was always someone around to make sure that ties got properly trimmed. When executives visited stores, they went alone, not with an entourage. Most worked on the floors in the beginning and knew the business from the ground up. They were approachable and employees frequently came forward with ideas and suggestions.

Nonconformity was evident in many different areas of the company—from the initial warehouse concept to the size and variety of merchandise to human resource practices. Both Marcus and Blank "flout conventional corporate rules that foil innovation." Training employees at all levels was one of the most powerful means of transmitting corporate culture, and Home Depot used it extensively. One analyst noted that Home Depot (in a reverse of the "top-to-bottom" training sequence in most organizations) trained the carryout people first: "The logic is that the guy who helps you to your car is the last employee you come in contact with, and they want that contact to be positive."[16]

Company management perception of what the customer finds on a visit to a Home Depot store is a "feel good" store. The company defined a feel good store as "a place where they *feel good* about walking in our doors, *feel good* about consulting our knowledgeable associates, *feel good* about paying a low price, and *feel good* about returning time after time."[17]

The Home Depot was built on a set of values that fostered strong relationships with its key constituencies. The company's management embraced the values of taking care of its people, encouraging an entrepreneurial spirit, treating each other with respect, and being committed to the highest standards. For the customers, management believed that excellent customer service was the key to company success, and that giving back to the communities it served was part of its commitment to the customer. Importantly, management believed that if all employees lived all of these values, they would also create shareholder value.

The Home Depot's long-term growth planning was taking place with full recognition of the importance of the company's culture to its future success. Its goal was for each associate to not only be able to explain the company's culture of respect, trust, ownership, and entrepreneurial spirit, but most importantly, to believe it and live it.

The management of Home Depot was often asked how the company had managed to grow so fast for as long as it had and still be successful, both financially and with its customers. They responded that aggressive growth required adapting to change, but continued success required holding fast to the culture and values of the company as the company grew.[18]

In addition, Home Depot recognized its role in the community, and strove to be known as a good "corporate citizen." In one community, a woman lost her uninsured home and teenaged son to a fire. Home Depot's management responded, along with other residents, by providing thousands of dollars of free materials and supplies to assist in the rebuilding effort. In another incident, a community organization sponsored a graffiti cleanup, and the Home Depot store in the area donated paint and supplies to assist in the project. These were just a few of the stories that communities told about Home Depot, which also participated in Habitat for Humanity and Christmas in April, and had provided over $10 million to help fund many community projects in the United States and Canada. The company also was active in environmental activities and promoted environmentally healthy building and home improvement practices.

Merrill Lynch stated about Home Depot's culture that its "entrepreneurial culture and heavy dedication toward customer service, combined with its large merchandise selection, has resulted in a retailer that leads its industry by almost every performance measure."[19]

Corporate Governance

Board of Directors

The Board of Directors of Home Depot were as follows[20]:

Bernard Marcus (68) had been Cofounder, Chairman, and Chief Executive Officer since the inception of the company in 1978 until 1997, when he passed the title of CEO to Arthur M. Blank and remained as Chairman. He had served on many other boards. He owned 21,842,890 shares (2.98%) of the company's stock.

Arthur M. Blank (55) had been Cofounder, President, Chief Operating Officer, and Director since the company's inception, and was named Chief Executive Officer in 1997. He had served on many other boards. He owned 12,182,614 shares (1.66%).

Ronald M. Brill (54) had been Executive Vice President and Chief Financial Officer since March 1993. He joined the company in 1978 and was elected Treasurer in 1980. He owned 872,392 shares of the company's stock.

Frank Borman (70) had been a Director since 1983. He had been a NASA astronaut and was a retired U.S. Air Force colonel. He was the retired Chairman and Chief Operating Officer of Eastern Airlines and presently was the Chairman of Patlex Corporation. He was a major investor in 1983 and owned 265,782 shares of the company's stock. He served on many other boards.

Barry R. Cox (44) had been a Director since 1978. For the past 20 years, he had been a private investor. He owned 1,650,243 shares of stock.

Milledge A. Hart, III (64) had been a Director since 1978. He served as Chairman of the Hart Group, Chairman of Rmax Inc., and Chairman of Axon, Inc. He served on many other boards. He owned 1,733,185 shares of the company's stock.

Donald R. Keough (71) had been a Director since April 1993. He was President and Chief Operating Officer and Director of Coca-Cola Company until his retirement in April 1993. He owned 20,304 shares of the company's stock. He served on many other boards.

John I. Clendenin (63) had been a Director since 1996. He had been Chairman and Chief Executive Officer of BellSouth Corporation for the last five years until his retirement in 1996 and remained Chairman until 1997. He owned 5,477 shares of the company's stock.

Johnnetta B. Cole (61) had been a Director since 1995. Dr. Cole served as President of Spelman College in Atlanta, Georgia, from 1987 until July 1997. She served on many other boards and foundations. She owned 4,803 shares of the company's stock.

Kenneth G. Langone (62) had been Cofounder and Director since the company's inception. He had served as Chairman, President, Chief Executive Officer, and Managing Director of Invened Associates, Inc., an investment banking and brokerage firm. He served on many other boards. He owned 6,850,243 shares of the company's stock.

M. Faye Wilson (60) had been a Director since 1992. She had been Executive Vice President of Bank of America NT&SA since 1992. She owned 16,743 shares of the company's stock.

The Directors were each paid $40,000 per annum, of which $10,000 was in the form of restricted shares of common stock, and an additional $1,000 fee and expenses for each meeting. The Executive Committee included Marcus, Blank, and Langone. The Audit Committee included Borman, Cox, Hart, and Keough. The Compensation Committee included Borman, Clendenin, Cox, and Keough. The Human Resource Committee included Cole, Langone, and Wilson.

FRM (Fidelity) Corporation owned 55,991,937 (7.65%) shares of common stock.

Top Management

Key executive officers of Home Depot, besides Bernard Marcus, Arthur M. Blank, and Ronald M. Brill, who served on the Board, were as follows[21]:

Mark R. Baker (40) has been President of the Midwest Division since December 1997. Mr. Baker first joined the company in 1996 as Vice President—Merchandising for the Midwest Division. Prior to joining Home Depot, from 1992 until 1996, Mr. Baker was an Executive Vice President for HomeBase in Fullerton, California.

Bruce W. Berg (49) has been President–Southeast Division since 1991. Mr. Berg joined the company in 1984 as Vice President–Merchandising (East Coast) and was promoted to Senior Vice President (East Coast) in 1988.

Marshall L. Day (54) has been Senior Vice President–Chief Financial Officer since 1995. Mr. Day previously served as Senior Vice President–Finance from 1993 until his promotion to his current position.

Bill Hamlin (45) was recently named Group President and continues to serve as Executive Vice President–Merchandising. Prior to being named Executive Vice President–Merchandising, Mr. Hamlin served as President–Western Division from 1990 until 1994.

Vernon Joslyn (46) has been President–Northeast Division since 1996. Mr. Joslyn previously served as Vice President–Operations for the Northeast Division from 1993 until his promotion to his current position.

W. Andrew McKenna (52) was named Senior Vice President–Strategic Business Development in December 1997. Mr. McKenna joined Home Depot as Senior Vice President–Corporate Information Systems in 1990. In 1994 he was named President of the Midwest Division and served in that capacity until he assumed the duties of his current position.

Lynn Martineau (41) has been President–Western Division since 1996. Mr. Martineau most recently served as Vice President–Merchandising for the company's Southeast Division from 1989 until his promotion to his current position.

Larry M. Mercer (51) was recently named Group President and has been Executive Vice President–Operations since 1996. Mr. Mercer previously served as President–Northeast Division from 1991 until his promotion to his current position.

Barry L. Silverman (39) has been President of the Southwest Division since July 1997. Mr. Silverman previously served as Vice President–Merchandising of the Northeast Division from 1991 until his promotion to his current position.

Bryant W. Scott (42) has been President of the EXPO Design Center Division since 1995. Since 1980, Mr. Scott has served in a variety of positions, including Vice President–Merchandising for the Southeast Division.

David Suliteanu (45) was named Group President–Diversified Businesses in April 1998. Mr. Suliteanu previously served as Vice Chairman and Director of Stores for Macy's East, a position he held from 1993 until he joined Home Depot in April 1998.

Annette M. Verschuren (41) has been President of The Home Depot Canada since 1996. In 1992, Ms. Verschuren formed Verschuren Ventures Inc. and remained there until joining Michaels of Canada Inc. in 1993, where she served as President until joining the company.

In 1997, Bernard Marcus, who had been CEO since the company's inception in 1978, passed the title to Arthur M. Blank. Blank now served as President and CEO.

Exhibit 3 shows all the officers of Home Depot.

Exhibit 3 Officers: Home Depot, Inc.

Corporate

Bernard Marcus
Chairman of the Board

Arthur M. Blank
President and Chief Executive Officer

Ronald M. Brill
Executive Vice President and Chief Administrative Officer

Bill Hamlin
Executive Vice President Merchandising and Group President

Larry M. Mercer
Executive Vice President Operations and Group President

David Suliteanu
Group President, Diversified Services

Alan Barnaby
Senior Vice President, Store Operations

Marshall L. Day
Senior Vice President, Chief Financial Officer

Pat Farrah
Senior Vice President, Merchandising

Bryan J. Fields
Senior Vice President, Real Estate

Ronald B. Griffin
Senior Vice President Information Services

Richard A. Hammill
Senior Vice President, Marketing

W. Andrew McKenna
Senior Vice President Strategic Business Development

Stephen R. Messana
Senior Vice President, Human Resources

Dennis Ryan
Senior Vice President, Merchandising

Lawrence A. Smith
Senior Vice President, Legal and Secretary

Terence L. Smith
Senior Vice President, Imports/Logistics

Richard L. Sullivan
Senior Vice President, Advertising

Robert J. Wittman
Senior Vice President, Merchandising

Mike Anderson
Vice President, Information Services

Ben A. Barone
Vice President, Credit Marketing

Dave Bogage
Vice President, Management and Organization Development

Patrick Cataldo
Vice President, Training

Gary C. Cochran
Vice President, Information Services

Charles D. Crowell
Vice President, Distribution Services

Kerrie R. Flanagan
Vice President, Merchandise Accounting

Mike Folio
Vice President, Real Estate

Frank Gennaccaro
Vice President, Merchandising

Paul Hoedeman
Vice President, Information Services

Ted Kaczmarowski
Vice President Construction/Store Planning

(continued)

Exhibit 3 *(continued)*

Bill Peña
Vice President/General Manager
International Development

William K. Schlegal
Vice President, Imports

Kim Shreckengost
Vice President, Investor Relations

Don Singletary
Vice President, Human Resources—
North American Stores

Grady Stewart
Vice President, Operations

Carol B. Tome
Vice President, Treasurer

DeWayne Truitt
Vice President
Compensation and Benefits

Gregg Vickery
Vice President, Controller

Edward A. Wolfe
Vice President, Loss Prevention

Ken Young
Vice President, Internal Audit

Midwest Division

Mark Baker
President

H. George Collins
Vice President, Store Operations

Robert Gilbreth
Vice President, Store Operations

Steven L. Mahurin
Vice President, Merchandising

Michael J. Williams
Vice President, Human Resources

Northeast Division

Vern Joslyn
President

Jeff Birren
Vice President, Store Operations

Carol A. Freitag
Vice President, Human Resources

William G. Lennie
Vice President, Merchandising

Michael McCabe
Vice President, Store Operations

Pedro Mendiguren
Vice President, Store Operations

Southeast Division

Bruce Berg
President

Tony Brown
Vice President, Store Operations

Dennis Johnson
Vice President, Merchandising

Eric Johnson
Vice President, Store Operations

H. Gregory Turner
Vice President, Store Operations

John Wicks
Vice President, Merchandising

Southwest Division

Barry L. Silverman
President

Jerry Edwards
Vice President, Merchandising

Frank Rosi
Vice President, Human Resources

Tom Taylor
Vice President, Store Operations

Western Division

Lynn Martineau
President

Terry Hopper
Vice President, Store Operations

Ethan Klausner
Vice President, Merchandising

Bruce Merino
Vice President, Merchandising

Timothy J. Pfeiffer
Vice President, Store Operations

Thomas "Buz" Smith
Vice President, Store Operations

Greg Lewis
Division Controller

The Home Depot Canada

Annette M. Verschuren
President

John Hayes
Vice President, Merchandising

Dennis Kennedy
Vice President, Store Operations

EXPO Design Center Division

Bryant Scott
President

Christopher A. McLoughlin
Vice President, Division Controller

Steve Smith
Vice President, Merchandising

Maintenance Warehouse

Jonathan Neeley
President

Jim Ardell
Vice President, Merchandising

Mike Brown
Vice President, Information Systems

Bill Luth
Vice President, Marketing

Steven L. Neeley
Vice President, Sales

Kevin Peters
Vice President, Logistics

Ron Turk
Vice President
Chief Financial Officer

Jeffrey R. Wenham
Vice President, Human Resources

National Blind & Wallpaper Factory

David Katzman
President

Rick Kovacs
Senior Vice President, Merchandising

David Littleson
Chief Financial Officer

Steve Kaip
Vice President, Information Systems

Debra Russell
Vice President, Operations

Bob Shepard
Vice President
Installation/Retail Development

Source: The Home Depot, Inc., 1997 Annual Report, p. 36.

Organizational Structure

The official organizational structure of Home Depot (see **Exhibit 4**) was much like that of other retail organizations, but according to a human resources spokesperson, the environment was so relaxed and casual that people felt like they could report to anyone. Marcus and Blank presided at the top of Home Depot's organizational chart and were supported by Executive Vice Presidents: Executive Vice President and Chief Administrative Officer; Executive Vice President of Merchandising and Group President; and Executive Vice President of Operations and Group President.

There were 3 Group Presidents, of whom 2 were also Executive Vice Presidents. The other was the Group President of Diversified Businesses. These executives were supported by 13 Senior Vice Presidents (see **Exhibit 4**). The company had 21 Vice Presidents at the corporate level.

The organization was divided into seven divisions:

1. Southeast Division,
2. Western Division,
3. Northeast Division,
4. Midwest Division,
5. Home Depot Canada Division,
6. Southwest Division, and
7. EXPO Design Centers.

Each division was headed by a President, who was supported by Vice Presidents of Merchandising and Store Operations. Under each Vice President in a division was a group of regional managers responsible for a number of stores. There were a number of Vice Presidents at the division level, some of which included Legal, Information Services, Logistics, Advertising, the Controller, and Human Resources.

At the store level, Home Depot was set up much as would be expected—with a Manager, Assistant Managers, and Department Managers. The average Home Depot store had one Manager whose primary responsibility was to be the master delegator. Four to six Assistants usually presided over the store's 10 departments. Each Assistant Manager was responsible for 1 to 3 departments. One Assistant Manager was responsible for receiving and the "back end" (stock storage area), in addition to his or her departments. The Assistant Managers were supported by Department Managers who were each responsible for one department. The Department Managers reported directly to the Assistant Managers and had no firing/hiring capabilities. Assistant Managers normally handled ordering and work schedules, and so on. Department Managers handled employees' questions and job assignments. In a recent change, human resource officers were made responsible for recruiting, staffing, employee relations, and management development for each division.[22]

Home Depot Canada (Aikenhead's)

On February 28, 1994, Home Depot acquired a 75% interest in Aikenhead's Home Improvements Warehouse chain of seven warehouses in Canada for approximately $161,584,000. It was a joint venture with Molson Companies, Ltd.; Home Depot served as the general partner. Stephen Bebis, a former Home Depot officer, developed the chain along the Home Depot concept. He initially served as President of this unit and was replaced by Annette M. Verschuren in 1995.

Exhibit 4 Organizational Chart: The Home Depot, Inc.

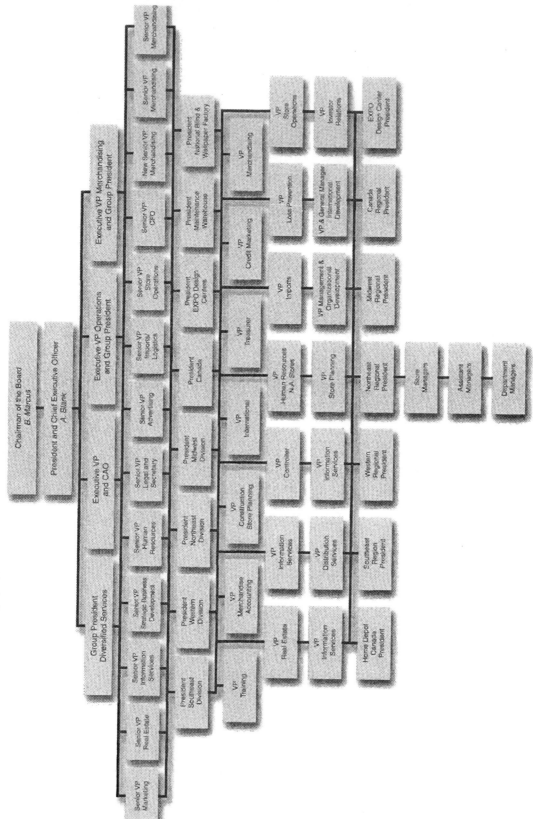

Note: This does not include the company's wholly owned subsidiaries (1) National Blind & Wallpaper Factory and (2) Maintenance Warehouse.

Source: Company records.

Operations[23]

Home Depot stores and their merchandise were set up so that all of the stores were very similar. The company's corporate headquarters was responsible for the "look," but individual managers could change a display or order more or less of a product if they could justify the change. The Managers within individual stores made decisions regarding their employees, such as firing and hiring, but they looked to headquarters in areas such as training. One Manager of a store in Georgia said that if he did not like a particular display or promotion, it was at his discretion to change it or drop it. The Manager went on to say that he and other store managers work hand in hand with corporate headquarters, and that if he wanted to make "major" changes or had a significant store or personnel problem, he would deal with headquarters.

During 1994, Home Depot introduced a prototype store format, which offered about 32,000 more square feet of selling space and a significantly broader and deeper selection of products and services, as well as a more convenient layout than the traditional stores. These "Type V" stores were designed around a design center, which grouped complementary product categories.

Operational efficiency had been a crucial part of achieving low prices while still offering a high level of customer service. The company was assessing and upgrading its information to support its growth, reduce and control costs, and enable better decision making. From the installation of computerized checkout systems to the implementation of satellite communications systems in most of the stores, the company had shown that it had been and would continue to be innovative in its operating strategy.

By fiscal year 1994, each store was equipped with a computerized point-of-sale system (POS), electronic bar code scanning systems, and a minicomputer. These systems provided efficient customer checkout with approximately 90% scannable products, store-based inventory management, rapid order replenishment, labor planning support, and item movement information. In fiscal year 1994, faster registers were introduced along with new check approval systems and a new receipt format to expedite credit care transactions.

Home Depot's attitude of complete customer satisfaction has led the company to constantly seek ways to improve customer service. When the company was faced with clogged aisles, endless checkout lines, and too few salespeople, it sought creative ways to improve customer service. Workers were added to the sales floor. Shelfstocking and price tagging were shifted to nighttime, when the aisles were empty. The changes were worth the expense because now employees were free to sell during the day. In an effort to ease customer crowding, Home Depot used a "clustering" strategy to locate new stores closer to existing ones.

The company also operated its own television network (HDTV). This money-saving device allowed Home Depot's top executives to get instant feedback from local managers and also allowed training and communications programs to be viewed in the stores. Management's operating philosophies and policies were more effectively communicated because information presented by top management could be targeted at a large audience. This addition had increased employee motivation and saved many dollars by making information available in a timely manner.

Home Depot was firmly committed to energy conservation and had installed reflectors to lower the amount of lighting required in a store. The reflectors darkened the ceiling but saved thousands of dollars a year in energy bills. Further, the company had pursued a computerized system to maintain comfortable temperatures, a challenge due to the stores' concrete floors, exposed ceilings, and open oversized doors for forklift deliveries. The system also had an automated feedback capability that could be used for equipment maintenance.

The adoption of the POS technology had improved each store's ability to identify and adapt to trends quickly. The information provided by this technology was transferred to computer centers in Atlanta and Fullerton, California, where consumer buying trends were traced.

This allowed Home Depot to adjust its merchandising mix and track both buyer trends and inventory.

In 1987, the company had introduced an advanced inventory management system that allowed it to increase inventory turnover significantly, from 4.1 in 1985 to 5.7 in 1994. This let Home Depot carry $40 million less in inventory, tying up less working capital to finance it. This efficiency allowed a cost structure that was significantly lower than the competition's.

In 1994, the company introduced phone centers to serve its customers who called to inquire about pricing and availability of merchandise. Adding experienced salespeople to a phone bank to answer calls quickly and efficiently had increased weekly phone sales. Without having to respond to phone calls, the sales staff could better concentrate on serving in-store customers.

The company continued to see greater efficiency as a result of its Electronic Data Interchange (EDI) program. Currently over 400 of the company's highest volume vendors were participating in the EDI program. A paperless system, EDI electronically processed orders from stores to vendors, alerted the store when the merchandise was to arrive, and transmitted vendor invoice data.

In fiscal year 1994, stores were outfitted with Electronic Article Surveillance (EAS) detectors, which triggered an alarm if a person exited the store with merchandise that had been affixed with an EAS label that had not been desensitized at the cash register. The system was proving to be a deterrent to theft, with many stores reporting reductions in shoplifting offenses.

Home Depot continuously experimented with new operating concepts, such as CrossRoads and EXPO Design Centers. Its investment in new retail technology and its willingness to streamline operations for the benefit of the customer and employees had paid off in areas such as inventory turnover, in-stock turnover, in-stock inventory positions, querying problems, employee motivation, and information flow from the company's buyers to its store-level managers and employees.

Merchandising[24]

If Home Depot's advertising strategy of creating awareness of the company's stores and encouraging do-it-yourselfers (DIYs) to tackle more at-home projects was getting people into the stores, the merchandising mix was aimed at getting people to buy. According to Marcus, "We could sell them anything . . . but we don't. We don't want the customer to think we're a discounter, food store, a toy store, or anything else, because it would confuse [them]."[25] Home Depot wanted to be thought of as the DIY warehouse, nothing less.

Advertising

The company maintained an aggressive campaign, using various media for both price and institutional policy. Print advertising, usually emphasizing price, was prepared by an in-house staff to control context, layout, media placement, and cost. Broadcast media advertisements were generally institutional and promoted Home Depot "the company," not just pricing strategy. These advertisements focused on the "You'll feel right at home" and "Everyday Low Pricing" ad slogans, name recognition, and the value of Home Depot's customer service. Although the company had grown over the years, the goal of its advertising was still to project a local flavor. The Western Division maintained its own creative department because of its different time zone and unique product mix. The company attempted to use information for the field in the various markets and put together an effective advertising campaign. The company still relied heavily on print media.

Home Depot sponsored the 1996 U.S. Summer Olympic Games in Atlanta. Through the sponsorship, Home Depot had hoped to further its ties with the home improvement customer, create sales opportunities, further differentiate itself from competitors, maintain its corporate culture, and support key businesses in the community. Home Depot began 1994 by unveiling a program to help pave the Olympic Park in Atlanta with engraved bricks, hiring athletes to work in the stores and office while they trained for the Games, and continuing a cooperative partnership with vendors in the Home Depot Olympic Family. This partnership had grown to include 29 key suppliers in the United States and 26 in Canada. Each member of the "Family" represented a specific home improvement product category and could participate in many of Home Depot's Olympic Games promotions.

The company participated in the Olympic Job Opportunities Program, in which Home Depot provided part-time jobs for 100 hopeful Olympic athletes as they trained for the Olympics. Twenty-six of the American and Canadian athletes participated in the Olympic Games and 6 earned medals. The company planned to remain a sponsor for at least the next six years for the Olympic Games in 2000, 2002, and 2004. The company also acted as a sponsor for the 1998 Winter Olympic Games.

Customer Target Market

Home Depot stores served primarily do-it-yourselfers, although home improvement contractors, building maintenance professionals, interior designers, and other professionals had become increasingly important customers. DIY customers continued to be the core business and made up approximately two thirds of the total home improvement segment. DIY customers bought materials for the home and installed them personally.

Due to the increasing home improvement activity, buy-it-yourself (BIY) customers began to emerge. BIY customers chose products, made the purchase, and contracted with others to complete the project or install the furnishings. Home Depot was catering to this segment by expanding its installed sales program companywide.

Home Depot also continued to target the professional business customer. It had set up a commercial credit program, provided commercial checkout lines in the stores, and had hired additional associates with experience in various professional fields.

The typical DIY customer was a married male homeowner, aged 25 to 34, with a high school diploma or some college, and had an annual income of $20,000 to $40,000. Projections through 1999 indicated that households headed by 25- to 35-year-olds with earnings over $30,000 would increase 34% to 38% by 1999. The 45-to-54 age group was earning over $30,000 and was expected to increase by 40%.

Economics

The DIY industry exhibited a demand pattern that was largely recession-proof. Because a mere 15% of Home Depot's business came from contractors, a downturn in home construction had only a modest impact on Home Depot sales. In addition, analysts pointed out that, during hard times, consumers could not afford to buy new or bigger homes; instead they maintained or upgraded their existing homes. Home improvement spending had declined in one recession during the past 20 years. The new strategy to penetrate the professional market might affect the company's sales more in future recessions.

Merchandising Strategy

The company's *1994 Annual Report* stated that Home Depot's goal was to be "The Do-It-Yourself Retailer." Merchandising included all activities involved in the buying and selling of goods for a profit. It involved long-range planning to ensure that the right merchandise was available at the right place, at the right time, in the right quantity, and at the right price. Success depended on the firm's ability to act and react with speed, spot changes, and catch trends early.

During 1994, Home Depot refined its merchandising function to be more efficient and responsive to customers. The new structure gave Division Managers responsibility for specific product categories, and specialists in each of these categories made sure the business lines were kept current. There were also field merchants who worked with the stores to ensure proper implementation of new programs as well as the maintenance of any ongoing programs. This approach strengthened product lines, got the right merchandise to the customers, reduced administration costs, and prepared Home Depot to expand into additional product lines.

The merchandising strategy of Home Depot followed a three-pronged approach: (1) excellent customer service, (2) everyday low pricing, and (3) wide breadth of products.

Each Home Depot store served 100,000 households with a median income of $45,000. Of those households, 75% were owner-occupied. In 1997, Home Depot responded to the demographics of certain markets by expanding its service hours to 24 hours a day in 15 store locations.

Home Depot continued to introduce or refine several merchandising programs during fiscal 1997. Key among them was the company's ongoing commitment to becoming the supplier of choice to a variety of professional customers, including remodelers, carpenters, plumbers, electricians, building maintenance professionals, and designers. According to management, the company had reacted to the needs of this group by enhancing and increasing quantities of key products for professional customers. In addition, the company was testing additional products and service-related programs designed to increase sales to professional customers, including expanded commercial credit programs, delivery services, and incremental dedicated staff.

The company's installed sales program was available, with varying services offered, in all of the company's stores. The company authorized approximately 3,500 installed sales vendors who, as independent licensed contractors, provide services to customers. This program targeted the BIY customer, who would purchase a product but did not have the desire or ability to install it.

Construction on the company's new Import Distribution Center (IDC), located in Savannah, Georgia, was completed in fiscal 1997. Built with the intention of servicing the company's stores located east of the Rocky Mountains, the IDC began shipments in April 1997, and by the end of fiscal 1997 was servicing all targeted stores. The 1.4-million-square-foot facility was staffed with approximately 600 associates. The IDC enabled the company to directly import products not currently available to customers or offer products currently sourced domestically from third-party importers. Other benefits included quicker turnaround deliveries to stores, lower costs, and improved quality control than would be possible if the products were purchased through third-party importers.

The company sponsored the "1997 National Home and Garden Show Series." Bringing together 16 of the nation's most successful consumer shows under one national sponsorship provided maximum exposure and support to the shows. Through this sponsorship, the company played a key role in bringing the most innovative lawn and garden, interior design, and home improvement products and services to the attention of the general public.

Homer TLC, Inc., an indirect, wholly owned subsidiary of The Home Depot, Inc., owned the trademarks "The Home Depot" and "EXPO," as well as the "Homer" advertising symbol and various private-label brand names that the company uses. The company's operating subsidiaries licensed from Homer TLC, Inc., the right to use this intellectual property. Management believed that the company's rights in this intellectual property were an important asset of the company.

Home Depot was the only big-box retailer to offer a number of other exclusive, high-quality products such as Pergo® laminate flooring, Ralph Lauren® paints, and Vigoro® fertilizer. Each of these products made Home Depot unique from its competitors and provided its customers with a better selection of products. Home Depot's proprietary products included Behr Premium Plus paints, Hampton Bay ceiling fans and lighting products, Husky tools, and Scott's lawnmowers. These proprietary products provided Home Depot customers with a quality product at a value price and often filled a needed void in the product offerings.

Following the success of Home Depot's best-selling *Home Improvement 1-2-3*™ book, the company recently released *Outdoor Projects 1-2-3*™, the company's latest how-to book sold in Home Depot stores and bookstores. For the past three years, Home Depot has sponsored *HouseSmart with Lynette Jennings*™, one of the highest-rated shows on The Discovery Channel®. The company planned to extend its reach to tomorrow's homeowners in 1998 through *Homer's Workshop*™, the first how-to, project-oriented television program for children.

Clustering Strategy

The clustering strategy had been employed to allow Home Depot's aggressive expansion program. Home Depot had intentionally cannibalized sales of existing stores by opening two other stores in a single market area. The short-run effect was to lower same-store sales, but a strategic advantage was created by raising the barrier of entry to competitors. It reduced overcrowding in the existing stores. It also allowed the company to spread its advertising and distribution costs over a larger store base, thereby lowering selling, general, and administrative costs. The company's 1997 gross margin was 28.1%.

Customer Service

The availability of sales personnel to attend to customer needs was one clear objective of the Home Depot customer service strategy.

Customer service differentiated Home Depot from its competitors. The provision of highly qualified and helpful employees, professional clinics, and in-store displays had developed into a customer service approach referred to as "customer cultivation." It gave DIY customers the support and confidence that no home project was beyond their capabilities with Home Depot personnel close at hand.

Home Depot employees went beyond simply recommending appropriate products, tools, and materials. Sales personnel cultivated the customer by demonstrating methods and techniques of performing a job safely and efficiently. This unique aspect of the company's service also served as a feedback mechanism—employees helping the next customer learn from the problems and successes of the last one.

All of the stores offered hands-on workshops on projects such as kitchen remodeling, basic plumbing, ceramic tile installation, and other activities in which customers in a particular locality had expressed interest. Offered mainly on weekends, the workshops varied in length, depending on complexity. Only the most experienced staff members, many of them former skilled craftsmen, taught at these workshops. Promotion of the workshops was done through direct mail advertising and in-store promotion.

At many Home Depot stores, customers could rent trucks by the hour through Load 'N Go™, Home Depot's exclusive truck rental service. The company also expanded a tool rental service to more stores during fiscal 1998. In addition, the company's special order capabilities should improve, due in part to the acquisition in November 1997 of National Blind & Wallpaper Factory and Habitat Wallpaper & Blinds stores, which became wholly owned subsidiaries of Home Depot. When integrated with the stores beginning in fiscal 1998, the innovative ordering systems of these companies should give Home Depot the capability to handle wallpaper and window covering special orders in a more efficient, cost-effective, and convenient manner for customers.

Pricing Strategy

Home Depot stressed its commitment to "Everyday Low Pricing." This concept meant across-the-board lower prices and fewer deep-cutting sales. To ensure this, Home Depot employed professional shoppers to check competitors' prices regularly.

One of the major reasons that Home Depot was able to undercut the competition by as much as 25% was a dependable relationship with its suppliers. The company conducted business with approximately 5,700 vendors, the majority of which were manufacturers. A confidential survey of manufacturers conducted by Shapiro and Associates found that Home Depot was "far and away the most demanding of customers." Home Depot was most vocal about holding to shipping dates. Manufacturers agreed that increased sales volume had offset concessions made to Home Depot.

Products

A typical Home Depot store stocked approximately 40,000 to 50,000 products, including variations in color and size. The products included different kinds of building materials, home improvement products, and lawn and garden supplies. In addition, Home Depot stores offered installation services for many products. Each store carried a wide selection of quality and nationally advertised brand name merchandise. The contribution of each product group was as follows[26]:

Product Group	Percentage of Sales		
	Year Ending February 1, 1998	Year Ending February 2, 1997	Year Ending January 28, 1996
Plumbing, heating, lighting, and electrical supplies	27.1%	27.4%	27.7%
Building materials, lumber, floor, and wall coverings	34.2	34.0	33.9
Hardware and tools	13.5	13.4	13.2
Seasonal and specialty items	14.8	14.7	14.8
Paint and others	10.4	10.5	10.4
	100.0%	100.0%	100.0%

The company sourced its store merchandise from approximately 5,700 vendors worldwide, and no single vendor accounted for more than 5% of total purchases.

Average Store Profile

According to Bob Evans in the Store Planning Division of Home Depot, all of the stores were company owned, not franchised, and most were freestanding, built to Home Depot's standards.

Home Depot owned 74% of its buildings in 1997, leasing the remainder. Marcus planned to increase the company owned percentage. In 1989, the company had owned only about 40% of its stores. Although the company preferred locations surrounded by shopping centers, Marcus insisted that the company was not interested in being attached to a shopping center or mall. Stores were placed in suburban areas populated by members of the Home Depot target market. Ownership provided Home Depot with greater operational control and flexibility, generally lower occupancy loss, and certain other economic advantages. Construction time depended on site conditions, special local requirements, and related factors. According to Evans, depending on "if we have to move a mountain, fill a canyon, level a forest, or how many gopher turtles are in the ground that we have to relocate," building a store can take up to a year.

Current building standards were 108,000 square feet for each store itself and 16,000 to 28,000 square feet of outside selling space for the garden department. Stores did vary, however, because the company "will make the store fit the land," and many of the original stores were located in leased strip-center space. Home Depot had increased its average store size from about 97,000 to 108,000 square feet, with an additional 20,000 to 28,000 square feet of outside (garden) selling space. The average weighted sales per square foot was $406, $398, $390, $404, and $398 for 1997, 1996, 1995, 1994, and 1993, respectively. The weighted average weekly sales per operational store was $829,000; $803,000; $787,000; $802,000; and $764,000 for 1997, 1996, 1995, 1994, and 1993, respectively. Although Marcus would like to see stores averaging 120,000 square feet, Evans said that "the hundred [thousand square-foot size] is what we're building most of." Some stores had thousands of customers a week and "just get too crowded," according to Evans. Marcus had estimated that "in some cases, we have 25,000 to 30,000 people walking through a store per week."

Because of the large number of customers, older stores were being gradually remodeled or replaced with new ones to add room for new merchandise, to increase selling space for what is already there, and sometimes even to add more walking room on the inside—and more parking space.

Because merchandising and inventory were centrally organized, product mix varied slightly from store to store. Each, however, sported the Home Depot look: warehouse-style shelves, wide concrete-floored aisles, end displays pushing sale items, and the ever-present orange banners indicating the store's departments. Most stores had banners on each aisle to help customers locate what they're looking for. Regional purchasing departments were used to keep the stores well stocked and were preferred to a single, strong corporate department "since home improvement materials needed in the Southwest would differ somewhat from those needed in the Northeast."

Information Systems

Each store was equipped with a computerized point-of-sale system, electronic bar code scanning system, and a UNIX server. Management believed these systems provided efficient customer check-out (with an approximately 90% rate of scannable products), store-based inventory management, rapid order replenishment, labor planning support, and item movement information. Faster registers as well as a new check approval system and a new receipt format had expedited transactions. To better serve the increasing number of customers applying for credit, the charge card approval process time had been reduced to less than 30 seconds. Store information was communicated to the Store Support Center's computers via a land-based frame relay network. These computers provided corporate, financial, merchandising, and other back-office function support.

The company was continuously assessing and upgrading its information systems to support its growth, reduce and control costs, and enable better decision making. The company continued to realize greater efficiency as a result of its electronic data interchange (EDI) program. Most of the company's highest volume vendors were participating in the EDI program. A paperless system, EDI electronically processed orders from buying offices to vendors, alerted the stores when the merchandise was to arrive, and transmitted invoice data from the vendors and motor carriers to the Store Support Center. In addition, during fiscal 1997 the company continued to develop new computer systems to facilitate and improve product order replenishment in Home Depot stores.[27]

The Year 2000 Problem

The company was currently addressing a universal situation commonly referred to as the "year 2000 problem." The year 2000 problem related to the inability of certain computer software programs to properly recognize and process date-sensitive information relative to the year 2000 and beyond. During fiscal 1997, the company developed a plan to devote the necessary resources to identify and modify systems impacted by the year 2000 problem, or implement new systems to become year 2000 compliant in a timely manner. The cost of executing this plan was not expected to have a material impact on the company's results of operations or financial condition. In addition, the company had contacted its major suppliers and vendors to ensure their awareness of the year 2000 problem. If the company, its suppliers, or vendors were unable to resolve issues related to the year 2000 on a timely basis, it could result in a material financial risk.[28]

Human Resources[29]

Home Depot was noted for its progressive human resources policies, which emphasized the importance of the individual to the success of the company's operations.

Recruitment/Selection

Throughout its entire recruiting process, Home Depot looked for people who shared a commitment to excellence. Also, management recognized that having the right number of people, in the right jobs, at the right time was critical. Employee population varied greatly among stores, depending on store size, sales volume, and the season of the year. In the winter, a store could have had fewer than 75 employees and in the spring would add another 25 to 40 employees. Some of the larger northeastern stores had as many as 280 employees. Full-time employees filled approximately 90% of the positions.

When a store first opened, it attracted applications through advertisements in local newspapers and trade journals such as *Home Center News*. A new store would usually receive several thousand applications. When seasonal workers and replacements were needed, help-wanted signs were displayed at store entrances. Walk-in candidates were another source, and applications were available at the customer service desk at all times. There was no formal program to encourage employees to refer their friends for employment. At the management level, the company preferred to hire people at the Assistant Manager level, requiring them to work their way up to store Manager and beyond. Historically the company often hired outside talent for senior positions. Now that the company had grown, Home Depot believed that, whenever possible, executives should come up through the ranks, although management from the outside was occasionally brought in. To support its growing infrastructure, Steven Messana served as Senior Vice President for Human Resources.

Interviews were scheduled one per day per week; however, if someone with trade experience applied, an on-the-spot interview might be conducted. "Trade" experience included retail, construction, do-it-yourself, or hardware. The company tended to look for older people who brought a high level of knowledge and maturity to the position. In addition to related experience, Home Depot looked for people with a stable work history who had a positive attitude, were excited, outgoing, and hard workers.

The selection process included preemployment tests (honesty, math, and drugs). The stores displayed signs in the windows that said that anyone who used drugs need not apply. Interviews were conducted with three or four people—an initial qualifier, the Administrative Assistant in operations, an Assistant Manager, and the store Manager. Reference checks were completed prior to a job offer. More in-depth background checks (financial, criminal) were conducted on management-level candidates.

To help ensure that Home Depot selected the best qualified people, during fiscal 1997 the company designed a proprietary automated system for identifying the best candidates for store sales associate positions. This system, which had been through extensive validation testing, screened candidates for competencies and characteristics inherent to Home Depot's best sales associates. The company planned to use this system to evaluate additional positions in the future.

Retention

Employee turnover varied from store to store. In the first year of operations, turnover could run 60% to 70% but would fall below 30% in future years. The company's goal was to reduce turnover to below 20%. The major causes of turnover were students who returned to school, employees who were terminated for poor performance, and tradespeople who considered Home Depot an interim position (often returning to their trade for a position paying as much as $50,000 per year). Very few people left the organization looking for "greener pastures" in the retail industry.

Career development was formally addressed during semiannual performance reviews, with goals and development plans mutually set by employees and managers. The company was committed to promotions from within and had a formal job-posting program. Vacancy lists were prepared at the regional level and distributed to the stores. Store managers were promoted from within. Affirmative action plans were used to increase female and minority representation.

Compensation

Employees were paid a straight salary. Bernard Marcus said, "The day I'm laid out dead with an apple in my mouth is the day we'll pay commissions. If you pay commissions, you imply that the small customer isn't worth anything." Most management-level employees were eligible for bonuses that were based on such factors as a store's return on assets and sales versus budget. Assistant Managers could receive up to 25% of their base salary in bonuses, and store Managers could earn up to 50% if their stores' performance warranted. Store managers could earn $50,000 to $120,000. The typical employee earned $10 to $14 per hour.

During fiscal year 1988, the company established a leveraged Employee Stock Ownership Plan (ESOP), covering substantially all full-time employees. In 1989, the company made its initial contribution to the ESOP of $6 million, which represented about $0.05 per share. Fully funded by the company, the ESOP was established to provide additional retirement security for the employees, while simultaneously reducing taxable income and discouraging hostile takeover attempts. At February 1, 1998, the ESOP held a total of 10,161,272 shares of the company's common stock in trust for plan participants. The company made annual contributions to the ESOP at the discretion of the Board of Directors. All employees eligible for the ESOP were entitled to receive a substantial portion of their annual salary in profit sharing. Tim Sparks, 31, who started out loading customers' cars in the lot at the age of 19 and managed a store in Jacksonville, Florida, said, "My father was a peanut farmer in Alabama. Dirt poor. Where else could a son go from that to being a millionaire?"

Recognition programs emphasized good customer service, increased sales, safety, cost savings, and length of service. Badges, cash awards, and other prizes were distributed in monthly group meetings.

Communication was the key by which Home Depot perpetuated its culture and retained its people. That culture included an environment in which employees were happy and where they felt productive and secure. The company sold employees on their role in Home Depot's success—they were giving the company a return on its assets. The environment avoided bureaucracy, was informal and intense, and encouraged honesty and risk taking. Each store maintained a strong open-door policy, and a Manager would spend two or three hours discussing a concern with an employee.

Top management was equally accessible to employees through frequent visits to the stores. An in-house TV broadcast, "Breakfast with Bernie and Arthur," was held quarterly. Impromptu questions were solicited from the employees. Department Managers met with employees weekly to provide new information and solicit feedback. Worker opinions also mattered at the top. When the company planned to open on New Year's Day, the employees voted to close and prevailed. When the company wrote a check-out training manual, a store cashier from Jacksonville helped write it. Internal sales charts were posted on bulletin boards so that employees would know how their store compared with others in the area.

Training

Home Depot believed that knowledgeable salespeople were one of the keys to the company's success and spent a great deal of time training them to "bleed orange." Callers to the home office found that corporate executives spent most of their time in the stores training employees. "We teach from the top down, and those who can't teach don't become executives," said one top executive. Training costs to open a new store were about $400,000 to $500,000.

Regular employees went through both formal and on-the-job training. Classes were held on product knowledge (giving the employee "total product knowledge . . . including all the skills a trade person might have"); merchandising concepts, and salesmanship (so that they could be sure that a customer has available, and would purchase, everything needed to complete a project); time management; personnel matters; safety and security; and how to interpret the company's various internally generated reports.

Each new employee was required to go through a rigorous week-long orientation, which introduced new hires to Home Depot's culture. To ensure that employees were convinced of the company's commitment, Bernard Marcus, Arthur Blank, and Ron Brill conducted many of the management training sessions. New employees were then paired with experienced associates in the stores to gain first-hand knowledge of customer service and general store operations. They trained an average of four weeks before working on their own. Even then, when there were no other customers in the department, newer employees would watch more experienced employees interact with customers to learn more about products, sales, and customer service. Employees were cross-trained to work in various departments, and even the cashiers learned how to work the sales floor.

The Home Depot Television Network allowed the company to disseminate policies and philosophies, product upgrades, and so on. With the ability to target special or mass audiences, the training possibilities were endless. The fact that the programs were broadcast live, with telephone call-ins, enhanced their immediacy and made interaction possible.

According to management, Home Depot's training programs were key to arming associates with the knowledge they needed to serve customers. During fiscal 1997, the company made several changes to its human resources and training programs to prepare for and support Home Depot's future growth plans. To address the unique growth needs of its divisions, new human resources officers were responsible for areas such as recruiting, staffing, employee relations, and management development in their divisions. They were also responsible for implementing the store training programs that take entry-level sales associates from the basics to becoming project experts and, ultimately, masters in their respective departments.

Employees

As of the end of January 1998, the company employed approximately 125,000 people, of whom approximately 7,900 were salaried and the remainder were on an hourly basis. Approximately 76% of the company's employees were employed on a full-time basis. There were no unions. The company has never suffered a work stoppage.

Industry and Competitors

Retail Building and Supply Industry

The retail building supply industry was moving rapidly from one characterized by small, independently run establishments to one dominated by regional and national chains of vast superstores. Home Depot developed the concept of the all-in-one discount warehouse home improvement superstore, designed to be all things to all people. The main rival to Home Depot was Lowe's, which had been replacing its older, smaller stores with new superstores. Other companies in the industry were facing the challenge by reconfiguring their stores and by targeting niche segments, but some were being forced to close stores in the face of increased competition.

In 1997, the retail building supply industry showed mixed results. The stronger companies (Home Depot and Lowe's) got stronger, and the weak struggled. The largest two operators, Lowe's and Home Depot, extended their dominance, especially in the Do-It-Yourself (DIY) segment of the market (see **Exhibit 5**). Small regional operators such as Grossman in the Northeast were liquidated.

In 1997, Leonard Green & Partners bought out both Hechinger and Builders Square, formerly owned and started by Kmart, in an effort to turn the two struggling chains into one profitable chain.[30]

The retail building supply industry served two distinct clients—the professional building contractor and the DIY homeowner. The DIY customer had grown in importance over the past few years. Home Depot's main competitors were:

- **Hechinger** was located in the mid-Atlantic states and was recently acquired by Leonard Green & Partners. Hechinger had financial problems for several years before it was acquired.

- **Lowe's** was located in 22 states with 442 stores and had recently moved into large metropolitan areas—Dallas and Atlanta. The company had developed regional distribution centers to better serve its growing markets. Lowe's 1997 sales were estimated to be $10,190,000,000 and second to Home Depot, with sales of $24,156,000,000 for 1997 (see **Exhibit 5**).

- **BMC** was renamed Building Materials Holding Corporation. The company had over 50 stores in 10 western states and was focusing on the professional/contractor market segment.

- **Hughes Supply** had 310 stores, principally in Florida, Georgia, and other southeastern states. The 1997 sales were estimated to be $1,810,000,000. The company made 13 acquisitions in 1996, which added about $340 million to its sales base. After these acquisitions, Hughes was in new territories—upper New York and California. The company focused on the professional/contractor market segment (see **Exhibit 5**).

- **Wolohan Lumber** had 58 stores located in Illinois, Indiana, Kentucky, Ohio, and Wisconsin. The company strategy was to focus on the professional/contractor market segment. The 1997 sales were estimated to be $425,000,000 (see **Exhibit 5**).

Exhibit 5 provides a summary of the key information on these companies.

The industry did not have barriers to entry in the form of patents or special technology. There was a major learning curve on efficiently managing a 100,000-square-foot store. The superstore warehouses tried to serve all market segments, but they had become increasingly consumer oriented. Because of this, smaller competitors were focusing their strategies on the professional constructor segment of the market.[31]

Eagle Hardware & Garden of Seattle, Washington, operated 24 home improvement stores. Its founder, David Heerensperger, viewed Home Depot's entry into Seattle as a "war."

Exhibit 5 Retail Building Supply Industry

A. Competitors

Company	Number of Stores		Sales in Millions ($)			
	2000–2002	1997	2000–2002	1998	1997	1996
Homebase, Inc.	105	84	$ 1,900.0	$ 1,500.0	$ 1,465.0	$ 1,448.8
Home Depot	**1,050**	**624**	**54,000.0**	**30,100.0**	**24,600.0**	**19,535.0**
Hughes Supply	362	310	2,500.0	1,960.0	1,810.0	1,516.1
Lowe's Companies	620	442	17,500.0	11,900.0	10,190.0	8,600.2
Woloham Lumber	75	58	620.0	410.0	425.0	430.4
Industry totals and averages			$66,000.0	$42,000.0	$38,050.0	$33,287.0

Company	Net Profit in Millions ($)				Net Profit Margins %			
	2000–2002	1998	1997	1996	2000–2002	1998	1997	1996
Homebase, Inc.	$ 38.0	$ 24.0	$ 21.0	$ 21.4	2.0%	1.6%	1.4%	1.5%
Home Depot	**2,790.0**	**1,455.0**	**1,160.0**	**937.7**	**5.2**	**4.8**	**4.7**	**4.8**
Hughes Supply	70.0	50.0	40.0	32.5	—	2.6	2.2	2.1
Lowe's Companies	645.0	405.0	345.0	292.2	3.7	3.4	3.4	3.4
Woloham Lumber	12.5	6.0	5.0	6.7	—	1.5	1.2	1.6
Industry totals and averages	$2,310.0	$1,510.0	$1,330.0	$1,287.2	3.6%	3.6%	3.5%	3.5%

B. Industry Indicators

	2000–2002	1998	1997	1996
Sales in millions ($)	$66,000.0	$38,050.0	$33,287.0	$27,152.0
Number of stores	2,350	1,980	1,860	1,922
Net profits in millions ($)	$ 2,310.0	$ 1,510.0	$ 1,330.0	$ 1,287.0
Net profit margin (%)	3.6%	3.6%	3.5%	3.6%

Note: Figures for 1998–2002 are projections.

Source: Value Line *(January 16, 1998), pp. 884, 888–892.*

He said, "They are aiming for us, but we're a thorn in their side. Eagle is the first home center they haven't completely run over."[32]

Eagle's stores averaged 128,000 square feet, compared to Home Depot's 103,000 square feet. Eagle offered other services, namely, a custom-design section, free chain-cutting station, fences, and an idea center where customers could watch videotapes and live demonstrations of home improvement techniques. Heerensperger began preparing for Home Depot's onslaught six years ago. He came up with a design for new stores that were brighter and more elegant than Home Depot's stores. He took into consideration women customers by reducing rack-type displays.[33] Eagle was building the largest stores in the industry in the West Coast and Northwest markets. Eagle planned to maintain a managed-growth strategy.

According to Ronald Pastore, real estate expert, "Between 1992 and 1994, 55% of all new retail square footage was built by big-box retailers (like Wal-Mart and Home Depot)."[34] In 1994, these retailers accounted for 80% of all new stores.

There had been a rampant construction of new retail space over the past 20 years. The supply of retail space nationally was 19 square feet for each person, and this was more than double the level of 20 years ago. The supply had far exceeded the population in growth for the same period. Christopher Niehaus, real estate investment banker, said, "That number is too high. It needs to come down."[35] He predicts that the discount sector is heading for the "'biggest shake-out' in retailing because of overbuilding."[36] Don McCrory, real estate expert, said, "Our question is, if the big-box tenants go out of business, what do you do with the enormous box?"[37]

The Professional Business Segment[38]

Early in fiscal 1997, Home Depot began a formal study of the professional business customer market. The findings of this study clearly indicated that there were many opportunities to grow its presence in the pro market that fit within the company's core business. The study also indicated that many of these opportunities could be captured inside its stores.

Estimated professional business customer sales across all channels in the United States were approximately $265 billion in 1997, substantially higher than the $100 billion Do-It-Yourself market. Excluding the heavy industrial sector, the majority of which was outside Home Depot's core business, the pro market opportunities for the company totaled approximately $215 billion. Home Depot's share of this market was less than 4% in 1998.

The initial focus for growing sales in the professional market was on the professional business customer who already shopped in Home Depot stores, but also made purchases at other retail and wholesale outlets. By listening and responding to his or her needs, the company intended to make Home Depot this customer's supplier of choice.

Late in fiscal 1997, Home Depot began a test in its stores in the Austin, Texas, market designed to increase professional customer sales while continuing to serve the strong and growing do-it-yourself customer market.

The test in Austin included incremental associates primarily responsible for serving and building relationships with the professional business customer. Professional business customers in these stores were assisted at a Pro Service Desk to more quickly meet their product and service needs. In addition, customized services, such as enhanced ordering and credit programs and a menu of product delivery options were available to the pro customer. The test, which was to be expanded to additional stores in fiscal 1998, was helping the company to successfully develop and refine its formula for serving the professional business customer inside its stores.

There were other ways to reach the professional customer, too. During fiscal 1997, Home Depot distributed its ProBook™ professional equipment and supply catalog to professional customers across North America. The ProBook contained over 15,000 products from its stores chosen especially for facility maintenance managers and the building trades. In addition, the company's longer term growth initiatives included exploring opportunities for serving professional customers with more specialized needs through distribution channels outside Home Depot stores.

The total professional business customer market was estimated to be $265 billion in 1997 (see **Exhibit 6**). The heavy industry market, with an estimated $50 billion in sales, was treated as a separate sector. The professional business market ($215 billion) consisted of four subsectors: (1) tradesmen ($85 billion), (2) builders/general contractors ($75 billion), (3) repair and remodeling ($40 billion), and (4) property maintenance ($15 billion).

In 1996, the $215 billion professional business customer target market could be further separated by volume of expenditures. The typical Home Depot pro customer was a repair and remodel professional who purchased up to $200,000 of products annually, but tended to buy less than 10% of this amount from the company. Home Depot planned to capture more of this

**Exhibit 6
Professional
Business Customer
Market**

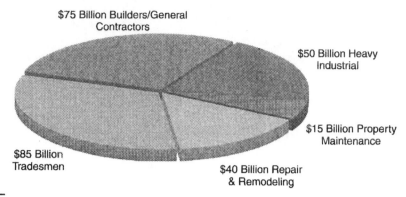

$265 Billion Market

$75 Billion Builders/General
Contractors

$50 Billion Heavy
Industrial

$15 Billion Property
Maintenance

$85 Billion
Tradesmen

$40 Billion Repair
& Remodeling

Source: The Home Depot Inc., 1997 Annual Report, p. 4.

customer's sales by responding to the distinct product and service needs of this professional. (See **Exhibit 7**.)

The company purchased Maintenance Warehouse as part of its strategy to penetrate the professional market.

Do-It-Yourself (DIY) Industry

The Home Depot occupied the number one position in the DIY industry, with sales of $24.1 billion, more than twice the sales of its nearest competitor, Lowe's Companies. Home Depot had approximately 24% market share. Clearly the $100 billion industry was extremely fragmented. The industry remained dominated by small- to mid-sized stores, with only a handful of the top retailers operating stores about 100,000 square feet in size. The trend was clearly moving in the direction of bigger stores, however, as companies such as Lowe's and Home Depot enjoyed success with their large-store formats. As these companies continued to roll out their superstores at an aggressive rate, industry analysts expected the industry to consolidate over time, with the major retailers gaining their share at the expense of the smaller, less efficient DIY chains.

Home Depot was regarded as the premier operator in the DIY industry. The following list shows the six top competitors in 1996. However, based on competitors' announced expansion plans, Home Depot believed that the level of direct competition would increase to 22% of its total store base. The largest and most formidable foe facing Home Depot was the North

**Exhibit 7
U.S. Professional
Business Customer
Profile—$215
Billion Total Target
Market**

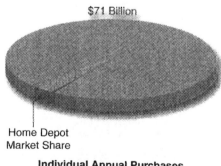

$71 Billion

Home Depot
Market Share

**Individual Annual Purchases
Less Than $200,000**

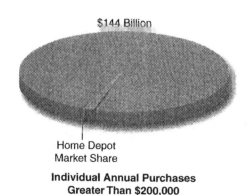

$144 Billion

Home Depot
Market Share

**Individual Annual Purchases
Greater Than $200,000**

Source: The Home Depot, Inc., 1997 Annual Report, p. 7.

Carolina chain, Lowe's. Since 1995, Lowe's had gone into more direct competition with Home Depot in more cities as both companies expanded. As Home Depot added more stores in Lowe's market, analysts believed that Lowe's could face increased margin pressure. Lowe's had been able to maintain its profit margin at 3.4% since 1996. Because Home Depot was more geographically dispersed than Lowe's and had a more balanced portfolio of stores, Home Depot was better able to be price competitive in these markets. The top six retail building supply companies in 1996 were as follows:

1. Home Depot
2. Lowe's Companies
3. Payless Cashways
4. Builders Square
5. Menard's
6. Hechinger

Other competitors were Sutherland Lumber, Wickes Lumber, and Scotty's.

America's do-it-yourselfers spent approximately $100 billion in home improvement products in 1997, up more than 6% from the previous year. This all-important customer group was getting larger in number and more confident and capable to take on home improvement projects every year. In addition, demographic changes were taking place within the do-it-yourself customer group that had important implications for the future of the home improvement industry. Home Depot was positioning itself to continue to grow its share of this industry segment as these changes took place.

The rate of home ownership in the United States continued to grow as first-time buyers entered the housing market at a rapid pace and baby-boomers moved in force to more expensive homes and second homes. During 1997, existing single-family home sales reached their highest point on record, and new single-family home sales showed strong increases from the previous year. In addition, studies showed that the average age of existing homes continued to increase, and people were staying in their homes later in life. All of these trends enhanced Home Depot's opportunities to add new stores across North America as well as to increase sales in its existing stores.[39]

The $100 billion DIY market breaks into six market segments: (1) lumber and building materials, (2) lawn and garden, (3) plumbing and electrical, (4) hardware and tools, (5) paint and supplies, and (6) hard surface flooring. **Exhibit 8** shows their market segment shares.

Exhibit 8
$100 Billion Do-It-Yourself Market

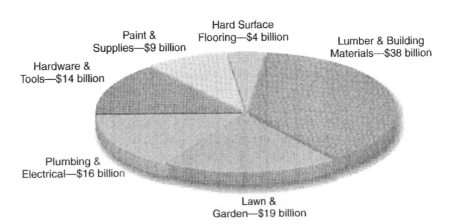

Paint & Supplies—$9 billion

Hard Surface Flooring—$4 billion

Lumber & Building Materials—$38 billion

Hardware & Tools—$14 billion

Plumbing & Electrical—$16 billion

Lawn & Garden—$19 billion

Source: The Home Depot, Inc., 1997 Annual Report, p. 8.

HomeBase, formerly HomeClub, was acquired by Zayre Corporation, a discount retail chain, in 1986. It was consolidated with BJ's Wholesale Club and renamed Waban, Inc. Zayre spun the company off to shareholders on June 14, 1989. In July 1997, Waban spun off the company to shareholders and was renamed HomeBase. In 1997, the company had to write off $27 million to cover store closings. The company was changing its strategy from being defensive to a more aggressive stance, such as accelerating store remodeling program. Analysts said, "This is an extremely competitive industry, and profit margins are small, so only the well-managed companies prosper and survive." They went on to say, "Look at Kmart; the company could not effectively manage Builders Square. They had to sell it off."[40]

Finance

The 10-year performance of Home Depot in selected key growth financial indicators is as follows:

Financial Indicator	Compound Growth Rate	
	5-Year Annual	10-Year Annual
Net sales	27.6%	32.5%
Earnings before taxes	28.3	35.6
Net earnings	27.5	36.6
Total assets	23.4	35.8
Working capital	19.9	33.6
Merchandise inventory	30.8	32.8
Net property and equipment	32.3	38.8
Long-term debt	9.1	37.9
Shareholders' equity	25.2	36.3
Capital expenditures	28.4	32.8
Number of stores	23.9	23.6
Average total company weekly sales	27.6	32.5
Number of customer transactions	23.8	27.6
Average sale per transaction	$3.00	$3.70
Weighted average sales per square foot	$1.00	$4.40

These compound growth rates had provided Home Depot shareholders with 48 consecutive quarters of growth in sales and earnings. Fiscal year (FY) 1997 was from February 3, 1997, to February 1, 1998.

Exhibit 9 shows that the average sale per transaction had increased from $33.92 in 1990 to $43.63 in 1997, or 28.7%. During the same period, average total company weekly sales had increased from $72,000 to $465,000, or 545.8%. The weighted average weekly sales per operating store had increased from $566,000 in 1990 to $829,000 in 1997, or 464.7%. The weighted average sale per square foot had increased from $322 in 1990 to $406 in 1997, or 26.1%.

If someone had invested $1,000 on June 30, 1982, in Home Depot, on June 28, 1997, the investment would have been worth $152,479. Only two stocks surpassed Home Depot's performance: Keane ($321,022) and Mark IV Industries ($269,265).

Exhibits 9, 10, and **11** provide the company's 10-year selected financial and operating income highlights, consolidated statement of earnings, and balance sheet.

Exhibit 9 Ten-Year Selected Financial and Operating Highlights: Home Depot, Inc.
(Dollar amounts in thousands, except where noted)

	5-Year Annual Compound Growth Rate	10-Year Annual Compound Growth Rate	Fiscal Years[3]									
			1997[1]	1996[1]	1995	1994	1993	1992	1991	1990[1]	1989	1988
Statement of Earnings Data												
Net sales	27.6%	32.5%	$24,156	$19,535	$15,470	$12,477	$9,239	$7,148	$5,137	$3,815	$2,759	$2,000
Net sales increase—%	—	—	23.7	26.3	24.0	35.0	29.2	39.2	34.6	38.3	38.0	37.6
Earnings before taxes[2]	28.3	35.6	2,002	1,535	1,195	980	737	576	396	260	182	126
Net earnings[2]	27.5	38.6	1,224	938	732	605	457	363	249	163	112	77
Net earnings increase—%[2]	—	—	30.5	28.2	21.0	32.2	26.1	45.6	52.5	46.0	45.9	41.9
Diluted earnings per share ($)[2-5]	24.4	31.0	1.64	1.29	1.02	0.88	0.67	0.55	0.39	0.30	0.21	0.15
Diluted earnings per share increase—%[2]	—	—	27.1	26.5	15.9	31.3	21.8	41.0	30.0	42.9	40.0	36.4
Weighted average number of common shares outstanding assuming dilution[3,4]	1.7	4.6	762	732	717	714	711	699	662	608	574	519
Gross margin—% of sales	—	—	28.1	27.8	27.7	27.9	27.7	27.6	28.1	27.9	27.8	27.0
Store selling and operating—% of sales	—	—	17.8	18.0	18.0	17.8	17.6	17.4	18.1	18.2	18.3	17.8
Pre-opening expense—% of sales	—	—	0.3	0.3	0.4	0.4	0.4	0.4	0.3	0.4	0.3	0.4
General and administrative expense—% of sales	—	—	1.7	1.7	1.7	1.8	2.0	2.1	2.3	2.4	2.5	2.4
Net interest income (expense)—% of sales	—	—	—	0.1	0.1	(0.1)	0.3	0.4	0.3	(0.1)	(0.1)	(0.1)
Earnings before taxes—% of sales[2]	—	—	8.3	7.9	7.7	7.8	8.0	8.1	7.7	6.8	6.6	6.3
Net earnings—% of sales[2]	—	—	5.1	4.8	4.7	4.8	5.0	5.1	4.8	4.3	4.1	3.8
Balance Sheet Data and Financial Ratios												
Total assets	23.4%	35.8%	$11,229	$9,342	$7,354	$5,778	$4,701	$3,932	$2,510	$1,640	$1,118	$699
Working capital	19.9	33.6	2,004	1,867	1,255	919	994	807	624	301	274	143
Merchandise inventories	30.8	32.8	3,602	2,708	2,180	1,749	1,293	940	662	509	381	294
Net property and equipment	32.3	38.8	6,509	5,437	4,461	3,397	2,371	1,608	1,255	879	514	332
Long-term debt	9.1	37.9	1,303	1,247	720	983	874	844	271	531	303	108
Shareholders' equity	25.2	36.3	7,098	5,955	4,988	3,442	2,814	2,304	1,691	683	512	383
Book value per share ($)[3]	22.9	31.2	9.70	8.26	6.97	5.06	4.17	3.46	2.67	1.29	0.99	0.75
Long-term debt to equity—%	—	—	18.4	20.9	14.4	28.6	31.1	36.6	16.0	77.7	59.1	28.1
Current ratio	—	—	1.82:1	2.01:1	1.89:1	1.76:1	2.02:1	2.07:1	2.17:1	1.73:1	1.94:1	1.74:1

(continued)

Exhibit 9 *(continued)*

	5-Year Annual Compound Growth Rate	10-Year Annual Compound Growth Rate	Fiscal Years[3]									
			1997	1996[1]	1995	1994	1993	1992	1991	1990[1]	1989	1988
Inventory turnover	—	—	5.4x	5.6x	5.5x	5.7x	5.9x	6.3x	6.1x	6.0x	5.9x	5.8x
Return on beginning equity—%	—	—	19.5	18.8	21.3	21.5	19.9	21.5	36.5	31.9	29.2	23.9
Statement of Cash Flows Data												
Depreciation and amortization	32.4%	38.8%	$283	$232	$181	$130	$90	$70	$52	$34	$21	$15
Capital expenditures	28.4	32.8	1,525	1,248	1,308	1,220	900	437	432	400	205	105
Cash dividends per share ($)[3]	28.6	43.5	0.19	0.15	0.13	0.10	0.07	0.05	0.04	0.02	0.02	0.01
Store Data[6]												
Number of stores	23.9%	23.6%	624	512	423	340	264	214	174	145	118	96
Number of states	16.6	17.8	41	38	31	28	23	19	15	12	12	10
Number of Canadian provinces	—	—	4	3	3	3	—	—	—	—	—	—
Square footage at year-end	26.0	26.8	66	54	44	35	26	21	16	13	10	8
Increase in square footage (%)	—	—	23.1	21.6	26.3	33.2	26.3	26.8	24.1	27.4	26.9	33.4
Average square footage per store (in thousands)	1.6	2.6	106	105	105	103	100	98	95	92	88	86
Store Sales and Other Data[6]												
Comparable stores sales increase—%[7]	—	—	7	7	3	8	7	15	11	10	13	13
Average total company weekly sales	27.6%	32.5%	$465	$369	$298	$240	$178	$137	$99	$72	$53	$38
Weighted average weekly sales per operating store (in thousands)	2.7	7.1	829	803	787	802	764	724	633	566	515	464
Weighted average sales per square foot ($)[7]	1.0	4.4	406	398	390	404	398	387	348	322	303	282
Number of customer transactions	23.8	27.6	550	464	370	302	236	189	146	112	84	64
Average sale per transaction ($)	3.0	3.7	43.63	42.09	41.78	41.29	39.13	37.72	35.13	33.92	32.65	31.13
Number of associates at year end (actual)	26.2	29.9	124,400	98,100	80,800	67,300	50,600	38,900	28,000	21,500	17,500	13,000

Notes:

1. Fiscal years 1996 and 1990 consisted of 53 weeks; all other years reported consisted of 52 weeks.
2. Excludes the effect of the $104 million nonrecurring charge in fiscal 1997.
3. All share and per-share data have been adjusted for a 3-for-2 stock split on July 3, 1997.
4. Share and per-share data have been restated for the adoption of SFAS 128 "Earnings per Share."
5. Diluted earnings per share for fiscal 1997, including the $104 million nonrecurring charge, were $1.55.
6. Excludes Maintenance Warehouse and National Blind and Wallpaper Factory.
7. Adjusted to reflect the first 52 weeks of the 53-week fiscal years in 1996 and 1990.

Source: The Home Depot, Inc. 1997 Annual Report, *first page fold-out.*

**Exhibit 10
Consolidated
Statement of
Earnings: Home
Depot, Inc.[1,2]
(Dollar amounts in
millions, except
per share data)**

Fiscal Year Ending	February 1, 1998	February 2, 1997	January 28, 1996
Net sales	$24,156	$19,535	$15,470
Cost of merchandise sold	17,375	14,101	11,184
Gross profit	6,781	5,434	4,286
Operating expenses			
Selling and store operating	4,287	3,521	2,784
Pre-opening	65	55	52
General and administrative	413	324	270
Nonrecurring charge	104	—	—
Total operating expenses	4,869	3,900	3,106
Operating income	1,912	1,534	1,180
Interest income (expense)			
Interest and investment income	44	25	19
Interest expense	(42)	(16)	(4)
Interest, net	2	9	15
Minority interest	(16)	(8)	—
Earnings before income taxes	1,898	1,535	1,195
Income taxes	738	597	463
Net earnings	$1,160	$938	$732
Basic earnings per share	$1.59	$1.30	$1.03
Weighted average number of common shares outstanding	729	719	709
Diluted earnings per share	$1.55	$1.29	$1.02
Weighted average number of common shares outstanding assuming dilution	762	732	717

Notes:
1. Fiscal year (FY) 1997 was February 3, 1997, to February 1, 1998.
2. Notes were deleted.

Source: The Home Depot, Inc., 1997 Annual Report, *p. 21.*

Fiscal Year Ending	February 1, 1998	February 2, 1997
Assets		
Current assets		
Cash and cash equivalents	$172	$146
Short-term investments, including current maturities		
of long-term investments	2	413
Receivables, net	556	388
Merchandise inventories	3,602	2,708
Other current assets	128	54
Total current assets	4,460	3,709
Property and equipment, at cost		
Land	2,194	1,855
Buildings	3,041	2,470
Furniture, fixtures, and equipment	1,370	1,084
Leasehold improvements	383	340
Construction in progress	336	284
Capital leases	163	117
	7,487	6,150
Less accumulated depreciation and amortization	978	713
Net property and equipment	6,509	5,437
Long-term investments	15	8
Notes receivable	27	40
Cost in excess of the fair value of net assets acquired, net of amortization		
of $18 at February 1, 1998 and $15 at February 2, 1997	140	87
Other	78	61
Total assets	$11,229	$9,342
Liabilities and shareholders' equity		
Current liabilities		
Accounts payable	$1,358	$1,090
Accrued salaries and related expenses	312	249
Sales taxes payable	143	129
Other accrued expenses	530	323
Income taxes payable	105	49
Current installments of long-term debt	8	2
Total current liabilities	2,456	1,842
Long-term debt, excluding current installments	1,303	1,247
Other long-term liabilities	178	134
Deferred income taxes	78	66
Minority interest	116	98
Shareholders' Equity		
Common stock, par value $0.05. Authorized: 1,000,000,000 shares;		
issued and outstanding—732,108,000 shares of February 1,		
1998 and 720,773,000 shares at February 2, 1997	37	36
Paid-in capital	2,662	2,511
Retained earnings	4,430	3,407
Cumulative translation adjustments	(28)	2
Total shareholders' equity	7,101	5,956
Less: shares purchased for compensation plans	3	1
	7,098	5,955
Total liabilities and shareholders' equity	$11,229	$9,342

Notes:
1. Fiscal year (FY) 1997 was February 3, 1997, to February 1, 1998.
2. Company consolidated balance sheet showed **Commitments and contingencies** instead of **Total liabilities and shareholders' equity**.

Source: The Home Depot, Inc., 1997 Annual Report, *p. 22.*

Notes

1. This section is based on P. M. Swiercz's case "The Home Depot, Inc.," as it appears in *Cases in Strategic Management*, 4th ed., Thomas L. Wheelen and J. David Hunger (Reading, Massachusetts: Addison-Wesley, 1993), pp. 367–397. Any information beyond 1989 is new to this case.

2. B. Sharav, "Home Depot," *Value Line* (July 21, 1995), p. 888.

3. R. Jacob, "Corporate Reputation," *Fortune* (March 6, 1995), pp. 54–55.

4. E. Lesser and A. Sharpe, "Home Depot Charges a Rival Drummed Up Opposition to Stores," *Wall Street Journal* (August 18, 1995), p. A-1.

5. *Ibid.*

6. C. Roush, "Home Depot Reaches a Cross Roads," *The Atlanta Journal* (July 16, 1996), p. P6.

7. *Ibid.*

8. The Home Depot, Inc., *1996 Annual Report*, p. 5.

9. The Home Depot, Inc., *1997 Annual Report*, p. 16.

10. *Ibid.*

11. *Ibid.*

12. *Ibid.*

13. *St. Petersburg Times* (December 24, 1990), p. 11.

14. *Business Atlanta* (November 11, 1988).

15. *Ibid.*

16. *Chain Store Executive* (April 1983), pp. 9–11.

17. The Home Depot, Inc., *1995 Annual Report*, p. 3.

18. The Home Depot, Inc., *1997 Annual Report*, p. 13. This was directly quoted, with minor editing.

19. *Ibid.*, p. 5.

20. The Home Depot, Inc., *Form 10-K* (February 1, 1998), pp. 8–9. The material was abstracted from The Home Depot, Inc., *1997 Annual Meeting of Shareholders Notice*, pp. 3–6.

21. The Home Depot, Inc., *1997 Form 10-K*, pp. 8–9.

22. The Home Depot, Inc., *1997 Annual Report*, p. 35.

23. P. M. Swiercz, "The Home Depot, Inc.," *Cases in Strategic Management*, 4th ed. (Reading, Massachusetts: Addison-Wesley, 1993), pp. 367–397.

24. *Ibid.*, The Home Depot, Inc., *1996 Annual Report*, p. 13, and The Home Depot, Inc., *1997 Form 10-K*, pp. 4, 10–11. Some paragraphs in this section are directly quoted with minor editing.

25. S. Caminiti, "The New Champs of Retailing," *Fortune* (September 1990), p. 2.

26. The Home Depot, Inc., *1997 Form 10-K*, p. 3. The table is directly quoted.

27. *Ibid.*, The Home Depot, Inc., *1997 Form 10-K*, pp. 6–7. This section was directly quoted with minor editing.

28. The Home Depot, Inc., *1997 Annual Report*, p. 20. This section was directly quoted with minor editing.

29. P. M. Swiercz, "The Home Depot, Inc.," *Cases in Strategic Management*, 4th ed. (Reading, Massachusetts: Addison-Wesley, 1993), pp. 367–397; The Home Depot, Inc., *1997 Annual Report*, pp. 12–13.

30. B. Sharav, "Retail Building Supply Industry," *Value Line* (January 16, 1998), p. 884.

31. B. Sharav, "Home Depot," *Value Line* (July 21, 1995), p. 884.

32. R. LaFranco, "Comeuppance," *Forbes* (December 4, 1995), p. 74.

33. *Ibid.*, pp. 74–75.

34. M. Pacelle, "Retail Building Surge Despite Store Glut," *Wall Street Journal* (January 17, 1996), p. A-2.

35. *Ibid.*

36. *Ibid.*

37. *Ibid.*

38. The Home Depot, Inc., *1997 Annual Report*, pp. 6–7. The first five paragraphs were directly quoted with minor editing.

39. *Ibid.*, p. 80.

40. R. Berne and W. M. Bulkeley, "Kmart and Waban Consider Combining Home Improvement Chains in New Firm," *Wall Street Journal* (February 4, 1997), p. A-3.

CASE 20

Gap Inc.:

A Specialty Apparel Retailer

Joanna Tochowicz, Robert J. Mockler, and Marc Gartenfeld

ON SEPTEMBER 26, 2002, GAP INC. ANNOUNCED THAT PAUL PRESSLER, 15-YEAR VETERAN of The Walt Disney Company and Chairman of its Global Theme Park and Resorts Division, had been named President and Chief Executive Officer of the company. Pressler succeeded outgoing CEO Millard Drexler, who had announced in May his plans to retire as soon as his replacement was hired.[1] Earlier that month, Gary Muto, former President of the Banana Republic division, was appointed as new President of the Gap division of Gap Inc. They were both faced with the inevitable task of developing an effective differentiating enterprisewide strategy if Gap was to survive and prosper against aggressive competition in the intermediate and long-term futures.

Gap Inc. sold its private-label clothing in its own retail stores only and to no other retailer, wholesaler, or independent distributor. The three main brands/divisions were Banana Republic, Gap, and Old Navy, as shown in **Exhibit 1**.

The three divisions had a presence in Japan, the United Kingdom, France, Canada, and Germany, but the majority of the stores were based in the United States. Each brand targeted different types of customers, with varying income levels and lifestyles. Each division was an independent strategic business unit. Gap Inc. had had major problems for more than two years, after an ill-fated foray into trendy clothes in early 2000 that had alienated its traditional customers. In September 2002, it reported its 28th straight month of declines in sales at stores open at least one year. The company's problems were reflected in its stock price. The stock reached its highest price of $51.68 on February 4, 2000. On October 8, 2002, the stock closed at $9.59, as shown in **Exhibit 2**.

The three divisions were having problems, but the Gap division was in the worst condition. For the past two years, since 2000, it had been struggling with problems resulting from overexpansion and misjudgment of fashion trends. The Gap division's stores went from

Exhibit 3
Divisions Gap Inc.

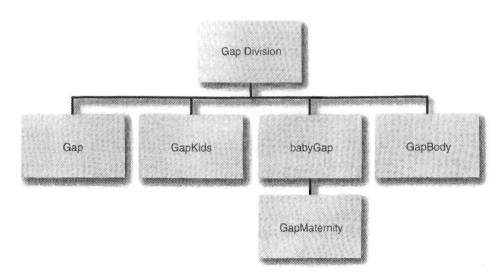

Exhibit 4 Structure of Gap Division

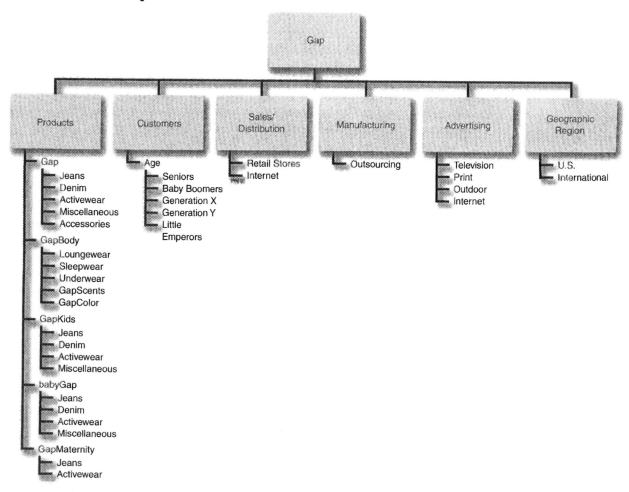

shelving. Products' labels were clear and understandable, and they provided sufficient product information. Gap often marked down the prices of different products. The company had some problems with inventory management, low-turnover products occupied shelf space for too long, and there were cases of inadequate inventory of high-turnover items.

The Gap

Gap, or Gap Adult, as some sources referred to it, offered activewear, denim products, accessories, jeans, and miscellaneous products to both men and women, all of which came in a variety of fits, colors and washes, and fabrics:

- **Jeans and pants:** This is what made Gap famous. Gap offered a variety of jeans and pants. They came in a variety of styles, fabrics, and colors. Women's jeans included boot cut, long and lean, lowrise boot cut, flare, modern boot cut, classic, loose fit, square pocket, utility, sidewinder, carpenter, and patch pocket. They were available in dark faded, light faded, stretch brown tinted, stretch faded, stretch black, stretch rinsed, stretch sandblasted, sandblasted, stonewashed, khaki, dark khaki, dark cement, and black. The men's selection included boot fit, easy fit, standard fit, relaxed fit, loose fit, wide leg, carpenter, worker, and straight fit. They came in vintage, faded, antiqued, brown tinted, rustic, black tinted, stonewashed, rinsed, black, dark blasted, black blasted, dark sandblasted, tinted rinsed, and black.

- **Denim:** Denim products included shirts, blouses, jackets, skirts, dresses, accessories, and shoes.

- **Activewear:** Activewear included sweatshirts, hooded sweatshirts, fleece sweatshirts, sweatpants, t-shirts, and tops.

- **Miscellaneous:** Miscellaneous products included sweaters, turtlenecks, v-necks, blouses, shirts, dresses, jackets, coats, peacoats, trench coats, vests, tops, t-shirts, and polos.

- **Accessories:** Accessories included bags, handbags, backpacks, tote bags, belts, hats, scarves, gloves, mittens, socks, shoes, flip-flops, and slides.

GapBody

With a focus on everyday essentials, GapBody offered loungewear, sleepwear, and underwear; GapScents; and GapColor:

- **Loungewear, Sleepwear, and Underwear:** GapBody offered loungewear, sleepwear, women's bras and panties, and men's underwear. One of the most popular products was the GapBody seamless-style t-shirts, tanks, and camisoles, with no seams or bulky edges. They were created on a cylinder, which made it possible to eliminate side seams.

- **GapScents:** Body lotions, body mists, and eau de toilette were available in "So Pink," "Dream," and "Heaven" fragrances. Gap also introduced "G," a men's fragrance composed of crisp white cotton, juniper, and musk. "G" eau de toilette, aftershave balm, hair and body wash, body lotion, soap on a rope, and gift sets were available. Gap also introduced "Simply White," a new women's fragrance with floral top notes of honeysuckle and jasmine and warm, woodsy bottom notes. Eau de toilette, shower gel, moisturizing soap, body mist, body lotion, intensified fragrance lotion, shimmer lotion, and gift sets were available in this fragrance line.

- **GapColor:** GapBody introduced GapColor, a new line of wearable, high-quality cosmetics. Offered in a range of versatile colors for lips, eyes, face, and nails, some of the products included lip glaze, lip gloss in 10 shades, lip color in 25 shades, lipstick in 10 shades, lip care in 4 shades, lip liners in 5 shades, nail color in 12 shades, eye color in 20 shades, face powder in 8 shades, and 5 kinds of brushes.

GapKids

GapKids' products included activewear styles, jackets, sweaters, pants, and jeans. As always, the emphasis on quality was shown in the details: from embellished denim for girls and knit tops for boys, to expanded washes in jeans and bright, simple colors across the assortment. Highlights for girls included flare, boot cut, and classic jeans; embellished jeans were also available—glitter flares, glitter patch pockets, charm and heart styles—as were polos, cotton cardigans, yoga pants, zip hoodies, velour and tricot track suits, boots, clogs, and slip-ons. Some highlights for boys included jeans (basic five-pocket jeans, carpenter, and cargo, all in stonewash blast, antique blast, dark sandblast, and whisker antique), basic tops, polos, Oxford shirts, track suits, hooded sweatshirts, sneakers, and slip-ons. GapKids also offered bags, small backpacks for younger kids, premier backpacks for older students, and messenger-style bags.

babyGap

babyGap offered products for little kids, from newborns up to age 5. Products included bodysuits, playwear, overalls, tops, cardigans, sweaters, socks, and shoes, in denim and cozy fabrics.

GapMaternity

GapMaternity did not have its own separate stores. It was a section of babyGap stores and sold online. The products for moms-to-be included jeans and activewear. According to Rachel DiCarlo, vice president of fashion public relations for Gap, "These are the same jeans women wear when they're not pregnant."[3] The favorite items from Gap were translated into maternity wear so women could maintain their sense of style throughout their pregnancy. A wide range of fits and washes were available. Maternity jeans took on a modern look in different styles. Jeans included stretch patch pocket, a worker-inspired jean with front patch pockets, a sandblasted stretch long-and-lean style that fit slim through the leg and had a demi belly panel that sat slightly lower at the waist, and stretch boot cut. The stretch fabric in all the jeans styles improved fit, maximized comfort, and provided ease of movement. GapMaternity also offered activewear, which included stretch hoods, pants, and jackets. Stores carried sizes from XS to XL. Styles were designed for comfort throughout pregnancy, with stretch fabrics and special features such as four comfortable belly panels (the new demi panel, no panel, side panel, and full panel) to ensure that jeans fit perfectly at every stage.

Customers

Gap catered to women and men of almost all ages. Different Gap brands targeted different age groups. Gap paid close attention to the age distribution and priorities of potential customers in its markets. Gap targeted women and men through all its store concepts. Women accounted for 80% of household spending and 83% of all purchases.[4] Most women worked full time, which for apparel retailers such as Gap was good news because it meant not only more income at the disposal of the most important customer but also a need to buy new clothing suitable for their work. Women bought not only clothes for themselves but also for their kids. In addition, they had a great influence on what their husbands were buying. Men were spending a growing percentage of their apparel money on casual wear because of the changes in the dress codes for many white-collar workers. This was a good change for specialty retailers such as Gap that specialized in casual clothing.

Management classified its customers into five generation clusters: seniors, baby boomers, Generation X, Generation Y, and the little emperors.

Seniors

Seniors comprised individuals 65 years and older. They were born before or during World War II and they accounted for more than 12% of the U.S. population in 2002. By 2015, this age group was expected to comprise nearly 15% of the U.S. population. Gap and GapBody targeted seniors.

Baby Boomers

The baby boom generation, comprising individuals born between 1946 and 1964, constituted some 77 million Americans. In 2002, the boomers were in their 40s and 50s. Gap and GapBody targeted these consumers.

Generation X

This group comprised approximately 45 million people born between 1965 and 1976. These individuals had reached adulthood in the mid-1980s and were in their 20s and 30s in 2002. Products from Gap, GapBody, and GapMaternity targeted this group.

Generation Y

This group included individuals born between 1977 and 1994, representing about 25% of the population in 2002. Gap, GapBody, and GapKids targeted this segment.

The Little Emperors

This group included the population of children born after 1994. Gap sold to these markets via its GapKids and babyGap stores.

Gap sold high-quality products at competitive price levels. Consumers were able to shop whenever it was convenient for them, by either going to a physical store or to the Gap web sites. Gap also offered a store credit card for its customers. Gap offered products in sizes 0–14, a limited selection of products in plus-sizes, and no extended plus-sizes. Another important strength of Gap was the customer service the company provided. The division's stores had bright lighting, and products were attractively displayed on shelves. A sufficient number of cash registers provided speedy checkout for customers. Sales associates and other store personnel were trained to answer customers' questions about fabric, fit, and fashion, and to help them select merchandise that would be perfect for them.

Sales and Distribution

The Gap division was headquartered with Gap Inc. in the San Francisco Bay area, Gap Inc.'s product development offices were in New York City, and its distribution operations and offices coordinating sourcing activities were located around the globe. Third-party manufacturers shipped merchandise to distribution centers, which sorted and redistributed it to the stores. Strategically placed throughout the United States, Canada, the United Kingdom, the Netherlands, and Japan, the distribution centers were the backbone of Gap Inc.'s worldwide operations. The company used bar coding and electronic data interchange systems in inventory management. The company operated all its stores, did not franchise or enter into joint ventures, and did not wholesale its products or serve as a supplier to other companies.

Retail Stores

Gap's stores were attractively located. Gap used stand-alone stores and mall locations. Gap leased most of its store premises. Store layout and design was strategic, and products often bought together were placed in close proximity. Products were attractively displayed on white shelving, and mannequins provided ideas and inspiration for customers. Sales associates and other store personnel were trained to answer customers' questions about fabric, fit, and fashion, and to help them select merchandise that would be perfect for them.

Internet

Gap products were available through Gap web sites, including gap.com, gapbody.com, gapkids.com, and babygap.com. Shopping on those web sites was safe, quick, and simple. Customers were able to return products bought online to the company's retail stores. Ordered products were sent to the customer directly from one of the distribution centers. However, customers were not able to pick up their online orders in retail stores.

Manufacturing

Gap Inc.'s goods were produced in approximately 3,600 factories in more than 50 countries. The company did not manufacture any of the goods itself; it neither owned nor operated any garment factories. Instead, it was almost always one of a manufacturer's many customers. Gap Inc. was a designer and marketer.

Gap Inc. developed a set of principles and operating standards for garment manufacturers that reflected its values, beliefs, and business ethics. These standards were set out in its Code of Vendor Conduct, which was first written in the early 1990s and updated in 1996. The Code focused on compliance with local labor laws, working conditions, and the natural environment. It also spelled out to vendors Gap's expectations regarding wages, child labor, health, and safety issues; respecting the right of workers to unionize; and much more. It was written in order to help vendors understand and apply these standards to their day-to-day operations and adopt them as "company policy." Few factories, if any, in the United States or anywhere else were in total compliance all the time.

Gap Inc.'s Global Compliance department comprised more than 90 full-time employees dedicated exclusively to working with potential and current vendors to help them understand and achieve compliance with the Code. Before Gap approved or placed an order with a vendor, the Global Compliance team was involved. First, before any orders were placed, a manufacturer and the factories it intended to use were subjected to a comprehensive approval process to make sure they could operate under the Code of Vendor Conduct. Second, if a garment factory was eventually approved, the Global Compliance team monitored compliance on an ongoing basis. In addition, other Gap employees visited factories—from quality assurance and production experts to employees who determined whether a vendor was capable of producing a specific kind of garment.

Advertising/Promotion

Gap, Inc. advertised its products in a number of ways. Each of the three main brands, including Gap, had its own marketing team headquartered in the San Francisco Bay area. In-house marketing teams created everything from hangtags and in-store posters to billboards and TV commercials. One recent campaign was titled "For Every Generation." This global campaign included television, print, outdoor, and online initiatives.

Television

Gap TV spots were aired in the United States, the United Kingdom, Canada, and Japan. TV spots in the United States were shown during primetime programs, including *Friends, Will & Grace, West Wing, Law & Order, Ed, Scrubs*, and *ER* on NBC; *Alias, The Practice*, and *My Wife & Kids* on ABC; *CSI* and *Survivor* on CBS; and *Malcolm in the Middle* and *Boston Public* on Fox. In those TV spots Gap turned to celebrities such as Lauren Hutton and Bridget Hall to serve as spokespersons.[5]

Print

Print ads appeared in more than 40 international magazines, including *Vogue, Harper's Bazaar, Marie Claire, InStyle, Details, Vanity Fair, W, ESPN, GQ, Spin, Sports Illustrated, Rolling Stone*, and *Interview*. Ads also appeared in major newspapers.

Outdoor

Gap used major-market outdoor billboards, walls, and transit posters in high-visibility markets throughout the United States, Canada, Europe, and Japan.

Internet

Gap pop-up ads and banners appeared on various popular web pages, such as *www.aol.com* and *www.yahoo.com*. Those ads were used not only to promote the Gap brand name but also to announce new product lines and sales. Although Gap took advantage of various channels of promotion, some customers complained that the message of the advertisements was sometimes unclear and confusing. This highlighted another problem in the company: It took a long time for Gap to react to the negative customer feedback and reaction.

Gap worked hard to earn a good reputation and establish a strong brand name. To enhance and exceed the expectations of every customer, Gap store designers were constantly evolving everything that touched the customers—from store signage and merchandise displays to dressing rooms and inventory systems. Their goal was to create a relaxed shopping environment that intensified Gap's bold brand expression and enhanced the sales associates' ability to provide outstanding service. These design changes were designed to help support Gap's growth and future vision and to make the customers' experiences the best of any retailer. Gap wanted its customers to know that when they visited a Gap store, they were not just walking into a store, they were walking into a brand.

High-quality products, good customer service, and a distinct shopping environment ensure a company a good reputation, but these things are often not enough. In 1977, Gap Inc. established a charitable arm, Gap Foundation. In order to make a name for itself, Gap, through the Gap Foundation, engaged in a number of partnerships. It funded two national organizations that shared a commitment to helping underserved youth: Boys & Girls Clubs of America and the Lorraine Monroe Leadership Institute aim to help students develop self-esteem, stay in school, and succeed academically so they can lead more rewarding and fulfilling lives. To help teens make sound educational decisions, explore career opportunities, and prepare for the workforce, Gap funded a career exploration and mentoring program for more than 2,600 Boys & Girls Clubs nationwide. Gap Inc. employees were also in charge of workshops, conducted Career Day sessions at their local Boys & Girls Clubs, and provided job-shadowing opportunities for youth at headquarters and store locations. Dr. Lorraine Monroe acknowledged the challenges of education in underserved urban areas. By embracing these challenges—adding a mix of first-rate teachers, a creative but disciplined environment, and the expectation of perfection—Monroe has helped transform the future of public urban education. This is the premise of the Lorraine Monroe Leadership Institute, which focuses on developing leaders for public schools who are committed to educating underserved youth. Through funding from Gap Foundation, the Institute created Demonstration Schools to train teachers and administrators in Dr. Monroe's extraordinary leadership principles. In addition to the major partnerships with Boys & Girls Clubs of America and the Lorraine Monroe Leadership Institute, Gap Inc. supported nonprofit organizations serving kids in local communities around the world. Although it focused primarily on education and youth development, Gap, Banana Republic, and Old Navy supported many other organizations in areas such as health and human services, civics and arts, and the environment.[6]

Geographic Region

Gap stores were located in five countries outside the United States—the United Kingdom, Canada, France, Japan, and Germany—as shown in **Exhibit 5**. The company had been successful in expanding into international markets. It was not present in any emerging markets, such as Eastern and Central Europe or Asian or South American countries.

Because it was a sole owner of all its subsidiaries, and it operated its stores by itself, Gap was able to avoid any problems associated with loss of control. Because it did not enter into joint ventures or franchises, its expansion was slower than it could have been.

Exhibit 5
Division Stores in Operation as of August 3, 2002: Gap, Inc.[1]

Domestic Stores	
Gap Adult	1,024
GapKids	819
babyGap	193
GapBody	154
Gap Outlet	133
Total Gap Domestic Stores	**2,323**
International Stores	
Canada	192
United Kingdom	235
France	54
Japan	155
Germany	20
Total Gap International Stores	**656**
Total Stores Worldwide	**2,979**

Note:
1. For the past two years, Gap Inc. reported store count based on the number of concepts for Gap brand. This means that any Gap, GapKids, babyGap, or GapBody meeting a certain square footage threshold was counted as a separate store, even when residing within a single physical location.

Source: Gap Inc., company web site www.gapinc.com (2002).

Exhibit 6 Domestic Location by States, as of August 3, 2002: Gap, Inc.

State	Number of Concepts	State	Number of Concepts	State	Number of Concepts
Alaska	29	Louisiana	35	Ohio	89
Arkansas	20	Massachusetts	105	Oklahoma	27
Arizona	35	Maryland	39	Oregon	27
California	235	Maine	12	Pennsylvania	132
Colorado	36	Michigan	51	Puerto Rico	12
Connecticut	50	Minnesota	39	Rhode Island	18
District of Columbia	5	Missouri	37	South Carolina	25
Delaware	8	Mississippi	14	South Dakota	5
Florida	145	Montana	6	Tennessee	38
Georgia	61	North Carolina	51	Texas	179
Hawaii	16	North Dakota	4	Utah	31
Iowa	31	Nebraska	11	Virginia	47
Idaho	8	New Hampshire	17	Vermont	6
Illinois	97	New Jersey	86	Washington	40
Indiana	34	New Mexico	14	Wisconsin	31
Kansas	23	Nevada	19	West Virginia	10
Kentucky	20	New York	212	Wyoming	1
Total stores 2,323					

Source: Gap Inc., company web site, www.gapinc.com (2002).

Gap operated 2,323 store concepts domestically, 235 in the United Kingdom, 192 in Canada, 155 in Japan, 54 in France, and 20 in Germany, as shown in **Exhibit 5**. The actual number of stores was lower because in some instances multiple concepts were located in a single store.

Although Gap was present in all states of the United States, it concentrated mostly on highly populated areas, such as in California, Florida, New York, and Texas, as shown in **Exhibit 6**.

Financial Position

Exhibit 7 shows Gap Inc.'s consolidated statement of operations, and **Exhibit 8** shows Gap Inc.'s consolidated balance sheet. See Gap's 2001 *Annual Report* at *www.gapinc.com*, for complete financial statements.

Due to misjudgment of fashion trends in 2000 and 2001, Gap's revenue grew more slowly than the cost of goods sold, as shown in **Exhibit 7**. Between January 2001 and January 2002, revenues grew less than 2%. At the same time, costs of goods sold grew more than 10%. As a result, gross profit margin fell from more than 41% to 35.8%, as shown in **Exhibit 7**.

Comparable store sales by division for the second quarter of 2002 were as follows: Gap Domestic reported –13% versus –8% in 2001, and Gap International reported –12% versus –6% in 2001.

Total sales by division for the second quarter of 2002 were as follows: Gap Domestic reported $1.1 billion versus $1.2 billion in 2001, and Gap International reported $374 million versus $388 million in 2001.

Comparable store sales by division, year-to-date 2002, were as follows: Gap Domestic reported –17% versus –6% in 2001, and Gap International reported –15% versus –7% in 2001.

**Exhibit 7
Consolidated
Statement of
Operations: Gap,
Inc. (Dollar
amounts in
thousands, except
per share data)**

Year Ending	February 2 2002	February 3 2001	January 29 2000
Net Sales	$13,847,873	$13,673,460	$11,635,398
Cost and expenses			
Cost of goods sold and occupancy expenses	9,704,389	8,599,442	6,775,262
Operating expenses	3,805,968	3,629,257	3,043,432
Interest expenses	109,190	74,891	44,966
Interest income	(13,315)	(12,015)	(13,211)
Earnings before income taxes	241,641	1,381,885	1,784,949
Income taxes	249,405	504,388	657,884
Net earnings (loss)	($7,764)	877,497	1,127,065
Weighted-average number of shares—basic	860,255,419	879,810,658	853,804,176
Weighted-average number of shares—diluted	860,255,419	879,137,194	895,029,176
Earnings (loss) per share—basic	($0.01)	$1.03	$1.32
Earnings (loss) per share—diluted[1]	($0.01)	1.00	1.26

Note:

1. Diluted losses per share for the 52 weeks ended February 2, 2002, are computed using basic weighted average number of shares outstanding and exclude 13,395,045 dilutive shares as their effects are antidilutive when applied to losses.

Source: Gap Inc., "2001 Annual Report," p. 27.

Total sales by division for year-to-date 2002 were as follows: Gap Domestic reported $2.1 billion versus $2.4 billion in 2001, and Gap International reported $692 million versus $765 million in 2001, as shown in **Exhibit 9**.

Comprehensive earnings included net earnings and other comprehensive earnings (losses). Other comprehensive earnings (losses) included foreign currency translation adjustments and fluctuations in the fair market value of certain derivative financial instruments. **Exhibit 10** presents comprehensive earnings for the 13 and 26 weeks ended August 3, 2002, and August 4, 2001, respectively.

Although Gap, Inc. was still able to raise capital, the worsening situation has made doing so more expensive. On February 14, 2002, Moody's reduced Gap's long- and short-term senior unsecured credit ratings from Baa to Ba and from Prime-3 to Not Prime, respectively, with a negative outlook on long-term ratings. Standard & Poor's reduced the long- and short-term credit ratings from BBB+ to BB+ and from A-2 to B, respectively, with a stable outlook on long-term ratings. On February 27, 2002, Moody's reduced the long-term senior unsecured credit ratings from Ba2 to Ba3 and stated that its outlook on the long-term ratings was stable. On May 9, 2002, and May 24, 2002, the outlook on Gap's credit ratings was changed from stable to negative by Standard & Poor's and Moody's, respectively.

As a result of the downgrades in the long-term credit ratings, effective June 15, 2002, the interest rates payable by Gap, Inc. on $700 million of outstanding notes increased by 175 basis points to 9.90% per annum on $200 million of outstanding notes due in 2005 and to 10.55% per annum on $500 million of outstanding notes due in 2008. The interest rates payable on these notes would be decreased only upon upgrades of long-term credit rating by these rating agencies. Any further downgrades of those ratings by these rating agencies would result in further increases in the interest rates payable on the notes.

Exhibit 8
Consolidated
Balance Sheets:
Gap, Inc.
(Dollar amounts in
thousands, except
per share data)

Year Ending	Feb. 3, 2002	Feb. 3, 2001
Assets		
Current Assets		
Cash and equivalents	$1,035,749	$ 408,794
Merchandise inventory	1,677,116	1,904,153
Other current assets	331,685	335,103.0
Total current assets	3,044,550	2,648,050
Property and Equipment		
Leasehold improvements	2,127,966	1,899,820
Furniture and equipment	3,327,819	2,826,863
Land and buildings	917,055	558,832
Construction-in-progress	246,691	615,722
	6,619,290	5,901,237
Accumulated depreciation and amortization	(2,458,241)	(1,893,552)
Property and equipment, net	4,161,290	4,007,685
Lease rights and other assets	385,486	357,173
Total assets	$7,591,326	$7,012,908
Liabilities and Shareholder's Equity		
Current Liabilities		
Notes payable	$ 41,889	$ 779,904
Current maturities of long-term debt	—	250,000
Account payable	1,105,117	1,067,207
Accrued expenses and other current liabilities	564,115	505,279
Total current liabilities	2,056,233	2,799,144
Long-Term Liabilities		
Long-term debt	1,961,397	780,246
Deferred lease credits and other liabilities	564,115	505,279
Total long-term liabilities	2,525,512	1,285,525
Total Liabilities	4,581,745	4,084,669
Shareholders' Equity		
Common stock $.05 par value		
Authorized 2,300,000,000 shares: issued 948,597,949 and		
939,222,871 shares; outstanding 865,726,890 and		
853,996,984 shares	47,430	46,961
Additional paid-in capital	461,408	294,967
Retained earnings	4,890,375	4,974,773
Accumulated other comprehensive losses	(61,824)	(20,173)
Deferred compensation	(7,245)	(12,162)
Treasury stock, at cost	(2,320,563)	(2,356,127)
Total shareholders' equity	3,009,581	2,928,239
Total liabilities and shareholders' equity	$7,591,326	$7,012,908

Source: Gap Inc., "2001 Annual Report," p. 18.

Exhibit 9
Second Quarter
Store Sales for
Domestic and
International Units:
Gap, Inc.

	Gap Domestic		Gap International	
	2002	2001	2002	2001
Comparable Store Sales for Second Quarter	(13%)	(8%)	(12%)	(6%)
Total Sales for Second Quarter	$1.1 billion	($1.2 billion)	$347 million	($388 million)
Comparable Store Sales for Year-to-date	(17%)	(6%)	(15%)	(7%)
Total Sales for Year-to-date	$2.1 billion	($2.4 billion)	$692 million	($765 million)

Source: Gap Inc., "2002 Form 10-Q," p. 13.

**Exhibit 10
Comprehensive
Earnings: Gap, Inc.
(Dollar amounts in
thousands)**

	13 Weeks Ended		26 Weeks Ended	
	August 3, 2002	August 4, 2001	August 3, 2002	August 4, 2001
Net earnings	56,780	89,751	93,458	205,231
Other comprehensive earnings (losses)	18,664	(7,488)	25,433	(19,647)
Comprehensive earnings	75,444	82,263	118,891	185,584

Source: Gap Inc., Form 10-Q *(2002).*

As a result of the downgrades in the short-term credit ratings, Gap Inc. no longer had meaningful access to the commercial paper market. In addition, it was expected that both the recent and any future lowering of the ratings on Gap Inc.'s debt would result in reduced access to the capital markets and higher interest costs on future financing. The increase in interest expense in the second quarter and first half of fiscal 2002 as compared to the same periods in fiscal 2001 was primarily due to an increase in long-term borrowings and higher interest rates on new debt issuance. Long-term debt as of August 3, 2002, was equal to $2,873,132,000, up 46% from $1,961,397,000 on August 4, 2001.[7]

Corporate Management and Strategy

Gap Inc.'s management has demonstrated that it is very proactive, especially when it comes to looking for opportunities for growth. For example, in 1983 the company seemed to have become stagnant, so Drexler was brought in as president. Since then, Gap Inc. has grown tremendously, the store's image has changed, and new store concepts have been started, such as GapKids, babyGap, and Old Navy. The firm has also expanded, with the acquisition of Banana Republic in 1983.

Gap Inc. opened 663 new stores between October 1999 and October 2000 but had slowed new-store openings in 2001 and 2002, as it continued to be plagued by the merchandising, marketing, and logistical problems that had wreaked havoc since spring 2000. Long accustomed to spectacular growth and flashy television advertising, Gap Inc. revamped its strategies in 2001, as competition in the apparel industry continued to increase and the absence of new merchandise offerings and new trends turned up the heat even more.

Gap Inc. pursued a hybrid strategy containing elements of both cost leadership and differentiation, as defined by Michael Porter. It relied on strong brand differentiation and had made considerable investment in brand image as well as customer service. At the same time, the strategy also involved several characteristics affiliated with the cost-leadership approach, including economies of scale and scope, simple product designs, and low-cost distribution. Because of all the problems, which involved mainly the Gap division, changes in management were made. On August 8, 2002, Gap Inc. announced that Gary Muto, President, Banana Republic, had been named President of Gap U.S. On September 26, 2002, it was announced that Paul Pressler had been named President and Chief Executive Officer of Gap Inc., effective immediately.[8]

Looking Toward the Future

Although Gap had strong and well-established brand recognition in the specialty apparel retailers' market, the mistakes that were made within the company, the increasing competition, and changing consumer groups and tastes all put pressure on this division to reevaluate its strategies in order to remain competitive. The new CEO of Gap Inc., Pressler, and the new President of Gap U.S., Muto, were faced with various alternatives in order to put the company ahead of the competition. Both alternatives focused on customers and the mix of products offered to them. Both maintained that changes were needed. Each one, however, had a different view on what exactly needed to be done.

The **first alternative** was to extend the customer base. It proposed that Gap target the plus-sizes (sizes 16–26) and extended plus-sizes (sizes 28–34) markets. In a sense, Gap would offer the same mix of products, such as clothing, accessories, and body care products to an expanded customer base. The benefit of this alternative was that Gap would get into major unsaturated markets with substantial growth opportunities.

The alternative was feasible because of the brand recognition Gap had in the market, which could be extended into new customer groups. It was also feasible because of the widely recognized high quality of Gap products. This alternative could win against competition, because Gap had good relationships with its vendors and would be able to produce the goods in the new sizes, which would not differ from existing ones as far as quality and the fabrics of the products were concerned. Gap monitored its vendors closely and had high standards when choosing new ones. This could also be a winning strategy for Gap because the competition present in that market, including H&M; some discounters, such as Wal-Mart and Target; and department stores, such as Macy's, offered only a limited selection of those products, often of poor quality and style, while Gap was known for classic and comfortable styles and high-quality, durable fabrics. Gap was also better than the competition because among those offering plus-sizes it was the only one with a widely recognized, strong brand name, while others were either just beginning to build a brand name, such as H&M, or did not sell products under private labels, such as department stores or discounters. The drawback of this alternative was that creating clothes in plus-sizes would be difficult. The same trajectory of sizing up could not be continued; it required drawing new patterns because necks, for example, don't get larger above a certain weight, but backs, thighs, and tummies do. A way around this drawback was to utilize the good relationships with vendors and pay extra attention to the new designs by hiring designers with experience in this area. With good designs prepared by Gap employees and close monitoring by the Global Compliance department, the quality could be achieved.

The **second alternative** was to maintain the same customer base but to extend the product line offered. Besides jeans, casual wear, activewear, loungewear, sleepwear, underwear, accessories, and body care products, Gap could also offer various home goods, such as picture frames, throw rugs, pillows, sheets, pillowcases, comforters, and towels. The benefit of this alternative was that Gap would be stretching the brand that was widely known and identified with quality.

This alternative was feasible because Gap could use the experiences of its sister division Banana Republic to better plan and execute this strategy. It was also feasible because through Banana Republic, Gap would also have access to already tested and reliable vendors that were selected using high standards and that were monitored by the Global Compliance department.

Gap would be able to win against the competition because the company would be able to offer a broader range of products than most of its competitors. The only competitors that offered a substantially wider product range were discounters and department stores. The goods offered by discounters, such as Target and Wal-Mart, often lacked the quality that Gap was able to provide. Gap was also better than most department stores, such as JCPenney or Macy's, because through extensive data gathering, it was able to establish a one-to-one relationship with its customers and offer them reliable customer service and product information. Through its efforts at getting to know the customers, Gap was able to develop customer loyalty, which would help persuade customers that the new product lines offered by Gap were as good as the ones they had already gotten used to and trusted. Gap would also be using a recognized brand name and image to market the products, while competitors, such as H&M, were only beginning to build their brand names. The drawback of this alternative was that creating a new product line could stretch the brand too much and diminish the quality brand image that Gap had worked hard to create. It could also use valuable store space currently given to apparel. Or the store size would need to be expanded, which is not always possible. The way around this drawback was to continue using the highest-quality materials and designs, using the same high standards when choosing the vendors as with other Gap products, and then to ensure close monitoring by the Global Compliance department.

Both alternatives seemed to make sense. They both seemed to have advantages and disadvantages. Both presented views about how to achieve the same result of maintaining and increasing the market share and getting ahead of competitors. Muto and Pressler decided to study both alternatives further, especially within present financial situations, as well as other alternatives in other strategic areas, in order to decide which would be most appropriate. The only sure thing at this point in time was that if Gap was to stay competitive, immediate action needed to be taken.

Notes

1. E. Kaiser, "Interview—New Gap CEO Starting at the Bottom," *MarketWatch, http://cbs.marketwatch.com* (2002).
2. Standard & Poor's, "Retailing: General," *www.netadvantage. standardpoor.com* (2002).
3. Gap Inc., company web site, *www.gapinc.com* (2002).
4. S. Reyes, "Tapping Girl Power," *Brandweek*, Vol. 43, No. 16 (April 22, 2002), pp. 26–30.
5. S. Brown, "Gap Customers Get Reassurance; Ads Emphasize Store's Classic Style," *Denver Post* (August 22, 2002), p. F1.
6. Gap Inc., company web site, *www.gapinc.com* (2002).
7. Gap Inc., *Form 10-Q* (2002).
8. S. Day, "The Gap Chooses Next Chief," *The New York Times* (September 27, 2002).

References

S. Barta, M. Jason, J. Frye, and M. Woods,"Trends in Retail Trade," Oklahoma State University, *www.agweb.okstate.edu/pearl/agecon/resource/wf-565.pdf* (November 1999).
Board of Governors of the Federal Reserve System, "Monetary Policy Report to the Congress," *www.federalreserve.gov/boarddocs/hh/2002/July/FullReport.pfd* (July 16, 2002).
C. DeNavas-Walt and R. Cleveland, "Money Income in the United States: 2001," *Current Population Reports, U.S. Census Bureau* (September 2002).
L. Downes, "Perpetual Strategy: Building an Information Supply Chain," *Presentation, Foresight on the Future: An Executive Form, New York: Business Objects and IBM DB2* (October 3, 2001).
S. Ellison, "Obese America: Retailer Bets Super-Size Women Will Buy Clothes That Fit—Catherine's Expands Plus Line for Those Who Need A 28 or 34; Studying How Body Gets Larger," *Wall Street Journal* (June 21, 2002), p. B1.
Gap Inc., *Annual Report* (2000).
Gap Inc., *Annual Report* (2001).
S. Hansell, "A Retailing Mix: On Internet, in Paint and in Store," *The New York Times* (December 14, 2002), p. C1.
D. Hazel, "Is Branding Working? Developers Hope the Name Game Will Pay Off," *Shopping Centers Today, www.icsc.org/srch/sct/current/sct9909/02.html* (September 1, 1999).
Hoover's Online, "Company Profiles," *www.hoovers.com* (2002).
T. Howard, "Gap Counts on Known, New Stars; Chain Puts Fresh Face on Classic Clothing," *USA Today* (August 8, 2002), p. B2.
T. Howard, "Gap Goes Back to Basics; Turnaround Plan Is About a Lot More Than Fashion," *USA Today* (August 8, 2002), p. B1.
L. Huff, "Apparel Specialty Stores: A Year to Forget," *Chain Store Age*, Vol. 78, No. 8 (August 2002), pp. A14–A15.
S. Konicki, "Sophisticated Supply," *InformationWeek* (December 10, 2001).
L. Lee, "Buried Alive in Khakis," *BusinessWeek*, Vol. 3747, No. 40 (July 9, 2002), p. 40.
D. Lipke, "Mystery Shoppers," *American Demographics* (December 2002), pp. 41–43.
S. Murray, "The Second Coming," *American Demographics* (April 2001), pp. 28–30.
J. Rendon, "The Supply Chain's RFID Gambit," *Mbusiness* (March 2002).
Standard & Poor's, "Retailing: Specialty," *www.netadvantage. standardpoor.com* (2002).
A. Stein, "The Money in the Middle: Step Right Up to the Roaring 2000s," *American Demographics* (April 1, 2000).
J. Strasburg, "Gap Gets Ready to Try On a New Leadership Style," *San Francisco Chronicle* (August 11, 2002), p. G1.
B. Tadeschi, "As Women Start to Use Internet More for Shopping, the Prospects Sharply Improve for On-line Retailers," *The New York Times* (July 12, 1999), p. 4.
V. Valkin, "Gap Taps Ex-Disney Executive As CEO," *Financial Times* (September 26, 2002).
J. Waters, "Gap Finds a New Leader from Disney," *MarketWatch, http://cbs.marketwatch.com* (2002).

CASE 21

Tiffany & Co.:
A Specialty Fine Jewelry Retailer

Marcia Chan, Robert J. Mockler, and Marc Gartenfeld

ON JANUARY 31, 2003, TIFFANY & CO. (COMMONLY KNOWN AS TIFFANY) ANNOUNCED that William R. Chaney would retire as Chairman of the Board but would continue to serve on Tiffany's Board of Directors. Michael J. Kowalski would assume the role of Chairman of the Board and continue as Chief Executive Officer (CEO). As Chairman and CEO, Kowalski faced the continuing pressures to implement strategies that would better position Tiffany and continue to create long-term shareholder value in an increasingly competitive environment. In such leadership roles, he faced the pressures of developing an effective differentiating enterprisewide strategy for Tiffany if the company was to survive and prosper against growing global competition over the intermediate and long-term futures as the world's premier luxury brand of fine jewelry.[1]

Fine jewelry was known for its quality, craftsmanship, value, price, and brand. Its quality was nearly perfect, with minimal flaws. The craftsmanship was characterized by excellence because time and patience were required to create each fine jewelry piece. The value was determined by the fine jewelry's quality and craftsmanship. If these criteria were strong and superior, then the value was strong. The prices of fine jewelry were usually high because of its quality, craftsmanship, and value attributes. Fine jewelry brands were well known because they offered the highest standard of these attributes.

Tiffany was a retailer, designer, manufacturer, and distributor of luxury fine jewelry. As of January 31, 2003, Tiffany had 44 company-operated stores in the United States and 82 company-operated international stores. Jewelry represented approximately 79% of its net sales in 2003, followed by 6% for tableware and 4% for timepieces, with all other categories aggregating to 11%. Tiffany's jewelry designs sold under the Tiffany brand, exclusively at company-operated stores, online, and via catalog. In 2003, Tiffany had the following fine jewelry collections: 1837, Atlas, Elsa Peretti, Etoile, Garland, Paloma Picasso, Return to Tiffany, Schlumberger, The Tiffany Mark, Tiffany Biscayne, Tiffany Bubbles, Tiffany Lace, Tiffany Pearls, and Tiffany Roundel.[2] In addition to having stores in the United States, Tiffany had stores in Canada, Mexico, Brazil, England, France, Germany, Italy, Switzerland, Australia, China, Guam, Hong Kong, Japan, Korea, Malaysia, Singapore, and Taiwan. The United States represented approximately 59% of Tiffany's net sales. Tiffany's international presence brought in net sales of 28% from Japan, 6% from other Asia-Pacific countries, 4% from Europe, and the remainder from Canada, Latin America, and the Middle East. However, its international presence produced less than 42% of net sales, even though the number of company-operated stores outside the United States was nearly double the number of U.S stores.[3]

With international stores nearly doubling the number of domestic stores but producing less net sales, Tiffany had to incorporate into its enterprisewide strategy ways to increase its international net sales. One way was to explore developing potential overseas markets. As China became a member of the World Trade Organization (WTO) in 2002, for example, every major organization in the fine jewelry industry positioned itself for the emerging fine jewelry trade in China. China's membership to the WTO had opened an opportunity for the fine jewelers both because of its growing consumer market and because it had low-cost production for custom work and fine craftsmanship.[4] Tiffany tried to capitalize on the market share by establishing one company-operated store, in December 2001, at The Palace Hotel in Beijing, China. It was also to take advantage of the growing trend in high-end luxury brands desired by the Chinese with sales growing during 2000 and 2001. However, Tiffany quickly realized that it took more than just one company-operated store to be successful in the promising fine jewelry market of China, as well as in other potentially strong markets, such as Brazil and Canada.

Besides China, Brazil was also a potential market because the fine jewelry industry was growing there due to lower design and operation costs. This caused fine jewelers to migrate to Brazil and position themselves in the growing market to utilize the low costs. Tiffany opened a company-operated store in San Paolo, Brazil, where it was able to tap the market's potential to help increase net sales. However, similarly to the case in China, Tiffany needed to do more than just open one company-operated store there. Canada was another growing market in the fine jewelry industry because of the growing popularity of diamonds. Most of the thriving diamond industry mines were in this area. Fine jewelers were looking to invest in Canada by investing in Canadian diamond mines. Being a pioneer in the fine jewelry industry by investing in diamond mines was expected to help enhance a specialty fine jeweler's diamond holdings and help streamline its sourcing process. As a result of having larger holdings of diamonds, this generally also meant a larger portion of the market share could be obtained in Canada.[5]

**Exhibit 1
Five-Year Stock
Price: Tiffany & Co.**

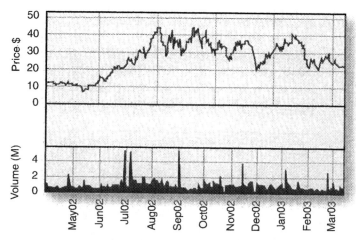

Source: Hoover's Online, "Tiffany & Co. 5 Year Quote," http://quotes.hoovers.com/thomson/chart.html?p=&t= TIF&n=Tiffany+%26+Co.&e=NYSE&c=1481&templ=4&frame=5+Year&index=&ticker=TIF&threed=2&x=5& y=7. Accessed February 25, 2003.

As Tiffany started to make its way into potential overseas markets, its competitors' proactive efforts in expansion and innovation became increasingly aggressive in these potential markets, as well as in the existing markets. Tiffany's competitors' aggressiveness in the industry was taking a toll on Tiffany's stock price. As shown in **Exhibit 1**, Tiffany's stock price had dramatically declined to a price of $23.06 per share as of March 2003, from a high of $41.38 per share in January 2003. This decline was attributed to factors such as increased competition, economic recession post–September 11, and, most recently, severe acute respiratory syndrome (SARS). The SARS epidemic spreading from China in 2003 affected retail sales from tourists because many people were hesitant to travel.

In light of these internal problems and increasing competition, the strategic question that Tiffany needed to resolve was how to expand on its product designs, customer base, manufacturing operations, retail stores, and international presence while enhancing, not hurting, its brand image. In doing this, Tiffany's most important focus of strategic concern was how to differentiate itself from its competitors in the global arena and ultimately achieve a winning edge over its competitors in the immediate, intermediate, and long-term time periods.

History

Tiffany & Co. was a retailer, designer, manufacturer, and distributor of fine jewelry. Its product category had expanded since it originated in 1837 as a stationery store in downtown Manhattan, New York. Established by Charles Lewis Tiffany and his schoolmate John Young, Tiffany's first day of sales in 1837 totaled $4.98. By 2002, fine jewelry made up about 79% of its sales. Other products included timepieces, stationery, chinaware, crystal, sterling silverware, fragrances, and gifts and accessories. It had stores in the United States as well as in international markets around the world. With Charles Tiffany's vision of establishing the grandest preeminent house of design and the world's premier jewelry house, his vision has held true even over a century later.[6] Tiffany had hit the "2001 Top 40 Plus," the National Jeweler's Annual Report that ranks the largest U.S. and Canadian retail jewelry chain sales. With a strong number of retail locations and four new stores in the United States, Tiffany's rank increased five notches, to 17th place.

Exhibit 2 shows Tiffany's organizational chart.

Products

Fine jewelry made up about 79% of Tiffany's sales. Other products included timepieces, stationery, chinaware, crystal, sterling silverware, fragrances, and gifts and accessories.[7] Known for its quality, craftsmanship, and value, Tiffany had established a brand name for itself in the specialty fine jewelry retail sector of luxury goods. Through its strong advertising campaigns, diversified portfolio of products, and license arrangements with third-party designers such as Elsa Peretti and Paloma Picasso, Tiffany was able to produce innovative designs that were signature Tiffany style brands. These signature products contributed to its established brand name and success.

Its quality and durable pieces helped project a positive brand name. However, its small use of celebrity sponsors only modestly supported the Tiffany brand name. With its strong utilization of different metals and stones, and detailed designs and styles with minimal flaws, Tiffany was able to offer quality and durable pieces. Simultaneously, it provided a brand name and long-term value synonymous with the Tiffany name. Its differentiated products through signature products such as the Return to Tiffany collection that were highly trendy and fashionable pieces, offered as everlasting pieces for every occasion to its customers. Tiffany also offered effective competitive pricing at various price ranges to compete in the industry. It offered a sterling silver collection that

Exhibit 2 Organizational Chart: Tiffany & Co.

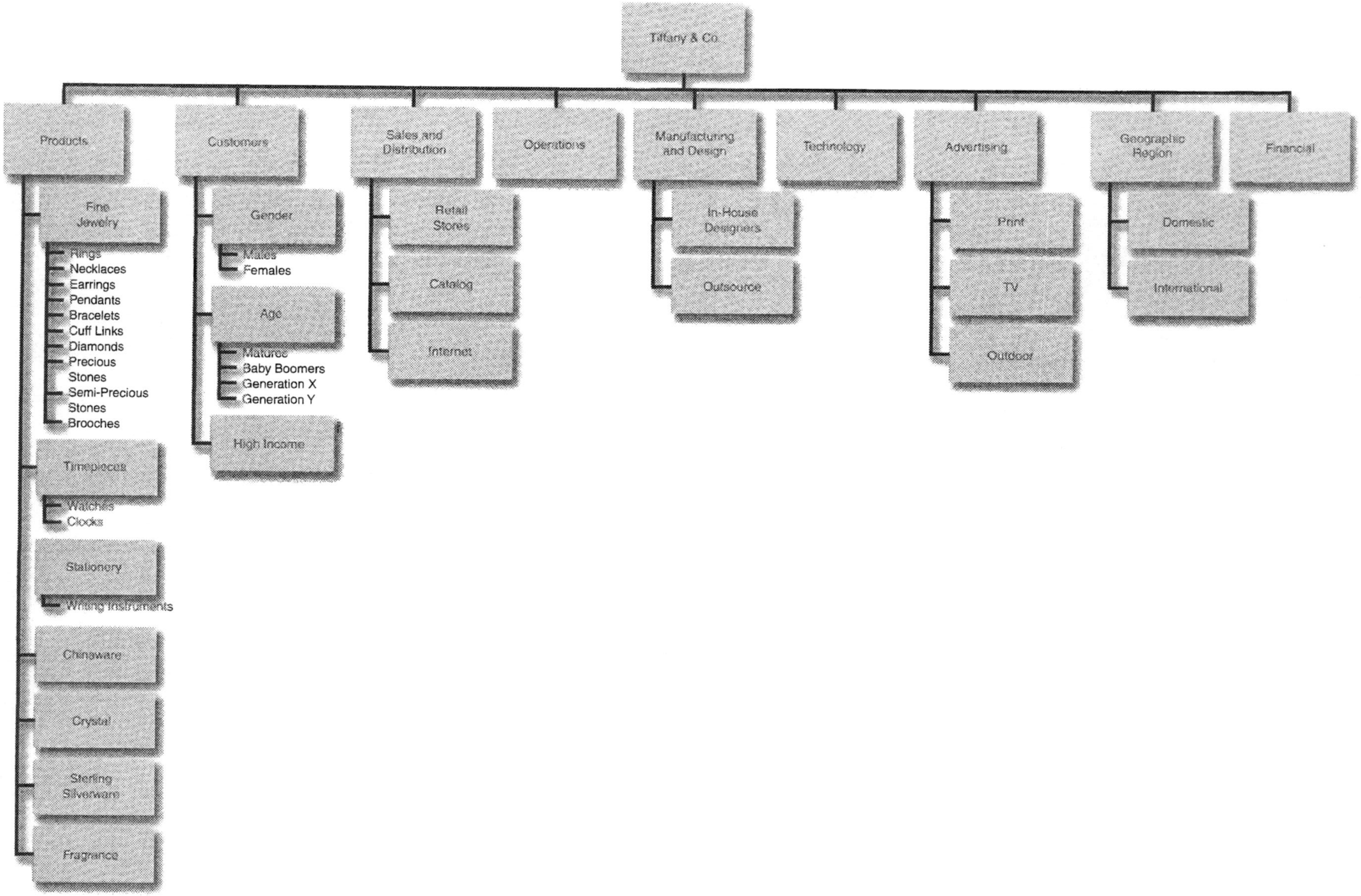

Exhibit 3
Top Purchase
Motivators for
Luxury Goods

Top Purchase Motivators for LuxuryGoods/Services	Respondents Rating Among Their Top 5
To buy things I know would last	76.65%
For my well-being	61.10%
To enjoy my favorite brands	51.74%
To feel good about myself	50.47%
To indulge myself	49.53%
To express myself	46.37%
To be able to rationalize my purchase	36.28%
To feel successful	30.60%
To be optimistic	29.97%
To be lighthearted	23.34%
To make an impression	17.03%
To be impulsive	12.62%
To be fabulous	7.89%
As a status symbol	6.00%

Source: Advertising Age, www.adage.com/news.cms?newsId=34174 (2002). Accessed February 26, 2003.

was priced less than its other fine jewelry pieces. This attracted a market that made purchase decisions based on price. Tiffany offered different product collections and lines at different prices. However, its very weak attempt to expand the men's product categories was hurting its overall sales and potential revenue. It currently had a limited selection of products for men.

Tiffany's effective inventory management allowed it to deliver its products in a timely manner. A well-stocked inventory on hand was a strength of Tiffany's because this allowed it to cater to customers and deliver the goods its customers desired. When Tiffany's fine jewelry pieces were worn, they maintained their luster through the years and fulfilled the desire for well-being. **Exhibit 3** shows the Top Purchase Motivators for Luxury Goods, as surveyed by *Advertising Age*, and conducted by Ziccardi Partners' Frierson Mee.

Customers

Tiffany catered to the wealthiest segments of all age groups. By capturing those segments, Tiffany could strategically position itself to be a brand representing preeminence for years to come for men, women, and all generations. Tiffany's reacted to new market trends that strategically helped position itself in the market by developing products desired by its target market. Its strong customer relations had helped it succeed with these genders and age groups.

Gender

Tiffany targeted both males and females.

Males
Males purchased jewelry pieces for themselves as well as expensive fine jewelry as gifts for others. Also, men were more involved in shopping because they grew up in households where their mothers were often successful career women. Their mothers would send them to purchase their own clothes, buy groceries for the house, and run errands. Men also became

more involved with shopping for apartment furniture and selecting items for the bridal registry. This was an opportunity for Tiffany to cater to this market. Tiffany's weak attempt to expand on men's product categories had reduced the potential revenue to be made. However, even with its limited men's products, its effective use of different metals and stones had helped it maintain partial market share in the men's line.

Females

Females were entering the workforce and relied more on convenience when shopping. They enjoyed purchasing fine jewelry to lavish themselves and decorate to their style. More women were entering the workforce and had little time to shop. This opportunity encouraged Tiffany to use Internet technology to cater to this group with effective shopping convenience efforts. Tiffany was strong in offering various price ranges, the latest trends, beautiful and detailed styles, an easy return and exchange policy, and availability of products at stores, online, and via the catalog to make it easier for working women to shop. However, Tiffany's weak efforts in offering later store hours of operation to accommodate working women drove more women to shop online or via catalog if they could not make it to a retail store in time.

Age

Matures

The age group composed of those 60 years and older was expected to comprise nearly 15% of the U.S. population by 2015. Tiffany was effective in catering to this group with features such as bright lighting, large signs, convenient parking, mass transportation near retail stores, and store layout. Because classic and antique jewelry designs were very popular with this age group, Tiffany offered antique-looking designs such as its Tiffany Bubbles collection

Baby Boomers

This generation, currently in their 40s and 50s, focused on luxury, travel, and leisure. With their kids not living at home, this generation was also known as "empty nesters." They also represented 40 million credit card users, which was about 50% of credit card owners in the United States.[8] Tiffany was strong in catering to their discretionary income and focused on luxury with the different Tiffany collections, diamonds, and gemstones by offering exclusive fine jewelry items and diversified products. Tiffany was also strong in offering store credit cards to reach the baby boomer generation since they preferred to make purchases with credit cards.

Generation X

Generation Xers, currently in their 20s and 30s, were born in the dawning of the Information Age. Specialty retailers gave the Generation Xers experiences that fit their lifestyle and aspirations, and information that kept them informed. Purchases via the Internet were high in this age group. Tiffany was strong in offering sales via the Internet for this age group and others for the convenience and ease of shopping. Its strong security online and in store made it safe and easy for customers to shop with confidence. Also, its sterling silver collections (i.e., Return to Tiffany and Elsa Peretti) were priced accordingly to cater to this age group. This made its collections more price competitive with other specialty fine jewelry retailers in this market.

Generation Y

Generation Y was composed of those primarily in their teens and early 20s. They made their own purchase choices but were influenced by their parents' spending habits. This age segment, which was starting to work, was price conscious and made many purchase decisions based on price. Tiffany targeted this group with its lower-priced collections, such as Return to Tiffany sterling silver jewelry and gifts, while still offering the Tiffany brand that represented quality, craftsmanship, value, and brand in each fine jewelry piece. Tiffany's strength with Generation Y was offering trendy and fashionable pieces, shopping convenience through availability of products online, secure online and store purchases, and strong customer relations.

Income

High-income individuals were affluent and enjoyed luxury items. Because of their taste for luxury, Tiffany offered diamonds, gemstones, and higher-karat metals to these individuals. The Tiffany brand provided status that high-income individuals sought. Also, the pricing of products denoted quality, craftsmanship, and value synonymous to its price range that high-income level individuals looked for in the Tiffany name. In addition, Tiffany's offered this segment convenient shopping through the acceptance of credit cards, easy payment transactions, and great customer service.

Sales and Distribution

Tiffany operated three channels of sales and distribution: (1) U.S. and international retail through company-operated retail stores, (2) Internet sales within the U.S. and wholesale sales to independent retailers and distributors in certain markets, such as in Japan, and (3) direct marketing via catalog sales and Internet sales in the United States.[9] By offering product quality, craftsmanship, value, and innovative designs, as well as expanding its channels of sales and distribution, Tiffany had strategically positioned itself in both the domestic and international markets. However, there was always room for expansion in new sales and distribution channels.

Retail Stores

Tiffany stores were located in prime retail space areas that had high visibility and high traffic. This contributed to the convenience factor for working women and for other target markets. The locations of the stores were in high-end areas to support the high-income individuals targeted. The stores were company operated with knowledgeable sales staffs. With Tiffany's effective decor and layout, excellent lighting, attractive merchandising of "Tiffany Blue" displays, beautiful packaging, excellent inventory on hand, and elegant store atmosphere, customers were attracted to the positive shopping experience Tiffany offered. This meant expanding selections of products, presented in an elegant, warm environment that celebrated the Tiffany name. This experience was offered to increase revenue per square foot of retail selling space and to increase repeat customer purchases.

Besides selling its products in company-operated retail stores, Tiffany also sold to independent retailers and distributors in certain markets, such as in Japan. Some of these independent retailers in Japan and stores such as Macy's and Tourneau carried Tiffany fragrances or timepieces. However, Tiffany's core operations of selling fine jewelry remained in its company-operated retail stores, where its knowledgeable sales staff could respond to all of its clients' questions, needs, and concerns.

Catalogs

Tiffany offered a Tiffany Business catalog, a Tiffany Diamond and the Measure of Brilliance catalog, and a Tiffany Selections catalog. Tiffany's catalogs contained appealing pictures, quality paper stock, and product lines that fell into the category that fit the individual customer or customer's choice of purchase. The Tiffany Business catalog offered business-related products such as writing instruments, business cardholders, and the like. These were gifts designed for clients or for colleagues. The catalogs had limited inventory compared to shopping in the retail store. However, there were items offered in the catalog that were exclusive, giving customers an incentive to shop via the catalogs. Tiffany's strong efforts in the collection of customer data through its customer purchases via the catalogs helped Tiffany understand its customers. If certain customers sought lower-priced items, Tiffany's effective way to reach these customers was to offer various price ranges by sending catalogs with its sterling silver collection, one of its lower-priced collections. The convenient policy of returning catalog purchases at retail stores was a key to its catalogs' success. Customers sought hassle-free returns and exchanges when making purchases, and Tiffany offered this through either returning the item via mail where postage was paid by Tiffany or by bringing the item to a Tiffany retail store.

Internet

Tiffany offered its products via the company web site, *www.tiffany.com*, for shopping convenience. The highly effective security, easy search feature and navigation, and a strong availability of products online offered its customers choice on where to shop and when. The site was divided into collections as well as product categories, so searching for a particular product was made easy. The online shop also provided the VeriSign secure logo, which indicated that shopping on the Tiffany web site was secure. To further ensure secure credit card payments online, Tiffany's encryption codes helped protect identity as well as credit card numbers. After an order was placed online, each fine jewelry piece purchased was individually wrapped and delivered in the famous "Tiffany Blue" packaging. The shopping experience online, from the quality product being purchased down to the last little detail of individually wrapped items in the "Tiffany Blue" box and bag, were things that kept customers satisfied and coming back for repeat purchases.

When a customer visited the Tiffany web site, the technology allowed for effective efforts in an automatic collection of information about the customer. For instance, the web server automatically recognized only the visitor's domain name (not the email address) and recorded the visitor's browser and platform type (such as Netscape browser or Microsoft platform). Cookies were used to record the visitor's session, such as the visitor's shopping selections, when ordering. User-specific information was also recorded, such as the pages the visitor selected for viewing. Also, visitor-keyed information, such as registrations and transaction information, was kept to build its customer database, to later reach the customers through other means such as via catalog, or to send them notifications of promotions. All this data was helpful to Tiffany and was key in helping it improve its Internet web site, promote brand image, promote brand recognition, and understand customer needs.

Tiffany acquired an approximate 5.4% equity interest in *Della.com* Inc. in February 2000. *Della.com* was a provider of online wedding gift registry services. After the acquisition, the company entered into a gift registry service agreement, and the company offered its products through Della's site. Della developed an online wedding gift registry for Tiffany. Later in 2000, *Della.com* merged with the *WeddingChannel.com*. Tiffany saw the growing bridal trend and was proactive in developing a gift registry for this segment. Noticing the growing trend in the bridal market, Tiffany had tried to incorporate products that were relevant to this category. For instance, Tiffany's signature solitaire engagement ring had made the Tiffany brand more popular. The "Tiffany Solitaire" name was a universal name used for a six-prong, solitaire diamond ring setting in the fine jewelry industry. By establishing a popular, signature product, Tiffany was able to help promote its brand image through this product in an industry that equated brand to quality, craftsmanship, and value.

Tiffany's various price ranges offered its customers a selection of different products. Its sterling silver collection was its lower-priced collection, to target the younger age groups in Generations X and Y.

Operations

Tiffany's linked communication between suppliers and personnel had enabled a strong relationship to be built. This helped in its sales operation by replenishing inventory and meeting customer demands through its effective real-time data. The supplier relationship had been built using total quality management, inventory control, and just-in-time operations. Feedback and constant communication helped build the relationship stronger, and, as a result, create quality products effectively and in the most cost-effective manner. Once the products were produced, the timely delivery of the products (just-in-time) was important. Tiffany's inventory management and schedule were timely and effective so that inventory would always be on hand. When products were received by the retail store, the knowledgeable sales force sold the fine jewelry. Besides purchasing a fine jewelry piece, customers received information about what they were purchasing through the trained sales force.

Manufacturing and Designing

Tiffany had manufacturing and design plants domestically and internationally.

In-House Manufacturing and Design

Tiffany recently set up a diamond-cutting factory in the tundra town of Yellowknife, Canada, to cut part of the mine's production, which it sourced through an agreement with junior partner Aber Resources. The $70 million cost of the investment in Aber was a strategic move because Aber held a 40% interest in the Diavik Diamonds Project in Canada's Northwest Territories, an operation developed to mine gem-quality diamonds. In addition, Tiffany had entered into a diamond purchase agreement with Aber. This strong relationship with its vendor helped Tiffany secure a good portion of its future diamond needs.

Outsourcing

Tiffany's strong ability to outsource helped it reduce costs since this process was less costly compared to in-house operations. Tiffany's licensed agreements with designers, such as Elsa Peretti and Paloma Picasso, who specifically designed for Tiffany, had helped it create signature, innovative products synonymous with Tiffany. Their innovative designs, which sold exclusively at Tiffany, provided additional leverage in the competitive environment.

Technology

Tiffany's strength in real-time data capability helped enhance its operations. With real-time data, suppliers and the company could communicate with each other and had up-to-the-minute data regarding production and operations. This information not only would help Tiffany's weak collaboration with its suppliers but also better serve and meet the demands of the customers. In early 2003, Tiffany's software was upgraded, and it was looking to incorporate QAD software into its processes. Its technology, however, had been upgraded to better collect customer data at retail stores and online. Its strong use of the Internet for business and reaching customers had been effective in reaching an audience and delivering a convenience factor.

Advertising

With its marketing and advertising programs that promoted the quality, craftsmanship, value, and design of its products, Tiffany enhanced customer awareness through various forms of advertising media and markets that it served. The shade of blue known as the trademark "Tiffany Blue" symbolized elegance and exclusivity available only at Tiffany stores. This was a key to its success in establishing its brand image and awareness. Tiffany's main advertising media were print, television, and outdoor. These media were used for visibility of brand awareness and helped sustain long-term sales growth.

Print

Tiffany's strength was advertising in high-end, luxury, and fashion magazines with large circulation. Print ads appeared in *InStyle, New Yorker, Cigar Aficionado*, and the like. Print ads included advertising in newspapers. Large and attractive ads were taken out in newspapers for greater visibility, such as a quarter of the page in *The New York Times*. The affluent market, the market that Tiffany catered to, read *The New York Times* and high-end, luxury, and fashion magazines.

Television

Since TV was the largest and usually the most expensive medium, financial resources had to be available for this type of advertising. Tiffany spent about $68.1 million on media (including television), $65.4 million on production, and $57.3 million on catalogs in 2002. Media was the most expensive because it caused the most impact on the target market. Production costs were the costs associated with producing television ads and print advertising, such as drawing the ad, using quality paper stock, and using quality photography. Since costs associated with advertising were high, choosing the right medium that had the largest reach and frequency was important. Research was implemented in choosing the right medium. This was based on the target market's lifestyle and interests. Tiffany's use of Nielsen television ratings data maximized its advertising dollars by researching its target market's television programming choices and networks based on its lifestyle and interests. It offered demographic information for all television shows and network views, indicated the type of shows the targeted demographic watched, indicated what commercials were watched by the specific demographic, and specified the ratings data for that demographic during certain time slots. Tiffany's strength in reaching its market through these high-rated shows and selection of networks had helped it reach its target market as well as making this medium effective for advertising. However, Tiffany's weak use of celebrity sponsors wearing Tiffany jewelry at galas and award shows reduced Tiffany's visibility to the public.

Outdoor

Tiffany advertised on billboards where there was high traffic and strong visibility. Bus depots were another place where Tiffany effectively advertised in the United States, as well as abroad. This helped with promoting the brand image and Tiffany's products by conditioning the consumer's mind with the messages or pictures advertised.

Geographic Region

Tiffany had 44 U.S. company-operated retail stores and 82 international company-operated retail stores. Its U.S. sales were greater, even though the number of international company-operated stores was nearly double. Tiffany's biggest concern was how to increase sales revenue in its international stores.

Domestic

Tiffany's strength was its presence in major U.S. cities, such as New York, San Francisco, and St. Louis. Tiffany's focus on expanding its retail locations both domestically and internationally was a strength in helping it increase its revenue, brand image, and respectable reputation. Its presence in target demographic areas, such as its flagship store on Fifth Avenue in New York, helped reach its clients and catered to their fine jewelry needs. The flagship store was a model store. For example, the flagship store was a lot larger than most of its regular retail stores. The Fifth Avenue flagship store was 124,000 square feet, with 40,000 devoted to retail selling and the remainder to executive and administrative offices, jewelry manufacturing, storage, and product services. Tiffany's U.S. stores totaled approximately 385,000 gross square feet. Individually, other stores were smaller than its flagship store. As a result, these smaller stores were not able to offer as much as the flagship store. For instance, some merchandise might not be displayed, but if asked for, would be brought out from inventory storage. Another strength of Tiffany was its location within major U.S. cities. Its domestic retail stores were located in prime retail space that was accessible by mass transit or driving based on nearby infrastructure. Tiffany's large presence in targeted demographic areas allowed for its target market to easily shop. However, most of the high-income individuals lived in suburbs, but Tiffany had limited presence in these areas. Its stores were mainly located in urban areas, similar to its competitors.

International

Tiffany had 82 company-operated retail stores internationally. Its presence in international markets and in a large number of locations had helped it build brand image as well as generate revenues to help with future expansion. Its largest international market, generating the highest international sales, was Japan. The total approximate gross square feet of its international stores was 224,000 compared to 385,000 square feet per store in the United States. Japan offered a greater shopping experience per square foot of selling space through its product offering, sales staff, store layout and decor, and its "Tiffany Blue" packaging. All these factors contributed to the higher purchase per visit by a customer per square foot of selling space in its Japanese store.

Tiffany opened company-operated stores in markets with strong potential, such as China, Brazil, and Canada. Since China's membership in the WTO in 2001, expansion of free trade had reduced the global cost of production and caused rising global trade. Since rising global trade increased economies of scale, Tiffany looked for low-cost sources of production in China and in Brazil. China was excellent for custom designing and cheap labor, while Brazil was great for its low design and operation costs. This new collaboration with the Brazilians and Chinese helped Tiffany with low-cost sources of production and producing innovative products. Tiffany's strength was not only producing innovative and fashionable pieces to cater to its market but also its streamlined process. With Canada's growing trend in diamonds, Tiffany purchased a diamond mine in Canada to help it gain a hold on the diamonds in the industry and to cater to the growing trend. As new trends developed in the future, Tiffany would explore other potential markets.

Financial Position

Exhibit 4 is Tiffany's financial highlights of 2002 and 2001. Its liquidity needs were expected to remain the same because of its seasonal working capital and capital expenditures, which had increased due to its expansion. Working capital and the corresponding current ratio were $612,978,000 and 2.8:1 at January 31, 2003, compared to $667,647,000 and 3.0:1 on January 31, 2002. See Tiffany's 2002 *Annual Report* for complete financial statements online at *www.tiffany.com*.

Capital expenditures and payment of a capital lease purchase obligation were $210,291,000 in 2002 and $108,382,000 in 2001. A portion of the capital expenditures was related to the renovation and expansion of stores and investment in new systems, office facilities, and internal jewelry manufacturing. Tiffany suffered a loss in 2001 due to economic conditions, especially post–September 11 results. Many retailers suffered due to people being out of jobs and having very little discretionary income, especially for luxury goods. Tiffany's stock price had decreased. However, Kowalski was to improve Tiffany's financial position, increase its stock price, and build brand image. His ongoing strategy was to help Tiffany maintain competitiveness as well as produce greater presence in the fine jewelry retail industry by offering a greater shopping experience per square foot of retail selling space; building brand image through vivid television, print, and outdoor advertising; and offering more products to its customers through detailed, innovative designs. As a specialty

Exhibit 4
Financial Highlights of 2002 and 2001: Tiffany & Co.[1] (Dollar amounts in thousands, except per share data)

Year Ending January 31	2003	2002	Increase (Decrease)
A. Earnings Data			
Net sales	$1,706,602	$1,605,535	6%
Worldwide comparable store			
Sales (on constant exchange rate basis)	$1,282,808	$1,393,836	(1)%
Gross profit	1,011,448	943,477	7%
Earnings from operations	$319,197	$309,897	3%
Net earnings	$189,894	$173,867	9%
B. Ratio Analysis and Other Data			
Net earnings per diluted share	$1.28	$1.15	11%
Cash dividends per share	$0.1600	$0.1606	
Weighted average number of diluted common shares	146,591	150,517	
Earnings from operations as a percentage of net sales	18.7%	19.3%	
Net earnings as a percentage of net sales	11.1%	10.8%	
Return on average assets	10.7%	10.9%	
Return on average stockholders' equity	16.9%	17.7%	
Net–debt as a percentage of total capital	13.8%	8.6%	

Note:
1. The company's fiscal year ends on January 31 of the following calendar year. All references to years relate to fiscal rather than calendar year.

Source: Tiffany & Co. (2002). Annual Report, p. 20.

fine jewelry retailer, the company's business was seasonal in nature. This meant that typically the fourth quarter represented a greater percentage of annual sales and earnings from operations and cash flow.

Management and Strategy

Tiffany's management strategy had grown and continued to evolve in the luxury goods and specialty fine jewelry retailer sector. With new stores opened in 2002, Tiffany was making a presence domestically as well as abroad. With its recent acquisition of Little Switzerland, Tiffany would have a wholly owned subsidiary. Little Switzerland was headquartered in St. Thomas, U.S. Virgin Islands, and was a specialty retailer of luxury items. It had operating stores in the Caribbean and Alaska, which helped cater to the tourists in those areas.[10] Tiffany had recently renovated its New York flagship store, opened four more company-operated stores, and expanded into potential markets such as Brazil, China, and Canada. Additionally, the investment in Aber Resources would help Tiffany secure a portion of its future diamond needs, giving it control over some of the resources.

When China entered the WTO in 2001, China became the newest potential market for specialty fine jewelry retailers. This market had the greatest potential for expansion as well as the fastest-growing fine jewelry market in Asia due to its low-cost production. Considerations of expanding in potential markets such as China, Brazil, and Canada were part of management's strategy. Expanding on the number of company-operated retail stores in untapped markets and expanding per square foot of retail space in already existing stores were considerations in the growth of Tiffany and its management.

While tapping into potential markets might have been a big step, building brand image and brand recognition were very important when dealing with international markets. International customers needed to be able to recognize the Tiffany name in order to be successful in that market. New products and designs catering to the markets' culture would help the customers realize that Tiffany was sensitive to the markets' culture and its needs.

Looking Toward the Future

Although Tiffany had increased its brand awareness that stood for luxury brand quality, craftsmanship, and value jewelry, it still faced increasing competition and environmental pressures. As Tiffany continued to expand the number of company-operated retail stores in domestic and international markets, it continued to face decisions that needed to be made to improve its strategy in order to remain competitive. Decisions regarding product, customers, sales and distribution, operations, manufacturing and design, technology, advertising, and geographic scope were in the hands of Kowalski. His decisions would determine the fate of Tiffany as a specialty fine jewelry retailer.

The *first alternative* considered was to expand the number of stores and square feet of gross international selling space in potential markets like Brazil, Canada, and China.

The benefit of this alternative was that these were growing markets for precious and semi-precious jewelry with innovative designs. Canada had diamond mines that could be beneficial to operations, and China's membership in the WTO made it a potential market for low-cost sourcing. Tiffany also had one company-operated store in each of these potential markets, giving it leverage in obtaining a larger market share since other competitors had not shown much presence in the areas. Also, the benefit of expanding the number of stores and square feet of gross international selling space would help increase its total international sales.

This alternative was feasible because Tiffany had brand recognition in these areas, which was needed to be successful when expanding in potential markets. Tiffany wanted its customers to be proud to wear the fine jewelry purchases branded with the Tiffany name. This not only helped promote brand image and recognition for Tiffany, but it gave the customers a sense of "status" and "well-being" when the fine jewelry piece was worn. The "Tiffany Blue" symbolized exclusive luxury fine jewelry, which was a brand already recognized by all markets, both potential and in which it operated. Because of Brazil and China's low-cost manufacturing and production facilities, Tiffany could use its financial position to help expand its operations and utilize its resources to its advantage. Besides cost-effectiveness in these markets, the fine jewelry trend was vastly growing in these areas as well as Canada. Tiffany had the ability to outsource some of its processes if needed in these areas since it was cost-effective in these areas. So catering to the potential markets was easy because of outsourcers and manufacturing facilities in these areas.

This alternative could win against competition because competitors, like David Yurman, had little international presence. Its major presence was in New York and California. Zales Corporation had a large presence in North America, while Harry Winston had stores in major cities such as New York, Paris, Beverly Hills, Geneva, and Tokyo. Since Tiffany retail stores were company-operated stores, its close relationships with the customers helped management better understand the customers' needs in those markets. Unlike its competition, which sold a larger portion of fine jewelry through major department stores or other independent retailers, Tiffany used company-operated retail stores. Therefore, the high prices that department stores were forcing some of Tiffany's competitors to pay were holding Tiffany's competitors from producing innovative fine jewelry pieces that were important in staying ahead in the industry. Tiffany already had one company-operated store in each of the potential markets of Brazil, Canada, and China. Tiffany's head start in these potential markets gave it a strong leverage to win over the competition. Many of its competitors did not have any presence in these markets or even strong international presence for that matter.

The drawback with this alternative was that Tiffany had to be prepared to face competitive pressures if it decided to expand in the Brazil, Canada, and China markets. Tiffany needed more than one company-operated store in each of these regions. Even though Tiffany was one of the earlier fine jewelers to grab the market share in the potential markets, this would not prevent competitors like Harry Winston and David Yurman from reacting to Tiffany's expansion. In addition, Tiffany would face competition from local competitors in the potential markets. The local competitors had been established for many years, and the residents of those areas recognized the local competitors' brands.

A way around this drawback was to expand per square foot in each of the stores it already had established. With a flagship store already established with the brand name, customers would recognize and feel the experience that Tiffany had to offer. The product lines, customer relations, value, quality, craftsmanship, and experience would be offered to the customers all under one roof. The local competitors would find it hard to compete with Tiffany because of its enormous size and offerings per square foot of selling space.

The *second alternative* was to collaborate with international local competitors in existing and potential markets.

The benefit of this alternative was to decrease or eliminate local competitors by working together with them. Tiffany could use these local competitors as independent retailers of Tiffany fine jewelry. Tiffany would utilize the local competitors to its advantage by building a reputation with their loyal customers.

This alternative was feasible because Tiffany would not only increase revenues in international existing markets but also in potential markets. With the help and recognition of the local competition, Tiffany would be able to use the competition's leverage to gain presence and customer loyalty through selling its fine jewelry in local competitors' stores. In addition, local competitors could use the introduction of Tiffany jewelry into their product lines as a way to promote customers to look at their new merchandise. New merchandise usually drew the attention of customers to a retail store.

Tiffany would be able to win against competition because it would be able to offer its merchandise in additional areas and stores in the international and potential markets through its local competitors as independent retailers. With its additional local competitors selling the Tiffany brand products, this would help increase gross international square feet of selling space.

The drawback of this alternative was that it would take huge efforts to come to agreements with local competition to sell Tiffany fine jewelry at their stores. The way around this drawback was for Tiffany to pay a certain percentage of sales to local competitors for each piece of Tiffany jewelry sold at their store. Usually, commission was an incentive to sell a product.

Notes

1. Tiffany & Co., *Annual Report* (2001).
2. Tiffany & Co., *www.tiffany.com*.
3. Tiffany & Co., *www.tiffany.com*.
4. V. Gomelsky, "China: The Once and Future Kingdom," *National Jeweler Online, www.nationaljeweler.com*.
5. V. Gomelsky, "China: The Once and Future Kingdom," *National Jeweler Online, www.nationaljeweler.com*.
6. Tiffany & Co., *www.tiffany.com*.
7. Tiffany & Co., *Annual Report* (2001).
8. E-Com Profits, "Baby Boomer Facts," *http://e-comprofits.com/babboomfac.html*.
9. Tiffany & Co., *Annual Report* (2001).
10. Tiffany & Co., *www.tiffany.com*.

References

About.com, *http://jewelry.about.com/cs/costumejewelry/index.htm*.

Advertising Age, *www.adage.com/news.cms?newsId=34174* (2002).

The Business Journal, "Holiday Sales Fall Flat for Specialty Stores," *http://tampabay.bizjournals.com/tampabay/stories/2003/01/06/daily7.html* (January 6, 2003).

P. Danziger, "The Tabletop Report, 2002: The Market, the Competitors, the Trends," *http://retailindustry.about.com/library/bl/02q4/bl_um101002.htm* (2002).

P. Danziger, "Today's Jewelry Market," *www.refresher.com/!umi.html* (2002).

Diamonds International, "Couples Confirm 'Love Is in the Air,'" *www.diamondsintl.com/about.cfm?page=press* (2003).

Ernst & Young, "Retail Newsletter," *www.ey.com* (2002).

Federal Trade Commission, *www.ftc.gov*.

B. Green, "Tiffany Granted Preliminary Injunction Against Counterfeit Jewelry Sales," *National Jeweler Online, www.nationaljeweler.com/nationaljeweler/search/search_display.jsp?vnu_content_id=1798850*.

J. Harris, "What Is Retailing?" *www.fiu.edu/~retail/whatis.html* (2000).

Harry Winston, *www.harrywinston.com*.

G. E. Hoover, "What Happens After All the Categories Are Killed?" *Arthur Anderson—Retailing Issues Letter.* Vol. 8, No. 4 (1996), pp. 1–4.

Hoover's Online, "Company Capsule," *www.hoovers.com/co/capsule/1/0,2163,11481,00.html*.

Hoover's Online, "Tiffany & Co. 5 Year Quote," *http://quotes.hoovers.com/thomson/chart.html?p=&t=TIF&n=Tiffany+%26+Co.&e=NYSE&c=11481&templ=4&frame=5+Year&index=&ticker=TIF&threed=2&x=5&y=7*.

LVMH, *www.lvmh.com*.

R. Molofsky, "FBI Raids Manhattan for Fake Tiffany Jewels," *www.nationaljeweler.com/nationaljeweler/search/search_display.jsp?vnu_content_id=1871560* (April 23, 2003).

Nielsen Media Research, *www.nielsenmedia.com*.

Professional Jeweler, "Jewelry Store Sales by Products Stats," *www.professionaljeweler.com/archives/features/stats/stats_prod.html*

QAD Inc., "David Yurman Selects QAD to Make Its Worldwide Manufacturing Operations Sparkle," *http://biz.yahoo.com/bw/021202/20232_1.html* (2002).

Retail Industry, "Catalog Sales Growth Continues to Outpace Overall Retail Growth," *http://retailindustry.about.com/library/bl/q2/bl_dma060401a.htm* (June 4, 2001).

Retail Industry, "The Global Luxury Retailing Sector," *http://retailindustry.about.com/library/bl/02q1/bl_ri020602.htm* (2002).

Retail Jewelers Organization, "Buying Fine Jewelry," *www.rjo.polygon.net/docs/buyingfine.html* (2002).

T. Rozhon, "Squeezed, a Jewelry Designer Closes Shop," *The New York Times www.nytimes.com/2003/04/04/business/04GEMS.html* (April 4, 2003).

R. S. Russell and B. W. Taylor III, *Operations Management*, 4th edition (New York: Prentice Hall, 2003), pp. 33–53.

Standard & Poor's, "Stocks Remain in the Red," *www.standardandpoors.com*.

Tiffany & Co., *Annual Report* (2002).

Unity Marketing, "Consumers' Appetite for Jewelry Is Vigorous in the First Half of 2002," *www.unitymarketingonline.com/reports/jewelry/pr1.html* (2002).

U.S. Census Bureau, "1992 Census of Retail Trade, Definitions of Industries," *www.census.gov/epcd/www/rc92sics.html* (1992).

M. Vargas, "Jewelry Sales Reach $39.8 Billion," *http://retailindustry.about.com/library/bl/q2/bl_um041701.htm* (April 17, 2001).

WetFeet, "Retail Industry Profile," *www.wetfeet.com/asp/industryprofiles_overview.asp?industrypk=28*.

WSL Strategic Retail, "Convenience Is Key," *http://retailindustry.about.com/library/uc/02/uc_wls1.htm*.

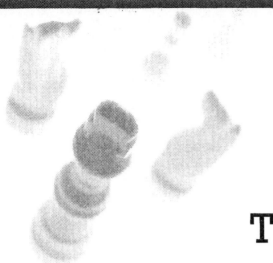

CASE 22

The Vermont Teddy Bear Co., Inc.:

Challenges Facing a New CEO (Revised)

*Joyce P. Vincelette, Ellie A. Fogarty, Thomas M. Patrick,
and Thomas L. Wheelen*

"**A TEDDY BEAR IS ALMOST A 100-YEAR-OLD PRODUCT THAT HAS BEEN MADE IN EVERY**
conceivable size, style, fabric, and price combined with a saturated market. Yet the teddy bear
industry stands as a model of strength and durability. Every year, bear makers create and market hundreds of original models."[1]

Vermont Teddy Bear Company was founded in 1981 by John Sortino, selling handsewn
teddy bears out of a pushcart in the streets of Burlington, Vermont. Since this time, the company's focus has been to design, manufacture, and direct market the best teddy bears made in
America using quality American materials and labor.

Until 1994, Vermont Teddy Bear experienced a great deal of success and profitability.
Problems arose in 1995. Since 1995, the company has had two CEOs. It changed its name to
The Great American Teddy Bear Company and then changed it back to The Vermont Teddy
Bear Company when customers got confused. From its inception, Vermont Teddy Bear had
been known for its Bear-Gram delivery service. In 1996, the company decided to shift emphasis away from Bear-Grams to other distribution channels. By 1998, the company decided to
renew its emphasis on Bear-Grams. Vermont Teddy has always been proud of the fact that its
teddy bears were made in America with American materials and craftsmanship. In 1998, the

This case was prepared by Professor Joyce P. Vincelette, Ellie A. Fogarty, Business Librarian, and Professor Thomas
M. Patrick of the College of New Jersey, and Professor Thomas L. Wheelen of the University of South Florida. They
would like to thank Matthew Tardougno for his assistance on this project. Copyright © 1998 and 2005 by Thomas L.
Wheelen. This case was edited for SMBP and Cases in SMBP–9th and 10th Edition. The copyright holder is solely
responsible for case content. Reprint permission is solely granted to the publisher, Prentice Hall, for the books,
Strategic Management and Business Policy–10th Edition (and the International version of this book) and Cases in
Strategic Management and Business Policy–10th Edition by the copyright holder, Thomas L. Wheelen. Any other
publication of the case (translation, any form of electronics or other media) or sold (any form of partnership) to
another publisher will be in violation of copyright law, unless Thomas L. Wheelen has granted an additional written
reprint permission.

company changed this philosophy by exploring the offshore sourcing of materials, outfits, and manufacturing in an effort to lower costs.

Elisabeth Robert assumed the titles of President and Chief Executive Officer in October 1997 and began to cut costs and position the company for future growth. According to Robert, there were many reasons to invest in The Vermont Teddy Bear Company:

> I believe that there is growth potential in this company. We are going to regain our balance this year. This is a rebuilding year. We are taking key steps to reposition the company. The move off-shore is going to provide this company an opportunity to become more profitable. We will gain additional flexibility with price points. There is opportunity for us to expand from a regional brand to a national brand. While we continue to emphasize the premium teddy bear gift business, we intend to expand into larger markets. There is now a whole new opportunity for us in the corporate incentives and promotions market as well as the wholesale market. We have weekly inquiries from companies who recognize our brands. These companies would love to buy and resell our product or use our product as a corporate gift. Our growth will come not only from expansion of our radio markets but in the corporate and wholesale markets as we use off-shore manufacturing alternatives to move to broader price points.[2]

According to Robert, "our competitors are the people who sell chocolates, flowers, and greeting cards. We target the last minute shopper who wants almost instant delivery."[3] Gift purchases account for 90% of the Company's sales.[4] "We thought we were in the teddy bear business," said Robert. "In fact we are in the gift and personal communications business. Our competition isn't Steiff [the German toy manufacturer]: it's 1-800 Flowers."[5]

On one beautiful June day in Vermont in 1998, Elisabeth Robert reflected on the enormous tasks to be accomplished. She wondered if she could successfully reposition her company and return it to profitability. Was she making the correct strategic decisions?

History: Why a Bear Company?

The Vermont Teddy Bear Co., Inc., was founded in 1981 by John Sortino. He got the inspiration for the teddy bear business shortly after his son Graham was born. While playing with his son, he noticed that Graham had many stuffed animals, but they were all made in other countries. Sortino "decided that there should be a bear made in the United States."[6]

He decided to design and manufacture his own premium-quality teddy bears. To turn his concept into reality, Sortino taught himself to sew and enrolled in drawing classes. In 1981, his first creation, Bearcho, was a bear whose thick black eyebrows and mustache resembled those of Groucho Marx. His first bear line included Buggy, Fuzzy, Wuzzy, and Bearazar, the bear with super powers. In 1982, Vermont Teddy Bear Company began limited production of Sortino's early designs using five Vermont homesewers. In 1983, Sortino took his operation to the streets where he sold his handmade bears from a pushcart on the Church Street Marketplace in downtown Burlington, Vermont. Four days later he sold his first bear. By the end of 1983, 200 bears were sold. He concluded from his selling experiences that customers "want bears that are machine washable and dryable. They want bears with joints. They want bears that are cuddly and safe for children. They want bears with personality."[7]

In 1984, Vermont Teddy was incorporated under the laws of the State of New York and Sortino's pushcart business had turned into a full-time job. To facilitate bear manufacturing, local homeworkers were contracted to produce an assortment of the founder's original designs. Even though the company opened a retail store in Burlington, Vermont, in 1985, the majority of the company's products were sold through department stores such as Macy's and Nieman Marcus during the 1980s. As the retail industry consolidated through mergers and store closings during the late 1980s, Sortino realized that a new market needed to be found for his bears. In search of a new customer base, Sortino turned to a local radio station and began advertising the company's products. This advertising strategy paved the way for the "Bear-Gram," where customers could send the gift of a Vermont Teddy Bear by placing an order through the company's 800 number.

The company initiated its Bear-Gram marketing strategy in 1985 in the Burlington, Vermont area. Local radio advertisements aired on WXXX in Burlington and customers called an 800 number to order the product. It was not until shortly before Valentine's Day in 1990 that the company introduced radio advertising of its Bear-Gram product on radio station WHTZ ("Z-100") in New York City, positioning the Bear-Gram as a novel gift for Valentine's Day and offering listeners a toll-free number to order from the company's facility in Vermont. The test proved to be successful, and the Bear-Gram concept was expanded to other major radio markets across the country. These radio advertisements were generally read live by popular radio personalities. John Sortino believed that the radio had been a successful medium for the Bear-Gram for several reasons. He believed that the use of popular radio personalities lent credibility to the product. In addition, because the disc jockey could give away a few bears, more air-time was spent on the product than the paid "60 seconds."[8] He also believed that radio advertising allowed for flexibility in the use of advertising copy, which could be adjusted as the company changed its marketing focus.

Due to the success of the Bear-Gram concept, Vermont Teddy's total sales of $400,000 in 1989 rose to $1.7 million in 1990 and over $5 million in 1991.[9] As sales increased, a larger manufacturing facility was needed. In 1991, the company leased and moved into a new factory space and guided factory tours began. The larger production facilities made it possible for Vermont Teddy Bear to begin producing bears in bulk and to enter into larger sales agreements with retail establishments. In 1992, *Inc.* magazine listed Vermont Teddy as the eightieth fastest growing company in the United States with sales totaling $10.6 million.[10]

Vermont Teddy Bear went public on November 23, 1993. By this time, sales totaled $17 million.[11] In 1993, the company was named the first national winner of the Dun & Bradstreet "Best of America" Small Business Award and was ranked as the fastest growing company in the United States by *Inc.* magazine.[12] Also in 1993, the company was the recipient of the Heritage of New England Customer Service Award. Previous recipients of the award included L.L.Bean, Inc., Boston Beer Company, and Ben & Jerry's Homemade, Inc.[13]

In 1994, construction began on a new factory and retail store in Shelburne, Vermont, which opened for business in the summer of 1995. In 1994, *Inc.* magazine listed Vermont Teddy Bear, with sales totaling $20.5 million, as the twenty-first fastest growing small, publicly owned company in the United States and named the company "Small Business of the Year."[14]

Prior to 1994, Vermont Teddy Bear had experienced a great deal of success and profitability, with sales growth in excess of 50% for three consecutive years.[15] However, 1994 marked the beginning of the company's financial troubles. The company's expenses increased in accordance with its anticipated growth, but sales did not increase as rapidly.

Vermont Teddy Bear's rapid growth during the 1990s taxed the organizational structure and efficiency of the company's operations. Due to the company's declining financial situation, on June 20, 1995, the company's Founder, President, and Chief Executive Officer, John Sortino, resigned. Sortino recognized that the future success of the company "depends on the transition from an entrepreneurial company to a professionally managed organization." He further stated, "I wanted to assist the company in positioning itself for the arrival of a new CEO. I will provide guidance to the company in a consulting role, and I will retain my position on the Board of Directors."[16]

On August 2, 1995, R. Patrick Burns was appointed as President and CEO. Also in 1995 Elisabeth Robert joined the company as Chief Financial Officer. Outside observers wondered if the company could successfully make the transition to a new CEO and generate enough sales to pull itself out of debt and remain profitable.

In its attempts to turn the company around, the new management team eliminated several unprofitable marketing ventures (such as its sponsorship of a NASCAR circuit race car and driver) and reduced general and administrative cost. By 1996, the new team had generated a profit of $152,000.[17]

During the later part of 1996, Vermont Teddy Bear took on a new trademarked name, "The Great American Teddy Bear Company," in an attempt to broaden brand appeal and take advantage of national and international distribution opportunities. Even though the "Vermont" name gave good name recognition in the Northeast, the company felt that it had less impact in other parts of the country. They were wrong. Customers became confused, and Disney's entry into the personalized teddy bear gift market with their "Pooh-Grams" added to the confusion. The confusion contributed to a decrease in Bear-Gram sales. By Valentine's Day, the company returned to its established mark, The Vermont Teddy Bear Company.

Late in 1996, the new management team began to explore opportunities for growth. They believed that the emphasis of the company should shift from the Bear-Gram business to other distribution channels. Their new five-year plan included opening new retail stores and expanding the catalog.

By 1997, retail sales were the fastest growing part of Vermont Teddy's business. Sales for the factory retail store in Shelburne for the fiscal year ending June 30, 1996, were 19% ahead of 1995.[18] It appeared obvious to top management that retail was a growing profit center for the company. The company's factory store had become a major Vermont tourist destination and had averaged 130,000 visitors a year since opening in July 1995.[19] As a result, the company became interested in high tourist traffic areas for retail expansion, hoping to duplicate this success at other retail locations.[20]

The location for the company's second retail store was North Conway, New Hampshire, a major tourist destination in both winter and summer months. The store opened in July 1996. The third retail location opened at 538 Madison Avenue in New York City in February 1997. The New York City location was chosen because it had been the number one market for Bear-Grams since the company began advertising on radio in 1990. The company believed that the New York store would benefit from the millions of dollars of radio advertising that the company had invested in this market. The fourth store opened in Freeport, Maine, on August 16, 1997, two doors down from L.L.Bean.

Fiscal 1997 was a disappointing year for Vermont Teddy. After a year of controlling costs and a return to profitability in 1996, they had set out in pursuit of revenue growth in 1997. The 1997 initiatives included an expanded catalog and the new retail stores. As part of the shift away from Bear-Grams, the company downsized their radio media buying department. The company lost money on their catalog programs, and the new retail stores were not as profitable as expected. Resources diverted to expanding secondary marketing channels, coupled with accelerating changes in the radio industry, contributed to a decline in Bear-Gram sales. The end result was a loss of $1,901,795 in fiscal 1997.[21]

Because of Vermont Teddy Bear's declining performance, R. Patrick Burns chose to step down as President and CEO in October 1997. Elisabeth Robert assumed the title of President and CEO and retained the title of Chief Financial Officer.

According to CEO Robert:

When we made the decision to expand our distribution channels in the areas of retail and catalog, our focus was on being a teddy bear category killer. We thought we were in the teddy bear business. Now what I believe is that we are in the Bear-Gram business, the gift business, and the impulse business. This is a completely different marketplace. Our competitors are the people who sell chocolates, flowers, and greeting cards. We target the last-minute shopper who wants almost instant delivery.[22]

She further stated that "the primary focus of the company would return to maximizing returns in the radio Bear-Gram business, which constituted the majority of the company's annual revenue."[23]

In 1998, the management team began seriously looking at the profitability of their various retail locations. They also began looking at the catalog, intending to optimize its size and product offerings to ensure its future profitability.

Corporate Governance

As of June 30, 1998, The Vermont Teddy Bear Co., Inc., had a total of seven Board members and two Executive Officers, both of whom were also members of the Board of Directors.

Board of Directors and Executive Officers[24]

The Board members, Executive Officers, and their experience and qualifications were as follows:

R. Patrick Burns (53) had been President and CEO of Vermont Teddy Bear from 1995 until 1997. He had been a Director of the company since 1995. He planned to remain active as a consultant to the company focusing on developing strategic marketing partnerships for the next two years. Prior to joining the company, he was the Chief Executive Officer of Disney Direct Marketing. He had also held senior management positions at J. Crew, Inc., and at L.L.Bean, Inc.

Joan H. Martin (74) was a private investor who had been a Director of the company since 1991. Martin had no business experience during the past eight years apart from managing her private investment portfolio.

Fred Marks (70) became a Director of the company in 1987 and became its Treasurer and Chairman of the Board in 1989. He served as the company's Chief Financial Officer until January 1995 and Treasurer until 1996. Previously Marks had served as Chairman of the Board of two privately held companies: Selection, Ltd., a manufacturer of remote controls for computers and televisions; and Contaq Technologies, a manufacturer of ultrasonic instruments.

Elisabeth B. Robert (43), Director, Chief Executive Officer, President, Treasurer and Chief Financial Officer, joined the company in 1995 as the Chief Financial Officer replacing Stephen Milford. She was appointed a Director of the company in January 1996 and Treasurer of the company in April 1996. She assumed the titles of CEO and President from R. Patrick Burns who stepped down from the positions in October 1997. Before joining Vermont Teddy, Robert served as the Chief Financial Officer for a high-tech startup company specializing in remote control devices, where she was also a founding partner.

Spencer C. Putnam (52), Director, Vice President, and Secretary, joined the company as its Chief Operating Officer in June 1987 and continued in this role. He had been a Director of the company and Secretary of its Board since 1989. Before joining the company, Putnam was the director of the Cooperative Education Program at the University of Vermont.

David W. Garrett (55) had been a Director of the company since 1987. He was a Vice President of First Albany Corporation, an investment banking and brokerage firm. Garrett was also President of the Garrett Hotel Group, a private hotel development and management firm and President of The Black Willow Group, Ltd., a private company which owned and operated The Point, a luxury hotel in Saranac Lake, New York.

Jason Bacon (64) became a Director of the company in 1997. He was a consultant to nonprofit organizations and a private investor focusing on real estate and securities with international perspective. Prior to his involvement with Vermont Teddy Bear, he served as a Managing Director at Kidder, Peabody & Company.

Ownership

As of June 30, 1998, there were 5,183,733 shares of the company's common stock outstanding, held by 1,553 shareholders.[25] Approximately 2,551,300 shares, or approximately 49.2%, of the stock was owned beneficially by the current directors and officers of the company. These figures did not include options or warrants held by current directors and officers, their spouses or minor children to purchase shares of the company's Common Stock or Series B Preferred Stock.[26]

In November 1993, the company made an Initial Public Offering (IPO) of 5,172,500 shares of common stock. The stock ranged from $17.19 to $11.44 from offering to December 31, 1993. Prior to the IPO, 4,000,000 shares of common stock were outstanding and held by nine shareholders. Ninety shares of nonvoting Series A Preferred Stock were held by shareholder Joan H. Martin. This preferred stock had an 8% cumulative dividend and liquidation value of $10,000 per share. On July 12, 1996, the company privately placed 204,912 share of Series B preferred stock. This stock was held by 12 shareholders and was not entitled to any dividends or voting rights. The 204,912 Series B shares were convertible into 482,441 shares of common stock.[27]

The following individuals owned more than 5% of the company's stock as of June 30, 1998[28]:

Beneficial Owner	Number of Shares	Percentage Owned
Joan H. Martin	1,840,975	35.5%
Fred Marks	600,500	11.6
Margaret H. Martin	267,000	5.2
Spencer C. Putnam	84,000	1.6
R. Patrick Burns	17,625	0.3
Jason Bacon	5,500	0.1
Elisabeth B. Robert	2,700	0.1
Notes were deleted.		

Vermont Teddy has never paid cash dividends on any of its shares of common stock. The high and low stock prices for 1998 were[29]:

Quarter Ending	High	Low
June 30, 1998	$1.63	$1.06
March 31, 1998	$1.63	$0.75
December 31, 1997	$2.13	$0.88
September 30, 1997	$2.56	$1.06

Company Philosophy

From its founding by John Sortino in the early 1980s until 1998, the company's focus has been to design and manufacture the best teddy bears made in America, using American materials and labor. The company believed that apart from its own products, most of the teddy bears sold in the United States were manufactured in foreign countries, and that the company was the largest manufacturer of teddy bears made in the United States. The company's mission statement can be seen in **Exhibit 1**.

This philosophy was modified significantly in 1998 with the company's decision to explore the offshore sourcing of materials and manufacturing alternatives in an effort to lower the company's cost of goods sold and to broaden its available sources of supply. Company customer surveys revealed that price was more important to potential customers than the "Made in America" label.[30] During 1998, the company began purchasing raw materials for bear production and some

Exhibit 1
Mission Statement:
The Vermont Teddy
Bear Co., Inc.

The Vermont Teddy Bear provides our customers with a tangible expression of their best feelings for their families, friends, and associates. We facilitate, communicate, and therefore participate in caring events and special occasions that celebrate and enrich our customers' life experiences.

Our products will represent unmatchable craftsmanship balanced with optimal quality and value. We will strive to wholesomely entertain our guests while consistently exceeding our external and internal customer service expectations.

The Vermont Teddy Bear brand represents the rich heritage of the "Great American Teddy Bear" begun in 1902. We are the stewards of a uniquely American tradition based on the best American virtues including compassion, generosity, friendship, and a zesty sense of whimsy and fun.

teddy bear outfits from offshore manufacturers. Vermont Teddy felt that plush materials from offshore were of better quality and less costly than those produced in the United States. They felt that importing these materials would enable them to produce a better, lower cost product and would provide the flexibility to meet a broader range of price points in response to customer needs.[31] The company planned to continue to handcraft the 15-inch "classic" teddy bear in Vermont for those customers interested in an American-made product. The new label read "Made in America, of domestic and foreign materials."[32] The company also planned to explore opportunities to introduce new teddy bear products made offshore to their design specifications at significantly lower cost points for sale initially into the wholesale and corporate channels.

With this change in philosophy, the company was committed to understanding its potential offshore partners and to ensuring that its partners provided decent, lawful working conditions. It required that all offshore vendors sign a written statement to this effect prior to any business dealings.[33]

Exhibit 2 details Vermont Teddy's statement of Stakeholder Beliefs. The company believed that the quality, variety, and creativity of the company's products, and its commit-

Exhibit 2
Stakeholder
Beliefs: The
Vermont Teddy
Bear Co., Inc.

Our customers are the foundation of our business. Exceeding their expectations everyday will form the backbone of our corporate culture. Zealous pursuit of "world class" customer service will build a self-fulfilling cycle of pride, partnership, team spirit, and personal commitment in every player in our company.

Our employees are our internal customers. The philosophy that applies to our external customers extends also to our internal associates. We will cultivate a results-oriented environment that encourages fairness, collaboration, mutual respect, and pride in our organization. Pro-active, positive, open-minded confrontation among well-intentioned colleagues will ensure innovation, reject complacency, and stimulate individual growth. Our company supports employee diversity and provides clear opportunities for each of us to reach our full personal and professional potential.

Our investors provide capital in good faith, and we are accountable for creating a realistic return while protecting the assets of our company. Our financial strength and profitability are essential to fulfilling all of our stakeholder commitments.

Our vendors provide a partnership opportunity for innovative product development, unsurpassed external customer service, and mutual prosperity. This is based on exceeding our customers' expectations for unique, innovative, high-quality communications and products delivered to our customers where and when they want them at a price that reinforces our reputation for perceived value.

Our community deserves our commitment to being ethically, legally, and environmentally responsible while remaining fiscally sound. We will support organizations and individuals with values similar to ours and participate actively in those enterprises that seek to improve local and world conditions for future generations. We will seek to maintain a dynamic balance between meeting our commitment to our community and maintaining the viability of our own enterprise.

ment to customer service, were essential to its business. Its manufacturing practices were environmentally sound. The company sought to use the best available materials for its bears. Customer service policies rivaled those of L.L.Bean. Each bear was sold with a "Guarantee for Life," under which the company undertook to repair or replace any damaged or defective bear at any time, even if eaten by the family dog or destroyed by a lawn mower.[34]

Products and Services

Vermont Teddy Bear made old-fashioned, handmade, jointed teddy bears ranging from 11 to 72 inches tall, in 6 standard color selections, including tan, honey, brown, and black. More than 100 different bear outfits were available for customers to outfit and individualize their bears or to emphasize certain relevant characteristics of the receiver such as policewoman, gardener, doctor, or racing car driver. Some of the more popular outfits included tutus, wedding gowns, tuxedos, business suits, and sports uniforms. Bears could also be dressed in a wide variety of outfits that personalized the bear for significant life events, such as a new baby, get well, birthdays, graduations, weddings, and "I love you." A collection of bears could also be designed for schools, sports teams, businesses, and other organizations. New "edgier" products were added in 1997 such as "Shredder, the Snowboarder Bear," targeted primarily at radio customers. As of June 30, 1998, 40% of the outfits were outsourced to overseas contractors.[35] Prices for the bears in standard outfits ranged from $40 to more than $200. Custom-made clothing was available at an additional cost.

Until 1997, bear materials were mostly American made, though mohair fur used for the premium bears came from Europe. All other fur was hypoallergenic, plush polyester. Bears were stuffed with virgin Dacron 91, a fire retardant filler for safety. Vermont teddy bears had movable joints, a feature associated with traditional, high-quality teddy bears. These joints were made from recycled Ben & Jerry's ice cream containers. In keeping with the company's attempt to produce the bears with domestic materials, the bears' eyes had come from the only eye maker left in America. Noses and paw pads were ultrasuede, also 100% American made.[36] Using American-made materials had been one of the methods by which Vermont Teddy Bear differentiated its products from those of its competitors. The company's 1998 move to the offshore sourcing of raw materials represented a significant departure from the company's historical position as an American manufacturer using almost exclusively American materials.[37]

In addition to the products it manufactured, Vermont Teddy Bear sold items related to teddy bears, as well as merchandise from other manufacturers featuring the logo of Vermont Teddy Bear. It did a small amount of licensing with Tyco, Landmark, and a manufacturer of children's and women's sleepwear. Some items such as clothing, jewelry, and accessory ornaments were available primarily at the company's retail stores and through its direct mail catalog. The company also sold stuffed toys that had been manufactured by other companies, such as Gund and Steiff.[38] Vermont Teddy Bear planned to alter this strategy in 1999 to focus more attention on the sale of the company's own manufactured products, including those manufactured offshore.

In addition to manufacturing and selling bears and bear-related merchandise to individual consumers, the company's Corporate Division provided unique and original customized products for corporations. Vermont Teddy also silk-screened or embroidered bears on clothing with the customer's logo, slogan, or team name. In 1998, the company planned to offer a line of offshore-manufactured ancillary products for corporate customers and outlets such as QVC.[39] Information about products offered through the company's Corporate and Wholesale Programs could be found on the company's web site.

Marketing Strategies and Distribution Methods

Vice President of Sales was Katie Camardo. Robert D. Delsandro was appointed Vice President of Marketing and Design in May 1998. He had been employed by The Vermont Teddy Bear Company as Creative Director since 1996 and had been responsible for developing a completely new look for the company's products, retail stores, printed promotional materials, and catalog. He was credited with creating the new "edgier" look of Vermont Teddy Bear.[40]

Although many teddy bear producers defined their product as a toy and marketed solely to children, Vermont Teddy Bear marketed its bears as an attractive gift or collectible for both children and adults. The company defined its target market as "children between the ages of 1 to 100."[41]

The company was primarily known for its Bear-Gram delivery service. Bear-Grams were personalized teddy bears that were delivered directly to recipients as gifts for holidays and special occasions. Bear-Grams were gift boxed in unique containers complete with "air-holes" for the bear. The bears were accompanied by a personal greeting from the sender.

Orders for Bear-Grams were generally placed by calling a toll-free number (1-800-829-BEAR) and speaking with company sales representatives called "Bear Counselors." Customers could also visit the company's web site, *www.vtbear.com*, and place their orders online. "Bear Counselors" entered an order on a computer, which was part of the company's computer network of approximately 250 workstations that linked order entry with sales and accounting systems. The company had plans to upgrade, expand, and integrate its computer systems, including the purchase of an inventory control system. In 1994, the company installed a new telephone system, which improved its telemarketing operations and was designed to accommodate future growth in telephone call volume. The company strove to provide rapid response to customer orders. Orders placed by 4 P.M. EST (3 P.M. on the Internet) could be shipped the same day. Packages were delivered primarily by UPS and other carriers by next day air or ground delivery service.[42] The company also sought to respond promptly to customer complaints. The company believed that, as a result of the quality of its products and service, it had established a loyal customer base.

The company attributed its success to this direct-marketing strategy. Since 1990, when the Bear-Gram was introduced to prime-time and rush-hour audiences in the New York City market, the company had continued to rely primarily on Bear-Gram advertising. It had also continued to focus its advertising on morning rush-hour radio spots, with well-known personalities such as Don Imus and Howard Stern, promoting the bears.

For the fiscal year ending June 30, 1998, Bear-Grams accounted for 70.2% of net revenues of $17.2 million. The percent of net revenues for the company's primary distribution methods can be seen in **Exhibit 3**. Included in Bear-Gram revenues were sales from the company's Internet web site. Other principal avenues of distribution included company-owned retail stores, direct mail catalogs, and licensing and wholesale agreements. The company's

**Exhibit 3
Primary
Distribution
Methods: The
Vermont Teddy
Bear Co., Inc.**

Year Ending June 30	1998	1997	1996	1995
Bear-Grams[1]	72.0%	70.0%	75.8%	78.7%
Retail Operations	18.0%	17.7%	12.9%	9.2%
Direct Mail	9.2%	10.9%	7.2%	8.8%
Other	0.8%	1.4%	4.1%	3.3%

Note:
1. Excludes Bear-Gram revenues from retail operations.

Source: The Vermont Teddy Bear Co., Inc., 1998 Annual Report, *p. 3.*

Exhibit 4
Vermont Teddy Bear's Largest Markets (Percentage of Bear-Grams for the 12 months ending June 30)

Markets	1998	1997	1996	1995
New York City	37.8%	40.8%	35.5%	38.6%
Boston	13.4%	13.2%	9.5%	9.5%
Philadelphia	8.9%	11.6%	8.9%	7.3%
Chicago	6.5%	8.9%	7.3%	8.5%
Los Angeles	6.3%	5.8%	4.0%	3.8%

Source: The Vermont Teddy Bear Company, Inc., 1998 Annual Report, *p. 4.*

sales were heavily seasonal, with Valentine's Day, Christmas, and Mother's Day as the company's largest sales seasons.[43] For Valentine's Day 1998, more than 47,000 bears were sent out by people across the country who wished to say "I love you."[44]

During the summer of 1997, Vermont Teddy Bear Company began doing business on the Internet with a new web site designed to inform and entertain Internet subscribers. The web site provided a low-cost visual presence and was developed for the purpose of supporting the radio advertising of Bear-Grams. Pictures of the product and other information could be accessed. A total of 396,000 hits to the web site were recorded during fiscal 1998, more than double the 195,000 hits recorded during fiscal 1997.[45] By August 1998, 10 to 20% of Vermont Teddy's business was being handled online.[46] All radio advertisements were tagged with a reference to the web site, which, in turn, provided visual support for the radio advertising and the opportunity for customers to place orders online.[47]

Since 1990, the company had extended its Bear-Gram marketing strategy beyond New York City to include other metropolitan areas and syndicated radio programs across the United States. During the fiscal year 1998, the company regularly placed advertising on a total of 44 radio stations in 12 of the 20 largest market areas in the United States.[48] **Exhibit 4** shows the company's largest markets. **Exhibit 5** shows the most frequent reasons given by customers for purchasing a Vermont Teddy Bear-Gram. The company was featured on Dateline NBC, Tuesday, December 17, 1996. Newsbroadcaster Stone Phillips interviewed R. Patrick Burns, President and CEO, on the subject of American companies that manufactured products in the United States.[49]

In 1998, the company was planning to expand its radio advertisements into new markets including Minneapolis, Dallas, and Milwaukee and to examine opportunities to consolidate radio advertising buys through annual contracts with major stations.[50]

The company had explored additional methods to market Bear-Grams and to publicize its toll-free telephone number. In June 1993, the company's toll-free number was listed for the first time in the AT&T toll-free telephone directory. Before then, the toll-free number was not readily available to customers, except in radio advertisements. Vermont Teddy Bear also expanded its listings in metropolitan phone book Yellow Pages and initiated the use of print advertising in magazines and newspapers, as well as advertising on billboards and mass transit panels.

Exhibit 5
Most Frequent Reasons for Purchasing Bear-Grams: Vermont Teddy Bear Co., Inc. (Percentage of Bear-Grams for the 12 months ending June 30)

Reasons for Purchases	1998	1997	1996	1995
Valentine's Day	27.7%	22.1%	20.8%	19.2%
Birthdays	11.8%	11.6%	13.4%	15.9%
New Births	11.6%	10.3%	12.8%	9.9%
Get Wells	11.0%	9.7%	12.0%	10.4%
Christmas	8.4%	5.6%	8.6%	10.4%

Source: The Vermont Teddy Bear Company, Inc., 1998 Annual Report, *p. 4.*

Vermont Teddy Bear believed that the popularity of Bear-Grams created an opportunity for catalog sales. For the fiscal year ending June 30, 1998, direct mail accounted for 9.2% of net revenues.[51] In addition, repeat buyers represented 33% of sales, giving the company an opportunity to use its customer database in excess of 1,500,000 names.[52] The company introduced its first catalog for Christmas in 1992. By 1994, catalog sales accounted for 16.7% of sales.[53] Vermont Teddy planned to prepare three catalogs in 1995, but the management shakeup that resulted in Patrick Burns' becoming CEO caused the company to scale back its plans. Instead it mailed just 165,000 copies of an eight-page book to previous customers. The small-size book kept up the company's presence but did not have the pages nor the product range to boost holiday sales. Quarterly sales dropped 24% below December 1994 levels.[54]

In 1996, to compensate for the decline in radio advertisement effectiveness, the company increased December 1996 catalog circulation to approximately one million. To increase its catalog circulation, Vermont Teddy Bear acquired additional mailing lists from prominent catalog companies, including Disney, FAO Schwarz, Hammacher-Schlemmer, Saks Fifth Avenue, and Harry & David. To strengthen its retail and catalog offerings, Vermont Teddy broadened the scope of its product line. New items included lower priced teddy bears, company-designed apparel, toys, books, and jewelry, as well as plush animals from other manufacturers such as Gund and Steiff.

Its Valentine mailing in 1997 amounted to 600,000 catalogs. Direct mail revenues increased from 1996, but they did not meet expectations due to the poor performance of rented mailing lists. In addition, the company incurred higher than anticipated costs due to the outsourcing of the order fulfillment process and was left with inflated inventories due to lower than expected sales.

During fiscal 1998, more than 15 million circulated pages were mailed to prospective customers. CEO Robert believed that Vermont Teddy's in-house list, which stood at 1.4 million names, would be a profitable future source of business. The company planned to increase the number of circulated pages during 1999, primarily though renting and exchanging of additional names from other catalogs and mailing to more names on the in-house mailing list.[55] It planned to handle all catalog fulfillment at company facilities in Shelburne. It also planned to continue to develop its own internal systems to adapt to the requirements of its catalog customers as the catalog business grew.[56]

During fiscal 1998, sales from retail operations accounted for 18.0% of net revenues.[57] Due to the continued unprofitability in its retail stores, the company reversed its retail expansion strategy in fiscal 1998. Vermont Teddy Bear's New York City retail outlet was closed to the public on December 7, 1997, due to structural problems. A sales profile for the store reaffirmed the company's core market. Bear-Grams accounted for 60 to 70% of the store's purchases—the same product that was being sold through the radio advertisements, without the overhead of New York rents.[58]

The company planned to close its retail location in Freeport, Maine, in August 1998 and its North Conway, New Hampshire, store in October 1998. CEO Robert commented:

> After two successful holidays at Valentine's Day and Mother's Day, it is more clear than ever, that focusing on radio Bear-Grams is the right strategy. Retail apart from our highly successful factory store here in Shelburne, is not a distribution channel that fits our current business. We are in the Bear-Gram business, offering a convenient, creative and expressive gift delivery service. It makes no sense to ship out a Bear-Gram from an expensive retail store front.[59]

The Shelburne factory store had continued to be successful as the company added new merchandise. To make the store more entertaining and interactive, the company invested $100,000 in its renovation in 1996.[60] Programs such as "Make a Friend for Life," which enabled customers to stuff, dress, and personalize their own bear and "virtual" factory tours, using video and theatrical demonstrations of teddy bear making received favorable responses from customers.[61]

In November 1996, the company announced that it had joined forces with Gary Burghoff to produce a video that promoted the company's new "Make a Friend for Life" products.[62] Burghoff was known for playing the character Radar O'Reilly in the *M*A*S*H* television show and was famous for his relationship with his teddy bear.

Vermont Teddy Bear had also targeted children's literature as a way of generating name recognition. A children's book, *How Teddy Bears Are Made: A Visit to the Vermont Teddy Bear Factory,* was available for purchase and could be found at libraries. The company also began to publish other children's books in order to develop characters for their teddy bears.

Beginning September 1, 1997, The Vermont Teddy Bear Co., Inc., introduced nationally a line of officially licensed NFL Teddy Bears. The NFL Bear was offered in 14 different teams and wore NFL Properties' uniforms and gear, including officially licensed jerseys, pants, and Riddell helmets.[63] NFL Properties, Inc., was the licensing and publishing arm of the National Football League. To advertise this new product, Vermont Teddy enlisted Wayne Chrebet, wide receiver for the NY Jets, and Mark Chmura, tight end for the Green Bay Packers, to be spokespeople for the NFL Teddy Bears. Chrebet and Chmura were featured in radio and print advertisements in New York and Milwaukee, respectively. The company believed that officially licensed NFL Bears would be a popular choice for sports fans, especially during the football and Christmas seasons. The company advertised the bear on sports-talk radio in metropolitan areas around the country.[64]

Vermont Teddy Bear conducted business almost exclusively in the United States. Bears could be shipped abroad, but it was very expensive. Some bears were shipped into Canada, and some radio advertising was done in Montreal. The added shipping charges, along with unfavorable exchange rates, caused price resistance to the products in Canada. In 1995, the company test marketed both the Bear-Gram and the use of the 800 number via radio advertising in the United Kingdom. Test results indicated that both were successful, but the program had to be eliminated because the company did not have the corporate infrastructure or the financial resources to support it.[65] The company had some trademarks registered in Great Britain and Japan and had discussions with companies in both of these countries. According to Robert, "These are the two countries that seem to have the most interest in Vermont Teddy's products."[66]

Vermont Teddy Bear's management believed that there were a number of opportunities to increase company sales. The company's strategy for future growth included increasing sales of Bear-Grams in existing markets, expanding sales of Bear-Grams in new market areas, increasing direct-mail marketing of teddy bears through mail-order catalogs and similar marketing techniques, increasing sales of premium teddy bears through wholesale channels to unaffiliated retail stores, and increasing the company's retail store sales through increased factory tours and visits.[67] Management was also interested in expanding sales through its Corporate Division.

Facilities and Operations

In the summer of 1995, in an effort to consolidate locations and improve manufacturing efficiency, the company relocated its offices, retail store, and manufacturing, sales, and distribution facilities to a newly constructed 62,000-square-foot building on 57 acres in Shelburne, Vermont. The new site was approximately 10 miles south of Burlington, the state's largest city. The new buildings were designed as a small village, the Teddy Bear Common, to promote a warm and friendly atmosphere for customers as well as employees. The new facility was estimated to have cost $7,900,00.[68] The company intended to minimize lease costs by subleasing any unused space. On September 26, 1995, the company had entered into a $3.5 million commercial loan with the Vermont National Bank. Repayment of the mortgage loan was based on a 30-year fixed-principal payment schedule, with a balloon payment due on September 26, 1997.[69]

On July 18, 1997, Vermont Teddy completed a sale-leaseback transaction with W. P. Carey and Co., Inc., a New York–based investment banking firm, involving its factory headquarters and a portion of its property located in Shelburne. W. P. Carey bought the 62,000-

square-foot headquarters facility and its 15-acre site, leaving the company with ownership of the additional land. W. P. Carey was not interested in acquiring the other building lots on the site due to their zoning restrictions. This financing replaced the company's mortgage and line of credit, which was about to come due on September 26, 1997.[70]

The company had a three-year lease on 10,000 square feet of inventory space at a separate location in Shelburne for $56,000 annually.[71] The company also had the following lease agreements for its retail stores[72]:

Location	Square Footage	Annual Rent	1999 Rent Obligation	End of Lease Obligation
North Conway, NH	6,000	$ 49,608	$ 28,938	1/31/1999
New York City, NY	2,600	$300,000	$300,000	10/23/2006
Freeport, ME	6,000	$240,000	$ 25,644	8/6/1998

For in-house manufacturers, all production occurred in the Shelburne manufacturing space, which included state-of-the-art packing and shipping equipment. The plant manager was Brad Allen. Visitors and guests were given the opportunity to take guided or self-directed tours that encompassed the entire teddy bear making process. The factory tour had become such a popular tourist attraction that approximately 129,000 visitors toured the factory and retail store in fiscal 1998. Since moving to its new location in 1995, more than 390,000 visitors had toured the facilities.[73]

In 1994, when the company was looking for a new location, it purchased only the 15-acre parcel it built on in Shelburne. Then the company bought the surrounding property because it wanted some control in the kind of neighbors it would have. As of June 30, 1998, plans to sell or lease the other lots had not been successful due to stringent zoning restrictions on the site. The zoning restrictions required that less than a quarter of the space be devoted to retail, effectively ruling out any kind of direct retail or outlet mall approach, which is the kind of business that could take advantage of the visitor traffic to the teddy bear factory. The company proposed a project for this unused space involving an attempt to bring together up to 50 Vermont manufacturers in a cooperative manufacturing, demonstration, and marketing setting—a made-in-Vermont manufacturing/exhibition park. Investors expressed concerns about the capital investment requirement.[74]

Vermont Teddy Bear began using Sealed Air Corp's Rapid Fill air-filled packaging (air bags) system to protect its teddy bears from damage during shipping in 1997. Previously it had used corrugated cardboard seat belt inserts to package the bears during shipping, but found that there were drawbacks, including minor damage to the products and the high cost of postage. Sealed Air's inflatable plastic bags were lighter than the corrugated inserts resulting in savings in postage costs and the plastic bags did not damage the bears with plush fur. Vermont Teddy Bear saved $150,000 in postage costs in 1997 and could realize $30,000 to $40,000 in additional savings in 1998.[75]

Vice President of Data Processing was Bonnie West. According to CEO Robert, Vermont Teddy Bear's desktop computers were in need of updating. However, West believed the company's call centers had state-of-the-art technologies, including PC terminals and very-high-tech telephone switching equipment that allowed the company to handle significant call volume. The company also had a high-tech shipping system, including state-of-the-art multicarrier software so that if a major carrier like UPS went on strike, it could immediately make adjustments.

Human Resource Management

Vermont Teddy Bear employees were known as the "Bear People," a term that expressed management's appreciation and respect for their dedication. Beth Peters was Vice President of Human Resources. As of June 30, 1998, the company employed 181 individuals, of whom

94 were employed in production-related functions, 67 were employed in sales and marketing positions, and 20 were employed in administrative and management positions.[76] None of the employees belonged to a union. Overall, the company believed that favorable relations existed with all employees.[77]

The company supplemented its regular in-house workforce with homeworkers who performed production functions at their homes. The level of outsourced work fluctuated with company production targets. As of June 30, 1998, there were 21 homeworkers producing product for the company. Homeworkers were treated as independent contractors for all purposes, except for withholding of federal employment taxes. As independent contractors, homeworkers were free to reject or accept any work offered by the company.[78] Independent contractors allowed the company flexibility in meeting heavy demand at holiday periods such as Christmas, Valentine's Day, and Mother's Day. This relationship also allowed the homeworkers flexibility in scheduling their hours of work.

Bear Market

The teddy bear was first created in the United States in 1902. The Steiff Company of Grengen/Brenz, Germany, displayed one at a fair in Leipzig in 1903. Thomas Michton of Brooklyn, New York, was credited with creating the name "Teddy Bear" in honor of President Theodore Roosevelt. At the time of the naming, President Roosevelt had been on a well-publicized hunting trip in Mississippi while negotiating a border dispute with Louisiana. When he came up empty-handed from his hunting, his aides rounded up a bear cub for the President to shoot. His granddaughter, Sarah Alden "Aldie" Gannett, said, "I think he felt he could never face his children again if he shot anything so small. So he let it go."[79]

The incident was popularized in cartoons by Clifford Berryman of the *Washington Post*. Michton and his wife stitched up a couple of honey-colored bears and then displayed them in their novelty store window along with a copy of Berryman's cartoon.

The bears sold in a day. Michton made another stuffed bear and sent it to President Roosevelt, requesting his permission to use his name. Roosevelt replied with a handwritten note: "I doubt if my name will mean much in the bear business, but you may use it if you wish." It was simply signed "T. R."[80]

Teddy bears today fall into one of two broad categories: either to a subsegment of the toy industry, plush dolls and animals, or are part of the collectibles industry. Although no one knows exactly how many teddy bears are sold each year, it is known that teddy bears accounted for 70 to 80% of the $1 billion plush toy industry in 1997.[81] "Bears sell across every season, occasion, and holiday," said Del Clark, Director of Merchandising for Fiesta, a Verona, California, maker of stuffed animals.[82] Not only have bears historically been a steady seller, but returns of teddy bears are almost nonexistent.[83]

The U.S. toy industry (including teddy bears, dolls, puzzles, games, action figures and vehicles, and preschool activity toys) was estimated to be worth $25 billion in sales and had been growing at an annual rate of more than 3%.[84] With its combination of a large demographic base of children and a population with a high level of disposable income, the U.S. toy market was larger than those of Japan (the number two market) and Western Europe combined.[85] Most toys that are sold in the United States were made in foreign countries. Chinese-produced toys represented about 30% of all U.S. toy sales due to inexpensive labor and favorable duty rates on imports.[86] The big toy manufacturers were buying each other's operations and those of smaller toy makers. In 1997, the number one toy manufacturer, Mattel (maker of Fisher-Price toys and Barbie dolls), bought Tyco Toys, formerly ranked number three. Hasbro (maker of G.I. Joe, Monopoly, and Milton Bradley toys) was the number two toy maker. Some games and toys maintained popularity over time, others were passing fads. It was difficult to predict which would remain popular over time. In the 1990s, marketing appeared to be the key to success. Toy production and marketing were regularly integrated with movies and television programs. For example, Star Wars action figures and other merchandise accounted for about one third of number 3 toy make Galoob Toys' 1997 sales of $360 million.[87] Small toy makers found it difficult to compete with the multimillion-dollar marketing campaigns and the in-depth market research of companies like Mattel, although there was always an exception such as Beanie Babies.

During 1997, manufacturers' shipments of plush products rose 37.5%, from $984 million to $1.4 billion, largely as a result of the Beanie Baby craze.[88] Designed by Ty Warner, the owner of Ty, Inc., Beanie Babies had been the big sales item since 1996 when they generated sales of $250 million. The $5 toys were produced in limited numbers and sold through specialty toy stores rather than through mass-market retailers. Beanie Baby characters no longer in production fetched up to $3,000 among collectors. Some retailers reported a decline in the sales of other plush toys due to the demand for Beanie Babies.[89]

Competitors of Vermont Teddy Bear were of various types. Major plush doll manufacturers such as Mattel and Hasbro were considered competition in this subsegment of the toy industry. More direct competition for Vermont Teddy came from other bear manufacturers including Steiff of Germany, Dakin, Applause, Fiesta, North American Bear, and Gund, the leading maker of toy bears. Information about some of these direct competitors is presented in **Exhibit 6**.

In general, these competitors relied on sales though retail outlets and had much greater financial resources to drive sales and marketing efforts than did Vermont Teddy Bear. Unlike Vermont Teddy Bear, these companies depended on foreign manufacturing and sources of raw materials, enabling them to sell comparable products at retail prices below those currently

**Exhibit 6
Competition: The
Vermont Teddy
Bear Co., Inc.**

Steiff
High-quality bears are manufactured in Germany and the Far East. The bears are not individually customized. The company's trademark is a button sewn into the ear of each bear. Prices of Steiff bears range from $50 for a 6-inch-tall bear to several thousand dollars for a life-size model. The bears are sold in a variety of outlets from discount stores and supermarkets to high-end specialty shops and antique stores.

Gund
This mass producer of a wide range of plush animals established an Internet Web site, allowing users to view and purchase products. Bears are manufactured overseas, primarily in Korea. Appearance of the bears is different from Vermont Teddy Bears', with shorter noses and limbs. They offer a broad range of styles and prices.

Teddy Bear Factory
This is the only other American manufacturer of teddy bears. The company is located in San Francisco and highly regional in its sales and marketing efforts. Vermont Teddy Bear advertises in the San Francisco Bay area but does not consider the Teddy Bear Factory to be strong competition because of the size and because its market is so regional.

North American Bear Company
This middle-sized company manufactures all of its bears in the Orient, primarily in Korea. Appearance of the bears is different from Vermont Teddy Bears, with shorter noses and limbs. The company advertises in trade magazines and has begun to do consumer advertising. It sells to retailers in Europe and Japan and collectors and gift shops in the United States.

Applause Enterprises, Inc.
This company focuses on manufacturing plush toy versions of Sesame Street, Looney Tunes, Star Wars, Muppets, and Disney characters as well as nonplush toys. Company was formed by the 1995 merger of plush toy maker Dakin and a company founded by Wallace Berrie.

offered by Vermont Teddy. In addition, small craft stores had begun to sell locally produced all-American-made teddy bears, and publications had been developed to teach people to craft their own bears.

The collectible market in bears had recently been booming with people seeking bears as financial investments. Collectible bears are those that are meant to be displayed, not drooled or spit up on by their owners. "In the past 5 to 10 years we've seen a tremendous growth in the upscale bear, the limited editions, and the artist-designed bears," said George B. Black, Jr., director of the Teddy Bear Museum in Naples, Florida.[90] The "collectible" segment of the plush market generated $441 million in consumer sales for 1996, up from $354 million in 1995. Collectible plush sales for 1997 were expected to reach nearly $700 million. This would make plush one of the fastest growing categories in the $9.2 billion collectibles industry.[91] Collectible bears started at about $25 but could cost $1,000 or more. This number was somewhat misleading, considering that the value of a collectible bear can be in excess of $50,000. A 1904 Steiff "Teddy Girl" bear sold at a Christie's auction in 1994 for a record $171,380.[92]

Two trade magazines, *Teddy Bear and Friends* and *Teddy Bear Review*, targeted the collectibles market. These magazines tell bear collectors where they can buy and sell old bears. In 1998, major bear shows and jamborees were held in at least 25 states, as well as hundreds of bear-making retreats and workshops.[93]

The concept of Bear-Grams lent itself to two distinct groups of competitors. Vermont Teddy Bear competed not only with soft plush stuffed animals, especially teddy bears, but also with a variety of other special occasion greetings such as flowers, candy, balloons, cakes, and other gift items that could be ordered by phone for special occasions and delivered the next day. Many of these competitors had greater financial, sales, and marketing resources than Vermont Teddy Bear.[94]

Patents, Trademarks, and Licenses

The company's name in combination with its original logo was a registered trademark in the United States. In addition, the company owned the registered trademarks in the United States for "The Vermont Teddy Bear Company," "Bear-Gram," "Teddy Bear-Gram," and "Make a Friend for Life." The company also owned the registered service marks "Bear Counselor," "Vermont Bear-Gram," and "Racer Ted," and had applications pending to register the company's second and third company logos, "Bearanimal," "Coffee Cub," "Vermont Bear-Gram," "Vermont Baby Bear," "The Great American Teddy Bear," "All-American Teddy Bear," "Beau and Beebee," "Teddy-Grams," and "Vermont Teddy Wear."[95]

Vermont Teddy Bear also owned the registered trademark "Vermont Teddy Bear" in Japan and had an application pending to register "The Great American Teddy Bear" in Japan.[96]

Although the company had continuously used the "Bear-Gram" trademark since April 1985, its initial application to register the mark on June 13, 1990, was rejected by the U.S. Patent and Trademark Office due to prior registration of the mark "Bear-A-Grams," by another company on June 7, 1988. The company reapplied to register "Bear-Gram," and its application was approved on November 5, 1996.

The company also claimed copyright, service mark, or trademark protection for its teddy bear designs, its marketing slogans, and its advertising copy and promotional literature.

On May 16, 1997, Vermont Teddy Bear sued Disney Enterprises, Inc., for injunctive relief and unspecified damages claiming that Disney copied its bear-by-mail concept with Pooh-Grams based on Disney's Winnie-the-Pooh character. The complaint accused Disney of unfair competition and trademark infringement saying the Pooh-Gram is "confusingly similar" to Bear-Grams in name, logo, how it is personalized, how it is delivered, and even how it is marketed.[97] Disney introduced Pooh-Grams in its fall 1996 catalog and escalated its promotion of the product using the Internet, print, and radio advertising. Disney disagreed saying that the Vermont Teddy lawsuit was without merit because Winnie the Pooh has been a well-known Disney character for 25 years and there are all kinds of grams—mail-grams, candy-grams, money-grams, telegrams, flower-grams—not just Bear-Grams.

On September 9, 1997, Vermont Teddy announced that it had entered into an agreement to resolve its dispute with Walt Disney Co. Under the agreement, Disney would continue to offer its Pooh-Gram products and services but would voluntarily limit its use of the Pooh-Gram mark in certain advertising and would adequately distinguish its trademarks and service marks from those of Vermont Teddy Bear. Vermont Teddy in turn would be allowed to offer certain Winnie-the-Pooh merchandise for sale in its mail-order catalogs but could not offer the merchandise with its Bear-Gram program.[98]

Finance

On November 23, 1993, Vermont Teddy Bear Co., Inc., sold 1.15 million shares of stock at $10 a share through an underwriting group led by Barrington Capital Group L.P. The stock rose as high as $19 before closing the day at $16.75, an increase of 67.5% in its first day of trading. The market's reaction to the IPO signaled that investors thought the stock was undervalued at $10 and that the company had a great deal of growth potential. During fiscal 1998, the company's stock price fluctuated between $2.56 and $0.75 a share. This was an indication that investors reconsidered the growth potential of Vermont Teddy Bear.

Vice President of Finance was Mark Sleeper. **Exhibits 7** and **8** detail Vermont Teddy Bear's financial situation. Prior to 1994, Vermont Teddy Bear had experienced a great deal of success and profitability. The company's net sales increased 61% from $10,569,017 in 1992 to $17,025,856 in 1993, while the cost of goods sold decreased from 43.1% of sales to 41.8% during the same time period. Net income increased 314% from $202,601 in 1992 to $838,955 in 1993.

Sales reached a peak in 1994 at $20,560,566. This represented a 21% growth over 1993. Unfortunately, profits did not experience similar growth. Had it not been for an almost $70,000 tax refund, the company would have experienced a net loss in 1994. The company's net profit fell to $17,523 after taxes in 1994 due to a substantial increase in both selling expense and general and administrative expenses. These two items combined for an increase of 35% over comparable figures for 1993.

In 1995, sales fell to $20,044,796. Although this represented only a 2.5% decline, this decline in sales painted a picture for the next two years. While sales were decreasing, selling and general and administrative expenses continued to climb. These expenses grew by 10% to $13,463,631 in 1995. These two items represented 67% of sales in 1996, whereas they were 53% of sales in 1993.

After three years of declining sales, Vermont Teddy Bear's sales grew by 4.4% in 1998 to $17,207,543. Vermont Teddy Bear experienced a loss of $2,422,477 in 1995. It returned to profitability in 1996, earning $151,953. Unfortunately, that was the last profitable year for the company. Losses were $1,901,745 in 1997 and $1,683,669 in 1998. Interest expense had risen dramatically for the company, from $35,002 in 1995 to $608,844 in 1998.

The company included in its quarterly report to the SEC (filing date: 5/14/98) that it had been operating without a working capital line of credit since July 18, 1997. On that date, the company completed a sale-leaseback transaction involving its factory headquarters and a portion of its property located in Shelburne, Vermont. This financing replaced the company's mortgage and line of credit. The company received $5.9 million from this transaction. Of this amount, $3.3 million was used to pay off the mortgage and $600,000 was used

Exhibit 7 Consolidated Balance Sheets: The Vermont Teddy Bear Co., Inc.

Year Ending June 30	1998	1997	1996	1995	1994[1]	1993[1]	1992[1]
Assets							
Current assets							
Cash and marketable securities	$ 1,527,052	$ 441,573	$ 1,121,500	$ 1,070,862	$ 2,379,760	$ 8,561,525	$ —
Accounts receivable, trade	51,538	46,304	131,550	122,679	142,029	103,762	77,815
Inventories	2,396,245	3,302,313	1,974,731	3,042,484	4,024,247	2,425,233	1,135,940
Prepaid expenses	444,229	386,947	277,502	213,236	568,680	123,886	10,681
Due from officer	—	—	—	—	565,714	—	—
Deferred income taxes	233,203	259,016	240,585	126,393	322,106	194,082	—
Total current assets	4,652,267	4,436,153	3,745,868	4,575,654	8,002,536	11,408,488	1,224,436
Property and equipment	8,844,475	9,845,935	10,300,318	10,493,214	3,052,002	861,419	589,196
Construction in progress	—	—	—	—	3,275,527	—	—
Due from officer	—	—	—	—	128,008	128,008	102,480
Deposits and other assets	903,110	272,348	98,086	102,676	121,640	97,400	14,356
Notes receivable	87,500	95,000	95,000	190,000	190,000	—	—
Total assets	$14,487,352	$14,649,436	$14,239,272	$15,361,544	$14,769,713	$12,495,315	$1,930,468
Liabilities and shareholders' equity							
Current liabilities							
Cash overdraft	$ —	$ —	$ —	$ —	$ —	$ —	$ 148,048
Line of credit	—	550,000	—	—	—	—	—
Notes payable, bank	45,603	—	—	—	36,748	108,748	180,748
Current installments of							
Long-term debt	231,133	3,443,096	187,095	27,805	21,981	22,793	19,075
Capital lease obligations	225,738	103,759	104,146	126,306	99,901	45,604	41,795
Accounts payable	1,846,042	2,562,536	1,353,698	2,513,468	3,336,558	1,319,499	1,604,066
Accrued expenses	916,191	657,347	449,048	860,440	442,467	381,146	156,777

Income taxes payable	—	—	37,365	90,889	117,810	117,810	—
Total current liabilities	3,264,707	7,316,738	2,131,352	3,618,908	4,055,465	1,995,600	2,150,509
Construction loan payable	338,317	372,999	3,505,812	3,252,379	60,408	82,411	81,401
Long-term debt	5,748,182	209,054	312,814	347,874	398,220	58,883	61,350
Capital lease obligations	—	—	84,430	204,430	—	—	—
Other liabilities	—	—	—	—	—	—	958,219
Accrued interest payable, debentures	233,203	259,016	240,585	—	—	—	—
Deferred income taxes	—	—	—	126,393	105,992	47,492	—
Total liabilities	9,584,409	8,157,807	6,274,993	7,549,984	4,620,085	2,184,386	3,251,479
Shareholders' equity							
Preferred stock $.05 par value:							
Authorized 1,000,000 shares	1,044,000	900,000	900,000	900,000	900,000	900,000	—
Series A							
Cumulative dividends at 8%							
Preferred stock $.05 par value:							
Authorized 375,000 shares							
Series B	10,245	10,245	—	—	—	—	—
Common stock, $.05 par value:							
Authorized 20,000,000 shares	259,787	258,638	258,638	258,625	258,625	258,625	200,000
Additional paid-in capital	10,587,316	10,565,482	10,074,595	10,073,842	10,073,842	10,073,842	185,868
Treasury stock at cost	(106,824)	(106,824)	(106,824)	(106,824)	(106,824)	—	—
(12,000 shares)							
Accumulated deficit	(6,891,581)	(5,135,912)	(3,162,130)	(3,314,083)	(976,015)	(921,538)	(1,706,879)
Total shareholders' equity	4,902,943	6,491,629	7,964,279	7,811,560	10,149,628	10,310,929	(1,321,011)
Total liabilities and shareholders' equity	$14,487,352	$14,649,436	$14,239,272	$15,361,544	$14,769,713	$12,495,315	$1,930,468

Note:
1. Fiscal year ending December 31.

Source: The Vermont Teddy Bear Company, Inc., 1998 Annual Report.

Exhibit 8 Statement of Operations: The Vermont Teddy Bear Co., Inc.

Year Ending June 30	1998	1997	1996	1995	1994[1]	1993[1]	1992[1]
Net sales	$17,207,543	$16,489,482	$17,039,618	$20,044,796	$20,560,566	$17,025,856	$10,569,017
Cost of goods sold	7,397,450	7,068,549	7,309,038	9,101,028	8,619,580	7,123,930	4,555,424
Gross margin	9,810,093	9,420,933	9,730,580	10,943,768	11,940,986	9,901,926	6,013,593
Selling expenses	7,866,843	7,961,003	6,287,208	9,121,023	8,907,440	6,862,328	4,454,891
General and administrative expenses	3,031,716	2,938,251	2,954,601	4,342,608	3,311,306	2,184,500	1,266,770
Total expenses	10,898,559	10,899,254	9,241,809	13,463,631	12,218,746	9,046,828	5,721,661
Operating income (loss)	(1,088,466)	(1,478,321)	488,771	(2,519,863)	(277,760)	855,098	291,932
Interest income	26,126	53,267	41,092	192,156	248,987	27,887	2,152
Miscellaneous income	29,243	(11,973)	63,236	1,620	1,620	25,000	—
Interest expense	(650,572)	(464,768)	(441,146)	(35,002)	(24,848)	(97,810)	(91,483)
Income (loss) before taxes	(1,683,669)	(1,901,795)	151,953	(2,361,089)	(52,001)	810,175	202,601
Income tax provision (benefit)	—	—	—	61,388	(69,524)	(28,780)	—
Net income (loss)	$(1,683,669)	$(1,901,795)	$ 151,953	$(2,422,477)	$ 17,523	$ 838,955	$ 202,601
Preferred stock dividends	(72,000)	(72,000)	—	(72,000)	(72,000)	(53,614)	—
Net earnings (loss) common shareholders	(1,611,669)	(1,829,795)	151,953	(2,350,477)	89,523	892,569	202,601
Net earnings (loss) per common share	(0.34)	(0.38)	0.03	(0.48)	(0.10)	0.19	0.05
Weighted average number of shares outstanding	5,172,475	5,160,750	5,160,583	5,160,500	5,164,057	4,210,070	4,024,140

Note:
1. Fiscal year ending December 31.

Source: The Vermont Teddy Bear Company, Inc., 1998 Annual Report.

to pay off the line of credit. A $591,000 transactions cost was associated with the sale-lease-back. The lease obligation was repayable on a 20-year amortization schedule through July 2017.

On October 10, 1997, Vermont Teddy received a commitment from Green Mountain Capital L.P. whereby it agreed to lend the company up to $200,000 for up to five years at 12% interest. The loan was secured by security interest in the company's real and personal property. Green Mountain Capital also received warrants to purchase 100,000 shares of common stock at an exercise price of $1.00. The warrants could be exercised any time from two years from the date of the loan to seven years from the date of the loan.

To reduce costs, the company closed its retail store in New York City and planned to close the Freeport, Maine, and North Conway, New Hampshire, stores before the end of 1998 because the revenue increases necessary to support the annual lease obligations would not be achievable in the short run. The company's lease obligation of $300,000 per year on the New York City store would continue until a replacement tenant was found.

On May 22, 1998, it was announced that The Vermont Teddy Bear Co., Inc., had signed a letter of intent with the Shepherd Group, a Boston-based private equity investment firm, for a proposed $600,000 equity investment with the company. The Shepherd Group invested in venture and existing small- to middle-market companies focusing on companies with high-growth potential and unique market-ready quality products and services. In return for the $600,000 investment, the Shepherd Group received 60 shares of Series C Preferred Stock as well as warrants to purchase 495,868 shares of Common Stock at $1.21 per share. The transaction was subject to final agreements and various approvals and conditions.

The Series C Convertible Redeemable Stock carried a 6% coupon, and each share was convertible into 8,264,467 shares of the company's Common Stock. The Preferred had voting rights, and the Shepherd Group was entitled to two seats on the company's Board of Directors.

Elisabeth Robert noted:

> The additional funds will provide working capital for the company to pursue growth in the Bear-Gram channel and to maximize the benefits of importing raw materials. Additionally Tom Shepherd has strong financial and operations experience and will bring a valuable perspective to the Board of Directors. Tom's strong suit has been working with companies that have not yet realized the full potential of their brand.[99]

According to some analysts, the survival of this company was going to depend on maintaining a source of working capital, cost containment, and a rebound in sales back to their 1995 level. The company had taken an aggressive approach to ensuring survival, but this was not done cheaply. High interest rates were paid, and warrants to purchase stock, at what might turn out to be a bargain price, had been issued.

Notes

1. C. Crossen, "Isn't It Funny How a Bear Makes Money, Year After Year?" *Wall Street Journal* (February 17, 1998), p. B-1.
2. "Vermont Teddy President and CEO Interview," *The Wall Street Journal Corporate Reporter, Inc.* (January 21, 1998).
3. *Ibid.*
4. The Vermont Teddy Bear Co., Inc., *1997 Annual Report.*
5. R. Levy, "Ursine of the Times: Vermont Teddy Bear Company Pulls Back from Catalog Sales," *Direct Marketing* (February 1998), p. 16.
6. M. L. Calta, "Cub Scout," *Detroit News* (March 5, 1995), pp. 22-D, 23-D.
7. *Ibid.*
8. P. Hise, "Making Fans on Talk Radio," *Inc.* (December 1993), p. 62.
9. The Vermont Teddy Bear Co., Inc., *1994 Annual Report*, p. 3.
10. The Vermont Teddy Bear Co., Inc., *Company Time Line*, Information Packet, p. 2.
11. *Ibid.*
12. *Ibid.*
13. The Vermont Teddy Bear Co., Inc., *Form 10-KSB* (June 30, 1995), p. 1.
14. *Company Time Line*, p. 2.
15. The Vermont Teddy Bear Co., Inc., Press Release (April 17, 1995).
16. The Vermont Teddy Bear Co., Inc., *1994 Annual Report* (Letter to Shareholders), p. 2.
17. *The Wall Street Journal Corporate Reporter, Inc.* (January 21, 1998).
18. Vermont Teddy Bear Co., Inc., "The Vermont Teddy Bear Company Roars into New York City," Press Release (October 9, 1996).

19. The Vermont Teddy Bear Co., Inc., "The Vermont Teddy Posts Year-End Results, Closes Equity Deal," Press Release (September 29, 1998), p. 1.

20. The Vermont Teddy Bear Co., Inc., "The Vermont Teddy Bear Company Expands Retail Activities," Press Release (June 20, 1996).

21. The Vermont Teddy Bear Co., Inc., *1997 Annual Report* (Letter to Shareholders), p. 3.

22. *The Wall Street Journal Corporate Reporter, Inc.* (January 21, 1998).

23. The Vermont Teddy Bear Co., Inc., *1997 Annual Report* (Letter to Shareholders), p. 3.

24. The Vermont Teddy Bear Co., Inc., *1997 Annual Report,* p. 22, and *1997 Proxy Statement* (October 28, 1997), pp. 6, 10, 21–23.

25. The Vermont Teddy Bear Co., Inc., *Form 10-KSB* (September 28, 1998), p. 10.

26. The Vermont Teddy Bear Co., Inc., *1997 Proxy Statement* (October 28, 1997), pp. 4–5.

27. The Vermont Teddy Bear Co., Inc., *Form 10-KSB* (September 28, 1998), p. 10.

28. The Vermont Teddy Bear Co., Inc., *1998 Proxy Statement* (July 23, 1998), p. 5.

29. The Vermont Teddy Bear Co., Inc., *Form 10-KSB* (September 28, 1998), pp. 9–10.

30. The Vermont Teddy Bear Co., Inc., *1997 Annual Report*, p. 4.

31. *Ibid.*

32. *Ibid.*

33. The Vermont Teddy Bear Co., Inc., *Form 10-KSB* (September 28, 1998), p. 6.

34. M. L. Calta, "Cub Scout," *Detroit News* (March 5, 1995), pp. 22-D, 23-D.

35. The Vermont Teddy Bear Co., Inc., *Form 10-KSB* (September 28, 1998), p. 6.

36. The Vermont Teddy Bear *Gazette* (Summer 1995 edition), p. 7.

37. The Vermont Teddy Bear Co., Inc., *Form 10-KSB* (September 28, 1998), p. 6.

38. *Ibid.*

39. R. Levy, "Ursine of the Times: Vermont Teddy Bear Company Pulls Back from Catalog Sales," *Direct Marketing* (February 1998), p. 16.

40. "Vermont Teddy Bear Appoints Vice President of Marketing and Design," The Vermont Teddy Bear Co., Inc., Press Release (May 5, 1998).

41. M. L. Calta, "Cub Scout," *Detroit News* (March 5, 1995), pp. 22-D, 23-D.

42. The Vermont Teddy Bear Co., Inc., *Form 10-KSB* (September 28, 1998), p. 3.

43. *Ibid.*

44. The Vermont Teddy Bear Co., Inc., "Vermont Teddy Bear Posts Quarterly Profit on Increased Revenues," Press Release (May 14, 1998), p. 1.

45. The Vermont Teddy Bear Co., Inc., *Form 10-KSB* (September 28, 1998), p. 4.

46. J. Kerstetter, "Setting Up Mom and Pop," *PC Week On-Line* (August 24, 1998), p. 1.

47. The Vermont Teddy Bear Co., Inc., *Form 10-KSB* (September 28, 1998), p. 4.

48. *Ibid.*

49. The Vermont Teddy Bear Co., Inc., "Vermont Teddy Bear Company to be Featured on Dateline NBC, December 17, 1996," Press Release (December 17, 1996).

50. The Vermont Teddy Bear Co., Inc., *1997 Annual Report*, p. 10.

51. The Vermont Teddy Bear Co., Inc., *Form 10-KSB* (September 28, 1998), p. 3.

52. *Ibid.*, p. 5

53. The Vermont Teddy Bear Co., Inc., *1994 Annual Report*, p. 3.

54. M. Dowling, "Vermont Teddy Bears the Pressure," *Catalog Age* (May 1996), p. 12.

55. The Vermont Teddy Bear Co., Inc., *Form 10-KSB* (September 28, 1998), p. 5.

56. The Vermont Teddy Bear Co., Inc., *1997 Annual Report* (Letter to Shareholders), p. 4.

57. The Vermont Teddy Bear Co., Inc., *Form 10-KSB* (September 28, 1998), p. 3.

58. R. Levy, "Ursine of the Times: Vermont Teddy Bear Company Pulls Back from Catalog Sales," *Direct Marketing* (February 1998), p. 16.

59. The Vermont Teddy Bear Co., Inc., "Vermont Teddy Bear Announces Second-Quarter Results," Press Release (February 13, 1998).

60. The Vermont Teddy Bear Co., Inc., *1997 Annual Report.*

61. The Vermont Teddy Bear Co., Inc., *1997 Annual Report* (Letter to Shareholders), p. 4.

62. The Vermont Teddy Bear Co., Inc., "Vermont Teddy Bear Company Joins Forces with America's Most Famous Teddy Bear Person," Press Release (November 5, 1996).

63. The Vermont Teddy Bear Co., Inc., "NFL Football Soft and Cuddly? The Vermont Teddy Bear Company Introduces Officially Licensed NFL Teddy Bears," Press Release (August 27, 1997).

64. The Vermont Teddy Bear Co., Inc., "The Vermont Teddy Bear Company Kicks Off NFL Bear-Grams," Press Release (September 30, 1996).

65. *The Wall Street Journal Corporate Reporter* (January 21, 1998).

66. *Ibid.*

67. *Ibid.*

68. The Vermont Teddy Bear Co., Inc., *1997 Annual Report*, p. 13.

69. The Vermont Teddy Bear Co., Inc., *Form 10-KSB* (September 28, 1998), p. 8.

70. The Vermont Teddy Bear Co., Inc., "Vermont Teddy Bear Refinances Factory Headquarters," Press Release (July 21, 1997).

71. The Vermont Teddy Bear Co., Inc., *Form 10-KSB* (September 28, 1998), p. 5.

72. *Ibid.*

73. *Ibid.*

74. E. Tenney, "A Teddy Bear's Modest Proposal," *Business Digest* (October 10, 1997), pp. 1–3.

75. B. Abrams, "Switch to Air Bags Bears Watching," *Packaging Digest* (March 1998), pp. 50–52.

76. The Vermont Teddy Bear Co., Inc., *Form 10-KSB* (September 28, 1998), p. 7.

77. "Bear Necessities," *Direct Marketing Magazine* (July 1998), p. 18.

78. *Ibid.*

79. M. L. Calta, "Cub Scout," *Detroit News* (March 5, 1995), pp. 22-D, 23-D.

80. *Ibid.*

81. C. Crossen, "Isn't It Funny How a Bear Makes Money, Year After Year?" *Wall Street Journal* (February 17, 1998), p. B-1.

82. *Ibid.*

83. "Bullish for Bears," *The Tampa, Florida Times* (February 18, 1998), pp. E1–E2.

84. S. Hampton, *Hoovers Online: Toys and Games Industry Snapshot*, 1998, p. 1.

85. J. S. Krutick, et al., "Salomon Smith Barney Toy Industry Update," *Investext Report*, No. 2715626 (June 23, 1998), p. 6.

86. S. Hampton, *Hoovers Online: Toys and Games Industry Snapshot*, 1998, p. 2.

87. D. Leccese, "Growth at a Price," *Playthings* (June 1998), p. 30.

88. *Ibid.*
89. The Vermont Teddy Bear Co., Inc., *1997 Annual Report*, p. 11.
90. D. Leccese, "Growth at a Price," *Playthings* (June 1998), p. 30.
91. M. L. Calta, "Cub Scout," *Detroit News* (March 5, 1995), pp. 22-D, 23-D.
92. C. Crossen, "Isn't It Funny How a Bear Makes Money, Year After Year?" *Wall Street Journal* (February 17, 1998), p. B-1.
93. The Vermont Teddy Bear Co., Inc., *1997 Annual Report*, p. 11.
94. The Vermont Teddy Bear Co., Inc., *Form 10-KSB* (September 28, 1998), p. 7.
95. *Ibid.*
96. B. Horovitz, *USA Today* (May 27, 1997), p. B-2.
97. The Vermont Teddy Bear Co., Inc., "Vermont Teddy Bear and Disney Settle Suit," Press Release (September 9, 1997).
98. The Vermont Teddy Bear Co., Inc., *1994, 1995, 1996, 1997 Annual Reports* and *Form 10-KSB* (September 28, 1998).
99. The Vermont Teddy Bear Co., Inc., Press Release (May 22, 1998), pp. 1–3.

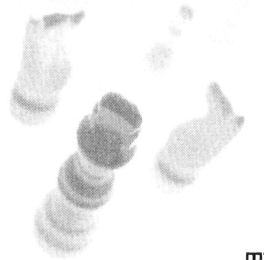

CASE 23

Oprah Winfrey:

The Story of an Entrepreneur

A. Mukund and A. Neela Radhika

"Oprah Winfrey arguably has more influence on the culture than any university president, politician, political or religious leader, except perhaps the pope."

Vanity Fair magazine, in 1994

"[Oprah] may be uncomfortable talking about [money], but when it comes to making it, she sure knows what she's doing."

Fortune magazine, in March 2002

The Mad Cow Controversy: A Talk Show Queen in Trouble

IN MID-1996, OPRAH WINFREY, ONE OF THE WORLD'S MOST WELL-KNOWN MEDIA PERSON-alities and the host of *The Oprah Winfrey Show*, was entangled in a major controversy. The controversy arose because of statements made by Oprah and Howard Lyman (Lyman, a founder/member of the Humane Society of the United States) during an episode of *The Oprah Winfrey Show* telecast on April 16, 1996.[1] The show, based on the theme "Dangerous Food," talked about the mad cow disease[2] and the threat it supposedly posed to beef consumers in the United States.

On the show, Lyman blamed the practice of feeding rendered livestock (protein derived from cattle remains) to cattle for outbreak of the disease in Europe, which resulted in the death of more than 1.5 million cattle and 20 people in 1996. Lyman's statements suggested that beef consumers in the United States could also contract the human form of the mad cow disease as a similar practice of feeding livestock was followed in the United States. On the show, Oprah swore that she would never eat a hamburger again in her life.

In May 1996, some cattle producers filed a $10.3 million suit against Oprah and Lyman in the Texas state court, under the Texas False Disparagement of Perishable Food Products Act,[3] claiming business disparagement, negligence, and defamation. They said Oprah created fear regarding the consumption of beef, when she vowed that she would never again eat a burger in her life. David Mullin, an Attorney representing cattle producers, said, "The message of the show was never meant to be where opinions are shared. The show was meant to be scary."

The cattle producers claimed that Oprah knowingly aired false and defamatory comments about the threat of mad cow disease in the United States. The show reportedly had a devastating impact on cattle prices and sales in the United States. Prices fell to a 10-year low within a week of the show, causing losses exceeding $12 million to the cattle producers. However, Chip Babcock, Oprah's Attorney, claimed that the show in question was fair and did not suggest that beef was unsafe. Commenting on the decline in cattle prices following the show, Oprah's attorneys said that the decline in prices was due to factors such as drought and oversupply.

Oprah soon aired a second show on the mad cow disease, with cattle industry representatives on the discussion panel to arrive at a balanced perspective on the issue. Commenting on this, Bill O'Brien, a co-owner of the Texas Beef Group, said, "I do not think it repaired the damage. She did not go on the program and eat a hamburger before the world." In February 2000, a federal court dismissed the suit against Oprah, stating that though Oprah's show melodramatized the issue, it did not give false information to defame cattle producers. The court also acquitted Lyman, stating that his statements, though strongly stated, were based on established facts.

The issue attracted media attention all over the world, highlighting Oprah's immense popularity and influence over her viewers. Oprah, with a business empire worth over $1 billion in 2002, was unarguably the most successful female media personality ever. How this lady overcame her disturbed, troubled childhood and several other problems to become so popular and successful is essentially a story of her entrepreneurial and leadership skills.

Oprah's Rags-to-Riches Journey

The *talk show Queen*, Oprah was born out of wedlock to Vernon Winfrey and Vernita Lee on January 29, 1954, in Kosciusko, Mississippi. Named Orpah Gail Winfrey, she became Oprah after Orpah was misspelled in her school records. Her parents separated when she was very young. Following this, she was sent to live with her grandmother, Hattie Mae Lee, on a small farm. Hattie laid the foundation of Oprah's career when she taught her to read the Bible. At the age of three, Oprah spent hours reading Bible stories to the animals on the farm. Hattie also taught her many lessons about God and faith. These lessons inspired her (at that tender age) to become strong and help people in need. She believed that she had a higher calling and she was sent to "do good" to others.

Public speaking skills were evident in Oprah right from her childhood. In 1957, at less than four years of age, Oprah recited sermons from the Bible at her local church. Oprah loved the attention and applause she received after her recitals. Oprah was an intelligent child who reportedly asked her teachers to advance her to higher grades.

At the age of six, Oprah was sent to live with her father in Nashville, Tennessee. Her father and her stepmother, Zelma, noticed her interest in reading and encouraged her by buying more books. Her voracious reading helped her always stay ahead of her classmates.

Later that year, she was sent to her mother in Milwaukee. Oprah led a few painful years of her childhood at her mother's. She was sexually abused by her male relatives and acquaintances. These experiences had a profound effect on her, and she turned into a promiscuous and problematic teenager. Her mother tried to admit her to a home for troubled teens, but as the home was full, Oprah was sent to live with her father again. The shift to her father's place was a turning point for Oprah. It reportedly put her life back on track. Oprah referred to the reunion with her father as "my saving grace."

Oprah said that her father was a tough taskmaster, insisting on hard work and discipline. This attitude helped her improve herself in all aspects. In Oprah's words, "As strict as he was, he had some concerns about me making the best of my life, and would not accept anything less than what he thought was my best."

Oprah's father encouraged her to participate in various competitions. Participation in such activities helped her develop self-confidence and improved her communication skills. Oprah organized and directed a series of presentations (especially on *God's Trombones*, written by James Weldon Johnson) at various local churches. Oprah used these presentations to raise funds to buy new robes for the youth choir of her church. She actively participated in Sunday church activities and spoke frequently in church. She also worked hard at her studies and, as a result, won a scholarship to attend Tennessee State University, where she specialized in speech communications and performing arts.

In 1971, at the age of 17, Oprah got her first broadcasting job. She worked as a part-time radio announcer for WVOL radio station (targeting mainly African-Americans) in Nashville. In 1972, she won the "Miss Black Tennessee" title. In 1973, after graduating from Tennessee State University, she joined WTVF-TV in Nashville as a reporter. In 1976, she joined WJZ-TV, a major affiliate of ABC[4] in Baltimore, as a news anchor. She worked at WJZ-TV until 1983. During her tenure at WJZ-TV, she got a chance to host a talk show.[5] She was the co-host for *People Are Talking*, a popular talk show in those days.

In 1984, Oprah moved to WLS-TV Chicago (an affiliate of ABC) to host a local TV talk show, *A.M. Chicago*. Oprah deviated from the general talk show format, referred to as "report talk." She introduced a new format, referred to as "rapport talk," that involved back-and-forth conversation between the host and the audience. Oprah's show became an instant hit with women, mostly in the 30–50 age group. According to analysts, Oprah's show was a success because the conversational mode formed the basis of female bonding. Many of the people in her audience felt that Oprah had made the talk show more personal and confessional.

By the end of the year, the talk show became very successful. As a result of the show's success and Oprah's increasing popularity, the show was renamed *The Oprah Winfrey Show*, and its duration was increased from 30 minutes to one hour. In 1986, the show went national and became the country's number one talk show within one year of being nationally syndicated.

During the mid-1980s, Oprah began her acting career with a role in Steven Spielberg's *The Color Purple* (1985). For her performance in the movie, Oprah was nominated for an Oscar and a Golden Globe Award in the category of Best Supporting Actress. Her performance in her second movie, *Native Son* (1986), also won applause from critics.

Oprah's love for acting and her desire to offer quality entertainment led to the establishment of Harpo Productions Inc. (Harpo is Oprah spelled backward). With Harpo, Oprah became the third woman in U.S. history to own a movie production studio (the pioneers were Mary Pickford and Lucille Ball). In October 1988, Harpo Productions acquired the ownership and production rights to *The Oprah Winfrey Show* from ABC. This made Oprah the first woman in the history of TV to own and produce her own talk show.

In 1992, Oprah got engaged to Stedman Graham, a former basketball player and a public relations executive, with whom she had been living since 1986. During the late-1980s and 1990s, Oprah won many awards and garnered recognition for her work in TV and films. In 1994, she was included in the TV Hall of Fame. (Refer to **Exhibit 1** for details of the awards won by Oprah.)

For over a decade, Oprah's talk show, like other talk shows, focused on dysfunctional families and their problems. However, in 1994, Oprah announced a change in her program format. She decided to stop the dysfunctional-group–based shows and began focusing on positive shows that inspired people to rise above their limitations and achieve their dreams. The

**Exhibit 1
Awards Won By
Oprah**

Year	Award
1971	Crowned Miss Fire Prevention, Nashville, TN
1971	Won Miss Black Tennessee pageant
1987	Daytime Emmy (Outstanding Talk/Service Show Host, *The Oprah Winfrey Show*)
1988	International Radio and Television Society, Broadcaster of the Year; youngest recipient
1989	Daytime Emmy (Outstanding Talk/Service Show, *The Oprah Winfrey Show*)
1991	Daytime Emmy (Outstanding Talk/Service Show Host, *The Oprah Winfrey Show*)
1991	Daytime Emmy (Outstanding Talk/Service Show, *The Oprah Winfrey Show*)
1991	NAACP Image (Outstanding News, Talk or Information Series, *The Oprah Winfrey Show*)
1992	Daytime Emmy (Outstanding Talk/Service Show Host, *The Oprah Winfrey Show*)
1992	Daytime Emmy (Outstanding Talk/Service Show, *The Oprah Winfrey Show*)
1993	Daytime Emmy (Outstanding Talk/Service Show Host, *The Oprah Winfrey Show*)
1993	Daytime Emmy (Outstanding Children's Special, *Shades of a Single Protein*, ABC after-school special)
1994	Daytime Emmy (Outstanding Talk/Service Show Host, *The Oprah Winfrey Show*)
1994	Daytime Emmy (Outstanding Talk/Service Show, *The Oprah Winfrey Show*)
1995	Daytime Emmy (Outstanding Talk/Service Show Host, *The Oprah Winfrey Show*)
1995	Daytime Emmy (Outstanding Talk/Service Show, *The Oprah Winfrey Show*)
1996	George Foster Peabody Individual Achievement Award
1996	Daytime Emmy (Outstanding Talk/Service Show, *The Oprah Winfrey Show*)
1997	People's Choice Award, Favorite Female Television Performer
1997	Daytime Emmy (Outstanding Talk Show, *The Oprah Winfrey Show*)
1997	NAACP Image (Outstanding News, Talk or Informational Special, *Dinner with Oprah: A Lifetime Exclusive—Toni Morrison*; shared award)
1997	NAACP Image (Outstanding News, Talk or Informational Series, *The Oprah Winfrey Show: Oprah's Book Club—Dinner with Maya Angelou*; shared award)
1998	People's Choice (Favorite Female Performer in a TV Series, *The Oprah Winfrey Show*)
1998	Daytime Emmy (Lifetime Achievement; presented by the National Academy of Television Arts and Sciences)
1998	Daytime Emmy (Outstanding Talk Show Host, *The Oprah Winfrey Show*; tied with Rosie O'Donnell)
1999	National Book Foundation's 50th Anniversary Gold Medal (for influential contribution to reading and books).
2001	Woman of the Century Award from *Newsweek*
2002	Emmy (Bob Hope Humanitarian Award)

Source: www.eonline.com

aim of this new format was to entertain, enlighten, and empower the millions of viewers who watched the show around the world.

The new format thus offered direction, advice, and help to people through entertainment mixed with therapy. Oprah introduced Dr. Phil McGraw, a renowned psychologist, as a weekly guest on the show, to help guests and the audience gain insights into their problems. Thus, while other talk shows continued to focus on entertainment and shock value, Oprah's shows (and her various ventures) helped change lives for the better.

The Oprah Harpo Empire

During the 1990s, Oprah expanded her business into many areas besides television. She entered various fields, such as publishing, music, film, health and fitness, and education. In 1994, Oprah's initiatives for the protection of children against abuse were rewarded when then U.S. President Bill Clinton signed the "Oprah Bill," a new law designed to protect children against abuse.

In 1996, Oprah headed the list of Forbes' highest-paid entertainers with earnings of $171 million, beating even celebrities such as Steven Spielberg, Michael Jackson, Arnold Schwarzenegger, and Jim Carrey. In September 1996, Oprah launched *Oprah's Book Club* on TV, which was aimed at inculcating and encouraging reading among people. *Oprah's Book Club* was a great success; most of her fans chose to read the books she selected for the Book Club. Reportedly, sales of all the books selected for the club increased substantially (on average by 10 times) and found a place in the bestsellers lists.

Harpo Films Inc., Oprah's film production division, signed a long-term agreement with the ABC television network in the mid-1990s to produce the *Oprah Winfrey Presents* series of telefilms. Some of the major projects under the *Oprah Winfrey Presents* banner were "Amy and Isabelle," "Tuesdays with Morrie," "David and Lisa," "The Wedding," and "Before Women Had Wings." Oprah even acted in some of these telefilms (such as "The Women of Brewster Place," "Before Women Had Wings," and "There Are No Children Here") and received critical acclaim for her performance. The telefilms venture met with reasonable success and generated $4 million in revenues in 2001.

Oprah also signed an exclusive agreement with the Walt Disney Motion Picture Group in the mid-1990s to produce feature films for Disney. The first film produced by the Harpo Group for Disney was Touchstone Pictures' *Beloved*, in which Oprah played the lead role. By the end of the 1990s, Oprah had reportedly become one of the very few people in the world who were recognized immediately by their first name alone. She had become so popular that in 1998, she was voted the second most admired woman in the United States, next only to President Clinton's wife, Hillary Rodham Clinton.

In November 1998, the Harpo Group launched Oxygen Media LLC in partnership with Geraldine Laybourne's GBL LLC, an entertainment company, and Carsey Werner Mandabach (CWM) LLC.[6] Harpo had a 25% stake in Oxygen. Oxygen Media, aimed at women, was an integrated media company that combined the advantages of both cable television and the Internet. Geraldine Laybourne was the chairman and CEO of Oxygen Media. The company's cable network featured a range of programs that included talk shows, music, health, news, comedy, movies, cartoons, and sports. *Oxygen Goes Online*, the first program featured on the Oxygen cable network, was a 12-episode course on using the Internet. Oprah also produced and hosted the show *Use Your Life* on Oxygen Media. Oxygen Media's web sites included *Oxygen.com*, *Oprah.com*, and *ThriveOnline.com*. Oprah's web site, *www.oprah.com*, which offered the latest information regarding *The Oprah Winfrey Show* (and later the Angel Network and *O* Magazine), was reportedly viewed over 7 million times every month in 1999 and received more than 2,000 e-mails every day.

Oprah's popularity and ratings had surged ahead of those of other talk show hosts, including veterans such as Phil Donahue (the pioneer of talk shows), Regis Philbin (*Live with Regis*), Kelly Ripa (*Kelly*), Sally Jessy Raphael (*The Sally Jessy Raphael Show*), Jerry Seinfeld, Jerry Springer, and David Letterman. (See **Exhibit 2** for details of popular TV personalities in the United States from 1993 to 2000.) The Harpo empire entered the magazine business in early 2000. By 2002, Oprah headed Harpo Inc., Harpo Productions Inc., Harpo Video Inc., Harpo Films Inc., and Harpo Studios Inc. as the Harpo Group's Chairman.

In April 2000, Harpo Entertainment and Hearst Magazines jointly launched *O, The Oprah Magazine*, in New York City. The magazine was positioned as a personal growth guide for women in the 21st century. *O* addressed various aspects of a woman's life, such as her inner well-being, fashion, health and fitness, relationships, self-discovery, books, home design, and food, among others. The magazine, targeted at women between 25 and 49 years of age, was circulated across the country. Speaking about *O*, Oprah, who was also its editorial director, said, "I believe you are here to become more of yourself, to live your best life. The magazine will present articles and stories of other people to help women look at their lives differently."

Exhibit 2
A. Favorite TV Personalities: Ranks: Harris Poll

	1993	1994	1995	1996	1997	1998	1999	2000	2001
Drew Carey	*	*	*	10	6	8	1	3	1
Regis Philbin	*	*	*	*	*	*	*	2	2
Oprah Winfrey	2	2	3	3	3	1	2	1	3
David Letterman	6	6	4	5	7	*	*	6	4
Ray Romano	*	*	*	*	*	*	*	7	5
Jay Leno	*	8	10	10	8	6	*	7	6
Bill O'Reilly	*	*	*	*	*	*	*	*	7
Kelsey Grammar	*	*	8	8	9	5	5	5	8
Katie Couric	*	*	*	*	*	*	*	*	9
Rosie O'Donnell	*	*	*	8	5	6	8	9	10

Note:
*Not rated in that year.

Source: www.harrisinteractive.com

B. Favorite TV Personalities Among Different Groups: Harris Poll[1]

Gender-Based

Men	Drew Carey
Women	Oprah Winfrey

Age-Based

Age 18–24	Drew Carey
Age 25–29	David Letterman
Age 30–39	Drew Carey
Age 40–49	Regis Philbin
Age 50 and over	Regis Philbin

Race-Based

White	Regis Philbin
African-American	Drew Carey
Hispanic	David Letterman

Note:
1. The Harris Poll was conducted (online) in the United States between December 20, 2001, and January 1, 2002. The sample size of the poll was 2,098 adults from a cross-section of audiences across the country.

Source: www.harrisinteractive.com

Columns in *O* included "Live Your Best Life," "Make Your Dreams Come True" (a step-by-step planning guide), and "Tell it Like It Is" (by Dr. Phil), "Dream Big" (a profile of a person who took steps to live out his or her dream), and "My Journal" (a profile of a celebrity's intimate thoughts).

O was reportedly the most successful startup in the magazine industry. In 2001, its revenues amounted to over $140 million. According to Cathleen Black, President, Hearst Magazines, most successful magazines took nearly five years to become as profitable as *O* did in only two years. Analysts noted that though the market was down and many magazines had posted losses in 2001, *O*'s advertising revenues increased by 43% over its revenues in 2000. *O*'s paid-up circulation amounted to an estimated 2.5 million copies, which was more than those of leading magazines such as *Vogue* and *Martha Stewart Living*. *O* targeted the premium segment, which had an average income of $63,000 and patronized premium brands such as Lexus, Coach, and Donna Karan (which were key advertisers for *O*).

Oprah described *O* as a personal growth manual and took an active part in the content development of the magazine. Analysts remarked that *O* was a reflection of Oprah's personality. The success of *O* was primarily attributed to Oprah's popularity. Commenting on the high revenues earned by the magazine in terms of advertising revenue, Black said, "Advertisers have unanimously responded to the powerful presence of Oprah. The magazine is a new voice for a new time—a lifestyle magazine with heart and soul."

However, Oprah's talk show continued to be her biggest success, generating revenues of over $300 million annually. The show was aired in over 107 countries in the world and was watched by 26 million people in the United States alone. It remained the number one talk show in the daytime slot for 16 years, despite competition from over 50 rivals. According to Bob Iger, President of Walt Disney, the Oprah show contributed significantly to the company's profits (Walt Disney's ABC Network syndicated *The Oprah Winfrey Show* in many major markets). The show appealed primarily to women in the age group 30–50 years. Since most of the audience was from the middle class, the show attracted huge advertising revenues from companies such as Wal-Mart, Procter & Gamble, and Sears.

Oprah, the Entrepreneur

Despite the fact that she was the owner of a huge business empire, Oprah reportedly did not even know how to read a balance sheet and did not follow any corporate models. She had declined offers from many companies such as AT&T, Intel, and Ralph Lauren to be on their boards, stating that "she did not understand what she would do on their boards." Oprah was once reported to have hoarded $50 million in cash, which she called her personal "bag-lady fund," as she was afraid of investing in the stock market, being totally ignorant about it.

Interestingly, she did not like being referred to as a businesswoman. Commenting on her ignorance of doing business the usual way, she said, "If I called a strategic-planning meeting, there would be dead silence, and then people would fall out of their chairs laughing."

According to analysts, Oprah was not in the "business of business"; she was in the "business of soothing souls." The kind of intimacy Oprah enjoyed with her audiences was something that reportedly no other talk show host had ever achieved. Oprah's message, "You are responsible for your own life," acted as her unique selling proposition (USP), just like "convenience" and "everyday low prices" were the USPs of McDonald's and Wal-Mart, respectively.

The Harpo empire, however, did not function purely on Oprah's personal skills. She had put in place a team that dedicatedly worked toward keeping the business running. Dennis Swanson[7] and Jeff Jacobs,[8] President, Harpo Group, contributed greatly to Oprah's success as a talk show host as well as a businesswoman over the years. Explaining Oprah's business, Jacobs said, "We bet on ourselves. We are an intellectual property company, and our partners [ABC, Hearst, Oxygen] are distributors. Core content is developed here and has never left our home base."

Jacobs said that controlling content was a difficult task as Oprah was not only the chief content creator but also the chief content itself. For instance, every issue of *O* sported a bold and winning picture of Oprah on its cover page; in her columns in *O*, she gave details of her personal life, such as her battle against abuse, her triumph over adversity, and her attempts at losing weight. She also discussed her painful experiences as a victim of child abuse and racism. Commenting on the content, Oprah said, "I bring all my stuff with me."

Analysts felt that Oprah's life was central to her brand. They believed that by making herself and her struggle against adversity the central theme of her messages, she successfully touched the American psyche and motivated Americans to become self-reliant. Oprah won the audience's trust by sharing her personal experiences with them on daytime TV to help them deal with their problems and become accountable for their own lives. This strategy reportedly kept Oprah ahead of her competitors.

Analysts believed that Oprah was reluctant to lose control of her brand because she was aware of its power. Oprah consistently refused requests from major companies to use her name on their products, such as perfumes, clothing, books, and food. One of the Oprah's friends remarked that everybody wanted "a part of Oprah's brand," but she was not ready to cede control over it. Analysts said that though some of her competitors (such as Martha Stewart) had lent their names to various products, Oprah firmly refused to do so. Since many of the products marketed by celebrities had failed in the market, analysts felt that Oprah was right in refusing to dilute her brand equity.

Oprah was also against taking the Harpo Group public. She held 90% of the Harpo Group herself. She claimed that by selling her name or a part of her business, she would be selling herself. In Oprah's words, "If I lost control of the business, I would lose myself or at least the ability to be myself. Owning myself is a way to be myself." This clearly indicated how Oprah perceived her businesses and the extent to which her businesses were based on Oprah herself.

Analysts felt that Jacobs' business acumen also contributed greatly to Harpo's success. Oprah and Jacobs were rather an odd pair to be running a business as they had very different management styles. According to analysts, Oprah followed a management-by-instinct technique and took all her decisions on the basis of her gut feelings, while Jacobs believed in careful planning and execution. While Jacobs described Harpo's strategy as multipurposing the content in various media, Oprah explained it as reaching out to a larger audience (through different media) to help people better their lives. However, the success of Harpo Group made it evident that the relationship worked.

According to company sources, Jacobs acted as Oprah's strategic advisor and dealmaker. In Oprah's words, "He is a piranha and that is a good thing for me to have." Remembering his meeting with Jacobs and his commitment towards Oprah, Iger said, "I remember being put off initially, but Jeff Jacobs has one thing in mind: his client. And he serves her very well."

Despite his many contributions to the company, Jacobs preferred to remain in the background and referred to himself as a "behind-the-scenes guy." Besides being the President of Harpo, he also acted as Oprah's personal agent, making her deals and agreements. This arrangement resulted in a saving of over 25% on Oprah's income, which would have gone in payments to agents and managers. Commenting on the financial success of Oprah, Jacobs said, "We understand it is not just how much you make but how much you keep."

Oprah was known for making sudden decisions on the basis of gut feelings. Oprah decided to launch *O*'s first international edition (in early 2002) when watching a documentary on Africa that showed some women in a beauty parlor in Nairobi reading *True Love* and *Hello* magazines. Commenting on this, Oprah said, "I thought, 'African women have no business sitting in a beauty shop reading *Hello!* and *True Love.*" Soon after, she launched *O* in Africa!

Interestingly, Oprah's business decisions (based on her gut feelings) were often successful. Her decision to place the table of contents of *O* on page 2 was not common business practice. Most publishers placed it in the middle of the magazine so that readers had to go through a couple of advertisements in search of the table of contents. This practice was aimed at benefiting advertisers, but Oprah, in her own words, wanted to "put the readers first."

The fact that *O* was an instant success proved Oprah's decision right. Commenting on the magazine's success, Oprah said, "I am most proud of the magazine, because I did not know what I was doing." Media reports claimed that *O*, which was mostly developed by Oprah, reflected her ability to balance practicality and preaching. Analysts believed that Oprah knew that such balance would sell—and it did. According to them, this was the same strategy that made her talk show such a success. Oprah maintained a balance between the issues or persons she chose for her show. For example, if one day she discussed the entertainment industry with a celebrity, the very next day she examined a grave issue such as the problems of women in Afghanistan.

Reportedly, Oprah followed the same balanced approach with her finances. Though she did not track her costs closely, she was aware of their magnitude and was sure to draw the strings when necessary. For instance, when Oprah found that the production costs of her show amounted to $50 million annually (which was double the expenditure incurred by other day-time talk shows), she called up Doug Pattison, Harpo's CFO, and said "That is okay, but that is also enough. I think we can keep it at $50 million."

As far as her employees were concerned, Oprah paid them well and expected quality for the money. Reportedly, she did not care about ratings as long as her shows and magazines achieved their objectives. Commenting on this, she said, "Ratings go down when we do an Oprah's Book Club show, but that does not matter. We are getting people to read." Thus, Oprah did not pressure her employees to achieve ratings; instead, she emphasized creativity and quality. According to her employees, Oprah took care that her staff did not measure its success on the basis of media reports. She showered praises on her staff once a project was completed; but when that project was recognized by the world and won ratings or awards, her staff received no special treatment from her. In the words of Kate Forte, President, Harpo Films, "But if it wins big ratings or awards, the boss is mum. It is her reminder that we should not do anything for the external reward."

Though there was great demand for Harpo-produced movies and television films, Oprah did not bend her rules to exploit that demand. According to Iger, though Disney wanted Harpo to produce more films, Oprah's standards and rules limited Harpo's output to one film per year. Commenting on this, Iger said, "Just because there is a buyer does not mean she is a seller."

Oprah's business decisions were based largely on trust (she referred to this as taking leaps of faith). It was reported that she asked only one question before she made a decision: "Can I trust you?" Commenting on this, Nancy Petersman, Executive Vice President, Allen & Co. (an investment banking firm), said "It is all about character with Oprah. We investment bankers do the same sort of thing—try to figure out what people are made of—but with Oprah, it is like someone is looking into your soul."

Trust and control over a project were major factors in Oprah's decision-making process. Hearst succeeded in winning Oprah's assent for *O* despite competition from AOL Time Warner and Conde Nast by winning Oprah's trust. Hearst promised her that the magazine would reflect her values and would work toward translating her message into the written word. To ensure this, Hearst entrusted Oprah with total editorial control of the magazine.

It was the same story with Oprah's investment decisions. Geraldine Laybourne, Co-founder of Oxygen, won Oprah's trust by telling her that she was planning a cable network aimed at providing content and service to women. The idea appealed to Oprah—in fact, she had something similar in her mind—and on an impulse, she invested $20 million in the project and also transferred certain rights to *The Oprah Winfrey Show* library. In return, she received a 25% stake in Oxygen Media.[9]

Oprah, Serving the People

Since Oprah had been a victim of child abuse, she constantly raised the issue in her show and made constant efforts to protect children from such abuse. In 1991, she demanded that the government pass a new law (The National Child Protection Act) against child abuse. Oprah even testified before the Senate Judiciary Committee of the United States to help establish a database of convicted child abusers in the United States. In December 1993, Oprah's efforts were rewarded, when the Oprah Bill (The National Child Protection Act) was made a law.

On principle, Oprah had donated at least 10% of her annual earnings to charity during her adult life. Reportedly, most of these donations were made anonymously. However, in the

5. A talk show is an interactive session between two or more people. Such shows generally involve interaction between a host, guest(s), and the audience.

6. CWM LLC is one of the major independent production studios in America, distributing programming content in over 175 countries.

7. Dennis Swanson was the head of WLS-TV, Chicago. He appointed Oprah as a talk show host and convinced her that she could succeed even though she was overweight and an African American. Such was his belief in Oprah's capability that he ran her show opposite Chicago's number one talk show hosted by Phil Donahue. Within one month, Oprah's show replaced Donahue's in ratings.

8. Jeff was an entertainment lawyer in Chicago. He helped Oprah handle legal formalities regarding her contracts. However, by 1986 he convinced Oprah to establish her own company instead of lending her talent to outsiders. This led to the formation of Harpo Entertainment Inc., in which Jeff was given 5% share. Jeff joined Harpo as President in 1989. In recognition of his contribution to the company, Jeff's stake in the company was increased to 10% later on.

9. In March 2002, it was reported that Oprah regretted her decision to impart certain rights to *The Oprah Winfrey Show* library to Oxygen Media. She felt that by doing so, she had traded her soul. To undo this mistake, Oprah acquired her rights back and in return she agreed to do a special program on Oxygen Media, "Oprah After the Show."

10. *www.christianitytoday.com*, April 1, 2002.

Additional Readings and References

www.achievement.org

www.auditionagency.com

B. Bridget, "Oprah Going, Sally Gone," *www.eonline.com* (March 11, 2002).

B. Byrne, "Oprah Heading to PrimeTime," *www.eonline.com* (June 11, 2002).

"Cattleman: 2nd Oprah Show 'Too Little, Too Late,'" *www.cnn.com* (January 26, 1998).

"Creating *Oprah: The Magazine*," *http://foliomag.com* (September 1, 1999).

"Court Upholds Dismissal of Oprah Lawsuit Without Testing 'Veggie Libel' Law," *www.mediainstitute.org* (February 2000).

"Hearst Magazines Introduces *O, The Oprah Magazine*," *www.broadcast.com* (April 2000).

www.jumptheshark.com

www.leatherquest.com

www.mcspotlight.org

www.oprah.com

"Oprah Accused of Whipping Up Anti-Beef 'Lynch Mob,' " *www.cnn.com* (January 21, 1998).

"Oprah's Angel," *www.etonline.com* (June 18, 2001).

O. Winfrey, *The African American Almanac*, 7th edition (Gale, 1997).

"Oprah Winfrey," *www.businessweek.com* (January 14, 2002).

"Oprah Winfrey," *www.forbes.com* (December 13, 2001).

"Oprah Winfrey: The Well Rounded Interview," *www.well-rounded.com* (July 1998).

"Oprah Wraps Up 'Life,' " *www.etonline.com* (July 2, 2001).

P. Sellers, "The Business of Being Oprah," *Fortune* (March 17, 2002).

"Shut Up and Eat," *www.prwatch.org* (Second Quarter 1997).

H. Taylor, "Oprah Winfrey Recaptures Top Spot As Nation's Most Popular TV Personality," *www.harrisinteractive.com* (December 27, 2000).

CASE 24

Inner-City Paint Corporation (Revised)

Donald F. Kuratko and Norman J. Gierlasinski

History

STANLEY WALSH BEGAN INNER-CITY PAINT CORPORATION IN A RUN-DOWN WAREHOUSE, which he rented, on the fringe of Chicago's "downtown" business area. The company is still located at its original site.

Inner-City is a small company that manufactures wall paint. It does not compete with giants such as Glidden and DuPont. There are small paint manufacturers in Chicago that supply the immediate area. The proliferation of paint manufacturers is due to the fact that the weight of the product ($52\frac{1}{2}$ pounds per 5-gallon container) makes the cost of shipping great distances prohibitive. Inner-City's chief product is flat white wall paint sold in 5-gallon plastic cans. It also produces colors on request in 55-gallon containers.

The primary market of Inner-City is the small- to medium-sized decorating company. Pricing must be competitive; until recently, Inner-City had shown steady growth in this market. The slowdown in the housing market combined with a slowdown in the overall economy caused financial difficulty for Inner-City Paint Corporation. Inner-City's reputation had been built on fast service: it frequently supplied paint to contractors within 24 hours. Speedy delivery to customers became difficult when Inner-City was required to pay cash on delivery (C.O.D.) for its raw materials.

Inner-City had been operating without management controls or financial controls. It had grown from a very small two-person company with sales of $60,000 annually five years ago, to sales of $1,800,000 and 38 employees this year. Stanley Walsh realized that tighter controls within his organization would be necessary if the company was to survive.

Equipment

Five mixers are used in the manufacturing process. Three large mixers can produce a maximum of 400 gallons, per batch, per mixer. The two smaller mixers can produce a maximum of 100 gallons, per batch, per mixer.

Two lift trucks are used for moving raw materials. The materials are packed in 100-pound bags. The lift trucks also move finished goods, which are stacked on pallets.

A small testing lab ensures the quality of materials received and the consistent quality of their finished product. The equipment in the lab is sufficient to handle the current volume of product manufactured.

Transportation equipment consists of two 24-foot delivery trucks and two vans. This small fleet is more than sufficient because many customers pick up their orders to save delivery costs.

Facilities

Inner-City performs all operations from one building consisting of 16,400 square feet. The majority of the space is devoted to manufacturing and storage; only 850 square feet is assigned as office space. The building is 45 years old and in disrepair. It is being leased in three-year increments. The current monthly rent on this lease is $2,700. The rent is low in consideration of the poor condition of the building and its undesirable location in a run-down neighborhood (south side of Chicago). These conditions are suitable to Inner-City because of the dusty, dirty nature of the manufacturing process and the small contribution of the rent to overhead costs.

Product

Flat white paint is made with pigment (titanium dioxide and silicates), vehicle (resin), and water. The water makes up 72% of the contents of the product. To produce a color, the necessary pigment is added to the flat white paint. The pigment used to produce the color has been previously tested in the lab to ensure consistent quality of texture. Essentially, the process is the mixing of powders with water, then tapping off of the result into 5- or 55-gallon containers. Color overruns are tapped off into 2-gallon containers.

Inventory records are not kept. The warehouse manager keeps a mental count of what is in stock. He documents (on a lined yellow pad) what has been shipped for the day and to whom. That list is given to the billing clerk at the end of each day.

The cost of the materials to produce flat white paint is $2.40 per gallon. The cost per gallon for colors is approximately 40% to 50% higher. The 5-gallon covered plastic pails cost Inner-City $1.72 each. The 55-gallon drums (with lids) are $8.35 each (see **Exhibit 1**).

Selling price varies with the quantity purchased. To the average customer, flat white sells at $27.45 for 5 gallons and $182.75 for 55 gallons. Colors vary in selling price because of the

Exhibit 1
Paint Cost Sheet:
Inner-City Paint
Corporation

	5 Gallons	55 Gallons
Sales price	$ 27.45	$ 182.75
Direct material	(12.00)	(132.00)
Pail and lid	(1.72)	(8.35)
Direct labor	(2.50)	(13.75)
Manufacturing overhead ($1/gallon)	(5.00)	(5.00)
Gross margin	$ 6.23	$ 23.65
Gross profit ratio	22.7%	12.9%

variety in pigment cost and quantity ordered. Customers purchase on credit and usually pay their invoices in 30 to 60 days. Inner-City telephones the customer after 60 days of nonpayment and inquires when payment will be made.

Management

The President and majority stockholder is Stanley Walsh. He began his career as a house painter and advanced to become a painter for a large decorating company. Walsh painted mostly walls in large commercial buildings and hospitals. Eventually, he came to believe that he could produce a paint that was less expensive and of higher quality than what was being used. A keen desire to open his own business resulted in the creation of Inner-City Paint Corporation.

Walsh manages the corporation today in much the same way that he did when the business began. He personally must open *all* the mail, approve *all* payments, and inspect *all* customer billings before they are mailed. He has been unable to detach himself from any detail of the operation and cannot properly delegate authority. As the company has grown, the time element alone has aggravated the situation. Frequently, these tasks are performed days after transactions occur and mail is received.

The office is managed by Mary Walsh (Walsh's mother). Two part-time clerks assist her, and all records are processed manually.

The plant is managed by a man in his twenties, whom Walsh hired from one of his customers. Walsh became acquainted with him when the man picked up paint from Inner-City for his previous employer. Prior to the eight months he has been employed by Walsh as Plant Manager, his only other experience has been that of a painter.

Employees

Thirty-five employees (20 workers are part-time) work in various phases of the manufacturing process. The employees are nonunion, and most are unskilled laborers. They take turns making paint and driving the delivery trucks.

Stanley Walsh does all of the sales work and public relations work. He spends approximately one half of every day making sales calls and answering complaints about defective paint. He is the only salesman. Other salesmen had been employed in the past, but Walsh felt that they "could not be trusted."

Customer Perception

Customers view Inner-City as a company that provides fast service and negotiates on price and payment out of desperation. Walsh is seen as a disorganized man who may not be able to keep Inner-City afloat much longer. Paint contractors are reluctant to give Inner-City large orders out of fear that the paint may not be ready on a continuous, reliable basis. Larger orders usually go to larger companies that have demonstrated their reliability and solvency.

Rumors abound that Inner-City is in difficult financial straits, that it is unable to pay suppliers, and that it owes a considerable sum for payment on back taxes. All of the above contribute to the customers' serious lack of confidence in the corporation.

Financial Structure

Exhibits 2 and **3** are the most current financial statements for Inner-City Paint Corporation. They have been prepared by the company's accounting service. No audit has been performed because Walsh did not want to incur the expense it would have required.

Exhibit 2
Balance Sheet for the Current Year Ending June 30: Inner-City Paint Corporation

Current assets

Cash	$ 1,535	
Accounts receivable (net of allowance for bad debts of $63,400)	242,320	
Inventory	18,660	
Total current assets		$262,515
Machinery and transportation equipment	47,550	
Less accumulated depreciation	15,500	
Net fixed assets		32,050
Total assets		**$294,565**

Current liabilities

Accounts payable	$217,820	
Salaries payable	22,480	
Notes payable	6,220	
Taxes payable	38,510	
Total current liabilities		$285,030
Long-term notes payable		15,000

Owners' equity

Common stock, no par, 1,824 shares outstanding		12,400
Deficit		(17,865)
Total liabilities and owners' equity		**$294,565**

Future

Stanley Walsh wishes to improve the financial situation and reputation of Inner-City Paint Corporation. He is considering the purchase of a computer to organize the business and reduce needless paperwork. He has read about consultants who are able to quickly spot problems in businesses, but he will not spend more than $300 on such a consultant.

The solution that Walsh favors most is one that requires him to borrow money from the bank, which he will then use to pay his current bills. He feels that as soon as business conditions improve, he will be able to pay back the loans. He believes that the problems Inner-City is experiencing are due to the overall poor economy and are only temporary.

Exhibit 3
Income Statement for the Current Year Ending June 30: Inner-City Paint Corporation

Sales		$1,784,080
Cost of goods sold		1,428,730
Gross margin		$ 355,350
Selling expenses	$ 72,460	
Administrative expenses	67,280	
President's salary	132,000	
Office Manager's salary	66,000	
Total expenses		337,740
Net income		**$ 17,610**

CASE 25

The Comeback
of Caterpillar, 1985–2002

Isaac Cohen

FOR THREE CONSECUTIVE YEARS, 1982, 1983, AND 1984, THE CATERPILLAR COMPANY lost $1 million a day. Caterpillar's major competitor was a formidable Japanese company called Komatsu. Facing a tough global challenge, the collapse of its international markets, and an overvalued dollar, Caterpillar had no choice: It had to reinvent itself or die.

Caterpillar managed to come back as a high-tech, globally competitive growth company. Over a period of 15 years, and throughout the tenure of two CEOs—George Schaefer (1985–1990) and Donald Fites (1990–1999)—Caterpillar transformed itself. George Schaefer introduced cost-cutting measures and employee involvement programs; outsourced machines, parts, and components; and began modernizing Caterpillar's plants. Donald Fites diversified Caterpillar's product line and reorganized the company structurally. He also completed Caterpillar's plant modernization program, revitalized Caterpillar's dealership network, and radically altered Caterpillar's approach to labor relations.

When Donald Fites retired on February 1, 1999, Glen Barton was elected CEO. Barton was in an enviable position. The world's largest manufacturer of construction and mining equipment, and a *Fortune 100* company, Caterpillar generated $21 billion in revenues in 1998, the sixth consecutive record year. Leading its industry while competing globally, Caterpillar recorded a $1.5 billion profit in 1998, the second best ever.

Notwithstanding Caterpillar's dramatic comeback, Barton could not count on the continued prosperity of the company because the U.S. construction industry was moving into a grinding economic downturn. At the time that Barton completed his first year as CEO, on February 1, 2000, the company announced its 1999 results: Sales declined by 6% and earnings by 37%. In March 2000, Caterpillar's share price was trading close to its 52-week low ($36, compared to a high of $66), and one industry analyst declared, "The stock for the foreseeable future is dead money."[1]

What should Barton do? Should Barton follow the strategies implemented by Schaefer and Fites to enhance Caterpillar's competitive position relative to its principal rivals, Komatsu, John Deere, and CNH Global (CNH was the product of a 2000 merger between Case Corporation and New Holland)? Should he, instead, reverse some of the policies introduced by his predecessors? Or should he, rather, undertake whole new strategies altogether?

The Heavy Construction Equipment Industry

The heavy construction equipment industry supplied engineering firms, construction companies, and mine operators. The industry's typical product line included earthmovers (bulldozers, loaders, and excavators), road-building machines (pavers, motor graders, and mixers), mining-related equipment (off-highway trucks, mining shovels), and large cranes. Most machines were offered in a broad range of sizes, and a few were available with a choice of wheels or crawler tracks. Most were used for the construction of buildings, power plants, manufacturing plants, and infrastructure projects such as roads, airports, bridges, tunnels, dams, sewage systems, and water lines. On a global basis, earthmoving equipment accounted for about half of the industry's total sales in the 1990s (see **Exhibit 1**). Among earthmovers, hydraulic excavators accounted for 45% of the sales. Excavators were more productive, more versatile, and easier to use in tight spaces than either bulldozers or loaders. Off-highway trucks that hauled minerals, rocks, and dirt, were another category of fast-selling equipment.[2]

Global demand for heavy construction machinery grew at a steady rate of 4.5% per year in the 1990s. The rate of growth, however, was faster among the developing nations of Asia, Africa, and Latin America than among the developed nations. In the early 2000s, North America and Europe were expected to account for 25% each of the industry's sales, Japan for 20%, and the developing nations for the remaining 30%.[3]

The distinction between original equipment and replacement parts was an essential feature of the industry. Replacement parts and "attachments" (work tools) comprised over a quarter of the total revenues of the heavy construction equipment industry (see **Exhibit 1**) but accounted for a substantially larger share of the industry's earnings for two reasons: First, the sale of replacement parts was more profitable than that of whole machines, and second, the market for replacement parts was less cyclical than that for original equipment.[4] As a rule of thumb, the economic life of a heavy construction machine was 10 to 12 years, but in many cases, especially in developing countries, equipment users kept their machines in service

Exhibit 1
Global Demand of Heavy Construction Equipment by Major Categories, 1985–2005[1] (Dollar amounts in billions)

Item	1985	1994	2000	2005[1]
Earthmoving Equipment	50%	49%	49%	49%
Off-Highway Trucks	8%	7%	7%	7%
Construction Cranes	9%	11%	10%	10%
Mixers, Pavers, and Related Equipment	6%	6%	7%	7%
Parts & Attachments	27%	27%	27%	26%
Totals	100%	100%	100%	100%
Total Demand	$38	$56	$72	$90

NOTE:
1. Percentages do not add up to 100 due to rounding.

Source: A. Gross and D. Weiss, "Industry Corner: The Global Demand for Heavy Construction Equipment," *Business Economics* (July 1996), p. 56.

much longer, perhaps 20 to 30 years, thus creating an ongoing stream of revenues for parts, components, and related services.[5]

Another characteristic of the industry was the need to achieve economies of scale. According to industry observers, the optimal scale of operation was about 90,000 units annually. Up to a production level of 90,000 units a year, average equipment unit cost declined as output increased. Therefore, capturing a large market share was critical for benefiting from economies of scale.[6] The relatively low volume of global sales—200,000 to 300,000 earth-moving equipment units per year (1996)[7]—further intensified competition over market share among the industry's leading firms.

Successful marketing also played an important role in gaining competitive advantage. A widespread distribution and service network had always been essential for competing in the heavy construction equipment industry because downtime resulting from the inability to operate the equipment at a construction site was very costly. Typically, manufacturers used a worldwide network of dealerships to sell machines, provide support, and offer after-sales service. Dealerships were independent, company owned, or both, and were normally organized on an exclusive territorial basis. Since heavy construction machines operated in a tough and inhospitable environment, equipment wore out and broke down frequently, and parts needed to be rebuilt or replaced often. Therefore, manufacturers placed dealers in close proximity to equipment users, building a global service network that spread all over the world.

Manufacturers built alliances as well. Intense competition over market share drove the industry's top firms to form three types of cooperative agreements. The first were full-scale joint ventures to share production. Caterpillar's joint venture with Mitsubishi Heavy Industries was a notable case in point. The second were technology-sharing agreements between equipment manufacturers and engine makers to ensure access to the latest engine technology. The joint venture between Komatsu and Cummins Engine and between Case Corporation and Cummins provided two examples. The third type of agreements were technology-sharing alliances between major global firms and local manufacturers whereby the former gained access to new markets and in return supplied the latter with advanced technology. Caterpillar utilized such an arrangement with Shanghai Diesel in China, and Komatsu did so with the BEML company in India.[8]

History of Caterpillar

At the turn of the 20th century, farmers in California faced a serious problem. Using steam tractors to plow the fine delta land of the San Joaquin Valley, California farmers fitted their tractors with large drive wheels to provide support on the moist soil; nevertheless, despite their efforts, the steamers' huge wheels—measuring up to 9 feet high—sank deeply into the soil. In 1904, Benjamin Holt, a combine maker from Stockton, California, solved the problem by replacing the wheels with a track, thereby distributing a tractor's weight on a broader surface. In addition, Holt replaced the heavy steam engine with a gasoline engine, thus improving the tractor's mobility further by reducing its weight (a steam tractor weighed up to 20 tons). He nicknamed the tractor "Caterpillar," acquired the Caterpillar trademark, and applied it to several crawler-type machines that his company manufactured and sold. By 1915, Holt tractors were sold in 20 countries.[9]

Outside agriculture, crawler tractors were first used by the military. In 1915, the British military invented the armor tank, modeling it after Holt's machine, and during World War I, the United States and its allies in Europe utilized Holt's track-type tractors to haul artillery and supply wagons. In 1925, the Holt Company merged with another California firm, the Best Tractor Company, to form Caterpillar (Cat). Shortly thereafter, Caterpillar moved its corporate headquarters and manufacturing plants to Peoria, Illinois. The first company to introduce a diesel engine on a moving vehicle (1931), Caterpillar discontinued its combine manufacturing during the 1930s and focused instead on the production of road-building, construction, logging, and pipe-laying equipment. During World War II, Caterpillar served as the primary supplier of bulldozers to the U.S. Army; its sales volume more than tripled between 1941 and 1944 to include motor graders, diesel engines, and electric generators, in addition to tractors and wagons.[10]

Demand for Caterpillar products exploded in the early postwar years. Cat's equipment was used to reconstruct Europe, build the U.S. interstate highway system, erect the giant dams of the Third World, and lay out the major airports of the world. The company managed to differentiate itself from its competitors by producing reliable, durable, and high-quality equipment; offering quick after-sales service; and providing speedy delivery of replacement parts. As a result, during the 1950s and 1960s, Caterpillar emerged as the uncontested leader of the heavy construction equipment industry, far ahead of any rival. By 1965, Caterpillar had established foreign manufacturing subsidiaries—either wholly owned or joint ventures—in Britain, Canada, Australia, Brazil, France, Mexico, Belgium, India, and Japan. Caterpillar's 50/50 joint venture with Mitsubishi in Japan, established in 1963, had become one of the most successful, stable, and enduring alliances among all American–Japanese joint ventures.[11]

Caterpillar's distribution and dealership network also contributed to the company's worldwide success. From the outset, the company's marketing organization rested on a dense network of independent dealers that sold and serviced Cat equipment. Strategically located throughout the world, these dealers were self-sustaining entrepreneurs who invested their own capital in their businesses, derived close to 100% of their revenues from selling and supporting Cat equipment, and cultivated close relationships with Caterpillar customers. On average, a Caterpillar dealership had remained in the hands of the same family—or company—for over 50 years. Indeed, some dealerships, including several located overseas, predated the 1925 merger that gave birth to Caterpillar.[12] In 1981, on the eve of the impending crisis, the combined net worth of Cat dealers equaled that of the company itself, and the total number of employees working for Cat dealers was slightly lower than the company's own workforce.[13]

The Crisis of the Early 1980s

Facing weak competition both at home and abroad, Caterpillar charged premium prices for its high-quality products, paid its production workers union-scale wages, offered its shareholders high rates of return on their equity, and enjoyed superior profits. Then, in 1982, following a record year of sales and profits, Caterpillar suddenly plunged into three successive years of rising losses totaling nearly $1 billion. "Quite frankly, our long years of success made us complacent, even arrogant,"[14] Pierre Guerindon, an executive vice president at Cat, conceded.

The crisis of 1982–1984 stemmed from three sources: a global recession, a costly strike, and unfavorable currency exchange rates. First, the steady growth in demand for construction machinery, dating back to 1945, came to an end in 1980, as highway construction in the United States slowed to a halt while declining oil prices depressed the worldwide market for mining, logging, and pipe-laying equipment. Second, Caterpillar's efforts to freeze wages and reduce overall labor costs triggered a seven-month strike (1982–1983) among its U.S. employees. Led by the United Auto Workers (UAW) union, the strike accounted for a sizable portion of the company's three-year loss. The third element in Caterpillar's crisis was a steep rise in the value of the dollar (relative to the yen and other currencies) that made U.S. exports more expensive abroad and U.S. imports (shipped by Caterpillar's competitors) cheaper at home. "The strong dollar is a prime factor in Caterpillar's reduced sales and earning . . . [and]

is undermining manufacturing industries in the United States,"[15] said Cat's annual reports for 1982 and 1984.

Taking advantage of the expensive dollar, Komatsu Limited had emerged as Caterpillar's principal rival. Komatsu (which means "little pine tree" in Japanese) had initially produced construction machinery for the Japanese and Asian markets, then sought to challenge Caterpillar's dominance in the markets of Latin America and Europe, and eventually penetrated the United States to rival Caterpillar in its domestic market. Attacking Caterpillar head-on, Komatsu issued a battle cry—"Maru C," meaning "encircle Cat." Launching a massive drive to improve quality while reducing costs, Komatsu achieved a 50% labor productivity advantage over Caterpillar and in turn underpriced Caterpillar's products by as much as 30%. The outcome was a dramatic change in market share. Between 1979 and 1984, Komatsu global market share more than doubled, to 25%, while Caterpillar's fell by almost a quarter, to 43%.[16]

Turnaround: George Schaefer's Caterpillar, 1985–1990

Competition with Komatsu and the crisis of 1982–1984 forced Caterpillar to reexamine its past activities. In 1985, Caterpillar's new CEO, George Schaefer, was a congenial manager who encouraged Cat executives to openly admit the company's past mistakes. "We have experienced a fundamental change in our business—it will never again be what it was," Schaefer said as he became CEO. "We have no choice but to respond, and respond vigorously, to the new world in which we find ourselves."[17] Under Schaefer's direction, Caterpillar devised and implemented a series of strategies that touched on every important function of the company, including purchasing, manufacturing, marketing, personnel, and labor relations.

Global Outsourcing

Traditionally, Caterpillar functioned as a vertically integrated company that relied heavily on in-house production. To ensure product quality as well as an uninterrupted supply of parts, Cat self-produced two-thirds of its parts and components and assembled practically all of its finished machines. Under the new policy of "shopping around the world," Caterpillar sought to purchase parts and components from low-cost suppliers who maintained high quality standards. Working closely with its suppliers, Caterpillar moved toward the goal of outsourcing 80% of its parts and components.[18]

An additional goal of the policy was branding—that is, purchasing of final products for resale. Through its branding program, Caterpillar sold outsourced machines under its own brand name, taking advantage of its superior marketing organization and keeping production costs down. Beginning in the mid-1980s, Cat contracted to buy lift trucks from a Norwegian company, hydraulic excavators from a West German manufacturer, paving machines from an Oklahoma corporation, off-highway trucks from a British firm, and logging equipment from a Canadian company, and it resold them all under the Cat nameplate. Ordinarily, Caterpillar outsourced product manufacturing but not product design. By keeping control over the design of many of its outsourced products, Caterpillar managed to retain in-house design capability and ensure quality control.[19]

Broader Product Line

For nearly a decade, the DC10 bulldozer had served as Caterpillar's signature item. It stood 15 feet tall, weighed 73 tons, and sold for more than $500,000 in 1988. It had no competitors. But as demand for highway construction projects dwindled, Caterpillar needed to reevaluate its product mix because heavy equipment was no longer selling well. Sales of light construction equipment, on the other hand, were fast increasing. Between 1984 and 1987, accordingly, Caterpillar doubled its product line from 150 to 300 models of equipment, introducing many small machines that ranged from farm tractors to backhoe loaders (multipurpose light bulldozers), and diversified its customer base. Rather than focus solely on large clients—i.e., multinational engineering and construction firms like the Bechtel Corporation, a typical user of heavy bulldozers—Cat began marketing its lightweight machines to a new category of customers: small-scale owner–operators and emerging contractors. Still, the shift in Cat's product mix had a clear impact on the company's bottom line. Unlike the heavy equipment market, where profit margins were wide, intense competition in the market for light products kept margins slim and pitted Caterpillar against John Deere and Case Corporation, the light equipment market leaders.[20]

Labor Relations

To compete successfully, Caterpillar also needed to repair its relationship with the union. In 1979, following the expiration of its collective bargaining agreement, Caterpillar had experienced an 80-day strike, and three years later, in 1982, contract negotiations had erupted in a 205-day strike, the longest companywide work stoppage in UAW history.[21] Named CEO in 1985, George Schaefer led the next two rounds of contract negotiations.

Schaefer's leadership style was consensual. In contrast to the autocratic style of his predecessors, Schaefer advocated the free flow of ideas between officers, managers, and production workers, and he promoted open communication at all levels of the company. A low-key CEO who often answered his own phone, Schaefer possessed exceptional people skills. Asked to evaluate Schaefer's performance, John Stark, editor of *Off Highway Ledger*, a trade journal, said, "Schaefer is probably the best manager the construction machinery industry has ever had."[22]

Schaefer's social skills led to a significant improvement in Cat's relations with the UAW. Not a single strike broke out over contract negotiations during Schaefer's tenure; on the contrary, each cycle of bargaining was settled peacefully. Under Schaefer's direction, furthermore, the union agreed to reduce the number of labor grades and job classifications, and to streamline seniority provisions—a move that enhanced management flexibility in job assignment and facilitated the cross-utilization of employees.[23] More importantly, improved labor relations contributed to the success of two programs that played a critical role in Caterpillar's turnaround strategy—namely, an employee involvement plan based on teamwork and a reengineering effort of plant modernization and automation.

Employee Improvement

An industrywide union famous for its cooperative labor-management efforts at Saturn Corporation, the NUMMI plant (a GM–Toyota joint venture in Fremont, California), and elsewhere, the UAW lent its support to Caterpillar's employee involvement program. Called the Employee Satisfaction Process (ESP) and launched by Schaefer in 1986, the program was voluntary. ESP members were organized in work teams, met weekly with management, and offered suggestions that pertained to many critical aspects of the manufacturing process, including production management, workplace layout, and quality enhancement. Implemented in a growing number of U.S. plants, by 1990, the program had resulted in productivity gains, quality improvements, and increased employee satisfaction. At the Cat plant in Aurora, Illinois, for example, the local ESP chairman recalled that the ESP program had "changed everything: the worker had some say over his job . . . . [and] top management was very receptive. We zeroed in on quality, anything to make the customer happy." Management credited the ESP teams at Aurora with a steep fall in the rate of absenteeism, a sharp decline in the number of union grievances filed, and cost savings totaling $10 million.[24] At another ESP plant, a Cat assembly-line worker told a *Fortune* reporter in 1988: "Five years ago the foreman wouldn't even listen to you, never mind the general foreman or plant supervisor. . . . Now everyone will listen." Caterpillar applied the ESP program to outside suppliers as well. Typically, ESP teams made up of Caterpillar machinists visited suppliers' plants to check and certify equipment quality. The certified vendors received preferential treatment, mostly in the form of reduced inspection, counting, and other controls. Only 0.6% of the parts delivered by certified suppliers were rejected by Caterpillar, compared to a reject rate of 2.8% for noncertified suppliers.[25]

Plant with a Future

Caterpillar's employee involvement plan went hand in hand with a $1.8 billion plant modernization program launched by Schaefer in 1986.[26] Dubbed "Plant with a Future" (PWAF), the modernization program combined just-in-time inventory techniques, a factory automation scheme, a network of computerized machine tools, and a flexible manufacturing system. Several of these innovations were pioneered by Komatsu late in the 1970s. The industry's technological leader, Komatsu had been the first construction equipment manufacturer to introduce both the just-in-time inventory system and the "quick changeover tooling" technique, a flexible tooling method designed to produce a large variety of equipment models in a single plant.[27]

To challenge Komatsu, top executives at Caterpillar did not seek to merely imitate the Japanese. This was not enough. They studied, instead, the modernization efforts of several manufacturing companies and arrived at two important conclusions: It was necessary (1) to change the layout of an entire plant, not just selected departments within a plant, and (2) to implement the program companywide—that is, on a global basis both at home and abroad. Implementing such a comprehensive program took longer than expected, however, lasting seven years: four under Schaefer's direction and three more under the direction of his successor, Donald Fites.[28]

The traditional manufacturing process at Caterpillar, known as "batch" production, was common among U.S. assembly plants in a number of industries. Under batch production, subassembly lines produced components (radiators, hydraulic tanks, etc.) in small lots. Final assembly lines put together complete models, and the entire production system required large inventories of parts and components due to the high level of "work in process" (models being built at any one time). Under batch production, furthermore, assembly tasks were highly specialized, work was monotonous and dull, and workers grew lax and made mistakes. Correcting assembly mistakes, it should be noted, took more time than the assembly process itself because workers needed to disassemble components in order to access problem areas. Parts delivery was also problematic. Occasionally, delays in delivery of parts to the assembly areas forced workers to leave the line in order to locate a missing part. Occasionally, the early arrival of parts before they were needed created inefficiencies.[29]

To solve these problems, Caterpillar reconfigured the layout of its manufacturing plants into flexible work "cells." Grouped in cells, workers used computerized machine tools to perform several manufacturing steps in sequence, processing components from start to finish and sending them "just-in-time" to an assembly area. For example, to manufacture steel tractor-tread under the batch production layout, Cat workers were required to cut, drill, and heat-treat steel beams on three distinct assembly lines. Under cellular manufacturing, by contrast, all three operations were carried out automatically in single tractor-tread cells linked together by computers.[30]

In addition, Caterpillar reduced material handling by means of an automated electrified monorail that delivered parts to storage and assembly areas, traveling on a long aluminum track throughout the modernized plant. When parts arrived at the delivery point, a flashing light alerted the assembly-line workers, semi-automatic gates (operated by infrared remote

Exhibit 2
Caterpillar Versus
Komatsu
(Dollar amounts
in billions)

| | Cat | | Komatsu | |
	Sales	Income As % of Sales	Sales[1]	Income As % of Sales
1985	6.7	2.9	—	1.8
1986	7.3	1.0	—	2.8
1987	8.2	3.9	5.1	1.3
1988	10.4	5.9	6.2	0.4
1989	11.1	4.5	6.0	2.6

Note:
1. Sales are available only in yen: 1985, 796 billion yen; 1986, 789 billion yen.

Source: For Caterpillar, Hoover's Handbook of American Business *(1995), p. 329; For Komatsu,* Hoover's Handbook of World Business *(1995–1996), p. 291.*

control) opened, and a lift lowered the components directly onto an assembly line. Don Western, a manufacturing manager at the Cat Aurora plant, observed: "Materials now [1990] arrive at the assembly point only when required—and in the order required. At most, we hold about a 4 hour supply of large parts and components on the line."[31]

Finally, Caterpillar improved product quality. Formerly, components moved down the assembly line continuously, not intermittently, and therefore workers were unable to respond quickly to quality problems. Managers alone controlled the speed of the line. Under the new assembly plan, on the other hand, components moved automatically between work areas and remained stationary during the actual assembly operation. More important, under the PWAF plan, managers empowered production workers to change the speed of the assembly line at will, granting them the flexibility necessary to resolve quality and safety problems.[32]

The PWAF program resulted in productivity and quality gains across the board in many Caterpillar plants. At the Aurora plant in Illinois, for instance, factory workers managed to reduce the assembly process time fourfold, building and shipping a customer order in 4 rather than 16 days, and cutting product defects by one-half in four years (1986–1990).[33] At the Cat plant in Grenoble, France, to mention another case, workers slashed the time it took to assemble machinery parts from 20 to 8 days in three years (1986–1989). Companywide changes were equally impressive: Collectively, Caterpillar's 30 worldwide plants cut inventory levels by 50% and manufacturing space by 21% in three years.[34]

During Schaefer's five-year tenure, Caterpillar had reemerged as a globally competitive company, lean, flexible, and technologically advanced. Caterpillar's world market share rebounded from 43% to 50% (1984–1990),[35] revenues increased by 66% (1985–1989), and the company was profitable once again. As Caterpillar prospered, Komatsu was retrenching. In 1989, Caterpillar's sales totaled over $11 billion, or nearly twice the sales reported by Komatsu, Caterpillar's profit margins exceeded Komatsu's, and the gap between the two companies—in terms of both market share and income on sales—was growing (see **Exhibit 2**).

The Transformation Continues: Donald Fites' Caterpillar, 1990–1999

Notwithstanding Schaefer's achievements, the transformation of Caterpillar was far from over. For one thing, the company stock lagged far behind its earnings; Cat shares underperformed the S&P 500 index by over 50% for five years (1987–1992).[36] For another, Caterpillar was facing an industrywide downturn in both its domestic and international markets. Partly as a result of the cyclical nature of the construction equipment industry, and also

Exhibit 3
Financial Results During the Labor Disputes of the 1990s: Caterpillar (Dollar amounts in millions, except per share prices)

Year	Sales	Net Income	Income As % of Sales	Stock Price FY Close
1991	$10,182	$(404)	—	$10.97
1992	10,194	(2,435)	—	13.41
1993	11,615	652	5.6%	22.25
1994	14,328	955	6.7%	27.56
1995	16,072	1,136	7.1%	29.38
1996	16,522	1,361	8.2%	37.63
1997	$18,925	$1,665	8.8%	$48.50

Source: Hoover's Handbook for American Business *(1999), p. 329.*

as a result of an increase in the value of the dollar (a weak dollar in the late 1980s helped Caterpillar's foreign sales), Caterpillar revenues and profits fell. During the two years following Schaefer's retirement, the company actually lost money (see **Exhibit 3**).

Replacing Schaefer in the winter of 1990, Donald Fites viewed Caterpillar's financial troubles as an opportunity to introduce change: "I certainly didn't count on . . . [a] recession . . . but [the recession] made it easier to accept the fact that we needed to change."[37] "It's hard to change an organization when you're making record profits."[38]

Leadership

Fites' leadership style stood in a stark contrast to Schaefer's. "George was . . . a consensus builder" while "[Don] expects people to challenge him forcefully,"[39] one Cat executive said, and another (former Cat CEO Lee Morgan) described Fites as "one of the most determined men I've ever met."[40] Fites was a hard-line executive, feared by his subordinates, respected by his peers, and cheered by Wall Street. An imposing man standing 6'5", Fites led by explicit command rather than persuasion, asserted the company's "right to manage" in the face of mounting union opposition, and did not hesitate to cut thousands of management and production jobs at a stroke.

The son of a subsistence corn farmer, Fites had joined Caterpillar in 1956, rose through the ranks, and spent 16 years overseas. A career marketer, he worked for Cat in South Africa, Germany, Switzerland, Brazil, Japan, and other countries. In 1971, Fites had earned an MBA from MIT, writing a thesis titled "Japan Inc.: Can U.S. Industry Compete?" Soon thereafter, he received an assignment in Japan, where he served nearly five years as the Marketing Director of the Caterpillar–Mitsubishi joint venture. Fites' Japanese experience resonated throughout the remainder of his career. He was impressed, first of all, by the ways in which the Japanese trained their managers, rotating executives through functional departments in order to educate them in all aspects of the business. Returning from Japan to Peoria, Illinois, in the mid-1970s, Fites revamped Cat's product development process, utilizing an integrated approach based on Japanese-style functional teams. He also admired Japanese labor relations. Historically, American unions had been organized on an industrywide basis and therefore labor relations in the United States were often adversarial. Trade unions in Japan, in contrast, were company-based organizations, loyal, cooperative, and, in Fites' words, "deeply dedicated to the success of the [firm]."[41] Leading Caterpillar in the 1990s, Fites sought to bring Caterpillar's labor relations closer to the Japanese model.

Reorganization

A marketing manager, Fites was convinced that Caterpillar did not pay sufficient attention to customer needs because global pricing decisions were made at the company's headquarters in Peoria, with little knowledge of the local market conditions around the world. In 1985, as he took charge of Cat's worldwide marketing organization, Fites delegated district offices the authority to set prices, thereby pushing responsibility down the chain of command to the lowest possible level. Promoted to President in 1989, Fites applied the same principle to Caterpillar's entire structure, developing a companywide reorganization plan under Schaefer's direction.[42]

Caterpillar's old organizational structure was archaic. It was a functional structure suitable for a small company that operated just a few plants, all located within the United States. A centralized body with only four primary functions—engineering, manufacturing, marketing, and finance—the old structure had served Caterpillar well until World War II, but as the company had expanded globally in subsequent decades, the limitations of such a structure had become apparent. First, decisions were made at the top of each functional unit, and executives were reluctant to delegate authority to midlevel or low-level managers. Second, each functional unit tended to focus on its own goal rather than the enterprise's objectives (marketing was preoccupied with market share, engineering with product safety, manufacturing with assembly problems, etc.), making it difficult for top management to coordinate functional goals.[43] Third, the bureaucratization of the decision-making process impaired effective communication. Under the old structure, Fites recalled, the flow of information upward was "so filtered with various prejudices—particularly functional prejudice[s]—that you didn't know whether you were really looking at the facts or looking at someone's opinion."[44]

To equip Caterpillar with the flexibility, speed, and agility necessary to operate in the global economy, Fites broke the company into 17 semi-autonomous divisions, or "profit centers," 13 responsible for products (tractors, engines, etc.) and 4 for services.[45] He then required each division to post a 15% rate of return on assets, and threatened to penalize any division that fell behind. He stood by his words. When Caterpillar's forklift division failed to improve its return on assets in 1992, Fites transferred it into an 80%–20% joint venture controlled by Mitsubishi.[46]

Caterpillar's new divisional structure facilitated downsizing. Under the new structure, Caterpillar cut 10,000 jobs in three years, 1990–1993 (see **Exhibit 4**). Of the 7,500 employees who lost their jobs between January 1990 and August 1992, 2,000 were salaried managers and 5,500 hourly workers.[47] As Caterpillar's sales grew from $10 billion to $15 billion in the first half of the 1990s, the number of managers employed by the company fell by 20%.[48] In addition, the move from a functional into a divisional structure, coupled with the drive for profit making, brought about a change in the methods of managerial compensation. Traditionally, Cat managers were paid in proportion to the size of the budget they controlled

Exhibit 4
Donald Fites'
Caterpillar:
Employment and
Sales (Dollar
amounts in
billions)

Years	Number of Employees	Sales
1990	60,000	$11.4
1991	56,000	10.2
1992	52,000	10.2
1993	50,000	11.6
1994	54,000	14.3
1995	54,000	16.1
1996	57,000	16.5
1997	60,000	18.9
1998	64,000	$21.0

Source: For 1990–1997: Hoover's Handbook of American Business *(1999), p. 329; for 1998: Caterpillar Inc., 1999* Annual Report, *p. 1.*

or the number of employees they supervised. Under the new plan, Caterpillar based all its incentive compensation schemes on return on assets.[49] Finally, Caterpillar decentralized its research and development activities. With each division controlling its own product development programs and funding, R&D activities under the new plan were more customer driven than they had been in any other period in the past.[50]

Marketing and Dealerships

Caterpillar's reorganization plan affected the company's distribution network as well. Under the new structure, dealers seeking assistance could contact any of the 17 product and service profit centers directly, saving time and money; they no longer needed to call the general office in their search for assistance within the company.[51] The new structure also facilitated more frequent interaction between Caterpillar's managers and dealers, a development that resulted in "virtually everyone from the youngest design engineer to the CEO" having "contact with somebody in [a] dealer organization," wrote Fites. Ordinarily, low-level managers at Caterpillar communicated daily with their counterparts at Cat dealerships; senior corporate executives did so several times a week.[52]

Caterpillar's network of dealerships was extensive. In 1999, 207 independent dealers served Caterpillar, 63 of which were stationed in the United States and 144 abroad. The number of employees working for Cat dealers exceeded the company's own workforce (67,000) by nearly one-third; the combined net worth of Cat dealers surpassed Caterpillar's stockholders' equity ($5.5 billion)[53] by nearly one-quarter (see **Exhibit 5**). Many of Caterpillar's dealerships were privately owned, and a few were public companies. On average, the annual sales of a Caterpillar dealership amounted to $150 million (1996); several of the large dealerships, however, generated annual revenues of up to $1 billion.

To Caterpillar, the informal relationships between the company and its dealers were far more important than the formal contractual relations. Dealership agreements ran only a few pages, had no expiration dates, and allowed each party to terminate the contract at will, following 90 days' notice. Notwithstanding the open-ended nature of the contracts, turnover among Cat dealerships was extremely low. Caterpillar actively encouraged its dealers to keep the business in their families, running seminars on tax issues and succession plans for dealers, holding regular conferences in Peoria for the sons and daughters of "dealer Principals" (dealership owners), and taking concrete steps to encourage a proper succession from one generation to another.[54]

While Caterpillar had always protected its dealers against failure, under Fites' direction, Caterpillar did so more aggressively than before, assisting individual dealers who were subjected to intense price competition by rival manufacturers. To help a dealer, Caterpillar sometimes offered discounted prices, sometimes helped reduce the dealer's costs, and occasionally

**Exhibit 5
Caterpillar
Dealerships, 1999
(Dollar amounts
in billions)**

	Inside U.S.	Outside U.S.	Worldwide
Dealers	63	144	207
Branch Stores	382	1,122	1,504
Employees	34,338	54,370	88,708
Service Bays	6,638	5,529	12,167
Estimated Net Worth	$3.22	$3.54	$6.76

Source: Caterpillar Inc., "1999 Annual Report," p. 43.

launched a promotion campaign in the dealer's service territory, emphasizing the lower lifetime cost of a Cat machine relative to a competitor's. Caterpillar also protected dealers during recessions. Despite the company's losses during the industry slump of 1991–1992, Fites' Caterpillar helped vulnerable Cat dealers survive the downturn, stay in the business, and order equipment in advance of the 1993 upturn. Caterpillar's competitors, in contrast, saw several of their dealers go out of business during the recession.[55]

Fites' Caterpillar cooperated with dealers in other ways. During the 1990s, Caterpillar worked together with its dealers to conduct surveys among customers in order to improve customer service and parts delivery. Sending out 90,000 survey forms annually, Cat received a response rate of nearly 40%. Through its "Partners in Quality" program, Caterpillar involved dealers in quality control discussions, linking personnel at Cat plants and dealerships and sponsoring quarterly meetings. Periodically, Caterpillar invited its entire body of independent dealers to week-long conferences in Peoria to review corporate strategy, manufacturing plants, and marketing policies. A firm believer in strong personal business ties, Fites explained:

> Dealers can call me or any senior corporate officer at any time, and they do. Virtually any dealer in the world is free to walk in my door. I'll know how much money he made last year and his market position. And I'll know what is happening in his family. I consider the majority of dealers personal friends. Of course, one reason I know the dealers so well is that I rose through our distribution organization.[56]

Caterpillar's worldwide distribution system, according to Fites, was the company's single greatest advantage over its competitors. It was a strategic asset whose importance was expected to grow in the future: "until about 2010," Fites predicted, "distribution"—that is, after-sales support, product application, and service information—"will be what separates the winners from the losers in the global economy."[57] Contrasting American and Japanese manufacturing firms, Fites elaborated:

> Although many Japanese companies had the early advantage in manufacturing excellence, U.S. companies may have the edge this time around. . . . They know more about distribution than anyone else. . . . Quite frankly, distribution traditionally has not been a strength of Japanese companies. Marketing people and salespeople historically have been looked down upon in Japanese society [58]

Information Technology

Fites' Caterpillar invested generously in expanding and upgrading Caterpillar's worldwide computer network—a system linking together factories, distribution centers, dealers, and large customers. By 1996, the network connected 1,000 locations in 160 countries across 23 time zones, providing Caterpillar with the most comprehensive and fastest parts delivery system in the industry. Although Caterpillar had long guaranteed 48-hour delivery of parts anywhere in the world, by 1996, Cat dealers supplied 80% of the parts a customer needed at once; the remaining 20%—not stocked by the dealers—were shipped by the company on the same day the parts were ordered. With 22 distribution centers spread all around the world, Caterpillar serviced a total of 500,000 different parts, keeping more than 300,000 in stock and manufacturing the remainder on demand.[59]

A critical element in Caterpillar's drive for technological leadership was an electronic alert information system the company was developing under Fites. The new system was designed to monitor machines remotely, identify parts that needed to be replaced, and replace them before they failed. Once fully operational in the mid-2000s, the new IT system was expected, first, to help dealers repair machines before they broke down, thereby reducing machine downtime and saving repair costs; and, second, to provide Caterpillar and its dealers with the opportunity to slash their inventory costs. In 1995, the value of the combined inventories held by Caterpillar and its dealers amounted to $2 billion worth of parts.[60]

Diversification

Fites' Caterpillar expanded its sales into farm equipment, forest products, and compact construction machines, introducing new lines of products, one at a time. Between 1991 and 1999, Caterpillar entered a total of 38 mergers and joint venture agreements, many of which contributed to the company's efforts to diversify.[61]

The growth in Caterpillar's engine sales was the company's largest. Caterpillar had traditionally produced engines for internal use only, installing them on Cat machines, but beginning in the mid-1980s, as the company was recovering from its most severe crisis, Cat embarked on a strategy of producing engines for sale to other companies. In 1999, engine sales accounted for 35% of Cat's revenues, up from 21% in 1990, and Cat engines powered about one-third of the big trucks in the United States. Apart from trucking companies, Caterpillar produced engines for a variety of other customers including petroleum firms, electric utility companies, and shipbuilding concerns (see **Exhibit 6**). Only 10% of the diesel engines manufactured by Caterpillar in 1999 were installed on the company's own equipment.[62]

Two important acquisitions by Caterpillar helped the company compete in the engine market. In 1996, Donald Fites purchased the MaK Company, a German maker of engines for power generation. Partly because governments of developing countries were reluctant to build large power plants, and partly because the utility industry in the United States deregulated and new electrical suppliers entered the market, worldwide demand for generators was fast increasing. The rise in demand helped Caterpillar increase its sales of power generators by 20% annually between 1995 and 1999.[63]

Similarly, in 1998, Fites bought Britain's Perkins Engines, a manufacturer of engines for compact construction machinery, for $1.3 billion. The new acquisition contributed to Caterpillar's efforts to increase its share in the small equipment market, which was growing at a rate of 10% a year. Perkins' best-selling engine powered skid steer loaders. A compact wheel tractor operated by one person and capable of maneuvering in tight spaces, the skid dug ditches, moved dirt, broke up asphalt, and performed a wide variety of other tasks.[64]

Labor Relations

Under Fites, perhaps no other areas of management had received more attention than Caterpillar's labor relations. For nearly seven years, 1991–1998, Fites fought the UAW in what had become the longest U.S. labor dispute in the 1990s. On the one side, a union official described the UAW relationship with Fites as "the single most contentious . . . in the history of the union"; on the other, a Wall Street analyst called Fites "the guy who broke the union, pure and simple."[65]

In part, Fites' opposition to the UAW was ideological: It "[was] not so much a battle about economics as it [was] a battle about who's going to run the company."[66] Yet economics did matter, and Fites was determined to ensure Caterpillar's global competitiveness by cutting the company's labor cost. His principal target was a UAW "pattern" agreement, a collective bargaining contract modeled on agreements signed by the UAW and Caterpillar's domestic competitors, John Deere, Case Corporation, and others. (A pattern agreement tied separate labor contracts together so that changes in one led to similar changes in others within the same industry.) Fites rejected pattern bargaining because Caterpillar was heavily dependent on the export of domestically manufactured products, selling over 50% of its American-made equipment in foreign markets, and thus it competed head-to-head with foreign-based, global companies like Komatsu. Cat's U.S.-based competitors, by contract, exported a far smaller proportion of their domestically made goods. Because Cat's global competitors paid lower wages overseas than the wages paid by Cat's American-based competitors at home, Fites argued, Caterpillar could not afford to pay the UAW pattern of wages.[67]

The first Caterpillar strike erupted in 1991, at a time when Caterpillar's 17,000 unionized employees were working under a contract. The contract was set to expire on September 30, and Fites was prepared. He had built up enough inventory to supply customers for six months, giving Cat dealers special incentives to buy and stock parts and equipment in case a strike shut down the company's U.S. plants. Caterpillar's contract offer included three principal demands: no pattern on wages, flexible work schedules, and a two-tier wage system. The union rejected the offer outright and staged a strike. About 50% of the strikers were within six years of retirement, and as the strike prolonged, 30% of the strikers crossed the picket line. Five months into the strike, Fites threatened to replace the strikers permanently if they did not return to work within a week. Shortly thereafter, the union called off the strike, the strikers went back to work "unconditionally," and Cat's unionized employees continued working without a contract under the terms of the rejected offer.[68]

One casualty of the 1991–1992 strike was Caterpillar's Employee Satisfaction Process. The strike effectively put an end to Cat's ESP program, which George Schaefer had launched in 1986 and had striven so painstakingly to preserve. As the climate of labor relations at Caterpillar deteriorated, the number of unresolved grievances increased. At the Aurora plant in Illinois, the number of grievances at the final stage before arbitration rose from fewer than 20 prior to the strike to more than 300 in the year following the end of the strike. When Cat employees began wearing their own ESP buttons that read "Employee Stop Participating," Caterpillar terminated the program altogether.[69]

During 1992–1994, Caterpillar's unionized employees continued to resist Fites' hard-line stand against the UAW. They organized shop-floor disruptions ("informational picketing"), slowdowns ("work to rule"), wildcat strikes in selected plants, and picket lines at Cat's dealerships.[70] Fites, in the meantime, trained managers and office workers to operate factory machinery and reassigned many of them to the shop floors of plants undergoing short-term work stoppages. Once again, he was fully prepared for a long strike. The 1994–1995 strike broke out in June 1994, lasted 17 months, was bitterly fought by the striking unionists, and came to an abrupt end when the UAW ordered its members to return to work "immediately and unconditionally" in order to save their jobs.[71] During the strike, Caterpillar supplemented its workforce with 5,000 reassigned white-collar employees, 3,700 full-time and part-time new hires, 4,000 union members who crossed the picket line, and skilled workers borrowed from its dealerships. The company, furthermore, shifted work to non-union plants in the South. Additionally, Caterpillar supplied the U.S. market with equipment imported from its plants in Europe, Japan, and Brazil.[72] Operating effectively all through the strike, Caterpillar avoided massive customer defection, and managed to keep up production, expand sales, increase profits, and drive up the company stock price. In 1995, the company earned record profits for the second year in a row (see **Exhibit 3**).

During the two years following the end of the strike, the shop-floor struggle between Cat management and the union resumed. Caterpillar issued strict rules of workplace conduct, limiting employees' behavior as well as speech. Union activists, in response, launched a work-to-rule campaign in Cat's unionized plants. The UAW, in addition, filed numerous charges with the National Labor Relations Board (NLRB), alleging that the company had committed unfair labor practices. Accepting many of these charges, the NLRB issued formal complaints.[73] Meanwhile, in 1997, Caterpillar racked up record profits for the fourth year in a row (see **Exhibit 3**).

In February 1998, at long last, Caterpillar and the union reached an agreement. The terms of the 1998 agreement clearly favored Caterpillar. First and most importantly, the contract allowed Caterpillar to break away from the long-standing practice of pattern bargaining.

Second, the contract allowed Caterpillar to introduce a two-tier wage system and pay new employees 70% of the starting union scale. A third clause of the contract provided for a more flexible work schedule, allowing management to keep employees on the job longer than eight hours a day and during weekends without paying overtime. The contract also granted management the right to hire temporary employees at certain plants without the union's approval and reduce the number of union jobs below a certain level. Running for six years rather than the typical three years, the contract was expected to secure for Caterpillar a relatively long period of industrial peace.[74]

Several provisions of the contract were favorable to the union. The contract's key economic provisions included an immediate wage increase of 2%–4% and future increases of 3% in 1999, 2001, and 2003; cost of living allowances; and substantial gains in pension benefits (the average tenure of the 1994–1995 strikers was 24 years). Another provision favorable to the UAW was a moratorium on most plant closings. But perhaps the most significant union gain was simply achieving a contract, as AFL-CIO Secretary Treasurer Rich Trumka observed: "The message to corporate America is this: Here's one of the biggest companies, and they couldn't walk away from the union."[75]

Why, then, was Fites willing to sign a contract? Why had a company that had operated profitably year after year without a contract, and operated effectively during strikes, suddenly sought to reach an agreement with the UAW?

Fites' decision was influenced by two developments. First, Caterpillar's record revenues and profits during 1993–1997 came to an end in 1998–1999, as the industry was sliding into a recession. Revenues and profits were declining as a result of a strong dollar coupled with a weak demand for Cat products. Caterpillar therefore needed a flexible wage agreement, stable employment relations, and a more cooperative workforce in order to smooth its ride during the impending downturn. Another reason Fites sought accommodation with the union was the need to settle some 400 unfair labor practice charges filed by the NLRB against the company during the dispute. These charges were not only costly to adjudicate but could have resulted in huge penalties, which the company had to pay in cases where the NLRB ruled in favor of the UAW. One of Caterpillar's principal demands in the 1998 settlement—to which the UAW agreed—was dropping these unfair labor practice charges.[76]

The Future: Glen Barton's Caterpillar, 1999–

When Fites retired in February 1999, Glen Barton, a 39-year Cat veteran, assumed the company's leadership. During his first year in office, Barton lost two potential allies on the Cat Board of Directors, Glen Schaefer and Donald Fites. In January 2000, Caterpillar's Board of Directors revised the company's corporate governance guidelines to prohibit retired Cat employees from sitting on the Board. The move was intended to safeguard the interests of stockholders and prevent the company's inside Directors from opposing swift actions proposed by the Board's outside members.[77] For a complete list of Board of Directors and top management members, see the *2000 Annual Report* at *www.caterpillar.com.*

Barton faced other difficulties. In 1999, Caterpillar's profits fell 37%, to $946 million, the worst results since 1993, and its North American market, which accounted for half of Cat's sales and nearly two-thirds of its profits, was in a slump.[78]

Barton believed that the downturn in the construction industry could be offset by an upturn in the international market. He thought that Caterpillar could take advantage of its global positioning to cushion the U.S. decline by increasing sales in Asia and Latin America, whose economies were rebounding. But being cautious, Barton also realized that he needed to

Exhibit 6
Cat Engine Sales to
End Users

End Users	1999	2000
Trucks	34%	27%
Electric Power Generators	26%	33%
Oil Drilling Equipment	20%	19%
Industrial Equipment	11%	13%
Ships and Boats	9%	8%
Total	100%	100%

Source: Caterpillar Inc., 1999 Annual Report, p. 24; Caterpillar Inc., 2000 Annual Report.

ensure the future of Caterpillar in the long run. He therefore embarked on four growth strategies: expansion into new markets; diversification; the development of a new distribution channel; and a build-up of alliances with global competitors.

New Markets

In 1999, 80% of the world's population lived in developing countries, and Caterpillar's sales to developing nations accounted for only 23% of the company's total sales. Developing countries had limited access to water, electricity, and transportation and therefore needed to invest in building highways, bridges, dams, and waterways. Under Barton's leadership, increased sales of Caterpillar's equipment to the developing nations of Asia, Latin America, Eastern Europe, and the Commonwealth of Independent States (the former Soviet Union) was a top strategic priority.[79]

Diversification

Just as globalization protected Caterpillar from the cyclical movements of boom and bust, so did diversification. Cat's expansion into the engine business is a case in point. In 1999, Caterpillar's overall sales fell by 6%, yet its engine sales rose by 5%. Cat's engine business itself was further diversified, with truck-engine sales making up just over one-third of all Cat's engine sales in 1999 (see **Exhibit 6**).

Such a diversification, according to Barton, ensured the company that any future decline in truck engine sales could be offset, at least in part, by an increase in sales of non-truck engines. By 2010, Caterpillar's total engine sales were expected to double, to nearly $14 billion.[80]

Of all Cat engine sales, the growth in sales of electric diesel generators—20% a year since 1996—had been the fastest (see **Exhibit 7**). Caterpillar's energy business clearly bene-

Exhibit 7
Caterpillar's Sales
of Power
Generators
(Dollar amounts in
billions)

Year	Power Generator Sales	Power Generator Sales As % of Total Revenues
1996	$1.2	7.3%
1997	$1.3	6.9%
1998	$1.6	7.6%
2000	$1.8	9.1%
2001	$2.3	11.4%

Source: D. Barboza, "Cashing In on the World's Energy Hunger," New York Times (May 22, 2001).

fited from the energy crisis. Large corporations, manufacturing facilities, Internet server centers, and utility companies had installed backup diesel generators for standby or emergency use; in the nine months ending May 2001, Cat sales of mobile power modules (trailers equipped with generators) quadrupled.[81]

The world's largest manufacturer of diesel generators, Caterpillar nevertheless faced a serious challenge in its efforts to transform itself into an energy technology company: Diesel generators produced far more pollution than other sources of power. To address this problem, Barton's Caterpillar accelerated its shift toward cleaner micro power. In 2001, only 10% of Caterpillar's generators were powered by natural gas; in 2011, the corresponding figure was expected to climb to 50%.[82]

To diversify the company in still another way, Barton planned to double its farm equipment sales in five years (1999–2004).[83] In the agricultural equipment market, caterpillar needed to compete head-to-head with John Deere Co. and CNH Corporation (formerly Case Corporation and New Holland), the leading U.S. manufacturers.

A New Distribution Channel

Under Barton's direction, Caterpillar expanded its rental equipment business, reaching a new category of customers both at home and abroad. Formerly, Caterpillar had sold or rented equipment to rental centers, and these centers, in turn, had re-rented the equipment to end users. Rarely had Caterpillar rented directly to customers. Now Barton was making aggressive efforts to help Cat dealers diversify into rentals. Nearly half of all Cat's machines sold in North America in 2000 entered the market through the rental distribution channel, and the fastest-growing segment of the business was short-term rentals. Implemented by Barton in 1999–2000, the Cat Rental Store Program was designed to assist dealers in operating a one-stop rental shop that offered a complete line of rental equipment, from heavy bulldozers and tractors to light towers, work platforms, and hydraulic tools.[84]

Joint Ventures

Increasingly, Caterpillar had used joint ventures to expand into new markets and diversify into new products. In November 2000, Barton's Caterpillar announced a plan to form two joint ventures with DaimlerChrysler, the world's leading manufacturer of commercial vehicles. One was for building medium-duty engines, and the other was for manufacturing fuel systems. The combined share of the two companies in the medium-duty engine market was only 10%, yet the medium-duty engine market generated worldwide sales of $10 billion annually. The sales of fuel systems were even more promising. Fuel systems were designed to increase the efficiency of diesel engines and thereby reduce diesel emissions. Participating in the two joint ventures were Cat and DaimlerChrysler plants in four U.S. states (South Carolina, Georgia, Illinois, and Michigan) and at least five other countries.[85]

Future Prospects

Notwithstanding their initial prospects, Barton's strategic initiatives failed to address adequately two major concerns that could affect the company's future. One had to do with the state of labor relations, particularly Cat's Employee Satisfaction Program, which Schaefer had introduced and Fites had terminated. Implemented effectively by Schaefer, the ESP program contributed to increased labor productivity, improved product quality, enhanced employee satisfaction, and reduced employee absenteeism. Should Barton, then, reintroduce

Exhibit 8 Five-Year Financial Summary: Caterpillar (Dollar amounts in millions, except per share data)

Year Ending December 31	2000	1999	1998	1997	1996
Sales and Revenues	$20,175	$19,702	$20,977	$18,925	$16,522
Profits	1,053	946	1,513	1,665	1,361
Profits As % of Sales and Revenues	5.2%	4.8%	7.2%	8.8%	8.2%
Profits per Share	$3.04	$2.66	$4.17	$4.44	3.54
Dividends per Share	$1.345	$1.275	$1.150	$0.950	.775
Return on Equity	19.0%	17.9%	30.9%	37.9%	36.3%
R&D Expenses	$854	$814	$838	$700	$570
As % of Sales and Revenues	4.2%	4.1%	4.0%	3.7%	3.4%
Wage, Salaries & Employee Benefits	$4,029	$4,044	$4,146	$3,773	$3,437
Number of Employees	67,200	66,225	64,441	58,366	54,968
Total Assets Consolidated	$28,464	$26,711	$25,128	$20,756	$18,728
Machinery & Engines	16,554	16,158	15,619	14,188	13,066
Financial Products	14,618	12,951	11,648	7,806	6,681
Long-term Debt Consolidated	$11,334	$9,928	$9,404	$6,942	$5,087
Machinery & Engines	2,854	3,099	2,993	2,367	2,018
Financial Products	8,480	6,829	6,411	4,575	3,069
Total Debt Consolidated	$15,067	$13,802	$12,452	$8,568	$7,459
Machinery & Engines	3,427	3,317	3,102	2,474	2,176
Financial Products	11,957	10,796	9,562	6,338	5,433

Source: Caterpillar Inc., 2000 Annual Report, p. 39; Caterpillar Inc., 2001 Annual Report, p. 25.

Cat's employee satisfaction program and thereby improve the climate of labor relations at the company's U.S. plants? Would Barton be able to cooperate closely with the local union leadership to persuade shop-floor employees to join the program?

Another challenge Barton faced pertained to the impact of e-commerce. How could Caterpillar take advantage of the opportunities offered by e-commerce without undermining its distribution system? How, in other words, could Caterpillar benefit from utilizing the Internet for the marketing, distribution, and service of its products without weakening its strong dealers' networks?

Financial Position

Exhibit 8 shows selected financial information for five years (1996–2000). For complete financial statements, see www.caterpillar.com.

Notes

1. M. Arndt, "This Cat Isn't So Nimble," BusinessWeek (February 21, 2000), pp. 148+; M. Tatge, "Caterpillar's Truck-Engine Sales May Hit Some Braking," Wall Street Journal (March 13, 2000).
2. A. Gross and D. Weiss, "Industry Corner: The Global Demand for Heavy Construction Equipment," Business Economics, Vol. 31, No. 3 (July 1996), pp. 54–55.
3. Ibid., p. 54.
4. Ibid., p. 55.
5. D. Fites, "Making Your Dealers Your Partners," Harvard Business Review (March–April 1996), p. 85.
6. U. S. Rangan, "Caterpillar Tractor Co.," in C. Bartlett and S. Ghoshal, Transatlantic Management: Text, Cases, and Readings in Cross Border Management (Homewood, Illinois: Irwin, 1992), p. 296.
7. D. Fites, "Making Your Dealers Your Partners," Harvard Business Review (March–April 1996), p. 85.

8. A. Gross and D. Weiss, "Industry Corner: The Global Demand for Heavy Construction Equipment," *Business Economics*, Vol. 31, No. 3 (July 1996), p. 58.

9. W. L. Naumann, *The Story of Caterpillar Tractor Co.* (New York: The Newcomen Society, 1977), pp. 7–9.

10. "Caterpillar Inc.," *Hoover's Handbook of American Business 1999* (Austin: Hoover Business Press, 1999), p. 328; "The Story of Caterpillar," *www.caterpillar.com*.

11. M. Yoshino and U. S. Rangan, *Strategic Alliances: An Entrepreneurial Approach to Globalization* (Boston: Harvard Business School Press, 1995), p. 93; W. L. Naumann, *The Story of Caterpillar Tractor Co.* (New York: The Newcomen Society, 1977), pp. 12–14; W. Haycraft, *Yellow Power: The Story of the Earthmoving Equipment Industry* (Urbana, Illinois: University of Illinois Press, 2000), pp. 118–122, 159–167, 196–203.

12. D. Fites, "Making Your Dealers Your Partners," *Harvard Business Review* (March–April 1996), p. 94.

13. U. S. Rangan, "Caterpillar Tractor Co.," in C. Bartlett and S. Ghoshal, *Transatlantic Management: Text, Cases, and Readings in Cross Border Management* (Homewood, Illinois: Irwin, 1992), p. 304; J. Risen, "Caterpillar: A Test of U.S. Trade Policy," *Los Angeles Times* (June 8, 1986).

14. Cited in K. Deveny, "For Caterpillar, the Metamorphosis Isn't Over," *BusinessWeek* (August 31, 1987), p. 72.

15. Cited in D. Hutchins, "Caterpillar's Triple Whammy," *Fortune* (October 27, 1986), p. 9? See also R. Eckley, "Caterpillar's Ordeal: Foreign Competition in Capital Goods," *Business Horizons* (March–April 1989), pp. 81–83.

16. J. Abegglen and G. Stalk, *Kaisha, the Japanese Corporation* (New York: Basic Books, 1985), pp. 62, 117–118; M. Yoshino and U. S. Rangan, *Strategic Alliances: An Entrepreneurial Approach to Globalization* (Boston: Harvard Business School Press, 1995), pp. 94–95; "Komatsu Ltd.," *Hoover's Handbook of World Business*, 1999, p. 320.

17. M. Yoshino and U. S. Rangan, *Strategic Alliances: An Entrepreneurial Approach to Globalization* (Boston: Harvard Business School Press, 1995), p. 96.

18. *Ibid.*, p. 97; R. Eckley, "Caterpillar's Ordeal: Foreign Competition in Capital Goods," *Business Horizons* (March–April 1989), p. 84.

19. R. Eckley, "Caterpillar's Ordeal: Foreign Competition in Capital Goods," *Business Horizons* (March–April 1989), p. 84; K. Deveny, "For Caterpillar, the Metamorphosis Isn't Over," *BusinessWeek* (August 31, 1987), p. 73; M. Yoshino and U. S. Rangan, *Strategic Alliances: An Entrepreneurial Approach to Globalization* (Boston: Harvard Business School Press, 1995), p. 97.

20. R. Henkoff, "This Cat Is Acting Like a Tiger," *Fortune* (December 19, 1988), pp. 67, 72, 76; K. Deveny, "For Caterpillar, the Metamorphosis Isn't Over," *BusinessWeek* (August 31, 1987), p. 73.

21. R. Eckley, "Caterpillar's Ordeal: Foreign Competition in Capital Goods," *Business Horizons* (March–April 1989), pp. 81, 83.

22. Quoted in R. Henkoff, "This Cat Is Acting Like a Tiger," *Fortune* (December 19, 1988), p. 76.

23. *Ibid.*; R. Eckley, "Caterpillar's Ordeal: Foreign Competition in Capital Goods," *Business Horizons* (March–April 1989), p. 84; A. Kotlowitz, "Caterpillar Faces Shutdown with UAW," *Wall Street Journal* (March 5, 1986).

24. B. Bearak, "The Inside Strategy: Less Work and More Play at Cat," *Los Angeles Times* (May 16, 1995).

25. R. Henkoff, "This Cat Is Acting Like a Tiger," *Fortune* (December 19, 1988), p. 76.

26. B. Bremner, "Can Caterpillar Inch Its Way Back to Heftier Profits?" *BusinessWeek* (September 25, 1989), p. 75.

27. J. Abegglen and G. Stalk, *Kaisha, the Japanese Corporation* (New York: Basic Books, 1985), p. 118.

28. R. Henkoff, "This Cat Is Acting Like a Tiger," *Fortune* (December 19, 1988), pp. 72, 74; B. Bremner, "Can Caterpillar Inch Its Way Back to Heftier Profits?" *BusinessWeek* (September 25, 1989), p. 75.

29. K. Auguston, "Caterpillar Slashes Lead Times from Weeks to Days," *Modern Materials Handling* (February 1990), p. 49.

30. B. Dutton, "Cat Climbs High with FMS," *Manufacturing Systems* (November 1989), pp. 16–22; Cited in K. Deveny, "For Caterpillar, the Metamorphosis Isn't Over," *BusinessWeek* (August 31, 1987), p. 73; B. Bremner, "Can Caterpillar Inch Its Way Back to Heftier Profits?" *BusinessWeek* (September 25, 1989), p. 75.

31. Quoted in K. Auguston, "Caterpillar Slashes Lead Times from Weeks to Days," *Modern Materials Handling* (February 1990), p. 49.

32. *Ibid.*, pp. 50–51.

33. *Ibid.*, pp. 49, 51.

34. B. Bremner, "Can Caterpillar Inch Its Way Back to Heftier Profits?" *BusinessWeek* (September 25, 1989), p. 75.

35. M. Yoshino and U. S. Rangan, *Strategic Alliances: An Entrepreneurial Approach to Globalization* (Boston: Harvard Business School Press, 1995), p. 98.

36. J. Reingold, "CEO of the Year," *Financial World* (March 28, 1995), p. 68.

37. Quoted in "An Interview with Caterpillar Inc. Chairman and CEO Donald V. Fites," *Inter-Business Issues* (December 1992), p. 32.

38. Quoted in T. Benson, "Caterpillar Wakes Up," *Industry Week* (May 20, 1991), p. 36.

39. Quoted in J. Reingold, "CEO of the Year," *Financial World* (March 28, 1995), p. 74.

40. Quoted in K. Kelly, "Caterpillar's Don Fites: Why He Didn't Blink," *BusinessWeek* (August 10, 1992), p. 56.

41. *Ibid.*, pp. 56–57.

42. *Ibid.*, p. 57.

43. Quoted in T. Benson, "Caterpillar Wakes Up," *Industry Week* (May 20, 1991), p. 32.

44. Quoted in "An Interview with Caterpillar Inc. Chairman and CEO Donald V. Fites," *Inter-Business Issues* (December 1992), p. 32.

45. Quoted in T. Benson, "Caterpillar Wakes Up," *Industry Week* (May 20, 1991), p. 33.

46. K. Kelly, "Caterpillar's Don Fites: Why He Didn't Blink," *BusinessWeek* (August 10, 1992), p. 56.

47. J. P. Donlon, "Heavy Metal," *Chief Executive* (September 1995), p. 50.

48. A. Zadoks, "Managing Technology at Caterpillar," *Research Technology Management* (January 1997), pp. 49–51.

49. K. Kelly, "Caterpillar's Don Fites: Why He Didn't Blink," *BusinessWeek* (August 10, 1992), p. 56.

50. J. P. Donlon, "Heavy Metal," *Chief Executive* (September 1995), p. 50.

51. Quoted in T. Benson, "Caterpillar Wakes Up," *Industry Week* (May 20, 1991), p. 36.

52. D. Fites, "Making Your Dealers Your Partners," *Harvard Business Review* (March–April 1996), p. 93.

53. Caterpillar Inc., *1999 Annual Report*, p. 34.

54. D. Fites, "Making Your Dealers Your Partners," *Harvard Business Review* (March–April 1996), pp. 89, 91–92, 94.

55. *Ibid.*, pp. 92–93.

56. *Ibid.*, pp. 90, 93, 94.

57. Quoted in J. P. Donlon, "Heavy Metal," *Chief Executive* (September 1995), p. 50.

58. Quoted in D. Fites, "Making Your Dealers Your Partners," *Harvard Business Review* (March–April 1996), p. 86.

59. M. Magnet, "The Productivity Payoff Arrives," *Fortune* (June 27, 1994), pp. 82–83; T. Benson, "Caterpillar Wakes Up," *Industry Week* (May 20, 1991), p. 36; D. Fites, "Making Your Dealers Your Partners," *Harvard Business Review* (March–April 1996), pp. 88–89.

60. S. Prokesch, "Making Global Connections in Caterpillar," *Harvard Business Review* (March–April 1996), pp. 88–89; J. P. Donlon, "Heavy Metal," *Chief Executive* (September 1995), p. 50.

61. Caterpillar Inc., "Caterpillar's Growth Strategies" (1999), *www.caterpillar.com.*

62. M. Tate, "Caterpillar's Truck-Engine Sales May Hit Some Braking," *Wall Street Journal* (March 13, 2000); D. Barboza, "Aiming for Greener Pastures," *New York Times* (August 4, 1999).

63. D. Weimer, "A New Cat on the Hot Seat," *BusinessWeek* (March 9, 1998), p. 61; M. Tatge, "Caterpillar's Truck-Engine Sales May Hit Some Braking," *Wall Street Journal* (March 13, 2000).

64. D. Weimer, "A New Cat on the Hot Seat," *BusinessWeek* (March 9, 1998), p. 61; M. Tatge, "Caterpillar's Truck-Engine Sales May Hit Some Braking," *Wall Street Journal* (March 13, 2000).

65. The quotations, in order, are from J. Reingold, "CEO of the Year," *Financial World* (March 28, 1995), p. 72; and C. Quintanilla, "Caterpillar Chairman Fites to Retire," *Wall Street Journal* (October 15, 1998). Online. ABI data base.

66. Quoted in J. Reingold, "CEO of the Year," *Financial World* (March 28, 1995), p. 72.

67. "An Interview with Fites," *Inter Business Issues*, pp. 34–35; "What's Good for Caterpillar?" *Forbes* (December 7, 1992). Online. ABI data base.

68. M. Cimini, "Caterpillar's Prolonged Dispute Ends," *Compensation and Working Conditions* (Fall 1998), pp. 5–6; K. Kelly, "Cat May Be Trying to Bulldoze the Immovable," *BusinessWeek* (December 2, 1991), p. 116; "Cat vs. Labor: Hardhats, Anyone?" *BusinessWeek* (August 26, 1991), pp. 48+.

69. M. Verespej, "Bulldozing Labor Peace at Caterpillar," *Industry Week* (February 15, 1993), pp. 19+.

70. "Caterpillar: Union Bull," *Economist* (January 9, 1993), pp. 61+; M. Cimini, "Caterpillar's Prolonged Dispute Ends," *Compensation and Working Conditions* (Fall 1998), pp. 7–9.

71. M. Cimini, "Caterpillar's Prolonged Dispute Ends," *Compensation and Working Conditions* (Fall 1998), p. 9; R. Rose, "Caterpillar Contract with UAW May Be Tough to Sell to Workers," *Wall Street Journal* (February 17, 1998). Online. ABI data base; J. Reingold, "CEO of the Year," *Financial World* (March 28, 1995), p. 72.

72. M. Cimini, "Caterpillar's Prolonged Dispute Ends," *Compensation and Working Conditions* (Fall 1998), pp. 8–9.

73. *Ibid.*, pp. 9–10.

74. C. Quintanilla, "Caterpillar Touts Its Gains As UAW Battle Ends," *Wall Street Journal* (March 24, 1998); D. Johnson, "Auto Union Backs Tentative Accord with Caterpillar," *New York Times* (February 14, 1998).

75. Quoted in P. Dine, "Gulf Remains Wide in Caterpillar's Home," *St. Louis Post Dispatch* (March 29, 1998). Online. ABI data base. See also M. Cimini, "Caterpillar's Prolonged Dispute Ends," *Compensation and Working Conditions* (Fall 1998), p. 11.

76. "The Caterpillar Strike: Not Over Till It's Over," *Economist* (February 28, 1998).

77. M. Arndt, "This Cat Isn't So Nimble," *BusinessWeek* (February 21, 2000), pp. 148+.

78. *Ibid.*

79. Caterpillar Inc., "Growth Strategies," *www.caterpillar.com*, p. 2.

80. M. Tate, "Caterpillar's Truck-Engine Sales May Hit Some Braking," *Wall Street Journal* (March 13, 2000).

81. D. Barboza, "Cashing In on the World's Energy Hunger," *New York Times* (May 22, 2001).

82. *Ibid.*; "Energy Technology: Beyond the Bubble," *Economist* (April 21, 2001).

83. H. Landy, "Putting More Cats Down on the Farm," *Chicago Sun Times* (March 28, 1999).

84. M. Roth, "Seeing the Light," *Rental Equipment Register* (January 2000); N. Tait, "Cat Sharpens Claws to Pounce Again," *Financial Times* (November 8, 2000).

85. J. Hallinan, "Caterpillar, DaimlerChrysler Team Up," *Wall Street Journal* (November 23, 2000).

CASE 26

Eastman Kodak:

The Photography Segment
of the Infoimaging Industry

Jossett Trewick, Robert J. Mockler, and Marc Gartenfeld

IN HIS MESSAGE TO SHAREHOLDERS, KODAK'S CHAIRMAN AND CEO, DANIEL A. CARP, commented:

> 2001 was an extraordinary and difficult year for the nation, for the world and for nearly every business, including Kodak. The continuing worldwide slump, coupled with the events of September 11, severely impacted industries important to our business, including travel, theme parks, lodging, advertising and entertainment.[1]

In 2001, Kodak's net worldwide sales decreased by $760 million (5%). This was caused mainly by a decline in photography sales of $828 million (8%). In spite of the sluggish U.S. economy, which had affected photography sales both in the United States and worldwide, the company was poised for growth in Digital and Applied Imaging Technology. However, competition was strong, and competitors were working relentlessly to capture market share in this area. In light of this, Carp and his management team needed to develop an effective strategy if Kodak was to survive and prosper against aggressive competition over the intermediate and long-term futures.

Kodak was traditionally known for its quality products in photography. However, over the years, Kodak had been continuously innovating new products and making acquisitions and strategic alliances throughout the world so as to maintain its market leadership in key segments of its business. In an effort to keep its products competitive in the world market, Kodak had integrated technology in many of its product offerings. The company was not just about pho-

Exhibit 1
Stock Price
History: Eastman
Kodak Company

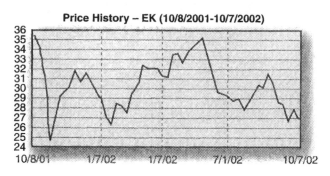

Price History – EK (10/8/2001-10/7/2002)

Source: Adapted from Moneycentral.com, http://moneycentral.msn.com/investor/charts/chartdl.asp?Symbol=ek (2002).

tography; rather, it described itself as an infoimaging company. Its strategic focus was to drive the convergence of images and information beyond traditional boundaries and into new image applications and business opportunities, a major move to create a new kind of company. According to an analyst at MSN's Moneycentral.com, Eastman Kodak Company, a large-cap value company in the consumer nondurables sector, was expected to underperform the market over the coming six months.[2] As shown in **Exhibit 1**, the company's stock received a rating of 5 (out of 10) and had a 52-week high of $35.65 and a 52-week low of $24.40. As of October 11, 2001, Zacks Investment Research recommended a strong sell for the company's stock.[3]

The U.S. economic conditions throughout the year 2001 and the events of September 11 adversely impacted Kodak's sales, particularly in the consumer film product groups within the photography segment. The decrease in photography sales was driven by declines in consumer, entertainment origination, and professional film products as well as consumer and professional color paper and consumer and professional digital cameras. The company's gross profit declined 19%, with margins declining 5.7 percentage points, from 40.2% in 2000 to 34.5%, in 2001. The decline in margin was driven primarily by lower prices across many of the company's traditional and digital product groups within the photography segment and a decline in the margin in the health imaging segment. This was caused by declining prices and the negative impact of exchange rates.[4]

As shown in **Exhibit 2**, analysts expected the earnings growth rate for the industry over the next five years to exceed 20%. However, Standard & Poor's (S&P) projected this growth rate to be less than 10%.[5] The S&P outlook on the photographic products industry was, however, generally negative. This was based on the economic downturn, terrorism threats, and massive layoffs at some of the world's largest companies. With less money to spend, consumers were hesitant to purchase travel and leisure products. Product distribution channels in the industry were constrained, due to Kmart's recent bankruptcy filing, and retailers' ordering patterns were conservative. During 2001, the industry index slumped 27.5% against an 11.8% drop for the S&P 500.[6] U.S. industry film sales declined steadily through the first three quarters of 2001, but at a slower rate in the fourth quarter.

Exhibit 2
Earnings Growth
Rates (2002–2007)

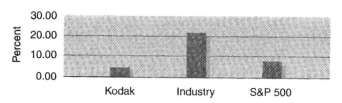

Source: Adapted from Moneycentral.com, http://moneycentral.msn.com/investor/invsub/analyst/earnest.asp?Page=EarningsGrowthRates&Symbol=ek (2002).

The industry faced opportunities and threats from digital imaging versus traditional silver-halide photography. Although the photography industry was mature, the introduction of digital and applied technology applications had changed the shape of the industry. The photography industry had a new way of describing itself. This industry, shaped by various technological developments, was now characterized as the infoimaging industry. Although traditional film would remain important for some time, digital imaging was clearly the way of the future. Demand for digital cameras was strong as they became less expensive, offered higher quality, and became much easier to use. This showed great growth potential for the industry. However, competition would be intense, as companies pumped huge investments into research and development to improve their technology in digital imaging. This would make profitability challenging in the near future.[7]

With the growing importance of digital imaging, competition within the industry was intense. Kodak was faced with lower sales, declining profit margins, pricing pressures, and low investor confidence. Only companies that were able to innovatively convert R&D efforts into profits would be able to survive and prosper. In light of these problems, Kodak's Daniel Carp had some tough decisions to make in such areas as extending the product life of film products and leveraging the company's R&D efforts into digital technology so as to increase global revenues and profits. The main question to be resolved, however, was how to differentiate Kodak from its competition and so achieve a winning edge over competitors within intensely competitive, rapidly changing immediate, intermediate, and long-term time frames.

History of Eastman Kodak

Over a century ago, in 1880, George Eastman began the commercial manufacture of dry plates. Back then, the young company was known as the Eastman Dry Plate Company. It was out of this venture that the Kodak camera had been developed. In 1883, Eastman startled the trade with the announcement of film in rolls, with the roll holder adaptable to nearly every plate camera on the market. With the Kodak camera in 1888, he made photography available to everyone. Since 2000, the company has redefined itself to capitalize on the tremendous opportunities in the marketplace as the transformation of a fairly well-defined and narrowly defined industry called photography moved into the infoimaging space. In late 2002, Kodak ranked as a premier multinational corporation and one of the 25 largest companies in the United States.

Kodak's historical strengths in image and materials science had put the company in the forefront within its industry. The company was definitely a market leader in many aspects. Through R&D, it had been able to continuously provide the market with new product innovations. The Kodak brand was known worldwide, and the company's aim was to leverage a brand that was second to none. Market penetration was extensive, with products bearing the company's name on almost every continent. In 2001, the company maintained a leading market share in the U.S. consumer film business and increased it slightly worldwide. Net worldwide sales in 2001 were $13,234 million, with more than 50% of net sales outside the United States. This market accounted for $6,775 million, while sales within the United States accounted for $6,459 million.[8] The company had consistently produced high-quality products and services, which had enabled it to stay at the top of its industry for a very long time. It continued to invest in R&D as a critical path to its future success in delivering innovative, customer-focused imaging products, systems, and services.

The continuing economic slump triggered by the September 11, 2001, terrorist attacks adversely affected Kodak's sales in industries important to its business. This included travel, theme parks, lodging, advertising, and entertainment. Although the company was still making profits and returning dividends to its shareholders, its sales from 2000 to 2001 decreased by 5%. This was attributed to a decline in sales in the consumer film product groups within the photography segment. The decrease in photography sales was driven by declines in consumer, entertainment origination, and professional film products; consumer and professional color paper; photofinishing revenues; and consumer and professional digital cameras. In addition, threat of strikes in the entertainment industry advanced most production schedules into the first half of the year, creating a slower demand during the second half. Also, film sales for television commercials were impacted as advertisers reduced their spending due to the economy and the aftermath of September 11.

Although the traditional film business was still healthy, the company did realize that some digital substitution was happening. The film and photo imaging segment of the company wasn't the only business affected by the economy; the health imaging business suffered pricing pressures and operating issues that led to margin declines. Despite the decline in sales, the company made some internal changes to offset the impact on profits. It reduced worldwide employment by 9% and inventories by 34%. It also reduced receivables and continued to restrain on capital expenditures. These efforts contributed to a strengthened cash position. **Exhibit 3** shows Kodak's business groups and units.

Services

Kodak provided services in three different categories: photography, commercial, and components. The photography group was the largest business unit in the company. It captured net worldwide sales of $9.43 million in 2001 and $10.23 million in 2000. The health imaging business group, the second largest in the company, offered digital equipment and devices used in health care facilities around the world. Sales of health imaging devices in emerging markets increased slightly in 2001.[9]

Photography Group

The photography group combined traditional and digital photography with photographic services in all its forms. Kodak's U.S. film sales declined steadily through the first three quarters of 2001 but at a slower rate in the fourth quarter.[10] This group consisted of three subgroups: Consumer Imaging, Digital and Applied Imaging, and Kodak Professional. Kodak's Consumer Imaging and Digital and Applied Imaging groups provided a host of services. Improved photofinishing services, such as online processing, APM kiosks, Digital Express stores, Kodak PhotoNet online, Kodak Picture, and photo CDs, as well as joint ventures with AOL's "You've Got Pictures" and the Kodak Picture Center Online at CVS.com helped to create a market presence globally for digital picture processing. Having the presence and expertise in helping customers print, share, and archive pictures were among the biggest factors contributing to customer satisfaction and loyalty. The Kodak professional group was geared toward the needs of professional photographers who relied on photographic devices and other peripherals to drive their businesses. Product knowledge and functionality were very important in determining which camera to use to get the best effect on portraits and pictures. This group was reported to be among the fastest growing in terms of adapting to digital cameras.

Commercial Group

The commercial group derived revenues from microfilm equipment and media, printers, scanners, other business equipment, and media sold to commercial and government customers, as well as from graphics film products sold to the Kodak Polychrome Graphics joint venture. Since 1997, Kodak had become the market leader in document scanning and preservation, building on its heritage of microfilm. The commercial group consisted of Document Imaging, Commercial and Government Systems, Graphics, and Wide-Format Inkjet.

Exhibit 3 Business Groups and Units: Eastman Kodak Company

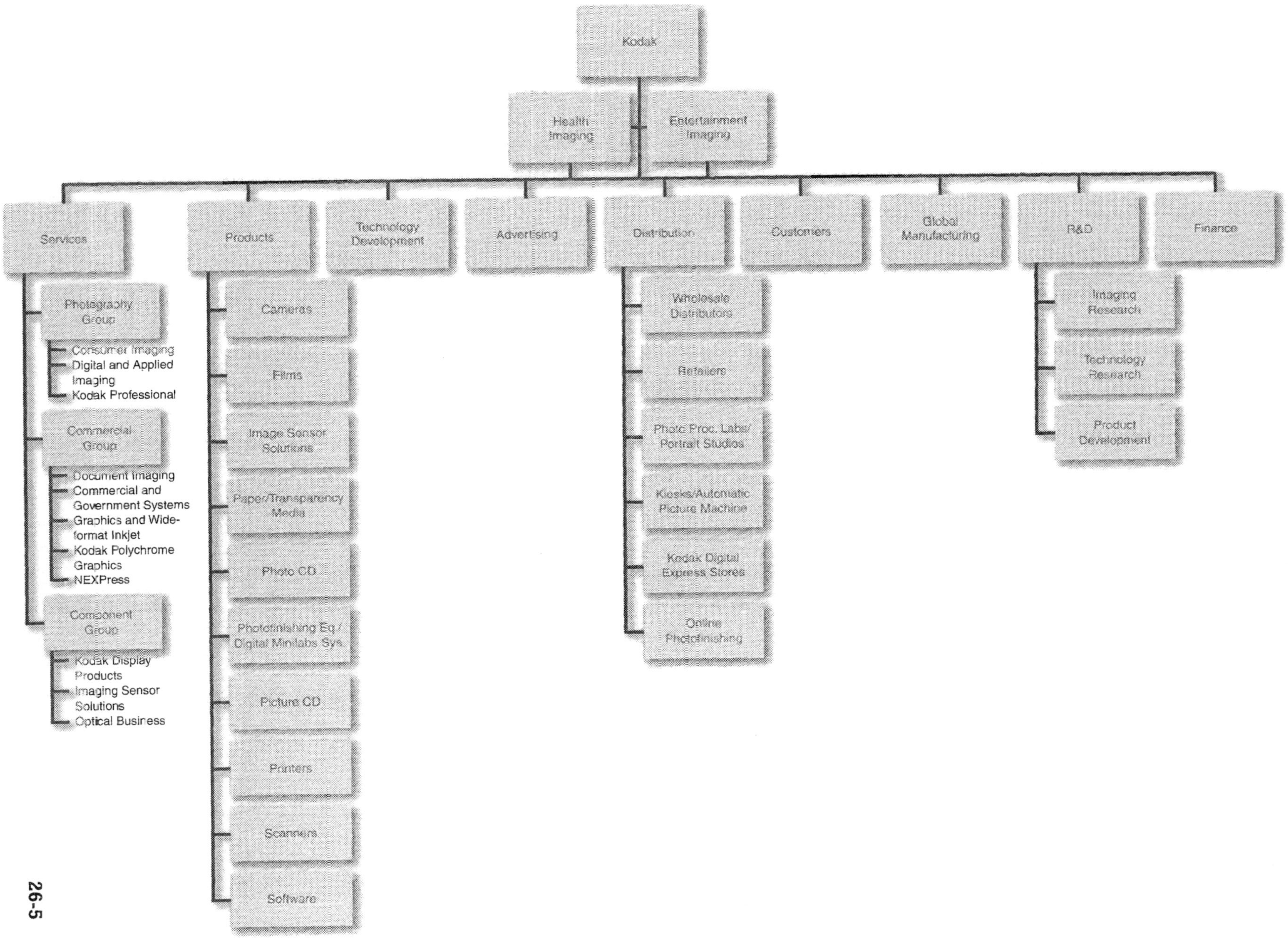

Kodak
- Entertainment Imaging
- Health Imaging
- Finance
- R&D
  - Imaging Research
  - Technology Research
  - Product Development
- Global Manufacturing
- Customers
- Distribution
  - Wholesale Distributors
  - Retailers
  - Photo Proc. Labs/Portrait Studios
  - Kiosks/Automatic Picture Machine
  - Kodak Digital Express Stores
  - Online Photofinishing
- Advertising
- Technology Development
- Products
  - Cameras
  - Films
  - Image Sensor Solutions
  - Paper/Transparency Media
  - Photo CD
  - Photofinishing Eq./Digital Minilabs Sys.
  - Picture CD
  - Printers
  - Scanners
  - Software
- Services
  - Photography Group
    - Consumer Imaging
    - Digital and Applied Imaging
    - Kodak Professional
  - Commercial Group
    - Document Imaging
    - Commercial and Government Systems
    - Graphics and Wide-format Inkjet
    - Kodak Polychrome Graphics
    - NEXPress
  - Component Group
    - Kodak Display Products
    - Imaging Sensor Solutions
    - Optical Business

Included in the group were two joint venture operations, Kodak Polychrome Graphics and NexPress. The Wide-Format Inkjet business had been consolidated into its acquisition of ENCAD, Inc.

Components Group

The components group derived revenues from the sale of OLED displays, imaging sensor solutions, and optical products to other manufacturers. The group included other businesses, such as Kodak's Display Products, Image Sensor Solutions, and the Optical business. These businesses would spearhead the company's diversification into high-growth product areas consistent with its historical strengths in image and materials science.

Products

Kodak offered various products that supported its businesses, which included cameras, digital minilabs systems, films, image sensor solutions, paper/transparency media, photo CDs, photofinishing equipment, Picture CD, printers, scanners, and software.

Cameras

Kodak manufactured a wide range of Point-and-Shoot Film cameras in addition to digital cameras for the consumer market and for professional photographers. Kodak consumer Point-and-Shoot film cameras were the Kodak Advantix, 35mm, One-Time-Use, and more. The company also made digital Point-and-Shoot cameras and accessories for consumers and professional photographers. Its newest line of digital cameras, EasyShare systems, had been doing very well on the market since its introduction in 2002. This new EasyShare line provided the industry's broadest number of integrated printing options, allowing consumers simplicity in transferring images from a camera to a computer at the touch of a button. Customers might choose to upload to either the EasyShare print service or another retail online photofinisher of choice, or at a retail store by using Kodak digitally enabled kiosks or over-the-counter. The new EasyShare software simplified how picture-takers printed, e-mailed, edited, and organized their digital pictures. The software's "One Touch to Better Pictures" feature, combined with premium Kodak inkjet paper, delivered hassle-free, stunning prints from any inkjet printer. For printing online, the software connected seamlessly to the Kodak EasyShare print service or any other online photofinisher, reflecting Kodak's commitment to consumer choice, open systems, and services.

The 2-megapixel Kodak EasyShare CX4230 Zoom Digital camera was the first EasyShare camera with a "share" button that allowed users to tag pictures for printing, e-mailing, or as favorites right on the camera's preview screen. When the camera was docked and images were transferred, the Kodak EasyShare software automatically opened the print screen for printing at home or online. It also had on-camera e-mail tagging and stored up to 32 e-mail addresses directly in the software. Users simply tagged an image for e-mailing and selected an address. This was the only camera in the world that automatically rotated pictures on the camera so pictures taken vertically appeared correctly. The CX4230 and all current Kodak EasyShare cameras were compatible with the improved Kodak EasyShare camera dock, which allowed consumers to upload digital images at the touch of a button and benefited from enhanced battery charging.[11]

Films

One of Kodak's core competencies was film and film accessories. The company manufactured films for various uses; the most notable were consumer films for cameras. In addition to consumer films, Kodak manufactured other kinds of film, including but not limited to aerial films, dental x-ray films, radiographic films for hospitals, motion picture films, mammography films, overhead transparency films, professional black-and-white films, and color negative films.

Image Sensor Solutions

Kodak manufactured image sensors for a number of different product categories, including digital cameras, scanners, medical and scientific equipment, and other applications. Sensors ranged from full-frame/low-noise, high-sensitivity imagers with resolutions up to 16 million pixels; to interline–progressive-scan sensors with electronic shutters for real-time imaging; to CMOS (camera-on-a-chip sensors), which offered a cost-effective, high-volume alternative to high-performance CCDs. Applications included consumer still cameras, video cameras, PC and videoconferencing, cell phones, etc.

Paper/Transparency Media

Kodak offered consumer photographic paper for printing color as well as black-and-white negatives. It also manufactured fast-graded paper for commercial, industrial, press, and professional use, in addition to desktop publishing hardware, software, and media. Kodak also manufactured overhead transparency films and papers for ultrasound recording.

Photo CD

This remarkable format combined the best of 35mm film imaging and digital technology, so consumers could show pictures on a television screen. Images could be transferred to a photo CD disc from newly developed 35mm film, older 35mm negatives that had already been used for conventional prints, and 35mm slides.

Photofinishing Equipment/Digital Minilabs Systems

Kodak DLS software supported a variety of digital minilab systems by a number of leading manufacturers that shared its high quality and performance standards. The easy-to-use system featured Kodak DLS LA software, which offered flexibility to input images from virtually any source. Designed for maximum efficiency, it increased order throughput and digital output. Its high-resolution, high-speed film scanner used proprietary Kodak technology to read and automatically correct images from most popular film types.

Picture CD

With Kodak Picture CD, consumers could easily turn film into pictures they could e-mail. Customers had the option to have film processed and printed on photographic paper in addition to having the images stored on a CD. Customers received their prints and negatives as usual—plus a CD that contained pictures along with software that allowed them to view, enhance, share, and print pictures from their computers.

Printers

Kodak offered desktop inkjet printers that were manufactured by Lexmark. It also manufactured film printers, high-speed digital paper printers, medical laser printers, microfilm printers, and thermal printers.

Scanners

Kodak scanners included document scanners, personal scanners, and rapid film scanners.

Software

The company offered various imaging software, including color image management systems; desktop publishing hardware, software, and media; a film-based management retrieval system; and document retrieval software.

In the face of intense industry competition, any delay in the development, production, or marketing of a new product could decrease the advantage Kodak might have had to be the first or among the first to market. The process of developing new products and services was complex and often uncertain due to the frequent introduction of new products that offered improved performance and pricing. Kodak's ability to successfully transition products and deploy new products required that Kodak made accurate predictions of the product development schedule as well as volumes, product mix, customer demand, and configuration. Also, Kodak stood at risk when anticipating demand and perceived market acceptance that might have differed from the product's realizable customer demand and revenue stream. Kodak's failure to carry out a product rollout in the time frame anticipated and in the quantities appropriate to customer demand could adversely affect the future demand for its products and services and have an adverse effect on its business.

Technology Developments

Through the efforts of its scientists and engineers, Kodak had consistently been among the top 10 U.S.-based companies for patents issued. In 2001, some breakthroughs included a revolutionary new way to double the image-amplifying ability of silver-halide film. The company called it "two-electron sensitization." Kodak also developed MEMS (micro-electro-mechanical systems) technology to produce smaller ink droplets for higher-quality color inkjet printing.

In 2001, Kodak and Sanyo Electric Co., Ltd., formed a global business venture to manufacture OLED displays for consumer devices and portable entertainment machines. Kodak owned the key patents to this technology. In late 2002, Kodak held more than 50 OLED patents. This new full-color display required no backlighting—unlike LCD displays. Therefore, new OLED displays were flatter and lighter than comparably sized LCD displays. They also consumed much less energy. OLED technology was being used in the manufacturing of flat-panel displays in digital cameras and personal handheld devices (PDAs and cell phones). OLED also offered an unlimited viewing angle, faster response, a brighter display, a high-contrast picture, and a wide operating-temperature range. Also in 2001, Kodak introduced Kodak EasyShare digital cameras with docking stations. This product truly reflected the company's motto, "You Press the Button, We Do the Rest." Since its launch in May 2002, sales of the EasyShare digital cameras had been doing well. This award-winning system set a new standard for ease-of-use in digital photography. The camera came with software, a docking station, and more, but what set it apart from other cameras was the EasyShare's one-touch simplicity.

Advertising

Kodak used a combination of print, television, and sponsorship events to promote its brand. In June 2002, the company released new television and print ads to support its premium consumer products and services. The ads were designed to inform consumers about more and better ways to take and share pictures and build off the successful, highly acclaimed "Share Moments. Share Life" campaign, which was designed to continually strengthen the Kodak brand and communicate powerful, emotional messages about the benefits of Kodak products and services. In addition to the new television ads, the national print campaign was to be expanded in 2003 to include Kodak Picture Maker, Kodak Max Versatility Plus film, Kodak processing, and Kodak Picture CD.

Distribution

Kodak distributed its products through wholesale distributors, retailers, photo processing labs, kiosks, Kodak Digital Express stores, and its web site.

Wholesale Distributors

The company used a network of global distributors to market its products worldwide. Costco, a nationwide wholesale club, was among Kodak's list of customers. Costco sold Kodak's films and cameras and had co-branded online services with Kodak. Kodak acquired Spector Photo Group's wholesale photofinishing and distribution activities in France, Germany, and Austria, and ColourCare Limited's wholesale processing and printing operations in the United Kingdom. The company believed that these acquisitions would facilitate its strategy to enhance photofinishing activities, provide access to a broader base of customers, create new service efficiencies, and provide consumers with technologically advanced digital imaging services.

Retailers

Kodak's consumer imaging products, devices, and films were sold at pharmacies, convenience stores, and photo studios. Kmart, CVS, and Rite-Aid were among the retail chains/pharmacies Kodak conducted business with.

Photo Processing Labs/Portrait Studios

Kodak films were used and sold in many photo processing labs worldwide. Photo labs provided an excellent source for all photographic needs. Professional photographers provided product knowledge, use, and functions of devices, and they took portraits. Consumers could customize orders and add special effects, different sizes, and color to their photos.

Kiosks/Automatic Picture Machines

Kodak Picture Maker digital station kiosks were located in high-traffic areas so that consumers could make high-quality photographs from digital cameras, CDs, or floppy disks. A consumer could simply go to a kiosk, insert a memory card or disk, and use a touch screen monitor to crop, adjust color of, and enhance pictures, then make photo-quality 4 × 6-inch prints on the spot.

Kodak Digital Express Stores

The company was strengthening its position in the digital camera business with the introduction of Kodak Digital Express stores. Kodak, through its extensive distribution network, operated more than 14,000 Kodak Express photo stores in greater Asia, including China. In addition, it launched a new concept called Photoshops in India. The company was exploring various digital market opportunities in the hope of stemming competition from other computer and audiovisual firms. The company had also begun a new marketing strategy with an innovative web site that allowed customers to order personalized digital photos online. The Kodak Digital Express store and the web site worked in tandem. Kodak Digital Express labs could sell not only traditional film and cameras but also digital-related products and mobile phones.

Online Photofinishing

On June 4, 2001, the company completed its acquisition of Emeryville, California-based, Ofoto, Inc., a leading online photography service. It was hoped that the acquisition of Ofoto would accelerate Kodak's growth in the online photography market and help drive more rapid adoption of digital and online services. Similarly, Kodak customized and co-branded online services with key retailers and wholesalers such as Kmart, CVS, Costco, and Rite-Aid. Ofoto offered digital processing of digital images and traditional film; top-quality prints; private online image storage and sharing; editing and creative tools; frames; cards; and other merchandise. Ofoto would operate as a wholly owned subsidiary of Kodak. It would serve as a critical connection between Kodak's film scanning and uploading services and Kodak's output capabilities through labs operated by its Qualex Inc. subsidiary. In addition to continued growth in digital printing services through Ofoto, Kodak foresaw the launch of services from its Phogenix joint venture helping to drive even greater popularity for printing digital photo files. These capabilities would give customers and consumers unlimited flexibility in storing, sharing, enhancing, and printing pictures.

Customers

Kodak's customers included regular consumers, professional photographers, retail outlets, wholesale distributors, commercial customers, the health industry, and the entertainment/film industry.

Consumer purchases of film and photographic devices accounted for a majority of Kodak's sales. However, increased competition had been driven somewhat by consumers' conservative spending behaviors during times of economic weakness. Consumers had passed over branded products to buy private-label products. Failure to successfully manage the consumers' return to branded products if and when the economic conditions improved could adversely impact Kodak's revenue and growth rate. In the consumer retail environment, there was a movement from small, individually owned retailers to larger and better-known mass merchants. In the commercial environment, there was a continuing consolidation of various group-purchasing organizations. The resellers and distributors might elect to use suppliers other than Kodak. Professional photographers as well as those in the entertainment/film industry relied on Kodak's products because of their reliability and quality. On the health and commercial side, aggressive pricing tactics intensified during the contract negotiations as competitors were vying for customers and market share domestically.

Global Manufacturing

The company had manufacturing operations in Canada, Mexico, Brazil, the United Kingdom, France, Germany, Australia, and the United States. Kodak products were marketed by subsidiary companies to people in more than 150 countries. The company's failure to successfully manage operational performance factors could delay or curtail planned improvements in manufacturing productivity. Delays in Kodak's planned improvement in manufacturing productivity could negatively impact the gross margins of the company. A continued weak economy could result in lower volumes in the factory than planned, which would negatively impact the gross margins of the company. If Kodak was unable to successfully negotiate raw materials costs with its suppliers or incurred adverse pricing on certain of its commodity-based raw materials, reduction in the gross margins could occur.

Research and Development

Kodak was constantly seeking and finding new ideas and better solutions to improve its products. Its R&D efforts were a major factor in its global success. Kodak researched and developed electronic imaging hardware and media, as well as new techniques for exploiting the versatile characteristics of silver halide–based systems and products that bridged both realms. The company's R&D efforts spanned a broad spectrum. In late 2002, the company was placing great emphasis on digital science and technologies such as OLED, image sensors, and invisible watermarking. Behind all Kodak products was its wealth of expertise in—and its deep commitment to—R&D in imaging science and technology. Kodak employed more than 5,000 engineers and scientists, including more than 600 Ph.D.s. It had R&D laboratories in the United States, United Kingdom, France, Japan, China, and Australia. Kodak's R&D's core competencies included: image science; silver halide imaging materials; non-silver imaging materials; precision thin-film coating and finishing; optomechatronics; imaging electronics; imaging solutions; solid-state sensors; image processing; and space imaging systems. Although most people associated Kodak with photographic film and paper—two of its flagship product categories—it was also a leader in digital and hybrid imaging technologies. Its three primary R&D areas were imaging research, technology research, and product development.

Imaging Research

Imaging science involved the effort to analyze, understand, model, simulate, and optimize all aspects of imaging media and imaging systems. This encompassed all methods that induced or emulated a visual response in a human observer. Kodak R&D had more than a century of experience in imaging science, yielding an extraordinarily large body of knowledge.

Technology Research

Kodak researched practical applications of technology that could reach beyond imaging. This *base-building* research covered areas such as chemistry, photographic media, electronic sensors, image communications, inkjet printing, scanning technologies, display technologies, and wireless networks.

Product Development

Kodak's strength in R&D was in the development of innovative products. In product development, the company translated the intellectual property obtained through its imaging and technology research efforts (together with communities of practices established within

R&D) into new imaging products and/or services. Kodak's R&D efforts encompassed design and usability, future product concept development, and manufacturing process development. R&D expenses decreased by $5 million from $784 million in 2000 to $779 million in 2001.

Financial Position

As part of Kodak's strategy to sharpen its focus on growth areas that were key to its survival in the photo and imaging industry, Kodak pursued aggressive cost reduction programs, which produced a strong balance sheet and a healthy dividend payout in 2001. Kodak's strategies included a number of initiatives to improve operating efficiencies throughout the company. These included charges of $830 million related to the restructuring programs implemented in 2001 as well as a restructuring charge of $350 million related to worldwide manufacturing and photofinishing consolidation in 1999. Restructuring charges were primarily for the rationalization of the U.S. photofinishing operations, the elimination of excess capacity, the exit of certain operations, and reductions in R&D positions and selling and general administrative positions worldwide. Additionally, during 2001, the company recorded asset impairments relating to the Wolf Camera bankruptcy, Kmart bankruptcy, and relocation costs in connection with a closed manufacturing site in addition to investments in strategic and nonstrategic ventures.

From a liquidity and capital resource perspective, the company expected to generate $46 billion in cash flow after dividends by 2007, with approximately $400 million of this being achieved in 2002. This would enable the company to maintain its dividend, pay down debt, and make acquisitions that promoted profitable growth. In 2002, the company expected to reduce its capital spending, excluding acquisitions and equipment purchased for lease, to a range of $550 million to $600 million. Kodak expected to fund expenditures for capital requirements, dividend payments, and liquidity needs from cash generated from operations. Cash balances and financing arrangements would be used to bridge timing differences between expenditures and cash generated from operations. As shown in **Exhibit 4**, earnings from operations in 2001 took a sharp decline by 84% from the prior year, as did net earnings, which declined by 95% in 2001. However, earnings from operations for the nine months ended September 30, 2002, were $1.009 billion as compared with $614 million for the nine months ended September 30, 2001, representing an increase of $395 million, or 64%. The increase in earnings from operations was primarily the result of $506 million of restructuring costs, other nonrecurring items, costs associated with the exit of an equipment manufacturing facility in the first nine months of 2001, and lower overall spending. **Exhibit 5** shows Kodak's financial information. See Kodak's *2001 Annual Report* for complete financial statements at *www.kodak.com*.

Kodak's photography segment's net sales were $1.051 billion within the United States and $1.358 billion outside the United States for the third quarter of 2002, representing 31%

Exhibit 4
2001 Earnings Report: Eastman Kodak (Dollar amounts in millions, except per share data)

	2001	Change	2000	Change	1999
Net sales	$13,234	–5%	$13,994	–1%	$14,089
Earnings from operations	345	–84%	2,214	+11%	1,990
Net earnings	76	–95%	1,407	+1%	1,392
Basic earnings per share	.26	–94%	4.62	+5%	4.38
Diluted earnings per share	.26	–94%	4.59	+6%	4.33

Source: Adapted from Kodak, Annual Report *(2001).*

Exhibit 5   Company's Financial Information: Eastman Kodak Company (Dollar amounts in millions)

1. Balance Sheet

	2001	2000	1999	1998	1997	1996	1995
Cash	$ 448	$ 251	$ 393	$ 500	$ 728	$1,796	$1,811
Current Assets	4,683	5,491	5,444	5,599	5,475	6,965	7,309
Total Assets	13,362	14,212	14,370	14,733	13,145	14,438	14,477
Current Liabilities	5,354	6,215	5,769	6,178	5,177	5,417	4,643
Long Term Debt	1,666	1,166	—	504	585	559	665
Common Equity	2,894	3,428	3,912	3,988	3,161	4,734	5,121
Total Capital	4,560	4,655	3,971	1,108	3,746	5,395	5,812
Capital Expenditures	743	945	1,127	4,561	1,485	1,341	1,034
Cash Flow	$ 995	$2,296	$2,310	$2,243	$ 833	$1,914	$2,168

2. Other Financial Information

	2001	2000	1999	1998	1997	1996	1995
Current Ratio (%)	0.9	0.9	0.9	0.9	1.1	1.3	1.6
Long Term Debt/Capitalization (%)	36.5	25.0	Nil	11.1	15.6	10.4	11.5
Net Income of Revenues (%)	0.6	10.1	9.9	10.4	0.0	6.4	8.4
Return on Assets (%)	0.6	9.8	9.6	10.0	0.0	7.0	8.5
Return on Equity (%)	2.4	38.3	35.2	38.9	0.1	20.6	27.4

3. Per Share Data

	2001	2000	1999	1998	1997	1996	1995
Tangible Book Value	6.71	8.56	9.45	8.54	8.09	12.51	13.25
Cash Flow	3.42	7.48	7.19	6.84	2.51	5.68	6.34
Earnings	0.26	4.59	4.33	4.24	0.01	3.00	3.67
Dividends	1.77	1.76	1.76	1.76	1.76	1.60	1.60
Payout Ratio (%)	NM	38%	41%	42%	NM	53%	44%
Prices: High	49.95	67.50	80.37	88.93	94.75	85.00	70.37
Prices: Low	24.40	35.31	56.62	57.93	53.31	65.12	47.12
P/E Ratio: High (%)	NM	15	19	21	NM	28	19
P/E Ratio: Low (%)	NM	8	13	14	NM	22	13

4. Income Statement Analysis

	2001	2000	1999	1998	1997	1996	1995
Revenues	$13,234	$13,994	$14,089	$13,406	$14,538	$15,967	$14,980
Operating Income	1,923	3,103	2,908	2,783	2,431	3,107	2,841
Depreciation	919	889	918	853	828	903	916
Interest Expense	219	178	142	110	98	83	78
Pretax Income	97	2,132	2,109	2,106	53.0	1,556	1,926
Effective Tax Rate (%)	33%	34%	34%	34%	34%	35%	35%
Net Income	$ 76.0	$ 1,407	$ 1,392	$ 1,390	$ 5.0	$ 1,011	$ 1,252

Source: S&P, "Industry Surveys," www.standardandpoors.com (2002).

and 40% of total net sales, respectively. Net worldwide sales of consumer film products for the same period, including 35mm film, Advantix film, and one-time-use cameras, decreased slightly, while net sales from the company's consumer digital products and services, which included Picture Maker kiosks/media and consumer digital services revenue from Picture CD, "You've Got Pictures," and Retail.com, remained essentially unchanged in the third quarter of 2002 as compared with the third quarter of 2001.[12]

However, net worldwide consolidated sales were $3.354 billion for the third quarter of 2002 as compared with $3.308 billion for the third quarter of 2001. For the third quarter of 2002, the company's gross profit was $1.288 billion, an increase of $156 million, or 14%. The increase was primarily attributed to improved manufacturing productivity/cost, which increased gross profit margins by approximately 4.5 percentage points due to increased volumes, reduced labor expense, favorable materials pricing, and improved product yields. Other contributing factors resulting in this increase were the costs incurred in the prior-year quarter in connection with the company's restructuring programs, which negatively impacted third quarter 2001 gross profit margins by approximately 1.8 points. These increases were partially offset by product shifts, primarily in the Photography segment, which reduced gross profit margins by approximately 2 percentage points.[13]

Analysts continued to downgrade Kodak's stock due to the company's sluggish performance. The stock was rated high risk and was a strong sell in late 2002. Since 1999, the stock had gone from a high of $80 to a low of $24, while return on equity had plummeted to 2.4 from 35.2 three years before. Cash flow had consistently been decreasing, and so had the capital outlay of the company. Declining revenues and decreased earnings per share had investors worried about the future of the company.

To renew investor confidence and return the company to greater profitability, Kodak's management team had to implement a winning strategy to differentiate itself from competitors so as to survive in this competitive market.

Strategy

In response to the challenges he faced, Kodak's CEO Daniel Carp had begun to implement strategic initiatives that would make the company stronger, more flexible, and more efficient. These initiatives were designed to enhance Kodak's position in key product categories and geographic markets as well as drive revenue growth and realize significant cost savings.

The company's business model had changed significantly since 1997, when Daniel Carp became CEO. Back then, the company had primarily been a product company that sold film, cameras, and x-ray film. Kodak had begun moving away from the heavily capital-intensive company it had been into an era that revolved more around systems. Instead of building new film machines and new material plants, the company was investing in the development of various systems, such as Kodak Perfect Touch, part of the photofinishing systems, the medical laser imaging systems, and the EasyShare systems.

Although 2001 had been a challenging year for the company, Kodak was bent on remaining focused on strengthening its value as an investment and also on maintaining market share in key segments of its business. It was poised for future growth and had made several initiatives to ride the wave of the newest technology in the industry—digital imaging. Digital imaging was changing the way Kodak operated in almost every aspect of its business. As such, management wanted to explore the opportunities available in the digital arena. Currently, many of Kodak's products were being digitized in some way or another, either through Kodak's own product development or through acquisitions. Due to the changing nature of the company, Kodak's key strategy was to manage the transition from photography to infoimaging and change the company in terms of its operating model to ensure that significant investments were made in cash-generating areas of the business.

On September 18, 2002, the company addressed investors at Kodak's 2002 Institutional Investor Meeting. At this meeting the company assured investors that it would continue to build on its long-term business strategy as the economy strengthened. It would continue to invest in R&D as a critical path to its future success and deliver innovative, customer-focused imaging products, systems, and services. In addition, management would work to maintain or increase share positions in all its businesses and pay close attention to costs and managing the business for maximum cash. The company hoped to generate at least $6 billion in cash over the next six years. The company did not expect any real upturns in the economy until 2003, but it expected that the balance of 2002 would reflect some of the cost-cutting efforts and operational improvements it had made in 2001. It also anticipated a gradual return to consumer spending habits and behavior that would positively affect its business growth.

Beginning in the fourth quarter of 2001, the company changed its operating structure, which had previously been composed of seven business units, to be centered around strategic product groups. The strategic product groups from existing businesses and geographies were integrated into segments that shared common technology, manufacturing and product platforms, and customer sets. The company believed this new alignment would reduce complexity, provide key managers with more decision-making authority, and enable business groups and product managers to concentrate on processes and decisions that had the greatest influence on generating profitable growth. These initiatives and others were expected to allow the company to sharpen its focus on the customers and markets it served by restructuring into specific business groups. Kodak's business units and groups included three business groups, two business units, global manufacturing, R&D, and the Kodak ventures group.

As a result of the decision to refocus Kodak based on strategic product groups, three strategic actions were:

- Continued investment in fundamental research and development
- Strategic acquisitions that would position the company going forward
- Disposition of manufacturing facilities and business segments that no longer fit the company profile

As part of its ongoing process to streamline the company's operations worldwide by improving operating efficiencies and asset utilization, Kodak implemented several cost-saving programs to maximize cash flow and enhance profitability. To achieve the target of cost reductions, the plan involved:

- Reducing headcount
- Streamlining the organization
- Reducing inventories
- Reducing receivables and tightly restraining capital expenditures

While its revenue and earnings were down in 2001, Kodak strengthened its balance sheet by implementing aggressive cost-reduction programs. Sales had been impacted by the slowdown of the economy. As a result, Kodak reduced its cost base and increased its focus on cash generation. Worldwide employment was reduced by about 9%. Kodak also reduced inventories by 34%, or $581 million. Receivables were also reduced as the company continued to tighten up on capital expenditure.[14] Daniel Carp thought these and other initiatives had to be implemented so that Kodak would be better positioned in its industry.

Looking Toward the Future

Although the company experienced a tumultuous year in 2001, it was still able to project decent profits in its consolidated statements. In addition, sales had decreased, and so had the stock value. Opportunities were looming within the industry, and Kodak was poised to take advantage of them. However, competition was strong; therefore, Kodak's Chairman and CEO Daniel Carp had to find ways to effectively differentiate the company from its competitors.

Michael Davis, Marketing and Global Strategist, had been in the business for over 25 years and had traveled to all the continents, visiting countries and various markets where Kodak had a presence. Through his knowledge and experience, he understood the market dynamics of various regions of the world very well and could easily predict customer purchasing patterns. Davis expressed his thoughts on what the company should do to differentiate itself from the competitors. His thoughts were to preserve the benefits of traditional film in the current and intermediate market environments since film sales were still healthy, but the company should also do some research in developing digital technology in the photography segment for the intermediate and long-term time frames, thereby positioning itself to compete effectively in both markets so as not to neglect one area over the other.

The benefits of the Davis alternative were that it would allow Kodak to remain the market leader in traditional film sales and allow the company to expand on new innovations in film as far into the future as possible. Despite digital substitution in some areas of the business, he believed the traditional film business was still healthy and developing in new markets around the world, such as Latin America, China, and some parts of Asia. He believed that film and digital photography would coexist in the market for a long time, especially in developing countries. This strategy was feasible as Kodak had recently made very large investments in developing the Kodak Advantix and Kodak Max film lines. These investments would diminish if sales fell off before the patents expired. Besides, Kodak held the highest number of patents in the industry. This strategy could be developed through the application of digital technology in such areas as wholesale and retail photofinishing and by expanding the company's presence in emerging film markets.

This alternative could win against the competition because in 2001, Kodak reached its highest worldwide consumer film market share position in the past nine years. Also, the company maintained the leading U.S. consumer film market share for the fourth consecutive year. Besides, Kodak's brand was recognized around the world and had an extensive global reach and was continuing to expand into emerging markets. The company had also been making strategic alliances around the world so that it could improve on its products and manufacturing processes. In addition, Kodak competed in both the film and devices segments. Not all competitors were able to offer both. Some competed either in film only or devices only.

The main drawbacks to this alternative were the market, financial, and economic risks involved in setting up operations in emerging markets. As a result of its global operating and financing activities, it was exposed to changes in foreign currency exchange rates, commodity prices, and interest rates which might adversely affect the results of operations and financial position. To bypass this drawback, the company could seek to minimize the risks of cost associated with such activities by entering into derivative contracts used to hedge foreign currency.

As Michael Davis concluded his final statement, Marty Meyers, Photography Group Executive Vice President, carefully thought through the proposal just presented. Although

Michael Davis' proposal seemed feasible, implementing it might result in a further decline in profits due to a continued decrease in the sales of film. Moreover, the company's available financial resources would not be sufficient to allocate equal investment in both areas. As a result, Marty Meyers felt that the company should no longer invest heavily in film but should divert its resources to the development of innovative digital devices. He strongly believed that Kodak should continue with its current film business as far into the future as possible but with very little investment in this area. He proposed that the company should position itself to compete effectively in photography's newest technology—digital imaging. The company's R&D efforts would be mostly concentrated on digital technology, with emphasis on producing high-quality digital devices such as digital cameras, digital camcorders, personal digital assistants (PDAs), and state-of-the-art health imaging equipment in the immediate, intermediate, and long-term time frames. The devices segment represented one of the fastest-growing areas in the digital photography industry. Therefore, building on Kodak's expertise in R&D and product innovation, the company could capture market share from its competitors if it were to compete in the digital devices market. Besides, its newest line of digital cameras (EasyShare) was doing very well in the market and was gaining market share over similar brands.

The benefits of the Meyers alternative would be to ensure that Kodak would be the market leader in this new technology and preempt the market with new features and functions for digital devices. By leveraging its strong brand name, Kodak could gain a substantial market share of the early adopters, who were eager to try new gadgets, thus increasing its revenues from global sales of these devices. In essence, the company would not be left behind with obsolete products that over time had the possibility of becoming antique items, as in the case of the computer replacing the typewriter. This strategy was feasible since Kodak had already invested a substantial amount of money in researching and improving these products. The company had also made strategic alliances within the industry to position itself ahead of the rest. Kodak's infrastructure offerings included online imaging networks, photofinishing networks, imaging protocols, and transmission and imaging software. In addition, Kodak had a large portfolio of next-generation digital photography offerings, and initiatives were under way in all areas of infoimaging. Given these attributes, the possibility of entering and succeeding in the camcorder market and the markets of other digital devices seemed very strong.

This alternative could win against the competition because in the digital still camera market, Kodak held a leadership position. One of the brightest spots in the digital imaging arena was OLED technology, in which Kodak owned more than 50 key patents. Because of the many benefits offered in this product, more and more manufacturers would be integrating this technology into their digital devices, therefore creating a stronghold for Kodak in this technology until the patents expired. Besides, Kodak already derived revenues from the sale of OLED displays, imaging sensor solutions, and optical products to other manufacturers. Therefore, this technology would provide a new stream of income for the company and would provide a major advantage to Kodak over its competitors. Also, because Kodak had expertise in developing innovative products, it could use this technology to form joint ventures with manufacturers of camcorders, PDAs, and other devices in the future. Its strength in R&D would allow it to accomplish this feat. In addition, Kodak's entertainment imaging was on its way to becoming the next generation of motion picture production and delivery. At the Kodak Technology Center in Hollywood and in the company's research laboratories in Rochester, Kodak was developing a complete digital cinema system. Kodak entertainment was also developing high-quality, affordable digital projection systems.

The main drawback to this alternative was the inability of Kodak to utilize the Common Picture Exchange Environment (CPXe), which was in progress in late 2002. Consumers would not be able to fully appreciate the benefits of its digital devices until all the kinks were ironed out. This included the convergence of broadband Internet access to wireless devices and accessibility to a majority of consumers' homes. With regard to digital camcorders, the company might have to engage in market and product research in this area. Financial resources might not be readily available at the moment. A way around the drawback was for Kodak to continue to participate in any initiatives that would aid in the development of common standards within the industry so that its product features could be enhanced.

After listening to both alternatives, Daniel Carp remained undecided. Both alternatives seemed feasible and could eventually lead the company toward winning against its competitors in the immediate, intermediate, and long-term futures. This was indeed a very difficult decision for him to make. However, making this and other enterprisewide strategic decisions was Carp's ongoing assignment as CEO, and now was the time for him to make that decision.

Notes

1. Eastman Kodak Company, *Annual Report* (2001).
2. Moneycentral.com, *http://moneycentral.msn.com/investor/charts/chartdl.asp?Symbol=ek* (2002).
3. Zacks Investment Research, *http://moneycentral.msn.com/investor/invsub/analyst/recomnd.asp?Symbol=ek* (2002).
4. Eastman Kodak Company, *Annual Report* (2001).
5. Standard & Poor's, "Industry Surveys," *www.netadvantage.standardpoor.com* (2002).
6. *Ibid.*
7. *Ibid.*
8. Eastman Kodak Company, *Annual Report* (2001).
9. *Ibid.*
10. Eastman Kodak Company, *10-Q Report* (2002). *www.sec.gov/Archives/edgar/data/31235/000003123502000016/ek10q0209.txt* (2002).
11. *Business Wire* (May 21, 2002).
12. Eastman Kodak Company, *10-Q Report* (2002). *www.sec.gov/Archives/edgar/data/31235/000003123502000016/ek10q0209.txt* (2002).
13. *Ibid.*
14. Eastman Kodak Company, *Annual Report* (2001).

References

Agfa, *Annual Report* (2001).

D. Carp, "Infoimaging—A New Platform for Economic Expansion," IDC Imaging Convergence Forum (August 2002).

C. Carrington, "CT Advances Win Converts in Cardiac Imaging," *Diagnostic Imaging Supplement*, *www.dimag.com/digitalradiography* (2001).

Consumer Reports, *www.consumerreports.org*.

M. Coyne, "Presenter—Photokina 2002," *www.kodak.com/US/en/corp/pressCenter/presentations/020926photokina2.shtml* (Cologne, Germany, September 25, 2002).

R. Guth, "Canon, Sharp Log Strong Profit," *Wall Street Journal* (October 30, 2002).

D. Harding, "IDC Conference Highlights the Changing Infoimaging Landscape," *www.kodak.com/US/en/corp/infoImaging* (2002).

L. Heller, "Competition and Low Prices Set Stage for 4Q Digital Boom," *DSN Retailing Today* (August 26, 2002).

Hoover's, *www.hoovers.com/premium/profile/6/0,2147,59626,00.html* (2002).

Infotrends Research Group, "Mass Market Scanner Revenue for North America Expected to Reach $1 Billion in 2002," *www.infotrendsrgi.com/press/2002082027001.html* (2002).

International Data Corp., "Infoimaging—A $225 Billion Industry Created by the Convergence of Image Science and Information Technology," whitepaper (2001).

J. Libbon, "APS Still Seeks Perfect Shot in Wake of Digital Imaging," *DSN Retailing Today*, *http://proquest.umi.com/pqdweb?TS=1035761130&RQT=309&CC=2&Dtp=1&Did=000* (March 19, 2001).

J. Libbon, "Photo Industry Focuses Message on Tech-Generation Teens," *DSN Retailing Today*, *http://proquest.umi.com/pqdweb?TS=1035761130&RQT=309&CC=2&Dtp=1&Did=000* (March 5, 2001).

J. Sculley, "IDC Conference Highlights the Changing Infoimaging Landscape," *www.kodak.com/US/en/corp/infoImaging* (2002).

The Seybold Group, "CPXe as a Web Services Business Framework for Printing Digital Photographs," whitepaper, *www.kodak.com/US/en/corp/infoImaging/infrastructure.shtml* (2002).

M. Slater, "Soon Digital Technology Will Rule," *Fortune*, Vol. 144, No. 10 (2002).

Standard & Poor's, *www.standardandpoors.com*.

CASE 27

The Carey Plant

Thomas L. Wheelen and J. David Hunger

THE GARDNER COMPANY WAS A RESPECTED NEW ENGLAND MANUFACTURER OF MACHINES and machine tools purchased by furniture makers for use in their manufacturing process. As a means of growing the firm, the Gardner Company acquired Carey Manufacturing three years ago from James Carey for $3,500,000. Carey Manufacturing was a high quality maker of specialized machine parts. Ralph Brown, Gardner's Vice President of Finance, had been the driving force behind the acquisition. Except for Andy Doyle and Rod Davis, all of Gardner's Vice Presidents (**Exhibit 1**) had been opposed to expansion through acquisition. They preferred internal growth for Gardner because they felt that the company would be more able to control both the rate and direction of its growth. Nevertheless, since both Peter Finch, President, and R. C. Smith, Executive Vice President, agreed with Brown's strong recommendation, Carey Manufacturing was acquired. Its primary asset was an aging manufacturing plant located 400 miles away from the Gardner Company's current headquarters and manufacturing facility. The Gardner Company was known for its manufacturing competency. Management hoped to add value to its new acquisition by transferring Gardner's manufacturing skills to the Carey Plant through significant process improvements.

James Carey, previous owner of Carey Manufacturing, agreed to continue serving as Plant Manager of what was now called the Carey Plant. He reported directly to the Gardner Company Executive Vice President, R. C. Smith. All functional activities of Carey Manufacturing had remained the same after the acquisition, except for sales activities being moved under Andy Doyle, Gardner's Vice President of Marketing. The five Carey Manufacturing salesmen were retained and allowed to keep their same sales territories. They exclusively sold only products made in the Carey Plant. The other Carey Plant functional departments (Human Resources, Engineering, Finance, Materials, Quality Assurance, and Operations) were supervised by Managers who directly reported to the Carey Plant Manager. The Managers of the Human Resources, Engineering, Materials, and Operations Departments also reported indirectly (shown by dotted lines in **Exhibit 1**) to the Vice Presidents in charge of their respective function at Gardner Company headquarters.

This case was prepared by Professors Thomas L. Wheelen of the University of South Florida and J. David Hunger of Iowa State University. Names and dates in the case have been disguised. An earlier version of this case was presented to the 2000 annual meeting of the North American Case Research Association. This case may not be reproduced in any form without written permission of the two copyright holders, Thomas L. Wheelen and J. David Hunger. This case was edited for SMBP–9th and 10th Editions. Copyright © 2001 and 2005 by Thomas L. Wheelen and J. David Hunger. The copyright holders, are solely responsible for case content. Any other publication of the case (translation, any form of electronics or other media) or sold (any form of partnership) to another publisher will be in violation of copyright law, unless Thomas L. Wheelen and J. David Hunger has granted an additional written reprint permission.

Exhibit 1 Gardner Company Organization Chart

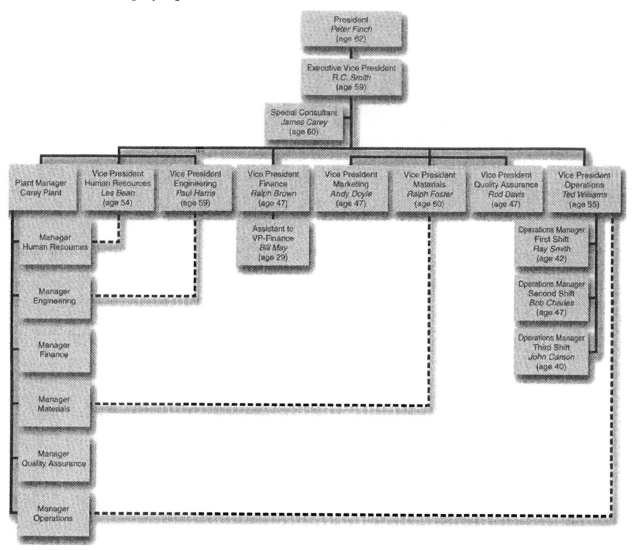

Note: Dotted lines show an indirect reporting relationship.

Until its acquisition, Carey Manufacturing (now the Carey Plant) had been a successful firm with few problems. Following its purchase, however, the plant had been plagued by labor problems, increasing costs, a leveling of sales, and a decline in profits (**Exhibit 2**). Two years ago, the Carey Plant suffered a 10-week strike called by its union in response to demands from the new management (Gardner Company) for increased production without a corresponding increase in pay. (Although Gardner Company was also unionized, its employees were represented by a different union than were the Carey Plant employees.) Concerned by both the strike and the poor performance of the Carey Plant since its purchase two years earlier, Ralph Brown initiated a study last year to identify what was wrong. He discovered that the poor performance of the Carey Plant resulted not only from its outdated and overcrowded manufacturing facility, but also from James Carey's passive role as Plant Manager. Gardner's Executive Committee (composed of the President and eight Vice Presidents) had been aware of the poor condition of the Carey Plant when it had agreed to the acquisition. It had therefore initiated plans to replace the aging plant. A new state-of-the-art manufacturing

Exhibit 2
Carey Plant: Recent
Sales and Profit
Figures

Year	Sales	Profits
5 Years Ago	$12,430,002	$697,042
4 Years Ago	13,223,804	778,050
3 Years Ago	14,700,178	836,028
2 Years Ago	10,300,000	(220,000)[1]
Last Year	13,950,000	446,812

Note:
1. Ten-week strike during October, November, and December.

facility was being built on available property adjacent to the current plant and should be completed within a few months. The information regarding James Carey was, however, quite surprising to the Committee. Before Gardner's purchase of Carey Manufacturing, James Carey had been actively involved in every phase of his company's operations. Since selling the company, however, Carey had delegated the running of the plant to his staff, the Department Managers. One of his Managers admitted that "He was the driving force of the company, but since he sold out, he has withdrawn completely from the management of the plant."

After hearing Brown's report, the Executive Committee decided that the Carey Plant needed a new Plant Manager. Consequently, James Carey was relieved of his duties as Plant Manager in early January this year and appointed special consultant to the Executive Vice President, R. C. Smith. The current staff of the Carey Plant was asked to continue operating the plant until a new Plant Manager could be named. Vice Presidents Brown and Williams were put in charge of finding a new Manager for the Carey Plant. They recommended several internal candidates to the Executive Vice President, R. C. Smith.

The Offer

On January 31 of this year, Smith offered the Plant Manager position of the Carey Plant to Bill May, current Assistant to Ralph Brown. May had spent six years in various specialist capacities within Gardner's Finance Department after being hired with an MBA. He had been in his current position for the past two years. Brown supported the offer to May with praise for his subordinate. "He has outstanding analytical abilities, drive, general administrative skills and is cost conscious. He is the type of man we need at the Carey Plant." The other executives viewed May not only as the company's efficiency expert, but also as a person who would see any job through to completion. Nevertheless, several of the Vice Presidents expressed opposition to placing a staff person in charge of the new plant. They felt the Plant Manager should have a strong technical background and line management experience. Brown, in contrast, stressed the necessity of a control-conscious person to get the new plant underway. Smith agreed that Gardner needed a person with a strong finance background heading the new plant.

Smith offered May the opportunity to visit the Carey Plant to have a private talk with each of his future staff. Each of the six Department Managers had been with the Carey Plant for a minimum of 18 years. They were frank in their discussions of past problems in the plant and in its future prospects. They generally agreed that the plant's labor problems should decline in the new plant, even though it was going to employ the same 405 employees (half the size of Gardner) with the same union. Four of them were concerned, however, with how they were being supervised. Ever since the acquisition by the Gardner Company, the Managers of the Operations, Materials, Human Resources, and Engineering Departments reported not only to James Carey as Plant Manager, but also to their respective functional Vice Presidents and staff at Gardner headquarters. Suggestions from the various Vice Presidents and staff assistants often conflicted with orders from the Plant Manager. When they confronted James Carey about the situation, he had merely shrugged. Carey told them to expect this sort of thing after an acquisition. "It's important that you get along with your new bosses, since they are the ones who will decide your future in this firm," advised Carey.

Bill May then met in mid-February with Ralph Brown, his current supervisor, to discuss the job offer over morning coffee. Turning to Brown, he said, "I'm worried about this Plant Manager's position. I will be in a whole new environment. I'm a complete stranger to those Department Managers, except for the Finance Manager. I will be the first member of the Gardner Company to be assigned to the Carey Plant. I will be functioning in a line position without any previous experience and no technical background in machine operations. I also honestly feel that several of the Vice Presidents would like to see me fail. I'm not sure if I should accept the job. I have a lot of questions, but I don't know where to get the answers." Looking over his coffee cup as he took a drink, Brown responded, "Bill, this is a great opportunity for you. What's the problem?" Adjusting himself in his chair, May looked directly at his mentor. "The specific details of the offer are very vague in terms of salary, responsibilities, and authority. What is expected of me and when? Do I have to keep the current staff? Do I have to hire future staff members from internal sources or can I go outside the company? Finally, I'm concerned about the lack of an actual job description." Brown was surprised by his protégé's many concerns. "Bill, I'm hoping that all of these questions, except for salary, will soon be answered at a meeting Smith is scheduling for you tomorrow with the Vice Presidents. He wants it to be an open forum."

The Meeting

The next morning, May took the elevator to the third floor. As he walked down the hall to the Gardner Company Executive Committee conference room, he bumped into Ted Williams, Vice President of Manufacturing, who was just coming out of his office. Looking at Bill, Ted offered, "I want to let you know that I'm behind you 100%. I wasn't at first, but I do think you may have what it takes to turn that place around. I don't care what the others think." As the two of them entered the conference room, May looked at the eight Gardner Vice Presidents. Some were sitting at the conference table and working on their laptops while others were getting some coffee from the decanter in the corner. R. C. Smith was already seated at the head of the table. Ralph Brown, sitting on one side of the table, motioned to May to come sit in an empty chair beside him. "Want some coffee?" Brown asked. "Good idea," responded May as he walked over to the decanter. Pouring cream into his coffee, May wondered, "What am I getting myself into?"

CASE 28

Panera Bread Company:
Rising Fortunes?

Ted Repetti and Joyce P. Vincelette

BREAD, ESSENTIAL AND BASIC, BUT NONETHELESS SPECIAL, TRANSCENDS MILLENNIA. A master baker combines simple ingredients to create what has been an integral part of society and culture for over 6,000 years. Sourdough bread, a uniquely American creation, is made from a "culture," or "starter." Sourdough starter contains natural yeasts, flour, and water and is the medium that makes bread rise. In order to survive, a starter must be cultured, fed, and tended to by attentive hands in the right environment. Without proper care and maintenance, the yeast, or the growth factor, would slow down and die. Without a strong starter, bread would no longer rise.

Ronald Shaich, CEO and Chairman of Panera Bread Company, created the company's "starter." Shaich, the master baker, combined the ingredients and cultivated the leavening agent that catalyzed the company's phenomenal growth. Under Shaich's guidance, Panera's total systemwide (both company and franchisee) revenues rose from $350.8 million in 2000 to $977.1 million in 2003. However, new unit expansion fueled this growth. In total, 419 Panera bakery-cafes were opened between 1999 and 2003. New unit growth masked a slowdown in the growth of average annualized unit volumes (AUVs) and year-to-year comparable sales. In 2000, systemwide comparable sales and AUVs increased 9.1% and 12.0%, respectively. Growth of these two key metrics declined in each consecutive year thereafter. In 2003, systemwide comparable sales and AUVs increased only 0.2% and 0.5%. Clearly, growth has slowed. In order to continue to rise, Panera's "starter" needs to be fed and maintained. In addition to new unit growth, new strategies and initiatives must be folded into the mix.

History

Panera Bread Company's roots began with the company that could be considered the grandfather of the fast casual restaurant concept: Au Bon Pain. In 1976, French oven manufacturer Pavailler opened the first Au Bon Pain (a French colloquialism for "where good bread is") in Boston's Faneuil Hall as a demonstration bakery.[1] Struck by its growth potential, Louis Kane, a veteran venture capitalist, purchased the business in 1978.[2] Between 1978 and 1981, Au Bon Pain struggled; it had opened 13 and subsequently closed 10 stores in the Boston area and piled up $3 million in debt.[3] Kane was ready to declare bankruptcy when he gained a new business partner in Ronald Shaich.[4]

A recent Harvard Business graduate, Shaich had opened the Cookie Jar bakery in Cambridge, Massachusetts, in 1980.[5] Shortly after opening the Cookie Jar, Shaich befriended Louis Kane. Shaich was interested in adding bread and croissants to his menu to stimulate his morning sales. Shaich recalled that "50,000 people a day were going past my store, and I had nothing to sell them in the morning."[6] In February 1981, the two merged the Au Bon Pain bakeries and the cookie store to form one business, Au Bon Pain Co., Inc. The two served as Co-CEOs until Kane's retirement in 1994. They had a synergistic relationship that made Au Bon Pain successful: Shaich was the hard-driving, analytical strategist focused on operations, and Kane was the seasoned businessman with a wealth of real estate and finance connections.[7] Between 1981 and 1984, the team expanded the business, worked to decrease the company's debt, and centralized facilities for dough production.[8]

In 1985, the partners added sandwiches to bolster daytime sales, as they noticed a pattern in customer behavior: "We had all of these customers coming and ordering a baguette cut in half. Then they'd take out these lunch bags full of cold cuts and start making sandwiches. We didn't have to be marketing whizzes to know that there was an opportunity there," recalled Shaich.[9] It was a "eureka" moment and the birth of the fast casual restaurant category.[10] According to Shaich, Au Bon Pain was the "first place that gave white collar folks a choice between fast food and fine dining."[11] Au Bon Pain became a lunchtime alternative for urban dwellers who were tired of burgers and fast food. Differentiated from other fast food competitors by its commitment to fresh, quality sandwiches, bread, and coffee, Au Bon Pain attracted customers who were happy to pay more money ($5 per sandwich) than they would have paid for fast food.[12]

In 1991, Kane and Shaich took the company public. By that time, the company had $68 million in sales and was a leader in the quick service bakery segment. By 1994, the company had 200 stores and $183 million in sales, but that growth masked a problem. The company was built on a limited growth concept, what Shaich called, "high density urban feeding."[13] The main customers of the company were office workers in locations like New York, Boston, and Washington, DC. The real estate in such areas was expensive and hard to come by. This strategic factor limited expansion possibilities.[14]

Au Bon Pain acquired the St. Louis Bread Company in 1993 for $24 million.[15] Shaich saw this as the company's "gateway into the suburban marketplace."[16] The acquired company was founded in 1987 by Ken Rosenthal and consisted of a 19-store bakery-cafe chain located in the St. Louis area. The concept of the cafe was based on San Franciscan sourdough bread bakeries.[17] The acquired company would eventually become the platform for what is now Panera.

Au Bon Pain management spent two years studying St. Louis Bread Co., looking for the ideal concept that would unite Au Bon Pain's operational abilities and quality food with the broader suburban growth appeal of St. Louis Bread.[18] Scott Davis, Panera's Chief Concept Officer, recalled the time spent trying to figure out what the new business should look like. "We didn't just look at restaurants and coffee houses," he stated. "We spent a lot of time looking at retailers. That's where our front-of-the-house bakery displays came from. We knew that people buy with their eyes, so we wanted them to walk in and crave baked goods."[19]

The restaging and development of the St. Louis Bread Co. concept was also affected by the management team's understanding of a consumer backlash against the commoditization of food service—a trend that began in the 1950s and spawned a coast-to-coast sameness (e.g., McDonald's).[20] The management team understood that a growing number of consumers wanted a unique expression of tastes and styles. Shaich and his team wrote a manifesto that spelled out what St. Louis Bread would be, from the type of food it would serve to the kind of people behind the counters and the look and feel of the physical space.[21]

Au Bon Pain began pouring capital into the chain when Shaich had another "eureka" moment in 1995. He entered a St. Louis Bread store and noticed a group of business people meeting in a corner. The customers explained that they had no other place to talk.[22] This experience opened Shaich's eyes to the fact that the potential of the neighborhood bakery-cafe concept was greater than that of Au Bon Pain's urban store concept. The bakery-cafe concept capitalized on a confluence of current trends: the welcoming atmosphere of coffee shops, the food of sandwich shops, and the quick service of fast food.[23]

While Au Bon Pain was focusing on making St. Louis Bread a viable national brand, the company's namesake unit was faltering. Rapid expansion of its urban outlets had resulted in operational problems, bad real estate deals,[24] and debt over $65 million.[25] Operating margins were on a steady decline. For example, from 1993 to 1994, margins fell from 11.5% to 8.5%.[26] Margins continued to contract because of higher food costs, stagnant sales, and decreased comparable store sales. Stiff competition from bagel shops and coffee chains such as Starbucks compounded operational difficulties. Another concern was that the fast food ambiance of the stores was not appealing to customers who wanted to sit and enjoy a meal or a cup of coffee.[27] On the other hand, the cafe-style atmosphere of St. Louis Bread, which was known as Panera (Latin for "time for bread") outside the St. Louis area, was proving to be successful. In 1996, comparable sales at Au Bon Pain locations declined 3%, while same-store sales in the Panera unit were up 10%.[28]

Lacking the capital to overhaul the ambiance of the Au Bon Pain segment, the company decided to sell the unit. This left the company the time and resources to strategically focus solely on the more successful Panera chain. Unlike Au Bon Pain, Panera was not confined to a small urban niche and had greater growth potential. Panera's per-store profit of $1.3 million over Au Bon Pain's $1 million (at the time of the sale) also proved more promising. On May 16, 1999, Shaich sold the Au Bon Pain unit to investment firm Bruckman, Sherrill, and Co. for $73 million. At the time of the divestiture, the company changed its corporate name to Panera Bread Company. The sale left Panera Bread Company debt-free, and the cash allowed for the immediate expansion of its bakery-cafe stores.[29]

General Business

From what was once a small chain acquired by Au Bon Pain, Panera Bread Company grew into the leader in the fast casual dining industry. The Panera concept combined and exploited several food service qualities: (1) the casual atmosphere of coffee shops, (2) the quality food of sandwich shops, and (3) the quick service of fast food chains. The company specialized in meeting five consumer-dining needs: breakfast, lunch, daytime "chill-out," lunch in the evening, and take-home bread. Daytime chill-out is the time between breakfast and lunch and between lunch and dinner when customers stop in to take a break from their daily activities. This niche of consumers included seniors, matineegoers, shoppers, business and sales people, and students.[30] Panera provided diners with high-quality foods, including fresh baked goods, made-to-order sandwiches on fresh baked breads, soups, salads, custom roasted coffees, and other cafe beverages. Panera targeted suburban dwellers and workers by offering a premium specialty bakery and cafe experience with a neighborhood emphasis.[31] Panera was the first in the bakery-cafe segment, and its unique concept and operational strengths led it to its leading position in the fast casual dining category.

Panera's concept was designed around meeting the needs and desires of consumers, specifically the need for efficient, time-saving service and the desire for a higher-quality dining experience—something not delivered by traditional fast food chains. The company's goal was to make Panera Bread a nationally dominant brand. Its menu, quality of operations, and design and real estate strategies were vital to the company's success.

Fast Casual

Panera's predecessor Au Bon Pain was a pioneer of the fast casual restaurant category. Fast casual, also known as quick casual, emerged to fill the gap between fast food and full-service restaurants. Technomic Information Services originally coined the term to describe restaurants that offer the speed, efficiency, and inexpensiveness of fast food with the hospitality, quality, and ambiance of a full-service restaurant. Technomic defined a fast casual restaurant by whether it met the following four criteria. *One*, the restaurant had to offer a limited-service or self-service format. *Two*, the average check had to be between $6 and $9, whereas fast food checks averaged less than $5. This pricing scheme placed fast casual between fast food and casual dining. The *third* criterion was that the food had to be made-to-order. Consumers perceived newly prepared, made-to-order foods as fresh. Fast casual menus usually also had more robust and complex flavor profiles than the standard fare at fast food restaurants. The *fourth* criterion required that the decor had to be upscale or highly developed. Decor inspired a more enjoyable experience for the customer as the environment of fast casual restaurants was more akin to that of a neighborhood bistro or casual restaurant. The decor also created a generally higher perception of quality.[32]

The fast casual market had enjoyed double-digit aggregate growth since 1999 and was expected to continue to grow by double digit figures.[33] Fast casual chain sales were expected to reach $50 billion in the next decade.[34] This large growth in fast casual was expected to come at the expense of the fast food industry.

Diverse dining offerings and higher profitability contributed to the industry's growth. Food concepts within the fast casual category ranged from Mexican, to bakeries, to Chinese. Unlike fast food restaurants that construct stand-alone stores, fast casual chains locate in strip malls, on small-town main streets, and in preexisting properties. As a result, the opening costs of a fast casual store are about a third of its average annual sales volume of $1.5 million.[35] The diversity and profitability of fast casual allowed many new players to enter the market offering new concepts and menu items.

The maturation of two large segments of the U.S. population, baby boomers and their children, was largely responsible for the growth in fast casual. Both segments had little time for cooking and grew tired of fast food, and they desired a high-quality, fresher, healthier dining experience, but did not have the time for a full dining experience. Dining trends caused fast casual to emerge as a legitimate trend in the restaurant industry as it bridged the gap between casual dining and the burgers-and-fries fast food industry.

Corporate Governance

Panera's corporate headquarters was located in St. Louis, Missouri.

Board of Directors

Shaich was the only internal board member. The biographical sketches for the board members are shown below[36]:

Ronald M. Shaich (age 50), Director since 1981, Co-Founder, Chairman of the Board since May 1999, Co-Chairman of the Board from January 1988 to May 1999, Chief Executive Officer since May 1994, and Co-Chief Executive Officer from January 1988 to May 1994. Shaich has served as a Director of Lown Cardiovascular Research Foundation.

Larry J. Franklin (age 55), Director since June 2001. Franklin has been the President and Chief Executive Officer of Franklin Sports, Inc., a leading branded sporting goods manufacturer and marketer, since 1986. Franklin joined Franklin Sports, Inc., in 1970 and served as its Executive Vice President from 1981 to 1986. Franklin has served on the Board of Directors of Bradford Soap International, Inc., The Sporting Goods Manufacturers Association, The Retail Industry Leadership Association, and The New England Chapter of the Juvenile Diabetes Research Foundation.

Fred K. Foulkes (age 62), Director since June 2003. Professor Foulkes has been a Professor of Organizational Behavior and the Director of the Human Resources Policy Institute at Boston University School of Management since 1981 and has taught courses in human resource management and strategic management at Boston University since 1980. From 1968 to 1980, Professor Foulkes was a member of the Harvard Business School faculty. Foulkes has served on the Board of Directors of Bright Horizons Family Solutions and the Society for Human Resource Management Foundation.

Domenic Colasacco (age 55), Director since March 2000. Colasacco has been President and Chief Executive Officer of Boston Trust & Investment Management, a trust company formed under Massachusetts state law, since 1992. He joined Boston Trust in 1974, after beginning his career in the research division of Merrill Lynch & Co. in New York City.

Thomas E. Lynch (age 44), Director since June 2003. Lynch has been a Senior Managing Director of Mill Road Associates, a financial advisory firm that he founded in 2000. From 1997 through 2000, Lynch was the founder and Managing Director of Lazard Capital Partners, a private equity firm affiliated with the investment bank Lazard. From 1990 to 1997, Lynch was a Managing Director at the Blackstone Group, where he was a senior investment professional for Blackstone Capital Partners. Prior to Blackstone, Lynch was a senior consultant at the Monitor Company. Lynch has served on the Board of the City Center.

George E. Kane (age 99), Director since November 1988. Kane was also a company Director from December 1981 to December 1985 and a Director Emeritus from December 1985 to November 1988. Kane retired in 1970 as President of Garden City Trust Company (now University Trust Company) and served as an Honorary Director of University Trust Company from December 1985 to January 2000. Kane became a nonvoting Honorary Director Emeritus after May 2004.

The Compensation Committee included Franklin, Foulkes, and Colasacco. The Committee on Nominations included Franklin, Lynch, and Kane. The Audit Committee included Foulkes, Colasacco, Lynch, and Kane.

Directors who were not employees received a quarterly fee ranging from $3,000 to $3,500 for serving on the Board, plus reimbursement of out-of-pocket expenses for attendance at each Board or committee meeting. Under the Directors' Plan, each Director who is not an employee or a principal stockholder received a one-time grant of an option to purchase 10,000 shares of Class A Common Stock when he or she was first elected. Each independent Director in office at the end of the fiscal year also received an option to purchase an additional 10,000 shares of Class A Common Stock.

Exhibit 1 shows the common stock ownership in the company. There were two classes of stock: (1) Class A Stock with 28,345,754 shares outstanding and one vote per share, and (2) Class B Common Stock with 1,761,521 shares outstanding and three votes per share.

Top Management

Key Executive Officers of Panera who did not also serve on the Board (as did Shaich) were as follows[37]:

Paul E. Twohig (age 50), Executive Vice President, Chief Operating Officer since January 2003. From 1993 to 2003, Twohig served as an executive at Starbucks Coffee Company, most recently as

Exhibit 1 Stock Ownership: Panera Bread Company

Name and, with Respect to Owner of More Than 5%, Address	Class A Common		Class B Common		Combined Voting Percentage
	Number	Percent	Number	Percent	
Ronald M. Shaich c/o Panera Bread Company 6710 Clayton Road Richmond Heights, MO 63117	601,660	2.1%	1,666,381	94.6%	16.5%
Domenic Colasacco	48,862	<1%	—	—	<1%
Larry J. Franklin	40,000	<1%	—	—	<1%
George E. Kane	45,912	<1%	—	—	<1%
Fred K. Foulkes	24,000	<1%	—	—	<1%
Thomas E. Lynch	20,000	<1%	—	—	<1%
Paul E. Twohig	1,000	<1%	—	—	<1%
Mark A. Borland	—	—	—	—	—
Michael E. Hood	—	—	—	—	
Michael J. Nolan	—	—	—	—	—
All directors, director nominees, and executive officers as a group (14 persons)	818,771	2.8%	1,666,381	94.6%	17.0%
Brown Capital Management, Inc. 1201 N. Calvert Street Baltimore, MD 21202	2,014,695	7.1%	—	—	6.0%
FMR Corp 82 Devonshire Street Boston, MA 02109	4,209,696	17.9%	—	—	12.5%

Source: Panera Bread Company, Inc., 2004 Notice of Annual Meeting of Stockholders, pp. 16–17.

Senior Vice President responsible for retail operations development and human resources for more than 1,200 Starbucks stores in 17 states and 5 Canadian provinces. From 1986 to 1991, Twohig was a franchisee and owned and operated four Burger King units in West Palm Beach, Florida. From 1968 to 1986, Twohig was with Burger King Corporation, serving in a variety of roles, including regional manager in New England.

Neal J. Yanofsky *(age 46), Executive Vice President, Chief Administrative Officer, and Corporate Staff Officer since June 2003. From June 1999 to June 2003, Yanofsky was an independent business consultant with a practice focused on strategy development for high-growth firms, including Panera. From April 1990 to June 1999, Yanofsky was Vice President of Fidelity Ventures, the private equity arm of Fidelity Investments, and served in additional capacities with Fidelity Capital, including Chief Financial Officer at Boston Coach.*

Mark A. Borland *(age 51), Senior Vice President, Chief Supply Chain Officer since August 2002. Borland joined the company in 1986 and held management positions within Au Bon Pain and Panera Bread divisions until 2000, including Executive Vice President, Vice President of Retail Operations, Chief Operating Officer, and President of Manufacturing Services. From 2000 to 2001, Borland served as Senior Vice President of Operations at RetailDNA and then rejoined Panera as a consultant in the summer of 2001.*

Scott G. Davis *(age 40), Senior Vice President, Chief Concept Officer since May 1999. Davis joined the company in 1987 and from May 1996 to May 1999 served as Vice President, Customer Experience. From June 1994 to May 1996, Davis served as Director of Concept Services and Customer Experience.*

Mark E. Hood *(age 51), Senior Vice President, Chief Financial Officer since April 2003. Hood joined the company in August 2002, and from August 2002 to April 2003 served as Senior Vice President, Finance and Administration. From August 2000 to April 2002, Hood served as the*

Chief Financial and Administrative Officer of the U.S. Loyalty Corporation. From June 1995 to September 1999, Hood served as an executive at Saks Fifth Avenue, most recently as Executive Vice President and Chief Financial and Administrative Officer. Prior to joining Saks, Hood held a number of financial positions with the May Department Stores Co. from 1983 to 1995.

Michael J. Kupstas *(age 46), Senior Vice President, Chief Franchise Officer since September 2001. Kupstas joined the company in 1996. Between August 1999 and September 2001, Kupstas served as Vice President, Franchising and Brand Communication. Between January 1996 and August 1999, Kupstas was Vice President, Company and Franchise Operations. Between April 1991 and January 1996, Kupstas was Senior Vice President/Division Vice President for Long John Silver's, Inc.*

John M. Maguire *(age 38), Senior Vice President, Chief Company and Joint Venture Operations Officer since August 2001. Maguire joined the company in April 1993. From April 2000 to July 2001, Maguire served as Vice President, Bakery Operations. From November 1998 to March 2000, Maguire served as Vice President, Commissary Operations. From April 1993 to October 1998, Maguire was a Manager and Director of Au Bon Pain/Panera Bread/St. Louis Bread.*

Michael J. Nolan *(age 44), Senior Vice President, Chief Development Officer since he joined the company in August 2001. From December 1997 to March 2001, Nolan served as Executive Vice President & Director for John Harvard's Brew House, L.L.C., and Senior Vice President, Development, for American Hospitality Concepts, Inc. From March 1996 to December 1997, Nolan was Vice President of Real Estate & Development for Apple South Incorporated, and from July 1989 to March 1996, Nolan was Vice President of Real Estate and Development for Morrison Restaurants Inc. Prior to 1989, Nolan served in various real estate and development capacities for Cardinal Industries, Inc., and Nolan Development and Investment.*

Exhibit 2 shows the executive compensation for the five highest-paid principal executives.

Exhibit 2 Summary Compensation Table for Executives: Panera Bread Company

| | | Annual Compensation | | | Long-Term Compensation |
| | | | | | Securities Underlying |
Name of Principal Position(s)	Year	Salary ($)	Bonus ($)	Other Annual Compensation ($)	Options (#)
Ronald M. Shaich	2003	397,616	—	$49,881[2]	100,000
Chairman and Chief	2002	331,500	—[1]	$144,909[2]	40,000
Executive Officer	2001	338,000	375,000		—
Paul E. Twohig	2003	306,250	68,250	—	50,000
Executive Vice President,	2002	—	—	—	130,000
Chief Operating Officer	2001	—	—	—	—
Mark A. Borland	2003	238,462	47,304	—	—
Senior Vice President,	2002	120,536	30,777	—	50,000
Chief Supply Chain Officer	2001	—	—	—	—
Mark E. Hood	2003	243,365	35,551	—	5,000
Senior Vice President,	2002	83,077	18,300	—	80,000
Chief Financial Officer	2001	—	—	—	—
Michael J. Nolan	2003	238,462	51,684	—	5,000
Senior Vice President,	2002	196,153	40,000	—	—
Chief Development Officer	2001	6,539	15,821	—	80,000

Notes:
1. Shaich declined his $375,000 bonus for 2002 earned under the bonus plan approved by the Compensation Committee, in light of the chartered plane benefits he received during 2002.
2. Shaich received $144,909 in personal chartered air travel (based on the aggregate incremental cost of such travel to Panera), $5,500 in matching contributions to the 401(k) plan, and $1,947 in life insurance premiums.

Source: Panera Bread Company, Inc., 2004 Notice of Annual Meeting of Stockholders, p. 10.

Concept and Strategy[38]

The company's concept focused on the Specialty Bread/Bakery-Cafe category. Its artisan breads, which were breads made with all-natural ingredients and an artisan's attention to quality and detail, and overall award-winning bakery expertise were at the heart of the concept's menu. The concept was designed to deliver against the key consumer trends, specifically the need for a responsive and more special dining experience than that offered by traditional fast food. The company's goal was to make Panera Bread a nationally dominant brand name. Its menu, prototype, operating systems, design, and real estate strategy allowed it to compete successfully in several sub-businesses: breakfast, lunch, PM chill-out, lunch in the evening, and take-home bread. On a systemwide basis, annualized AUVs increased 0.7%, to $1,852,000, for the 52 weeks ended December 27, 2003, compared to $1,840,000 for the 52 weeks ended December 28, 2002 (see **Exhibit 3**).

Exhibit 3 Selected Financial Information: Panera Bread Company (Dollar amounts in thousands)

A. Systemwide Bakery-Cafe Revenues

	For Fiscal Year Ending			
	December 27, 2003	December 28, 2002	December 29, 2001	December 30, 2000
Systemwide	$977,100	$755,400	$529,400	$350,800

B. Year-to-Year Comparable Sales

	Fifty-Two Weeks Ending				
	December 27, 2003	December 28, 2002	December 29, 2001	December 30, 2000	December 25, 1999
Company-owned	1.7%	4.1%	5.8%	8.1%	3.3%
Franchise-operated	–0.4%	6.1%	5.8%	10.3%	2.0%
Systemwide	0.2%	5.5%	5.8%	9.1%	2.9%

C. Annualized Unit Volume (AUVs)

	For Fiscal Year Ending				
	December 27, 2003	December 28, 2002	December 29, 2001	December 30, 2000	December 25, 1999
Company-owned	$1,831,000	$1,764,000	$1,636,000	$1,471,000	$1,330,000
Franchise-operated	$1,860,000	$1,871,000	$1,800,000	$1,710,000	$1,568,000
Systemwide	$1,850,000	$1,840,000	$1,748,000	$1,617,000	$1,444,000

D. Year Percentage Change in AUVs

	For Fiscal Year Ending			
	December 27, 2003	December 28, 2002	December 29, 2001	December 30, 2000
Company-owned	3.8%	7.8%	11.2%	10.6%
Franchise-operated	–0.6%	3.9%	5.3%	9.1%
Systemwide	0.5%	5.3%	8.1%	12.0%

Sources: Panera Bread Company, Inc., Media Kit *and* 1999 Form 10-K *through* 2003 Form 10-K.

Exhibit 4 Company-Owned and Franchise-Operated Bakery-Cafes: Panera Bread Company

	For Fiscal Year Ending				
	December 27, 2003	December 28, 2002	December 29, 2001	December 30, 2000	December 25, 1999
Number of bakery-cafes:[1]					
Company-owned:					
Beginning of period	132	110	90	81	70
Bakery-cafes opened	29	23	21	11	12
Acquired from franchisee	15	3	—	—	—
Bakery-cafes closed	(3)	(4)	(1)	(2)	(1)
End of period	173	132	110	90	81
Franchise operated:					
Beginning of period	346	259	172	102	47
Bakery-cafes opened	102	92	88	70	56
Sold to company[2]	(15)	(3)	—	—	—
Bakery-cafes closed	(4)	(2)	(1)	—	(1)
End of period	429	346	259	172	102
System-wide:					
Beginning of period	361	252	145	66	—
Bakery-cafes opened	131	115	109	81	68
Bakery-cafes closed	(7)	(6)	(2)	(2)	(2)
End of period	485	361	252	145	66

Notes:
1. Includes majority-owned.
2. In January 2002, the company purchased the area development rights and 3 existing bakery-cafes in the Jacksonville, Florida, market from franchisees. During fiscal 2003, the company acquired 15 operating bakery-cafes' area development rights in the Louisville/Lexington, Kentucky, Dallas, Texas; Toledo, Ohio; and Ann Arbor, Michigan, markets from franchisees.

Sources: Panera Bread Company, Inc., 2003 Form 10-K, *p. 2, and* 2001 Form 10-K, *pp. 2–3.*

The distinctive nature of the company's menu offerings, the quality of its bakery-cafe operations, the company's signature cafe design, and the prime locations of its cafes were integral to the company's success. The company believed its concept had significant growth potential, which it hoped to realize through a combination of company and franchise efforts. Franchising was a key component of the company's success. Utilization of franchise operating partners enabled the company to grow more rapidly because of the added resources and capabilities they provided to implement the concepts and strategy developed by Panera. As of December 27, 2003, there were 429 franchised bakery-cafes operating and signed commitments to open an additional 409 bakery-cafes. In addition, there were 173 wholly or majority-owned company bakery-cafes operating at December 27, 2003. **Exhibit 4** shows the number of bakery-cafes for the last five years.

Competition[39]

The company experienced competition from numerous sources in its trade areas. The company's bakery-cafes competed based on customers' needs for breakfast, lunch, daytime chill-out, lunch in the evening, and take-home bread sales. The competitive factors included location, environment, customer service, price, and quality of products. The company competed for leased space in desirable locations. Certain competitors had capital resources that exceeded those available to the company. Primary competitors included specialty food and casual dining restaurant retailers, including national, regional, and locally owned concepts.

Menu[40]

The menu was designed to provide the company's target customers with products that built on the strength of the company's bakery expertise and met customers' new and ever-changing tastes. The key menu groups were fresh baked goods, made-to-order sandwiches, soups, and cafe beverages. Included within these menu groups were a variety of freshly baked bagels, breads, muffins, scones, rolls, and sweet goods; made-to-order sandwiches; hearty, unique soups; and custom roasted coffees and cafe beverages such as hot or cold espresso and cappuccino drinks. The company's concept emphasized the sophisticated specialty and artisan breads that supported a take-home bread business.

The company regularly reviewed and revised its menu offerings to satisfy changing customer preferences and to maintain customer interest within its target customer groups, the "bread loving trend-setters" and the "bread loving traditionalists." Both of these target customer groups sought a quality experience that reflected their discriminating tastes. The major characteristic that set these two groups apart was the more enthusiastic embrace of new and nutritional menu items by the *trend-setters*. New menu items were developed in test kitchens and then introduced in a limited number of the company's bakery-cafes to determine customer response and verify that preparation and operating procedures maintained product consistency, high quality standards, and profitability. If successful, they were then introduced in the rest of the company's bakery-cafes and franchise bakery-cafes.

Franchises[41]

Panera management believed that its specialty bakery-cafe concept had significant growth potential, which it hoped to realize through a combination of owned, franchised, and joint venture–operated stores. Franchising was a key component of the company's growth strategy. Expansion through franchise partners had enabled the company to grow more rapidly as the franchisees contributed the resources and capabilities necessary to implant the concepts and strategies developed by Panera.

The company began a broad-based franchising program in 1996. The company was actively seeking to extend its franchise relationships beyond its current franchisees and annually filed a Uniform Franchise Offering Circular to facilitate sales of additional franchise development agreements. The company offered two types of franchise opportunities: independent third-party franchisees and Area Development Agreements (ADAs). ADAs transferred all development rights within a specified geographic area to the owner of that contract and required the developer to adhere to a predetermined development time line. Franchisees were required to develop a specified number of bakery-cafes on or before specific dates. If franchisees failed to develop bakery-cafes on schedule, the company had the right to terminate the ADA and to develop company-owned locations or develop locations through new ADA developers in that market.

The franchise agreement typically required the payment of an up-front franchise fee of $35,000 (broken down into $5,000 at the signing of the ADA and $30,000 at or before the bakery-cafe opened) and continuing royalties of 4%–5% on sales from each bakery-cafe.

Franchise-operated bakery-cafes followed the same standards for product quality, menu, site selection, and bakery-cafe construction as did company-owned bakery-cafes. The franchisees were required to purchase all of their dough products from sources approved by the company. The company's fresh dough facility system supplied fresh dough products to most franchise-operated bakery-cafes. The company did not finance franchisee construction or ADA purchases. In addition, the company did not hold an equity interest in any of the franchised bakery-cafes.

The company had entered into franchise ADAs with 32 franchisee groups as of December 27, 2003. Also, as of December 27, 2003, there were 429 franchised bakery-cafes open and commitments to open 409 additional franchised bakery-cafes (see **Exhibit 5**). The company did not have any international franchise development agreements.

The high volume of franchise applicants allowed Panera to be very selective in granting franchises. Panera preferred executives with retail and restaurant franchising experience. The

**Exhibit 5
Panera Bread/St.
Louis Bread Co.
Bakery-Cafes**

State	Company Bakery-Cafes	Franchise-Operated Bakery-Cafes	Total Bakery-Cafes
Alabama	4	—	4
Arkansas	—	2	2
California	—	5	5
Colorado	—	14	14
Connecticut	1	4	5
Delaware	—	1	1
Florida	5	43	48
Georgia	8	6	14
Iowa	—	13	13
Illinois	34	32	66
Indiana	3	15	18
Kansas	—	14	14
Kentucky	4	1	5
Massachusetts	2	18	20
Maryland	—	18	18
Maine	—	2	2
Michigan	32	8	40
Minnesota	—	20	20
Missouri	36	16	52
North Carolina	1	17	18
Nebraska	—	7	7
Nevada	—	2	2
New Hampshire	—	7	7
New Jersey	—	25	25
New York	5	3	8
Ohio	6	55	61
Oklahoma	—	15	15
Pennsylvania	7	27	34
Rhode Island	—	3	3
South Carolina	—	2	2
Tennessee	1	9	10
Texas	2	9	11
Virginia	20	1	21
West Virginia	—	2	2
Wisconsin	—	15	15
Totals	**173**	**429**	**602**

Source: *Panera Bread Company, Inc.*, 2003 Form 10-K, *p. 8.*

company chose only very strong and capable franchising partners, many of whom had experience with well-known chains, such as McDonald's and Burger King.[42] Franchisees needed to have access to financing since the company did not finance franchisee construction or ADA purchases.

Panera also saw potential in implementing a joint venture structure as an alternative to company-owned or franchised bakery-cafes to facilitate the development and operation of bakery-cafes. Unlike with franchise agreements, Panera was the major financier (where a specified interest is invested by the joint venture partner) of the bakery-cafes and earned revenues from operations. The joint venture partner managed the bakery-cafes and was entitled to a specified percentage of cash flows. The joint venture agreements forbade the partner from transferring or selling its interest to another party without the consent of Panera. After a specified term, the company had the right to purchase the joint venture partner's interest at a determined value, and the joint venture partner had the right to sell its interest back to the company at a lower value. The company saw the joint venture structure as an opportunity to attract and retain experienced and motivated operators who would want the opportunity to participate in the success of the bakery-cafes.

In 2001, Richard Postle, Panera's former Chief Operating Officer and President, left the company and through an indirect subsidiary entered into a joint venture agreement to develop 50 bakery-cafes in northern Virginia and central Pennsylvania. Under this agreement, there were 27 bakery-cafes operating in these markets at December 27, 2003. After October 2006, the company and the minority-interest owner would each have rights that could, if exercised, permit/require the company to purchase the bakery-cafes at contractually determined values based on multiples of cash flows.

Bakery Supply Chain[43]

According to Ronald Shaich, "Panera has a commitment to doing the best bread in America."[44] Freshly baked bread made with fresh dough was integral to honoring this commitment. Systemwide, bakery-cafes used fresh dough for sourdough and artisan breads and bagels. The company's fresh dough facility system supplied fresh dough to both company-owned and franchise-operated bakery-cafes daily. The company supplied both company-owned and franchise-operated bakery-cafes with fresh dough daily through its commissary system. The company's 16 commissaries (see **Exhibit 6**) prepared fresh, preservative-free dough daily.

The commissaries assured product quality and consistency at both company-owned and franchised bakery-cafes. Panera's master artisan baker, Mile Marino, had been with the company since 1987 and oversaw all baking operations at the fresh dough facilities. A fleet of 98 temperature-controlled trucks leased by Panera and driven by Panera employees distributed the fresh dough to bakery-cafes. The optimal distribution limit was approximately 200 miles. An average distribution route delivered dough to 6 bakery-cafes. The fresh dough was then baked overnight in a $50,000 stone-bottom oven, standard in all bakery-cafes.

The company focused its expansion in areas served by commissaries in order to continue to gain efficiencies through leveraging the fixed cost of its current commissary structure. Panera selectively entered new markets that required the construction of additional facilities until a sufficient number of bakery-cafes could be opened to permit efficient distribution of the fresh dough.

The remaining baked goods that were not prepared with fresh dough (sweet goods) were prepared with frozen dough. In 1996, the company constructed a state-of-the-art frozen dough facility in Mexico, Missouri. In 1998, the company sold the facility and its frozen dough business to Bunge Food Corporation for approximately $13 million in cash. At the time of the

**Exhibit 6
Leased Fresh
Dough Facilities:
Panera Bread
Company**

Facility	Square Footage
Franklin, MA	40,300
Chicago, IL	30,900
Cincinnati, OH	14,000
Washington, DC (located in Beltsville, MD)	17,900
Warren, OH	16,300
St. Louis, MO	30,000
Orlando, FL	16,500
Atlanta, GA	18,000
Greensboro, NC	9,600
Kansas City, KS	17,000
Detroit, MI	13,500
Dallas, TX	7,800
Minneapolis, MN	8,900
Ontario, CA	13,900
Fairfield, NJ	20,200
Denver, CO	10,000

Source: Panera Bread Company, Inc., 2003 Form 10-K, p. 8.

sale, Panera entered into a five-year contract with Bunge for the supply of substantially all of its frozen dough. In November 2002, the company signed an agreement with Dawn Food Products, Inc., to prepare and deliver frozen dough from 2003 through 2007. The agreement was structured as a cost-plus agreement.

All frozen dough and related food materials were distributed to the bakery-cafes through independent distributors. Contract vendors delivered virtually all food products and supplies for retail operations (i.e. paper goods, coffee, smallwares) to the distributors, which then delivered to the individual bakery-cafes. Franchised bakery-cafes operated under individual contracts with either the company's distributor or other regional distributors. As of December 27, 2003, there were three primary distributors serving the Panera Bread system.

Marketing[45]

Panera did not rely heavily on advertising to promote its stores. In 2001, the company spent only $700,000 on media, a low 2.1% ad-to-sales ratio compared to the category average of 4%.[46] The company attempted to increase its per-location sales through menu development, product merchandising, and promotions at everyday prices and by sponsorship of local community charitable events. Advertising was intended to promote the company but not to create an identifiable image that would be synonymous with Panera, such as the McDonald's golden arches.

Franchised bakery-cafes contributed 0.4% of sales to a company-run national advertising fund and 0.4% of sales as a marketing administration fee and were required to spend 2.0% of sales in their local markets on advertising. The company contributed similar amounts from company-owned bakery-cafes toward the national advertising fund and marketing administration fee. The national advertising fund and marketing administration fee contributions received from franchised bakery-cafes were consolidated with company amounts in the company's financial statements. Liabilities for unexpended funds were included in accrued expenses in the consolidated balance sheets. The company's contributions to the national advertising fund and marketing administration fee, as well as its own media costs, were recorded as part of other operating expenses in the consolidated statements of operations. The company utilized external media when deemed appropriate and cost-effective in specific markets.

Most marketing was done through product promotion and word-of-mouth marketing. According to Shaich, "when a new store is opened in an established market, the new store benefits from the buzz and consumer familiarity created by existing locations."[47] This was akin to the "Krispy Kreme Phenomenon," which occurred when consumers greatly anticipated a new store opening in their neighborhood due to word-of-mouth praise for the quality of the food products.

Another way Panera used word-of-mouth marketing was through local charity and community work. Panera strove to add value to its surrounding neighborhoods through its products, service, employment opportunities, and citizenship and believed it had a responsibility to participate and sponsor local events. The company's most well-known program began in 1992. The "Operation Dough-Nation" program ensured that every purchase at Panera would give back in some way to the community. Cash donations could be made inside the store, with the amounts matched with fresh baked bread donated to local food drives. In addition, the company donated all unsold bread to local hunger relief agencies. The company's second community outreach program, "Dough for Funds," gave nonprofit groups a means to raise funds by profiting from the sales of Panera coupons.

The company did not compete on the basis of pricing only; its main selling point was its specialty dining experience. Yet pricing was key to promoting the company's concept. Pricing was structured so customers perceived good value with high-quality food at reasonable prices to encourage frequent visits. The company's average check per transaction at company-owned bakery-cafes for 2003 was $6.61. The average check per transaction varied by the time of day: breakfast, $4.86; lunch, $7.65; PM chill-out, $6.67; and lunch in the evening, $7.42 (see **Exhibit 7**).

The company used its store locations to market its brand image. When choosing a location to open a new store, the company carefully selected the geographic area. Better locations needed less marketing, and the bakery-cafe concept relied on a substantial volume of repeat business. Management used demographic and competitive information to identify areas with the best opportunity for success and that best promoted Panera's neighborhood concept. Location, real estate, and marketing teams worked in conjunction to select ideal locations. In evaluating a potential location, the company studied the surrounding trade area, obtained demographic information within that area, and examined information on breakfast and lunch competitors. Based on analysis of this information, including utilization of predictive modeling using proprietary software, the company determined projected sales and return on investment. The Panera concept had proven successful in a number of different types of real estate (i.e., in-line strip centers, regional malls, and freestanding) in 35 states.

The company also used the actual bakery-cafe as a marketing tool to promote its brand image. The company designed each bakery-cafe to provide a differentiated environment and

Exhibit 7
Average Check per Transaction: Panera Bread Company

	2003	2002	2001	2000	1999
Breakfast	$4.86	$4.49	$4.30	$4.03	$3.76
Lunch	7.65	7.32	7.26	6.89	6.41
PM "Chill Out"	6.67	6.30	5.39	N/A	N/A
Evening lunch	7.42	7.02	N/A	N/A	N/A
Overall	6.61	6.26	6.19	5.80	5.44

Sources: Panera Bread Company, Inc., 1999 Form 10-K through 2003 Form 10-K.

Exhibit 8
Average Opening
Costs and Square
Footage: Panera
Bread Company

	2003	2002	2001	2000	1999
Opening Costs	$850,000	$737,000	$760,000	$700,000	$656,000
Square Footage	4,330	4,400	4,250	4,000	3,500

Sources: Panera Bread Company, Inc., 1999 Form 10-K through 2003 Form 10-K.

in many cases used fixtures and materials complementary to the neighborhood location of the bakery-cafe. Many locations incorporated the warmth of a fireplace and cozy seating areas and groupings that facilitated utilization as a gathering spot. The design visually reinforced the distinctive difference between the company's bakery-cafes and other bakery-cafes serving breakfast and lunch. Many of the company's cafes also featured outdoor cafe seating.

The average construction, equipment, furniture and fixture, and signage cost for the 29 company-owned bakery-cafes opened in 2003 was $850,000 per bakery-cafe after landlord allowances (see **Exhibit 8**). The average bakery-cafe size was 4,330 square feet (see **Exhibit 8**).

All company-owned bakery-cafes were in leased premises. Lease terms were typically 10 years, with one, two, or three 5-year renewal option periods thereafter. Leases typically had charges for minimum base occupancy, a proportionate share of building and common area operating expenses and real estate taxes, and contingent-percentage rent based on sales above a stipulated sales level.

Management Information Systems[48]

Each company-operated bakery-cafe had computerized cash registers to collect point-of-sale transaction data, which was used to generate pertinent marketing information, including product mix and average check. All product prices were programmed into the system from the company's corporate office. The company allowed franchisees who elected to do so to have access to certain proprietary bakery-cafe systems and systems support.

The company's in-store information system was designed to assist in labor scheduling and food cost management, to provide corporate and retail operations management quick access to retail data, and to reduce managers' administrative time. The system supplied sales, bank deposit, and variance data to the company's accounting department on a daily basis. The company used this data to generate weekly consolidated reports regarding sales and other key elements, as well as detailed profit and loss statements for each company-owned bakery-cafe every four weeks. Additionally, the company monitored the average check, customer count, product mix, and other sales trends. The fresh dough facilities had computerized systems that allowed the fresh dough facilities to accept electronic orders from the bakery-cafes and deliver the ordered product to the bakery-cafes. The company also used network/integration systems, encompassing e-mail and all major financial systems, such as general ledger database systems, and all major operational systems, such as store operating performance database systems.

Human Resources[49]

From the beginning, Panera realized that the quality of its employees was a critical part of a successful product and a unique company. It was the company's belief that the key ingredients in the successful development of Panera ranged from the type of food served to the kind of people behind the counters. Employees included full-time associates in general or administrative positions, commissary operators, bakers, and associates at the bakery-cafes. As of December 27, 2003, the company had 3,924 full-time associates (defined as associates who averaged 25 hours or more per week), of whom 344 were employed in general or administrative functions principally at or from the company's support centers (executive offices); 676 were employed in the company's fresh dough facility operations; and 2,904 were employed in the company's bakery-cafe operations as bakers, managers, and associates. The company also had 4,078 part-time hourly associates at the bakery-cafes. There were no collective bargaining agreements. The company considered its employee relations to be good. The company placed priority on staffing its bakery-cafes, fresh dough facilities, and support center operations with skilled associates and invested in training programs to ensure the quality of its operations. Incentive programs and bonuses were available to salaried employees. Employees also received product discounts and were invited to join employee stock ownership plans. Panera believed that providing bakery-cafe operators the opportunity to participate in the success of the bakery-cafe enabled the company to attract and retain experienced and highly motivated personnel, which resulted in a better customer experience. The company developed a program and began implementation in certain markets in 2003 to allow unit general managers and multi-unit managers to own a minority interest in a bakery-cafe. Prior to full implementation of the program, the company modified the program from an ownership structure to a multi-year bonus structure, which allowed operators to participate in the success of a bakery-cafe. The company expected to continue implementation of this bonus structure where appropriate as an alternative to its traditional company-owned or franchised bakery-cafes to facilitate the development and operation of bakery-cafes.

Finance[50]

Exhibits 9 through 11 show the consolidated statement of operations, common size income statement, and consolidated balance sheets, respectively, for the company for the fiscal years ended 1999 through 2003.

The company's revenues were derived from company-owned bakery-cafe sales, fresh dough sales to franchisees, and franchise royalties and fees. Fresh dough sales to franchisees were the sales of dough products to franchisees. Franchise royalties and fees included royalty income and franchise fees. The cost of food and paper products, labor, occupancy, and other operating expenses related to company-owned bakery-cafe sales. The cost of fresh dough sales related to the sale of fresh dough products and sweet goods to franchisees. General and administrative, depreciation, and pre-opening expenses related to all areas of revenue generation.

Systemwide bakery-cafe sales for the 52 weeks ended December 27, 2003, for the company increased 29.3%, to $977.1 million from $755.4 million, for the 52 weeks ended December 28, 2002. Comparable sales increases and increases in AUVs were lower during the 52 weeks ended December 27, 2003, than during the 52 weeks ended December 28, 2002 (see Exhibit 3).

Total company revenues for the 52 weeks ended December 27, 2003, increased 28.1%, to $355.9 million compared to $277.8 million, for the 52 weeks ended December 28, 2002 (see Exhibit 9). The growth in total revenues for the 52 weeks ended December 27, 2003, as compared to the prior year, was primarily due to the opening of 131 new bakery-cafes in 2003, as well as the increase in systemwide average weekly sales (excluding closed locations) of 0.7% for the 52 weeks ended December 27, 2003.

Bakery-cafe sales for the 52 weeks ended December 27, 2003, for the company increased 25.1%, to $265.9 million from $212.6 million, for the 52 weeks ended December 28, 2002. Bakery-cafe sales increased primarily due to the impact of a full year's operations of the 23

Exhibit 9 Consolidated Statement of Operations: Panera Bread Company
(Dollar amounts in thousands, except per share information)

Year Ending	December 27, 2003	December 28, 2002	December 29, 2001
Revenues:			
Bakery-cafe sales	$265,933	$212,645	$157,684
Franchise royalties and fees	36,245	27,892	19,577
Fresh dough sales to franchisees	53,708	37,215	23,856
Total revenue	355,886	277,752	201,117
Costs and expenses:			
Bakery-cafe expenses:			
Cost of food and paper products	73,727	63,255	48,253
Labor	81,152	63,172	45,768
Occupancy	17,990	14,619	11,345
Other operating expenses	36,804	27,971	20,729
Total bakery-cafe expenses	209,673	169,017	126,095
Fresh dough cost of sales to franchisees	47,151	33,959	21,965
Depreciation and amortization	19,487	13,965	10,839
General and administrative expenses	28,140	24,986	19,589
Pre-opening expenses	1,531	1,051	912
Nonrecurring charge	—	—	—
Total costs and expenses	305,982	242,978	179,400
Operating profit	49,904	34,774	21,717
Interest expense	48	32	72
Other expense (income), net	1,227	287	213
Minority interest	365	180	8
Income before income taxes	48,264	34,275	21,424
Income taxes	17,616	12,510	8,272
Income (loss) before cumulative effect of accounting change and extraordinary items	30,648	21,765	13,152
Cumulative effect of accounting change, net	(239)	—	—
Extraordinary loss from early extinguishments of debt, net	—	—	—
Net Income (loss)	**$ 30,409**	**$ 21,765**	**$ 13,152**
Per share data:			
Basic earnings per common share:			
Before cumulative effect of accounting change	$ 1.03	$ 0.75	$ 0.47
Cumulative effect of accounting change	(0.01)	—	—
Net income (loss)	$ 1.02	$ 0.75	0.47
Diluted earnings per common share:			
Before cumulative effect of accounting change	$ 1.01	$ 0.73	$ 0.46
Cumulative effect of accounting change	(0.01)	—	—
Net income (loss)	$ 1.00	$ 0.73	$ 0.46
Weighted average shares of common and common equivalent shares outstanding:			
Basic	29,733	28,923	27,783
Diluted	30,423	29,891	28,886

Sources: Panera Bread Company, Inc., 2003 Form 10-K, *p. 30, and* 2001 Form 10-K, *p. 28.*

Exhibit 10 Common Size Statement: Panera Bread Company (Dollar amounts in thousands, except per share information)

Year Ending	December 27, 2003	December 28, 2002	December 29, 2001	December 30, 2000	December 25, 1999[1]
Revenues:					
Bakery-cafe sales	74.7%	76.6%	78.4%	82.9%	91.5%
Franchise royalties and fees	10.2%	10.0%	9.7%	8.0%	4.3%
Fresh dough sales to franchisees	15.1%	13.4%	11.9%	9.1%	4.2%
Total revenue	100.0%	100.0%	100.0%	100.0%	100.0%
Costs and expenses:					
Bakery-cafe expenses:[1]					
Cost of food and paper products	27.7%	29.7%	30.6%	32.7%	33.4%
Labor	30.5%	29.7%	29.0%	28.9%	29.0%
Occupancy	6.8%	6.9%	7.2%	7.4%	9.9%
Other operating expenses	13.8%	13.2%	13.1%	12.8%	12.9%
Total bakery-cafe expenses	78.8%	79.5%	80.0%	81.8%	84.3%
Fresh dough cost of sales to franchisees[2]	87.8%	91.3%	92.1%	88.6%	89.7%
Depreciation and amortization	5.5%	5.0%	5.4%	5.6%	3.7%
General and administrative expenses	7.9%	9.0%	9.7%	10.8%	10.0%
Pre-opening expenses	0.4%	0.4%	0.5%	0.3%	0.0%
Non-recurring charge	0.0%	0.0%	0.0%	0.3%	3.2%
Operating profit	14.0%	12.5%	10.8%	7.1%	2.2%
Interest expense	0.0%	0.0%	0.0%	0.1%	1.6%
Other expense (income), net	0.3%	0.1%	0.1%	(0.3%)	0.4%
Minority interest	0.1%	0.1%	0.0%	0.0%	0.0%
Income before income taxes	13.6%	12.3%	10.7%	7.3%	0.2%
Income taxes	4.9%	4.5%	4.1%	2.8%	0.3%
Income (loss) before cumulative effect of accounting change and extraordinary items	8.6%	7.8%	6.5%	4.5%	(0.1%)
Cumulative effect of accounting change, net	(0.1%)	0.0%	0.0%	0.0%	0.0%
Extraordinary loss from early extinguishments of debt, net	0.0%	0.0%	0.0%	0.0%	0.2%
Net Income (loss)	8.5%	7.8%	6.5%	4.5%	(0.4%)

Notes:
1. As a percentage of bakery-cafe sales.
2. As a percentage of fresh dough facility sales to franchisees.

Sources: Panera Bread Company, Inc., 2003 Form 10-K, p. 14, and 2001 Form 10-K, pp. 12–13.

company-owned bakery-cafes opened in 2002, the opening of 29 company-owned bakery-cafes in 2003, and the 1.7% increase in comparable bakery-cafe sales for the 52 weeks ended December 27, 2003.

Franchise royalties and fees rose 29.7%, to $36.2 million, for the 52 weeks ended December 27, 2003, from $27.9 million for the 52 weeks ended December 28, 2002. The increase in royalty revenue was attributed to the impact of a full year's operations of the 92 franchised bakery-cafes opened in 2002 and the addition of 102 franchised bakery-cafes in 2003.

Fresh dough facility sales to franchisees increased 44.4%, to $53.7 million, for the 52 weeks ended December 27, 2003, from $37.2 million for the 52 weeks ended December 28, 2002. The increase was primarily driven by the increased number of franchise bakery-cafes opened, as well as a shift in certain products being distributed through the fresh dough facility system rather than third parties.

The cost of food and paper products included the costs associated with the fresh dough operations that sell fresh dough products to company-owned bakery-cafes, as well as the cost of food and paper products supplied by third-party vendors and distributors. The costs associated with the fresh dough operations that sell fresh dough products to the franchised bakery-cafes were excluded and are shown separately as fresh dough cost of sales to franchisees in the consolidated statements of operations. The cost of food and paper products decreased to 27.7% of bakery-cafe sales for the 52 weeks ended December 27, 2003, compared to 29.7% of bakery-cafe sales for the 52 weeks ended December 28, 2002. This decrease in the cost of food and paper products as a percentage of bakery-cafe sales was primarily due to the company's improved leveraging of its fresh dough manufacturing and distribution costs as it opened more bakery-cafes in fiscal 2003. For the 52 weeks ended December 27, 2003, there was an average of 32.7 bakery-cafes per fresh dough facility compared to an average of 27.3 for the 52 weeks ended December 28, 2002. Additionally, lower ingredient costs, including the benefits of a new sweet goods contract that commenced during the first quarter of fiscal 2003, further benefited food cost.

Labor expense was $81.2 million, or 30.5% of bakery-cafe sales, for the 52 weeks ended December 27, 2003, compared to $63.2 million, or 29.7% of bakery-cafe sales, for the 52 weeks ended December 28, 2002. The labor expense as a percentage of bakery-cafe sales increased between the 52 weeks ended December 27, 2003, and the 52 weeks ended December 28, 2002, primarily as a result of customer service initiatives in fiscal 2003 related to quality and speed of service as well as table delivery service testing and the continued commitment to training and staffing at bakery-cafes.

Occupancy costs were $18.0 million, or 6.8% of bakery-cafe sales, for the 52 weeks ended December 27, 2003, compared to $14.6 million, or 6.9% of bakery-cafe sales, for the 52 weeks ended December 28, 2002. The occupancy cost as a percentage of bakery-cafe sales declined for the 52 weeks ended December 27, 2003, due to the leveraging of these costs over higher sales volumes.

Other bakery-cafe operating expenses, which included advertising, retail field overhead, utilities, and other cafe expenses, were $36.8 million, or 13.8% of bakery-cafe sales, for the 52 weeks ended December 27, 2003, compared to $28.0 million, or 13.2% of bakery-cafe sales, for the 52 weeks ended December 28, 2002. The increase in other bakery-cafe operating expenses as a percentage of bakery-cafe sales for the 52 weeks ended December 27, 2003, was primarily due to increased organizational costs for field management, costs associated with new markets opened that did not yet have multi-unit leverage, and increased recruiting and training, repair and maintenance, and advertising costs.

For the 52 weeks ended December 27, 2003, fresh dough facility cost of sales to franchisees was $47.2 million, or 87.8% of fresh dough facility sales to franchisees, compared to $34.0 million, or 91.3% of fresh dough facility sales to franchisees, for the 52 weeks ended December 28, 2002. The decrease in the fresh dough cost of sales rate in fiscal 2003 was pri-

Exhibit 11 Consolidated Balance Sheets: Panera Bread Company (Dollar amounts in thousands, except per share information)

Year Ending	December 27, 2003	December 28, 2002	December 29, 2001	December 30, 2000	December 25, 1999
ASSETS					
Current assets:					
Cash and cash equivalents	$ 42,402	$ 29,924	$ 18,052	$ 9,011	$ 1,936
Investments in government securities	5,019	4,102	—	—	—
Trade accounts receivable, net	9,646	7,462	4,559	3,105	2,686
Other accounts receivable	2,748	2,097	597	—	—
Inventories	8,066	5,191	3,459	2,442	1,880
Prepaid expenses	1,294	1,826	1,649	1,027	484
Refundable income taxes	—	—	—	474	98
Deferred income taxes	1,696	8,488	7,289	5,193	5,473
Other	—	172	399	—	—
Total current assets	70,871	59,262	36,004	21,252	12,557
Property and equipment, net	132,651	99,313	79,693	59,857	47,191
Other assets:					
Notes receivable	—	—	—	—	35
Investments in government securities	4,000	5,047	—	—	—
Goodwill	32,743	18,970	17,530	17,790	18,779
Deferred financing costs	—	—	—	24	88
Deposits and other	5,678	5,554	5,020	4,731	3,960
Deferred income taxes	—	294	5,687	8,035	8,419
Total other assets	42,421	29,865	28,237	30,580	31,281
Total assets	$245,943	$188,440	$143,934	$111,689	$91,029

LIABILITIES AND STOCKHOLDERS' EQUITY

Current liabilities:					
Accounts payable	$ 8,072	$ 5,987	$ 5,271	$ 5,396	$ 3,535
Accrued expenses	35,552	24,935	16,433	12,086	12,237
Current portion of deferred revenue	1,168	1,403	677	—	—
Current portion of computer equipment financing	—	—	—	374	—
Total current liabilities	44,792	32,325	22,381	17,856	15,772
Deferred income taxes	328	—	—	—	—
Other long-term liabilities	1,115	262	1,125	2,245	2,011
Total liabilities	46,235	32,587	23,506	20,101	17,783
Minority interest	3,771	2,197	556	—	—
Stockholders' equity:					
Common stock, $.0001 par value: Class A, shares authorized 75,000,000; issued 28,296,581 and outstanding 28,187,581 in 2003 and issued 27,446,448 and outstanding 27,337,448 in 2002	3	3	3	1	1
Class B, shares authorized 10,000,000; issued and outstanding 1,847,221 in 2003 and 1,977,363 in 2002					
Treasury stock, carried at cost	(900)	(900)	(900)	(900)	—
Additional paid-in capital	121,992	110,120	98,101	82,971	70,581
Retained earnings	74,842	44,433	22,668	9,516	2,664
Total stockholders' equity	195,937	155,853	120,428	91,588	73,246
Total liabilities and stockholders' equity	**$245,943**	**$188,440**	**$143,934**	**$111,689**	**$91,029**

Sources: Panera Bread Company, Inc., 2003 Form 10-K, p. 29, and 2001 Form 10-K, p. 27.

marily due to favorable ingredient costs and the impact of the favorable change in the sweet goods supply agreement, which took effect during the first quarter of fiscal 2003.

Depreciation and amortization was $19.5 million, or 5.5% of total revenue, for the 52 weeks ended December 27, 2003, compared to $14.0 million, or 5.0% of total revenue, for the 52 weeks ended December 28, 2002. The increase in depreciation and amortization as a percentage of total revenue for the 52 weeks ended December 27, 2003, compared to the 52 weeks ended December 28, 2002, was primarily due to the impact of a full year's depreciation of the prior year's capital expenditures and increased capital expenditures in the current year.

General and administrative expenses were $28.1 million, or 7.9% of total revenue, and $25.0 million, or 9.0% of total revenue, for the 52 weeks ended December 27, 2003, and December 28, 2002, respectively. The decrease in the general and administrative expense rate between 2003 and 2002 resulted primarily from higher revenues, which helped leverage general and administrative expenses, and from decreased bonus costs.

Pre-opening expenses, which consisted primarily of labor and food costs incurred during in-store training and preparation for opening, exclusive of manager training costs, which were included in other operating expenses, of $1.5 million, or 0.4% of total revenue, for the 52 weeks ended December 27, 2003, were consistent with the $1.1 million, or 0.4% of total revenue, of pre-opening expenses for the 52 weeks ended December 28, 2002.

Profit for the 52 weeks ended December 27, 2003, increased to $49.9 million, or 14.0% of total revenue, from $34.8 million, or 12.5% of total revenue, for the 52 weeks ended December 28, 2002. Operating profit for the 52 weeks ended December 27, 2003, rose as a result of operating leverage that results from opening 29 company bakery-cafes in 2003 as well as the factors described above.

Other expenses for the 52 weeks ended December 27, 2003, increased to $1.2 million, or 0.3% of total revenue, from $0.3 million, or 0.1% of total revenue, for the 52 weeks ended December 28, 2002. The increase in other expense resulted primarily from increased operating fee payments to the minority interest owners. Minority interest represented the portion of the company's operating profit that was attributable to the ownership interest of the minority interest owners. The provision for income taxes increased to $17.6 million for the 52 weeks ended December 27, 2003, compared to $12.5 million for the 52 weeks ended December 28, 2002. The tax provisions for the 52 weeks ended December 27, 2003, and December 28, 2002, reflects a consistent combined federal, state, and local effective tax rate of 36.5%.

Net income for the 52 weeks ended December 27, 2003, increased $8.6 million, or 39.7%, to $30.4 million, or $1.00 per diluted share, compared to net income of $21.8 million, or $0.73 per diluted share, for the 52 weeks ended December 28, 2002. The increase in net income in 2003 is consistent with the factors described above.

Notes

1. Hoover's Inc., "Overview: Panera Bread Company."
2. Hoover's Inc., "Overview: Panera Bread Company."
3. L. Tischler, "Vote of Confidence," *Fast Company*, No. 65 (December 2002), pp. 102–112.
4. P. O. Keegan, "Louis I. Kane & Ronald I. Shaich: Au Bon Pain's Own Dynamic Duo," *Nation's Restaurant News*, Vol. 28, No. 37 (September 19, 1994), p. 172.
5. *Ibid.*
6. Quoted in L. Tischler, "Vote of Confidence," *Fast Company*, No. 65 (December 2002), pp. 102–112.
7. P. O. Keegan, "Louis I. Kane & Ronald I. Shaich: Au Bon Pain's Own Dynamic Duo," *Nation's Restaurant News*, Vol. 28, No. 37 (September 19, 1994), p. 172.

8. R. L. Allen, "Au Bon Pain's Kane Dead at 69; Founded Bakery Chain," *Nation's Restaurant News*, Vol. 34, No. 26 (June 26, 2000), pp. 6–7.
9. Quoted in P. O. Keegan, "Louis I. Kane & Ronald I. Shaich: Au Bon Pain's Own Dynamic Duo," *Nation's Restaurant News*, Vol. 28, No. 37 (September 19, 1994), p. 172.
10. L. Tischler, "Vote of Confidence," *Fast Company*, No. 65 (December 2002), pp. 102–112.
11. Quoted in *Ibid.*
12. P. Kemp, "Second Rising," *Forbes*, Vol. 166, No. 13 (November 13, 2000), p. 290.
13. L. Tischler, "Vote of Confidence," *Fast Company*, No. 65 (December 2002), pp. 102–112.

14. *Ibid.*
15. Hoover's Inc., "Overview: Panera Bread Company."
16. *Ibid.*
17. *Ibid.*
18. L. Tischler, "Vote of Confidence," *Fast Company*, No. 65 (December 2002), pp. 102–112.
19. *Ibid.*
20. *Ibid.*
21. *Ibid.*
22. C. Y. Kwok, "Bakery-Café Idea Smacked of Success from the Very Beginning; Concept Gives Rise to Rapid Growth in Stores, Stock Price," *St. Louis Dispatch* (May 20, 2001), p. E1.
23. *Ibid.*
24. R. L. Allen, "Au Bon Pain Co. Pins Hopes on New President, Image," *Nation's Restaurant News*, Vol. 30, No. 47 (December 2, 1996), pp. 3–4.
25. P. Kemp, "Second Rising," *Forbes*, Vol. 166, No. 13 (November 13, 2000), p. 290.
26. R. L. Papiernik, "Au Bon Pain Mulls Remedies, Pares Back Expansion Plans," *Nation's Restaurant News*, Vol. 29, No. 34 (August 28, 1995), pp. 3–4.
27. "Au Bon Pain Stock Drops 11% on News That Loss Is Expected," *Wall Street Journal* (October 7, 1996), p. B2.
28. *Ibid.*
29. A. Caffrey, "Heard in New England: Au Bon Pain's Plan to Reinvent Itself Sits Well with Many Pros," *Wall Street Journal* (March 10, 1999), p. NE.2.
30. M. Sheridan, "Time Trials," *Restaurants & Institutions*, Vol. 112, No. 12 (May 15, 2002), pp. 93–102.
31. G. LaVecchia, "Fast Casual Enters the Fast Lane," *Restaurant Hospitality*, Vol. 87, No. 2 (February 2003), pp. 43–47.
32. *Ibid.*
33. M. Pethokoukis, "Bye-Bye Burgers," *US News & World Report*, Vol. 133, No. 21 (December 2002), p. 36.
34. *Ibid.*
35. S. Brooks, "Feeling Hot, Hot, Hot," *Restaurant Business*, Vol. 101, No. 15 (September 2002), p. 36.
36. Panera Bread Company, Inc., *2004 Notice of Annual Meeting of Stockholders*, pp. 4–6.
37. *Ibid.*, pp. 7–8.
38. Panera Bread Company, Inc., *2003 Form 10-K*, p. 3. This was directly quoted, with minor editing.
39. *Ibid.*, p. 5.
40. *Ibid.*, p. 4.
41. Panera Bread Company, Inc., *2003 Form 10-K*, pp. 6–7. Some sentences in this section were directly quoted, with minor editing.
42. B. R. Hook and A. Stevenson, "Rising Dough," *Kiplinger's Personal Finance*, Vol. 56, No. 1 (January 2002), p. 71.
43. Panera Bread Company, Inc., *2003 Form 10-K*, pp. 5–6. Some sentences in this section were directly quoted, with minor editing.
44. L. Tischler, "Vote of Confidence," *Fast Company*, No. 65 (December 2002), pp. 102–112.
45. Panera Bread Company, Inc., *2003 Form 10-K*, pp. 4–5. Some paragraphs and sentences in this section were directly quoted, with minor editing.
46. B. Sperber, "Fast Casual Dining Ahead," *Brandweek*, Vol. 43, No. 31 (September 2, 2002), pp. 16–20.
47. J. Peters, "No Loafing Around: Panera Bread Raises Projections for Unit Growth," *Nation's Restaurant News*, Vol. 36, No. 23 (June 10, 2002), p. 12.
48. Panera Bread Company, Inc., *2003 Form 10-K*, p. 6. This section was directly quoted, with minor editing.
49. Panera Bread Company, Inc., *2003 Form 10-K*, pp. 3, 6. Sentences 4 through 8 of the first paragraph and the entire second paragraph were directly quoted, with minor editing.
50. Panera Bread Company, Inc., *2003 Form 10-K*, pp. 13–19. This section was directly quoted, with minor editing.

CASE 29

Arm & Hammer:
Church & Dwight Grows Up (2002)

Roy A. Cook

AS MANAGEMENT STEPPED FIRMLY INTO ANOTHER NEW CENTURY, AN EXCITING NEW chapter in the company's history was opened. "2001 was an exciting and eventful year for Church & Dwight Co., Inc., during which major consumer brands and businesses were acquired, directly and through our new Armkel affiliate, creating a $1.5 billion consumer packaged goods and specialty chemicals company."[1] Had the pieces finally been put in place for the company to compete in the consumer products arena successfully?

Background

For over 156 years, Church & Dwight Co., Inc., worked to build market share on a brand name that is rarely associated with the company. This brand name became so pervasive that it can now be found on a variety of consumer products in 95% of all U.S. households. As the world's largest producer and marketer of sodium bicarbonate–based products, Church & Dwight had achieved fairly consistent growth in both sales and earnings as new and expanded uses were found for sodium bicarbonate. Although Church & Dwight may not be a household name, the name on the company's ubiquitous yellow box of baking soda was: ARM & HAMMER.

Shortly after its introduction in 1878, ARM & HAMMER Baking Soda became a fundamental item on the pantry shelf as homemakers found many uses for it other than baking, such as cleaning and deodorizing. It could also be used as a dentrifice, a chemical agent to absorb or neutralize odors and acidity, a kidney dialysis element, a blast media, an environmentally friendly cleaning agent, and a pollution control agent. It also showed promise in the area of odor control/elimination.

From the 1980s through the early 1990s, average company sales increased almost 15% annually. However, the stated strategy of "selling related products in different markets all

Exhibit 1
Consolidated
Statements of
Income: Church &
Dwight Co., Inc.
(Dollar amounts in
thousands, except
per share data)

Year Ending December 31	2001	2000	1999
Net sales	$1,080,864	$795,725	$740,181
Cost of sales	680,211	450,321	414,486
Gross profit	400,653	345,404	325,695
Advertising, consumer, and trade promotion expenses	195,960	178,614	176,123
Selling, general, and administrative expenses	111,832	92,718	87,047
Impairment and other items	(660)	21,911	6,617
Gain on sale of mineral rights	—	—	(11,772)
Income from operations	93,521	52,161	67,680
Equity in earnings (loss) of affiliates	(6,195)	3,011	6,366
Investment earnings	2,224	2,032	1,216
Other income (expense)	(269)	(187)	201
Interest expense	(11,537)	(4,856)	(2,760)
Income from minority interest and taxes	77,744	52,161	72,703
Minority interest	3,889	287	525
Income before taxes	73,885	51,874	72,178
Income taxes	26,871	18,315	26,821
Net income	$ 46,984	$ 33,559	$ 45,357

Source: Church & Dwight Co., Inc., 2001 Annual Report, and "SEC 10-K" (March 28, 2002), p. 12.

linked by common carbonate and bicarbonate technology"[2] faltered, and sales growth plateaued. As the Chairman of one investment company said, "The only thing they had going for them [was] their uniqueness and they lost it. They made poor marketing and operating decisions that cost them a lot of money."[3] These decisions proved to be a mistake as consumer products were launched in major competitors' markets when the company was operating from a much smaller financial base.

Faced with investment community concerns and a string of disappointing financial results, Robert A. Davies III was brought in as President and Chief Executive Officer (CEO). His primary goals were to reshape the company while raising sales and operating profit margins. The results of his efforts can be seen in the financial statements shown in **Exhibits 1** and **2**. In six years, he reshaped the company from a $500 million into an $1.08 billion business entity with an objective of achieving earnings growth of 12% to 15% per year through 2005.

Management

The historically slow but steady course Church & Dwight had traveled over the decades reflected top management's efforts to focus the company's activities. The ability to remain focused may be attributable to the fact that about 25% of the outstanding shares of common stock were owned by descendants of the company's Co-Founders. Dwight C. Minton, a direct descendant of Austin Church, actively directed the company as CEO from 1969 through 1995 and remained on the Board as Chairman Emeritus. He passed on the duties of CEO to the first non-family member in the company's history, Robert A. Davies III, in 1995. Davies assumed the additional duties of Chairman of the Board from Minton in 2001.

Although Davies was a non-family member, he had a long history of service with Church & Dwight. He served as Vice President, General Manager of the Arm & Hammer Division and then as President/Chief Operating Officer from 1969 through 1984. Davies continued to expand his experiences by serving as President and CEO of California Home Brands (a group of canning companies). In 1995, he returned to Church & Dwight as President of the Arm & Hammer

**Exhibit 2
Consolidated
Balance Sheets:
Church & Dwight
Co., Inc. (Dollar
amounts in
thousands)**

Year Ending December 31	2001	2000	1999
Assets			
Current assets			
Cash and cash equivalents	$ 52,446	$ 21,573	$ 19,765
Short term investments	—	2,990	4,000
Accounts receivable	106,291	64,958	64,505
Inventories	101,214	55,165	72,670
Deferred income taxes	19,849	11,679	8,221
Note receivable and portion of long-term note receivable	5,803	—	—
Prepaid expenses	7,604	4,136	6,622
Total current assets	293,207	160,501	175,783
Property, plant, and equipment, net	231,449	168,570	182,219
Notes receivable	11,951	—	3,000
Equity investment in affiliates	115,121	19,416	20,177
Long-term supply contract	7,695	8,152	4,105
Trade names	136,934	29,699	—
Goodwill and other intangibles	127,320	53,140	83,744
Other assets	25,408	16,154	7,278
Total assets	$949,085	$455,632	$476,306

Year Ending December 31	2001	2000	1999
Liabilities and stockholder's equity			
Current liabilities			
Short-term borrowings	$ 3,220	$ 13,178	$ 25,574
Accounts payable and accrued expenses	176,176	129,268	106,109
Current portion of long-term debt	8,360	685	685
Income taxes payable	8,260	6,007	8,240
Total current liabilities	196,016	149,138	140,608
Long-term debt	406,564	20,136	58,107
Deferred income taxes	27,032	17,852	20,416
Deferred and other long-term liabilities	19,164	15,009	11,860
Nonpension postretirement & postemployment benefits	15,880	15,392	15,145
Minority interest	2,126	3,455	3,437
Stockholders' equity			
Common stock—$1 par value	46,661	46,661	46,661
Additional paid-in capital	28,414	22,514	18,356
Retained earnings	312,409	276,700	253,885
Accumulated other comprehensive income (loss)	(9,728)	(9,389)	(4,599)
	377,756	336,486	314,303
Less common stock in treasury, at cost	(95,453)	(101,836)	(87,021)
Due from shareholder	—	—	(549)
Total stockholders' equity	282,303	234,650	226,733
Total liabilities and stockholders' equity	$949,085	$455,632	$476,306

Source: Church & Dwight Co., Inc., 2002 Annual Report.

Division to put the division "back on track."[4] According to Davies, future growth would be accomplished with "a well-balanced portfolio of household, personal care, and specialty products."[5]

Many companies with strong brand names in the consumer products field have been susceptible to leveraged buyouts and hostile takeovers. However, a series of calculated actions spared Church & Dwight's management from having to make last-minute decisions to ward off unwelcome suitors. Besides maintaining majority control of the outstanding common stock, the Board amended the company's charter, giving current shareholders four votes per share, but required future shareholders to buy and hold shares for four years before receiving the same privilege. The Board of Directors was also structured into three classes, with four directors in each class serving staggered three-year terms. According to Minton, the objective of these moves was to "give the Board control so as to provide the best results for shareholders."[6]

As a further deterrent to would-be suitors or unwelcome advances, the company entered into an employee severance agreement with key officials. This agreement provided severance pay of up to three times the individual's highest annual salary and bonus plus benefits for three years if the individual was terminated within one year after a change in control of the company. Change of control was defined as "the acquisition by a person or group of 25% or more of Company Common Stock; a change in the majority of the board of directors not approved by the pre-change board of directors; or the approval by the stockholders of the Company of a merger, consolidation, liquidation, dissolution, or sale of all the assets of the Company."[7]

As Church & Dwight pushed more aggressively into the consumer products field, several changes were made in key management positions. **Exhibit 3** shows the company's directors and executive officers. Several of these individuals, including Davies, Henry Kornhauser, and Larry Koslow, brought extensive marketing experience to the top management team. The marketing team has continued to be strengthened with the addition of Bradley Casper and Joseph Sipia. With over 40 years of combined domestic and international experience ranging from Procter & Gamble to FMC Corporation, Casper and Sipia brought extensive experience in marketing a variety of consumer and industrial products to the top management team.[8]

In addition to the many changes that had taken place in key management positions, changes had also begun to be made in the composition of the Board of Directors. Although 7 of the 11-member Board had served for 20 years or more, 3 have served for 5 years or less. One woman served on the board, and ages of the current members ranged from 52 to 70. Although in a less active role as Chairman Emeritus, Dwight Minton continued to provide leadership and a long legacy of "corporate memory."

A Change in Direction

Entering the 21st century, management recognized a major challenge to overcome the company's small size compared to its competitors in basic product lines of household and personal care. They also recognized the value of a major asset, the company's pristine balance sheet, and made the decision to grow the business with two decisive transformational moves:

1. On April 2, 2001, a tender offer was made to acquire USA Detergents, Inc. (NASDAQ:USAD), its partner in the Armus joint venture. With this acquisition, Church & Dwight's laundry business became the third largest in the $7 billion retail U. S. laundry category. XTRA and NICE'N FLUFFY brands were part of the acquisition and Church & Dwight acquired the consumer products business of Carter-Wallace, Inc., purchasing outright the ARRID Anti-Perspirant and the LAMBERT KAY Pet Care businesses. Armkel, LLC, Church & Dwight's 50-50 joint venture with the private equity group Kelso & Company, acquired the remainder of Carter-Wallace consumer products businesses, including such brands as TROJAN Condoms, NAIR Depilatories and FIRST RESPONSE Home Pregnancy and Ovulation test kits. Combining these products with

Exhibit 3
Key Officers and Their Management Positions: Church & Dwight Co., Inc.

Corporate Governance: Church & Dwight Co., Inc.

A. Directors

William R. Becklean
Managing Director
SunTrust Equitable Securities
Director since 1980

Robert A. Davies, III
Chairman and CEO
Church & Dwight Co., Inc.
Director since 1995

J. Richard Leaman, Jr.
Retired President and CEO
S.D. Warren Company
Director since 1985

John D. Leggett III, Ph.D.
President
Sensor Instruments Co., Inc.
Director since 1979

Robert A. McCabe
Chairman
Pilot Capital Corporation
Director since 1987

Burton B. Staniar
Chairman and CEO
Knoll, Inc.
Director since 1999

Robert H. Beeby
Retired President and CEO
Frito-Lay, Inc.
Director since 1992

Rosina B. Dixon, M.D.
Physician and Consultant
Director since 1979

Richard D. LeBlanc
President and CEO
Handy & Harman
Director since 1998

John F. Maypole
Managing Partner
Peach State Real Estate Holding Co.
Director since 1999

Dwight C. Minton
Chairman Emeritus
Church & Dwight Co., Inc.
Director since 1965

John O. Whitney
Professor and Executive Director
The Deming Center for Quality Management,
Columbia Business School
Director since 1992

B. Executive Officers

Robert A. Davies, III
Chairman and CEO

Raymond L. Bendure, Ph.D.
Vice President, Research & Development

Mark A. Bilawsky
Vice President, General Counsel, and Secretary

Mark G. Conish
Vice President, Operations

Steven P. Cugine
Vice President, Human Resources,
Acting President and Chief Operating Officer,
Specialty Products Division

Zvi Eiref
Vice President, Finance, and Chief Financial
Officer

Henry Kornhauser
Vice President, Advertising

Dennis M. Moore
President, ARMUS, LLC
Vice President, Sales,
Arm & Hammer Division

C. Principal Accounting Officers

Gary P. Halker
Vice President, Controller, and Chief Information Officer

Steven J. Katz
Assistant Controller

Source: Church & Dwight Co., Inc., Notice of Annual Meeting of Stockholders and Proxy Statement *(2002), p. 5.*

the company's existing product lines makes Church & Dwight one of the leading consumer packaged goods companies in the United States.

2. On September 28, 2001, the company completed the acquisition of the consumer products business of Carter-Wallace, Inc., in a partnership called Armkel, LLC, with the private equity group Kelso & Company. These two acquisitions doubled the company's size and almost tripled the number of employees, and set the stage for several years of growth.[9]

This change led to a restructuring of the company. What had once been a small company focusing on a few consumer and specialty products had emerged as a much larger competitor. Consumer products now encompassed a broad array of personal care, deodorizing and cleaning, and laundry products, while specialty products offerings were expanded to specialty chemicals, animal nutrition, and specialty cleaners.

Consumer Products

Prior to its acquisition spree, the company's growth strategy had been based on finding new uses for sodium bicarbonate. Using an overall family branding strategy to further penetrate the consumer products market in the United States and Canada, additional products were introduced displaying the ARM & HAMMER logo. This logoed footprint remains significant as the ARM & HAMMER brand controlled a commanding 85% of the baking soda market. By capitalizing on its easily recognizable brand name, logo, and established marketing channels, Church & Dwight moved into such products as laundry detergent, carpet cleaners and deodorizers, air deodorizers, toothpaste, and deodorant/antiperspirants. This strategy worked well, allowing the company to promote multiple products using only one brand name.

From the company's founding until 1970, it produced and sold only two consumer products: ARM & HAMMER Baking Soda and a laundry product marketed under the name Super Washing Soda. In 1970 under Minton, Church & Dwight began testing the consumer products market by introducing a phosphate-free, powdered laundry detergent. Several other products, including a liquid laundry detergent, fabric softener sheets, an all-fabric bleach, tooth powder and toothpaste, baking soda chewing gum, deodorant/antiperspirants, deodorizers (carpet, room, and pet), and clumping cat litter have been added to the expanding list of ARM & HAMMER brands. However, simply relying on baking soda extensions and focusing on niche markets to avoid a head-on attack from competitors with more financial and marketing clout limited growth opportunities.[10] So, in the late 1990s, the company departed from its previous strategy of developing new product offerings in-house and bought several well-known consumer brands such as Brillo, Parsons Ammonia, Cameo Aluminum & Stainless Steel Cleaner, Rain Drops water softener, SNO BOWL toilet bowl cleaner, and TOSS 'N SOFT dryer sheets from one of its competitors, The Dial Corporation. (See **Exhibit 4**.)

Church & Dwight faced the same dilemma as other competitors in a mature domestic market for consumer products. New consumer products had to muscle their way into markets by taking market share from current offerings. With the majority of company sales in the United States and Canada, it was well-equipped to gain market share with its low-cost strategy. However, in the international arena, where growth was more product driven and less marketing sensitive, the company did not possess the in-house expertise to capture market share.[11] To compensate for this weakness, Church & Dwight relied on acquisitions to improve its international footprint and reach. The breadth of its expanded consumer product offerings can be seen in **Exhibit 4**.

Exhibit 4 Consumer Product Breakdown

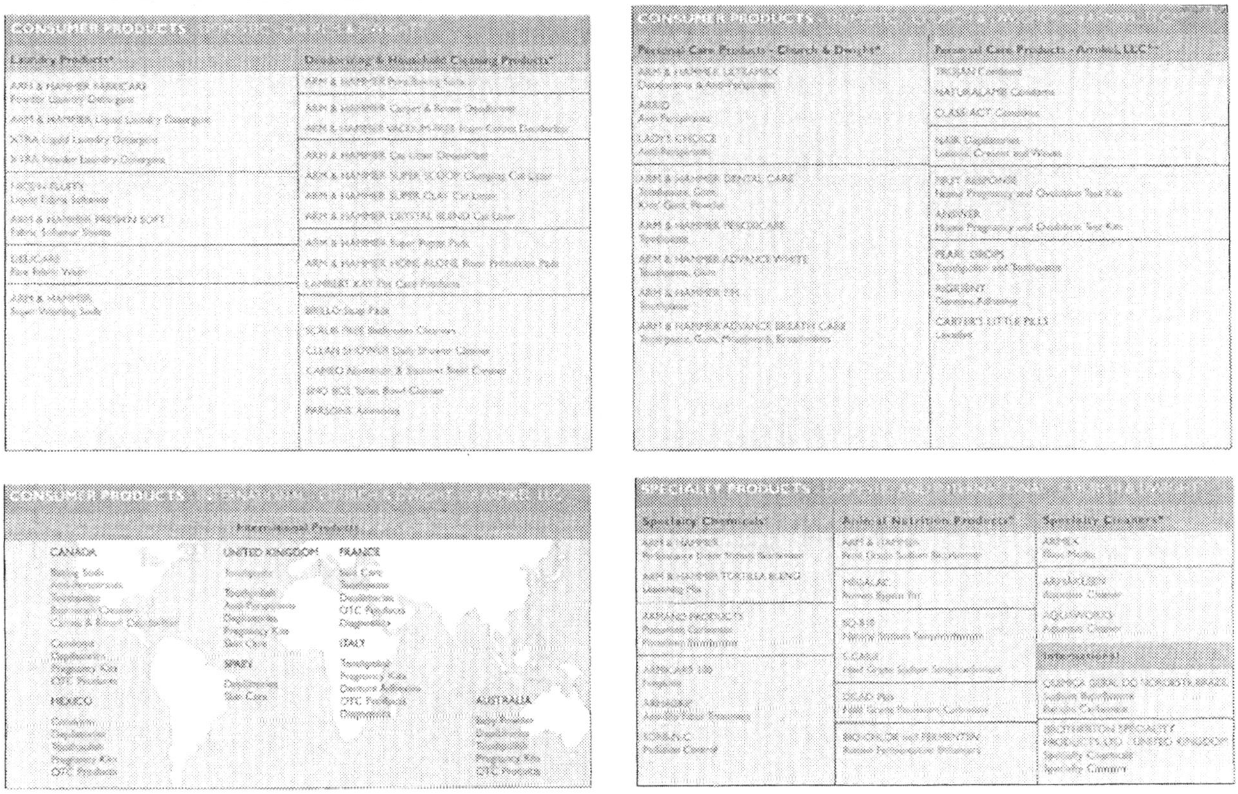

Notes:
* All trademarks are owned by Church & Dwight Co., Inc., or by one of its wholly owned subsidiaries or affiliates.
**All trademarks are owned by Armkel, LLC, a 50–50 joint venture between Church & Dwight Co., Inc., and Kelso & Company.

Source: Church & Dwight Co., Inc., 2001 **Annual Report,** *pp. 8–9.*

According to Minton, as the company had grown, "We have made every effort to keep costs under control and manage frugally."[12] A good example of this approach to doing business can be seen in the Armkel partnership. "Armkel borrowed money on a non-recourse basis so a failure would have no impact on Church & Dwight, taking any risk away from shareholders."[13]

With its new stable of products and expanded laundry detergent offerings, Church & Dwight found itself competing head-on with consumer product giants such as Procter & Gamble, Clorox, Lever Brothers, and Dial. Church & Dwight's market share positions in key product categories can be found in **Exhibit 5**.

As more and more products were added to Church & Dwight's consumer line-up, the need for additional marketing expertise had grown. Along with the addition of Henry Kornhauser to the top management team in 1997, Church & Dwight brought many of its marketing tasks in-house. Kornhauser brought 17 years of senior management and advertising agency experience with him to Church & Dwight.

The first major project undertaken by this new in-house function was the $15 million launch of ARM & HAMMER Dental Care Gum.[14] Although it entered a crowded field of specialty products, Church & Dwight planned to ride the crest of increasing interest of both dentists and hygienists in baking soda as an important element in a regimen for maintaining dental health.[15] Church & Dwight was able to sneak up on the giants in the industry and moved rapidly from the position of a niche player in the toothpaste market (along with products such as Topol, Viadent, Check-Up, Zact, and Tom's of Maine) to that of a major competitor.

Exhibit 5
U. S. Market Share
Position

Product Category	Position
Laundry Detergent	#3
Cat Litter	#2
Bathroom Cleaner	#1
Antiperspirants	#5
Condoms	#1
Depilatories	#1
Home Pregnancy Test Kits	#2

For the most part, Church & Dwight's entries into the consumer products market have met with success. However, a potential marketing problem may be looming on the horizon for its ARM & HAMMER line of consumer products. The company could be falling into the precarious line-extension snare. Placing a well-known brand name on a wide variety of products could cloud its position and cause it to lose marketing pull.[16] Will the addition of such well-known brand names as XTRA, Nair, Trojan, and First Response provide sufficient avenues for growth?

Specialty Products

The stated strategy for the Specialty Products division was "to solidify worldwide leadership in sodium bicarbonate and potassium carbonate, while broadening our product offerings to other related chemicals . . . to build a specialized high-margin specialty cleaning business, allying carbonate technology, the ARM & HAMMER trademark and environmental position."[17] Management's apparent increased focus on consumer products had somewhat affected the growth of specialty products, as is shown in the company's product mix in **Exhibit 6**.

Church & Dwight was in an enviable position to profit from its dominant niche in the sodium bicarbonate products market since it controlled the primary raw material used in its production. The primary ingredient in sodium bicarbonate was produced from the mineral trona, which was extracted from the company's mines in southwestern Wyoming. The other ingredient, carbon dioxide, was a readily available chemical that could be obtained from a variety of sources.

The company maintained a dominant position in the production of the required raw materials for both its consumer and industrial products. It manufacturered almost two-thirds of the sodium bicarbonate sold in the United States and, until recently, was the only U.S. producer of ammonium bicarbonate and potassium carbonate. The company in 2002 had the largest share (approximately 75%) of the sodium bicarbonate capacity in the United States and was the largest consumer of baking soda as it filled its own needs for company-produced consumer and industrial products.[18]

To meet these needs and solidify market dominance, product capacity had been raised by 80,000 tons, to 520,000 tons, in 2000.[19-21] Even though it was the dominant player in the field, additional competition was on the horizon. "The playing field in the sodium bicarbonate industry is broadening with two nahcolite solution mining producers on the horizon. This alternative to trona processing involves extracting nahcolite, or naturally occurring sodium

Exhibit 6
Percentage of Net
Sales: Church &
Dwight Co., Inc.

	2001	2000	1999	1998	1997
Consumer Products (%)	82	77	77	79	80
Specialty Products (%)	18	23	23	21	20
Totals (%)	100	100	100	100	100

bicarbonate, embedded in oil shale."[22] The nahcolite extraction process appeared to be more cost-effective than the trona mining process used by Church & Dwight.

The Specialty Products Division of Church & Dwight consisted of the manufacture and sale of sodium bicarbonate for three distinct market segments: specialty chemicals, animal nutrition products, and specialty cleaners (see **Exhibit 4**). Manufacturers utilized sodium bicarbonate performance products as a leavening agent for commercial baked goods; an antacid in pharmaceuticals; a chemical in kidney dialysis; a carbon dioxide release agent in fire extinguishers; and an alkaline in swimming pool chemicals, detergents, and various textile and tanning applications. Animal feed producers used sodium bicarbonate nutritional products predominantly as a buffer, or antacid, for dairy cattle feeds and made a nutritional supplement that enhanced milk production of dairy cattle. Sodium bicarbonate had also been used as an additive to poultry feeds to enhance feed efficiency. Just like the Consumer Products Division, the Specialty Products Division focused on developing new uses for the company's core product, sodium bicarbonate. Additional opportunities continue to be explored for ARMEX Blast Media. This was a sodium bicarbonate–based product used as a paint-stripping compound. It had gained widespread recognition when it had been utilized successfully for the delicate task of stripping the accumulation of years of paint and tar from the interior of the Statue of Liberty without damaging the fragile copper skin. It was now being considered for other specialized applications in the transportation and electronics industries and in industrial cleaning because of its apparent environmental safety. ARMEX had been introduced into international markets.

Specialty cleaning products were found in blasting (similar to sand blasting applications) as well as many emerging aqueous-based cleaning technologies, such as automotive parts cleaning and circuit board cleaning. Safety-Kleen and Church & Dwight had teamed up through a 50–50 joint venture, ARMAKLEEN, to meet the parts cleaning needs of automotive repair shops. Safety-Kleen's 2,800-strong sales and service team marketed Church & Dwight's aqueous-based cleaners as an environmental friendly alternative to traditional solvent-based cleaners.[23]

The company's ARMAKLEEN product was also used for cleaning printed circuit boards. This potentially promising product may have an enormous potential market because it may be able to replace chlorofluorocarbon-based cleaning systems. "ARMAKLEEN, a carbonate and bicarbonate technology, is the first nonsolvent-based system for this market."[24] Sodium bicarbonate also had been used to remove lead from drinking water and, when added to water supplies, coated the inside of pipes and prevented lead from leaching into the water. This market could grow in significance with additions to the Clean Water Bill. The search for new uses of sodium bicarbonate continued in both the consumer and specialty products divisions.

International Operations

Church & Dwight had traditionally enjoyed a great deal of success in North American markets; however, until the 2001 acquisition of the Carter-Wallace line of products, only about 10% of sales had come from outside the United States. The Specialty Products Division established small footholds in the South American markets through investments in Venezuela and Brazil and was also exploring opportunities in Asia. According to Eugene Wilcaukas, Vice President, "We've been a little late in Asia. We have a strong desire to be there and the financial ability to accomplish it."[25]

The company's first major attempt to expand its presence in the international consumer products markets was with the acquisition of DeWitt International Corporation, which manufactured and marketed personal care products, including toothpaste. The DeWitt acquisition not only provided the company with increased international exposure but also with much-needed toothpaste production facilities and technology.

At the same time the company was testing the international waters for its consumer products, it was also continuing to pursue expansion of its specialty products into international markets. Attempts to enter international markets have met with limited success, probably for two reasons: (1) lack of name recognition and (2) transportation costs. Although ARM & HAMMER was one of the most recognized brand names in the United States (in the top 10), it did not enjoy the same name recognition elsewhere. In addition, "international transportation represented 40%–45% of Church & Dwight's sales expense, versus 5 to 10% domestically."[26] However, export opportunities continued to present themselves as 10% of all U.S. production of sodium bicarbonate was exported.

Church & Dwight's Future

According to Davies, recent acquisitions had advanced the company's objective "to build a well-balanced, high-growth consumer packaged goods company with a related specialty chemicals business."[27] And, now, "the Company will conduct a major strategic business review."[28]

The core business and the foundation on which the company had been built remained the same after more than 156 years. However, as an expanded management team at Church & Dwight looks to the future, the team must reflect on the successes and mistakes of the past as the team planned for the future. In the extremely competitive consumer products market, can management continue to pursue a "growth strategy based around the modernization of long-standing uses of sodium bicarbonate"[29] while realizing the "synergies that can be achieved by combining its operations with those of ARMAKLEEN, particularly in the areas of sales, manufacturing, and distribution, and most service functions"?[30]

Notes

1. Church & Dwight Co., Inc., *2001 Annual Report*, inside cover.
2. "C&D Sees Growth Despite Competitions," *Chemical Marketing Reporter* (December 11, 1989), p. 9.
3. A. Adelson, "Arm and Hammer Names a New President," *New York Times* (February 2, 1995), p. D3.
4. *Ibid.*
5. Church & Dwight Co., Inc., "Church & Dwight Co., Inc. Reports Second Quarter EPS Rose 36% to $0.45 on 13% Sales Increase; Adjusted EPS Rose 18% to $0.40 for Quarter and 22% to $0.82 for First Half," *Company Press Release* (August 5, 2002).
6. D. C. Minton, Personal Interview (October 2, 2002).
7. Church & Dwight Co., Inc., *Annual Meeting Report* (May 2002), p. 1.
8. Church & Dwight Co., Inc., "Church & Dwight Co., Inc. Names Bradley A. Casper as President, Personal Care and ARMKEL Domestic," *Company Press Release* (April 25, 2002).
9. Church & Dwight Co., *Annual Meeting Report* (May 2002), p. 1.
10. C. M. Wainwright, "Church & Dwight: Slow but Steady into Personal Care," *Drug & Cosmetic Industry* (February 1987), p. 28.
11. P. Weisz, "Church & Dwight in Need of Next Big Idea," *Brandweek* (November 13, 1995), p. 8.
12. D. C. Minton, Personal Interview (October 2, 2002).
13. *Ibid.*
14. J. Pollack, "Arm & Hammer Spending Soars to Back Dental Gum," *Advertising Age* (March 23, 1998), p. 49.
15. D. Kiley, "Arm & Hammer Mixes Its Own," *Adweek's Marketing Week* (July 4, 1988), p. 3.
16. R. Alsop, "Arm & Hammer Baking Soda Going in Toothpaste as Well as Refrigerator," *Wall Street Journal* (June 24, 1998), pp. 2–24.
17. Church & Dwight Co., Inc., *Annual Report* (1997), p. 13.
18. L. Jarvis, "Church & Dwight Builds Sales Through Strength in Bicarbonate," *Chemical Market Report*, Vol. 257, No. 15 (April 10, 2002).
19. J. Adams, "Church & Dwight Completes Bicarb Upgrades," *Chemical Week*, Vol. 161, No. 18 (May 12, 1999).
20. J. Adams, "Church & Dwight Completes Expansion in Ohio," *Chemical Week*, Vol. 161, No. 44 (November 24, 1999).
21. L. Jarvis, "Church & Dwight Builds Sales Through Strength in Bicarbonate," *Chemical Market Reporter*, Vol. 257, No. 15 (April 10, 2000).
22. *Ibid.*, p. 6.
23. H. Harvilicz, "C&D's Industrial Cleaning Business Continues to Grow," *Chemical Market Reporter*, Vol. 257, No. 20 (May 15, 2000).
24. R. Mullin, "Soaps and Detergents: New Generation of Compacts," *ChemicalWeek* (January 27, 1993), p. 29.
25. R. Westervelt, "Church & Dwight Takes Brazilian Stake," *Chemical Weekly* (June 18, 1997), p. 15.
26. R. J. Bowman, "Quality Management Comes to Global Transportation," *World Trade* (February 1993), p. 38.
27. Church & Dwight Co., Inc., *Annual Report*, 2002, p. 7.
28. *Ibid.*
29. L. Jarvis, "Church & Dwight Builds Sales Through Strength in Bicarbonate," *Chemical Market Report*, Vol. 257, No. 15 (April 10, 2002).
30. Church & Dwight Co., Inc., *2001 Annual Report*, p. 2.

CASE 30

JetBlue Airways' Success Story

Sanjib Dutta and Shirisha Regani

"JetBlue has been put together as no other airline has ever been put together before. It has the most capital. It has the best product. So now the question is, can you continue it? And that's what worries me. That's what keeps me up at night. How can we continue what we have started?"

David Neeleman, Founder and CEO of JetBlue

"JetBlue will continue to eat out of the major carriers' rice bowls for quite some time. While they struggle to repair their balance sheets and become more liquid and financially flexible, low-cost airlines like JetBlue will expand into the vacuum the majors have created."

Robert Mann, airline analyst and consultant at R.W. Mann & Co.

JetBlue Beats the Biggies

IN EARLY 2003, JETBLUE AIRWAYS, THE THREE-YEAR-OLD NO-FRILLS U.S. AIRLINE, posted a profit of $17.6 million for the first quarter of 2003. In the same period, the U.S. airline industry announced losses of around $2 billion. JetBlue was one of the few bright spots in an industry that had been reeling under the woes of overcapacity and losses for over two years. The company managed to succeed in a period when big names of the U.S. airline industry, like American Airlines, United Air Lines, US Airways, and others, suffered huge losses and were a few steps from bankruptcy.

The U.S. airline industry was in a bad state owing to the effects of terrorism, war, and economic downturn. The major carriers alone were estimated to have an outstanding debt of over $100 billion, as against a combined stock market value of $13 billion in 2002. Passenger traffic was also falling consistently. In early 2003, air traffic was 17% lower than in the same period of 2002 (which was itself 10% lower than the traffic in early 2001).

In this scenario, a number of low-cost airlines began to make their presence felt in the industry. (See **Exhibit 1** for a note on low-cost airlines in the United States.) Southwest

Exhibit 1
A Note on Low-Cost
Airlines

No-frills, low-cost carriers seem to be the answer to the problems of the American airline industry. In 2002, when the industry was estimated to have made losses to the tune of $9 billion, Southwest Airlines and JetBlue Airways were the only two major carriers to post profits. Low-cost carriers seemed to be gaining popularity with passengers for short point-to-point trips in the United States. The main features of low-cost carriers are:

- They operate only one kind of aircraft, such as the Boeing 737 or the Airbus 319/320.
- They are one-class carriers that offer standardized treatment to all the passengers.
- They do not offer benefits like lounges, free meals, or drinks.
- Normally there is no seat allocation (JetBlue is an exception).
- Tickets are normally booked over the Internet.

Most low-cost airlines also make efforts to simplify check-in processes by introducing electronic check-ins and simplifying baggage handling.

In 2002 it was estimated that low-cost airlines accounted for 25% of short-haul bookings in the United States.

Some of the prominent low-cost carriers in the United States are:

- Airtran
- American West
- American Trans Air
- Delta Express' Song
- I-Jet
- JetBlue
- Frontier Airlines
- Midwest Express
- Southwest
- Spirit Airlines
- Suncountry
- USA-3000

However, low-frills airlines are not all benefits. Observers say that low-cost carriers charge low fares only when tickets are booked far in advance. Late bookers are penalized with prices equal to or higher than those for premium flights. Analysts also say that the idea that people choose only on the price dimension is wrong. They say that a number of people are willing to pay a premium to be able to fly from good airports and have a comfortable travel experience.

The difference between low-cost and premium airlines, however, is narrowing. The high-cost, full-service airlines are making efforts to control costs, while the low-cost carriers are trying to expand to longer hauls and provide better flight experiences.

Source: Adapted from various newspaper and magazine articles.

Airlines, the highly successful 30-year-old discounter, was the inspiration for most of the low-cost startups. However, not all the startups succeeded. The most important cause for failure was the inability of these low-cost airlines to bring about a balance between cost-cutting and quality of service. The most successful exception to this condition was JetBlue.

JetBlue, which was modeled on Southwest Airlines, managed to succeed in a depressed and highly competitive industry because of its innovative approach to business and its efforts in becoming a cost leader by cutting down on unnecessary frills and wasteful expenses. The airline managed to cut costs without compromising the quality of service. In fact, it provided more amenities than other airlines, including a personal television set for every flyer and comfortable leather seats, creating a feeling of luxury. JetBlue's strategy was to identify and eliminate non-value-adding costs and use the money so saved to provide service of better quality.

Background

JetBlue is the brainchild of David Neeleman, the son of a Mormon missionary, who grew up in Salt Lake City, Utah. Neeleman was a poor student and dropped out of the University of Utah after his freshman year. After dropping out, he spent two years in Brazil as a missionary. Upon returning to the United States, he took up a career in sales, selling condominiums in Hawaii. To boost his business, he started his own travel agency by chartering flights to transport prospective clients to the Hawaiian islands. Neeleman was a hard-seller who even tried to push honeymoon packages onto couples during their weddings.

His reputation as a salesman caught the attention of June Morris, who owned one of Utah's largest travel agencies. Together, they started a Utah-based charter operation in 1984 called Morris Air. Neeleman modeled Morris Air on Southwest Airlines,[1] run by his idol Herb Kelleher. He took ideas from Southwest and tried to improve on them. He adopted a strategy of keeping costs low to increase margins by turning around[2] the planes quickly and having reservationists work from home to save on office rentals. He also developed the industry's first electronic ticketing system, which was easier to operate than manual ones and did not cost much. By 1992, Morris Air had developed into a regular scheduled airline and was poised for an IPO.

Herb Kelleher, impressed with the airline's low-cost, high-revenues strategy, offered to take it over. Southwest bought Morris Air for $129 million. Neeleman gained $22 million from this sale and went to work at Southwest as an Executive Vice President. This arrangement, however, did not work out. Neeleman, accustomed to running his own airline, was unable to adjust to working in a team. Within a year, he parted ways with Southwest. Before he could leave, Kelleher made him sign a non-compete agreement that would be valid for five years.

Neeleman then moved to Canada, where he co-founded a discount airline called West Jet. He also fine-tuned the online reservations system he developed at Morris Air, called it *Open Skies*, and sold it to Hewlett-Packard[3] in 1999, for a reported $22 million.

After his non-compete agreement with Kelleher expired in 1998, Neeleman, along with his lawyer, Tom Kelly, started developing business plans for a new airline that was to be called JetBlue. He raised capital from the same five people who had invested in Morris Air and millionaire investor George Soros. He blew through $30 million before the first plane flew and went back for more capital. But the investors, who were impressed with the success he had made of Morris Air, were ready to lend him more.

Next, he started studying the current scenario in the airline industry to make strategic decisions about his airline. He decided to base his airline in New York's John F. Kennedy International Airport (JFK) rather than the two nearby airports LaGuardia and Newark because he reasoned that, since JFK mostly flew international flights, he would have very little competition from domestic flights at that airport.

He then identified routes that were poorly served by other airlines and decided to concentrate on those. JetBlue would not serve too many routes. Instead, it would concentrate on certain areas, like the West Coast, Northeast, and Florida, flying key routes that were not taken by competitors.

From the beginning, Neeleman was sure that his airline would be a low-cost operator. He studied the price structures of the major airlines over different routes from New York and found that they would not be difficult to undercut, provided that he had the right technology and equipment. To achieve his objective, he used capital equipment that had high initial outlay but was easier on the maintenance side.

He then went after the best people in the industry to work with him for the airline. He roped in Dave Barger, who had led a turnaround at Continental Airlines, to function as

Exhibit 2
Income Statement:
JetBlue (Dollar
amounts in
millions, except
per share amounts)

Particulars	December 2002	December 2001	December 2000
Revenue	$635.2	$320.4	$104.6
Cost of Goods sold	212.0	159.4	63.6
Gross Profit	423.2	161.0	41.0
SG&A Expense	291.3	134.3	62.2
Depreciation & Amortization	26.9	—	—
Operating Income/Loss	105.0	26.8	(21.2)
Total Net Income/Loss	$ 54.9	$ 38.5	$ (21.3)
Net Profit Margin	8.6%	12.0%	—
Gross Profit Margin	66.6%	50.3%	39.2%
Operating Margin	16.5%	8.4%	—
Diluted EPS	$ 0.84	—	—

Source: www.hoovers.com.

President and COO. He also took two of Southwest's top people to manage finance and human resources at JetBlue.

JetBlue started with initial capital of $160 million. Operations began on February 11, 2000. The inaugural flight was between New York's JFK and Fort Lauderdale, Florida. In early 2002, JetBlue came out with an initial public offer of about 5.5 million shares. The shares, traded on NASDAQ, were offered at a price between $22 and $24 but shot up to around $45 on the first day. The capital raised through the issue was used to buy new planes and to supplement working capital.

In 2002, JetBlue recorded a total net income of $55 million on revenues of $635 million (**see Exhibit 2**). This occurred in a year when the major airlines in the industry were estimated to have lost about $9 billion (**see Exhibit 3**). After posting a 35% increase over the previous year in the first quarter earnings for 2003, the company placed an order for 65 new Airbus A-320 planes, with Airbus Industries, adding to the 41 planes already in the fleet. See the company's *2003 Annual Report* for complete financial statements, at *http://investor.jetblue.com/ireye/ir_site.zhtml?ticker=jblu&script=700.*

Exhibit 3
Loss Position of
Airlines in America

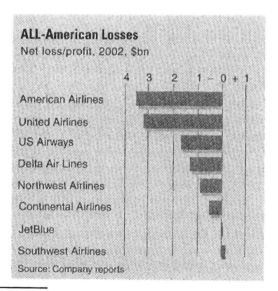

Source: "Flying Dinosaurs," The Economist *(February 6, 2003).*

In its three years of operation, JetBlue flew more than 12 million passengers. The airline received a number of awards for the quality of its service and its success in operations. (**See Exhibit 4** for a list of awards received by JetBlue.)

JetBlue's Success Model

JetBlue succeeded because of its cost advantages and no-nonsense approach to business. The company adopted aggressive cost-cutting measures by doing away with most of the frills other airlines provided that only increased their costs and did not improve customer value, without compromising on quality or comfort. Said Neeleman, "You can be efficient and effective and deliver a great experience at the same time."[4] JetBlue's aim was to create a cost structure that would support low fares without lowering service standards. The fares JetBlue charged for a round trip averaged between $98 to $498, which was more than 50% less than those charged by the majors in the industry. (For instance, a round trip from New York to Florida cost about $500 on the major airlines; JetBlue charged about $140 for the same trip with a seven-day advance purchase.) To support its decision to become a cost leader, JetBlue adopted a number of innovative measures on its flights.

Effective Cost Management

JetBlue decided not to serve meals on its flights, no matter what the distance or duration. Neeleman identified food as an area in which major cost-cutting was possible. He realized that since airline food was notoriously bad, no one was likely to miss it. He, therefore, did away with meals altogether. Instead of meals, JetBlue served light snacks like chips, cookies, and crackers, which cost a fraction of what a regular meal did and also pleased the passengers. All the snacks were piled in a basket, and the customers could help themselves to whatever they wanted. The airline also served coffee and canned drinks, which did not cost much. Neeleman calculated that a normal airline meal cost about $4 per passenger. By choosing to serve snacks that cost 12–14 cents, JetBlue saved a huge amount.

Not serving meals on flights did not affect JetBlue in any way. In fact, analysts felt that JetBlue had identified a very good area for reducing expenses. This innovative approach helped JetBlue save over $3 per passenger, at the same time ensuring that no one went hungry on flights. Passengers also seemed to prefer this kind of snacks to regular, insipid meals, and serving items like chips and animal crackers went well with JetBlue's image as an innovative, fun airline.

The money saved on food was put to better use elsewhere. It was spent mainly on providing personal television sets to all the passengers on the flight. Every passenger was given an individual TV, with a set of headphones. The TV was fixed to the back of the seat in front of each passenger, and passengers could watch 24 channels of satellite television. This idea was a great hit with passengers, who seemed to enjoy the freedom of being able to watch whatever they wanted without having to compromise. (In other airlines, there was normally only one television screen, which all the passengers had to watch together. This left no scope for individual preferences.) There were instances of people choosing JetBlue over other airlines only because of the personal TVs.

Personal TVs provided JetBlue with a good point for differentiation. The company used this feature like a weapon against other domestic airlines, as it was the only one offering personal TVs. The personal TV feature was played up, mentioned in most of the brochures, and it was emphasized in all the advertisements. JetBlue even acquired Live TV, the television

Exhibit 4 Awards Received: JetBlue

Award	Conferred By
1. 2003 Awards	
Top 5 Domestic Airline	Departures, 2003 Readers' Favorite Survey
Best Low Cost Airline	*Entrepreneur* magazine
Best Low Cost Airline	Skytraxx, 2003 Airline of the Year Survey
Airline of the Year	*Airfinance Journal*, 2003 Deal of the Year Awards
North American Corporate Finance Deal of the Year	*Airfinance Journal*, 2003 Deal of the Year Awards
IPO of the Year	*Corporate Finance*
Editors' Choice	Travel-Holiday
Outstanding Inflight Entertainment	*Onboard Services*, 2003 Onboard Services Awards
Outstanding Safety Video	*Onboard Services*, 2003 Onboard Services Awards
2. 2002 Awards	
Best Domestic Airline	*Conde Nast Traveler*, 2002 Readers' Choice Awards
Best Domestic Airline—Coach	*Conde Nast Traveler*, 2002 Business Travel Awards
Best Domestic Airline—Value for Cost	*Conde Nast Traveler*, 2002 Business Travel Awards
Best Domestic Airline	North American Travel Journalists Association, Five-Star Award
#2 Domestic Airline	*Travel and Leisure*, 2002 World's Best Awards
Best Low-Cost Carrier (runner-up)	*Business Traveler*, 2002 Best in Business Travel Awards
"It" Airline	*Entertainment Weekly*, 2002 It List
Editor's Choice	*Worth*
Marketer of the Year	*Advertising Age*
#4 Brand of the Year	*www.brandchannel.com*, 2002 Readers' Choice
Finance Award	*Airline Business*, 2002 Airline Strategy Awards
Market Development Award	*Air Transport World*, 2002 Industry Achievement Awards
Best Overall Airline	*Onboard Services*, 2002 Onboard Service Awards
Best Inflight or Onboard Service	*Onboard Services*, 2002 Onboard Service Awards
Best Onboard Entertainment	*Onboard Services*, 2002 Onboard Service Awards
Best Uniforms (2nd place)	*Onboard Services*, 2002 Onboard Service Awards
3. 2001 Awards	
Best Domestic Airline—Coach	*Conde Nast Traveler*, 2001 Business Travel Awards
#2 Domestic Airline	*Conde Nast Traveler*, 2001 Reader's Choice Awards
#2 Domestic Airline	Zagat, 2001 Airline Survey
Best Domestic Airline	North American Travel Journalists Assn., 2001 Five-Star Award
Best New Airline	*Money*
Favorite U.S. Airline	*Orange County Register*/Knight Ridder
Seal of Approval	*Diversion*
"A" Rating	Planetfeedback, leading online consumer feedback service
#2 Airline	Epinions.com
4. Awards Won by David Neeleman	
Best & Brightest (2003)	*Esquire*
Atlas Award for Guerilla Marketing (2003)	Association of Travel Marketing Executives
Best Visionary (2001)	*Sales & Marketing Management*
Top 20 Most Influential People In Aviation (2001)	*Aviation Daily*
Winners' Circle (2001)	*Travel Agent*
Top Ten Entrepreneurs (2000)	*BusinessWeek*
Travel Industry Innovator (2000)	*Time*
25 Most Influential Executives of 2000	*Business Travel News*
Top 20 Most Influential People in Aviation (2000)	*Aviation Daily*
Winners' Circle (2000)	*Travel Agent*

Source: www.jetblue.com.

station that broadcast the 24 channels onboard, to be able to maintain its advantage over rivals.

The television sets cost about $1 per passenger per flight. That was less than one-third the cost of a meal, so JetBlue did not have to incur any additional expenditure in providing the service. It only diverted resources from an unproductive function to a productive one, which gave the company a competitive advantage over its rivals.

JetBlue did not try to cut costs in all areas. Neeleman realized that cost-cutting must be balanced with good quality for an airline to succeed. Cutting costs in all areas only brought down the quality of service and sometimes turned out to be counterproductive. To avoid this, he sometimes chose items that involved a high initial cost but provided a greater advantage in the long run. For instance, he chose to fit his planes with leather seats instead of cloth ones. Leather furnishings cost twice as much as cloth ones, but they also lasted twice as long. Besides, leather seats were more comfortable for passengers and therefore improved customer value. Passengers really liked the new leather seats, which were also wider and offered more leg room. JetBlue managed to combine luxury with economy. Said Neeleman, "It's different with JetBlue. And people feel different. They don't feel like they are flying on a start-up airline."[5]

Unlike a number of other startup airlines, JetBlue did not use old, cheap planes. By choosing to operate Airbus[6] flights, it dispelled the image of a startup operator functioning on a shoestring budget and created an image of smart efficiency. Neeleman chose the Airbus A-320 over the more popular Boeing 737[7] because he calculated that, although the Airbus cost more initially, it was easier on the maintenance side and was also more fuel-efficient. Fuel-efficiency was an important variable in the decision, in light of rising fuel prices around the world. The planes also came with a five-year warranty, which reduced the maintenance costs drastically and more than made up for the higher initial expenditure.

JetBlue's cost per passenger mile was 6.43 cents, which was only slightly higher than the 6.33 cents of Southwest and much lower than US Airways' 12.45 cents.

Operational Advantage

JetBlue operated only a single fleet of planes, and there was no division into first class, business class, and economy class, unlike with other airline majors. JetBlue figured out that it could save more by offering standard treatment to all passengers and providing good service without distinctions. Flying a single fleet worked to the advantage of the airline as it involved fewer scheduling and maintenance problems. It also helped control costs, as spare parts, furnishings, and crew were interchangeable.

One of the critical factors in the success of JetBlue was that it was able to identify a niche market and cater to it. It did not try to fly too many routes, instead concentrating on New York, Florida, and California. It also flew to secondary airports that did not handle too much air traffic. Neeleman reasoned that he could gain more passengers by flying out of airports his competitors did not use. Secondary airports also offered better business terms than the larger ones, and JetBlue was able to get more terminals and flight slots, enabling it to fly more planes. As a result, JetBlue was able to fly more planes per day than its competitors and, consequently, be more profitable.

Like Southwest, JetBlue also chose point-to-point flights[8] over a hub-and-spoke network.[9] Point-to-point flights were faster and cheaper for the airline as they involved lower travel time and could be accomplished with minimum expenses. (**See Exhibit 5** for JetBlue's route map.)

Another important cost-cutting factor was that JetBlue managed to reduce the turnaround time of flights, which reduced the time spent on the ground. JetBlue flights were ready for their next trip in about 35 minutes, unlike other airlines, whose flights took an hour or more to get ready. This way, JetBlue managed to fly more flights per day than its competitors.

**Exhibit 5
Route Map:
JetBlue[1]**

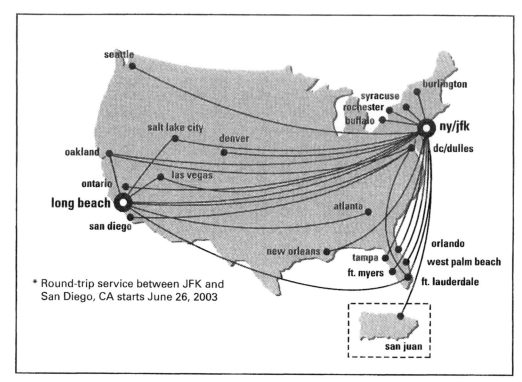

* Round-trip service between JFK and
San Diego, CA starts June 26, 2003

Note:
1. New York and Long Beach are the focus cities.

Source: www.jetblue.com.

Harnessing Technology

To bring about effective cost control and the accomplishment of functions with minimum wastage of time and resources, JetBlue decided to harness the advantages of information systems. Neeleman, who had earlier developed an electronic reservation system, decided to minimize time and costs by allowing the airline's 600-odd reservationists to work from home, using VoIP (Voice over Internet Protocol). Electronic ticketing reduced the hassles of booking tickets and also had the advantage of saving on office rentals. JetBlue also avoided use of travel agents completely by encouraging booking of tickets over the Internet.

JetBlue was also the first airline to introduce the concept of a paperless cockpit by equipping pilots with laptops to access electronic flight manuals and make requisite calculations before take-off. Because of this, they managed to save between 15 and 20 minutes in take-off. First Officer Kevin Carney said, "I used to work for US Airways, and they didn't have anything like this. None of the airlines do."[10]

JetBlue appointed Jeff Cohen as the Chief Information Officer in the first year of business, with a mandate from Neeleman to automate everything. Neeleman wanted a paperless office and highly simplified processes that could be accomplished with minimum manpower. Automation was the key to saving on labor charges and also to completing tasks with a minimum of fuss and delay. Said Cohen, "From the beginning, I've basically had to wake up everyday and figure out how we stay a low-cost airline, without bringing in huge ideas that will cost a huge amount of money and aren't aligned with our business model."[11]

Toward this end, Cohen and his team worked on projects to minimize the CASM (cost per available seat mile, which is the airline industry equivalent of ROI). In 2002, JetBlue's

CASM was 7 cents, which was 25% less than that of other major carriers. Neeleman also tried to avoid outsourcing technologies and programs, preferring instead to develop them in-house. The in-house developers developed a program to track information flight-by-flight and post it on the airline's intranet to keep employees updated about the happenings in the airline. Programs were also developed to enable electronic baggage tagging and automatic check-in, which saved huge amounts of time. Information technology made things easier for customers and also helped JetBlue work with a lean employee force. Having fewer employees allowed the airline to take better care of them and keep them happy.

Customer Focus

JetBlue adopted a proactive, customer-oriented approach to service. Neeleman believed that most airlines did not succeed because they did not give customers their due importance. They looked on them as an annoyance, and subjected them to all kinds of inconveniences and rudeness, without understanding their importance to the business.

JetBlue's philosophy was to keep passengers happy and comfortable. This was reflected in every aspect of the company. Neeleman himself flew in his planes at least once a week and spent time interacting with customers. He also helped the crew serve snacks, handed out baggage, and helped the plane get ready for its next trip. It made customers feel special when the CEO of the airline took the trouble to interact with them and see to their comfort. He also noted customer suggestions and saw that they were attended to as soon as possible.

The airline also made an effort to avoid inconveniencing passengers whenever possible. JetBlue had the best on-time record in the industry, but even when the planes were delayed due to weather or other uncontrollable conditions, the airline ensured that passengers were not put to trouble. There was an instance when Neeleman and his staff called passengers at their homes at 3:00 A.M. to tell them that their 6:00 A.M. flight was delayed so that they did not have to bother coming to the airport early.

Jennifer Klyse, who once flew JetBlue to find out what all the hullabaloo was about, was full of praise for the airline's customer service. She recollected how, when her flight was delayed for two hours in Oakland, the crew apologized to all the passengers at the airport and arranged snacks and drinks. Later, when the plane had to be diverted to San Jose because of weather problems, they gave lunch vouchers to all the passengers. The biggest surprise, however, came when the plane was unable to depart from San Jose because of weather problems. The captain announced that all the passengers would be provided with a free flight segment, which could be redeemed on their next JetBlue flight. All this was done when there was a delay because of the weather, about which there was nothing the airline could have done. This kind of customer orientation won JetBlue a number of loyal customers. The airline estimated that almost 74% of its passengers used this airline for the first time because of good word-of-mouth.

It also helped that JetBlue had an on-time performance record of 80%, as against the 72% for the top 10 airlines in the United States. Luggage-handling errors were also considerably lower, at 2.54 per 1,000 bags handled, compared to the 5.2 of the top 10. On an average, JetBlue received less than 1 complaint for every 100,000 customers flown.

Picking the Right People

To support its customer-centric approach, JetBlue was very careful about the people it employed. Neeleman ensured that the company employed only people who were genuinely service oriented and liked interacting with others. Said Neeleman, "We don't want jaded people working here. If you don't like people, or can't deal with rude customers, you'll be fired."[12] He also ensured that he recruited people who were open-minded and did not hesitate to do things that may not fall into their job descriptions. Only at JetBlue did pilots emerge from the cockpit after every flight to help clean up the plane for the next trip.

Initiative in employees was encouraged and rewarded. Once, when a flight was delayed, the pilot came out from the cockpit and offered his cell phone to customers to use. There were instances when the crew ordered pizza for everyone when a flight was canceled. Employee initiative was recognized. They were usually given free tickets or a vacation to show appreciation.

JetBlue also had a profit-sharing program and attractive bonuses, which motivated employees to contribute their best. New recruits or trainees were also taken care of like regular employees. At other airlines, new recruits were paid a stipend but were asked to look after their own expenses for hotel rooms, food, etc. At JetBlue, those expenses were also taken care of, so new people also came to work grateful and motivated, instead of disgruntled and resentful.

Neeleman motivated his employees by example. Whenever he flew on his flights, he helped clean up the plane and ready it for the next trip. This attitude was adopted by his employees as well. There were no rules at JetBlue except that the customers had to be kept happy at any cost. Every employee knew what was happening in the organization. There was no interdepartmental rivalry, and nobody looked down on any work. Everybody was given equal importance, whether their work was to fly the plane or keep it clean.

Positioning for Fun

JetBlue positioned itself as a fun airline. It used creative advertising to cut through clutter and get its message across effectively. The marketing department at JetBlue, headed by Amy Curtis-McIntyre (who had earlier worked in Virgin Atlantic's marketing department), came up with the hip image JetBlue has. It created advertisements that were "cheap and cheeky" and appealed equally to the affluent and to bargain-seekers. One advertising project included a road show in which cars, painted bright blue, drove through certain identified areas in sets of three, distributing t-shirts and other souvenirs to passers-by to create awareness about JetBlue. Oranges were once distributed in Washington, DC, to promote the airline's flights to Florida. Billboards in New York promised free TVs with every purchase. In Los Angeles, the airline promoted its flights to San Francisco with a "Smog to Fog" punchline. Television spots continued this same theme of fun.

The name JetBlue itself connoted fun and freedom to passengers. It gave an impression of being cool. Naming the airline, however, had not been easy. Neeleman and his team had gone over a number of names, ranging from New Air, to Taxi, to True Blue, before lighting on the name JetBlue. They chose JetBlue because it sounded unique and also conveyed the "young, smart, uncluttered image" the company wanted to maintain. "It works so well for an airline—the blue skies, the wild blue yonder and the idea of openness. Blue creates a happy connotation for the travel experience," said David Polinchock, a branding expert at Location Based Branding in New Jersey.[13] Most of the flight names also have the word *blue* in them, carrying the idea further. The concept was so successful that Virgin Atlantic Airways[14] started an Australian service under the name VirginBlue. Southwest was also planning to paint all its planes blue.

However, JetBlue was not all fun. Customer safety was given utmost importance. After the September 11, 2001, terrorist attacks on America, JetBlue was the first airline to introduce safety measures in planes. It installed monitors in the cockpits so that pilots could see what was happening in the passenger cabins from behind heavy titanium bolted doors.

Looking Ahead

JetBlue succeeded where a number of other airlines had failed. The primary reason for this success was that the airline tried to be different. It built its success on low cost and high standards, which attracted and kept passengers and at the same time helped the airline remain solvent in times when the majors were crumbling to dust.

However, analysts wondered whether this magnitude of success could be sustained for a longer period. JetBlue's cost-leader approach succeeded when the airline was in its growing stage and could yet exercise close control over the business. There were no labor problems because the airline was small enough for all the employees to feel involved and for the management to look after employees well. Things could not be the same forever. With JetBlue growing at a very rapid pace, its real success would be in replicating the same model successfully on a larger scale.

An important factor in JetBlue's success was that it operated in a niche market where it had no competition. It had adopted the Southwest model, but it did not operate in the same markets as Southwest. However, competitors were catching up with JetBlue. Delta Air Lines launched a new discounted fleet called *Song* in April 2003, in direct competition with JetBlue. Song was flying everyday to West Palm Beach from all three airports in New York, which was an advantage over JetBlue (JetBlue still flew only from JFK). Delta was also likely to introduce personal satellite TV, Internet access, and multichannel MP3 audio at a later stage. Virgin Airways was also eyeing the U.S. markets after its success as an inter-city carrier in Europe and Australia. Southwest had better costs than JetBlue and was expected to become JetBlue's biggest competitor, although, in 2003, they were not competing in the same markets.

Another drawback of JetBlue was that it operated only a single fleet of jets. It offered standard treatment to all flyers, without the luxury of first class or business class. It also had more seats than galley space, which made it an essentially short route choice, or the choice of economy class travelers. Business travelers were more likely to prefer airlines that had more space between seats, which was an important factor in comfortable travel. Also, travelers who preferred business class or first class were likely to choose other airlines. The service at JetBlue may have been comparable to first class service, but analysts wondered whether travelers who had the opportunity and means to travel in greater luxury would like traveling with an airline better known for functionality than luxury.

JetBlue's success could well prove to be an example for other airline carriers to emulate. It was one of the very few startups to succeed in the U.S. airline industry from among over 100 that mushroomed after the industry was deregulated in 1978. JetBlue was growing very rapidly. In three years of operations, it had more than 40 planes in its fleet, with more to come. On average, it was adding a plane per month. Its main distinction, however, was that it was one of the few airlines able to remain solvent in difficult times.

Notes

1. Herb Kelleher's Southwest Airways is America's most successful discount airline. The airline has been profitable for a straight 30 years. It is headquartered in Dallas, Texas.
2. Turning aircraft around as fast as possible at the gate is important to minimize the time that aircraft spend on the ground as ground time is non-revenue-producing time for an airline.
3. Hewlett-Packard is a leading provider of IT products, including computing, imaging, and printing. It is headquartered in California.
4. *www.cio.com.*
5. *www.cbsnews.com.*
6. Airbus is a leading manufacturer of aircraft in the world. It was established in 1970 and is headquartered in France.
7. Boeing is a U.S.-based manufacturer of aircraft.
8. In the point-to-point system, the planes have a simple flight route and fly from the origin to the destination.
9. A hub-and-spoke system uses a strategically located airport (the hub) as a passenger exchange point for flights to and from outlying towns and cities (the spokes).
10. *CIO Magazine* (July 1, 2002).
11. *www.cio.com.*
12. *Forbes* (January 31, 2001).
13. *Fortune* (June 19, 2001).
14. Virgin Atlantic Airways is a part of Richard Branson's Virgin group of companies.

Additional Readings and References

"Amazing JetBlue," *Fortune* (April 23, 2003).

M. Arndt and W. Zellner, "American Draws a Bead on JetBlue," *BusinessWeek* (June 24, 2002).

R. Barker, "Is JetBlue Flying Too High?" *BusinessWeek* (April 29, 2002).

J. Boorstin, "Final Boarding Call," *Fortune* (April 29, 2002).

E. Brown, "Neeleman; A Smokeless Herb," *Fortune* (May 22, 2001).

L. DiCarlo, "JetBlue Skies," *Forbes* (January 31, 2001).

S. DiFranco, "Learning from JetBlue," *www.funfactspublishing.com.*

S. Donnelley, "Blue Skies for JetBlue," *Time* (July 10, 2001).

"Flying Dinosaurs," *The Economist* (February 6, 2003).

www.foxnews.com.

www.hoovers.com.

www.jetblue.com.

"JetBlue: Flying Higher?" *www.cbsnews.com,* (October 23, 2002).

"JetBlue Reports More Paying Passengers, Fuller Planes," *South Florida Business Journal* (December 6, 2002).

J. Keeney and D. Neeleman, "JetBlue," *Business 2.0* (March 2001).

J. Keeney, "JetBlue; Cleaning Up," *Fortune* (April 24, 2003).

S. J. Klien, "Naming Your Baby," *Fortune* (June 19, 2001).

http://news.airwise.com.

S. Overby, "JetBlue Skies Ahead," *CIO Magazine* (July 1, 2002).

A. Tsao, "Thinking of Taking Off on JetBlue?" *BusinessWeek* (April 5, 2002).

"A Way Out of the Wilderness," *The Economist* (May 1, 2003).

C. Woodyard, "JetBlue: The Cool Factor," *www.usatoday.com.*

C. Woodyard, "JetBlue Soars on CEO's Creativity," *www.usatoday.com.*

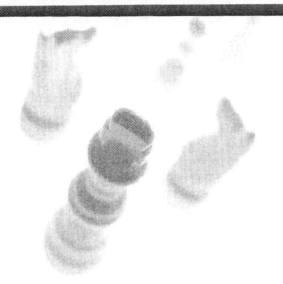

CASE 31
A.W.A.R.E.

John K. Ross III and Eric G. Kirby

IT WAS A TYPICALLY BEAUTIFUL MORNING IN CENTRAL TEXAS AS SHERRY STOOD AT THE office door watching the bustle of activity in the arena. It was just before the first client arrived and Bobby, the Lead Instructor, and several volunteers were getting Duke ready for Cindy. Duke was a 1,000-pound horse that would be led from his stall, groomed, tacked, and then provide Cindy an hour of physical and emotional therapy. Cindy was a beautiful nine-year-old girl with cerebral palsy who used a small walker and leg braces to walk and would, for a short time, allow Duke to be her legs—and her friend.

With a grin and a bang, Cindy opened the screen door to the office and entered as fast as she could. Sherry turned to help her put on her helmet, and within minutes Cindy was being assisted into the arena and onto the mounting blocks, where Bobby and Duke waited. Cindy's smile grew wider as she approached Duke and carefully climbed the mounting blocks. With the help of Bobby and the volunteers, Cindy lifted one leg up and over the saddle, and she was ready to ride. After carefully leaving the mounting blocks Cindy excitedly said "Walk on" and Duke, Cindy, Bobby, and the volunteers began an hour of intense physical therapy, which for Cindy would seem to pass like minutes and would be the highlight of her week.

History

This was A.W.A.R.E. (Always Wanted A Riding Experience). Located in San Marcos, Texas (30 miles south of Austin), A.W.A.R.E. was a not-for-profit therapeutic horseback riding center under the provisions of Section 501(c)3 of the U.S. Internal Revenue Service. Cathy Morgan founded A.W.A.R.E. in October of 1986, using her personal horse, four horses borrowed from friends, and a small arena borrowed from another friend. Cathy was a certified special education teacher and horse-riding expert. For years she had dreamed of combining

The authors wish to thank the fine people at A.W.A.R.E. for their cooperation and assistance. Although A.W.A.R.E. is real, the names used in this case have been changed. This case was prepared by Professors John K. Ross, III and Eric G. Kirby of Southwest Texas State University. This case was edited for SMBP and Cases in SMBP–9th and 10th Editions. The copyright holders are solely responsible for case content. Reprint permission is solely granted to the publisher, Prentice Hall, for the books, Strategic Management and Business Policy–10th Edition (and the International version of this book) and Cases in Strategic Management and Business Policy–10th Edition by the copyright holders, John K. Ross, III and Eric G. Kirby. Any other publication of the case (translation, any form of electronics or other media) or sold (any form of partnership) to another publisher will be in violation of copyright law, unless John K. Ross, III and Eric G. Kirby have granted an additional written reprint permission.

her love for special children and horseback riding. There was a ready clientele for her specialized type of therapy and growth occurred quickly.

Horseback riding as physical and emotional therapy began in Europe, probably in the 1600s. The modern therapeutic benefits were not realized until Liz Hartel of Denmark won the silver medal for dressage at the 1952 Helsinki Olympic Games—despite having paralysis from polio. Within a short period of time, medical and equine professionals had begun riding centers for rehabilitation purposes in England and then in North America by the 1960s. The first professional organization, North American Riding for the Handicapped Association (NARHA), was formed in 1969 for educational purposes and later to accredit active centers. Today, the number of NARHA-affiliated centers totals more than 550, providing more than 30,000 individuals with riding experiences (*www.narha.org*).

Within two years of founding A.W.A.R.E., Cathy had moved to a larger outdoor arena with nine stalls and lights for night riding. By then she had found three additional riding experts to become instructors and was soon "riding" clients from 9:00 A.M. until 9:00 P.M. She was charging $10 for a one-hour riding lesson and providing scholarships (discounted rates or free-of-charge) for some clients. A small Board of Directors, comprised of Cathy's acquaintances, had been formed and they provided some assistance. For the most part they were not a strong Board, being comprised of well-meaning individuals who were not members of the community's "movers and shakers" and not particularly savvy at running a business. Cathy was able to continue offering the therapeutic riding services, but, as in many small not-for-profits, cash flow was a continual problem. In fact, some weeks her instructors did not get paid until a client paid.

In 1992 Cathy began a letter-writing campaign for donations to help support A.W.A.R.E. with operating expenses, to provide scholarships, and to move to a covered arena. Their facilities were unusable when it rained, at which time the arena turned into a quagmire. Additionally, riders and volunteers were suffering from the heat and sun during the long Texas summers when afternoon temperatures in the 100s were not uncommon. The fund-raising campaign paid off when two locally owned corporations joined together and donated 20 acres with a covered arena, worth about $250,000. For the next year Cathy and a group of volunteers worked to refurbish the land and arena to meet NARHA accreditation standards.

During that same time A.W.A.R.E. put on a successful fundraiser dinner-dance-auction that netted approximately $19,000, and Cathy decided to return to teaching. The Board searched to replace Cathy but was unable to successfully find a long-term Executive Director. After two Executive Directors left within a short time because of the long hours, hard work, and meager salary, one of the volunteers, Sherry Ross (a local CPA who was working as a full-time volunteer), took over the functions of Executive Director and began exercising tight fiscal control of the operation.

Current Situation

A.W.A.R.E. was located on donated property seven miles south of San Marcos, approximately one-quarter mile off an interstate highway and directly behind one of the country's largest outlet malls. Recently the property across the street had begun to be developed into an upscale residential community. A.W.A.R.E. had 13 horses, over 100 clients per session (a 16-week period of time equivalent to a university semester), an unpaid Executive Director, two full-time paid instructors, four part-time paid instructors, and over 200 volunteers per session. A typical day began when Yvonne (who lived in a mobile home on the A.W.A.R.E. property as part of her salary) fed the horses at 7:00 A.M. Classes then began sometime after 8:00 A.M. and continued throughout the day, ending around 9:00 P.M.

For a typical lesson, the instructor began preparations 30 minutes prior to its start by reviewing previous lessons and goals for that client, organized aids (toys for fine motor skills, etc.), then assisted the volunteers as they groomed and tacked the horse. Once the client arrived, they donned a helmet and mounted their horse. During the lesson, one volunteer would be the "horse handler" and also had responsibility for observing and controlling the horse. One or two other volunteers would walk beside the horse as "sidewalkers" (spotters) for safety reasons and to interact with the client. The instructor then guided the class, leading the client through a series of activities designed to focus on verbal, gross or fine motor skills, balance, flexibility, or some other specific goal. Frequently these activities were disguised as games or play and may have included singing, interactions with other riders, and other "fun" activities. All of this was accomplished while the client was sitting, lying, or standing on the horse's back. At the conclusion of the hour lesson, the client was dismounted and returned with the instructor to the office area, returned his or her helmet, and talked briefly with the instructor. The volunteers untacked the horse and returned it to its stall. The instructor would then make notes about the current lesson in the client's file for future reference. Up to six clients may have ridden in a group lesson and been supervised by one instructor.

The Executive Director was also an instructor and, with the help of the Lead Instructor, performed all of the office work necessary to keep A.W.A.R.E. operating. This included preparing financial records, correspondence, payroll, schedule preparation, and the like. To begin a typical semester session, A.W.A.R.E. must contact previous riders to confirm continuing riding, select others who might want to ride from a waiting list, advertise for volunteers and conduct volunteer training, schedule lesson times that match both rider and instructor needs, perform routine maintenance on the facilities, and so forth. The workload was very heavy and the Executive Director generally worked 60 to 70 hours per week. **Exhibit 1** shows the current organizational structure for A.W.A.R.E.

The Lead Instructor typically worked 40 to 50 hours per week, and the one other full-time instructor worked a 40-hour week (both were paid about $10/hour). All other instructors were part time and were paid $8 per hour. Instructors had to be trained in the dual disciplines of horsemanship and physical therapy. A.W.A.R.E. would not ride a client unless a physician had approved horse riding as a beneficial therapy and the instructors had been able to provide not just a pony ride, but a therapeutic riding experience. The instructors continuously supported each other with ideas to improve their lessons and the sharing of knowledge about instructional pedagogy. Additionally, A.W.A.R.E. supported instructors attending specialized conferences on therapeutic horseback riding. However none of the instructors were certified physical therapists.

**Exhibit 1
Organizational
Structure:
A.W.A.R.E.**

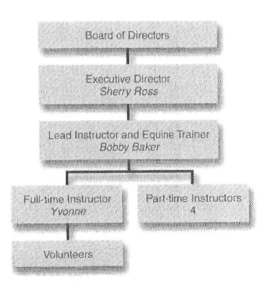

The Board of Directors for A.W.A.R.E was comprised of six volunteers from the local community and included two physicians, a university business professor, the wife of the local newspaper editor, the spouse of a local prominent lawyer, and a local businessperson. Although the Board members were good, well-intentioned individuals, the Board, as a whole, was not strong. They had put on two successful fund-raising events and seemed prepared to attempt another. However, the average tenure of the current Board member was well over five years, which was much too long to remain effective in a not-for-profit such as A.W.A.R.E. With only six members, the work of the Board could be demanding, and burnout could occur.

A.W.A.R.E. had a very good reputation in the local community as a well-run, efficient, and caring organization. The staff and volunteers were active in community affairs, A.W.A.R.E. received funds from the United Way, participated in local and state equestrian Special Olympics (where their riders generally took home most of the gold medals), and cooperated with other not-for-profits in local events. A.W.A.R.E. also had an excellent reputation amongst the equestrian community throughout the state.

Financials

When A.W.A.R.E. was located in a small arena, the majority of the expenses concerned involved payroll and horses. These were still the two largest expense items, however, maintenance and upkeep on the much larger facility had increased expenses dramatically. Additionally, expenses from several other items, like insurance, taxes, and veterinary care, had also increased drastically. Revenues came almost entirely from client fees, supplemented by donations. (See **Exhibits 2** and **3**.)

The contributors of the land placed a stipulation that for the first five years, only therapeutic horseback riding was to be allowed on the property. That time had now expired; however, no other revenue sources had been attempted. Clients were charged $25 for a one-hour

Exhibit 2
Balance Sheet:
A.W.A.R.E.

Year Ending December 31	1999	1998	1997	1996	1995
Assets					
Current assets					
Checking and savings	$ 17,336	$ 20,229	$ 20,312	$ 8,608	$ 19,961
Accounts receivable	(864)	(1,189)	(659)	(362)	(187)
Total current assets	16,472	19,040	19,653	8,246	19,774
Fixed assets					
Buildings and land	265,419	265,000	265,000	265,000	265,000
Horses	10,551	10,850	7,550	4,401	4,400
Equipment	32,486	31,485	18,622	27,195	28,073
Accumulated depreciation	(85,195)	(70,622)	(24,087)	(22,034)	(11,329)
Total fixed assets	223,261	236,713	267,085	274,562	286,144
Total Assets	$239,733	$255,753	$286,738	$282,808	$305,918
Liabilities and equity					
Liabilities					
Current liabilities	$ 157	$ 0	$ 0	$ 0	$ 124
Total liabilities	157	0	0	0	124
Equity					
Retained earnings	239,576	255,753	286,738	282,808	305,794
Total equity	239,576	255,753	286,738	282,808	305,794
Total liabilities and equity	$239,733	$255,753	$286,738	$282,808	$305,918

Note: Rounding errors on total.

**Exhibit 3
Profit and Loss
Statement:
A.W.A.R.E.**

Year Ending December 31	1999	1998	1997	1996	1995
Ordinary income/expenses					
Income					
Rider fees	$ 50,097	$49,703	$44,894	$ 28,863	$42,184
Donations	10,670	12,716	8,056	4,051	6,579
United Way	7,653	423	5,550	3,982	3,924
Other income	4,095	1,451	3,275	4,367	25,089
Total income	72,515	64,293	61,775	41,263	77,767
Expenses					
Hay and feed	5,097	5,832	6,094	8,866	1,685
Facility maintenance	2,555	2,015	1,229	1,214	1,602
Insurance	3,294	1,875	1,900	1,864	1,265
Payroll	38,381	29,615	22,780	26,194	31,057
Other expenses	37,938	25,034	26,053	17,074	27,156
Total expenses	87,265	64,371	58,056	55,212	62,765
Net ordinary income	(14,750)	(78)	3,719	(13,949)	15,002
Other income/expenses					
In-kind donations	3,960	2,500	7,400	0	350
Net other income	3,960	2,500	7,400	0	350
Net income	$(10,790)	$ 2,422	$11,119	$(13,949)	$15,352

riding session with one of A.W.A.R.E.'s instructors. A modified fee could be charged for group lessons, and some clients were given scholarships. Hippotherapy, horseback riding with a certified physical therapist (PT), billed out as physical therapy and was covered by insurance. Currently, a local physical therapist brought a group of her clients to A.W.A.R.E. once a week. A.W.A.R.E. charged only the regular riding fees, and the PT billed the insurance companies at her regular rates.

Decision Time

Sherry, still standing at the door to the arena, frowned as she began to ponder several recent events that had placed A.W.A.R.E. in a precarious position. She was worried about, and unsure of, both the short-term and long-term viability of the organization. Over the past several years, the summer session had been very profitable for A.W.A.R.E. During the summer, a diagnostic camp for children was run by a national social organization that had brought 12 to 14 riders per day as part of their planned activities. This cash flow paid the summer salaries for the instructors, bought a year's supply of hay for the horses, and allowed A.W.A.R.E. to net around $7,000 for the summer. The camp had informed A.W.A.R.E. only weeks before the summer session was to begin that they were not participating this summer. The loss of cash flow could severely impact both the summer and fall programs. The loss of additional future revenues could force A.W.A.R.E. to scale back operation significantly.

Cash flow would also be impacted when Sherry stepped down as Executive Director. Sherry had been the volunteer Executive Director for over six years, and a medical condition was forcing her to retire. It would be expensive to replace her with a paid Executive Director (a typical salary range might be $36,000 per year) and an additional full-time instructor.

While these problems could be overcome, Sherry was worried about the future. What would A.W.A.R.E. be in 5 to 10 years? Would it even be in existence, operating as it did at present, or would it be something completely different? What would be best for the short- and long-term viability of A.W.A.R.E.? As volunteer Executive Director, Sherry realized there were a number of alternatives, ranging from closing A.W.A.R.E. to creating a nationwide network of similar programs. More realistically, A.W.A.R.E. could offer profit-generating activities such as riding camps for well children or perhaps holding another fund-raiser and hiring a new Executive Director. Other options might include partnering with the local hospital or other not-for-profits in the surrounding area. Sherry realized that due to the success and proximity of the outlet mall, the current property could be sold for about $750,000.

When Cathy Morgan first began A.W.A.R.E., she envisioned the eventual development of an entire therapy complex with staff physicians, live-in clients, and extensive therapy programs. However, Cathy was no longer with the program, and Sherry was unsure what direction A.W.A.R.E. should take and how to get there.

References and Sources for Additional Information

North American Riding for the Handicapped Association, *www.narha.org*.

San Marcos home page, *http://ci.san-marcos.tx.us*.

San Marcos Chamber of Commerce, *www.sanmarcostexas.com*.

CASE 32

AirTran Holdings, Inc.

Maryanne M. Rouse

AIRTRAN AIRWAYS' ABILITY TO GROW, IN WHAT HAS ARGUABLY BEEN THE WORST ENVIRON-
ment in years for airlines, adds an unexpected new chapter to one of the most unlikely turn-around stories in the airline industry. In 1996, when the carrier was known as ValuJet, it grounded all flights for three months after the crash of its Flight 592 in the Everglades killed all 110 people on board. Fortunately, the carrier had floated a package of $150 million in junk bonds just prior to the Everglades crash, and these cash resources proved critical as the company addressed safety concerns during the shutdown and the 11 successive loss quarters that followed. In 1997, ValuJet merged with AirTran Airways Corporation to form AirTran Holdings, Inc. (AAI).

At the end of December 2004, AirTran operated 508 daily flights to 48 destinations, primarily in the eastern United States, making it the second-largest "affordable-fare" scheduled airline in the United States in terms of departures (just behind Southwest).

Although the company moved its headquarters from Atlanta to Orlando, Florida, after the 1996 crash, it still flies most of its flights to and from Atlanta, providing both point-to-point and one-stop flights through its Hartsfield hub. AirTran offers a business class any business can afford, all-assigned seating, a generous frequent flier program, and a corporate program dubbed "A2B"; unlike its competitors, the carrier never requires a round-trip purchase or a Saturday night stay.

The company's regional jet operation, AirTran JetConnect, operated by joint-venture partner Air Wisconsin, flies 50-seat Canadair Regional jets in short-haul markets to and from the airline's hub at Hartsfield Atlanta International Airport. AirTran JetConnect serves Greensboro, North Carolina; Pensacola, Florida; and Savannah, Georgia—all of which were previously served by AirTran. The new service will allow the company to redeploy its 717s to increase frequencies in longer-haul, more profitable markets and facilitate growth in larger markets not currently served. In addition, AirTran JetConnect will allow the airline to expand into other short-haul markets as well as increase frequencies in underserved markets.

Marketing and Operations

AirTran's marketing strategy is to develop an innovative brand identity that sets it apart from its low-fare and full-service competitors. The company targets two primary segments: price-sensitive business travelers and leisure travelers, primarily in the eastern United States. To attract business travelers, the carrier launched a business class product that is, in terms of comfort, the equivalent of the first class service offered by its full-service rivals. The business class cabin is configured with 2×2-foot oversized seats, providing considerably more leg and seat room than a typical coach cabin. Targeted to the price-sensitive business flier, upgrades to business class from coach are just $25.

AirTran offers a range of fares based on advance purchases of 14 days, 7 days, 3 days, and "walk-up" fares. All fares are one-way, and most are nonrefundable; however, reservations can be changed prior to departure, with a service charge.

The company also offers a popular frequent flier program, A+ Rewards, that allows members to earn free travel more quickly than its competitors and, for twice the number of flight credits, will even buy members a free domestic ticket on any major carrier. The A+ Rewards program offers a number of ways to earn free travel, including the use of the AirTran Visa card, Hertz car rentals, and bonus earnings for Business Class.

In spring 2003, AirTran introduced a new standby program targeted broadly to young travelers (and specifically to college students) between the ages of 18 and 22. Dubbed the X-Fares Standby Program (*www.xfares.com*), this marketing initiative allows those who are eligible to fly standby to almost any AirTran destination for $55 per segment ($75 per "long-haul" segment.).

In addition to targeting individual business travelers, AirTran has focused on developing travel partnerships with companies of all sizes, from one- and two-person small businesses to such large corporations as BellSouth, State Farm, and John Deere. Under the terms of its A2B corporate travel program, employees of registered companies get free confirmed upgrades to business class when paying full coach fares, fee waivers for ticket refunds or changes, and advance seat assignment. Unlike rival Southwest, AirTran has established interline ticketing and baggage agreements with Delta, United, US Airways, and American Trans Air and has ticketing arrangements with major online travel services such as Orbitz, Priceline, Expedia, and Travelocity.

AirTran has been aggressive in lining up corporate and community support via public–private partnerships that allow the carrier to shift more of the risk of expansion to communities and businesses expected to benefit from overall lower fares in their markets. The "public" part comprises revenue guarantees by cities, counties, or other municipal entities to protect AirTran against losses during the initial phase of operations; the "private" part builds "travel banks" in which businesses pledge to spend a specified amount on tickets. Both elements help to build a loyal following and serve as a cushion against the early losses of expanding into a new city and the invariable backlash from bigger competitors, which often respond by slashing their own fares and expanding service. Because AirTran's arrival in a market typically drives down fares by as much as 50%, both cities and businesses view the partnership guarantees as money well spent. For example, when AirTran began service to Wichita, Kansas, in May 2002, the average full fare on the Wichita–Washington, DC, flight dropped from $1,667 to $460. Wichita, which was competing with other cities to lure AirTran, estimates that the entry of the low-fare carrier could lead to annual airfare savings of $43 million for business and leisure travelers.

In December 2004, AirTran lost a bidding war to buy leases on 14 gates at Midway Airport in Chicago from ATA Holdings, a company now in bankruptcy. The company, which added seven daily flights from Midway to Florida destinations in January 2004, had planned to create a Midwestern hub and diversify its route system by adding more east–west flights. Despite the disappointing loss of gates to Southwest, AirTran believes it can grow profits by adding new destinations—Sarasota, Indianapolis, and three unnamed cities—and by adding flights to connect cities already in its system.

Named "Best Low-Fare Airline" for 2001 and 2002 by *Entrepreneur* magazine, AirTran's cost structure is among the lowest in the domestic airline industry in terms of cost per Average Seat Miles (ASM). The company's low-cost position is supported by an emphasis on cost controls, lower distribution costs (reservations, ticketing), and high employee productivity. The company's labor costs are equivalent to approximately 25% of revenue—the same percentage as Frontier and JetBlue—below Southwest's 30% and significantly below the full-service carriers' 40+%. An award-winning web site that makes it easy to book flights online has helped AirTran shift 52.5% of its sales to the site—one of the highest percentages in the industry—with an additional 13% of bookings coming from other travel sites. The company estimates its cost per booking online at less than $1—a significant saving over the $8.50 average cost of booking through a travel agent.

In September 1999, the company became the launch customer for the new Boeing 717, an innovative, cost-efficient, and environmentally friendly commercial aircraft that has reduced the higher fuel and maintenance costs associated with the DC-9s with which it had begun operations. (The company's current fleet comprises 77 Boeing 717-200s and 5 Boeing 737-700s.) AirTran has also forged close ties with Boeing and Boeing Capital Corporation, a full-service provider of financial services, including asset-based lending and leasing. Boeing Capital, an indirect wholly owned subsidiary of the Boeing Company, refinanced $201 million of AirTran's junk bonds in 2001 (and also agreed to finance the 20 Boeing 717s to be delivered in 2002, 22 used and 1 new 717 in 2003, and 5 737-700s delivered through June 2004), enabling AirTran to continue its rapid fleet modernization.

Finance

AirTran was one of the few domestic airlines to report profitable operations for the year ended December 31, 2003, recording operating income of $86.3 million and net income of $100.5 million. The company also strengthened its balance sheet by issuing $145.9 million in common stock and $125.0 million of convertible debt at 7% while paying down $76.5 million of long-term debt at 11.27%, paying down $12.7 million of long-term debt at 13%, and converting $5.5 million of 7.75% convertible debt to equity, all of which greatly improved AirTran's debt-to-equity ratio.

Despite a sea of red ink, overcapacity, and threatened bankruptcies in the industry, the company overcame intense fare wars and weak October bookings to eke out a profit of $1.1 million, or 1 cent per share for fourth quarter 2004. Although this was down from $21.7 million or 24 cents a share in fourth quarter 2003, AirTran beat analysts' consensus estimate of a 9 cent loss. Both domestic fare wars and escalating fuel costs hurt the company's profit yield. (The company reported a 70.3% increase in fuel costs.) AirTran's load factor for the period declined 0.5%, to 69.3, compared with fourth quarter 2003; however, revenue passenger miles increased 22.6% as capacity rose 23.4%.

The four hurricanes that struck the state of Florida in 2004 have had and will continue to have a major economic impact on the state in the affected area, which represents about 51% of the airline's normal traffic flows and seriously disrupted flights over the normally busy Labor Day holiday. Both the company's Orlando headquarters and its aircraft hangar in Orlando suffered damage that further hampered operations. The impact of the hurricanes, coupled with a weak revenue environment and record high fuel costs, affected AirTran's financial results for both the third and fourth quarters.

For the full year, AirTran reported a profit of $12.3 million, or 14 cents per share, to become one of only two U.S. airlines (the other was Southwest) to post an overall profit for the year.

Complete annual and quarterly financial information is available from the company's web site (*www.airtran.com*), *The Wall Street Journal* (*www.wsj.com*), and FreeEdgar.

The Industry

On the morning of September 11, 2001, terrorist attacks shut down the U.S. airline industry. The Federal Aviation Administration (FAA) suspended all commercial flights within hours after the attacks on the World Trade Center's Twin Towers and the Pentagon and, although some flights resumed three days later, on September 14, the industry still had not recovered nine months later. Continuing concerns about the safety of flying, a weaker-than-expected economic recovery, and delays resulting both from tighter security and fewer flights led to a passenger traffic year-over-year decline of approximately 12% among the nine major U.S. airlines in the first three quarters of 2002.

Major airlines, many of which deferred or cancelled new aircraft deliveries, pared down flight schedules, and furloughed employees in the wake of 9/11, have been slow to increase capacity to previous levels. Some majors have permanently retired up to 5% of their total capacity, mostly large, older, gas-guzzling planes such as DC-10s and 727s. And, while analysts and airline financial officers agree that retiring inefficient aircraft is a positive step toward profitability in an industry that had suffered from overcapacity, a great deal of that capacity is being replaced by low-fare startups, most of which are still growing, and by small-jet regional carriers. For example, New York–based JetBlue Airways, while still small (500 million revenue passenger miles in April 2002, about 10% of what Continental carried in the same period), has won over a significant number of business travelers on the long-haul routes that have been the province of big, full-service carriers for years. JetBlue is strongly capitalized and well run, and analysts predict that it can grow at an aggressive 25% per year for the next five years by taking market share from the majors. Similarly, both Frontier Airlines and American Trans Air have made traffic gains at the expense of United Airlines in Denver and other western cities.

The airline industry is highly competitive in terms of fares, frequent flier benefits, routes, and service. Profit levels in the industry are highly sensitive to changes in operating and capital costs and the extent to which competitors attempt to match each other's fares and services, as well as to general economic trends. Energy prices continue to be unpredictable: Favorable prices in the first quarter of 2002 were followed by sharp increases in April and May. The airlines have racked up higher costs for the security tax assessed on tickets; for the monthly security fees paid to the Department of Transportation (DOT); for a war-risk insurance premium; for implementing federally mandated directives such as stronger cockpit doors; and for the first class seats dedicated to federal air marshals. Recently testifying before a Congressional committee, airline executives noted that if the United States does strike Iraq, the results will be disastrous for the industry because travel, particularly international travel, will fall off sharply at the same time that oil prices surge.

Of increasing concern to carriers is the number of business travelers who are practicing what one industry analyst calls "Airline Avoidance." Poor service and complex pricing, further exacerbated by arcane rules, regulations, and restrictions on reservation changes, have created an environment in which companies and individuals are purchasing planes, purchasing fractional ownership in planes, or choosing to drive. So many travelers are choosing the latter that Delta Air Lines (DAL) launched a fare sale at the end of March 2002 specifically to provide additional customer incentive to fly rather than drive. The short-haul market is crucial to profitability for full-service carriers because, in general, travelers pay more per mile to fly short trips.

Increasing numbers of travelers are using web sites to book airline tickets, hotel rooms, and car rentals. According to the Internet analysis group Jupiter Media Metrix, consumers were expected to spend about $36.8 billion on travel sites in 2004, up from $24 billion in 2001. Concerned about prices and practices of online travel services, Congress created a nine-member commission to investigate the pricing, practices, and exclusive marketing agreements of various airline and independent sites.

The industry is subject to regulation by a number of federal, state, and local departments and agencies. The DOT has regulatory jurisdiction over passenger airlines, with the FAA regulating aircraft maintenance and operations, including equipment, ground facilities, licensing, and communications. The Aviation and Transportation Security Act of 2001 established a new Transportation Security Administration (within the DOT) with responsibility for aviation security functions including passenger and baggage screening.

CASE 33

Boise Cascade/ OfficeMax

Maryanne M. Rouse

BOISE CASCADE CORPORATION (BCC), LONG AN INTEGRATED FOREST PRODUCTS COM-pany, had been attempting for some time to shift its emphasis from manufacturing to distribution. In a move that surprised many who thought Boise would move more gradually, the 91-year-old paper and lumber products company announced in late July 2004 that it would sell its land and plants, its headquarters building in Boise, Idaho, and even its name to Madison Dearborn Partners, a Chicago equity investment firm. When the $3.7 billion deal was completed, probably by mid-November, what was then Boise Cascade would take the name OfficeMax (OMX).

When Boise acquired office supplies catalog/retailer OfficeMax late in 2003, many industry analysts thought the acquisition sent a clear signal that the company might eventually leave the volatile and regulated timber market and key segments of the paper business altogether—but thought it would do so gradually. At the same time that Boise announced the OfficeMax acquisition, the company revealed that it would review alternatives for its non-retail paper and building products businesses, which have combined annual sales exceeding $3.6 billion. Although Boise's best-performing line of business had been its office solutions segment, which alone accounted for $4.022 billion of the company's total sales in 2003, it was thought unlikely that Boise would pursue an immediate sale of its other businesses. Boise had argued for a "mill-to-desktop" model for its paper business, giving the company a good reason not to sell. And, although net income for the paper business had declined substantially over the past few years, it had contributed $1.9 billion to sales and $38.6 million to Boise's bottom line in 2003.

The Company

Boise had been a major distributor of office products and building materials and an integrated manufacturer and distributor of paper, packaging, and wood products. The company currently competed in three segments: Boise Office Solutions, Boise Building Solutions, and Boise Paper Solutions. Although there were significant intersegment transactions, each was managed as a separate business because products, services, markets, and competitive factors differed. Once the acquisition was complete, the company planned to report results for two segments: contract sales and retail sales.

Boise Office Solutions (formerly Boise Cascade Office Products) was a multinational distributor of products for the office, including office supplies and paper, technology products, and office furniture. While office papers were sourced from Boise Paper Solutions, substantially all other products were purchased from outside manufacturers or industry wholesalers. The Office Solutions segment sold directly to large and small businesses and government purchasers in the United States, Canada, Mexico, Australia, and New Zealand. This segment served customers via 63 distribution centers, 2 outbound sales centers, 4 customer service centers, and more than 100 retail stores. This segment included the operating results for OfficeMax. Boise Office Solutions accounted for 48.4% of the company's sales and 58.6% of the company's operating segment profits in 2003, compared to 47.8% of the company's sales and 61% of the profit of the three operating segments in 2002.

Boise Paper Solutions manufactured and sold free-sheet papers, containerboard, corrugated containers, newsprint, and market pulp. This segment operated five pulp and paper mills, two paper converting facilities, six paper distribution facilities, and five corrugated container plants in the United States. Boise Paper Solutions accounted for 34.6% of the company's sales and 48.4% of segment profits in 2003 versus 18.9% of the company's 2002 sales and 19.1% of the profit of the three operating segments. Uncoated free sheet represented 57% of the segments revenue for 2002. Approximately 38% of the segment's free sheet (including 74% of office papers) was sold through Boise Office Solutions; the equivalent of 54% of containerboard was transferred to the company's corrugated container plants. With the exception of newsprint, sales were made by the company's own sales force.

Boise Building Solutions manufactured plywood, oriented strand board (OSB), lumber, laminated veneer lumber (LVL), particleboard, and engineered wood products at 25 manufacturing facilities in the United States, Canada, and Brazil. The segment also operated 28 distribution facilities that provided a broad line of building materials, including wood products manufactured by Boise, to retail lumber dealers, home centers, home improvement "big box" stores, and industrial customers. Boise Building Solutions accounted for 16.45% of Boise's segment sales and a loss of 7% for fiscal 2003, compared to 33% of the company's 2002 sales and 19.7% of the profit of the three operating segments.

Boise owned or controlled approximately 2.4 million acres of timberland in the United States. The timberland was managed as part of the company's Building Solutions and Paper Solutions segments, with the impact on operating results included in those segments. Although Boise's timber resources represented a relatively small part of the company's overall operations, this aspect of the business had been the source of continuing public relations problems for the company. And, while the company's competitors in forest products had also been the target of environmental groups, Boise had been the environmental movement's "poster child" for forest mismanagement and environmental irresponsibility. Because much of the criticism related to the company's logging operations in old-growth forests, Boise's recent announcement that it would no longer engage in this practice was expected to mitigate the negative publicity.

The OfficeMax Acquisition

In December 2003, Boise paid approximately $1.4 billion in cash, stock, transaction costs, and debt assumed for the number-three U.S. office supply chain, OfficeMax. The acquisition created an $8.3 billion company that was expected to be better able to battle rivals Staples and Office Depot. On the plus side, analysts agreed that the combined OfficeMax and Boise Office Solutions would be a much stronger competitor. Although there was some concern that the acquisition, which was financed with a combination of 40% cash and 60% equity, would result in significantly higher debt, an increase in intangible assets and goodwill, much higher lease payments (reflecting OfficeMax's principal mode of financing), and heightened business risk, it was hoped that the recent announcement of the deal with Madison Dearborn Partners would allay many of those concerns.

OfficeMax sold discount-priced office supplies and equipment through nearly 1,000 stores in the United States, the U.S. Virgin Islands, and Puerto Rico, as well as via a majority-owned subsidiary in Mexico. The company also sold more than 40,000 name-brand and private-label office products online and via catalogs. The stores combined office supplies with in-store FurnitureMax (office furniture) and CopyMax (printing services) outlets. Through an alliance with Hewlett-Packard, OfficeMax sold computers and related products in most of its stores. As part of its strategy to focus on meeting the needs of small businesses, OfficeMax offered Internet connection services through EarthLink and shipping services through Airborne. The company's retail operations were supported by 3 PowerMax inventory distribution facilities, 17 delivery centers, and 2 national customer service centers.

The company's financial performance had reflected both a weak economy and strong competitors. OfficeMax reported net income of $76.165 million on sales of $4.775 billion for 2002; however, $57.5 million of earnings resulted from the use of tax loss carryforwards. For Quarter 3 2003, the company reported a loss of $26.7 billion on sales of $1.046 billion. OfficeMax reacted to a string of quarterly losses by developing new store formats to boost sales and reach new markets. OfficeMax PDQ (Pretty Darn Quick) was a smaller-format store that featured CopyMax. OfficeMax's current plans included using its Mexican stores as a platform for expansion into other Spanish-speaking countries.

Financial Position/Performance

Boise's 2003 net income of $17.1 million on total sales of $8.245 billion was an improvement over the company's disappointing $11.34 million in profit on $7.412 billion in sales for 2002. Approximately 90% of the company's sales were in the United States. Analysts believed that Boise's restructuring would leave the company in a stronger financial position, with low debt levels and adequate cash to fund aggressive store and supply-chain improvement as well as growth in its retail and contract segments. However, Boise was seen as lacking the marketing expertise and merchandising strategies of its two larger rivals. Information about Boise's financial position and performance is available in the company's annual reports, quarterly reports, and 10-K forms (*www.officemax.com*).

Key Competitors

International Paper

International Paper (IP) was the world's largest forest products company. It had significant global businesses in paper and paper distribution, packaging, and forest products, including building materials. The company had operations in nearly 40 countries, employed more than

90,000 people, and exported its products to more than 120 nations. Sales of $24.976 billion for 2002 were derived from businesses located primarily in the United States, Europe, Latin America, Asia/Pacific, and Canada; the company reported a net loss of $880 million for 2002. In International Paper's Quarter 3 2003 results, released September 27, the company reported earnings of $122 million on sales of $6.4 billion.

International Paper produced plywood, paper, pulp, and packaging, and it processed chemicals such as crude tall oil and crude sulfate turpentine (byproducts of the paper making process). Arizona Chemical, an International Paper subsidiary, produced resins and inks. International Paper controlled approximately 9 million acres of forest in the United States and 1.5 million in Brazil; it also held interests in forests in New Zealand. The company distributed paper products via its xpedx subsidiary in North America and its subsidiaries Papeteries de France, Scaldia (the Netherlands), and Impap (Poland). About 75% of International Paper's sales were in the United States.

International Paper had pursued an aggressive restructuring strategy, divesting approximately $3 billion of non-core operations from mid-2000 through year-end 2002. The company had also announced that it would sell 1.5 million of the 9 million acres of U.S. timberland it owned in the Southern United States before 2009. (International Paper had planned to sell its Industrial Paper and Arizona Chemical businesses, but it had not received what it considered to be acceptable offers.) International Paper planned to exit the cellulose pulp business and close its mill in Natchez, Mississippi, by the end of 2003. At the same time, International Paper had made a number of acquisitions, including Union Camp, Shorewood Packaging, and Champion International.

Georgia-Pacific

Georgia-Pacific (GP) was the world's second-largest forest products company. Georgia-Pacific operated in two key lines of business: building products (plywood, lumber, OSB, gypsum, wallboard, particleboard, adhesives) and consumer products (Brawny, Coronet, Dixie, Quilted Northern). The company's on-again, off-again portfolio realignment strategies had confused investors and analysts alike.

In a move that would allow the company to develop a sharper focus on its core businesses, Georgia-Pacific announced on September 22, 2003, that it was exploring strategic alternatives for its building products distribution business, including a possible sale. Divesting this segment would allow the company to focus on operating its established building products manufacturing businesses and maintaining its leading supplier role in the wholesale distribution channel. And, although Georgia-Pacific had noted a desire to create shareholder value by sharpening focus on its more stable, consumer-oriented businesses and its goals of reducing debt and strengthening its balance sheet, the company contemplated and then withdrew a planned $1 billion spinoff of its consumer products and packaging businesses, citing poor market conditions.

Georgia-Pacific had reported a loss of approximately $735 million on $23.271 billion in sales for 2002. On October 16, 2003, the company reported quarterly earnings of $1.369 million on $1,369 million in sales (*www.gp.com*).

Weyerhaeuser

One of the largest U.S. forest products companies and North America's largest producer of softwood lumber, Weyerhaeuser (WY) managed 8 million acres of timberland, mainly in the Southern United States and Pacific Northwest. The company also held cutting licenses on about 35 million acres in Canada and had holdings in New Zealand, France, Ireland, and Uruguay. The company had grown both internally and via acquisition. It had bought rival

Willamette Industries for $6.1 billion in early 2002. In addition to timberlands, Weyerhaeuser's operating segments included Wood Products, Containerboard, Packaging and Recycling, Pulp and Paper, and Real Estate.

The wood products segment produced lumber, plywood, OSB, and engineered wood. Weyerhaeuser's real estate operations (home building and master-planned communities) were conducted through its Weyerhaeuser Real Estate Company subsidiary, principally in selected metropolitan areas of southern California, Maryland, Nevada, Texas, Virginia, and Washington.

Weyerhaeuser had reported 2002 net income of $241 million on sales of $18.521 billion. On October 24, 2003, the company reported quarterly earnings of $82 million on revenues of $5.2 billion.

Staples

Staples (SPLS), the largest office supply superstore in the United States and the largest global competitor in this segment, targeted small businesses, home office professionals, and consumers. It sold office products, furniture, computers, and printing and photography services at over 1,500 Staples and Staples Express stores in the United States, Canada, Belgium, France, Germany, Italy, the Netherlands, Portugal, Spain, and the United Kingdom. The company's superstores, which average 20,000 square feet, offer approximately 7,500 SKUs, including computers, other business machines and equipment, office furniture, and office supplies, as well as complementary services, including printing, binding, and copying.

Although Staples superstores generated most of the company's revenues and profits, Staples also operated Staples Business Delivery (a combination of its Staples Direct small business catalog and staples.com), Quill Corporation (catalogs and related web sites), and Staples Contract (contract office supplies). The company's market penetration strategy had focused on opening superstores in city suburbs and smaller Staples Express stores in urban areas. The company had also pursued growth via acquisition in its European operations.

Staples reported earnings of $446.10 million on $11.596 billion in sales for the fiscal year ended February 1, 2003. On August 17, 2003, the company reported Quarter 2 earnings of $139.353 million on quarterly sales of $2.878 billion.

Office Depot

Office Depot (ODP) was the second-largest global chain of office supply stores. In addition to office supplies, Office Depot's 1,000+ company-owned and licensed stores offered computer hardware and software, furniture, and art and engineering supplies, as well as printing and copying services. Most of the warehouse-type stores' sales were to small firms, home offices, and individual customers. Ink Depot, a "corralled" shop dedicated to ink, toner, and fax supplies, currently operated at over 500 Office Depot superstores and would soon be added to all Office Depot locations. In 2002, OPD formed a two-year alliance with the U.S. Chamber of Commerce that would provide members a 5% discount on most office supplies.

Office Depot had closed its concept chains, including Furniture at Work, to focus on aggressively growing its retail stores in North America. Although Office Depot planned to add some stores in Europe and Asia, the company was concentrating on Internet and catalog sales to serve those markets because the operational costs of doing so were significantly lower. In response to a growing concern about ecological issues, Office Depot had entered into an alliance with the environmental consulting firm Green Order to help customers comply with environmental standards in their procurement practices.

Retail sales accounted for just under 60%, with more than 40% of Office Depot's sales generated by its business services group via delivery and contract services to medium and large companies. The company also sold through its Office Depot and Viking Office Products catalogs. (Viking sold office products worldwide.) Office Depot had reported net income of $310.7 on overall sales of $11.357 billion for 2002; 3rd quarter earnings of 2003 were $91.666 million on sales of $3.2 billion.

Industry Environment

Growing and harvesting timber were subject to numerous federal and state government laws and policies to protect the environment, water resources, and wildlife. Most competitors operated under the Sustainable Forestry Initiative (SFI), a certification standard designed to supplement government regulatory programs with voluntary landowner initiatives to further protect public resources. SFI certification was also a key element in repairing the poor social responsibility ratings timber and logging operations had earned for their lack of environmental concern. SFI was an independent standard overseen by a governing board comprising conservation organizations, academia, the forest products industry, and large and small forest landowners. Regulatory and nonregulatory initiatives had increased operating costs, resulted in changes in the valuation of timber, and had made it more difficult to respond to rapid changes in markets, extreme weather, or other unexpected circumstances. The industry faced a protracted squeeze on profits as global competitors flooded the market with lumber and other commodity wood products. Cyclical factors such as the current global recession and the relative strength of the U.S. dollar had negatively affected sales and profits, while other factors, including the increased demand for lumber, plywood, and OSB as a result of the expansion of home building and the increase in repair/remodeling activity in the United States, had had positive effects on demand.

The slowing global economy had resulted in a decreasing demand for pulp and uncoated free sheet, while the strength of the U.S. dollar had made pulp products less competitive overseas, especially in Europe. The demand for paper was expected to lag behind historical rates as a result of electronic substitution in some paper applications. In the containerboard segment, the global recession had reduced manufacturers' demand for corrugated containers, particularly in the United States. In addition, costs for old corrugated containers, a primary raw material for containerboard production, had increased during 2002 and 2003 as a result of increased demand as Asian competitors increased containerboard capacity.

Weak prices, high energy costs, and increased cheap paper imports from Europe had negatively affected the paper sector. For the balance of 2003 and 2004, demand and prices were expected to be flat because competitors may not be able to sustain previously announced price increases. As business levels and employment increase, the demand for certain grades, including uncoated free sheet, were expected to improve.

The business-to-business and business-to-consumer office products markets were highly competitive. Competition was based principally on price and service. Although business demand was strongly influenced by economic conditions and employment levels, consumer demand was considerably less volatile. If market research by Office Depot was any indication, all three companies had ground to make up in brand building/differentiation. Office Depot had found that about half of customers who bought office supplies were uncertain afterward which of the three chains' stores they had shopped in.

CASE 34

Eli Lilly & Company

Maryanne M. Rouse

A LEADING U.S. PHARMACEUTICAL COMPANY, ELI LILLY AND COMPANY (LLY) PRODUCED a wide variety of ethical drugs (approximately 94.2% of 2003 revenues) and animal health products (just over 5.8% of 2003 revenues). The company history began with Colonel Eli Lilly, a Union officer in the Civil War, who invented a process for coating pills with gelatin. Lilly's principal activities were to discover, develop, manufacture, and market pharmaceutical-based health care solutions. The company's two business segments are Pharmaceutical and Animal Health. The company's pharmaceutical product lines comprised neuroscience, endocrine, anti-infective, cardiovascular agents, oncology, and animal health. Lilly manufactured and distributed its products through owned or leased facilities in the United States, Puerto Rico, and 26 other countries; the company's products were sold in approximately 160 countries.

In the United States, Lilly's pharmaceutical products were distributed through approximately 35 independent wholesalers that served physicians, pharmacies, hospitals, and other health care professionals. Three wholesalers in the United States, AmeriSource Bergen Corporation, Cardinal Health, and McKesson, each accounted for between 19% and 23% of 2001 consolidated net sales. Products were promoted through sales representatives who called on physicians, wholesalers, hospitals, managed-care organizations, retail pharmacists, and other health care professionals. The company supported sales representatives' efforts with advertising in medical and drug journals and distributed literature and samples of products to physicians at medical meetings. Like its competitors, Lilly also advertised certain products directly to consumers, a practice coming under increased criticism from public health and cost-containment advocates. Marketing methods and product emphasis were adapted to meet local needs and regulations in markets outside the United States.

Lilly's patents were critical to maintaining its competitive position. Current patents for major products included:

Drug	Year Introduced	Purpose
Alimta	2004	Malignant mesothelioma and advanced lung cancer
Symbax	2004	Bipolar depression
Cialis	2003	Erectile dysfunction
Straterra	2003	ADHD
Forteo	2002	Osteoporosis
Xigris	2001	Severe sepsis
Actos	1999	Type 2 diabetes
Evista	1998	Osteoporosis
Zyprexa	1996	Schizophrenia, bipolar maintenance
Humalog	1996	Type 1 and type 2 diabetes
Gemzar	1995	Pancreatic, bladder, breast, and lung cancers
ReoPro	1995	Prevention of cardiac ischemia
Humatrope	1987	Human growth hormone
Humulin	1982	Type 1 and type 2 diabetes

For a number of these products, in addition to the compound patent, the company held patents on the manufacturing process, formulation, or uses that may extend beyond the expiration of the product patent. Although industry analysts had concerns about Lilly's performance as it moved beyond the "Prozac era" (the company lost patent protection for its blockbuster antidepressant in August 2001, after a Federal Circuit Court reversed a part of a Federal Court decision upholding Lilly's patents), the introduction of six major drugs between 2001 and 2004 plus a strong pipeline and solid performance had secured the company's ranking as one of the top 10 global pharmaceutical firms, with most analysts rating the company's stock as "outperform."

As part of an inspection related to regulatory reviews of Lilly's Zyprexa intramuscular and Forteo products in 2001, the Food & Drug Administration (FDA) found quality problems at several of the company's manufacturing sites. Although Lilly appeared to be moving in the right direction in resolving these quality issues, they were still a concern several years later. The bottom-line implication from this manufacturing mess was that several new product approvals, including Forteo and Straterra, were delayed. Lilly's margins were likely to remain under pressure from lower volumes and costs associated with resolving its manufacturing problems. The company expected to resolve most manufacturing problems to the satisfaction of the FDA by year-end 2004.

Legislative-Related Activity and Litigation

In early October 2002, Lilly and Bristol-Myers Squibb settled over 300 lawsuits accusing them of failing to stop Kansas City pharmacist Robert Courtney from diluting cancer drugs over a period of years. Plaintiffs had maintained that both companies were complicit in the pharmacist's actions, based on internal documents showing they knew as early as 1998, three years before the arrest, that cancer drugs were being diluted but failed to act. In 2004, Lilly still faced a number of consumer lawsuits related to Prozac and was involved in patent litigation involving both Prozac and Zyprexa. Lilly was also expected to face charges of deceptive marketing in connection with its osteoporosis drug Evista. Critics noted that Lilly had attempted to position Evista as a means of lowering the risk of cardiovascular events (heart attack, heart-related chest pain, and other coronary events) based on data gathered in a study designed solely to assess Evista's effects on osteoporosis. Questions were also raised about financial support provided by Lilly to the authors of the study.

Financial Position/Performance

The loss of patent protection for Prozac had a significant effect on Lilly's sales and profitability in both 2001 and 2002; however, worldwide sales for 2003 increased 14%, due primarily to the strong performance of more recently introduced drugs, including Zyprexa, Evista, and Gemzar, as well as growing sales of Cialis, Straterra, and Forteo. Net income for 2003 declined approximately 5.5%, from $2.71 billion in 2002, due to increased spending on research and development, revamping of manufacturing facilities, and an increase in marketing costs from 30.9% of revenue in 2002 to 32.23% of revenue in 2003. Impairments, restructurings, and other special charges (principally as a result of the Isis joint venture) resulted in a $382.2 million write-down for 2003. Complete financial information, including links to Eli Lilly's annual and quarterly reports and SEC filings, is available via the company's web site *www.lilly.com* or at *www.wsj.com*.

The Industry

In the United States, the largest segment of the global pharmaceutical market, demographic trends, including the baby boom population bulge and longer average life spans, drove industry growth. At the turn of the 21st century, although approximately 12% of the U.S. population was over 65 years of age, over 33% of all U.S. prescriptions were written for those over 65. Patients generally considered prescription medicines necessary purchases which, together with a third-party payment system, tended to reduce the price elasticity of demand.

Despite near-term uncertainties with respect to pricing and patent expirations, the pharmaceutical industry was still one of the healthiest and widest-margin industries in the United States. U.S. prospects for the longer term were enhanced by demographic growth in the elderly segment of the population (accounting for about one-third of industry sales), as well as by new therapeutic products resulting from discoveries in genomics and biotechnology. However, drugs generating over $40 billion of industrywide sales in 2001 were going to lose patent protection over the next four years. The flood of patent expirations offered major opportunities for the generic manufacturers, especially for those obtaining 180 days of "first to file" marketing exclusivity.

On the regulatory front, the FDA had become much tougher on new drug approvals. Regulatory compliance was costly both in out-of-pocket application, establishment, and product fees and in time required to gain approval. Major new drug therapies took an average of 14 years to develop, at an estimated cost of $500 million. Only about 1 applicant in 20 makes it through Phase 3 trials to FDA approval. The FDA was also cracking down on drug manufacturing, with some plants closed as a result of quality problems.

Three key developments were expected to act as a ceiling on profits for pharmaceutical firms: (1) Managed care plan buyers, who accounted for 70.4% of prescription drug purchases, had made drug cost containment a priority, (2) the Medicare Prescription Drug Improvement and Modernization Act was signed into law in December 2003, and (3) states had become very aggressive in pushing for new legislation aimed at obtaining greater drug discounts for Medicaid and other state-run programs. Many HMOs used a three-tiered copay system to discourage the use of expensive drugs and encourage the use of generics.

Outside the United States, the competitive landscape was quite different. Although the standardization of regulatory requirements among European Union member countries was expected to create a simpler operating environment, the EU imposed stringent price controls and banned most direct-to-consumer marketing; similar price controls and advertising bans existed in Japan. The operating and competitive environments in developing nations were characterized by a high degree of uncertainty and, while they represented significant opportunities for revenue growth, they lacked the strong intellectual property protection pharmaceutical companies relied on to justify huge investments in R&D.

Recent Developments

A growing challenge to U.S. pharmaceutical firms came from increased out-of-country purchases. On October 12, 2002, the largest U.S. health insurer informed members of the senior citizens lobbying group AARP that it would reimburse them for prescriptions filled in Canada and elsewhere abroad where governments cap drug prices. UnitedHealth Group, Inc., sent a letter to 97,000 people who bought insurance with a drug benefit through AARP about the coverage. Although buying prescription drugs outside the United States for use in the country violated federal regulations, it was a growing practice among older Americans seeking relief from high-priced name-brand drugs. UnitedHealth and AARP appeared to want to keep the announcement low key; however, thousands of AARP members, as well as other senior citizens, regularly purchased prescription medicines in Canada and Mexico—in person or via the Internet—where the drugs are significantly cheaper, even if not reimbursed. By October 2003, industry lobbyists, who had mounted a campaign against reimportation of prescription drugs based on purported safety concerns, were pressing Congress to set harsh penalties for those facilitating the practice.

In early October 2002, the U.S. Office of the Inspector General warned drug companies that offering incentives, such as concert tickets and vacations, to physicians could lead to civil or criminal charges. The policy came after years of concern about drug industry marketing practices that critics said influenced doctors to prescribe certain drugs that led to higher costs for consumers. Although the policy did not bar nominal-cost gifts, golf balls, or bags emblazoned with company logos, meals other than those in conjunction with medical education, concert and other entertainment tickets, cash payments, and a wide range of other incentives were not allowed. The policy also prohibited drug companies from reporting average wholesale prices that differed substantially from what was actually charged—and touting those prices in marketing. The government's concern stemmed from the use of average wholesale prices in determining reimbursement for the drugs Medicare currently covered. There had been some concern that if drugs were sold to doctors for less, doctors could bill for the higher amount and keep the difference. Critics said this was a tactic drug makers used to lure doctors to their products and further inflate consumer drug costs by more than $1 billion annually.

To continue generating the returns enjoyed by the industry over the past decade, pharmaceutical companies would be forced to rethink how they identify and exploit opportunities to gain a competitive edge in an increasingly complex market.

Hershey Foods Corporation

Maryanne M. Rouse

HERSHEY FOODS (HSY), PRINCIPALLY THROUGH HERSHEY CHOCOLATE U.S.A., HERSHEY International, and Hershey Canada, Inc., produced and distributed a broad line of quality chocolate, confectionery, and grocery products. In a related diversification move that it hoped would help overcome the seasonality of the chocolate/confectionery segment, Hershey acquired San Giorgio Macaroni and Delmonico foods, both pasta manufacturers, in 1968. Acquired brands included San Giorgio, Ronzoni, Skinner, P&R, Light 'n Fluffy, and American Beauty. In January 1999, Hershey completed the sale of 94% of its U.S. pasta business to New World Pasta for $450 million in cash. The divestiture was intended to allow Hershey to refocus on its core businesses. Hershey also divested its two main European businesses, Gubor in Germany and Spelari in Italy, and its Canadian Planters business as well as its Luden's throat drops business.

Hershey manufactured, imported, marketed, sold, and distributed chocolate products in Brazil under the Hershey's brand name. In China, Japan, Korea, and the Philippines, the company imported and/or marketed selected confectionery and grocery products. Although Hershey marketed confectionery and grocery products in over 60 countries worldwide, almost 90% of Hershey's sales were currently in North America (the United States, Mexico, and Canada).

Products and Brands

Hershey grew from a small, one-product company in 1894 to a global company with fiscal year 2001 sales of $4.17 billion. The company's products included chocolate and non-chocolate confectionery products consisting of bar goods (both candy and snack bars), bagged items, and boxed items; and grocery products, including baking items, peanut butter, chocolate chips, chocolate syrup, cocoa drink mixes, dessert toppings, and beverages. Hershey's chocolate milk was produced by independent dairies throughout the United States, using chocolate milk mix manufactured by Hershey.

In December 2004, Hershey planned to introduce four varieties of chocolate-covered cookies in single-serving four-cookie packs expected to retail for $.99. The company planned to position its Hershey's, Reese's, Almond Joy, and York Peppermint cookies as a premium-priced snack that would compete against Campbell Soup's Pepperidge Farm brand. The new line of cookies was in line with Hershey's strategy to move into categories that were "adjacent to" its existing confectionery products, building on company confectionery expertise and channel relationships.

Hershey's Chocolate and confectionery products were marketed under more than 50 brands, including Hershey, Kit Kat, Mr. Goodbar, Reese's, Kisses, Mounds, Almond Joy, Skor, Twizzlers, and Amazin' Fruit gummy bears fruit candy. In addition to its traditional confectionery products, Hershey offered a range of products specifically developed to address the nutritional interests of health-conscious consumers, including Hershey's Sugar-Free candy as well as Hershey's 1g Sugar Carb bars for people living a low-carb lifestyle.

Hershey significantly increased its participation in the non-chocolate side of the confectionery industry through its late-1996 acquisition of Leaf North America, whose major brands included Jolly Rancher, Whoppers, Milk Duds, and Good & Plenty. In December 2000, the company purchased the intense and breath-freshener mints and gum businesses of Nabisco for $135 million. The acquired brands included Breath Savers mints and Ice Breakers, Carefree, Stickfree, Bubble Yum, and Fruit Stripes gums. In September 2003, Hershey sold a number of gum brands, including Fruit Stripes gum, Rain Blo gum balls, and Super Bubble to Farley and Sathers Candy Company, Inc. Industry observers thought that Hershey may have considered an offer for Kraft Foods' Life Savers and Altoids breath mint product lines, both of which were reportedly up for sale; however, Hershey refused to comment.

Marketing Strategies

Hershey's marketing strategies were based on the consistently superior quality of its products, mass distribution, and the best possible consumer value in terms of price and weight. Hershey devoted considerable resources to the development, manufacturing, and distribution of new products. Because the significant power of buyers, intense competition, and low inflation made it difficult to raise prices, the company sought to adjust the prices and weights of its products to accommodate changes in manufacturing costs and profit objectives while at the same time maintaining consumer value. Recent product strategies included focusing on big brands and improving the marketing mix with a stronger emphasis on promotion.

The company's products were distributed in over 2 million retail outlets in the United States, including grocery wholesalers, chain stores, convenience stores, mass merchandisers, drugstores, vending companies, wholesale clubs, and food distributors. In 2004, Hershey stepped up its focus on the convenience and vending channels, two channels in which Mars had traditionally done well. A single customer, McLane Company, a former subsidiary of Wal-Mart, accounted for approximately 22% of Hershey's total sales.

Labor Relations

Approximately half of Hershey's full- and part-time employees were covered by collective bargaining agreements. On April 27, 2002, nearly 3,000 workers at two Hershey Foods plants went on strike two days after negotiations between the company and a union broke down. The workers, who made chocolate and other confections in Hershey, Pennsylvania, began picketing at about 9 A.M., in the first strike at the company in 22 years. The chocolate workers' Local 464 had been at odds with the company, based in Hershey, over wages and health care costs.

The striking workers represented about one-fifth of the company's employees. Although company–union relations then improved, they remained less than cordial.

A Summer of Discontent

In an unexpectedly swift reversal of its plans to diversify its holdings of Hershey Foods Corporation stock, by a vote of 10–7 in summer 2002, the Hershey Trust Company, which was legally responsible for overseeing the Milton Hershey School, rejected Wrigley's $12.5 billion offer and announced that its 77% stake in Hershey was no longer for sale. The next morning, September 19, the Commonwealth Court upheld 4–1 an earlier injunction against any sale conducted without full public hearings.

The school, which was created for orphans, served a wide array of 1,200 disadvantaged youngsters; it was the sole beneficiary of Mr. Hershey's charitable trust as it grew into the multibillions on the success of Hershey Foods. The 17 trustees, who ultimately controlled Hershey Foods, the school, and other Hershey entities, maintained that their concern for the school and community as well as advice from Pennsylvania Attorney General Michael Fisher led to the Trust's initial decision to put the company up for sale. Trustees maintained that because more than half its $5.4 billion portfolio was in Hershey stock, the Trust—and school—were quite vulnerable to business downturns.

When the town and alumni heard of the possible sale of the highly profitable candy company, they were aghast. Despite assurances that jobs would be protected and that the company would maintain its presence in the town, Hershey employees and school alumni banded together in a "Derail the Sale" campaign that ultimately had the Attorney General filing an injunction in Orphan's Court to overturn the very sale he had counseled. The rift between the Trust and other Hershey stakeholders would be difficult to heal: A petition with 6,500 signatures was hand-delivered to Attorney General Fisher on Monday, September 23, calling for the removal of the 17 trustees.

Finance

Hershey's financial results strengthened between 2001 and 2003, driven by divestitures, the elimination of marginal product lines, Hershey's ability to integrate a number of complementary acquisitions, and an extraordinarily high rate of new product success. The company also appeared to have recovered from the flawed implementation of an enterprisewide information system that led to an inability to meet demand during Halloween and Christmas 1999 (because of increased order cycle time and decreased fill rates). However, while cost of goods sold showed a slight decrease, selling and administrative expenses increased as a percentage of sales, reflecting increased promotional spending.

Net sales increased approximately 1% in 2003, compared with 2002 net sales, which were down slightly from 2001. The increase in 2003 reflected the selling price increase announced in December 2002, effective in January 2003, and the introduction of new products. Net sales in 2003 and 2002 were reduced considerably as a result of business divestitures and product line rationalization as part of the company's business realignment initiatives. Growth in sales during the three-year period resulted from accelerating the introduction of innovative new products and limited-edition items and from leveraging the company's selling capabilities. Hershey gained market share during the period in key growth channels, reflecting its value-enhancing strategies, including the introduction of new products.

Net sales for the first six months of 2004 increased $104.5 million, or 6% from the comparable period in 2003. Sales increases were driven by increased volume, especially in the

United States, strong sales of single-serving snack and bar candies, higher prices, and the introduction of innovative new products and product line extensions. Net sales in the company's Canadian, Mexican, and Brazilian businesses also increased as a result of increased sales volume and favorable foreign currency exchange rates, particularly in Canada. Sales were unfavorably affected by the divestiture of certain gum brands in September 2003, lower sales of remaining gum brands, and higher promotion allowances and returns, discounts, and allowances, relating primarily to the sales volume growth. The results of the company's Asian operations, particularly in China, continued to be below expectations through the first half of 2004. Consequently, management changes were made, and the company began reexamining its business model for that part of the world. (Note: Hershey's annual and quarterly reports and SEC filings are available via the company's web site *www.hersheys.com* and at *www.wsj.com*.)

The Industry

The $10+ billion U.S. confectionery industry is dominated by five major competitors that control over 70% of the market: Hershey, M&M Mars, Brach and Brock, Nestlé, and RJR Nabisco; the remaining 30% was shared by local and regional candy manufacturers. The U.S. market leader for many years, Hershey slipped to number two, behind Mars, in 1999 and had remained there. Hershey dominated the U.S. chocolate segment with a 43% share, followed by M&M Mars with 27% and Nestlé with just 12%.

Nestlé, which acquired Carnation in the late 1990s, was the largest food company in the world and the strongest global competitor in the chocolate and confectionery segment, with 98% of its sales outside its home country, Switzerland. Nestlé manufactured in 23 countries in highly automated plants. Although Mars was privately held and family controlled, analysts estimated the company's sales to be in excess of $7.5 billion. Mars had a much stronger presence outside the United States than Hershey and was able to gain over 12% market share in Mexico only one year after entering the market. In its grocery products segment, Hershey competed against such processed foods giants as Kraft, ConAgra, Heinz, General Mills, and Kellogg.

The confectionery segment of the processed foods industry was characterized by manufacturing economies of scale and high transportation costs for moving milk and sugar, the principal raw materials. Cocoa beans, the primary ingredient in chocolate, were imported from West Africa, South America, and equatorial regions in Asia. West Africa accounted for about 70% of the world crop. During 2001–2004, cocoa prices had been subject to wide fluctuations attributable to the effects of weather on crop yield, imbalances between supply and demand, political unrest, currency exchange rates, and speculative influences. Hershey used commodities futures contracts to hedge the prices of cocoa, sugar, corn sweeteners, and dairy products. U.S. import quotas and import duties to support the price of domestic sugar had resulted in domestic sugar prices being substantially higher than those in the world market.

Industry analysts expected the mature, competitive confectionery segment of the global processed foods industry to grow by 5% to 8% per year. Consumption of chocolate appeared to be closely correlated with national income; however, the Far East was an exception to this rule as Asian consumers had shown a preference for non-chocolate confections at all income levels. Americans consumed about 22 pounds of candy per person per year, while Europeans consumed approximately 27 pounds. Chocolate accounted for approximately 54% of all candy consumption. Among European countries, Switzerland, Norway, and the United Kingdom consumed the most chocolate.

Tech Data Corporation

Maryanne M. Rouse

The Company

TECH DATA CORPORATION'S (TECD) AGGRESSIVE GROWTH HAD TAKEN THE COMPANY from 10 employees and $2 million in sales in 1983 to approximately 8,000 employees and $15.7 billion in sales for fiscal 2002 (fiscal year ended January 31, 2003) and secured the company's position as a leading distributor of information technology (IT), logistics management, and other value-added services to "solution providers," including value-added resellers (VARs), direct marketers, retailers, corporate resellers, and Internet resellers. Ranked 117 on the *Fortune 500* list, the company and its subsidiaries served more than 100,000 technology resellers in the United States, Canada, the Caribbean, Latin America, Europe, and the Middle East.

Tech Data was incorporated in 1974 to market data processing supplies, including tape, disk packs, and custom and stock tab forms for mini and mainframe computers directly to end users. With the growing popularity of microcomputers and the emergence of microcomputer dealers, the company withdrew entirely from end-user sales and made the transition to wholesale distribution in 1984.

The company's flexible structure comprised five major product divisions (components, systems, peripherals, networking, and software) plus Strategic Business Units (SBUs) designed to address specific market, channel, customer, or product opportunities. Tech Data's current SBUs included digital imaging/CAD, mobile solutions, security, storage, and telephony. Fiscal 2002 sales by product category were peripherals, 46%; components and systems, 24%; networking, 15%; and software, 15%. On a channel basis, VARs accounted for 58% of the company's $17.2 billion 2002 sales, with direct marketers, retailers, and Internet resellers comprising 24% and corporate resellers accounting for the remaining 18%. No single customer accounted for more than 5% of sales during fiscal 2002.

Tech Data's broad vendor base included such manufacturers and publishers as Adobe, Apple, Cisco, Computer Associates, Creative Labs, Epson, Hewlett-Packard/Compaq, IBM, Intel, Iomega, Lexmark, Microsoft, Nortel Networks, NEC, Palm, Seagate, Sony, Symantec, 3Com, Toshiba, Viewsonic, and Western Digital. With the exception of Hewlett-Packard/Compaq, no vendor accounted for more than 10% of the company's sales. Sales of HP/Compaq products accounted for 38% of Tech Data's net sales in 2002, 39% in 2001, and 35% in 2000.

Strategies

Tech Data was the second largest global IT distributor, and its business model was based on a four-point strategy of excellence in execution, proactive initiatives, cost leadership, and e-business, with each element focused on enhancing the company's relationships with its business partners. The company defined excellence in execution as the promotion of six key elements for ensuring customer/partner satisfaction and loyalty: accessibility, availability, pricing, shipping metrics and service-level agreements, planning and execution, and people. Proactive initiatives, such as customer relationship management and comprehensive business development, were designed to support internal growth via market penetration and product development. The company's SBU initiative was a good example of its proactive initiatives strategy. Cost leadership, based on centralized purchasing, benchmarking, continuous improvement, and capacity management, was considered critical to profitability and return on investment in an industry characterized by increasingly thin profit margins. Tech Data's strategic emphasis on e-business supported the first three key elements by increasing efficiency and transaction speed, reducing costs, and supplying information that was critical to identifying and developing proactive initiatives.

Acquisitions

Tech Data had grown both internally via market penetration and product/market development and externally through acquisition:

- **May 1989:** The company entered the Canadian market via the acquisition of a privately held distributor that was subsequently named Tech Data Canada.
- **March 1994:** Tech Data entered the European market through the acquisition of a second privately held company that was renamed Tech Data France, SA.
- **February 1997:** The company expanded its Miami-based Latin American export business by opening a sales and logistics office in Sao Paolo, Brazil.
- **July 1998:** Tech Data completed acquisition of 83% of the voting stock of Computer 2000 AG, Europe's leading technology products distributor; in April 1999, all the shares of Computer 2000 were integrated into Tech Data Germany AG. This acquisition gave Tech Data a presence in important markets in Europe, the Middle East, and Latin America and expanded the company's presence to 29 countries worldwide.
- **May 1999:** The company acquired Globelle Corporation, a leading publicly held Canadian distributor, which almost doubled Tech Data's Canadian presence.
- **March 2003:** Tech Data agreed to acquire UK-based Azlan Group PLC, a distributor of networking and communications products.

Financial Performance

Reflecting an uncertain economy, tight-fisted business technology buyers, the aftermath of 9/11, and severe pricing pressure, Tech Data's sales decreased from $20.4 billion in fiscal 2001 to $17.2 billion for the same period in 2002; however, the company's quick action in cutting costs salvaged what could have been a disastrous year. Among other steps, Tech Data reduced its headcount from 10,500 to approximately 8,000, scaled back on infrastructure, and aggressively pursued efficiency in operations. Although net income declined just under 38%, from $178.3 million to $110.8 million for fiscal 2002, Tech Data was a bright spot in an industry full of calamity.

In a conference call with analysts on March 17, 2003, Chief Executive Steve Raymund reported that sales for the fiscal year ended January 31 had further eroded to $15.7 billion. The company's $199.8 million loss for the year was entirely due to a $334.6 million write-off of goodwill associated with Tech Data's 1998 acquisition of Computer 2000 AG.

The Industry

Distribution channels for IT products had changed substantially over the past two decades, as the wholesale distribution model had evolved to serve the needs of both vendors and resellers; the large number and diversity of resellers made it cost-efficient for manufacturers and publishers of IT products to rely on wholesale distributors to serve this customer base, while the large number of vendors and products allowed resellers access to broad product lines without requiring them to establish direct purchasing relationships. In addition to cost-efficiency, large two-tier wholesalers such as Tech Data and Ingram Micro could offer their customers special pricing, credit, financing, and other valued-added services not available to small and midsized business from manufacturers.

Direct sales initiatives by IBM and the recently merged Hewlett-Packard/Compaq posed a growing threat, luring systems integrator and end-user customers from distributors. In 1998, the then "Big Three" distributed approximately 90% of their products via indirect channels; that number was estimated at less than 50% in 2004. Among the factors cited for the growing emphasis on direct distribution were the commoditization of technology, which had placed a ceiling on prices; the increased sophistication of end users, which translated into a greater willingness to purchase IT products via web sites; and pressures to reduce costs. At the other end of the value chain, distributors were concerned that an increasing number of VARs might choose to focus on services and drop hardware because they could no longer afford to support it.

Overall weak sales in the technology sector and increasing pressure on margins had channel members at least discussing alternatives to the current model. Many solution providers were concerned that distributors would eventually have to sell directly to end users to squeeze more revenue from the small/medium-sized business and corporate markets. In addition, some channel observers believed that sales gains by direct marketers, such as CDW, would increase the pressure for direct sales. And, while few thought such major players as Tech Data and Ingram Micro would abandon their solution provider businesses altogether, increased competitive pressures could cause distributors to reexamine their reluctance to break the existing value chain. To some extent, two-tier distributors had heightened concerns among solution providers by offering their logistics, back-end capabilities, and broad product lines to such e-tailers as Buy.com, Amazon.com, and auction sites such as eBay and by giving large IT purchasers reseller status (as Ingram Micro did with Lockheed-Martin).

Competitors

Tech Data's key competitors in the industry included Ingram Micro, Arrow Electronics, Avnet, and Pioneer Standard. Tech Data also competed with manufacturers that sold directly to resellers and end users. As the company had diversified into new products and related industries, it had had to face new competitors and master new critical success factors.

Ingram Micro was the world's largest distributor of IT products. It offered more than 280,000 products, including desktop and notebook PCs, servers, storage devices, CD-ROM drives, monitors, printers, and software, to approximately 175,000 reseller customers around the world. The company also provided its business partners a wide range of services for both resellers and suppliers, including contract manufacturing and warehousing, customer care, financing, logistics, and enterprise network support services. The Ingram family controlled more than 70% of the company's voting stock. Ingram's revenue declined 10.8% from 2001 to 2002, and its profit declined 10.3% for the same period; this reflected both industry conditions and Ingram's low price strategy.

Arrow Electronics was the world's largest distributor of electronic components and computer products. Arrow sold semiconductors, computer peripherals, passive components, and interconnection products from over 600 suppliers to more than 200,000 computer manufacturers and commercial customers. Arrow distributed products made by such vendors as 3Com, Computer Associates, Intel, Hitachi, Motorola, and Texas Instruments. Arrow also provided value-added services such as component design, inventory management, and contract manufacturing.

Avnet was the second-largest distributor of electronic components and computer products in the United States. Avnet's suppliers included more than 250 components and systems manufacturers; the company distributed these suppliers' products to more than 100,000 other manufacturers. Avnet's Electronics Marketing Group handled semiconductors and other components, while its Computer Marketing Group provided computer products and services to resellers and large end users. A third unit, Avnet Applied Computing, marketed system-level components such as motherboards. Avnet also provided services such as logistics, integration, and consulting.

Pioneer Standard sold thousands of products to manufacturers, resellers, research laboratories, government agencies, and end users. The company supplemented its product offerings with a range of services, including design engineering, connector and cable assembly, logistics support, integration, and outsourcing.

Recent Developments

In 2003, industry observers expected weak demand for IT products as economic uncertainty and a less-than-robust global economy had put a damper on technology spending by businesses and consumers. The potential interest rate and currency fluctuations, as well as the impact of geopolitical instability and continued downward pressure on pricing, were expected to contribute to a lackluster 2003.

Analysts in the PC industry, which had been racked by customer indifference for the past two years, expected only a modest rebound of 6% to 8% in 2003. However, with aggressive price-cutting, revenue was expected to be flat. On a more positive note, falling prices for components created opportunities to shift customers to alternative tablet and notebook PCs, and Microsoft's recent announcement that it would cease providing support for Windows 98 was expected to create an opportunity for third-party service providers and to shore up demand as users shifted to computers that would support later software editions. Analysts expected somewhat stronger demand in several segments, including servers, digital imaging/CAD, mobile solutions, security, and storage.

Computer disposal was becoming a serious problem, particularly because a new machine had an average life expectancy of two years. According to the U.S. Environmental Protection Agency, 20 million computers were taken out of service in 1998 alone, and the number continued to grow. Of these, 12% were recycled; an estimated 75% were stored in closets, garages, etc.; and the remaining 13% were sent out with the trash. Environmentally, PCs still rated poorly, despite ongoing improvements in manufacturing. While electronics in landfills leached toxins into groundwater and incinerated ones polluted the air, manufacturers, distributors, and end users disagreed over who bore the burden of seeking out responsible means of disposal.

The Challenge

As technology had become a commodity, the role of the "pure-play" distributor had disappeared. In this new environment, the challenge facing Tech Data and its competitors would be to continually develop and provide their partners with attractive, value-adding technology solutions in new and developing markets characterized by intense competition and declining prices.

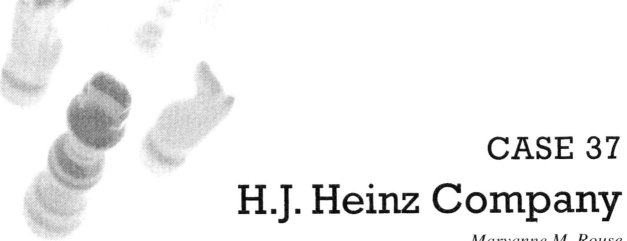

CASE 37

H.J. Heinz Company

Maryanne M. Rouse

H.J. Heinz Company (HNZ) and its subsidiaries manufactured and marketed an extensive line of processed and minimally processed food and related products throughout the world. The company's products were organized into two core businesses: meal enhancers and meals and snacks. Heinz distributed its products via its own sales force, independent brokers, agents, and distributors to chain, wholesale, cooperative, and independent grocery accounts; mass merchants and superstores; pharmacies; club stores; food service distributors; and institutions, including schools and government agencies.

The Del Monte Merger

In June 2002, Heinz announced that it would spin off and then merge its slower-selling products with Del Monte Foods, Inc., in an effort to simplify its business. After positive votes by both Heinz and Del Monte shareholders and approval by the IRS, the transaction, completed on December 21, 2002, gave Heinz shareholders approximately 75% of the new, much larger Del Monte. The product lines/segments shifted to Del Monte included Heinz's U.S. and Canadian pet food and pet snacks businesses; U.S. tuna; U.S. private-label soups and gravies, as well as College Inn soups; and U.S. infant feeding. The affected brands included StarKist, 9 Lives, Kibbles 'n Bits, Nature's Goodness baby food, and College Inn soups. The merger was expected to reduce Heinz's annual revenue by approximately 20%, or $1.8 billion, while doubling Del Monte's size.

Under the terms of the merger, Heinz shareholders received 0.45 share of stock in the new Del Monte for every share of Heinz stock owned, while Del Monte assumed approximately $1.1 billion of Heinz's debt (about 21% of Heinz's total debt). Heinz also announced that it would reduce its dividend by 33%. (The dividend reduction was expected to free up substantial cash flow, which Heinz planned to use to pay down debt and underwrite additional marketing.) The merger was effected in several steps, including the transfer of Heinz assets to a temporary entity, SKF, which was then merged, along with the existing Del Monte, into a "new Del Monte." The complicated deal, referred to as a *reverse Morris Trust*, resulted in a tax-free transfer because Heinz shareholders would ultimately own a majority of shares in the new Del Monte.

In addition to allowing Heinz to sell its sluggish brands on an essentially tax-free basis, the company noted that the smaller, less-diverse Heinz would become a more flexible, faster-growing company focused on two strategic food platforms: meal enhancers (ketchup, condiments, sauces) and meals and snacks (frozen and shelf-stable meals and snacks, food service frozen products, and infant feeding in non-U.S. markets). The new Heinz would have a global structure, which the company believed would enhance its ability to compete outside the United States. Reducing debt would enable Heinz to better support its core businesses with added investments in product development and advertising.

Investors reacted coolly to the merger announcement, sending Heinz shares down and resulting in only modest gains for Del Monte. By year-end 2002, both companies' stock prices had posted further declines, reflecting weakness in the broader market. (Some industry observers believed the merger could be win–win for Heinz shareholders *only* if there was an end game that involved selling the slimmer and more attractive Heinz.) By mid-January 2005, however, Heinz's stock price had recovered to just under $38, $3 below its 52-week high of $40.67, and Del Monte had managed to regain some strength, closing at $11.17 on January 13, 2005.

The New Growth Strategy

Shortly after the completion of the Del Monte merger, Heinz announced an aggressive growth strategy based on four key initiatives:

- Drive profitable growth through superior products and packaging, everyday price/value, accelerated innovation, and creative marketing
- Remove the "clutter" both by focusing on core businesses and products and by creating a simplified business structure
- Reduce costs (especially fixed costs) by creating a more efficient supply chain, improving cash and working capital management, and making focused capital expenditures
- Measure and recognize performance through a "balanced scorecard" that tied management compensation to key financial and non-financial performance measures and drivers

As part of the company's emphasis on core products, Heinz realigned its SBUs into two core businesses:

- **Meal enhancers:** This segment comprised key brands from the former Ketchup and Condiments unit. Although sales in this segment had been driven by ketchup, which had always been the company's flagship brand, acquisitions and new product development (Jack Daniel's grilling sauces and Mr. Yoshida's marinades, Classico pasta sauces) had given Heinz a growing presence both on the grill and in the kitchen. With global ketchup sales in excess of $1 billion, Heinz had over 50% of the domestic ketchup market and approximately 34% of the global market. Packaging innovations such as the E-Z Squirt bottle had helped drive Heinz's global market share in ketchup up 15%, to 60%. (Heinz had a 75% share in the United Kingdom; the company claimed that 5 points were directly related to the new bottle.) As U.S. fast food chains increased in global popularity, Heinz expected strong growth in both single-serving packet and bulk ketchup and condiment (barbecue sauce, soy sauce, steak sauce, etc.) sales. However, Heinz ketchup faced challenges from other brand-name ketchups, private-label ketchups, and salsa. The increased popularity of salsa and other ethnic condiments, as well as the lower cost structures for private-label brands, were expected to threaten Heinz's market share.

- **Meals and snacks:** This segment brought together branded shelf-stable and frozen meals and snacks from the previous Soup, Beans, and Pasta Meals and Frozen Foods units as well as non-U.S. infant feeding and frozen or shelf-stable products for the institutional market.

  The company's growing frozen meal/snack product line included such best-selling U.S. brands as Ore-Ida potatoes, Boston Market HomeStyle Meals, and Weight Watchers and Smart Ones entrees and desserts. (Heinz, which had acquired Weight Watchers in 1978, sold the international weight control segment of that business in 1999 as part of an initiative to focus on core businesses; however, the company retained the processed food segment.) Popular U.S. snack brands, including Bagel Bites, T.G.I. Friday's, Delimex, and Poppers, were being managed as part of this segment.

  Heinz expected its UK and other non-U.S. brands in this category, such as Weight Watchers from Heinz and Main Street Bistro entrees and Linda McCartney meat-free meals, to drive growth outside the United States. For example, Wattie's was among the most powerful brands in New Zealand, offering a wide range of meal solutions; and the Honig and HAK brands provided Dutch consumers a wide variety of dried soups, meals, and vegetables. And, while Heinz included its U.S. tuna business in the spin-off, it retained such European brands as John West and Petit Navire and the Australian Greenseas tuna brand.

  The company was developing a strong presence in food service frozen products, with varieties such as Chef Francisco and Quality Chef soups and Alden Merrill frozen desserts. Although Heinz's retail private-label soups and gravies and College Inn broths were spun off to Del Monte, the company hoped to grow market share in both U.S. and global markets via such innovations as microwaveable Soup Cups—a convenience concept imported from Australia.

  Also included in this segment was infant feeding. Although Heinz included its U.S. infant feeding business in the spin-off to Del Monte, the company retained both its Heinz branded baby foods, which held top positions in the United Kingdom, Canada, Venezuela, Australia, and China, and Plasmon, its Italian infant feeding business.

A New Organizational Structure

In the first quarter of fiscal 2004, Heinz changed its segment reporting to reflect changes in organizational structure and management:

- **North American Consumer Products:** This segment manufactured, marketed, and sold ketchup, condiments, sauces, pasta meals, frozen potatoes, entrees, snacks, and appetizers to grocery channels in the United States and Canada. North American Consumer Products accounted for approximately 24.5% of sales and 31.6% of profits in fiscal 2004.

- **U.S. Foodservice:** This segment manufactured, marketed, and sold branded and private-label products (including ketchup, condiments, sauces, frozen soups, and desserts) to commercial and non-commercial food outlets and distributors. U.S. Foodservice accounted for approximately 17% of sales and 14.1% of profits in fiscal 2004.

- **Europe:** This segment sold products across categories and channels in Europe; it accounted for approximately 39% of sales and 42.6% of profits in fiscal 2004.

- **Asia/Pacific:** This segment included operations across product categories and channels in New Zealand, Australia, Japan, China, South Korea, Indonesia, Singapore, and Thailand; it contributed approximately 15% of sales and 9.7% of profits in fiscal 2004.

- **Other Operating Entities:** This segment sold products across categories and channels in Africa, India, Latin America, the Middle East, and other geographic areas. This segment accounted for approximately 4.5% of sales and 2% of profits in fiscal 2004.

Financial Position/Performance

In accordance with generally accepted accounting principles, Heinz's financial statements for prior years had been restated to reflect the merger (show revenues, expenses, assets, and liabilities, excluding the entities that were later spun off to Del Monte) and the new segment reporting structure. On that basis, revenues for fiscal 2004 (fiscal year ended April 28, 2004) of $8.41 billion showed an increase of just under 2.2% over the prior year compared to an 8.2% revenue increase from 2002 to 2003. However, gross profit performance improved to 36.7% of sales in 2004 compared to 35.4% of sales in 2003. (Despite cost-cutting initiatives, Heinz's gross profit as a percentage of sales had decreased from 36.93% in 2001 to 35.4% in 2003.)

Net income for fiscal 2004 reflected discontinued operations of the company's Northern Europe bakery business as well as write-downs and reorganization costs; net income for fiscal 2003 reflected both income from discontinued operations ($88.74 million) and the cumulative effect of a change in accounting principles related to goodwill (–$77,812), and it represented a 6.88% return on sales, significantly below 2002's 10.95% but slightly ahead of 2001's 6.84%. In a less positive development, S&P downgraded the company's long- and short-term debt ratings to reflect Heinz's increased financial leverage.

Sales for the six months ended October 27, 2004, increased $216.6 million, or 5.4%, to $4.20 billion. Sales volume increased 1.2% over the same period in the previous fiscal year, while exchange translations added 4.2% to sales. Acquisitions, net of divestitures, increased sales by 0.5%, while lower pricing decreased sales by 0.5%. Despite cost-cutting initiatives, gross profit as a percentage of sales decreased to 36.6% from 37.3%, mainly due to lower pricing and increased product costs in Europe and Latin America. SG&A increased $65.5 million, or 8.3%, to $855.7 million, and increased as a percentage of sales to 20.4% from 19.8% for the six-month period. Operating income decreased $15.0 million, or 2.1%, to $683.1 million, and decreased as a percentage of sales to 16.3% from 17.5%. Income from continuing operations for the first six months of fiscal 2005 (ended on October 27, 2004) was $392.1 million compared to $378.3 million in the same period a year earlier, an increase of 3.6%. On a segment basis, North American Consumer Products accounted for 25% of sales and 34.5% of operating income; U.S. Foodservice contributed 17% of sales and 15.7% of operating income; Europe contributed 38% of sales and 39.2% of operating income; Asia/Pacific contributed 14% of sales and 10.5% of operating income. (Complete SEC filings are available via a link from the company's web site *www.heinz.com* or *www.wsj.com*.)

Acquisition Strategies

Heinz had pursued global growth via market penetration and product/market development achieved principally via acquisition. In September 1999, Heinz acquired a 19.5% interest in The Hain Food Group, Inc., for nearly $100 million, forming a strategic alliance for global production of natural and organic foods and soy-based beverages. Hain was the leading U.S. natural and organic foods company, with more than 3,500 products sold under such brands as Health Valley cereals, bakery products, and soups; Terra Chips snacks; and Westsoy, the largest soy beverage marketer. As part of the alliance, Heinz was to provide procurement, manufacturing, and logistics expertise, with Hain providing marketing, sales, and distribution services.

Other recent acquisitions included the Borden Food Corporation's pasta sauce, dry bouillon, and soup business; the Linda McCartney and Ethnic Gourmet brands; and Anchor Food Products' branded retail business, which included the licensing rights to the T.G.I. Friday's brand of frozen snacks and the Poppers brand of appetizers. The company also completed its acquisitions of Delimex, a leading maker of frozen Mexican food products. Heinz had financed its acquisition strategy principally via debt (in 2004, approximately $5.6 billion), resulting in a total debt to equity ratio of 3.63, twice the industry average.

In fiscal 1999, the company began a growth and restructuring initiative named "Operation Excel." This multiyear program established manufacturing centers of excellence, focused on the product portfolio, realigned the company's management teams, and invested in growth initiatives. The total cost of Operation Excel was estimated at $1.2 billion; pretax savings generated from the program were estimated to be $70 million in fiscal 2000 and $135 million in fiscal 2001. Cost savings were projected to grow to approximately $185 million in 2002 and $200 million in fiscal 2003 and thereafter. In the fourth quarter of fiscal 2001, the company announced a restructuring initiative, named "Streamline," designed to decrease overhead and other operating costs via such steps as closure of the company's tuna operations in Puerto Rico, consolidation of the company's North American pet food production, and the divestiture of the company's U.S. fleet of fishing boats.

The Food Service Market

Heinz was the largest prepared food supplier (ketchup and condiments, salad dressings, frozen foods, soup concentrate, etc.) to the U.S. food service market, which comprised restaurants and other away-from-home eating places. The food service industry, which had seen flat growth as the U.S. economy stalled in recession, was expected to improve as U.S. economic growth strengthened and U.S. families increased the proportion of food dollars spent away from home (slightly over 50% in 2003, up from about 33% in the 1970s). Industry analysts expected strong growth in global food service demand (especially in Europe and Asia) over the next five years. Key competitors included Kraft, Unilever, Sara Lee, Campbell Soup Company, and Dole Food Company, Inc. Because Heinz drew approximately 17% of its revenues from food service operations (restaurants, stadiums, airports, etc.), the company had suffered more than most processed food firms from the after-effects of September 11.

Processed Food Industry

As a whole, the packaged food industry outperformed the S&P 500 for the first seven months of 2004, posting a 5.7% versus a 2.1% decline for the broader index. Cost pressures were a key concern for the industry, primarily from increased commodity, pension, and fuel costs. While many commodities were below recent highs, they remained above 2003 levels. An additional concern was the vulnerability of input prices to weather and export demand. However, industry profit margins were expected to benefit from cost reductions resulting from mergers and acquisitions and the aggressive restructurings undertaken by most major companies in the previous several years.

Sales of frozen and prepared foods in the United States had grown significantly over the previous three years, driven by quality improvements and convenient packaging, factors that promised to make those products still more attractive in the future. Retailers' adjustments virtually guaranteed this: In the previous three years, Wal-Mart and Albertsons had increased their frozen food departments by 25%–40% throughout their chains.

Key competitors in this industry segment included Kraft, Kellogg Company, ConAgra, General Mills, Unilever, Dole, and Sara Lee. Eighty percent of total food, drug, and mass merchandiser sales in the United States went to national brands and, according to one recent study, 46% of Americans were "national brand loyalists" who gravitated strongly to national brands. However, brand loyalty was eroding in all age groups. The benchmark annual index from Interbrand, a brand consultancy, showed 41 of the top brands a year earlier declining in value in 2004.

The industry had experienced aggressive consolidation (13 mergers among publicly traded packaged food companies since the beginning of 2000), which had eliminated all the obvious takeover targets. Industry consolidation plus the maturity of the U.S. market for processed foods (1% growth, low inflation, increasing popularity of generics) made competition for market share intense and left little latitude for price increases. Continued consolidation in the grocery industry via the acquisition of niche players and the emergence of super-stores and wholesale clubs would also exert downward pressure on prices.

The Westernization of eating habits, together with rising incomes in developing countries and the appeal of American brand names abroad, was expected to contribute to increased growth among U.S. processed food companies; however, new dietary guidelines from the U.S. Department of Agriculture, which cautioned consumers about the consumption of trans fats, could negatively impact sales of some shelf-stable products.

Heinz has created a special link for students: *www.heinz.com/jsp/students.jsp*.

CASE 38

Lowe's Companies, Inc.

Maryanne M. Rouse

LOWE'S COMPANIES (LOW), THE SECOND LARGEST U.S. HOME IMPROVEMENT RETAILER, competed in the highly fragmented $400+ billion home improvement industry. Capitalizing on historically high rates of home ownership, the company had grown from 15 stores selling commodity-type products to new home builders in 1962 to a chain of almost 1,000 stores in 45 states with over 99.5 million square feet of selling space in 2004. (The total includes 46 stores opened between January 31, 2003, and August 1, 2004, the end of the second quarter of Lowe's fiscal year.) In 1989, the company redefined its business and positioned itself as a "big-box" home-improvement retailer, selling a wide array of higher-margin merchandise. Lowe's opened its first 100,000+ square-foot big-box store in 1992. Between 2003 and 2004, the company developed two prototype stores: the larger had 116,000 square feet of selling space plus an additional 31,000 square feet dedicated to lawn and garden products, while the store developed for smaller markets provided 94,000 square feet of selling space plus an additional 26,000 feet devoted to lawn and garden product lines. A typical store stocked more than 40,000 SKUs, with hundreds more available through the company's special order system. Product lines included plumbing and electrical products, tools, building materials, hardware, outdoor hardlines, appliances, lumber, mill work, paint and decorative products, cabinets, furniture, and nursery and gardening products.

Lowe's served both retail and commercial business customers. Retail customers were primarily do-it-yourself homeowners and others buying for personal and family use. Commercial business customers included repair and remodeling contractors, electricians, landscapers, painters, plumbers, and commercial and residential building maintenance professionals. Approximately 73% of the company's sales were to retail customers, with the balance to commercial customers.

Growth Strategies

With no plans for international expansion in 2004, Lowe's planned to grow domestic square footage at an annual rate of 16%–17% over the next two to three years, with 150 store openings planned for 2005 and another 150–160 store openings for 2006. The company was aggressively targeting metropolitan markets with populations of 500,000 or more, noting that currently the company's highest-volume stores were in metropolitan markets. Stores in these larger markets accounted for approximately 65% of the company's new store openings in 2003 and 2004. In line with this strategy, Lowe's announced plans to add more than 40 stores in the New York/New Jersey metro market as well as in Chicago by year-end 2005. Through September 30, 2004, Lowe's opened over 48 new stores, bringing the company's total above 1,000:

	2003	2002	2001	2000	1999
Number of stores, beginning of year	854	744	650	576	520
New stores opened	125	112	101	80	60
Relocated stores opened	5	11	14	20	31
Stores closed (including relocated stores)	(6)	(13)	(21)	(26)	(35)
Contractor yards sold	(26)	—	—	—	—
Total number of stores, end of year	952	854	744	650	576

The company believed there were significant product/market growth opportunities in three key areas: installed sales, special order sales, and commercial business customers. Additional growth strategies included increasing sales per square foot and adding high-quality product lines.

In 1998, Lowe's began a major expansion into the Western United States, with plans to build 100+ new stores in three to four years. In early 1999, the company acquired Eagle Hardware and Garden, a 41-store chain of home improvement and garden centers, accelerating Lowe's West Coast expansion and providing a stepping-stone to 10 new Western states, including a number of key metropolitan markets.

Finance

Net earnings for 2003 increased 27%, to $1.9 billion, or 6.1% of sales, compared to $1.5 billion, or 5.6% of sales, for 2002. Return on beginning assets, defined as net earnings divided by beginning total assets, was 11.7% for 2003, compared to 10.7% for 2002 and 9.0% for 2001. Return on beginning shareholders' equity, defined as net earnings divided by beginning shareholders' equity, was 22.6% for 2003, compared to 22.0% for 2002 and 18.6% for 2001. The company recorded sales of $30.8 billion in 2003, an 17% increase over 2002 sales of $26.1 billion. Sales for 2002 were 20% higher than 2001 levels. Average ticket amounts increased 4.2%, from $56.80 in 2002 to $59.21 in 2003, due in part to the success of the up-the-continuum initiative as well as the Lowe's credit programs. Comparable-store sales in 2003 increased by 6.7%, with the strongest sales increases in lumber, building materials, outdoor power equipment, paint, flooring, and home organization.

The company reported consistent sales gains across all categories, from appliances to outdoor plants. Percentage contributions to sales by product line are summarized below (dollar amounts in millions):

Category	2003	2002
Appliances	11%	11%
Lumber/Plywood	9	9
Outdoor Fashion	7	7
Millwork	7	7
Nursery	6	6
Flooring	6	6
Fashion Electrical	6	6
Fashion Plumbing	6	6
Paint	7	7
Tools	5	5
Hardware	6	6
Building Materials	5	5
Cabinets/Furniture/Shelving	4	4
Outdoor Power Equipment	3	4
Rough Plumbing	3	3
Walls/Windows	3	3
Rough Electrical	3	2
Home Organization	2	2
Other	1	1
Total sales (millions)	$30,838	$26,112

Sales in the second quarter of fiscal 2004 exceeded $10 billion for the first time in the company's history, increasing 17.3% over sales in the second quarter of fiscal 2003. For the six months ended July 30, 2004, sales increased 19.4%, and comparable-store sales increased 7.2%. Net earnings increased 17.9%, to $704 million, compared to the previous year's second quarter results. The gross margin was 33.3% of sales for the quarter ended July 30, 2004, compared to 30.3% for the previous year's comparable quarter. The gross margin for the six months ended July 30, 2004, was 33.2% versus 30.7% for the first six months of 2003. The company's aggressive new store growth gave Lowe's additional leverage with vendors, which, together with improved inventory management, resulted in a decline in cost of goods sold as a percentage of sales for fiscal 2003 and the first two quarters of 2004. (Lowe's annual and quarterly reports and SEC filings are available via the company's web site *www.lowes.com* or *www.wsj.com*.)

Logistics

To help maintain appropriate inventory levels in stores and to improve distribution efficiency, Lowe's operated 10 highly automated regional distribution centers (RDCs). In 2004, the RDCs were strategically located in North Carolina, Georgia, Indiana, Pennsylvania, Texas, California, Ohio, Wyoming, and Florida. Each Lowe's store was served by one of these RDCs. The company also operated nine smaller support facilities to distribute merchandise that required special handling due to size or type of packaging, such as lumber, various imports, and building materials. Approximately 50% of the merchandise purchased by the company was shipped through its distribution facilities, while the remaining portion was shipped directly to stores from vendors.

Promotion

Lowe's reached target customers through a promotional mix that included television, radio, direct mail, newspaper, event sponsorships, and in-store programs. The company had developed a strategic alliance with the HGTV network, one of a half-dozen media partnerships created to build the image and equity of the Lowe's brand while complementing core media and marketing programs. Lowe's also hosted customer hospitality events through its Team 48 NASCAR sponsorship, supported the wide-ranging activities of Lowe's Home Safety Council, and used its proprietary credit programs to drive customer traffic and purchases. The easy-to-navigate Lowe's web site was a key element in its promotional strategy. The site allowed customers to search the company's inventory on a store-by-store basis, compare products and prices, and order online or for store pickup.

Other Marketing Initiatives

In response to significant growth in the "buy-it-yourself" (BIY, or "do-it-for-me") market, Lowe's developed an installed sales program that allowed customers to arrange for installation of products in over 30 categories. A BIY customer chose and purchased the product but relied on professionals to handle installation. Lowe's had added kiosks in departments such as appliances, home decor/flooring, electrical, lighting, millwork, hardware, seasonal, plumbing, and tools to facilitate special orders. Some of these kiosks were technology based and some were literature based, but all facilitated the ability of the customer to special order to fit their home improvement needs. Special order sales allowed Lowe's to offer a variety of unique items without the investment in inventory.

The design of Lowe's stores had attracted customers, particularly women, who disliked the warehouse shopping layout of rival Home Depot. Lowe's featured wider aisles, brighter lighting, and more signs, and it stocked a larger selection of products for home decorating, including lamps, window treatments, and designer towels, than is found in a typical Home Depot.

In both 2003 and 2004, Lowe's developed a series of initiatives to better serve commercial business customers, including enhanced ordering and credit programs, increased delivery options, an increase in professional-preferred brands, and a policy of increasing in-stock quantities for bigger jobs in an effort to win the loyalty of commercial customers. Analysts estimated potential sales to this segment of the market at almost three times sales to the traditional DIY market.

Suppliers

Excluding special order vendors, Lowe's sourced its products from approximately 7,000 merchandise vendors worldwide, with no single vendor accounting for more than 4% of total purchases; however, the company had begun to develop vendor alliances with key partners under a vendor certification program. Lowe's used its Global Sourcing Division to purchase directly from foreign manufacturers and avoid higher-cost third-party importers. Growing demand for steel, plywood, and other building products, especially from China and other developing economies, had placed pressure on both suppliers and prices.

The Industry

According to the Home Improvement Research Institute (HIRI), the total retail home improvement market in the United States reached $187.6 billion in 2001 and was expected to climb to $236.7 billion in 2006. Industry sales were sensitive to a number of factors, including interest rates, housing turnover, consumer debt levels, and concern about job security. Although new housing starts were important, the sales opportunity from housing turnover was three times larger than from the sales of new homes. Even when a weakening economy forced some homeowners to delay the purchase of new homes, industry research showed that they were likely to continue to invest in improving their existing homes. Aggressive interest rate cuts during 2001, 2002, and 2003 and continued low fixed and variable first and second mortgage rates had allowed consumers to borrow more to fund home improvement projects.

Homeowners spent more to maintain and improve their living spaces than did renters. The U.S. Census Bureau estimated that home ownership increased to 69.2% in third quarter 2004, up from 65% in 1995. In addition, as baby boomers spent more time at home with their families, they were likely to spend a larger portion of disposable income on their homes than in prior years. With the bulk of the U.S. population entering the post-40 age group, demand for household products and remodeling/renovation were likely to experience strong growth.

Competition

The home improvement industry was highly fragmented, with the two largest players, Home Depot and Lowe's, controlling approximately 32% of the $192 billion do-it-yourself market and less than 5% of the $245 billion professional/commercial market. Key competitive factors in the home improvement retailing business were price, location, customer service, product and brand selection, and name recognition. As Lowe's and Home Deport pursued aggressive growth strategies, industry analysts expected consolidation, with less competitive players closing, being acquired, or merging with other retailers.

The industry leader was Home Depot, with 1,788 stores in 50 states, the District of Columbia, 5 Canadian provinces, Puerto Rico, and Mexico and an overall market share estimated at 18%, compared to 9% for Lowe's. The company's stores marketed a wide range of building materials, home improvement supplies, and lawn and garden products; EXPO Design Center stores offered interior design products and installation services.

Home Depot targeted the same three customer groups as Lowe's and, although Home Depot and Lowe's pursued many of the same competitive strategies, Home Depot's size provided the company with significant economies of scale and cost advantages. In September 2004, Home Depot opened a 105,000-square-foot superstore just off Broadway on West 23rd street, replete with such big-city touches as doormen and home delivery. After two lackluster years, Home Depot's stock had rebounded, nearly doubling to around $40 from January 2003 to mid-October 2004. Although profits at Lowe's were rising faster, Home Depot's shares were cheaper.

Other direct competitors included Building Materials Holdings, House 2 Home, Inc., Wolohan Lumber Company, Wickes, Inc., and Payless Cashways. Lowe's also competed with traditional hardware, plumbing, electrical, appliance, and home supply retailers, and with lumber yards in most of its market areas. In addition, Lowe's competed in some product categories with discount stores and membership warehouse clubs.

CASE 39
Nike, Inc.

Maryanne M. Rouse

CAN NIKE (NKE) FIND ENOUGH SHELF SPACE TO MAKE UP FOR LOWER SALES TO ITS TOP customer? In February 2002, Foot Locker told Nike that it wanted to reduce the number of Nike's marquee shoes—the Air Jordans, Shox, and others that sell for well over $100— because the retailer believed that consumers were turning more to midpriced shoes. Because Nike refused to change its product mix to support Foot Locker's product line reshuffling, Foot Locker, the dominant global footwear retailer, with over 3,600 stores, cancelled approximately $150 million in Nike orders. (Nike's premium segment accounts for approximately 15%–20% of total global revenues and although neither company discloses details of total orders, Nike noted in its 2002 10-K form that sales to Foot Locker represented approximately $1 billion of Nike's $9.9 billion worldwide sales.)

According to Foot Locker, Nike retaliated by cutting the retailer's allotment of key products, including the highly popular Air Force One. The feud escalated in December, when Nike announced that Foot Locker would no longer be its launch customer for marquee products and, in fact, gave rival FootAction access to high-end basketball shoes that had been exclusive to Foot Locker. In mid-February 2003, Nike's "Hall of Hoops" displays in Foot Locker stores came down and were replaced by Reebok's "Above the Rim" campaign. In 2004, Nike was aggressively lining up new outlets, while Foot Locker faced a significant challenge in maintaining a broad, attractive, and profitable product line (for 2002, Nike comprised 47% of Foot Locker's sales).

The Company

Nike designed, developed, and marketed athletic and casual footwear, active sports and leisure apparel, sports equipment, and accessories under the Nike, Bauer, Cole-Haan, and Hurley brands. Nike was the largest seller of athletic footwear and apparel in the world, with a U.S. market share exceeding 40%. The company's products were sold through approximately 18,000 retail accounts in the United States, including footwear stores, department stores, and sporting goods stores. Nike, with the broadest product line of all competitors, also distributed to specialty, skate, tennis, and golf shops. The company operated several retail formats in the United States: 78 Nike Factory Stores (primarily close-out merchandise), 4 Nike stores, 13 Niketown "showcase" stores, 4 employee-only stores, and 61 Cole-Haan stores. Sales in the United States accounted for 53% of total revenues in 2002. Nike sold its products outside the United States through independent distributors, licensees, and subsidiaries in 140 countries.

In addition to performance equipment (sports balls, timepieces, eyewear, skates, and other equipment designed for sports activities), Nike sold hockey equipment and related accessories under the Bauer and Nike brand names. In April 2002, Nike acquired Hurley International LLC, a California-based designer and distributor of sports apparel for surfing, skateboarding, and snowboarding as well as youth lifestyle apparel. Footwear accounted for 58% of fiscal 2002 revenues; apparel, 29%; equipment, 8%; and other, 5%.

Almost all Nike brand apparel was manufactured by approximately 700 independent contractors, 99% of which were located in Southeast Asia. The reasons for locating shoe production in Southeast Asia were many, but the most important was the cost of labor. In addition to having lower labor costs, Asia provided access to the raw material suppliers and satellite industries (tanneries, textiles, plastics) necessary in athletic shoe manufacturing. A third important factor driving the location of athletic shoe production was the current complex system of differential tariffs.

Working conditions and wages, as well as allegations of harassment and abuse, had been a source of heated debate between Nike and a broad array of special interest groups and journalists for a decade. Critics accused Nike of abandoning countries as they developed better pay and employment rights in favor of countries such as China with lower wages and little regulation of employment practices. In several cases relating to physical or verbal abuse and child labor, Nike agreed that employment practices were problematic, and the company responded with what the Global Alliance agreed were serious and reasonable remediation plans. The company's argument that many of the charges were based on old and/or inaccurate information and did not reflect current operations had done little to satisfy activists. Although Nike had implemented a series of social and environmental initiatives and Nike's largest competitors had pursued almost identical manufacturing strategies, Nike continued to be the focus of activists opposing manufacturing practices in developing countries.

Because Nike didn't actually produce shoes, the company's focus was on R&D and marketing. Nike considered its product design and ability to quickly take advantage of technological advances key sources of competitive advantage. Celebrity spokespersons (Michael Jordan, Tiger Woods, Lance Armstrong, Mia Hamm, etc.) and team endorsements (such as the long-term agreement with Manchester United) were important elements of what had been a very successful promotional strategy. According to the company's annual report, Nike's spending for "demand creation" was $1,027.9 million for 2002—10.4% of revenue. R&D costs, estimated at close to $1 billion, were not separately disclosed.

While Nike was fairly well diversified across price points, the company's marquee shoes, which accounted for 15%–20% of global revenue, had been a strong contributor to profits and had created the "buzz" to move lower-priced models. Declining demand for these premium sneakers was exacerbated by growing unemployment rates, a worsening economy, uncertain geopolitical events, falling consumer confidence, and competition from other teen and young adult "must haves," such as cell phones, PDAs, and other new gizmos; fickle consumer tastes and preferences and the spat with Foot Locker were factors as well.

Although Nike's fiscal 2002 revenue of $9,893 million was the highest in company history, top-line growth was slower (4.3%) than in the previous year (5.5%). Slower sales of athletic shoes in the U.S. region were balanced by increases in footwear sales in other regions and increases in apparel and equipment sales in all regions. Despite downward pressure on prices and markdowns, the company was able to increase gross margin as a percentage of sales to 39.3% for the year. Selling and administrative expenses increased from 28.3% of sales in 2001 to 28.5% in 2002, reflecting both lower sales and increased marketing costs. Operating profit showed definite improvement in 2002, at 10.2% of sales, versus 9.3% in the prior year. Complete financial information is available in Nike's 10-K form for 2002 (*www.nike.com*).

The Industry

In 2003, growth in sales of athletic footwear in the United States could best be described as sluggish. The one bright spot in an otherwise dismal year was the women's segment. In 2003, women's casual tennis footwear was the hottest category, driven by both the retro fashion trend and growth in the casual lifestyle segment. As footwear providers focused on international demand to grow revenue, it was hoped that a continued weak U.S. dollar would prop up global sales.

The non-athletic shoe segment had experienced a major shift away from dress to casual shoes, reflecting the more casual dress environment of the workplace. Lower-priced competition in this segment would make overseas sourcing, effective marketing, and operating efficiencies keys to profits in the near term. According to SportscanINFO, the following trends were expected to continue to influence global sales growth in both shoe segments in 2003:

- Continued growth in the casual, non-performance athletic footwear segment
- A decline in the demand for premium-priced performance athletic shoes
- Price deflation as the middle-range price points continued to shift down and casual styles increased in importance
- Decent but not spectacular growth in basketball shoes (the huge increases predicted for 2002 never did materialize), coupled with better-than-expected growth in running shoes
- The implosion of White/White Retro shoes, which had been aggressively overpromoted, especially by mall retailers

Analysts expected weak growth in equipment, with potentially strong growth in casual apparel.

Competition

The athletic footwear, apparel, and equipment segments were intensely competitive both in the United States and globally. Key competitors included Reebok, New Balance, and Adidas in athletic footwear and sports apparel.

New Balance

Privately held New Balance Athletic Shoe, Inc., headquartered in Boston, Massachusetts, was a leading manufacturer of technically innovative, width-sized footwear and athletic apparel for women, men, and children. The range of product categories included running, walking, cross-training, basketball, tennis, adventure sports, and kids. In 1998, New Balance acquired Dunham Bootmakers to expand into work and hiking boots, sandals, boat shoes, and rugged casuals without diluting the New Balance brand. In 2001, the company acquired PF Flyers to pursue the comfort/casual market.

The company, which has remained committed to a domestic manufacturing strategy, employed more than 2,400 people around the globe. New Balance, long a staple in such outlets as Sports Authority, Foot Locker, and Champs, expanded its distribution channels in 2000 to include independently owned retail stores that would provide the opportunity to showcase the full brand and were to carry New Balance apparel, accessories, and the Dunham line of casual shoes. At the end of 2001, 55 of these independently owned stores, which generated about $46.4 million in sales—4% of New Balance's $1.16 billion in revenue—had opened. By the end of 2002, the company was distributing to over 90 independent retailers. New Balance surprised analysts and industry watchers alike with its vault to the number three spot both worldwide and in the United States, with a 25% year-over-year sales increase from 2001 to 2002, estimated athletic shoe market share of more than 11%, and full line sporting goods market share of 19%.

Adidas

German-based Adidas-Salomon AG held the number four spot in the United States in 2002, with an estimated 11% market share. With global sales of almost $7 billion, a 7.7% increase from 2001 and a record for the company, Adidas was the number two footwear and apparel company worldwide, behind Nike. Industry analysts noted that double-digit sales increases in both North American and Asian markets helped fuel the company's growth. Although analysts expected a sales boost in Asia (the World Soccer Cup matches were played in Japan and South Korea), the company's gains in the North American market were interpreted as a strong indicator of Adidas' success.

Adidas suffered a setback in 2002, when its most important endorser, Kobe Bryant of the L.A. Lakers, bought out his contract (he was expected to sign with either Nike or Reebok). Although the company's new "marquee endorser," Tracy McGrady, was a popular NBA player, he played for the Orlando Magic, a losing team in what was considered a small market. The Adidas group comprised three distinct divisions: Adidas Sports Performance, Adidas Sports Heritage, and Adidas Sports Style. The Sports Performance group housed the current footwear and apparel lines and accounted for 80% of the business; Sports Heritage was the retro division that put out the classic, old-style sneakers targeted to the urban audience; Sports Style, introduced in February 2003, was an upscale sportswear collection to be sold in 150 retailers, including Barney's New York, where the launch was held. Although it accounted for just 20% of the company's revenue, Adidas Sports Style was expected to make significant contributions to both the top and bottom lines.

Reebok

Reebok International, with a 12.2% market share, was the number two U.S. maker of athletic shoes, behind Nike, and ranked fourth globally. In addition to athletic shoes, sportswear, and accessories, Reebok's product lines included the Greg Norman line of men's casual wear, Rockport walking and casual shoes, and Ralph Lauren and Polo dress and athletic shoes. An athletic shoe powerhouse in the mid-1980s and early 1990s, Reebok couldn't compete with Nike when the emphasis shifted from fitness to team sports.

Reebok reached its low point in 1999, when its share price fell to about $7; however, industry observers believed that, with the return of Paul Fireman, the company was once again on the move and appeared to be gaining market share on several fronts. In December 2000, Reebok signed a 10-year licensing contract with the NFL that gave the company the exclusive right to sell "authentic, on-field stuff." Reebok's marketing budget for 2003 was reported to be

$40 million, a 38% increase from the previous year. That increase was expected to help cover the cost of endorsement deals with a roster of younger basketball stars, such as Steve Francis of the Houston Rockets. In 2003, Reebok had deals with 17 of the 26 NBA teams and, by November 2004, was expected to have signed all 26.

The Challenge

Although Nike's 2002 acquisition of Hurley had further diversified its product line, it was essentially still an athletic shoe company. Aggressive competition from Reebok, New Balance, and Adidas; the Foot Locker fiasco; Michael Jordan's retirement—which was expected to seriously impact the company's $350 million Jordan business; increasingly fickle consumers; and a worsening economy all posed significant threats to the growth of Nike's top and bottom lines. What is the company's next strategic move? Can Nike continue to "Just do it"?

CASE 40

Stryker Corporation

Maryanne M. Rouse

STRYKER CORPORATION (SYK), A LEADING MAKER OF SPECIALTY MEDICAL AND SURGICAL products, could trace its origins to a business founded by Dr. Homer S. Stryker, an orthopedic surgeon with a talent for invention and a desire to improve the tools that physicians use to treat patients. At the end of September 2004, Stryker comprised two reportable business segments and three lines of business, Orthopedic Implants (approximately 60.4% of sales for the first nine months of the 2004 fiscal year), MedSurg Equipment (33.6%), and Physical Therapy Associates (6%). The company had grown via internal venturing, acquisition, and strategic alliances. Recent acquisitions and alliances included:

Date	Acquisition/Alliance
July 2004	Stryker entered into a definitive agreement to acquire by merger all the outstanding stock of SpineCore, Inc., a privately owned Summit, New Jersey, developer of artificial lumbar and cervical discs.
October 2002	The company purchased the DEKOMPRESSOR product line from Pain Concepts, Inc. DEKOMPRESSOR was a single-use disposable device used by surgeons for the removal of disc nucleus material in spinal surgery.
April 2002	Stryker Japan entered into an agreement with Integrated Surgical Systems, a pioneer in medical robotics for surgical applications, to develop software for the Stryker knee prostheses. While the agreement was with Stryker Japan, the software would be made available worldwide.
November 2001	Stryker acquired the business of an independent Italian distributor of the company's products to consolidate the distribution of substantially all of Stryker's products in Italy.
August 2000	Stryker completed the acquisition of Image Guided Technologies, Inc., a manufacturer of three-dimensional optical devices.

(continued)

| *(continued)* | |
Date	Acquisition/Alliance
June 2000	Stryker acquired Colorado Biomedical, the developer and manufacturer of the Colorado Microdissection Needle, a device used for precision electrosurgery.
November 1999	Stryker acquired all the outstanding common stock of InfoMeddix Communications, a developer and manufacturer of video communications hardware and software that enabled telecommunication of surgical images.
December 1998	Stryker acquired Howmedica, the orthopedic division of the global pharmaceutical competitor Pfizer.

Operating Divisions

Orthopedic Implants

The Orthopedic Implants segment produced and sold orthopedic reconstructive (hip, knee, shoulder) devices, trauma fixation devices and spinal implants, bone cement, and a bone growth factor osteogenic protein (OP-1) through its Stryker Orthopedics, Stryker Trauma, Stryker Spine, and Stryker Biotech operating divisions. Made of cobalt chromium, titanium alloys, ultra-high-molecular-weight polyethylene, or ceramics, artificial joints were implanted in patients whose natural joints were damaged by arthritis, osteoporosis, other diseases, or injury. In 2001, Stryker received FDA approval for the OP-1 bone growth factor. Composed of recombinant human osteogenic protein-1 and a bioresorbable collagen matrix, OP-1 induced formation of new bone. Key competitors in the orthopedic implant segment included Biomet, the Swiss medical technology firm Sulzer Medica, Zimmer Holdings, Orthofix International, and Johnson & Johnson.

This segment offered a variety of hip systems for the global reconstructive market, each of which comprised both implants and associated instrumentation. Stryker's extensive clinical history with hip implant technology and products and long-term clinical results were important factors in the company's ability to market hip implants.

The company offered five major knee systems under the Stryker name, including the Global Modular Replacement System (GMRS), which was launched in 2003. GMRS was a global product that offered a comprehensive approach for radical bone loss in oncology, trauma, and surgery patients. Knee Navigation 2.0, a product that Stryker promoted as the next generation of surgical navigation software for total knee replacement, was introduced in 2003 as a replacement for the company's previous software product, introduced in 2002. Other reconstructive products included shoulder and elbow implants and related instruments offered under the Stryker name.

Many of Stryker's technologically advanced reconstructive implants were suited to minimally invasive procedures that were intended to reduce soft tissue damage and pain while hastening healing and return to functionality. During 2003, the Orthopaedic Implants segment introduced the Scorpio Total Knee Minimally Invasive Instrumentation and began development of instrumentation for minimally invasive hip arthroplasty.

Stryker manufactured several variations of Simplex bone cement, the most widely used bone cement in the world. Simplex had more than 40 years of clinical history, longer than any Stryker competitor. In 2003, the company received FDA clearance to market Simplex P with Tobramycin, an antibiotic bone cement that had been previously approved for use in Europe. Stryker's OP-1 was a proprietary bone growth factor that induced the formation of new bone when introduced into bony defect sites. Currently approved for use in long bone fractures,

OP-1 was being studied for use in spinal stenosis, a degenerative condition widespread among those over 65.

Through Stryker Trauma, the company developed, manufactured, and marketed trauma-related products, including nailing, plating, hip fracture, and external fixation systems used primarily in the fixation of fractures resulting from sudden injury. Stryker Spine developed, manufactured, and marketed spinal implant products (plates, screws, rods, connectors, cages, and instrument systems) for a growing U.S. and European market.

MedSurg Equipment

MedSurg (medical and surgical) Equipment products included powered surgical instruments, endoscopic products, hospital beds and stretchers, and microimplant and surgical navigation systems.

The Stryker Instrument unit designed, manufactured, and sold powered surgical instruments, operating room equipment, interventional pain products, and surgical navigation systems. Surgical instruments included drills, saws, fixation, and reaming equipment, as well as other surgical instruments used for drilling, rasping, or cutting bone, wiring or pinning bone fractures, and preparing hip or knee surfaces for the placement of artificial hip or knee joints. In 2002, Stryker Instrument introduced the PainPump2, a disposable system that offered electronically controlled flow rates of pain medication directly to the surgical site. The company acquired the DEKOMPRESSOR single-use, disposable product line from Pain Concepts, Inc. The product offered an early, less invasive approach to relieving leg and back pain.

Stryker Endoscopy designed and manufactured a broad range of medical video imaging equipment and instruments for arthroscopy and general surgery. Arthroscopic procedures, in which the surgeon removes or repairs damaged tissue through several small punctures rather than an open incision, are less invasive than traditional surgical procedures. Patients experience reduced trauma and pain, less time in the hospital, and a quicker return to health. Arthroscopic procedures also have a lower total cost than traditional surgical procedures. Pioneering engineering work in miniaturization had enhanced Stryker's position as a leader in the development of medical video imaging systems: It was the first company to offer surgeons full-color, broadcast-quality imaging. This unit also made laparascopes, powered surgical instruments, and disposable suction/irrigation devices.

Stryker Leibenger Micro Implant Systems manufactured plating systems and related products for craniomaxillofacial and hand surgery. The Stryker Medical unit designed, developed, and manufactured specialty stretchers and beds customized to fit the needs of acute care and specialty surgical facilities. Among the products Stryker Medical had developed in consultation with hospitals and surgeons was a line of innovative stretchers, Trio Mobile Surgery Platforms, that reduce the number of patient transfers (from bed to stretcher, to operating table, and back again). This unit also produced accessories such as bedside stands and overbed tables.

Physiotherapy Associates

Through a network of 374 outpatient centers in 25 states and the District of Columbia, the Physiotherapy Associates division provided physical, occupational, and speech therapy to patients recovering from orthopedic or neurological illness or injury. This division generally operated multiple facilities within a single area, offering patients a choice of locations. This grouping of facilities also allowed sharing of administrative and other functions, resulting in substantial operating efficiencies.

Marketing

Product Development

New products and product improvements played a key role in supporting Stryker's aggressive growth strategy. The company took a decentralized approach to research and development, allocating research funds to each of the three manufacturing divisions. Stryker's close working relationships with physicians, surgeons, and medical personnel in hospitals and universities strengthened customer relationships and helped R&D engineers better understand customers' product needs. Total expenditures for product R&D were $180.2 million in fiscal 2003, $141.4 million in 2000, and $142.1 million in 1999. Stryker owned patents covering a broad range of products and processes and also maintained licensing and cross-licensing agreements. Its patents were significant because they prevented competitors from duplicating unique designs and features.

Promotion/Distribution

In the United States, most of Stryker's products were marketed directly to more than 6,000 hospitals, other health care facilities, and physicians by approximately 2,100 sales and marketing personnel. About 70% of the company's 2003 U.S. sales were to large individual accounts and hospital cooperative buying groups.

Stryker's products were sold in over 100 countries through over 1,900 local dealers and direct sales relationships. Sales outside the United States accounted for 36% of the company's total revenue in 2003. The company's second-largest geographic market was Europe, comprising 58% of international sales, followed by Japan, with 24%; sales in all other countries accounted for 18% of the company's international sales.

Manufacturing

Stryker both purchased and manufactured components and finished products. Approximately 11% of the company's cost of sales in 2003 represented finished products that were purchased complete from outside suppliers. The company also purchased parts and components, such as forgings, castings, gears, bearings, casters, and electrical components, and used outside sources for certain finishing operations, such as plating, hardening, and coating of machined components and sterilization of certain products. The principal raw materials used by Stryker's various operating units were stainless steel, aluminum, cobalt chrome, and titanium alloys. In all, purchased parts and components from outside sources were approximately 33% of the total cost of sales in 2003.

Although the company relied on single sources for certain purchased materials and services, it believed alternate sources were available if needed; Stryker had not experienced any significant difficulty in the past in obtaining the materials necessary to meet its production schedules.

Substantially all products manufactured by the company were stocked in inventory, while certain products manufactured within the company's MedSurg segment were assembled to order.

Finance

Stryker's results for third quarter 2004, released on October 14, showed that the company posted a 16% increase in sales over the same period in 2003. Excluding the impact of foreign currency, net sales increased 13% for the third quarter and 15% for the first nine months. Net income for the third quarter was reduced by a $120.8 million write-off of purchased R&D

costs associated with the SpineCore acquisition. Excluding that one-time charge, reported net income would have been $135.2 million for the quarter.

Stryker Corporation's net sales increased 20% in 2003, to $3,625.3 million, from $3,011.6 million in 2002. Net sales grew by 12% as a result of increased unit volume and changes in product mix; 2% related to higher selling prices; 5% due to changes in foreign currency exchange rates; and 1% as a result of acquired businesses.

Domestic sales were $2,333.4 million for 2003, representing an increase of 18% as a result of strong shipments of Orthopedic Implants and MedSurg Equipment and higher revenue from Physical Therapy Services. International sales were $1,291.9 million for 2003, representing an increase of 24% as a result of higher shipments of Orthopedic Implants and MedSurg Equipment. The impact of foreign currency comparisons to the dollar value of international sales was favorable by $145.9 million for 2003. Excluding the impact of foreign currency, international sales increased 10% in 2003:

| | (Dollar amounts in millions) | | | | | |
| | 2003 | | 2002 | | 2001 | |
	$	%	$	%	$	%
Business Segment sales						
Orthopedic Implants	$2,093.0	58%	$1,704.8	56%	$1,447.2	56%
MedSurg Equipment	1,309.3	36	1,105.3	37	974.2	37
Physical Therapy Services	223.0	6	201.5	7	180.9	7
Total	$3,625.3	100%	$3,011.6	100%	$2,602.3	100%
Domestic/international sales						
Domestic	$2,333.4	64%	$1,973.7	66%	$1,688.4	65%
International	1,291.9	36	1,037.9	34	913.9	35
Total net sales	$3,625.3	100%	$3,011.6	100%	$2,602.3	100%

The Industry

Overall, analysts expected industry revenue to grow by 15% in 2002, with more robust growth in 2003; total sales in the global orthopedics business were estimated at $12 billion for 2002. In orthopedics, the demand for hip, knee, and shoulder replacements was expected to remain strong, reflecting both favorable demographic trends in both the U.S. and global markets and continued technological innovation; the spinal repair segment was expected to grow at a 25% annual rate during 2002. Positive long-term fundamentals included expanding global demand for sophisticated diagnostic equipment and quality health care and an aging population. The global medical device industry has not been subject to the economic cycles that affect most other industries. Emerging markets were expected to grow rapidly and to account for as much as 25% of worldwide demand by 2005. New product introductions, although hampered by long approval times in the United States, would be spurred by the development of engineered raw materials (polymers, alloys, and compounds) and shorter approval times in non-U.S. markets.

Hospital mergers would result in a decline in the number of acute care facilities in the United States. Health care cost-containment efforts by government programs (Medicare, Medicaid), third-party payers (e.g., Blue Cross/Blue Shield), and large employers would limit total medical device expenditures. The industry was expecting further downward pressure on prices as more purchasing decisions were shifting from physicians and hospitals to managed care providers. A strong U.S. dollar over the past several years had made U.S. medical devices more expensive, while an unfavorable exchange rate of the U.S. dollar relative to the euro and the Japanese yen had negatively impacted revenue and earnings.

Competition

The global market for diagnostic and therapeutic medical devices had grown increasingly concentrated over the last decade, with most major segments dominated by three to five key competitors. Stryker was one of five leading global companies in the orthopedic and reconstructive products segment. The others were Depuy Orthopaedics (a subsidiary of Johnson & Johnson), Zimmer Holdings, Inc., Biomet, Inc., and Sulzer Medica.

In the trauma segment, the company's three key competitors were Synthes-Stratec, Smith Nephew Richards, and DePuy. In the spinal implant segment, Stryker competed against Medtronic Sofamor Danek (a unit of Medtronic), DePuy AcroMed (a subsidiary of Johnson & Johnson), Synthes-Stratec, and Spine-Tech (a subsidiary of Sulzer Medica). In the powered surgical instruments segment, the company was one of three leaders, the others being Linvatec (a subsidiary of Conmed Corporation) and Midas-Rex (a subsidiary of Medtronic). Aesculap-Werke AG, a large European manufacturer, was a strong competitor in this segment in international markets. Principal competitors in the arthroscopy segment were Smith Nephew Endoscopy and Linvatec. In laparoscopic imaging, Stryker was one of four global leaders, with the principal competitors being Karl Storz GmbH (a German company), Circon Corporation (a subsidiary of Maxxim Medical), and Olympus Optical Company (a Japanese company). In the craniomaxiofacial segment, Stryker competed against Synthes-Stratec and Walter Lorenz (a subsidiary of Biomet).

Stryker was a new competitor in the rapidly growing surgical navigation segment. The company's five principal competitors were Medtronic Surgical Navigation Technologies (a unit of Medtronic), BrainLAB, Inc., Radionics, Inc. (a subsidiary of Tyco International), Surgical Navigation Network, Inc. (a division of Cedara Software), and Visualization Technology, Inc.

The company's primary competitor in the hospital bed segment was Hill-Rom, a division of Hillenbrand Industries. In the specialty stretcher segment, Stryker's main competitors were Hausted, Hill-Rom, and Midmark Hospital Products. Stryker's principal competitors in the physiotherapy segment were independent practitioners, medical groups, and hospital-based services. Competitors also included such national rehabilitation companies as HealthSouth, NovaCare/RCI, and Rehability.

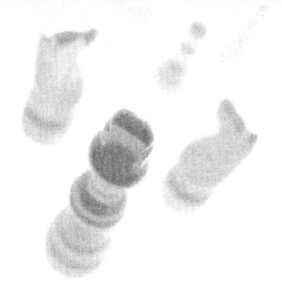

CASE 41
Walter Industries

Maryanne M. Rouse

Had Walter Industries (WLT) begun to find its focus? The company had had a hard time making its diverse portfolio of businesses, ranging from homebuilding and coal mining to manufacturing of petroleum coke and ductile pipe, pay off for shareholders and an equally difficult time explaining its mix of businesses to analysts and potential investors. WLT, classified by analysts as a "domestic industrial conglomerate," narrowed its mix of businesses in 2003 by selling three subsidiaries: AIMCOR, a marketer and distributor of petroleum coke; JW Aluminum, a manufacturer of specialty aluminum products; and Southern Precision, a supplier to the casting and foundry industries. The company's remaining businesses were structured as five independent segments: Homebuilding (21% of revenue in 2003), Financing (18%), Industrial Products (34%), Natural Resources (19%), and Other Products (8%). WLT considered Homebuilding, Financing, and Industrial Products the company's core businesses.

Homebuilding

Homebuilding was the company's original business. Begun by James W. Walter in 1946 as Jim Walter Homes (JWH), its business concept was to build affordable, unfinished "shell" homes for American families who owned their own property but did not have the cash necessary for a down payment. In its "on your lot" product line, JWH built on property owned by the customer, with the value of the land substituting for the traditional down payment required by lending institutions; financing was provided through WLT's Mid-State Homes subsidiary. The leading on-your-lot homebuilder in the United States, JWH had historically concentrated on the low- to moderately-priced segment of the housing market, with an average 2003 home price of $66,200. JWH's broad product line comprised over 50 models of conventionally built homes and over 50 modular home models sold through 111 branch offices serving 18 states. Substantially all the branch offices also served as "display parks" designed to allow customers to view the actual models.

In 1997 and 1998, JWH acquired Neatherlin Homes and Dream Homes, both Texas-based on-your-lot builders, and in 1999, the company acquired Crestline Homes, a manufacturer and distributor of system-built modular homes located in Laurinburg, North Carolina. Crestline homes were sold by a network of independent dealers, primarily in the Southern United States.

Although historically JWH had not owned land and functioned as a developer, during 2001 the company began to grow its Homebuilding segment through the construction of speculatively built homes and subdivisions on company-owned land. In 2001, WLT created Walter Mortgage Company (WMC) to provide new-home financing to customers of JWH and its affiliated homebuilding companies. Through WMC, homebuyers had the option to finance both land and home purchases, allowing the Homebuilding segment to expand its target market beyond those who already owned buildable property and also to support sales efforts in the company's first two subdivisions in Houma, Louisiana, and Brookwood, Alabama. WMC was expected to be a key component in achieving the Homebuilding segment's growth and profit objectives.

The single-family residential housing industry was highly competitive. JWH competitors ranged from regional and national firms such as Centex, Pulte, and Lennar to small local companies. Competitive variables included price, design, finishing, options, and accessibility to financing. In 2003, sales of new single-family site-built homes had been at an all time high, with the homebuilding index recording 32.7% compound annual gains over the past five years. Growth in home sales had been aided to a great extent by historically low mortgage rates. After moving down to 5.4% in March 2004, rates on 30-year conventional mortgages rose as high as 6.4% in mid-June but fell to 5.8% in early October. Industry analysts predicted that a lackluster economy and rising interest rates would slow the fast-paced growth in single home sales; however, they had also been predicting that the housing "bubble" was about to burst for several years.

The Homebuilding segment reported operating income of $1.5 million for fiscal 2003 but disappointing losses in the first two quarters of 2004. However, because most homes sold by JWH were purchased with financing provided by WLT's Financing subsidiary, home sales were the key to driving profitability in the Financing segment.

Financing

The Financing segment included Mid-State Homes (MSH), Walter Mortgage Company (WMC), and insurors Best Insurors and Cardem Insurance Company, Ltd. MSH was established in 1958 to purchase and service mortgage installment notes originated by JWH's on-your-lot Homebuilding segment. In 2001, WLT established WMC to broaden its market to include purchasers who needed financing to purchase land and those who wanted to finance both the land and the home. WMC also made loans to those who owned land jointly and wanted to buy out their partners and those who wanted to remove liens from existing parcels. Existing MSH customers also had the option of refinancing their mortgages with WMC. From inception through December 2003, 1,152 mortgages totaling approximately $79.6 million were originated, purchased, or funded through WMC. WMC's growth strategy included a program to buy seasoned mortgage loans. Best Insurors provided fire and extended insurance for homeowners who financed through JWH or WMC. Cardem functioned as a reinsurer for Best and provided captive coverage for WLT's other segments.

The Financing segment reported operating income of $51.9 million for fiscal 2003 and remained in positive territory for both quarters one ($13.8 million) and two ($16.6 million).

Industrial Products

The Industrial Products division comprised United States Pipe and Foundry (U.S. Pipe), a leading manufacturer of ductile iron pressure pipe, fittings, valves, and hydrants, with a 29% share of a two million ton market. Ductile iron pressure pipe was used primarily for potable water distribution systems and water and wastewater transmission and collection systems. Acquired by Walter Industries in 1969, Birmingham, Alabama–based U.S. Pipe offered a broad line of pipe systems and restrained joint pipe and fittings adaptable to a variety of industrial applications and field conditions. Ductile iron pipe was manufactured at four of the company's five plants (Bessemer and Birmingham, Alabama; Burlington, New Jersey; and Union City, California), and a factory in Chattanooga, Tennessee, produced complementary fittings and hydrants. Because freight costs for pipe were high, having locations close to important markets lowered transportation costs and contributed to U.S. Pipe's low cost position.

U.S. Pipe's products were sold primarily to contractors (22%), distributors (58%), municipalities (9%), and private utilities and other customers (9%) via a nationwide network of sales offices. International sales were handled directly by U.S. Pipe's sales force as well as via an extensive network of representatives in Central and South America and the Middle East. During 2003, a single customer accounted for 21% of U.S. Pipe's sales, while foreign sales accounted for approximately 4% of sales. Key competitors were American Cast Iron Pipe, a privately held company; McWane, Inc.; and Griffin Ductile Iron Pipe Company.

The ductile iron pressure pipe industry was concentrated and highly competitive. Because of its dependence on the level of new construction activity and state, municipal, and federal spending to fund water projects, the industry was generally sensitive to economic conditions. Demand in the replacement market had grown significantly, however, driven in part by the Safe Water Drinking Act. (New construction accounted for approximately 65% of U.S. Pipe's revenues, with replacement sales accounting for the balance.)

Rapidly escalating scrap iron prices, driven by increased demand from China and Japan, had put pressure on U.S. Pipe's margins. However, the subsidiary's strong position as a high-quality, low-cost producer had allowed it to successfully implement a series of price increases that had at least partially offset high materials costs. U.S. Pipe, which reported operating losses of $11.9 million for fiscal 2003 and $1.5 million for first quarter 2004, returned to profitability in second quarter 2004.

Natural Resources

In the Natural Resources segment, the operations of Jim Walter Resources (JWR) were conducted through its Mining division, which mined and sold coal from three mines in Alabama; and its De-Gas division, which extracted and sold methane gas from coal seams owned or leased by JWR. The Mining division sold steam and metallurgical coal to a diverse base of domestic and foreign customers in markets including the United States, Europe, Latin America, and the Middle East. Operating and safety problems, including explosions at the Brookwood mine in 2001 that left 13 miners dead and led to millions of dollars of fines and a critical report from federal safety officials, were a continuing problem.

Natural Resources, which reported an operating loss of $25.6 million for fiscal 2003, turned a surprising but welcome $14.8 million profit for the second quarter of 2004. WLT put JWR up for sale in March 1999, but a slump in coal prices at the time dampened enthusiasm among potential buyers, and the company took it back off the market the following year. A significant increase in demand for coal, coupled with tight supply conditions, allowed JWR to raise prices a number of times in 2003–2004. JWR's improved profitability caused WLT to shelve plans for divesting this non-core business.

Other

The Other segment included Sloss Industries, the company's land groups, and corporate expenses. Sloss Industries manufactured and distributed furnace and foundry coke (a coal-based fuel used to melt iron and steel) to the domestic steel industry as well as to ductile iron foundries. The company also manufactured specialty chemicals and slag fiber. In mid-2003, Sloss was slapped with the biggest environmental penalty in Alabama history for discharging up to 22 times the legal amount of cyanide per day into Five Mile Creek. The cost of non-compliance was $675,000 in cash, the donation of more than 300 acres of company-owned land for conversion to jogging trails, and the planting of 25,000 trees.

Although WLT had put Sloss on the market, efforts to sell the subsidiary were impeded more by the state of the U.S. steel industry than by the environmental challenges, which were well known and widespread in the industry. A growing demand in non-U.S. markets, especially in China, and favorable demand/supply conditions had enabled Sloss to post consistent profits in excess of $2 million for each of the first two quarters of 2004. Prospects for continued profitability were strong, and WLT took Sloss off the market. (Note: Because the reported loss for the Other segment included unallocated corporate charges and because WLT did not separate out the financial results for Sloss, the segment appeared to be unprofitable.)

Risks and Challenges

WLT was subject to interest rate and commodity price risks. Interest rate risk exposure related to the risks associated with installment notes receivable, short-term investments, long- and short-term borrowings, and pension and other postretirement liabilities. Commodity risk related primarily to raw materials prices.

WLT and its subsidiaries were subject to a wide range of environmental laws and regulations. Compliance and remediation costs totaled $10.8 million in 2003, $5.8 million in 2002, and $7.8 million in 2001. Natural Resources, U.S. Pipe, and Sloss Industries had all been sources of environmental problems and fines.

Asbestos lawsuits, resulting from the operations of WLT's former Celotex division, and high levels of debt forced the company into bankruptcy in 1989. After millions of dollars of settlement costs, WLT emerged from bankruptcy in 1995 with immunity from asbestos litigation. However, the Asbestos Settlement Trust, created by the bankruptcy court and funded by WLT for the purpose of paying lawsuit awards, owned approximately 8% of the company's stock at December 31, 2003. Analysts believed that the trust ownership might be off-putting to potential investors and might serve to keep the company's stock price artificially low.

Finances

Fiscal 2003 was a disappointing year for WLT. The company reported a consolidated operating loss of $26.8 million and a net loss of just over $29 million. Restructuring of the sales force and ERP system implementation problems in the Homebuilding segment led to a 92%

drop in operating income, from $17.1 million in fiscal 2002 to $1.45 million in 2003, while Industrial Products and Natural Resources delivered losses of $11.9 million and $25.6 million. The bright spot for the year was Financing, with reported operating income of $51.9 million. Losses related to discontinued operations totaled $32.7 million for the year.

Despite the strong demand for single-family housing, the Homebuilding segment posted disappointing losses of $8.8 million in the first quarter and $6.7 million in the second quarter of 2004. WLT's Financing segment delivered strong results in both quarters, $13.8 and $16.6 million, while Industrial Products returned to profitability in the second quarter, with operating income of $1.4 million. Favorable spot coal and gas pricing and increased coal production resulted in $14.7 million operating income for Natural Resources, a significant increase over the prior year same quarter and up sharply from the first quarter of 2004.

Total revenues for the nine months ending September 30, 2004, increased 8.8% over the same period in the prior year as gains in Financing, Industrial Products, and Natural Resources outweighed a decline in Homebuilding revenues. Anticipation of significantly

CASE 42

Sykes Enterprises

Maryanne M. Rouse

AND THEN THERE WERE FIVE. IN LATE SUMMER 2004, SYKES ENTERPRISES (SYKE) informed city and state officials that it planned to close both its Marianna and Palatka, Florida, call centers by October 2. The two Florida closings brought to nine the number of U.S. call centers the Tampa-based company would close in 2004. By the end of the year, just five of the company's U.S.-based centers would remain: Bismarck, North Dakota; Wise, Virginia; Morganfield, Kentucky; Ponca City, Oklahoma; and Sterling, Colorado. Like many of its competitors, Sykes was shifting its operations to lower-wage countries in an attempt to remain competitive and to meet client demands for reduced costs. Palatka and Marianna would face challenges not unlike those that still plagued Milton-Freewater, Oregon.

Like many similar small towns desperate to add jobs and maintain both population and tax bases, Milton-Freewater, Oregon, was willing to take significant risks to survive. In 1998, town officials signed a multimillion-dollar agreement with Sykes Enterprises in which the town promised land, roads, utilities, and tax abatement. Although the company refused to guarantee a minimum number of jobs, minimum length of stay, or salary levels, Milton-Freewater negotiated a $2.2 million loan with the Baker-Boyer National Bank of Walla Walla, Washington, to meet the company's cash incentive requirements. In early March 2004, Sykes announced that it would close the Milton-Freewater center and lay off its remaining workers by May 2.

In her March 9, 2004, letter to the company, Milton-Freewater city Manager Delphine Palmer asked that Sykes donate its 42,000-square-foot building and land parcel back to the city. She noted:

> You asked us to dig deep into our pockets to provide Sykes with generous incentives to entice you.
> I am asking you personally to (help) our small rural American city to cope with this major loss.[1]

Sykes had previously refused a similar request from Eveleth, Minnesota. In that case, CEO John Sykes said it was not his building to give away and noted that he was obligated to give shareholders the highest possible return on their investment, including assets obtained through legitimate government contracts. Sykes sold the Eveleth center for $2.3 million.

In a surprise announcement in January 2005, the company disclosed that it would lay off staff and close yet another call center—this time in Bangalore. Rising costs and competition for skilled workers in that southern Indian city, together with what the company termed inadequate rates of return, led Sykes to hand off a number of remaining contracts to other company call centers in the Asia/Pacific region—most likely China or the Philippines—where Sykes had had operations since 1997.

The India layoffs did not suggest that Sykes was retreating from its aggressive relocation strategy. More likely, the move reflected a growing disillusionment with the economics of operating in large Indian cities. Perceived advantages of the Philippines included lower attrition rates, closer cultural ties to the United States, and less noticeable accents. Filipino workers were also thought to be more service-minded than their Indian counterparts.

Company Overview

Sykes Enterprises provided outsourced customer management solutions and services to *Fortune 1000* companies worldwide via two geographic segments: the Americas (U.S., Canada, Latin America, India, and the Asia/Pacific Rim area) and EMEA (Europe, the Middle East, and Africa). For the six months ended June 30, 2004, the Americas segment contributed between 60% and 61% of consolidated revenues, with the balance coming from EMEA.

Operating Segments

Customer support outsourcing accounted for 91% of consolidated revenue for the company's 2002 fiscal year. Sykes' core business, this segment comprised primarily inbound technical support services (installation support, "up and running" support, troubleshooting, and usage support), customer support (order status, account maintenance, service dispatch, and customer relations), marketing support (inbound and outbound sales, lead generation, up-sell and cross-sell programs), and speech solutions. The company's customer support contacts included product information requests, description of product features, activation of customer accounts, resolution of complaints, and handling of billing inquiries. Sykes delivered customer support services via a number of communications channels, comprising telephone, e-mail, web, and chat.

At the close of 2002, Sykes operated 15 stand-alone customer support centers in the United States; 3 centers in Canada; 15 in Europe, the Middle East, and South Africa; and 7 offshore in the Peoples' Republic of China, the Philippines, India, and Costa Rica. The company's strategy in the United States had been to locate centers in smaller and rural communities with lower labor (wage plus turnover) and infrastructure costs. A weak economy, pricing pressures, and the need to reduce costs had led to the company's gradual relocation from rural America to more cost-effective locations overseas. Communities that had met all the company's requirements (cash and land grants, site preparation, and tax abatement)—including Ada, Oklahoma; Eveleth, Minnesota; Hazard, Kentucky; Pikeville, Kentucky; Bismarck, North Dakota; Greeley, Colorado; Klamath Falls, Oregon; Milton-Freeman, Oregon; and Scottsbluff, Nebraska—were stunned and angry at the closures, which many regarded as a breach of trust.

Fulfillment and enterprise support services accounted for approximately 11% of the company's revenue for fiscal 2002. Fully integrated with its customer support services in Europe, fulfillment services provided multilingual sales, order processing via the Internet and telephone, inventory control, kitting and assembly, product delivery, and product returns handling, multi-currency payment processing, and financial services, as well as vendor management and warehousing. In the United States, Sykes provided a range of enterprise support services for client internal support operations, including technical staffing, IT services, IT help desk services, and corporate help desk services.

Financial Performance

Results for the quarter ended June 30, 2004, were uninspiring. Consolidated revenues were down 4.6% from the same period a year earlier, while net income for the quarter was down significantly. By mid-August 2004, the company's stock was trading near an all-time low of $4.76 in response to disclosures that:

- Sykes expected to lose 7 to 10 cents per share in the third quarter, even after including one-time gains from the sale of closed call centers. Analysts had expected a positive 5 cents per share.

- The company planned to cancel underperforming contracts with a number of leisure industry clients.

- The "migration" of some clients, including SBC, from U.S. to offshore locations was lagging, which was expected to lead to higher short-term costs.

- A recent FCC decision that was expected to drive AT&T and other providers from the long-distance business was expected to increase the company's costs.

Sykes' revenue growth in 2003 benefited from diversification into new markets, including financial services and the travel and leisure industries, growth in offshore markets, and the strength of the euro. For the 12 months ended December 31, 2003, the company reported total revenues of $480.4 million, a 6.1% increase over the prior year, together with operating income of $11.6 million and net income of $9.3 million. Operating results reflected a number of special items, including a $2.1 million gain related to the sale of two U.S. customer contact management centers and a reversal of prior-year restructuring accruals.

A weakening global economy as well as the company's decision to exit certain business segments had negatively impacted consolidated revenues for the two previous fiscal years. For fiscal 2002, Sykes reported consolidated revenue of $452.7 million, a decrease of $44 million, or 8.9%, from the prior year. The company's reported $18.6 million net loss reflected $20.8 million of restructuring charges related to the closure and consolidation of two U.S. and three European customer support centers, $1.5 million in intangible asset impairments, and $13.8 million in charges associated with the settlement of litigation related to a shareholder suit. For 2001, the company reported consolidated revenues of $496.72 million, a decrease of $106.9 million, or 17.7%, from 2000. Sykes' reported $406,000 net income reflected a $14.6 million restructuring charge related to the closure and consolidation of two U.S. customer support centers, two U.S. technical staffing centers, and one European fulfillment center, as well as $1.5 million in intangible asset impairments. Revenues and reported profits for the third quarter were flat; fourth quarter results were expected to be disclosed in late February 2005.

For 2002, SBC Communications and its affiliates accounted for 15.8% of the company's consolidated revenue, while Microsoft accounted for 12.1%; final results for 2003 were expected to show a similar revenue pattern. (Sykes' top 10 customers, including SBC and Microsoft, accounted for approximately 60% of total consolidated revenues.)

Complete financial statements, including management's discussion and analysis, as well as SEC filings, can be accessed via the company's web site *www.sykes.com*.

Key Competitors

Convergys Corporation

Industry leader Convergys (CVG) provided a broad range of outsourced services to clients via its two operating groups. Convergys' Customer Management Group provided customer service, technical support, and telemarketing services for clients in the financial services, telecommunications, Internet services, and other industries through more than 45 contact centers worldwide. The company's Information Management Group (IMG) processed over 50 million bills a month from its data centers, provided business process consulting services, and licensed its data processing software. Convergys had grown both internally and through acquisition, expanding its European presence with the acquisition of UK billing services from Geneva Technology. A more recent acquisition of Avaya, Inc.'s, global employee service operations was expected to allow the company to expand its human resources support segment.

The company's third quarter revenues were $570.7 million compared to $561.2 million for third quarter 2002—an increase of approximately 1.7%. (Although the Customer Management Group's revenue increased 13.4% for the quarter, the Information Management Group's revenue declined 16.3% compared to the prior year; operating margins for both operating groups were down.) CVG was engaged in a restructuring effort designed to streamline operations and reduce costs, which was expected to benefit both operating and net margins. Top-line performance was expected to benefit from efforts to expand human resource services, such as the five-year contract Convergys signed with Fifth Third Bancorp in late October.

TeleTech Holdings, Inc.

TeleTech, the number two U.S. teleservices/business process outsourcing company, provided a variety of customer relationship management (CRM) services in over 50 "customer interaction" centers worldwide. TeleTech offered customer acquisition, service, and retention programs; customer satisfaction and loyalty programs; customer data and management services; and consulting and marketing services to clients including American Express, Blockbuster, Citigroup, AT&T, and Microsoft.

The company had grown principally through acquisitions, moving into Australia and New Zealand in 1996 with its purchase of Acccess24 and into Mexico in 1997 by acquiring Telemercadeo Integral. Acquisitions of Intellisystems (automated support systems) and Digital Creators (Web-based education and training) in 1998 helped diversify the company's customer base and broaden its expertise. In 1999, TeleTech expanded into Argentina and Singapore, acquired Newgen Results (which offered CRM services to automakers and dealerships), and entered a CRM joint venture named Percepta with Ford Motor Company. The company acquired the customer care division of Boston Communications (which served wireless operators, carriers, and resellers) in 2000.

The company reported third quarter 2003 revenue of $244.9 million, a decline of $7 million, or 2.8%, from the comparable quarter in 2002. TeleTech's operating margin for the quarter declined from 4.3% in 2002 to 3.7% for 2003, while net income declined from $6.3 million in third quarter 2002 to $2.1 million in third quarter 2003.

West Corporation

Formerly West TeleServices, West Corporation (WSTC) was the number three U.S. provider of outsourced teleservices, with over 30 call centers and 7 automated voice and data centers. The company provided inbound (customer service, product support, order processing) and outbound (product sales, customer acquisition and retention) call handling for such clients as AT&T, Dell, and Microsoft. West generated almost half its revenue from the inbound call segment, nearly a third of revenue from outbound calls, and the remainder from computerized call processing services such as processing of automated product information requests, prepaid calling services, and credit card activation. West, which had pursued both internal and external growth strategies, had recently announced it had agreed to acquire ConferenceCall.com, a provider of Internet-based conferencing. The acquisition would be integrated into West's InterCall unit but maintain its own brand name and presence.

For the quarter ended September 30, 2003, West reported consolidated operating revenues of $263.2 million, a 32% increase over the same quarter in 2002. The company's operating income for the period was $40.4 million, a 93.2% increase over the comparable quarter in 2002, while net income increased 79.1%, to $24.4 million.

SITEL Corporation

SITEL (SWW) provided inbound call handling for customer service requests, technical support, and order taking. The company also offered outbound telemarketing, database and list building services, and direct response marketing. The company served over 300 corporate clients from 84 contact centers in 20 countries; four units of General Motors accounted for nearly 25% of SITEL's sales. With consumers becoming more and more web savvy, SITEL had begun building a new business around offering e-services, such as inbound e-mail handling, real-time customer service chat support, and automated customer service support. The company also was trying to leverage its international expansion efforts to capture global clients. (The United States accounted for almost 60% of sales.)

SITEL's third quarter 2003 revenue was $208.8 million, a 16% increase over the comparable quarter in 2002; however, the company reported an operating loss of $396,000 and a net loss of $3.9 million, a significant decline from the prior year's quarter three operating income of $2.6 million and breakeven net income.

The Industry

The customer management services industry was extremely competitive and highly fragmented with firms providing different combinations of outsourced business process services, from outbound telemarketing to customer relationship management and human resources consulting, to clients on a global basis. Industrywide pricing pressures, reflecting a lingering economic weakness and continuing pressures on MNCs to control costs, had compelled competitors to walk a fine line between aggressive cost cutting and revenue growth.

One way firms had sought to provide attractive value propositions to their clients was by moving customer service centers offshore to India, the Philippines, Costa Rica, and other low-cost locations. In addition to lower wage costs, competitors cited educated employees and significantly lower turnover as key reasons to relocate service centers. Although the cost of routing calls to offshore locations had been considered a barrier several years earlier, the decline in telecommunications costs over the past three years made overseas operations not only viable but competitive. Strengthening economies in these locations could, however, make service center jobs less attractive and drive up wage and turnover costs. And public perception in the United States continued to be a problem for firms shifting manufacturing or service jobs out of the country. International outsourcing was a subject that made U.S. business leaders and elected officials clearly uncomfortable, especially in the jobless economic recovery of the early 2000s.

On a positive note, the same weak economy, rapid changes in technology, global competition, and pricing pressures that afflicted competitors in the customer management services industry made outsourcing customer management as well as other business processes an attractive option for clients. Although clients had traditionally turned to service companies to reduce costs, more and more companies had begun to view outsourcing as a means of enhancing service while allowing a sharpened focus on core competencies rather than on non-revenue-producing activities. The expectation of 24-hour-a-day, seven-days-a-week customer service, especially in the United States—a level that many in-house contact centers would have trouble reaching—was a key trend driving growth in the industry.

Note

1. D. Palmer, Letter to the Company, *St. Petersburg (FL) Times* (March 27, 2004).

CASE 43

Outback Steakhouse, Inc.

Maryanne M. Rouse

WITH 1,185 RESTAURANTS IN 50 STATES AND 21 FOREIGN COUNTRIES IN 2004, OUTBACK Steakhouse, Inc. (OSI), was one of the largest casual dining restaurant companies in the world. Founded in 1988 with a single restaurant in Tampa, Florida, OSI now comprised eight unique themed concepts: Outback Steakhouse (884 company-owned, franchised, and development joint venture units), Carrabba's Italian Grill (171), Bonefish Grill (66), Fleming's Prime Steakhouse and Wine Bar (31), Roy's (18), Lee Roy Selmon's (2), Cheeseburger in Paradise (11), and Paul Lee's Chinese Kitchen (2).

At the end of January 2005, 1,120 of the existing restaurants were company owned. The balance were more joint ventures—the preferred route to entering new markets—than franchises. Because OSI continued to buy back franchises, only three geographic franchises remained.

In August 2004, OSI acquired designation rights for the 76-unit Chi-Chi's restaurant chain from the then-defunct Prandium for $42.5 million. The properties included 23 locations with owned land and buildings, 15 sale-leaseback properties with reversion rights and purchase options, 23 ground leases, and 15 leases. Included in the price were real property, furniture, fixtures, equipment, and liquor licenses. OSI had not disclosed final disposition, but the company had noted that it might convert the sites to one of its existing concepts under its current expansion plans.

Not all of OSI's concepts had been successful. The company shut down its two-location southern Louisiana-themed Zazarac concept because it appeared to lack broad appeal. The per person tab at Zazarac had grown to more than $46, an average higher ticket than OSI had planned for but which was required to make the concept reasonably profitable.

Outback Steakhouse

The atmosphere at an Outback Steakhouse, OSI's Australian-themed flagship brand, was casual and fun, with generous portions, moderate prices (average check per person of $17.50–$20.00), and great service. In addition to its popular beef menu items, Outback offered a continually evolving menu of chicken, fish, seafood, and salad choices, as well as such signature appetizers as "Shrimp on the Barbie" and the "Bloomin' Onion." Alcohol accounted for approximately 13% of Outback Steakhouse revenues.

Two recent initiatives, Call-Ahead Seating and Curbside Take-Away, were designed to enhance the customer experience while increasing same-store sales. Although Outback did not use a conventional reservation system, Call-Ahead Seating had shortened wait times that could exceed an hour on busy weekend nights. Curbside Take-Away rooms plus convenient designated parking places for take-out customers were introduced to capitalize on a growing meal replacement trend across all demographics.

The Outback Steakhouse concept was the company's revenue driver. For the nine months ended September 30, 2004, the Outback Steakhouse segment contributed just over 75% of OSI's company-owned restaurant sales. In 2004, 723 of the 884 Outback locations were company owned. International operations, principally in Asia, comprised a growing percentage of the concept's overall revenue.

Carrabba's Italian Grill

Once considered ethnic, flavorful Italian cooking had become firmly a part of the mainstream of American dining, both at and away from home. OSI's popular Carrabba's Italian Grill concept, designed around an open kitchen, offered a wide range of Italian classics, including pasta, chicken, seafood, and wood-fired pizza, complemented by a versatile wine list. The average per person check at a Carrabba's was $18–$20; alcoholic beverages comprised approximately 16% of revenue. Call-Ahead Seating and Carside Carryout were available at every Carrabba's location.

OSI purchased half interest in Carrabba's Italian Grill, two somewhat upscale Italian-themed restaurants in Houston, Texas, in 1993 and, two years later, acquired sole rights to develop the concept. The company bought back 47 franchised units for $138 million in stock, closed several less successful locations, and began a major remodeling effort in 1998. In 2004, OSI operated 171 Carrabba's Italian Grill restaurants; all were company owned.

Fleming's Prime Steakhouse and Wine Bar

Acquired by OSI in 1999, Fleming's Prime Steakhouse and Wine Bar (31 company-owned units) offered a menu featuring aged USDA prime corn-fed beef, chops, fresh seafood, chicken, salads, sides, and desserts plus a creative wine list in an upscale casual setting. The average check was $55–$65 per person; 33% of the 2003 revenues at Fleming's came from alcohol. With wines categorized by grape variety and each section arranged from lighter to more full-flavored choices, the Fleming's wine list was anything but intimidating. Each of the Fleming's concept restaurants had dining rooms that could be configured in a variety of ways to accommodate large and small groups as well as private dining functions.

In addition to regular menu choices, Fleming's had created three unique four-course menus and wine pairings for parties of six or more. Each of these "Discovery Dinners" was offered at three different price levels—$75, $100, and $150 per person.

Bonefish Grill

Founded in St. Petersburg, Florida, by Tim Curci and Chris Parker in 2000, this "polished casual" concept based on fresh grilled fish and other uniquely prepared seafood was acquired by OSI in 2001. The Bonefish Grill menu offered a wide choice of fresh seafood with unique sauces (lemon butter, lime-tomato-garlic, warm mango salsa, pan-Asian) and toppings plus beef, pork, and chicken entrees at prices ranging from $14 to $25. At the end of January 2005, Bonefish Grill comprised 62 company-owned and 4 development joint venture or franchise units.

Roy's

Roy's featured Hawaiian fusion cuisine with sauces and Asian spices developed by Chef Roy Yamaguchi. Innovative entrees at the 18 company-owned restaurants ranged in price from $21 to $65; the average per person check was $50–$60. Liquor sales accounted for approximately 29% of revenue. In 2003, Roy's debuted a prix fixe menu that was an immediate hit with guests and was expected to build dining frequency at this more sophisticated concept. Chef Yamaguchi's "Hawaii Cooks" series, aired on PBS, together with its companion cookbook, had created positive buzz for Roy's.

Lee Roy Selmon's

Developed by OSI in 2000, Lee Roy Selmon's was a family sports restaurant—a new category of dining experience that reflected the evolving role of sports entertainment in the American family lifestyle. Selmon's offers generous portions of "soul-satisfying Southern comfort cooking," with entrees such as Twisted Southern Chicken, the House Filet, and Firecracker Shrimp, priced from $12.79 to $18.99. Both locations—Tampa-Westshore and New Tampa—were company-owned joint ventures.

Cheeseburger in Paradise

Developed as a partnership between OSI and Jimmy Buffet's Margaritaville Holdings, Inc., the 11-unit Key West–themed Cheeseburger in Paradise concept restaurants offered a wide selection of American and island favorites, from giant cheeseburgers, shrimp fritters, and authentic key lime pie to Caribbean-flavored jerk chicken wraps, onion six strings, and chocolate nachos. Nightly live music, "frozen concoctions" from the Tiki bar, and special events, including Full Moon Parties and Sunset Celebrations, attracted a multigenerational customer base.

Paul Lee's Chinese Kitchen

Paul Lee's Chinese Kitchen was a partnership between OSI and Paul Fleming, the innovator behind both Fleming's Prime Steakhouse and Wine Bar and the successful publicly held P.F. Chang's China Bistro. In addition to positioning itself as a neighborhood restaurant, Paul Lee's had made take-out a key priority. The strategy for Paul Lee's, which opened its second location in November 2004, was based on a few key elements: dual kitchens, each with its own chefs, equipment, and ingredients, to more efficiently serve both take-out and dine-in customers; a separate take-out entrance to improve traffic flow; and the use of woks and deep fryers to reduce cooking time and expense and speed up customer turnover.

The core of Paul Lee's menu was traditional Chinese food: There was almost nothing on the menu customers would not have seen in their neighborhood restaurants, from Hot & Sour Soup and Crab Rangoon to Sweet & Sour Pork and Moo Goo Gai Pan. The extensive menu featured soups and salads, chicken, seafood, meat and pork, and noodles, rice, and freshly prepared vegetables. Aside from the traditional tea, Paul Lee's beverage menu offered beer, wine, and what are billed as "far east spirit concoctions." The average per person check at Paul Lee's Chinese Kitchen was $14, with children's entrees at $3.99.

Some industry observers questioned whether Paul Lee's could deliver the 25%–30% return on investment that OSI demanded with the lower average menu prices required to compete as a neighborhood Chinese restaurant. They also questioned whether the concept could match the percentage of revenue derived from alcohol delivered by the company's other restaurants.

Operations

For a company its size, OSI was surprisingly decentralized. The company's lean corporate structure shifted responsibility for key personnel and operating decisions to unit-level managers who, because of OSI's unique ownership structure, had their own money on the line. For most restaurant managers, the dream was to own a restaurant, so OSI designed a creative compensation system that made the general manager or proprietor a limited entrepreneur, requiring him or her to make a $25,000 investment and sign a five-year contract in exchange for a base salary plus 10% of the restaurant's cash flow. OSI did, however, centralize such key functions as purchasing. With almost 1,200 restaurants across eight concepts, the company's centralized purchasing team could bargain for the best quality and prices for meats, vegetables, and non-food items.

OSI's "one-shift culture" (with few exceptions, OSI's themed restaurants served dinner only) had been a key element in attracting and retaining top employees while keeping labor costs reasonable. A lunch and dinner concept required at least one additional management person per restaurant and created competition among servers for desirable time slots. An added benefit of dinner-only was that it provided more of a chance for employees to work hard but still enjoy life.

Financial Performance/Position

OSI's overall sales (restaurant sales plus other revenue) increased by 16.2% in 2003 compared to 2002 (11% in 2002, 11.6% in 2001, and 15.8% in 2000), while gross margin as a percentage of restaurant sales continued to improve. A number of factors, including higher health insurance and other employee benefit costs, resulted in higher labor costs that were only partially overcome by productivity increases. Other restaurant operating expenses increased from 19.9% of restaurant revenues in 2001 to 20.4% in 2002 and 21% in 2003. Operating income as a percentage of sales declined from 9.8% in 2002 to 9.6% in 2003, still significantly ahead of the 8.8% reported for 2001.

Restaurant sales for the first nine months of 2004 increased by 20.9% over the same period in the prior year, while cost of sales showed a slight increase (from 36.2% to 36.5%). Labor and labor-related costs increased 0.2%, to 24.8%, while other restaurant operating expenses increased 0.5%, to 21.5%, for the first nine months of 2004.

OSI's principal source of cash was operations. Operating activities contributed positive cash flow of $269.08 million for fiscal year 2003, $294 million for 2002, and $192.9 million for 2001; however, increases in inventories, income taxes payable, and the current portion of long-term debt negatively impacted liquidity for fiscal 2003. Details of OSI's financial position and performance are available in the company's annual report and SEC filings (*www.outback.com*).

Key industry measures included average unit volume, store operating margin, systemwide sales, and same-store or comparable sales. Average unit volume was a per store calculated average sales amount. This measure was used to assess changes in consumer traffic, pricing, and brand development. Per store operating margin was calculated as store revenue less store-level operating costs that were controlled or significantly influenced by store managers (cost of sales, restaurant operating expenses, and labor and related costs). Systemwide sales was a non-GAAP revenue measure that included total sales volume for all stores, regardless of ownership structure (company owned, franchise, joint venture). Same-store or comparable sales was a measure used across retail concepts to eliminate the impact of new store openings and to allow year-over-year comparison of existing stores.

Competition

Outback's eight restaurant concepts faced stiff competition from both single-location casual and fine dining restaurants and from other casual dining chains. Key competitors in the latter category included Brinker International and Darden International Restaurants, Inc.

With over 1,325 locations in the United States and Canada, Florida-based Darden was the leading operator of casual dining restaurants, including Red Lobster, Olive Garden, Smoky Bones BBQ, Bahama Breeze, and Seasons 52. Red Lobster, with just over 680 units, was the number one seafood chain, while Olive Garden, with approximately 543 locations, led the Italian dining segment. Both chains catered to families with midpriced menu items, themed interiors, and primarily suburban locations. With growth at both Red Lobster and Olive Garden restaurants slowing, Darden appeared to be counting on a national rollout of Smoky Bones BBQ (69 locations at the end of 2004) to jump-start revenue growth. The Bahama Breeze concept had been a disappointment to Darden, which was attempting to reposition the concept and turn financial performance around. Seasons 52, Darden's latest venture, comprised a single-location casual wine bar and grill.

Brinker International, owner and operator of Chili's Grill and Bar, Romano's Macaroni Grill, On the Border Mexican Grill and Cantina, Maggiano's Little Italy, Rockfish Seafood Grill, and Corner Bakery Cafe, was the number two casual dining operator, behind Darden. Named for its founder, casual dining pioneer Norman Brinker, the company had been able to successfully capitalize on America's love of ethnic and regional foods with its Chili's and Romano's Macaroni Grill restaurants, but it continued to struggle with its other concepts: Rockfish Seafood Grill had underperformed against expectations, while On the Border development had slowed to a halt. In October 2004, the Executive Vice President with responsibility for emerging brands resigned; the company subsequently eliminated that position.

The Industry

The highly fragmented restaurant industry was characterized by high initial investment, high labor costs as a percentage of overall costs, and intense competition across segments. As a whole, the restaurant industry outperformed the S&P 500 for the first 11 months of 2004, posting an 11% 5-year annual growth rate versus a 7% rate for the broader index. Year-to-date through December 23, 2004, the S&P restaurants index was up 29.7% (versus a 9.7% increase for the S&P 500), after rising 41% in 2003 (versus 27.4%).

Cost pressures were a key concern for the industry, primarily from increased beef, poultry, and dairy costs; labor costs; and uncertain fuel costs. While many commodities were below recent highs, they remained above 2003 levels. An additional concern was the vulnerability of input prices to weather and export demand. Competition for the lower-cost "B" sites that were part of the location strategy for OSI and its key competitors, had intensified, leading to higher prices and a scarcity of good locations.

A growing awareness of the consequences of unhealthy lifestyles—the U.S. Centers for Disease Control and Prevention in its recently revised statistics, estimated that more than 300,000 obesity-related deaths occurred each year—had spurred consumer demand for high-protein, low-carb dining options and created opportunities as well as threats for industry competitors. In addition to adding menu choices to accommodate diners' health and nutrition concerns, more individual and chain restaurants had begun to move beyond the standby "plateful of steamed vegetables" to offer innovative and flavorful vegetarian options.

Other trends included "global tapas," or small plate, menus as a way of giving diners more latitude in terms of ordering. This strategy of serving several small dishes at appetizer prices instead of the more traditional appetizer–entree model, was picking up around the country.

For two decades, a growing percentage of U.S. food dollars had been spent away from home. Factors contributing to this growth included an increase in the number of dual-income households, positive demographic trends, strong economic growth, and low unemployment rates. The casual dining sector in the United States continued to gain share from fast-food chains as a more affluent and somewhat older population favored full-service restaurants; this trend was expected to accelerate as the population ages.

In 2004, the National Restaurant Association was backing several legislative measures to curb frivolous lawsuits, increase the business-meal tax deductibility, and help shift the responsibility for tip reporting back to the Internal Revenue Service.

The cases in *Strategic Management and Business Policy–10th Edition* (and international version of this book) and *Cases in Strategic Management and Business Policy–10th Edition* were edited by the publisher and the book authors.